History of the Arabic Written Tradition

Supplement Volume 3-i

Handbook of Oriental Studies

Handbuch der Orientalistik

SECTION ONE

The Near and Middle East

Edited by

VOLUME 117/S3-1

The titles published in this series are listed at *brill.com/ho1*

History of the Arabic Written Tradition

SUPPLEMENT VOLUME 3-I

By

Carl Brockelmann

Translated by

Joep Lameer

BRILL

LEIDEN | BOSTON

Originally published as *Geschichte der Arabischen Litteratur* in 1898 and 1902.
Subsequent editions by Brill between 1937 and 1943, and in 1996.

Library of Congress Cataloging-in-Publication Data

Names: Brockelmann, Carl, 1868–1956, author. | Lameer, Joep, translator. | Witkam, J. J., writer of preface.
Title: History of the Arabic written tradition / by Carl Brockelmann ; translated by Joep Lameer ; with a preface by Jan Just Witkam.
Other titles: Geschichte der arabischen Litteratur. English | Handbook of Oriental studies. Section one, Near and Middle East (2014) ; vol. 117.
Description: Leiden ; Boston : Brill, 2016. | Series: Handbook of Oriental studies. Section one, The Near and Middle East ; volume 117 | Originally published as Geschichte der Arabischen Litteratur in 1898 and 1902 — Title page verso of volume 1. | Includes bibliographical references.
Identifiers: LCCN 2016032425 (print) | LCCN 2016041105 (ebook) | ISBN 9789004323308 (hardback : alk. paper) | ISBN 9789004326262 (E-book) | ISBN 9789004323308 (hardback) | ISBN 9789004326316 (hardback) | ISBN 9789004334618 (hardback) | ISBN 9789004335806 (hardback) | ISBN 9789004335813 (hardback)
Subjects: LCSH: Arabic literature—History and criticism.
Classification: LCC PJ7510 .B713 2016 (print) | LCC PJ7510 (ebook) | DDC 892.7/09—dc23
LC record available at https://lccn.loc.gov/2016032425

Typeface for the Latin, Greek, and Cyrillic scripts: “Brill”. See and download: brill.com/brill-typeface.

ISSN 0169-9423
ISBN 978-90-04-33581-3 (hardback)
ISBN 978-90-04-36979-5 (e-book)

Contents

Preface XVII
Note to the Reader XVIII
Translator's Note XIX
Transcription XX

FOURTH BOOK
Modern Arabic Literature

Chapter 1. Egypt Since the British Occupation 3
1 *Poetry* 7
1 Sāmī al-Bārūdī 7
2 Ismāʿīl Ṣabrī 14
3 Aḥmad Shawqī 16
4 Walī al-Dīn Yegen 36
5 Ḥāfiẓ Ibrāhīm 41
6 Muṣṭafā Ṣādiq al-Rāfiʿī 51
7 Aḥmad Muḥarram 55
8 Aḥmad al-Kāshif 57
9 Aḥmad Nasīm 58
10 Ḥasan al-Qāyātī 58
11 Muḥammad Tawfīq ʿAlī 59
12 Tawfīq al-Bakrī 59
13 Muḥammad ʿAbd al-Muṭṭalib 60
14 Other Poets 60
15 Khalīl Maṭrān 63
16 Aḥmad Zakī Abū Shādī 72
17 ʿAbd al-Raḥmān Efendi al-Shukrī 93
18 Aḥmad Rāmī 96
19 ʿAbd al-Ḥalīm Ḥilmī al-Miṣrī 97
20 Aḥmad Abu ʾl-Najāh and Muḥammad Badawī 98
21 Maḥmūd Abu ʾl-Wafāʾ 99
22 Muḥammad Muṣṭafā al-Māhī, Maḥmūd Efendi ʿImād, and Muḥammad al-Harawī 99
23 Ismāʿīl Ṣabrī the Younger 100
24 Al-Banhāwī 102
25 Khalīl Shaybūb 102

26 The *Apollo* Magazine 103
27 ʿUthmān Ḥilmī 105
28 ʿAbbās Maḥmūd al-ʿAqqād 105
29 Al-Māzinī 119
30 Young Poetical Talent 125
31 Ḥasan Kāmil al-Ṣīrafī 126
32 Bishr Fāris 128
33 ʿAlī Maḥmūd Ṭāhā 129
34 Maḥmūd Ḥasan Ismāʿīl 130
35 ʿAlī al-Jārim Bek 131
36 Provincial Poets 133
37 Female Poets 133
a. *Zaynab bint ʿAlī* 133
b. *Āmina Najīb* 134
c. *Jamīlat Muḥammad al-ʿAlāʾilī* 134
d. *Munīra Ṭalʿat* 134
38 Poets in the Popular Genre 134
a. *Khalīl Naẓīr* 135
b. *Muḥammad ʿAbd al-Nabī* 135
c. *Muḥammad Bek ʿIzzat Saqr* 136
d. *Al-Wafāʾ Maḥmūd Ramzī Naẓīm* 136
e. *Muḥammad ʿAbd al-Munʿim* 137
f. *Varia* 137
39 Religious Poets 137
40 Poetry in the Sudan 138
2 *Narrative and Essayistic Prose* (*Novels, Short Stories, Essays*) 140
1 The *Maqāma* 141
2 Jamīl Nakhla b. Mudawwar 142
3 Jirjī Zaydān 143
4 Aḥmad Ḥāfiẓ ʿIwaḍ al-Damanhūri 146
5 Faraḥ Anṭūn 148
6 Muḥammad Ibrāhīm al-Muwayliḥī 149
7 Al-Manfalūṭī 151
8 Muḥammad Ḥusayn Haykal 156
9 Manṣūr Fahmī 163
10 Muḥammad ʿAbdallāh ʿInān 164
11a Shiblī Ibrāhīm Shumayyil 164
11b Salāma Mūsā 165
11c Fuʾād Ṣarrūf 166
12 Muḥammad and Maḥmūd Taymūr 168
13a Nīqūlā al-Ḥaddād 175

13b Muḥammad Farīd Abū Ḥadīd 176
14 Other Authors 176
(*15.–23a.*) *Short Stories, Mostly Involving the Lower Classes* 182
15 Ibrāhīm al-Sayyid Abū Kurāt 182
16 Shaḥḥāta ʿUbayd 182
17 Aḥmad al-ʿĀṣī 183
18 Khayr al-Dīn al-Zarkalī 183
19 Muṣṭafā ʿAlī al-Hulbāwī 184
20 Ḥusayn Shafīq al-Miṣrī 185
21 ʿAbdallāh Ḥabīb 185
22 Ḥasan Aḥmad Abu ʾl-Dhahab 186
23 ʿAbd al-ʿAzīz ʿUmar al-Sāsī 186
23a Muḥammad Amīn Ḥassūna 187
24 Tawfīq al-Ḥakīm 188
25 Maḥmūd Ṭāhir Lāshin 195
26 Ḥusayn Fawzī 196
27 Al-ʿAqqād, Recent Work 197
28 Maḥmūd Taymūr, Recent Work 198
(*29a.–f.*) *Female Authors* 199
29a Malak Ḥifnī Nāṣif 199
29b Alexandra de Avierino 201
29c Labība Hāshim Māḍī 202
29d Mayy Ziyāda 202
29e Bint al-Shāṭiʾ 205
29f Hudā Shaʿrāwī 205
3 *Drama* 206
1 The Theatre in Egypt 207
2 Muḥammad Taymūr 211
(*3.–5.*) *Other Plays* 213
3 Jūrj Abyaḍ and Zakī Tulaymāt 213
4 Muḥammad Rashād Ḥāfiẓ et al. 214
5 Aḥmad Shawqī et al. 214
(*6a.–m.*) *Miscellaneous Playwrights* 214
6a Muḥammad Luṭfī Jumʿa 215
6b Ibrāhīm Ramzī 215
6c Aḥmad Ḥāʾirī Saʿīd 215
6d Maḥmūd Efendi Khalīl Rāshid 216
6e ʿUthmān Ṣabrī 217
6f Ibrāhīm al-Miṣrī 217
6g Anṭūn Yuzbak 218

6h Maḥmūd Badawī 218
6i Maḥmūd Shukrī 218
6k Ibrāhīm ʿAbd al-Qādir a-Māzinī and Maḥmūd Kāmil 218
6l Jūrjī Sharqī 219
6m Zaynab Fawwāz 219
7 Folk Theatre 219
4 *Philology, Literary Criticism and History* 220
1 Aḥmad Zakī 220
2 Ṭāhā Ḥusayn 222
3 Zakī Mubārak 236
(*4.–7.*) *Other Philologists* 239
4 Aḥmad Amīn and Aḥmad Ḍayf 239
5 Muḥammad Ṣabrī 239
6 Aḥmad Farīd Rifāʿī 240
7 Ḥasan Efendi al-Sandūbī and Ḥasan Ṣāliḥ al-Jiddāwī 241
8 Historians 241
5 *Modernists, Reformists, and Politicians* 244
1 Jamāl al-Dīn al-Afghānī 244
2 Muḥammad ʿAbduh 247
3 Muḥammad Rashīd Riḍā 252
4 Muḥammad Tawfīq Ṣidqī 254
5 Muḥammad Farīd Bek Wajdī 254
6 Aḥmad Fatḥī Zaghlūl Pāshā 256
7 Ṭanṭāwī Jawharī 256
8 Muṣṭafā & ʿAlī ʿAbd al-Rāziq 258
9 Muṣṭafā al-Marāghī 259
10 Qāsim Amīn 260
11 Al-Nadīm 260
12 Aḥmad Luṭfī Bek 261
13 Muṣṭafā Kāmil Pāshā 261
14 Muḥammad Bek Farīd 262
15 Saʿd Bāshā Zaghlūl 262

Chapter 2. Syria 264
1 *Poetry* 265
(*1. & 2.*) *Forerunners* 265
1 Before the [First] World War 265
A *The Lebanon and Beirut* 265
a Jirjīs al-Lubnānī al-Mārūnī 265
b Manṣūr al-Hamsh al-Mārūnī 266

c Miṣbāḥ Efendi Ramaḍān 266
d Ḥannā Bek al-Asʿad al-Lubnānī 266
e ʿAṭiyya Jirjī Shāhīn 266
f Asʿad Shudūdī 266
g Bashīr Efendi Ramaḍān 267
h The Brothers al-Mallāt 267
i Amīn Fatḥallāh Ṣabbāgh al-Lubnānī 268
k Al-Khūrī Wadīʿ 268
l Muṣawbaʿ Rashīd Ḥannā al-Lubnānī 268
B *Damascus* 269
a ʿAbd al-Salām al-Shaṭṭī 269
b Muḥammad Salīm al-Qaṣṣāb 269
c Salīm ʿAnḥūrī 269
d Ṣāliḥ b. Ṭāhā 270
e Sulaymān al-Ṣawla 270
C *Aleppo* 270
a Qāsim al-Bakrajī 270
b Mīkhāʾīl al-Ṣaqqāl 270
c ʿAbd al-Fattāḥ al-Ṭarābīshī 272
d ʿAbd al-Masīḥ al-Antākī 272
E *Hama* 272
F *Latakia* 273
G *Tripoli* 273
a ʿAbd al-Qādir al-Ṭarābulusī 273
b Abū ʿAbdallāh al-Shahhāl al-Ṭarābulusī 273
c Taqī al-Dīn al-Rāfiʿī 273
d ʿAbd al-Qādir al-Adhamī al-Ṭarābulusī 274
e Muḥammad Rashīd al-Rāfiʿī 274
2 Adult Witnesses of the [First] World War 274
a *Jirjis Shalḥat* 274
b *Ḥalīm Dammūs* 275
3 Sulaymān al-Bustānī 275
4 Poets of Damascus 279
a *Fāris Bek al-Khūrī al-Dimashqī* 280
b *ʿAbd al-Raḥmān Shāhbandar* 280
c *Muḥammad al-Bizm* 281
d *Shafīq Jabrī* 281
e *Khalīl Mardam Bek* 282
f *Khayr al-Dīn al-Zuruklī (Zarkalī)* 283
g *Muḥammad al-Shurayqī* 283

f *Poets included in the* Dīwān al-thawra 284
h *Munīr al-Ḥusāmī al-Dimashqī* 285
i *Aḥmad ʿUbayd* 285
k *Aḥmad al-Najafī* 285
5 Nuṣayrīs 285
a *Muḥammad Sulaymān al-Aḥmad* 285
b *Kāmil Shuʿayb al-ʿĀmilī* 286
c *Al-Ḥawmānī* 287
d *Muḥammad Najīb Marwa* 287
e *ʿAbd al-Raʾūf al-Amīn* 287
6 Poets from the Lebanon 287
a *Nasīb Arslān* 287
b *Ilyās Fayyāḍ* 287
c *Bishāra al-Khūrī* 288
d *Felix Fāris* 288
e *Ilyās Abū Shabaka* 289
f *Mīshāl Abū Saḥlā and Khalīl Taqī al-Dīn* 293
g *Ṣalāḥ Labkī* 294
h *Poets whose Works were Not Available at the Time of Writing* 294
7 Iskandar al-Khūrī al-Bitjālī 295
8 Aleppo 297
9 Hama 297
a *ʿUmar Yaḥyā* 297
b *Badr al-Dīn al-Ḥamīd* 299
10 Folk Poetry 299
2 *Narrative and Debating Prose (Novels, Short Stories, and Essays)* 301
1 Forerunners 301
2 ʿAbd al-Raḥmān al-Kawākibī 302
3 Nakhla Qalfāṭ 303
4 Prose under the Ottomans 304
a *Mīkhaʾīl ʿAwrā* 304
b *Muḥyi ʾl-Dīn b. Ibrāhīm al-ʿAṭṭār* 304
c *Najīb Mīkhāʾīl Gharghūr* 304
d *Ibrāhīm Bek al-Aswad* 304
e *Muḥammad Amīn al-Sukkarī* 305
f *Fāʾiz Khalīl Hammām and other Historical Novelists* 305
g *Shākir Bek al-Khūrī* 305
h *Najīb al-Lādhaqānī* 305

i *Amīn al-Khūrī al-Lubnānī* 305
k *Amīn Efendi al-Ghurayyib* 306
l *Ṭāhir b. Ṣāliḥ b. Mawhūb al-Waghlīsī* 306
m *Muḥammad Efendi ʿIzz al-Dīn ʿArabī Kātibī al-Ṣayyādī* 306
n *Aḥmad Fawzī al-Sāʿātī* 307
5 Prose After the [First] World War 307
(*a–x*) *Forerunners*
a *Yūsuf Ṣufayr* 307
b *Muṣṭafā al-Ghalāʾīnī* 307
c *ʿĪsā Iskandar Maʿlūf* 307
d *Jirjī Niqūlā Bāz* 308
e *Ṭanyūs Abū Nāḍir, Ilyās Niqūlā Ẓāhir, and Jamīl al-Baḥrī* 309
f *ʿAbd al-Ḥasīb Efendi* 309
g *Abū Ghanīma* 309
h *Najīb Efendi Naṣṣār* 310
i *Ḥannā Khabbāz* 310
k *Wajīh Efendi Bayḍūn and ʿĪsā Mīkhāʾīl Sābā* 310
i *Rafīq al-ʿAẓm* 310
k *Al-Khūrī Mārūn Ghuṣn* 311
l *Aḥmad al-Dimashqī* 311
m *Khurfisqufūs Yūsuf Rabbānī* 311
n *Fuʾād Afrām al-Bustānī* 312
o *Tawfīq Ḥasan al-Sharnūbī and Other Writers on Literature and Sociology* 312
p *Yūsuf Ghaṣūb* 312
q *Muṣṭafā al-Arnāʾūt* 312
r *Iskandar al-Riyāshī* 312
s *Ḥārith Nakht and Muḥammad al-Najjār* 313
t *Tawfīq Ḥasan al-Sharṭūni and Tawfīq Yūsuf ʿAwwād* 313
u *Karam Malḥam Karam* 313
v *Sāmī al-Kayyālī* 314
w *Muḥammad Isʿāf al-Nashāshībī* 315
x *Ḥannā al-Khūrī al-Fighālī* 316
6 Amīr Shakīb Arslān 316
7 Amīn al-Rayḥānī 320
8 Female Authors 332
a *Maryam Naḥḥās* 332
b *Hannā Kasbānī Kūrānī* 332
c *Labība bint Mīkhāʾīl b. Jirjis Ṣuwāyā* 333

d *Farīda ʿAṭiyya* 333
e *Mārī ʿAjamī* 333
f *Alice Abkāryūs* 333
g *Naẓīra Zayn al-Dīn* 333
h *Wadād al-Sakākīnī* 333

3 *Drama* 333
1 Anṭūn Rabbāṭ al-Yasūʿī 333
2 Mīshal al-Ḥāʾik 334
3 Al-Khūrī Yūḥannā Ṭūbī Ṭannūs 334
4 Saʿīd Efendi Taqī al-Dīn 334
5 Al-Khūrī Būlus al-Bustānī 334
6 Jamīl al-Baḥrī 334
7 Asmā al-Ṭūbī 334
8 Al-Khūrī Niqūlā Ḥannā 334
9 Wadīʿ Abū Fāḍil 335
10 Aḥmad Maky 335
11 Al-Muqannaʿ 336

4 *Historiography (general), Literary Criticism, and Local History* 337
(1.–13.) Historiography 337
1 Yūsuf Dibs 337
2 Jirjī Yannī al-Ṭarābulusī 337
3 Ṣādiq Pāshā al-ʿAẓm 338
4 Rashīd Duʿbūl al-Baʿabdawī, Ṣāliḥ al-Madhūn al-Yāfī and Adīb Efendi Luḥūd 338
5 Aḥmad b. Ibrāhīm al-Ṣābūnī and Aḥmad ʿĀrif al-Zayn 338
6 Rūḥī Bek al-Khālidī 338
7 ʿAbd al-Razzāq Bayṭār 339
8 Ḥusayn Kāẓim Bek and Umayl al-Ḥabashī 339
9 Memoirs of the Druze Revolt: Muḥammad Saʿīd al-ʿĀṣ and Others 339
10 Taysīr Ẓabyān et al. 340
11 Amīn Khalīfa et al. 340
12 Anīs Zakariyyāʾ al-Naṣūlī 341
13 Muḥammad Jamīl Bahum and Muʿammar Riḍā Kaḥḥāla 341
(14a.–15.) Literary Criticism 341
14a Anīs al-Khūrī al-Maqdisī 341
14b ʿUmar Aḥmad Farrūkh 342
14c Shafīq Jabri and Khalīl Mardam Bek 342

14d Jabr Ḍūmaṭ and Qusṭakī Bek al-Ḥimṣī 343
14e Jamīl Bek al-ʿAẓm 344
14f Edwār Murqus 344
14g L. Cheikho 344
14h Qusṭākī Ilyās ʿAṭṭāra al-Ḥalabī 345
15 Muṣṭafā Farrūkh 345
(*16a.–18.*) *Local History* 345
16a Jūrj Yuzbek et al. 345
16b Ṣāliḥ al-Burghūthī et al. 345
16c Muḥammad Adīb al-Ḥiṣnī et al. 346
16d Mīkhāʾīl Mūsā Allūf al-Baʿlabakkī 346
16e ʿAbdallāh Ḥabīb Namal and Salīm Sarkīs 346
16f Muḥammad Amīn Ghālib al-Ṭawīl 346
16g Al-Khūrī Būlus Qarʾallī et al. 346
16h Salmān Būlus 347
17 Muḥammad Kurd ʿAlī 347
18 ʿUmar Abu ʾl-Naṣr 350
5 *Reformist Theologians* 351

Chapter 3. The Syrians in the Americas 353
1 *Poetry* 355
(*1.–10.*) *Poets in North America* 355
1 Mīkhāʾīl Efendi Asʿad Rustum al-Shuwayrī 355
2 Asʿad Muḥammad Rustum 355
3 Amīn Ẓāhir Khayrallāh 357
4 Ilyās Manṣūr al-Farrān al-Lubnānī and Mitrī Jirjīs Kafurī 357
5 Maḥbūb al-Khūrī al-Shartūnī 358
6 Ilyā Abū Māḍī 358
7 Nasīb ʿArīḍa 359
8 Niʿma al-Ḥājj 359
9 Rashīd Ayyūb 360
10 Three Inaccessible *dīwāns* 361
(*11.–13.*) *Poets in South America: Brazil* 362
11 Beginnings: Qayṣar Bek Maʿlūf et al. 362
12 Rashīd Salīm al-Khūrī 362
13 Fawzi Maʿlūf 363
(*14.–15.*) *Poets in South America: Argentina* 367
14 Jurjī Ṣuwāyā 367
15 Elias Konsol 367

2 *Prose* 368
- 1 Sulaymān Sarkīs 368
- 2 ʿAfīfa Karam 369
- 3 Jabrān Khalīl Jabrān 369
- 4 Mīkhāʾīl Nuʿayma 381
- 5 ʿAbd al-Masīḥ Ḥaddād et al. 385
- 6 Shukrī al-Khūrī 386
- 7 Yūsuf Saʿd Naṣr 386
- 8 Ilyā al-Khūrī Abū Rizq et al. 387

Chapter 4. Iraq 388

1 *Poetry* 388
- 1 Najaf and Karbala 389
  - a *Ḥaydar b. Sulaymān al-Ḥillī* 389
  - b *Al-Sayyid Muḥammad Saʿīd al-Najafī* 389
  - c *Muḥammad b. Ṭāhir al-Samāwī* 389
  - d *Muḥammad Ḥasan Abu ʾl-Maḥāsin* 390
  - e *Muḥammad Riḍā al-Shabībī* 390
- 2 Baghdad 390
  - a *Jamīl Ṣidqī al-Zahāwī* 390
  - b *Maʿrūf al-Ruṣāfī* 394
  - c *Muḥammad b. ʿAlī al-Kāẓimī* 395
  - d *Muḥammad Mahdī al-Baṣīr al-Baghdādī* 395
  - e *Muḥammad b. Yaḥyā al-Hāshimī* 396
  - f *Nasīm Mallūl* 396
  - g *ʿAbd al-Ḥamīd al-Rāḍī* 396
  - h *Nuʿmān Thābit ʿAbd al-Laṭīf* 397

2 *Prose* 397
- 1 Storytelling 397
  - a *Yūsuf Efendi Hurmuz and Anwar Shāʾūl* 397
  - b *Maḥmūd Aḥmad al-Sayyid al-Baghdādī* 398
  - c *Muḥammad ʿAlī al-ʿĀmilī* 398
- 2 Popular Science 398
  - a *Sulaymān Ghazāla* 398
  - b *Mīkhāʾīl Yūsuf Taysī* 398
  - c *Muḥammad Efendi al-Mawṣilī* 398
  - d *ʿAṭāʾ Efendi Amīn* 399
  - e *Ṭāhā al-Hāshimī* 399
  - f *Makkī Jamīl* 399
  - g *Muḥammad ʿAbd al-Ḥusayn al-Kāẓimī* 399

3 Philology 399

a *Rafāʾīl Buṭṭī* 399

b *Anastase Marie de St. Élie al-Kirmilī* 399

4 Historiography 400

a *Ḥusayn b. Aḥmad al-Burūqī al-Najafī, et al.* 400

b *Āl al-Muṣīb al-ʿUmarī* 401

c *Adīb al-Taqī al-Baghdādī* 401

d *Kāẓim al-Dujaylī* 401

e *Yūsuf Rizqallāh Ghanīma* 401

f *Raʾūf Bek al-Jadarjī* 402

g *Al-Sayyid ʿAbd al-ʿAzīz al-Rashīd* 402

h *ʿAlī Ẓarīf al-Aʿẓamī al-Baghdādi* 402

i *Muḥammad Ṣādiq al-Ḥusaynī* 402

k *Muḥammad Ṣāliḥ Abu ʾl-Barakāt* 402

l *Al-Sayyid ʿAbd al-Razzāq al-Najafī* 402

n *ʿAbbās al-ʿAzzāwī* 403

o *ʿAbd al-Sattār al-Qurghūlī* 403

p *ʻMuʾallif Fāḍilʼ* 403

Chapter 5. Arabia 404

Chapter 6. The Maghreb 405

Addenda & Corrigenda 407

Supplement Volume 1 407

Supplement Volume 2 495

Supplement Volume 3 637

Abbreviations 649

Preface

This third volume continues the history of Arabic literature up to the outbreak of the Second World War, which will probably also signal the beginning of a new chapter for it. In view of the economic uncertainties of the Autumn of 1939, the publisher asked me to limit this volume's last two chapters, which did not seem to be of great importance anyway, to their bibliographical sections alone.

I have included as much detail in the indices as possible. At the request of the publisher, there is an Index of Names and a separate Index of Works. Since these are often cited in various places, it is always good to follow an imaginative searching strategy.

In the Addenda I have once again included everything available at the time of writing. This material has also been included in the indices.

Apart from the gentlemen mentioned in the foreword to Supplement II and who also contributed greatly to the aforementioned addenda, I likewise owe a debt of gratitude to my colleagues Messrs Heffening and Spitaler, to all the authors from Egypt and Syria who sent me their works or informed me of recent publications that had come to their attention, especially to Messrs Maḥmūd Taymūr, Bishr Fāris, Ḥasan K. el-Syrafi, and Sāmī al-Kayyālī, and last but not least to Mr H.G. Farmer, who was kind enough to send me the pages of his *The Sources of Arabian Music* in 1939 before it had appeared in print.

Halle/S
January 1942
C. Brockelmann

Note to the Reader

The references to GAL (Ad p …) have been revised and now refer to the pagination of the English translation of GAL. Rather than merely updating the referenced page numbers to the numbers of the English translation, the place of reference has also been adapted to the new situation. Keeping in mind Brockelmann's original intention of closely linking GAL S to GAL, references may have been moved, deleted or created in order to optimally match the English translation of GAL.

Translator's Note

The structure of GAL's third Supplement volume has been made more transparent by the addition of section and entry headings, especially in Chapter 2 on Syria. For even if there is no denying that the literary production of modern Egypt until the late 1930s was very important, it was judged more appropriate to grant Syrian authors the same kind of visibility as their Egyptian colleagues in the table of contents and the layout of the present work.

In order to improve user experience, this English translation of GAL has been enriched with a list of abbreviations, which has been placed at the end of this volume, after the Addenda et corrigenda to the three Supplement volumes. As a result, this third Supplement volume has become too large to publish in a single tome.

Joep Lameer
Rozendaal, January 2018

Transcription

Transliteration Table of Arabic and Persian Characters

Consonants						Short vowels	
ء	ʾ	ز	z	ك	k	َ	a
ب	b	ژ	zh	گ	g	ُ	u
پ	p	س	s	ل	l	ِ	i
ت	t	ش	sh	م	m		
ث	th	ص	ṣ	ن	n	Long vowels	
ج	j	ض	ḍ	ه	h	اى	ā
چ	ch	ط	ṭ	و	w	و	ū
ح	ḥ	ظ	ẓ	ى	y	ي	ī
خ	kh	ع	ʿ				
د	d	غ	gh			Diphtongs	
ذ	dh	ف	t			َو	aw
ر	r	ق	q			َي	ay
ة	-a (pausa) / -at (construct state)						
ال	al- (article)						

|FOURTH BOOK 1

Modern Arabic Literature

 | DOI:10.1163/9789004369795_002

Chapter 1. Egypt Since the British Occupation

When Britain occupied Egypt, it initially believed that it was simply securing its authority in India by keeping open the Suez canal. However, one of the positive side-effects of the occupation was that it saved Egypt from political and economic collapse. Indeed, even the greatest champion of the freedom of nations will have to admit that it was only thanks to the British administration that the majority of the Egyptian population, the fellahs, could have a decent life in the first place. And even though they did lose some of their personal freedoms, the higher classes, too, did not pay too high a price for the unmistakable progress in their daily lives, both from a material and an intellectual point of view.[1] In fact, it is above all thanks to the British that a sense of national pride has taken possession of all layers of Egyptian society, irrespective of class or creed.

In the beginning, intellectual life did not keep pace with the unmistakable improvements in material prosperity. Even after the British occupation, the assimilation of European standards initiated by Muḥammad ʿAlī | and attempts 2
to put the achievements of modern technology into the service of the country had no impact on the attitude of the population at large. In his book on modern Egypt,[2] the longtime British consul-general there, the Earl of Cromer, dismisses any criticism that is based on claims that his government deliberately kept the Egyptian population in a state of ignorance so as to be better able to control it. But the fact that, under Cromer, too little has been done in the way of national education is even admitted by his successor, Lord Lloyd,[3] although the latter blames it only on failing resources and on a general policy on the part of the British government to prevent the country from being influenced by British culture. As a result of this, French culture remained dominant even under British rule, as can be seen from the fact that young Egyptians wishing to have first-hand experience of Europe always went to Paris. This is also why local writers always based their works on French literature whenever they wanted to renew their art. It is only since the [First] World War, and then only incidentally, that the influence of British education can be detected, notably in the works of Abū Shādī.

In the beginning, the Egyptian nation focussed all its energy on assimilating European technology and on its struggle for independence. It is, therefore, only

1 Cf. the appraisal of Lord Cromer in Walī al-Dīn Yegen, *al-Maʿlūm wal-majhūl* I, C. 1327/1907, 105ff.

2 German by M. Plüddemann, II, Berlin 1908, 493; cf. K. Vollers' criticism of it in *Hist. Zeitschr.* 102 (1909), p. 69ff.

3 *Egypt since Cromer* I, London 1933, 159.

natural that developments in literature should have fallen short of the more
3 general changes in lifestyle for a considerable period of time. Tellingly, | all
the leading figures in Egyptian literature were, until recently, for the most part
foreigners: poets like Sāmī al-Bārūdī, Aḥmad Shawqī and Walī al-Dīn Yegen
were products of the Turkish ruling class;[4] in journalism, it was the Syrians
who led the way, among them the founder of the modern novel, Jurjī Zaydān,
and Khalīl Maṭrān, who redefined modern lyrics. In the beginning there were
very few indigenous writers who shared the limelight with them, such as the
poet of the Nile, Ḥāfiẓ Ibrāhīm, and Zakī Abū Shādī. This foreign dominance
was also the result of the material conditions of the lives of writers in general.
Those whose needs were not met by the kind of personal wealth that is handed
down among members of the ruling class were dependent on a job in journalism to be able to ply their trade. Outside of the press, a writer would have
almost no audience, let alone material support. In his *Thawrat al-adab* of 1933,
Muḥammad Ḥusayn Haykal complains about the indifference of the Egyptian
people when it comes to literature of any kind, in particular among women,
and this despite all the efforts spent on their intellectual emancipation.

In such circumstances, poets could only address themselves to a restricted
circle of admirers at the court or to their fellow-literati. This is also why, for
a long time, they felt no incentive to step outside the well-trodden paths of
tradition. As poetry served only to embellish peoples' lives, deeper issues remained deliberately untouched. It was enough for classical forms and themes
to receive a modern varnish while the poetry's essence remained untouched.
With his political fervour, Ḥāfiẓ Ibrāhīm was the first to succeed in revitalis-
4 ing poetry in Egypt. | Yet it was Khalīl Maṭrān who led poetry along new av-
enues of artistic expression. His student Abū Shādī, once an ardent follower
of his, lost sight of all this when he started pursuing the naive goal of leading
his people—over many intermediate stations—towards some undiluted kind
of humanism.

Religion is, however, still at the root of each and every intellectual movement in Egypt. This is also what prevented it, twice, in its pursuit of European technology, from losing life's sacred dimension through an undue emphasis on material culture, in the way in which this did occur in Europe around the turn of the twentieth century. This is also why a history of Arabic literature cannot help but mention the founders of Egyptian modernism, Jamāl al-Dīn

4 The fact that, even in the countryside, these felt intellectually superior is borne out by Tawfīq al-Ḥakīm's *'Awdat al-rūḥ*; the mother of his hero is a Turkish woman who constantly reminds her husband of the fact that it is only thanks to her, so to speak, that he can claim to be a human being.

al-Afghānī and his student Muḥammad ʿAbduh, even though it is more appropriately the task of the history of religion to come to a full appreciation of their merits.

A new and particularly fertile field of literature is the short story, a field in which local tradition was combined with foreign elements. For a long time, the educated classes of the country had found their entertainment only in foreign, mostly French, novels. These had been translated into Arabic in large numbers, but their choice was often infelicitous.[5] However, following the example of Jurjī Zaydān, many local writers soon adopted the techniques of these foreign novels, among them Maḥmūd Taymūr, who soon outclassed all others with his tales taken from the lives of the common Egyptians.

Less fortunate were the attempts at | writing Arabic drama. The first effort 5
towards the creation of an Arabic theatre in Syria (II, 754) were imitated in Egypt. But neither the translations and adaptations of classical French tragedies and comedies, nor the historical pieces of Aḥmad Shawqī or the romantic operas of Abū Shādī, were able to assert themselves permanently on stage. It is simply that theatre had no local tradition, while the audiences, too, were used to light forms of amusement and not yet capable of appreciating the stage as an artistic or even moral institution. But who knows if the company founded by Khalīl Maṭrān will be granted success in changing this situation.

Literary criticism, which in its highest form goes hand in hand with a scientific analysis of its subject matter, has also played an important role in the development of modern literature. In this domain, too, French scholarship has assumed a leading role through a number of scholars who were educated in Paris, although some of them have tried their best to liberate themselves from the intellectual tutelage associated with it.

In literature, classical Arabic maintained its leading position. The translators did a good thing when they adapted the literary language of old to satisfy the demands of modern times, and the press followed them in this. But it was of course inevitable that the Arabic language should acquire an international character by incorporating many loanwords and calques.[6] | In order 6
to protect the purity of the language, some of the literati made a serious

5 Cf. the inventory in H. Pérès, *Annales de l'Institut d'Etudes orientales*, Algiers III, 1937, 289/311, and Alexandria, *Fihris al-qiṣaṣ wal-riwāyāt* 1–88.

6 M. Brugsch and G. Kampffmeyer, Arabische Technologie der Gegenwart, in *MSOS* 1929/30, G.S. Collin, *Pour lire la presse arabe*, Rabat 1937, E. Mainz, *Zur Grammatik des heutigen Schriftarabisch*, Hamburg 1931, H. Wehr, Die Besonderheiten des heutigen Hocharabischen, in *MSOS* 1934, II, 1/64; some information may also be found in W. Braune, ibid. 1933, 132ff. Relevant questions, also on matters of style, are discussed in detail in Bichr Fares, Des

study of the spirit of *ʿarabiyya*. Leaders in this domain were P. Anastase al-Karmalī in Iraq, with his magazine *Lughat al-ʿArab*, and, in Syria, the *Majallat al-majmaʿ al-ʿilmī al-ʿarabī*, founded in 1922 by Muḥammad Kurd ʿAlī. These were followed in Egypt by the foundation (on 13 December 1932) of the Royal Academy, the *Majmaʿ al-lugha al-ʿarabiyya al-malikiyya*, whose publications are, however, limited to matters concerning the decontamination of the language, in contradistinction to the other two magazines mentioned earlier. Yet besides influences of a lexical character, the general style of modern literary Arabic, too, is continually exposed to the risk of foreign infiltration. In his essays, al-Manfalūṭī resisted this trend more than anyone else, showing that the classical language does possess the necessary means to deal with modern issues. Classical Arabic is indeed invaluable as a binding force between all Arabs, liberated from foreign occupation or still struggling to achieve this, even though the special characteristics (*tamṣīr al-lugha*) of the national language of Egypt, the cultural leader, predominate through its press and, lately, the radio.

In contrast to the classical language, local dialects will always play merely a secondary role. The attempt by Muḥammad ʿUthmān Jalāl to conquer the
7 theatre | with the Egyptian dialect failed fifty years earlier. Just like the regional dialects of Germany and rare exceptions aside, Arabic dialects, too, will always be confined to the entertainment of local communities, even though its artistic level is quite elevated. It is only in narrative poetry that the local dialect has penetrated the higher literary arts. However, wise artists only use it as a means to carve out their heroes rather than for its own sake. But the relationship between classical Arabic and its dialects is not such—as was still the opinion of W. Spitta—that the Arabs should have to wait for their own Dante to appear and promote a dialect, by his works, to the level of a literary language, degrading *ʿarabiyya* in the process to the rank of a language of the church and of scholarship, as happened to Latin.

difficultés d'ordre linguistique culturel et social que rencontre un écrivain arabe moderne, spécialement en Égypte, in *REI* 1936, 221/45.

1 *Poetry*

1 Sāmī al-Bārūdī

By the middle of the last century, poetry was on the brink of extinction in Egypt. It then found new life with Sāmī al-Bārūdī,[7] the son of a family of government officials among whom Islamic culture had apparently always been cultivated with loving care.

His forebear, Murād, had been *multazim* of Bārūd in the Buḥayra, from which the family derived its name. They traced their pedigree to the Circassian Nawrūz al-Atābekī, brother of Barsbāy Qara al-Muḥammadī, meaning al-Bārūdī was of Mamlūk stock. His father, Ḥasan Ḥusnī, originally an officer in the artillery, was the *mudīr* of Dongola, in the Sudan. It is there that Maḥmūd was born on 27 Rajab 1255/7 October 1839. | He lost his father when he was 8
just seven years old. After being schooled at home, he went to the military academy in Cairo in 1267/1851. He completed his studies there in 1271/1854, having obtained the rank of *başçavuş*. He then went to Istanbul to complete his education. There, he worked in the offices of the Sublime Porte, where he learned Turkish and Persian, and even tried his hand at Persian verse. When the new ruler of his native country, Ismāʿīl, came to pay his respects to the sultan after his ascent to power, he returned with him to Egypt, in Ramaḍān 1279/February-March 1863. On 23 Muḥarram 1280/11 July 1863 he was promoted to the rank of *binbaşı* in the cavalry of the homeguard and sent to take part in military excercises in France, and then on to England. He then swiftly climbed the ranks, and, now in the rank of adjutant-general, in Rabīʿ I 1282/August 1865 he was dispatched to Crete with the Egyptian troops to help suppress the rebellion there. When he returned, he became aide-de-camp to the khedive and to Crown Prince Tawfiq. He also acted as the privy secretary to Ismāʿīl. During the war with Russia he commanded the Egyptian troops that had been sent to the assistance of Turkey. In Rabīʿ II 1295/April 1878 he became *mudīr* of Sharqiyya province and, soon after, head of the police in Cairo. After the ousting of Ismāʿīl, he was appointed to the council of ministers on 6 Rajab 1296/27 June 1879, and entrusted with the management of the *awqāf*. In this position, he attached special importance to buying mosque libraries, thereby laying the foundations of what would become al-Maktaba al-Khidīwiyya. In Rabīʿ I 1298/February 1881, when ʿArābī and his officers' party had brought about the downdall of ʿUthmān Rifqī, al-Bārūdī took charge of the Ministry of War. Even though he resigned on 25 Ramaḍān/22 August because people had accused him to the khedive of conniving with the mutineers, he resumed

---

7 "He resuscitated oratory when decomposition had already penetrated its bones and its efflorescence had already come to an end," *Dīwān Muḥarram* I, 184, 12 (*marthiya*).

his office as soon as 14 Shawwāl/10 September, this time under the new prime minister Sharīf Pāshā. When the latter was brought down on 15 Rabīʿ II 1299/8 March 1882, al-Bārūdī himself became prime minister, but resigned as early 9 Rajab/28 May. Then, when the war with Britain broke out, he participated—as was his duty—in the defence of his country, and then was taken prisoner and sent into exile on Ceylon after ʿArābī's defeat on 14 December 1882. It was there, near Colombo, that he was forced to spend 17 of the best years of his life as a planter. It was not until 18 Muḥarram 1318/17 May 1900 that he was allowed to return to his native country. From then on he devoted himself entirely to his
9 literary work, | which included an edition of Abū Tammām and the compilation of an anthology (*mukhtārāt*) of Arabic poetry from Bashshār b. Burd until Ibn ʿUnayn. He died on 6 Shawwāl 1322/15 December 1904.

His collected poems, which his wife published after his death, are dominated by classical poetry. Despite his eventful career as a military and official, he must have found the time for serious linguistic studies long before his involuntary period of leisure in Ceylon. He was a master of *ʿarabiyya* in all its forms and every detail.[8] Accordingly, he mostly shows strict respect for the thematic universe of classical poetry, uses ancient proverbs all around (I, 109,9, 267,2, 407,1, II, 428), and only refers to personalities from pre-Islamic times or early Islam (Zayd al-Fawāris I, 121 bottom, Sulayk 58 bottom, al-Ḥajjāj 56 bottom). Even when talking about his personal life, he only rarely allows himself to refer
10 to contemporaneous events.[9] | Of all modern inventions, electricity was the

---

8 His language is only rarely in conflict with classical usage. For instance, in I, 264 ult., where he says of a she-camel: *fa-rāḥat wahya khāwiyatu 'l-wifāḍi* (in rhyme) 'being exhausted at night,' even though *wifāḍ*, neither in the sense of the support of a handmill, which is how the commentary understands it, nor as a plural of *wafḍa* ('travelling bag'), makes any sense here. And even the commentary cannot make sense of the verse *yamshī ʿalā sāḥatiya 'l-janafu* in I. 490, 1. When, in II, 46, he characterises the escape from fate as *wathāqu* or 'bond', this is only because the rhyme forces him to do so, in the same way in which he characterises the lovers as *dhāki 'l-aḍluʿi*, in the sense of *dhakiyyu 'l-qalbi* (I, 369,2). *Metri causa*, he sometimes also embellishes his verses with ancient lexical lore, such as *shaydhāq* ('falcon'), and with *aqāḥat* as a plural of *uqḥuwān* ('camomile'). On the other hand, he only makes use of his *licentia poetica* when he ventures to use neologisms such as *nahmān* ('avaricious') II, 40, 1, or *ahāzij al-ḥamām* ('dove songs') I, 384, 1. He rarely condones modern Arabic, such as in the language of the *zajal zamzimi 'l-ka'sa* ('proffer the beaker') I, 50,11 (cf. Dozy s.v.).

9 "The steamer blared farewell, and thus they sailed, having saddled nor bridled a mount. She abducted them as in a cloud, as if she really meant to cause friends to be separated", I, 79, 12, 13.

only one that impressed him so much that he weaved it time and again into his poetical imagery.[10]

In metrics, too, he strictly follows classical patterns. Only rarely does he use the *rajaz*, as in no. 69 (I, 67), no. 99 (I, 113) and no. 242 (II, 519ff). Only once, in no. 212 (I, 466), does he allow himself to use an unusual short form of the *mutaqārib* (⏑- -, ⏑- -, ⏑-), and once even a metre invented by himself, in no. 63, I, 63/4, whose light and joyful rhythm is a perfect fit with the playful tone of the poem.

The extent to which his art depends on examples from classical lore may be inferred from the fact that he characterises quite a number of his poems as mere exercises by prefacing them with the words *yarūḍu 'l-qawl* or *yarūḍu 'l-shiʿr*. These are indeed wholly imitations of the austere style of the *qaṣīda* (no. 18, I, 35/5, no. 86, 85/8, no. 190, 270/291). Thus, he practices the description of a hunt (no. 14, I, 22/5), of the falcon, the lion, and the snake (no. 219, II, 3/64), and of various other themes (no. 241, II, 472/518). In passing, he boasts in 512, 1 of having avoided all the mistakes that can possibly be made when writing a poem. Like the masters of old, he likes to endlessly spin out his comparisons, without any concern for the theme with which it all started (cf. Zakī Mubārak, *al-Muwāzana*, 190).

Al-Bārūdī characterises an imitative poem of the kind described above as simply *ʿalā ṭarīqat al-ʿArab* (no. 240, II, 446/470). | Yet it often happens that he 11
takes the metre and rhyme of a specific poem as his example. Take the first poem of his *Dīwān* (I, 9/11), which is modelled on al-Mutanabbī's *qaṣīda* in praise of Secretary Abū ʿAlī al-Awārijī (Diet. 191ff). A hunting poem, which he himself characterises as a juvenile exercise (no. 14, I, 22, 5), is based on a *qaṣīda* by al-Sharīf al-Riḍā. Even in Ceylon he was still able to compose a counterpart to al-Mutanabbī's famous *qaṣīda* in praise of Kāfūr al-Ikhshīdī (Diet. 640ff) and whose opening verse he even copies with a minor change, only to part ways with him for the remainder of his poem. From al-Nābigha al-Dhubyānī he borrows, in no. 73 (I, 74/79), metre and rhyme for one his *qaṣīda*s which, following the patterns of old, depicts scenes of war, drinking bouts, and amorous adventures. At the request of a friend he made an imitation of

---

10 "The electricity of the morning threw strands of light", I, 123, 13. "Through every kingdom passes a wave of electricity and through every gathering, the voice of happy tidings", 133, 4. "Under the sun, the horses walk in a wave of electricity" (*sic*), 177, 2. ("The stars are like) balls (*ukar*, misinterpreted in the commentary as 'holes') in the ceiling of a room, charged with electric fire", 376. "The secret of love is unfathomable, like electricity, whose nature defies cognition", II, 587, 1.

a *qaṣīda* by Ibn al-Nabīh (no. 62, I, 61/3). In no. 118 (I, 129/132),[11] he took the *qaṣīda* by Abū Nuwas on the emir of Egypt, al-Ḥaṣīb (Āṣāf, 98/101), as his example, and in no. 120 (I, 134/5), something similar from Ibn Firās (Beirut 1873, p. 85/87). In all these imitations he shows himself very independent, borrowing a specific turn of phrase never more than once, such as *shīmatuhu 'l-ghadru* (I, 135, 10 = Abu 'l-Firās 85, 13), and even then only *metri causa*. In many *luzūmiyyāt*, he tries to imitate the artificialities in the rhyme of al-Maʿarrī (no. 6, 7, I, 16/7, no. 65, 65/6, no. 91, I, 101, no. 100, I, 113 etc.). It is only rarely that he imitates a famous verse directly, such as in I, 529, 1 Dhu 'l-Rumma. Of his
12 studies of Persian in Istanbul there is only a single trace, in | two hemestichs translated from the Persian in no. 214, I, 517/8. In view of his close ties with the court of the khedive, it is only natural that he should have put his art at its service. In 1279/1862, so probably while still in Istanbul, he greeted Ismāʿīl when the latter acceeded to the throne (no. 15, I, 25/8). He offered similar congratulations to Muḥammad Tawfīq in 1297/1880 (no. 71, I, 68/70). While still in Ceylon, he sent a short *taʾrīkh* verse to ʿAbbās Ḥilmī, congratulating him on the ʿĪd al-fiṭr of 1314/1896. After his invited return to Egypt, he praised its ruler in two spirited *qaṣīdas* (no. 2, I, 12, no. 239, II, 418/445), and also congratulated him on the birth of his son Muḥammad ʿAbd al-Qādir in 1319/1901.

Thus, one cannot really characterise him as a court poet. Instead, he exercised his art as a free man and of his own will. Love is one of the major motifs in his poetry. Nevertheless, his compliance with classical models is so strict that one can hardly believe that personal experience inspired any of it. In the social circumstances of his time, passionate relations were only possible with the *demi monde*. And sometimes, he does indeed allude to this, such as in no. 94 (I, 106, 6), in which he situates an *histoire galante* explicitly on the island of al-Rawḍa in the Nile (which he simply refers to as al-Miqyās), with its various places of amusement. In no. 197, (I, 327, bottom) he addresses his lover as *ẓabyat al-miqyās*. In an otherwise very long-winded *qaṣīda* that was composed during a period of recuperation in Helwan, he seems to allude to similar adventures (no. 235, II, 266/313).

Similarly, we do not know to what extent his drinking songs, of which there are quite many, are just exercises or whether they are based on his actual life-
13 style. | It is true that he likes to depict himself as a "friend of the goblet" and to wine as the "basis of all elegance" (I, 217, 1), but he must have been confident

11 Cf. Zakī Mubārak, *al-Muwāzana* 222ff.

that his reputation as a good Muslim would not be endangered by this kind of poetic licence.[12]

In his many depictions of nature he is rather more personal. Thus, he extols his residence near Candia at the time of the military campaign on Crete in no. 6, I, 16,[13] a forest in its vicinity (no. 179, I, 240/5), and later also a garden in Ceylon, enchanted by its tropical beauty and its many birds (no. 225, II, 128/47). The sea, too, left a deep impression on him, although in this case fear outweighs aesthetic charm (no. 243, II, 532/46). He strikes a warm tone in his praise of Spring and Autumn (no. 5, I, 15, no. 116, I, 123, no. 125, I, 152, no. 242, II, 519ff.). Still, in his description of Rawḍat al-Miqyās, he soon digresses into a praise of wine. But when he writes about the rain (no. 184, I, 262/5), the clouds (no. 69, I, 67), and even about the camel (no. 184, I, 495), he just imitates the ancients.

Nevertheless, real personal effusions are certainly not lacking. It is admittedly rather strange, though, that, having resigned from the ministry of war and being on his way to his estate, he should describe the steamvessel[14] that takes him down the Nile | and the fields along its banks through a longwinding 14
nasīb entirely in the style of Bedouin poetry (no. 13, I, 20/2). In comparison, the way in which he expresses his longing for home during the Russian war (no. 61, I, 57/60, no. 74, I, 79/83), and which overwhelms him especially during ʿĪd al-fiṭr (no. 75, I, 13/5), strikes one as much more natural. This theme is inexhaustible during his stay in Ceylon; the many wistful songs that he wrote there can certainly stand comparison with Ovid's *Tristia*.[15]

---

12 Such as the confession that "I never went there (i.e al-Rawḍa) in the morning without getting drunk the night before" (I, 214, 2). But when he recommends the morning drink (*ṣabūḥ*) in the manner of the ancients, he is immediately beyond suspicion.

13 According to Abū Shādī (*al-Imām*, March 1936, following al-Saḥartī, *Adab al-ṭabīʿa*), this poem alone was sufficient to render him immortal.

14 I, 21, 1: "I'm riding a black steed, which lightning could never compete with without stumbling; it crumples any distance like it was just another piece of paper, finding its way in any desert where even the Qaṭā bird would get lost. It moves on wheels, all day long, and never tires" etc.

15 I, 84, 12ff: "Who helps a stranger in Sernasov (?), beaten down by fate? A land from hell; only, with snow and ice, rather than a fiery glow. Bulgarians, Tatars and Greeks throng together there. Talking nonsense to each other, the earth teeters under the impact of their voices. Their hair and faces look horrible, as if they are from another than Adam's race. Their faces are shapeless, with eyes and jaws merely suspended on them, it seems. All around me, they howl like cattle and butcher the language when they try to speak. Wherever I look, I find no one to talk to. They are of no use to me, and neither me to them, for as long as I am with them."

No less genuine are most of his songs of mourning; not only the distich full of muted sorrow on the death of one of his daughters (no. 10, I, 18) and the verses that he wrote on the deaths of a son (no. 89, I, 96/7, no. 146, I, 192) and his foster mother (no. 145, I, 191), but also the artful ode on the occasion of the death of his wife, of which he was notified while still in Ceylon (no. 87, I, 88/95). The stiff tone of the poem that he wrote on the occasion of the death of his father (no. 98, I, 95) stands in stark contrast to these, but finds its explanation in his childhood. More dignified again are the elegies on ʿAbdallāh Pāshā Fikrī (no. 18, I, 18), another one on the same and on Ḥusayn al-Marṣafī from Ceylon (no. 17, I, 31/2), and one on Aḥmad Fāris Shidyāq (no. 207, I, 354/368).

He also cultivated all the other motifs of classical poetry with great zeal, with the *fakhr* or self-praise being the part in which his personality stands out
15 most. | Even as an adolescent, he boasted of the noble origins of his house (no. 64, I, 164/5). A highly-developed sense of self-awareness, untouched by the blows of fate, characterises the poems of his adult years (e.g. no. 230, II, 157). Indeed, in one of his final poems (no. 113, I, 121), he still puts himself on a par with the poets and heroes of the olden days. He is always willing to recognise the merits of his friends. For instance, he praises Shakīb Arslān (I, 389) in a letter (no. 208, I, 369/402) as a renewer of poetry, using an honorific title that al-Manfalūṭī was actually more justified in claiming as his own (*Mukhtārāt* 233 n). To ʿAbdallāh Pāshā Fikrī (no. 121, I, 141/5) he rendered homage with the most pompous *madīḥ* one can imagine.

Yet he was also capable of biting satire, even though he never discloses its true object, and this not only in distiches, tristiches, or quatrains (no. 44/481, 45/6, no. 159, I, 198, no. 176, I, 235), but also in longer discharges of discontent (no. 105, I, 117/8, no. 264, II, 596/604). The fact that he denounces one of his victims as an alcoholic must be taken to mean that his wine-songs should not be understood as representing his true opinions.

Moral and philosophical reflections are given ample space. They are frequently called *zuhd* (no. 49, I, 46 with *luzūm*, no. 55, I, 52, no. 60, I, 56, no. 111, I, 120, no. 161, I, 200, no. 266, II, 618, no. 267, II, 623) or *ʿitāb* (no. 202, I, 343), and quite often they reveal a very pessimistic view on life (no. 56, I, 53,[16] no. 105,
16 I, 116, II, 355). More often, however, he | indulges in reflections on life in general (no. 33, I, 42, no. 112, L, 98, no. 144, I, 189, no. 220, II, 65/83, no. 221, II, 84/9

16 "I sue God for having to live among humans to whom good and bad are equal, whose tongues invade the soul with their invented stories any time they like, who know of no bond of friendship—how could something so brittle last?—who have neither old nobility nor new virtue. I am sick and tired of them, they render my life repulsive, making me refuse to be happy. If God does not help me by His grace, then no-one will help me."

etc.), but these are sometimes very trivial (I, 248ff). Only rarely does he touch on matters of politics, like in his counsels for a ruler (no. 181, I, 250/2) or his complaint—though phrased ever so carefully—on the shortcomings of the administration under Ismāʿīl (no. 234, II, 207/66).

Religious feelings are only rarely to be found, making the heartfelt prayer of no. 162 (I, 202) stand in happy contrast with his usual pessimism, even though it was written under completely different circumstances.[17] His poem in praise of the Prophet, on the other hand, is probably just a case of paying respect to a living tradition (no. 59, I, 54/6).

His typical Egyptian patriotism, praised lavishly by his followers at times, makes its first appearance in his poem on the two pyramids of Giza (no. 124, I, 149/52). In this, he claims to have spent an entire month trying to get to the bottom of their secrets, turning his ire on the fortune-seekers by whom they had been damaged.

| Not being open to modern ideas, preferring to remain faithful to his clas- 17
sical paradigms, al-Bārūdī's intellectual horizon is obviously very restricted. This is also why it is sometimes difficult for him not to descend into the vulgar when he wants to try a new turn of phrase. It would be pedantic to come up with a list of such instances; still, some need to be pointed out. For example, in a poem on his stay in Giza mentioned previously (no. 4, I, 13), he lets the south wind etch letters onto a pond, each of which constitutes a song on the enjoyment of life, whose melody is entoned by pigeons. He was apparently so happy with this image that he uses it again in a poem written on Crete (I, 16 bottom): "The wind writes, the pond is a sheet of paper, the clouds do the dotting and the pigeons read." In the same poem from Giza he says (14, 7): "Rise for the morning drink! The white hair of dawn starts showing in the black hair of night." The exigencies of the rhyme seduce him, in a poem rhyming on *ẓāʾ* (notoriously difficult), to use the following turn of phrase: "You have banished sleep from my eyes, so that the only thing they will taste are insomnia and tears" (I, 295, 1). Once, he even describes (II, 137) the morning dew as "spittle in

17 "I praise Thee, for the Good issues from Thee, and I thank Thee, Lord of the heavens, for Your grace. You bestowed on me all that is good and You have purified me such that people welcomed me in their midst. So please, continue to grant me the good that I wish for, and please keep away the evil that I fear. Those whom You keep at bay, no one can help, and those whom You embrace, no one can hurt. Those to whom You reveal the Straight Path, no one can confound, and those whom You guide astray, no one can help. If only my soul attains its end and if only I do not break Thy command, then I need no guiding star to beshine my path at the top of my fame, nor good fortune at the summit of my power."

a camomile calyce." But it is likely that his readers were not peturbed by this as they were used to it from al-Mutanabbī.

Dīwān in 3 volumes, ordered alphabetically, with a very detailed commentary by Maḥmūd al-Manṣūrī (*aḥad ʿulamāʾ al-Azhar*), which, in the second volume especially, becomes ever more verbose as a result of excerpts from the *Lisān al-ʿArab* and other works. Cairo n.d. (the supplement, *Qayd al-awābid*, mentioned in the preface, was never published). *Mukhtārāt al-Bārūdī* (cf. above), in 7 chapters (*adab, madīḥ, rithāʾ, ṣifāt, nasīb, hijāʾ, zuhd*), pub-
18 lished by | his secretary Yāqūt al-Mursī; 4 vols, C. 1327/9. *Kashf al-ghumma fī madḥ sayyid al-umma* in *Majm.*, C. 1327. Muḥammad Ṣabrī (*khirrīj al-Surbun wa-muḥarrir bi-jarīdat al-Siyāsa*) *Maḥmūd Sāmī al-Bārūdī, ḥayātuhu wa-shiʿruhu*, Cairo (Maṭbaʿat al-Shabāb) 1341/1923. *Mukhtār al-zuhūr, nubdha ṣāliḥa lil-shuʿarāʾ Shawqī wa-Ḥāfiẓ wa-Maṭrān wa-Ṣabrī wal-Bārūdī*, C. n.d., ʿIzz al-Dīn Ṣāliḥ, *Muḥammad Bāshā al-Bārūdī*, in the series *Shuʿarāʾ al-jīl al-ʿishrīn*, Alexandria 1324/1911. Muḥammad ʿAbd al-Fattāḥ Ibrāhīm *Shuʿarāʾuna 'l-ḍubbāṭ* C. 1935. Zakī Mubārak, *al-Muwāzana bayna 'l-shuʿarāʾ* (C. n.d.), 186/94. Cheikho, *Mashriq* XXIII, 306. Khalīl Maṭrān, *Dīwān* 238/41, al-Manfalūṭī, *Mukhtārāt* 68/70. *Rithāʾ* in *Dīwān Muḥarram* I, 184/6. *Marthiya* by Muṣṭafā Ṣādiq, *Dīwān* III, 144/5. ʿAqqād, *Sāʿāt bayna 'l-kutub* 165ff, reports that al-Marṣafī cites verses by him more than once in his *al-Wasīla al-adabiyya ila 'l-ʿulūm al-ʿarabiyya* C. 1289/92, improving their phrasing afterwards in his *Dīwān*. Aḥmad Shādī, *al-Taṣwīr fī shiʿr al-Bārūdī*, in *Majallat al-Imām, al-ʿadad al-khāṣṣ bi-dhikra 'l-Bārūdī*, Cairo March 1936.—Five notebooks with notes by him, Landb.–Br. 29, a manuscript related to the edition of Abū Tammām, ibid. 200. Compilations for a new *Ḥamāsa*, ibid. 201. *Risāla fī 'l-ṣarf*, ibid. 202, *Risāla fī 'l-ṭabīʿa*, ibid. 203, *Sharḥ al-Ajurrūmiyya*, cf. II, 344,$_{22}$.

2 Ismāʿīl Ṣabrī

Where al-Bārūdī succeeded in resuscitating a joy in poetry that had almost become extinct along the Nile, the sensitive yet sophisticated poems of his younger contemporary Ismāʿīl Ṣabrī played a role in improving the artistic judgement of his readers. Even though his writings were never printed collectively after his death, many of his poems live on among the people in the form of songs.

Ismāʿīl Ṣabrī was born on 16 February 1855. Graduating from the Madrasat al-idāra at the age of 16, he was sent to France by the government. He got his *baccalauréat* in Aix-en-Provence on 29 November 1876 and his *licence* on 13 April 1879. On his return to Egypt he became an acting judge at the mixed
19 court in al-Manṣūra. During his career as a judge he was promoted | to *qāḍī*

in Cairo in 1891, made representative of the khedive at the courts of Cairo on 21 April 1895, appointed *muḥāfiẓ* in Alexandria on 27 February 1896, and *wakīl* in the ministry of justice on 3 November 1899. He retired on 28 February 1907 and died on 21 March 1923.

A student at the Madrasat al-idāra, he tried his hand at congratulatory poems for the khedive, poems that were published in *Rawḍat al-madāris*. And later, too, he continued to practise this courtly art. For instance, on 24 April 1893 he published a congratulatory work for Khedive ʿAbbās, on the occasion of ʿĪd al-Fiṭr, in *al-Waqāʾiʿ*. But even in these poems, where he expressed an unadulterated kind of patriotism, he rose above the traditional style of the *madīḥ*. Such was the case, for instance, in his congratulations offerered at the time of the khedive's accession to the throne in 1908, at which moment those who had been incarcerated after the mishap of Dinshawāy[18] were released from prison. On this day, he tried to outdo Aḥmad Shawqī and Ḥāfiẓ Ibrāhīm. On the other hand, he did not shrink from intervening in current political affairs either. When Buṭrus Ghālī formed a new cabinet on 11 November 1908, he published a series of satirical epigrams (*maqṭūʿāt*) on each of its ministers under the sobriquet Pentaur (the name of the putative author of an ancient Egyptian 'epos' on Ramses II). His Egyptian patriotism also expressed itself in an ardent love for all his brothers in the Islamic faith, a love that he poured into an overwhelming poem on the battle of Tripoli.

Besides patriotism, his love for women and religion take centre stage in his poems. | A Sufi tone, refined by his studies in philosophy, is clear in his poem 20
on God's goodness.[19]

Ṣabrī's language is inspired by al-Buḥturī, just as al-Bārūdī's is, although he conveys al-Buḥturī's spirit with more success than the latter. Following the fashion of his time, he also liked to imitate poets other than al-Buḥturī. So, when Aḥmad Shawqī published a counterpart to Abu 'l-Ḥasan al-Ḥuṣrī's *qaṣīda* in '*dih*', he soon followed with one of his own.

---

18 This event caused a lot of political excitement and contributed greatly to the rise of Egyptian nationalism. See Hasenclever, *Gesch. Ägyptens* 453.

19 "Oh Lord, where shalt Thou establish hell for the evildoers and bad characters, tomorrow? (*ghadan*, like Persian *fardā* = the Day of Judgement). Your forgiveness has not left an inch of space for the fire of hell to burn in, not in the highest heavens, nor anywhere on earth. Lord, bestow Your grace upon me, and spare me the effort of reason and the pains of thought. Let the drapes of the universe be aired by Your essence, allowing me to see the ire of the Benign and the Ruler's grace."

The influence of his melodious strophic poems (*adwār*), of which Muḥammad Ṣabrī unfortunately cites only one (p. 35), was even greater than that of his *qaṣīda*s in the style of the ancients.

Even though Ṣabrī was very well-read in French literature, he never imitated foreign examples. There is no indication that the poem by Lamartine, which Muḥammad Ṣabrī compares with the religious poem cited in the previous footnote, served as a source of inspiration for it.

Ṣabrī's poetry was drowned out by the sound of war. From that time on, he left it to the younger generation, with whom he entertained a lively literary correspondence, to express themselves on the things that were destroying his world.

Muḥammad Ṣabrī, *Ismāʿīl Ṣabrī, Muḥāḍara adabiyya fī ḥayātihi wa-shiʿrihi ulqiyat bil-Jamʿiyya al-Miṣriyya, mudhayyala bi-ajwad qaṣāʾidihi wa-maqāṭīʿihi*, C. 1341/1923; idem, *Adab wa-taʾrīkh*, 1st ed. 1923, 2nd ed. 1927, p. 111/79, 289/92.
21 *Rithāʾ* by | Ḥāfiẓ Ibrāhīm, *Dīwān* ²11, 208/14. Aḥmad ʿUbayd, *Mashāhīr shuʿarāʾ al-ʿaṣr fī ʾl-aqṭār al-ʿarabiyya al-thalātha*, I, *Shuʿarāʾ Miṣr* 158/67 (with a portrait). He wrote a *taqrīẓ* on the *Dīwān* of the Ibāḍī Sulaymān b. ʿAbdallāh al-Bārūnī al-Nafūsī, C. 1326.

3 Aḥmad Shawqī

Before it had to make way for a new artform, the poetry of the classics resuscitated by al-Bārūdī found a brilliant representative in the much-celebrated 'king of the poets,' Aḥmad Shawqī.[20]

Born in 1868, he hailed from a distinguished Cairene family that had Turkish, Kurdish, Greek, and Arab blood.[21] In 1885 he enrolled in a lawschool at the Sūq al-Zalat, whose director D. al-Basyūnī is said to have assisted him in writing poems in praise of the khedive Tawfīq.[22] In 1887 he was sent to France, with other students, to complete his law studies there. Studying for two years in Paris and Montpellier, he also took time to read French literature, although it had no noticeable influence on his authorship.[23] After his return to Egypt,

20 A portrait of him in old age may be found in *Apollo* I, 278.

21 His great-grandfather was a Kurd who married a Greek prisoner of war, Timzār, whom Ibrāhīm Pāshā had captured in Morea when she was ten years old and then set free. Alluding to a verse by al-Mutanabbī, he calls her (*Shawq.* III, 43, 8) the best Arab mother because she had begotten him.

22 Aḥmad Zakī Pāshā in *Dhikrā al-shāʿirayn* 326, *Apollo* I, 382.

23 H. Pérès, Aḥmad Shawqī, Années de jeunesse et de formation intellectuelle en Égypte et en France, in *Annales de l'Institut d'études orientales* II (1936), 313/40 (transl. from the

he joined the French Desk of the khedive in 1891. Together with Luṭfī Bek and Aḥmad Zakī Pāshā, he participated in the Congress of Orientalists, held London in 1891[24] and in Geneva in 1894, on behalf of the Egyptian government. When ʿAbbās II, who had spent his youth in Vienna, came to power, Shawqī initially kept himself in the background. Yet with the passing of time the khedive became more and more | interested in Arabic literature, and Shawqī, who 22
had meanwhile married a daughter of the wealthy Ḥusayn Bey Shāhīn, succeeded in gaining this khedive's favour as well. His imitation of the *Burda*, the *Nahj al-Burda*, which he wrote in 1327/1909 on the occasion of the pilgrimage of the khedive, aroused the interest of a highly-respected specialist of tradition, Selīm al-Bishrī; indeed, the latter even wrote a commentary on it.[25] When the British installed Ḥusayn Kāmil as sultan on 18 December 1914—after the war had already begun—he, too, believed in Shawqī. Notwithstanding the fact that the British commander ruthlessly suppressed any demonstration of nationalism, Shawqī had the boldness to confront the khedive with his famous *qaṣīda* on the shameful state of the country (*Diw.* I, 214/8, "The kingdom is yours, oh sons of Ismāʿīl; may your house beshadow the Nile forever!" etc.). The following lines particularly, raised the suspicion of the military authorities of the British to such an extent that he was banished from the country: "God knows the weeping of my heart, like a mother bereft of her children, over the cruel fate that has struck my people's sons, the Fertile Crescent, its kingdoms, and its tribes. Should I betray Ismāʿīl through his sons while I was born at his court and so abundantly enjoyed the munificence of his house?" He went to Spain with his sons, and it was only with difficulty that his friends succeeded in ensuring that at least part of his income was transferred there. In Spain, he immersed himself in the history and culture of the Arabs there, which he extolled in several *qaṣīda*s. It was only after the war ended that he could return to Egypt. There, he was richly compensated by an unrivalled popularity and by the warm sun of royal grace. During a festive gathering at the Royal Operahouse, in which delegations from the entire Arab world took part, he was proclaimed 'Prince of the Poets' (*amīr al-shuʿarāʾ*) on 29 April 1927.[26]

---

preface to *al-Shawqiyyāt* I, C. 1898, 1/24, 2nd ed. C. 1329/1911, 1/24, fragment in *Karmat b. Hāniʾ*, C. 1923, 4/16).

24 When he set sail, Ibrāhīm Ḥāfiẓ sent him a poetic farewell, on which cf. the latter's *Dīwān* [1] I, 185, [2]201.

25 According to Zakī Mubārak's *al-Muwāzana bayna ʾl-shuʿarāʾ*, 173, his son ʿAbd al-ʿAzīz was its real author; a preface was written by Muḥammad Bek al-Muwayliḥī.

26 See the account in *al-Siyāsa* of 30 April 1927 and, especially, M. Guidi, Le onoranze al poeta egiziano Shawqi e il loro significato politico, in *Oriente Moderno* VII, 346/53.

23 His *qaṣīda*s were widely sung by all the famous | singers, like Muḥammad ʿAbd al-Wahhāb, Abū ʿUyūn, Umm Kulthūm and others.[27] After this, he wanted to move from being the poet of the khedive and the caliph to the songwriter of the people; indeed, of the Muslim world and the whole Orient. But, at the age of 50, he did not have the strength for it anymore. When he saw his influence dwindle at court, he tried to acquire new fame as a dramatist, but due to a lack of experience on the stage and the fact that theatre in Egypt was still very underdeveloped at the time, he was unable to achieve any lasting success. In 1932 he greeted the *Apollo* magazine founded by Abū Shādī with a *taṣdīr*. But, on the night of 13–14 October 1932, he died after a brief dietetic illness.

Aḥmad Shawqī started his literary career as a prose writer. In 1897, he published his first historical novel, while he was still officially employed at the *dīwān khidīwī: Riwāyat ʿadhrāʾ al-Hind aw tamaddun al-Farāʿina* (Alexandria: Maṭbaʿat al-Ahrām).

In the preface, he says he was inspired by Ferdinand de Lanu (oix?)'s "Ramses the Great or Egypt 3,300 years ago" and by the work of the Egyptian inspector of antiquities, Aḥmad Najīb Bek. But the only real historic persons in Shawqī's book are Ramses and his son, Crown Prince Āshīm (for Kmyum or Shmyum), who died at the age of 30 when his father was in the 55th year of his reign, the king's sister Atart, and the court poet Pentaur. Everything else is pure fantasy, which he exercised quite unrestrainedly. In accordance with the late Greek tradition, he identifies Ramses with Sesostris, crediting him with the conquest of the whole of Asia, Indochina included. Indochina's King Dhnish is re-employed by him in this new empire. When Dhnish is consecrated by his conqueror, Crown Prince Āshīm meets the Indian princess and they fall in
24 love. | Not wanting to give his daughter's hand to the hated conqueror, Dhnish sends her off to a remote island for a period of seven years, together with 100 other virgins. There an old priest looks after them, with 101 leopards mounting the guard. When her seven years of banishment are almost over, a prince by the name of Tharthar—the son of a vassal of Dhnish, he has been in love with the princess for a long time—decides to get her off the island with his fleet in the hope of winning her hand. However, an Egyptian fleet confronts him and orders all his pilots off his ships, leaving him no other option than to return empty-handed. In contrast, an Egyptian by the name of Tūs succeeds in reaching the island and abducting the princess. The second part of the story then plays out in Egypt, where there is a power struggle between the party of the crown prince, under the leadership of his tutor, the poet Pentaur, and the party of the priests. Following a plot by the priests, who want to obstruct any

---

27 Cf. E. Ḥunayn, in *al-Mashriq* XXXIII, 68.

marrriage between the crown prince and the princess from Indochina, the head of the guards, Radris, comes under suspicion of treason. He is incarcerated but, thanks to the fortunate retrieval of some documents that had gone missing, he is acquitted. Receiving news of the abduction of his daughter, Dhnish sends a delegation to Egypt to ask the pharaoh to ensure that she is brought back unharmed. Meanwhile, the girl has arrived in Egypt where preparations for her marriage to the prince are in full swing, the pharaoh having dropped his initial reservations against their union in matrimony. However, during the marriage celebrations a small black bird flies by, shedding its feathers onto the pair. The prince drops dead on the spot and, behind him, his rival Tharthar emerges and kills himself with a dagger. After all this, the princess from Indochina drowns herself in the sea.

The author mobilises all the marvels of the 1001 Nights, of sailor's tales and traditional folklore to add plenty of imagination to his tale; in this he succeeded, even though the unity of the composition suffers because of it. As a result, the reader often wonders what the connection between some of its episodes could be, even though, individually and with their lively depictions, these episodes are often very well written. His prose is thoroughly classical, frequently rhymed, and often enlivened by the insertion of poetry (see A.H.R., Gibb in *BSOS* VII, 6).

| In his novel *Dall wa-Taymān aw ākhir al-Farāʿina*, published in 1899 and 25
on the title page of which he already allows himself to be called *Shāʿir Miṣr fī hādha 'l-ʿaṣr*, he gives a very free rendering of the plot of G. Ebers' *Eine ägyptische Königstochter*.

He does not mention his source; in the preface he just refers to a German work that a Syrian friend had supposedly translated into Arabic. But he added an entirely new element to Ebers' tale by juxtaposing Nitetis, who appears with him under the name of Dall, with a suitor in the person of the palace guard Taymān. The Greek element, which plays such a prominent role in the story by Ebers, has been completely removed, save for Phanes, the leader of the mercenaries, and his supporters. Bardiya and his love story have disappeared entirely, while several newly-invented episodes have been added. One of the latter is the tale of the Arab border guard Munjāb and his son Jādī, who is exposed as a traitor by Taymān. The tale of Cambyses is much simplified, and there is no mention of his illness. The largest changes were made at the end. In the battle against the Persians following their invasion of Egypt, Taymān leads the Egyptian forces. On the battlefield he suddenly runs into Nitetis; he lifts her onto his chariot, after which both are killed in the fighting. The book ends with the escape of Psammetichus. Even though individual episodes do have suspense, the novel is not very imaginative and lacks colour. The author uses a lot of rhyming prose, both in his dialogues and in the general narrative. In the love scene between Dall and Taymān on pages 89/90 he even switches to outright poetry in *basīṭ*. He also lets Munjāb the Arab use *ṭawīl* verse to utter his indignation at being accused of treason. The narrative of the final battle on page 147 begins with a poem, while the book concludes with a quotation from his *qaṣīda Taʾrīkh Miṣr*, called *Kibār al-ḥawādith fī Wādi ʾl-Nīl* in *Shawqiyyāt* I (see there 6/7).

In 1914, when he could already call himself the court poet of the khedive,
26 Shawqī allowed himself to be talked into writing a third historical novel by |
the owner of *al-Shiʿb wal-Musāmarāt* printing house. He chose the story of the fall of Hatra following the treason of the daughter of Sāṭirūn Ḍayzan, calling it *Riwāyat waraqat al-Ās*.

He starts with an impressive teichoscopy, which is a motif that was sometimes used in ancient Arabic narrative technique. The king's daughter al-Naḍīra looks from the ramparts of the beleagered city of al-Ḥaḍr onto the army of the Persians when she sees King Sābūr and instantly falls in love with him. The unfolding of the remainder of the story, well known from al-Ṭabarī, was, however, too simple for his taste. He enhanced it by adding a number of new motifs in order to better explain the attitude of the Persian king. He lets the king's daughter visit the enemy in his own encampment, and, instead of through a spell, the city falls as a result of the surprise capture of a tower whose guards had drank themselves into a stupor when it was rumoured that the Persians were going to pull out the next day. One of king Ḍayzan's faithful companions, who had warned him earlier against the treachery of women in the guise of a *hātif*, now repeats this warning outside the chamber of Sābūr. King Ḍayzan does not die and hides himself in his father's stronghold in a subterranean vault equipped for such emergencies. Shawqī introduces a new character in the person of the king's brother Ardashīr, who is entrusted with the administration of the newly-conquered province. Al-Naḍīra falls in love with him and tries to make him betray his brother, the king. When he refuses, al-Naḍīra takes revenge by accusing him of treason to the king. The latter immediately orders his incarceration, together with al-Naḍīra's friend Hind, with whom the prince had fallen in love. During the night, when the fire that is going to consume the supposed traitor next day is being stoked, al-Naḍīra awakes, as in the original story, because of a myrtle leaf in her bed. When the king asks her what her father had given her to eat that she looks so pampered, she answers: "honey and gazelle's brains," as in the original version. But this is not enough to arouse the king's rage against this spoiled creature to the extent that he is prepared to kill her. In the first instance, he lets himself be softened once more by her beauty; however, when
27 this happens, the voice of the *hātif* resounds once again, | warning him of the

ruses of women. Emerging from his hideout, Ḍayzan appears in front of him, describing his ungrateful daughter's treason for a last time, at the moment at which the king is going to let the execution of his innocent brother and his lover go forward. Now Sābūr has al-Naḍīra and her treacherous friend Asmā' tied to the tails of the horses of the person who sounded the alarm and his friend, in order for them to be trampled when the horses gallop away. Ḍayzan, on the other hand, he takes as his adviser. While Shawqī may unconsciously have introduced the twin motif that we often find in popular storytelling in his line-up of the story's characters, the tale as a whole fits the *musāmara* quite well without lapsing into the annoying kind of wordiness found in Jurjī Zaydān. At the end of this work we find the first printing of a *marthiya* for the two Ottoman pilots Fatḥī and Nūrī, who were killed in action over in Egypt in 1913 (*Shawq.* III, 126/30).

Shawqī's true talent lay in the composition of *qaṣīdas*. The first collection of his poems, *al-Shawqiyyāt*, was published—with an autobiography that was not included in later editions—in Cairo in 1898, and a second edition in Cairo in 1911/1329. Below, we shall cite from the two-volume edition with a preface by Dr. Muḥammad Ḥusayn Haykal, Cairo (Maṭba'at Miṣr) n.d., later followed the publication (Cairo: Maṭba'at lajnat al-ta'līf wal-tarjama wal-nashr, 1936/1354) of a third volume, *al-Marāthī*. The *dīwān* is ordered by subject: volume one contains *Bāb al-ḥawādith al-kibār*, volume two the *Bāb al-waṣf*, p. 1/137, *Bāb al-nasīb* 139/80, varia 181/243; a series of thus far unpublished poems was brought out in *Dhikra 'l-shā'irayn* 609/72. Unfortunately, the *dīwān* is not ordered chronologically, and the date of composition for the individual poems, insofar as they do not relate to a specific event, is only rarely indicated.

In connection with his intentions as a poet, Shawqī himself once declared, in the preface to the *dīwān* of Khalīl Shaybūb (*al-Fajr al-awwal*, Alexandria 1921; see also *Dhikra 'l-shā'irayn* 671): "There are two kinds of poetry, one of which outlives the author while the other | evaporates at the very moment of 28
its conception. In true poetry, old or new have no place, it is beyond time. It consists of words and thoughts, so you must try to hit upon some noble expression or (*sic*) some grand idea. Write whenever you can. Sometimes our imagination can work miracles. The aridity or fecundity of his imagination alone is what makes the lesser or the better poet. When a poet describes a camel, he will besing a mount that can go for a thousand miles. Ask your contemporaries, who among them wore the laurel wreath after al-Khalīl or who created unrivalled proverbs like those of al-Mutanabbī? By God! Neither Musset in his *Nuits*, nor Lamartine or Girzille (?) have sung the praise of love more beautifully than Qays al-Majnūn or Jamīl. He described love's workings in the heart of the timid and submissive person in such a way that its images will remain

with us forever." If we may take the poet by his word—never mind the careless phrasing of the above verses, jotted down in haste[28]—he believes that form and content are of equal importance; indeed, form actually ranks higher than content, while ancient Arabic poetry as a whole is superior to things written in France.

Shawqī was absolutely convinced that he had created eternal values for his people.[29] His contemporaries must often have told him as much, with him being
29 the most influential poet of the court. | Indeed, even Ṭaha Ḥusayn (*Dhikrā* 708, *Ḥāfiẓ wa-Shawqī* 203), despite many issues of interpretation, inclines towards calling Shawqī the greatest poet of Muslim Egypt, indeed of Arabic literature since al-Maʿarrī, ever. Ḥalīm Dammūs and Khalīl Mardam Bek, too, talk in *Dhikrā* p. 545 of his immortal fame. Even Aḥmad Zakī Abū Shādī expressed his admiration of him in verse (*Nakbat Navarīn* 44). And in one of his juvenile poems (*Shiʿr al-wijdān* 74/5) Abū Shādī even used the following hyperbole: "If he had lived at the time of Error (i.e. pagan times), he would have risen to the rank of prohethood without ever spreading error. If Einstein could have been able to measure his greatness, he would have found no contradiction in its unique emergence."[30] In *al-Shafaq al-bākī* $322,_{12}$ he equates him with al-Maʿarri, al-Mutanabbī and Abū Nuwās, and at $1236,_{5}$ he calls him the best lyricist on condition that he follow his nature, while at $1212,_{3}$ he says that his *Uns al-wujūd* ranks among the very best products of modern poetry. But it is also true that he criticises him—deservedly—for his use of language in *Waṭan al-farāʿina* 81n.

In other ways, too, sharp criticism has not been lacking even during his lifetime. People reproached him a certain fickleness and an egotistic thirst for power, and not without reason.[31] Despite his incessant talk about patriotism,

---

28 In the penultimate verse, *aw jal* is apparently a misprint for *aw wajīl*, which he uses against the tradition in place of *wajil*. But in the last verse he simply puts (*metri causa*) *jalīl* 'great' instead of *jīl* 'people', which would be the true opposite of *dahr*.

29 "Even though the stupid do not recognise its value, my pen will withstand the test of time. My wisdom reaches beyond that of the ancient Greeks, in the same way in which Ghāzī beat the Byzantines" (I, 200, 7, 8). "My panegyric puts Zuhayr to shame when I praise him (the Prophet); there is no comparison between my generosity and that of Ḥarīm" (I, 244, 8). "You, unrivalled beacon of Islam, I am the greatest poet of your times. The songs I sang to your eternal glory, put distant Sirius to shame (II, 46, 10, 11; a play on words involving *shiʿr* 'poetry' and *shiʿrā* 'Sirius'). "My poetry is the song of joy of the Orient and a comfort in its sorrow" (II, 243, 12). There are many more instances of this self-consciousness which leaves even Horace's "Exegi monumentum" lagging far behind.

30 *Mā qāla fi 'l-fadhdhi 'l-nubūghi jidālā*, a rather vague image.

31 When, during the beginning of the constitutional movement, he took an ambiguous political position, a youthful Abū Shādī emboldened himself to alluding to this by the words

he never gained the trust of the Fatherland party (*al-Ḥizb al-waṭanī*). | People 30
reproached him by saying that his patriotism was just meaningless platitudes aimed at obtaining the approval of the masses without enthusing them for some higher goal.[32]

But his art, too, was not spared criticism, with his sharpest critic being the young poet and editor of *al-Ahrām* newspaper, ʿAbbās Maḥmūd al-ʿAqqād.

In a series of critiques that he published together with Ibrāhīm ʿAbd al-Qādir al-Māzinī with the title *al-Dīwān* in April of 1921 (I, 3/45, II, 33/84: *Shawqī fi ʾl-mīzān*), he maliciously tore to pieces a whole series of his most famous *qaṣīda*s, his *marāthī* on Farīd, the botanist ʿUthmān Ghālib, on Muṣṭafā Kāmil and princess Fāṭima, as well as the prizewinning Egyptian national anthem or *nashīd*. In the first *marthiya*, he had vainly entered into competition with al-Maʿarrī, while in the second he had only been capable of describing the profession of the deceased by compiling a tasteless catalogue of plants. The *marthiya* on Muṣṭafā Kāmil he finds insipid, just an inventory of triviality and bad taste. And even though his critique of the national anthem is rancorous, exposing all kinds of scandalous events surrounding the work of the jury, he certainly rightly accuses Shawqī of suffering from a lack of ideas. In his *Sāʿāt bayna ʾl-kutub* 109/11 he makes mincemeat of Shawqī's *Song of spring* (*Dīw.* II, 240), which formed the opening part of the *qaṣīda* that he had recited during the festivities in his own honour at the Royal Operahouse. In it, he finds just crooked
images and not | a trace of that genuine kind of feeling that the awakening of 31
nature should evoke in any and every real poet. The *qaṣīda* he dedicated to the khedive on the occasion of ʿĪd al-aḍḥā 1908—a rival one was written by Ismāʿīl Ṣabrī—was critiqued by E. Marcus in *Fatāt al-sharq* II, 367/61, pointing out the shortcomings of this attempted imitation of al-Buḥturī's *qaṣīda* for al-Mutawakkil. We shall deal with al-ʿAqqād's criticisms of Shawqī's plays when we get to him later on. All this led to a steadily-increasing movement away from

---

anīn wa-ranīn in a *qaṣīda* called *al-Kawkab al-tāʾih*. Shawqī took his revenge by setting the local press against him, on which see al-Jiddāwī in *al-Shafaq al-bākī* 1265n. In spite of his wealth, he did not escape being accused of being led by commercial motives; after all, he once even consented to writing a poetic advertisement for a steel pen, on which cf. ʿAbbās Maḥmūd al-ʿAqqād, *Dīwān* II, 37.

32 Cf. al-Jiddāwī, *al-Naẓarāt al-naqiyya*, C. 1344/1925, p. 171/2. In a footnote to Abū Shādī's *al-Shafaq al-bākī* 769, he attacks him most viciously because, in his *qaṣīda al-Khilāfa*, he had radically altered the position on the opposition movement that he had advocated thusfar. Anṭūn Jumayyil then defended him by pointing out that despite frequent changes in his political views, he had always stood up for human freedom. ʿAbbās Maḥmūd al-ʿAqqād, *Dīwān* I, 4/5 reproaches him for having solicited the favour of the press in an unworthy manner.

Shawqī by the younger generation. Even Muḥammad Ḥusayn Haykal, the very same who had written the preface to the *Shawqiyyāt*, now joined his colleagues at the newspaper and moved to the critics' camp.

In the beginning, his contemporaries must hardly have thought his being under the spell of classical and post-classical poetry—more than al-Bārūdī even—as something objectionable. Like the poets of old, Shawqī seeks to prove his mastery not in the composition of the poem as a whole, but in a single verse.[33] Zakī Mubārak (*al-Muwāzana bayna 'l-shuʿarāʾ*, 180 ff.) and Ṭalaba Muḥammad ʿAbduh (*Apollo* I, 457/69) compared a number of his *qaṣīda*s with their models (al-Ḥuṣrī, al-Buḥturī, al-Būṣīrī). Even though they leave it to the reader to pass his own judgement, there can be no doubt that they do not award the imitator the laurel wreath. However, we should not forget, for instance, that Shawqī, when he describes his trip through Spain in the same metre and using the same rhyme as al-Buḥturī in his famous *sīniyya* that describes the Īwān-i Kisrā,[34] or when he imitates a famous *dāliyya* of al-Ḥuṣrī
32 | (II, 152), he merely exercises a time-proven art rather than perpetrates acts of plagiarism. He also practised the pastime *tashṭīr* from time to time (for instance on a verse by Abū Nuwās, *Dīw.* II, 142 and by Bahāʾ Zuhayr, ibid. 163). Yet not only had he carried out a detailed study of the ancient *dīwān*s, he often also had recourse to the *Kitāb al-wasīla al-adabiyya ila 'l-ʿulūm al-ʿarabiyya*, a work on philology by Shaykh Ḥusayn b. Aḥmad al-Marṣafī (d. 1307/1889, cf. II, 727,$_7$ Sarkīs 1137).[35] In comparison with the examples taken from Arabic tradition, influences from French literature are minimal. Muḥammad Luṭfī Jumʿa dedicated *Dhikrā* 440/60 to an analysis of this influence and recognised in Victor Hugo's[36] *Légendes des siècles* the model for Shawqī's *qaṣīda*s on ancient Egypt, especially about Tutankhamun (*Dīw.* I, 334ff); but this influence only expresses itself in a stronger tendency to use rhetoric, which is something that characterises his poetry anyway through his Arabic archetypes. There can be no doubt that, in his *qaṣīda* on Muṣṭafā Kamāl's victory over the Greeks, Victor

33 ʿAbbās Maḥmūd al-ʿAqqād has shown this in a very dramatic manner in *Dīwān* 48/54, where he presents Shawqī's *marthiya* on Muṣṭafā Kāmil first in its original order, and then in a re-arangement of the verses that has no impact whatsoever on the poet's original train of thought.

34 Cf. the nasty but basically justified criticism of al-ʿAqqād, *Sāʿāt bayna 'l-kutub*, 113/9.

35 This is why people reproached him for depicting contemporary life using the imagery of the ancients, such as when he lets a lady driving a car appear as if seated in a camel's litter (Zakī Mubārak, op. cit., 19).

36 Whom he praised in a special *qaṣīda* which Abū Shādī (ad *Mahā* 87) considers as outright blasphemy.

Hugo does not present himself to the mind of the reader with the same intensity as Abū Tammām's song on al-Muʿtaṣim's victory at Amoria (cf. Ṭāhā Ḥusayn, *Ḥāfiẓ wa-Shawqī*, 89). English literature offered absolutely nothing of interest to him. His *qaṣīda* on Shakespeare (II, 5/7) is very artificial in its exaltation, while his effort to pour over in pessimism like Hamlet is not very successful, spoiled darling of fortune that he was (*Dhikrā* 627).[37] | His rela- 33
tions with the poet Hall Cayne, whose praise he sang when the latter came to Egypt (*Dīw.* II, 23/6), were apparently purely social. As such, we find much fewer Europeanisms in his works than in al-Bārūdī's. There are some smaller poems, probably dating back to his adolescence, in which he praises the beauty of Paris (Bois de Boulogne, II, 30, Place de la Concorde, II, 75, the flower and vegetable market in the year 1901, II, 97, Napoleon's grave, I, 312/8). When the German army's march against Paris during the war inspired him to a tearful elegy[38] on the places of his youthful happiness and of his studies, we can, given the mentality of the times, hardly be surprised. But typically, in this poem, too, in which he sings the praises of Paris as the cradle of poetry and learning,[39] he follows his Arabic models. It is only rarely that one encounters a European neologism, such as when he refers to the Nile as Egypt's "lifeline" (*warīd al-ḥayāt*) I, 332, 8, or when he goes so far as to let life "experiment" on man, just like the medical profession experiments on rabbits (II, 184, 8). From the world of antiquity he only invokes the spirit of Nero to use him as the backdrop for the cruelty of the sharif of Mecca, who in 1914 perpetrated acts of violence against pilgrims from Egypt (I, 263 penult.), and of Lord Cromer for the death sentences over Dinshawāy (ibid., 301, | 10),[40] Alexander as the hero who was 34
outclassed by ʿAbd al-Ḥamīd and, indeed, even Socrates and Homer as the backdrop for the eloquence and determination of the sultan (I, 31/2), while, finally, there is of course also Icarus as the predecessor of the French pilots

37 Maybe Zakī Mubārak (*Muwāzana* 21) is not wrong when he invokes this aspect of his personality in order to defend him against the criticism that he had compared the dead to "crying corpses" in his *marthiya* on Muḥammad Taymūr.

38 "I say this with tears running down my cheeks: Paris, whoever fights against you knows you not", *Dīw.* II, 99, 10.

39 "You give birth to the royal masters of oratory, who pour out their poetic wisdom, over all nations, fizzling like the fount of life. Young scholars flock in your direction, from the East and from the West," II, 99, 14/16.

40 This catastrophe was the subject of a play by Ḥasan Marʿī (C. 1907), but it was soon banned by the British authorities (see *Revue du Monde Mus.* III, 504/9).

(II, 108 penult. ff).[41] Modern Turkish poetry, which he must have known well, only inspired him to translate a line or two here and there (II, 147, 5, 6; 151, 3, 4).

Aḥmad al-Iskandarī (*Dhikrā* 320) regards its richness of ideas as the greatest merit of Shawqī's poetry, a richness that, in his view, even surpasses the power of his language. According to him, there is hardly any poem that does not contain an original idea. Unfortunately, one must also admit that his obsession with new ideas sometimes makes him go against good taste, for instance when he lets Muṣṭafā Kamāl's subjects string the bow of their backs with the tendons of submisssiveness (I, 138 bottom). In a grotesque use of imagery he once describes his breath as a boiler (he probably means the boiler of a steamboat) and his heart as a sail, sailing and anchoring with these as his tears pour down. And probably his countrymen were not much offended by his image of Muṣṭafā Kamāl's cavalry as "saddled winds, carrying the helmeted lions of al-Sharā, dressed in armour" (I, 50 penult.). He remains entirely within the
35 boundaries of classical | poetry[42] when he borrows his imagery from scripture, such as when, talking about the Bosporus, he refers to all the other beauties in the world as to the *wāw* that concludes the name of ʿAmr (II, 51, 5), or when he compares the columns of the Alhambra with the alifs of the great calligrapher al-Wazīr (Ibn Muqla, ibid. 59, 1).

The poet's true character and feelings stand out most clearly in those poems that were written on minor occasions, such as when, returning from abroad by boat, he sees a Greek girl that reminds him of his little daughter Amīna who had stayed behind in Helwan, which makes his sentiment as a father want to express itself (II, 126), or when he asks Ḥusayn Wāṣil Pāshā for some rare plants

---

41 His critic ʿAbbās Maḥmūd al-ʿAqqād (*Riwāyat Qambīz fi ʾl-mīzān*, 50/1) reproaches him for failing to introduce Solon as a way to enliven the epoch referred to in this piece. At the same time, al-ʿAqqād shows that Muslim culture is much closer to the heart of the Egyptians than the Classics when he replaces Croesus by Qārūn of the Qurʾān, i.e. the Korah of the Israelites, like in *Hilāl* XXXIII, 91 (*Mashriq* XXI, 156).

42 In this context it may be worthwhile to study the role of handwriting in the imagination of the poets of the Arabs, starting with the pre-Islamic poets who like to recognise letters in the faded traces of the encampment of the beloved, until the time of the classics and those who emulated them, and what, if any, connection there is with the importance of calligraphy as a replacement of painting in Islamic culture. To mention just a few examples, there are the three dots of the letter *thāʾ* which seem to Ibn al-Muʿtazz as if they were three hearthstones (*Dīw.* I, 12, 11), and the cup-bearer between the boozers as a letter *alif* that rises above the line (II, 63, 14, cited in *Ḥalbat al-Kumayt* 30, 8, al-Juzūlī, *Maṭāliʿ* I, 186, 7), and of course the obligatory image of the forelock as the letter *nūn* (I, 72, 1, 14, II, 58, 12 etc.). See also Abū Tammām 233, 21, 234, 29, al-Waʾwāʾ I, 3, II, 13, VIII, 1, 3, 9, 4, 34, 3 etc. etc.

for his garden in al-Maṭariyya (II, 137). His love poems, on the other hand, leave a strong impression of artificiality, especially because time and again he uses the old motifs of the envious and the slanderer, while at one point (II, 157) he elaborates on a *maṭlaʿ* by Sāmī al-Bārūdī. We find real poetry again in his descriptions of nature, such as when he depicts the rising moon while out at sea (II, 37/8), or when he lets himself be taken in by the charms of Lebanon (II, 187/9, Zaḥle, ibid. 225/6) or the landscape surrounding Istanbul (Gök Ṣū II, 62/4, Bosphorus | II, 48/51). But even in these cases he sometimes has dif- 36
ficulties in resisting his penchant for oratory, as in the case where he describes Geneva and its surroundings, or his trip through the Alps and the Balkans, back to Istanbul (II, 39/47).[43]

His oratory reaches its highest point when he puts it into the service of Islam and contemporary history. His imitation of the *Burda* was already mentioned and it is equalled by his long *Hamziyya nabawiyya* (I, 21/9) and also by two poems on the occasion of the *mawlid* of the Prophet. In his poem for the New Year of 1329/1911, he talks for the first time as if he was meant to be the spokesperson for his people and Islam as a whole (I, 231/3). And it is from then on that he provides all the happenings in politics and society at large with a personal comment; comments that carried a much greater weight—because of his position at the court—than they would have deserved to have by their mere content or by a show of political backbone.

When Egypt lost its independence to Britain, its khedives again sought to establish closer ties with their suzerain in Istanbul, whom their ancestors had tried to get away from as much as possible. This attempt, which in light of the true balance of power was more Platonic than anything else, Shawqī tried to support with his publications. In two long poems, he celebrates the brilliant feats of arms of the Turks in the Greek War, which had raised new hopes throughout the Muslim world. While the first of these (I, 30/47) begins with a bootlicking glorification of ʿAbd al-Ḥamīd before quickly striking a more popular tone, | the second (I, 352/7) poem was conceived entirely to appeal to the 37
masses through its strophic form alone, and, according to its publisher, it did indeed meet with enormous success throughout the Arab world. For as long as ʿAbd al-Ḥamīd was in power, Shawqī never got tired of paying homage to him. In 1904, he also sent him a petition in rhyme, asking him to lend his support to the Egyptian pilgrims who had been exposed to violence on the part of the sharif of Mecca (I, 263/6). And when, in reward for his homages to the sultan, he is received as one of his guests when he visits Istanbul, he can hardly find the words

43 "Then the shroud was torn off Tirol, its nature showing itself without a veil. I likened her to Bilqīs on her throne, in all her glory and surrounded by her maidens", II, 43, $_{7,8}$.

to express the feelings of gratitude by which he is overwhelmed (I, 296/302). But with the shiftiness that was his own, very quickly after the revolution he succeded in adapting himself to the new situation. Even though he begins his long *qaṣīda* in celebration of that occasion (I, 136/41) by lamenting to Yildiz that everything earthly is ephemeral, he commends ʿAbd al-Ḥamid nonetheless to the grace of the Lord, while showering the new strongmen Enver, Niyāzī and Shewket with praise, and offering the homage of the Egyptian people to the new sultan, Meḥmed. He praises the new Turkish constitution while adding a cautious reference to Egypt, still deprived of its blessings (I, 358/62). A sincere enthusiasm fills the verses with which he celebrated the incorporation of SMS Breslau and SMS Goeben into the Turkish fleet (I, 282/6). Being in Istanbul at the time, he even emboldened himself to demand of India, Egypt and North Africa that they contribute to its enlargement. The fact that he was really fond of Istanbul is not only apparent from his farewell song (I, 182/5), but also from his congratulations to Ankara on the occasion of its designation as the country's new capital (I, 198/203), which is followed by wistful memories
38 of the beauties of Istanbul now dethroned. | The victories of Ghāzī over the Greeks then inspire him again with a spirited hymn (I, 48/53).

Of course his greatest interest goes out to his fatherland. There is probably hardly a single event in its history that he did not accompany with some poetic outpouring. But, as we have seen, national politicians had a point when they criticised him for letting his opinion on contemporary politics too often be determined by personal interests. True, he could have defended himself by pointing at the brutal administration of the British, who had made him pay for his admonishment of the khedive with four years of banishment in the past. As such, his poems will provide future historians with but little material, which even then will have to be used with the greatest circumspection, taking care to not overrate his influence on his contemporaries. Nevertheless, he could regard himself as the voice of public opinion when he confronted Lord Cromer on his departure with the dubious effects of his policies, especially in Egypt. In matters of national politics, too, he was too little involved for his statements on the issue of women's rights (I, 102, 219, 1213), the reform of higher education (al-Azhar I, 175/9, the university I, 180), or the constitution (II, 190/3, of 19 February 1926)[44] to have any influence.[45] Social issues were really something

44 Also published by Kampffmeyer in *MSOS* XXI, 115/8.

45 At one point he does not even shrink from launching covert attacks on Saʿd Zaghlūl Pāshā by publishing an anonymous *qaṣīda* on Dr. Maḥjūb Bek Thābit in *Kashkūl*, which was

he was not concerned about. This is illustrated in an exemplary manner by his poem for the workers (I, 85/7), which ends with an admonishment to be thrifty.

| In contrast, in his courtly poems he is truly in his element, not only in 39
a panegyric on Muḥammad ʿAlī (I, 110/3) or in a consolation in verse for the mother of ʿAbbās II (I, 319/23), but also and especially in the poems that he wrote for festive occasions at the court (II, 8/12, 13/7, 111/5) and whose slightly exhilarated *ramal* rhythm fits the atmosphere of a formal dance so well.

It is only natural that he should lay claim, in the name of his people, to the merit of the culture of the ancient Egyptians, as all of his contemporaries did.[46] Accordingly, he, too, regards Pentaur as one of his predecessors (I, 6,$_{3}$, 199,$_{13}$), enticing him to a dialogue on the welfare of Egypt in his prose work *Ḥadīth Pentaur*, while looking at Imhotep as the forebear of the Egyptian physicians (II, 237,$_{13}$). The excitement caused by the exacavation of the grave of Tutankhamun (I, 116, 294, II, 107/9), especially, is reflected in two long *qaṣīda*s (I, 334/343, II, 107/9).

Ṭāhā Ḥusayn wrote a long critique on the first of these poems (*Ḥāfiẓ wa-Shawqī* 93/103). He seems to be right in saying that, even though Shawqī did try to express how the Egyptians in general felt about this discovery—a discomfort about how the present time compares to Egypt's brilliant past—he was not very successful in it. He criticises many of Shawqī's artificialities and plays on words, and with good reason. But it is most of all Shawqī's preference for amalgamations, in this case the sad ending of Lord Carnarvon—to whom he dedicates a special obituary (I, 79/84)—with happenings in recent history (the presumed abduction of Sultan Waḥīd al-Dīn, threatened by Kemalists, on a British warship to Malta in November of 1922), which Ḥusayn finds absolutely tasteless. Naturally, the ending of the poem, in which Fuʾād is asked to provide
Egypt with a constitution, is liked by the nationalists, | while the verve of his 40
language is certainly appropriate for the subject. More unusual still is the amalgamation of contradictory sentiments in the second poem, 'Tutankhamun and the Parliament', in which the pharaoh, grudgingly aroused from the sleep of death, bemoans the sad situation that his country is in.

Apart from feeling destined to comment on the fortunes of his country with his songs, Shawqī also likes to draw events of global importance into his poetic universe. In 1902, he composed a poem on the occasion of the coronation

---

in turn answered (anonymously) by Ḥāfiẓ Ibrāhīm in *Nawwāb*, and by Abū Shādī in *al-Shafaq al-bākī* 209/11.

46 Aḥmad Ḥasan al-Zayyād criticised the excesses of Egyptomania in his essay *Firʿawniyyūn wa-ʿArab* in *Aḥsan mā katabtu* 44/5.

of King Edward VII, which had been postponed because he suffered from a furuncle, and where it is not quite clear whether we are dealing with a somewhat indelicate courtly flattery or with some kind of covert glee (I, 75/8). When President Roosevelt of the United States visits Egypt, he honoured him with a welcome poem preceded by an introduction in prose (II, 65/70) and in which there resounds at least a faint hope that the distinguished guest will intercede with the League of Nations on behalf of the Egyptian people. The earthquake in Tokyo, on the other hand, elicites no more than cool rhetoric (II, 103/5). Apart from the poem on Paris mentioned earlier, the war only inspired a poem on the sinking of the RMS Lusitania (II, 135) and the death of Kitchener (II, 200, 4); in view of the fact that he lived in exile at the time, it is of course understandable that he underwent this event with mixed feelings.

The *rajaz* poem *Duwal al-ʿArab wa-ʿuẓamāʾ al-Islām*, Cairo 1933 (109 pp., fragments also in *Dhikra ʾl-shāʿirayn* 611/9) was written during his exile in Spain. It starts with a glorification of the Arab language, followed by a reflection on the task of the historian, a song on his fatherland and on Mecca, to continue with a history of the Prophet, followed by an account of the caliphs
41 until the Umayyads. | Then comes the *muwashshaḥ* on ʿAbd al-Raḥmān, the Ṣaqr Quraysh, the first of the Spanish Umayyads, and which had been published earlier in his *Dīwān* (II, 214/20). After an interlude he turns to the first ʿAbbāsids and then concludes with the Fāṭimids. The fact that he did not publish this work during his lifetime—save for the *muwashshaḥ*—is almost certainly due to his own (justified) dissatisfaction with it. He must have felt that simple historiography debased his art and that he was not capable of historico-philosophical contemplation.

It would be doing an injustice to the author if one were to look for philosophical issues in his works, as Dr. Manṣūr Fahmī does in *Dhikrā al-shāʿirayn* 494/502. True, in one case he ventured to compete with Ibn Sīnā's *Urjūza* on the soul (*Dīw.* II, 71/5), but he can hardly have been serious in this; and as regards his poem in praise of ʿAbdallāh Luṭfī Bek's translation of Aristotle's *Nicomachen Ethics*, Ṭāhā Ḥusayn justly observes that he can hardly have read the work, since otherwise he would not have ascribed any Platonic ideas to it. Fahmī is, therefore, right to emphasise the poet's practical optimism. We see it, for instance, in his *qaṣīda* on the beehive (*Dīw.* I, 167/71), which to him is exemplary for mankind. Abū Shādī, himself an apiculturist, calls it one of his most valuable creations (*al-Shuʿla*, 92).

After Shawqī had died, a collection of his *marāthī* was published as an addendum to his *dīwān* (*al-Shawqiyyāt*, III, C. 1936).

The *marathī* date from various periods. Unfortunately, they were not ordered chronologically but by rhyme. They include strictly personal effusions

on the occasion of the death of some member of his family, such as the touching elegies on the death of his father in 1897 | (p. 169), on his great-grandmother 42
Timzār (cf. above p. 21 n. 2) and on his mother, whose death he heard about when he was in exile in Spain (156/9). In the latter *marthiya*, which was apparently written in the first hour after the arrival of the telegram, the pain over her death dissolves into cold reflections on the speed of communications (156, 5ff). A series of *marthiya*s is dedicated to friends who were mourning over losses in their own families, like Sāmī al-Bārūdī (123). But most of them are dedicated to people from public life, to princesses from the royal family, such as Fāṭima Ismāʿīl, who rendered outstanding services through the foundation of Cairo University (1920, p. 96ff), or the mother of Khedive ʿAbbās, Umm al-muḥsinīn, who died in Istanbul in 1931 (173f), to Turkish generals such as Edhem and ʿUthmān Pāshā (150, 164), to the former king of the Hijaz, Ḥusayn (160/6), to almost all of the important politicians and men of state of Egypt, to leading intellectuals such as his old rival Ḥāfiẓ Ibrāhīm, Jirjī Zaydān, Muḥammad al-Muwayliḥī, Ismāʿīl Ṣabrī, the Shaykh al-shuʿārāʾ (d. 1923, 133/8), al-Manfalūṭī—whom he compares to Homer (102/4)—and to the champion of women's emancipation, Qāsim Amīn.[47] Characteristically, he only finds three lines for Muḥammad ʿAbduh (45) but provides long outpourings on the transitory fame of singers like ʿAbduh al-Hamūlī (80/2), ʿAbd al-Ḥayy (56/7), Ḥasan Bek Enver (171/2) and Salāma Ḥijāzī (148/9). As for Europe's intellectual heroes, he is inspired by the 100th anniversary of the death of Victor Hugo (78/9) and by the deaths of Tolstoy (87/90) and Verdi (1901, 192). The phraseology of these *marāthī* is not much different from that of his other poems. It is, of course, not up to European critics to pass judgement when Shawqī's publisher believes that a comparison of the warriors at Badr with those of al-Nābigha and the acclaimed botanist ʿUthmān Pāshā Ghālib (54, n. 1) is particularly beautiful. But when the poet tells himself, in 1925, that a song bemourning his death must certainly overflow with tears, or rather with great maxims so as not to look like a wailing woman who just mourns for the money and not for grief (105, 7, 8), then we can only conclude that these are signs of mental fatigue. | We are 43
surely much more touched by the elegy on ʿUmar Bek Luṭfī that was written just hours after his death (in 1911, 91/2) than by the *marthiya*, brimming with rhetoric, which was written on the occasion of the commemorative service held on the 40th day after Luṭfī's passing (93/5).[48] Disturbing are bizarre images such as: "when the soul is not liberated from the body, then Hippocrates blows into the ashes" (63, bottom), or trivialities like: "At the last gasp, even

47 Against whom he nevertheless defends the veil indirectly in 86, 2, 3.

48 On the *Ḥaflat al-arbaʿīn*, cf. E.W. Lane, *Manners and Customs*, London 1899, 532.

the negligent wakes up, the one who spits out life like a coloquint, where it was sugar in his mouth first; but this ball goes ever further, from hand to hand" (98, 4, 6), such in the *marthiya* on princess Fāṭima Ismāʿīl. This is especially so when they occur in a form that was more dictated by rhyme than reason, as in: "The nights are only short and the world is nothing but the dreams of a sleeper, the teeth of someone happy after sleep exposed by lips until the teeth of the rueful (*sic*). One year brings happiness, another misery, the dreamer stays not in bliss nor in distress" (160, 6/8 on the former king Ḥusayn).

An evaluation of the plays of this Prince of Poets is much more difficult than a survey of his lyrics. But we must give it a try here, before we start talking about the history of Egyptian theatre. In Paris in 1893, Shawqī had tried his hand at historical drama with *ʿAlī Bek*.[49] True, in this case a Mamlūk setting is merely used as the backdrop for a romantic love story about a brother and a sister who both are slaves. Unaware of their blood relationship, they fall in love, only to be saved from incest in the nick of time. But already in this early work the poet does not rest content with a simple *rajaz* like Muḥammad b. ʿUthmān Jalāl did.
44 | Instead, he often uses different metres, even within the discourse of a single person. In the absence of the success that he had hoped for, Shawqī appears to have shelved his plans for the theatre for the time being. It was only during his exile that he took them up again. In 1916, he published the play *Majnūn Laylā* (with pen drawings by W. Strekalovsky, 2nd ed. C. 1931),[50] based on the famous ancient Arabic love story, adding the hero of another romance, Qays b. Dharīḥ (cf. I, 87), to the first. In order to preserve the atmosphere of the time, he used verses from the *Dīwān* of Majnūn for some of the latter's monologues. It is difficult to judge whether he really did succeed in turning something which is not rich in drama in the first place into something that could convince the public on stage.[51] In 1917 he published the play *Cleopatra* (2nd ed. 1929) in an audacious effort to revive a chapter from ancient history.

The first act takes us to the Library of Alexandria, where Zeno and his collegues are all at work and studying. Then, hearing the clamour of the crowds in the steets outside, they realise that the Egyptian fleet has just returned from the battle of Actium. Next, the queen appears on stage to give an account of

---

49 The drama is mentioned—without a year of publication—in the appendix to *Duwal al-ʿArab*. Kampffmeier (MSOS XXIX, 198/206) refers to a detailed review by Ḥasan Maḥmūd in *al-Siyāsa* of 13 July 1926, citing some samples.

50 *Majnun Laila*, a poetical drama in five acts, transl. into English verse by Arthur John Arberry, Cairo 1933.

51 See the critique by Muḥammad Salīm Kmeid in *Lughat al-ʿArab* VIII, 201/8.

events. While Antonius and Octavianus are doing battle, the author introduces us to the inevitable lovers, the assistant-librarian Habi and the slave Helena, a scene that continues until Antonius' arrival and report of his victory to Cleopatra. This victory is celebrated by a raucous party in the second act. In the third act, the author lets Antonius commit suicide after Olympus the physician brings him the false tiding that Cleopatra had killed herself. This is supposed to absolve her from the guilt with which she has been saddled by history, by pushing her lover to commit suicide by sending him this false message. Inside the temple, at the door of which he | had inflicted his deadly 45
wound, Cleopatra finds her lover in his death throes. Earlier, she had made Anubis the priest promise to send her some poisonous snakes. At the bier she is surprised by Octavian. In the fourth act Cleopatra receives from Habi, who is disguised as a peasant, the poisonous snakes that had been promised her by Anubis, hidden in a basket under some figs, and these have already done their job by the time that Octavian enters the scene. Thus, she did not, like the historical Cleopatra, try to seduce him, but dies only to prevent herself from falling into enemy hands. Like a real woman, she is worried about keeping her beauty even in death, surrendering only to the deadly snakebite after the priest assures her that it will have no adverse effect on her appearance. Despite its shallow psychology and some lengthy dialogues, it seems to me as an outsider that this piece must have been quite attractive on stage.

In his theatrical experiment *Qambīz*, which premiered in the Ramsīs theatre in December 1931, he returned to his country's ancient history. It is certainly not unintentionally that, once again, he chose an era in which his country suffered under foreign occupation.

The piece begins in the palace of Amasis, who is summoned by Persian envoys to send his daughter Nefrit to the court of Cambyses in order to become his wife. Instead, he sends Nitetis, daughter of his deposed predecessor Apries. The second act takes us to the palace in Susa, where Nitetis, by now a queen, tells her female slave how much she loves her husband. But Cambyses threatens to harm her when Phanes, a Greek, tells him about the ruse that the Egyptians have played on him. The third act starts in Egypt where Nefrit commits suicide because she dreads the thought of falling into Cambyses' hands now that he has seized Egypt following her father's death. A popular scene then tells us of his wholesale destruction of the country. Next, the king himself appears on stage, in a scene in which he kills Apis in the temple at Memphis. From a dramatic point of view, this piece is certainly not as good as the one about Cleopatra.
| It was the object of a thorough critique by ʿAbbās Maḥmūd al-ʿAqqād 46
(*Riwāyat Qambīz fi 'l-mīzān*, C. n.d., 88 pp.; with illustrations, 1931, 125 pp.).

As is characteristic of al-ʿAqqād, he does not examine the work's dramatic qualities; the only thing he wants is to judge the author by common standards. For instance, he criticises his constant change of metre, even within one and the same dialogue. But Shawqī used this technique in one of his early works, most likely as a way to increase the dramatic energy of the play. And one will hardly criticise him either, as al-ʿAqqād does, for using the Greek forms of the names of the poet Apries and [the sacred bull] Apis rather than their ancient Egyptian forms, even though he is right in disapproving of Shawqī's spelling of the name Phanes, which constantly varies. Even pettier seems al-ʿAqqād's reproach that the poet uses the hamza too freely, merely to satisfy the metre; in his defence, Shawqī could have cited many classical and post-classical poets. More serious are Shawqī's apparent breaches of the rules of grammar and lexicology. Al-ʿAqqād even shows that he commits plagiarism in two instances (16/7), pointing out some cases of poor taste as well, as we also found in his lyrics. But when he compares the Cambyses of history with the one of the play, al-ʿAqqād is again really pedantic to criticise the author for letting Apis' *metri causa* be injured at the horns rather than the shoulder (21) because this would render the whole scene impossible. In his representation of the death of Bardiya, too, Shawqī deviated from history for no good reason. And he also confused Atossa, the later wife of Darius, with one of her sisters, killed by Cambyses. Also, and entirely against the accepted tradition, Shawqī lets Cambyses die in Egypt. In connection with the secondary characters of the play he points out another series of mistakes. Al-ʿAqqād finds it especially shameful that Shawqī calls the Egyptians cowards, just like the foreign occupiers always did, and which, to him, is nothing but an act of treason (30/45). On the other hand, one will hardly let him criticise the author for not having done enough to bring to life the atmosphere of the time just because he could not justify the staging of Solon (see above p. 34, n. 2) in light of the economy of the
47 play. | One can agree with him, on the other hand, where he finds the description of the Persian envoy dishonorable. (64/5), while his criticism of the representation of the death of Cambyses, too, is certainly justified. But was it really in good taste, after his harsh criticism of the Prince of Poets, to make a laughing stock of him in 'An Undramatic Scene Involving Shawqī before Cambyses'? Al-ʿAqqād seems to have forgotten that Shawqī's failure at drama was not just his own shortcoming; it was the product of the culture of his time.

In 1932 and 1933 there followed two more plays: *Amīrat al-Andalus*, in prose, and *ʿAntara*, his last work, in verse. The Spanish princess is Buthayna, daughter of al-Muʿtamid b. al-ʿAbbād, the emir of Seville, who meets the rich merchant Ḥassūn b. Abi 'l-Ḥasan in the book market in Cordova and falls in love with him. The end of the ʿAbbādids and al-Muʿtamid's incarceration under the Almoravids in Aghmāt, in Morocco, provide the poet with the dramatic suspense that he needs. Al-Muʿtamid's daughter's lover follows him there and pays the ransom, upon which al-Muʿtamid gives him his daughter in matrimony. The ancient Arab poet ʿAntara appears in the role of the lover of ʿAbla. The son of a black female slave, ʿAbla's father does not consider him a match for his daughter, no matter how many heroic feats he has and will have to his name. When the girl is engaged to Ṣakhr, the leader of the Banū ʿĀmir, ʿAntara elopes with her, forcing Ṣakhr to marry Naqiyya, who really loves him. In imitation of *Antar*, a French play by Ghānim, the hero is also hailed as a protagonist of the unity of the Arab nation.

Apart from the works discussed just now, the appendix to *Duwal al-ʿArab* also lists a collection of aphorisms, *Aswāq al-dhahab* (cf. *Apollo* I, 44/5), an imitation of al-Zamakhsharī's *Aṭwāq al-dhahab*, and two plays, *al-Bakhīla* and *al-Sitt Hudā*, which are said to be in press. Sarkīs | 1158 mentions as private editions 48
Aʿmālī fi 'l-muʾtamar (the *hamziyya* and some fables in *rajaz*), Būlāq 1895, *Ṣada 'l-ḥarb* (*Dīw.* I, 30/47), C. 1897, *Qaṣīda taʾrīkhiyya* in *Majallat Miṣr* I, 545/65, *Karmat b. Hāniʾ min majmūʿ al-qaṣāʾid mukhtāra min ʿuyūn al-shiʿr wa-ghurra fi 'l-qarīḍ min naẓm amīr al-shuʿarāʾ Aḥmad Shawqī Bek* [*sic*], ed. Tawfīq al-Rāfiʿī, C. 1923/1342. Kampffmeyer MSOS XXIX, 204 mentions also: *al-Mukhtār min shiʿr amīr al-shuʿarāʾ Aḥmad Shawqī Bek ikhtārahu adīb Miṣrī*, C. (al-Maktaba al-Miṣriyya) n.d., Saʿd Mīkhāʾīl, *Ādāb al-ʿaṣr fī shuʿarāʾ al-Shaʾm wal-ʿIrāq wa-Miṣr* (Cairo: Maṭbaʿat al-ʿUmrān), 7/22, (idem, *Samīr al-udabāʾ* I, 13/5). Aḥmad ʿUbayd, *Mashāhīr shuʿarāʾ al-aṣr fi 'l-aqṭār al-ʿArabiyya al-thalātha Miṣr wa-Sūriyya wal-ʿIrāq*, I, *Shuʿarāʾ Miṣr*, Damascus 1922, 62/99. Further: *al-Shayṭān al-jasūr, al-mukhtār min shiʿr amīr al-shuʿarāʾ Aḥmad Shawqī Bek.*, C. n.d. (Maṭbaʿat al-Saʿāda).—Aḥmad ʿAbd al-Wahhāb Abu 'l-ʿIzz, *Ithnā ʿashar ʿāman fī suḥbat Amīr al-shuʿarāʾ*, C. 1933. Muḥammad Isʿāf al-Nashāshībī, *al-ʿArabiyya wa-shāʿiruha 'l-akbar Aḥmad Shawqī* C. 1928, *al-Baṭal al-khālid Ṣalāḥ al-Dīn wal-shāʿir al-kabīr Aḥmad Shawqī*, Jerusalem 1932. Ṭāhir al-Ṭannāḥī, *Shawqī wal-Mutanabbī fī thawb*, *Apollo* I, 447/57. Muṣṭafā Ṣādiq al-Rāfiʿī, *al-Shiʿr al-fannī fī naẓm Shawqī B.*, in *Apollo* I, 534/5.—Special issue of *Apollo* in commemoration of Shawqī dated December 1932, January 1933, 510/35, February 1933, 604/23, March 713/23.—E.F. al-Bustani, *Shakhṣiyyat Aḥmad Shawqī, al-Mashriq* XXXIV, 17/75, Edward Ḥunayn, *Shawqī ʿala 'l-masraḥ*, Beirut 1935.—Anṭūn al-Jumayyil Bek, *Shawqī Shāʿir al-umarāʾ* C. 1932, idem *Shawqī, dirāsāt taḥlīliyya ʿanhu wa-ʿan shāʿiriyyatihi*, C. 1933 (see *Apollo* I, 649). A.J. Arberry, Hafiz Ibrahim and Shawqi, in JRAS 1937, 41/58 (with sample translations). Ph. Bochi in *Rev. Egypt.* I, 471ff, Khalīl Maṭrān in al-Manfalūṭī, *Mukhtārāt* 65/6 (see also his *Dīwān* 54/5, *taqrīẓ* of November 1898, 256/7, laudatory poem dated 1905), Muḥammad

Bek al-Muwayliḥī ibid. 138/58 (hateful and pedantic critique), Muḥammad Khurshīd, *Amīr al-shuʿarāʾ Shawqī bayna ʾl-ʿāṭifa wal-taʾrīkh* C. 1935. F.H. Ali-Assiut, Shawqī, in *Or. St. Littmann*, Leiden 1935, 139/48 (phrases). ʿAlī Maḥmūd Ṭāhā, *Mīlād shāʿir, Apollo* I, 289/95.—*Marthiya* by Abū Shādī in *al-Shuʿla* 129/30, *Dhīkrā Shawqī* in *Aṭyāf al-rabīʿ* 103/4. Further literature in Ḥāfiẓ Ibrāhīm no. 5 and in H. Pérès in *Annales de l'Institut d'Études or.* (Faculté des lettres de l'Université d'Alger) I, 1936, 315n. His son Ḥusayn Shawqī was also active as a poet, see *Mā lil-gharām wa-mā lī*, in *Apollo* I, 1034/5.

49 | 4 Walī al-Dīn Yegen

Like Shawqī, Walī al-Dīn Yegen[52] came from a distinguished Turkish family. But life took him in an altogether different direction from that of the pampered poet of the court. He got involved in the political struggles of his country, campaigning for its freedom in the press. Being extremely committed as a person, he developed a passionate and sparkling style of writing, prose much more than poetry.

Walī al-Dīn Yegen was born in Istanbul in 1873. He was the son of Ḥasan Sirrī Pāshā Yegen—a grand nephew of Muḥammad ʿAlī—and the daughter of a Circassian officer. His father took him along when he moved to Cairo, dying when Walī al-Dīn was only six years old. His legal guardian, ʿAlī Ḥaydar Pāshā, chancellor of the exchequer at the time, sent him to the Madrasat al-Anjāl, which was the royal school Khedive Muḥammad Tawfīq had founded for the education of his children. His literary inclinations soon made him enter the press corps, working for *al-Qāhira*, *al-Nīl* and *al-Miqyās* newspapers. He also worked briefly as a government official for *al-Niyāba al-ahliyya* and *al-Māʾiyya al-saniyya*. When he was 24 years old he went to Istanbul, where he lived for a year in the household of his uncle Fāʾiq Bek Yegen, who was a member of the Council of State. But he fell out with his family when he married a Greek woman. Back in Cairo, he founded *al-Istiqāma* newspaper, which he was soon forced to close down as the Turkish government blocked its import. He then continued his criticism of ʿAbd al-Ḥamīd's dictatorship in *al-Muqaṭṭam* and *al-Mushīr* newspapers. When he returned to Istanbul a year later he was initially given a job in the customs department, at the same time becoming a member of the Supreme Council on Education (*Majlis al-maʿārif al-aʿlā*). But it was not long before ʿAbd al-Ḥamīd banished him to Sīwās, where he remained for seven years, until he was liberated following the Turkish revolution of 1908. He then

52 I.e. 'cousin'. His family was named thus after his great-grandfather, who was a cousin of Muḥammad ʿAlī. Kračkovsky in Ode Vasilieva XIV and *EI*. Oddly enough, Erg. 291 spells Yekun. A portrait is contained in vol. I of *al-Maʿlūm wal-majhūl*.

returned to Cairo by way of Istanbul. There, he worked initially for *al-Muʾayyad* and *al-Rāʾid al-Miṣrī* newspapers. For some time, he was also chief editor of *al-Iqdām*, the newspaper that had been founded in Alexandria by | princess 50
Alexandra de Avierino, née Constantin Vizniewska Huri, publisher of *al-Anīs al-jalīs*. His essays and poems were also published by *al-Zuhūr* magazine and later published in collective form. In 1327/1909 he translated Aḥmad Niyāzī's[53] *Khawāṭir*, being his memoirs on the Turkish revolution. Soon after, he published his own memoirs of his exile in Sīwās (in the second volume of his *al-Maʿlūm wal-majhūl*), as well as sketches from Ottoman history, under the titles *al-Ṣaḥāʾif al-sūd*[54] and *al-Tajārib*. Then he joined the ministry of justice. When Ḥusayn Kāmil ascended to the throne in 1914 he was nominated secretary of the Arabic desk in al-Dīwān al-ʿAlī al-Sulṭānī. Soon after, he started suffering from emphysema, an illness from which he died in Helwan on 6 March 1921.

While he was still alive, his poems were only published in newspapers and magazines. Two years before his death he took up the plan to bring them together in a *dīwān*, but this project was only completed by Anṭūn Jumayyil in 1924 (see Khalīl Mardam Bak, in *RAAD* v 289/92). His attitude towards classical poetry is much freer than that of Shawqī. Nowhere does he lapse into imitations of the ancient *qaṣīda* style. Even though he has a perfect command of literary Arabic, he avoids all manner of artificiality and any showing off with outrageous expressions. Occasionally, he boasts of his distinguished background, but then in a naïve kind of language in poems of his adolescent years.[55]

| Even though the tone of his love songs (*Dīw.* 94ff) rarely rises above the 51
ordinary,[56] his brief occasional poems, such as the one written following the death of his favourite dog (119), show pure, human feelings of a kind that is hard to find among his contemporaries. The poems bemourning the deaths of

53 Born around 1290/1873 in Resna, he joined the military academy in 1310/1892. In August of 1312/1894 he was promoted to the rank of officer. He participated as lieutenant in the Greek war and commanded an infantry battalion that fought the Comitatchi in Monastir. With Enver, he participated in the march against ʿAbd al-Ḥamīd in Istanbul. In 1329/1911 he was murdered by an Arnaut in Valona. Cf. *Türk Yurdu* II, 467/71. The Turkish text of *Khāṭirāti Niyāzī* was published in Istanbul in 1326.

54 A sample from it, *al-Marʾa*, is in *Fatāt al-sharq* v (January 1911), 140/4.

55 "Do not try to humiliate a member of the noble Yegen tribe, whose ancestors subjugated the world while themselves, they were never conquered" *Dīw.*, 100 penult. "By my nobility as a member of the Banū Yegen, and by my fame; let these two, my nobility and my fame, suffice you" 101,16.

56 Like the beautiful distich: "She was created from rays emanating from the soul and therefore above any and every filth or defect. Her pure, chaste image radiates in the soul of her lover, in the same way in which the scent of a rose makes the soul light up."

his son Muḥammad Jān and his brother Maḥmūd Saʿīd distinguish themselves from those of others writing in this same genre if only by their conciseness. But it is also true that, later on, he could not always avoid dressing an obituary in a poetic garb, as was customary in his time. He wrote these, for instance, for the Turkish general Edhem Pāshā, for the khedive Ḥusayn Kāmil and for Edward VII, as well as for Jirjī Zaydān and Ḥasan Ḥusnī al-Ṭuwayrānī (no. 13a).

His songs from the time of his exile in Sīwās (*Dīw.* 25, 34, 36, 53, 55) are full of longing for the throb of life of Istanbul and Cairo. Onboard the steamvessel that took him from Istanbul in 1902, the pangs of farewell induced him to compose a poetic lament on his fate, the horrors of which he can only express by excessive imagery.[57] The climate of his exile weighed heavily upon him,[58] more even than the lack of company or books (*Dīw.*, 56, 8). But in a poem (Pref. 7) that was not included in his *dīwān*, but which was published in *al-*
52 *Zuhūr*, | he admittedly tries to downplay his suffering in exile, in which his enemies rejoice.[59]

More than with Shawqī, his feelings of belonging were divided between Cairo and Istanbul. Even though he not only had an eye for the beauties of Istanbul, but also for the places of its misery ('The Bosporus on a Winter's Night,' 60)[60] and oppression ('Čirāghān Castle,' ibid., 'Čirāghān Burning,' 57), he still feels a very intimate bond with the city where he passed a happy childhood. A member of the Young Turks, he took a very active part in the political ups and downs of the Ottoman empire. As early as 1898, he expressed his longing for freedom in his 'Song for the Fatherland' (*Dīw.* 22, from *al-Mushīr*), letting the city of Istanbul herself (*Dīw.* 24, from *al-Qānūn al-asāsī*) present her grievances to the sultan. After the Balkan war, he wrote his 'On the Ruins of our Fatherland' (16/19) in the same manner in which he, during the war for

57 "Write up your pain; let the sun's rays be your plume, the sea the ink, and let paper be the skies" 55, 11.

58 "We live in a sunless land and only see its skies beclouded. Its stars are hidden in the dark and your (!) brother, the moon, has disappeared behind the horizon. There is no garden there and no nightingale, and it is only ravens that we hear. We walk through dung and live in houses that one could mistake for kraals. In winter, we only see snow, in spring, just dust", 36 bottom.

59 "Sīwās feels very much like home, it is not as bad as all that. People have sinned against the city, and this is why she has become a wasteland."

60 "Fārūq (Istanbul), your beauty is magic and I always succumb to magic. However, you are not only a joy to see, but an admonition for the understanding" 54, 12–13. The chronological relation between this fragment and the prose version in *al-Udabāʾ al-khams* 82/5, Ode-Vasilieva 113/6, *al-Kuttāb al-thalātha* 55/59, which at any rate has more dramatic suspense, remains unknown.

Tripoli, expressed his hope for a happy ending (48) with great enthusiasm. At the inauguration of the Ottoman parliament he greeted the representatives from around the nation, those who are supposed to lead the country—after the dark days of tyranny—towards the light of freedom (53/4). When Shawqī published his 'Tears of the Times' in 1909, in which he expressed his mixed feelings at the | deposition of ʿAbd al-Ḥamīd, Yegen countered this with a *qaṣīda* 53 bearing the same title in which he highlights the sins of the fallen tyrant without mercy (*Dīw.* 20/2). But, like Shawqī, he salutes Meḥmed V when he ascends to the throne.

The valley of the Nile was, to him, a beloved home as well. In 1315/1897, he dedicated some heartfelt verses to it, even though these oscillate between pride in ancient glory and hope for political freedom.

On a different note, he also shared the political ups and downs of his adoptive country with great energy. In 1909, he celebrated the freedom of the press that he missed so much in Sīwās and Istanbul. In January 1910 he composed a *qaṣīda* for a meeting in the Continental Hotel, in which he demanded that the Egyptian people, too, get a constitution approved by parliament (39). Despite his close ties with the ruler and his family, it was only on special occasions that he tried to outdo Shawqī as one of the poets of the court. Thus, he saluted ʿAbbās Ḥilmī on his return from Europe on 12 August 1912, Ḥusayn Kāmil on his ascent to the throne and on the ʿĪd of 1916, and also during his visit to Tanta (78/82).

He is also conerned about neighbouring Syria. In an ode that was not included in his *dīwān* (but published in Kampffmeyer, MSOS XXXI, 165 from *al-Āthār*, vol. 5. fascicle 8, October 1928, p. 403), he calls on the youth of Syria to restore the ancient glory of their fatherland by serving justice and freedom by their acts, since pamphlets and speeches alone will never be able to accomplish such a task.

He follows the happenings in Egypt with a critical eye, too. 'How the Eastern Writers Die' (in Ode-Vasilieva 106/10, from *al-Tajārib* 51/9) sketches a disconcerting image of the plight of the literati, who find no understanding among their countrymen, focused as these are on material pleasures and | political 54 phraseology, let alone that they could hope for any encouragement from them. He believed that the Egyptians were still not ready to govern themselves, as is apparent from his vision in 'The Occupiers Withdraw from Egypt' in *al-Ṣaḥāʾif al-sūd*, C. 1910, 45/51. After the murder of Buṭrus Ghālī, he deplored the fanatic hatred of the Copts to which this minister had fallen a victim (ibid. 101/7). He was also enthusiastic about the champions of intellectual and political freedom in Europe. Following the execution by the firing squad of the Spanish reformer and revolutionary G. Ferrer, after the *Semana trágica* of Barcelona, in

July 1909, he raised a fiery protest in the name of humanity (see *al-Ṣaḥāʾif al-sūd* 52/6, *al-Kuttāb al-thalātha* 50/4).

At the beginning of the war he complained about the imminent decline in culture because of the return of the heathen wars, something for which he wants to make the supposedly trigger-happy German Emperor responsible (49). Yet, he also celebrates Tommy Atkins as the friend and defender of freedom (44), however strange that may seem from the mouth of an Egyptian. And when General Maxwell takes his leave from Cairo in 1916 he pays him homage (84). But, otherwise, he is careful to avoid taking a stand on the British occupation. Nonetheless, it is only natural that he had to pay homage to the great Shakespeare once, comparing him to Imraʾ al-Qays and Homer.

His last major piece was a monologue of Cleopatra in her final hour, which he wrote in 1920 and which was probably inspired by the play by Shawqī. It is uncertain whether he had the intention of trying to outdo the latter and that it was only due to an increasing loss of strength that he was unable to do so.
55 But whatever the case, in this piece, which was only | followed by a few shorter poems from his sickbed, his fatigue is already present in his language.

Shortly before his death, he started to write a novel, *Dikrān wa-Rāʾif*, of which only the first two parts were published (C. n.d., 96 pp.). The work was going to draw an image of the youth of Turkey under the dictatorship of ʿAbd al-Ḥamīd. The heroes are two young physicians who had just obtained their degree, one an Armenian by the name of Dikrān (the east-Armenian form of Tigran), the other the son of a Turkish schoolteacher who had worked with the leaders of the Young Turks and who dies during an attempt to liberate Murād from the Čiraghān palace in which he had been kept prisoner. Drawn against his will into a conspirary in which Rāʾif takes part, the emotional hardship of the young Armenian is further aggravated by his love for one of his cousins, which in his religion is regarded as a form of incest. The work being unfinished, it is difficult to say how the author would have brought this first attempt at narrative prose to an end. Stylistically, the part that was published shows all the qualities of his art. A fragment of it, *Nashīd al-bulbul* (42/7), was also published in *al-Kuttāb al-thalātha* 60/4.

Mansī (loc. cit.) praised the style of his prose extensively, stating that some of his countrymen regarded the strict manner in which he develops his thought as something almost European. There can be no doubt that he was familiar with European prose. After all, towards the end of his life he had worked on a translation of P. Bourget's *Divorce*. Even though real Europeanisms such as 'firmament' (*Dīw.* $61_{,9}$) or 'house of cards' (*al-Kuttāb al-thalātha* $16_{,10}$) are relatively rare in his works, his syntax sometimes leaves the impression of being a

translation from a European language, | though far from clumsy.[61] The original- 56
ity and boldness of his imagery are only rarely grotesque[62] because his similes are mostly taken from real life and very accessible to the reader.

In her *Ṣaḥā'if*, 88ff, Mayy compared the poet to P. Loti, and in this al-ʿAqqād (*Muṭālaʿāt* 220) agrees with her because their fortunes explain their shared pessimism. But when he feels obliged to disagree with her, denying that Yegen had a great sense of humour, he merely confirms the well-known insight that nothing is more difficult than appreciating the sense of humour of a stranger.

Ismāʿīl ʿAbd al-Ḥamīd, *al-Udabā' al-khams*, Cairo n.d. Aḥmad Abu 'l-Khidr Mansī, *Walī al-Dīn Yegen kātiban wa-shāʿiran*, C. 1921/1339. E.F. Bustānī, *al-Rawā'iʿ*, no. 23, Beirut 1929, Mayy, *al-Ṣaḥā'if* 88/93. 1. *al-Tajārib*, Alexandria 1913.—2. *Khawāṭir Niyāzī*, C. 1327.—3. *al-Ṣaḥā'if al-sūd*, essays from *al-Muqtaṭaf*, C. 1910.—4. *Fukāhat dhawi 'l-fiṭan, Sharḥ sīniyyat Abi 'l-Ḥasan* (Zurayq, see I, 133 ad 82), C. 1311.—5. *al-Maʿlūm wal-majhūl*, 2 vols, C. 1327/8.—6. *Dīwān*, C. 1343/1924 (on p. 43 reference is made to *Mi'at burhān wa-burhān ʿalā ẓulm ʿAbd al-Ḥamīd al-sulṭān*).—7. *Dikrān wa-Rā'if*, Cairo n.d., 97 pp.—8. Lecture held during the last annual meeting of the *Jamʿiyyat al-ittiḥād wal-iḥsān al-Sūrī* in Ṭanṭā on 11 February 1912, in *Fatāt al-sharq* VI, 211/4.—Samples of his prose in Ḥusayn Ḥasanayn, *al-Kuttāb al-thalātha*, Cairo n.d., pp. 1/64.

| 5 Ḥāfiẓ Ibrāhīm 57

Among Aḥmad Shawqī's contemporaries there was only one serious competitor for the favour of the Egyptian public: Muḥammad Ḥāfiẓ Ibrāhīm. People liked to call him Shāʿir al-Nīl, this in distinction from Shawqī, who was called Amīr al-shuʿarā'. But where Shawqī had been a spoiled kid from the day that he was born, Muḥammad Ḥāfiẓ Ibrāhīm had to struggle his whole life and never had the leisure to really enjoy his fame.

Ḥāfiẓ Ibrāhīm was born in Dhahabiyya near Dayrūṭ in 1871. Having lost his parents at an early age, he started as an apprentice lawyer in Tanta in 1305/1887

61 "A vast, endless plain, flat like the palm of your hand, with tree nor shrub, water nor pasture, stone nor pebble, hill nor valley, a lake of sand whose surface had been caressed by the winds, until these had polished it to near perfection, where all traces of animal presence, bird or beast, had completely vanished; and in the middle of this plain stood Rā'if, all alone and without a guide," *Dikrān wa-Rā'if* 75.

62 "He wore a turban like Saturn, a cane in his hand, like the red of dawn (*ʿamūd al-ṣubḥ*), and was dressed in a green heavy jacket, as if bedecked by spring; on his feet, he wore two yellow shoes like brass ships and around his neck, a rosary that was even longer than Ibn Mālik's *Alfiyya*," *al-Maʿlūm wal-majhūl*, I, 72 (Mansī 19). A similar kind of descripton of a shaykh is found in *al-Ṣaḥā'if al-sūd* 46/7.

(see ʿAbd al-Wahhāb al-Najjār in *Apollo* I, 1322/7). From there, he went to the military academy in Cairo. In 1309/1891 he was sent to the Sudan, at the rank of lieutenant. After a considerable period in service he became involved in a conspiracy against the supreme command of the British armed forces. The khedive overturned the conviction of Ibrāhīm and his friends and called them back to Egypt. In Cairo, Ibrāhīm joined Muḥammad ʿAbduh, whom he had already congratulated once with a poem on the occasion of his appointment as a *muftī* (*Dīw.* I, 34). He attended his lectures and accompanied him on various inspection tours through the provinces. In 1911, he was appointed as a librarian at the National Library and on 4 February 1932 he retired. He died on 21 July that very same year. Despite his great social gifts and an ever-growing recognition of his art, the last years of his life were overshadowed by hypochondria, his feeble constitution adding countless imaginary afflictions to the ones that he already had.[63]

Even though his education was defective, his keen mind and extraordi-
58 nary memory—an inexhaustible source of anecdotes | that won him many friends—gave him a perfect command of the classical language. He had started writing poetry while still an officer in the Sudan, taking Sāmī al-Bārūdī as his example. Back in Cairo, he started reading the *Kitāb al-aghānī* and ancient *dīwān*s, of which he liked those by Abū Tammām and Muslim b. al-Walīd the most. Like Shawqī, he is said to have found much inspiration in al-Marṣafī's *Wasīla* (*Dhikrā* 102). But where Shawqī came more and more under the spell of the ancients over the course of his life, Ḥāfiẓ Ibrāhīm was able to gradually liberate himself from his models as his personality matured.[64]

When he copies a verse straight out of al-Farazdaq (*Dīw.*^{1}, II, 75 penult. ff, ^{2}I 225), this has of course a literary purpose. On other occasions, too, he borrows, for example when, in a somber mood in the Sudan, he writes an adaptation of the famous verse by al-Maʿarrī in which he reproaches his father for having brought him into this world (*Dīw.*^{1} I, 92,$_2$ ^{2}II 121,$_{10}$). Muṣṭafā Ṣādiq al-Rāfiʿī (*Dhikrā* 110ff) examined a whole series of verses by al-Mutanabbī and Ibn Nubāta that Ḥāfiẓ surpassed by his imitations, while in one case he fell short of Ibn al-Jahm (ibid. 112), while Ṭāhā Ḥusayn (ibid. 122) was right to find his imitation of a *dāliyya* by al-Maʿarrī not altogether successful. Aḥmad Muḥarram

63 On the occasion of one of his laments, Aḥmad Shādī consoles him admiringly in *al-Shafaq al-bākī* 906/8.

64 Characteristic of him is the fact that he left no more than three out of four volumes of the Būlāq edition of the *Aghānī*, one or two works on the French language, and a whole collection of Arabic translations of modern novels, of which he would put one in his pocket each time that he went out so that he could read it on his way (*Apollo* 1312).

wrote a sharp review of many of his other borrowings from ancient poets in *Apollo* 1279/96.

The first part of his *Dīwān*, which was published for the first time in 1319/1901, is, for the most part, dominated by imitations.[65] | While still in 59
the Sudan he addressed a poem to Muḥammad Bek Bayram, bemoaning the difficult situation that was awaiting him after his discharge from active service ([1]I, 50/63, [2]I, 162/6). From the Sudan he tried to get in touch with Muḥammad ʿAbduh by sending him a letter in ornate, rhyming prose ([1]I, 102/11, [2]I). At this same time he also tried his hand at *madīḥ*, which he believed was the only artform that could bring him personal gain. Thus, he congratulated the adjutant general of Khedive ʿAbd al-Ḥalīm Pāshā ʿĀṣim on his appointment as Amīr al-ḥajj in 1313/1895 ([1]I, 67/9, [2]I, 3/4). In Cairo, he dedicated a poem on the occasion of ʿĪd al-fiṭr 1900 to Khedive ʿAbbās II and another one on the occasion of his ascent to the throne in 1901. In 1908 he competed against Ismāʿīl Ṣabrī and Aḥmad Shawqī with a *qaṣīda* on the occasion of ʿĪd al-aḍḥā (*Fatāt al-sharq* II, 179/85; cf. the detailed critique of all three poems by E. Marcus, ibid. 329/37, 367/84). But in those days he had not yet succeeded in getting near the court. Perhaps it really was Shawqī's influence that stood in the way of his recognition by the khedive, as claimed by Aḥmad Muḥammad in *Apollo* I, 1268. But later, too, at the height of his fame, he never was a poet of the court, even if he could not help himself in joining the throngs of well-wishers on celebratory occasions. His poem in praise of the venerated master of his art Sāmī al-Bārūdī ([1]I, 40/9, [2]I, 7/11) was apparently much appreciated by the latter, who wrote a *taqrīẓ* on the former's first *dīwān* that bestows almost too much honour on the emerging poet.[66]

| In the first volume of the *Dīwān*, one can already find the beginnings of his 60
endeavours in a domain that the poet and his public would later call his own: his critique of the social situation of his country—which is why he was also called *al-Shāʿir al-ijtimāʿī*. Nevertheless, it is also true that his opinions and demands hardly ever rose above the level of an appeal to brotherly love, such as when he, after the fire of Mayyit Ghamr, sent out a cry for help to the wealthy (*Dīw.*[1] II, 33/6, [2]I, 250/2), or when he, on 8 April 1910, addressed a poetical greeting

65 Our understanding of his development is complicated by the fact that many of his poems have been lost or only fragmentarily preserved, such as his *marthiya* on the daughter of al-Bārūdī, *Dīw.*[1] II, 59/64, [2]II 246/7.

66 "No one can compare himself to Ḥāfiẓ but for his namesake from Shīrāz" (*Dīw.*I, 186, 1). But it is true that criticisms have not been lacking either; in *Shiʿr al-wijdān* 23, Abū Shādī defends him in particular against the accusation that his poems are just 'rhymed editorials'.

to the attendees of a meeting of the Society for the Fostering of Children in Distress (*Dīw.* [1]III, 66/73, [2]I, 275/9). On the issue of women's rights he does not take a definitive position either, even though, in a *qaṣīda* written on the occasion of the opening of a girls' school in Port Said on 1 February 1911 ([1]III, 73/85, [2]I, 279/83), he voices an eloquent defence of the intellectual liberation of the female sex. And earlier, too, in the first volume of the *Dīwān* ([1]I, 85/90 missing in the second edition), he strongly deplores the initial lack of success of Qāsim Amīn's efforts to liberate the women of Egypt from the bondage of the veil.

But the political problems of his country are even more important to him than all its social issues. Most important of these is the humiliating feeling of being at the mercy of a foreign power. Of course, one may not expect a poet to come up with a clear political vision, but the heartfelt poems with which he accompanied the events of his time did probably more to awaken and sustain the national feelings of the Egyptians than Shawqī's courteous declarations. In his first *Dīwān* ([1]I 72/9, [2]II 116/91) he raises a loud complaint against the
61 Ottomans |—brothers in the faith of the Egyptians—for leaving Egypt in the hands of strangers with another faith, other morals, and another kind of education. In his poem 'Two Banners on the Ruins of Khartoum' (I, 158/160, [2]II, 5/6) he talks as if victory lies just around the corner only to see it escape him again. "Just wait and see, when two banners fly. Egypt is not like the Sudan, a morsel for the hungry; it forfeited its freedom but momentarily. Leave me alone with your nonsense. Despite all the intrigues, I am the prophet[67] of my times. I see how the lord and the viscount compete in Egypt, in the Sudan, and in India especially. I believe that the day of their ousting and the day of resurrection will coincide, which is the day when the waters of the oceans will recede, the day when the animals of the Zodiac will incline themselves before the happenings of the End of Time, the day when the time of the bearer of the lance is turned around and when the sword will rule supreme yet again. On that day, remember that the time of the ousting has come and rouse the sleepers of the pyramids!" But this desperate mood of the days that he was an officer in godforsaken Sudan changes to hope of a better future when finds himself in Cairo once more, sharing the lives of his own people. Just like Shawqī, he first sets his hope on the Turks, addressing several congratulatory poems to ʿAbd al-Ḥamīd on the occasion of his ascension to the throne (*Dīw.* [1]II, 65/8, [2]I, 15/8). As he himself stated (*Dhikrā* 32/3), his patrons in Istanbul had recommended him to the sultan, suggesting that he should make him his poet
62 for the Arabic-speaking world, | which was then prevented from happening by

---

67 He calls himself Shiqq here, just as he introduces Satīḥ in *Layālī Satīḥ*, after the two *kāhin*s of pre-Islamic times (Ibn Hishām, *Sīra* I, 9ff, Bahāʾ al-Dīn Zuhayr, ed. Palmer $38_{,4}$, $48_{,11}$).

al-Muwayliḥī's machinations.[68] But he had enough class to keep on venerating the sultan even after the latter had been toppled ([1]III, 30/7, [2]II, 43/7). After all, with his construction of the Hijaz railway, ʿAbd al-Ḥamīd had secured the eternal gratitude of all the Muslim peoples (cf. *Dhikrā* 92/3), which is also why Ḥāfiẓ reminds him consolingly of the much harsher fates of Napoleon and of his own predecessor, Bāyezīd. All this does not stand in the way of him paying homage, in this very same poem, to ʿAbd al-Ḥamīd's successor Meḥmed V, of intoning a song of freedom in celebration of the Ottoman constitution (ibid. [1]37/44, [2]II, 48/53), or of honoring Enver and Niyāzī in a poem for the New Year ([1]III, 53, 7/10, [2]II, $38_{,3}/39_{,1}$). In the same way in which he had lamented the shelling of Beirut by the Italian fleet in 1912 (*Dīw.* [1]III, 161/70, [2]II, 69/76, in the form of a conversation between Laylā, a wounded person, a doctor, and an Arab), he now greets the restructured Ottoman fleet as the carrier of all his hopes for the Muslims and Islam. Like so many of his contemporaries, he believes that the imminent rise of the Orient is confirmed by the happenings in Japan. In a famous poem ([1]II, 1/6, [2]II, 7/10) he praises Japanese women as an example for their oriental sisters. And in a poem on the occasion of the New Year, addressed to the khedive and dated 19 March 1904 ([1]II, $105_{,1}$, [2]I, $33_{,2}$), he voices the hope that Egypt may soon follow Japan in its course to freedom, as had earlier been done by the Turks ([1]III, $24_{,8}$, [2]I, $46_{,2}$). He wishes for the Turkish fleet to have commanders just as successful as Togo and Oyama ([1]III, $91_{,4}$, [2]II, 65 bottom). But when he addresses a poem to Edward VII on the occasion of his ascension to the throne, | still full of reverence for Britain's might, he 63
probably justified this by pointing at the festive mood throughout the empire, Egypt being no exception. It was not long, however, before the catastrophe of Dinshawāy and Lord Cromer's farewell to Egypt ([1]II, 36/9, 94/98, [2]II, 20/30) elicited from him expressions of noble indignation over the kind of serfdom which arrogant imperialists had imposed upon a civilised nation. Time and again, across religious boundaries separating Muslims from Copts, and across state frontiers, separating Egyptians from Syrians, he urges his people to unite (cf. *Dhikrā* 90). Just like Shawqī, Ḥāfiẓ, too, welcomed Roosevelt to Egyptian soil in hopes of his intercession (*Dīw.* [1]III, 91/3 missing in the second edition). It was only from the time that he started working in the khedival library that he almost entirely abandoned his earlier activism as a political poet.

68 From Istanbul, he had instigated Ḥāfiẓ to write a satire against the Sufis addressed to a certain Shakīb. Al-Muwayliḥī then showed this piece to the all-powerful imam of the court, Abu 'l-Hudā (cf. II, 868), who associated it with a friend of his by the same name. Feeling embarrassed on the latter's behalf, he withdrew his support for Ḥāfiẓ.

During the final years of his life he liked to use the *marthiya* in his comments on world affairs. Thus, he expressed the gratitude of the Egyptian nation towards all major figures of his time in obituaries that were full of admiration. From this first period there is also a strophic *marthiya* on Queen Victoria (*Dīw.* ^{1}I, 155/6, ^{2}II, 136/8). These obituaries became a part of his nature, so much so that he even wrote a lament on his own death (*Dhikrā* 270, *Dīw.* ^{2}II, 83/5).

Apart from two poems in homage of Ḥusayn Kāmil on the occasion of his ascent to the throne (*Dīw.* ^{2}I, 67ff), he seems to have fallen almost completely silent during the war, just like Shawqī. A hate-filled poem addressed to Emperor Wilhelm II (*Dhikrā* 303/4, *Dīw.*^{2} 83/5) is the only proof we have that he could
64 not altogether | avoid paying tribute to the wartime propaganda. Entirely objective, on the other hand, is a poem from July 1915 (*Dīw.* ^{2}II, 86) in which he condemns the abuse of science for the purposes of war.

After the war, by now at the height of his fame, he puts his art—not counting the many obituaries—into the service of public life with unchanged vigour. Thus, he salutes King Fu'ād on his ascent to the throne (*Dīw.* ^{2}I, 144/8) and his old rival Shawqī when the latter returns from exile (ibid. 98/102), and also at the festivities in his honour in 1927 (ibid. 119/130). He congratulates Saʿd Zaghlūl on surviving an attempt on his life (ibid. 109/14) while celebrating the sisterly bond between Egypt and Syria in his *qaṣīda* 'A Salute to Syria', recited at the American University of Beirut on 2 June 1929 (ibid. I, 133/40).[69]

He rarely used his talents to write lighter forms of poetry;[70] the fourth *bāb* of the first volume of his *Dīwān* contains only six winesongs (^{1}I, 12/43. ^{2}I, 239/45). All the same, Muḥammad Ḥusayn Haykal (*Dhikrā* 30) believes that he is the best of all Arab poets in this particular genre, outshining even Abū Nuwās. The love poetry that he wrote was usually in the format of the *nasīb* (cf. *Dhikrā* 114/5); indeed, in a poem addressed to the khedive on the occasion of New Year
65 (*Dīw.* ^{1}II, 102/3, ^{2}I, 31/2) | he even says that he does not at all like making his feelings public.[71]

---

69 Both his poems for the Welfare Federation of Aleppo, quoted in translation from the Federation's magazine by Kampffmeyer in *WI* XVff, are missing in the *Dīwān*.

70 At the recommendation of al-Muwayliḥī he wrote an elegant poem for a curtain belonging to Princess Nāzilī, daughter of Muṣṭafā Fāḍil (on this princess see Walī al-Dīn Yegen, *al-Maʿlūm wal-majhūl* I, 155/60), for which he was paid 100 Guineas. See al-Jiddāwī on Abū Shādī, *al-Shafaq al-bākī* 1278/9.

71 "When I concealed (my love), they called me a poet who denies its existence. But is there anyone other than me who really knows what passion is? If I wanted, I could dislocate the stars from their orbits and the skies in which they circle, I could lay out anew. I could set the night ablaze with just one passionate sigh, letting sparks fly. But instead, I hide my feelings; for passion is always censured, something for which one must always apologise.

The language of his *qaṣīda*s is noble and rhythmic.[72] He only rarely gave in to the temptation of impressing the reader with far-fetched embellishments. Yet in a poem on the occasion of the pilgrimage of the khedive (*Dīw.* [1]III, 80, [2]I, 50), he pushed his courtly flattery so far that his words sound almost blasphemous: "The Kaʿba of the world came to the Kaʿba of the right guidance; the majesty of power and religion emanates from them, both." Really tasteless things rarely flowed from his pen, like: "The Orient has become estranged from refined education and its ears reject poetry; like a dyspeptic, who tolerates no fat" ([1]II, 56, [2]II, $142_{,2}$); or: "The cooks of public opinion hand them over to time, to let them quietly ripen" ([1]III, $127_{,7,8}$, [2]II, $159_{,2}$). Much more rarely than among his contempories do images of the present find their way into his genuinely oriental mind, | as when he praises the Ottoman state, saying that any act of 66
injustice is felt by her as if it were an electric shock ([1]II, $62_{,3,4}$, [2]II, $17_{,10}$). He once assures his teacher and friend Muḥammad ʿAbduh that: "My heart is a magnetic needle (*tamaghṭasat*) in its love for you, swerving back to you when I am far from you" ([1]II, $74_{,5,6}$, [2]II, $21_{,7}$). In a poem on the occasion of New Year he expresses the hope that his people, still anaesthetised by the morphine of adversity, may finally come round ([1]III, $57_{,11}$, [2]II, $41_{,6}$). The miracle of the phonograph, which also gave rise to legal debates when it made its appearance in the Muslim world (cf. Snouck-Hurgronje, *Verspr. Schr.* II, 419ff), only elicits his opinion that the world will probably be swamped by more lies, like the newspapers already do well enough and whose news items often sound rather like April fool's jokes ([1]I, 161, [2]I, 207).

In the last years of his life, he tried to overcome the traditional form of the *qaṣīda* in two longer poems:

In his *ʿUmariyya*, he attempted to create a large work on an Islamic subject. It was presented for the first time when he recited it on 8 February 1918 during a meeting convened by the Ministry of Education, following which it was published at the expense of the former *mudīr* of al-Buḥayra, Muḥammad Maḥmūd

---

I find love and those who bemoan it ignominious, and my sense of dignity requires of me that I shun all ignominy. My love poems are of two kinds: one type I publish, while the other I keep in my heart. If it were not for a constant pressure by those who envy me, no one would ever have learned of the passion hidden within me, and never would I have touched a quill to pen down a complaint. But I do not parade my despair, do not increase my pain, when it is there." And, indeed, a love for women played no significant role in his life, on which see Zaynab Salīm, *Apollo* 1424/7; he was only married once, for four months, when he had just returned from the Sudan, see his *Dīwān*[1], *muqaddima* 15.

72 However, Abū Shādī, in *al-Shafaq al-bākī* $1236_{,12}$, is only prepared to concede that he has the gift of *bayān*, but not of *balāgha fanniyya*; see also Zakī Mubārak, *Ḥāfiẓ wal-lugha al-faṣīḥa*, in *Apollo* 1319/21.

Pāshā, and then once more under the title *ʿUmariyyat Ḥāfiẓ fī taʾrīkh sayyidinā ʿUmar wa-sīratihi wa-manāqibihi wa-akhlāqihi*, with a foreword by Muḥammad Bek al-Khuḍrī and a brief historical commentary by ʿAbd al-Ḥamīd Ḥamdī, Cairo (al-Maktaba al-Maḥmūdiyya al-Tijāriyya) n.d.; see also *Dīwān* ^{2}1 77/97.

Instead of being a coherent account of the life and deeds of this great caliph, it offers a series of isolated scenes which, together, give a fine illustration of the
67 personality of its hero. | As such, he starts with the murder of ʿUmar, because it was only through the loss of their leader that the followers of Islam understood his real importance. Then follow his conversion to Islam, followed by his homage to Abū Bakr as the first caliph and his personal relationship with individual Muslims of note. He lets the installation of the *shūrā* be followed by examples of ʿUmar's piety, charity, and asceticism, to conclude with his ordinance to take down the Shajarat Riḍwān when the people's veneration of it threatened to deteriorate into tree-worship. In a short *khātima*, he expresses the hope that this great man's example may inspire a generation in Islam which, by following him, will obliterate the blemishes of its past.

His 'Italian Journey,' which was only published in 1923 (*Dhikrā* 237/40, *Dīw.* ^{2}1, 226/33), strikes a completely different tone. It is from A to Z a product of his own fantasy, just as is his 'Tribute to Lebanon,' which al-Saḥartī, in *Adab al-ṭabīʿa* 91, calls a "classic." It begins with a very lively description of the terror of a voyage at sea (justly admired by al-Saḥartī, op. cit., 90), then praises the ship that takes him safely across it, to continue with a glorification of Italy as the country of beauty in nature and the arts, but also of awe-inspiring outbursts of nature's violence, shocking the world recently with the earthquakes that hit Reggio, Messina[73] and Calabria. It then draws a comparison between Egypt and Italy, which appears to conclude in favor of the latter.[74] It is probably

73 Shādī, *al-Shafaq al-bākī* 1212,$_{5}$, views his *qaṣīda* on the Messina earthquake of *Dīw.* ^{2}1 215/20 as among the best in modern poetry.

74 "Its sun is like a veiled virgin, an oriental woman then, who is kept inside the house; our sun, on the other hand, is like a virgin who does not want to hide herself; a European woman, therefore, who goes without the veil. Its climate fluctuates, although stability predominates; our climate is the most stable of all, but we can't stand it! In the arts, they possess the pith, we just the skin. Its laws know no *waqf*, which is why every square inch of land is cultivated there. There are no swamps there, and no walls that are at the point of toppling over, no deserted dwellings. Wherever you look, you see high buildings, gardens, and ponds. Their days are divided between serious work and pastimes, following a fixed order. Everyone starts working for his livelihood in the early hours of the morning, and then relaxes when the time of distraction has come. There, no morning-players of backgammon with a circle of betters around them, and no bums who, sound of limb, waste

typical of him and his cultural environment | that here, too, he gets no deeper 68
than the surface, making no effort to learn the true distinction separating East from West.

It was only late in life that Ḥāfiẓ became aqcuainted with European literature, at the time that his poetic style had already become fixed. He translated a scene from Shakespeare's *Macbeth* (*Dīw.* [1]II, 115/19, [2]I, 234/6) for example, paying homage to his memory in a *qaṣīda* dated 1 March 1916 and of which *Dhikrā* 287 only cites the beginning and the end (complete in *Dīw.* [2]I, 72/5). He also translated a poem by Rousseau ([1]I, 161, [2]II, 114). In November 1910, he dedicated
| a *marthiya* to Tolstoy on the occasion of his passing, just after the publication 69
another one by Aḥmad Shawqī ([1]III, 150/4, [2]II, 164/7); he asks the deceased writer to go and visit al-Maʿarrī in the Hereafter, who, like him, had preached a universal humanitarian religion and who will understand his life's sufferings. Even in the *qaṣīda* in praise of his favourite writer Victor Hugo (*Dīw.* [1]II, 30/3, [2]I, 38/40, from 1907), all he is able to say is that he reached the same level of fame as al-Maʿarrī. Zakī Mubārak (*al-Muwāzana*, 58) is right when he says that Ḥāfiẓ's attempt to describe Victor Hugo is lacklustre.

Ḥāfiẓ also translated Victor Hugo's *Les miserables*, giving it the title *al-Bu'asā'*. No matter whether one agrees with Ṭāhā Ḥusayn or not when he says that the theme was not well-chosen, one will at least share his opinion that the translation itself is a failure, as is also the view of al-ʿAqqād (*al-Fuṣūl*,

their time in the coffee house, one time in the morning and another time at night. No clouded sky will reduce their joy in life. They don't care about nature, whether it is merciful or whether it commits acts of violence against them, whether storms are raging or a southerly breeze blows. They are prepared for natural disasters and they even cultivate the rocky soil high up in the mountains, while in our country, even the fertile lowlands lay barren. We are trapped in the past, while they march to perfection, month after month. Along the Nile, nothing has changed in the education of girls since Pharaonic times. People like cleanliness, whether they be rich or poor. When I walk around the streets in the daytime, I believe I am walking on mirrors. People are very attached to tidiness, a quality which I believe is widespread. When their joy in life degenerates, they are unstoppable. If you ask me, I would say: as a people, they are free, but as individuals, bound. This is my opinion, and if no-one should agree with me, then it is the harmless talk of a poet. In the mountains of Tirol the summers are beautiful; and when the summer moves out, it is cold. This reminds me of something said by a Ṭāriqī Arab in Schlier (?): "In this country one may neglect one's prayers; instead, wine is allowed us here. The inside of hell shows us more clemency than Schlier does; what is hell to us anyway?" I have tried life, in the East and in the West. In life, nothing is easy. If one persists in it, weariness is inevitable, but saying goodbye is very difficult."

58/70). While in his poetry Ḥāfiẓ always escaped the danger of turning it into a showpiece for his command of Arabic (a trap into which Shawqī fell so many times), this translation is dressed in an impossible number of outlandish expressions. At the same time, he put in a tremendous effort to produce it, the more so since he was a very slow worker (*Dhikrā* 105). This same overworked style is also found in his adaptation of a French work on economy, *al-Iqtiṣād*, which he produced together with Khalīl Maṭrān, as well as in his *Layālī Satīḥ*, C. 1324/1906. In this work,[75] he used the *maqāma* for his conversations with other 'sons of the Nile' and with Satīḥ, the pre-Islamic sage (see above p. 61n),
70 as a way to criticise the social and intellectual conditions in Egypt and | to do some suggestions for their improvement.[76] According to him, the country's major problem lies in the poor education of its youth, whose only ambition is to land a job as a civil servant. One could redress this situation by establishing modern universities, while, thusfar, the newspapers had failed completely in their task of educating the people. Ḥāfiẓ was right to point out that the main obstacle in the educational benefit of the literary language is its impenetrability to the common man. Yet he did not take a clear position on reforms either, which seem impossible if one is not prepared to listen to the proposals of W. Spitta and Willmore.

Muḥammad Kurd ʿAlī, *Ḥayāt Ḥāfiẓ Ibrāhīm*, *RAAD* XIII, 744/9, idem in *al-Siyāsa* of 20 and 27 October 1923, *al-Hilāl* 40/1 (October-November 1932), Aḥmad b. Muḥammad ʿAysh, *Sīrat Ḥāfiẓ*, *Apollo* 1382/94, ʿAbd al-Wahhāb b. al-Najjār, *Ṣafḥa majhūla min ḥayāt Ḥāfiẓ* ibid. 1322/7. Ḥasan al-Ḥātim, *Ḥāfiẓ Ibrāhīm bayna ẓarfihi wa-mujūnihi*, ibid. 1315/9. Ḥasan al-Jiddāwī, reminiscences about him (especially his relation with Shawqī), ibid. I, 74/7. *Marthiya* by Shawqī, ibid. I, 165/7, by Aḥmad Zakī Abū Shādī in *al-Shuʿla* 126/8 (*Apollo* I, 32/3), commemoration of the first anniversary of his death in *Aṭyāf al-rabīʿ* 69/70, a *qaṣīda* in his honour on the occasion of his visit to a therapeutic institution in Port Saʿīd on 27 July 1926 in *al-Shafaq al-bākī* 930/7. A tribute to him in the Academy of Damascus, *RAAD* IX (1929), 363/74. A *marthiya* by ʿAbbās Maḥmūd al-ʿAqqād in *Waḥy al-arbaʿīn* 171/2.—Muḥammad b. ʿAbd al-Wahhāb in *Shuʿarāʾuna ʾl-ḍubbāṭ*, C. 1935.—A comparative appreciation of Ḥāfiẓ and Shawqī in Abū Shādī, *Qaṭra min al-yarāʿ* I, 256, exalted eulogy, ibid. 259/61.—Ḥasan al-Sandūbī, *al-Shuʿarāʾ al-thalātha Shawqī, Maṭrān, Ḥāfiẓ* (only samples), C. 1341.—Ṭāhā Ḥusayn, *Ḥāfiẓ wa-Shawqī*, C. 1933.—Aḥmad ʿUbayd,

75 In which he tried to imitate Muḥammad al-Muwayliḥī's *ʿĪsā b. Hishām*; see H.A.R. Gibb, *BSOS* VII, 6.

76 In *al-Shafaq al-bākī* 1236,$_{10}$, Abū Shādī praises his sense of humour as a major part of his criticisms.

Mashāhīr shuʿarāʾ al-ʿaṣr, I, *Shuʿarāʾ Miṣr*, C. 1922, 181/216. *Dhikra ʾl-Shāʿirayn Shāʿir al-Nīl wa-Amīr al-shuʿarāʾ dirāsāt wa-marāthin wa-muqāranāt*, Damascus 1351.—Khalīl Maṭrān in al-Manfalūṭī, *Mukhtārāt* 66/7. Ch.C. Adams, *Islam and Modernism*, London 1933, p. 216.—al-ʿAqqād, *Shuʿarāʾ Miṣr*, 8/20.—al-Ustadh al-Maghribī, *Ḥāfiẓ Ibrāhīm wal-lugha al-ʿArabiyya*, RAAD XIII, 750/9.—*Dīwān Ḥāfiẓ li-nāẓim ʿiqdihi Ḥāfiẓ Ibrāhīm | wa-shāriḥihi Muḥammad Ibrāhīm Hilāl*, in 71
3 vols, first printing C. 1901, second printing C. 1922 (Maṭbaʿat al-Maʿāhid, used here). *Dīwān Ḥāfiẓ Ibrāhīm, ḍabaṭahu wa-ṣaḥḥaḥahu wa-sharaḥahu wa-rattabahu Aḥmad Amīn, Aḥmad al-Zayn, Ibrāhīm al-Abyārī*, C. 1937, Maṭbaʿat Dār al-Kutub al-Miṣriyya (referred to here as *Dīw.*[2], including the many poems that were added since and information on when these were written).—*al-Buʾasāʾ muʿarrab ʿan V. Hugo*, C. 1903 and n.d. (critique by al-Aqqād, *Fuṣūl*, 58/70).—*al-Tarbiya al-awwaliyya aw kutayyib fi ʾl-tarbiya al-ūlā*, 2 vols, C. 1300/1, *Layalī Saṭīh* C. 1324/1906.—*al-Mūjiz fī ʿilm al-iqtiṣād taʾlīf li-Roi Beaulieu, ʿarrabahu bi-muʿāwanat Khalīl Bek Maṭrān*, 5 vols, C. 1913.

6 Muṣṭafā Ṣādiq al-Rāfiʿī

Muṣṭafā Ṣādiq al-Rāfiʿī (d. 1937)[77] was one of the poets who were close to the circle of Sāmī al-Bārūdī. When the first volume of his *Dīwān* was published in 1320/1902, the ageing poet accompanied it with a *taqrīẓ* in which he celebrated its merits exuberantly, comparing him to Kaʿb and Zuhayr; indeed, in the *nasīb* he ranked him even higher than Jamīl. And the sharp critic Muṣṭafā Luṭfī al-Manfalūṭī, too, welcomed him as the new hope for Arabic poetry, which had become completely ossified. Al-Bārūdī wrote a short *taqrīẓ* to the second volume, too. When the third volume was published in 1333, al-Bārūdī's place was taken by Ḥāfiẓ Ibrāhīm with a *taqrīẓ* that, later, he also included in his own *Dīwān* ([1]II, 123/4), which, additionally, contains a *marthiya* for al-Bārūdī (144/5), who had meanwhile died.

The preface he wrote to the second volume of his *Dīwān* is typical of al-Rāfiʿī's attitude towards art. Once again, he examines the difference between intentional plagiarism and accidental similarities of ideas, a subject that had often been debated among the ancient *udabāʾ*. The third volume, too, is preceded by theoretical reflections on poetry, reflections which he resumes one more time in Rufaʿīl Buṭṭī's *Siḥr al-shiʿr* I (C. 1922/1342), 199/208. He seems entirely | 72
under the spell of the classical tradition. His models are mainly: al-Mutanabbī, whose verses he imitated in II, 77 and II, 91; Ibn Zaydūn, in whose style he composed a *qaṣīda* in I, 113/5; Abu ʾl-Fatḥ al-Bustī, of whom he adopts a verse as *taḍmīm* in I, 17,4; and the ancients, such as al-Nābigha in I, 50, and ʿAntara, adapting two unauthentic verses in III, 85. He also cultivated the newer form of

77 *Hilāl* 15, 1906/7, a portrait in *Apollo* I, 970, Rufaʾīl Buṭṭī, *Siḥr al-shiʿr* I, 206.

the *muwashshaḥ* now and then (II, 87, III, 109, 120/1, for Sulaymān al-Bustānī, the translator of the *Iliad*, 123/5 in a wedding song). He tried to give the quatrain a new, popular form in a song called 'The farmer's morning,' in which the rhyme in the second hemistich holds the song together. He dedicated this song to the publisher of *al-Muqtaṭaf*, Ṣarrūf. He wanted to praise all Egypt's social classes in this manner, but apparently he never got round to publishing the small *dīwān* that he had intended for this purpose. With a play on proverbs (III, 136/7) he tried to offer a new form of the *badīʿ*.

His earliest poems had their origin at school, the environment in which he worked. They are exalted poems on the caliphs ʿUmar (I, 14) and al-Maʾmūn (I, 15), on the fatherland and on educational ideals, including declamations for students at school functions, all of which are written as if they were exercises in style (I, 24ff, II, 28ff). He had a special penchant for the love song, the *ghazal*, and the *nasīb* (I *Bāb* IV, 67/117, II *Bāb* V, 76/119, III *Bāb* IV, 83/114), genres in which he wrote many charming though not very original poems, especially in his early adolescence, such as one about meeting one's lover in a streetcar (I, 115/7).

Like all his contemporaries, he assiduously cultivated the oldest genre of Arabic poetry, the panegyric. In 1901 and 1903 he paid homage to Sultan ʿAbd al-Ḥamīd on the occasion of his ascent to the throne (I, 33, II, 69/71), as well as to the ruler of his own country, the khedive (II, 77ff). And to his master Sāmī al-Bārūdī (I, 40) and the great theologian Muḥammad ʿAbduh (I, 38, on the occasion of ʿĪd al-fiṭr 1321, II, 72), too, he paid his respects. In the third volume (145), he mourns simultanuously the deaths of ʿAbduh and of his successor as Grand Mufti, his uncle ʿAbd al-Qādir al-Rāfiʿī, who died soon after him. And on family occasions, too, his inspiration does not falter, such as the birthday
73 of his little daughter Wahība (III, 50f) and also those of his friends | (II, 119,
113/4). Yet, mostly, he has higher things in mind. Like Ḥāfiẓ Ibrāhīm, he wants to serve his people with his art. Accordingly, he marked national disasters with his songs, like the fire of Mayt Ghamra (I, 63/6) and the Dinshawāy incident (III, 20, 133). Often he admonishes, putting his finger on social problems in the lives of Egyptians.

Especially important to him is the issue of women's rights. The second *bāb* of volume III is entirely dedicated to *Nisāʾiyyāt*. He opens with a *qaṣīda* on Napoleon's repudiation of Josephine, which is preceded by an historical introduction. Although he would like to see the women of Egypt rise above the intellectual feebleness of their mothers, he also warns them against an exaggerated imitation of the faithless women of Europe (III, 51/2) and of the damages of a superficial "Frankisation" (III, 82). He is all the more zealous in his struggle against superstition, such as the cult of the *zār* and the belief in magic, which were particularly widespread among women and which derived from negro culture.

He does not hide his admiration for the technical achievements of Europe. For instance, he praises electrical lighting (II, 78), describing the deep impression it left on children and peasants in a manner just as vivid as Manṣūr Fahmī in one of his essays. In an essay from his *Malakat al-inshāʾ* (III, 80/2), he takes up the very same theme. It goes without saying that, in all this, he does not forget the cinema or the phonograph (III, 117, 2); he even extols the railways several times.

He was also delighted by the dances of Europe, of which he gives a description (II, 63/5) whose bouncing rhythm can compete with one of Aḥmad Shawqī's songs (*Dīw*. II, 8ff). While he sang the praises of wine with great enthusiasm in his younger years (I, 54/8, II, 58/63), as he has got older, he warned against the dangers of alcohol. Throughout his country he sees its ravages, making him wish that he had the riches of Rockefeller to redress this situation (III, 25/7). His bitter feelings over the social situation in Egypt, feelings which he laid down in a long *qaṣīda* in 1905, are only exacerbated at the sight of the many European tourists (III, 20/2): "We are a people that have always lived under some oppressor, in some state of humiliation" (23,2). Yet his people share this weakness with all the peoples of the East: "Because of the weakness of the East, | for us, every kind of human justice was suspended. Brahma, 74
there is something which they have wrongly attributed to you (the creation of the caste system), but it actually applies to every oriental. My people is so despised among its fellow humans, that one would hardly consider it as human" (III, 30). Like all his contemporaries, he tries to raise the image that his countrymen have of themselves by citing the example of Japan. An original marriage notice of a Japanese lady gives him the opportunity to glorify the power of Japan, which has just shown itself in an agreement signed with the UK (125/7). He then praises it outright for its conduct in the battle of Port Arthur and after its peace agreement with Russia (III, 128f), without, however, withholding his compassion from the ailing Russian Tsar (ibid. 130). Many of his poems are in the style of the *waṣf*, giving him the opportunity to set off the fireworks of his rhetoric. Together with a description of the sea and the sky (II, 66), he shares a piece of prose about a Sunday at the beach in Alexandria with his readers, reproduced from his *Malakat al-inshāʾ*.

Al-Rāfiʿī also has a high opinion of his own abilities: "The thoughts that dwell in my heart enlighten even the remotest spot with their rays; the world feeds on the splendour of their wisdom, in the same way in which the flowers of the earth partake of beauty through the sun's rays, through the wind, and through rain. In my time, I have revealed secrets using a type of description that people

call poetry. In it, words become concrete, ideas consolidated; one in the form of a pearl, another as something magic. When they consider a half-verse, half the revelation will enter their hearts. In its deceptiveness, this magic will make them wonder whether it is drops on flowers or lines of text that they are looking at. My quill is, so to speak, made out of x-rays; it can see what is hidden behind the ink" etc. (III, 76/7). When asked by a newspaper, he characterised himself some months before his death as *Imām al-bayān wa-Ḥujjat al-ʿArab wa-Mālik nāṣiyat al-balāghah*. He always liked bizarre images such as these. For example, he can look at the morning as a long, flowing dress, attached to the skies with two stars. "Withered are the flowers on the starry meadow, the morning bird has fled its cage. Mounting the skies, it flaps its wings, the horizon to its eyes being where all ends. There, the sun built its nest, like thoughts that
75 nest in the heart" (III, 109/10). "Her sigh | was just that spark of passion, which set off the bomb of love in my heart" (ibid. 112, 1), etc. He was not lacking in recognition on the part of his contemporaries. In *Waḥy al-qalam*, Muḥammad ʿAbduh expressed the wish that his poetry could render the same kind of service to Islam as did Ḥassān to the Prophet. And in a *taqrīẓ* to *Iʿjāz al-Qurʾān*, Saʿd Zaghlūl compared his language to the language of revelation. Abū Shādī, on the other hand, views him as one of the major representatives of modern writing (ad *Mahā* 79, bottom), while al-Manfalūṭī praised him extensively in his *Mukhtārāt* 67/104.

A second *dīwān*, entitled *al-Naẓarāt*, was published in Cairo in 1908. A sample of it ('The beauties and poetry') was published in *Fatāt al-sharq* II (1908), 353/4. He also published individual *qaṣīda*s in *Fatāt al-sharq* VI (1912), 209/11, VII (1913), 128/30 ('The beauty and the mirror'), ibid. 351 (dedicated to the publisher) and in *Apollo* I (1932), 239 (*Ila 'l-ḥazīn*), *Waṣf al-mayyit* ibid. 661, *Ilā* … ibid, 823. Competing with Shawqī, he wrote *al-Nashīd al-Miṣrī al-waṭanī* in 1339/1920.

In the second half of his life, he turned more and more to prosewriting. Nevertheless, in *Ḥadīth al-qamar* (1330/1911), we still find poems between pieces of prose containing descriptions of nature that often degenerate into hollow rhetoric. His *Kitāb al-masākīn* (1335/1917) was meant to be the oriental counterpart to Victor Hugo's *Les misérables*. His *Rasāʾil al-aḥzān fī falsafat al-jiwāz wal-ḥubb* (1343/1924, with *al-Saḥāb al-aḥmar* as a *takmila*), on the other hand, are entirely dedicated to the question of women's rights. He also took part in the heated discussions around Ṭāhā Ḥusayn's book on classical Arabic poetry. In his *Taḥta rāyat al-Qurʾān, al-maʿrika bayna 'l-qadīm wal-jadīd* (1926) he stands up for his classical ideals. His *Taʾrīkh ādāb al-ʿArab* (cf. I, 12) was written with the same purpose in mind. In his *Iʿjāz al-Qurʾān wal-balāgha al-nabawiyya* (3rd ed. 1928), he brings all the skills of the ancient philologists to bear. In his

ʿAla ʾl-saffūd, naqd taḥlīlī, he attacks modern poetry in an extremely rude and coarse manner. He does not shrink from calling Salāmā Mūsā an infidel and a traitor of his nation, while he insults al-ʿAqqād by calling him a "poet from the sewers" (*shāʿir al-marāḥīḍ*). His own poetical ideals he developed once again in two essays: *Sharḥ al-nubūgh fi ʾl-adab* in *Muqtaṭaf* of January 1933, and *Naqd al-shiʿr wa-falsafatuhu* in *Apollo* I, 970/81. In the end, | he wrote mainly 76
on politics. Together with Muḥammad ʿAbdallāh ʿInān (see T. Khemiri and G. Kampffmeier, *Leaders* 22f), he published *al-Siyāsa al-Miṣriyya wal-inqilāb al-dustūrī* n.d. *Waḥy al-qalam* I, II, C. 1936 (Lajnat al-taʾlīf wal-tarjama wal-nashr; with a third volume announced as forthcoming), is a collection of essays that were previously published in *al-Risāla* magazine. The first volume deals mainly with the issue of women's rights, on which he takes a conservative stance. He dressed his defence of ancient Islamic ideals in the garb of scenes from the lives of traditionists and Sufis, something in which his great familiarity with theological literature stands out prominently. In the *qaṣīda*s of the devil and the angel, he juxtaposes (I, 279/91) a description of what goes on at the beaches of Alexandria (*luḥūm al-baḥr*) with an admonition (*iḥdhārī*) of the women of Egypt. The second volume is dominated by discussions of daily politics. In an appeal to the Egyptian youth, and in another one to all Muslims to take part in the struggle of the Arabs in Palestine, he defended his nationalist ideals with passionate rhetoric. In his sketches from the life of a pasha and his secretary he depicts the situation of the country under the British occupation with scathing irony. His prose is extremely polished and avoids any slavish imitation of the classics. He therefore rarely needs to explain outlandish expressions. It is also only in very exceptional cases that he takes the liberty of introducing neologisms for new or modern things (e.g. *dakhīna* for cigarette, I, 297, n. 1, *karkara* for the waterpipe, II, 233, n. 1). See also the obituary by Asʿad Ḥusnī in *al-Ḥadīth*, June 1927, 493/98. Samples in Ismāʿīl ʿAbd al-Ḥamīd, *al-Udabāʾ al-khams*, Cairo n.d.

7 Aḥmad Muḥarram

Another person belonging to the circle of al-Bārūdī was Aḥmad Muḥarram. The son of a Turkish father, he was born in Cairo on 25 Muḥarram 1294/10 February 1877. He received his education from a scholar who worked at al-Azhar. After a time at the *Madrasat al-ḥukūma*, he began working in journalism, representing the ideas of al-Ḥizb al-waṭanī. As a poet, he came forward when he was just 18. In 1904, an article in *Majallat al-muḥīt* ranked him, together with Ḥāfiẓ Ibrāhīm, among the second-best poets of Egypt, | right after al-Bārūdī. With 77
his well-known modesty, Ḥāfiẓ is said to have placed Muḥarram above himself (see Abū Shādī, *al-Shafaq al-bākī*, 1236 bottom). In 1901, a *qaṣida* by Muḥarram

was given first prize by the Lajnat al-iḥtifāl that was responsible for the festivities around the khedive's ascent to the throne—presided over by ʿAbd al-Qādir Ḥilmī and Aḥmad Zakī—and included in *al-Majmūʿa al-dhabiyya*, published specially for the occasion. In 1908 he published the first volume of his *dīwān*, dedicated to the Nile.

The *dīwān* also contains a number of pieces that had been published earlier, such as a *khāṭira* (p. 294), which had been published in 1899 in the women's magazine *Anīs al-jalīs*, October no. 381/2; on pp. 267/70 there is a poem from the same magazine of April 1903, p. 1385/7. His poetry lacks personal warmth, due to the fact that he sticks closely to the panegyric in the way in which it had been reintroduced by al-Bārūdī. But there is no lack of self-confidence, since on page 272, 5 he praises himself with the words: "My books are a treasure that has no equal among the wise." He begins his *dīwān* with poems in praise of ʿAbd al-Ḥamīd; then follows the poem that was writen for the festivities around the khedive's ascent to the throne mentioned earlier, while he also sends him his good wishes when he leaves for Istanbul following the Ṭashyūz (Thasos) incident of 1902, as well as his congratulations on his return. Besides, he also writes for smaller potentates, such as the sultan of Zanzibar and the emir of Dārayn, Muḥammad b. ʿAbd al-Wahhāb, as well as for Egyptian officials and for his own friends. While, in the second chapter, called *al-Waṭaniyyāt*, his 'At the Tomb of Muḥammad ʿAlī' and also the poems that he dedicated to Muḥammad ʿAlī's College of the Arts, are still very much in the previous vein, he tries to educate his compatriots—like Ḥāfiẓ Ibrāhīm did—where he lashes out at curious onlookers at public executions (64), at the number of suicides among high-school students, or when he laments national disasters such as the cholera pandemic of 1902. But he also writes on political issues, such as his lament for the decline of the East (88/73) and the "disease" of the orientals (91/4). For him, being a patriot, the root of all trouble is British supremacy over Egypt. Even though in only one case does he refer directly to the British (in a letter to Aḥmad Kāshif [225, 8–9]: "You are worked up over the fact that our country was shared out like booty among the sons of the Thames"), it was the
78 Boers who fueled his | hopes for the liberation of Egypt, warmly praising their courage in the Boer war (86/90). And even after their defeat, he still held them up as an example to his people, praising the courage of L. Botha and Delarey in refusing to take up a seat in the South African parliament, or the Boer girl who turned down her fiancé when she learns that he betrayed his people to England (pp. 130, 139/41). The third chapter, 'Religion and virtue' (116/43), only contains some small pieces. In the fourth chapter, 'Ethics and education' (116/43), he not only denounces the social injustices in his country (such as the lack of liberty for women), but even uses the unhappy affair between Princess

Louise of Saxonia and the Swiss-Roman Giron as an opportunity to glorify the idea of free love ('Love and nobility', 141/3). Chapters five and six deal with reverence for one's parents, the government, and the law. These chapters also contain a number of very pessimistic pieces that sketch a lively picture of all of Egypt's social sufferings. The love poems of chapter seven (167/83), on the other hand, are very conventional. He even has recourse to the motifs of ancient poetry, trying to place himself fully in the position of the Bedouin poet (180, 12). Therein also originates the lightning motif (170, 174). He opens his elegies (185/220) with *marāthī* on al-Bārūdī and Ibrāhīm al-Yāzijī, followed by the same for other writers. It is only in a poem on the death of his mother that he strikes a personal note. The work ends with *Musājalāt wa-khawāṭir*, poetic correspondence and reflections. They are addressed to his friends Aḥmad Kāshif, Amīn al-Ḥaddād and Nīqūlā Rizqallāh, and are partly about contemporary events. The claim that Mars is inhabited leads him to express his weltschmerz loud and clear. Afterwards, he added two more love poems to this last chapter.

Outside of his *dīwān*, his poems can also be found in *Anīs al-jalīs* 1902 (*Takhayyul al-shāʿir*, which received an answer by Amīn al-Ḥaddād in the same magazine, in April 1903, 1399/1401), ibid. March 1903, p. 1359/62, *Tabshirat al-shāʿir* ibid. May 1904, 1841/3, a poem on the war in *Aḥsan mā katabtu* 40/1, a *taqrīẓ* in Abū Shādī's *Iḥsān* 25/7, *Min humūmī* in *Apollo* I, 19/20, *Quwwa wa-ḍaʿf* ibid. 87, *Dhikrā Muṣṭafā Kāmil* ibid. 769/71, *Qaṣīdat asmāʾ ukhrā* in *Majallat al-Azhar* VIII, | 14/6. *Urjūzat Muḥarram aw qawl al-rawī fī ḥādithat al-Mnsawi* (to 79
be read as Dinshawāy?) Alex. Adab 7.

For an evaluation of his work, see also the foreword in Abū Shādī, *Shiʿr al-wijdān* 27/34. Al-Saḥartī, in *Adab al-ṭabīʿa* 95, detects samples of real, natural art in his Islamic *'Iliad'*, but regrets that these have been pushed into the background by Muḥarram's political agenda. A biography with a portrait and samples of his work can be found in Aḥmad ʿUbayd, *Mashāhīr shuʿarāʾ al-aṣr* I, 114/44, Saʿd Mīkhāʾil, *Samīr al-udabāʾ* I, 22/3.

8 Aḥmad al-Kāshif

Al-Bārūdī's art produced a whole series of admirers and imitators, among whom special mention must be made of Aḥmad b. Dhi 'l-Fiqār b. ʿUmar al-Kāshif, whose *Dīwān* was published in 2 volumes: vol. I, Cairo 1315, vol. II, Cairo 1321 and 1338.

The grandson of a Caucasian who had gone to Cairo as a child and who had been adopted by Katkhudā Dhu 'l-Fiqār in Mamlūk times, al-Kāshif was born in Muḥarram 1295/January 1878 in al-Qurashiyya, a village in al-Mudīriyya al-Gharbiyya. In his youth he applied himself to music and painting. After the victory of the Turks over the Greeks, he came forward as a poet, writing a *qaṣīda* for the *mushīr* Aḥmad Mukhtār Pāshā. As a politician, he was, for a time, suspected of working for the foundation of an Arab caliphate in Egypt, and was banished to his village for this, but later allowed to return to Cairo. His publication in *al-Ahrām* of a *qaṣīda* on the independence of Egypt—reprinted in Aḥmad ʿUbayd—did away with any remaining suspicion regarding his loyalty to the ruling dynasty. Afterwards, he avoided politics for a time, his poetry generally emphasising the human element with a pessimistic undertone.—Aḥmad ʿUbayd, *Mashāhīr shuʿarāʾ al-ʿaṣr* I, 110/13 (with a portrait); al-Saḥartī, *Adab al-ṭabīʿa* 95. A political poem dedicated to prime minister Muḥammad Maḥmūd Pāshā from *al-Siyāsa* of 2 October 1928 is cited in Kampffmeyer, MSOS XXXI, 143.

9 Aḥmad Nasīm

Al-Saḥartī (*Adab al-ṭabīʿa*, 95) also views Aḥmad Nasīm as belonging to al-
80 Bārūdī's school. He is right in this insofar as his | art follows the rigid style of the classics, even when he raises his voice in harmony with the nationalist mood.

Born in Cairo on 30 August 1878, he lost his father when he was six years old. He was raised by an uncle who was the director of the Cairo observatory. A grave illness forced him to break off his studies at a Turkish school, after which he dedicated himself to the study of philology at al-Azhar. From that time on he lived as an independent author until he departed this life in March 1938. His *dīwān* was published in two volumes in 1326/1908 and 1328/1910. The animated political scene of the post-war period fascinated him as well. He published political pieces for al-Ḥizb al-Waṭanī in the newspapers *al-Liwāʾ*, *al-Ṣāʿiqa*, and *Miṣr al-fatāt*. A collection of these was published with the title *Waṭaniyyāt Aḥmad Nasīm* in Cairo in 1910. To the Wafd he dedicated a poem that expressed the hopes of the Egyptian people. He also made his mark as an author of *marāthī* (see his poem on the occasion of the death of Sarwat in *al-Siyāsa*, 24 September 1928, cited in Kampffmeyer, MSOS XXXI, 125). In the last years of his life he was not able to avoid completely the influence of the new artform, introduced by Khalīl Maṭrān. This is shown by the impressionist song 'The dancing girl,' and even more so by his *Nafathāt shāʿir* in *Apollo* I, 734/7.—Aḥmad ʿUbayd, *Mashāhīr shuʿarāʾ al-ʿaṣr* I, 144/57, Sarkīs 404.

10 Ḥasan al-Qāyātī

Like Aḥmad Nasīm, Ḥasan al-Qāyātī was a graduate of al-Azhar and, like him, had liberated himself from the rigid school tradition.

He was born in 1300/1882 in the village of Qāyāt, in Mudīriyyat al-Minya. His family traced its lineage back to the Daws tribe of Yemen and also to the famous traditionist Abū Hurayra. Like his father and grandfather before him, he studied theology at al-Azhar but then quit, dissatisfed as he was with its outdated teaching methods. In a series of poems in his *Dīwān* (C. 1328/1910), he speaks out strongly in favour of the emancipation of the peasants.—Aḥmad ʿUbayd, *Mashāhīr* 207/23. For a description of a turtle, see *Apollo* I, 15/6.

| 11 Muḥammad Tawfīq ʿAlī 81

Muḥammad Tawfīq ʿAlī, too, prided himself on his true Arab lineage. His somewhat sobre songs extol the quiet joy of a life in the country while railing against the guilty pleasures of modern times. However, as an adolescent he took pride in praising the untamed lifestyle of his Bedouin forefathers.

His family, hailing from the ʿAsīrāt tribe, prided itself on its ʿAbbāsid lineage. It had settled in Upper Egypt. After a conflict with his relatives, ʿĀmir, his forefather six times removed, had moved to Zāwiyat al-Maṣlūb, in the Mudīriyyat Banī Suwayf in Central Egypt. This is where he was born in 1887. After his graduation from the military academy, he became an officer and served in the Sudan. He retired in the rank of captain, after which he applied himself at home to agriculture and trade. His *dīwān* was published in 1327/1909.—Aḥmad ʿUbayd, *Mashāhīr shuʿarāʾ al-ʿaṣr* I, 280/95, Saʿd Mīkhāʾīl, *Samīr al-udabāʾ* 91/6.

12 Tawfīq al-Bakrī

One of the final representatives of a type of poetry that was dominated by the classics was Muḥammad b. ʿAlī Tawfīq al-Bakrī al-Ṣiddīqī al-ʿUmarī (d. 1351/1932), the Earl Marshal of the ʿAlids (Naqīb al-shurafāʾ) and head of the Sufi orders of Egypt, and who was also famous as an author on theological subjects.

He was born in Cairo on 27 Jumādā II 1287/24 September 1870. He received his education in the royal school that had been founded by Khedive Tawfīq, until that institution was abolished in 1895. Following an exam in the ministry of education in 1887, he received a Bachelor of Arts and requested and obtained an *ijāza* from the Shaykh al-Azhar, al-Anbābī. When his brother ʿAbd al-Bāqī died in 1892 he was appointed by Khedive ʿAbbās II to the rank of *naqīb* and a member of the Mashyakha al-Bakriyya, positions that were traditionally held by his family. In May that year he was appointed a lifelong member of the legislative council. On his way back from a trip to Europe he also visited Istanbul, where ʿAbd al-Ḥamīd awarded him the title of chief military judge for Anatolia. In 1312/1895 he lost all of his posts as a result of slander, but after he had vindicated himself he was reinstated as *naqīb* in 1903.

82 | Even though he had some knowledge of European culture, he immersed himself so much in ancient literature that echoes of the classics from the time of the ʿAbbāsids keep surfacing in his poems, as has also been shown in detail by Aḥmad Muḥarram in his obituary of him in *Apollo* I, 68/74. And even when he ventures upon a new form—distiches with alternating rhyme—inside of a strophic poem (*dhāt al-qawāfī*), he does not step outside the frame of reference of the ancients. In his *Ṣahārīj al-luʾluʾ* (C. 1907) he offers, as well as poems, *maqāmas* in the style of Ḥarīrī, in which philosophical contemplation is dressed in the colourful garb of ancient rhetoric (see Ṭāhir al-Ṭannāḥī, *Apollo* I, 155/9, who defends this work against its critics). His meritorious *Arājiz al-ʿArab* was mentioned in I, 90. Entitled *Fuḥūl al-balāgha*, in 1313 he published a selection of the poems of Muslim b. al-Walīd, Abū Nuwās, al-Ḥasan b. Hāniʾ, Abū Tammām, al-Buḥturī, Ibn al-Rūmī, Ibn al-Muʿtazz, al-Mutanabbī and from the *Rasāʾil* of al-Maʿarrī. In 1323 he published, in Cairo, the genealogies of the masters of his order and of his own family, under the titles *Bayt al-sādāt al-wafāʾiyya* and *Bayt al-Ṣiddīq* respectively. In his *al-Mustaqbal lil-Islām* (C. 1310) he offers some very uninspiring ideas for reforms.—Aḥmad ʿUbayd, *Mashāhīr shuʿarāʾ al-ʿaṣr* I, 168/80, Sarkīs 581/2, al-ʿAqqād, *Shuʿarāʾ Miṣr* 54/75.

13 Muḥammad ʿAbd al-Muṭṭalib

Just like Tawfīq al-Bakrī, Muḥammad ʿAbd al-Muṭṭalib (b. 1870 in Baṣūna in Mudīriyyat Jirjā, d. 1931 in Cairo) was entirely under the spell of the ancients.

He prided himself on his descent from the Arab tribe of Juhayna. Like his father, who was a follower of the Khalwatiyya order, he received his education at al-Azhar, to which he added an extra four years of study at the Dār al-ʿulūm. Being a zealous Muslim, he was a member of the Jamʿiyyat al-muḥāfaẓa ʿala ʾl-Qurʾān al-karīm, of the Jamʿiyyat al-shubbān al-Muslimīn, and the Jamʿiyyat al-hidāya al-Islāmiyya. His *dīwān*, which was published by al-Sikandarī, mainly contains *madīḥ*. In one case, he believes he pays tribute to the moderns (outwardly at least) when he describes an aeroplane rather than a camel. In his *ʿAlawiyya*, too (a counterpart to Ḥāfiẓ Ibrāhīm's *ʿUmariyya*), he remains faithful to the conventions of the classics. ʿAbbās Maḥmūd al-ʿAqqād, *Shuʿarāʾ Miṣr* 42/52.

83 | 14 Other Poets

Before we turn to the latest developments in poetry, we should briefly mention a number of authors who committed themselves to the preservation of the literary tradition of the ancients during the half century between 1880 and 1930. They represent all classes of society: scholars from al-Azhar, officials who had received their education in one of the modern institutions of the country, some journalists, and also a Copt, all of whom we shall mention now, in chronologcal order.

An overview of the poetic production of the time is provided by the anthology *ʿUkāẓ al-adab*, published in 3 volumes by Abū Naṣr Muḥyī b. ʿAbd al-Ghanī al-Salāwī (Istanbul 1335/7). The first volume only contains *qaṣīda*s on ʿAbd al-Ḥamīd, to whom the compiler himself dedicated his *Ḥilyat al-ʿaṣr al-jadīd fī shamāʾil al-malik al-ḥamīd*.

a. ʿAlī al-Laythī (d. 1896) was a court poet in the style of old, one who poured all his talent into poems for special occasions and *marāthī*. He enjoyed the favour of the khedives Ismāʿīl and Tawfīq, but never offered his *dīwān* for publication. Apart from imitating the ancient *nudamāʾ*, he could also improvise in public, even though he did not neglect to carefully polish the songs that he recited on festive occasions. The last glimmerings of a bygone literary era, only the few creations that were preserved in the memories of friends have historical value. ʿAbbās Maḥmūd al-ʿAqqād, *Shuʿarāʾ Miṣr* 100/9.

b. Of the journalists who were also active as poets, we can mention here the publisher of the *Jarīdat al-Nīl*, Ḥasan Ḥusnī b. Ḥusayn ʿĀrif b. Ḥasan Suhrāb b. Maḥmūd b. Masīḥ b. ʿAlī Bāshā al-Ṭuwayrānī.

He was born in Cairo on 6 Dhu ʾl-Qaʿda 1266/24 September 1850. Having proved himself in various literary fields, he founded *al-Nīl* newspaper in December 1891. He died on 11 June 1897 in Istanbul. His *dīwān*, *Thamarāt al-ḥayāt*, was published in Cairo in 1300 (351, 218 pp.). His later poems and *rasāʾil* have only been preserved in manuscript form: *Lawāḥiq al-thamarāt*, dated 1299, Cairo² II, 320, *al-Nathriyyāt*, collected by Ḥasanayn Nājī b. Ibrāhīm, ibid. IV, b. 83. | His *Lāmiyyat al-Turk* was published with other *ṣuḥuf mansiyya* in 84 *Fatāt al-sharq* III (1909), 371/4. He showed himself as an author of theological subjects in his *Dalīl ahl al-īmān fī ṣiḥḥat al-Qurʾān*, C. 1309, and *al-Ḥaqq, rūḥ al-fāḍila* ibid. 1309.

c. Maḥmūd b. Muḥammad al-Qūsī, *Dīwān sulṭān al-ʿāshiqīn al-musammā bil-Tuḥfa al-durriyya fī ʾl-taghazzulāt al-Muḥammadiyya*, Būlāq 1309.

d. al-Nashshār, *Dīwān*, C. 1310.

e. Aḥmad ʿAbd al-Bāqī al-Daqqāq, *Masarrāt al-khawāṭir fī ʾl-tawshīḥ wal-nawādir*, C. 1312.

f. Ibrāhīm Barakāt al-Qibṭī, *Bāb al-samīr, Dīwān*, C. 1313.

g. Maḥmūd al-Iskandarī, *Dīwān*, Alexandria 1319.

h. Maḥmūd Shukrī Efendi Raʾīs qism idārat mudīriyyat al-Sūdān, *Sahl al-qarīḍ, Dīwān* in 5 vols, C. 1322/46.

i. Aḥmad Bek al-Majīdī, editor of the *Jarīdat al-Muʿtaṣim* in Cairo, *Dīwān al-Durra al-Miṣriyya* with *al-Nafāʾis al-durriyya* by ʿAbd al-Raḥīm b. ʿAbd al-Raḥmān b. Muḥammad b. ʿAlī al-Makkī al-Suyūṭī (b. Rajab 1281/December 1864, d. 1342/1923), C. 1325/1907.

j. ʿAbd al-Laṭīf Bek al-Ṣayrafī was born in Alexandria on 8 Rabīʿ I 1257/1 May 1841. He served as a judge and official, last as *wakīl* in Mudīriyyat al-Buḥayra, then turned to private practice before dying in 1322/1904. *Dīwān* with a biography, published by his son ʿAbd al-ʿAzīz, Alexandria 1325/1908; see Cheikho, *al-Mashriq* XXIII, 817, Sarkīs 1219.

k. Amīn b. Sulaymān al-Ḥaddād, a grandson of Nāṣif al-Yāzījī by his mother, lived in Beirut and Cairo, where he was an editor at several newspapers. He died in 1912. *Muntakhabāt Amīn al-Ḥaddād al-Shāʿir*, Alexandria 1913; individual poems in *Anīs al-jalīs*, February and March 1904, 1708/9, 1783/6, *Zalāzil Ṣiqilliyya, Fatāt al-sharq* January 1909, 129/31.

l. Muṣṭafā Mumtāz, around 1910, *Dīwān*, Alexandria n.d.

m. ʿAbd al-Majīd Efendi Shawqī, d. 1324/1906, *Dalāʾil al-ashwāq, Dīwān*, C. 1325.

n. Mūsā Shākir al-Ṭanṭāwī, *Nafaḥāt al-rabīʿ, Dīwān* C. n.d. (Maṭbaʿat al-Riwāyāt al-Adabiyya), whence *Taʿlīm al-fatāt* in *Fatāt al-sharq* 1911, 240.

o. ʿAlī (b.) Yūsuf b. Muḥammad b. Yūsuf al-Balṣaffūrī al-Azharī al-Mālikī was born in 1863 in Balṣaffūra, in Mudīriyyat Jirjīs. After studying at al-Azhar he founded *al-Adab* magazine in 1887, and in 1890, together with Shaykh Aḥmad
85 Māḍī, *al-Muʾayyad*, which, after 1893, he ran on his own, turning it into | an Islamic magazine of global renown. He died on 25 October 1913.—*Nasīm al-saḥar, Dīwān*, C. 1304.—*Maqālāt qaṣr al-Dūbārā* C. n.d.—*Ayyām janāb al-khadīwī al-muʿaẓẓam ʿAbbās al-thānī fī Dār al-saʿāda*, C. 1311.—Hartmann, *Ar. Press* 12/3, Sarkīs 1371.

p. Nicola Rizqallāh al-Sūrī, b. 12 March 1869 in Beirut, d. 20 April 1915 in Cairo: *Munājāt al-arwāḥ, Dīwān* C. n.d. (Maṭbaʿat al-Riwāya al-jadīda); individual poems: *ʿIbrat ḥāditha* (on the assassination of the king and queen of Serbia), *Anīs al-jalīs* July 1903, 1582/3, *Ghādat al-mirʾāt* ibid. August 1522/3, *Malika ʿalā ʿarsh al-Farāʿina* (from the French) ibid. 1536, *Fitnat shāʿir* ibid., December 1903, 1846/7.

q. Ḥāmid al-Qirdāwī, an official in the ministry of war, *Nafathāt maḥzūn fi ʾl-ḥubb al-ṭāhir*, C. 1336/1918.

r. Maḥmūd Rāshid Efendi in Alexandria. 1. *Maqāmāt al-ḥaqīqa wal-khayāl*, lectures, C. 1913.—2. *Dīwān*, Alexandria 1323/1914.

s. ʿAbd al-ʿAzīz Ṣabrī, son of the mayor (*ʿumda*) of al-Khiyāriyya in al-Wajh al-qiblī, around 1919 (Sarkīs 1285). 1. *Anfās al-aʿlāq fī makārim al-akhlāq*,

C. 1313.—2. *Zahrat al-ṣibā fī rawḍat al-ḥayāt*, C. 1327.—3. *Dīwān* (fables, panegyrics, nationalist texts) C. 1329.

t. Aḥmad Shākir al-Karmī, *al-Karmiyyāt*, C. 1921.

u. Aḥmad al-Zayn al-Azharī, *Qalāʾid al-ḥikma* (*rajaz* poems), C. 1918. *Rāḥat al-suluww*, *Apollo* I, 8/9; Abū Shādī turns against one of his critics from *al-Ahrām* in *al-Naqd wal-mithāl*, ibid. 61/5.

v. Aḥmad Bek Jālal al-Dīn al-Ḥusaynī, *mustashār bil-maḥākim al-ahliyya*, *Ḥadīth al-nafs*, *dīwān*, C. 1345.

w. Muḥammad Ṭāhir al-Jiblāwī al-Dimyāṭī, *Dīwān Multaqa ʾl-ʿibārāt*, C. 1925, on which is a *taqrīẓ* by al-ʿAqqād in *Hadiyyat al-karawān*, 137.

x. Iskandar Quzmān, *al-Rawḍ al-ʿarīḍ fī mā naẓamahu min al-qarīḍ*, C. 1926.

y. Aḥmad b. Muḥammad al-Kinānī al-Abyārī, formerly professor at a Madrasa amīriyya, *Dīwān* with an appendix, *Īnās al-jullās fī sharḥ qaṣīdat Abī Firās*, C. 1344/1926.

z. ʿUmar Muṣṭafā al-Bahnasawī, *Dīwān al-Bahnasawī*, C. 1927/1346.

aa. Thābit b. Faraj b. ʿAbd al-Raʾūf b. Aḥmad b. ʿAbd al-Raḥmān b. ʿAbd al-Raʾūf al-Jirjāwī al-Azharī, around 1345/1926, *Dīwān* C. 1323.

| 15 Khalīl Maṭrān 86

The Syrian Khalīl Maṭrān[78] was the pioneer of a new kind of Arabic poetry that expressed attachment to modern culture. Like so many of his compatriots, he found his readership as a journalist in Cairo.

As he emphasised in the preface, his *Dīwān* (Cairo, Maṭbaʿat al-Maʿārif, n.d. 1908 or 1910, new edition with a foreword by Ṭāhā Ḥusayn, C. 1932) contains no more than a selection of his poetical production. It starts with the only poem from his childhood that he deemed worthy of being preserved, a *qaṣīda* about the cities of Jena and Sedan from the year 1888, and ends with a *marthiya* on the great national leader Muṣṭafā Kāmil Pāshā (d. 8 Muḥarram 1326/12 February 1908), which he had recited during the ceremony held 40 days after his death (*Ḥaflat al-arbaʿīn*; see Lane, *Manners and Customs* 532). In between there are, in a strictly chronological but no other order, meticulously dated samples of his poems. At their head, we find an elegy on the death of an anonymous young European, whose flower-strewn coffin he had seen by accident, somewhere on the streets, and dated January 1894. While, in spite of its foreign subject, he had adhered to the style of the ancient *qaṣīda* in this poem from his youth, this elegy is a pure effusion of feelings, it being the metre alone that it shares with ancient poetry. At the same time, this poem is a programme. True,

78 Or Muṭrān; for a portrait see *Apollo* 703/4, *Fatāt al-sharq* VII, 306.

later also, Khalīl has shown—in some of his panegyrics and *marthiya*s especially—that he is an outstanding master of the *qaṣīda* genre, as he was in his youth. The difference is, however, that it is no longer an ideal to him, something which he states very clearly in his preface. And even though there is always the risk that people will turn him down with an arrogant smile merely because he is 'modern,' this does not deter him. This is because he does not want to be a slave to ancient poetry anymore, no longer let himself be distracted from his train of thought by mere considerations of metre and rhyme. He does not want to hunt for fame with a single verse like the ancients did, but rather to offer a coherent work of art. In all this, he never overestimates himself. In a dedication
87 to Rizqallāh Efendi Khūrī inserted on pages 290/4, | he expresses himself with great modesty on his own work: "These ideas, anecdotes and examples were merely lined up by me; I'm not saying that I forged them together like pearls.[79] I just lined them up in the order in which they came to me, between the past and the present, as short-lived verses which I never meant to immortalise. I do not flatter myself with the idea that they will secure my immortality when I shall no longer be alive,[80] like all those who came up with a line of poetry once or maybe wrote some prose in their time and then, full of pride, believe they have conquered eternity … Never have I, as you know well, my dear friend, entertained such high hopes; never have I cared about fame … I followed the advice of one of my friends, who told me: let the past be the past, and only concentrate yourself on the present. Describe to your friends whatever shines and blooms, the way you see it. Sing of what makes them happy and what dispels their pain. Warn them against the hardships and the danger of the way. Appease the heart of the frightened and do not help the sinner; admonish, sometimes in a friendly manner, while on other occasions, you must scold."

The poet followed this principle faithfully, even though the brighter side of life always attracted him more than the other,[81] feeling no urge to act as a judge of morals or a politician. Nevertheless, he also cultivated the *marthiya* genre assiduously, lamenting the deaths of numerous relatives and friends, as well as figures from public life, such as the poet al-Bārūdī (238/41), and, as stated earlier, the politician Muṣṭafā Kāmil. The language of these poems is of an unadulterated classicality. This fact notwithstanding, he is convinced that it will only be able to unfold itself in all its richness once it has been liberated from

---

79 For once, a crooked image escapes him.

80 Compare with this Shawqī's arrogant self-assurance.

81 One must know how he lived in order to understand how Khalīl Maṭrān, with his happy constitution, could mention the bubbles rising in a glass of champagne in a *marthiya* for Ismāʿīl Ṣabrī (not in the *Dīwān*), see Zakī Mubārak, *Muwāzana* 20.

the heavy bonds that still weigh down upon it (cf. the preface to *Nero* in Abū Shādī, *Nakbat Navarīn* 51).[82] Only rarely does he | allow European phrases such 88
as "our (the lovers') throne floats high above the clouds" at $183_{,5}$, or "(when our happiness was complete,) fate, in its envy, lunged at it" at $183_{,12}$. But his way of thinking is fully modern and only rarely reminiscent of ancient poetry, as in the case where he extols the beloved: "If a praying monk would see her, he would be confused" ($177_{,10}$, cf. also $204_{,8}$), which uses an image that was very common among the early poets (cf. Nābigha, Ahlw. 7, 26, 27, Wellhausen, *Reste*² 232), or when, in a love song, he introduces guardians or banners that also happen to be common in European love poetry (Ecker, *Ar. prov. u. deutscher Minnesang*, Bern and Leipzig 1934, 22ff.). Direct influences from western poetry are hardly to be found, although he once translated a poem from French, which, however, itself came from the Orient since it was by Jeanne, the daughter of Niqula al-Quṣayrī (107/8, of June 1901). But he was certainly familiar with French literature, as is shown by the poem on A. de Musset with which he accompanied a volume of the latter's poems that he gave as a present to a lady in June of 1903 (141). Modern images or ideas, which al-Bārūdī liked to use, are only rarely found, as in the great love cycle (cf. below), in which he brings in X-rays in order to convince the beloved | of the immutability of his love (168/9). His many long 89
*qaṣīda*s bear witness to his absolute mastery of this ancient form, although he does not look down upon the later varieties either. He likes the *muwashshaḥ* very much and at times he even invents a type himself, as in the case where, in a wedding poem, passing the congratulations of the flowers on to the bride,

---

82 Only rarely do improper word forms escape his attention, as in the case of *ḥinya* ad *aḥnū* in $87_{,12}$, or the use of an expression like *raythamā* ('for a time') $95_{,3}$, unless a verse following it was dropped. A constraint of rhyme in a long *qaṣīda* is the only reason for him to use bizarre expressions sometimes, which he then has to explain, such as *buham* = *abṭāl* at $149_{,5}$ or even to use ancient words in a sense that is not theirs, like *adam* = *taṣallub al-jism* at 148,6, or *ziyam*, which otherwise only means 'pebbles' (*Hudh.* $275_{\cdot 29}$. Kaʿb, *Bānat Suʿād* 27) or 'herd of camels or horses' (*Agh.* ²XIV, $28_{,14}$, ʿAskarī, *Ṣin.* $43_{,6}$), for *ghārāt* at $150_{,5}$, or *irtaṭam*, which otherwise only means 'to fall into the dung' (Abū Nuwās $393_{,3}$ Jāḥiẓ, *Ras.* $14_{,9}$), for 'to perish' at $151_{,2}$. This happens only in rare cases outside of the rhyme, such as *ahāba*, which otherwise only means 'to yell at horses or camels' (Ṭarafa, *Muʿall.* 15 *Muf.* $54_{\cdot 31}$ *Hudh.* $250_{,1}$ 4), for a simple *takallama* at $180_{,2}$, in the way in which Abū Shādī, *Aḥnatūn*, preface $13_{,5}$, $37_{,7}$, and al-Māzinī, *Hilāl* 1934, $1162_{,15}$ use it as 'to call out to,' and then as 'to urge, to invite' (cf. Dozy); see also Rajab al-Iskandarī *ad* Abū Shādī, *Mafkharat Rashīd* $26_{,5}$. Surely he would raise the same kind of objection to this criticism as did Muḥammad ʿAṭiyya Yūsuf in the preface to Abū Shādī, *Fawq al-ʿubāb* 14 and argue that, when a language is as rich as Arabic, the poet must sometimes be given the freedom to step outside the boundaries of linguistic usage.

he lets the roses recite verses in *ramal* in the middle of a *qaṣīda*, verses that rhyme at the hemistich and in which the rhyme perdures over three syllables (252/3).[83] He has a special liking for the Persian *dubayt*, a verse form that was later rejected as un-Arabic by his student Abū Shādī. He uses it, for instance, in a caption under a portrait of himself (104), for the glorification of the Ottoman coat of arms (230, on the occasion of a celebration in the Continental Hotel in Istanbul in January 1904), in his praise for the philanthropist Emilie Sarsaq (115) and the singer Laylā (132), but especially for flatteries (34, 44, 82, 111) and jokes (on the heart-shaped swelling on the eyelid of a beautiful woman, 141); being too tight, he sometimes lets the form burst, like in his quatrain on the same thing that was just mentioned (*Shaḥḥādh* 256), or in the tristich with which he offered a bunch of flowers to a European lady (110). Of the older verse forms, he occasionally practised the *taʾrīkh* (congratulations on the birth of a child, 261, 272), the riddle ('*Anti* and Annette,' 196) and once the tenso ('Heart and Eye,' dated 1896, 28/30). In his preface he emphasizes the fact that he does not feel bound by the old artistic rule that prohibited every form of enjambment; for instance, he once lets a sentence run over five lines (130, 11–15), or through the entire strophe of a *muwashshaḥ* (210.10–12).[84] Free verse—'*vers libre*,' the
90 invention of which was disputed between Gustave Kahn and Emile | Dujardin in France, practised by Walt Whitman as its unrivaled master in America[85] and later used by Maṭrān's student Abū Shādī, but in particular, under Whitman's influence, by the American Syrians—Maṭrān only used once, during a memorial ceremony organised by Yūsuf Bek Numayr in honour of Ibrāhīm al-Yāzījī, in January 1907, in a *shiʿr manthūr* (276/8) that starts as follows: "Release your tears from the domination, by the metre, of the verse, and from the bonds of rhyme; let your sigh do the talking, broken by no metre, and by no order bound."

Al-Manfalūṭī brought Maṭrān's views on contemporary poets together in *al-Mukhtārāt* 69/75. Maṭrān looks upon Ismāʿīl Pāshā Ṣabrī as the poet of short *qaṣīdas* of 2 to 6 verses, which are polished with endless care. Aḥmad

83 For once, he may have imitated the rhyming technique of A. de Musset; cf. the latter's 'Stances' in *Premières poésies*, Paris 1885, 7, or 'Réponse à M. Ch. Nodier' in *Poésies nouvelles*, Paris 1887, 266/71. Abū Shādī used the same rhyme in the opera *Aḥnatūn* 57/8 as an ending to three-verse strophes, and Khayr al-Dīn Ziriklī in the strophic poem in *Aḥsan mā katabtu* 71/2. It is not very likely that the *radīf* of Persian and Turkish poetry, of which he must have had as little knowledge as of their incidental imitations in ancient Arabic poetry, served as his example.

84 Apparent breaches of metre turn out to be simple printing errors; he seems to have failed just once, in a half verse in the *mutaqārib* metre (155, 1a).

85 Fr. Wild, *Die englische Literatur der Gegenwart*, Wiesbaden 1928, p. 19.

Shawqī was always writing, on any occasion, be it for himself or for others, at home or on the move. When he follows ancient examples (*muʿāraḍāt*), he surpasses them often. Next to him and al-Bārūdī, the poet of the perfect form, there is Ḥāfiẓ, who often sat writing in the gardens of al-Azbakiyya: the three great masters. He adores al-ʿIzzī as his teacher, while he judges the language of Tawfīq al-Bakrī, who often drew on al-Shinqīṭī for advice, as too far-fetched.

Yet his own career as a poet was not free from difficulties. In November 1898 he had written a *taqrīẓ* for the *Dīwān* of Aḥmad Shawqī, the Prince of Poets, that was almost exuberant (54/5), and which he ended with the words: "A scholar should let his choice fall on your book, a noble friend and a wise and rightly-guided judge." No less sonorous were the verses that he dedicated to Shawqī ("our honoured brother") in 1905 (256). Nevertheless, he was not able to avoid the hostility of this man, who couldn't tolerate any potential rival. According to Abū Shādī (*al-Shafaq* al-*bākī* 1272), Shawqī tried to raise people's suspicions against him by calling him a "business-oriented poet" (*shāʿir tijārī*), even though he himself had once praised Khalīl as the benefactor of literature and the intermediary between European literature and Arabic style (Abū Shādī, *Nakbat Navarīn* 51 bottom). Ḥāfiẓ Ibrāhīm (ibid. 1236, 14), too, appears to have disparaged and spoken critically of Khalīl's language from time to time. But such criticism was always related to Maṭrān's efforts to emulate the other two—favourites of the public—in their own area of expertise. And it is true, | 91 Khalīl did try to do this from time to time, this in disregard for his true nature (see Ṭāhā Ḥusayn, *Ḥāfiẓ wa-Shawqī* 148), but this has nothing to do with the essence of his art.

His art unfolds in its purest manner when in the service of love. The pinnacle of his creative production is represented by the great cycle of love, amorous bliss, and broken-heartedness of *Ḥikāyat al-ʿāshiqayn* of 1898/1903 (159/195). It begins with a distich about his first encounter with his beloved, in a garden, where she had been stung by a bee, taking us, in the form of *qaṣīda*s and *muwashshaḥ*s, through the ups and downs of a happy union ('Adam and Eve' 165/6) and the occasional separation due to some misunderstanding all the way up to the death of the beloved, which he laments at the end ('*Kāna*') in an overwhelming manner, transcending all conventions. There can be no doubt that the poet draws fully upon personal experience, even though he introduces the beloved by various pseudonyms so as to protect her memory from indiscrete investigations. Besides this showpiece, the *Dīwān* contains a number of shorter love poems, some of which show that he was still under the spell of older verse forms (e.g. 'My moon, the moon in the sky' of May 1894, 14/5), but also charming genre images like 'The Little Bird' (79/82), which found refuge near the beloved and thus allowed him a peek into the innermost part of her heart.

The poet likes to spin out such genre images and knows very well how to describe even the most inconspicuous scenes in a charming manner, like the girl in a garden in Giza who is arranging her hair and using her mother's eye as her mirror (13/4, of Apri 1894), or when he observes his beloved while she is busy preparing sweets for a feast (November 1903, 227/8). Once, as if it were with the brush of an impressionist painter, he depicts a young girl in a white dress who separates herself from her companions during an evening walk along the Nile, and how the light of the moon plays upon her dress and on its reflection in the river. He starts this image with two verses which are composed of adjectives and nouns only, like individual spots of colour, and which start melting into a single image from the third verse onward, its soft tone underlining the dandling rhythm of the *mutaqārib* (140, of April 1903).

But his art does not exhaust itself in these miniatures. He wrote a large num-
92 ber of epic works, | which until then did not exist in Arabic literature, at least not in verse form. He derives his subjects from ordinary life more readily than from history's great events. In August 1894 he recounts the story of a young man from a village, somewhere in Lebanon, who, pretending to be dead in order to attract a girl's attention—this at the advice of a friend—is surprised by death itself (16/7). In July 1899 he recounts, in *rajaz* verses which rhyme in pairs, how a young man from a Syrian village, while killing a rabid wolf is bitten and infected himself, whereupon he kills his fiancée and then himself (64/74). In March 1900 he recounts—in the form of a *qaṣīda*—the sentimental story of a female luteplayer suffering from fainting fits and her lover, who follows her in death (84/88). In December of that same year he recounts—using the same format—the story of the extinction of a rich family, whose last heir kills himself out of heartache (92/7). In July of that same year he chose the form of the *muwashshaḥ* for a long-winded description of a prostitute who forces an abortion (199/218). This preference for sentimental subjects, which he shares with the essayist al-Manfalūṭī, is probably due to the influence of the French Romantics. He may also have borrowed his narrative technique from them, a technique in which the impressions of the onlookers—directly involved in the event or not—are given preference over a direct account. In the story of a naïve pair of lovers from September 1903 (223/6) the application of this technique is taken so far that not much is left of the original story itself. But he also tried his hand at historical subjects. In the story of the coffee cup, which he recited in person during a social gathering in August of 1902, he recounts how a king has the lover of his daughter poisoned, without, however, specifying time or place (123/8). It has a strange metre, a *kāmil* which rhymes at the hemistich

like a *rajaz*. Similarly timeless is the story of an Arab poet who bewitches a Bedouin girl with his verses (37/41, of October 1896). The ballad of the execution of the vizier Bozorgmehr[86] of March 1901 (99/102) takes us to the time of the Sāsānids. As an adolescent, he had been fascinated by the personality of Napoleon I. | Thus, he tells us in November 1895 how this emperor decorated a 93
soldier who lay dying out on the battlefield. And here, too, he is so immersed in the emotions of the moment that he leaves his reader completely in the dark about all the surrounding circumstances. Finally, the wars lost by Turkey provided him with the material for a series of longer tales in verse. The peasant girl praying for her father going out to war (March 1903) is entirely sentimental (137/9). The unfair and uneven war between a large and a small nation, likewise of March 1903 (147/153), does not rise above mere clichés, just like the poem of April 1907 in which he addressed this theme once more (262/3). It is only his 'Girl of Montenegro' (154/8, undated) that sounds like a real ballad.

The poet does not tell us much about his personal life. His attachment to Syria, the country of his family's origin, shows itself in 'Farewell' (to Egypt) and 'A Salute' (to Syria) from August 1899 (74/6), and in his memories of a happy childhood among the ruins of Baalbek, in a poem of November 1899 (76/9). In July of 1902 he lay in quarantine in Alexandria and, from his sickbed, wrote of the anxiety with which he said goodbye to his childhood years (119/121). But a moment later he shows himself as a witty and able man-of-the-world once more (122); for example when he, after his convalescence from said disease, inviting his friends for dinner in recognition of their moral support, embellished the menu cards of the ladies with distiches on the flowers placed in front of them. The sentimental tale of a rose in *Apollo* I, 109/12 shows that, even at the height of his career, he remained a youthful dreamer.

In the poems that were written for special occasions and of which his *Dīwān* has many, his amiable side stands out most. In October 1903 he sent a Syrian friend enjoying the summer coolness of the Lebanon a funny epistle in *rajaz* (144/6). His poetic congratulations on weddings and births are countless; in one case, he strikes a more serious tone when he congratulates a father simultaneously on the birth of his first child and on the formal recognition of his union, which had been threatened by religious discord (242). On one occasion, he failed in his attempt to lend the happy tone of a wedding song a sense of history, when, in his description of a banquet of the gods, he presents Jupiter

86 Whom he, in a learned whim, designates with the supposedly real Persian 'Buzarjumuhr'.

94 Ammon as the principal god | of the Greeks (116).[87] In his panegyrics and many elegies (among them, one for Queen Victoria, 112) and consolatory poems, he tries, as we mentioned already, to outdo the two masters Aḥmad Shawqī and Ḥāfiẓ Ibrāhīm. These attempts were not always successful. But as a poet of the court he did not intrude upon their territory very often, such as in the case of his congratulations for ʿAbbās II after his conquest of the Sudan, after the latter's safe return from his trip to Europe in November (25/6), and also in his salute to him of December 1898 on the occasion of the happy outcome of a political crisis, in which he pushed his flattery to the point of saying: "When a cloud passes in front of the moon, it does not light up, nor is the moon shadowed by it." He much prefers to move in a literary environment, congratulating his patron, Princess A. De Avierino Visniewska, on her decorations (April 1901, October 1902, 102/4, 132), or paying homage to his fellow-poet Shukrī Ghāni on the occasion of a party organised in honour of his French play *Antara* (February 1906, 262/4). And here, too, he enjoys employing his gentle wit, for instance when he praises his dentist for the painless extraction of a tooth (143).

Only twice did he venture into politics, with allegories whose object and context he concealed in such a way that only the best informed of his contemporaries could understand their meaning. And in the dialogue between the emperor and the poet on the planned construction of the Chinese wall of January 1897 (41/3), an enterprise that is strongly discouraged by said poet, he was probably thinking of the radical nationalists and their demand for an 'Egypt for the Egyptians.' The danger of the British, on the other hand, he invokes in a *qaṣīda*—dedicated to the lawyer Maḥmūd Bek Abū Naṣr—in which "the old man from Athens" warns his fellow-citizens against the invasion of the Romans (March 1906, 264/6). The *Malḥamat Nīrūn* (*qaṣīda*)—which he recited in al-Jāmiʿa al-Amirīkiyya in Beirut in 1924—I only know from Abū Shādī's reference to it in *Nakbat Navarīn* 54, but it seems that it was a similar kind of allegory.

Every now and then Maṭrān also pays tribute to the Egyptian nationalists' infat-
95 uation with their ancestors. | In February 1900 he extols the pyramids after a visit to Saqqara (83). He opens a festive address to the leader of the nationalists Muṣṭafā Kāmil (233) with the following verse: "If only Mina could see from his grave how his sons are afflicted by ruin." His *Waqfa fī ẓill timthāl Raʿmsīs al-kabīr*, which was published in *al-Muqtaṭaf* 11, no. 64, p. 132 and reprinted in *Aḥsan mā katabtu*,

87 Leaving Ṭāhā Ḥusayn's learned studies aside, antiquity lay far beyond the cultural horizon of his social milieu. In a similar vein, Abū Shādī is quite happy to let the Olympic Games take place at the foot of Mount Olympus (*al-Shafaq al-bākī*, 346, n. 3).

Cairo (Idārat al-Hilāl) 1934, 12/7, is praised by Aḥmad Shādī in *Waṭan al-Farāʿina* 74 and *al-Shafaq al-bākī* 1212, 5.

At the height of his fame as a poet he embarked upon the gratifying task of introducing his people to European drama. He transformed Shakespeare's *Othello* into prose as *ʿUthayl* (first showing 30 March 1912 at the al-Khidīwiyya opera house, by the theatre company of Jurj Abyaḍ, Maṭbaʿat al-Maʿārif) and likewise his *Merchant of Venice* (see the critique by Ibrāhīm ʿAbd al-Qādir al-Māzinī in *Ḥasād al-hāshīm* ^{2}31/50). In 1927, he produced an adapted version of Schiller's *Kabale und Liebe*, giving it the title *al-Ḥubb wal-dasīsa*, while he also adapted a modern British play called *Topaz*. Since 1934 he has been the director (*mudīr*) of al-Firqa al-qawmiyya al-Miṣriyya li-rafʿ shaʾn al-Masraḥ al-Miṣrī which, in the first period (*dawra*) of its third season (*mawsim*), commissioned three pieces from Egyptian writers and two translations from foreign languages (see *al-Ahrām*, dated 14 December 1937, p. 14).

Ḥasan al-Sandūbī, *al-Shuʿarāʾ al-thalātha Shawqī, Maṭrān, Ḥāfiẓ*, C. 1344. A critique of his *Dīwān* by Anṭūn al-Jumayyil in *al-Hilāl* was published in *Fatāt al-sharq* II, 385/94. In addition to the pieces that have already been mentioned but which were not included in his *Dīwān*, Abū Shādī, *al-Shafaq al-bākī* 1279/81 mentions a poem entitled *al-Barāʾa*, from *al-Nawwāb* magazine of 30 September 1926; al-Bustānī, in *al-Mashriq* XXV, 623 mentions the tales in verse *al-Ṭifl al-ṭāhir* and *al-Janīn al-shahīd.* His *Khuṭba shiʿriyya fī adwāʾ al-sharq*, pronounced during the annual meeting of the *Jamʿiyyat al-ittiḥād wal-iḥsān al-Sūriyya*, in Tanta on 11 February 1912, was printed in *Fatāt al-sharq* VI, 221/4; for a poem recited during the commemorative ceremony for Ibrāhīm al-Yāzijī at the Cairo railway station on 4 June 1913, see ibid. 355/5; a *Marthiya* on Aḥmad Shawqī, *al-Nīl al-khālid*, was published in *Apollo* I, 487/9, on Ḥāfiẓ Ibrāhīm ibid. 1298/1306; *Mafākhir al-hadāyā*, a wedding song in 9 strophes, ibid. 724/7; *Ḥikāyat warda*, ibid. 109/12; *al-Kashshāf al-aʿẓam*, a salute to Crown Prince Fārūq in his capacity as *kashshāf aʿẓam* ibid. 1187/90. Poetic *Muḥāwara* with Ḥāfiẓ Ibrāhīm on the occasion of the foundation of the *Jamʿiyyat riʿāyat al-ṭifl* on 31 March 1913, in Ḥāfiẓ, *Dīwān* ^{2}I, 295/6; *Fi 'l-Dustūr al-ʿUthmānī: al-nisāʾ yaḥmilna rasāʾil al-Fidāʾiyyīn, nashīd* in 6 strophes in the *mujtathth* metre | with 96
a continuous rhyme in *iyyi*, each time preceded by two verses in a changing rhyme, published in *al-Hilāl* of 1 November 1934, 25/7. From his prose works, other than what he wrote for the daily press we only mention: the translation of Roi Beaulieu's work on national economy, which he made together with Ḥāfiẓ Ibrāhīm, together with a French study on national economy and sociology by Yūsuf Efendi Naḥḥās al-Fallāḥ (Cairo n.d., see Sarkīs, *Jāmiʿ al-taṣānīf al-ḥadītha*, no. 570); *Mirʾāt al-ayyām fī mulakhkhaṣ al-tadrīs al-ʿāmm*, Cairo 1897,

1905 (dedicated to ʿAbbās Ḥilmī, *Dīwān* 266/7); *Nāʾif wa-Ṣāliḥa*, a tale in prose on the origin of a popular song (*dawr*), published in *Fatāt al-sharq* I, 249/56.

16 Aḥmad Zakī Abū Shādī

The most prolific poet of Egypt, Aḥmad Zakī Abū Shādī, showed himself in his early works a student of Khalīl Maṭrān, although it did not take long for him to go his own way.

He was born in Cairo on 9 February 1892. His father was Muḥammad Abū Shādī, who had rendered great service to the national movement, while his nephew was the poet Muṣṭafā Najīb. He grew up amidst the literati, and at an early age a talent for poetry had started to show itself. His *dīwāns Anīn wa-ranīn* and *al-Shafaq al-bākī* contain a number of poems from when he was 14, 15 years old (cf. *al-Shafaq* 73, 676, 680, n. 1, 684), some of which had been published earlier in *Fatāt al-sharq*, from 1910 onward (December 1910 *Baʿd al-firāq* V, 96, January 1911 *Damʿa ʿalā qabr* ibid. 130/2, *al-Shāʿir wal-jamāl* ibid. 273/7, *Shiʿr al-ghināʾ*, 1. *Kalimāt ʿawāṭif* ibid. 384, *Ilā Shāʿir al-ummatayn Khalīl Maṭrān*, of February 1912, ibid. VI, 189/91, in answer to a letter by Khalīl Maṭrān, *Fī Sharsharṣū* [on the Bosporus], of March 1912, ibid. 215, *Fī shabāb rāḥil* ibid. 252, *Shiʿr al-ghināʾ* ibid. 253, *Yaʿqūb* ibid. 239).

In 1326/1908, that is to say, at just 16 years old, he published a collection of essays and poems of an unusual maturity, titled *Qaṭra min yarāʿ fi ʾl-adab wal-ijtimāʿ*, in 1 *juzʾ* (the only one available to me).

97 | In this work, we already see the brilliant stylist that he was, with an absolute command of the Arabic language.[88] And almost all the subjects that he will consistently engage with in later years, are already touched upon in this volume. The work opens with a *Muqaddima fi ʾl-mūsīqī wal-shiʿr wal-naẓm wal-nathr*, a passionate defence of the ideals of classical literature that also predicts an upsurge in the appreciation of Arabic music. The self-assurance with which this sixteen-year-old discusses issues in parenting and education is just amazing, although surely the shortcomings in these areas must have been so evident that it was impossible even for him not to notice. Together with the foundation of a university, in those days a hotly-debated issue, he also demanded a thorough reform or, rather, a re-establishment from scratch of the public school system and, also, education for girls. When he talks about happiness or duty, or about the merits of a profession, he is of course not capable of anything more than commonplaces. So much more must we admire the boldness with which he tackles the issue of women's rights, outlining its history

88 Blunders are rare, such as in *wal-izāru kamīsh* at $335_{,6}$, from the correct form *rajulun kamīshu ʾl-izār*, Labīd 50, 4 and elsewhere.

in Islam on pages 398/416, candidly exposing the wrongs of married life, for knowledge of which he had, of course, to rely on his informants. In the process, he weaves a number of tales into his argument so expertly that they make us almost regret that he entirely neglected this genre in later times. A keen analyst, he understands that it is not just traditional Islamic culture that is responsible for this situation, but also, and at least in equal measure, the corruptive influence of European civilisation. Although he certainly does not close his eyes to the advantages of European, especially British, culture, he claims that Cairene society has so far just assimilated its excesses, such as the abuse of alcohol, debauchery and gambling, something in which he is probably right. On the other hand, he also attacks superstition with great vigour, such as the cult of the *zār* (316). He refers to the Coptic system of education as an example for his fellow Muslims (p. 450). But most of all, he draws their attention to the advances made in modern Turkey (305, 440), where they had been much smarter in their use of Western ideas. One could almost forget that a sixteen-year-old is behind all this, and so one is happy to encounter some youthful sensitivity in his beautiful descrriptions of the Mediterranean coast (150ff, 320ff). His poems also show an extraordinary versatility of form for his age.

| Just like his models Muṣṭafā Ṣādiq al-Rāfiʿī (150), Ḥāfiẓ and Shawqī—whom 98
he once (256) ventures to weigh against each other in 8 verses, with Ḥāfiẓ (cf. 259/60) emerging the winner—he prefers the classic form, without rejecting the *muwashshaḥ* (381/2) altogether. Despite his admiration for Turkey, he once pays tribute to ʿAbd al-Ḥamīd with a conventional panegyric (262ff). Following the example of Ḥāfiẓ Ibrāhīm, he emboldens himself, in elegies for Ibrāhīm Yāzījī (255), Qāsim Amīn Bek (357), and Muṣṭafā Kāmil Pāshā (249), to come forward with his own views on literary and political matters. There are very few love poems, even though one would expect these more than anything else, especially in view of his age ('A Sigh of Love' 258/9, 'Inner Voices' 377/81); instead, he prefers to lay out his (still bookish) wisdom in the form of trenchant *ḥikam*.[89] His later love for English literature also shows itself in his reproduction of the verses of an unknown British poet (248), of a maxim from J. Stilton's (1630/94) *Advantages of Truth and Sincerity* (385), and in his recommendation of R. Herrick's *Together* (436). In view of all of the above, it does not come as a surprise when—in a New Year's greeting to the youth of Egypt—he contrasts his own social, political and aesthetic ideals with those of the past, urging for their immediate implementation, with he himself being resolved to devote

89 Here, as in later works, he cannot resist the temptation to show off his knowledge of physics, something for which he was often criticised in later times (247, 6: "When the acid of death is poured over it, the compound dissolves with the sweet (*sic*) turning black").

his entire career to this. According to Edhem, the second volume of this work (1909)—not acessible to me—shows an even greater maturity.

In April of 1912 he went to England to study medicine. After finishing his studies in 1915, he worked as a 'Webb scholar in bacteriology,' as director of the clinical laboratory in Ealing, and finally as a private tutor in Binson, near Oxford. It was also in England that he became interested in apiculture. He became a member of the Apisclub, which honoured him with a portrait when he left, and stood at the cradle of *Bee World* magazine.

99 He delved into English literature, | with which he had become acquainted in 1909 through Bradley's *Poetry for Poetry's Sake* (Oxford 1901). Via Georgian poetry, the dominant trend in British poetry in those days (he had a special liking for the work of W.H. Davies), he was led to its precursors in Romanticism, Shelley and Keats in particular. Wanting to immerse himself completely in Western thought, he absorbed the theories of Liberalism and Marxism, showing a special interest in the work of H.G. Wells. In the process, English became a second language to him, so much so that he not only occasionally wrote poetry in English, but even explained unusual terms in his Arabic works with the help of the English language (e.g. *al-Shafaq* 1183, 8). In spite of all this, he did not forget his homeland or his people, either. Still, of the things that he wrote in Arabic while in England not much remains; a poem on a snow shower from when he was 25 years old (*al-Shafaq* 74), of which a fragment was included in *Shiʿr al-wijdān* 101/8 ('Winter in the West,' ibid. 111), a piece from a longer *qaṣīda* full of weltschmerz from the time shortly before his return (*al-Shafaq* 451), and some short poems ('Faithfulnes to Egypt', 'For Science and Fatherland', 'Beautiful Egypt', 'Memories of my Fatherland', in *Shiʿr al-wijdān*, 80/1, 83). He also followed the intellectual movements in his homeland with great interest, and through his articles in *al-Muʾayyad* and *al-Ahālī* he tried to influence debates. In London he founded the *Jamʿiyyat adab al-lugha al-ʿarabiyya*, which was presided over by Margoliouth. Furthermore, he rallied his fellow-Egyptians around him in *al-Nādī al-Miṣrī*. These activities drew the attention of the political police, which regarded him as a sponsor of an undesirable Egyptian nationalism; in the preface to *al-Shafaq* 59, Abū Shādī's friend Ḥasan Ṣāliḥ al-Jiddāwī even intimates that the former's return to his homeland may not have been entirely voluntary. Whatever the case, when he crossed the border into Egypt his belongings drew a lot of attention from customs and the police, and much of what he had written in England is reported to have been seized.

After his return to Egypt in December 1922, he founded the *Nādī al-naḥl al-Miṣrī* in February 1923. During its inaugural meeting, Aḥmad Shawqī honoured him with the *qaṣīda Mamlakat al-naḥl* (see p. 41). In April 1923 he assumed the directorship of the bacteriological unit of the Institute of Hygiene Matters

in Cairo, | in April 1924 of the Bacteriological Institute in Suez, in 1925/6 in 100
Port Said, and then in Alexandria. In 1928 he moved back to Cairo. Besides his professional activities, he also dedicated himself to agriculture and apiculture. In Port Said he was a member of the local lodge of the Freemasons (*al-Badr al-munīr*), whose ideals he exalted in a lecture (*al-Māsūniyya wa-aʿmāl al-insāniyya*) and in a series of poems. To achieve his practical objectives he founded a whole series of societies: *Rābiṭat mamlakat al-naḥl, al-Ittiḥād al-Miṣrī li-tarbiyat al-dajāj, Jamʿiyyat al-ṣināʿāt al-zarʿiyya, al-Majmaʿ al-Miṣrī lil-thaqāfa al-ʿilmiyya, al-Jamʿiyya al-Baktīriyūlūjiyya al-Miṣriyya* and the magazines *Mamlakat al-naḥl, al-Dajāj* and *al-Ṣināʿāt al-zarʿiīya* (*Apollo* I, 4).

His leisure hours were spent on writing, something he had done from his early youth. Muḥammad Ḥāfiẓ Ibrāhīm is said to have advised his father in those days to not encourage him to develop his poetical talents because his nervousness had thrown him into a crisis after a romantic mishap. However, this pessimistic poet's advice turned out to be mistaken because, in reality, poetry helped Abū Shādī surmount all of life's difficulties (see Muḥammad Ṣubḥi, on *Shiʿr al-wijdān* 12). He had enormous respect for Khalīl Maṭrān as his teacher in poetry, celebrating him in a *qaṣīda* dated 14 March 1911 as the *Shāʿir al-ummatayn* (*al-Shafaq*, 685/91, with a note by Khalīl, see p. 86). In his poetic correspondence with him he once declares: "If there is anyone to whom I owe a debt of gratitude as my teacher in poetry, then it is you, Khalīl" (ibid. 91/3). His obligation towards him is stated in even stronger terms in *Shiʿr al-wijdān* 68: "I am just a wisp of you which, despite its weakness, keeps on thirsting, even if forever you're my model." But he certainly does not want to be taken as a mere imitator (*al-Shafaq*, 1236), even though Maṭrān bequeathed the most precious of things to his people, which is freedom in poetry (*al-ḥurriyya fī 'l-naẓm*).

One of his earliest works, *Nakbat Navarīn*, was published by his friend Ḥasan Ṣāliḥ al-Jiddāwī,[90] accompanied by extensive historical, biographical,
and critical notes (C. 1924/1343). In 1925/1344 he published | the counterpiece 101
Mafkharat Rashīd, on the defence of Rosetta against the British in Ṣafar 1222/April 1807.

These poems, whose precursors were partly preserved in *Shiʿr al-wijdān*, 82, 96 ('The martyrs of Navarino'), show a whole series of characteristics by which his art distinguishes itself from that of his predecessors. The heroism of the defenders of Rosetta and of the marines who sacrificed themselves for the sultan's honour and, thereby, for Islam, he celebrates in glowing terms as the

90 Author of the critical study *al-Adab al-jadīd fī 'l-shiʿr wal-shāʿir min taʾlīf wa-jamʿ* C. 1925 (cf. *al-Mashriq* XXIV, 797).

highest expression of patriotism. In *Nakbat Navarīn* he gives a lively description of the fate of the fleet, from the moment that it weighed anchor until its final destruction; at the same time, he views the glory of Egypt against the backdrop of its history, calling upon Sesostris to lament those killed in action.

In the same year and from Suez, the same publisher brought out a selection from his adolescent poems, entitled *Zaynab, nafaḥāt min shiʿr al-ghināʾ mukhtāra min shiʿr al-ṣibā li-Abī Shādī*, C. 1924/1343.

The main themes of these poems are love and nature, themes to which he remained faithful throughout his live. The title of this collection refers to a love poem for Zaynab. Although, in this poem, he broke with all conventional forms, he still expresses his feelings without any sensuality (16). In the champagne song (21) his sensuality starts to show itself. In 'A Farewell to Childhood' (26), we discern the first traces of the 'weltschmerzy' mood that often dominates his later poems. This poem is followed by a translation of a maxim on childhood by Rückert. Similar translations of maxims on love by Bouvée, Pascal, A. de Musset, Southey and Dr. Parker are found on pp. 26 and 40. Apart from *qaṣīda*s, there is also a series of strophic *muwashshaḥ*s ('The Plover as a Messenger' 34) and some *dubayt mustazād* ('Just Punishment' 36).

Other poems from his youth were published in 1925 by Ḥasan Ṣāliḥ al-
102 Jiddāwi (*Anīn wa-ranīn*) and | Muḥammad Ṣubḥī (*Shiʿr al-wijdān min naẓm al-duktūr Abī Shādī*). These were later all included in his great *dīwān*, *al-Shafaq al-bākī*. In this same year he also published a guide to apiculture and a tale in verse, entitled *ʿAbduh Bek, qiṣṣa Miṣriyya ijtimāʿiyya*.

The tale (a mere 240 verses in *kāmil* in paired rhyme, embellished with primitive drawings by Aḥmad Ghazāle) relates the marital experiences of a young Egyptian who, through the offices of a female intermediary, marries a girl he has never met before. The marriage breaks down very quickly. The man falls first for the charms of a cocotte, but it is only with an educated lady from his own country that he finds real marital bliss. The publisher, Ḥasan Ṣāliḥ al-Jiddāwī, greatly added to its historical value as a witness of the literary movements of its time by providing a booklet with numerous appendices, among which we find: an exposition of the Arab tale by ʿAbd al-Qādir ʿĀshūr; a very detailed and critical analysis by ʿAbdallāh Bakrī; a refutation—by the publisher—of a critique by Qudāma (a pseudonym of one of the editors of *al-Siyāsa al-uṣbūʿiyya* magazine), in which he also published a *qaṣīda* by Abū Shādī on ʿAbd al-Karīm with the title *al-Asad al-asīr*; a detailed appreciation of Abū Shādī as a poet by ʿAbd al-Qādir ʿĀshūr; and a dissertation by the publisher on poetry as a mirror onto its age. An extremely spiteful critique of this tale by a follower of Shawqī—rebutted by the publisher—was printed in the preface to *al-Shafaq al-bākī* and refuted in detail.

Ever since composing the *qaṣīda*s of his adolescence Abū Shādī has talked way too much about his art. He is very conscious of its great value for the nation: “Poetry is the archive of all great nations and we are all willingly led to it. Poetry is the key to sentiments and reason. It is on poetry, that a culture and a nation rest. Poetry is the mirror of life in all its aspects, life being thus immortalised” (p. 71). As in later times, here, too, love provides him with his most productive motifs. “If it were not for love, there wouldn't be a poet who'd lift his finger and fly | around the stars (Spica) at dawn. Virtue would not rule and 103
nature would not be worshipped. There is an amazing power in the weakness that makes life go limp and falter” (‘The power of love’ 65). In these poems, his talent, carried by genuine emotions, produces absolute beauty (‘When my mouth tastes yours’ 71, ‘Memories of the first love,’ 101, and elsewhere). But nature, too, inspires him to real effusions of genuine emotions (‘The sun of Nīsān’ 100, ‘The beauty of nature’ 103). As well as this, his more rational side shows itself quite strongly. Surely one will not question the substance of his patriotic feelings; but when he extols loyalty to Egypt (80), he overindulges in rhetoric and does so even more when he addresses political issues like freedom (87), democracy (99), or sovereign and subject (103) in verse. In his patriotism, he likes to invoke the glories of ancient Egypt (‘The great pyramid’ 84/5, ‘Eternal Egypt’ 97/8), but he also celebrates its hard-working farmers (106) with an admittedly still covert reference to the oppressive rule of the British (“On their shoulders, they carry our history, from the time of the Pharaohs until the robbers of its waters” 106, 10) and to those who struggle for its freedom (‘The immortal Saʿd’ 83/4). From early on, he had to defend himself against attacks on this aspect of his work: “People criticise me by saying that my poetry seduces, as if we are dealing here with a competition between Arabs and the past. They do not know that nationalist poetry is poetry, and that a dialogue with the Nile Valley can be art. When I was young, I derived my hopes from this valley, and when it blossomed, my joy increased. In its paradisiac world, I never stumbled in my love without her bringing me unabated comfort. She generously supported me in my amorous sentiments and rendered me pure. I therefore consider it my duty to remain faithful to her like to a parent” (*Nationalist poetry* 78). In metrics he initially stuck with the traditional patterns. Only once did he try to create something new on the basis of the *muwashshaḥ*. The poem *Laylat al-ams* (67) is composed of seven distiches, each with its proper rhyme. The first two employ *ramal* and *kāmil* alternatively, then follow 5 strophes in *kāmil*, while the | 104
final strophe is again entirely in *ramal*. He reprimands the admirers of ancient poetry for condemning any and all change: “Oh, descendants of Arab glory, do not get stuck in self-praise, the world is not just words. Do justice to the past with your present, for today and for tomorrow, and not with empty love. When

you look pained upon its ruins (*aṭlāl*), then please see that its inhabitants live in bondage. When you consent, you will be just like those dilapidated ruins and your lives will be changed. While the memory of our forebears is, in itself, a beautiful thing, it should not become an object of ostentation. The only way to glory lies in ceaseless striving, so don't be like sluggish water" etc. etc. On one occasion he turned against the nagging criticism of his language. Against a *qāḍi 'l-bayān*, who had reproached him for confusing *azhār* and *zuhūr*, he says: "This is part of the language of beauty and obeys the inspiration of the fairest speaker ... do not seek to improve upon the language of love as it is infallible etc." (89/90). Later on, he came more and more under the spell of English literature, though in this work he still pays homage to Anatole France: "You, prince of poets and the arts, which know no master other than you, you steer insight and emotion; how could anyone refuse to give you his allegiance?" etc. (77). In an article from *al-Muqtaṭaf* from the year 1917, which is reprinted in the preface, he even confesses that his former admiration for Kipling was dampened somewhat by the excessiveness of his later imperialist writings (p. 22).[91] His interest in Persian literature shows itself in the free adaptation of three *rubāʿiyyāt* by Ḥāfiẓ.[92] To modern life in Europe, to which he was later so receptive, he dedicated just one elegy here, on Lenin (94). This elegy, typical of Abū Shādī, vacillates strangely between admiration and dismay: "Lenin, you erect-
105 ed the Idea in the Empire of Destruction, | tending to a wound which, though healing, still does not cease to bleed. Seeing that you saved man from committing an injustice against himself, how could you say that piety is wrong? While you, a despot, suppress justice, you don't see that injustice breeds injustice" etc.

From 1926 onward, the quality of Abū Shādī's poetic production was so high that its originality started to suffer, the more so since his official activities took up so much of his time. To begin with, 1926 was the year of publication of his great *dīwān*, *al-Shafaq al-bākī*, again by his friend Ḥasan Ṣāliḥ al-Jiddāwī (1333 pp.).

Even though he does complain about the burden of his profession as a physician (his first inclination being towards the arts, 197/201), at the same time he recognises (p. 1198) that the faculty of observation which he honed in medicine does certainly contribute to his art. He thus dedicates an enthusiastic song of praise to his old friend the microscope (p. 356).[93] As in his younger years, nature

---

91 In *al-Shafaq al-bākī* 746 too, he turns against Kiplings "East is East and West is West".

92 In *Apollo* I, 63/7, he defends himself against Aḥmad Zayn's criticism of these adaptations.

93 When people reproach him sometimes for giving his profession too much place in his poetry (like in the poem 'My Life' 465/73), he refers to R.C. Trevelyan, who, in his book *Thamrys* (63/4), demanded that the poetry of the future should even give an artistic

and love are still very much at the heart of his poetic production. In addition, his nationalist and political inclinations come more and more to the fore. Time and again he tries to awaken and raise the self-awareness of his people, be it by resuscitating the memory of the day of Tell al-Kabīr or Dinshawāy (901/5, 711/3) or by celebrating Zaghlūl's visit to the almost-finished monument to the 'uplifting of Egypt' on 9 January 1927 (997/1000), having defended him against the covert attacks of Aḥmad Shawqī (209). When Egypt's national hero passed away on 24 August 1927, | he dedicated to him a *marthiya* that was published as 106
a separate booklet, together with the poem *al-Turāth al-khālid*, which he had written in commemoration of the first 40 days following his death. Despite his grief, which was undoubtedly genuine, these poems also contain some icy rhetoric. From then on, he expressed himself emphatically on events regarding the unity of the Arabs, be it by celebrating the Moroccan freedom fighter ʿAbd al-Karīm (247/54) or by condemning the bombardment of Damascus that took place on 20 October 1925 (p. 280/4). At the same time, he does not shrink from accompanying the less important happenings of the time with his poetic effusions, such as when he defends ʿAlī ʿAbd al-Razzāq against attacks from the ranks of the Ittiḥād party (767/70), urging him to stand up for the truth like Luther did and to reconcile the Qurʾān with the Gospels. Like his predecessors, he likes to use the format of the ancient panegyric *qaṣīda*, for instance when he glorifies Dr. Haykal as a champion of democracy (360). But he also used this format to pay homage to his friends at *Apollo* magazine (Shakīb Arslān 417/9, Ḥāfiẓ Ibrāhīm 930, the poetess Mayy 367) or the Indian Tagore when he visits Egypt in November of 1926 (988/90). The Egyptian sculptor Mukhtār (who had an exposition in Paris in 1926) and the pilot Ḥasan Anīs Pāshā (742/5) he also celebrates as the bearers of the hopes of his country; just like the opera singer Munīra al-Mahdiyya, when her name was inscribed in the Golden Book of the Arts in Italy (1050/54). A counterpart to this was constituted by *marāthin* on contemporary persons of merit, including one on the tragic death of the British beekeeper R. Wright (601). But he really transgressed the boundaries of his art when he wrote about *faits divers*, such as the suicide attempt of the former sultana Saniyya (309/313), about Clémenceau in exile (707/9), the incident at Mina (stones being thrown at the Egyptian *maḥmal* on 11 Dhu 'l-Ḥijja 1344, p. 770), or even the woman dancer at the Parthenon (366).[94] Occasional poems

treatment to mathematics, medicine, and the practical professions (cf. ʿAbbās Maḥmūd al-ʿAqqād in *Sāʿāt bayna 'l-kutub*, C. 1929, 61/65).

94 Monna Paiva, whom he believed to have been intoxicated by its beauty when she performed there naked, although it soon became clear that it had been only for the purpose of promoting the Parthenon.

and personal effusions are not lacking either, not only on the occasion of festivities such as the opening of the University of Egypt (212/28),[95] the anniver-
107 sary of *al-Muqtaṭaf* (376/80), or | the opening of the Bank of Egypt (1055/61), but also in playful dialogues with good friends (713, 860, 958/60) as well as on days of remembrance within the family (926/9), in his memories of his father (320), his farewell to Suez (133), at the tomb of his brother (672), or on the occasion of the birth of his son Anīs (555/7). His discussions of world affairs take up much space but the only thing they share with his poetry is the fact that they are in verse. In Egypt, his views remained influenced by the liberal ideas he had picked up in England and which culminated in a generalised kind of humanitarianism.[96]

Thus, he is even able to celebrate the Prophet Muḥammad himself as the precursor and actual founder of the modern scientific outlook (142); but Socrates (307/8) and Aristotle (753/7), too, he worships as his spiritual fathers. He preaches a futuristic religion (778/780) which, though based on Freemasonic ideas,[97] is claimed to owe its best part to science (890). Even though, in the first part of his poem 'The Spirit of the Creator' (553/4)—which he calls a *qaṣīda taṣawwufiyya*—he still plays with pantheistic ideas, in the second part, he changes this into an acknowledgement of nature and the embodiment of its beauty in the female sex.

Here, too, the poet keeps on wrestling with the question of the meaning of his art. In vain does he try to capture the notion of beauty in words (149, 870, 1078/8). In his opinion, poetry, the most sublime of the arts (703), should be a mirror of life, forever create anew, yet let itself be guided by science (343/4). A gifted poet is a leader of his people, and he feels like one in a poem on the occasion of *al-Muʾtamar al-waṭanī* of 19 February 1926 (p. 506/511); and when
108 he boasts of its taking place, | he merely echoes the nationalist upsurge of his people. Even though he once speaks out against mindless adulation (569/71), he nevertheless has a great sense of ego ("I am quite content with the merit

---

95 He had supported the idea of its foundation as early as April 1907, in a lecture entitled *Tashyīd al-jāmiʿa am nashr al-katātīb?* (see *Anīs al-jalīs* 118/23).

96 "The most beautiful religion is to think humbly of your family, striving towards the victory of tomorrow, and to connect the future to the present, thus taking a step towards tomorrow, your companion for life. Remember this and make every and any sacrifice on its behalf, everything good and true to heart and mind etc." (141).

97 He did not only develop these ideas in his lecture *Rūḥ al-Māsūniyya* because he put his muse more often in the service of celebrations in Lodges, as in the case of the opening of the Lodge of Port Said (203/5), or on the occasion of the commemoration of the foundation of the Grand Lodge of Egypt on 8 October (1876, 228/30), or for a celebration of the Freemasons (277).

of affecting people with my emotions and with their praise of my songs" etc. 816/7). Even though Reason keeps pushing itself into the foreground, he emphasises time and again that the real foundation of his art is formed by his sensations and emotions (291). After a conversation with Ḥāfiẓ Ibrāhīm and others, at the beach in Port Said, he summarises his view as follows: "Poetry rests on deep and genuine emotions; always in search of hidden bliss, it wanders like a beam of light, all through the universe, painting everything in the colours that are hers etc." (940, 5ff). He regards Ibn Khafāja and Ibn Ḥamdīs as his predecessors, but he also believes that he was inspired by the work of the British painter Romney (1734/1802, 306, 13–14). He does not want to copy Ibn Sīnā, al-Maʿarrī, al-Mutanabbī, Ibn Hāniʾ or Shawqī, but only be led by nature (322). Those who criticise his poetry fail to see that it is about the world of the living and not about the realm of the dead (921). "I do not live in the past but only in this beautiful fatherland. Even though I have not forgotten the glory of my ancestors, I shape my life according to the present and with an eye to a better future" (263). This is also why he wants to speak the language of the present[98] but, like America and Britain, which have remained connected by a common language despite their cultural | differences, the Arabs must remain 109
united too (46); his ideal, however, is a *tamṣīr al-lugha* (48, 1172, 12), which would certainly not endanger the unity just mentioned.

98 "Speak up to him who does not know that my language is the vehicle of the feelings and the thinkings of my soul, who brands me a heretic just because of my language, and say: Tone down your blaming and don't rush your judgment etc." (747ff). "Don't think I'm confused or delirious; I adore the beauty of the past and incline myself towards it. In what is new, too, I see two strands: the artificial and the naturally beautiful. Forgive my taste for sometimes taking the past as its model in a poem, and for showing itself, at other times, according to the way it is naturally disposed. In both cases, however, it brings forth beauty by its language, a beauty which affects the whole. You can criticise my art as much as you like but don't call it artificial" ('Old and New' 499/500). Yet here, and certainly in his later poems, such criticism is not altogether misplaced. Like the British poets Miss Edith Sitwell and S. Sassoun, he wants to write poetry in a language that is easily accessible and avoid the eccentricities of Arabic that were so dear to Shawqī and his contemporaries. In this context, he praised the services rendered by Taymūr and Spiro with their inventories of the Egyptian language (1237ff). In his later works, too, he often discussed the issue of language. In the preface to *al-Shuʿla*, 10, he refers to Bahāʾ Zuhayr, Ibn Qalāqis, Ibn al-Nabīh and Ibn Nubāta as his examples, but affirms at the same time that it is impossible to keep the language of literature free from European ideas (*rūḥ al-tafarnuj*). Muṣṭafā Jawād made a detailed analysis of his language in the epilogue to *al-Yanbūʿ* (164/204). Still, he had to admit that his criticisms only concerned small things and that the poet had never sinned against the spirit of the classical language.

Even though he emphasises the nationalistic basis of his poetry, he is nevertheless entirely alive to the beauty of European art. When (1202ff) he wants to cite samples of real poetry, he prefers to take them from English literature. Thus we find, here and in his later collections of poems, numerous translations and adaptations from English, such as Stevenson's 'Youth and Love' (656), G. Goldsmith's 'Woman' (611), H. Wolfe's 'The Dead Fiddle' (657), F.W. Harvey's 'Stars' (727). W.H. Davies' 'Come, Come my Love' (758), Matthew Arnold's 'Time' (835), R. Kipling's 'If' (923), H. Coleridge's 'Night' (1001), and Shakespeare's 'O Conspiracy!' (1014/5).[99] French literature is much less conspicuous. Chateaubriand's 'Le dernier Ebn Cerragen' inspired the poem on pages 176/8. He transposed a poem by J. Richepan ('To Her') into verse from a prose version by al-Jiddāwī (809).[100] His rendering of 'Chorus of Angels' by the Dutchman Joost van den Vondel is based on an English translation from *The International Library of Famous Literature* (801).

Here, as also in his later *dīwāns*, his description of paintings, in which he takes great delight, is based on British examples (G. Dante Rosetti, Gordon Bottomley, *Sonnets for Pictures:* 'A lady of Paris Bordone' 1898, 'L'Apparition' by Gustave Moreau 1899, with drawings by C.H. Shannon, 'The white watch'
110 1900/4). | Here, he extols G.F. Watt's 'Mammon' (p. 545/7), Lord Lytton's 'Bathing Psyche' (669), 'The winner' by an anonymous painter (698/702), 'La vérité' by A. Faugeron (719/20), and 'Waterfall' and 'Forest stream' by unnamed artists (761/975/7).

Apart from European painting, music also inspired his art, even though he has a preference for Egyptian musicians: Sayyid Darwīsh (394), the female singer Umm Kulthūm (318), the singers Sālim al-Kabīr (319) and ʿAbd al-Wahhāb (818), and the violonist Shāmī al-Shawwāʾ (363); during a musical soirée, which counted Khurshīd Bek, founder of *al-Nādī al-Mūsīqī al-Sharqī*, among its contributants, Abū Shādī improvised a poem, *Fitnat al-ʿūd*, in which he included numerous references to his impressions of that evening (692/5). In a poem called 'The Kiss of Nature' (273/4), on the other hand, he takes both Turner's paintbrush and the works of Beethoven as his sources of inspiration.

While, in his youthful poems, he stuck closely to the schemes of classical verse—some rather timid attempts at other things aside—he now seeks to enhance the expressiveness of his poetry by resorting to free verse (cf. above p. 90). It started with his occasional easing of the constraints of a continuous rhyme in the classical metres, still prominent: *basīṭ* (658/68, 1023/34), *khafīf*

---

99 On page 1091 there is an English translation of his poem *ʿInda l-shāṭiʾ* by the Palestinian poet Hānī Qibṭī.

100 He rejects Beaudelaire's *Fleurs du mal* as morbid art on pages 1218/9.

(721/803), *mutaqārib* (802), *ṭawīl* (923, 1001), and *kāmil* (1014). Besides, he sometimes also employs the stropic *muwashshaḥ* (344, 349, 483/4, 564). In his translation of a poem by W.H. Davies (758), he tried to imitate the English verse form as precisely as he could, and in the poem 'The Artist' (535/7) he not only skips the rhyme but also uses a new metre which is only remotely reminiscent of Arabic metres. In his epilogue to *Mahā* (80ff) he predicts that Arabic poetry will be dominated by free verse and the *muwashshaḥ*, dismissing the Persian *dubayt* and *rubāʿiyyāt*—at which he had tried his hand in the last part of *Shiʿr al-wijdān*—as contrary to the spirit of the Arabic language.

In *al-Shafaq al-bākī* we find some minor attempts at the kind of narrative verse with which he later tried to enlarge the scope of subjective poetry. | He 111
thus recounts the tale of a pair of lovers who had fallen victim to the tyranny of al-Ḥākim, in 17 episodes with changing rhyme, based on an article in *al-Muṣawwar* from 27 August 1926 (402/22). Inspired by Voltaire, he narrates the story of the philosopher Memnon in a rhymeless *khafīf* (626/39). A bizarre tale in rhymeless *basīṭ*, entitled 'The Empire of the Devil,' he describes as a 'philosophical *qaṣīda'* (1023/34). Finally he recounts, apparently from an English source, the story of Aeschylus' death (1093/5).

Even in *al-Shafaq al-bākī*, he tried to raise the self-esteem of his people by pointing out their glorious past, just as some of his contemporaries did. It thus contains a poem on Tell al-Amarna (618/24) and a translation of Achtanon's ode to the sun in free verse after Breasted (963/72). In the same year he also published a collection of poems on that theme with the title *Waṭan al-farāʿina* I.[101] In it, he first extols the Nile, the desert, the fellahs, the shepherds, life in the countryside, the Suez canal, the sea resort of Ra's al-Barr, and the New Year celebrations; he then turns to the monuments of antiquity: the pyramids, the Sphinx, the Wādi 'l-mulūk, Uns al-wujūd, the temple of the Ḥatāsū in Dayr al-Baḥrī, Karnak, the Ramesseum and the ruins at Saqqara. In between, there is a poem about the nights of Ramaḍān, and then follow songs on the castle of Saladin, the Sinai, and the Colossi of Memnon. Although he takes care not to overburden the reader with his erudition in ancient history, this succession of related subjects is a bit tiresome all the same.

In 1926 he published another tale in verse, a rather assertive one this time, called *Mahā, qiṣṣa gharāmiyya sharqiyya*, which was—revealingly—printed at the expense of the al-Badr al-Munīr Lodge of Port Said, together with a number of somewhat naïve drawings by ʿInāyatallāh Ibrāhīm.

---

101 I know of no further volumes.

He owed the subject to his friend Jāmātī, who told him about the publica-
112 tion of an apparently true story in *al-Muṣawwar* magazine. | It was about a British officer by the name of Graves who, while on assignment in al-ʿAqaba during the war, met a Bedouin girl of the Huwayṭāt tribe. They fell in love, and the officer deserted to his lover's tribe, but was turned down by the girl's father. The lovers then eloped into the desert, where they perished. The story is told in five cantos in rhymed *kāmil* verse. In a very elaborate epilogue (p. 59/90) Abū Shādī explains that he tried to remain as close as possible to his source, defending the character, language and structure of this poem against every objection imaginable.

Kalimāt dāʾiʿa, which was apparently published in 1926 as well, was written as part of his wider attempt to resuscitate classical Arabic. In it, he tried to reintroduce ancient vocabulary into the everyday language of the educated.

In the year 1927, his ambition set him even higher goals. Until then, and we shall see this later on, the Egyptian theatre had remained at a rather low level, with light operas and floorshows alone. As such, he wanted to make it comply with European artistic standards by contributing a series of operas. Unfortunately, he did not realise beforehand that this is a job for a composer and not for a poet. He thus tells us that he couldn't find any composer willing to accept his work; and if he did find someone, this person would demand such a high fee that it would be impossible to come to an agreement. His first attempt in this discipline was *Iḥsān, maʾsāt Miṣriyya talḥīniyya* (Maṭbaʿat al-Salafiyya, 1927), which was accompanied by a foreword by the playwright Luṭfī Jumʿa, a *taqrīẓ* by Aḥmad Muḥarram, a detailed epilogue on the history of the opera by the author himself,[102] a critique by Muḥammad ʿAlī Ḥammād, and its rebuttal
113 by the poet. | The action unfolds during the war between Egypt and Abyssinia. The female hero is the lover of an officer by the name of Amīn Bek, and the first act shows us him taking his leave of his beloved when he goes off to war. In the second act we are with the Egyptian army in Qurʿa, where the commanding officer receives an Abyssinian envoy. In the third act, his traitorous friend Ḥasan, who also has his eye on the girl, deserts him on the battlefield and thus Amīn

102 Verdi's *Aïda*, ordered by Ismāʿīl, passed unnoticed in Egypt, while talented songwriters such as Najīb Ḥaddād and Ṭanyūs ʿAbduh were unable to write operas. Based on the needs and limitations of the singers, the first attempts by the lawyer Anṭūn Yūzbek (*ʿĀṣifa fī bayt* and *al-Dhabāʾiḥ*) and Ismāʿīl Bek ʿĀṣim (*Ḥusn al-ʿawāqib*) gave so much room to the common vernacular that they had no lasting artistic success. On the other hand, the theatre companies of al-Qardāḥī, Faraḥ, Shaykh Salīma, Ibrāhīm al-Iskandarī, Aḥmad al-Shāmī and others, which dominated the scene around 1900, produced pieces that could lay no claim to being works of art at all.

Bek is taken prisoner by the enemy. After he successfully escapes, he first hides with his former servant Ḥājjī Riḍwān. When he returns to his beloved, he finds her on her deathbed in her uncle's house, as the message of his heroic death on the battlefield by the traitorous Ḥasan had caused her to die of consumption. With this sentimental theme, Abū Shādī not only wanted to offer text material for mellifluous arias, but also and at the same time, and he alludes to this on page 106, pursue the political objective of promoting the reunification of the countries of the Nile: Abyssinia, Egypt, and the Sudan. As in his later operas, he tried to cater for the tastes of the general public, which expected a ballet in every opera, although in this case it is done a bit artificially through a dance by some Abyssinian slave girls who are presented to the Egyptian commander as a gift. The piece is written in different metres (mostly *kāmil*, *ramal* and *mujtathth*) and changing rhyme. Of course, it is not for us to pass a judgement on its adaptability to music or the potential that it might have had for the stage.

He wrote his second opera, *Ardashīr wa-ḥayāt al-nufūs* (Alexandria 1928), at the instigation of the director of the *Shirkat tarqiyat al-tamthīl al-ʿArabī*, who wanted to bring material from the 1001 Nights onto the stage.

In the fourth Cairene printing he decided to adapt the story of Prince
Ardashīr and his artful 'conversion' of the male-unfriendly | Princess Ḥayāt al- 114
Nufūs, acquitting himself of this task in four acts that exploit the pliable material through an effective escalation of emotions. In form, the piece is similar to *Iḥsān*.

After his completion of the above work in May 1927, he followed it up, in August that year, with the much more ambitious *al-Āliha*, *The Goddesses*, a symbolic opera in three acts (Dār al-ʿUṣūr).

The hero of the piece is a poet-philosopher. In the first act, which takes place in the forest, he is awakened by the singing of the goddess of beauty. Pretending to be the ruler of the world, she promises him true bliss. She permits him to have commerce with her sister, the goddess of love. But he lets himself be betrayed into renouncing both of them by the goddesses of lust and power. He thus wanders about unhappily in the material world, a prey to doubt and remorse. When he begs the goddesses of beauty and love to help him, he awakens as if from a bad dream; they forgive him, lead him back into their world, and grant him eternal bliss. Perhaps only the master of the *Zauberflöte* would have been able to render this brittle material into musical form. Yet, actually, it was the young composer Maḥmūd Ḥilmī who undertook this task in 1932, telling the author about it in a letter that was published in *Apollo* I, 51/2.

We continue immediately with two further operas which, though written in the same year, were only published four years later. In these, Abū Shādī turned to history, as he must have understood that he could only win the heart of the public by offering stageable subject matter.

In the first act of *al-Zabbāʾ, malikat Tadmur, opera taʾrīkhiyya kubrā dhāt arbaʿat fuṣūl*, he introduces Queen Zenobia at the height of her power, during the conquest of Alexandria. The second act depicts the mobilisation of the Roman army against her. In the third act we learn how her Roman general, whom she had refused in marriage, betrayed her. The fourth act shows her in
115 | Roman captivity and the punishment of the Roman general, whose treason
she had reported to the emperor.

He embarks upon national history with *Akhnatūn Firʿawn Miṣr, opera taʾrīkhiyya dhāt thalāthat fuṣūl*, C. n.d. (1931), dedicated to Khalīl Maḥmūd and H.G. Wells, and with a foreword signed "Alexandria, 26 June 1927." He mentions as his sources Breasted's *History of Egypt* and H. Weigall's *The Life and Times of Akhnaton*, London 1922. Even more so than the previous one, this opera lacks real drama. In the first act, we see an old sun-worshipper amidst his family. The second act takes us to a tavern in Beirut, where the consequences of his reign—weak because it shuns all violence—become apparent. The third act takes place in Egypt again, this time at the court of the king while he suffers a stroke on his thirtieth birthday. This takes place at the very instant in which a bearer of bad tidings arrives at the palace door, bringing news of the loss of Syria. Yet the king will not hear it. Abū Shādī does not succeed in describing Akhnaton: he values the king as one of the greatest thinkers in the history of mankind and a real democrat, but because of this he is unable to use the dissolution of his power—which only bears a superficial relation to his death—as a lesson in politics on the subject of poor leadership. It is this same unworldliness, which makes him say in the preface (p. 9) that, to his mind, the [First] World War showed how right all great thinkers of humanity are when they talk about brotherhood and the evilness of war.

Both operas were the object of violent criticism. ʿAbd al-Ḥamīd Ṣāliḥ sharply criticised *Zabbāʾ* in *al-Akhbār* newspaper, even going so far as to compare it to the negro poetry of America. He was particularly offended by the piece's language, which he (unjustly) blamed for having made concessions to the common vernacular. The poet defended himself against this charge in the preface to *Akhnaton*, saying that although he did aim for a language that is easy to sing and understand, nowhere did he sin against the conventions of the classical language. In that same preface he also tried to defend himself against the criticism by P. Anastase Karmalī in *Lughat al-ʿarab*, who had criticised him espe-
116 cially for his blending of different metres. In answer to this charge, | Abū Shādī
drew attention to the requirements of modern music, while at the same time referring—typically—to R.F. Brewer in asserting his right to poetic freedom.

The opera *Nofretet*, a counterpart to *Akhnaton* which he announced as forthcoming, has not been published yet.

Since then, Abū Shādī must surely have understood that all his efforts to conquer the stage are doomed to failure. But however this may be, over the last couple of years he has returned to his own field again, that is to say, lyrical and didactic poetry. In 1928 a small collection of poems was published, *Mukhtārāt waḥy al-ʿām* (Dār al-ʿUṣūr, 80 pp.), which bears all the characteristics of *al-Shafaq al-bākī*.

In that work, he reprinted his elegy on Saʿd Zaghlūl (published earlier in a collection of *marāthī*), followed by a song that was written on the occasion of the *arbaʿīn* celebrations for Muṣṭafā Naḥḥās Pāshā (18/21). Apart from this theme, so typical of the Egyptian way of thinking and which he likes to cultivate in other places, too, his attachment to European culture stands out more clearly here than ever before. He glorifies Einstein and Schopenhauer (in a didactic poem in 7 chapters, 61/79) and bemoans the death of the Spanish revolutionary Blasco Ibañez (50). He states his commitment to the modern worldview in 'My Answer.' But he also extols the female dancer Vanessi (58) and describes Ingres' painting 'The Source' (42/3), seen in the Louvre. Here, too, he tries out new forms on more than one occasion. In a ceremonial elegy on Saʿd Zaghlūl, written in Alexandria on 5 October 1927 (12/14), he uses the *muwashshaḥ*, and his strophic poem 'Saʿd Forever' is really very artistic. On page 35, in 'Me and the Others,' he uses free verse, as he does in a genre scene (European women bedecked with flowers in front of a mirror); in 'The Light from Hell' (59) he imitates the sonnet.

In 1928 he also completed an adaptation of ʿUmar Khayyām's *Rubāʿiyyāt*. He did this on the basis of a literal prose version by the Iraqi poet Jamīl Ṣidqī
al-Zahāwī, who had already complemented it with | a rendering in verse. This 117
adaptation was published in 1931: *Rubāʿiyyāt ʿUmar al-Khayyām, naẓamahā bil-ʿarabiyya Aḥmad Zakī Abū Shādī. The Rubaiyat of Omar Khayyam, rendered into Arabic Verse by* A.Z. Abushady (Maṭbʿat al-Muqtaṭaf). As a complement to it he published an adaptation of 10 *rubāʿiyyāt* after Fitzgerald in *Apollo* I, 222/3. In 1929, he translated Shakespeare's *The Tempest* (*al-ʿĀṣifa*), having already expressed his reverence for this great Briton in his *Dhikrā Shakespeare* of 1926.

In 1928 he published a new collection of poems, *Ashiʿʿa wa-ẓilāl, Rays and Shadows*, collected poems (Maṭbaʿat al-Shabāb, 145 pp.). Then followed: *al-Shuʿla, The Torch*, collected poems, in 1933 (139 pp.), *Aṭyāf al-rabīʿ, Spring Phantoms*, collected poems (200 pp.), *al-Yanbūʿ, The Fountain*, collected poems (218 pp.), 1935 *Fawq al-ʿuqāb* (158 pp., 147 *qaṣīda*s and *maqṭūʿāt* in 2248 verses).

The poet's style being firmly settled now, we can examine these five *dīwān*s at the same time. The poet, who regards himself as the pioneer of a new intellectual movement, proudly voices his self-assurance time and again: "When my voice is heard, I need no further fame. I don't understand people who live for fame alone and get exited by applause, as if they were entertainers … My friend said: 'I see that people are not happy with your poems and even disparage them', whereupon I answered: 'It is enough for me if they are concerned about them; the judgement of my poems, I leave up to time'" (*al-Shuʿla*, 86/7).

A special trait of his art, his description of paintings, continues as before. Thus, he writes of 'Silent Watchers' by A. Wardale in *al-Shuʿla* 5, 'Eva' by an known artist, ibid. 10, 'The Mediator,' also by an unknown artist, ibid. 26, 'Sleep' by the Egyptian illustrator Shaʿbān Zakī, ibid. 31, 'The Gleaners' by J.F. Millet, ibid. 32, 'The Banker and his Wife' by Quentin Matsys 35, a drawing of his daughter and 'Misery' by Shaʿbān Zakī 37, 39, 'l'Inpriration' by J.H. Fragonard 41,
118 'The Gypsy Girl' by Frans Hals 43, 'Muraqqash' | and 'Charivari' by Laura Knight 47, 49, 'Good Bye, Old Man' by F. Matania 51, 'In al-ʿArīsh' by Shaʿbān Zakī, 'A Hunter's Dreams' by an unnamed artist 58, 'The Old Man and his Grandson' by Domenico 61, 'The Sad Castle' by an unnamed artist 71, 'Love Locked Out' by Anna Lea Merrett 73, 'Meditating' by an unnamed artist 77, 'The Surprise' by Caban 80, 'Summer Moon' by F. Layton 85, 'The Prisoner' by an unnamed artist 96, 'Christmas Morning' idem 101, 'The New Echo' idem 116, and 'The Vale of Leutha' by H. Spead 121. This list is enough to show that the poet had a preference for genre paintings and that he was especially charmed by nude women. This would show itself even more in his later *dīwāns*. For instance, in *al-Shuʿla* p. 36 he extols 'The Harp' by Pierre Jules, 'The Enchanted' by an unnamed artist 44, 'The Moonworshipper' idem 123/4, 'Crown of Thorns' idem 132, in *Aṭyāf al-Rabīʿ* 'The Farewell' by L. Riedel, 'Sunbathing,' 'The Bath,' and 'Life', all by unnamed artists 90, 94, 97, in *al-Yanbūʿ* 'Lilies of the Nile' by Henri Manuel 19, 'The Beauty and the Skeleton' by an unnamed artist 57, 'A Summer's Night' by Albert Moore 89; indeed, on page 16 he even provides his poem 'Noble Beauty' with a nude photograph (*min taṣwīr sex appeal*).

He further demonstrates his attachment to English literature with an impressive number of translations, among these of W. Gibson's 'The Fowler' in *Ashiʿʿa* 25, 'Twins' by Longfellow 30, 'New Times' by J. Russel Lowell 97, 'Growth of Love' by R. Bridges 120, 'Philosophy of Love' by P.B. Shelley in a free adaptation in *Yanbūʿ* 125. He notes English translations of various works by fellow poets, such as 'The Pipe' and 'The Crows and the Gardener' by Muḥammad ʿAbdallāh Muṣṭafā in *Ashiʿʿa* 93, 138, and 'The Mother' by the Palestinian poet Hānī Qibṭī ibid. 129. In contrast to this, French literature is again almost absent. He only versified two poems by E. Rostand ('The Future' and 'Nobility,' rendered accessible to him in prose by Ḥasan Ṣāliḥ al-Jiddāwī), in *Ashiʿʿa* 94, 107.

Egypt still inspired him very much. Thus, he extols the passageway in the
temple at Edfu based on a drawing by Shaʿbān Zakī in *Ashiʿʿa* 11, ʻNofretete and
the Sculptor' after a painting by Matania in *al-Shuʿla* 46, and ʻIn the Temple,'
following a painting by an unnamed artist in *Aṭyāf* 4. Furthermore, antiqui-
ty becomes more prominent in his later poems. | Whereas in *Ashiʿʿa* 67ff, in 119
his panegyric on Alexandria, he was content with some learned innuendos,
later he does not shrink from adapting ancient myths and sagas. In *al-Shuʿla*
62/66, he recounts the tale of Psyche and Cerberus, in *Aṭyāf* 5 that of Zeus and
Europa, on page 7 of this same work that of Aphrodite and Adonis, and on page
55 the tale of Pluto and Proserpina. In *Yanbūʿ* 22, he tells the tale of Orpheus
and Euridyce, on page 37 that of Deianira and Heracles and the one of Phryne
on page 91. But he also used biblical themes, such as Elias and Samuel in *Aṭyāf*
6, Daniel in the lions' den in *Yanbūʿ* 50, and Moses on the Nile on page 73 of
the same work. It speaks for itself that he also takes great interest in each and
every aspect of modern life. A special characteristic of *al-Shuʿla* is that it bears
witness to his rising interest in medicine. For example, he lauds a number of
famous physicians from among his compatriots, and celebrates the foundation of the Order of Physicians of Egypt in 1928 with a satirical poem (113). In
Apollo I, 1175/6, his critic ʿAbd al-Raḥīm Ṣāliḥ had special praise for his *qaṣīda
al-Muṣāb* (p 113), which criticises the exploitation of the Egyptian people by
foreign quacks, in *zajal* in the common vernacular.

While joyous in his younger years, it must have been the approach of old
age that made him indulge more and more in pessimistic thoughts. In *al-Shuʿla*
22/3, he criticises the baseness and the foolishness of mankind, fighting each
other like animals while they, being mere guests in this world, should gratefully
enjoy the brief spell that they are granted. It is very well possible that the uncertain political situation of Egypt in the post-war era favoured these moods.
In *al-Shuʿla* 27, we read: "Let me talk to despair. I live in a country that has been
sacrificed to the wrath of devil and doom. There is no hope for us anywhere.
Should we entertain any hope in a country that all others lunge at in covert
or open animosity? They are only all too happy to run it aground, but ever so
slow when its welfare is at stake—hostile to its soul. They boast of the damage they inflict on it, as if they are rivals, battling ʿAntara. I am surprised that
the sun should still shine here, given that they are the arch enemies of the sun
and of light." These moods are recurrent in this volume: pp. 52/3 (ʻDisavowal'),
58/9 (ʻA General Suspicion'), | 59 (ʻFutile Admonitions': "From among Saʿd's ad- 120
monitions, there isn't one whose pertinence we, inhabitants of Egypt, did not
disregard" etc.), 63 (ʻLoneliness,' 8ff: "I went ahead of my people, time welcomed
me, but disavowal is in the nature of welcoming. A country, in which baseness
rules supreme, in which the vandal is praised, in which tragedies border on the

burlesque, and in which nothing magic seems what it is" etc.), 116 ('A Hostile World'), and 118 ('Revenge'). In one case, he is even obliged to address a poem to the prime minister Ismāʿīl Ṣidqī Pāshā, complaining about the obscurantists who oppose his working towards enlightment ('The Guilty Environment or the Diclosure of an Injustice': "Can time abandon me while you protect me, can my people despise me while you defend my cause?" etc.). In *Aṭyāf al-rabīʿ* he raises a similar complaint ('Morning breeze' 51, 16ff: "My whole life is nothing but hardship and misery. I cry and I laugh, but laugh like a drunken sailor is all they'll see me do. With my vessel, I sailed the seas of suffering and all I want to do, is to sit and drink. Only God knows if my drunken me is in the hands of a surgeon or a bloodletter. I don't know if His hand will heal or kill me. So I play and jest, wrestling against the surf like swimmers do. The sea refuses me its shores, despite my bravery; this, then, is where bravery ends." 'The Prisoner' 52: "I beg of you, forgive me my fears, for I live in a windowless prison" etc. 'A Song of Pain,' ibid. 52, 'The Monk, a Vision,' ibid. 53, 'Exile' 73, 'The Avengers' 88: "Sure, you can take revenge; in class, pupils always go missing. My sin is to live in a place of ignorance, a desert, which disavows, misleads and infects. I gave you a reason yesterday, by teaching you what you did not know. You then lapidated me in pure envy, as if I wanted to enrich myself with that which I gave you out of generosity"). But even in moods like these, his self-assurance resurfaces again. For instance, right after the passage just quoted he says: "Too bad, all this time lost. But even though I complain, I have no regrets. Once
121 you understand that it is all a farce, you just keep on giving | and laugh at the foolishness of the blind. You give and want nothing in return, even though they misconstrue your merits and lapidate you."). In *al-Yanbūʿ*, these complaints may still be heard: 'Tedium Vitae' p. 42: "Why be merry, why sing, if life in Egypt equals disillusionment, a life suffused by ignobility, a life whose damages no one can ignore? A nation that has been brought down to the level of animals, so that you can't speak of humans anymore; connected to its soil, but whose share in crops and produce steadily dwindles; a worker , enslaved, and without pay." etc., and on p. 82, 'Dancing on a Volcano.' But every bit of success restores the author's courage. Thus, he greets the first female Egyptian pilot Luṭfiyyat al-Nādī as a pioneer of progress (84: "Oh, day of joy! You have overcome my faintheartedness! Already I began to despair of my fellow countrymen!").

A selection of Abū Shādī's poems was published 1933 under the title *Aghānī wa-anāshīd*. Most of these had been published earlier in *Shiʿr al-wijdān* and *al-Shafaq al-bākī*, although some of them are more complete when compared to their earlier version.

Of the 6 verses of *al-Ṭīb wal-zahr* (p. 3), only numbers 3 and 4 were included in *Shiʿr al-wijdān* 104; the 'Champagne Song' (ibid. 100/1) has a new introduction of four verses here, etc. We learn nothing about the reasons behind these changes.

In the preface to his penultimate *dīwān*, *Fawq al-ʿubāb* (C. 1935), dated November 1934, he once more feels obliged to defend his art against his critics. While these expected the poet above all to reproduce the music of the language, he defends himself with a reference to some lines of Ibn al-Rūmī, inimitable in the vividness with which they express the desert's scorching midday heat. And while he admits that the language of these verses is brutal, such language was clearly in keeping with the topic. He does not care much about public approval, convinced as he is that he writes for the future. A poet should not flatter the ear but serve the highest ideals of mankind. His art is, more
than anything, akin to philosophy, he says, referring | to G. Ingram Bryan's *The* 122
Philosophy of English Literature.

'The Poets,' a small poem on page 135 of this *dīwān*, expresses the same kind of sentiment: "How many fools among you are there not, who take pride in their foolishness, as if it were a sign of prophethood? Instead, one should honour the few who are really wise, and who lead our race towards a golden age." In this *dīwān*, the sound of his younger years is rarely heard any more, only when he envies his lover's necklace hanging around her neck (92), or when he praises a lady's beautiful cleavage (111). Even though he still professes to be in the service of beauty (43), the demoralisation of old age makes him reject Spring as it has nothing more to offer him (4). And, time and again, pessimism rears its ugly head; he sees himself in endless strife, surrounded by people who envy him, and by spies (74, 4). But he is not so much troubled by his own fate as by that of his people. More than ever before, he puts his poetry in the service of politics. In compelling language he points out the miserable situation of the Egyptian farmers (116). He praises ʿAbbās Ḥalīm, who was thrown into jail for his courageous defence of the workers (108). He still expects the Wafd to save the situation and does not tire of repeating his admiration for its leader, al-Naḥḥās (10, 57, 71 etc.). And the Copts, too, he wants to become a genuine part of his people, assuring them of his esteem for their ancient culture (127).

At the same time, he also keeps on plying his ancient trade when he translates verses by Byron (8) or O. Goldsmith (76), or when he lets himself be inspired to descriptions and contemplations by a work of art such as the Nile sculpture by E. Zakī Khalīl (26), paintings like Marc Simon's 'Paradise' (49), Urbino's 'Diana and Aktaion' (77) and 'The Act' by a modern French painter (89). The discoveries of the sciences, astronomy in particular, he continues to admire (with poems on the person who discovered Pluto 62, on the wonders of the Milky Way 63, or of Mars 66). Well represented are the poems that he wrote for his friends, like the one for Zakī Mubārak on the occasion of a soirée

in his honour at the Alhambra on 29 April 1934 (38), or for the 'orator of Egypt' Mukarram 'Ubayd at the opening of a conference of lawyers (6), and especially the *marāthī* he wrote, such as the one on the sculptor Maḥmūd Mukhtār (17, 45), the one on his teacher 'Abdallāh al-Anṣārī (53) and the one on Aḥmad Zakī
123 Pāshā (86). Among these, his elegy | for Hindenburg (102) has a special place; for it shows to what extent the poet was able to immerse himself in the feelings of a foreign nation, allowing him to fully understand the historical importance of the victor of the Battle of Tannenberg. He also tried his hand (again) at narrative poetry, a genre that was not very suited to his talents. Nevertheless, he made some lucky choices that gave him the opportunity to indulge in reflections, for instance on the story of Abélard and Héloïse (105/8), and notably on Egyptian mythology, such as the epic cycle around Isis and Osiris (39/45). Of course, these Egyptian themes were a way to arouse patriotic feelings, like the Solar Ship's visit to the fourth pyramid, a project which he carried out with the Society for the Advancement of Science that he founded, and which is described on page 14.

This *dīwān* distinguishes itself from the others because his bond with nature comes more and more to the fore. It is thus not by accident that he signs the preface from his country estate in al-Maṭariyya. Apart from philosophical contemplations, such as the one on man and nature (125), we find unpretentious descriptions of the lives of birds ('The Return of the Caravan' 9, 'Abū Qirdān' 16, 'The Hoopoo Bird' 22, 'Zummaj, The Sea Swallow' [called the white-winged tern in English] 31, 'The Peacock' 52), but also of the spider (128) and of the bat (135). He also records scenic impressions from a trip through the countryside (93ff), such as his gaze over waving fields, the beauties of a garden or of a beach. And the joy derived from the colourful dress of a peasant woman (94), too, belongs in this category, no less than the pleasure of the bustle of the crowd at a popular celebration (*Mawlid al-Sayyida Zaynab* 122).

He brought out two more sequels of poems called *Anbā' al-fajr*, C. n.d. (1355), and *al-Insān al-jadīd*. He only used free metre once here, in the poem 'At the Beach' (113/4). He somewhat arbitrarily calls a ditty for the female dancer Bība a sonnet (96), but its shortened *rajaz* is well adapted to the dancing mood.

Apart from his *dīwān*s, the poet also worked for a number of magazines as a way to advance his ideals. After *Imām* magazine, he worked from September
124 1932 to July 1933 | for *Apollo*, Majalla adabiyya li-khidmat al-shi'r al-ḥayy lisān ḥāl Jam'iyyat Apollo (also with the English title *Apollo*, a monthly review devoted to the interests of Arabic poetry, official organ of Apollo's Society), and then, since July 1936, *Adabī*.

Apart from Abū Shādī's own creations, *Apollo* also published the works of many other, younger poets who followed in his footsteps, including from other

Muslim countries, such as Aḥmad Tawfīq Bakrī from the Sudan with his *Sarāb al-amal* and *al-Nahr al-mutadaffiq* (551/2) or Muḥammad ʿAlī Maḥjūb's *Qiṣṣat al-ḥubb* (1131/2) (both portraits show strong negroid traits); from Tunis, there are Abu 'l-Qāsim al-Shābī's *Ṣalawāt fī haykal al-ḥubb* (848/51), *al-Saʿāda* (868), and *al-Janna al-ḍāʾiʿa* (1022/5); and from Baghdad, there is Ḥusayn al-Ẓarīfī's *Masraḥ al-tamthīl* (877/8).—There are also translations: from the English there is Wordsworth's *al-Narjis al-māʾī* by Mutawallī Najīb (1009/11), from the French A. de Musset's *al-Wadāʿ yā Sūsū* by Aḥmad Kāmil ʿAbd al-Salām 1011/2, and A. Lambert's *Laytak bi-jānibī* by Aḥmad Yāsīn in free metre (1012/5).—Abū Shādī's own contributions are very numerous, among them a *marthiya* on Muḥammad Ḥāfiẓ Ibrāhīm (32/4), 'Night in the Desert' (39), 'In the Oasis' (128), and another series of descriptions of paintings: *al-Mashūra* (129), *Nifirtītī wal-maththāl* (251), *Fi 'l-maʿbad* (577), 'Zeus and Europa' (652), 'Aphrodite and Adonis' (900/3), *al-Aḥdab* (1032/3), and *Bulūtū wa-Birsifūn* (1180/2).—In *Adabī* of 1937, 520/22 he was forced to answer critics who did not shrink from accusing him of plagiarising the poems of ʿAbd al-Raḥmān Shukrī. In an open letter to Aḥmad al-Shāʾib in *al-Ḥadīth* of July 1938, 518/9, he announced his intention of bidding farewell to the ungrateful world of Arabic literature and to write only in English from then on, adding that his book *At Random* was already in press.—Ḥasan Kāmil al-Ṣīrafī, *Fī ṣuḥbat Abī Shādī* in his *Aṭyāf al-rabīʿ* 120/77. J.A. Edhem (on the author, who is a specialist of theoretical physics by training, cf. *Adabī* 1936, 435/60), *Abushady the Poet, A critical study with specimens of his poetry*, London 1936, Ḥasan Ṣāliḥ al-Jiddāwī, *Naẓariyyāt naqdiyya fī shiʿr Abī Shādī maʿa taʿqīb*, C. 1925, Aḥmad Muḥarram, *Aḥmad Zakī Abū Shādī shiʿruhu fī dīwān al-Shuʿla*, C. 1933, Muḥammad ʿAbd al-Ghafūr, *Abū Shādī fi 'l-mīzān* C. 1934, ʿAbd al-Hādī al-Ṭawīl, *Waṭaniyyāt Abī Shādī* in *Adabī* 1937, 514/20, Muḥammad ʿAbd al-Ghafūr, *al-Rīf fī shiʿr Abī Shādī* is cited | in al-Saḥartī, *Adab* 125
al-ṭabīʿa 101, Ibrāhīm Nājī, *al-Shiʿr al-ḥadīth* in *al-Ḥadīth* 764/765 (a defence of Abū Shādī and his school).—His son Muḥammad Muḥammad Abū Shādī also published a poem in *Apollo* 731/2.

17 ʿAbd al-Raḥmān Efendi al-Shukrī

Of the poets in the circle of Khalīl Maṭrān and Abū Shādī, the first champion of the new poetry to be mentioned here is ʿAbd al-Raḥmān Efendi Shukrī.

The son of a civil servant working for the company that runs the Suez Canal, Shukrī was born in Port Said in 1304/1886, went to school in Alexandria and in 1909 completed his studies with a diploma from the Madrasat al-muʿallimīn. He then went to England, where he studied history and linguistics at the University of Sheffield. Since then he has worked as a teacher at the Ra's al-tīn and ʿAbbāsiyya secondary schools in Alexandria.

In 1909 he published the first volume of his *dīwān* (*Ḍawʾ al-fajr*) in Alexandria. It was followed by six further volumes, in 1913, 1915, 1916, 1918, and 1919 (*Laʾālīʾ al-afkār, Anāshīd al-ṣibā, Zahr al-rabīʿ, Azhār al-kharīf, Khaṭarāt, Dīwān al-afnān*).

Miftāḥ al-qulūb, from the unpublished eighth volume of the *dīwān*, was printed in *Lughat al-ʿarab* V, 650. In the beginning, al-Shukrī was strongly influenced by the French symbolists, and had a penchant for inner contemplation (*munājāh*) of a strongly pessimistic nature. Having heard of Lobroso's *Genio e follia*, he liked to think of himself as a lunatic: "The ingenious poet is possessed, making him want to go over and over every thought." His philosophical background is, however, insufficient to permit him to come up with anything new on the subject. As such, the theme of erotomania, much used in all kinds of ways in ancient poetry, turns up time and again, mounting to a murderous frenzy: "In my heart, mistreated by you, madness rages. It would not feel any remorse if one day it wanted to kill you. Let my madness swallow your blood,
126 for murder heals a wounded | heart." In 'Delusions of a lunatic,' he describes himself as haunted by fears and a sense of guilt and inferiority. This mental condition, he believes, can be seen in all: "Every face shows clear signs of madness, signs that speak to you." This dark side of the human condition is also the theme of the play *al-Ḥallāq al-majnūn* which (following a Russian piece) tells the story of a barber who cuts the throat of a client because he believes it is the head of a sheep.

These strange moods could not, of course, endure, and in his sixth *dīwān* they give way to more objective contemplation. True, in his long 'Ode to the sun' he does once strike a buoyant, joyful tone ("You, dreams of the soul, go out and fly, sing! The sun is calling you to the most beautiful feast of all!"). More often, however, it is fatalistic pessimism that speaks ("Even though my life is brightened by joy, still the shadow of death keeps looming"). He pays homage to his newly-awakened interest in nature in poems on the Sphinx and on the pyramid of Cheops. According to al-Saḥartī in *Adab al-ṭabīʿa* 98/9, his talent for describing scenes from nature is especially visible in the poems 'Winter in England' and 'The sea,' which were both published in *Majallat al-Risāla* III, no. 129, 23 December 1935. By contrast, he never pronounces himself on current affairs. As for the form of his poetry, several times he tried out a new rhyming technique, inspired by the popular *muzdawija*.

Abū Shādī views his *qaṣīda al-Shallāl* as one of the best specimens of true, modern poetry (*al-Shafaq al-bākī* 1212_1). And his friend Muḥammad Ibrāhīm Saʿīd even wants to regard him as one of the greatest living poets (ibid., 1194). Still, Ibrāhīm ʿAbd al-Qādir al-Māzinī, who Ḥasan Kāmil al-Ṣīrafī says was his student (Abū Shādī, *Aṭyāf al-rabīʿ*, 122,$_{17}$), attacked him extremely aggressively in *Ṣanam al-alāʿīb*, in his *Dīwān* I, 48/62 and II 85/95. But this criticism shows great agitation and may, therefore, have been triggered by ʿAbd al-Raḥmān Shukrī's criticism of his poems in *al-Muqtaṭaf*. Abū Shādī tried to mediate between the two in an article that was reprinted in *Shiʿr al-wijdān* 20/6. His high esteem for this poet is also shown by the fact that he dedicated his opera *al-Āliha* to him and that he defended him from his critics once more in *al-Yanbūʿ* 215/6.

| In his essays, which he brought together in various collections—*Kitāb al-thamarāt* C. 1335/1916, *Kitāb ḥadīth Iblīs* Alexandria 1335/1916, *Kitāb al-iʿtirāfāt, Kitāb al-ṣaḥāʾif* C. 1918, *Kitāb adab al-shiʿr, Kitāb al-madāris, Kitāb rasāʾil al-ḥubb, Kitāb maẓāhir al-quwwa fī 'l-ḥayāt*—he develops a philosophy of life that is based more on emotion than on reason, and this in a style that is fluent and elegant at one and the same time and which clearly draws more upon the works of al-Manfalūṭī than on the classics. 127

The masters to whom he refers are, apart from classical poets (mostly Abu 'l-ʿAlāʾ al-Maʿarrī, Ibn al-Rūmī and al-Mutanabbī), the British Romantics Shelley, Wordsworth and Byron—as well as a philospher like Berkeley—and besides, V. Hugo and, at times, E. Zola. So, with him, one cannot expect any systematics. He is, instead, an exponent of the level of education of the first decades of the twentieth century, which was a period when people were still looking for some kind of new ideal, without yet having a fixed objective before them. Al-Shukrī is very much aware of this. It is also why he wants to be judged more mildly than someone representing a closed culture and a mature art; he wants similar treatment for his friends. The pessimism that so often rings through in his poems is present here as well; for instance, when, in his *Kitāb al-ṣaḥāʾif*, he speaks of the lies of life and society and of life's sacrifices. He draws on Schopenhauer here, who regards love as man's greatest sacrifice, made for the preservation of mankind. *Ḥadīth Iblīs* is written in a similar vein. In it, the author establishes direct communication with the devil (just like Dante and al-Maʿarrī in his *Risālat al-Ghufrān*), who teaches him his lessons in life, now in Hell itself, and then on the streets of Cairo or somewhere along the Nile. And even though he does, in one case, try to enliven his gloomy philosophy with some fun, talking about the animal parliament under the chairmanship of man, in the end this parliament can only conclude that the law of the strongest will always prevail. Also, he is not capable of defining happiness in anything other than negative terms, such as one's elation when, passing under a window, | one is only hit by some dirty water rather than a piece of steel. 128
The maxims from his *dīwān* with which he ends the book strike a similar

tone. In his *Iʿtirāfāt*—published before *Ḥādīth Iblīs* but in the same year—he preaches this same decadent philosophy of life. This work contains the putative confessions of a friend of his who had fallen victim to the man-eaters of the Sudan, and which he now publishes in unadulterated form, even though he cannot agree with each and every one of the opinions they contain. At the same time, the book is probably meant to hold up a mirror to the youth of Egypt of his time, making them see the contradictions in their culture. Even though the alleged author of these confessions praises the youth for its aspirations, he also finds that they are still not free from the evil products of superstition. He revels in the memory of a poet's joy when he sees his first poem published, and tells us about a young man being torn between religious ecstasy and unrestrained abandonment to the pleasures of life. But because of his upbringing, his will crumbles as soon as he goes out into the world, his only answer to life's problems being an absolute resignation to fate, making life seem as if it were a drawing in the sand, blotted out by the ocean surf. He articulated his thoughts on modern poetry once more in *Naqd al-ṭarīqa al-ramziyya wa-sharḥ atharihā fī asālīb al-shiʿr wa-maʿānīhi* in *Apollo* 1194/1204, in *al-Shiʿr* and in his *Faṣl fī anna 'l-shuʿarāʾ kamāliyūn* in Rufāʾīl Buṭṭī, *Siḥr al-shiʿr* 216/29.—Aḥmad ʿUbayd, *Mashāhīr shuʿarāʾ al-ʿaṣr* 249/67 (with a portrait; a later photograph in *Apollo* 1195), al-Saḥartī, *Adab al-ṭabīʿa* 98 (who counts him as one of the *Arkān al-nahḍa al-adabiyya al-ḥadītha fī Miṣr*).

18 Aḥmad Rāmī

Even though Aḥmad Rāmī does not belong to Khalīl Maṭrān's circle proper, he, too, did derive quite a lot of inspiration from the moderns.

The son of Muḥammad Rāmī, a physician, and the grandson of Emir Alāy Ḥasan, of Circassian stock and killed in action during the conquest of the Sudan on 11 August 1885, he was born in Cairo in August 1892. As a child, he spent two
129 wonderful years on | the island of Ṭashyūz (Thasos) in the Aegean archipelago, which once belonged to Muḥammad ʿAlī and where his father had been sent by ʿAbbās II. He went to school in Cairo. In 1914 he graduated from Teachers' College and got a job at al-Madrasa al-Gharbiyya al-Amīriyya, and in 1921 he was appointed librarian at the Madrasat al-muʿallimīn al-sulṭāniyya al-ʿāliya. Because his father had been sent to the Sudan, where he was accompanied by Aḥmad's mother, he was raised in the house of his maternal grandfather. Rāmī explains his penchant for melancholy through this generally unhappy childhood.

His *dīwān* was published in two volumes in Cairo in 1916/7 and 1918/20, and reprinted in 1928 (*al-Mashriq* XXX, 397). Ḥāfiẓ Ibrāhīm wrote a preface to the second volume, while Aḥmad Shawqī attached a *taqrīẓ* in verse. Rightly, both praise the fluent and versatile language of his verses whose sound, Ḥāfiẓ says, flatters itself into your ear even before your brain can make sense of them. Rāmī himself says that his readings in the works of English and French poets greatly influenced his poetry. And indeed, his repertoire is quite limited. He is at his best in love songs, like 'The first kiss' (II, 94), and in narrative form ('The peasant girl from the Fayyūm' II, 103/7, and 'A stranger's love' ibid., 107/10). His complaint about his vanishing youth and his attempts to solve the mysteries of life leave no impression worth mentioning. He is more moving when—like some of his contemporaries—he writes about the railway accident in Udine in which Italian students perished (cf. p. 145).[103]

For a considerable period of time he practiced his verse technique on foreign material. The *Rubāʿiyyāt* of ʿUmar Khayyām, for instance, which he had come to know through the translation by the Iraqi Jamīl al-Zahāwī, inspired him to imitate it (C. 1923/4; see al-Māzinī, *Ḥaṣād al-hashīm*, C. 1932, 97ff). In the narrative poem *Semiramis* (C. n.d. 96 pp.) he tried his hand at the creation of pseudo-historical material, but in the love songs that he wrote for Umm Kulthūm in colloquial Arabic he returned to what he was really gifted at. | 130
(*Aghānī Rāmī* C. 1928, see J. Lecerf, Littérature dialectale et rénaissance arabe moderne, in *Bulletin d'Études Orientales de l'Institut Français de Damas*, II, III, 93, n. 1).

He thinks he is justified in equating his poems with the voice of nature and in expecting them to become immortal (see his description of himself in *Aḥsan mā katabtu* 83).—Aḥmad ʿUbayd, *Mashāhīr shuʿarāʾ al-ʿaṣr* I, 45/62 (with a portrait), Muḥammad Amīn Ḥassūna in *al-Hilāl* 1933, 333ff, Trowbridge Hall, *Egypt in Silhouette*, New York 1928 (verses by him, together with those by ʿAqqād, Shawqī, Ḥāfiẓ Ibrāhīm and an English translation of numbers 2 and 7 of Muḥammad Taymūr's *Mā tarāhu 'l-ʿuyūn* by him). A poem, *Aḥlāmī*, from Geneva, was printed in *al-Ahrām*, 5 January 1939.

19 ʿAbd al-Ḥalīm Ḥilmī al-Miṣrī

Even at a time when modern poetry had gained much in popularity, some poets still preferred to remain faithful to the style of al-Bārūdī and Shawqī. Among them was ʿAbd al-Ḥalīm Ḥilmī al-Miṣrī, who died at an early age. Initially, he put his art into the service of politics, but later became a protégé of King Fuʾād.

Born in Damanhūr in 1887, he made a living as a journalist in Cairo. At one point, he was thrown into jail because he had written a *qaṣīda* that was

---

103 *Shuhadāʾ al-ʿilm wal-ghurba wa-hum al-ṭalaba alladhīna qutilū fī Īṭalya fi 'ṣṭidām al-sikka al-ḥadīdiyya* by Faraj Sulaymān, Tyre 1910.

much too critical of the British occupation. He died on 2 June 1922. After a first attempt with his *Nasamāt al-ṣabāḥ* (C. 1325/1907), in which he looked for a freer rendering of the traditional formats, he published his *Dīwān fi 'l-madā'iḥ wal-awṣāf wal-tawārīkh* in Cairo in 1909 and 1328/1916. Abū Shādī published a *taqrīẓ* of it in *Fatāt al-sharq* IV, 229. In his *Bakriyyat al-Miṣrī, ṣaḥīfa min sīrat awwal al-khulafā' al-rāshidīn* (C. 1919), Ḥilmī tried to render a historical subject in verse, following the example of Ḥāfiẓ Ibrāhīm's *'Umariyya*. He gained the king's favour with his narrative poem *Muḥammad 'Alī al-kabīr, munshi' Miṣr al-ḥadītha*, C. 1338/1919. He was then invited to accompany him on a trip during which he wrote his *al-Riḥla al-sulṭāniyya wa-ta'rīkh al-salṭana al-Miṣriyya*, C. 1339/1921; see Cheikho, *al-Mashriq* XXIV, 865. A *marthiya* is contained in *Dīwān al-Māḥī* 205.

20 Aḥmad Abu 'l-Najāh and Muḥammad Badawī

During the difficult days of Egypt's struggle for freedom, Aḥmad Abu 'l-Najāh
131 and Muḥammad Badawī | bravely defended the rights of the people in an unpretentious kind of verse. Their *dīwān*s were both published in 1924, one in Alexandria and the other in Cairo, the latter under the title *al-Badawiyyāt* (al-Maṭba'a al-'Arabiyya), vol. II, 1925.

a. Having graduated from the Madrasat Dār al-'ulūm in 1915, Aḥmad Abu 'l-Najāh joined the Wafd party in 1919. He followed Sa'd Zaghlūl's struggle in poems that were read at party gatherings in Desouk, Fuwwa and Tanta. The bold language in which he addressed himself to the British authorities stands in stark contrast to the meek polemics of Shawqī and Ḥāfiẓ Ibrāhīm. But it is also true to say that Britain had considerably lessened its grip on Egypt in the wake of the war. The poetical value of these witnesses of their time, interesting as they are from a historical point of view, is not very great. And his other poems, too, are quite unremarkable, such as his *marāthī* on Ismā'īl Ṣabrī and al-Manfalūṭī, some descriptive creations, and several pieces of a more religious nature. The novel on the life of the ancient Arabs, and from which he cites an example on page 86 (*fī 'Ukāẓ*), was apparently never published.

b. Muḥammad Badawī 'Abduh was born in Bīlā in al-Gharbiyya on 18 May 1898. After high school in Alexandria he went to al-Azhar and then worked in his father's business. As a journalist he sympathised with the Nationalist Party (al-Ḥizb al-Waṭanī). Apart from traditional love songs, the two volumes of his *dīwān* contain *qaṣīda*s on the issue of women's rights, on social evils ('The player' I, 8) and on current affairs, such as the abolition of the caliphate (II, 49), a call for elections (I, 24/1), the opening of parliament (II, 27), general issues in Muslim politics ('Turkey or the Sick Man' I, 9, the Suez canal and its fruits I, 8, *Miṣr tunāji 'l-Sūdān* II, 38, *al-Sūdān yastanjid Miṣr*, ibid., 48), and several attempts at a national anthem. The form of his poems is classical ("My poetry is inspired by a loyalty to history" I, 7, 1), but the constraints of metre and rhyme prompted him—precisely in this poem, which is in fact a manifesto—to permit himself a number of rare liberties; he closes with the words *fa-khayru 'l-sayri an nataʾākhayā* ("the best way forward is in brotherhood", i.e. me and time), in which the first person dual (I, 7, 14) was probably not intentional.

| 21 Maḥmūd Abu 'l-Wafāʾ 132

The art of Maḥmūd Abu 'l-Wafāʾ flourished in secret for a long time, until his friends in the Rābiṭat al-adab al-ʿarabī made it possible for him to go to Paris, a trip which gave him a new impulse and resulted in the publication of his *dīwān* entitled *Anfās muḥtariqa*, C. 1933.

In *al-Ḥadīth* 1932, 248/9, Muḥammad Amīn Ḥassūna tells us about the celebration in Abu 'l-Wafāʾ 's honour that was held on 19 February 1932. Abū Shādī, *Aṭyāf al-rabīʿ* 200, has particular praise for his two *qaṣīdas Rithāʾ nafsī* (*al-Ḥadīth* 1931, 52) and *Ḍaḥiyyat al-ʿīd*. A love song, *Fi 'ntiẓār al-rabīʿ*, was published in *Apollo* 94/5. Two poems in his honor, *Baʿth shāʿir* and *Āyat al-shāʿir al-mabʿūth*, were published in *Dīwān al-Māḥī* 97ff.

22 Muḥammad Muṣṭafā al-Māhī, Maḥmūd Efendi ʿImād, and Muḥammad al-Harawī

Art, free from any political connotations, only served to embellish the lives of three highly-placed government officials: Muḥammad Muṣṭafā al-Māḥī (who had started his career in an office under the directorship of Muḥammad al-Muwayliḥī), Maḥmūd Efendi ʿImād (born on 7 August 1897 on his father's estate near Fāriskūr), and Muḥammad al-Harawī (an accountant in the Dār al-kutub al-Miṣriyya, born in Cairo in 1885).

a. The *Dīwān Muḥammad Muṣṭafā al-Māḥī* (C. 1934) opens with some verses by Khalīl Maṭrān and by three prefaces: by the author himself, by ʿAbdallāh al-ʿAfīfī, and by Maḥmūd ʿImād. Apart from a poem he wrote when he was nineteen years old and which recounts some episode from his youth (144), the work contains poems on events from his family life, a couple of *marthiyas*, and some of the products of his interactions with his friends who were poets. Among the latter is *Ṣada 'l-ḥanīn*, which is his answer to verses by Shawqī in which the latter expressed his longing for his fatherland when he was in Spain, together with an answer in three verses by Ḥāfiẓ Ibrāhīm. One can see that he studied the classics very well, and not merely through his song on the *Kitāb al-aghānī* (129/32) and a longwinding *muʿāraḍa* on a famous *Nūniyya* by Ibn al-Rūmī in *Aḥlām al-shabāb* (172/204). The poet's good taste protects him from an all too slavish | imitation and his language is free from archaic rarities and disturbing 133 modernisms. Only on the outside does his *Waqfa bayna ʾl-aṭlāl* remind us of the style of the ancients with its typical *khalīlayya* (153/4), to turn immediately towards the usual complaint about a bygone youth. Since the poet—like his friends—has few pretentions, Ḥabībī's hateful criticism of ʿAfīfī's preface to Ḥabīb al-Ziḥlāwī's *Udabāʾ muʿāṣirūn* (C. 1935, 63/7) is somewhat misplaced.

b. In his poems, Maḥmūd Efendi ʿImād wants to serve philosophy and the sciences. He does this, for instance, by means of abstract contemplations, which supposedly reflect the condition of his soul. They are for the most part quite colourless memories of thwarted dreams and a happy childhood lost, in a language which has liberated itself even more from classical paradigms than has al-Māḥī's; see Aḥmad ʿUbayd, *Mashāhīr shuʿarāʾ al-ʿaṣr* I, 307/19. His contributions to *Apollo* are similar in tone, with just one (p. 772) positive exception for the forceful language with which he appeals to the conscience of Egypt's effeminate youth.

c. Muḥammad al-Harawī likes to discuss social themes, like the issue of women's rights or the influence of European civilisation. His mastery of the language gives his writings a special charm and assures his poems a high regard in the press. The festive gathering in his honour, organised by the Arab Academy of Damascus on 28 August 1933, during which he recited a *qaṣīda* in praise of that city, shows that his work also found recognition outside of Egypt, RAAD, XIII, 438/41. Aḥmad ʿUbayd, *Mashāhīr shuʿarāʾ al-ʿaṣr*, 296/306.

23 Ismāʿīl Ṣabrī the Younger

Ismāʿīl Ṣabrī the Younger, a former teacher at the Madāris al-Awqāf al-Khuṣūṣiyya al-Malikiyya, i.e. at an art school, presented the fruits of 30 years of poetic activity in his four-volume *Dīwān* I, *Muhadhdhib al-aghānī* (published from 1353/1935 onwards), in which he holds firm to the classical tradition, untouched by the squabbles of his contemporaries.

His strongest creation is the philandering lovesong in the style of Bahāʾ al-
134 Dīn, samples of which make up the majority of volume one | (66–110) with the subtitle *Sitrīs ʿAdhrāʾ Manf*. Here, the whole repertoire of classical *ghazal* poetry is mobilised again and skilfully diversified, though not enriched with new expressions. In this, he draws on the oldest theme in Arabic love poetry, namely when he (115, 8) compares the fingers of the beloved to the fruit of the *ʿanam*, i.e. the Loranthus tree, as al-Muraqqish the Elder had done (*Mufaḍḍ.* 54, 6), an image which was copied over and over again by his successors (e.g. ʿUmar b. Abī Rabīʿa 13, 11, Abū Nuwās 394, 6). But he goes further than his models as he also calls the fingers themselves *anʿām* (14). The south wind's regular association with the beloved (87, 8; 91 penult.; 97 ult., 99 penult.) is just as natural as the poet's sleepless nights ($85_{,313}$, $92_{,9}$). But lions and gazelles (89,

13), and the crushing war (90, 11), too, all make their appearance in his work. Entirely against the prevailing sentiment of his time, he does not shrink from reproducing the archaic tone of his models, for instance when he refers to astrologers on page 80, 9. There are also plenty of learned allusions, such as in the passage (81, 3) where he says that his heart is weighed down by a burden which even Mount Raḍwā, near Yanbūʿ, would not be able to bear. But, just as in ancient poetry, these allusions are sometimes occasioned by the rhyme. One example are Kisrā and Tubbaʿ as the backdrop for his joys of love (108, 1), or even Kisrā and Alexander, who smilingly shake hands in an extremely bizarre image of the eyebrow of the beloved. But such gaffes are actually rare, like his amusing observation that the arrows of love are brainless (76, 5). Allusions to ancient Egypt, so popular among the Moderns, are only found in the person of Hathor (100, 3). He uses no inflated archaisms, even though his language is definitely classical in style, which does not, however, preclude the occurrence of an occasional Egypticism.[104] He only rarely sins against the rules of classical
Arabic.[105] | He employs many different metres and handles all forms with great 135
skill.[106] Every now and then he also uses a strophic form that he calls a *maqṭūʿa* (p. 111ff). His songs must be popular, since for many of them he can name a composer and the record company marketing the song.

In the first volume of his *Dīwān* these *ghazaliyyāt* are surrounded by religious poetry and poems written for special occasions. The first poem, by way of *iftitāḥiyya*, is a *mawʿiẓa* (17/45), which reminds the reader admonishingly of the Last Judgement, and of Paradise and Hell, taking him through a history of the prophets all the way down to Muḥammad. He gives an overview of the history of human culture under the title of *Mirʾāt al-zamān*, in which he does not look down upon the use of archaic forms like the *ayna*-scheme on page 50ff. The occasional poems at the end were in part written for musical gatherings, like the one in the Ezbekiyya garden of 5 June 1930, the one in honour of the musical specialist in the ministry of education, Dr. Maḥmūd al-Ḥifnī, on 26 March of 1931, and also on the occasion of the opening of the municipal

---

104 Like *tawaʿʿaka* for 'to be unwell' (104, 4), which Maḥmūd Taymūr also uses a lot, but which in the Middle Ages was known to the Egyptians Ibn Ayās (IV, 463, 6) and Ibn Taghrībirdī (VI, 9, 18, VII, 71, 112); see also v. Berchem, *Mat.* I, 201, 3; 309, 3.

105 Like *al-karīmi ʾl-muzni* 'the generous clouds' at 48, 12, the accusative without ending in rhyme 109, 11; 119 penult., and (probably intended as poetic licences) *lasta rāḍin* at 78, 15, and *kunta bāghin* at 110, 13. The constraints of rhyme let him lose the construction at 100, 14.

106 He only rarely takes liberties with the metre, such as at 77, 7 from below, 82, 13; 90, 7; 104, 5; 108, 8.

library of Alexandria. In these, he also cites some excerpts from operas that will be published shortly, such as *Ḥanīn al-arwāḥ* ('Music and the sick man' on page 119, and a duet between Jubal, the inventor of music of the Old Testament, and the Greek inventor of the musical scale on pages 127/37), *al-Shaykh al-abyaḍ* on page 123, *Majd Miṣr* on page 24, and the duet between prosperity and music on page 124.

Following established custom, the first volume is concluded with *taqārīẓ* by his friends.

24 Al-Banhāwī

Abū Darsh Muṣṭafā Ḥasan al-Banhāwī was a regional poet who belonged to Abū Shādī's circle of friends in Port Said. His *Dīwān al-ʿabarāt* (C. 1332/1914) is mostly about precious objects. See Abū Shādī, *al-Shafaq al-bākī* 995 n., *al-Shuʿla* 112, 116.

25 Khalīl Shaybūb

Of the poets who followed Khalīl Maṭrān in his total abandonment of the
136 ancient models | special mention must be made of Khalīl Shaybūb,[107] even though he published just one *dīwān*, *al-Fajr al-awwal* (Alexandria 1921), which contains a chronologically-ordered collection of his poems from the years 1912/20.

Khalīl Maṭrān wrote the preface to this work by his disciple. And Aḥmad Shawqī, too, contributed some verses in which he equates Arabic to French poetry so long as the goals of true poetry are not lost from sight, goals which he feels are equally well represented by al-Mutanabbī, Qays al-Majnūn and Jamīl as by Musset and his *Nuits*, and Lamartine and his *Girzil*.[108] It almost sounds like a protest when the poet in his preface declares himself to be a supporter of the Moderns, expecting more benefit from the French for Arabic poetry than from the British, who in any case depend on them. The poet shows that he has an extraordinary talent for form. Apart from the *qaṣīda*, of which he has complete mastery, he also likes to use the *muwashshaḥ*, of which he creates multiple variants, like in 'A glance at the past' (59/63) and the more elaborate *Law* (202/6). Among the feelings that he wants to express lyrically, love has pride of place; not its happy moments, although he does praise love as the light of life (140/4), but rather the pain of the torments of jealousy (178/80), which he increases by listing—in the style of the ancients—the charms of his

107 A bank clerk from Alexandria, whose portrait was published in *Apollo* I, 83.

108 See above, p. 28. In it, our colleague W. Mulertt recognised Lamartine's lover Graziella from his well-known autobiographical novel that was named after her.

beloved in a catalogue of beauty, or by imagining her in the arms of a dancer (109), or in the premonition of an imminent separation after a brief flirtation (77/83), or through a voice coming from a grave (57). Even though he often goes down the well-trodden path of tradition here, he does strike a new chord when he celebrates Creation as the temple of God (84/7) or when he praises the beauty of the seaside near Alexandria, rediscovered recently by his fellow Egyptians (68, 173). But when he sometimes indulges in economic and biological ruminations, comparing the sea to the mirror of life (88), he quickly loses his inspiration.

| The fact that, in his *dīwān*, he allotted little space to the children of his 137
muse, victims of their marriage, only testifies to his good taste. By contrast, modern life does elicit critical observations from him, such as on the make-up of women. But more often it triggers his enthusiastic acclaim, for instance when he talks about the charms of the cinema (134/6).

In several cases, he also ventured into longer accounts. In the poem "Salīm and Salmā" (117/25), which he dedicated to Khalīl Maṭrān, he recounts an unhappy love story in 125 lines of *ṭawīl* verse. But he did not have the creative power necessary to give its heroes a life of their own, above and beyond the typical victims of the Egyptian marital tradition. And his reminiscences of the battle of Abukir (49/56), too, which were most likely inspired by Abū Shādī's *Nakbat Navarin*, do not reach the level of their model, even though they succeed in calling forth some forceful images of the past. His review of the year 1916 (dated 8/10 January 1917), on the other hand, is very boring (126/9).

In one case he tried his hand at free verse, championed by his master, in an atmospheric description of the seashore in *al-Shirāʿ* (*Apollo* 227/31). There are ten strophes of varying length with artfully entwisted rhymes, but in which only the theme *wa-badā fīhi shirāʿu*, in the second strophe, stands out, in a free metre, which, at the end of the fifth and tenth strophes, has a distich in *mutaqārib* and *ṭawīl* respectively.

His language is strictly classical; only in one case does he hazard an unusual *taṣghīr al-jamʿ* (cf. Fück, ZDMG 90, 629) in *al-uṭayfālu 'l-jiyāʿu*, 'the hungry little children,' *Dīw*. 24, 9.

26 The *Apollo* Magazine

From the circle of Abū Shādī's literary magazine *Apollo*, there are only a few people who can be qualified as his disciples in the narrow sense of the term.

a. Among these, and the most important, is the physician Dr. Ibrāhīm Nājī (b. 1998), whom we met earlier as a champion of the literary endeavours of Abū Shādī (p. 125). In 1934, he published his *dīwān Warāʾ al-ghamām* (see Shafīq Jabrī, *al-Ḥadīth* 1934, 410/3, Abū Shādī in *Fawq al-ʿubāb*, 42, 56). | Personally, he 138 may consider his poetry primarily as romantic. Like his master, he is influenced by British literature. His poem *al-Ḥayāt fi 'l-shāriʿ* is a recreation of a poem by D.H. Lawrence (*min shubbāk al-kulliyya*) (see Abū Shādī, *Aṭyāf* 199). He wrote an *istiʿrāḍ* on it, entitled *al-Ḥayāt*, which was published in *Apollo* 235/7. Like in many other places, here, too, he uses strophes of four lines with a rhyme of the type a-b-a-b. In his wistful reminiscence of the places of his childhood that he finds changed upon his return (*al-ʿAwda*, *Apollo* 1084/6), he brings the quatrain back again to strophes of four pairs each. He also published a number of *qaṣīdas* in *Apollo*: *al-Nāy al-muḥtariq* 536, *Ẓalām wa-nūr* 854, and *al-Khitām* 1143. In *al-Ghad* (ibid. 754/6, with a portrait) he divided this form again into strophes of four verses each, bound by a single rhyme. On page 883, he translated Shelley's famous 'Ode to the West Wind', using free metre. Apart from being a romantic, he also has a sense of humour, as is shown by his satirical poems, ibid. 907/8. He also wrote a biographical essay on W. Scott, ibid. 647/50. In *al-Ḥadīth* magazine he published the poems *Qibla*, 1933, 668, *Ṣakhrat al-liqā'*, 1934, 72/4, and a romantic episode from the life of a doctor, written in prose and entitled *al-Ḥulm* ibid., 1933, 461/73, *Qiṣṣat al-Ḥurmān* ibid. 307/13, *al-Manbaʿ, qiṣṣa ʿālamiyya li-Charles Morgan, talkhīṣ* ibid. 225/37. See Ibrāhīm Miṣrī, Ibrāhīm Nājī, *Hilāl* 1933, 225/37, Muḥammad Amīn Ḥassūna, ibid. 1933, 41/3.

b. Muḥammad ʿAbd al-Muʿṭī's (who died young in 1938) *al-Hamshahrī Shāṭi' al-aʿrāf*, in *Apollo* 627/44, was probably inspired by Abū Shādī's romantic opera *al-Āliha*, even though al-Saḥartī (*Adab al-ṭabīʿa* 108) is reminded of A. de Musset. But whatever the case, it bears testimony to an independent imagination and great linguistic talent, even though the poet thinks that he still needs the props of ancient mythology. And his smaller poems in *Apollo*, too, betray his great talent: *ʿĀṣifa fī sukūn al-layl* 554/6, *al-Farrāsh al-aṣfar* 871 and the epigram-like *Lamaḥāt* 1038/41. His study of the beauty of symbolism (*Jamāl al-ibhām al-ramzī*), 1204/7, was initially inspired by Abū Shādī. Obituary by Kāmil al-Shannāwī in *al-Ahrām* of 15 December 1938, p. 10.

c. Ṣāliḥ Jawdat, who published his *dīwān* (C. 1934) at the age of 20, was
139 even more influenced by Abū Shādī. | His *qaṣīda al-Insān al-awwal* infuriated theologians so much that they wanted to take him to court over his disavowal of God's Creation (see Abū Shādī, *Fawq al-ʿubāb*, preface 10). Al-Saḥartī (110) praises the true sense of nature in his poem *ʿAhd al-miyāh*, which was inspired by the seashore of Alexandria. Apart from *qaṣīdas* he also wrote elaborate strophic poems, such as *al-Safīna al-ḥā'ira* in *Apollo* 1135, while other poems by him can also be found on pages 663, 749/52, 875/6, 882, and 1028/9. Samples in Saʿd Mīkhā'īl, *Samīr al-udabā'* 82/3.

27 ʿUthmān Ḥilmī

In his *dīwān Nasīm al-saḥar* (Alexandria 1937), ʿUthmān Ḥilmī reconnected with the ancient lyrical tradition of Ṣafī al-Dīn al-Ḥillī, possibly under the influence of Walī al-Dīn Yegen.

His simple language and uncomplicated technique serve to express a pure joy in life and nature in his *Āyat al-ṣubḥ*, *Apollo* 11/3, his *Waṭan al-ḥusn*, ibid. 744, and in his *Bustān al-ṣuḥba*, ibid. 240. But when he attempted to philosophise in *al-ʿUmr wal-amānī* and *Safīnat al-ʿumr* (ibid. 1056) it seems more artificial. Taking his inspiration from a Persian allegory, he created a new type of verse in his narrative poem *Qiṣṣat al-bakht al-nāʾim* (ibid. 888/96, 1048/60, 1097/1120), using strophes of five verses with an internal rhyme in the final verse. In this, he propagated a rather mundane philosophy of life without any aspiration for a more elevated, artistic kind of creation. See also Abū Shādī in *Adabī*, 533/6.

28 ʿAbbās Maḥmūd al-ʿAqqād

During the war, a new and rich talent that would truly enrich Arabic literature, mostly in the field of lyrics but also in other areas, made its appearance: ʿAbbās Maḥmūd al-ʿAqqād.[109]

Born in Aswan in 1889 as the son of an Egyptian and a mother with Kurdish blood, he received a rather poor education in his hometown, which he compensated in the most excellent manner, through self-study. The main | elements 140
of his education came from Arabic and English literature. He had read Carlyle by the age of 14. In Cairo, he worked as an editor at *al-Ahrām*, *al-Muʾayyad*, and *al-Dustūr* newspapers and also joined the Wafd party, becoming friends with Saʿd Zaghlūl. As punishment for his involvement in a plot against prime minister Muḥammad Ṣidqī Pāshā—in which his brother was also implicated—he was incarcerated between 13 October 1930 and 8 July 1931. He used this period to learn French. After his release he wrote the poem 'At Saʿd's Grave' (*Waḥy al-arbaʿīn* 173/4), and he recorded his time in prison in a work called *ʿĀlam al-sudūd wal-quyūd* (C. 1937).

He had no direct connection with Muḥammad ʿAbduh (cf. Ch. Adams, *Islam and Modernism in Egypt*, 250). On what grounds Ḥasan Kāmil al-Ṣīrafī (Abū Shādī, *Aṭyāf al-Rabīʿ* 122/7) calls him a student of ʿAbd al-Raḥmān Shukrī remains to be seen.[110]

---

109 A portrait was published in *Apollo* 285.

110 Muḥammad Qābīl and Ramzī Miftāḥ identify some (partly literal) echoes of ʿAbd al-Raḥmān Shukrī in his works in *Apollo* 926/32, 995/1002, and 1208/17.

Initially, he collected his poems in a one-volume *Dīwān*, C. 1916/1334 (Maṭbaʿat al-Busfūr), then in three volumes, C. 1921 (Maṭbaʿat al-Maʿāhid),[111] and finally in four volumes, 1928 (al-Muqtaṭaf al-Muqaṭṭam). He called the four volumes of this last edition: *Morning's Awakening*, *Afternoon Heat*, *Evening*, and *Nocturnal Meditations*. By his own admission, he was unable to order his poems chronologically because he had forgotten the date of composition of most of them. Their ordering is therefore somewhat arbitrary, with some of his most beautiful love poems included in the last volume.

There is no doubt whatsoever that al-ʿAqqād is the most original poet in modern Arabic literature. His language being strictly classical, he feels obliged to provide lexical annotations on almost every page. What one could hold against him is that he sometimes goes too far in his search for obscure
141 expressions.[112] | But in suppleness and pregnancy of meaning there is hardly anyone who can compare to him. Ṭāhā Ḥusayn (*Ḥāfiẓ wa-Shawqī*, 148) is right to constrast him and the Iraqi Jamīl Ṣidqī al-Zahāwī with the Ancients as two broadly-educated representatives of the Moderns.

Like his language, his metrics, too, are strictly classical. He is averse to any free use of it, as some of the ʿAbbāsid poets ventured to do, and, in Egypt, ʿAbd al-Ḥalīm Ḥilmī (in his *Nasamāt al-Ṣabāḥ*, see p. 130) and Abū Shādī did too (see al-Jiddāwī, *Naẓarāt*, 177 n). In his 'Voyage to Khazzān' (93/6) he employs a *rajaz* in continuous rhyme, although once he lets go of the constraints of rhyme (128/9). He is just as versatile in the strophic forms as in the classical metres: *ramal* with a resounding, paired rhyme (141/3), *rajaz* with interchanging rhyme a-b-a-b (148/50), and the *muwashshaḥ* in various forms 173/4, 184/6, 188/90. He employs a new kind of *ramal* verse in strophes of 4 to 6 verses with interchanging rhyme a-b-a-b-a-b or a-b-a-b in *Waḥy al-arbaʿīn* 19/21, 121/4, and 136/8.

The intellectual horizon of al-ʿAqqād stretches far beyond that of ancient poetry but at the same time it cannot be said to suffer from an excess of foreign elements. Yet it is also true that he sometimes likes to show off his British education somewhat. For example, in the preface to the second volume of his *dīwān*

---

111 It is this second edition that he must be referring to when he says (*Sāʿāt bayna 'l-kutub* 136,$_{16}$) that the first volume of his *Dīwān* sold out in less than 14 days.

112 Thus, he tries to bring new life to ancient expressions such as *uyām* 'smoke' (Abū Dhu'ayb 2,$_{25}$), 115,$_{10}$, or *ri'bāl* 'lion' (*Hudh.* 98,$_{6}$, Jāḥiẓ, *Ḥay.* I, 173,$_{6}$ and often in ancient poetry) 233 bottom, while, on the other hand, he also does not shrink from investing old expressions with new meanings—he uses *aḍāt* 'puddle, pond' as 'mirror', 145,$_{10}$,—or even from coining new terms altogether, such as *nūṭatu 'l-qalbi* 'aorta' 201,$_{10}$, although classical Arabic only has *nūṭ* as a plural of *niyāṭ* (*LA* IX, 296,$_{21}$). Rarely does a vulgar term escape him, such as *dibq* 'birdlime' 98,$_{5}$.

(10), he quotes from "The four ages of poetry" by the British critic Th.L. Peacock (d. 1866) and from V. Hugo's essay on Shakespeare. Sometimes, he also tries to imitate British poetry, such as strophes 185/91 from Shakespeare's *Venus and Adonis* under the title 'Venus and the Corpse of Adonis' 21/3, I, 3/4, the lines on the morning from *Romeo and Juliet* 34, I, 17, his verses about honour, 63, W. Cooper's 'To the Rose' 113, I, 108, Pope's 'On destiny'; at 137$_{,12}$ he alludes to "and Brutus is an honorable man". On pages 233/6 he celebates Shakespeare as the greatest intermediary between nature and mankind, referring to Hazlitt and Emerson in the footnotes. | For particular poems, al-Hamshahrī identifies 142
examples from Shelley and others in *Apollo*, 823.

But all these are mere insincere frivolities, the foundation of his thinking and emotions remaining genuinely Arab. He almost completely liberated himself from the classical paradigms to which his predecessors are so indebted. Nevertheless, in a contest with his friends al-Māzinī and ʿAlī Shawqī he once tried his hand at a *muʿāraḍa* on two verses by Ibn al-Rūmī (37/46); on another occasion, he writes on mystical love in the style of Ibn al-Fāriḍ (74/5); finally, he lets al-Maʿarrī's son complain to his father for never having dared to engender him, out of pure pessimism (184/6, II, 65/7). In one case he also sings of Khumārawayh and his lion (34) and Shahrzād of the 1001 Nights (100).

His self-confidence vis-à-vis the material superiority of European civilisation is not only founded on Muslim pride (as is the case for many of his compatriots), but also on the high level of civilisation of ancient Egypt. Thus he extols the timelessness of the columns of the pharaoh (33), the image of Ramses at al-Badrshīn which the authorities wanted to bring to Cairo (191/3, II, 73/6), the graves of the pharaohs (344), and the temples at Edfu (136/141, *Dīw.* II, 2/8) and Karnak (268, *Dīw.* III, 101). While he does not want to remain altogether unmoved by the religion of the ancient Egyptians, he regards the splendour of their monuments, more than anything, as a symbol of hope for an eternal youth of his country.

In his thinking, these oriental elements are matched by as many elements taken from Europe. Thus, he adapts classical motives to poetry, such as the river Lethe (342), and the virgin of Athens from Plutarch's *Life of Alexander* (87/8); Ovid's tale of Echo and Narcissus he discusses in an essay (reprinted in Muḥammad Zakī al-Dīn 155/8). Yet he also tries to reconstruct Columbus' thoughts while out on the ocean (47/8, I, 32). The phenomenon of the cinematograph inspires him to an ode to modern technology (58, I, 45).

As a lyricist, al-ʿAqqād is at his best when he writes on nature and love. The changing of the seasons inspires him each time to beautiful images. Thus, he greets the clouds of autumn as bringing a new lease of life to nature, exhausted by the summer's sun (23), or winter in Aswan (67/9, I, 55/7) as bringing a new

143 | zest for life, no less than spring (263) which does, however, render him melancholic too (76). The splendour of the moon enthuses him (71, 114, 178) just as much as do the wonders of the sea, which, to him, inlander that he is, are frightening at first (222/3, III, 20/8), but whose vast expanses do give wing to his thought (74); at the same time, he praises the Nile as the bearer of all beauty and joy for life (264/7, III, 29/33). No less familiar to him is nature in the form of living things. In his flower poems (295/7) he extols the rose first and foremost, but also the French daisy as a symbol of abstinent love. His concern with small birds is no less than his compassion for the antelope of Kurdufan in the zoo (216, II, 19).

As a theme, love, too, is inexhaustible for him. True, at times we hear an echo of the boundless splendour of classical and post-classical love poetry. But he is also capable of sketching attractive genre scenes which are sometimes reminiscent of Catullus.[113] But feelings of a more profound character he also expresses in no less apposite terms.[114] But it is not only these cute little things that he pulls off well. In an ode to Venus, he praises love as the quintessence of life; but he also knows its pains and he once juxtaposes birth and death with love (299/301). Only rarely does he lapse into trivialities, such as in his advice for lovers or in the cure for love (60, 76).

144 | Yet it is possible that such poems are not serious because he does have a great sense of humour. For instance, he congratulates the dog Flora (77/8, *Dīw.* I, 65) with a song in praise of her litter;[115] he praises the cosy bubbling of the water pipe (118); he congratulates a black friend from the Sudan on his new

---

113 'The maiden's envy' (49): "How charming was the little one, if only she had not been so outrageous! When I smiled at her, she leaned forward, her locks flying. I hoped she would kiss me, but she refused, coquettishly. I was getting tired of her, first turning towards me, then turning away. So I took an old mirror which I showed her; I let her look into it and said: 'Look at her face, is she more beautiful, or you?' To this, she answered indignantly: 'I look much more beautiful! When will you stop forgetting real beauty, when will you recognise it again?' I then said: 'Which one of you two should I then call forward and kiss?' Hearing these words, she threw herself into my arms, for jealousy makes every lover submissive."

114 303: "Give me your hand! Today, a handshake, no quick kiss on the hand. You refuse me it? Out of anger or are you just being coquettish? Or is it because of your chaperon that you prudishly stay away from me? Hesitantly she stretched out her left arm. Was this gallantry or was she, rather, just being mean? She feared her entourage and yet she trusted me; this, then, is how she turned away from me yet approached me at the same time. But the left hand is more pious and more generous, and I consider it closer to the heart. She is certainly closer to the heart than the right hand, so she is more than welcome to me!"

115 *Apollo* 282/6, al-ʿAqqād's answer to a poem by Muḥammad Ṭāhir al-Jiblāwī on his dog which had gone astray.

suit under the title 'Sartor resartus,' *Dīw.* I, 115; and the wish list of the avaricious he dresses up as a prayer (46). In his prose works, too, he likes satire, as in the sketches 'The idiots' conference' (Muḥammad Zakī 141/4), 'The willpower store' (ibid. 159/68, Ode Vasilieva 171/6), and 'Peace' (Ode-V. 169/71).

But, on the whole, seriousness prevails in his writings. On the one hand, he likes to discuss general issues in ethics and morals, like when he weighs the pros and cons of patience (35/6), tries to put a name to hatred (96), or praises hope as a positive element in life (103). On the other hand, he also ventures into more profound issues in philosophy, like the question of the relation between our subjective image of the world and reality ('The dead world' 167/9), or music as the sister of philosophy (201/3, II, 12/5). At the same time, however, he warns against the "cold sublimeness" of the latest advances in human knowledge (206, III, 7). Despite his humour and penchant for irony, his philosophical outlook is basically one of weltschmerz.[116] He does not merely complain about the personal fate of the poet who abjures the world (83),[117] since fame and poverty are siblings after all (49), but rather the whole era in which he lives, one in which the culture of the East is in a constant struggle with the civilisation of the West.[118] He calls modern life the new Hell (214, III, 16/8). And, most of all, he does not tire of warning Egypt's youth, which has lost all sense of morality, be it in the upper classes | or among the poor; so much so, that it should fear for 145
its survival were it not for the peasants who still possess a healthy core (151/5, II, 21/4). He points at the huge mission the youth have ahead of them, saying that they should confidently embark on it, for "God did not change heaven and earth, the Nile still is Egypt's neighbour, and the reward of glory still beckons the ambitious, until the end of time" (194/7, II, 77/80). He laments the misery that the war brought to Egypt and the rest of the world in a long strophic poem (238/54, III, 48/84) about the devil who, having converted, was admitted into Paradise by God but who, weary of his uneventful existence there, rebelled against God who then changed him into a stone whose beauty has continued to fascinate mankind ever since.

The many elegies contribute in no small part to the serious undertone of his *dīwān*: on a young girl (53), on a brother who was drowned (130), on Sultan Ḥusayn (d. 18 December 1914, p. 218, III, 22), on Muḥammad Farīd Bek (228/31,

---

116 194, 6: "My poems are my tears, yet they cannot compensate the tears which the sad eye is denied."

117 Compare the complaint by Walī al-Dīn Yegen, above p. 53.

118 'Our Time' (III, 9ff.): "We are living at a time in which the great are only great in sin; if the solid foreheads of the upper classes would only soften, they would bathe in sweat for shame. These are evil times; its air has spoiled my health and its seas seem polluted to me" etc.

III, 34/7, on his funeral 266), or on the death of the Italian students who perished in the trainwreck at Udine (231, III, 38/41 see above p. 129). Yet he also knows how to console his friends, such as his teacher Wajdī on the death of his father (98), or al-Māzinī on the death of a daughter of his (122). And for himself, he also wants to take the sting out of death; not in the hopes of the joys of Paradise, but rather of a love that will surround his grave (99). That is also why he does not want his burial to be a sad occasion; rather, he wants songs to be heard one last time (55), death after all being a sweet drink, and where there is drinking, there is singing.

Politics is only an indirect source of inspiration, such as when he welcomed his friend Saʿd Zaghlūl when the latter returned from exile on the Seychelles (1923) (277/80), and then when he gave him a special welcome on his return to his native Aswan (347). Later, he dedicated a whole cycle of poems to the memory of this patriot (281/92: 'Fourty Days', 'Attendance at the Funeral', 'At the Grave's Pulpit', 'Saʿd and the Poor', 'The Stations to Eternity', 'Saʿd Writes History', 'Images on the Blackboard of Time', 'The Day of Banishment', 'Greeting', 'An Escort for his Homecoming', 'The Seychelles and Gibraltar', 'The Assassination',
146 'The National Congress', 'Farewell'). | One should probably forgive his friend his slightly exalted tone.[119]

In 1933, he presented a new collection of poems, called *Waḥy al-arbaʿīn* because most of the poems which it contains were written around the age of 40. In 8 chapters, entitled *Taʾammulāt fi ʾl-ḥayāt, Khawāṭir fi shuʾūn, Qiṣaṣ wa-amāthīl, Waṣf wa-taṣwīr, Ghazal wa-munājāh; Qawmiyyāt wajtimāʿiyyāt, Fukāha, Mutafarriqāt*, we find *qaṣīda*s and fragments (*maqṭūʿāt*). In the preface he criticises all those who are merely imitators of the classics, demanding that poetry "express genuine thinking in a beautiful way." The philosophy of life which he proposes in his poems has the same kind of pessimism as that championed by Abū Shādī around the same time. "Nothing in life withstands the force of thought. Whichever way I turn, I feel like an uprooted tree," "Death rattles at the door like a beggar; it takes all, so take from life whatever you can" (26). Like Abū Shādī, he also tries to work with ancient motifs, such as the story of Icarus (60/71), which begins with the admonishment given by Daedalus to his son before the latter commences his flight and then recounts the story's prologue, before concluding with the account of Icarus' fall. Among the descriptions, the one of the beach resort Khalīj Stanley (88/95) takes pride of place. With a three-times repeated *Yā wayḥa qalbika min hadaf*, it shows the strong impact that the baring of female beauty had had on the poet. In the

119 285 bottom: "Kemal rose through the army, Mussolini through the Blackshirts; I am the people and the army in one, sword and justice united."

chapter 'Things National and Social' he excluded poems that deal with matters of daily politics so as not to disrupt an existing party truce (*riʿāyatan li-ʿahd al-iʾtilāf*, 152). Yet he shows clearly whose side he is on in his poem 'At Saʿd's Grave' (173/4), which he wrote on the day that he was released from prison. He joins the Syrians in celebrating their "independence" (146) and follows Ghandi's hungerstrike (38, 145) with the same interest as Abū Shādī (*Aṭyāf al-rabīʿ*, 98). In two instances, he refers to European literature here, insofar as his reading of Th. Hardy's poem 'Shelley's Skylark' (54) and the French poet Dugeral's 'If I were God' (132) inspired him to write on similar themes.

| See the critique of Abū Shādī in *Apollo* 691/4, in which he criticises par- 147
ticular expressions/turns of phrase, and al-ʿAqqād's defence, ibid. 707/11; see further also ʿAbd al-Ḥamīd Shukrī, ibid. 801/8, Maḥmūd al-Khawalī, ibid. 912/5, Ismāʿīl Maẓhar, 918/25.

In the third collection of his poems, *Hadiyyat al-karawān* (C. 1933)—named after the first section, the *Karawāniyyāt*—he shows himself as heralding a new attitude towards life. The roots of this new attitude he finds in nature, and he hears its voice especially in the song of the plover (*Charadrius oedicnemus* or *Alexandrinus*), the emblematic bird of the Delta.[120] He had sung the praise of this bird twenty years earlier, but the singing of his favorite bird sounds, of course, different to the ear of the mature man than to that of the young man in love. Where the latter heard passion, the former hears the call to go out into the world. But more important than this, says al-ʿAqqād, is to reflect on the true joys of existence and to let oneself be led by the magic of the nightly voices of nature. This introductory *bāb* is followed by other samples of his writing, first *Ghazal wa-munājāh* (41/113), among which we find, besides the tender products of yearning ('The kiss-less kiss', p. 65), the funny song for the postman (p. 60). Under the title *Ṣifāt wa-taʾammulāt* (114/132) we find, besides picturesque descriptions of the seashore, philosophical contemplations on the struggle for being and happiness. In *Mutafarriqāt* (133/40) a number of poems for special occasions and *taqārīẓ* have been put together. The work is concluded with *hijāʾ* (141/4, including the *Hijāʾ al-dahr*) and *rithāʾ* (145/53), where we find a beautiful elegy for his childhood friend, the physician Ḥusayn, who belonged to a group of poets in Qena.

120 In a postscript he defends himself against the criticism that he would have dethroned the nightingale by it; after all, the European and Persian Bulbul are not indigenous to Egypt at all, while their relatives that hibernate in Egypt do not sing while they are there. And apropos, before him Abū Shādī, in one of his early poems, had extolled the plover as the harbinger of love (*Zaynab* 34, *Shiʿr al-wijdān* 102/3).

His most recent collection of poems, *ʿĀbir al-sabīl* (C. 1937/1355), is called after its first chapter, in which he tries out a new kind of poetry. It depicts his daily surroundings—as is also shown on the frontispiece by the illustrator
148 Shaʿbān Zakī—as if passing in front of him. | Thus, the house, the mosque, the bank, the tavern, the street, the railway carriage, each of these has its say in proclaiming the poet's new attitude to life. He juxtaposes the haste of the machine era (*ʿaṣr al-surʿa*) with the peace of the mosque and the people praying in it, picturing both with just a few strokes of the pen, e.g. an ironer at work or a beggar. He no longer feels bound as strongly to classical form as he did in the past. In his five strophes on the Bank (p. 37/9), three two-footed *kāmil* verses take turns with three four-footed ones. In his six-strophe 'Merchandise in a shop on a holiday' (46/8), one-footed and two-footed *ramal* verses take turns. The second chapter, *Anāshīd wa-aghānī*, first brings a national anthem in six strophes of six two-footed *mutadārik* verses each, with the rhyme pattern 1–4, 2–5, 3–6. In answer to a competition for just such a national anthem, organised by the ministry of education, but in which he could not participate because of his political leanings, he wrote a bitter satire called 'Retreat!' which was again written in the form of a very elegant *muwashshaḥ* in *rajaz*. To accompany some movies, he wrote a number of songs in the Egyptian dialect for the female singer Nādira. The *Qawmiyyāt* that follow were written on the occasion of national commemorations and holidays, such as the final interment of Saʿd Zaghlūl, the jubilee of the Bank of Egypt, and others. The work is concluded with *Taʾammulāt, Rabīʿiyyāt* and *Mutafarriqāt*, among which we find some fine occasional poems, such as 'The call of the child to a young couple' and 'To my friend Muwaffaq Jalāl, in celebration of his eighteenth month.' The *rithāʾ* for Ghānim Muḥammad is followed by *ʿAlā aṭlāl al-dunyā*. The whole *dīwān* shows that the poet feels freer than before vis à vis the classical models that he once venerated, creating a kind of poetry that is more suitable for the personality of his nation.

Maybe one should evaluate al-ʿAqqād's prose even higher than his poetry. Under the influence of British writers, he further developed the easy and fluid style of the essay introduced by al-Manfalūṭī, subjecting it to a rigid style of argumentation. In all this, his language and vocabulary remain truly Arabic, with calques or Europeanisms only rarely tolerated.

149 These qualities can be found in his earliest prose writing, | *Majmaʿ al-aḥyāʾ*, first ed. Cairo (Maṭbaʿat Muḥammad Muḥammad Maṭar) n.d., second ed. Cairo (al-Maṭbaʿa al-Raḥmāniyya) n.d. (with a long preface dated 8 January 1920). In this highly imaginative allegory, first written during the [First] World War and then stylistically reworked for the second edition, he takes the reader to an animal parliament convening somewhere in the African jungle. It was convoked

by Life itself to put an end to the discontent amongst its children. Life opens the discussions and gives the floor first to the pigeon. The pigeon pleads for mutual compassion and a general clemency. She is soon shouted down by the fox, who defends the law of the strongest. The monkey's objections to this latter position are answered, in turn, by the lion. When the animals dare not stand up against the latter, it is the woman who comes forward in order to assert her freedom and the equality of her rights compared to the man; the latter immediately puts her in her place with a reference to the power of her beauty. And he tells the monkey, who wants to proclaim the law of the jungle again, that faith in justice is the only thing that can render him victorious, and that faith alone can determine what justice is. The animals are ready to agree with him on condition that he give up his power over them. At this point Nature in person breaks off the hearing. For it was only out of fear of Death that Life had convened this parliamentary meeting. So now Nature summons Death to do battle with Life, which is to come out of it all the more complete. All the animals immediately obey the call of Nature and the struggle begins anew. The value of his political ideology, which boils down to asserting that war is a step towards freedom, may in itself be very disputable, but this has no negative impact on the literary attractiveness of the work itself, the only reproach that one could make of it being a certain weakness in the structure of its conclusion.

Under the title *al-Dīwān*,[121] al-ʿAqqād and his friend al-Māzinī (no. 29) published in February and April of 1921 a sharp critique of the work of Shawqī, to which al-ʿAqqād opposes new approaches in poetry, based on European models.

| He published the best of his collected newpaper articles in several vol- 150
umes. The most important of these is that entitled *Sāʿāt bayna 'l-kutub*.[122] Even though literary criticism makes up the core of this work, it is not restricted to this. The articles brought together in the first volume date from 1926/7. In it, he criticises, among others, Muṣṭafā Ṣādiq al-Rāfiʿī and his book *Fī iʿjāz al-Qurʾān*, while paying homage to the Iraqi writer Jamīl Ṣidqī al-Zahāwī, whom he believes is more of a scholar than a philosopher or a poet. In a series of essays he analyses the situation of poetry in Egypt, warning time and again against the wrong tracks down which poetry had been led by Shawqī and his followers, and against the spiritless copycats of European, especially French, models. He calls for a literature that is truly Arab and based on true emotions, yet entirely

121 From the ten fascicles announced on the title page only these two were published.

122 In 1914 he had started printing a work with this title but never got further than five sheets. After his move to Aswan his publisher published these five sheets, disappearing with the rest of the manuscript. These five sheets were later reprinted as *al-Fuṣūl* on pages 87/127.

modern and free from any rhetoric. He turns resolutely against all efforts aimed at introducing the common vernacular into the literary language as this would endanger the unity of Arab culture, which has not yet been brought into being in the first place. But he is also interested in foreign literature. He not only pays tribute to the works of Tagore, but is also especially fond of discussing English literature. He makes a detailed analysis of Trevelyan's new ambitions for poetry in the latter's *Thamyris*; at the same time, he also praises Shakespeare and above all Thomas Hardy, whose lyrics he says are the best of modern times, even though they do not stand comparison with the very best literary achievements of the past.

He published further selections from his essays in *al-Fuṣūl* (C. 1922/1341), *al-Muṭālaʿāt* (C. 1924/1343) and *al-Murājaʿāt fī 'l-ādāb wal-funūn* (C. n.d. [1926]). Of his many studies, all of which bear witness to his lively interest in Arabic literature, as well as modern intellectual life in general, special mention must here be made of, on the one hand, his analysis of the philosophy of al-Maʿarrī
151 (*F.* 1/23), in which he is against J. Zaydān and the *EI*, | as well as his description of Ibn Zaydūn's unpretentious love poetry (which was actually meant to be published as part of *Sāʿāt bayna 'l-kutub*) (*F.* 97/113), and, on the other, his critique of V. Hugo's *Les misérables* and Ḥāfiẓ Ibrāhīm's translation of it (*F.* 58/70), and the account by Gabriele Reuters of her visit to an ailing Nietzsche (*F.* 258/264). In the *Murājaʿāt* he moves on several occasions to discuss issues of general aesthetics, like in his essay on form and content (*al-Ashkāl wal-maʿānī*) of May 1925, p. 60/9. In 'Sayyid Darwīsh' of September 1925 (ibid. 185/95), he turns the obituary of this dead young musician into an epitome of the history of oriental music in which he also makes a warm plea for the national music of the Turks, outlawed by the moderns. Excellent descriptions are given of the classic al-Bashshār and Ibn al-Rūmī as well as of the founder of modern prose in Egypt, al-Manfalūṭī, whom he rightly regards as a *munshiʾ* and not as a *kātib*. Here, too, he returns once more to the issue of women's rights (in October 1925), championing the weak sex's right to intellectual education in the warmest of terms, while at the same time warning about the dangers of women's emancipation.

The studies brought together in the collection *Muṭālaʿāt fī 'l-kutub wal-ḥayāt* (C. 1924/1343) show an ʿAqqād at the height of his literary achievement. The collection opens with a discussion of the question of how people understand art. He calls for an art that is connected to life, yet at the same time rises above it. In two further articles on exhibitions—dated 23 May 1922 and 11 March 1924—he questions the position of art in the life of the modern Egyptian. He warmly welcomes the efforts of young Egyptians to make their country enter

the community of civilised nations in this area as well. But he is very negative about efforts to create an Egyptian theatre. The only thing he sees are theatre companies that aim for the lowest kind of entertainment, and he is right to not even discuss any of the pieces written by leading authors. Two large studies deal with the liveliest representatives of classical poetry, viz. Abu 'l-ʿAlāʾ al-Maʿarrī and al-Mutanabbī. He assesses the creative imagination of al-Maʿarrī's *Risālat al-ghufrān* and is right where he says that its main importance lies in | the 152
caustic irony with which it criticises the ideals of Arabhood. Al-Mutanabbī's extraordinary command of the Arabic language enthralled him so much that he overrated him somewhat as a thinker where he regards him as a precursor of the ideas of Nietzsche or Darwin. Of the contemporary poets this work only speaks about Faraḥ Anṭūn, of whom he wrote a deeply-felt obituary on 5 March 1924, eight months after Anṭūn had passed away. He describes him as the leader of modern Arabic literature who liberated it from the bonds of the classics and who tried to bring it back to things natural, following the example of the French. Apart from this, he valued Muḥammad Kurd ʿAlī's *Gharāʾib al-gharb* as a serious attempt by an oriental to come to grips with modern Europe, a continent that he had visited three times, the last occasion being after the war.

His receptiveness to European culture is borne out by his studies on Max Nordau, Anatole France and Immanuel Kant. If he wanted to show that he was familiar with intellectual life in Europe in all its manifestations, then he could hardly have chosen people farther apart than these. In one case, he even ventured to pay homage to the genius (*ʿabqariyya*) of Goethe, while he only knew *Werther* (*Ālām W.*) in the translation (from the French) of Aḥmad Ḥasan Zayyāt (C. 1342/1924) and *Faust*. He also tried to awaken people's interest in European painting and music. What his friend Abū Shādī had tried to achieve through his poems on paintings, al-ʿAqqād did with greater success in a number of sophisticated essays. He celebrated Rubens, for instance, as a political painter, while praising G. Romney's portrait of Lady Hamilton as a bacchante. On the other hand, he also attempted to identify modern trends in British painting by a study of the works of H. Draber and G. Watts. Moreover, he tried to introduce his readers to Beethoven and German music, and to familiarise them with G. le Bon's critique of culture and with Nietzsche's concept of the 'Übermensch', which he and Abū Shādī had come to know through Shaw's *Man and Superman*.

In several articles he made a genuine effort to take a personal stance on particular philosophical issues, above all in aesthetics. In his *Rasāʾil al-aḥzān* he elaborates on Muṣṭafā Ṣādiq al-Rāfiʿī's *Falsafat al-jamāl wal-ḥubb*. Having tried to define | corporeal beauty in the past, he now wanted to elevate beauty to a 153 higher level by regarding it as being rooted in freedom. Al-ʿAqqād believes that, in Egypt, culture suffers the most from a lack of sincerity among the youth. As such, he calls for new methods in education which aim at a healthy balance between the powers of body and soul.

Next to all these important issues of modern life, ancient Egypt naturally recedes into the background a bit. Nevertheless, he still ponders melancholically the temple of Isis, crumbling away on the island of Philae, but not without a spirited declaration on the rightful claims of the present and a discussion of the superstitious belief in Tutankhamun's revenge as explanation for the death of Lord Carnavon.

Al-ʿAqqād does not limit himself to literary and aesthetic criticism. In addition, he also writes about the social conditions in his country. In an essay on public education in Egypt (Ḥusayn Ḥasanayn, *al-Kuttāb al-thalātha* 228/235), he takes a stance on the burning issue of women's rights. Prudently, he warns against the excesses of an all-too-hasty emancipation, without denying the fact that it would not be to the advantage of society if the medieval station of women were to be maintained. Despite his British education, he protects the values of the East from the influences of European civilization. From M. Nordau's *Paradoxe* (1885) he translates selected passages from the chapter on success (*Erfolg*), in which his own, critical attitude on the teachings of this author clearly shines through (ibid. 200/228).

Whatever he does is motivated by his sense of freedom and truth. Only, for him, freedom does not exhaust itself in the concepts of political liberalism; indeed, what he calls for is an intellectual freedom based on a conscious fostering of beauty, in life as well as in the arts.

Together with Ḥusayn Haykal and Ṭāhā Ḥusayn, al-ʿAqqād is in the frontline of those who have tried to make Egypt (and with it, the Arab world as a whole) join the ranks of the civilised nations, authors who will all be reviewed in the chapters to come. At the same time, he is very much aware of the fact that he and his comrades-in-arms stand only at the beginning of an evolution, and that his people will have to go through a long and arduous process of education
154 before they can lay claim to | being regarded as a bearer of human standards that have fully matured.

In his *Shuʿarāʾ Miṣr wa-biʾātuhum fī ʾl-jīl al-māḍī* (C. 1937/1355), al-ʿAqqād brings together a series of brilliant essays that had earlier been published in the press. This is probably the first time that an Arab author tries to apply the methods of modern Western literary criticism. But he also exercises his rights as a poet insofar as he drops the chronological order to pick out poets on whom he has something to say instead. He starts with Ḥāfiẓ Ibrāhīm as the intermediary between the old school that wrote for the public at large and the younger generation that writes for the press. This old school he exemplifies by its eminent representatives Ḥifnī Nāṣif anf Ismāʿīl Ṣabrī. These are followed by two exponents of a style that consists of blindly following the ancients, viz. Muḥammad ʿAbd al-Muṭṭalib and Tawfīq Bakrī, of whom the first is a mediocre copycat of the classics, and who are all he knows, while the second is a faithful admirer who was also receptive of Western ideas. He then returns once more to the *nudamāʾ* of old, with ʿAbdallāh Nadīm and ʿAlī al-Laythī. In the person of Muḥammad ʿUthmān Jalāl he acclaims a die-hard Egyptian patriot who was merely ahead of his time. Sāmī al-Bārūdī is celebrated as the founder of a new era in Arabic poetry. ʿĀʾisha al-Taymūriyya, on the other hand, is the only woman in Arabic literature whom he is willing to recognise as possessing the qualities of a writer. His overview terminates with Aḥmad Shawqī, whom he exposes mercilessly as a shallow populist, as in his *dīwān* of fifteen years before. The part dedicated to the period after Shawqī (190/6) is unfortunately rather short. In it, he emphasises the influence of the British conception of the arts, which had spread in Egypt through the works of Hazlitt in particular. In his epilogue, he defends himself against the accusation that he did not give proper consideration to the work of Khalil Maṭrān by pointing out his foreign origin. At the same time, he calls on the younger generation of Egyptian poets to let true national sentiments bear witness to their patriotism, without borrowing from socialism or other exotic ideas.

After his time in prison for political crimes in 1930/1, | his book *ʿĀlam al-* 155
sudūd wal-quyūd (1937/1355) offered him the opportunity, as a follow-up to his account of that experience, to discuss the prisons of Egypt and the foundations of penal law. Because six years had passed since that experience, sufficient distance had been created for al-ʿAqqād to be able to look at the funny side of things, especially where he describes his faithful though mentally challenged cook. He is very good at describing the different human types found in the prison's population of common criminals. Needless to say that his proposals to reform the Egyptian prison system take their inspiration from the latest Russian and American authors.

In one case, al-ʿAqqād ventures into theorising about politics, a domain that he had often served practically as a journalist. He does this in *al-Ḥukm al-muṭlaq fī ʾl-qarn al-ʿishrīn* (C. n.d.: Maṭbaʿat al-Balāgh al-Usbūʿī, 110 pp.), which he dedicated to Saʿd's successor Muṣṭafā al-Naḥḥās Pāshā. It is a 'Song of songs' on democracy in which he tries to prove that, even though apparently weak today, democracy has a great future ahead of it. Being an Egyptian nationalist who sees his country robbed of any and all political freedom under the British occupation, his position is understandable. In the Introduction, his fiercest attacks are directed at Prof. Sarulya because, in his lectures at the University of

Egypt, the latter had stated that a parliamentary democracy is only feasible in Britain, where he was born, and that it could not be exported to other states without adverse consequences. Al-ʿAqqād first tries to disprove this by taking a negative line of reasoning, stating that Primo de Rivera's dictatorship in Spain has only caused greater chaos to this country without improving any of its social shortcomings. In opposition to this he characterises the Turkish republic under Mustafa Kemal as a paradise of popular freedom which, under his vigorous leadership, had liberated itself from a much-weakened government in Istanbul and, at the same time, from the nefarious tutelage of the Entente powers. With this, he juxtaposes the Italy of Mussolini, whom he characterises entirely along the lines of his political adversary Nitti, which means that he has no understanding whatsoever of Mussolini's historical greatness. The two final chapters fall slightly outside the general scope of the work. In the
156 first of these, he tries to understand Bismarck's | place in history, regarding him as something of a despot (*mustabidd*). Given that he makes no effort to explain Bismarck's achievements against the backdrop of German history, a subject that he could hardly assume his readership to have any knowledge of, the image that he sketches remains rather dull and lacklustre. He juxtaposes Bismarck with Napoleon I and III, showing that the former, despite all his military achievements and after his return from Elba towards the end of his life, believed that he could only regain the sympathy of the people by promising them a democratic government, and that the latter came to power by making similar promises. He then concludes his book by voicing the hope that democracy may see another blossoming, in which all her blessings to mankind will entirely unfold. All in all, this is a work that is certainly worthy of this writer-cum-idealist and which may never be subjected to the cold judgement of a realpolitiker or historian.

Ṭāhā Ḥusayn, in *al-Ḥadīth* 1934, 377/81, praises him as the greatest Arab poet of modern times.—H.R. Gibb in BSOS V, 460/3, Kračkovsky on Ode-Vasilieva XVIII, XIX (German MSOS XXXI, 194/5), Khemiri and Kampffmeyer, *Leaders* 13/6 (with a portrait), Sarkīs 1347, Ismāʿīl ʿAbd al-Ḥamīd, *al-Udabāʾ al-khamṣa* C. n.d. (from which *al-Rāḥa wa-quwwat al-irāda* in Ode-Vas. 169/76), selected prose fragments in Ḥusayn Ḥasanayn, *al-Kuttāb al-thalātha*, C. n.d., 130/232.—Works, other than the *Dīwān*: 1. *Majmaʿ al-aḥyāʾ*, second ed. C. 1920.—2. *al-Shudhūr*, C. 1915, 1926.—3. *al-Dīwān, kitāb fī ʾl-naqd wal-adab* (together with al-Māzinī), 2 fascicles, C. 1921, against which *Thimār al-qalam li-ʿAzīz Naṣrallāh wa-huwa Radd ʿalā kitāb al-Dīwān taʾlīf al-ʿAqqād wal-Māzinī*, C. 1922.—4. *al-Fuṣūl* (see MSOS XXIX, 241/2).—7. *Sāʿāt bayna ʾl-kutub*, C. 1929.—8. *Waḥy al-arbaʿīn, qaṣāʾid wa-maqṭūʿāt*, C. 1933 (from which *Laylat al-ward* in *Aḥsan mā katabtu* 52/3).—9. *Hadiyyat al-karawān*, C. 1933.—10. *Ibn al-Rūmī ḥayātuhu min shiʿrihi*, C. n.d. (1931). *ʿAbqariyyat Ibn al-Rūmī* preface to Kāmil Kīlānī's selection (I, 125).—11. *Riwāyat Qambīz fi 'l-mīzān*, see above, p. 46.—12. *al-Ḥukm al-muṭlaq fi 'l-qarn al-ʿishrīn*, C. n.d.—13. *Khulāṣat al-yawmiyya*, C. n.d.—14. *Tidhkār Goethe*, C. n.d. (from which *ʿAbqariyyat G.* in *Aḥsan mā katabtu* 20/2).—15. *Saʿd Zaghlūl*, C. n.d.—16. *Shuʿarā' Miṣr*, C. n.d. (1937).—17. *ʿĀbir al-sabīl*, C. 1937.—18. *ʿĀlam al-sudūd wal-quyūd*, C. 1937.—Unfortunately I had no chance to see his latest work, *Rajʿat Abi 'l-ʿAlā'*, C. 1939 (274 pp.).

| 29 Al-Māzinī 157

One of the most brilliant humourists of Arabic literature is Ibrāhīm ʿAbd al-Qādir al-Māzinī. He graduated from a teachers' college, then worked for about ten years as a teacher,[123] after which he started to work full-time for the press.[124] Even though, in 1325/1917, he published a *dīwān* (to which his friend ʿAbbās al-ʿAqqād wrote a preface), he soon recognized that his main strengths lie in the column and the short essay.

Al-Māzinī's *dīwān* (two volumes, first edition Cairo 1917, with a preface by ʿAbbās al-ʿAqqād in volume one, reprinted in Rufā'īl Buṭṭī, *Siḥr* 134/56, and by the author himself in volume two) shows that he lacks creative genius, despite his mastery of the Arabic language. He employs the different metres of the old *qaṣīda* with great assurance. In a few cases, he also uses the strophic form ('The deserted house' I, 3/6, 'A storm in the soul' I, 30/5) and in one case he tries a new kind of rhyme (ababacc I, 115/6). As a poet, he quite often takes his inspiration from British models (which he also admits in the preface to volume II), such as Shelley and Byron, and in volume II he even imitates the poems of James Russell Lowell (II, 161/5), Oscar Wilde (ibid., 165) and Maurice (168), as well as Shakespeare (169), Milton's *Paradise Lost* (170), and Fitzgerald's adaptations of ʿUmar Khayyām's *Rubāʿiyyāt* (172/3). But all these models had only a superficial influence on his style, the core of which remained untouched. His poetry is actually a kind of rhetoric, even though, at times, real emotions shine through, as when he bemoans the loss of someone's little daughter. But other than that, as he is still a young man, his weltschmerz is quite unconvincing, despite his long-winded laments ('Tedium vitae' p. 156, 'The poet on his deathbed' 245/53, 'The soul's balance-sheet' 263/8, 'My life's harvest' 331/40, etc.). Certainly, the situation that the Egyptian people were in at the time, and whose youth he criticizes (I, 1), as did so many of his contemporaries, | must have favoured 158
such negative feelings. Fortunately, his later prose writings show that the tone

123 He recounts some delightful episodes from this period in *Fātiḥat ʿahd* in *Khuyūṭ al-ʿankabūt*, 393/401.

124 In 1930 he was present at the coronation of Ibn Saud on behalf of *Jarīdat al-Siyāsa*.

of these poems in no way corresponds to his true feelings. However, romantic love induces him to no more than some disdainful reflexions. The samples of his correspondence with his poet-friends al-ʿAqqād, ʿAbd al-Raḥmān Shukrī and ʿAbd al-Raḥmān Ṣidqī all have the character of spirited dalliances. It appears, however, that al-Māzinī soon understood that poetry was not his strong point, for, as far as I know, he never tried his hand at it again.

The first time that he played the role of literary critic was in the *Dīwān* that he published, together with al-ʿAqqād, in 1921 (cf. above p. 149), and to which he contributed a critique of ʿAbd al-Raḥmān Shukrī's *Ṣanam al-alāʾīb* and a detailed, analytic description of al-Manfalūṭī.

Al-Māzinī discovered that his true talent lay in writing columns and short essays which he published from 1919 onward in various newspapers in Cairo, Damascus, and Baghdad. In 1924/5 he published a collection of these pieces with the title *Ḥaṣād al-hashīm* (second printing 1932, Cairo, Elias, Modern Press). In August 1919 he published *al-Madīna al-fāḍila*, a brilliant satire on Woodrow Wilson, whose political ideals he compares with those of Thomas Moore in the latter's *Utopia*. In 1921 he wrote a piece in praise of the *dīwān* of his friend al-ʿAqqād, which he hails as a welcome interlude in the political turmoil of the times and as the inspiration for a new kind of Arabic poetry, identifying al-ʿAqqād's artistic agenda point-by-point in the latter's *qaṣīda* on Satan's fall (cf. above p. 145). The First Cairene Artshow, which put 13 foreign and 18 Egyptian artists on display in the Dār al-funūn wal-ṣanāʾiʿ al-Miṣriyya in April and May of 1922, provided him with an opportunity to broach the subject of the place of the visual arts within his own culture for the very first time. Significantly, he derived his aesthetic viewpoint from poetry, seeking counsel from a British connoiseur.

The year 1923 was all European: Khalīl Maṭrān's translation of the *Merchant of Venice* obliged him to come to grips with that work, and all the problems of the nineteenth century were presented to him when he tackled the writings of Max Nordau, the biography of the Russian anarchist Kropotkin, and Dumas' *Dame aux camélias*. Impressed with these, he compared Aḥmad Rāmī's re-
159 cently published translation of ʿUmar Khayyām's *Rubāʿiyyāt* with | al-Sibāʿī's prose-rendering of that same work, and with Fitzgerald's English adaptation of it; in the second edition, he removed some of his sharper criticisms of al-Sibāʿī. He devoted an in-depth study to the works and the person of al-Mutanabbī, whom he sought to cleanse of all the imperfections that the literary tradition had imputed to him. This is followed by a detailed analysis of the importance of the metaphor in both spoken and written language—a much-discussed subject among linguists in medieval times—on which he tried to cast a new

light with a passage from Locke's *An Essay Concerning Human Understanding*. This even led him to delve into the origins of human language. Stylistically and otherwise, the two essays from September and October 1923 (*al-Ṣaḥrā'* and *Ṣafḥa sawdā' min mudhakkarātī*), put at the head of this collection, have nothing to do with the rest. They are personal confessions whose tone belies his uneasiness with his professional life thus far. The mood of the second piece is summed up in a poem whose last line is: "O moon! Did you see her in my arms, counting the stars, or were you in this beautiful night just too busy painting the clouds? How come you shone so beautiful, although you were enwrathed?" These lines contrast sharply with the strophic poem that follows it, dedicated to a lover who has died (*Fī jiwāriha*), and whose sincerity does not contain any traces of the rhetoric of his *dīwān*.

In 1924, he writes again about aesthetics. He tries to provide a new answer to the question of the meaning of nature in ancient poetry by bringing in a quotation from Rider Haggard's *Allan Quatermain*, the juxtaposition of the scene with the gravedigger from Shakespeare's *Hamlet* with a *marthiya* on his son by Ibn al-Rūmī, and two poems by Ibn al-Rūmī and Thomas Hardy. The longest chapter in this book is devoted to Ibn al-Rūmī: *Kalima 'an Ibn al-Rūmī wa-ḥayātihi* (from *al-Bayān* 1913/4). Remarkable here is his recognition of the fact that Ibn al-Rūmī owes his special place in Arabic literature to his Greek roots (p. 341)—al-Māzinī being unprejudiced enough to grant the Arians a greater talent for poetry than the Semites.[125] | He even goes so far as to admit that the 160
greatest weaknesses of Arabic poetry are bad taste and bad manners (p. 34). The chapter is followed by a detailed appreciation of the personality of Ibn al-Rūmī as a poet, this on the occasion of the publication of Kāmil al-Kīlānī's selected poems from al-Rūmī's *Dīwān* (cf. I, 125) in 1924.

In *Qabḍ al-Rūḥ* (Cairo 1928, al-Maṭba'a al-Aṣriyya), he deals once more with literary issues; in this case those that were raised by Ṭāhā Ḥusayn's *al-Adab al-Jāhilī* and *Ḥadīth al-arba'ā'*. After this, he only wrote funny stories, starting with *Ṣundūq al-dunyā* (Maṭba'at al-Taraqqī) in 1348/1929.

His model, or rather, the master who is the most suitable for him in light of his talents, is Mark Twain, whose *Memoirs of Adam* he countered with his *Muqtaṭafāt min mudhakkirāt Ḥawwā'* (92/112). But rather than contenting himself with the funny effects of the all-too-human sentiments of our forefather, he also wanted to increase our understanding of the female soul and the tasks of motherhood. He creates the best effect with reminiscences of his childhood,

125 Among the Arab literati of Arian descent he wrongly mentions Abu 'l-Faraj al-Iṣfahānī (p. 344), probably because of his *nisba*.

both in his ludicrous adventures, like in 'The nightmen' or 'How I came to be a daemon' (221/8), and especially in the story of his first love. That he is also perfectly capable of writing something serious is shown not only by his obituary for Saʿd Zaghlūl, but also in the story of the widow who, in a state of increasing madness, awaits the return of her husband, dead while on pilgrimage—apparently another recollection from his childhood (133/140). He also tries to solve problems of a more serious character with satire, such as in his analysis of fatherly feelings (276/90) or when he speaks out on the issue of women's rights (192/8). But in satire unrestrained by reality he is truly like a fish in the water, for example when he solves the issue of women's rights for the year 2230 by simply reversing the current relation between the sexes (143/9). In his mockery he does not spare his colleagues either, be they poets or journal-
161 ists, but he is never offensive and seems to trigger the kind of liberating | roar of laughter among his fellow countrymen that removes every needle from even the sharpest criticism. The fact that he does not look down upon playing the role of the protagonist in his own comical stories 'Horsemanship' 86/91) must surely have had a conciliatory effect. But genuine humour is just as scarce in the Orient as it is in the West because, in both places, derision and scorn rule supreme. That is why al-Māzinī's influence does not seem to go much beyond a limited readership. But whatever the case, needless to say that he did not create much of a following.

In his second book of short stories, called *Khuyūṭ al-ʿankabūt* (Cairo 1354/1935, Maṭbaʿat ʿĪsā al-Bānī wa-Shurakāʾihi), al-Māzinī wants to hold a mirror up to his fellow countrymen. In his preface (*al-Fātiḥa*) he does not shrink from putting his finger on the problems of their social lives: their inclination to enjoy life with the minimum of effort, their unwillingness to carry responsibility, and their adoption of the achievements of European civilization without the slighest inquiry into its rootedness in the development of its underlying culture. He tries to familiarize his readership with these difficult issues in two series of essays: *Ṣuwar min al-ams* and *Ṣuwar min al-yawm*. The reminiscences of his childhood brought together in the first of these could well have the greatest impact. They give a brilliant and humorous account of life among the middle classes of Cairo which, around the turn of the twentieth century, had still preserved many elements of their former, established lifestyle before they were blasted out of their peace and comfort and hurled into the modern age. For his two boys, to whom the book is dedicated, there is no better way to imagine the happines of that era than to read their father's account of his childhood pranks and his memories of his schooldays. The only piece that is a bit out of sync with the rest is *al-Rāʿiyāni, ṣūra waṣfiyya min al-ʿahd al-qadīm*

(148/54), which is a timeless buccolic idyll that depicts a nascent love between two young people with a tenderness that is plainly poetic. The second series opens with a humorous description of the old-fashioned household of his parents (*al-Qadīm wal-ḥadīth*) and recounts in a delightful manner how his mother was upset about his mentioning of her in a slightly disrespectful manner in *Ṣandūq al-dunyā*, before she was reassured again. The pieces after that one introduce us to modern life among the sophisticated people of Cairo; *Ḍārra nāfiʿa* and *Layla wa-lā* | *kal-layālī* are merely recordings of comic situations 162
in everyday life. In many of these stories, a sentimental, or even a sensuous and erotic, mood dominates, but not without his humour eventually breaking through. In the highly amusing story *Māh* (305/18, first published in *Hilāl* 38, 1057/63), for instance, we read how a young couple's clash over traditional and modern lifestyles is solved by the natural sensibility of the woman. Several times he addressed the difficult issue of death, in each case trying to remove its sting. In *Shaykh Quffa* (175/81), he tells us how the happy disposition of a working-class man can even surmount the fear of death; in *Ibtisāmat al-īmān* (329/37), he imagines that he washes corpses for a living, covering the agonies of death with layers of cosmetics; and in *Fi 'l-ḥayāh wal-mawt* (353/9) he tries to shed light on the attitudes towards this issue among different generations.

On the other hand, he does not shrink from dealing with our fear of the grave. In *Bayna 'l-ḥayāh wal-mawt* (118/24), he tells of one night in Ramaḍān in which he got lost in a graveyard and fell straight into an open tomb; in *Layla sawdāʾ* (402/11), he tells how his gloomy ruminations on the majesty of death in a graveyard were suddenly disturbed when he stumbled upon a couple in a loving embrace.

These pieces are of a sparkling liveliness that is never vulgar, and written in an authentic kind of Arabic that is rarely influenced by European expressions and then, tellingly, only in the second series: *shāʾa ḥusnu ḥaẓẓikunna*, "you had the good fortune to …" (193,$_{15}$); *mizāḥ ʿamalī*, "practical joke" (232,$_{4}$); and *an tunqidha 'l-mawqif*, "to save the situation" (306,$_{11}$ and 436,$_{18}$).

Several of these pieces were published previously in *al-Hilāl: Miṣr baʿd miʾat ʿām* 38 (1929), 10/13, *Anā wa-ḍamīrī* ibid. 165/9, *Khawāṭir fi 'l-ikhāʾ* ibid. 305/8, *Fī ṭarīq al-ḥayāh* ibid. 785/8, *Tūḥa, qiṣṣa* ibid. 910/5, *Nādi 'l-raʾm al-ʿāmm* ibid. 39 (1930), 57/9, *al-Baqara, al-fukāha fi 'l-adab al-Rūsī* following Arkadij Awerčenko, ibid. 190/5, *Zayyān al-wāḥid* ibid. 40 (1931), 73/7, *Waladāni ṭayyib wa-sharīr* ibid. 42 (1933), 270/1, *Lāʾiḥat al-Farāʿīn* ibid. 518/21, *Layla hādiʾa* ibid. 781/7, *Ummī* ibid. 43 (1934), 17/21.

At the same time, al-Māzinī also tried his hand at serious stories about social issues, for which the people of Egypt had a greater liking. | In 1925 he 163 started working on his first novel, *Riwāyat Ibrāhīm al-kātib*, which he finished in 1926 and which was published in 1931 (Cairo, Maṭbaʿat al-Taraqqī); the book's second half had to be partly rewritten in haste when it was already in press because the manuscript had gone missing. In his preface he defends the Egyptian novel's right of existence against Ḥusayn Haykal, calling for the use of modern Arabic in the dialogues instead of the dialect. Even though the story is not well structured and the personality of the protagonist not well carved out, the storyline is fluid and the dialogues are lively. Having been a widower for a considerable period of time, while in hospital the story's main character, Ibrāhīm, a writer, gets to know a nurse, herself a widow, with whom he falls in love. Being unable to decide whether he should marry again, he escapes to a relative in the countryside as a way to regain his health. There, he runs into one of his sister-in-laws, Shūshū, whom he had known as a child. She now is a grown-up, modern, educated lady and it is not long before he falls in love with her, and she with him. However, the wife of his host tries to prevent their union in matrimony because she wants to marry off another, older sister first. In order to escape her meddling, Ibrāhīm leaves the house and goes to Luxor, where he makes the acquaintance of a woman of the world who soon becomes his lover. Taking care of him during an illness, she chances upon the amorous correspondence between him and Shūshū. She immediately backs out of the relationship in favour of the other. Eight months later, she writes to tell him that she has married a doctor, concealing the fact that originally, she had gone to see the latter in order to have a pledge of her love to him, Ibrāhīm, removed. In this same letter, he also learns that Shūshū is happily married now. He thus returns to his first love, the nurse, but soon leaves her again because he can't stand the sight of her sleeping. He then goes to the tomb of his wife, in search of consolation for all his disappointments.

Even though the author rejects any suggestion of a link with his personal life, it cannot be denied that the protagonist of this novel has some of his own characteristics, notably a penchant for cynical irony. The artistic quality of this novel derives mainly from the author's analysis of the human psyche, which takes place through juxtapositions in the storyline. Cf. the thorough analysis
164 by E. Saussey in *Bull. d'Etudes Orientales* II, Damascus, 1932, 145/78. | The language of this novel contains a lot of Europeanisms and is strongly influenced by Artzybaschev's *Sanin*, which he himself (?) had translated into Arabic from a shortened English version by P. Pinkerton, and which had been published as a serial story in one of the newspapers, under the title *Ibn al-ṭabīʿa*.

In his *al-Muwāzana bayna 'l-Māzinī wa-khuṣūmihi* (*al-Ḥadīth* 1932, 359/66), ʿUmar Abū Naṣr defends the former against al-ʿAqqad's accusations of plagiarism (*al-Ḥadīth* 1932, 194/201)—which were not only directed against this novel but also against his *Riḥlat al-Ḥijāz* (not accessible to me)—just because he had been inspired by some scenes from Mark Twain's *The Innocents Abroad.*

In 1934, *al-Hilāl* awarded a prize to his short story *Nidāʾ al-ubuwwa* (see August 1934, 1154/64). This story relates the tale of a reckless young man, estranged from his family, who remembers his duties and former affections through his son being threatened by a blaze.

In 1937, he brought 34 stories together in one volume entitled *al-Ṭarīq*.

Gibb, in BSOS V, 460/4, 466, VII, 19/20, T. Khemiri and G. Kampffmeyer, *Leaders* 27/9.

30 Young Poetical Talent

In the wake of al-ʿAqqād, there were several young poets who were quite successful in their lyrical descriptions of nature and life in general.

a. Here, special mention must be made of ʿAbd al-ʿAzīz ʿAtīq, who published the first volume of his *Dīwān* (with a foreword by Sayyid Quṭb) in Cairo (1932/1350) at the age of 24. True, complaints about his disappointments in love and friendship still dominate, complaints that sometimes culminate in a general *tedium vitae* (*Malūl*, p. 60/2). But at the same time, he also tries to relativise his feelings, such as in *Shawqat al-jamāl* (29/31), which is the complaint of a woman who is married to a man she does not love, and in an elegy on al-ʿAbbās b. al-Aḥnaf (p. 49). He seeks inspiration from W. Wordsworth in his lament of happiness bygone (96/7). There are some nationalist songs that escape the general mood: in *Li-man?* (p. 25) he still complains that his country is in the hands of foreigners, but in his greetings to the Palestinian delegation of the year 1928 (143/5) he expresses with great passion his hope that all Arabs
may soon | be freed from servitude. Besides the dominant form of the *qaṣīda*, 165
he also writes *dūbayt*s that he weaves into longer compositions, embellished with inner rhyme or changing verse lengths (e.g. 83/5). Yet he is also capable of composing verses of greater artistic value (18, 52). Later, he turned more to descriptions of nature. In his *Adab al-ṭabīʿa* 111, al-Saḥarti gives particular praise to his poem *Shāṭiʾ al-baḥr*. In a second *dīwān*, *Aḥlām al-nakhīl*, he shows a preference for celebrating country life.

b. In his *al-Shāṭiʾ al-majhūl*, the poems of his friend Sayyid Quṭb, a teacher in Helwan, move along similar lines. Al-Saḥartī (112) has special words of admiration for the dialogue between two palms, *al-ʿAwda ila ʾl-rīf*, and for *Laylāt fi ʾl-rīf*. A second *dīwān*, *Muhimmāt al-shāʿir fi ʾl-ḥayāt wa-shiʿr al-jīl al-ḥāḍir*, was published in Cairo in 1932.

c. Fāʾid al-ʿAmrūsī's *Alḥān al-ālām* is a great *dīwān* (see al-Saḥartī 114). With its 17 verses that all begin with *sa-aqsū*, his *qaṣīda Qaswa* (*Apollo* 1029) revolts against man's yielding to life's temptations, still a rarity in the East.

d. Apart from these, al-Saḥarti (114) also mentions Mukhtār al-Wakīl, the poet of the *dīwān* called *al-Zawraq al-ḥālim* (Cairo 1935), and al-ʿIwaḍī al-Wakīl, whose small *dīwān Taḥiyyat al-ḥayāh* sounds a lot like Abū Shādī (see *Apollo* 665, 738).

31 Ḥasan Kāmil al-Ṣīrafī

Having praised Abū Shādī extensively for the latter's *Aṭyāf al-rabīʿ* (120/770), the young Ḥasan Kāmil al-Ṣīrafī,[126] from the *Apollo* circle of poets, published his own *dīwān*, *al-Alḥān al-ḍāʾiʿa*, in 1934.

He started publishing his own poems in *al-Muqtaṭaf* from 1930 onward: the strophic poem *Jifāʾ al-ṭabīʿa* (78, 679/80), *Manaʿūki* (ibid., 79 [1931], 196/7), *Ḥayāt al-fannān* (80 [1932], 346), *al-Shāʿir* (ibid., 454,) *Mawt ʿAzrāʾīl* (ibid., 331/2), *Shawqī* (ibid., 89, 385/97), *Laḥn al-ḍāʾiʿ* (ibid., 82 [1933], 332. In his *Dīwān* he reprinted his *Mawt al-bulbul* from *al-Muqataṭaf* 82 (1933), 409, *Taḥta ḍawʾ*
166 *al-qamar* (57) from *al-Ḥadīth* 1934, 556, *al-Rabīʿ* | *al-bāhit* (78) from *Apollo* 739, *al-Laghz* (30/2) from *Apollo* 864, *ʿAynuki* from *al-Ḥadīth* 1934, 683, and *Waḥy al-shiʿr* (65) from *Apollo* 89/91. His *dīwān* bears testimony to his being a determined representative of the symbolist movement (*al-shiʿr al-ramzī*), as do the poems *Qalbī*, *Apollo* 225, *al-Qalb al-hāʾim*, ibid. 544, *Ijaʿlīnī ḥulman*, ibid. 661, *al-Ḥurmān*, ibid. 1016/8, and *al-Nūr al-jadīd*, ibid. 1037. The only poem that differs in tone is his satirical "King of the Misers" (*Dīwān* 118). The best expression of his ideals may be found in his long allegorical poem 'The poet' (33/42), which lets us experience the creation of the poet as a dream of happiness, lost in Paradise. When the poet quarrels with God about his loneliness after the ousting of Adam and Eve, God sends him down to earth to keep man's memory of a lost happiness alive. His 'The death of the Angel of Death' (45/7), too, shows great imagination. It is characteristic of this poet that he avoids the usual poetical topoi almost entirely. Love only shows itself in melancholic musings ('The end of the cigarette smoked by him", 54) or in tender longing ('The handkerchief', 76). Nature only speaks to him through the withering of flowers (78) and the dying of autumn (53); to him, even spring is just decay in the making (80). It is only in his poem on the inventions of Thomas Edison (67/9) that a natural joy in life makes itself heard.

---

126 This is how he spells his name, and not Ṣayrafī.

In form, too, the poet explores new avenues. In order to achieve a certain musical effect, he takes the courageous step of combining half verses in different metres (65). He also likes free verse and strophic quatrains.

Apart from an introduction by Abū Shādī, this *dīwān* also contains an aesthetic appreciation of it by ʿAbd al-ʿAzīz ʿAtīq, who says that two further *dīwān*s, *Qaṭarāt al-nadā* and *al-Shurūq*, are planned for publication.

The poet was so kind as to let me have a look at the corrected typescripts of extracts from the two aforementioned *dīwān*s, as well as from his *dīwān Rajʿ al-ṣadā*. In the following, *Qaṭarāt al-nadā* is called no. 1, the printed *dīwān* no. 2, *al-Shurūq* no. 3, and *Rajʿ al-Ṣadā* no. 4. In these *mukhtārāt*, artful strophic poems far outnumber the *qaṣīda*s. The pictorial language of the poet is dominated by sound and rhythm. "In the temple of emotions, in the grove of memory, there is just one melody by which a song rings forth; a melody that, | while 167
rhythmic, has no metre, but whose music stirs the emotions all the same; the language of love to the soul is life; it is of a magnitude that elevates us above the world of death and decay," which is how he puts it in *Dhikrāki*, which is no. 6 of *Qaṭarāt al-nadā*. His soul only rings out when she can retreat into herself. "In the nest, oh my heart, in the nest are your dreams; there you may embrace what in the song is disclosed to you. By the majesty of love and in your dreams all your troubles will come to an end. In your heart, your songs rise up as in a soliloquy. When the world puts a spell on you, your sins will be awakened, when you leave your nest, and are fooled by your delusions"[127] (no. 3 in *Rajʿ al-ṣadā*). The external word is almost entirely excluded from these songs; the only thing we hear is the sound of ocean waves and the murmur of a stream: "A melody on the lips of some female singer, a stream, bordered by beauty, gushes forth from its source, life itself, to feed the torrential stream of passion. On its banks I find a calm and majesty as if in front of a prayer niche, embracing the light of the Transcendent and Sublime, forgetting myself and my small desires. I dissolve into Him, like an echo of a beautiful song, still hanging in the air. On its banks, I and all my vain wishes melt away."[128] (*Thawrat al-jadwal*,

127 *Fī haykali ʾl-wijdān—fi maʿbadi ʾl-dhikrā—ḍarbun min al-alḥān—yuʿaẓẓimu ʾl-shiʿrā—yuwaḥḥidu ʾl-awzān-wa-yajhalu ʾl-baḥrā—lākinna mūsīqāh—tastaʾthiru ʾl-iḥsās—al-ḥubbu fī najwāh—kal-ʿumri fi ʾl-anfās—yasmū binā maʿnāh—ʿan ʿālami ʾl-armās* (*Dhikrāki* str. 2). *Ilā wakrika yā qalbī—fa-fī wakrika aḥlāmuk—tuʿāniqu fīhi mā yūḥī—hi min shiʿrika ilhāmuk—wa-tafnā fī jalāli ʾl-ḥubbi wal-aḥlāmi ālāmuk—wa-tazkharu fīhi aṣdāʾu—ka bil-najwā wa-anghāmuk—fa-qad tasḥaruka ʾl-dunyā fa-tastayqiẓu āthāmuk—idhā mā ḥidta ʿan wakrika aw gharratka awhāmuk* (*Rajʿ al-Ṣadā* no. 3).

128 *Yasīlu wa-fī ḍiffatayhi ʾl-jamālu—ka-laḥnin ʿalā shafatay ghāniyah—manābiʿuhu min jināni ʾl-ḥayāti—ʿalā talaʿāti ʾl-hawa ʾl-sāmīyah. Sakantu ilayhi sukūna ʾl-muṣallī—amāma jalālati miḥrābihi—yuʿāniqu nūra ʾl-jalāli ʾl-baʿīda—wa-yansa ʾl-raghāʾiba fī*

al-Shurūq, no. 3). Yet he is also familiar with the art of the *qaṣīda*; a good example of this is his "Farewell to the Alhambra" (no. 2 in *Rajʿ al-ṣadā*), in which he
168 | lets Boabdil cry out his anguish on the 'Hill of Tears'. In time, we may expect many more beautiful products from this talented young poet, duly recognised by al-Saḥartī in his *Adab al-ṭabīʿa* 117/8.

32 Bishr Fāris

Basing himself firmly on the French symbolists P. Verlaine and Beaudelaire, Dr Bishr Fāris tries to lead Arabic poetry down new paths.

He completed his studies in Paris (about which he tells us in *Kayfa ṣadamatnī Bārīs, al-Hilāl* 42 [1933] 460/3) in 1933 with a brilliant dissertation on sociology, entitled *l'Honneur chez les arabes*, testifying to his great knowledge in the field of ancient Arabic poetry. Back in Egypt, he devoted himself to literature. He presented a follow-up to his earlier studies on the *makārim al-akhlāq* at the Congress of Orientalists, in Rome in 1935 (cf. *Atti*, 1938, 593, *Rend. R. Act. dei Lincei*, s. VI, 213 [1937] 411/25). So far, his poems have only been published in various magazines, notably in *al-Muqtaṭaf* (*Khaymāt amal* 79 [1931] 396, *Makānaka yā ʿishq* ibid. 82 [1933], 418, *Unshūdat al-fajr* ibid. 83, 279, *Fī jibāl Bāwaryā* of August 1935 ibid. 90 [1937], 218), *al-Hilāl* (*Iḥtiḍār al-shabāb* 42, 1933, 847) and *al-Ḥadīth* (*al-Ḥarīq fī Bārīs*, 1934, 33). He explains the background of all these in his *Fi 'l-Madhhab al-ramzī* in *al-Risāla* 1938, 711/3 and in a review of Mayy's *Risālat al-adīb ila 'l-ḥayāt al-ʿarabiyya*, ibid. 734/5; he then applied his theories in detail in his interpretation of the poem *al-Fujūr* in *Majallat al-ṣabāḥ* of 28 April 1938.

Earlier, he published short pieces on various aspects of life in general: in 1927 in *al-Muqtaṭaf* 380/6 (*Jullanār*), in 1928, 522/30 (*Haydā*), in 1930, 145/51 (*al-Qahqaha*), and in 1931, 417/21 (*Ṭabaq al-fūl*). In 1934, *al-Hilāl* (vol. 42, 1165/72) awarded him a prize for his story *Qiṭʿat al-laḥm*; H. Melzig made a German translation of it that was published in the *Frankfurter Zeitung* of 17 September 1937.

The author decided that the play *Mafriq al-ṭarīq* (Cairo, 1938) would be the most appropriate form for him to realise his ambitions as an artist. In it, he wanted to "… seize the perceptibles, once they have passed the senses
169 (*mā warāʾ al-ḥiss min al-maḥsūs*), | to bring out their inner meaning and to record whatever comes to mind without having to bother about the phenomenal world, in an effort to find the true world in which, like it or not, we are thrown hither and thither, and in the discovery of which the hidden senses,

---

bābihi.—Tafānaytu fīhi ka-ughniyyatin—maḍā fi 'l-āthīrī ṣadāha 'l-jamil—wa-dhubtu ʿalā ḍiffatayhi kamā—tadhūbu 'l-raghāʾibu fi 'l-mustaḥīl.

pure reason, and unhemmed imagination each have an equal part." All this unfolds in a symbolic exchange between Samīra, the searching soul that remains bound to the sublunar world, the absolute fool, unable to speak but of unfailing intuition, and "him", a product of society who, caught in its conventions, is unable to grasp the significance of life, even if he stumbles on it; all this in a language of inimitable transparency. It is thus one of those typical plays for reading; being, in fact, poetry in another form. It seems that we are witnessing the early stages of a literary development, but intense efforts will be required for this to lead to renewal or even enrichment.

His latest work, *Mabāḥith ʿarabiyya* (Maṭbaʿat al-Maʿārif, 1939), is entirely devoted to scholarship again. It contains an augmented version of a study of the Muslims of Finland that had been published earlier in *REI*, as well as study on *makārim al-akhlāq*. A discussion of the basic concepts of social ethics in ancient Arabia is followed by some suggestions on terminology in music and philosophy.

33 ʿAlī Maḥmūd Ṭāhā

ʿAlī Maḥmūd Ṭāhā, too, is definitely inspired by French romanticism, but in his *dīwān al-Mallāḥ al-tāʾih* (Cairo, 1934) he inclined more and more to putting his art to the service of nationalist ideals.

Some of the poems in this collection had earlier been published in *al-Muqtaṭaf.* His memories of his childhood, spent in the countryside near Damietta, are the subject of *Fi ʾl-qarya*, which is about the vast expanses of rural northern Egypt, dominated by the Nile and the sea. In *ʿAla ʾl-ṣakhra al-bayḍāʾ* (50/2) he describes the struggle between land and sea around the Manzala lake. He returns the debt of gratitude that he owed to the inspired work of A. Lamartine with an adaptation of the latter's *Lac de B.* (*Les grands écrivains de France*, s. XXII, 1, p. 133) in *al-Buḥayra* (53/8), | a strophic poem in 170 batches of four *khafīf* verses each. His *Allāhu wal-shāʿir* (63/84), a long poem composed of batches of four half-verses each, in *sarīʿ* with the rhyme a-b-a-b, was inspired by a statement by Lamartine. It is an attempt to provide the modern world, whose beliefs were shaken in its struggle for the control of nature, with renewed access to God through the arts ("What is the true poet, other than a vehicle of God's mercy, bringing consolation to a world in mourning and relieving its heart from its pains?" 74, 3, 4). The first poem of this *dīwān*, *Mīlād al-shāʿir*, is similar in tone. Arranged strophically and written in the *khafīf* metre, its verses contain the following exhortation: "Thus, oh poet, have faith in your lyre and sing your song; let love and beauty be your motto; praise the Lord of Creation for His blessings, He who prides in the poet's birth." In *al-Fann al-jamīl* (105/6), he wishes for his country to have its proper share in the artistic

culture of the classics, inherited by the West. He is very much aware of the fact that, before this can happen, a gap still needs to be bridged, as is evident from *al-Mallāḥ al-tā'ih* (25/7), the title poem of the collection. When he wants to expand the horizons of his inner sensations, to the point of waxing lyrical about the polar world after having seen a movie on Amundsen and his expedition (*al-Quṭb* 93/9), one should not be confused into thinking that he betrays his own tradition. In *al-Ṭarīd* (143/7) he complains about the lack of understanding among his colleagues ("The poets of Egypt ramble through life as if they were roaming in the desert, blown off course by one storm after another"). But, on the other hand, he is also willing to give credit to those who deserve it. He thus mourns the loss of two Egyptian pilots who crashed on 28 November 1933 (*al-Ajniḥa al-muḥtariqa* 53/60) and celebrates the memory of minister ʿAdlī Yegen (148/50). And it is with the same sense of belonging that he expresses the nation's heartfelt gratitude towards two of Egypt's great poets, even if their art was far removed from his, viz. Ḥāfiẓ Ibrāhīm and Aḥmad Shawqī, at a commemorative ceremony organised by the actress Fāṭima Rushdī on 1 January 1933, that he celebrates the art of the Syrian Fawzī Maʿlūf, who died young.
171 Again, at the time of the death of King Fayṣal of | Iraq, when speaking for the entire Arab nation, he is able to find the right words to thank the man who was the first to chart the way to political independence.

34 Maḥmūd Ḥasan Ismāʿīl

Besides the overly-refined products of a blossoming international artistic scene, the local art of Egypt appears to hold its ground in he form of the *Aghāni 'l-kūkh* of the young Maḥmūd Ḥasan Ismāʿīl, from the village of al-Nukhayla on the left bank of the Nile in Upper Egypt (vol. 1, Cairo 1935, Maṭbaʿat al-Itimād).

In the hustle and bustle of city life, the poet is time and again overcome by a melancholic longing for the places of his childhood. He recalls the shepherd's flute (120/1), the charms of a moonlit night (34/41), and the quiet peace of the isolated village, a peace that is underscored by the mournful sound of the *sāqiya* (44/7) but also often rudely disturbed by a chorus of frogs ("the devil's organ", 112,$_{11}$). In *Damʿat al-baghī* (80/4) he depicts the mournful cries of a country girl who has landed in the gutter of the city. Yet he is also very much aware of the needs and concerns of the peasants and in no way seeks to depict their lives as some kind of ideal. But, for him, their connectedness to nature outweighs all their problems. His style is visibly influenced by Abū Shādī, even if he never refers openly to his *al-Shafaq al-bākī* (90,1). It is also under the latter's influence that he took to describing works of art ('Daughter of the Nile', describing a sculpture by Maḥmūd Mukhtār, 30/3, and 'The Drowned', on a painting by P. Delaroche in the Louvre, 106/9). When he conjures up the looming shadows of Pentaur and Cheops (89,4), he does what any nationalist poet would do. He has full control of the *qaṣīda* as a poetical form that is eminently suitable for expressing his melancholic moods, although he also likes to use all kinds of strophic structures for this. Next to four strophes of five catalectic *kāmil* dipodies in the a-b-a-b rhyme (*Tabassamī*, 42/3), we find, in *al-ʿAdhrāʾ al-shahīda* (106/9), shortened *kāmil* couplets in the rhyme abc-abc, while in *Maṭʿam al-ṭabīʿa* (*Apollo* 619/20) he even tries his hand at free verse.

| 35 ʿAlī al-Jārim Bek 172

Despite the appearance of all these modern literary trends, classical poetry, resuscitated by Sāmī al-Bārūdī and represented so brilliantly by Aḥmad Shawqī, still holds its ground. Its most important representative is ʿAlī Jārim Bek, whose *Dīwān* appeared in two volumes in Cairo in 1938 (Maṭbaʿat al-Maʿārif) and a third volume of which has been announced as forthcoming.

Born in Rashīd (Rosetta), he made his first appearance as a poet in 1895—when he was still in high school—with a poem on the cholera pandemic that had ravaged his native city (*Dīw.* II, 171/4). A short poem, *al-Fakhr* (of 1900), bears testimony to unrestrained ambition and a naïve sense of selfhood. In 1901 we find him as a student at al-Azhar, where he expresses his adoration for Muḥammad ʿAbduh in a poem in which he already refers to himself as to *fāris al-shiʿr* (I, 115). He completed his studies in Britain. All that remains of this period is a short satirical poem on the London fog, dated 1910 (I, 127). In 1913 he was back in Egypt, where he dedicated a wedding song to a friend (I, 128/34). The [First] World War inspired a lament on the looming loss of Western culture (II, 118/26) and on its effects on the private situation of the author (*al-Ḥubb wal-ḥarb* 196, II, 127/33). In 1915 he was given permission to greet Sultan Ḥusayn Kāmil with a few verses on the occasion of the latter's visit to the Dār al-ʿulūm (I, 135/6). In the same year, he sent his regards to a friend in England, warning him against romantic mis-steps in *Laylatun wa-layla* (II, 134/8). In 1917 he extolled the bliss of love in a beautiful strophic poem called *al-Ḥanīn al-ṭāʾir* (II, 88/93). The advice of a friend to his daughter, written in French, he rendered in a *Waṣiyya* (I, 94/5). After the war his name as a poet was already so firmly established that he was invited to recite a *marthiya* for Ismāʿīl Ṣabrī during a commemorative ceremony held in the Teachers' College in May 1923 (II, 116/26). In the general outpouring of mourning for the loss of the leader of the fatherland, Saʿd Zaghlūl, in 1927, his voice, of course, had to be heard (I, 45/57). In the same year he also took part in a ceremony for Aḥmad Shawqi that had been organised by Arab poets, | this time with a song of praise (*Min shāʿir ilā* 173
shāʿir II, 86/9). In 1932 he composed an elegy for this venerated model of his (II, 901/3). When King Fuʾād made a visit to the university in 1933, he saluted

him as the patron of the sciences (II, 58/63). In that year, he also sang the praises of the king's daughter Fawziya in a commemorative volume for a girls' school bearing her name (I, 55/7). In November of that same year he lamented the crash of two Egyptian pilots in France (I, 83/7). In 1934 he offered the king his congratulations on the occasion of the festivities surrounding his accession to the throne (II, 63/73), and during a festive gathering of the Royal Academy he praised him and Crown Prince Fārūq (ibid. 74/85). In 1936 he expressed the sorrow of the people at the passing of Fu'ād in the heart-rendering *Miṣr al-wāliha* (I, 35/44). At the same time, however, he gave expression to all the expectations that were raised by Fārūq's accession to the throne. When the latter visited Rosetta by ship in 1936, he welcomed him with an exuberant *qaṣīda*. Its metre, a lively *mujtathth*, captures the happy atmosphere in which this event took place, while the author does not miss out on the opportunity to recommend himself as the king's father's poet laureate (I, 21/9). When Fārūq, after attaining adulthood, assumed power on 29 July 1937, he dedicated *al-Tājiyya al-kubrā*, the poem which opens his *dīwān*, to him, along with another poem written on the occasion of the festivities surrounding Fārūq's accession to the throne in the Sudan (II, 11/20). On the occasion of his birthday (I, 12/21) and of the breaking of the fast, he congratulated him in that very same year (I, 45/54). Finally, in January of 1938, he glamourised the king's wedding in a reverberating song (I, 30/44). Since that time, his voice has been heard at every official occasion, such as the hundredth anniversary of the ministry of education (I, 22/34). He also wrote the national anthem of the boyscouts (*al-kashshāfa*) (I, 107/110). Currently, his fame reaches far beyond Egypt's borders. When the government of Iraq organized a commemorative service for the poet Jamīl Ṣidqī al-Zahāwī, on 12 December 1937, he was there, with other Arab poets, to read a *marthiya* (I, 104/17) that also contained words of praise for the young king Ghāzī. On the occasion of the Congress of Arab Physicians in Baghdad in February 1938, he paid homage to this old caliphal town on behalf of the intellectuals of the entire Muslim world. Apart from his *Dīwān*, other *qaṣīda*s were also published in *al-Ahrām*, such as a song on Egypt on 21 and 30 January 1939 (with a portrait) and a *Nashīd al-muʿallimīn*, on 25 September 1937, in which he gave up classi-
174 cal metres for the very first time, | composing seven strophes in a free metre. Otherwise, his language and metrics are so rigidly classical that he found it necessary to write an extensive philological commentary on his own *dīwān*, which he did with the help of three of his friends. His language is admittedly not as rich in *nawādir* as Aḥmad Shawqī's, but it is also true that restrictions of rhyme or metre only rarely cause his language to be non-standard. One case in point is II, 8, 5, where he uses *ghann* in the sense of 'singing'. His exaggerations, too, mostly remain within the boundaries of good taste, with the exception of

the case where he, in a poem on the occasion of the birthday of King Fārūq, credits the king with having studied and memorised the first printing of the Book of Nature from *alif* until *yāʾ* (I, 18,$_{6}$), or when he, in his national song for the boyscouts, designates Egypt as the *alif* of nature and existence (ibid. 107,$_{1}$). It seems that he attaches special significance to puns involving Kināna, the poetic name for Egypt (after the famous Bedouin tribe), in the sense of 'quiver' (as in I, 45,$_{3}$, 83,$_{2}$, II, 91,$_{6}$).[129] He only rarely allows Europeanisms, such as in his poem and *marthiya* on Aḥmad Shawqī, in which he uses the painter Raphael as a backdrop for his metaphors (II, 88, 94,$_{4}$).

36 Provincial Poets

In the provinces too, new poets keep appearing, such as Mūsā Shākir al-Ṭantāwī with *Ṣaḥāʾif al-damʿ* (Cairo, 1935) and Muṣṭafā ʿAlī ʿAbd al-Raḥmān, whose *dīwān Laḥn al-khulūd* (Maṭbaʿat al-Ahrām, Damanhūr 1938) is dedicated to King Fārūq (see *al-Ahrām* of 13 March 1939).

37 Female Poets

In Arabic literature, women have always had their place. However, over the last couple of hundred years they gradually lost it. Yet during the previous generation, this place was successfully reclaimed by the Eygptian ʿĀʾisha Taymūr, a Muslim (II, 724,$_{9}$, on whom al-ʿAqqād, *Shuʿarāʾ Miṣr* 150/4, *al-Shiʿr al-nisāʾī al-ʿaṣrī*, C. 1347, 11/8), and the Syrian Warda al-Yāzījī, a Christian (II, 767, on whom *Balāghat al-nisāʾ* II, 13/76, *al-Shiʿr al-nisāʾī* 5/10). | In the wake of the women's 175
liberation movement headed by Qāsim Amīn there appeared a whole series of women activists who stood up to men through poetry.

a *Zaynab bint ʿAlī*

In Egypt, the first of these was Zaynab bint ʿAlī b. Ḥusayn b. ʿUbaydallāh b. Ḥasan b. Ibrāhīm b. Muḥammad b. Yūsuf Fawwāz. Born in 1860 in Tibnīn, near Sidon in Syria, she moved to Alexandria when she was ten years old. One of her teachers there was Ḥasan Ḥusnī al-Ṭuwayrānī (cf. 14 b). She later dedicated herself entirely to literature, standing up for women's rights in all kinds of magazines. She died on 20 Ṣafar 1332/17 January 1914. While her poems were published in magazines (e.g. on the occasion of the festivities surrounding the accession to the throne of ʿAbd al-Ḥamīd of 1905), some of her essays were published in *al-Rasāʾil al-Zaynabiyya* I (there are no other volumes), Cairo n.d. In her *al-Durr al-manthūr fī ṭabaqāt rabbāt al-khudūr* (Būlāq 1312/3) she

129 The pun in the anonymous song in Littmann, *Äg. Nationallieder u. Königslieder* II, 5, 2, is not very clear, which is why it is better to understand Kināna there as a proper name.

gives an account of the history of women in politics and literature (from which *Tarjamat Jeanne d'Arc* was published in *al-Mashriq* XIX, 108/14). Besides this, she also wrote three novels (*riwāyāt adabiyya*): *Ḥusn al-ʿawāqib wa-ghādat al-zāhira*, C. 1316, *al-Hawāʾ wal-wafāʾ*, completed on 6 Rabīʿ II 1310/29 September 1892, C. 1310, and *al-Malik Qurūsh aw Mulūk al-Furs*, C. 1323. See *al-Mashriq* XIX, 555, *Fatāt al-sharq* I, 225/8, VIII, 152, Fatḥiyya Muḥammad, *Balāghat al-nisāʾ fī 'l-qarn al-ʿishrīn*, Cairo n.d. (Maṭbaʿat al-Saʿāda) I, 116/23, Sarkīs 989.

b *Āmina Najīb*

While Zaynab's successors Malak Ḥifnī Nāṣif and Mayy Ziyāda stood up for women's rights in prose, Āmina Najīb turned out to be a gifted poet. The daughter of Muḥammad Najīb and the sister of Muṣṭafā, she was born in Cairo in 1873, married in 1888, and died in 1917. She was especially successful in writing short impressions, such as *al-ʿUṣfūr* and *al-Nakhla al-munfarida* (*al-Shiʿr al-nisāʾī al-ʿaṣrī*, 19–23).

c *Jamīlat Muḥammad al-ʿAlāʾilī*

More successful as a poet was Jamīlat Muḥammad al-ʿAlāʾilī. Being politically active in the Wafd party, she was banished from Cairo to work as a teacher in Aswan for a time. Apart from passionate laments from exile, her 1936 *dīwān*,
176 *Ṣadā aḥlāmī*, | also contains lyrical effusions in free verse. In *al-Funūn al-jamīla* (*Apollo* 945/8, with a portrait), she talks about her ideals as an artist. See Abū Shādī, *Fawq al-ʿubāb* 117, *Adabī* I, 425/33 (with many samples).

d *Dr. Munīra Ṭalʿat*

Author of a series of dramatical prose pieces called *Riwāyat al-bāʾisa*, Alexandria 1930.

See also Maryam Naḥḥās Nawfal, *Maʿraḍ al-ḥasnāʾ fī tarājim shahīrāt al-nisāʾ*, Cairo 1879, Fatḥiyyat Muḥammad, *Balāghat al-nisāʾ fī 'l-qarn al-ʿishrīn*, Cairo n.d. (1344/1925), Muḥammad Salīm Bey, *Maṭāliʿ al-budūr fī maḥāsin rabbāt al-khudūr*, Cairo 1907, Qadriyyat Ḥusayn, *Shahīrāt al-nisāʾ fī 'l-ʿālam al-Islāmī*, Cairo (Maṭbaʿat Amīn al-Khānajī) 1334, *al-Shiʿr al-nisāʾī al-ʿaṣrī wa-shahīrāt nujūmihi* (*ʿuniya bi-jamʿihi wa-nashrihi Maktabat al-Wafd li-ṣāḥibihā Muḥammad Maḥmūd*) Cairo 1929/1347.

38 Poets in the Popular Genre

Compared to poetry in classical Arabic, poetry in the common vernacular still remains entirely in the background. Only the *zajal* ventures out into the open sometimes, and then only in the newspapers. Rare is the author who succeeds in publishing a collection. Some of these *zajal* poets deserve being mentioned here:[130]

a *Khalīl Naẓīr*

Khalīl Naẓīr was, like Muḥammad Imām and Muḥammad Faraj, a negro from the Sudan. His father, a slave, was bought by ʿAlī Pāshā Rifāʿa. When he was given his freedom, he got married. His son received a good education, but when his patron died he had to make a living from his writings. To do so, he turned to the *zajal*, just as Muḥammad Imān and al-Najjār had done before him. He also wrote a number of *qaṣīdas*, though, but these he sold to wealthy would-be poets who then published them under their own name in *al-Muqaṭṭam*, *al-Ahrām* and other newspapers. His *zajals* were first printed in *Jarīdat al-Sayf*, which also published them in collective form, under the title *Azjāl Naẓīr*, following his death in 1920.

| Easily understandable for the masses, his poems comment upon major so- 177
cial and political developments, and likely did more to awaken and strengthen Egyptian nationalism than established literature ever could. The Milner delegation, for example, he welcomed in the hope that it would restore Egypt's long-awaited independence (19/21 *Milner wa-Farīd*). Generally, he believes that the infiltration of European culture and its inventions (102.5) can only cause severe damage (97), which he then details in individual poems. But he also keeps telling the youth of Egypt that they need to have an active professional life if they are ever to stand their ground against the foreigners. Singing the praises of family life, he takes refuge in mystical contemplations. Despite the fact that his poetry has done much to promote the common vernacular, he has no intention of pushing classical Arabic out of the literary domain (36/8: "Take my advice, preserve it in your heart, don't forget it, even if you should live as long as Noah. It is the backbone of your native language, and I fear that it may vanish if we should commit a sin against the language of the Arab").

b *Muḥammad ʿAbd al-Nabī*

His endeavours were continued by Muḥammad ʿAbd al-Nabī, whose *Majmūʿat azjāl* appeared in three volumes in 1916, 1922 and 1923, having mostly been

---

130 From the older collections of popular poetry, the following can be mentioned: Manṣūr ʿAbd al-Mutaʿāl al-Kutubī, *Nuzhat al-ʿāshiq al-walhān fī 'l-aghānī wal-anāshīd wal-alḥān*, 2 vols, C. 1327 and Philippe Qaʿdān al-Khāzin, *al-ʿAdhāra 'l-māʾisāt fī 'l-azjāl wal-muwashshaḥāt* (from a North African manuscript belonging to the Ethiopian College in Rome), Jounieh 1902 (Sarkīs, 1299, 810).

published first in *Jarīdat al-Musāmir*. For him, too, the *zajal* mainly serves as a vehicle for his criticism of the social conditions in his country. In vol. II, 22/4, for instance, he depicts the deplorable situation of the average man of letters while scoffing at the obsession of the fellahs with sending their sons to the cities to receive a half-baked European education so they can find a job as a civil servant (ibid. 25/9). Many of his *zajal*s were meant to be sung in plays, such as *al-Aqraʿ b. Ḥābis* of vol. II, 42/44, or *Ādī ākhirathā* of vol. II, 52/6. Both pieces were printed in their entirety in volume III, together with *Hafawāt al-muḥibbīn*. Yet he also used the *zajal* for an elegy on his artist-friend Khalīl Naẓīr (II, 66/8) and, in December 1921, on the freemason ʿAbd al-Bāqī Ṣāliḥ Bek (ibid. 68/70), and in celebration of the *mawlid al-nabī* of the year 1338 in the lodge that was directed by Grandmaster Idrīs Rāghib Bek.

c *Muḥammad Bek ʿIzzat Saqr*

During his lifetime, the late Muḥammad Bek ʿIzzat Saqr was regarded as *Amīr al-zajal*. Unfortunately, I do not have access to the collection of his poems reviewed in *Apollo* 968 (on pages 948/52 of the same publication Muḥammad ʿAbd al-Rasūl discusses the *zajal* genre).

178 | d *Al-Wafāʾ Maḥmūd Ramzī Naẓīm*

In this position, Saqr was succeeded by al-Wafāʾ Maḥmūd Ramzī Naẓīm, who was born on 25 December 1889 in Qaryat Birkat al-Sabʿīn, in al-Mudīriyya al-Manūfiyya. His early poems were published with the titles *Muntakhabāt* (Cairo n.d.) and *Mubakkir al-ghayth* (ibid.) (Sarkīs 1709). Undated are his *Muwashshaḥāt*, in which he pronounces himself in classical Arabic on political issues, such as Saʿd's exile (p. 58) and return (50, 67). Twice, the establishment of the Bank of Egypt leads him to call on the people to be thrifty (39, 48). He uses the same form in an elegy for the early deceased Saʿīd Muḥammad al-Raffāʿ (ibid. 70). In 1918 he brought his *marāthī*, *madāʾiḥ* and *arājiz* together in one volume, calling it *Kaʾs al-ḥikma*. In 1921 he published (Maṭbaʿat al-Sufūr, n.d. [1921]) *Alḥān al-asā*, a small volume containing two essays, *al-Sāḥir al-jamīl* and *al-Munājāh*, and a series of mystical quatrains, the last five of which were given the separate title *Mathālith al-asā*. In 1343/1924, he published his *Dīwān* and *Azjāl Naẓīm*. Another collection of *zajal*s, together with some stories in classical Arabic, was published in 1929 under the title *Taḥt ẓilāl al-nakhīl*. *Apollo* 88 published a *qaṣīda* with the title *Ālām fannān* (with a portrait). In Kampffmeyer, *MSOS* XXXI, 134, 144 and 150, there are a number of poems on political affairs of the time that had earlier been published in *al-Siyāsa*. Littmann, *Or. Moderno* XVII (1937), 206/10, offers a transcription and translation of a so-called *manalugh* in the common vernacular on the capitulations in Egypt, which had earlier been published in a newspaper.

e *Muḥammad ʿAbd al-Munʿim*
Azjāl al-Buthayna, third collection, Cairo 1930

f *Varia*
17 songs, partly designated as nashīd and partly as *manalugh*, in classical Arabic and in the common vernacular, including two poems by Aḥmad Rāmī (cf. p. 128), were published by E. Littmann from newspapers and other sources, in transcription and translation, in *Ägyptische National- und Königslieder der Gegenwart, Abh. K.M.* XXIII (Leipzig 1938).

39 Religious Poets
Uninfluenced by modern developments, a number of poets have continued to write religious poetry in the old style in the last couple of decades. From among these, we mention:

a. Ḥusayn b. Aḥmad b. Bilāl Fawzī: 1. *ʿIqd jīd al-zamān bi-madḥ sayyid walad ʿAdnān*, a *qaṣīda* in 140 verses, lith. | Alexandria 1303, C. 1310.—2. *Rashf al-kuʾūs* 179
fī riyāḍ al-nufūs, *dīwān*, Alexandria 1314 (Sarkīs 771).

b. Maḥmūd b. Muḥammad al-Qūsī of Dongola, *khalīfa* of the Saʿdiyya order, wrote his *dīwān al-Tuḥfa al-durriyya fī ʾl-taghazzulāt al-Muḥammadiyya* in the common vernacular, Būlāq 1309 (Sarkīs 1703, see p. 84).

c. Aḥmad b. Aḥmad al-Najjārī al-Dimyāṭī al-Ḥifnāwi al-Shāfiʿī al-Khalwatī al-Musayliḥī composed, on 26 Shawwāl 1309/16 June 1890: *Saʿādat al-dārayn fī minḥat sayyid al-kawnayn*, a long *qaṣīda*, C. 1310 (Sarkīs 401/2, where 6 other theological and philological works are mentioned).

d. ʿAbdallāh al-ʿAlawī al-Ḥasanī al-Ghazzī wrote, on 1 Muḥarram 1320/10 April 1902: *Ṣubḥ al-dujā fī shawāhid ṣuwar al-maḥāsin al-shabīha bi-ḥurūf al-hijāʾ*, sample word-games involving various letters of the alphabet (see p. 35 n), in alphabetical order, with three *qaṣīdas* by the author (Cairo^2 III, 229) in an appendix, C. 1323.

e. ʿUrfān Bek Sayf al-Naṣr al-Raydī al-Mollawī (alive in 1345/1926): *Nukhabat* (Sarkīs 1320 mistakenly has *Taḥiyyat*) *al-ʿurfān fī tanwīr al-adhhān*, poems on God and the Prophet, *maqāmas*, *ḥikam*, and *mawāʿiẓ*, poems in praise of contemporary poets, jocular poems, *mawāwīl* and other items, such as the correspondence between Shaykh ʿAlī Abu ʾl-Naṣr and Rushwān Muḥammad al-Sawajī, Cairo 1321 (Cairo^2 III, 407).

f. ʿAbd al-Masīḥ al-Anṭākī, publisher of the *Jarīdat al-ʿUmrān* in Cairo and alive in 1338/1920: *al-Qaṣīda al-ʿAlawiyya aw Taʾrīkh shiʿrī li-ṣadr al-Islām*, dedicated to al-Sirdār Arfaʿ al-Shaykh Khazʿal Khān, the sultan of al-Muḥammara, C. 1338/1920 (Cairo² III, 286).

g. Maḥmūd ʿAbdallāh al-Qaṣrī, alive in 1345: *al-Qaṣīda al-ʿAlawiyya*, the life of ʿAlī in verse with an appendix in prose by Muḥammad ʿAbduh on the same subject, together with some verses ascribed to ʿAlī, C. 1337/1918 (Cairo² III, 286).

h. Karāma b. Hāniʾ: poems in the style of the *Burda*, a *hamziyya* and other poems on the Prophet, collected by Tawfīq al-Rāfiʿī, C. 1341/1924.

i. Aḥmad b. Muḥammad al-Shaykh Banbā: *Majmūʿ qaṣāʾid al-musammā Niʿmat al-rabb al-amīn fī khidmat khayr al-ʿālamīn*, C. 1345.

k. Muḥammad Bek Farghalī al-Anṣārī al-Tahṭāwī, Raʾīs al-taḥrīrāt al-ʿarabiyya bi-wizārat al-khārijiyya al-Miṣriyya (alive in 1345): *Dīwān rawḍat al-ṣafāʾ bi-madḥ al-Muṣṭafā*, a *takhmīs* on the *hamziyya* (*Umm al-qurā*) on the *Burda*, on which a *tashṭīr*, a *takhmīs* on *al-Lāmiyya al-kubrā* in the *dīwān* entitled *Ahna*
180 *ʾl-manāʾiḥ fī asna ʾl-madāʾiḥ* | by Shihāb al-Dīn Maḥmūd al-Dimashqī (see II, 43), a *takhmīs* on the *Rāʾiyya Hāʾiyya* by the same, at the end poems in praise of King Fuʾād, Crown Prince Fārūq, Rifāʿa Bek Rāfiʿ and others, Cairo n.d. (Cairo² III, 131).

l. Abu ʾl-ʿAbbās Aḥmad al-Bahlūl, *al-Durr al-aṣfā wal-zabarjad al-muṣaffā fī madḥ sayyidinā Muḥammad al-Muṣṭafā al-maʿrūf bi-Sirr bāb al-wuṣūl* C. 1311, in which every *qaṣīda* starts with the rhyme consonant in the style used in the Maghreb.

m. In his *Ṣafwat al-ʿArab*, Aḥmad Ramaḍān al-Madanī al-Shādhilī published an anthology of ancient and modern poets, together with exerpts from his books *Mā ata ʾl-shuʿarāʾ bi-madḥ sayyid al-anbiyāʾ*, *al-Salāsil al-dhahabiyya* (C. 1340) and *Musāmarat al-adīb wa-munājāt al-ḥabīb fi ʾl-ghazal wal-nasīb*, taken from 60, mostly contemporary poets (C. 1342).

40 Poetry in the Sudan

Since its conquest by Muḥammad ʿAlī, the Sudan has become one of the provinces of Egypt in a cultural sense as well. Outside Cairo, in cities like Helwan, Damanhur, or Tanta, there were always people engaged in imitating the style of the leading poets of the capital. In a similar way, we always find, in cities like Khartoum, Omdurman or El-Obeid, some theologian, teacher, or official who tries to uphold the banner of literature in more or less successful verse. Saʿd Mīkhāʾīl, a civil servant working for the post and telegraph services and who also wrote *Samīr al-adab*, which we refer to now and then, tells us about these people in his *Shuʿarāʾ al-Sūdān* I, Cairo n.d. (ca. 1930).

The first to be mentioned in Mīkhāʾīl's overview of Sudanese poets is Shaykh Ḥusayn Zahrāʾ of Wād Shaʿīr, who studied in Cairo at al-Azhar and who rallied behind the Mahdi after the latter's victory over Hicks Pāshā. ʿAbdallah, the Mahdi's *khalīfa*, put him in charge of teaching *ḥadīth* and inheritance law. Subsequently, he appointed him as *qāḍī*. In this capacity he soon came into conflict with the ruler and died in prison, having tried in vain to regain the favour of the Mahdi through a number of *qaṣīdas*.

Once Anglo-Egyptian rule had been re-established in the Sudan, local scholars | working for the government could turn their attention to things cultural. 181
At the head of these was the clan of Aḥmad Hāshim, who traced their pedigree back to al-ʿAbbās b. ʿAbd al-Muṭṭalib. It was this family that provided the first *Shaykh al-ʿulamāʾ* of the Sudan, Abū ʾl-Qāsim, who was born in 1278/1861 in a small village near Khartoum. Having worked as the secretary of the Mahdi and his *khalīfa*, he was appointed *qāḍī* in Sennār after the fall of Omdurman in 1899, in 1906 in Mudīriyyat al-Nīl al-Azraq, and in 1912 he was made *Shaykh al-ʿulamāʾ*. He published a *dīwān* entitled *Rawḍ al-ṣafāʾ fī madḥ al-Muṣṭafā*. His brother al-Ṭayyib Aḥmad Hāshim, born in Berber in 1273/1856, after working as the tutor of ʿUthmān, the son of the Mahdi's *khalīfa*, was appointed *muftī* of the Sudan by the Anglo-Egyptian government. Of him, we have a *tashṭīr* to a famous *qaṣīda* by Lisān al-Dīn b. al-Khaṭīb. Their brother Ibrāhīm, born in Berber in 1289/1872, was *bāshkātib* at the *sharīʿa* court in Wād Madanī and enjoyed some notoriety as the author of poems on the Prophet. Another member of this family is the most celebrated poet of the Sudan, ʿUthmān Efendī Hāshim, born in Berber in 1898. Having completed his education at Gordon College in 1915, he started working as a civil servant. From his many occasional poems, special mention must be made of his song celebrating the victory of Muṣṭafā Kamāl over the Greeks.

ʿAbdallāh Muḥammad ʿUmar al-Bannāʾ, born in Rifāʿa on 24 Shawwāl 1308/3 June 1898, received his education at Gordon College as well, where he has taught since 1922. In his poems he pronounced himself several times on contemporary issues such as the education of women and the problem of the Arabic language (*Damʿa ʿala ʾl-lugha al-ʿarabiyya*). The *Rāʾid al-Sūdān* newspaper gave a prize to one of his *takhmīs*.

One of his classmates was ʿAbdallāh ʿAbd al-Raḥmān, whose grandfather, al-Amīn b. Muḥammad al-Ḍarīr (d. 1302/1884), had been a high-school inspector in the Sudan before the fall of Khartoum and who was a well-known poet in his day. ʿAbdallāh ʿAbd al-Raḥmān works as a teacher in Omdurman and wrote a book called *al-ʿArabiyya fi ʾl-Sūdān* as well as countless occasional poems, especially for religious feasts.

As well as all these representatives from the teaching corps, we should also mention the shaykh of the Sāmāniyya order, Muḥammad Saʿīd al-ʿAbbāsī. Born in Ramaḍān 1298/August 1881 in al-Kūh in Mudīriyyat al-Nīl al-Abyaḍ, he belonged to the much respected Sudanese Jumūʿiyya tribe, which traced its
182 | origins back to ʿAbbās b. ʿAbd al-Muṭṭalib and to which Zubayr Pāshā, the conquerer of Darfur and Baḥr al-Ghazāl, also belonged. His father sent him in 1899 to the Military Academy in Cairo at the instigation of Lord Kitchener, but he returned after just two years, devoting himself to academic studies instead. After the death of his father, who had been on the payroll of Ismāʿīl, he succeeded him in all his religious offices in 1325/1907. Among his religious poems there is also a *qaṣīda* on the war in Tripoli.

People working in the free professions, too, some of them traders, dedicated themselves to poetry. One of these was ʿAbd al-Majīd Efendī Waṣfī, born the son of the commander of Dongola in 1288/1871. Having started his working career as a civil servant in 1897, he turned to trade in 1916. At the request of the government, he greeted King George V with a *qaṣīda* when the latter visited Port Sudan on 17 January 1912. Besides him, other poets that can be mentioned here are the traders ʿUthmān Ḥasan Badrī of Tandalti in Mudīriyyat al-Nīl al-Abyaḍ and ʿAlī al-Shāmī, whose father had arrived in Dongola as an immigrant in 1302/1884.

As was stated on page 124 (on Aḥmad Tawfīq Bakrī, see Saʿd Mīkhāʾīl 100/8), portraits of many of these poets show clear traces of negro blood.

A second volume of *Shuʿarāʾ Sūdān*, announced on the cover of the first volume, was apparently never published.

Among the poets selected for this overview, Ḥamza al-Malik Tunbul and Ibrāhīm Muḥammad ʿAbd al-ʿĀṭī have not yet been mentioned. The former published his *Dīwān al-ṭabīʿa* in Cairo in 1930 (Maṭbaʿat al-Raḥmāniyya), the latter *al-Rāwūq, Dīwān al-Ibrāhīmiyyāt* in Cairo in 1938.

2 *Narrative and Essayistic Prose* (*Novels, Short Stories, Essays*)

Maḥmūd Taymūr, *al-Nahḍa al-qiṣaṣiyya al-ḥāliyya* RAAD VI (1925), 263/8, expanded in the *muqaddima* of his *al-Shaykh Sayyid al-ʿAbīṭ wa-aqāṣīṣ ukhrā*, C. 1926/1344., transl. G. Widmer, On the beginnings and development of narrative prose in Arabic literature, in *WI* XIII, 8/54.

183 | Idem, *Nushūʾ al-qiṣṣa wa-taṭawwuruhā, al-muḥāḍara allatī alqāhā fī qāʿat Yūrt bil-Jāmiʿa al-Amrīkiyya yawm al-jumʿa 20 Māris 1936*, C. (al-Maṭbaʿa al-Salafiyya).

Muʿāwiya Lawz, *Baḥth fī uṣūl fann al-adab al-qiṣaṣī fī ʾl-qarn al-ʿishrīn*, in *al-Hilāl* 39 (1930), 1533/60.

Muḥammad Amīn Ḥassūn, *al-Thaqāfa al-qiṣaṣiyya fī Miṣr*, in *al-Ḥadīth*, 1931, 491/5.

Aḥmad Ḍayf, *al-Qiṣaṣ fī 'l-adab al-'Arabī*, in *al-Muqtaṭaf* 86 (1936), 145/8.

Ṣalāḥ al-Dīn Dhuhnī, *Miṣr bayna 'l-iḥtilāl wal-thawra*, C. (Maṭba'at al-Sharq al-Islāmiyya) n.d. (1939).

I. Kračkovsky, Der historische Roman in der neueren arabischen Literatur, in *Žurnal Minist. Narodnago prosvjäščeniya*, St. Petersburg 1911, 260/88, German trans. by G. v. Mende, in *WI* XII, 51/87.

H.A.R. Gibb, The Egyptian Novel, in *BSOS* VII, 1/31.

H. Pérès, Le roman, le conte et la nouvelle dans la littérature arabe moderne, in *Annales de l'Institut d'Etudes Orientales de l'Un. d'Alger* III, 1937, 266/337.

1 The *Maqāma*

In poetry, literary progress could take its inspiration straight from the past, which just had to be resuscitated and then continued. Yet authors wishing to provide their Arab readership with an alternative to the popular translations of European prose works had no examples that they could start from.

True, the people of the Orient still enjoyed telling stories, a pleasure that had expressed itself from the Middle Ages onward in pseudohistorical romances and in the stories of the 1001 Nights. This is confirmed by the tales that Spitta and others have written down from the mouths of popular storytellers and also by some publications in the common vernacular.[131] But this art was looked down upon by the literati and it is only recently that it has started to regain some of its former influence. These literati only accepted the *maqāma*, which developed into a story in Fikrī Pāshā's | *al-Maqāma al-Fikriyya* (cf. Gibb, 184
BSOS IV, 753, VII, 4n), but soon proved to be too cumbersome to suit the goals of modern literature. The countless translations from French and English (see above, p. 4 n), absorbed eagerly by the reading public, soon inspired local imitations. And it were the Syrians especially, many of whom worked in Egypt as journalists, who tried their hand at this. Following the example of Sir Walter Scott, historical plots had a special attraction for them, particularly since they had the advantage of passing unharmed through the hands of an unforgiving censor. Before the war, it would have been too dangerous to write about social, let alone political, issues. For a contemporary, true-to-life novel, one vital condition was still not satisfied, viz. a social position enabling women to feel

131 Of which I only have access to *Kitāb bulbul al-ṣayyāḥ fī 'l-ḥikāyāt wal-ḥawādīt al-milāḥ allatī (sic) ḥawā jumlat ḥikāyāt jadīda muḍḥika hazaliyya*, Cairo (Maṭba'at al-'Umūmiyya) 1320.

passionately about things that lay beyond the sensual and to act upon those feelings.

In the same way in which, in the previous section, we saw some poets who were also active in narrative prose, here, too, it is not possible to distinguish clearly between the various genres within the persons who practice them. Many of the authors who will be mentioned here were not only active as storytellers, but also as social critics, which is why it seems practical to let them be followed by those essayists who were neither writers of short stories nor novelists.

2 Jamīl Nakhla b. Mudawwar

The first work to be mentioned here, as a precusor of the historical novel, eminently represented by Jurjī Zaydān, is Jamīl Nakhla b. Mudawwar's (d. 1907) *Ḥaḍārat al-Islām fī Dār al-salām*, Cairo 1888, 1323/1905, 1932.[132]

185 | Apart from Barthélémy's *Lettres du jeune Anacharsis*, the author must also have found inspiration in the European academic novel. Of the first, he adopted the epistolary form, of the second, the obligation to provide a source reference for each and every piece of information. Despite these learned accoutrements, the author did succeed in writing a lively story, from which we also learn that he studied the sources of the cultural history of the heyday of the ʿAbbāsids with great success. The protagonist of the story is a young Persian who leaves his hometown of Nahrawān in 156 AH to go and complete his studies of *fiqh* under Abū Yūsuf, a friend of his father, and who carries on a correspondence with a friend in which he tells him of his adventures in Iraq. It starts with his departure from the port of Hormuz and an account of his passage by ship that is just as lively as his description of the Bedouins, whose lands he passes through while crossing the estuary of the Euphrates and the Tigris. After a short stay in Basra, whose then already-faded glory he brings back to life, he finally arrives in Baghdad. A fortunate idea related to a thorny question of *fiqh*, in which the crown prince al-Mahdi sought to revoke his impulsive divorce from his favourite wife Khayruzān, secures him the favour of the court. Appointed tutor to the household of the crown prince, he soon draws closer to the Barmakids. This gives the author the opportunity to give a vivid description of the splendour of the court, together with its flourishing cultural life. After al-Mahdī's accession to the throne, the hero of the story maintains his position of trust with the caliph, with the latter even sending him on one occasion to Khurāsān, to crush al-Muqannaʿ's revolt. But here the author fails to describe the lands of the East, possibly because his sources were lacking

---

132 See Kračkovsky in *WI* XII, 1930, 6/9.

in information about them. After his pupil Hārūn al-Rashīd's accession to the throne, he retains the latter's confidence. The new caliph sends him as an emissary to the emperor in Rome, a trip that gives the author the opportunity to describe the capital of Christianity as the counterpart of Baghdad, the capital of Islam, although because he had no sources available on this subject, he has to rely entirely on his own imagination. The hero's diplomatic mission, viz. the conclusion of an alliance with the emperor Charles against the Umayyads of Spain, is a failure. Passing through Tunisia and Egypt, he returns to the East, | 186
joining the caliph in Mecca. This gives the author the opportunity to describe the holy places and the customs surrounding the pilgrimage. After the hero's return to the caliphal palace, fate catches up with the Barmakids. The author describes their tragic downfall, and places the protagonist of the story as an Iranian in the camp of this great family of viziers, very much like the historical novel *al-Itlīdīs*. The work concludes with the gloomy prospect of the collapse of the empire following the ruin of the Barmakids. There can be no doubt that the author succeeded in providing his readers with an authentic representation of the heyday of Islam, and even though his language reproduces the diction of the period, he avoids artificial archaisms, thus remaining quite understandable to someone of average education.

3 Jirjī Zaydān

Jirjī (Jurjī) Zaydān is the real inventor of the historical novel and founded a historiography that was based on European standards.

Born in Beirut in January 1861, he rose by his own efforts from being a shoeshine boy to a student at the American University of Beirut. Due to a conflict with his teachers, he gave up his study of medicine there. He moved to Egypt, where he studied medicine and philology at the Madrasat Qaṣr al-ʿAyn. After holding the position of chief editor at *Jarīdat al-Zamān* for around a year, he joined Gordon's British expedition to the Sudan as a correspondent. He stayed there for about 14 months, until early 1885. He then returned to Beirut, where he studied Hebrew and Syriac. His first scholarly publication appeared in 1886 in Beirut, entitled *al-Alfāẓ al-ʿarabiyya wal-falsafa al-lughawiyya* (2nd printing Cairo, 1904). In this, he tried to trace all biliteral roots back to natural sounds. After a visit to London he returned to Cairo, where he first joined the editorial staff at *al-Muqtaṭaf*, which at the time was headed by Dr. Ṣarrūf. At the end of 1892 he founded his own magazine, *al-Hilāl*. At the same time, he had become a historian with his publication, in 1889/1306, of *Taʿrīkh Miṣr al-ḥadīth* (2nd printing Cairo, 1911), which was still mostly modelled on the work of Marcel. This work was then followed by a quick succession of | other historical works, 187
culminating in his five-volume *Taʾrīkh al-tamaddun al-Islāmī*, published in

Cairo in 1902/7. Although it is not very difficult to find all kinds of factual inaccuracies in his novels and historical works,[133] they do have the merit of having introduced the Arabic reader to the methods and findings of European historiography.

The influence of Zaydān's historical novels was far greater than that of his scholarly works. From 1891, he published, almost on a yearly basis, one novel after another, to the great joy of his fans. When he died, he had published a total of 22 novels. The only one that does not fit the general description is his romantic *Jihād al-muḥibbīn*; with Kračkovsky, all the others can be divided into two sequences. With the publication in 1891 of *al-Mamlūk al-shārid* (3rd printing 1931) and *Istibdād al-Mamālīk* (2nd printing Cairo, 1896), he began his description of the foundations of modern Egypt, something that was completed in 1892 with *Asīr al-mutamahdī* (later printings Cairo 1901, 1904), which deals with contemporary events. He began his historical depictions of the Muslim past with the publication of the two-volume *Fatāt Ghassān* (2nd printing Cairo 1903, 6th printing 1924). This cycle starts with the great conquests and runs, via the Umayyads and the ʿAbbāsids,[134] up to Ṣalāḥ al-Dīn and *Shajarat al-Durr* (1914). Only once did contemporary events induce him to return to the present with his *al-Inqilāb al-ʿUthmānī* (1912).

As well as being enormously popular among his fellow countrymen (as is
188 shown by a quick succession | of reprints),[135] his novels met with great success in other Muslim countries too. They were translated into Persian by Prince ʿAbd al-Ḥusayn Mīrzā, into Hindustani by Muḥammad Ḥalīm al-Anṣārī, and into Azeri by the *muftī* of Baku, Muḥammad Kerimov.

One should not judge the artistic value of Jirjī Zaydān's novels by European standards.[136] One would also do him an injustice by comparing his success

133 This was done, not without malevolence towards the Christians, by Amīn b. al-Ḥasan al-Madanī (II, 815, 13) in *Nabsh al-hadhayān* (not *hazayān*, as in *WI* XII, 75n, 56) *min taʾrīkh J. Z.*, Bombay 1307, Shiblī al-Nuʿmānī al-Hindī, professor in Aligarh, d. 1322/1904 (II, 862, 49), in his *Intiqād kitāb* Taʾrīkh al-tamaddun al-Islāmī, C. 1330, by Yūsuf Ṭabshī in his *al-Burhān fi ʾntiqād riwāyat ʿAdhrāʾ Quraysh*, C. 1900 and by an anonymous critic in *Intiqād kutub J. Z.* of 1330. Zaydān defended himself against the first of these in his *Radd rannān ʿalā* Nabsh al-hadhayān, C. 1891.

134 Here, the climax is obviously formed by the downfall of the Barmakids, something that had inspired other Arab authors and which had also stimulated Goethe's contemporary E.M. Klinger to write his "Dschaffer der Barmekide".

135 This fact, referred to by Zaydān himself, is at odds with Maḥmūd Taymūr's assertion (*al-Shaykh Sayyid al-ʿAbīṭ* [C. 1926], p. 43) that, in Egypt, people were hardly interested in his novels.

136 A study into traces of his European models would, however, certainly be rewarding.

with that of Karl May; after all, he did not write for young adolescents. His ability to write lively scenes, to create suspense in the development of the plot, and to powerfully depict key events, is undisputed. Even if the protagonists of his novels are types more than individuals, Zaydān is nevertheless very capable of motivating their actions by appealing to the situation that they are in.

One should not expect any poetical verve, as he never wrote any poetry. His language is cultivated without being cluttered. He avoids both the immoderation of the *ʿarabiyya* of old, with which al-Manfalūṭī liked to show off, and descending into a universe filled with Europeanisms, so common in journalism.

Jirjī Zaydān's range of activities did not stop at historiography and writing novels; he also tried to introduce his readership to other branches of European learning. Here we just mention his *Kitāb ṭabaqāt al-umam aw al-salāʾil al-bashariyya* (Cairo: Maṭbaʿat al-Hilāl, 1912), in which he ably expounds key notions in ethnology and anthropology, even if primarily through secondary sources alone. And if we then also consider the fact that he gave his opinions on many of the scientific and social issues of his time in the magazine he founded, then we cannot help but describe his legacy as rich in the extreme. Jirjī Zaydān died suddenly, in Cairo, on 22 July 1914.

| Al-Manfalūṭī wrote a heartfelt obituary in *al-Naẓarāt*, C. 1925, III, 131/45, 189
and Shawqī a *marthiya*, *Dīw.* III, 135/7, as did Ḥāfiẓ Ibrāhīm, *Dīw.* [2]II, 183/6; see also Cheikho, *al-Mashriq* XXIV, 446. Autobiography in *Taʾrīkh ādāb al-lugha al-ʿarabiyya* IV (C. 1914), 323/6, augmented in *al-Mukhtārāt* I (C. 1919), 7/16, see *RSO* VI, 1422/4, a biography by Ilyās Zakhūrā, *Mirʾāt al-ʿaṣr*, C. 1897, 457/64, *J. Z. 1861/1914 bi-qalam aḥad muḥarrirī majallat al-Hilāl*, C. 1915, Kračkovsky, *WI* XII 69/74, *EI* IV, 1294, M. Hartmann, *Die arab. Frage* 586, *Ausf.* 211, an inventory of his works in Sarkīs 985/7, with a portrait, *RMM* IV, 838/45.—*J. Z. Taʾrīkhuhu wa-ḥaflat taʾbīnihi wa-aqwāl al-shuʿarāʾ wal-jarāʾid* C. n.d.[137]

I. Linguistics.—1. See above, p. 186.—2. *Taʾrīkh al-lugha al-ʿarabiyya biʿtibār annahā kāʾin ḥayy tāmm khāḍiʿ li-nāmūs al-irtiqāʾ*, C. 1904.—3. *al-Bulgha fī uṣūl al-lugha*, C. n.d.

II. History. 4. *Taʾrīkh Ingilterra* (up to the House of York), C. 1899.—5. *al-Taʾrīkh al-ʿāmm mundhu ʾl-khalīqa ila ʾl-ān* I (the only volume to have been published), Beirut 1890.—6. *Taʾrīkh al-Māsūniyya al-ʿāmm*, C. 1889.—7. *Taʾrīkh al-Yūnān wal-Rūmān*, C. n.d.—8. *Taʾrīkh al-tamaddun al-Islāmī* 5 vols., C. 1902/6, from where *Umayyads and Abbasids, being the fourth part of J. Z.'s History of Islamic Civilisation*, transl. by D.S. Margoliouth, *Gibb Mem.* IV, Leiden 1907.—

137 We cannot guarantee the completeness of the inventory that follows, especially in regard to the various editions and translations.

9. *Tarājim mashāhīr al-sharq fi 'l-qarn al-tāsi' 'ashar*, 2 vols, C. 1907, 2nd printing 1911.—10. *Ta'rīkh Miṣr al-ḥadīth* (Sarkis *al-jadīd*), 2 vols, C. 1306/1911.—11. *Ta'rīkh ādāb al-lugha al-'arabiyya*, 4 vols. 1911/1914, Index 1922, *Mukhtaṣar* in 1 volume 1924 (cf. Cheikho, *Mashriq* XIV, 582–95, XV, 597/10, XVI, 792/4, Anastase, *Lughat al-'Arab* I, 392/7, II, 52/62, 139/146, 205/9, IV, 82/90, Muḥammad Ḥusayn Haykal, *Fī awqāt al-farāgh* p. 221/247).—12. *Ansāb al-'Arab al-qudamā'* (a critique of Robertson-Smith, *Kinship and Marriage*), C. 1906.—13. *al-'Arab qabla 'l-Islām* vol. I (the only volume to have been published), C. 1908.—14. *Ṭabaqāt al-umam aw al-salā'il al-bashariyya*, C. 1912.

III. Historical novels (see H. Pérès, *Le Roman* 70, no. 675/716).—15. *Jihād al-muḥibbīn*, C. 1894.—16. *Istibdād al-Mamālīk*, 2nd printing C. 1896.—17. *Riwāyat al-Mamlūk al-shārid*, 3rd and later printings C. 1904, 1928, 1931, German by M. Thilo, *G. Z. Der letzte Mameluck und seine Irrfahrten*, Leipzig
190 | 1917.—18. *Risālat asīr al-mutamahdī*, C. 1892, 1901, 1904.—19. *Fatāt Ghassān*, C. 1898/1903, 6th printing 1924/20, Persian C. 1900, *Kitāb khānum-i Sha'mī*, Tehran 1324, Hindustani C. 1900.—20. *Armanūsa al-Miṣriyya*, 2nd printing C. 1889, Persian C. 1889, Hindustani C. 1889.—21. *'Adhrā' Quraysh*, 2nd printing C. 1889, 1925.—22. *al-Sābi' 'ashara Ramaḍān*, C. 1900, Persian ibid.—23. *Ghādat Karbalā'*, C. 1901, 1926, Persian C. 1902.—24. *al-Ḥajjāj b. Yūsuf*, C. 1902, Persian 1903.—25. *Fatḥ al-Andalus*, C. 1904, Hindustani ibid.—26. *Shārl wa-'Abd al-Raḥmān*, C. 1904, 1910.—27. *Abū Muslim al-Khurāsānī*, C. 1905.—28. *al-'Abbāsa ukht al-Rashīd*, C. 1906, traduction française par M. Y. Bīṭār et Ch. Moulié avec une préface de Cl. Farrère, Paris 1912.—29. *al-Amīn wal-Ma'mūn*, C. 1907.—30. *'Arūs Farghāna*, C. 1908 (in which, on pages 1–2, there is a list of translations).—31. *Aḥmad b. Ṭūlūn*, C. 1909, 1921.—32. *'Abd al-Raḥmān al-Nāṣir*, C. 1909.—33. *al-Inqilāb al-'Uthmānī*, C. 1911, *J. Z. Allah veuille! Roman sur la révolution turque*, traduit de l'arabe par M. Y. Bīṭār et Thierry Sandre, Paris 1924.—34. *Fatāt al-Qayrawān*, C. 1912.—35. *Ṣalāḥ al-Dīn wa-makā'id al-Ḥashāshshīn*, C. 1913.—36. *Shajarat al-Durr*, C. 1914.—37. *Riwāyat Muḥammad 'Alī*, C. 1907.

IV. Varia.—38. *'Ajā'ib al-khalq*, C. n.d.—39. *Mukhtaṣar jaghrāfiyyat Miṣr*, C. 1891.—40. *'Ilm al-firāsa al-ḥadīth*, Beirut 1876, C. 1901.—41. *Mukhtārāt* I, II, C. 1919, 1921.—*Intiqād kutub Z.* (by Cheikho and others), C. 1320.—For his son Ibrāhīm, see below, no. 13, 1900.

4 Aḥmad Ḥāfiẓ 'Iwaḍ al-Damanhūri

While Jirjī Zaydān tried to captivate his readers with stories about the distant past, Aḥmad Ḥāfiẓ 'Iwaḍ al-Damanhūrī was the first to take material for his stories from contemporary life. Nevertheless, he was still far removed from realism, preferring instead to lose himself in sentimental romance.

His novel *Riwāyat al-yatīm aw tarjamat ḥayāt shābb Miṣri* (Cairo: Maṭbaʿat al-Tawfīq, 1898) takes the form of an autobiography and ends with the death of the protagonist in 1303. The hero of the story starts by telling us of his happy childhood in the house of his widowed father in the beach resort of al-Ramal, not far from Alexandria. His father, once a wealthy businessman, had moved there at the invitation of a former colleague after he had lost his entire fortune.
| There our hero grows up, together with the only daughter of his father's col- 191
league. From playmates they become lovers, growing aware of their true feelings when the boy is sent to school in Cairo and the girl accompanies her father to spend the winter there. Their bliss is brutally destroyed by the hero's father's untimely death. From his father's will he not only learns that he is now penniless, but also that he has a brother. This brother had been born during his father's pilgrimage to Mecca, and when their mother died the brother had been left in the care of a foster mother there. But after the foster mother had died, all trace of him was lost. Although his father's friend is willing to ensure the boy's further education, the young Amīn Farīd considers it as his duty to first go and find his brother. During his passage to Mecca by ship, he makes the acquaintance of a wealthy Indian trader who lives there and who accommodates him for a while as his guest. When his enquiries have no result, his patron sets him up in a small shop. One day, one of the Indian's servants tells him that his master wants an inconvenient suitor for his daughter, a son of the local dignitary Sharaf al-Dīn, to be assassinated. Our hero believes he recognises his brother in the servant's story, so decides to save him. When he gets to the Indian's house in the evening, two large men are busy carrying the body of the lover into the garden. He shoots one of them and then, dragging the lifeless body along with him, flees to the house of the mother of the servant, who had come along with him. There it turns out that the first victim, despite serious injuries, is still alive. While the protagonist is taking care of him, the servants of Sharaf al-Dīn burst onto the scene and carry him off in chains to their master's residence. It is only with the greatest difficulty that the hero succeeds in explaining the true state of things to the adoptive father and to tell him about the true background of his son, who dies in the arms of his lover Asmāʾ who had come running onto the scene. Even though he had fulfilled his duty, our hero stays on in Mecca, turning down the love that Asmāʾ now displays towards him. At the end of the story we read how he is murdered by Bedouins while defending a woman's honour on his way to Medina. One can see that the author likes to use coarse effects and is not interested in the actions' psychological underpinnings. He is all the more diligent in the depiction of love scenes in the style of ancient
popular romances. Just like these, | he likes to intersperse the story with lines 192
of poetry, which he also cites in the heading of each chapter. His Arabic is

classsical, without archaisms, but with the occasional loan word, such as 'revolver' instead of the later *musaddas*. It is not altogether free of Europeanisms, but these are not disturbing.[138]

The novel does not seem to have met with great success. A second printing appeared in 1905 in the first issue of *Musāmarāt al-shiʿb*, which also published some of his later works (*al-Jazāʾ al-ʿādil, al-Ḥāl wal-maʾāl, Ḥusn al-khitām, al-Ḥuṣūl ʿalā zawja, Fasḥat al-amal, al-Ḥuṣūn al-rūsiyya*; see Pérès op. cit., 322, no. 538).

5 Faraḥ Anṭūn

Like his fellow-countryman Jirjī Zaydān, it was only after he had gone to Egypt that Faraḥ Anṭūn's talents developed to their fullest extent. But in his case, his disagreements with the dominant Muslim culture and with the Jesuits of Beirut were much more pronounced than those of the multi-faceted polyhistor.

Born in Ṭarābulus al-Shām in 1861, he received his education at the prestigious school of Keftin, following which he worked for a time as a teacher. In the 1890s, he went to Alexandria, where he founded *al-Jāmiʿa* magazine. In it, he tried to promulgate his free-thinking but divided worldview, which had developed under the influence of Rousseau, Bernandin de St Pierre (transl. of *Paul et Virginie* in *al-Kūkh al-Hindī*, Alexandria 1902), Renan (transl. of his *Vie de Jésus*, Alexandria 1904),[139] Chateaubriand, Jules Simon, and Tolstoy. Five years after the conflicts resulting from his writings had erupted, he emigrated
193 to | the United States, freeing himself from them. There, he continued with his magazine. After the re-establishment of the constitution, he returned to Egypt. Together with ʿAbd al-Qādir Efendi Ḥamza, he published the newspapers *al-Ahālī* and *al-Maḥrūsa* in Cairo. When the war broke out, these were prohibited by the British. He died in Cairo on 6 June 1922. In *al-Dīn wal-ʿilm wal-māl aw al-mudun al-thalāth* (Alexandria 1902), his first work, he mainly talks about social issues. In 1903, he published a philosophical travelogue called *Kitāb al-waḥsh, al-waḥsh, al-waḥsh! aw siyāḥa fī arz Lubnān*. Inspired by Jirjī Zaydān, he wrote a historical novel called *Urushlīm al-jadīda aw fatḥ al-ʿArab Bayt al-maqdis* (Alexandria 1904; second printing Cairo 1919). It starts with a lively description

---

138 He shows off just once: "While I was building castles in the sky (according to the Arabs), towers in the air (according to the British) or castles in Spain (according to the French), ..." 99, 2/4.

139 As well as this, he translated *Athala* by Chateaubriand (New York 1908), *Nahḍat al-asad wa-wathbatuhu wa-farīsatuhu aw taʾrīkh al-thawra al-Faransawiyya* by A. Dumas (Alexandria 1900), *Melfa* by Gorki, *Zarathustra* by Nietzsche (new transl. by Felix Fāris), and *al-Samāʾ* by Flammarion (Mansī 27).

of Christmas Eve in Bethlehem. He tells the story in a captivating manner, blending it with the romantic tale of a beautiful Jewess, and concluding with the image of an immigrant who, when the city has fallen, sits on the Mount of Olives reading Jeremiah's laments. Clearly inspired by the French, his writing is much more attractive than the austerity of Jirjī Zaydān. But in fact, the story itself is not what the book is all about. Indeed, Anṭūn interrupts the story all the time with protracted discussions about his ideas on religious and social issues. As a result of this, he did not have the success of a born storyteller like Zaydān. In the previous year, Anṭūn had dealt with a subject that suited him better in *Ibn Rushd wa-falsafatuhu* (Alexandria 1903), followed by his *Falsafat Abī Jaʿfar b. Ṭufayl ustādh Muḥammad b. Rushd al-faylasūf al-ʿaẓīm* (Alexandria 1904). This is also the backdrop of his polemic against Muḥammad ʿAbduh and his circle in their magazine *al-Manār*, which he answered in his own magazine *al-Jāmiʿa*. In *Arwāḥ al-arwāḥ* (Alexandria 1908)[140] he defends the Turkish revolution. It is said that he wrote a number of successful plays in his final years, but as far as I know these were never published. His adaptations of two plays by Dumas, viz. *al-Burj al-hāʾil* (Alexandria 1904) and *Ibn al-shiʿb al-Latīn*, had already been staged before he emigrated to the United States. After his return, he published *Miṣr al-jadīda* and *Ṣalāḥ al-Dīn aw fatḥ Bayt al-maqdis*. Later, he
turned | to writing in the much more popular genre of vaudeville plays, like 194
al-Fatāt al-ḥasnāʾ Graziella,[141] in which he used the common Syrian vernacular as well as classical Arabic, and for which he launched a noisy commercial campaign.[142]—Biography by his sister Roza Ḥaddād: *Faraḥ Anṭūn ḥayātuhu wa-taʾbīnuhu wa-mukhtārātuhu*, C. 1923, a critical biography by Aḥmad Abu 'l-Khiḍr al-Mansī, C. 1923, al-ʿAqqād, *Muṭālaʿāt*, C. 1924, 61/6, (see above p. 152), Muḥammad Taymūr, *Ḥayātuna 'l-tamthīliyya*, 75/84 (*Muḥākamat Faraḥ Efendi Anṭūn*), Kračkovsky, *WI* XII, 79/82, Introduction to Ode Vasilieva, *Obr. nov. ar. Lit.* XII/IV, Cheikho, *al-Mashriq* XXV (1927) 115.

6 Muḥammad Ibrāhīm al-Muwayliḥī

In 1906, Muḥammad Ibrāhīm al-Muwayliḥī resurrected the *maqāma* genre as a vehicle of social criticism with great success.

---

140 Without providing any further bibliographical data, Mansī, 27 also cites *Maryam qabl al-tawba, al-Ḥubb ḥatta 'l-mawt, Tidhkār iftitāḥ al-mabʿūthān, al-ʿAthmana aw al-Tabarzul wal-taʾamruk* (against *al-Manāẓir* and *al-Muhājir* newspapers).

141 Based on the autobiographical novel *Graziella* by Lamartine, see p. 135, n. 2, and G. Niqolas, Graziella, *al-Muqtaṭaf* 83 (1934) 150/2.

142 Twelve more plays, some of which have never been staged, among them *King Oedipus*, are mentioned in Mansī, 27/8.

He was the great-grandson of the *sartujjār* in the days of Muḥammad ʿAlī. His father Ibrāhīm (b. 1262/1846, d. 1322/1906) accompanied the khedive Ismāʿīl on his travels and his exile to Naples. In Cairo, he founded the weekly magazine *Miṣbāḥ al-sharq*. He also published a series of essays under the title *Mā hunālika* (Maṭbaʿat Muqtaṭaf, 1896), mostly recollections of Istanbul. Muḥammad was born in 1868. He went to Ismāʿīl's Madrasat al-Anjāl and also studied at al-Azhar. Because of his participation in ʿArābī's revolt he had to go into exile, assisting Jamāl al-Dīn al-Afghānī in Paris with the renewed publication of the latter's *Mirʾāt al-sharq*. In Istanbul, he published al-Maʿarrī's *Risālat al-ghufrān* and other Arabic works. Back in Cairo, he started working for *al-Ahrām* and *al-Muʾayyad*. He died in 1930. His most important work is *Ḥadīth ʿĪsā b. Hishām*, which was first published as a serial in *Miṣbāḥ al-sharq* and then in one volume in 1324/1907 (Maṭbaʿat al-Maʿārif), third printing 1341/1923 (Maṭbaʿat al-Saʿāda, with a *taqrīẓ* by Jamāl al-Dīn al-Afghānī in a facsimile of the autograph), fourth printing n.d. (between 1928/30, Maṭbaʿat Miṣr). In the story, al-Hamadhānī's ʿĪsā b. Hāshim and a resurrected pasha from the time of Muḥammad ʿAlī get to know each other in Cairo, where together they start hunting for the latter's
195 fortune, | placed in a *waqf*, a hunt that takes them through every office and social class in Cairo. This gives him the opportunity to vehemently criticise Europe's negative impact on Egyptian society. Even if there is no real progress in the story, the author's depictions and descriptions are certainly entertaining (see the analysis in Ṣalāḥ al-Dīn Dhuhnī, *Miṣr bayna 'l-iḥtilāl wal-thawra* 8/64). He imitates al-Ḥarīrī's rhyming prose while avoiding the latter's obsession with far-fetched idioms. In the many dialogues that the story contains he gives up rhyme. The third edition concludes with a chapter on Western civilisation in which the storyteller announces that he and his protégé will travel to Europe to study matters there. This intention was then carried out in the fourth edition, inaccessible to me; a short appendix, entitled *al-Riḥla al-thāniya*, describes the World Fair in Paris of 1906.

A less successful imitation of the above work, Ḥāfiẓ Ibrāhīm's *Layālī Saṭīḥ*, was mentioned on page 69. Both works inspired Muḥammad Luṭfī Jumʿa (see below § 3) to write his *Layāli 'l-rūḥ al-ḥāʾir* (Cairo 1912). In it, he uses a ghost to voice his criticism of the social conditions in Egypt. He uses free verse (*shiʿr manthūr*) instead of rhyming prose; see the notice by Jirjī Zaydān in *al-Hilāl* XX (1912), 551/5.

The same form is also used by Shaykh Ṭanṭāwī Jawharī in his *ʿAyn al-insān*, which he dedicated to the International Congress of Peoples in London in 1911. In it, he uses a spirit from heaven to voice his opinions on human progress and brotherhood, in a language that is archaic and without the use of rhyme (see D. Santillana, *RSO* IV, 762/73 and Carra de Vaux, *Les penseurs de l'Islam* V, 281/4).

On Ibrāhīm al-Muwayliḥī, see *al-Hilāl* XIV, 383/8, Cheikho, *al-Mashriq* XXIII, 377/9, Hartmann, *Ar. Press* 79; on Muḥammad al-Muwayliḥī, al-ʿAqqād, *al-Murājaʿāt* 173, Gibb, *BSOS* VII, 5ff. As regards Ṭanṭāwī Jawharī, we also mention a large Qurʾān commentary, C. 1341—, until 1935 in 22 volumes up to sura 49, and his *Aḥlām fi 'l-siyāsa wa-kayfa yataḥaqqaq al-salām al-ʿāmm*, C. 1334/1935.

7 Al-Manfalūṭī

If there was anyone among the intellectuals of Egypt who responded positively to the impulses coming from journalism through Jirjī Zaydān, other Syrians, and father and son al-Muwayliḥī, | it was Muṣṭafā Luṭfī al-Manfalūṭī, the most 196
celebrated essayist of the twentieth century.

Son of an ʿAlid father and a Turkish mother, he was born in Manfalūṭ on 10 Dhū l-Ḥijja 1293/30 December 1876. In 1888, he began his studies at al-Azhar, and for ten years he lived in the circle around Muḥammad ʿAbduh. After the latter's death he initially returned to his native Manfalūṭ. He started his literary career in 1908 at *al-Muʾayyad* newspaper. He lived in Cairo until his death on 25 July 1924.

Even though he knew no foreign languages, he had a great interest in French literature, writing adaptations of Alph. Karr's *Sous les tilleuls*, Fr. Coppée's *Pour la couronne*, Bernardin de St. Pierre's *Paul et Virginie* and even of E. Rostand's *Cyrano de Bergérac* in the form of a novel. In his *al-ʿAbarāt* (C. 1915, fourth printing 1923), too, he intersperses his own stories with adaptations of French short stories and one from the United States. He has a special interest in women who, victims of male licentiousness, have the misfortune of being sacrificed on the altar of an inherently rotten social order. As the sentimental depiction of their misfortunes can hardly leave him satisfied, he must be intending to warn his compatriots against the dangers of adopting Western culture.

While the tearful atmosphere of these stories, whose defective psychology was justly criticised by al-ʿAqqād (*al-Murājaʿāt*, 178ff), becomes rather tedious with the passing of time, this is not so for the essays of his *Naẓarāt*,[143] which are often characterised by a deeply-felt male pathos. Still, sentimental stories—in part again based on French sources—are not lacking here either, like 'Little Yvonne' (III, 45/51), 'The Dead' (ibid. 103/10), and 'Revenge' (ibid. 135/87). In *ʿIbrat al-dahr* he draws the picture of a stranded marriage, the result of hedonism and total surrender to a Western lifestyle. Elsewhere, too, he does not tire

143 In his *al-Mukhtārāt*, 177, he reproduces an exalted critique from a letter by Ḥāfiẓ Ibrāhīm.

of warning against European culture (I, 196/203). He points to drinking (I, 70/8
197 = *al-Adabiyyāt al-ʿaṣriyya* 7/18), gambling (II, 17ff), | free love (I, 262/9, II 225/9), and suicide, especially by the young (I, 233/7), as its most dangerous manifestations. He even goes so far as to claim that marrying a fallen woman is no less than a service to mankind (I, 317/23). When he translates V. Hugo's obituary for Voltaire (II, 36/55, *al-Adabiyyāt al-ʿaṣriyya* 65/80), when he turns a poem by him into prose (II, 319/25), and when he translates the speeches over Julius Caesar's corpse from Shakespeare[144] (II, 202/18, with the revealing title *Siḥr al-bayān*), in all these cases he seems to have only one thing in mind, which is to prove that Arabic literary prose is of no less quality than anything coming from Europe. It is only in his 'Letter to Tolstoy' (II, 242/51) that he strikes a universal human chord. When he sets himself the task of describing the nations of Europe in 'Today and Yesterday' (III, 243/58), he is only able to do so in the darkest of colours.[145] Following G. Lebon's *Les lois psychologiques de l'évolution des peuples*, which he had read in the translation of Fatḥī Zaghlūl, he is convinced that the destinies of human societies, East and West, are governed by the same laws and that he should therefore not give up hope in the advancement of his country (*al-Adabiyyāt al-ʿaṣriyya* 81/91).

There is, according to al-Manfalūṭī, only one way of preventing the damage that threatens Egypt due to excessive foreign influence: people must stick to Islam. In a rebuttal of Lord Cromer's claim that Islam is not capable of any edu-
198 cation (I, 270/85), he argues that | originally Christian culture was an offshoot of Muslim culture, explaining its decline as the disastrous consequence of the later Christian civilisation. He thinks that Abu 'l-ʿAlāʾ al-Maʿarrī and ʿUmar al-Khayyām are ideals to be followed in Muslim culture. He wrote an imitation of al-Maʿarrī's *Risālat al-ghufrān* (I, 133/49) and the poet himself tells him in an

144 A translation of the whole play by Louis Ghannām Thābit was published in Cairo in 1925.

145 Page 249ff: "He sent his children to different schools in which they learned different languages. This is how one of them became a Briton, coarse and rude-mannered, the other a Frenchman, lewd and licentious, and the third a German, with his self-importance and pride." Page 25ff: "The house of the man looked like a gathering of foreign diplomats, the Turk insisting on his Turkhood and the Briton chanting 'Britannia rule the waves; the empire on which the sun sets not.' The Frenchman worships France and sings its praise; he calls it the mother of justice and mercy and the happiest land of all. The German quotes the speeches of the Kaiser and foretells that the future will belong to Germany, once England and France have been wiped off the map. Lovers of the French and Germanophiles haggle over Alsace-Lorraine, Germanophiles and Anglomaniacs over Waterloo and over who was the greater general: Blücher or Wellington." His hatred of the British is also apparent from the comparison "like British spies" in I, 110 bottom.

appearance (III, 327/356)[146] about his ideals regarding vegetarianism and true humanity. In the *Rubāʿiyyāt*, ascribed to al-Khayyām and translated into Arabic several times, al-Manfalūṭī sees (II, 235/41), strangely, the accomplishment of Islamic philosophy. Still, this does not prevent him from praising the *sīra* of the Prophet (I, 189/93) as the highest ideal for all Muslims, making all previous and modern wisdom redundant. One should not expect any consistency from al-Manfalūṭī. In a dream about Paradise (204/15) he overhears a conversation between Muḥammad ʿAbduh and Qāsim Amīn in which they accuse each other, the former reproving the latter for wanting to abolish the headscarf at a time when women were not ready for such a thing, the latter reproaching the former for killing Islam with his liberal Qurʾan interpretation instead of reviving it, turning unknowing Muslims into heretics. Now, even though we need not judge this as severely as Gibb does,[147] it does nevertheless contrast clearly with the enthusiastic words with which he, in 1913, praised Muḥammad ʿAbduh and ʿAlī b. Yūsuf as the two towering mountains that had prevented the people of Egypt from sinking into the abyss of unbelief and political chaos.[148] He opposes, in the same way, extremism, such as the murder of the Armenians in Adana in 1909 (I, 324/9) just as he opposes the cult of saints at the tomb of Aḥmad al-Badawī (II, 132/5) and in a Tamil work on Abd al-Qādir al-Jīlānī (II, 91/100). For him, too, the ideal is that Islam be one and united. This is also the spirit in which he greets Ismāʿīl Gaspirinski[149] at the Islamic Congress in Cairo (III, 208/17) and spurs on the Tripolitanians | in their war against Italy (II, 199
259/64). In an appeal to all the peoples of the East (*al-Ittiḥād* in *al-Adabiyyāt al-ʿaṣriyya* 108/12) he demands that all the religions of the East stand together in defending their freedom against the dangers coming from Europe, in the face of which their existing quarrels must cease.

Al-Manfalūṭī considers social questions, which had also arisen in Egypt as a result of Western influence, not just as a Muslim but also as a student of Rousseau. The city of bliss, which he sees in a dream (I, 101/13), is still dominated by a weak kind of socialism. And even though he pities women, as do the stories which he had adapted from the French, he still declares himself against any and all emancipation. He has no calling as a reformer whatsoever. He praises contentment as the happiness of the poor (‘Rich and Poor’ I, 96/100,

---

146 Reprinted in *al-Adabiyyāt al-ʿaṣriyya*, 19/50.

147 “Yet went out of his way to insult his master”, BSOS V, 317.

148 He celebrates him as a master of prose writing in II, 365.

149 See Kirimli Cafer Seydahmet, *Gaspirali Ismaʾil Bey*, Istanbul 1934, p. 119, in which the inauguration of the congress is said to have taken place on 25 Ramaḍān 1325/2 November 1907, while the fifth Cairo printing of this work mentions the year 1908.

'The Fisherman' I, 223/32), while he advises the wealthy man (III, 119/130) who complains of his taxload to engage in some real charity. He does not want to have anything to do with politics as it spoils one's character (II, 101/4). At the same time, however, he wholeheartedly takes part in the endeavours and aspirations of the people, as is shown by his obituaries for Muṣṭafā Kāmil (I 85/90), ʿAlī b. Yūsuf (III, 66/74) and Saʿd Pāshā Zaghlūl (III, 188/90). Like all his contemporaries, he not only regards himself as a Muslim, but also and before anything else as an Egyptian and, thereby, heir to the world's most ancient culture, which is why he mentions Pentaur in the same breath as Aḥmad Shawqī as belonging to the greatest poets of all times (II, 241).

His softest side he shows in personal effusions, such as his lament on approaching middle age ('The first white hair' I, 216/222, 'Forty' III, 357/81) and his fictional letters on matters of personal ethics and discretion.

He never forgets that, before anything else, he is a poet, even though he only rarely writes poetry. He detests the would-be poets, the *naẓẓāmūn*, in the extreme (I, 180/2). For him, too, the ideal is still the poetry of the ancient Arabs. Among the latter, he praises Abū Nuwās and Bashshār (II, 272/6). As such, his enemies focussed their criticism on his adoration of the classics (see Zakī Mubārak, *al-Nathr al-fannī* II, 71). He is right to apply the same standards to his own art as he does to *shiʿr* (II, 297/311). To him, metre and rhyme are embellishments of language, no more and no less than other kinds of embel-
200 lishment, | and have nothing to do with the inner value of that which is said. It was singing, alone, that produced rhythmic structure, a natural consequence of an exalted mood.[150] After the death of al-Bārūdī, master of the poets of his time, he was very pessimistic about those who remained (II, 365/8). The situation in the theatres was so bad that, in the second year of the [first world] war, he felt obliged to start writing again, even though he had sworn that he would not write a single word for as long as the war lasted (III, 52/65). In the very prolonged *Muqaddima* (I, 64), he talks about the characteristics of his own style of writing, as he also does in a number of his essays (*al-Bayān* II, 3/13, III, 3/15; *al-Lafẓ wal-maʿnā* III, 191/7). He claims to have been aware of his calling ever since he was thirteen years old and to have remained true to it despite the objections of his teacher at al-Azhar. He is right to pride himself on his personal style, which he developed without the benefit of any example

150 He documents these views with a series of samples from poetry, without ever mentioning their authors. He shows his literary taste in I, 239, 8, where he says: "(There are people) who have greater admiration for the poems of Ibn Fāriḍ, Ibn Maʿtūq and al-Burʿī than for those of Abu 'l-Ṭayyib, Abū Tammām and al-Buḥturī. They laugh when they should cry and vice-versa."

whatsoever. This does not prevent him, however, from recognising the great service that the Syrians have rendered to Egyptian literature, asking himself whether one should be happy for them to have gone back to a free Syria after the enactment of the new Turkish constitution, or be sad for Egypt to have lost them (I, 286/8). He is probably speaking the truth when he says that, in writing, he only follows his inspiration; and even if imagination plays an important role in it, his primary goal in writing is to be useful and not to entertain (160/4).

There is no room here for a full analysis of his style of writing, even though such would certainly be rewarding. His diction draws on the treasures of *ʿarabiyya*, which he then feels obliged to explain on almost every page.[151] More than any writer of the classics, his sonorous prose is dominated by parallel constructions, often making him lapse | into rhyme, although he actually disdains 201
it. In the same way in which he has no model, his art is inimitable. Nevertheless, it did sharpen the linguistic conscience of his contemporaries. After all, in III, 351/4, he calls for a congress with the aim of giving structure to the much-needed coining of new words and expressions, a mission that was then undertaken by the academies in Cairo and Damascus that have been founded since.

Marthiya in *al-Shawqiyyāt* III, 102/4, ʿAbbās Maḥmūd al-ʿAqqād, *al-Murājaʿāt fī ʾl-adab wal-funūn*, C. 1926, 174/84 (*al-Manfalūṭī ḥayātuhu wa-aqwāl al-kuttāb fīhi wal-mukhtār min nathrihi*), Aḥmad ʿUbayd, *Mashāhīr shuʿarāʾ al-ʿaṣr* I, 320/41 (with a portrait and sample poems), Saʿd Mīkhāʾīl, *Samīr* 115/6 (the same), Rufāʾīl Buṭṭī, *Siḥr al-shiʿr* 230/9 (*Nafs al-shāʿir*), Sarkīs 1805, Cheikho, *al-Mashriq* XXV, 868, Kračkovsky in Ode-Vasilieva *Obr.* XV (German in *MSOS* XXXI, 191), Gibb, Manfalūṭī and the 'New Style', in *BSOS* V, 311/21, Ch. C. Adams, *Islam and Modernism in Egypt* 215, Ibrāhīm ʿAbd al-Qādir al-Māzinī in *Dīwān* II, 1/32 (very sharp and partly undeserved criticism, but justified in condemning his exaggerated sentimentality), Dr. Manṣūr Fahmī, *Khaṭarāt al-nafs* 98/101, Ṭāhir al-Ṭannāḥī, *al-Sayyid Muṣṭafā Luṭfī al-Manfalūṭī bi-munāsabat murūr khams sanawāt ʿalā wafātihi*, in *al-Hilāl* 39 (1930), 20/6, idem, *al-Manfalūṭī al-shāʿir, baḥth wa-ṭarāʾif fī ṭayy al-khafāʾ* ibid. 41 (1932), 223/6, Muḥammad ʿAbd

151 Neologisms are very rare and mostly relate to matters to do with modern civilization, such as *qiṭār* 'train' I, 394,$_{7}$, *maḥaṭṭa* 'station' I, 295,$_{4}$, *makhfir* 'police station' I, 174,$_{12}$, *mustashfayāt* 'hospitals' II, 30,$_{3}$. Colloquialisms are even rarer, such as the apparently deliberate choice of *mutasawwil* for 'beggar' I, 289,$_{7}$. He is probably the one who coined the term *tamadyun* 'civilization' as a pejorative next to *tamaddun* 'culture', if Walī al-Dīn Yegen was not the first to do so in his *al-Kuttāb al-thalātha* 50$_{3}$; later, it was adopted by Abū Shādī (*al-Insān* 92,$_{1}$) and Khalīl Shaybūb (*al-Fajr al-awwal* 119,$_{13}$). He only rarely uses Europeanisms, as in 'The Olympus' III, 358,$_{12}$, "the crumbs that fall off the tables of the rich" (cf. Matt. 15,$_{27}$) I, 29,$_{2}$, III, 136,$_{2}$, "a miller awakens the moment the mill stops", I, 71,$_{9}$.

al-Majīd, *al-Kawākib wal-mawākib wal-durar* (*al-Manfalūṭī, Walī al-Dīn Yegen, Jabrān*), C. n.d., Muḥammad ʿAbd al-Ḥamīd al-Saḥartī, *al-Manfalūṭī ḥayātuhu wa-adabuhu*, C. 1930. *al-Adabiyyāt al-ʿaṣriyya wa-hiya majmūʿat maqālāt mukhtāra min āthār faqīd al-ʿilm wal-adab al-sayyid Muḥammad Luṭfī al-Manfalūṭī* by Muḥammad Muḥammad Zakī al-Dīn (Maṭbaʿat al-Saʿāda n.d. with a portrait). Ḥusayn Ḥasanayn, *al-Kuttāb al-thalātha, maqālāt muntaqāt min Walī al-Dīn Yegen wal-Manfalūṭī wal-ʿAqqād*, C. n.d. p. 66/127.—1. *Mukhtārāt al-Manfalūṭī* I, C. 1912, second printing 1923 (a selection of poems and prose pieces in two parts: *Bāb al-faṣāḥa wal-bayān* and *Bāb al-adab wal-ḥikma* from classical
202 and modern literature; | he refers to himself as *aḥad al-udabāʾ al-muʿāṣirīn.*—2. *al-ʿAbarāt*, C. 1916, second printing 1922.—3. *al-Naẓarāt*, 3 volumes, 1902/10, third printing 1920, fifth printing 1925.—4. *al-Shāʿir aw Cyrano de Bergérac wa-hiya khulāṣat al-riwāya al-tamthīliyya allatī waḍaʿahā al-shāʿir al-ʿaẓīm E. Rostand*, third printing C. 1925.—5. *Majdūlīn aw taḥt ẓilāl al-zayzafūn, taʾlīf al-kātib al-Faransī al-shahīr Alphonse Karr, mulakhkhaṣa*, fourth printing C. 1923, fifth printing 1928.—6. *Riwāyat Fī sabīl al-tāj wa-hiya khulāṣat riwāya tamthīliyya bi-hādha ʾl-ism lil-kātib al-Faransī al-shahīr François Coppée maʿa baʿḍ taṣarruf*, fourth printing 1925 (with a preface by Ḥasan al-Sharīf dated 1 June 1920).—7. *al-Faḍīla aw Paul wa-Virginie lil-kātib al-Faransī al-shahīr Bernardin de St. Pierre, mulakhkhaṣa*, second printing C. 1924, see E. Saussey, *Bull. d'Etudes de l'Institut Français de Damas* I, 49/80.—8. *al-Qaḍiyya al-Miṣriyya min sanat 1921 ilā sanat 1923*.—9. *al-Intiqām*, C. 1923.—10. *Kalimāt al-Manfalūṭī* selected by Aḥmad ʿUbayd, Damascus 1343.—An essay by him in English translation is in Trowbridge Hall, *Egypt in Silhouette*, New York 1928.

8 Muḥammad Ḥusayn Haykal

The first decisive impulse towards a narrative art that was European in technique but otherwise thoroughly Egyptian was given by Muḥammad Ḥusayn Haykal. Even though he went in different directions in his later works, he did show literature new avenues in this area as well.

Born on 20 August 1888, he studied in Cairo from 1905 to 1909, and in Paris from 1909 to 1913, where he obtained a doctorate in economics. He then settled as a lawyer in Cairo, but spent most of his energy on politics and the press. In 1922, he became editor-in-chief of *al-Siyāsa*, which he affiliated with *al-Siyāsa al-usbūʿiyya* in 1926. On 29 December 1937, he joined the cabinet of Muḥammad Maḥmūd Pāshā, first as minister without portfolio, and then as minister of education (portrait in *Apollo* I, 101).

As a way of dealing with his homesickness while a student in Paris, he wrote *Zaynab, manāẓir wa-akhlāq rīfiyya, bi-qalam Miṣrī fallāḥ*, C. Maṭbaʿat al-Jarīda n.d. (1914), which he published for a second time in 1929, but then under his proper name, C. n.d. (Maṭbaʿat al-Jadīd). It was the first ever attempt to describe peasant life as it really is.

| Perhaps the novel's female hero is a bit more sensitive than one would ex- 203
pect of a simple peasant girl (cf. K.V. Ode-Vasilieva in *Zap. Koll. Vost.* v, 300/1). Her male counterpart is a young man from the ruling class (Ḥāmid). At first he falls in love with a cousin, but custom prevents him from declaring his love. She then suddenly marries someone else. In the countryside, he seeks to console himself through his love for the beautiful Zaynab. However, his love is unrequited because Zaynab is bound in two ways: on the one hand, she is bound by her marriage vow to her husband Ḥasan, whom she does not love; on the other, she is bound by her secret love for Ḥasan's friend Ibrāhīm, who was the only one from the village to have been sent on military service to the Sudan. After endless sentimental reflections on the artificiality of the social order, Ḥāmid leaves his family to start a new, independent life in the city. Meanwhile, Zaynab dies of consumption, a disease which, following the example of French literature, was a popular means of liberating unhappy lovers from the burdens of life. In Turkish novels of the period, the same phenomenon can be seen.

Even though the characters of the novel remain somewhat sketchy, the author's lavish descriptions of nature in the countryside amply make up for this. Inspired by his longing for home, these romanticising descriptions can be found throughout the book. There are also the many depictions of village life, which succeed quite well. An example of this is the wandering dervish who invites himself to a sumptuous meal at the village inn, following which he organises a *dhikr* with the local population. He even impresses Ḥāmid for a time, who seeks healing from him for his broken heart but soon is disappointed by the endless incantations. The personalities of the secondary characters too, remain sketchy; this is not surprising, though, as the author, still young, could not have had much insight into human nature at that time.

After the book's second printing there arose a heated discussion in the press, reported by Gibb in *BSOS* VII, 12ff. The discussions were opened by al-Māzinī in the weekly issue of *al-Siyāsa*, and he summarised their outcome in two articles, dated 27 April and 4 May 1929, after Muḥammad Ḥusayn Haykal and Muḥammad ʿAbdallāh ʿInān had responded in the issues of 22 February and 1 and 8 March of that same year. Haykal is right to emphasise the fact that in Egypt, the novel had, thus far, been unable to develop | because the posi- 204
tion of dependence of women belonging to the higher classes did not permit the emergence of intellectual relationships with members of the opposite sex. Significantly, Dr Zaki Mubārak (see below § 4) concluded from this that, for now, the novel has no place in Arabic literature (*Ḥayātunā al-adabiyya* in *al-Maʿrifa* of March 1932, 1326/8).

It seems that Haykal came to the very same conclusion, continuing initually with essays alone. A book on J.J. Rousseau was published in 2 volumes in 1921 (Maṭbaʿat al-Wāʿiẓ) and 1924 (Maṭbaʿat al-Shabāb).

In the collection of essays that was edited by Ilyās Anṭūn Ilyās under the title *Fī awqāt al-farāgh* (C. 1925), he selected his best pieces, published earlier in newspapers and magazines. He divided these into three: 1. critiques; 2. things Egyptian; 3. reflections on history and literature. While his mind is very much open to Western, especially French, culture, his heart is wholly dedicated to the people and culture of Egypt. In his brilliant descriptions of Anatole France[152] and Pierre Loti[153] one can see how his love for France, the country where he had completed his academic studies, also inspired him with a deep respect for its writers. Even if he wishes that his people would produce works of the same quality, he knows only too well that there still is a very long way to go. As such, he is more than willing to stand up for anyone able to show the Egyptians how to find their way back to the top. He thus writes a heartfelt obituary for Qāsim Amīn (d. 1908), the champion of women's rights. In it, he shows how this patriot had always remained a good Muslim, in spite of his law studies in France, and that it is precisely because of this that he defended Islam against the Frenchman d'Arcour (*Les Egyptiens*, 1894), who wanted to explain the backwardness of the Orient solely through its religion.[154] The
205 defender | then turns into a reformer, first pointing out the damages, and then ways to repair them. His critique of the literary histories of Ṣādiq al-Rāfiʿī and Jirjī Zaydān (see Suppl. I, p. 12) has its origin in this same desire to see his compatriots do well compared to the West. He is right to argue that al-Rāfiʿī did not really write a history of Arabic literature, but rather a kind of introduction to Arabic linguistics while attempting to write a history of the Arabic language as well. His concern with the latter then confused his linguistic taste, leading him to use an unartistic mixture from different style periods instead of the literary language of his contemporaries, a style that was evolving along purely natural lines. Even though he recognizes that Muḥammad Farīd Wajdī had the best of intentions in familiarising the Egyptians with European culture through his *Dā'irat al-maʿārif*, he also criticises him with good reason for having undertaken a task that is beyond the capacities of any individual. Then again, he does welcome Ṭāhā Ḥusayn's book on Greek drama and Aḥmad Luṭfī's translation

152 Whose *Thaïs* and *Le lys rouge* were translated by Aḥmad al-Ṣāwī Muḥammad, C. 1924, 1926. Other translations in Pérès, op. cit., 298.

153 Translations in Pérès, 302.

154 At the invitation of a French newspaper, he discussed the same subject in a French article, published in Arabic translation in *al-Shabāb* of March–April 1936.

of Aristotle's *Nicomachean Ethics* as successful attempts at familiarising the Egyptians with the Hellenic roots of European culture. The fact that he regarded Woodrow Wilson as one of the most eminent representatives of this culture is explained by the fact that he got his knowledge from the media.

The essays of the second group make for lighter reading, their fluid style and powerful imagery making them very appealing. The first of them recounts a visit to the tomb of Tutankhamun made by journalists from Cairo. Noteworthy are the memories of his sufferings at primary school, which are at the same time a powerful denunciation of the shortcomings of the educational system in Egypt, and his defence of a woman who had killed the man who had robbed her of her honour, and in which he puts his finger on the fundamental damage inflicted by Egypt's social order. The third group contains two studies, one on language and literature and the other on the Arabs and Muslim culture. The first is a very good defence of the modern literary Arabic of Egypt, which steers a middle course between the bombast of an archaic style of writing and the literary licentiousness of 'Americans' like al-Rayḥānī and Jabrān Khalīl Jabrān.
| The second study ends with the justified hope that the great centres of Muslim 206
culture will stand their ground against the pressure coming from Europe, and even will go through a real renaissance.

His *'Asharat ayyām fī 'l-Sūdān* (C. 1927, Maṭbaʿat al-ʿAṣriyya) is a by-product of one of his assignments as a journalist in which he reported on the commissioning of a new dam on the Nile. A second series of newspaper articles, mostly from *al-Siyāsa al-usbūʿiyya*, was published in 1929 under the title *Tarājim Miṣriyya wa-Gharbiyya*. It contains descriptions of Egyptian rulers like Cleopatra and the khedives Ismāʿīl and Tawfīq, of political leaders like Muḥammad Qadrī Pāshā, Buṭrus Ghālī Pāshā, Muṣṭafā Kāmil Pāshā, Ismāʿīl Ṣabrī Pāshā, Maḥmūd Sulaymān Pāshā, ʿAbd al-Khāliq Tharwat Pāshā, and the social reformer Qāsim Amīn Bey. All these he juxtaposes with the Europeans Beethoven, Taine, Shakespeare and Shelley.

On 21 December 1930 the government of Ismāʿīl Ṣidqī Pāshā banned the newspaper *al-Siyāsa*, but at the same time allowed the Ḥizb al-Aḥrār al-Dustūriyyīn to found their own newspaper entitled *al-Aḥrār al-Dustūriyyīn*, the first issue of which was published on 2 January 1931. Yet on the 25th of that very same month, the new publication, too, was banned. Together with his colleagues Ibrāhīm ʿAbd al-Qādir al-Māzinī (see above p. 157) and Muḥammad ʿAbdallāh ʿInān, Haykal then used this enforced break to summarise their views on the political situation in a book called *al-Siyāsa al-Miṣriyya wal-inqilāb al-dustūrī* (Cairo: Maṭbaʿat al-Siyāsa, 1931/1349), which was published despite efforts by the government to suppress it. Because the three authors did not sign their contributions separately, we must use stylistic criteria to allow us to clearly distinguish Ḥusayn Haykal's legalistic 'European' prose from that of the others. Together, they address all outstanding questions of foreign policy (still dominated by Egypt's relationship with Britain and the aspiration to settle matters once and for all in a treaty), the constitution, party building, and economic hardship. They thus produced a rich source of information on one of the most important periods in the modern history of Egypt, although it should be used with care.

That same year of forced journalistic inactivity gave him the opportunity to write a book in memory of his son Mamdūḥ, who died of diphteria at the age of six, called *Waladī*. To the reader's surprise, who would have expected anything
207 but this, | the book contains an account of three trips that Haykal and his wife made through Europe during the summers of 1926/28 in an effort to console the mother in her grief.

Even though the book, written in a conversational style, has no ambition of throwing new light on life in post-war Europe, it bears witnesss to a keen sense of observation. His juxtaposition of Paris (which he still idealises, thinking of his time as a student there) and London, especially, has turned out well, and likewise, his descriptions of life in Geneva and the spas of Switzerland.

His depictions of Istanbul, Vienna, and Berlin are of special interest. His description of the essential characteristics of the former capital of Turkey, a country that is slowly being released from its lethargy by a strong government intent on letting modern life unfold in it without, however, giving up on the appeal of its impressive past, is careful, yet lucidly executed. In Vienna, on the other hand, the author sees nothing but the misfortune of the former capital of a huge empire, torn loose from its natural environment and condemned to slow, endless suffering. Biased by the political ideology of the Entente, he prefers to blame Vienna's fate on the Entente's co-signatories rather than on the delusions of the previous government. After all this, the 'deception' provided by the chapter on Berlin is all the more pleasant. Admitting that, before, he had avoided the capital of the German empire out of prejudice, he now is surprised by the powerful pulse of its economic life, ten years after its greatest humiliation. He gives fitting descriptions of its sights, and one will forgive this pupil of French culture that he sometimes misses the elegance of Paris in Berlin.

In his *Thawrat al-adab* of 1933 he outlines a new ideal for Arabic literature. He begins by defining the essence of poetry and then analyses the different periods in the modern literature of Egypt. While the 'Arābī revolt had given a great boost to the sense of national selfhood, the [First] World War was followed by an enormous setback, due to the fact that, in all areas of life, material concerns had become more important than anything else. In the wake of this, Haykal sees an all-time low in literary output, which in his view reflects the

indifference of the affluent classes, of women especially, | towards literature. 208
The only books that the public is still interested in, he says, are works of general entertainment. To counter this, he calls for a national literature of Egypt, departing from the fictional premise that there is a bond of blood that has bound the Egyptian people from its earliest times to the present day. This is a fantasy that has no life-bringing power in the world of letters, something which the development of Egyptian literature has, meanwhile, also amply demonstrated (see Dr Bishr Fāris in *al-Jihād* of 11 July 1933).

In the works mentioned above, this sharp jurist and critic makes it sufficiently clear that Western culture can never replace Islam, even though he would not like to see Egypt entirely deprived of its blessings. He points out several times that, like the modernists, he believes that a return to the sources of Islam in its original form is a necessity. In preparation for such a return he wrote his biography of the Prophet, *Ḥayāt Muḥammad*, the first printing of which (3000 copies) sold out in no time, and which was published in an improved and augmented edition in 1354, together with a foreword by Muḥammad Muṣṭafā al-Marāghī, dean of al-Azhar (607 pp., with maps and plates).

This was the first attempt ever at an objective, historical appraisal of the life of the Prophet. As such, Haykal complements his Arabic sources with information drawn from European accounts. Of P. Lammens, whose hateful and hostile studies of the life of the Prophet even appalled otherwise thoroughly Europhile Muslims, he only mentions the essay *l'Islam*. His main authorities are W. Muir and E. Dermenghem. He seems to have been unfamiliar with L. Caetani's foundational studies. His critical attitude is summed up by his attempt to save the historicity of Abraham and Ismael's migration to Arabia against the doubts voiced by Muir (p. 89/90). Then again, he rejects the *Qiṣṣat Gharānīq* as unhistorical, just like Muḥammad ʿAbduh does (p. 157/64). Stories involving miracles he tries to save from criticism by furnishing rational explanations. For instance, he believes that the birds that destroyed Abraha's army at the gates of Mecca actually transmitted the plague (p. 101). And the story of Muḥammad's ascent to heaven he seeks to explain by means of modern psychological theories about telepathy and magical sleep (p. 192). | Nobody will 209
be astonished about the fact that he defends Islam as the most perfect religion against attacks by "orientalists and missionaries," even if he only rarely does so openly, as in the case of *jihād* (p. 246).

Even as foreigners we can say that he has been successful in rendering the human aspects of his hero accessible to his readers, while fully maintaining his own religious attitude. The story, pleasantly wide in scope and with much theatrical momentum, is of a high artistic level. This impression is only rarely disturbed by attempts at being modern. One such example of this occurs where

Haykal declares the attack on the honour of a Muslim woman that led to the expulsion of the Banū Qaynuqāʿ as being at the same level of historical importance as the assassination in Sarajevo (p. 275).

In his earlier works, the author's language was sometimes at odds with the strict rules of *ʿarabiyya*; here, his language has been worked on more carefully, doubtless under the influence of his sources. He sometimes borrows literally from Ibn Hishām and then sees himself obliged to explain his archaisms in a footnote.

It is only natural that such an audacious work did not meet with the approval of some of the orthodox. In his *Naqd kitāb Ḥayāt Muḥammad*, which is a collection of articles that he wrote earlier for the *Jarīdat Kawkab al-gharrāʾ*, the Wahhābī ʿAbdallāh b. ʿAlī al-Najdī al-Qāsimī[155] directs his principal attack at Haykal's stance on miracles. After pointing out some minor errors, he directs all the force of his criticism at this particular point. He does not even want to give up the exact wording of the Surāqa miracle, which took place during Muḥammad's flight to Medina. It is small wonder that he has no sympathy for Haykal's mystico-psychological interpretation of Muḥammad's ascent to heaven, and he also holds fast to all the other miracles, most of which only appear in later legendary lore, trying to convince his readers of the possibility of their truthfulness by pointing at discoveries in modern science which had, likewise,
210 seemed impossible in the eyes of earlier generations. | He even wants to explain the tale in which Muḥammad's breast is split asunder through the miracles of modern surgery (p. 37). It is no surprise that he greatly criticises Haykal's other ideas about Islam as well. Even Haykal's language, which al-Qāsimī admits is, on the whole, quite beautiful, does not meet with his full approval. His main objection he saves for the end, where he says that while the book may satisfy the needs and expectations of politicians and generals, it does no justice to the Prophet. This is where the positions of Haykal and al-Qāsimī truly differ. All in all, together, the book and its critique are important in that they bear witness to the divisions between Muslim intellectuals, between tradition, on the one hand, and the spirit of European science, on the other.

His account of his pilgrimage (*Fī manzil al-waḥy*, Cairo: Maṭbaʿat Dār al-Kutub, 1356, 672 pp.), often planned but only performed in the spring of 1936, is a valuable supplement to his biography of the Prophet. This voluminous

---

155 Other works by him include: *al-Burūq al-Najdiyya fī ʾktisāḥ al-ẓulumāt al-dujawiyya*, C. 1931; *Shuyūkh al-Azhar wal-ziyāda fī ʾl-Islām*, C. 1351; *al-Faṣl al-ḥāsim bayna ʾl-Wahhābiyyīn wa-mukhālifīhim*, C. 1934; *Mushkilāt al-aḥādīth al-nabawiyya wa-bayānuhā*, C. 1935; *al-Ṣirāʿ bayna ʾl-Islām wal-Wathaniyyīn*, C. 1356; *al-Thawra al-Wahhābiyya*, C. 1936.

work has no intention of offering a history of the Hijaz and the holy places, and neither is it an alternative guidebook; rather, it seeks to describe the religious experiences of its author. Apart from its importance as a description of modern Islam, it offers a wealth of precious material on the situation in the Hijaz under the rule of Ibn al-Saʿūd, with whom the author could speak at great length, as well as with Philby, the king's political advisor. When the author sees the desert and the bustle of the caravans for the first time near al-Tanʿīm, he suddenly understands the motif of an old *qaṣīda*, which, before, he had always looked at through the prism of a satirical verse by Abū Nuwās. At the same time, however, he thinks of the poem on Lac Léman by Lamartine, which had sprouted from similar sentiments (p. 266/7). He had gone to al-Ṭāʾif in hopes of finding a purer Arabic than he had heard in Mecca (p. 291, 323); he feels, therefore, very disappointed when all he hears is a dialect that is just as difficult to understand as those of Lebanon or the Maghreb (p. 349). That is also why the contest between local poets that had been organised in his honour could not give him the kind of pleasure he had hoped for (p. 323/25). The author does not realise that he just missed an occasion to record valuable material for later research. | As a model of a sentimental journey, and notwithstanding its at 211
times tediously long-winded accounts of insignificant events, this work is, after the old *riḥla*-type of narration still cherished by al-Batanūnī, without doubt an important monument in the history of Arabic prose.

Gibb, BSOS V, 447, 450/4, 464, VII, 8, Khemiri and Kampffmeyer 20/3.

9 Manṣūr Fahmī

One of the most brilliant representatives of the essay genre is Dr. Manṣūr Fahmī, director of the Library of Egypt. Manṣūr Fahmi was born in 1886 in Talḥa near al-Manṣūra. After his studies at Law School in Cairo, he was sent to Paris to study philosophy. A student of Lévy-Bruhl, he earned his PhD in 1913 with a dissertation called *La condition de la femme dans la tradition et l'évolution de l'islamisme*. Because of its modern conception of history it was not well received in his native country, which is why he could not work as a civil servant for a while. Having taught philosophy at the University of Egypt, he was subsequently entrusted with the management of the National Library. Dealing mainly with social and ethical issues, his essays were published in *al-Jarīda* before the [First World] War, in *al-Sufūr* during the war, and, later, in *al-Ahrām*, *al-Hilāl*, and *Fatāt al-Sharq*. He published a selection from the years 1915/30 under the title *Khaṭarāt al-nafs*, Cairo n.d. (1930). These are, without exception, short pieces on the harms of social life in Cairo (*al-Qahwa wal-bayt*, 36/8), in which he also complains about the destruction of the traditional culture of the

Orient due to a superficial adoption of Western ways. But with his educational background it is not surprising that he still believes that European culture will be positive for his people, and in his farewell speech to the girls that were sent to study in Europe in October 1925, he emphasises this optimistic expectation. When he visits Athens, he gets a very real sense of the foundation of Western culture. He also knows how to convey the mood of a German forest (102/5) or describe the social shortcomings of a city like Vienna and the charm of Russian ballet (44/6). In this collection, he deals with politics just once, launching a
212 powerful | attack on the lack of engagement among the masses (146/9). It is
their language that makes these pieces really attractive. He owes much to al-Manfalūṭī, whose obituary—published in *al-Siyāsa* on 27 August 1924—he re-wrote while in Lyon in 1930 (Khemiri and Kampffmeyer, *Pr.* 15/7), but it is also true that he improved on the latter's style with great success. Even though he does not altogether eschew the use of rhyme, his language is generally free of artificiality of any kind; moving at a natural pace, it almost sounds as if it were a *qaṣīda*.

T. Khemiri and G. Kampffmeyer, *Leaders* 16 (with a portrait).

10 Muḥammad ʿAbdallāh ʿInān

From among the leading journalists of today, separate mention should be made of Muḥammad ʿAbdallāh ʿInān, referred to earlier in passing.

Born in 1896, he studied law in Cairo, practising there as a lawyer until 1924, when he turned to journalism. Besides numerous high-quality translations of European novels, he also wrote a number of historical studies: 1. *Taʾrīkh al-ʿArab fī Isbāniya*, C. 1924.—2. *Tarjamat kitāb* Falsafat Ibn Khaldūn *lil-Duktūr Ṭāhā Ḥusayn*, C. 1925.—3. *Qaḍāya ʾl-taʾrīkh al-kubrā*, C. 1925 (famous lawsuits).—4. *Taʾrīkh al-jamʿiyyāt al-sirriyya wal-ḥarakāt al-haddāma*, C. 1926.—5. *Taʾrīkh al-muʾāmarāt al-siyāsiyya*, C. 1928.—6. *Mawāqif ḥāsima fī taʾrīkh al-Islām*, C. 1928.

11a Shiblī Ibrāhīm Shumayyil

In the wake of liberal ideas, the materialism of the ideological hardliner L. Büchner also found its way, via Syria, to the educated classes of Egypt, something that had happened in the 1880s. However, Büchner's ideas met with great resistance among most Muslims in the same way they had rejected the evolutionary theories of Charles Darwin. The main representative of both materialism and evolutionism in Egypt was Dr. Shiblī Ibrāhīm Shumayyil.

Born around 1850 in Kafr Shīmā in Lebanon, he studied at the American University in Beirut and lived for a year in Europe, probably in 1875. He then
213 went | to Egypt, where he lived in Alexandria, Tanta and Cairo, where he
died towards the end of 1916. Even though the programme of studies at the

American University of Beirut was dominated by a religious and conservative way of thinking, the young Shumayyil became familiar with the ideas behind evolutionism—which would determine his life—when he was writing his dissertation *Les variations des animaux et de l'homme suivant le climat, la nourriture et l'éducation*. After completing his dissertation, he published the *Kitāb al-ahwiya wal-miyāh wal-buldān*, an Arabic translation of Hippocrates' *On Airs, Waters, and Places* (Cairo: Maṭbaʿat al-Muqtaṭaf, 1885). Büchner's *Kraft und Stoff* turned out to be crucial for his development. He then translated the latter's *Die Darwinsche Theorie von der Entstehung und Umwandlung der Lebewelt*, giving it the title *Sharḥ Büchner*[156] *ʿalā madhhab Darwīn*, Alexandria 1884. Objections to it he rebutted in his *Kitāb al-ḥaqīqa*, Cairo 1885. He tried to further disseminate and defend the theory of evolution in a series of articles for al-*Muqtaṭaf*. In politics, he wrote his *Shakwā wa-āmāl* (Cairo 1896), which he addressed to ʿAbd al-Ḥamīd and in which he tried to identify the causes of the backwardness of the Ottoman Empire. His *Majmūʿat al-Duktūr Shumayyil* (1910) contains a collection of his pieces on Darwinism, its first volume carrying the title *Falsafat al-nushūʾ wal-irtiqāʾ*. A hateful reference to his ideas by a critic of Khalīl Jabrān's *The Book of Khalid* gave him the opportunity to summarise and defend them once more in his *Ārāʾ al-Duktūr Shumayyil*, published in 1912. His *al-Rujḥān, manẓūma mashrūḥa lil-Duktūr Shiblī Shumayyil* contains a kind of philosophical testament in verse (Cairo: Musa Ruditi et Cie, n.d.). Shiblī Shumayyil's greatest influence was among the intellectuals of Syria; in Egypt, his ideas inspired heated debates in Muslim circles, debates that later spread to Iraq (see Suppl. II, 806, 82). He also caused a new translation of Darwin's *opus maior* to be written, the *Aṣl al-anwāʿ*, by Ismāʿīl Maẓhar, which was published in Cairo in 1928.—Mayy, *al-Duktūr Shiblī Shumayyil al-shāʿir*, in *al-Ṣaḥāʾif* 19/31, Sarkīs 1144/5, J. Lecerf, Shiblī Shumayyil métaphysicien et moraliste contemporain, in *Bull. d'Études Orientales de l'Institut de Damas* I (1931), 153/86.

11b Salāma Mūsā

In Egypt, his work was continued by the Copt Salāma Mūsā.

| Born in Zaqāzīq in 1888, he completed his studies at the University of 214
London, taking degrees in law and macro-economics. In 1908, he also attended an address by B. Shaw there. He then studied French literature in Paris, after which he returned to Cairo, where he founded the weekly *al-Mustaqbal* in 1914, but which did not get beyond issue 16. After the war he worked for *al-Hilāl* and *al-Balāgh*. In November of 1929, he founded *al-Majalla al-jadīda*. His interest in the works of B. Shaw resulted in a study entitled *Muqaddimat al-Suberman*

156 Corrupted to *Ykhbr* in Sarkīs.

(Cairo 1910, and again in *al-Yawm wal-ghad*, 12/31) and various articles, which were later brought together in *Mukhtārāt Salāma Mūsā* (Cairo: al-Maṭbaʿa al-ʿAṣriyya, 1924). He translated Dostoyevsky's *Crime and Punishment* as *al-Jarīma wal-ʿiqāb* (Cairo 1914). He published a collection of the most famous speeches and love stories from world literature and the best-known utopian schemes in *Ashhar al-khuṭab wa-mashāhīr al-khuṭabāʾ* (Cairo 1924), *Ashhar qiṣaṣ al-ḥubb al-taʾrīkhiyya* (Cairo 1925), and *Aḥlām al-falāsifa* (Cairo 1926). Then, he defended the theory of evolution in *Naẓariyyāt al-taṭawwur* (Cairo 1925) and freedom of thought in *Ḥurriyyat al-fikr wa-abṭāluhā* (Cairo 1927). His *al-Yawm wal-ghad* (Cairo 1927) is a collection of articles about literature, society and philosophy that had earlier been published in *al-Hilāl*. His attitude towards Western culture is exemplified by his book *al-ʿAql wal-bāṭin*, in which he tries to introduce the Egyptian public to the psychoanalytical theories of Sigmund Freud and his school, theories that had already been cast aside by European science at the time the book was written. He quite cleverly transmitted their terminology into Arabic, except for 'libido' which he transliterated as *libīd*, and 'psychology', for which he chose a terrible, hybrid *nafsulūjiyya*. In *al-Yawm wal-ghad* (123/31) he boldly claims that classical Arabic is no longer capable of accommodating modern culture and that it better be replaced by colloquial Arabic. When he says, in the same passage, that he feels alienated from the East, indeed, even harbours feelings of hatred towards it, this should probably not be taken literally but rather be understood as following the style of B. Shaw, whose social ideas he also adopts, as being dictated by an insatiable need to *épater les bour-*
215 *geois*. Even if his ultra-modern views did enthrall certain Muslim writers, | it is nevertheless hardly to be expected that they will find much resonance.—Gibb, *BSOS* V, 464/6, Khemiri and Kampffmeyer, *Leaders* 31/3, Sarkīs 1038.

11c Fuʾād Ṣarrūf

The works of Dr. Fuʾād Ṣarrūf show that it is possible to use classical Arabic when telling the educated classes of Egypt about the achievements of modern science.

His father, Yaʿqūb Ṣarrūf, was born in al-Ḥadath in the Lebanon in 1852. He studied at the American University in Beirut, after which he worked for two years as a teacher in Sidon and Tripoli. In 1876, he founded *al-Muqtaṭaf*[157] magazine in Beirut, moving its editorial staff to Cairo in 1888. There, it developed into the most influential periodical on modern Arabic literature. He was also interested in the monuments of the classics, and this created a bond of friendship

157 See also Ḥannā Khabbāz, *Mukhtārāt al-Muqtaṭaf*, Cairo 1931; *Aʿlām al Muqtaṭaf* 1. Cairo ca. 1920, 2. *al-Ruwwād* Cairo 1927.

between him and the booklover and patron of the arts Aḥmad Taymūr, who in the 1890s established one of the most important private libraries in Cairo. He died in 1927. When he was a young man, he translated *Thrift* of S. Smiles as *Sirr al-Najāh* (Beirut 1880, see also Mayy, *al-Ṣaḥāʾif*, 188/96). In this same period, he also translated a Greek mythology with his collaborator in *al-Muqtaṭaf* Dr. Fāris Nimr, giving it the title *Siyar al-abṭāl wal-qudamāʾ al-ʿuẓamāʾ* (Beirut 1883). As well as the countless contributions to his own magazine, he also wrote three historical novels during his years in Cairo: *Fatāt Miṣr* (Cairo 1905, fourth printing 1922), *Amīr Lubnān* (Cairo 1907), and *Fatāt Fayyūm* (Cairo 1908) (see Sarkīs 1206/8, Pérès 330, no. 633/5).

The author himself describes his novel *Fatāt Miṣr* (Mulḥaq al-Muqtaṭaf, al-ṭabʿa al-rābiʿa, Cairo 1922) as a *riwāya fukāhiyya ijtimāʿiyya tahdhībiyya*. It is indeed a very ambitious work, introducing the reader to life among the upper classes of Cairo, international politics, the media, the world of finance, and also to the background of the Russo-Japanese war, all at the same time. The story unfolds partly in the house of the owner of the *London News*, E. Browne, and partly in Japan. Just before the outbreak of the [First World] War, the media mogul E. Browne sends his children Henry and Dora | to Japan to take 216
charge of his business interests there. Once, in a dream, Henry had fallen in love with an oriental woman. When, during a ball at the khedive's palace at the time of their sojourn in Cairo, while on their way to Japan, he meets the daughter of the Coptic business tycoon Wāṣif Bey, he believes it is her. But rather than focus directly on the solution to this problem, which would have given him ample opportunity to talk about women's rights in Egypt, Cairene society, and the challenges that such an unlikely marriage would pose, the author only further complicates the situation by juxtaposing the aforementioned Coptic family with their friend Rāghib Pāshā, a Muslim business magnate, and with a rich Jew by the name of Levi. While the focus is initially on the romantic relationship, it is gradually overshadowed by events at the stock exchange and the crimes of a Jew named Ezra, who betrays the son of the Muslim magnate, and who also tries to bring the other Jew, Levi, to heel in the matter of the latter's daughter, by whom Ezra is rejected, first through an accident staged by him, and then even by means of a burglary. All this is interspersed with scenes from the Russo-Japanese war, which brother and sister witness as newspaper correspondents, long discussions between people from the London stock exchange on loans to Japan and British policy in the Far East, as well as the erratic appearances of a Jewish spy who shadows the two British correspondents on behalf of the Russian governement, but who is soon neutralised by the law enforcement agencies of Japan. At the end, brother and sister are even shipwrecked on their way home, off the coast of Socotra. It is only then that the author, Ezra's

crimes having meanwhile been exposed, rushes towards the story's end, which features the Briton and the Coptic woman as a married couple. Not a word is said about the difficulties that such a union would face. Enhanced by many unexpected developments, this unlikely story, though much appreciated by the public, as the number of printings shows, cannot be regarded as a work of art in the true sense. And this is even truer of *Fatāt Fayyūm*, in which the number of intrigues is compounded. It is about the adventures of a young man, related
217 in the first person, who is defrauded of his fortune but then retrieves it with | the help of a clever lawyer. After a housefire, he finds a cache of jewelry, hidden previously by his father to keep it out of the hands of a greedy Ismāʿīl Pāshā. These matters are interweaved with the adventures of a British lady. The only daughter of a wealthy man, she is abducted by a cousin of hers in a staged car crash after she had turned him down, and then made to live under an assumed name as a *dame de compagnie* in the house of a rich Egyptian by the name of Ibrāhīm, whose son falls in love with her. All this is enriched with stories about going public, buying and selling stocks, and the uncovering of a plot against the British occupying powers. In parallel, Ibrāhīm tells a British engineer about his adventures during the ʿArābī uprising.

His son Fuʾād took over *al-Muqtaṭaf* after his father's death in 1927. But before then, he had published a popular work on astronomy called *Basāʾiṭ ʿilm al-falak wa-ṣuwar al-samāʾ* (1923). His collected articles on scientific subjects were published in Cairo in 1934, under the title *Futūḥāt al-ʿilm al-ḥadīth, Asrār al-kawn wal-ḥayāt wa-maʿāqil ghuzātihā wal-ʿulamāʾ*. While the latter work introduces the reader to the latest developments in astronomy and physics, his *Asāṭīr al-ʿilm al-ḥadīth* (Cairo 1935) provides us with excellent portraits of the lives of leading scholars in astronomy, from Copernicus up to Einstein, in chemistry, nuclear physics, medicine, and engineering. There is no doubt that these two works will contribute greatly to the dissemination of true culture in the Orient. It is, of course, inevitable that he adopts European terminology, although he does try to Arabicise them whenever possible, such as *talfaza* for 'television'.

12 Muḥammad and Maḥmūd Taymūr

Muḥammad and Maḥmūd Taymūr, sons of the learned patron of the arts Aḥmad Taymūr,[158] opened new avenues in literature, aiming for a straightforward depiction of life the way it really is.

---

158 Died 26 April 1930, see M. Kurd ʿAlī, *RAAD* XI (1931), 129/47, Khayr al-Dīn Zarkalī in *al-Muqtaṭaf* 77 (1930), 129/32, Schacht in ZDMG N.T. 9 (1930), 225ff, Schaade in *OLZ* 1930, St. 854, Sarkīs 652/3.

a. Muḥammad Taymūr was born in Cairo in 1892. From 1912 onward he studied law in Paris. He was unable to complete his studies | because he could not 218
leave Egypt again after his vacation at the outbreak of the [First] World War. Being a fan of literature from his childhood, he now devoted himself entirely to it. He took a special interest in theatre. In the next section, we shall explain what he has done for the Egyptian theatre. Unfortunately, his untimely death in February 1921 put an end to his ambitions. His sharp sense of observation and his capacity to create memorable scenes are borne out by his plays and his sketches from life entitled *Mā tarāhu 'l-ʿuyūn* (of which the *Khawāṭir qiṣaṣṣiyya* are one part; second printing, Cairo: Maṭbaʿat al-Salafiyya, 1927/1345). His great example is Guy de Maupassant. One of Taymūr's stories, called 'Lord, why did you create this paradise?', is written in Egyptian Arabic. But he does not simply want to entertain the reader briefly; he also wants to enlighten him on the backwardness of his culture. Erotic elements just make an appearance once, in the story of the governess and her maturing pupil. The other stories criticise the rude manners and lack of education of the wealthy classes, as well as the total indifference of the people, just as he does in his plays (story no. 2 on adultery and the one about the governess and her pupil were translated into English by Aḥmad Rāmī in Trowbridge Hall, *Egypt in Silhouette*, New York 1928). The first printing of *Mā tarāhu 'l-ʿuyūn* was published in the first volume of his collected works *Mu'allafāt Muḥammad Taymūr*, Maṭbaʿat al-Iʿtimād 1922, *Kitāb wamīḍ al-rūḥ*, book 4; there, the *Riwāyat al-shabāb al-ḍā'iʿ al-qiṣaṣiyya* was added. This first volume also contains *Dīwān al-wijdān, majmūʿ qiṭaʿihi 'l-wijdāniyya, al-Adab wal-ijtimāʿ, majmūʿat maqālātihi 'l-adabiyya wal-ijtimāʿiyya, Khawāṭir, majmūʿat khawāṭirihi ʿani 'l-ḥayāt* and *Mudhakkirāt Bārīs, majmūʿat mudhakkirātihi ʿan ḥayātihi fī Bārīs*.

b. What had been left unfinished by Muḥammad's untimely death[159] was resumed and completed by his younger brother Maḥmūd (born on 16 June 1894), who had always adored him as his teacher. Initially he studied agriculture, but due to an illness he had to give up his studies and now dedicates all his time and energy to literary pursuits. Like his brother, he was initially influenced by Maupassant | and his like-minded Russian colleague Anton Chekhov, as well 219
as by the analytical realism of Paul Bourget. However, in the course of his development he liberated himself more and more from his masters, trying to express in his own words "… what had struck and touched him while observing the lives of his fellow countrymen." From his first three collections of short stories, viz. *al-Shaykh Jumʿa wa-aqāṣīṣ ukhrā* (Cairo: Maṭbaʿat al-Salafiyya,

159 He dedicated the *Marāthi 'l-marḥūm Muḥammad Taymūr* (Cairo, 1922/1340) to his memory.

1925/1343, second printing 1927/1345), *ʿAmm Mitwallī wa-qiṣaṣ ukhrā* (Cairo: Maṭbaʿat al-Salafiyya, 1925/1343), and *al-Shaykh Sayyid ʿAbīṭ wa-qiṣaṣ ukhrā* (Cairo: Maṭbaʿat al-Salafiyya, 1925/1343; Sarkīs, *Jāmiʿ al-taṣānīf al-jadīda* no. 1128 has a mistaken 1926/1344), he published a selection entitled *al-Wathba al-ūlā* in 1937. The introductions to these collections eloquently testify to the sense of purpose with which the author goes after his target, which is to provide his people with a narrative art that is commensurate with its cultural standing. In his introduction to *Shaykh Jumʿa*, he first has to explain to his readers what kind of art he practises. He wants it to be acknowledged as *uqṣūṣa*, the equivalent of '*conte*' and '*story*', in contrast to the *qiṣṣa* ('*roman*' or '*novel*'). He protests against the idea that his art is only there for the purpose of amusement; rather, it is meant to deepen our understanding of life. That is also why, in *al-Ujra*, he does not shrink from painting a raw, squalid, libidinous scene from city life, invoking Zola against any possible criticism.[160] The themes of two stories (the lost letter in *Khiṭāb min Munīr Bek* and the perpetually impeded traveller in *al-Sāʾiḥ*) were borrowed from two British works whose details are not mentioned, but then so well adapted to life in Egypt that there will hardly be any reader who will sense their foreign origin. The honest and God-fearing, but otherwise quite stupid, peasant in *al-Shaykh Jumʿa* and the man of the street who blindly submits to the influence of an insincere dervish in *Sayyidnā* are juxtaposed with a number of greedy, dim-witted, licentious and degenerate representatives of bourgeois society, whose ups and downs are not of the kind to impassion the reader, even if they take a dramatic turn in *Mashrūʿ Kafāfī Afandī*.

220 | The showpiece of the second collection is the first story, *ʿAmm Mitwallī* (translated by C. Nallino, *Oriente Moderno* VII 391/400), which is the tale of a former officer of the Mahdi from the Sudan. Eeking out a meagre existence as a peddler, everything changes the day that his stories, until then just amusement for local children, catch the attention of a wealthy man and his spouse. Thanks to their patronage, he attains a modest fortune, which allows him to daydream again about his past, daydreams in which he finally comes to the conclusion that he himself is none other than the Mahdi. During one of his ecstatic raptures, he dies a blissful death. This story—also published, pruned and stylistically improved in *al-Wathba al-ūlā*—provides a fine analysis of the problem of religious madness, a subject he adressed several more times in later works as well. He only considered three stories from bourgeois life worthy of inclusion in *al-Wathba*: *Fatāt al-jīrān*, published unaltered, is a comic account of a failed education by a mother who is much too severe. Its counterpart, *Ab wa-ibn*, sketches the conflict between a father and a son, ending tragically in

160 The ending of the story, which is especially offensive, was deleted in the second printing.

patricide. In this heavily condensed second edition of the story, the suspense has been greatly increased. Concluding this series of scenes from life, which are sometimes truly revolting, the innocent love story *al-Mughaffal* radiates harmony, and the shortened version in which it was published in *al-Wathba* is undoubtedly more attractive than the original. The black comedy *Muzhilat al-mawt* (translated from the manuscript by Widmer, *WI* XIII, 1932, 807), a story about the personnel of an upscale family whose lives are governed by the lowest greed, was reprinted almost unchanged in *al-Wathba*. With its ending rewritten, the story on things happening at a school called *Qalam al-abanūs* is surely more attractive in its second printing. The title story of *Shaykh Sayyid al-ʿAbīṭ* sketches a most lively image of daily life in a village, where a poor peasant has lost his mind due to an accident. Because the villagers regard him as a holy man in that state he is allowed to gratify all his lusts at their expense for a time, until the day that popular anger turns against him, sending him to a grisly end. The story has been artfully put together, | with ever-increasing dramatic 221
suspense. In *Abū Darsh* he adopts a theme from Guy de Maupassant, in this case the tragi-comedic story of an old fighting cock and its groom. Two masterpieces of satire are 'My friend as a classmate and an official' and 'Sallām Pāshā's aunt.' Both stories ridicule middle and higher officialdom in all its vain conceit.

The collection *Rajab Afandī, qiṣṣa Miṣriyya* (Cairo: Maṭbaʿat al-Salafiyya, 1928) is entirely dedicated to the dark side of human existence. The hero of the title story is a God-fearing *petit bourgeois* who falls victim to an Armenian spiritualist-cum-exorcist. The latter not only succeeds in bringing the former completely under his control and depossessing him of all his money, but in addition confuses him to such an extent that he finally murders his tyrant to end his days in an asylum. Appended to this is the story 'Death row', about a young man from the upper classes whose death a French soothsayer says will come four months later, and who then acts on this suggestion. Both stories have been put together with a great sense of suspense and give perfect descriptions of people who are unable to put up any resistance to the influence of others.

In 1930, Maḥmūd Taymūr returned to writing satirical pieces again with the collection *al-Ḥājj Shalabī*. The title story (first published in *al-Hilāl* 35, 718–28) is a fiery charge against the shameless exploitation of Muslim marital law by ill-intentioned men. In contrast, there is also the amusing tale of *al-Shaykh Naʿīm al-imām aw al-mizwāj*, which is about a pious man who is used by his fellow-villagers to repair broken bonds of marriage—divorce formulas having been rashly pronounced three times over—through marriages of convenience. But on one of these occasions he falls in love with the beauty led before him and, keeping her to himself, he refuses to dissolve their temporary bond (French translation in *Les amours de Sāmī* [Paris, 1938], 133/44). Next to the grotesque

al-Thālūth al-muqaddas, which is a satire on the obsesssion with easy fame as a writer among immature kids, we find the story *Salīm Afandī al-ṭālib al-adīb*, about a schoolboy who defrauds an editor of the school paper of his first liter-
222 ary achievements | but who is too well-behaved to call the person who robbed him of it to account, preferring to suffer the ridicule of his classmates instead. Next to these is another series of satires on the popular belief in ghosts (*ʿIfrīt Umm Khalīl*, first published in *al-Hilāl* 37, 1929, 1225/35) and the hollowness of society, as well as a tender love story, *Quwwat al-shabāb* which, in the collection mentioned earlier, was translated as 'Cruauté de la jeunesse' (185/94).[161]

The title story that closes the collection *Abū ʿAlī ʿĀmil artist wa-qiṣaṣ ukhrā* (Cairo, 1934) relates the tragi-comedic story of a young man who is mad about theatre and who leaves the safe haven of a bourgeois existence in his uncle's shop to become an actor, gets thrown out of the mosque after his first attempt as a preacher, and then squanders his entire inheritance on his own theatrical company. Apart from this small masterpiece, some more depictions of divine madness are worth mentioning: the story of a farmer who, in his yearning for paradise, engages someone to kill him (*Ila 'l-janna*, first published in *al-Ḥadīth* of 1934, 210/7), and the one about the schoolmaster who kills his own daughter to drive the devil out of her (*al-Shayṭān*, 67/88 translated into French as 'Le démon', in the same volume as *Les amours de Sāmī*). Similar are the stories of *Ṣābiḥa* (29/44, first published in *al-Hilāl* 1928, transl. Widmer, *WI* XIII, 1932, 55/66), who is killed by her lover because she refuses to marry him for a dowry stemming from theft, and the one about a grandmother's disappointment when her grandson, who she raised, comes to visit her in the countryside, but now as an urbanised man (*al-ʿAwda* 1/14, first published in *al-Majalla al-jadīda* 1929, 166/71, translated as 'Umm Zayyan' by Widmer, *WI* XIII, 1932, 72/80, and into French in the same volume as *Les amours de Sāmī*, 109/119). The story of the disoriented victim of a ditty in *Ila 'l-ḥadīd* was published initially in *al-Hilāl* 41 (1932), 467–78 with the title *al-Wabā'*.

The first, longer story of Maḥmūd Taymūr was published in 1934 as *al-Aṭlāl, riwāya qiṣaṣiyya Miṣriyya*, and translated as *Les amours de Sāmī, roman égyp-*
223 *tien*, Paris 1938. It is the | story of the youth of a man who, having lost his parents, grows up in the house of a brother who is much older than he. Written in the first person, it sketches the story of the young Sāmī in bold strokes. The affection of his sister-in-law serves as a substitute for a motherly love that is no

161 The volume opens with a translation of a talk by A. Schaade from the 17th International Congress of Orientalists in Oxford (German in *Hamburger Fremdenblatt* of 27 October 1928) and concludes with a lecture by Salāma Mūsā that had been published in *al-Hilāl* in January of 1929.

longer there, while his older brother replaces their father with outright reluctance. At school, the boy, who is pampered by the servants and whose younger cousin introduces the first juvenile excitement into his life, is confronted with his first real worries, but it is also there that he feels the comradeship of his classmates, while his teacher surrounds him with his good-hearted care. His friendship with the teacher's daughter, whose mother had died, first develops into affection, then catches fire to become a real passion when the girl, following her father's death, is invited to come and stay in the house of Sāmī's brother. As the liaison does not remain without consequences, Sāmī's brother marries the girl off to an elderly guard on the estate. The cousin, considering herself neglected by Sāmī, entangles his older brother in her webs, who then takes her as a second wife and sets her up in a separate household. Quietly, Sāmī penetrates this latter universe and, behind his brother's back, enjoys the love of his sister-in-law-cum-cousin in a consensual sadistic act. When his older brother is snatched away by an untimely death, Sāmī rejects the widow's attempts to get close to him; instead, he goes out looking for the lost love of his youth, only to find her son, his mother having died three years earlier, in the care of a great aunt, and now the only thing he wants is to fulfil his duties as a father. Next to the protagonist of the story, the brother's persona is not worked out well, leaving him somewhat obscure. The three women, on the other hand, the wife with motherly feelings for her little brother-in-law, the spontaneous, child-of-nature Fatḥiyya, and the coquette Tahānī, have all been drawn with firm strokes, as has life in the house of an affluent family, where there are no social duties and people are driven purely by pleasure. Even if the novel is lacking psychological depth (basically, it is just about the sex life of an immature adolescent), as a colourful image of life in a decadent society, it is a valuable record of the times.

This novel too, is accompanied by a number of short sketches that are not mentioned on the title page. Among these is *Abū ʿArab* (first published in *al-Hilāl* 37, 1928, 201/5, 145/50 in the French translation), which is about the triumph of an Arab's fatherly love over his thirst for revenge; *Ḥilm wanqaḍā*, about
the life of a minor civil servant in a | remote hamlet and where the Sudanese 224
wife of the stationmaster is the cause of brief excitement for the clerk of the post office.

With *al-Shaykh ʿAfa ʾllāh wa-qiṣaṣ ukhrā*, in 1936, he returned to his primary literary means of expression, the short story. The title story is about a conscience-stricken man who roams the countryside after having caused his brother's wife to commit suicide in order to cover up their adulterous affair. Besides a few love stories with their usual tragic edge (social constraints in Egypt being what they are), there is a story about a bookbinder who was maimed in a tragic accident in the workplace (*al-Kasīḥ*, 77ff, first published in *al-Hilāl* 39, 881/7) and whose aggressive behaviour weighs heavily on his dedicated assistant. This continues until the day the assistant suffers the same fate and, by his steadfast behaviour, moves his boss to take on a similar attitude. On the other hand, there is the story of *Shaykh ʿAlawān*, an incorrigible vagabond and freeloader who ends up inheriting his brother's estate, three wives included, but who refuses to give up his lifestyle (first published in *al-Hilāl* 37, 1929, 585/90). There is also the tale of the ambitious reformer who loses his job because of his obsession with improvement and then retires to the countryside with his savings; finding no satisfaction in agriculture, he spends his days doing nothing but waste his money, finally ending up as a tramp (*al-Iflās*). In *Nājiya bint al-fiqī* and *al-Takfīr* he juxtaposes a father who grants his dying daughter forgiveness for an adulterous affair, fifteen years after the fact, with a young man whose insults had sent his wife to her grave and then falls in love with a picture of her, to the point of violating her lifeless corpse. In between, there is the tender story of the little orphan girl, taken care of by a student (transl. Widmer, WI XIII, from *al-Majalla al-jadīda* I, 807/13).

The introduction to *Qalb ghāniya wa-qiṣaṣ ukhrā* contains a favourable appraisal of the narrative works of Ḥāfiẓ Ibrāhīm, of his translation of *Les misérables* of Victor Hugo, and of his *Layāli 'l-Satīḥ*. The work is almost entirely dedicated to things moving a woman's heart. Starting with the title story about a licentious woman who, in the final stages of tuberculosis, turns down the
225 advances of a young doctor, the work continues with *al-Sajīna*, | in which a woman, tied to an ailing husband after just a brief period of marital bliss, ends up releasing her pent-up desires with the husband's younger brother, and concludes with *Umm*, in which he tells us how the love for her niece resuscitates the emotions of a widow, numbed since the death of her grown-up son. In between, we find stories like *Ḥanīn*, about the uncontrollable longing for home of an elderly peasant who was made to come and live in the city by his son; the story of the conscientious beggar, translated from *Jarīdat al-Sharq al-Jadīd* of 1 January 1929 by Widmer in WI, XIII, 88/95; and the wondrous story *Ḥūriyyat al-baḥr*, about a teenage boy who, having read a French book of fairy tales, starts believing in mermaids and then, on a stormy night, is drowned when he goes out swimming looking for them (first published in *al-Hilāl* 41, 1933, 96/104).

Firʿawn al-sharq wa-qiṣaṣ ukhrā was announced for Spring 1938, but I have not seen it yet, the reason being that it will only be published in May of 1939, as the author was kind enough to let me know (see below no. 27). Apart from the stories included in the collections, *al-Hilāl* also published, among others, *Jārim al-ḥubb* 38, 1929, 73/8, *al-Munqidh* 40, 1930, 88/96, *al-Umūma* (ibid. 690/2),

Ḥazan ab (ibid. 983/6, now in *Firʿawn al-sharq* 65/74), *Inqilāb* 42, 188/92 (ibid. 101/14), and *al-Shabāb* of March 1936, 27/9, *al-Hazīma*. Apart from the stories mentioned earlier, the collection *al-Wathba al-ūlā* also features two new ones, *Ḍarīḥ al-arbaʿīn* and *Allāh yarḥamuh*, transl. of *Inqilāb* in *Les Amours de Sāmī* no. 8, conte égyptien: 'Volte face'.

Maḥmūd Taymūr's narrative skills having been honed through his readings of the great French masters, it is only natural that his language is not entirely free of Europeanisms. But these do not define his style. His ideal is a Classical Arabic modelled on the everyday language of the educated, without giving too much space to colloquialisms. He uses the Egyptian vernacular sparingly, just to mark out individuals from the lower classes in his dialogues. People have criticised his language for being sloppy, and it is true that there are numerous cases in which his phraseology goes against the rules of Classical Arabic. Yet all this serves a well-defined, artistic purpose, namely to lend his stories the colour of life itself. He once expressed himself on this issue | during a lecture 226
at the International Congress of Orientalists in Leiden, entitled *al-Nizāʿ bayna 'l-fuṣḥā wal-ʿāmmiyya fi 'l-adab al-Miṣrī al-ḥadīth*, which was published in *al-Hilāl* 41, 1931, 185/8.

13a Nīqūlā al-Ḥaddād

Besides Maḥmūd Taymūr, numerous journalists have attempted to satisfy the need for amusement among the Egyptian people. The first to be mentioned here is the Syrian Nīqūlā al-Ḥaddād, publisher of the magazine *al-Sayyidāt wal-rijāl*. Identifying himself entirely with the lives and ways of thinking of the Egyptians, his works are particularly loved by them (Maḥmūd Taymūr, *al-Shaykh Sayyid al-ʿAbīṭ*, 46/7).

He started in 1906 in *Musāmarāt al-shiʿb* II with *Asrār Miṣr, al-Ḥaqība al-zaqqāʾ, riwāya ʿaṣriyya* and *Ḥawwāʾ al-jadīda*, following the example of the French novel *Yvonne Monard*, Cairo 1900; next followed *ʿAhd al-jāsūsiyya*, in *Musāmarāt al-shiʿb* VII (1911), *al-Ṣādiq al-majhūl*, Cairo n.d., and *Ādam al-jadīd* Cairo 1914. He deals with contemporary history in *Fātinat al-Ambarāṭūr* (on Kaiser Franz Joseph II), Cairo 1922 and *Firʿawnat al-ʿArab ʿinda 'l -Turk*, Cairo n.d. (Maṭbaʿat al-Kawwāʾ), revised as *Jamʿiyyat Ikhwān al-ʿAhd*, on the history of the league of Arab officers in the Turkish army, Cairo n.d., 1923. A continuation of this is *Wadāʿan ayyuha 'l -sharq*, Cairo 1926, on the new Turkey under Muṣṭafā Kamāl. After a story from the New World in *al-ʿĀlam al-jadīd aw al-ʿAjāʾib wal-gharāʾib al-Amirīkiyya*, Cairo 1924/5, he turned in 1927 to the history of his native country in the years 1840/6 in *Nabiyyat Lubnān*. In *Min ʿArābī ilā Zaghlūl*, Cairo 1929, he sketches the history of the nationalist movement in his adopted country. Thanks to their being mentioned in Pérès 494/6, I now know

of the existence of the novels *ʿAyn bi-ʿayn, Kulluh naṣīb*, Cairo 1901 (Aʿlā Qiṣaṣ
63), *Zaghlūlāt Miṣr, al-Hānum al-muʿtaqala, Hawkār al-muḥtāl, al-Khuffāsh al-
basharī, al-Khātam al-sāḥir*, and his contributions to *al-Laṭāʾif al-muṣawwara:
al-Muntāḍ al-muntaqim, Zaghlūl Miṣr, Zaghālīl Miṣr, Fatāt Āl ʿUthmān, Taḥt
rāyat Muṣṭafā Kamāl, Fatāt al-Anaḍūl wanhizām al-Yūnāniyyīn*, as well as the
one to *Majallat al-Riwāyāt al-muṣawwara: Ibn al-maqādīr*. He calls his latest
227 work, *al-Muqaddas*, Cairo 1935, a *Riwāya khayāliyya*. Gibb, BSOS | VII, 18 is
probably right when he says that his influence on the development of storytelling in Egypt has not been very great. It is just through an occasional reference that I know of his play *Ṣalāḥ al-Dīn al-Ayyūbī*. Sarkīs, who refers to him
on page 745 as a *ṣaydalī fi ʾl-Qāhira*, mentions three more politico-sociological
works: *Taʾrīkh asās al-sharāʾiʿ al-Inklīziyya*, translated from the English original
of David Watson Rany, Cairo n.d., *al-Ḥubb wal-ziwāj*, Cairo 1901, and *Manāhij
al-ḥayāh*, Cairo 1904.

13b Muḥammad Farīd Abū Ḥadīd

According to Gibb, loc. cit., the historical novel *Ibnat al-Mamlūk* (Cairo: Maṭbaʿat al-Iʿtimād, 1926, 435pp.), the second book by Muḥammad Farīd Abū Ḥadīd, gives evidence of greater talent.

It is the story of a Wahhābī who fled from Saudi Arabia to Egypt at the time of Muḥammad ʿAlī and who, among other things, participates in the succesful defence of Damietta against the British in 1807. Having no other aim than to sketch a lively picture of the times, the author avoids copying J. Zaydān's at times bothersome habit of imparting historical information. Earlier, he had published *Ṣaḥāʾif min ḥayāt aw Mudhakkirāt al-marḥūm Muḥammad*, Cairo 1924 (Pérès 411). His play *Maysūn al-Ghajariyya* (*The gipsy girl Maysūn*, Cairo 1347/1928) was followed in 1937 by an historical novel about Egypt towards the end of the eighteenth century, called *Sīrat al-sayyid ʿUmar Makram* (Pérès, no. 413).

14 Other Authors

Besides the leading figures in narrative prose, there was a host of lesser authors who all tried to provide amusement for their readers, be it in the style of ancient *adab* or according to modern literary techniques. Of all these, only a summary overview can be given here, the order being chronological.

1874: Ibrāhīm b. Yūsuf al-Ṣādirānī, *Qiṣṣat Badr al-Naʿām bint al-malik al-Shahīd maʿa maḥbūbihā Jabr al-mazīd*, Alexandria 1291, Damascus 1319.

1887: Nīqūlā Efendi Bistris, *Fuʾād*, Alexandria.

1888: Muḥammad al-Tamīmī, Najl al-Shaykh al-Tamīmī Mufti ʾl-diyār al-Miṣriyya, *Ḥadīth Laylā aw al-Durr al-naẓīm*, Cairo.

1890: Aḥmad Efendi al-Ṣarrāf al-Ṣaghīr (in Alexandria), *Ẓabyat al-bān*, Alexandria.

| 1892: Ibrāhīm Efendi Ramzī, *al-Muʿtamad b. ʿAbbād*, Cairo.—Muḥammad 228
Ḥamdī al-Dimyāṭī, *Thamarāt al-afkār*, C. 1310.

1893: ʿAbd al-Raḥmān b. Ismāʿīl, *Ghādat al-Andalus*, C. 1311 (Pérès no. 534).

1894: ʿAbd al-Bāqī al-Daqqāq, *Musirrāt fi ʾl-tankīt wal-nawādir*, C. 1312.—Ḥannā Efendi Naqqāsh, *ʿAwāqib al-ghurūr*, Alexandria.—Marqūs Efendi Fahmī, *al-Marʾa fi ʾl-sharq*, Cairo.—Muḥammad Zakī al-Itribī, *al-Nukhaba al-zakiyya fi ʾl-nawādir al-fukāhiyya*, C. 1312.

1895: Sālim Efendi Sarkīs (editor of *Rajʿ al-ṣadā, al-Mushīr* and *Majallat Sarkīs*, Sarkīs 1021, d. 1926), *Sirr Mamlaka* I, second printing C. 1897 (from the history of the Ottomans under ʿAbd al-Ḥamīd), further *Gharāʾib al-Maktūbjī* (history of the Ottoman press, dedicated to ʿAbd al-Ḥamīd), C. 1896.—*Qiṣṣat Josephine* (the wife of Napoleon), New York 1901.

1897: Aḥmad Efendi Saʿīd al-Baghdādī, *Ghādat Jabal Anāṣyā*, C. 1315.—Khalīl Efendi Kāmil, Nāẓir maḥaṭṭat Ḥulwān, *Maẓālim al-ābāʾ*, C. 1315.—Muḥammad Efendi al-ʿIyādī, *Muqātil Miṣr Aḥmad ʿArābī*, Cairo.—Mīkhāʾīl Efendi Faraj (teacher at the American School of Cairo), *al-Muhandis al-Miṣrī*, Cairo.

1898: Rāghib Efendi Damyān, *ʿAjāʾib al-ḥadathān*, Cairo.

1899: Ayyūb Efendi, *Bahman Shāh*, Alexandria 1317.—Aḥmad Efendi Fahmī, *Āyāt al-ʿibar*, C. 1317.

1900: Aḥmad Efendi Ṣādiq (ṣāḥib *Jarīdat al-Ṣādiq*), *Thamarāt al-ghawāya*, Alexandria.—Ḥasan Efendi Rushdī al-Muhandis, *Ḥassān al-ʿArabī*, C. 1318.—Ḥasan Bāshā Ḥusnī al-Ṭuwayrānī (see p. 83), *Mudhishāt al-qadar*, C. 1318.—Aḥmad b. Khalīl al-Qabbānī, *Lubāb al-gharām*, C. 1318.—*Riwāyat ʿAntar b. Shaddād*, C. 1318.—*al-Amīr Maḥmūd, najl Shāh al-ʿAjam*, C. 1318.—ʿAlī Efendi Luṭfī, *Dhill al-gharām*, C. 1318.—Ibrāhīm Zaydān (the son of Jirjī Zaydān see p. 186), *Nawādir al-kirām fi ʾl-Jāhiliyya wal-Islām*, C. 1899; *Nawādir al-ʿushshāq*, C. 1900; *Nawādir al-udabāʾ*, C. 1901; *al-Mustaẓrafāt min al-nawādir wal-laṭāʾif wal-fukāha*, C. n.d.; *al-Nawādir al-muṭriba*, C. 1321.—*Durūs al-ashyāʾ*, C. 1903; *Salāsil al-inshāʾ*, C. n.d.; *Mabādiʾ al-handasa*, 2 vols., C. n.d. (Sarkīs 984).

1901: Maḥmūd Ḥāsib, *Khafāyā Miṣr*, C. 1319; *al-Qāʾimmaqām Naṣīb Bey* (situated in the era of ʿAbbās I, Pérès no. 516), C. n.d.—Khalīl Khayyāṭ, *Hannibal al-Fanīqī* (ibid. 516).—Niqulā Efendi Mīkhāʾīl ʿAṭiyya, *Shuhadāʾ al-būrsa*, Cairo.

| 1902: Aḥmad Rifʿat, *al-Ḥasnāʾ al-wafiyya*, C. 1320 (Pérès 601).—al-Amīr 229
Amīn Raslān (Turkish consul in Brussels, publisher of the *Kashf al-niqāb* in Paris, Sarkīs 931), *Asrār al-quṣūr*, Cairo.—*Ḥuqūq al-milal wa-muʿāhadāt al-duwal*, only vol. IV, Cairo 1900.—ʿAlī Efendi Nūr, *Shuhadāʾ al-ikhlāṣ*, C. 1322.—Sālim b. Khalīl al-Naqqāsh (editor of the *Jarīdat al-Maḥrūsa* in Alexandria, d. 1883 or 1884, Sarkīs 1886), *Miṣr lil-Miṣriyyīn*, ibid. 1302; *al-Ẓulūm*, Alexandria.

1903: Najīb Asʿad Jāwīsh, *Maghāyir al-jinn* (an historical novel on the Visconti), Alexandria (Pérès 473).—Muḥammad Ḥilmī Zayn al-Dīn, *Maḍārr al-zār*, Cairo (ibid. 718).—ʿIwaḍ Efendi Wāṣif (munshiʾ *Majallat al-Muḥīṭ*), *Iskandar wa-Draga*, Cairo; *ʿAdrāʾ al-Yābān*, C. 1906.—Ḥasan Efendi ʿAfīfī, *al-Fata ʾl-ṭāʾish*, C. 1321.—Khalīl Efendi Fahmī, *al-Qiṣāṣ al-ʿādil*, Alexandria.—Manṣūr Efendi Rifʿat, *al-Akh al-ghādir*, Cairo.

1904: Muḥammad Efendi Munjī Khayrallāh, *Majnūn Laylā*, Alexandria.—Kāmil Efendi Fahmī, *al-Sulṭān al-ʿĀdil maʿa waliyy ʿahdihi*, Cairo.

1905: Maḥmūd Khayrāt, *al-Fatāt al-rīfiyya*, Cairo; *al-Fata ʾl-rīfī* in *Musāmarāt al-shiʿb* 1; *al-Kanz al-Miṣrī* (detective stories), C. 1923 (Pérès 501).—al-Ḥājj Muḥammad al-Harāwī, *al-Ṭabīb al-Miṣrī*, Cairo (ibid. 513).—Dr. Khalīl Saʿāda, *Asrār al-thawra al-Rūsiyya*, Cairo (ibid. 613).—Muṣṭafā Ṣabrī, *Ghāniyat al-Jazāʾir*, C. 1322 (ibid. 615).—Muḥammad Efendi Aḥmad and Sayyid Rushwān Efendi, *al-Ḥubb al-ṭahīr*, Cairo.—Muḥammad ʿAbdallāh al-ʿAlāʾilī (al-mudarris bil-madāris al-ḥurra al-Islāmiyya), *Aḥsan al-maḥāsin*, maxims and proverbs in alphabetical order, C. 1323.

1906: ʿAbd al-Ḥalīm Dilāwar, *Dānishwāy*, Cairo (Pérès, 444).—Maḥmūd Ṭāhir Ḥaqqī, *ʿAdhrāʾ Dānishwāy*, Cairo n.d. (ibid. 511).—Muḥammad Kamāl Ḥilmī, *Ḥayāt shaqāʾ* (set in the period of the French Revolution), C. 1324 (ibid. 519).

1907: Muḥammad Efendi ʿAbd al-Ḥayy, *al-Ghazāl al-sharīd aw Amīr al-luṣūṣ*, C. 1324.—Muḥammad Efendi Sāmī, *Nawādir al-ḥamqā wal-mushaffalīn*, C. 1532.

1908: Khalīl Bek Saʿd, *al-Sharkasiyya al-ḥasnāʾ*, Cairo (Maṭbaʿat al-Maʿārif).

1909: Saʿādat Bey Mūrali (a Turkish civil servant), *al-Intiqām al-ḥāʾil aw Asrār al-Āsitāna*, 14 *juzʾ* in 2 vols., Cairo.—*Mahārat surūr aw Būlīs Dimashq al-sirrī bi-Miṣr*, 10 *juzʾ* in 2 vols., Cairo n.d.—*Fatāt al-Busfūr aw Asrār al-Āsitāna*, Cairo.—*Fatāt Erzerūm* (1 volume on the history of ʿAbd al-Ḥamīd), 9 *juzʾ* in 1 volume, Tanta 1911.—*al-Riwāyāt al-ʿUthmāniyya* (together with Jurjī Saʿāda), Cairo n.d.
230 and Tanta n.d. (6 short stories).— | Niqūlā Basyūr (a teacher at al-Madrasa al-Saʿīdīya), *al-Jihād fī nayl al-murād*, Cairo.—*Masāʾil fi ʾl-ṭabīʿa*, C. 1334 (Sarkīs 565).—ʿAbd al-Raʾūf Efendi Ibrāhīm, *al-Gharām wal-siyāsa aw Nābūlyūn* 1, C. 1327.—Ḥasan Tawfīq Efendi (*al-kātib bil-maḥkama al-ahliyya*), *Maḥasīn al-ʿaṣr*, C. 1327.

1910: Ṣāliḥ Ḥamdī Ḥammād, *Aḥsan al-qiṣaṣ* (3 short stories), C. 1328 (Pérès 507).—*Ḥayāt al-fuʾād aw ṣuwar al-shiʿr fī rawḍat al-baḥrayn*, Cairo n.d. (Maṭbaʿat Ramsīs, 1915).—Maḥmūd Jaʿfar Ismāʿīl, *Fatāt al-Nuʿmān b. al-Mundhir aw Shuhadāʾ al-wafāʾ*, Alexandria (ibid. 536).—Niqūlā Rizqallāh (mostly known for his translations), *Fikriyya Hānum*, Cairo n.d.—*Munājāt al-arwāḥ*, Cairo n.d.—*Dār al-ʿajāʾib*, 2 vols., Cairo n.d.—*François I*, Cairo n.d.—*Ḥūriyya*, Cairo n.d.—*al-Junūn funūn*, Cairo n.d. (ibid. 606/11).—Tawfīq Saʿīd al-Rāfiʿī, *Maṣraʿ al-ẓālimīn*, C. 1328.—*Ḍaḥiyyat al-wājib* (situated in Paris in 1905/6), C. 1913 (Pérès 596).

1911: Ismāʿīl ʿAbd al-Munʿim, *ʿAlā safḥ al-jabal*, C. 1329 (Pérès 404).—Amīn Ḥamdī, *al-Ḥubb al-ṭāhir*, Tanta 1329 (ibid. 506).—*ʿUjālat al-muta'addib*, C. 1330—*Luqaṭ al-ḥikam*, in *Majmūʿa*, C. 1331.—Muḥammad Efendi al-ʿInānī (an officer working in the Ministry of Defense), *al-Rawḍa al-adabiyya fi 'l-muntakhabāt al-nathriyya*, C. 1329.

1913: Amīn al-Ghurayyib, *Fī zawāya 'l-quṣūr*, Cairo (Pérès 478).

1914: Ḥasan Khaṭṭāb al-Wakīl, *ʿIbra min al-ta'rīkh aw Ayyām al-Rashīd*, Cairo (Pérès 515).

1915: Muḥammad Ṣabrī, *Dhikr al-māḍī aw Siyāḥāt fi 'l-jabal*, Cairo (Pérès 614).

1916: Zakariyyā' Nāmiq, *al-Fatāt al-Sharkasiyya fī ḥarb al-Dawla al-ʿAliyya*, Cairo (Pérès 580).—ʿAzmī Sulaymān Bek (formerly a teacher of history and geography), *al-Tuḥfa al-bahiyya fi 'l-adab wal-aḥwāl al-marḍiyya*, C. 1335.

1917: Muṣṭafā Maḥmūd al-Ṣayyād, *Jarīmat al-fu'ād aw ʿĀqibat al-ziwāj al-qahrī*, C. 1335 (Pérès 550).

1918: Kāẓim ʿAlī Ismāʿīl Efendi, *Samīr al-ṭālib* I, *al-Ṭufayliyyūn*, Cairo.

1919: Muḥammad ʿAlī Rizq, *Dawla* (on the revolution of 1919), Cairo (Pérès 605).

1920: ʿAbd al-Ḥamīd Muḥammad ʿIzzat, *Mudhakkirāt al-shabāb*, Cairo (Pérès 539).—Muḥammad Jamāl, *Kashkūl Jamāl*, C. 1339.—Zakī Wāṣif (professor at Madrasat Muṣṭafā Kāmil), *Zafarāt fi 'l-ḥubb, Rasā'il*, C. 1339.

1921: Zakariyya' Ibrāhīm, *Khawāṭir muntahir*, Cairo (Pérès 533).— | Najīb al- 231
Mandarāwī, *Mārī di Midīsīs aw Maqtal al-malika*, Cairo (ibid. 551).

1922: Muḥammad Yūsuf al-Mudrik, *al-ʿIffa wal-fāqa*, Cairo; *Āmāl al-muḥibbīn aw Min al-kūkh ila 'l-qaṣr*, Cairo (Pérès 565).—ʿAbduh Ḥasan Qashqūsh, *Nihāyat al-gharām aw Fī sabīl al-ḥubb al-ṭāhir*, Cairo (ibid. 588).—Aḥmad Abū Khiḍr Mansī (see p. 194), *Mukhtār al-nawādir*, C. 1340.—ʿĪsā ʿUbayd (d. 1922), *Iḥsān Hānum, majmūʿat qiṣaṣ Miṣriyya ʿaṣriyya*, C. 1921 (see Ode-Vasilieva 177/93, treated with disdain by Shaḥḥāta ʿUbayd, *Dars mu'lim* 6); *Thurayyā, majmūʿat qiṣaṣ Miṣriyya ʿaṣriyya*, Cairo, *ʿAlā ḍifāf al-Nīl*, Cairo n.d. (Pérès 681/3).—Muḥammad Ṣubḥī Abū Ghanīma, *Aghāni 'l-layl, Majmūʿat qiṣaṣ ijtimāʿiyya akhlāqiyya adabiyya* I, Cairo (Pérès 410).—Muḥammad Ra'fat Jamālī, *Qūt al-fātina aw Ālām al-ʿāshiqayn*, Cairo; *Mudhakkirāt baghī* (the life of a prostitute), Cairo (Pérès 465/6).—Aḥmad Muḥammad Ḥifnī, *al-Bā'iʿa al-ḥasnā'*, Cairo; *al-Armaniyya al-ḥasnā'*, C. 1925; *al-Insān wal-shayṭān*, C. 1344/1926 (ibid. 517).

1923: Maḥmūd Muḥammad al-Ṣayrafī, *al-Hawā al-ʿudhrī aw al-Wafā' fi 'l-ḥubb*, Cairo; *Mamlakat al-gharām*, C. 1345/1926; *Qātil abawayh*, Cairo n.d.

(Pérès 625/7).—Yūsuf Ḥamdī Yegen, *al-Layāli 'l-ʿashr*, Cairo.—Murquṣ Yannī al-Mīrī, *Mudhakkirāt laqīṭ*, Cairo.—ʿAbd al-Qādir Ḥamza, *Ḍaḥāya 'l-aqdār*, Cairo (on the victims of gambling addiction).

1924: Muḥammad ʿAbd al-Qādir Sirāj al-Dīn, *al-Shuhadāʾ aw al-Qulūb al-dāmiya*, 2 vols., Cairo, third printing C. 1927.—Muḥammad Zakī Shuʿayb, *Mathwa 'l-ḥabībayn aw al-ʿAdārā*, Cairo (Pérès, 650/1).—Khalīl Baydās, *Masāriḥ al-adhhān*, Cairo.—ʿAbd al-Ḥamīd Mutawallī al-Muḥāmī, *Khawāṭir fi 'l-shiʿr wal-nathr*, Cairo.

1925: Ḥusayn Shāhīn Shākir, *Shaqāʾ al-ʿarūsayn aw ʿAdhrāʾ Shubrā*, C. 1343 (Pérès 628).

1926: Aḥmad Rifʿat ʿAbd al-ʿAẓīm, *Shahīda aw Ḍaḥiyyat al-hawā*, C. 1345 (Pérès 399).—Aḥmad Kāmil al-Dīb, *al-Dumūʿ*, C. 1344 (ibid. 445).—Muḥammad Kāmil Farīd, *Iqbāl Hānum aw Masāriḥ al-ʿushshāq*, Cairo n.d.; *Taḥt al-rāyatayn*, Cairo n.d.; *Mudāʿabāt al-milāḥ fi 'l-talāhī wal-mizāḥ*, Cairo n.d. (ibid. 452/4).—Asʿad Ḥannā, *Basīma aw Majd fi 'l -hawān* (ibid. 510).—Ḥasan Ṣubḥī, *Qiṣaṣ al-bardī* (with a preface by Muḥammad Ḥusayn Haykal), C. 1345.—Ḥusayn Suʿūdī, *Aḥādīth wa-qiṣaṣ*, C. 1344; *Asrār al-hawānim*, Cairo (ibid. 661/2).—Aḥmad Imām ʿAṭiyya , *Mudhakkirāt ʿāmil fī biqāʿ al-ʿāhirāt*, Cairo (ibid. 434).—Yūsuf Iskandar Gharīs, *Abūnā Sarjiyūs wa-qiṣaṣ ukhrā*, Cairo; *Kunūz al-malik Sulaymān*, Cairo n.d. (ibid. 469/70).—ʿAbbās Muḥammad, *Sukayna*
232 *aw ʿAlā masraḥ al-khiyāna*, | C. 1345 (ibid. 566).—Aḥmad Mukhtār al-Ḥanbalī, *al-Riwāyāt al-qiṣaṣiyya* (10 short stories), C. 1345 (ibid. 570).—Ḥasan Ṣādiq, *al-Qiṣāṣ*, C. (ibid. 620).—ʿAlī Aḥmad al-Shāhid, a public servant at the Library of Egypt, *Zubayda*, C. 1345 (ibid. 623).—Aḥmad ʿAbd al-Munʿim, *al-Sharīd* (ibid. 403).—Abū ʿAbd al-Raḥmān Kamāl al-Dīn Muḥammad b. Muḥammad b. ʿAbd al-Raḥmān al-Ḥusaynī al-Adhamī, *Lawāmiʿ al-isʿāf fī jawāmiʿ al-ʿadād*, an anthology, Cairo.—Farīd Ḥubaysh, *al-Nafs al-ḥāʾira, qiṣṣa ijtimāʿiyya gharāmiyya*, Cairo; *Fazāʾiʿ al-thawb al-aswad* (stories from the [First] World War), Cairo n.d. (Pérès 520).

1927: Maḥmūd Abāẓa, *al-Jārimān* (anecdotes from the house of parliament), Cairo (Pérès 397).—Muḥammad ʿAbd al-ʿAzīz al-Ṣadr, *Iʿtirāfāt mūmis*, C. 1345 (ibid. 400).—ʿAbd al-Ḥalīm al-ʿAskarī, *Suʿād*, C. 1344 (ibid. 402).—ʿAbduh al-Shaʾmī, *Riḥlat Isḥāq al-aqdam aw al-Yahūdī al-mutajawwil*, C. 1345 (ibid. 408).—Yūsuf Abū Ḥajjāj, *Mudhakkirāt futuwwa*, C. 1345 (ibid. 414).—al-Ḥusayn ʿAlī, *al-Shaykh al-ṣāliḥ*, C. 1346 (ibid. 423).—ʿAbd al-Raḥmān ʿAlī Hilālī, *al-ʿĀṭifāt al-thāʾira aw al-Ḥubb al-khāliṣ*, Cairo (ibid. 518).—Jabrān Musūḥ, *Ghidhāʾ shahr*, Cairo (ibid. 572).—Yūsuf Ṣabrī, *Jarīmat al-mulāzim*, Cairo; *ʿAlā madhbaḥ al-shahawāt aw Ḍaḥāya 'l-tamaddun*, Cairo; *ʿAlā ajniḥat al-khayāl aw Bayn alsinat al-nīrān*, C. 1928 (ibid. 616/8).—Ṭāhir Aḥmad al-Ṭannāḥī (cf. p. 82), *al-Layālī*, Cairo (ibid. 677), poems *Apollo* 91, 258, *Shawqī wa-Mutanabbī fī thawb* (ibid.

447/57).—ʿAbdallāh al-ʿAlawī b. Muḥammad al-Ḥaddād, *al-Durr al-manẓūm li-dhawi 'l-ʿuqūl wal-fuhūm*, C. 1346.

1928: Muḥammad Ṣafwat, *al-Ḍaḥāyā*, Cairo (Pérès 622).—Arslān ʿAbd al-Ghanī al-Banbī, *al-Aqdār*, Cairo (ibid. 432).—Aḥmad ʿAbd al-Fattāḥ Budayr, *Ghādat Yildiz wa-ʿashhar qiṣaṣ gharām al-mulūk wal-umarāʾ*, Cairo (ibid. 439).—Ibrāhīm al-Miṣrī, *al-Adab al-ḥayy, majmūʿat maqālāt wa-buḥūth fi 'l-adab wal-intiqād mudhayyal bi-qiṣṣa wa-drāma kāmila*, Cairo (wherein *Sukhriyyat al-muyūl, mudhakkirāt ʿan qiṣṣat al-ḥubb*, 113/36, Pérès 529); *Qawī kal-mawt*, abbreviated from Guy de Maupassant, 'Fort comme la mort', *al-Hilāl* 39 (1930), 567/74; *bayna 'l-thulūj*, abbreviated from 'La neige sur les pas' by H. Bordeaux, ibid. 72/8; *al-ʿAdhāb* after 'Le calvaire' by O. Mirbeau, ibid. 905/13; *Fājiʿat al-buḥayra* after Blasco Ibañez, 'Tragédie sur le lac', ibid. 1079/80; *al-Adab al-ḥadīth*, C. 1931, wherein *al-Kharīf* in the spirit of Freud, p. 56/70 (Pérès 529); *al-Fikr wal-ʿālam*, Cairo 1932; *Ṣawt al-jīl* C. 1932; *Waḥy al-ʿaṣr* (essays, stories and translations), C. 1935.

1930: Maḥmūd Kāmil, *al-Ḥanīn qiṣṣa Miṣriyya, al-Hilāl* | 39, 265/72; *al-Shakk* 233
al-hāʾil, qiṣṣa Miṣriyya fī rasāʾil ibid. 383/7; *al-Qātila, qiṣṣa Miṣriyya* ibid. 745/51; *Ḥālāt junūn, qiṣṣa Miṣriyya* ibid. 1041/7; *al-Rujūla al-kāmila, qiṣṣa Miṣriyya* ibid. 1201/7; *Ab wa-ibn*, ibid. 1322/8; *Ṣayḥāt jadīda fi 'l-naqd fi 'l-fann wal-adab*, C. 1930; *al-Mutammarridūn, qiṣaṣ Miṣriyya*, C. 1931 (Maṭbaʿat al-Taraqqī) (Pérès 540); *al-Qātil, qiṣṣa taḥlīliyya, al-Hilāl* 40, 881/7; *Fi 'l-bayt wal-shāriʿ, majmūʿat qiṣaṣ Miṣriyya*, C. 1932 (Maṭbaʿat al-ʿAṣriyya) (Pérès 541).—Kāmil Kīlānī, *Mukhtār al-qiṣaṣ*, Cairo n.d. (on which a *taqrīẓ* by Abū Shādī, *Ashiʿʿa wa-ẓilāl*, p. 134); *Maṣāriʿ al-khulafāʾ, Maṣāriʿ al-aʿyān*, Cairo n.d.; *Tājir Baghdād*, previously *Qiṣaṣ al-aṭfāl* in 13 sequences (Pérès 543/4).

1931: Sayyid Jaʿfar: *Kitāb al-afdān aw ʿAtharāt al-qadar, qiṣṣa Miṣriyya*, Cairo.

1932: Ḥabīb Jāmātī, *Ḍaḥāyā, majmūʿat aqāṣīs*, Cairo (Pérès 467).—Ḥusayn Shawqī, *Ṣadīqī Rīnān, qiṣṣa ijtimāʿiyya*, Cairo, several short stories in *al-Risāla*, no. 14, 19, 23 (Pérès 644/5).—ʿAbdallāh ʿAfīfī, *Zaharāt manthūra fi 'l-adab al-ʿarabī wa-hiya tafṣīl lil-muḥāḍarāt allatī alqāhā bi-Kulliyyat al-Sharīʿa*, Cairo.

1933: Fikrī Abāẓa, *al-Ḍāḥik al-bākī, maqālāt adabiyya, fukāhiyya ijtimāʿiyya*, Cairo (see *al-Mashriq* XXXI, 798).

1934: Muḥammad ʿAbd al-Fattāḥ Ibrāhīm, *Qiṣaṣ al-ḥayāh*, Cairo.—Muḥammad ʿAlī Ibrāhīm, *al-ʿAṣaba al-ḥamrāʾ*, Cairo (Pérès 530/1).—Muḥammad Ṭāhā Maḥmūd, *Thamarāt al-qalam fi 'l-adab wal-ijtimāʿ* (in which three short stories; *Ḍaḥiyyat al-ikhlāṣ*, 48/81; *al-Risāla al-muṣṭanaʿa*, 106/24; *al-Khādimān al-wafiyyān* [set in Cordoba in around 327 AH], 150/89, Pérès 549).

1935: Amīn Ḥāfiẓ, *Sharaf al-thāʾira, riwāyat gharām wa-falsafa wa-ṣuwar shattā min muʿtarak al-ḥayāh*, Cairo (Pérès 631).

1936: Ibrāhīm ʿAbduh, *al-Ḥayāt al-thāniya*, Cairo (Pérès 406).—Abū Ṭawīl, *Taḥta 'l-nāmūsiyya*, Cairo (ibid. 419).—ʿAbd al-Wahhāb Amīn, *Majmūʿat qiṣaṣ*, Cairo (ibid. 424).—Ḥabīb Tawfīq, *Madīḥa wa-qiṣaṣ ukhrā*, Cairo n.d.; *al-Rabīʿ wa-qiṣaṣ ukhrā*, Cairo n.d. (ibid. 679/80).—ʿIzzat al-Sayyid Ibrāhīm, *Waḥy al-rimāl*, cf. *al-Ahrām* of 11 September 1937.

1937: Amīn Yūsuf Jurāb, *al-Ḍabāb*, Damanhūr (on life in the countryside, Pérès 477).—Karam Mulḥam Karam, *Riwāyat al-maṣdūr*, Cairo (ibid. 542).—Muḥammad ʿIwaḍ Muḥammad (who translated Goethe's *Faust*), *Min ḥadīth al-sharq wal-gharb* (22 short stories), Cairo (ibid. 567).—Yūsuf, *Min ghawr muḥīṭ*, Cairo n.d. (ibid. 693).—Ḥasan Kāmil, *al-Rūḥ al-sharīd*, Cairo.—Muḥammad b. Muḥammad al-Jundī, *Rasūl al-ʿawāṭif*, Cairo (cf. *al-Ahrām* of 5 May 1937).—
234 Tawfīq Ḥasan al-Shartūnī, | *al-Ḥakīm wa-Laylā*, problems in modern marriages (see *al-Ahrām* of 14 October 1937).

1938: Ibrāhīm Wahba, *Mudhakkirāt ʿimāra laqṭ fī aḥḍān al-radhīla ghurrat aʿwām fī Bārīs*, Cairo.—Karam Khalīl Thābit, *Ḍaḥāya 'l -ḥurriyya sanat* 1919, *riwāya Miṣriyya waṭaniyya*, Cairo.

1939: Amīn Yūsuf Badda, a teacher in Alexandria, *al-Wafāʾ, qiṣṣa* (on the social evil of marriages for money), with a preface by ʿAbd al-Bāsiṭ Shaḥḥātā, Cairo (see al-ʿIwaḍī al-Wakīl in *al-Ahrām* of 13 March 1939).

(*15.–23a.*) *Short Stories, Mostly Involving the Lower Classes*

15 Ibrāhīm al-Sayyid Abū Kurāt

An example of an average product from the provinces, inspired by the masters in the capital, is *al-Zafarāt, majmūʿat qiṣaṣ akhlāqiyya ijtimāʿiyya* by Ibrāhīm al-Sayyid Abū Kurāt, Port Said (Maṭbaʿat al-Qanāl) n.d. (Pérès 415).

There are short scenes from the lives of prostitutes, alcoholics, gamblers, victims of rural wedding customs, and a defence of the theft of food by the unemployed, all in an uninspired language that is not entirely free from Europeanisms ('crocodile tears' $21,_{2}$, 'pangs of conscience' $39,_{7}$).

16 Shaḥḥāta ʿUbayd

The images from life in the affluent circles of the capital that Shaḥḥāta ʿUbayd, brother of ʿĪsā ʿUbayd (see p. 233), has tried to eternalize in his *Dars mu'lim, majmūʿat qiṣaṣ ʿaṣriyya Miṣriyya* (Cairo: Maṭbaʿat al-Sufūr, 1922), are on a higher artistic level.

With cleverly developed suspense, the main story relates how a young *bon-vivant* is driven back into the arms of his wife when he understands that one of his acquaintences has fallen in love with her without even knowing her. Two other stories take us into Christian circles, where people have an altogether

different understanding of the priorities in life than do Muslims. In the first of these, the female protagonist is at first unable to marry the person she loves because she is too poor. Then, when her brothers get rich during the war, she finally has a dowry, but in the meantime she also lost her innocence to an officer from Australia. The second story centres on a charity bazaar, where a Copt succeeds in selling the works from the estate of | a poor author that nobody 235
wanted by appealing to people's vanity. The final part of the book contains a translation of two of the *Lettres de femme* by M. Prévost. Another collection of stories, *al-Aghlāl* (Cairo n.d.), details the things that keep Egyptian society from progressing.

17 Aḥmad al-ʿĀṣī

The story *Ghādat Lubnān* by Aḥmad al-ʿĀṣī (Cairo: Maṭbaʿat Jarīdat al-Ṣabāḥ, 1926, the same year in which he also published a *dīwān*) is lyrical rather than epic.

The story's protagonist, a young doctor, is suffering from a hopeless case of weltschmerz, which even the longwinded reflections of the author are incapable of explaining. His father then sends him to a village in Lebanon for treatment. During his stay there he meets a poor peasant girl, enjoys a brief period of amorous bliss with her and then leaves her—despite her being willing to come with him to Cairo—so as not to impede her from fulfilling her duties towards her family. The sentimental tone of the book, while made to match the weak character of the protagonist, will not arouse the reader's interest.

18 Khayr al-Dīn al-Zarkalī

A special place is occupied by the memoirs[162] of Khayr al-Dīn al-Zarkalī (Zuruklī), known particularly for his serial work *al-Aʿlām, qāmūs tarājim li-ashhar al-rijāl wal-nisāʾ min al-ʿArab wal-mustaʿriba fi ʾl-Jāhiliyya wal-Islām wal-ʿaṣr al-ḥāḍir*, which he began in 1927. In these memoirs, called *Mā raʾaytu wa-mā samiʿtu*, he recounts his adventures during the Syrian war of liberation and in the Hijaz (Cairo: al-Maṭbaʿa al-ʿArabiyya, 1923/1342).

| The book starts with a dramatic description of the fighting in Damascus in 236
July of 1920 and of his flight to Cairo by way of Haifa. In Cairo, a representative of Sharif al-Ḥusayn invites him to go to the Hijaz. He then gives a lively description of the court of this most unhappy ruler. But the main part of the work is

162 A valuable source of information, but with no literary pretensions, are the memoirs of Aḥmad ʿArabī Pāshā al-Ḥusaynī (d. 18 Ramaḍān 1329/24 June 1911): *Kashf al-sitār ʿan sirr al-asrār fi ʾl-nahḍa al-mashhūra bil-Thawra al-ʿArābiyya*, Cairo n.d. (published by his son; manuscript, in part autograph, Cairo[2] v, 308).

devoted to his stay in the city of al-Ṭāʾif, of which he gives a very detailed and precise description. Following the example of ancient travelogues written in Arabic, he attaches special importance to mentioning all the city's prominent people that he met there. He also conducted a detailed study of al-Ṭāʾif's surroundings during the many excursions he made. In this connection he also recounts seeing old inscriptions. Some of these, which are reminiscent of cuneiform script and seemingly belong to the South Arabian alphabet, could actually be quite valuable for European scholars. The last part of the book, which contains a detailed account of contemporary poetry in the Hijaz, is the most important of all. Leaving the Hijaz, he went to Amman to visit al-Ḥusayn's son ʿAbdallāh, the emir of Transjordan. His reflections on that country are detailed in his *ʿĀmān fī ʿAmmān* (Cairo: al-Maṭbaʿa al-ʿArabiyya, 1925). His poetical rendering of al-Manfālūṭī's translation of a French short story, *Majdūlīn wal-shāʿir aw Fī ẓilāl al-zayzafūn* (Cairo: Maṭbaʿat al-Taraqqī, Shawwāl 1339; ʿUbayd Ikhwān publishers, Damascus), is a juvenile work which bears testimony to his great linguistic skills. He moulded the story into 21 strophes of three verses each in *ramal* with changing rhyme and three catalectic *ramal* verses with a continuous rhyme a-a-b throughout, gaining the acclaim of no less than eight Syrian authors, whose views were added to that booklet.

19 Muṣṭafā ʿAlī al-Hulbāwī

While many people had previously written about the lives of the rural population of Egypt, some with stark realism, others idealizing it, in 1928 yet another author, a philosophy student this time, Muṣṭafā ʿAlī al-Hulbāwī, himself raised in the countryside, undertook to describe life there as it really is in his *Fi 'l-rīf al-Miṣrī*, a work that was prefaced by his teacher, Dr. Manṣūr Fahmī.

237 | Sometimes calling his work a *risāla*, and at others *aḥādīth*, one will not hold it against the author that he, being a novice, could not always find the proper form for his subject. He likes showing off slightly with his philosophical education, referring to Kant, Rousseau and Indian philosophy as gleaned from Tagore. His book begins with reminiscenses from his childhood, in which the inadequacies of the village school take centre stage. After a general description of the Egyptian countryside, which sometimes rises to lyrical heights, he juxtaposes the lives of men and women in the rural communities. In this, he focusses exclusively on the poorest class of Egypt's rural population, the peasant tenants, exploited by rich landlords from the cities. Disclosing the shortcomings of the leasehold system with merciless lucidity and bitter irony, he castigates the bureaucrats for their indifference towards the needs of the peasant class. However, more than just complain, he also gives lively descriptions of various aspects of popular life, such as the peasants' stance towards religion,

the way vagabonds are organised—at times causing the peasants more trouble than they already have in finding the money for their lease (120ff)—and also of rural wedding customs (164ff). But rather than just protest, he also makes some specific proposals for change at the end. Insofar as these proposals touch upon the economic situation of the leaseholders, they follow the ideas of Sir W. Willcock. Yet reforming the education system is much more important to him, a matter which, after a delay of ten years, is now about to be tackled seriously by the ministry of education under the leadership of Ḥusayn Haykal. And he is absolutely right when he says that the Egyptian peasant can only be the true backbone of Egyptian society on condition that he be freed from the fetters of ignorance.

20 Ḥusayn Shafīq al-Miṣrī

As a work of art, Ḥusayn Shafīq al-Miṣrī's *Ḥawādith wa-arāʾ al-Ḥājj Darwīsh wa-Umm Ismāʿīl* (Cairo: Maṭbaʿat al-Nahḍa, 1929) occupies a special place.

Very much inspired by the Turkish *meddāḥ*s, the work does not offer truly a coherent story; using a series of adventures and tableaus which they
themselves recount, it is rather a description of its protagonists, a man | and 238
a woman from Cairo's lowest classes. After his coffeehouse was closed down because of drug trafficking, the male protagonist tries his hand at all sorts of professions. However, as a merchant, a street performer with a monkey, and even as a husband of convenience, he only has bad experiences; and the same for the woman, whether as a servant in a European family, as a seller of lottery tickets, as the wife of a fellah, etc. etc. Both tell us about their adventures in a genuine colloquial language interspersed with swearwords. It seems that this attempt at lending the common vernacular literary prestige in its own area of competence was another failure, not repeated since. At any rate, the necessary combination between, on the one hand, familiarity with life among the lower classes and, on the other, ability at creative writing, will only rarely be found.

21 ʿAbdallāh Ḥabīb

In his collection of stories *al-Mughaffal wa-qiṣaṣ ukhrā* (Cairo: Maṭbaʿat al-Shabāb, 1930, with a flattering preface by ʿAbbās Maḥmūd al-ʿAqqād), ʿAbdallāh Ḥabīb pretends to offer *ṣuwar min al-ḥayāt al-Miṣriyya*.

It is true that the title story and most of the others are primarily scenes from the lives of the people of Cairo and its corrupted youth, whose pranks do not always end well, as in the case of the gasoline price racket (13/31). But in the lower strata of society, too, he finds interesting characters, such as the rich, blind beggar (49/54), the king of beggars, the washer of corpses who wants to get married (*Shaykh Muṣṭafā*, 135/9), or the schoolmaster in *Shaykh ʿAbdallāh*

(32/48) who gives a fiery denouncement of the neglect of the primary school system. Ethnologically interesting descriptions of the Sudan are given in a story about the Arabs living there, called *Laylā Majnūn Sūdānī* (85/9). Furthermore, there is *Mawt muḥaqqaq* (191/6), on how an Egyptian officer is saved from a difficult situation by a record player, and *al-Ma'mūr al-sāḥir* (222/6), on how false teeth help an officer assert his authority in the face of village sorcerers.

Several of the stories are based on real events, such as the escape of a politi-
239 cal prisoner | that took place in 1919 (216/21), and the story of someone who was shipwrecked during the [First] World War (197/208). Rather out of character with the rest of the stories is the portrait of the master violonist (*Malik al-rabāba*) Abū Ṣalāḥ (209/215), which is apparently meant to secure immortality for this virtuoso.

22 Ḥasan Aḥmad Abu 'l-Dhahab

In the title of his collection of short stories, *Ṣuwar min al-ḥayāt* (Cairo: al-Maṭbaʿa al-Miṣriyya, 1932/1330), Ḥasan Aḥmad Abu 'l-Dhahab makes a similar claim.

The book opens with *al-Shahīd*, a sketch from the Egyptian struggle for freedom in which a student—rather colourless in the author's description of him—is hit by a bullet in a riot and then comforted by a female comrade as he lays dying. The other stories, however, are, almost without exception, immersed in an unpleasant kind of pessimism. The author is especially focussed on doctors, private practitioners (*al-Ṭabīb*) and civil servants (*Mustashfā Amīrī*), whom he accuses of greed and unscrupulousness. Aside from this, he has a particular liking for victims of petty morals and narcotics. In his depictions of country life, which contrast sharply with its glorification among his contemporaries (84ff), he pretends to have observed its disastrous consequences even among the fellahs. In the few stories that distinguish themselves from these sinister pieces, such as 'The End of an Artist' (71/80), he is unable achieve his aim of being true to life.

23 ʿAbd al-ʿAzīz ʿUmar al-Sāsī

The way in which ʿAbd al-ʿAzīz ʿUmar al-Sāsī (lic. jur.) depicts images from Egyptian life in his *Min al-aʿmāq* (Alexandria: Maṭbaʿat Ṣalāḥ al-Dīn, 1352/1933) is much more mature.

His work, prefaced by Ḥusayn Haykal and Khalīl Shaybūb (in his capacity as Ra'īs Jamāʿat nashr al-thaqāfa), starts with a reminiscence from his youth (*baʿd ithnayn wa-ʿishrīn ʿāmman*) entitled *Abī*. In the happy childhood of a latecomer in an affluent household, the intitial shadows are cast during his first day at school, the deficiencies of which are painted, like so often, in stark colours,

| until the day on which the death of his elderly father kills all the joy there 240
was. We are led into the world of bourgeois society in stories like *Qalbān fī saʿīr*, about a young man who falls in love with the wife of his acquaintance, even though he had never met her; *Bint al-Bek*, about the spoilt daughter of an affluent family who wins back the love of her husband, a minor official, which she was on the verge of losing; *al-Ṣirāʿ*, about a young man's struggle with his family to make them accept his beloved; and, as a counterpoint to the latter, *Sharīʿat al-ḥubb*, about a young girl from an upper-class family who has to overcome the shyness of her lover, a young lawyer, who does not dare ask for her hand in marriage. Delightful is the story about *Sayyid al-qarya*, whose carnal appetite pushes him to introduce a young woman from the city into his existing household of elderly wives. But she causes him so much trouble that he divorces her, something which does not deter him from looking for someone to replace her some four months later. A counterpiece to this is the story of a poor schoolmaster from the countryside who is transferred to Alexandria where, having left his sickly wife behind, he is seduced into having an affair with a woman from that city. For his daughter, this lady turns out to be an evil stepmother, so the father returns repentantly to his wife during the summer vacation (*al-ʿAwda*). The story of Muṣṭafā takes us into the lives of the lower classes. The son of a newspaper vendor, his father sends him at the age of nine to become a plumber's apprentice. When he proves too weak for this, his father puts him to work in his own business, after which he is soon killed by a car. There is also *Ḥāʾir*, the story of an orphan whose stepfather finds him a job as a conductor on a bus after he failed his first school exam. Hating his work and his unloving stepfather, he runs away and becomes lost without a trace. The author's talent as a writer shows itself especially in his minute depiction of household scenes, even if the characters, in particular those of the younger protagonists, are somewhat underdeveloped. His language is very literary, but without a trace of affectation; he only uses the Egyptian dialect to mark out people from the lower classes.

23a Muḥammad Amīn Ḥassūna

The collection of short stories by the railway engineer Muḥammad Amīn Ḥassūna (see p. 183) entitled *al-Ward al-abyaḍ* (after the first story, as is common in France) (Cairo: Maṭbaʿat al-Shams, 1353/1933), | is called a *majmūʿat* 241
aqāṣīṣ Miṣriyya wa-ṣuwar min al-fann al-qiṣaṣī al-ḥadīth by him.

The book, prefaced by A.H. Baxton of the University of Egypt and by Maḥmūd Taymūr, is almost exclusively about the international scene in Cairo. Taking its example from French literature, like so many other books from that period, the leading roles are for ladies of easy virtue and the unsuspecting young men who get trapped in their webs. They are juxtaposed with the reckless seducers skimming the bathing crowds on the beaches of Alexandria. The unfaithful women of Egypt, on the other hand, are either depicted as the victims of local marriage customs, as in the title story, or as the fortunate beneficiary of native superstitions, as in story no. 11, *Ṣāḥib al-muʿjiza. Fi 'l-wāḥa*, which is a story about a love affair between an American lady and a Bedouin sheikh who has studied in England, stands more or less on its own. Unfortunately, the author missed the opportunity to describe the challenges facing a woman raised in the West when visiting a Bedouin encampment. Instead, he rests content with describing their honeymoon in Upper Egypt with a precision that would honour a travel guide like Baedeker's and then letting the lady perish in a sandstorm when she goes out riding alone soon after their arrival at the camp of her husband's tribe. The main character of the story *al-Adīb Abū Darsh*, a tragic figure who dreams of fame as a poet before becoming an alcoholic, has been sketched before by others; the author is not familiar enough with life in the countryside to be able to come up with new and original aspects to it. *ʿImrān* is just another variation on the much-used theme of deception and juvenile love. In his use of language, the author tries to steer a middle course between a lighthearted, conversational tone and the passionate language of love poetry. The stories are not free from breaches of syntax or Europeanisms, such as Cupido, several times designated as *Kyubid*, based on its English form. In his preface, Maḥmūd Taymūr also praises the volume *Ashbāl al-thawra*, which was not accessible to me.

242 | 24 Tawfīq al-Ḥakīm

Where, previously, the biggest event in the lives of the Egyptian people today, their struggle for freedom, had always remained in the background, in his *ʿAwdat al-rūḥ* (2 vols., written in Paris in 1927 but published in 1933 in Cairo, Maṭbaʿat al-Raghāʾib) Tawfīq al-Ḥakīm tried to sketch the social conditions surrounding this struggle while avoiding its political ramifications.

Both volumes are descibed as forming part of a cycle called *al-Kull fī wāḥid*, whose first and last volumes, entitled *al-Mawtā* and *Hunāka* respectively, though announced as being in press, have not yet been published. The novel seeks to describe life for the average Egyptian, governed by one and the same mentality, be it in the countryside or in the towns. It is the spirit of the farmers of ancient Egypt which, under the Pharaohs, produced a great culture and which, even today, offers the foundations for the advancement of the country. This is demonstrated by the story of three young men living with their elder sister and a black servant, somewhere in Cairo, who provide board and lodging to a young nephew coming to the town for school. The peace of the family is disturbed by the arrival, in the same building, of the pretty daughter of a

retired army doctor. Two of the older single men fall in love with her, but it is the musical talent of the little nephew alone that opens her heart. The boy's juvenile love, his revelling in impossible hopes and expectations, at the very moment at which the young lady herself, who, while full of imagination, is also a realist, is looking for a serious lover, is described in tender words. Such a lover announces himself in the person of the heir of a rich manufacturer who is renting an apartment nearby because, instead of taking over the factory from his father, he would prefer to have a comfortable job as a civil servant. The first to fall in love with him is the spinster, though. Having used all kinds of artifices in trying to conquer the elegant young man's heart, she finds out about the relationship between the younger girl and him and then upsets the peace of both households with an anonymous letter. Returning from a brief
holiday in the countryside, the little nephew is much distressed | at the sudden 243
estrangement of the person whom he secretly loves. As if by divine intervention, he is then snapped out of this by the indignation of the Egyptian people at the forced exile of Saʿd Zaghlūl. While, until then, there was no reason to suspect the family of political leanings of any kind, the five men are then suddenly sucked into the tumultuous events and arrested by the British. Thanks to the intercession of a British civil servant—a friend of the boy's father—they are fortunate enough to be housed in a military hospital. There they become reconciled again after all the problems that the pretty young lady had created. This simple story is seasoned with a number of delightful episodes. The goings-on in a small coffeehouse; the adventures from his years of service in the Sudan with which the retired army doctor entertains his friends; life at the country estate where the boy goes during the holidays and which is run by his Turkish mother, by whom his ethnic Egyptian father is totally outclassed; all of which is depicted with a fresh and sparkling kind of humour. The novel's language is almost entirely free of literary pretences. In the dialogues, which are often very long, everyone speaks in the common vernacular, which also pops up regularly in the story itself. The many Europeanisms leave no doubt that the work was first written in French and only then translated into Arabic.

The novel was re-translated into French by Maurice Berin (?) (see *al-Ahrām* of 12 October 1937, p. 3), reviewed by ʿAlī Ḥammād (*ʿAwdat al-rūḥ, naqd wa-taḥlīl*) in *al-Muqtaṭaf* 84 (1934) 326/36, 474/8), and extensively analysed and acknowledged for what it is in Ṣalāḥ al-Dīn Dhihnī's *Miṣr bayna 'l-iḥtilāl wal-thawra* vol. 2 (Cairo n.d., 1939), p. 67/166.

Even though the novel was written in Paris, it shows hardly any foreign influences in the way it is structured. Yet it is true that, later, Tawfīq al-Ḥakīm turns towards the symbolists, notably Maeterlinck and Jean Grandoux. This was already apparent in a few stories from 1933, such as *Montmartre* in *al-Ḥadīth*,

1933, 669/82, *al-Ḥulm wal-ḥaqīqa, aḥaduhumā shabīh al-ākhar* in *al-Hilāl* 42, 1235/8, and *al-Sāqūn al-thalātha* in *Aḥsan mā katabtu*, 57/60.

The four-act drama *Ahl al-kahf* (second printing Cairo: Maṭbaʿat al-Iʿtimād, 1933) is written along similar lines. It is the story of the Seven Sleepers, which he
244 relocates for the occasion to Tarsus. In the myth of the Islamic | and Christian
traditions, a myth that is no more than hinted at in the Qurʾān, the saints, having awoken from their 300-year sleep, simply die after the news of their miracle has reached the town. But here, in the second act of the play, the author lets them attempt a return to life. In the palace of the Christian king, Mashīlīna (*sic*), the former lover of Prisca, daughter of Decius (here Dekianus), meets the king's daughter, who carries the same name as her ancestor. The resurrected Mashīlīna believes that he has his beloved in front of him, but when his proposals are all rejected, he has to admit that there is an unbridgeable gap between them. His companions, one of whom, searching his family, has found out that his son has been dead for two hundred years, retreated into the cavity where they had slept all those centuries, seeing that it is impossible to pick up life where they left off. So, then, he joins them there, awaiting their death together. But before he departs from this life, Prisca, who has fallen in love with him after all, comes to find him—escorted by her teacher, Gallias—because she wants to die together with him. Before that, she explains the meaning of all this to her teacher by telling him the Japanese fable of the fisherman Ūrāshīmā, who had slept 400 years—rather than just 4, as he himself believed—in the palace of the daughter of the Sea King, and who, returning from the netherworld, had had the same experience as the Seven Sleepers, gaining life on the one hand, but losing all contentment on the other. The dramatic structure is very clever and efficient. The symbolism of the play is nowhere intrusive. Its language is classical throughout, but in a natural manner without any affectation.

His second play, *Muḥammad* (Cairo: Maṭbaʿat Lajnat al-taʾlīf wal-tarjama wal-nashr, 1354/1936), is altogether different. It carries the motto *Qul innamā anā basharun mithlukum yūḥā ilayya*. And, indeed, the intention to sketch a lively image of the appeal of the Prophet is much more important than any symbolism. After a *muqaddima*, which sketches the childhood of the Prophet from the moment of the announcement of his birth to his marriage to Khadīja in eight brief *manāẓir*, there follows a description of his life until the conquest of Mecca in four *faṣl*, to conclude with a *khātima* recounting his death. In
245 his description of the facts, | as well as in most of the dialogue, he copies Ibn
Hishām's account word-for-word, but where Ibn Hishām fails to provide any details, as in the case of the address of Muḥammad's envoy ʿAmr b. Umayya to the Najāshī, he lets the words arise from the situation itself. All this leads to a series of tableaux of unusual dramatic force, much more powerful in its

imagery than however fancy a tale. Following his sources to the letter in his dialogues and accounts, his talent is all the more conspicuous in his choice and structuring of the scenes.

In *Muḥammad*, Tawfīq al-Ḥakīm had kept his imagination in check because he respected religion and its traditions. In the play *Shahrazād* (Cairo: Dār al-Kutub al-Miṣriyya, 1934; French trans. G. Leconte, Paris 1936), on the other hand, it is given much freer reign. The frame-story of the 1001 Nights offered him pliable material which could be moulded freely along symbolist lines. He gives his work the motto of Isis which says: "I am all that was, all that is, and all that shall ever be; no mortal being has ever lifted my veil." In *Taḥta shams al-fikr* 108 he chooses man's struggle with space for a theme. While elsewhere the queen's virgins—spared thanks to Shahrazād's intrigues—are throwing a party, the king, looking in vain to gratify his unquenched lusts, is surprised near the house of some miracle worker by his former executioner, who has long since pawned his sword in some tavern. In another scene, Shahrazād confesses to the vizier Qamar that she did not heal the king out of love, but rather from motives of self-preservation. Meanwhile, the king himself had also understood this. While all the time falling for her charms, he nevertheless undertakes a long voyage in the company of his vizier in order to get away from the danger of his love for her. Fearing the same fate as her predecessor, which she wants to prevent from happening by shaking the king out of his indolence, the queen starts an affair with her male slave while her husband is away. However, on their return, Shahriyār and his vizier do not go to the palace straight away, but first enter the tavern where the executioner had pawned his sword | and where 246
they run into the latter. The vizier buys the sword from the innkeeper. When they later meet the queen, she keeps her slave hidden behind a curtain. When the kings tells his vizier that his sympathies for Shahrazād had been known to him for a long time, the vizier throws himself into the executioner's sword. The king leaves Shahrazād once again, but not before confessing that on his first trip he had let himself be pushed around like a rag doll with no resolve of his own. When the slave offers to go and fetch him back, Shahrazād says that she is convinced that he will return as another person, and terminates with the words: "It is just a white hair that was torn out." Even if some scenes do have some dramatic vigour, this is a play one must read and which is not likely to meet with much success on stage.

The play had a wonderful offspring in the form of *al-Qaṣr al-masḥūr*, a case history he wrote with his friend Ṭāhā Ḥusayn while they were spending the summer in Sallanches, in the Haute Savoie [in France] in 1937 (Cairo: Dār al-Nashr al-Ḥadīth, n.d.). During a hiking trip in the mountains, the author is abducted to Shahrazād's magic castle by one of her servants in order to answer a

series of complaints raised against him by the protagonist of his own play, king Shahriyār, by his vizier Qamar, and by the king's former executioner. When the queen entrusts him to the care of her female servants who are to take him to the baths and get him ready and worthy to meet her, he escapes. Meanwhile, the thought of Shahrazād induces the scholar to interrupt his work on al-Mutanabbī and to go look for her magic castle. When he enters the palace, he is surprised by the female servants who, taking him to be the author, lead him in front of the queen. He succeeds in making her decide to bring the case involving the aforementioned complaints before the court of Time. Meanwhile the female servants have also caught the author who, in turn, is brought before the queen, who hands him over to Time. Time then designates the tower of the church of Combloux as the remand centre. When the court convenes on top of Mont Blanc, the author succeeds in justifying himself, resulting in his acquittal and permission to go and attend the musical festivities in Salzburg. The authors, whose contributions are indistinguishable from one another, have
247 captured and mixed oriental myth | and mountain magic in such an intricate way that the reader is only too happy to follow them in their fantasies, which is another proof that a writer should never give in to philistine temptations.

After a book entitled *Ahl al-Fann* (Cairo: Maṭbaʿat Dār al-Hilāl, 1934), a collection of other plays, *Masraḥiyyāt Tawfīq al-Ḥakīm*, vol. I, *Sirr al-muntaḥira, Nahr al-junūn, Raṣāṣa fi 'l -qalb, Jinsuna 'l-laṭīf* (Cairo: Maṭbaʿat al-Iʿtimād, 1937); II. *al-Khurūj min al-janna, Amām shubbāk al-tadhākir, al-Zammār, Ḥayāt taḥaṭṭamat* (Cairo: Maṭbaʿat Lajnat al-taʾlīf etc., 1937), a story called *Yawmiyyāt nāʾib fi 'l-aryāf* (Cairo: Maṭbaʿat Lajnat al-taʾlīf etc., 1937), all of which are unfortunately not accessible to me, in 1938 he published four volumes of short sketches, the first of which, *ʿUṣfūr min al-sharq*, autobiographical in character, is already sold out.

The second of these four volumes is named after the title of its first story, *ʿAhd al-shayṭān* (Cairo: Maṭbaʿat Lajnat al-taʾlīf etc.). Having read Goethe's *Faust*, the author also wants to conclude a pact with the devil. But unlike Faust he craves not for youth and enjoyment, but for knowledge. When the devil grants him his wish, without any further obligation on his part, and having spent a certain period of time on intensive studies, he cannot help but conclude that he has surrendered his youth to him. In 'In a dream' he goes through the experience of a lover who is shoved aside without ceremony when his beloved's husband comes home a sudden millionaire. In 'Life's tavern' he finds himself, after a brief entanglement with both head waiters, Love and Satan, soon confronted with the last in line: Death. 'Duties towards myself' and 'The angry mistress' are two case histories around *Ahl al-kahf*, while in 'In front of the marble basin' he confronts Shahrazād for the last time. In 'Between dream and reality' we hear a conversation between the artist of Nefertiti and his wife. 'Over the clouds' depicts his experiences on a flight from Cairo to Alexandria. 'Be the enemy of women!' is the maxim of the artist who, like Beethoven, renounces carnal love for the sake of art. 'From eternity' is a satire on the indifference inside a funeral procession and concludes with an address he is considering playing by gramophone at his own funeral.

More earnest in tone is the collection of stories called *Taḥta shams al-fikr* (Cairo, Maṭbaʿat Lajnat al-taʾlīf etc.). | In the first chapter, called 'On religion', 248
he follows Muḥammad ʿAbduh in defending Islam against Hanotaux as a religion of pure reason. In the first of the essays that were brought together under the heading *Fi 'l-adab wal-fann wal-thaqāfa*, he discusses the question of the foundations of Egyptian culture, such as in a letter to Ṭāhā Ḥusayn from Damanhūr, dated May 1933. Like so many of his contemporaries, he is worried about the disconnect between the ancient culture of Egypt and the culture of the Arabs that dominates his country. He senses an affinity between the cultures of India and of ancient Egypt and believes that their opposition to Hellenism is borne out by their relationship to nature. In his understanding, the riches of Egypt and India explain why people there have a habit of turning away from life, while the Greeks, due to their struggle with the aridity of their lands, are much more attuned to it. In this sense, they are related to the Arabs, whom he justly denies the capacity of a total vision. In the footsteps of Nietzsche, he regrets the fact that Euripides chased the spirit of Dionisius from Greek drama, thinking that he was an Asian god. He wishes for the new art of his fellow-Egyptians to marry matter and spirit, movement and rest, and architecture and the decorative arts, in the same way in which this amalgamation had once come to maturity among the Greeks. In a letter about literary criticism, addressed to Ṭāhā Ḥusayn, written in Kūm Ḥammāda, and dated September 1933, he builds on this. Turning against the one-sided, sociological-evolutionary criticism of Spencer, Ruskin, and H. Taine, he insists on an amalgamation in Egyptian art, literary criticism included, between, on the one hand, the ancient Egyptian sense of harmony as incorporated by the pyramids and, on the other, the subjective sense of taste of the *udabāʾ* of ancient Arabic literature. In an interview with a journalist he develops the artistic aims of his *Ahl al-kahf* once more. This play, which he had never thought of bringing onto stage, was intended to express the ancient Egyptian theme of "man and time", in the same way in which ancient Greek drama represented man's struggle with fate, and his own *Shahrazād* represented man's struggle with space. He then continues by expressing his hope of finding another opportunity to write a play in which he can give a role to a choir in the manner of a Greek tragedy. And in the same way he wants to see the specific role of the Egyptian spirit

249 | safeguarded in the universe of human cultures, he also expresses the hope that the Orient as a whole can soon shake off the lethargy into which it has sunk due to its infatuation with European civilization. At the same time, he hopes that the Arab world, too, even if it follows a political and economical course of its own, will render its own spirit victorious over that of Europe.

The chapter *Fi 'l-siyāsa* opens with a letter to Manṣūr Fahmī dated March 1938 that contains a fictitious election address in parliament, in which he explains that democracy is, essentially, a system in which a crowd of hungry bare-footed people provide the arrogant rich with a monthly income of 40 guineas. Similarly bitter in tone is his description of the general tendency among the people to live on welfare instead of relying on their own strength. He lets two former ministers meet in Paradise, both visibly surprised to run into the other there. The only thing both miss in their eternal bliss is the arbitrary use of power which they enjoyed during their days on earth. He terminates the chapter with the song of Horus to Osiris from the *Book of the Dead*, and whose call to resurrection must be heard by all the people of Egypt.

At the end he holds a warm plea for women's rights in academia and the arts, although his earlier reservations have not disappeared altogether. Even if he believes that, in theory, it is possible for an artist to love both his art and his spouse, he still warns against the inconvenience: a beautiful woman has no other goal than to rob a man of his art or whatever profession he has, just to have him all to herself.

In *Ta'rīkh ḥayāt ma'ida* ('Biography of a stomach', Cairo: Maṭba'at Lajnat al-ta'līf etc., 1938), the reader is put into an entirely different situation. Using anecdotes on freeloaders and pimps, such as are well known from ancient *adab* works (al-Khaṭīb al-Baghdādī lists them in his fifth-century *Kitāb al-taṭfīl* I, 464), enriched with a series of amusing jokes, it tells the story of two of such characters, Ash'ab and Bunān, and in which a cheapskate called al-Kindī serves
250 as backdrop. He transfers the story to Medina and the time of | the caliph al-Ma'mūn. Enlivened with countless verses in the style of the 1001 Nights, it shows what a modern artist can achieve when drawing upon the rich mosaic of ancient literature. The language of the book is classic in its simplicity and it is just because of the inclusion of the names of numerous medieval dishes that it has this special ring.

In 1939, Tawfīq al-Ḥakīm returned to writing drama with *Prāksā aw mushkilat al-ḥukm* (Cairo: Maṭba'at al-Tawakkul). In this, he turns the subject of Aristophanes' *Ekklesiazousai* into a comedy on power in the state, in a way similar to how the *académicien* Maurice Donnay did in 1893, when he transposed

Aristophanes' *Lysistrata* to a modern ideological setting. The female protagonist, Prāksāgorā, whose name is mostly abbreviated to Prāksā, convenes a meeting of women, with beards and in men's cloths, in order to talk about saving the state of Athens, threatened by Lacedaemon. The author here follows the original in the scene with Blepyros and Chremes, but for the rest he goes his own way. The hero of the story has just been elected head of state when she immediately finds herself confronted with all kinds of nonsensical requests from her entourage. But when the Spartans attack, she defeats their commander Hieronymus and draws all state power to herself. The final act shows Prāksā's aide, Epikrates the philosopher, in jail. When Prāksā visits him there, she is surprised by Hieronymus. He throws her in jail as well because people in power must be unmoved by rational or sentimental considerations. More than in the work of the French author, Aristophanes' satire has here been amplified to a universal level of humanity. But it is precisely because of this that it has lost its sharp edges and thus allows its comical scenes to stand out better. The snappy dialogue would guarantee its success if put on stage, if only there were a theatre company with the guts to do so.

The same publisher announced another play, *Rāqiṣat al-maʿbad*, as forthcoming in this same year, 1939, but I have not seen it yet.

25 Maḥmūd Ṭāhir Lāshin

The economic conditions of today have led to changes in Egyptian society, bringing about a new phenomenon: the amorous spinster. | Chief-engineer in 251
the *tanẓīm* department Maḥmūd Ṭāhir Lāshīn is the first to have dealt with this subject in a novel entitled *Ḥawwāʾ bi-lā Ādam* (Cairo: n.d. [1934]). Before then, he had published two collections of short stories, *Sukhriyyat al-nāy* and *Yuḥkā an* …, the first of them in 1921.

The independent, economically active woman is a new phenomenon in Egypt, though it is not always easy for them to assert themselves. In this novel she is called Ḥawwāʾ and lives together with an uncle and her grandmother. Having lived in the protective embrace of her backward family until the age of 32, devoting herself entirely to the ideals of her profession and the advancement of female education, she falls for the charms of the first male creature that crosses her path. Brother of one of her female students and son of a pasha, yet a rather mediocre representative of his class and much younger than she, he unintentionally gains her heart. When he marries a woman of his own class not long after that, the teacher commits suicide with poison, wearing a bridal gown. The contrast between the poverty of her surroundings in which she could at least carve out a small realm for herself, and the richness of the pasha's house is developed with a sense of humour. However, the female hero of the story remains in the shadows, perhaps because the author felt he had no right to depict her as representative of her colleagues in her profession.

26 Ḥusayn Fawzī

Besides the travelogues on the Hijaz by al-Batanūnī, Ḥusayn Haykal and al-Māzinī, and the descriptions of Spain mentioned by H. Pérès[163] that will be discussed later, a work of high literary quality which must be mentioned here is the account of a scientific expedition in the Indian Ocean by Dr. Ḥusayn Fawzī, director of the Institute for Hydrology and Fishery in Alexandria, and which was published with the title *Sindbād ʿaṣrī, jawalāt fi 'l-muḥīṭ al-Hindī* (Cairo: Maṭbaʿat al-Iʿtimād, 1938).

252 | In this book, the author tells us that he wrote a play in verse when he was 24 years old (he mentions no title), but that the unsympathetic criticism of an older writer had discouraged him from any further attempts in this field. In 1925, when he was a civil servant working in the ministry of education, he had dedicated a book, *al-Marʾa wa-ārāʾ al-falāsifa*, to the leader of the movement for women's rights Hudā Hānum Shaʿrāwī (see 29c). After these detours outside his own specialism, in 1934 he participated as a physician and biologist in a nine-month expedition to the Indian Ocean, financed by the British government. Having reported elsewhere on the scientific aspects of this expedition, he now shares his memories of it with the general public (in four parts, called *ʿAbath, Ṣuwar, Jidd, Mashāʿir*), allowing him to express the sensations and reflections that this trip aroused in him. In colourful changing scenes, he first tells us about a strange Indian saint, an adventurous trip in a rickshaw, some characteristic types among the inmates, and a number of funny happenings onboard. The second part takes the reader along various stopovers on his route such as the African coast and the Perim and Khuria Muria islands, although he mainly focusses on places of worship in India, which inspire him to reflections on Indian religions, notably Buddhism. He concludes this part with a funny presentation of Ibn Baṭṭūta's report on the women of the Maldives. In the next part he resumes his reflections on Indian culture and Buddhism. A visit to a cinema in Karachi occasions him to voice his justified concern about the harmful influence of European civilization on the cultures of the Orient. A visit to the Seychelles awakens all the memories of the great leader of the Wafd party, Saʿd Zaghlūl, and his captivating description of this unforgettable character of contemporary Egypt constitutes one of the most beautiful

---

163 *L'Espagne vue par les voyageurs musulmans de 1610 à 1930*, Publ. de l'Institut d'Études Or. Faculté des Lettres d'Alger, VI, Paris 1937.

chapters of this book. Serious and funny reflections on nine months of his life in a small, all-male company of Europeans mixed with orientals, together with a description of the delight caused by some British ladies during a stopover in Mombasa and Kenia after a long period of austerity, finish the book. It shows, much better than many a novel, | how a European outlook can be a source of 253
inspiration for a Muslim remaining true to himself.[164] See also *MSOS* XXVIII, 307/8.

27 Al-ʿAqqād, Recent Work

One of the most brilliant prosewriters of modern Egypt, ʿAbbās Maḥmūd al-ʿAqqād, was discussed in great detail on pages 139ff. Here we just add two of his latest works.

In 1936/1355 he published his detailed biography of the father of the nation: *Saʿd Zaghlūl, sīra waṭaniyya* (Maṭbaʿat al-Ḥijāzī, 630 pp.). It is the work of a fervent patriot, which one should not always judge too harshly by historical criteria. Having supported the political career of this leader of the Wafd from day one through his journalism, al-ʿAqqād tries his best to correct and supplement his own reminiscences of him, both through friends and fellow party members, and through European sources, especially Lord Lloyd's *Egypt since Cromer*. All this leads to a very lively portrait of this statesman, throwing new light on many aspects of, notably, his childhood, the beginnings of his political career, family life, and his periods of exile on Malta and the Seychelles. But his judgement on his political legacy, too, is moderate and fair. At the same time, he tries to do justice to his adversaries as well. This is a work of high literary standing. There is no other work in Arabic literature, ancient or modern, which gives such a lively description of an historical person in the context of his time. It will keep the memories alive that the Egyptians have of their struggle for liberation.

The plan of the Syrian government, following the millennial celebrations around al-Mutanabbī, to also commemorate Abu 'l-ʿAlāʾ al-Maʿarrī by restoring his tomb, | inspired al-ʿAqqād, who had often busied himself with the ideas of 254
this blind poet-philosopher, to come up with the bizarre idea of resuscitating him from the grave and taking him on a trip around the world by aeroplane, with the explicit request that he give his opinion on the progress of humanity. This is the story behind *Rajʿat Abi 'l-ʿAlāʾ al-Maʿarrī* (Cairo: Maṭbaʿat Ḥijāzī,

164 One may also mention *Fī qalb Najd wal-Ḥijāz* by Muḥammad Shafīq Efendi Muṣṭafā, Maṭbaʿat al-Manār 1346/1927, and—not accessible to me—the travelogue by Muḥammad Thābit, *Jawla fī rubūʿ al-buldān al-Islāmiyya* (Cairo 1939), on his trips from the Hijaz to Afghanistan, Anatolia and North Africa, see *al-Ahrām* of 3 June 1939, p. 11.

1357/1939), which was published previously in *al-Balāgh* magazine, save for the last four stories. After a general description of the poet, he suddenly provides him with an escort from the delegation that has awakened him from his eternal sleep, calling the latter now a *rasūl* and then a *tilmīdh*, who informs him first of all about the existence of a military regime ruling the country where once he was born. A magical flying carpet then takes them from Syria straight to Germany. Here, the first to meet him are the orientalists, whose work he fully acknowledges. Then he meets some journalists, who are immediately ready to go out and ensure his fame among the Nordic race. When a Jew offers to present him instead to the whole world as the pride of the Semitic race, he laughs and says that he would like to leave that judgement to God. And the socialists of some unnamed country are no luckier when they try to use him as a reference for their teachings. While he does feel happy for a while in Sweden and Norway, he has to confront the Danes, despite a warm reception, with the shortcomings of socialism. In Spain, he witness all the terrors of the civil war, whose happy ending he could not foresee at the time. In an interlude, the poet invites his escort to inform him of Western views regarding the issue of women's rights and then has to endure an explanation involving the philosophy of Schopenhauer. In Britain, he is introduced to the blessings of parliamentary democracy, while in Italy G. d'Annuncio is introduced to him as the successor of Dante. The trip to the United States offers an opportunity for a critical discussion of the value of modern inventions for the happiness of mankind, and also to have a closer look at Roosevelt's 'New Deal.' In the Far East, Chiang Kai-Shek has his complete sympathy. When he lands in the port Jedda on the way home, he is prompted to a comparison between the asceticism of Ibn Saʿūd's Ikhwān and the Indians. In Egypt, the poet is greeted by al-ʿAqqād himself,
255 who has always advocated | the preservation of traditional Muslim values in modern culture. But after this long trip he is too tired to accept al-ʿAqqād's invitation to come with him to his hometown of Aswan. He declines the invitation with a verse from his *Luzūmiyyāt*, the whole book being full of quotations from al-Maʿarrī's works which serve as witty explanations of his comments on the issues of the day.

28 Maḥmūd Taymūr, Recent Work

Let me now briefly discuss the latest work by Maḥmūd Taymūr (cf. p.255), *Firʿawn al-ṣaghīr wa-qiṣaṣ ukhrā* (Cairo: Maṭbaʿat al-Maʿārif, 1939), which was kindly sent to me by the author.

The book acquires a special value because it opens with an autobiography, originally presented as a talk at the American University of Beirut, on 5 March 1938. From this autobiography we need to add on page 218 above that in the

years 1925/7 the author lived in Switzerland, where he studied European literature. This new book shows the author fully matured and at the summit of his art. The title story is about the adventures of a young Egyptian with a libidinous American woman in Heliopolis. Infatuated with ancient Egypt, she falls in love with the young man whom she regards as Tutankhamun restored to life. She passes a romantic night with him among the ruins of Saqqara, after which she disappears without a trace. The second story, *al-Jarīm*, is a kind of counterpart to it. It is about a man of a certain age who wins the heart of a young girl who is still mourning over the death of her childhood lover. Bringing this up in the wrong moment he almost loses her. Two showpieces in this work are again stories from the countryside, just as in his early days. *ʿAzrāʾīl al-qarya* is the story about the friendship between a peasant and a washer of corpses, which turns into fierce animosity when the peasant falls ill and foresees ending up in the other's hands. His hatred increases to such an extent that he burns his enemy in his own house, but then takes charge of his dead body, unwittingly embarking upon a new career. Like al-Hulbāwī (see p. 237), *Rajul rahīb* tells the story of organised gangs disturbing the peace in the countryside. An estate
owner neutralises one of their leaders | by appointing him as a guardian of his 256
estate. The latter takes his work so seriously that one day, when a stepdaughter wants to steal from his master while he is out stealing, he kills her with his own hands, but only after he has retrieved the stolen money. Besides two stories on the life of the demi-monde there are some delightful satires on the goings-on in bourgeois society, which sometimes hit hard, like *Zamān hanāʾ*, or in which satire is couched in friendly sentimentality, as in *Inqilāb*, the original of 'Volte-face' (see p. 225) and *Afdīk bil-rūḥ*. In this work, the book *Nidāʾ al-majhūl, riwāya qiṣaṣiyya*, is announced as being in press.

(29a.–f.) Female Authors

29a Malak Ḥifnī Nāṣif

It was not long before women, too, took possession of the new prose style introduced by men in an effort to assert their right to education. Their leader was Malak Ḥifnī Nāṣif, who wrote under the pen-name of Bāḥithat al-Bādiya.

Born in Cairo on 2 December 1886 as the daughter of Ḥifnī Bek Nāṣif (cf. II, 728), she was the first daughter of a family of standing to move from a French-language primary school to al-Madrasa al-Saniyya, which until then had only been frequented by girls who, because of their poverty, had no access to other education. When she was 16 years old she passed her final exam and obtained her teacher's diploma. From that time onward, she actively encouraged girls from her own social class to follow her example. At the time,

al-Mu'ayyad also published poems and essays by her, promoting better education for girls. In 1907, she married—in the Fayyūm—the sheikh of the al-Rummāḥ tribe, ʿAbd al-Sattār al-Bāsil, who later took part in the Tripolitanian war, which obliged her to run the household all alone for an entire year. Their marriage remaining childless, she started working for the improvement of the situation of women in her husband's tribe, at the same time broadening her own horizons through trips to Turkey and Europe. Furthermore, she continued her literary activity, often spoke at all-women meetings, and established contacts with feminists in England and France. She supported the efforts of Qāsim Amīn (see § 5, 11), even if she thought that his demands sometimes
257 went too far. | In 1911, she presented 10 demands on the subject of women to the legislative council, including the right of access to mosques, a right to the same education as boys, and reforms in marital law (*The Muslim World* XXI, 1926, 279ff). In October of 1918 her brother was arrested during unrest in Cairo and was about to be condemned to death. In spite of a severe flu, she hurried into town to help him. As a result of this, her illness got worse and she died on 12 October 1918.

After her death, her essays, which had mostly been published in *al-Jarīda*,[165] were collected in two volumes by her brother Majd al-Dīn and published under the title *al-Nisā'iyyāt* (Cairo, Maṭbaʿat al-Taqaddum; transl. O. Rescher, *Ueber die aegyptische Frauenfrage*, Constantinople 1926). She took a very moderate stand on the controversial subject of the abolition of the veil, seeing that even in modern life the veil often offers protection where it is needed. For this, she opposed all the more energetically the shortcomings in Muslim marital law, demanding an increase in the legal marriage age for girls while exposing the damages of polygamy with merciless candour. But she not only addressed herself to men; indeed, with the same sharpness she also opposed the backwardness of women and their indifference to education and progress. In all this, she did not look down upon talking in detail about women's clothing either. But, in her view, men are mainly responsible for the backwardness of Egyptian society. She did not shrink from finding fault with the upper classes for the deterioration of the race due to mixed marriages with Circassian women, which became fashionable under Ismāʿīl, and then, later, with substandard European women. But she was not only a sharp critic; in the deepest part of her soul she also was a poet. Even though she did not write much poetry (such as the *marthiya* on ʿĀ'isha Taymūr and her *Qaṣīda nisā'iyya* in answer to a poem by Aḥmad Shawqī), her praise of country life and her tribute to the beauty of the seaside

---

165 The newspaper of the Ḥizb al-Umma, founded in 1901 by Aḥmad Luṭfī Bey al-Sayyid, later minister of education and dean of the University of Egypt.

are genuine poetic effusions, even if there is no metre or rhyme. Her language is feminine, eloquent, and often mischievous in tone. It is therefore somewhat pedantic | for Ḥusayn Walī—in the *taqārīẓ* by leading men of letters (Ismāʿīl 258 Ṣabri, Aḥmad Zakī, Shiblī Shumayyil, and others) that were appended to this work—to criticize her for all kinds of breaches of style.

Mayy, *Bāḥithat al-bādiya, baḥth intiqādī*, C. 1920 (Maṭbaʿat al-Muqtaṭaf), *Khuṭba fī Ḥaflat Dhikrā Bāḥithat al-Bādiya*, in *al-Nisāʾīyāt* II, 39/42, *al-Mashriq* XVIII, 192ff, Cheikho ibid. XXIV, 860, Fatḥiyya Muḥammad, *Balāghat al-Nisāʾ* I, 31/60, *al-Shiʿr al-nisāʾī al-ʿaṣrī* 24/32, Muḥammad Rashīd Riḍā in *al-Manār* XXIII, 188ff. Ch. C. Adams, *Islam and Modernism in Egypt* 235ff.—Her work also inspired a lady from the family of the khedive, Qadriyya Ḥusayn, to write a study called *Shahīrāt al-nisāʾ fi ʾl-ʿālam al-Islāmī* C. 1343/1922, Maṭbaʿat al-Saʿāda, which ʿAbd al-ʿAzīz Amīn al-Khānajī translated from Turkish, as he did her *Malikat Qurṭuba*.

29b Alexandra de Avierino

What had been started by a determined and enthusiastic Muslim woman was continued more successfully and on a larger scale by some Christian women from Syria. The first of these was Alexandra de Avierino.

Born the daughter of Constantine Naʿūma Khūrī in Beirut, she was first educated by the Lazarist nuns in that city and then at the American University. When she was 14 years old she went to Alexandria, where she completed her education studying Arabic language and literature. When she was 16, she married Miltiade de Avierino, whose wealth enabled her to start the first successful women's magazine. While, before her, Hind bint Nawfal had founded the monthly *al-Fatāt* in 1892, followed by the weeklies *Mirʾāt al-ḥasnāʾ* of Maryam Mizhir (1896) and *al-Firdaws* of Louise Ḥabbalīn (1898), it was not long before these were overshadowed by Alexandra's monthly *Anīs al-jalīs*, established in 1898 and for which she secured the cooperation of Egypt's leading men of letters. On 26 March of that year, she presented her magazine to the mother and the spouse of the khedive in a private audience. During the Paris World Fair of 1903, she represented the women of Egypt. Following the fair she visited Istanbul, where she had been invited for the 25th anniversary of the reign of ʿAbd al-Ḥamīd. Back in Egypt, she started the French-language women's magazine *Lutèce*, though this soon closed. The chairwoman of the European Association of Women for Peace, princess | Visniewska,[166] induced her, having 259 remained childless, to add her own name to her family's name.

---

166 Cf. Aḥmad Zakī Bek, *al-Dunyā fī Bārīs* 85, n. 1.

Fatḥiyya Muḥammad, *Balāghat al-Nisāʾ* 81/94, Hartmann, *Ar. Press* 49. As well as articles for her magazine and some *qaṣīda*s, she also published a play called *Shaqāʾ al-ummahāt*.

29c Labība Hāshim Māḍī

From October 1906, *Anīs al-jalīs* received the editorial assistance of Labība Hāshim Māḍī, of Zahle in Lebanon, who had founded the magazine *Fatāt al-sharq* in 1905. Both magazines have often been used here, important as they are as sources on literary developments of the time.

Fatḥiyya Muḥammad, *Balāghat al-Nisāʾ* 96/102 (without biographical data, just the sample *al-Qimār wal-ziwāj*). Besides short stories such as *Jazāʾ al-khiyāna* (on the daughter of the king of Ḥaṭra) in *Fatāt al-sharq* VI, 1911, 30/40, she published *Shīrīn fatāt al-sharq* (Cairo n.d.) and *Qalb al-rajul* (Cairo n.d. [1904]), see Ḥannā Sarkīs in *Anīs al-jalīs* 1904, 1791/6.

29d Mayy Ziyāda

The fruits of the efforts of her predecessors were collected by the most successful female author in the Arabic language, the Catholic Mārī (Miryam) Ziyāda, known through her nickname of "Mayy".

Daughter of Ilyās Ziyāda, of the Keserwan district in Lebanon, who later founded *al-Maḥrūsa* magazine in Cairo, Mayy Ziyāda was born in al-Nāṣira (Nazareth) in 1895. She received her primary education from the Sœurs de la Visitation, which she then completed under the Lazarist nuns in Beirut. After her parents moved to Cairo, she published—using the pen name Isis Copia—a small collection of French poems, entitled *Fleurs de rêves* (1911). In the same year she started her career as a journalist by writing an article for her father's *al-Maḥrūsa* magazine, which was about a lecture held by Labība Hāshim. Initially, she developed and honed her style through translation work, translating a French novel by Brada as *Rujūʿ al-mawja*, and English novel by Conan
260 Doyle as *al-Ḥubb fi ʾl-ʿadhāb*, | and M. Müller's *Deutsche Liebe* as *Ibtisāmāt wa-dumūʿ aw al-Ḥubb al-Almānī* (second printing, Maṭbaʿat al-Hilāl, 1921). In 1915/16 she studied philosophy, literature and history at the University of Egypt. When she left the university again, she addressed—in April 1917 and January 1918—warm words of thanks to her teachers there, the Spanish philosopher de Galarza[167] and the philologists Muḥammad al-Khuḍrī and Muḥammad al-Mahdī. These were later published in *Kalimāt wa-ishārāt* under the titles *al-Baʿth al-ʿatīd* (77ff) and *Wadāʿ al-ustādhayn* (87ff). Her first major publication

167 Whose lectures on the history of philosophy were published as *Muḥāwarāt fi ʾl-ḥikma* (2 vols., Cairo: Maṭbaʿat al-Iʿtimād, 1924 and 1955).

was the biography of Bāḥithat al-Bādiya (Cairo: Maṭbaʿat al-Muqtaṭaf, 1920) which, as an appreciation of her great predecessor, was written with real female empathy and a true literary power of creation. On 29 April 1924 she held a lecture for the women's association Fatāt Miṣr al-Fatāṭ at the University of Egypt, entitled *Ghāyat al-ḥayāt* and published by Maṭbaʿat al-Muqtaṭaf wal-Muqaṭṭam (reprint in Fatḥiyya Muḥammad, *Balāghat al-nisāʾ*, 114/30). These first publications had already secured her fame, so much so that by the time she returned to her native Syria in the summer of 1922 she was enthusiastically received and fêted by the literary communities of Beirut, Zahleh and Damascus. There is a detailed account of this by the editors of *al-Marʾa al-jadīda* magazine, in a special issue entitled *Mayy fī Sūriyā wa-Lubnān*, Beirut 1924.

Walī al-Dīn Yegen wrote a commending foreword to her *Sawāniḥ fatāh* (Cairo: Maṭbaʿat al-Hilāl, 1922). This was her first attempt at narrative prose, which was not as suited to her talents as literary prose or social criticism. In the same year she published a collection of articles that had first appeared in *al-Hilāl*, giving it the title *Kalimāt wa-ishārāt*. Apart from an exposition on the role of women in the history of cultures—a lecture given at a meeting of al-Nādī al-Sharqī in April 1914—special mention must be made of her laudation of her compatriot Khalīl Maṭrān, entitled *al-Shāʿr al-Baʿlabakkī*. It was delivered in April 1913 at the University of Egypt, on the occasion of a festive gathering in honour of Khalīl Maṭrān, after which she also read a laudation by Jabrān Khalīl Jabrān. In 1922 she published a series of essays on the political and social history of mankind, entitled *al-Musāwāt* (Cairo, Maṭbaʿat al-Raḥmāniyya). In 8 chapters | she reviews various social systems, from aristocracy to nihilism. 261
Her learned pedantry in matters of small importance and her blind trust in outdated theories are more than compensated for by her lively style of writing, which is full of female empathy for all matters related to her own sex, even if it be just about some legal claim of ownership which a marriage may create or destroy. Of special interest is her account of the beginnings of the Democratic Party of Egypt and of the socialist movement, though still of minor importance (p. 82ff). She avoids judging the merits of the various theories that she reviews. She discusses them once more in her circle of family and friends and then concludes with a letter by one of these, which limits itself to some suggestions towards satisfying the needs of the lowest classes. In *Ẓulumāt wa-ashiʿʿa* (Maṭbaʿat al-Hilāl) and *Damʿa wabtisāma* (ibid.), she returned in 1923 once more to literary writing. A collection of short stories and essays, entitled *Qaṣāʾid manthūra*, contains among other things the piece *Anā wal-ṭifl*, which is ostensibly about a conversation she had with the 7-year old son of a British officer but which should perhaps be understood as a veiled complaint about

the damages wrought by militarism. In 1924 she published another series of pieces that she wrote as a journalist, called *al-Ṣaḥā'if* (al-Maṭba'a al-Salafiyya). After a collection of aphorisms (*Suṭūr*) on literature and life, there follows first of all *Ṣaḥā'if al-ashkhāṣ*, including an article in appreciation of Dr Shiblī Shumayyil—first published in *Majallat Sarkīs* in 1913—whom she had been able to meet because of his friendship with her father. Her observations on Walī al-Dīn Yegen, Ismā'īl Ṣabrī and the first native Egyptologist, Aḥmad Kamāl (see II, 484, Suppl. II, 735), are also very valuable. Her essays on the art of Michelangelo and on the time of Madame de Sévigné date from 1918. In 1919 she wrote about Jabrān Khalīl Jabrān's *Kitāb al-awākib*. In 1923 she wrote an article in praise of the manes of Pierre Loti and tells the story of the French officer Sèves, who organised the army of Muḥammad 'Alī under the name of Sulaymān Pāshā. A second series of *Ṣaḥā'if* opens with an often hilarious account of her four trips to Syria, and in which her description of a storm at sea shows that she has great creative powers.

A selection of articles she wrote for *al-Hilāl* magazine was published in 1924 (Maṭba'at al-Hilāl) under the title *bayna 'l-jazr wal-madd*. She stands up for the preservation of Classical Arabic as a literary means of expression in an essay
262 on the genesis and destruction of languages. | Then she comes to the defense of al-Majma' al-Lughawī, a precursor of the Academy of Egypt and founded by the director of the National Library Aḥmad Luṭfī Bek, against attacks in *The Egyptian Mail*. Even if she never published any poems herself, her critical observations on the national anthems by Aḥmad Shawqī and Muḥammad al-Harawī show that she has a very fine poetical sense. She was right to stand up for the Arabs, saying that one should not deny their talent for epic poetry, even if she finds that they lack in metres suitable to other moods. On a series of questions regarding the state of affairs in contemporary Arabic literature, by van Beer in the *Revue Belgique*, she answers with a fine sense for the current ambiguities, which she presents as potentialities.

Since then, she has published a great number of shorter articles, mostly in *al-Hilāl*. Among these there is an essay on 'Ā'isha Taymūr and Warda Yāzijī in *al-Muqtaṭaf* of February/May and June/August of 1924, aphorisms in *al-Hilāl* 39 (1930), 37/8, contributions to the language issue, *Taṭawwur al-lugha al-'arabiyya* in *al-Muqtaṭaf* 77 (1930), 249/55, but also short stories such as *al-Sham'a taḥtariq* in *al-Hilāl* 42, 257/62, *al-Ḥubb fī 'l-madrasa bayna tilmīdhayn*, ibid. 43 (1934), 5/10, in addition to all kinds of articles on current issues in literary criticism.

G. Nīqūlā Bāz, *Man hiya Mayy* in *al-Fajr*, Beirut 1923, 5/10, *Dār al-salām*, Baghdad, IV, 2, 17ff, V, 23, 192, E. Rossi in *Or. Mod.* V, 1925, 604/13, Kračkovsky, introduction to Ode Vasilieva, *MSOS* XXXI, 196/7, Kampffmeyer ibid. XXVIII 309, XXIX 256, 261, XXX 220, XXXI, 166, Khemiri and Kampffmeyer, *Leaders* 24/7.

29e Bint al-Shāṭi'

While female authors had thus far gone no further than to champion women's right to a proper education and to show that they, too, could write real literature, from 1936 onward, an anonymous woman, probably a teacher, calling herself Bint al-Shāṭi', | started writing about the most important political and 263
social question in Egypt: the fate of the fellah.

In 1936 she wrote a proposal for hygienic reforms in rural settlements, which she presented to the Lajnat al-mubārāt al-rasmiyya li-tarqiyat al-fallāḥ, in participation in an open contest that she also won. In her *Fi 'l-rīf al-Miṣrī*, she had given a general description of the situation among the people in the countryside in a manner similar to al-Hulbāwī (see p. 236). But in her *Qaḍiyyat al-fallāḥ* of 1938 (Maktabat al-Nahḍa al-Miṣriyya), she develops concrete, well thought-out propositions for the improvement of conditions in rural communities, based on a wealth of statistical data. After a brief sketch of the peasant's question from the days of Muḥammad 'Alī up to the present, followed by a listing of the most important causes of the backwardness of the countryside, she has another look at the government's position on the issue, and concludes that even though the fellah has rendered, and continues to render, invaluable services to the country, yet, right next to our doorstep, he lives a life unworthy of a human being. In a third work, she demonstrates this in detail with data on the material and intellectual standard of living among the fellahs. She discusses in detail how a yearly-increasing exodus from the countryside leads to the flooding of major cities, Cairo especially, with a proletariat that is a menace to its social structure. She plays on the conscience of the great landowners who, until then, had showed hardly any concern for the living conditions of their labourers, pointing time and again to the example set by the agricultural firm and model settlement in Bahtīm and also by the chief judge 'Abd al-'Azīz Pāshā on his estate at Kafr al-Muṣayliḥa, with its foundations for schools and care for the needy. After reminding the peasants how little their representatives have done for them so far, she addresses herself to King Fārūq in person, showing him how the government could lead the country towards a better future for its peasants.

29f Hudā Sha'rāwī

Instead of serving the rights of women through literary works alone, like Mayy and Bint al-Shāṭi', Hudā Sha'rāwī | continues the work of the movement for 264 the improvement of the social situation of women initiated by Malak Ḥifnī Nāṣif.

The daughter of Sulṭān Bāshā, the first president of the Egyptian parliament and representative of khedive Tawfīq, she was born in Minya in the tumultuous year of 1882. She was raised in Cairo and married ʿAlī Bāshā al-Shaʿrāwī who represented the Wafd party at Versailles in 1919 and who died on 14 March 1922. Having participated in many charitable initiatives when her husband was still alive (relief for the victims of the war in Turkey, for instance), she devoted herself entirely to the women's movement once she had become a widow, especially in the field of arts and crafts. In 1923 she founded the Union Féministe Égyptienne and represented Egypt at the International Women's Conference in Rome. At the International Conference Against the Trade in Girls in September of 1924, she presented a report on the efforts of the Egyptian goverment in this area. In October of 1938 she was president of the first Oriental Women's Conference in Cairo, whose acts were published as *al-Muʾtamar al-nisāʾī al-sharqī* in 1939 (Maṭbaʿat al-ʿAṣriyya).

Majd al-Dīn Ḥifnī Nāṣif in Fatḥiyya Muḥammad, *Balāghat al-nisāʾ* 61/85, *MSOS* XXXI, 107, Adams, 231, 236, 239. See also Iḥsān Aḥmad al-Qūṣī (of Beirut), *Lamḥa taʾrīkhiyya ʿani ʾl-nahḍa al-niswiyya al-Miṣriyya*, C. 1930, R. Fr. Woodsmall, *Moslem Women Enter a New World*, London 1936 (Publ. of the Amer. Un. of Beirut, Social ser. 14).

3 *Drama*

Muḥammad Taymūr, *Ḥayātuna ʾl-tamthīliyya* (*Muʾallafāt Muḥammad Taymūr* II), Maṭbaʿat al-Iʿtimād, 1922.

Curt Prüfer, Drama—Arabic, in *Encyclopaedia of Religion and Ethics* IV, 1911, 876/8.

Nevill Barbour, The Arabic Theatre in Egypt, in *BSOS* VIII, 1935, 173/87, 991/1012.

ʿUthmān Ḥamdī, *Fī ʿālam al-tamthīl, Taʿrīb* Cairo n.d. (Maṭbaʿat al-Saʿāda).[168]

168 This book, written for those who want to stage plays at schools or in theatrical societies, opens with directions for everything to do with technical and practical things on and around the stage, among other things 'The art of make- up' (translated from the English works of Cavendish Morton, Arthur Peerson and others), and then continues with some small pieces and individual scenes, 'The rehearsal' in one act, the scene between Hamlet and his mother, the monologue of the messenger from Oedipus, *al-Malāḥāt al-fiḍḍiyya* after Stuart Washing, a dialogue between a poet and an apparition (*Ṭayf*) after Kāmil Bek Ḥajjāj, and 'The blind man', a drama in one act by the author himself.

Maḥmūd Efendi Khalīl Rāshid, *Fann al-tamthīl* Alexandria, Maṭbaʿat al-Rashād n.d.

1 The Theatre in Egypt 265

The precursor of Arabic drama, the shadow play, which made its first appearance in the Muslim world during the Middle Ages and which has remained a popular amusement until today, will not be part of this account, which is only about drama as a literary category. The latter only made its appearance in the nineteenth century as a result of foreign—first Italian, then French—influence, and it is only in the twentieth century that it has become an artistic discipline at the national level.

For a general overview of the history of the theatre and the dramatic arts, I refer the reader to Taymūr and Barbour. Here, we can only highlight the most important data, necessary to understand the developments from a literary point of view. As was the case for the novel, drama too, was first introduced by the Syrians. In volume II, page 754, the founder of the first theatre in Beirut, Mārūn Naqqāsh, was mentioned. The opera of Cairo and the comedy house in the Ezbekiyya Gardens, founded by the khedive Ismāʿīl, were initially only used by the European military. It was not until around 1870 that a Jew by the name of Yaʿqūb (James) b. Rafāʾīl Ṣanūʿ—famous as al-Shaykh Ṣanūʿ Abū Naḍḍāra (b. 1839), who had studied in Italy and worked as a language teacher in Cairo—succeeded in drawing the khedive's attention to some of his plays in Italian and Arabic, which were then put on stage at the opera house. Later he was disgraced and banished, dying in France in 1912.

The only play by him to have been published is *Mūlyīr Miṣr wa-mā yuqāsīhi* (Beirut, 1912; Cairo[2] IV, 127). Written in the common vernacular, it is about the ups and downs of the director of a theatre in Egypt. He became very well-known with his comical magazine *Abū Naḍḍāra*, on which see Hartmann, *Ar. Press* 82, *MSOS*, 31, 176, *WI*, XI 181. 266

Together with his friend Adīb Isḥāq al-Dimashqī (II, 759), a nephew of Mārūn Naqqāsh named Salīm Khalīl Naqqāsh continued the efforts of his uncle in Beirut, bringing Arabic adaptations of French plays—of which only *Andromache* was preserved in print—and of Ghislanzoni's text to Verdi's Aïda[169] onto the stage. In 1876 they tried to introduce their art in Alexandria as well, but without success. After a tour of the provinces, one of the actors in their

---

169 *ʿĀʾīda, trājīda dhāt khamsat fuṣūl, taʾlīf Salīm Khalīl Naqqāsh*, Beirut, al-Maṭbaʿa al-Sūriyya, 1875, performed among others by the company of Iskandar Ṣayqalī in Beirut, on 13 February 1886 (notes in M. Hartmann's copy).

company, Yūsuf al-Khayyāṭ, went to Cairo in 1878, where the khedive put the opera house at his disposal. But the ruler did not like the piece that he put on, *al-Ẓalūm*, thinking that he was ridiculed in it, and so he had the unfortunate actor deported.

Khalīl al-Yāzijī's verse drama *al-Murūʾa wal-wafāʾ* was never put on the stage in Egypt.

One of the earliest attempts at Arabic drama was *Riwāyat Abi ʾl-Futūḥ al-Malik al-Nāṣir, tashkhīṣiyya dhāt khamsat fuṣūl min qalam Muḥammad al-Sikandarī al-Iyādī*, Alexandria n.d. (ca. 1880?).

The play unfolds in an imaginary world in which an Arab and a Persian kingdom are at war. The nephew of the Arab king Hishām, ʿAdī, is married to the daughter of the Persian king Irildām, whose name is Iksīr. ʿAdī was the next in line to the throne, provided that the marriage of his uncle remain childless. But then, when the latter fathers a son, he fears some act of betrayal on the part of ʿAdī and tries to cause his destruction. Against the advice of one of his viziers, he first has him incarcerated, but when Ildirām declares war on him, demanding that he hand over Iraq, he sees no other solution than to liberate his nephew, the most able of his commanders, and entrust him with the
267 command of the campaign. | However, the latter takes revenge by leading his army to the Persian king. Together with him, he defeats his uncle and when the latter is taken prisoner has him killed. But now the Persian king is overcome by fear of also being betrayed by him. At the suggestion of one of his viziers, he plans to have him poisoned. But ʿAdī learns about this and anticipates his father-in-law by having him disposed of. In the final act we see him at the height of his success, a king of two nations with a loving wife, even if she regrets her father's death. The play is not without dramatic excitement. The account in the first act, which takes place in the apartments of Iksīr, is not bad. And the scene in the second act, in which ʿAdī, imprisoned, still believes himself to have been mistakenly convicted, certainly contributes to the image of the typical hero, beloved by his people. Yet these beginnings are almost completely obscured by protracted dialogues in which prose and lyrical passages take turns. It seems these dialogues and the lyrics in between—just the melodies are given—were to the taste of the public, if the piece was ever brought onto stage at all. Even if the language is supposedly classical throughout, it mimics the style and phraseology of medieval romances.

It was only in 1882 that Khedive Tawfīq again opened the doors of the operahouse to a theatre company from Syria, one put together by Sulaymān Qardāḥī by adding new blood to some of al-Khayyāṭ's former colleagues in the art. He was the first who dared let women perform, one of whom was his wife. As

part of this group, Salāma Ḥijāzī of Alexandria, who had started his career as a *mu'adhdhin* and Qur'ān reciter, made his first appearance on stage. Later, he joined the company of Iskandar Faraḥ for 18 years. In spite of his efforts, he was not able to assert himself as an actor because the public only liked his voice. In 1904/5, he had his own theatre, the *Dār al-tamthīl al-ʿArabī* near the Ezbekiyya gardens, which was a great success, but he had to retire because of ill-health. | It was not until 1910 that he could perform again in Tunis. In 1914/6, he co- 268
operated with Jūrj Abyaḍ, dying in 1917. He was also active as a composer, his greatest successes being the operas *ʿĀʾida* and *ʿIẓat al-Mulūk*. (cf. Taymūr, 123/43).

After an interruption because of the ʿArābī uprising, al-Qardāḥī was only able to resume his activities at the operahouse in 1884, but then he had to leave for the provinces, leasing his own theatre in Cairo in later years. He died in Tunis in 1909.

In Cairo, it was not long before he was faced with competition from his compatriot Abū Khalīl al-Qabbānī. The latter had had to give up his theatre in Damascus because the notables there were offended by the representation of Hārūn al-Rashīd in Mārūn's *Abu 'l-Ḥasan al-Mughaffal*. In his new theatre in al-ʿAtaba al-Khaḍrāʾ he mostly staged musical comedies with ballet.

In 1886, the actor Iskandar Faraḥ parted ways with him and started his own theatre. For 18 years, this theatre was supplied with attractive plays by the translators Najīb and Amīn Ḥaddād, Tanyūs ʿAbduh and Ilyās Fayyāḍ, while the mainstay was Salāma Ḥijāzī. After the latter's departure he tried to stage plays without music, but without success.

On Amīn al-Ḥaddād, see p. 84 k., and Cheikho, *Mashriq* XXIV, 442. His brother Najīb, born in Beirut in 1867, went to Alexandria after the ʿArābī uprising, working as a journalist for *al-Ahrām*. Together with his brother Amīn he founded the *Jarīdat lisān al-ʿArab* in 1894 and, when that closed down again soon after, a weekly magazine. He later returned to Alexandria, where he became editor-in-chief of *Anīs al-jalīs*. His translations, among others of Corneille's *Le Cid*, were hailed by al-Manfalūṭī as real works of art. His play *Riwāyat Ṣalāḥ al-Dīn* was published in Alexandria in 1898. His collection of juvenile poems, *Tidhkār al-ṣibā*, was published in Beirut in 1899, and then in Baʿabda in 1906. He died at an early age in 1899. See J. Zaydān, | *Taʾrīkh al-ādāb al-ʿarabiyya* 269
II, 142, *Tarājim mashāhīr al-sharq* II, 325, Sarkīs 744, Hartmann, *Ar. Press* 26, 56 II 762.

Ṭānyūs ʿAbduh came from Lebanon, to where he returned during the [First] World War. As a journalist, he was amazingly productive. Apart from the daily newspaper *al-Sharq*, he also published the weeklies *al-Rāwī* and *Faṣl al-khiṭāb*.

It is said that he also translated and adapted no less than 700 plays.[170] Volume I of his *Dīwān* was published in Cairo in 1925 (Maṭbaʿat al-Hilāl), prefaced by Anṭūn Jumayyil and Khalīl Maṭrān, with a dedication to Jupiter in reference to the well-known parable. Apart from the usual occasional poems, it contains also a number of political songs, such as those on the Ottoman constitution and the Lebanese flag. While usually sticking rigorously to the *qaṣīda*, in *Rāḥat al-ʿāshiq* (p. 93) he instead uses the *radīf* rhyme (see Ṣāliḥ al-Jiddāwī, *Naẓarāt naqdiyya*, p. 204). He also wrote two stories, *al-ʿUlba al-mafqūda* (Cairo 1914) and *Murawwidāt al-usūd* (Cairo 1926).

Around 1900 the Egyptian theatre was still at such a low level that the government could only send a theatre company to the World Fair in Paris that, besides plays like *ʿAntar* and *Waqāʾiʿ Kisrā maʿa ʾl-ʿArab*, was also able to perform mostly oriental dance pieces in the fair's beautifully equipped theatre, such as the infamous belly-dance. See Aḥmad Zakī Bek, *al-Dunyā fī Bārīs*, 97/8, who could only praise this company for the strict measures that its director had taken to keep its male and female members separate before and after performances.

270 | The years 1910/25 saw the blossoming of the theatre companies of the three brothers ʿUkkāsha: ʿAbdallāh, ʿAbd al-Ḥamīd and Zakī (Taymūr, 198/212) and which only provided simple and plain entertainment, without any artistic objective. In 1924, they founded a theatre company that built its own theatre in the Ezbekiyya gardens with the support of Ṭalʿat Bāshā Ḥarb and the Société Miṣr. The theatre is currently leased by Zakī.

The most famous comedian in Cairo today is ʿAzīz ʿĪd, a Syrian by birth who has more than 30 years of experience on stage and who runs his own theatre company together with his wife Fāṭima Rushdī (Taymūr, 159/67). The latter enjoys the special affection of the youth as *ṣadīqat al-ṭalaba*, but is equally able to play tragic roles such as in Shawqī's *Cleopatra* and men's parts like Marcus Antonius in Shakespeare's *Caesar* or in Rostand's *Aiglon*. With her company she also made successful tours in Palestine, Syria and Iraq, and in the summer of 1932 across North Africa all the way to Morocco.

---

170 He adapted Schiller's *Kabale und Liebe* as *Riwāyat gharām waḥtiyāl, trājīda nathriyya shiʿriyya dhāt khamsat fuṣūl*, Cairo: Maṭbaʿat al-ʿUmūmiyya, n.d. On the whole, he sticks very closely to the plot and only removes some intermediary scenes. However, the dialogue has been completely rewritten and made to fit oriental understandings. In scenes that are more emotional he often breaks into lyrical effusion. Other translations are mentioned in Sarkīs, *Jāmiʿ al-taṣānīf al-ḥadītha* I, 18, 1102, 1104, II, 224.

She came from the Ramsīs theatre company, which was founded in 1923—together with ʿAzīz ʿĪd—by the affluent Yūsuf Wahbī, son of a Turkish pasha, on his return from Italy, where he had devoted much of his time to the theatre.

He made several successful tours in Syria and Palestine and in 1928 even went all the way to Buenos Aires, where he was almost more popular among the Spanish-speaking people than among the Syrians living there. Because of financial problems, both companies were dissolved in 1933. The government tried unsuccessfully to stimulate a merger between them, giving them a subsidy that was insufficient.

The first actress of purely Egyptian descent was Munīra al-Mahdiyya (see Taymūr, 174/86). She started her career as a singer in *Carmen*, then continued
with her own company with which she performed mostly romantic | pieces 271
such as *Ṣalāḥ al-Dīn* after Scott's *Talisman*, and in which she mostly played male parts.

2 Muḥammad Taymūr

A tragic episode in the history of Egyptian theatre was the end of Muḥammad Taymūr's (cf. p. 127) activities as a result of his untimely death. If he had been granted a longer life, he might have created the comic theatre that Muḥammad ʿUthmān Jalāl had vainly tried to start.

As a law student in Paris, he was already crazy about theatre. When he got stuck in Egypt due to the outbreak of the war, he joined the *Jamāʿat anṣār al-tamthīl* that had been founded in March 1914 by Muḥammad ʿAbd al-Raḥīm, who had received his theatrical education in England. He succeeded in overcoming his father's initial resistance to his hobby. At the opera, he played the role of the emir Sayf al-Dīn in *ʿAzza bint al-Khalīfa* in a showing that was attended by Sultan Ḥusayn himself, and also played the marquis in *al-ʿArāʾis*, based on P. Wolf's *Marionettes* in an adaptation by Ismāʿīl Bek Wahbī.[171] His real talent only revealed itself when he himself started writing comedy plays based on the daily lives of the Egyptians, entirely in the common vernacular. The only piece he wrote in Classical Arabic was *ʿUṣfūr fi ʾl-qafaṣ*.

The third volume of his *Muʾallafāt, al-Masraḥ al-Miṣrī* (Maṭbaʿat al-Salafiyya, 1341), contains three plays with a preface by Maḥmūd ʿIzzī. The first of these, *Riwāyat al-ʿuṣfūr fi ʾl-qafaṣ, kūmīdī Miṣriyya dhāt arbaʿat fuṣūl*, had its premiere in the Printania theatre on 1 March 1918, in a performance by the theatrical company of ʿAbd al-Raḥmān Rushdī. The hero of the story is a young man who, bullied by his tyrannical father, falls in love with the French maid Marguérite.

---

171 This is according to Zakī Ṭulaymāt in the preface to *Ḥayātuna ʾl-tanthīliyya* 46ff; this is contra Barbour, op. cit., 179.

When the latter becomes pregnant with his child, he sees a way to wrench himself loose from his father's grip. And at the end, even the tyrant, convinced of his son's happiness, becomes a loving grandfather.

272 | Much sharper is the satire of his second play, *Risālat ʿAbd al-Sattār Efendi, kūmīdī Miṣriyya akhlāqiyya, dhāt arbaʿa fuṣūl*, which had its debut in December 1918 in the Dār al-tamthīl al-ʿarabī of Ustādh ʿAzīz ʿĪd, in a performance by the theatrical company of Munīra al-Mahdiyya. The story is about the marital bliss of a young girl whom her brother wants to marry off to a confidence trickster who has promised him a rich bride in return. Totally dominated by his wife and son, the father, in an act of competition with the latter, makes a pass at the maid who, when she sees herself betrayed by the son, teams up with the janitor to thwart the marriage plans. The family is finally released from the many comical and embarrassing situations that the double intrigue brings about when the suitor of the girl's liking receives a large inheritance and the confidence trickster is unmasked. Both pieces, which portray the lives of the upper-middle classes with their exclusive interest in material gain, their hedonism, and their prejudices, at times in blatant scenes, are very well structured and must have had their desired effect on a public with a sense of humour. They are entirely in the common vernacular, but apparently not in an effort to distinguish social classes one from the other. Completely different is the third piece, *Risālat al-ʿashara al-ṭayyiba, ūbirā buff dhāt arbaʿa fuṣūl wa-thalātha manāẓir, wadaʿa azjālahā Badīʿ Efendi Khayrī, laḥanahā al-shaykh Sayyid Darwīsh*. It had its debut on 11 March 1920 in a performance by the Firqat al-Kazīnū de Bārīs under the leadership of ʿAzīz ʿĪd. The story unfolds at the time of the Mamlūks and is about the retrieval of the daughter of the *wālī* of Cairo who had disappeared immediately after her birth and grown up in the countryside. It is also about one of her father's notables, Sayf al-Dīn, who, disguised as a peasant, wins her heart and to whom she, after he brings her back to her parents, is about to be given in marriage, seemingly against her will. This piece employs much coarser means while its comic scenes are much more vulgar. It tries to bring out the atmosphere of the time by the use of the strongly Turkicised Arabic of the upper classes and with borrowings from peasant dialects. We are not in a position to judge the effect of all this on stage. In his fourth play, *al-Hāwiya, kūmīdī drām dhāt thalātha fuṣūl*, printed at the end of the second volume of his *Muʾallafāt* (331/451) and which had its premiere on 6 April 1921 in a performance by the
273 *Shirkat tarqiyat al-tamthīl* | *al-ʿarabī* (ʿUkkāsha and associates), Taymūr returns to social comedy, using even cruder means. The play describes the goings-on in the life of someone who inherited a fortune but is addicted to alcohol and cocaine. He is surrounded by freeloaders, one of whom not only cheats him out of a country estate but almost sleeps with his wife as well. The latter is spared

this disgrace only because her totally drunk husband visits her lover's apartment at the time of their rendezvous, even if he fails to sense her presence. When he learns from a friend about the true state of things he totally collapses and dies of a cocaine overdose. Even if this play, very coarse at times, will certainly have had a comic effect on stage, it is also rather exaggerated, especially because the characters remain entirely superficial.

Muḥammad Taymūr's studies on the history of drama among the Greeks, in French classicism and in Egypt—published in the second volume—show just how seriously he took his theatrical mission. The most informative of these is *Muḥākamat muʾallifi 'l-riwāyāt al-tamthīliyya*, which was first published in 1920 in *Jarīdat al-sufūr*. In this essay, the most well-known drama authors of Egypt are called to appear before a panel of classical authors from all times and all places, presided over by Shakespeare. They are then submitted to a comic interrogation and duly sentenced. The piece is followed by descriptions of the most important actors and some *munulūjāt* and *qaṣāʾid tamthīliyya*.

(3.–5.) *Other Plays*

3 Jūrj Abyaḍ and Zakī Tulaymāt

The government of Egypt has twice tried to raise the level of Egyptian drama by sending talented actors abroad to study. ʿAbbās II had noticed the talent of a Syrian named Jūrj Abyaḍ, who worked as a stationmaster in Alexandria, and sent him to Paris, to the famous actor Sylvain. After his return in 1910 he assembled a company around him with which he initially achieved great success, but which he was unable to perpetuate. When the foreign military was away during the war | he took possession of the opera house. In 1920 he made 274
a tour of the Maghreb that was especially successful in Tunis and Tripoli. The sophisticated Francophile audience of Algiers, on the other hand, did not approve of his art (Taymūr 131/42).

A second attempt was made in 1924, when Zakī Ṭulaymāt—secretary of the zoological garden—was sent for four years to Paris to study at the Théatre de l'Odéon. After his return, it was at his suggestion that the ministry of education founded the actor's academy *Maʿhad fann al-tamthīl* in 1930. At this academy, Ṭāhā Ḥusayn gave courses on the history of drama and Aḥmad Ḍayf on Arabic literature. But within a year of its opening, its opponents, especially offended by the mixed courses that it offered to its male and female students, succeeded in convincing the new minister, Ḥilmī ʿĪsā Pāshā, to close it down. Zakī Ṭulaymāt tried to compensate for this as best he could by organising lectures at the Qāʿat al-muḥāḍarāt of al-Madrasa al-Ibrāhīmiyya, which he did together with Jūrj Abyaḍ and others. When the theatrical companies of Fāṭima

Rushdī and Yūsuf Wahbī had gone bankrupt, the government entrusted him, in Autumn 1933, with the management of an *Ittiḥād al-mumaththilīn* that performed at the Alhambra cinema for the remainder of the season, but which was later dissolved due to lack of success.

4 Muḥammad Rashād Ḥāfiẓ et al.

The prize contests organised by the ministry of education in 1925 and 1932 were complete failures. The winning play of 1932, *Samīra* by Muḥammad Rashād Ḥāfiẓ, was refused by all theatre directors, and even the performance of it by Zakī Ṭulaymāt, which the ministry had made possible at the opera house, found no acclaim. The playwrights who received second place fared
275 no better. Of these, Fransīs Shiftāsī's *Ibnat al-shams* and | ʿĀdil al-Ghaḍbān's (who went to school with the Jesuits) *Ahmas al-awwal aw Ṭard al-rūʿāt* (i.e. the Hyksos) (Cairo: al-Maṭbaʿa al-ʿAṣriyya, 1933) were clumsy imitations of classical French plays (see Barbour, op. cit., 999) in old-Egyptian garb, while ʿAbdallāh ʿAfīfī's (see p. 233) *al-Hādī* (Cairo: Maṭbaʿat al-Maʿārif, n.d.) was situated in the ʿAbbāsid era and Muḥammad Khurshīd's *al-ʿAwāṭif* in modern times.

5 Aḥmad Shawqī et al.

While Aḥmad Shawqī's *Cleopatra* and *Majnūn Laylā* were at least met with consideration at the time of their performance, Abū Shādī's opera libretto's and his adaptation of Shakespeare's *The Tempest* never made it to the stage. A translation of *The Tempest* by Aḥmad Rāmī, on the other hand, was brought to stage by Fāṭima Rushdī. Tawfīq al-Ḥakīm's religious plays are, by their subject, excluded from the stage.[172] On page 98 we mentioned Khalīl Maṭrān's efforts in the dramatic arts, from 1934 onwards, as leader of his own ensemble. Merely by their language, these works are all totally incomprehensible to the larger public. In spite of this, Ṭāhā Ḥusayn again champions their unique presence on stage, this time in an article in *al-Ḥadīth* from 1934, p. 233ff.

(*6a.–m.*) *Miscellaneous Playwrights*

Here we should briefly mention some other playwrights who, like Faraḥ Anṭūn (see p. 192ff), catered to the taste of the masses, as well as some authors who set themselves higher goals.

---

172 When an Egyptian theatre company wanted to stage a piece that featured the Prophet, outside of the country, the clergy prevented this from happening by putting political pressure. See Ṭāhā Ḥusayn, *Min baʿīd*, 241.

6a Muḥammad Luṭfī Jumʿa

The lawyer Muḥammad Luṭfī Jumʿa is just as many-sided as Faraḥ Anṭūn. He studied in Lyon, France, and was a contributor to the *Jarīdat al-Ẓāhir*. In his plays he has a preference for | historical subjects, such as in *Nero*, but at 276
times he also tried his hand at psychological drama, as in *Qalb al-marʾa* (see Taymūr, 94/103). He started his literary activity with the political work *Taḥrīr Miṣr* (Cairo 1324/1906). This was followed in 1911 by the *Muḥāḍarāt fī taʾrīkh al-mabādīʾ al-iqtiṣādiyya wal-niẓāmāt al-ūrūbiyya*, vol. 1. In 1912 he published, besides *Layāli ʾl-rūḥ al-ḥāʾir* (p. 195), a translation of Macchiavelli's *The Prince*, titled *Kitāb al-amīr* (Maṭbaʿat al-Maʿārif), selections from Saʿdī's *Gulistān* and from a work by the Japanese philosopher Ednadigako (?) on the education of women (from an English version) with the title *al-Ḥikma al-mashriqiyya*, and *Ḥikam Nabulyūn* (Maṭbaʿat al-Taʾlīf). In 1926 he participated in the criticism of Ṭāhā Ḥusayn with the book *al-Shihāb al-rāṣid* (see Suppl. I, 32, note 1, on which see Muḥammad Kurd ʿAlī, RAAD VII, 89/90). His *Taʾrīkh falsafat al-Islām fi ʾl-mashriq wal-maghrib* (Maṭbaʿat al-Maʿārif, 1345/1927) was identified by Maḥmūd Muḥammad al-Khuḍarī as a plagiarism of S. Munk, *Mélanges de philosophie juive et arabe* (Paris 1859) in *al-Siyāsa* of 29 October 1927. Taymūr (op. cit., 96) mentions two novels, *Fī buyūt al-nās* and *Fī dār al-humūm*, which are missing in Sarkīs, 1692/3.

6b Ibrāhīm Ramzī

Ibrāhīm Ramzī, an official in the ministry of agriculture, had achieved a certain level of fame through his successful plays *al-Ḥākim bi-amri ʾllāh* and *Abṭāl al-Manṣūra*. This induced him to rush into the production of other plays; he is said to have brought out the plays *al-Badawiyya, Richelieu, al-Amīr Shalīm, al-Huwārī, Ḥanjal Būbū* and *Abṭāl al-Manṣūra*, all within the space of six months. He used the common vernacular in his *Dukhūl al-ḥammām mish zāy khurūguh*, which was first performed in 1917 and published in 1924 (Maṭbaʿat al-Salafiyya) (Taymūr, 85/93, Barbour, 998, n. 1).

6c Aḥmad Ḥāʾirī Saʿīd

Aḥmad Ḥāʾirī Saʿīd was born in 1894, studied medicine from 1912 onward and served in the British Red Cross during the [First] World War. In his plays *Asā* and *bayna ʾl-kaʾs wal-ṭās*, the latter of which was performed by Jūrj Abyaḍ in 1916, he used the common vernacular, just like Muḥammad Taymūr. He also defended this in a number of articles in *al-Fajr* magazine, which he had founded himself, all published in or after 1925 (see Muḥammad Amīn Ḥassūna in *al-Ḥadīth*, 1933, 153/160, who also mentions a study on poetry, *Fann als-shiʿr* and two stories, *ʿAbath al-shabāb* and *Zijāt al-shabāb*, but without any reference).

The leader of a literary circle called *al-Madrasa al-ḥadītha*, he founded *al-*
277 *Shabāb* magazine, | which nowadays champions the national struggle for freedom in countries that still remain occupied, under the chief-editorship of Muḥammad ʿAlī al-Ṭāhir.

6d Maḥmūd Efendi Khalīl Rāshid

Maḥmūd Efendi Khalīl Rāshid, Licencié fi ʾl-tarbiya wal-ʿulūm and teacher of chemistry and physics at al-Madrasa al-ʿAbbāsiyya al-Thānawiyya in Alexandria, acquired from the Ministry of the Interior the rights to perform the musical *Salāma wa-Salmā, riwāya tamthīliyya ghināʾiyya etc.* (Alexandria: Maṭbaʿat al-Rashād, 1922) on 30 April 1916. The plot is based on the famous story of Ṣaʿṣaʿa, the grandfather of al-Farazdaq, who, while looking for a stray camel, buys the newly-born daughter of a Bedouin, who would otherwise certainly die. The author enlarges the story insofar as he lets Ṣaʿṣaʿa raise the girl, Salmā, as if she were his own daughter, while letting her biological mother also have a son soon after her. Because his mother dies in childbirth, the boy is given to a foster mother, where he is swapped with the newborn son of the leader of the Qays at the instigation of his concubine. When he grows up, the boy, Hāshim, falls in love with his biological sister Salmā. Salmā herself, on the other hand, is in love with the prince's son who, found in the tent of the foster mother by a poor Bedouin, is raised by him as his own son, given the name Salāma, and becomes a famous poet. When this controversial situation is about to be resolved by means of an abduction, the two servants involved in the child-swapping confess what really happened. In an outburst of generosity Hāshim declares himself prepared to give up all his rights on behalf of the true heir, but the latter is content with taking his beloved home with him. The whole story has a certain dramatic force and is interspersed with songs, all of which are performed by Salāma. The language is meant to sound archaic, which is why the author feels obliged to provide all manner of learned comments, but the syntax and sometimes the vocabulary, too (like the word *ʿumda* for a Bedouin sheikh), clearly show its modern imprint. As well as a *dīwān* that was mentioned earlier, on page 85r, his *maqāma*s, the story *Ḥabāʾil al-shayṭān* mentioned in Pérès, no. 600 (which is no. 1 of the *Riwāyāt al-qarawī al-faylasūf* [Alexandria 1334]), Rashīd also wrote the stories *Mamlakat al-mutazawwijayn aw Madīnat Salmān, Saniyya aw Fatāt al-Iskandariyya, al-Liṣṣ al-faylasūf*, a col-
278 lection | of literary pieces with the title *al-Laḥẓ*, and several works on physics and technology, all of which are mentioned in the printed editions of his plays but with no further information, and finally also a work on writing plays, *Fann al-tamthīl* (Alexandria: Maṭbaʿat al-Rashād, n.d.) (Sarkīs, *Jāmiʿ al-taṣānīf al-ḥadītha*, no. 403, Cairo[2] IV, 82).

6e ʿUthmān Ṣabrī

In his *Shubbānunā fī Ūrubbā, maslāt ḥadītha dhāt 4 fuṣūl* (*Majmūʿat riwāyāt Ṣabrī al-tamthīliyya* 1, Cairo: al-Maṭbaʿa al-Salafiyya, 1922), ʿUthmān Ṣabrī (lic. *fī 'l-ḥuqūq*) tried to create an entirely modern kind of drama. The very sophisticated plot has a young Egyptian student who marries a girl from Paris behind his father's back. When his father comes to visit him, he surprises the couple in some café. The father, who is very much a traditional man, repudiates his son when the latter does not want to give up his beloved. Thus, the young couple start fending for themselves. However, the girl is the fruit of a love affair from his college days of an Egyptian judge who is a friend of the boy's father and who accompanies the latter on his visit to Paris. The judge's marriage having remained childless, he has been thinking about his child in France for years. One day, the judge is staying with friends from his student days in Dijon. This happens to be the same family to whom the girl had gone to ask for work, upon the advice of her mother, now dead. This is where the judge learns who she is. However, out of consideration for his wife he does not tell her that he is her father, while she, on her part, refuses to accept his offer of some discrete financial help. The wife of the judge's friend then breaks the deadlock by introducing his wife to the girl. The two women immediately become friends. The result of all this is that the judge can now openly recognise his daughter while the father of the boy no longer opposes the latter's marriage. The two Egyptian fathers are very well portrayed. The French characters, however, especially the woman, a hedonistic type, jealous of the fact that her husband has a professional life of his own and who is only happy when he sells his share in his father's factory to go live with her in Paris, give the audience a completely distorted picture of life in Europe and of women in France. Exceptions aside, the dialogue has no dramatic force. In most cases, they are so full of lengthy dissertations | on the issue of women's rights that the author himself suggests 279
that much of it be omitted should the play be brought to the stage. The remainder of the *Majmūʿa*, which was to contain modern pieces in volumes 2 to 6, dramas taken from the lives of the ancient Arabs in volumes 7 to 9, and a play about ancient Egypt in volume 10, was probably never published.

6f Ibrāhīm al-Miṣrī

On the construction of Egyptian society, Ibrāhīm al-Miṣrī was much more to the point. His first play, *al-Anāniyya* (Cairo: al-Adab al-ḥayy, 1930), written in the common vernacular and first performed in 1923, sketches the total breakdown of morality in an Egyptian family, estranged from Islam as a result of Western culture. When a rich pasha wants to take a young woman as his third wife, the second wife links her to her stepson, issued from her husband's first marriage. The two fall in love and it is only after countless conflicts that the father gives up on his initial idea. *Naḥwa 'l-nūr* (Cairo: al-Fikr wal-ʿālam, 1933) is even more gloomy in tone, so much so that no theatre director dared bring it to the stage. A young journalist discovers that his wife is betraying him with a rich media tycoon. The latter wants to silence him by giving him a well-paid job. At the same time, the journalist discovers that his younger brother, for whose education he had made great sacrifices, is in love with his wife as well. When the brother commits suicide, the journalist decides to continue his life alone in poverty, not giving up on his struggle for freedom and the truth.

6g Anṭūn Yuzbak

Al-Dhabāʾiḥ (Shirkat Maṭbūʿāt al-Qirṭās, n.d. [1927]) is a play in the common vernacular by the late lawyer Anṭūn Yuzbak (author of an earlier play, *ʿĀṣifa fi 'l-bayt*) that was first performed in 1925. This is the story of the unhappy ending of a marriage between a European woman and an Egyptian officer who had walked out on an Egyptian woman because of her. Because the European woman is not able to adapt herself to the limitations of life in the Orient, the marriage becomes a nightmare for both. When the husband, who has meanwhile been promoted to the rank of general, seeks the freedom to find refuge with his former love, his son commits suicide. See Barbour, p. 1001, *al-Mashriq* xxxv, 48, *Dīwān al-Māḥī* 66, 81.

6h Maḥmūd Badawī

The two historical dramas by Maḥmūd Badawī, *al-ʿAbbāsa ukht Hārūn al-*
280 *Rashīd* (Cairo, 1931) and *Shajarat al-Durr* | (Cairo, 1933; brought to the stage by the Ramsīs theatre company in 1932/33), were both written with a keen sense of theatrical effects. On both of these, see Barbour, op. cit., 998/9.

6i Maḥmūd Shukrī

It was only from a reference in Bishr Fāris, *Mabāḥith ʿarabiyya*, 34, n. 13, that I learned of the existence of the play *Riwāyat makārim al-akhlāq* by Maḥmūd Shukrī (Cairo, 1929), which seems to have been dedicated to the Raʾīs Idārat Mudīriyyat al-Buḥayra, who himself had published his *Kitāb al-ḥikma* in 1925 (Maṭbaʿat al-Iʿtimād) (Sarkīs, *Jāmiʿ al-taṣānīf al-ḥadītha*, no. 913).

6k Ibrāhīm ʿAbd al-Qādir a-Māzinī and Maḥmūd Kāmil

The problems of marriage are dealt with in a similar way in a series of plays inspired by modern life: a young woman from a good family withers away in a forced marriage, to die in one of two time-honoured ways, viz. tuberculosis or suicide. Such a plot is even used by Ibrāhīm ʿAbd al-Qādir al-Māzinī (see p. 157ff above) in his one and only play *Gharīzat al-mar'a*, of 1931 (Cairo: Maṭbaʿat al-Ṣabāḥ, n.d.). He was followed in the same year by Maḥmūd Kāmil with *Fāṭima* (Cairo: Maṭbaʿat al-Siyāsa, n.d.) and in 1933 by Rashād Ḥāfiẓ with *al-Samīra* (see 4, above). The play *Qulūb al-hawānim* (Cairo 1933) by Muḥammad Khurshīd (see p. 274) is more lively. Here, the problem of forced marriage is solved through the partners each going their separate ways in love. They agree on a divorce on friendly terms, so that the man can marry his beloved while the woman has great trouble in subjugating the man of her heart. See Barbour, p. 1000.

6l Jūrjī Sharqī

The plays *al-ʿIẓa* by Jūrjī Sharqī (Ṭanṭā, 1932) and Aḥmad Ṣabrī's *Kāhin Amūn, masraḥiyya Firʿawniyya* (Cairo, 1938), I only know by name.

6m Zaynab Fawwāz

The first woman to try her hand at drama was Zaynab Fawwāz, whose *Riwāyat al-hanāʾ wal-wafāʾ, dhāt arbaʿat fuṣūl* (Maṭbaʿat al-Jāmiʿa, 1310) deals with problems of marriage.

7 Folk Theatre

Besides serious drama and apart from the shadow play, several types of farce and vaudeville plays prosper as forms of popular amusement, in part inspired by existing local traditions, and for another part by models taken from the French.

In connection with Prüfer, loc. cit., I mention some printings from the first category: Aḥmad Ḥamdī al-Rashīdī, *Riwāyat hāt lī min da*, Cairo n.d., Muḥammad Efendi Ḥusnī, *Risālat Baʿgar*, anon. *Riwāyat al-zawāg bayn al-nabbūt wa-bakhīl al-ʿakrūt*, | Cairo n.d., Muḥammad Efendi Shafīq, *Faṣl al-* 281
bakhīl, Sayyid Aḥmad ʿAbd al-Wāḥid al-Zayyāt, *Ṣadr al-baghāsha*, Cairo n.d.

Yūsuf Wahbī also tried to make money by introducing a type of melodrama. Barbour's (op. cit., 996) account of the play *Awlād al-faqīr* gives some idea of it. As in Muḥammad Taymūr's *al-Hāwiya*, in this piece, adapted to the lowest common denominator, addiction to cocaine plays an important role, even if it is not at the centre as it is in the play *Kūkāyīn*. Predictably, the piece *al-Ṣalīb wal-hilāl*, about a love story between Muslims and Copts, was forbidden by the authorities. While most of these pieces, in which the director, the actors and the person with whom the idea originated all have equal parts, are not linked to any specific author, the farce *Kishkish Bek*, staged by Yūsuf Wahbī, was by the actor Najīb al-Rīḥānī (Taymūr, 115/22). Samples from a piece entitled *Banāt al-yōm* are given in J. Lecerf, Lit. dialectale, 86/92.

4 *Philology, Literary Criticism and History*

Under the influence of al-Azhar, the traditional Islamic sciences of *adab* and *taʾrīkh* continue to be practised in twentieth-century Cairo. Their representatives fall outside the scope of this volume; a future bibliography will have to list them.[173] Here, we only mention some scholars who have tried to develop these sciences according to Western standards.

1 Aḥmad Zakī

Besides Aḥmad Taymūr (see p. 217, n. 1), the first person to be mentioned here is Aḥmad Zakī Bek.

Born in 1283/1866 in Alexandria and coming from a rich and respected family whose founding father had immigrated there from the Maghreb after a stopover in Jaffa, Aḥmad Zakī Bek moved to Cairo at the age of twelve.
282 | There, he obtained a degree as lic. jur. He began his career in the civil service as a translator in the municipality of Suez and then became a teacher at al-Madrasa al-Khidīwiyya. Later, he became the secretary to the Egyptian Council of Ministers. He became interested in the culture of the Arabs of Spain at a young age, a fact that is borne out by his first work, *al-Arbaʿata ʿashara yawman saʿīdan fī khilāfat ʿAbd al-Raḥmān al-Andalusī* (Cairo, 1303/1885). Two works were the result of his professional activities as a translator: from the French he translated Muḥammad Saʿīd Bāshā's *Risāla fī 'l-maʿārif al-ʿumūmiyya bil-diyār al-Miṣriyya wa-bayān mā yalzam idkhāluhu fīhi min al-iṣlāḥāt al-ḍarūriyya*, Cairo 1305, and Aḥmad Bek Shafīq's *al-Riqq fī 'l-Islām*, Būlāq 1309. His interest in learned societies resulted in *Mawsūʿāt al-ʿulūm al-ʿarabiyya wa-baḥth ʿalā Rasāʾil Ikhwān al-ṣafāʾ*, Cairo 1308. He translated Maspéro's work on the early history of the peoples of the Orient as *Taʾrīkh al-Mashriq* (Būlāq, 1314/1897). A member of the Egyptian Geographical Society, he translated Fr. Banula Bek's book on the services to geography rendered by the khedival family as *Miṣr wal-jaghrāfiya* (Būlāq, 1310). And after that, his compact *Qāmūs al-jaghrāfiya al-qadīma bil-ʿarabī wal-faransāwī* (Cairo 1317/1899) also gave evidence of his interest in geography.

In his capacity as a representative of the Egyptian government, he participated in the 1893 Congress of Orientalists in London, an account of which is given in his *al-Safar ila 'l-muʾtamar* (Būlāq, 1311). After that congress he travelled from February 1892 to February 1893 around Spain to study the monuments of Arab culture in that country. His account of this trip is what makes the

---

173 On the history of education in Egypt, cf. J. Heyworth-Dunne, *An Introduction to the History of Education in Modern Egypt*, with Glossary, Bibliography, and 3 Indices, London 1938.

aforementioned book especially valuable and caused it to be often used by later travellers to Spain (see H. Pérès, *L'Espagne vue par les voyageurs musulmans de 1610 à 1930*, Publ. de l'Institut d'Études Or., Fac. des Lettres d'Alger VI, 1937, 72/87). He never carried out his plan to write a larger work on the same subject. After his death, some articles on Hispano-Arabic monuments of art were published in *al-Hilāl*, December 1934, January-May 1935. His interest in Spain is also borne out by his *Rapport sur les manuscrits arabes conservés à l'Escurial en Espagne* and his *Mémoire sur les relations entre l'Égypte et l'Espagne pendant l'occupation musulmane* in *Homenaje a Codera*. In 1900 he dedicated a second travelogue to his visit to the World Fair in Paris. The book, *l'Univers à Paris 1900*, | *al-Dunyā fī Bārīs aw ayyāmī al-thalātha fī Ūrubbā* (Cairo, 1900, illus- 283
tr.), starts out in a very pleasant conversational tone, with just the rhyme leaving an archaic impression here and there, first in the form of a quite personal diary, then switching to a very precise and matter-of-fact like account of things when it comes to the Egyptian pavillion itself, concluding with a description of the German section, which is full of praise for its patron, the German Kaiser Wilhelm II. He seizes the opportunity to draw the attention of his Egyptian readers to the merits of the German Arabists and the editions of the Arabic classics there, which he readily admits are of better quality than the products of the printing presses of Cairo.

Back home in Egypt, he dedicated himself entirely to philologico-historical studies. He laid out a grand programme for them in his *Mémoire sur les moyens propres à déterminer en Égypte une renaissance des lettres Arabes*, Cairo 1910. In 1910/11 he gave lectures at the newly-founded University of Egypt, entitled *al-Ḥaḍāra al-Islāmiyya*, which were printed by ʿAbdallāh Efendi Amīn in *Majallat al-Jāmiʿa*. A public address on the occasion of the inauguration of the memorial for Mouillard in Heliopolis, published in 1912 as *L'Aviation chez les musulmans* (Imprimerie des Pyramides), is a report on his research into the first attempts at flying in the Islamic world, those by al-Jawharī and by the Spanish philosopher Ibn Firnās. In the same year, he developed detailed proposals for a system of interpunction in printed works in Arabic, a system he had applied earlier in his own *al-Dunyā fī Bārīs*, and which were published as *al-Tarqīm wa-ʿalāmātuhu fi 'l-lugha al-ʿarabiyya* (al-Maṭbaʿa al-Amīriyya). In his house, the *Dār al-ʿurūba* in Giza, he assembled a library rich in manuscripts and photocopies, as well as an important collection of artwork. From this collection he published the works mentioned earlier in volumes I, 212, 3, 246D, 1; II, 28, 6; 175, 31 (see also I, 573). He also played a major role in the re-edition of al-Nuwayrī's *Nihāyat al-arab* and al-Qalqashandī's *Ṣubḥ al-aʿshā*. In the final years of his life he built a mosque next to his house, in whose court he was put to rest when he died on 5 July 1934. See ʿĪsā Iskandar al-Maʿlūf in *RAAD* XIII, 394/9, Dr. Aḥmad

ʿĪsā Bey in *Bull. de l'Inst. d'Égypte* XVII, p. vii/xix, Bishr Fāris, *REI* 1934, 383/94, Sarkīs 971/2, *al-Hilāl* 1934, 173f.

284 | 2 Ṭāhā Ḥusayn

While Aḥmad Zakī did much to introduce the people of Egypt to the philological method of European scholarship, Ṭāhā Ḥusayn, Dean of the Faculty of Philosophy at the University of Egypt, has the merit of having paved the way for a modern scientific approach to the history of literatures and cultures of the Orient. He could do this because as an artist he was exceptionally gifted, his creative work often being carried out in parallel with his scientific activities, the former inspiring the latter.

Ṭāhā Ḥusayn was born around 1891 (or, according to others, in 1889) in a village in Upper Egypt, not far from the town of Maghāgha on the left bank of the Nile. He was the seventh of thirteen children in a family of peasants. He lost his eyesight at a very early age. This disability, which is usually a great obstacle to anyone wishing to be active as a scholar, was compensated by exceptional powers of thought and a very good memory. All the other means of making a career being closed to him, his parents, following a time-honoured custom, sent him to al-Azhar in Cairo. He was then just 13 years old. After graduating in the traditional sciences he soon turned to *adab*, a field to which he was introduced—at al-Azhar still—in Ḥusayn al-Marṣafī's classes on Abū Tammām's *Ḥamāsa*, Mubarrad's *Kāmil* and al-Qālī's *Amālī*. But then new horizons appeared when he started attending the lectures of European orientalists at the newly-founded University of Egypt, especially those of Nallino. He completed his studies there in 1914 with a study on the life and teachings of Abu 'l-ʿAlāʾ al-Maʿarrī. On 5 May of that year this work was accepted as the newly-founded academy's first dissertation, after he successfully defended it in a public ceremony. It was published in the very same year as *Dhikrā Abi 'l-ʿAlāʾ*. Sharply criticised by some supporters of traditional culture (see Muḥammad Ḥusayn al-Walāʾ, *Fī naqd dhikrā Abi 'l-ʿAlāʾ li-Ṭāhā Ḥusayn*, Cairo 1917, and also I, 452, n. 2), it was reprinted in 1922.

The book already had all the hallmarks of the later writer: an admirable
285 erudition, aquired under difficult circumstances, | a healthy sense of history, a creative imagination, and a sharp judgement that does not shrink from drawing consequences where necessary. From among the many European studies on al-Maʿarrī he only had access to the works of Margoliouth, Nicholson and Salmon. His description of the life of his hero, for whom he must have felt a special sympathy since they shared the same fate, is self-confident and convincing, viewing it as he does in the wider context of the political and cultural circumstances of his time. His study into the political fate of al-Maʿarrī's

hometown, especially, is of great merit, even though he has to admit that his conclusion that al-Maʿarrī acted for a time as governor for the Mirdāsids there is questionable. The fact that his rather detailed study of the etymology of the name Maʿarra did not lead to any concrete result, finds its explanation in the inferior level of Semitic linguistics worldwide (see Suppl. I, 19, n. 1). His account of the literary climate at the time of al-Maʿarri and his immediate predecessors, on the other hand, is an early testament to his solid sense of judgement. But where he tends to overestimate the Indian influence in mysticism and philosophy, he relies on his European sources again. His interpretations of the poems with which he interspersed his text to enable the reader to appreciate al-Maʿarrī's art are first-rate, while his account of his religious and philosophical teachings—especially offensive to Ḥusayn's orthodox critics—bear witness to an independent judgement and a keen eye for the importance of contextuality in the history of thought. A special quality of the book is its brilliant style, which already foreshadows the great successes that he would later have as an author, public speaker and teacher. He has all the registers of the Arabic language at his fingertips but only once does he let himself be seduced into showing off with one of its *nawādir*,[174] while his language, lucid though it is, likes to sway to and fro in a *parallismus membrorum*.

| Towards the end of 1913 he went to France, where he first completed his 286
studies in Montpellier.[175] In Paris,[176] he was mostly interested in issues regarding philosophy and sociology, which led to his 1917 dissertation *Étude analytique et critique de la philosophie sociale d'Ibn Khaldoun*, which was rendered into Arabic by Muḥammad ʿAbdallāh ʿInān in 1343/1925 (see p. 212). He also acquired sound knowledge of modern French literature, which enabled him later to inform the Egyptian public on its latest publications, something which he did for a number of years in *al-Hilāl* magazine. Even though he only learned Greek and Latin in France, he took such a lively interest in the culture of classical antiquity, displaying such a good understanding of it, that when he

---

174 Which he has to explain in a footnote on page 241 n: *al-ghazrama al-ibtidāʾ bi-qawl al-shiʿr* of *Aghānī*[1] VII, 170, 18. Actually, it is probably a *taṣḥīf* of *yuqarzim*, which he uses in *Maʿa 'l-Mutanabbī* I, 61 in the form of *qirzām*, 'a bad poet', al-Quṭāmī 31,$_{15}$, ʿAmr b. Kulthūm 36,$_{7}$, al-Āmidī, *al-Muʾtalif* 57,$_{4}$.

175 When he was on holiday in Cairo, he had ostentatiously left a class by Shaykh Mahdī who, besides his own subject, *adab*, had also had to assume responsibility for the teaching of the history of literature, criticising him sharply in the press afterwards. In punishment for this, his name was to be taken off the list of grantee students abroad, but then his patrons succeeded in securing him a second trip to France (see *al-Adab al-jāhilī*, 4).

176 See Aḥmad al-Ṣāwī Muḥammad, *Ṭāhā Ḥusayn fī Bārīs* in *al-Hilāl* 1928, 1180/3.

returned from his second sojourn in France the University of Egypt initially asked him to lecture on this subject.

In the beginning he had great difficulties in giving these lectures because his audience was in no way prepared for them. As he tells us himself, it took him quite some time before he was able to arouse their interest in a subject which put them off by its foreignness or just bored them. But he overcame these obstacles by the sheer energy that he displayed, and in the end he could even motivate some of his students to start working on subjects to do with classical antiquity. Given that most of his audience had no knowledge of any European language, he had to create all the learning tools himself. Later, he published these so as to arouse the interest of a wider circle of educated Egyptians. This led to his translation of Aristotle's *Constitution of Athens*, titled *Niẓām al-Athīniyyīn* (Maṭbaʿat al-Hilāl, 1921), a book on the Greek religion called *Ālihat al-Yūnān* (Maṭbaʿat al-Manār, 1919), and his *Ṣuḥuf mukhtāra min al-shiʿr al-tamthīlī ʿinda 'l-Yūnān* I (Cairo: Maṭbaʿat al-Hilāl, 1339/1920). In this
287 latter work, he first gives a brief outline of the history | of Attica, accompanied by an overview of the genesis of Greek tragedy in the way in which this used to be set out in French handbooks at the time, handbooks which he does not mention. Then he recounts the lives of Aeschylus and Sophocles, listing the tables of contents, with sample translations, of the seven plays that we have of the former, and of *Aias*, *Antigone* and *Elektra* by the latter. The work bears witness to the deep understanding with which he put himself into the mindset of a foreign people. Even if he often emphasizes the difficulties that he ran into in the reproduction of his sources, this work also ennobled his speech, uplifted it from mere matter-of-factness to a noble kind of dignity, denuded of all the exuberance still found in his maiden publication.

This first attempt to introduce his fellow Egyptians to classical antiquity seems not to have fully satisfied him; its continuation, whose publication was announced as forthcoming, never saw the light of day. The situation of the Egyptian theatre, on the other hand, led him to believe that there was a need to familiarise the public with the essence of French theatre. He did this in his outline of fifteen French plays by Becque, H. Bataille, Kistemaeckers, P. Hervieu, Fr. De Curel, A, Capus and H. Bernstein in his *Qiṣaṣ tamthīliyya li-jamāʿa min ashhar al-kuttāb al-Fransiyyīn*, al-Maṭbaʿa al-Tijāriyya, 1924.

His lecturing activity caused him to gradually move away from classical antiquity to cover the intellectual history of Europe as a whole. In 1922 he translated G. LeBon's *Psychologie de l'éducation* under the title *Rūḥ al-tarbiya* (Maṭbaʿat al-Hilāl). In his *Qādat al-fikr*[177] (Maṭbaʿat al-Hilāl, 1925) he gave an account

177 *Leaders of thought*, translated by H.A. Lutfī, Beirut, 1932.

of the wider context of the rise and fall of intellectual currents in European culture, in which he recognises four stages: the poetical, the philosophical, the political, and the religious. The first stage he illustrates with Homer who, to him, is the proverbial poet. But because he did not consider the specific cultural situation of the Greek aristocracy which Homer's poems sought to express, the beginnings of Greek culture appear in a light that is not entirely historical. His portraits of the three greatest philosophers of antiquity, on the other hand, Socrates, Plato, and Aristotle, even if succinct, | nevertheless offer a bright and 288
generally accurate image of the zenith of Hellenic culture, while their importance for the progress of human thought is adequately explained. The reader will be slightly surprised to find that he lets Aristotle be followed immediately by Alexander the Great, the incarnation of the Greek model of the State, which the latter tried to propagate on a worldwide scale. What Alexander was not able to realize due to his untimely death, viz. the unification of the ancient world into one large empire, was achieved by Caesar, whose biography duly follows right after Alexander's. This empire provided the medium through which the religious movements which were to supplant philosophy and politics in the minds of the people could propagate. He characterises Christianity as a child of Hellenism and the idea of a global empire, while in Islam he discerns a reaction of the Semitic mind against the infiltration of foreign ideas, threatening its essence. After a brief sketch of the intellectual currents of the Middle Ages, he concludes with a description of modern times. Claiming that, in this case, it is not possible to come up with a consistent progression of events as it was for antiquity, he limits himself to a description of some of the leading thinkers of the seventeenth century. At the end, he expresses the hope that one day he will find the energy to supplement this outline—begun in London and Paris and completed in Cairo—with a detailed history of modern philosophy. There is no doubt that he would be better qualified than any other Egyptian intellectual to undertake such a task. As such, he could pave the way for a spiritual renewal of Islam, in many ways ready to come about, but which so far has not moved beyond its initial stage.

His studies of the intellectual history of the West in no way alienated him from Arabic literature. This is clear from a series of brilliant articles on the history of poetry at the time of the ʿAbbāsids that he published in 1922/4 in *al-Siyāsa*, and which he then published collectively in 1925 with the title *Ḥadīth al-arbaʿāʾ* (al-Maṭbaʿa al-Tijāriyya al-Kubrā), in imitation of St. Beuve's *Causeries de lundi*. These articles represent the first serious effort in Arabic literature to interpret the poetry of a certain era on its own terms. It was only to be expected that this entirely new approach would run into opposition. Thus, on pages 78 and subsequently, he has to respond to the Syrian | author Rafīq Bek al-ʿAẓm, 289 who criticized him for the fact that in his description of the era of Abū Nuwās he did not show the required level of respect for the sacrosanct personality of the ʿAbbāsid caliph. In answer to this, he emphasizes the right and duty of an objective historiography to let its criticism and representations not be bound by any dogmatic prejudice. This attack shows that it was still dangerous to work with and stand up for European methods in scholarly research. The above series of articles was opened by a description of the struggle between established and up-and-coming writers in Greek and Arabic literature. At the end, he returns once more to this subject, then of current interest with new struggles raging, such as in an opinion piece regarding a dispute that was being fought out on the pages of *al-Hilāl* magazine between Muṣṭafā Ṣādiq al-Rāfiʿī and Salāma Mūsā, and also between the Syrians Khalīl al-Sakākīnī and Shakīb Arslān. And of course he passionately defends the right of the up-and-coming generation, for whom he displays a great deal of sympathy, to pursue new artistic goals. Other essays are contained in a second volume (Dār al-Kutub, 1926, reprint Cairo, 1937/1356).

His research in the field of ʿAbbāsid poetry led him to the study of pre-Islamic poetry, the more so since he had accepted a professorship in the history of Arabic literature in 1925. Being overwhelmed by the impression made on him by the many verses that later transmitters and philologists had undoubtedly falsely attributed to the ancient poets, his sense for the authentic was disturbed. As a result, he could believe that the Qurʾān was the oldest literary monument of the Arabs and that everything transmitted in the name of the pre-Islamic poets had been falsely attributed to them in later times, for all kinds of reasons. One of his main arguments is the uniformity of language among the pre-Islamic poets and its similarity to the language of the Qurʾān. But he overlooks the fact that there are quite important differences between the two, which are to do with the Meccan dialect surfacing in a language that the Prophet otherwise sought to adapt to the Arabic language prevalent among the educated classes. But having taken this position, he has no trouble, being the dialectician that he is, identifying the many weak points in later reports
290 | on the lives of the pre-Islamic poets, and throwing suspicion on the many verses that were undoubtedly falsely attributed to them, verses he believed could serve as a criterion by which to judge an entire tradition. Even though he assures us time and again that the Qurʾān is the only source for the lives of the pre-Islamic Arabs, he never attempts to compare such a representation of things with the image that arises from pre-Islamic poetry so as to prove that it is all fake. Now, even though the book contains a number of fine observations towards a critical assessment of the received tradition, it came as no surprise that its first edition, entitled *Fi ʾl-shiʿr al-Jāhilī* (Cairo, 1925), triggered a

storm of indignation, leading to the rebuttals mentioned in Suppl. I, 32, n. 2. Reactionary circles in Cairo even went so far as to accuse him of launching an attack against religion. As such, he saw no other solution than to produce a new, adapted version of the book, entitled *Fi 'l-adab al-Jāhilī* (Cairo: Maṭbaʿat al-Iʿtimād, 1927/1345), in which he limited the scope of his original claims without, however, completely withdrawing any of them.[178]

This first struggle for academic freedom put him in a state of mental shock from which he cured himself by writing reviews of French books, which were published *al-Hilāl*. At the same time, this shock also drew his attention to his own development as a human being, which led to the story of his childhood, *al-Ayyām*, first published in *al-Hilāl* in 1926, and in 1929 (and again in 1933) as a book (Maṭbaʿat al-Iʿtimād). English translation by E.H. Paxton, *An Egyptian Childhood, The Autobiography of Taha Hussein*, London 1932, French translation by Jean Lecerf, *Le livre des jours, souvenirs d'enfance d'un égyptien*, Paris 1934 (a Hebrew translation by M. Kabiluk and Atamara, a Russian translation by Kračkovsky and a Chinese translation by Tsingtin are mentioned in *al-Ḥadīth* XII, 1938, 275, n. 1, 286). With incomparable tenderness, this work describes the childhood years of a delicate boy amidst his siblings, hindered by his handicap but loved and cared for all the more by his parents because of this, and how he, little by little, constructs an image of the outside world inside his developing mind. As in other cases, his childhood, too, was overshadowed by the shortcomings and backwardness of the educational system, which had nothing to offer his hungry mind other than the arduous memorisation of the Qur'ān.[179] Small wonder that he, besides the | Holy Book, reached out eagerly 291
for anything which the public readings of popular romances that his father and comrades used to listen to for their amusement had to offer him, so much so that he even abandoned himself to the magical beliefs of al-Dayrabī and his *Mujarrabāt* for a time. He tells us in moving language of the suffering that befell this happy family, first when a little sister of his passed away, and again, when its most gifted child of all, an elder brother who was a student of medicine, died of cholera in 1902. Not long after, at thirteen years old, he followed another elder brother of his to al-Azhar in Cairo, for which he must have prepared himself by memorising Ibn Mālik's *Alfiyya* and other *mutūn*. There, he witnessed the time-honoured system of teaching at the foot of the pillars of its venerable mosque, suffering the hardships that the Alma Mater expected the *mujāwirūn*—whose board and lodging she provided—to accept. At the end

178 He describes the political circumstances in this period in *Min baʿd*, 232ff.

179 See the review by J. Lecerf in *Mélanges publiés par la section des arabisants de l'Institut Français de Damas*, Beirut 1929, 54/5.

of the story, he is, therefore, all the happier to proudly tell his daughter that it was by divine grace that he was delivered from such hardship, onto the summit where he now stands. The language of the book is divested of any and all pretension that marked his earlier, scholarly works, and evolves with a simplicity worthy of its subject.

Reactionary forces, however, succeeded one more time in causing this famous university professor, whose influence on the youth they feared, to be removed from his post; at least for some time, that is. During the 1932 Term of the Egyptian House of Parliament, one of its members, Dr ʿAbd al-Ḥamīd Saʿīd, basing himself on denunciations by a number of students, accused Ṭāhā Ḥusayn of false teachings on the Qurʾān. This was because, during his lectures, he had told his audience about the results of European research into the history of the Qurʾān.[180] Even though the dean, Aḥmad Luṭfī, defended him in glowing terms, the government saw no other response than to transfer him to the Ministry of Education to shut him up. He used some of this time for journalistic work, publishing in the *Kawkab al-sharq* and *al-Wādī* newspapers, but, most of all, to write two belletristic works.

292 The result of his journalistic work was his collection | of articles *Ḥāfiẓ wa-Shawqī* (Maṭbaʿat al-Iʿtimād, 1933). Here, in a stark display of all its weaknesses, the critic holds up a mirror to modern literature. He opens with a discussion on literary taste, in the course of which Shawqī's poem on the victory of Mustafa Kemal over the Greeks is dissected, limb by limb, and in which he shows that the former's attempt to apply the style of the ancients to a modern theme was bound to be a travesty. He then shows his readers what living poetry really is by citing some examples from his own translations of the poems of Sully Prudhomme. He juxtaposes this with Beaudelaire's *Fleurs du mal*, asking whether art can ennoble the obnoxious. Then, after an exposition of the development of Arabic prose since the beginning of the nineteenth century, he offers a critical analysis of Ḥāfiẓ's translation of Victor Hugo's *Les Misérables* that justly exposes the agonizing affectation of it. Shawqī's *qaṣīda* on Tutankhamun (*al-Shawqiyyāt* I, 334/43) receives his unreserved approval, just after it was reprinted in *al-Ahrām*, while in one of Ḥāfiẓ's last poems, in honour of Fuʾād I from December 1922 (*Dīw.*[2] I, 106/8), he is sorry to note that his creative power was waning. Very instructive is his comparison between three poems by Shawqī, Ḥāfiẓ and Aḥmad Nasīm in praise of Aḥmad Luṭfī's

180 Cf. Muḥammad Aḥmad ʿArafa, *Naqd maṭāʿin fī ʾl-Qurʾān al-karīm, yataḍamman tafnīd mā alqāhu ʾl-Duktūr Ṭāhā Ḥusayn ʿalā ṭalabat kulliyyat al-ādāb fī ʾl-Jāmiʿa al-Miṣriyya*, ed. Muḥammad Rashīd Riḍā, ṣāḥib al-Manār, Cairo: Maṭbaʿat al-Manār, 1351.

translation of Aristotle's *Nicomachean Ethics*, concluding that none of them seems to have taken the trouble to actually read the work. In an open letter to its author, he deals with an article on poetry and prose in *al-Siyāsa* by Ḥusayn Haykal, a letter in which the continued lethargy of Egypt's contemporary youth is described as the real reason for its backwardness in the literary field. After this, he returns to the two persons whose names figure in the title of this book, paying an affectionate tribute to Ḥāfiẓ as an important author of *marāthī*, one in which he acted as a true spokesman for his people, juxtaposing him with Shawqī once more. In the same way in which his position at the court proved fatal for Shawqī's art, it was his job at the National Library that forced Ḥāfiẓ into silence for many years. Shawqī turned to genuine art only in his final years, although as a playwright | he really was a failure. This article, which ap- 293
peared in *al-Hilāl* 40, 1932, was criticized on several points by Sāmī al-Jarīdīnī, ibid., 330/2.

In 1928, he interrupted his scholarly work once more to write an account of a holiday trip to France, which appeared in 1933 under title *Fi 'l-ṣayf* (Maṭbaʿat al-Hilāl). The sea passage initially evokes memories of his first trip to France, and, with these, other images from his childhood come to surface in his mind. Again he sees himself as the poor relation of the austere Alma Mater al-Azhar, letting himself, like his comrades, be enthused by shaykh Muḥammad ʿAbduh with his ideas on freedom of thought and progress. Like his comrades, he is also scandalized by the schemes plotted against his master by reactionary forces in collusion with the court, and after ʿAbduh left the academy, he finds the spiritual fare that it had to offer meagre and stale. In the end, he has to admit that his classmates only realized very little of the ideals of their teacher in their private lives, which they had once hoped to fashion in his image (on this, see Gibb in *BSOS* VI, 433). His description of the English courses taken by some of his comrades with the aim of some day combatting the oppressors in their own language, and which he joined as an onlooker, is quite amusing. As soon as the aeroplane touches down in France, he is—as usual—immediately enchanted by his wife's native country. Revelling in his memories of his days as a student at the Sorbonne, he vainly looks for witnesses of the past. There is no end to his fascination with the theatre and the cabaret. Just as in the museum itself, he finds the art and life of France in Les Grands Magasins du Louvre. From Paris he travels to the Alsace, which he looks at with the eye of a Frenchman, although he does not fail to recognise its predominantly German character. His little boy's excitement about the cathedral of Strasbourg and the beauty of the Alsace takes hold of him as well. He juxtaposes the piety of the rural population participating in a procession to Mont St Odile with the blatant obsession with miracles at Lourdes and cannot help but conclude that the Alsace is ruled

by a totally different spirit. He is rudely awakened from his holiday reveries by
294 the news of Tharwat Pāshā's unexpected death in Paris. | Thus, it is with deep sorrow that he returns to his native country, mourning a friend who was also a great patriot.

According to Ismāʿīl Aḥmad Adham (*al-Ḥadīth* XII [1938], 288), Ṭāhā Ḥusayn's third narrative work, *al-Adīb* (Lajnat Tarjamat Dāʾirat al-Maʿārif al-Islāmiyya, 1935), is the very best *adab taṣwīrī* available in modern Egyptian literature. There can surely be no doubt that some parts of the book, in particular his description of his farewell to his native village on the eve of his trip to France, are on the same level as *al-Ayyām*. But the book does not have the same unified form as a work of art as the memoirs of his youth. The personality of the main character of *al-Adīb* remains unclear. It is difficult to understand how a young man, apparently so enthusiastic about the sciences that he even divorces the woman whom he had married without telling anyone because scholarships were only given to singles,[181] could be seduced by a chambermaid on his arrival in Marseille and then, in Paris, falls for a courtesan who finally seals his academic fate. If, apart from his experiences involving the difference between al-Azhar and the University of Egypt, the author also wanted to tell us about his years as a student in France without becoming too personal,[182] which one can understand, then there really was no need for such a plot. He published a series of smaller stories in a number of magazines, like *al-Qīthārā wa-jāzband* in *al-Ḥadīth* 1931, 14/19, and *Quyūd wa-aghlāl*, ibid. 1932, 21/4.

When Nasīm Pāshā of the Wafd party returned to power in 1934, Ṭāhā Ḥusayn was reinstated as a professor towards the end of that year. Soon after, he was named dean of his faculty. In June 1935, he published a second collection of magazine articles, entitled *Min baʿīd* (al-Maṭbaʿa al-Raḥmāniyya). The subjects vary widely and are organized in five sections. The first of these, *Min Bārīs*, of-
295 fers small talk on a vacation trip made in March 1923, | a piece in memory of Sarah Bernhard, and some thoughts about the piece *Pénélope* by G. Fauré and R. Fauchois which he had seen at the Opéra Comique; then also 'Doubt and certitude', following a book by Nordmann, *L'empire des cieux*, and 'Knowledge and wealth', in which he admonishes wealthy Egyptians to emulate the French and provide financial support for the sciences. In the second part, he gives a detailed report on the International Congress of Historians in Brussels in 1923 in which he rails, among other things, against L. Massignon's presentation on

181 What Saʿd Zaghlūl, the father of modern Egypt, when minister of education, thought of men who divorced for these motives, may be found in ʿAbbās Maḥmūd al-ʿAqqād, *Saʿd Zaghlūl*, 118.

182 Compare the article *Zawjatī* in *al-Hilāl* 43 (1934), 12/6.

the influence of Sufism on the development of dogmatics in Islam. The third part consists of memories of a vacation trip around France in 1924, which took him to Lourdes. This part terminates with detailed accounts of the plays staged in Paris at the time. The fourth part, *Bayna 'l-ʿilm wal-dīn*, is about the experiences that he had in his struggle against the reactionary forces of Egypt. In it, he makes another energetic plea for academic freedom. The fifth part, *Bayna 'l-jidd wal-hazal*, primarily serves the same purpose. Here, too, he is for the most part deadly serious when he defends his ideals, for instance when he speaks out against an article by ʿAllām Salāma in *al-Siyāsa al-usbūʿiyya* concerning a question raised by a faculty member at al-Azhar on whether there are limits to *adab* as a field of academic research. He dedicates kind words of recognition to Manṣūr Fahmī's *Khaṭarāt al-nafs*. In conclusion, he defends, once more, a passage from his *al-Shiʿr al-Jāhilī* in which he had promised that he would conduct the analysis in the spirit of Descartes' *Philosophie*. It was precisely this promise that had caused the ire of his adversaries, and now he takes his revenge with a brilliant piece of satire in which he depicts the life of Descartes in the style of the *1001 Nights* as a wondrous voyage through the Orient on which he discovers the secrets of mysticism.

In the two years during which he could not exercise his function as a university professor, Ṭāhā Ḥusayn gave a series of public lectures on Arabic literature, which he published in 1936 as *Min ḥadīth al-shiʿr wal-nathr* (Maṭbaʿat al-Ṣāwī). In the preface, he emphasises the fact that none of these lectures had been committed to paper before they were held and that he had not recorded them afterwards, either. Indeed, they represented what some of his listeners had written down as he spoke. These minutes of his lectures had not undergone any post-editing on his part either; the only thing he would check was
their general | agreement with his own ideas. This explains both the merits and 296
some of the shortcomings of these studies, most of all the unusual liveliness of his language[183] and the boldness of some of his ideas, which do not bear close examination. In the first of these lectures, held at the American University in Beirut in November 1932 and which was published for the first time in *al-Ḥadīth* 1938, 210/20, he tries to determine the place of Arabic literature in its relationship to the literatures of the world, limiting himself expressly to a comparison with Greek, Latin, and Persian literature alone. But it seems that this was not a good decision. For instance, in order to correctly judge the value of ancient Arabic prose as we know it from the *Ayyām al-ʿArab*, it would have been necessary to compare it, at the very least, with similar ancestral legends of the Jews

183 But which is still Classical Arabic, admitting only rarely of an isolated Europeanism such as *al-dushsh al-bārid* on 251,9.

in Hebrew prose. If he had, he would not have been offended as much as he is now by the article in *EI* on Arabic literature in which its beginnings were compared to the beginnings of the literatures of primitive peoples.[184] General value judgements, like that stating that Arabic literature is of a higher order than Latin and Persian literature and equal to that of the Greeks, are always questionable because they are based on different standards. And these even change with the author himself. On page 15, for instance, he praises the poems of Jarīr, Farazdaq and al-Akhṭal as living testimonies of the life of the ancient Arabs that can compare to the *Iliad* and the *Odyssey*; yet, on another occasion, he says he cannot read a single hour in their *dīwān*s without being overcome by a sense of weariness and boredom. He is right to emphasise that Islamic culture has the merit of having pulled Greek science through the Middle Ages and transmitting its knowledge to the West. But, more appropriately, he could have pointed out that there are no absolute standards when it comes to aesthetic values, and that the literary scholar has to determine which standards
297 apply during different periods. | This also applies to modern Arabic literature, which he cannot value yet but hopes will soon prove to have one. The next two lectures, of December 1930, are about the beginnings of Arabic prose. It was probably because of earlier experiences that his analysis leaves the Qur'ān aside, arguing that it is a literary monument *sui generis*. Instead, he tries to identify influences from Greek and Persian literature on the earliest stages of Arabic literature. Following W. Marçais, he emphasises that any influence from Persian literature is difficult to determine since there is nothing left of Ibn al-Muqaffaʿ's translations from Pahlevi works. But besides the *Shāhnāmeh*, enough related texts from this literature have been preserved for us to have an opinion about it and conclude that, even though Ibn al-Muqaffaʿ's syntax is different, the style and spirit of his writings are quite close to the originals on which they are based. In contrast, he inclines towards serious overestimation of the influence of Greek on the beginnings of Arabic literature. But, in this case, we have the possibility of comparing a considerable amount of scientific texts in translation with their Greek originals or the Syriac prototypes on which they were often based. And here we find that the language of the translators is, for the most part, rather clumsy and does not bear comparison with independent scientific prose in Arabic of the same period. Sībawayh is an exception here; being a Persian, he struggled with a language that he did not fully master,

184 If he really refused the comparison, he should not have referred exclusively to *zunūj* because the Bantu negroes are mentioned together with other primitive peoples in the article referred to.

in addition to all the difficulties that he must already have run into when trying to develop a new science from scratch. His attemps at identifying Greek influences in ʿAbd al-Ḥamīd and Ibn al-Muqaffaʿ do not withstand criticism. In a passage from a letter by ʿAbd al-Ḥamīd in which directions are given for the purchase of horses, which he later (p. 102) aptly compares with a *qaṣīda* by Aws b. Ḥajar, Ṭāhā Ḥusayn believes he sees the influence of a Greek style of writing in the accumulation of *ḥāl* constructions, which the subject imposes. But at the same time, he does not substantiate this with examples of an analogous use of participles in Greek. When, one day, ʿAbd al-Ḥamīd advises the caliph to have every hundred of his soldiers headed by a commander, Ṭāhā Ḥusayn believes he sees the example of the Roman centurion. But in the Byzantine army, which is the only army in ancient Roman territory that ʿAbd al-Ḥamīd could
have known, the centurion had become obsolete long before then. | Even more 298
vague are the traces of Greek influence he believes he found in Ibn al-Muqaffaʿ. When the latter recommends that every imam, when instated, issue a legal order binding all judges, Ṭāhā Ḥusayn is reminded of the *edicta praetorum*. But these were defunct at the time of Hadrian, and the Arabs could not have become familiar with them through Hellenic law as practiced by the Christian churches of the time. Even bolder is his claim that Ibn al-Muqaffaʿ followed a Greek example when he advised the caliph in Syria to appoint officials to positions similar to that of the later *muḥtasib*; unfortunately, we do not learn which institution under Greek or Byzantine constitutional law he has in mind. The fourth lecture is about Arabic prose in the third century of the Hijra. It was first delivered in January of 1931, then read again at the International Congress of Orientalists in London, and printed as the preface to Ibn Qudāma's *Naqd al-nathr* (Suppl. I, 407). It deals primarily with the work of al-Jāḥiẓ, whose artistic talent is illustrated with his *hijāʾ* work in prose, the *Kitāb al-tarbīʿ wal-dawāʾir*, and then tries to prove that this work depends on the treatise on Aristotelian *Rhetoric* ascribed to Ibn Qudāma. In his five lectures on the poetry of the third century of the Hijra, given in Beirut in March of 1933, he speaks with great authority on a subject in which he is fully at home. Analyzing a number of typical examples, he gives trenchant descriptions of an artform that was based on a deliberate and learned kind of craftmanship, rather than on poetical inspiration. He defends Abū Tammām against the criticism of the ancient philologists, while admitting, at the same time, that al-Buḥturī's art remained free of many of the negative aspects of his master's poetry.[185] Again, he cannot resist

185 That such judgements are very subjective, just like the old masters themselves, is shown at the bottom of page 220, where he criticises al-Buḥturī for his use of the word *shasūʿ*

the temptation of positing a Greek influence on the poetry of Abū Tammām and Ibn al-Rūmī. In this, he bases himself on reports on the supposedly Greek origin of Abū Tammām's father, although we only know that the latter's name was Tādūs (Thaddeus or Theodosius?), so he could also have been an Aramaic Christian, while Ibn al-Rūmī's descent from a Greek slave is clear from his
299 name alone. | But the stichomythia in Ibn al-Rūmī that he refers to in support of this on page 240 is to be found in a lovesong attributed to al-Waḍḍāḥ, while the personification of characteristics in that same poem can hardly be associated with the classical drama of the Greeks.

The year 1935 also saw the publication of the Arabic translation of an article on modern Arabic literature in present-day Arabia, published earlier in *Open Court* in Chicago and entitled *al-Ḥayāt al-adabiyya fī Jazīrat al-ʿArab* (Damascus: Maktabat al-Nashr al-ʿArabī, 1354; first in *al-Hilāl* 46, 514/604). Having established that Bedouin poetry is still alive in the Najd (as we also know from Socin's *Dīwān*), he describes the specific, religious outlook of the Zaydīs and Wahhābīs in their appreciation of literature, which in those regions still very much depend on Egypt as a centre of intellectual education.

Maʿa ʾl-Mutanabbī (2 vols., Cairo: Maṭbaʿat Lajnat al-taʾlīf wal-tarjama wal-nashr, 1936), written during a holiday in the French Alps, shows him at the summit of his literary creativity. Using al-Mutanabbī's *Dīwān* to trace his biography step by step, he interprets almost all of his poems with a great sense of what motivated and moved him. At the same time, he makes sound judgements on their value as works of art, without overlooking any weaknesses in their rhetoric. On several occasions, he opposes the book by R. Blachère, against whom he justly argues (e.g. at II, 327) that it is not right to qualify al-Mutanabbī's poems on Sayf al-Dawla's feats of war as half-baked attempts at an epic style, but that these should instead be seen as samples of a mature, Islamic poetry of war which, it is true, only a Muslim can really appreciate.

The book *al-Qaṣr al-masḥūr* (cf. p. 246), which he wrote together with Tawfīq al-Ḥakīm, is part of his work on al-Mutanabbī.

In the same way in which he gives free reign to his imagination in the work just mentioned, earlier he had woven a kind of historical novel around the life of the Prophet in his *ʿAlā hāmish al-sīra* (al-Maṭbaʿa al-Raḥmāniyya, 1933), which gave him the opportunity to display all his literary talents. He returned to
300 this in L'Écluse in the autumn of 1937, | leading to the second volume, which is about the life of the Prophet until his calling, while the first volume had closed

('removed') whose hissing sounds he says are meant to imitate Bedouin coarseness, without realizing that Abū Tammām, too, used the term, unintentionally for certain, at 191,$_{12}$.

with the Prophet's being entrusted to his foster mother in the countryside. In the preface, he emphasises that his book has nothing to do with history as it actually happened, but that it is meant to cater for the need for an attractive and imaginative kind of reading material among a youth that is primarily attuned to foreign literature for its intellectual amusement. Thus, the first volume started with ʿAbd al-Muṭṭalib's digging of the Zamzam well and continues with the story of the Prophet's parents until the death of his father in Yathrib. Here, the story is interrupted by an inspirational tale about the campaigns in conquest of the world by the Tubbaʿ of Yemen and the history of his descendants up to Dhū Nuwās, who elevated Judaism to a state religion. His imagination getting bolder all the time, the reader is next taken to an unnamed city in Greece, to the house of an affluent young man named Kimon, son of Archytas (?), who in a dream is led to go to Arabia, then hauled off as a slave to Najrān, where he is witness to the persecution of the Christians. With the aim of taking revenge, the emperor has an Alexandrian monk incite the Najāshī of Abyssinia to go out and conquer Yemen; all this is a prelude to his governor's campaign against Mecca, riding his elephant bull. At this point, we are taken back to the main theme of the story, where we learn about the Prophet's birth and his early childhood. In the second volume, the author lets the twines of his imagination envelop the meagre stem of tradition with even greater abundance. The Baḥīra legend is drawn out to become a novel: *al-Faylasūf al-ḥāʾir*. It depicts its Greek hero Kallikrates, a kind of counter-character to the Kimon of the first volume, as one of the last adherents of a hedonist paganism in a world already dominated by Christianity. In his case too, an acquaintance with a monk brings him to his senses. In order to find the truth, he travels to the East, is captured by a Bedouin tribe, spends his life among them a slave named Ṣābiḥ, and is taken to Mecca by Zayd b. ʿAmr after he learns that a new prophet has made an appearance there. The second book, *Rāʾiʿ al-ghanam*, continues the story of the Prophet until his marriage to Khadīja. The tradition concerning | the 301
reconstruction of the Kaʿba is described in *Ḥadīth Bākhūm* (Pachomius), in the form of the story of an Egyptian master builder who took part in it. The mood that reigned among the Quraysh prior to the Prophet's calling is described in a scene in the shop of a Greek wine merchant in *Ṣāḥib al-ḥān*. It appears that Renan's *Vie de Jésus*, which situates the life of the Saviour right in the middle of a Palestinian village idyll, served as the artistic model for this book. Even if some passages are slightly long-winded, the author's verbal powers captivate the reader time and again. Only rarely does he refer explicitly to his sources by quoting them directly, and then mostly to Ibn Saʿd's *Ṭabaqāt*. But still, at times they do provide his language with an archaic tone he then thinks he should explain to the reader.

His most recent work, *Mustaqbal al-thaqāfa fī Miṣr* (Cairo, 1939), is the product of his many years as the Dean of the Faculty of Philosophy of the University of Egypt. Time and again, he and his colleagues noticed that the intellectual level of high-school (*madrasa thanawiyya*) graduates enrolling at the university was sub-standard. This led him to conduct an investigation into the foundations of the entire school system in Egypt, criticized so often by his contemporaries for its shortcomings. Where, in the past, the British administration was accused of criminal neglect of the educational sytem, he now had to blame the rulers of an independent Egypt for being solely concerned about the material welfare of the country. He analyses the educational system of Egypt from antiquity onward, concluding that the intellectual future of the country can only be secured by resolute acknowledgement of European culture. To achieve this, he demands reform of the institutions that govern the educational system of the country to allow decisive imput by members of the academic community. In its passionate and uncompromising criticism, the boldness of its thinking and its captivating language, this work bears all the hallmarks of his earlier works; never mind whether it will achieve anything in practical or political terms. See the detailed review by Dr Aḥmad ʿAbd al-Salām al-Kardānī Bek, ʿAmīd Maʿhad al-tarbiya, in *al-Thaqāfa* I, no. 7, dated 14 February 1939, 9/14.

302 | See also Salāma Mūsā in *al-Hilāl* 1923, 516/20, 1936, 34/8, Zakī al-Maḥāsinī in *al-Ḥadīth* 1934, 513/5, a special issue of *Majallat Jamʿiyyat al-shubbān al-Muslimīn*, April 1932, Dr. Ism. Aḥmad Edhem in a special issue of *al-Ḥadīth* of April 1938 (including a detailed bibliography), Gibb in BSOS V, 454/8, Ch. C. Adams, *Islam and Modernism in Egypt*, 253/9.

3 Zakī Mubārak

Zakī ʿAbd al-Salām Mubārak shares Ṭāhā Ḥusayn's ideas and, like him, pursues his academic goals with great artistic talent. He was born around 1895 (?) in Sintrīs in Upper Egypt. He spent his childhood years there and in Asyut. He went to Cairo at an early age to study at al-Azhar. He greatly respected his teachers al-Marṣafī and Aḥmad al-Mahdī Bek. Around 1915, the former *wakīl al-Azhar*, Muḥammad Ḥasanayn al-ʿIdwī, founded a *jamʿiyya adabiyya* for students, in which the poetically gifted Zakī Mubārak soon played a leading role. He won a contest for the best poem that was organised by Sultan Ḥusayn, and his winning *qaṣīda* was printed in *al-Muʾayyad*. He started to study French at the University of Egypt as early as 1913, but his official registration only occurred in November 1916. He completed his studies in 1925 with the brilliant dissertation *al-Akhlāq ʿinda ʾl-Ghazzālī* (Maṭbaʿat al-Raḥmāniyya), to which his teacher Manṣūr Fahmī wrote a preface. The work not only places the ethics of

this great theologian in the larger framework of the development of Islam, it also provides detailed comparisons with the ethical ideas of European thinkers, from Descartes up to Carlyle. In the same year, he published a series of essays on literary criticism under the title *al-Badāʾiʿ* (2nd printing 1937). After his edition of al-Ḥuṣrī's *Zahr al-ādāb* (Cairo, 1344/1925; see Suppl. I, 472), he published a work that was wholly in the style of ancient *adab* works, entitled *Madāmiʿ al-ʿushshāq* (Cairo: al-Maṭbaʿa al-Raḥmāniyya, n.d., 2nd printing Cairo 1353). The work offers a compilation of all the expressions of love and their accompanying phenomena, including banners, in Arabic poetry from classical times until the present, for which he likes to quote from Ḥāfiẓ Ibrāhīm and Shawqī the most. He concludes the work with a juvenile poem he wrote himself, | which 303
was set to music by ʿAbd al-Samīʿ ʿĪsā al-Bājūrī. He does not shrink from referring to a sensational lawsuit in Berlin when he talks about lesbian love (p. 73). The historical aspect of things is not important to him; typical is his reference to al-Bahāʾ Zuhayr as *aḥad wuzarāʾ Miṣr fī ayyāmina ʾl-khawālī*. In one instance he also quotes a larger piece from Ibn Ḥajala's *Dīwān al-ṣabāba* (p. 67), and the famous *Nūniyya* by Ibn Zaydūn (p. 122/5) from al-Maqqārī's *Nafḥ al-ṭīb* he cites in its entirety. In his *al-Muwāzana bayna ʾl-shuʿarāʾ, abḥāth fī uṣūl al-naqd wa-asrār al-bayān* (Maṭbaʿat al-Muqtaṭaf wal-Muqaṭṭam, 1344/1926) he pursued higher scientific goals (Sarkīs, *Jamīʿ al-taṣānīf*, no. 707, has a mistaken 1924). Even if he still regards Arabic poetry as a unified whole, which is why he has no problem in comparing the poems of al-Buḥturī with those of Shawqī, he tries, and not without success, to work out aesthetic criteria that are more enduring than those available to the ancient *udabāʾ*; as such, this inspiring work was often gratefully used by the undersigned. His work *Ḥubb Ibn Abī Rabīʿa wa-shiʿruhu* was only published after his departure from Cairo (Cairo 1928).

In 1927 he went to the Sorbonne and the École des langues orientales vivantes in Paris to study European methods in philology. He completed his studies in 1931 with a thesis entitled *La prose arabe au quatrième siècle de l'Hégire* (*dixième siècle*). The book shows that he has learned to treat his teacher Ṭāhā Ḥusayn's at times extravagant theories with circumspection. But he still falls too often for the temptation to generalise individual observations, even if these observations are important in themselves, and to squeeze variegated historical developments into inflexible schemes. But these things aside, his descriptions of the leading figures of the glory days of Arabic prose are well taken. In his revised edition of the work, entitled *al-Nathr al-fannī fi ʾl-qarn al-rābiʿ* (2 vols, Cairo: Dār al-Kutub al-Miṣriyya, 1354/1934), we learn, somewhat to our surprise, that when he wrote his thesis he had often felt inhibited by the criticism of his teachers in Paris, and that it was only in the revised version that he could fully develop his ideas. And indeed, this is an entirely different work, which

begins with a general overview of Arabic prose until the fourth century, whose stylistic characteristics are analysed in every detail. The first volume concludes
304 with a comprehensive overview | of narrative prose, from the *maqāma* until the Ikhwān al-ṣafāʾ. The second volume first discusses the literary critics, then the historians of dogma, and terminates with a detailed appreciation of epistolography. The special attractiveness of this book, which is the first monograph on the literary history of the Arabs that is based on a rigid methodology, comes from Mubārak's literary views, which now have fully matured. A by-product of these studies is his work on *al-Risāla al-ʿadhrāʾ*, mentioned in Suppl. I, 153,$_{5}$. But apart from belles lettres, which took up most of his time, he did not look down upon sharpening his brains on problems concerning the transmission of religious texts, as may be inferred from his 1934 study on the *Kitāb al-umm* attributed to al-Shāfiʿī, and which was mentioned earlier in Suppl. I, 304.

In these years, Zakī Mubārak also contributed to belles lettres himself through the publication of his *Dhikrayāt Bārīs* (Cairo, 1931) and, most of all, by his *Dīwān* (Cairo: Maṭbaʿat Ḥijāzī, 1933/1352). In the latter, short *maqṭūʿa*s, some of them no more than two sharply phrased lines, predominate, besides the *qaṣīda*, which he had skillfully practiced in his younger years at al-Azhar in praise of his teachers there. Yet he does not look down upon older artforms either. An example of this is his juxtaposition of a poem by Aḥmad b. Muḥammad al-Anṭāṭī (d. 399), *Layla fī Tinnīs*, with a *qaṣīda* entitled *Layālī Sintrīs*, of which he had already quoted some lines in *al-Badāʾiʿ*, *Madāmiʿ al-ʿushshāq* and *Ḥubb Ibn Abī Rabīʿa*, and which was printed fully for the first time in *Jarīdat al-Ṣabāḥ* of 22 December 1929, to be reprinted in the present work from page 87 onward. In his younger years he also wrote on politics. His indignation at the pressure exercised by the British is still cautiously phrased in the *qaṣīda Ghaḍbat al-asad*, which was read by Maḥmūd Bāshā Sulaymān during a party meeting of the Wafd on 13 November 1919. On page 83 there is a *marthiya* in memory of the leader of the National Party, Muḥammad Bek Farīd. In 1919 he implores Wilson not to forget Egypt now that he is ill, but then cannot help poke fun at him because the multitude of presents in reward for his opposition to the Entente had caused the American customs to protest when he declared his luggage on his return (104/6). But, on the whole, sentimental feelings predomi-
305 nate, often directed towards a childhood love from Sintrīs. His art, which | he only engaged in occasionally, with long intervals and when inspired, earned him the friendship of Abū Shādī, with whom he once exchanged some verses (129 f) when they were travelling back to Cairo from the beaches of Alexandria one September. In Abū Shādī's magazine *Apollo* he published, in 1933/4, some verses on the statue of Muṣṭafā Kāmil Bāshā (p. 766/7) and some pieces on

al-Shiʿr al-ʿarabī bayna ʾl-yaqaẓa wal-khumūd (141/2, with a portrait), *Shawqī amāma ʾl-taʾrīkh* (369/79), and *Ḥāfiẓ wal-lugha al-faṣīḥa* (319/21).

During these years he spent all his energy on his scholarly activity, resulting in three important books: *al-Lugha wal-dīn wal-taqālīd fī ḥayāt al-istiqlāl* (Cairo 1937), *al-Taṣawwuf al-Islāmī* (2 vols, Cairo 1938), and *ʿAbqariyyat al-Sharīf al-Raḍī* (2 vols, Cairo 1938). Since 1937 he has been a professor at the École normale supérieure in Baghdad (cf. *Or. Mod.* 1938, 77), from where he still participates in the intellectual life of his country.

(4.–7.) *Other Philologists*

4 Aḥmad Amīn and Aḥmad Ḍayf

From among the scholars co-operating with Ṭāhā Ḥusayn on the re-establishment of Arabic philology, we also mention Aḥmad Amīn and Aḥmad Ḍayf.

Aḥmad Amīn was born in Cairo in 1887. In 1923 started his career as a writer with *al-Akhlāq*, followed by a treatise entitled *al-Balāgha al-gharrāʾ*, which was published in 1933. Together with Ṭāhā Ḥusayn and ʿAbd al-Ḥamīd al-ʿIbādī, he started in 1928 with an account of intellectual life in the early days of Islam, which was published under the title *Fajr al-Islām* (Maṭbaʿat al-Itimād). Its continuation, *Dūḥa ʾl-Islām* (2 vols. Lajnat al-taʾlīf wal-tarjama wal-nashr, 1351/1933 and 1953/1935), which continues the account into the ʿAbbāsid era, was translated into Persian as *Partaw-i Islām* by ʿAbbās Khalīl Iqdām (Tehran, 1315/1936).—See Muḥammad Ismāʿīl Ḥassūna in *al-Ḥadīth* VII, 1933, 650/6.

In 1924, Aḥmad Ḍayf published his *Kitāb balāghat al-Andalus*, and together with Ṭāhā Ḥusayn, Aḥmad Amīn and others worked on the handbook for the history of Arabic literature, *al-Mujmal fī taʾrīkh al-adab al-ʿarabī*, mentioned in Suppl. I, 13 (where one must read: ʿAbd al-ʿAzīz al-Bishrī).

5 Muḥammad Ṣabrī

From among the scholars who received their methodological schooling in France, | mention must also be made of Muḥammad Ṣabrī, professor of early 306
modern history at the Dār al-ʿulūm.

After completing his studies under Seignobos at the Sorbonne with a thesis called *La génèse de l'esprit national égyptien*, he published his *Taʾrīkh al-Miṣr al-jadīd min Muḥammad ʿAlī ila ʾl-yawm* in 1926. In it, he analyses the recollections of Muḥammad ʿAbduh, which, in the second edition, is supplemented by an appendix on the revolution of 1919. In 1927 he published a collective volume entitled *Adab wa-taʾrīkh* (Maṭbaʿat Dār al-Kutub al-Miṣriyya), containing a series of essays on literature and political history. The book opens with an excellent essay on Sāmī al-Bārūdī, his time, and his place in the history of Arabic literature. No less important is his biography of Ismāʿīl Ṣabrī, accompanied by a selection of his poems. These two essays had first been published (without indication of the year) by Maṭbaʿat al-Shabāb. With his terse but otherwise comprehensive account of the Italian freedom movement of 1815/1870, read on 10 and 20 May 1922 at the University of Egypt and to which Khalīl Maṭrān wrote a good preface, Ṣabrī rendered an important service to the political formation of his fellow Egyptians. This lecture was first published separately in 1922 by al-Maṭbaʿa al-Raḥmāniyya. The third part, *al-Fuṣūl*, features a number of articles on literature and politics which had previously been published in *al-Ahrām* and *al-Siyāsa*. As well as an essay on Molière and an obituary for Ismāʿīl Ṣabrī, special mention must be made of a critique of a *marthiya* by Shawqī on the occasion of the death of an infant son of Ḥusayn Haykal (cf. p. 206) (*al-Shawqiyyāt* III, 26/8), followed by a counter-critique by Shakīb Arslān that was first printed in *Kawkab al-Sharq*, and the political essay *Ilā ayyi ṭarīq naḥnu masūqūn, Muhzila fī maʾtam*. He published a counterpart to his study on the Italian freedom movement in *al-Hilāl* 35, 932/7, entitled *al-Ḥaraka al-istiqlāliyya fī Burūsiyya*. After his publication of a history of the French Revolution and Napoleon, entitled *al-Qarn al-thāmin ʿashar wal-thawra al-Faransawiyya wa-Nabūlyūn* (Maṭbaʿat Dār al-Kutub al-Miṣriyya, 1927), there followed in 1929 *al-Imbirāṭūriyya al-Miṣriyya fī ʿahd Muḥammad ʿAlī wal-masʾala al-sharqiyya*, French transl. *L'empire égyptien sous Muḥammad ʿAlī et la question d'orient 1811/49*, Paris 1930. Only in French: *Épisode de la question d'Afrique, l'empire égyptien sous Ismail et l'ingérence anglo-française 1863/79*, 1933.

307 | 6 Aḥmad Farīd Rifāʿī

Independent from ongoing research in academia, Dr. Aḥmad Farīd Rifāʿī tried to apply modern historical methods to his study on the heyday of the ʿAbbāsid Caliphate, published as *ʿAṣr al-Maʾmūn* (3 vols, Maṭbaʿat Dār al-Kutub al-Miṣriyya, 1346/1928).

A graduate of the University of Egypt, he first worked as a secretary for ʿAbd al-Khāliq Tharwat Bāshā, after which he was appointed *mufattish* in the Ministry of the Interior. His work is very well documented. After a detailed history of the Umayyads and the first ʿAbbāsids, pages 189/372 of volume 1 are dedicated to political history under al-Maʾmūn. The major part of this work is about the intellectual movements under that caliph. The poets of the age receive significant space, though for some of them he strictly follows the *Kitāb al-aghānī*. The third volume is almost entirely taken up by quotations of stylistic samples from the great prose writers of that age. After some smaller historical studies (*Imāma taʾrīkhiyya sādhaja bi-ʿaṣr Abī Bakr al-Ṣiddīq* in *al-Muqtaṭaf* 75, 376/83, 499/504, 76, 57/62, and *ʿUmar b. al-Khaṭṭāb* in *al-Hilāl* 38 [1929], 33/43), he published *al-Shakhṣiyyāt al-bāriza al-taʾrīkhiyya* in 1936, see *al-Ḥadīth* x, 1936, p. 371 and *al-Taʿqīb ʿala ʾl-Muqaddima* (Maktabat al-qirāʾa wal-thaqāfa al-adabiyya lil-jayb, no. 1), see *al-Shabāb* of 9 March 1936, p. 31.

7 Ḥasan Efendi al-Sandūbī and Ḥasan Ṣāliḥ al-Jiddāwī

The outstanding philologists Ḥasan Efendi al-Sandūbī and Ḥasan Ṣāliḥ al-Jiddāwī should also be mentioned here.

We know the former as the author of a work on al-Jāḥiẓ and the edition of his *Rasāʾil* (Suppl. I, 241), as well as from his study *Aʿyān al-bayān min ṣubḥ al-qarn al-thālith ʿashar al-hijrī ila ʾl-yawm* (Maṭbaʿat al-Jamāliyya, 1332/1914), and the latter as the editor of the poems of Abū Shādī (see above p. 100ff) and the author of a study called *al-Adab al-jadīd fī ʾl-shiʿr wal-shāʿir min taʾlīf wa-jamʿ* (Cairo 1925).[186]

| 8 Historians 308

From the many works in which the past and contemporary history are mostly still portrayed according to the methods of *taʾrīkh* of olden days, we can again only cite a selection here, in chronological order:

1892—Muḥammad Bek Diyāb (b. 1269/1853, d. early 1921), a teacher at al-Azhar and the Dār al-ʿulūm, later chief *mufattish* in the ministry of education, published a brief *Taʾrīkh Miṣr al-qadīm wal-ḥadīth*, Būlāq 1310, which runs until the year 1309. Then, in 1899, there followed his *Taʾrīkh ādāb al-lugha al-ʿArabiyya*, 2 vols, Maṭbaʿat al-Islām 1317, Maṭbaʿat al-Taraqqī 1318, and his *Taʾrīkh al-ʿArab bi-Isbāniyā*, Maṭbaʿat al-Jamāliyya 1913. Apart from a number of philological works (*Durūs al-ashyāʾ fī ʿilm al-naḥw*, C. 1303, *al-Durūs al-naḥwiyya*, together with Ḥifnī Bek Nāṣīf, Suppl. II, 728, among other places Būlāq 1305, 1309, *Durūs al-balāgha*, together with the same, Būlāq 1310, *Qalāʾid al-dhahab fī faṣīḥ lughat al-ʿArab*, Būlāq 1311, *Muʿjam al-alfāẓ al-ḥadītha*, Maṭbaʿat al-Raghāʾib 1337/1919), he also wrote some books on arithmetic, see Sarkīs 1653/4, Cheikho, *al-Mashriq* XXIV, 863.

---

186 In many ways interesting and informative about the background of newspaper journalism is the book by the bank clerk Ḥabīb al-Ziḥlāwi, *Udabāʾ muʿāṣirūn, mughālāt udabāʾ al-shabāb wa-ṭābiʿ udabāʾ al-shuyūkh fī kitābat muqaddimāt al-kutub wa-fuṣūl fī ʾl-naqd al-adabī*, Maṭbāʿat al-Ikhāʾ, 1935.

1897—In 1897 the Syrian Ilyās Zakhūra published his *Mirʾāt al-ʿaṣr fī taʾrīkh wa-rusūm akābir al-rijāl bi-Miṣr*, in 4 *juzʾ*, al-Maṭbaʿa al-ʿUmūmiyya (Sarkīs 965).

1901—Muṣṭafā Bek Najīb, an Egyptian civil servant who died in 1901/1319, started a series of biographies with the title *Ḥumāt al-Islām*. Its body, which runs into the sixth century, was published by Maṭbaʿat al-Liwāʾ in 1901 on the order of Muṣṭafā Kāmil Bāshā (Sarkīs 1756 says that Najīb died in 1320). In the same year, Ibrāhīm Bāshā Fawzī, who had spent his military career in the Sudan where he had been captured by the Mahdists, published his *al-Sūdān bayna yaday Gordon wa-Kitchener*, 2 vols, Maṭbaʿat al-Muʾayyad (see Cairo² IV, 222, Alexandria, *Taʾrīkh* 79; Sarkīs has a mistaken 1309).

1903—A description of the Turco-Greek war of 1898 was given in 1903 in Farīq al-Ṭubjī al-Miṣrī ʿAlī Bek Riḍā Shākir b. Muḥammad Shākir's *al-Qawl al-sadīd fī ḥarb al-dawla al-ʿUthmāniyya maʿa ʾl-Yūnān* (Cairo: Maṭbaʿat al-Mawsūʿāt, 1321; Sarkīs 1363).

1904—In 1904, Ṣāliḥ Jawdat published a brief history of Egypt in the nineteenth century entitled *Miṣr fī ʾl-qarn al-tāsiʿ ʿashar* (Maṭbaʿat al-Shaʿb). Earlier, in 1901, he had published *al-Dalīl al-ʿaṣrī lil-quṭr al-Miṣrī*, and in 1908 there fol-
309 lowed a history of the Malay states, | *Ummat al-Malāyū*, at Maṭbaʿat al-Shaʿb (see *al-Muqtaṭaf* 35, 1029, Sarkīs 1184).

1905—Basing himself on Turkish chronicles, Ibrāhīm Ḥalīm Bāshā, a former *mufattish al-awqāf* in Damanhūr, published *al-Tuḥfa al-Ḥalīmiyya fī taʾrīkh al-dawla al-ʿaliyya* (until 1923) in 1905, Maṭbaʿat Dīwān ʿumūm al-awqāf, 1322 (Sarkīs 14).

1913—In 1913, ʿAbd al-Fattāḥ Efendi ʿUbayda (d. 1928), secretary at al-Maḥākim al-ahliyya, published a naval history of Islam entitled *al-Usṭūl al-Islāmī* (Maṭbaʿat al-Hilāl), followed in 1915 by his *Intishār al-khaṭṭ al-ʿarabī fi ʾl-ʿālam al-sharqī wal-ʿālam al-gharbī* (Maṭbaʿa Hindiyya) (Sarkīs 1289).

1922—Amīn Saʿīd and Karīm Khalīl Thābit, *Sīrat al-ghāzī Muṣṭafā Kamāl wa-taʾrīkh al-ḥaraka al-Turkiyya al-waṭaniyya fī Anāḍūl*, Cairo.—Khalīl Karīm Thābit, *Ludendorf, al-qāʾid al-Almānī al-ʿaẓīm*, Cairo, Maṭbaʿat al-ʿArab; *Saʿd Zaghlūl fī ḥayātihi ʾl-khāṣṣa*, C. 1929; *al-Durūz wal-thawra al-Sūriyya*, C. 1925.—Ilyās al-Ayyūbī, *Taʾrīkh Miṣr fī ʿahd al-Khidīwī Ismāʿīl Bāshā min sanat 1863 ilā 1879*, Maṭbaʿat Dār al-Kutub al-Miṣriyya; *Muḥammad ʿAlī, sīratuhu wa-aʿmāluhu wa-āthāruhu*, Maṭbaʿat al-Hilāl, 1923.

1923—ʿAbd al-Raḥmān al-Barqūqī, *Ḥaḍārat al-ʿArab fi ʾl -Andalus*, C. 1341 (Sarkīs 551, who also mentions two philological works).

1924—Muḥammad Sharīf Salīm, *Mulakhkhaṣ taʾrīkh al-Khawārij*, Maṭbaʿat al-Taqaddum 1342.—Kāmil al-Kīlānī (see Suppl. I, 125, and page 233 above), *Naẓarāt fī taʾrīkh al-adab al-Andalusī* (based on his lectures at the University of Egypt), 1342; to his *Maṣāriʿ al-khulafāʾ* there is a *taqrīẓ* in Abū Shādī, *Ashiʿʿa* 125.—Muḥammad ʿAbd al-Jawād al-Aṣmaʿī, *Qalʿat Muḥammad ʿAlī lā qalʿat Nabūlyūn, baḥth taʾrīkhī, bi-nubdha taʾrīkhiyya ʿala ʾl-madāris al-ḥarbiyya wal-maʿāmil al-ʿaskariyya wa-ḥālāt al-jaysh al-Miṣrī fī ʿahd Muḥammad ʿAlī Bāshā bi-qalam al-amīr ʿUmar Tūsūn*, Maṭbaʿat Dār al-Kutub al-Miṣriyya, 1342.

1925—Aḥmad Ḥāfiẓ ʿIwaḍ , ṣāḥib *Jarīdat Kawkab al-sharq, Fatḥ Miṣr al-ḥadīth aw Nabūlyūn Būnabārt fī Miṣr; Min wālid ilā waladihi*, 2nd printing 1925; *Maʿa ʾl-raʾīs* (Saʾd Zāghlūl Bāshā) *fi ʾl-manfā*, Cairo n.d.—Muḥammad Qāsim wa-Ḥusayn Ḥusnī, *Taʾrīkh al-qarn al-tāsiʿ ʿashar fī Ūrūbā wa-mā yalīhā min al-ḥawādith ḥattā nihāyat al-ḥarb ʿuẓmā*, 3rd printing Maṭbaʿat Dār al-Kutub al-Miṣriyya, 1343.—Aḥmad Shafīq Bāshā, mudīr maṣlaḥat al-ḥūdūd al-Miṣriyya, *Ḥawliyyāt Miṣr al-siyāsiyya*, running from 4 August 1914 until 1924, with a brief overview from Muḥammad ʿAlī until the [First] World War, Cairo.—*Mudhakkirāt min ziyārat dayr Ṭūr Sīnā*, 1926, al-Maṭbaʿa al-Amirīkiyya.

1926—ʿAbd al-Wahhāb al-Najjār, *Taʾrīkh al-Islām wal-khulafāʾ* | *al-rāshidīn*, 310
C. 1345.—Muhammad Rifʿat, *Taʾrīkh Miṣr al-siyāsī fi ʾl-azmina al-ḥadītha*.—Zakī Fahmī, *Ṣafwat al-ʿaṣr fī taʾrīkh wa-rusūm mashāhīr rijāl Miṣr min ʿahd sākin al-janna Muḥammad ʿAlī Bāshā al-Kabīr* Cairo, 734 pp.

1927—ʿAlī Shukrī, *Taʾrīkh Miṣr qabla ʾl-iḥtilāl al-Barīṭānī wa-baʿdahu*.—Muḥammad al-Khuḍrī (d. 2 Shawwāl 1345/10 April 1927), teacher of Islamic law at Madrasat al-qaḍāʾ al-sharʿī and *wakīl* of that same institution, then inspector of Arabic language teaching at the ministry of education, *Itmām al-wafāʾ fī sīrat al-khulafāʾ*, Būlāq 1306, C. 1317.—*Taʾrīkh al-umam al-Islāmiyya* (based on his lectures at the University of Egypt), vol. I until the Umayyads, vol. II until the Mongol onslaught, Maṭbaʿat al-Jamāliyya, 1334/1916.—*Nūr al-yaqīn fī sīrat sayyid al-mursalīn*, Maṭbaʿat al-Jāmiʿa 1315, 1320, 1327, 1926.—*Taʾrīkh al-tashrīʿ al-Islāmī*, Maṭbaʿat Dār al-Kutub, 1339/1920.

1929—Muḥammad Rushdī al-Jarkasī, *Madaniyyat al-ʿArab fi ʾl-Jāhiliyya wal-Islām*.—ʿAbd al-Raḥmān Efendi al-Rāfiʿī al-Muḥāmī, *al-Jamʿiyyāt al-waṭaniyya* (in France, America, Germany, Poland, and Anatolia), Maṭbaʿat al-Muqtaṭaf, 1922.—*Taʾrīkh al-ḥaraka al-qawmiyya wa-taṭawwur niẓām al-ḥukm fī Miṣr*, 3 vols, 1929.—*ʿAṣr Ismāʿīl*, 2 vols, 1351/1931, *al-Thawra al-ʿArābiyya wal-iḥtilāl al-Inglīzī*, 1937.—Najīb Makhlūf, *Nūbar Bāshā wa-mā tamma ʿalā yadihi*.

1932—Aḥmad Faḍl b. ʿAlī Muḥsin al-ʿAbdalī, *Hadiyyat al-zaman fī akhbār mulūk Lahij wa-ʿAdan*, C. 1351.

1933—Amīn Saʿīd, editor of *al-Muqaṭṭam* (cf. 1922), *Mulūk al-Muslimīn al-muʿāṣirīn wa-duwaluhum; al-Thawra al-ʿArabiyya al-kubrā* in 3 vols (a documented account that was banned by the Syrian authorities, see *Oriente Moderno* XV, 1935, 157), Maṭbaʿat ʿIsā al-Bābī al-Ḥalabī wa-Shurakāʾihi, n.d.—Anon. *Thawrat al-ʿArab, muqaddamātuhā al-siyāsiyya, asbābuhā wa-natāʾijuhā bi-qalam aḥad aʿḍāʾ al-Jamʿiyya al-ʿArabiyya*, Cairo n.d., 246 pp. *Al-Nahḍa al-qawmiyya, wadaʿahā kātib kabīr Miṣrī*, Cairo n.d., 235 pp.

5 *Modernists, Reformists, and Politicians*

Ch.C. Adams, *Islam and Modernism in Egypt, a Study of the Modern Reform Movement Inaugurated by Muḥammad ʿAbduh*, London 1933, 2nd ed. 1936, Arabic trans. ʿAbbās Maḥmūd, *al-Islām wal-tajdīd*, C. 1935.

311 | H. Laoust, Le réformisme orthodoxe des 'Salafiya' et les caractères généraux de son orientation actuelle, *REI* VI, 1932, 173/224.

If literature and poetry could develop so freely in twentieth-century Egypt, despite there also being obstacles and setbacks, this was thanks to the work of some of its religious and political leaders. Even though their writings fall outside of the scope of the present volume, they nevertheless deserve to be briefly mentioned.

1 Jamāl al-Dīn al-Afghānī

On 22 March 1871, at the time when Egypt, as a result of the totally irresponsible financial policies of Khedive Ismāʿīl, was coming more and more under the influence of the European powers who were its creditors, and while, throughout the country, the first signs of a rejection of the traditional blind faith in its religious and political leaders started to make themselves felt, there arrived in Cairo a man who would give this nascent movement a real face and a genuine voice. At the time, Jamāl al-Dīn al-Afghānī[187] could not boast of any literary achievements, but he already possessed a turbulent political past in his homeland and Istanbul, where his bold appearance had caused a true sensation.

Born in Asʿadābād near Kabul, Afghanistan, in 1839, he came from a family of sharifs that traced its origin back to ʿAlī al-Tirmidhī (d. 279/892) and claimed to have been dispossessed of its lands by Dūst Muḥammad (see his biography in *al-ʿUrwa al-wuthqā*, p. 3). But people said that he had actually been born in Asʿadābād near Hamadan, in Persia, and that he had only claimed to be Afghan
312 to pass for a Sunnī. | After his studies in Persia, Afghanistan and India, and having made the pigrimage in 1857, he started to work for the emir of Afghanistan, Dūst Muḥammad Khān. After the latter's death in 1864, he joined the pretender, Muḥammad Aʿẓam. When the latter had conquered his brothers, he appointed Jamāl al-Dīn as Prime Minister. But soon Muḥammad Aʿẓam had to give way to his brother, Shīr ʿAlī, who was supported by the British, dying not long after. Even if Jamāl al-Dīn was not held to account for his deeds immediately afterwards, he believed it would be better for him to leave the country,

---

187 Portrait from *al-Hilāl* in *Tatimmat al-bayān*, p. 10.

pretending to go on pilgrimage. By way of India, where he was received with all honours but also kept under strict observation, he first went to Cairo where he contacted the scholars of al-Azhar. Having become fully acquainted with the ruinous consequences of British colonial policy in his adoptive country, he believed that his plans for the liberation of Islam would meet with the sympathy of ʿAbd al-Ḥamīd in Istanbul. And it is indeed true that he was initially well received, not just at the court, but in society at large as well. However, this aroused the jealousy of the Shaykh al-Islām and, after a careless remark on prophecy and human professions during a lecture at the Dār al-funūn, the University of Istanbul, the shaykh was able to throw suspicion onto him and have him expelled. This is how Jamāl al-Dīn went to Cairo.

Riyāḍ Pāshā gave him a stipend so he could spend all his time teaching. Because he tried to interest his students in philosophy, it was not long before the scholars at al-Azhar became suspicious. In the same way in which he tried to arouse pride in Islam in his students (instead of a national awareness that was still in its infancy), he also contested the influence of European powers by means of articles in the press, especially Britain's influence on the government of Ismāʿīl. When the latter had to cede the throne to his son Tawfīq, on 26 June 1879, Jamāl al-Dīn and his supporters expected the start of a new era. Thus, they were deeply disappointed when the khedive expelled Jamāl al-Dīn and his confidant Abū Turāb as early as September 1879.

Initially, he found refuge with the *niẓām* of Hyderabad. This was also where
he wrote his first work, | in Persian, which was a defence of Islam against the 313
'materialists' (lith. Bombay, 1298). It was first translated into Urdu (lith. Calcutta 1883), and then into Arabic by his student Muḥammad ʿAbduh under the title *Risāla fī ibṭāl madhhab al-Dahriyyīn wa-bayān mafāsidihim wa-ithbāt anna 'l -dīn asās al-madaniyya wal-kufr asās al-ʿumrān*, Beirut 1303, C. 1312. As clearly emphasised by him in *al-ʿUrwa al-wuthqā* 35/41 (*al-Dahriyyūn fī 'l-Hind*), the work was directed against the efforts of Aḥmad Khān Bahādur and his student Samīʿallāh Khān to reconcile Islam with Western values as they had come to know them through the British occupation. During the ʿArābī uprising he was detained in Calcutta, but when this uprising failed and he was allowed to go wherever he liked, he went to Europe.

After a brief stay in London he took up residence in Paris. There, for three years, he campained actively against Britain in the press. In 1883, the *Journal des débats* allowed him the possibility of writing a polemic against Ernest Renan, who had denied Islam any and all capacity to develop. When his student Muḥammad ʿAbduh came to visit him in Paris in 1884, they jointly undertook the publication of the magazine *al-ʿUrwa al-wuthqā*, of which 18 issues were distributed free of charge throughout the Muslim world with the aim of

consolidating their readership into an underground anti-British movement. Because they attached no value to copyright, it is impossible to determine which of the individual articles was written by whom. Nevertheless, the magazine's brilliant literary form was probably the work of Muḥammad ʿAbduh. It is one long, passionate indictment of British policy; not just in Egypt and the Sudan, but also in Ireland and India. The authors emphasise time and again that Islam unites all its followers, irrespective of nationality or race, and that they only need to become aware of their strength to repossess their former freedom. Besides short articles on current affairs, especially in the Sudan and on the advance of the Russians in Central Asia, we find detailed expositions in which Islam is defended against criticism from Europe. One of these articles, *al-Qaḍāʾ wal-qadar wa-uṣūl al-ʿaqāʾid al-Islāmiyya wa-ummahāt al-masāʾil al-tawḥīdiyya* (*al-ʿUrwa* 164/79), in which Islam is defended against the accu-
314 sation of blind fatalism and | in which predestination is presented as compatible with free will, was also published separately in al-Afghānī's name (Cairo: Maṭbaʿat al-Maḥmūdiyya, n.d.).[188] When Britain prohibited the magazine in Egypt and India, it was closed down but then reprinted in Beirut, Maṭbaʿat al-Tawfīq, in 1328 and 1928.

The British government must have believed that it could use him for its own political ends when it invited him to come to London to advise them in their campaign against the Mahdi in the Sudan. But Russia, too, tried to win him to its cause; thus, he spent four years in St. Peterburg and Moscow. There are reports claiming that in 1886 he was minister of war for Shāh Nāṣir al-Dīn, but that he latter soon lost trust in him, so that al-Afghānī went back to Russia. In 1889 he met the shah in Munich and accepted his invitation to come to Persia. Here, he soon had significant influence on public opinion, which was already unhappy about the foolish policies of the shah; as such, the shah had him expelled to Iraq in the winter of 1890/1. After a brief stay in London he went to Istanbul in 1892, where ʿAbd al-Ḥamīd gave him a house in Nišāntāš. The latter did not expel him to Persia when one of al-Afghānī's followers assassinated the shah on 1 May 1896. Al-Afghānī died on 9 March 1897, purportedly of cancer.

It remains unclear to what period of his life his most important literary achievement belongs: *Tatimmat al-bayān fī taʾrīkh al-Afghān*, ed. ʿAlī Yūsuf al-Kurdīlī (publisher of the *Jarīdat al-ʿAlam al-ʿUthmānī*), Cairo: Maṭbaʿat al-Mawsūʿāt, 1318/1901. It seems likely, however, that it was written in Istanbul. After a brief sketch of the early history of his country, he gives a quite detailed account of its development until the British-Afghan war of 1878. While he does

188 Adams 152 attributes this article to ʿAbduh, but provides no grounds for this.

not refer to his own experiences at the court of Dūst Muḥammad and his son, he does not tire of pointing out the deviousness of British policy. At the end, he gives a fairly detailed account of the ethnography and geography of the country, and includes an unidentified emir's instructions for his sucessor, probably Dūst Muḥammad's.

| Yet even more than his writings, it was Jamāl al-Dīn's charisma that galvan- 315
ised the Muslim world to fight for its independence, filling it with the awareness that Europe's civilisation could only be used as a means to this end, and that it could never replace the spiritual values of Islam.

Jirjī Zaydān, *Mashāhīr al-sharq* II, 55ff, Shakīb Arslān in Lothrop Stoddard, *Ḥāḍir al-ʿālam al-Islāmī*, C. 1343, 199/209, Ph. di Ṭarrāzī, *Taʾrīkh al-ṣiḥāfa al-ʿarabiyya* 293/9, E.G. Browne, *The Persian Revolution* 3ff, Adams, 4/17.—*Khāṭirāt Jamāl al-Dīn al-Afghānī al-Ḥusaynī wa-fīhā mujmal ārāʾihi wa-afkārihi wa-marqāhu fī ahl al-sharq wal-gharb khulqan wa-siyāsatan wajtimāʿan, taʾlīf Muḥammad Bāy al-Makhrūṣ*, Beirut 1939.

2 Muḥammad ʿAbduh

Jamāl al-Dīn's work was continued in Egypt by his most important student, Muḥammad ʿAbduh, who paved the way for the spiritual liberation of Islam.

He was born in a village near Tanta around 1849. His father was a peasant of Turkish stock who had given up his lands near Maḥallat Naṣr in al-Buḥayra province because the oppression of Muḥammad ʿAlī's officials had become too much for him. His mother came from a family that traced its origin all the way back to Caliph ʿUmar. When Muḥammad ʿAbduh was born, his father returned to his native province, where Muḥammad grew up as a true peasant boy. When he was thirteen years old, his father sent him to the madrasa of the Aḥmadī mosque in Tanta. An older stepbrother of ʿAbduh was a teacher there. Disgusted with the backward schooling system, he returned to his village in 1865 and got married. But it was not long before his father forced him to return to Tanta. On his way there, he escaped to his great-uncle in Kunayyisat ʿAdrīn. This uncle, a member of the Shādhiliyya order, succeeded in convincing him that he should really go and study. And it so happened that, when he returned to Tanta in October of 1865, he put such energy into his studies that it took just a couple of months before he could go to al-Azhar in Cairo.

At al-Azhar, he was especially interested in the lectures on philosophy by Ḥasan al-Ṭawīl. At the same time, he indulged in mystico-ascetic exercises to such an extent that his uncle, who had introduced him to them, had to warn
him against exaggeration. | These exercises produced his first work, *Risālat al-* 316
wāridāt (Cairo, 1290, 1874, reprint in *Taʾrīkh al-ustādh al-imām* II, 1/25 and Cairo

1344). A new world opened up for him when Jamāl al-Dīn al-Afghānī returned to Cairo, lecturing not only on Islamic philosophy based on Ibn Sīnā's *Ishārāt* but also introducing him to European thought through translations from the French. He became an unconditional follower of al-Afghānī, who also gave him guidance in writing and public speaking. All this resulted in four articles for the newly-founded newspaper *al-Ahrām*, in which he put all his youthful enthusiasm into propagating al-Afghānī's ideas, especially his warning that Islam could only assert itself by using modern scientific methods. On the surface, his second work, the *Ḥawāshī* to al-Dawwānī's commentary on *al-ʿAqāʾid al-ʿAḍudiyya* (cf. II, 292, ii) of 1876, still follows the traditional path of Islamic theology. However, it already shows his rational approach in distinguishing between various dogmas. This book, and even more so his private lectures on *al-ʿAqāʾid al-Nasafiyya*, made the orthodox, especially Shaykh ʿUllaysh (see Suppl. II, 738), suspect him of heresy. As a result of this he almost failed his final exam, were it not for the liberal-minded dean of al-Azhar, Muḥammad al-ʿAbbāsī, who spoke up in his defence.

He started lecturing at al-Azhar in 1877. In his classes, he lectured on Ibn Miskawayh's *Tahdhīb al-akhlāq* just as easily as on political philosophy using Guizot's *Histoire de la civilisation*. In 1878, Riyāḍ Pāshā appointed him Reader in History at the *Dār al-ʿulūm* (founded in 1873 by ʿAlī Pāshā Mubārak) and Reader in Arabic at the *Madrasat al-lughāt al-Khidīwiyya*. But when Tawfīq assumed power in 1879 and immediately expelled Jamāl al-Dīn, ʿAbduh too, was banished to his native village of Maḥallat Naṣr. But just a year later Riyāḍ Pāshā was back in charge, appointing ʿAbduh as editor-in-chief of *al-Waqāʾiʿ al-Miṣriyya* and granting him permission to recruit staff from among Jamāl al-Dīn's students. Among these, there also was a certain Saʿd Zaghlūl, who still was a student at al-Azhar at the time.

317 | Editor-in-chief of the official organ of the state, he controlled the rest of the press while at the same time promoting every possible kind of modern literary expression. Moreover, he was in a position now to stand up for the reform of the education system. A member of the department of education founded on 31 March 1881, he soon gained practical influence as well. But he certainly did not hesitate to criticise government policy when necessary. All these activities took place at a time when the first national movement of Egypt under Aḥmad ʿArābī (ʿUrābī) made itself heard. Even though the military revered him as a spiritual leader, he often had to warn them against rash demands, such as their call for the introduction of a parliamentary democracy, the masses not being ready for this at all. But he nevertheless sided with them so that, after the movement fell apart, he was court martialled and expelled from the country for thee years and three months.

He first went to Beirut. A year later, he followed his teacher to Paris. There, he helped him with the publication of *al-ʿUrwa al-wuthqā* and with the construction of the movement for which it was the mouthpiece. But then they parted ways. This was not just on practical grounds, but also because ʿAbduh preferred to work quietly towards a spiritual renewal of Islam instead of engaging in the violent kind of revolution that his teacher was preparing. Nevertheless, in 1884 he travelled to Tunis and also tried to infiltrate the Sudan by way of Egypt and cause the Mahdī to take up arms against the British. In early 1885, he returned to Beirut where he gave private lectures on the life of the Prophet and the interpretation of the Qurʾān. Towards the end of that same year he was appointed to a teaching position at al-Madrasa al-Sulṭāniyya. It was here that he translated al-Afghānī's treatise against the Dahriyya, while his commentaries on al-Murtaḍā's *Nahj al-balāgha* (cf. Suppl. I, 705) and the *Maqāmāt* of Badīʿ al-Dīn al-Hamadhānī were also written there. He presented each of the Shaykh al-Islām and the Wālī of Beirut with a memorandum on the improvement of the educational system in which he warned strongly against the dangers of foreign schools. Towards the end of 1884 he was able to return to his native country after Lord Cromer had interceded on his behalf.

The khedive, however, still feared his influence on the younger generation. As such, he merely gave him a judgeship at the | common trial court, first in 318
Banhā, then in Zaqāzīq and finally in Cairo, where he was appointed counsellor at the court of appeals (*maḥkamat al-istiʾnāf*) two years later.

Even though he did much to improve the judicial system when in these positions, teaching remained his calling. When ʿAbbās II Ḥilmī came to power in 1892, he submitted a plan for the improvement of the curriculum at al-Azhar, following which he was appointed a member of the committee that was to reorganise this institution of higher learning. It was not long before he gained a decisive influence in it, so that he could achieve important reforms. Having raised the salaries of the teaching staff and improved the living conditions of the students, he then reorganised the curriculum by supplementing the theological subjects with mathematics, geography, history, and philology. A teacher of *adab* he appointed started his lecture series with an interpretation of al-Mubarrad's *Kāmil*. ʿAbduh himself not only lectured on dogmatics and *tafsīr*, but also on logic and rhetoric. His reforms often met with passive resistance, though, and when ʿAbbās Ḥilmī turned to the reactionaries after his conflict with Cromer and tried to disengage himself from the endowments of the supporters of al-Azhar, ʿAbduh left the university's administrative board and resigned from his teaching post, both on 19 March 1905.

He was appointed muftī of Egypt on 3 June 1899. This post, too, was transformed by him; all of his fatwas breathe the spirit of liberal reform. Two of

them created a sensation, when he declared both the eating of meat slaughtered by Jews and Christians and the keeping of interest-bringing accounts in the National Savings Bank to be permissible. Being the *muftī*, the *sharīʿa* courts of the country—which he regularly went to inspect in person—came under his supervision, as did the administration of the religious endowments or *waqf*s. His plans to change the status of officials in places of worship, though, were frustrated by resistance from the khedive. As *muftī*, he was also appointed a member of the legislative council. Working within the narrow margins available to him, he tried to prepare for the future self-rule of the country. In *al-Jamʿiyya li-iḥyāʾ al-ʿulūm al-ʿarabiyya* (founded in 1900), he co-operated
319 with Muḥammad al-Shinqīṭī on the edition of | Ibn Sīda's *Mukhaṣṣaṣ* and Ibn Mālik's *Muwaṭṭaʾ*.

During his career as a civil servant, Muḥammad ʿAbduh often went to Europe on holiday. He was preparing for another such trip in the house of a friend in Ramla, near Alexandria, when a long illness saw him die on 8 Jumādā I 1323/11 July 1905.

Even if his work in Egypt often met with resistance, his Afghānī-inspired ideas left a strong impression on the spiritual development of the country, helping it to liberate itself from British rule despite seemingly insurmountable difficulties. Therefore, anyone criticising him with Horten for not having enriched philosophy with his own ideas completely misjudges his true intentions. The mere fact that a man of his background was able to identify with people like H. Spencer and Tolstoy, accepting polygenesis as an hypothesis to explain the existence of different human races, shows just how open he was to Western thinking.[189] In the same way in which his teacher Jamāl al-Dīn wanted to render all the material achievements of European civilization accessible to Muslims in order to prepare them for their struggle against its domination, ʿAbduh, too, only wanted to use European education as a way to defend the eternal truths of Islam.[190] Both as a dogmatist and a jurisconsult he felt no longer bound by any doctrine of the past, claiming the right to take the Qurʾān as the sole guideline for his teachings and moral actions. Insofar as he tried to cleanse the core of the Prophet's teachings of all later additions, he felt related to the aspirations of the Wahhābīs and their spiritual fathers Ibn Taymiyya and Ibn Qayyim al-Jawziyya, to whom his own students were even closer than he.

189 At the same time, his language is almost entirely free from Europeanisms, except, e.g. *rūḥ al-waqt* 'spirit of the age', in *Risālat al-tawḥīd*, 2nd printing, 1343, 11,$_{2}$.

190 That he could also go too far in his apologetical zeal is shown by his effort to explain the belief in *jinn*s in terms of bacteriology.

His position on the cult of saints is typical. Even though he does not deny that religious personalities can achieve such a closeness to God that they also have a very close bond with the Prophet, | he does not want to force anyone to be- 320
lieve in the miracles of the Awliyāʾ, so important to their followers among the masses.

Apart from the works mentioned above, he also published: 1. *Risālat al-tawḥīd*, the draft of which he had written for his lectures at the Sulṭāniyya in Beirut and which he later augmented and finalised, 1st printing C. 1315/1897; 2nd printing with notes by Muḥammad Rashīd Riḍā, 1326/1908, 2nd printing of the text alone 1343, Maṭbaʿat al-ʿUlūm al-Adabiyya, 5th printing C. 1346/1926, 6th printing C. 1353, French trans. by B. Michel and Cheikh Moustapha Abdel Razik, Paris 1925 (with a valuable introduction).—2. *Sharḥ Kitāb al-baṣāʾir al-Naṣīriyya fī ʿilm al-manṭiq taṣnīf al-qāḍī al-zāhid Zayn al-Dīn ʿUmar b. Sahlān al-Sāwī* (cf. Suppl. II, 830), C. 1316/1898.—3. *Taqrīr fī iṣlāḥ al-maḥākim al-sharʿiyya*, C. 1318/1900.—4. *al-Islām wal-radd ʿalā muntaqidīhi*, a reply to an article by G. Hanotaux titled 'Face à face de l'Islām et la question musulmane' in *Journal de Paris* 1900, transl. in *al-Muʾayyad*, included in *Taʾrīkh* II, 382/95, with Muḥammad ʿAbduh's answer on pages 395/411, a reply by Hanotaux dated 16 July and a rejoinder by Muḥammad ʿAbduh, together with extracts from the *Risālat al-Tawḥīd*, the *Radd ʿala ʾl-Dahriyyīn*, from Muḥammad Farīd Wajdī's *al-Madaniyya wal-Islām* and articles from *al-Muʾayyad* about the Muslim congress on education in Calcutta of December 1899, published in 1327/1909, 1343/1924, 1925, French transl. *L'Europe et l'Islam* by Ṭalʿat Bey Ḥarb, C. 1905.—5. *al-Islām wal-Naṣrāniyya maʿa ʾl-ʿilm wal-madaniyya*, a series of articles from *al-Manār* against Faraḥ Anṭūn's condemnations of Islam in his magazine *al-Jāmiʿa* (see p. 193), dated 1900, special issue, n.d. n.p. (with a portrait), C. 1320/1902, 1323, 1431/1922, 1923. In a postscript, he juxtaposes his rejection of Hanotaux's view on Islam with the attitude of the British, whose constitution he regards as commensurate with the ideals of Islam, something which he believes may be the fruit of the Crusades.—6. *Tafsīr sūrat al-Fātiḥa, wa-mushkilāt al-Qurʾān*, C. 1319, 1323/1905, 1330/1911.—7. *Tafsīr sūrat al-ʿAṣr*, a special issue of *al-Manār*, C. 1321/1903, 1345.—8. *Tafsīr juzʾ ʿamma* (p. 78/114), a special issue of *al-Manār*, C. 1322/1904.—9. *Tafsīr al-Qurʾān al-ḥakīm, Tafsīr al-Manār*, by himself only until sura $4_{,125}$, completed in Cairo in 1325/30, continued by Muḥammad Rashīd Riḍā until sura $9_{,93}$ in 10 volumes until 1350/1931; reprint of volume 1 in 1927.—10. *Palermo-Sizilien, die Reisenotizen des Scheich Muḥammad ʿAbduh*, with a preface by Prof. | A.E. Schmidt, Tashkent 1927 321
(see Kračkovsky MSOS XXXI, 186, n. 3).—11. *al-Iḍāʾa li-ṭālib al-kafāʾa taʾlīf al-shaykh ʿAbdallāh Manṣūr wa-Muhammad ʿAbduh*, Alexandria 1340 (*Jāmiʿ* I, 340).

I. Goldziher, *Die Richtungen der islāmischen Koranauslegung* 320/70, M. Horten, *Beitr. z. Kenntnis des Orients* XIII, 1915, 85/114. XIV, 1916, 74/128. Biography by Muḥammad Rashīd Riḍā in *al-Manār* VIII, 1905, *Taʾrīkh al-ustādh al-imām al-shaykh Muḥammad ʿAbduh* by the same.—II. Collected smaller works 1908.—III. Obituaries etc. 1910.—I, Biography 1134 pp., C. 1931, Maṭbʿat al-Manār, Jirjī Zaydān, *Mashāhīr al-ṣiḥāfa al-ʿarabiyya*, 287/93, H. Lammens, *l'Islam* 229/34, Carra de Vaux, *Les penseurs de l'Islam* V, Paris 1926, 254/67, Adams 18/176, M. el Baḥay, *Muḥammad ʿAbduh, Untersuchung seiner Erziehungsmethode zum Nationalbewusstsein und zur nationalen Erhebung in Ägypten*, Diss. Hamburg 1936.

3 Muḥammad Rashīd Riḍā

After Muḥammad ʿAbduh's death, Sayyid Muḥammad Rashīd Riḍā, mentioned earlier as the person who continued ʿAbduh's commentary on the Qurʾān, became the leader of his followers, trying to unite them into a political party.

He was born in Ṭarābulus al-Shām on 27 Jumādā I 1282/19 September 1865. In 1897, he completed his education there, with Shaykh Ḥusayn al-Jisr having been his teacher. Al-Jisr had written the *Risāla Ḥamīdiyya*, dedicated to ʿAbd al-Ḥamīd (ca. 1306/1889). In it, he defended Islam against the criticisms of missionaries while trying to demonstrate that it was entirely compatible with modern scientific insights, including Darwinism. Rashīd Riḍā was initially very much influenced by Sufi ideas, until he received a copy of Jamāl al-Dīn's *al-ʿUrwa al-wuthqā*. He then first tried to get in touch with him in Istanbul, but then went to Cairo where he joined Muḥammad ʿAbduh in Rajab 1315/December 1897, becoming his most trusted student. In Shawwāl 1315/March 1898 he founded the weekly *al-Manār* for the dissemination of ʿAbduh's ideas. The magazine was banned in Turkey, but it initially met with little response in Egypt itself. From the second year onward it became a monthly and it was only in its fifth year that it really started to catch on. In his editorial work, Rashīd was assisted by his brother Ḥusayn Waṣfī Riḍā (b. 1882, d. 1911, see *al-Mashriq* XXIV, 229). *Al-Manār* also published, among other things, Muḥammad ʿAbduh's interpretation of verses of the Qurʾān, pieces which were later brought together
322 in his | commentary. In the same way in which Jamāl al-Dīn al-Afghānī had once tried to unite his supporters around *al-ʿUrwa al-wuthqā*, Rashīd Riḍā founded *al-Jamʿiyya al-Islāmiyya* with the aim of uniting all Islamic states into a federation that was to be led by the caliph. Even if he renounced all forms of political agitation, he nevertheless found himself opposed to Muṣṭafā Kāmil's National Party (*al-Ḥizb al-waṭanī*) and its mouthpiece *al-Liwāʾ*, which advocated Egyptian nationalism. He had more success with his missionary society *Jamʿiyyat al-daʿwa wal-irshād*, which sought to start a missionary school.

In order to avoid any opposition from Egyptian nationalists, he set his hopes on the Young Turks and, once the Turkish constitution had been restored, he went to Istanbul, where he stayed for an entire year. Initially, he was indeed successful in creating interest in his plans, but as the political situation in Istanbul did not allow things to come to fruition he returned to Cairo. There, on the anniversary of the Prophet on 12 Rabīʿ I 1330/2 March 1912, he opened the *Dār al-daʿwa wal-irshād* on the island of Rawḍa. While the institution did indeed enroll students from Africa, Turkey, Turkistan, India, Java and the Malay Archipelago, it had to cease its activities at the outbreak of the war. A member of the *Ḥizb al-lāmarkaziyya al-idāriyya al-ʿUthmānī*, he also tried to support his fellow Egyptians in their aspirations for autonomy within the larger Ottoman empire.

After the collapse of the Ottoman Empire he opposed the new Turkey of Mustafa Kemal as a center of atheism. Instead, he set his hopes on the Arabia run by Ibn Saʿūd—whom he met personally in 1926—as the one and only independent Islamic state.

He opposed the cult of saints with great zeal, in one case even risking death at the hands of an angry mob in the al-Ḥasanayn mosque. But he also opposed the pretensions of individual *madhāhib* as obstacles to any kind of true progress, taking the Qurʾān and the Sunna as his sole guidelines in life. He advocated the strict separation of religion and civil law, which he wanted to be founded on modern insights. This is how he supplemented Muḥammad ʿAbduh's ideas on ethics. Since he held fast to religion as | the foundation of the state, he was 323
closer to the conservatives than to the liberals (al-Aḥrār) in political matters. He died on 23 Jumādā I 1354/ 24 August 1935.

Adams 177/204, G. Antonius, *The Arab Awakening* 109, 159/60, Sarkīs 934/6. Necrology in *al-Ahrām* of 14 July 1939. Works: 1. *Kashf shubuhāt al-Naṣārā wa-ḥujaj al-Islām*, Maṭbaʿat al-Manār 1322.—2. *Injīl Barnabā*, ibid. 1325.—3. *Muḥāwarat al-muṣliḥ wal-muqallid*, ibid. 1325.—4. *al-Muslimūn wal-Qibṭ wal-muʾtamar al-Miṣrī*, ibid. 1329.—5. *ʿAqīdat al-ṣalb wal-fidāʾ* ibid. 1331.—6. *Dhikra ʾl -mawlid al-nabawī wa-hiya khulāṣat al-sīra al-Muḥammadiyya wa-ḥaqīqat al-daʿwa al-Islāmiyya*, ibid. 1335.—7. *Tarjamat al-Qurʾān wa-mā fīhā min al-mafāsid wa-munāfāt al-Islām*, ibid. 1340.—8. *al-Khilāfa wal-imāma al-ʿuẓmā*, ibid. 1341, cf. H. Laoust, *Le califat dans la doctrine de Rashīd Riḍā*, trad. et annoté d'*al-Khilāfa wal-imāma al-ʿuẓmā*, Mém. de l'Inst. franç. de Damas VI.—9. *Majmūʿat al-ḥadīth al-Najdiyya ashrafa ʿalā taṣḥīḥihā Muḥammad Rashīd Riḍā*, 2nd printing, ibid. 1342/8.—10. *al-Wahhābiyyūn wal-Ḥijāz*, ibid. 1344.—11. *al-Waḥda al-Islāmiyya wal-ukhuwwa al-dīniyya*, ibid. 1346, see *REI* VI, 192, n. 1.—12. *Yusr al-Islām wa-uṣūl al-tashrīʿ al-ʿāmm*, ibid. 1347.—13. *al-Sunna wal-Shīʿa aw al-Wahhābiyya wal-Rāfiḍa*, ibid. 1347.—14. *Nidāʾ lil-jins al-laṭīf fī ḥuqūq al-nisāʾ fī ʾl-Islām wa-ḥaẓẓihinna min al-iṣlāḥ al-Muḥammadī al-ʿāmm*, ibid. 1351.—15. *al-Waḥy al-Muḥammadī*, ibid. 1352, see *al-Mashriq* XXXI, 954.—*Taʾrīkh* and *tafsīr* see p. 320ff.

4 Muḥammad Tawfīq Ṣidqī

One of Muḥammad Rashīd Riḍā's most faithful followers was a young physician at the state prison of al-Ṭurra, Dr Muḥammad Tawfīq Ṣidqī, who died in 1920 at the age of just 29.

Even as a student he was much interested in issues to do with religion, as he felt harassed by the pamphlets of Christian missionaries. When he started reading *al-Manār*, he was drawn into Muḥammad ʿAbduh's ideological universe. Under Rashīd Riḍā's guidance, he immersed himself in it more and more. This is how he wrote his first apology for Islam from a rational point of view, titled *al-Dīn fī naẓar al-ʿaql al-ṣaḥīḥ*, which was published in *al-Manār* VIII, 1905, and as a special issue at Maṭbaʿat al-Manār 1346/1927. He then continued by demonstrating the compatibility of the Qurʾān with the findings of modern science, notably astronomy, in his *al-Hayʾa wal-Qurʾān*, published in *al-Manār* XIV, 577/600. In *al-Manār* volumes XV and XVI he fulminated so vehemently
324 | against Christianity that the Christians were able to convince the government to ban his polemics. Following the *ʿAqīdat al-ṣalb wal-fidāʾ* of his teacher, he was an adherent of Docetism, in the version that holds that it was Judas Iscariot who died on the cross in place of Jesus Christ. In his *Naẓra fī kutub al-ʿAhd al-jadīd wa-ʿaqāʾid al-Naṣrāniyya*, Maṭbaʿat al-Manār 1331/1913, he wanted to demonstrate that the New Testament was a work by Paul, the enemy of the Apostles. Biography in *al-Manār* XXI, 483, *al-Majalla al-Ṭibbiyya* May 1923.

5 Muḥammad Farīd Bek Wajdī

The polyhistor Muḥammad Farīd Wajdī, born in Alexandria in 1875, was even more succesful in his continuation of Muḥammad ʿAbduh's apologetical work.

An amateur of French philosophy, he made it the topic of his first publication in 1895, *al-Falsafa al-ḥaqqa fī badāʾiʿ al-akwān* (Maṭbʿat ʿAbd al-Rāziq 1313). Just 22 years old, he wrote an apology of Islam in French, referring all the time to B. Constans and J. Simon, which he published in 1316 in Arabic translation as *Taṭbīq al-diyāna al-Islāmiyya ʿalā nawāmīs al-madaniyya*[191] at Maṭbaʿat al-ʿUthmāniyya.[192] From its second printing, he changed the title to *al-Madaniyya*

---

191 This is according to Sarkīs; Adams 244, n. 2 *al-Masīḥiyya*; in the fourth printing available to me the title is not mentioned.

192 Even though Muḥammad Rashīd Riḍā (*al-Manār* II, 110/1) praises its style as being in the same league as Muḥammad ʿAbduh's, its cumbersome syntax often betrays its French

wal-Islām, 3rd printing Maṭbaʿat al-Hindiyya 1331, 4th printing 1345/1927 ibid. In the preface he mentions a Serbian translation that was published in the Bosnian magazine *Bahār* and, among the Young Turks too, the work was extremely popular. He believes he can demonstrate that modern science can do no more than confirm the truths of the Qurʾān, as, with the advent of Islam, mankind has reached the ultimate stage of knowledge. He is in no way unsettled by the existence of slavery in Islam, which to him is in fact the highest form of humanity. After this work, with which he achieved his greatest success, he also wrote two theologico- | philosophical studies, *al-Ḥadīqa al-fikriyya fī ithbāt* 325
wujūd Allāh bil-barāhīn al-ṭabīʿiyya, Maṭbaʿat al-Taraqqī 1318, and *al-Islām fī ʿaṣr al-ʿilm*, 2 vols, Maṭbaʿat al-Shaʿb 1320. Despite his philosophical background, he turned out to be a champion of orthodoxy. As such, he criticised Qāsim Amīn's proposals with regard to women's rights in his *al-Marʾa al-Muslima*, Maṭbaʿat al-Taraqqī, 1319, Maṭbaʿat al-Hindiyya, 1331. In his *Ṣafwat al-ʿirfān* he gives a detailed account of the principles of Qurʾānic exegesis (1323/1905, printed earlier in lith.). He contributed to theology with his commentary on the Qurʾān entitled *al-Muṣḥaf al-muqassam*, for the third printing of which he commissioned a very beautiful manuscript in zincography. Having also published a *Majmūʿat al-rasāʾil al-falsafiyya* in 1333, he embarked upon writing his great encyclopaedia, the *Dāʾirat maʿārif al-qarn al-rābiʿ ʿashar al-ʿishrīn lil-mīlād*, which he completed in ten volumes in 1918 without the help of a single employee, and which was reprinted in 1924 (see Muḥammad Ḥusayn Haykal, *Fī awqāt al-farāgh* 164/81). A summary of it, entitled *Kanz al-ʿulūm wal-lugha*, was published in 1333/4, Maṭbaʿat al-Wāʿiẓ.[193] In his *Kitāb al-muʿallimīn* (Dāʾirat al-Maʿārif, 1918), he explained the curriculum for elementary schools prescibed by the ministry of education. He completed his studies in philosophy with the book *ʿAlā aṭlāl al-madhhab al-māddī* (Dāʾirat al-Maʿārif, 1921). In 1921, he also began the publication of his magazine *al-Wajdiyyāt*, of which only 15 issues were published, the last one on 15 April 1922. In it, he tried to popularise his views, sometimes by using conversations between birds. He also advocated spiritualism as a key witness for the Muslim worldview, as he did in places in his encyclopaedia. As such, he translated excerpts from C. Flammarion's *La mort et ses mystères*. In 1926, he also challenged Ṭāhā Ḥusayn with his book *Naqd al-shiʿr al-Jāhilī* (Maṭbaʿat Dāʾirat al-Maʿārif). Its quiet tone and the matter-of-fact nature of

origin, e.g. *ḥālata kawninā ṣārifīn al-naẓar ʿan tadabbur asrār al-Qurʾān*, "when we turn our vision away from the contemplation of the secrets of the Qurʾān," 4th printing $140_{,6}$.

193 His encyclopaedic interest went so far that he even published a dietetics from a medical point of view, entitled *Dustūr al-taghadhdhī*.

his critique contrast favourably with the rebuttals by others. Sarkīs 1451/2, Adams 243/5.

6 Aḥmad Fatḥī Zaghlūl Pāshā

Aḥmad Fatḥī Zaghlūl Pāshā made an outstanding contribution to the dissemination of Muḥammad ʿAbduh's ideas and their underpinning by similar works
326 | from European literature, which he rendered accessible through translations.

He was born into an distinguished family in 1863. After finishing high school, he went to Paris with the first group of students to be sent there by Ismāʿīl, where he studied law. Back in Egypt, he started work as a lawyer. He was successively *wakīl al-nāʾib* in Asyut and Alexandria, president of *al-maḥkama al-ahliyya* in Cairo, and minister of justice, dying in office in 1914. Apart from smaller essays of literary and sociological content, collected by ʿAbd al-ʿĀl Aḥmad Ḥamdān and published under the title *al-Āthār al-fatḥiyya* (Cairo: Maṭbaʿat Maṭar, n.d.) and *al-Muḥākamāt fī kulli zamān wa-makān* (Cairo 1900), he translated Bentham's *Spirit of Legislation* as *Rūḥ al-sharāʾiʿ* (Cairo, 1888) and his *Principles of Legislation* as *Uṣūl al-sharāʾiʿ* (Cairo 1309). He also translated G. Le Bon's *Psychologie des foules* as *Rūḥ al-ijtimāʿ* (Maṭbaʿat al-Shaʿb 1327, Maṭbaʿat al-Raḥmāniyya 1921), his *Les lois psychologiques de l'évolution des peuples* as *Sirr taṭawwur al-umam* (Maṭbaʿat al-Maʿārif 1331, Maṭbaʿat al-Raḥmāniyya 1921), *Jawāmiʿ al-kalim* (Cairo 1914), H. de Castries, *al-Islām, khawāṭir wa-sawāniḥ* (Maṭbaʿat al-Maʿārif 1315, 1329, 1911) and E. Desmoulins' *The Secret of the Advancement of the Anglo-Saxons* as *Sirr taqaddum al-Inglīz al-Saksūniyyīn* (Maṭbaʿat al-Maʿārif 1317, Maṭbaʿat al-Shaʿb 1326, 1901), as well as, from Turkish, Muṣṭafā Fāḍil Pāshā's memorandum for ʿAbd al-ʿAzīz dated 1866 under the title *Min amīr ilā sulṭān* (Cairo 1331). Rashīd Riḍā admits in *al-Taʾrīkh* I, 1006, that *al-Manār* magazine owed its success, to a large extent, on Zaghlūl Pāshā's endorsement of it in legal circles.

Sarkīs 1435/7, *al-Manār* XI, 528ff, Gibb, BSOS IV, 759, Adams 213.

7 Ṭanṭāwī Jawharī

Ṭanṭāwī Jawharī was also one of Muḥammad ʿAbduh's students. He connected ʿAbduh's ideas with the aesthetic view of nature found in Sir John Lubbock's *The Beauties of Nature* as well as with the insights of modern science.

Born in 1287/1870, he taught at the Dār al-ʿulūm and later also at the
327 University of Egypt in Cairo. | After two popular works, *al-Arwāḥ* (Maṭbaʿat al-Saʿāda, n.d.) and *Aṣl al-ʿālam* (Alexandria: Maṭbaʿat al-Funūn al-jamīla, n.d.), he published a schoolbook entitled *al-Farāʾid al-jawhariyya fī 'l-ṭuraf al-naḥwiyya* (Maṭbaʿat al-Islām, 1316). He published another work on philology, entitled

Mudhakkirāt fī adabiyyāt al-lugha al-ʿarabiyya (Maṭbaʿat al-Shaʿb, 1928). His first work in the field of popular physics, which was to be his speciality, was his *Mīzān al-jawāhir fī ʿajāʾib hādha ʾl-kawn al-bāhir* (Maṭbaʿat al-Taraqqī, 1318, 2nd printing Maṭbaʿa Hindiyya, 1322/3, 1913). He defended the ideals of Islam in his *Jawāhir al-taqwā* (1322), *al-Niẓām wal-Islām* (Maṭbaʿat al-Jumhūriyya, 1321, Maṭbaʿa Hindiyya, 1331), *al-Zahra fī niẓām al-ʿālam wal-umam* (1322), and *Niẓām al-ʿālam wal-umam awi ʾl-ḥikma al-Islāmiyya al-ʿulyā* (2 vols, Maṭbaʿat Wālidat ʿAbbās, 1324/4, 2nd printing 1931). In 1906, he presented a paper entitled *al-Tāj al-muraṣṣaʿ bi-jawāhir al-Qurʾān wal-ʿulūm* (Maṭbaʿat al-Muʾayyad, 2nd printing Maṭbaʿat al-Taqaddum) to the congress of religions in Tokyo that was dedicated to the Emperor. This text was also translated into Persian and Turkish. In it, he gives a detailed account of his studies at al-Azhar and of his efforts to reconcile the Qurʾān with Greek philosophy and the modern sciences. In his *Jamāl al-ʿālam* (1329), he returned once again to his favourite subject (2nd printing Maṭbaʿat al-Hidāya). In the same year, he presented his *Ayna ʾl-insān* (Maṭbaʿat al-Maʿārif, 1913) at the International Congress of Peoples. His *al-Nahḍa al-ʿArabiyya* (Cairo n.d.) probably belongs to this same period. In his *al-Sirr al-ʿajīb fī ḥikmat ʿadad azwāj al-nabī* (Maṭbaʿat al-Jamāliyya, 1333), he dealt with a particular subject regarding the biography of the Prophet. His *Rasāʾil* (Alexandria: Maṭbaʿat Jirjī Gharzūzī, 1915) contains a collection of essays (*al-Ḥikma wal-ḥukamāʾ*, following a talk at the *Nādi ʾl-Madāris al-ʿulyā, Mā al-maqṣūd min hādha ʾl-ʿālam, Wajhat al-ʿālam wāḥida wa-hiya ʾl-niẓām al-ʿāmm*), translations of English poems, and some *qaṣīda*s that he himself wrote. Other shorter essays were published under the title *Sawāniḥ al-Jawharī* (Cairo n.d). In his *Tafsīr sūrat al-Fātiḥa* (Cairo n.d.), he tried to prove that it contains all that we know in physics today. In 1341 he started his *opus maius*, entitled *al-Jawāhir fī tafsīr al-Qurʾān al-karīm* (Maṭbaʿat Muṣṭafā al-Bābī al-Ḥalabī), which had grown to comprise 22 volumes, running to sura 49, by 1935 (cf. *RAAD* x, 381). In his *al-Qurʾān wal-ʿulūm al-ʿaṣriyya* | (Maṭbaʿat ʿĪsā al-Ḥalabī, 1344) he 328
wrote once more about the compatibility of the Qurʾān and modern science. As early as 1911, Jawharī had presented his ideal of education in the form of a vision in which, while looking at the skies in search of Halley's comet, he is taken to another planet by some heavenly young creature who explains to him the state of eternal peace existing there. He did this in his *Ayna ʾl-insān*, presented to the Congress of Peoples in London. In 1932, he made the bold move of setting out an even more ambitious vision of the world in which he gives an account of the ideal condition of mankind. He wrote the work initially in English, but when he could not get it published in that language he translated it into Arabic under the title *Aḥlām al-siyāsa wa-kayfa yataḥaqqaq*

al-salām al-ʿāmm (Maṭbaʿat Muṣṭafā al-Bābī al-Ḥalabī, 1354/1935). While studying the Qurʾān in al-Zaytūn on the outskirts of Cairo in 1932, five shining figures made their appearance to him, inviting him to present himself to a tribunal of extra-terrestrial beings on a planet in the sign of Gemini, in order to pass an examination in arithmatic, atomic theory, the theory of sea currents, botany, the biology of bees and ants, the planetary system, and the anatomy of the brain. In a first dream, he is presented with a magical quadrant and, when he has explained it correctly, he is told that each people should be given its proper place in a manner corresponding to it. On the basis of the table of the atomic weights, he is told that every people has to discover and exploit its potential in a manner comparable to it. In a third dream it is explained to him that the potential of every people has to be channelled and used as if they were ocean currents. In a fourth dream he is led to a heavenly garden where the future order in human civilization is explained to him by the colours of its flowers. In the fifth dream this is supplemented by a closer look at the purposive structure of the leaves of plants in light of 'The mathematics of plants' in R. Brown's *Science for all*. The sixth dream considers the structure of the human brain and the capacities of the soul in light of Amīn Marsī Qandīl's (Professor at the Madrasat al-muʿallimīn al-ʿulyā) *Uṣūl ʿilm al-nafs wa-āthāruhu fī 'l-tarbiya wal-*
329 *taʿlīm* (al-Maṭbaʿa al-ʿArabiyya, 1925), praising the British | and the Americans for their use of psychological tests as a tool in career advice.

M. Hartmann, Ein moderner ägyptischer Theolog und Naturfreund, *Beitr. zur Kenntnis des Orients* XIII, 1916, 54/82, Goldziher, *Richtungen der Koranauslegung* 352, Adams 234/7.

8 Muṣṭafā & ʿAlī ʿAbd al-Rāziq

In his final works, Ṭanṭāwī Jawharī moved away significantly from Muḥammad ʿAbduh's theological viewpoint. The brothers Muṣṭafā and ʿAlī ʿAbd al-Rāziq, for their part, focussed their interest more and more on scientific subjects of a general character. As such, they were close to the endeavours of Ṭāhā Ḥusayn.

They were the sons of Ḥasan ʿAbd al-Rāziq Pāshā, a friend of Muḥammad ʿAbduh and, from 1907, the leader of the National Party (Ḥizb al-umma). Born in 1885, Muṣṭafā studied at al-Azhar under Muḥammad ʿAbduh. In 1909, he went to study in Paris, where he spent most of his time on sociology and ethics under Durkheim. Back in Egypt, he worked first as an inspector of the *sharīʿa* courts. In 1927, he was appointed as professor of philosophy at the University of Egypt. He wrote the introduction on Muḥammad ʿAbduh's life for the translation of the latter's *Risālat al-tawḥīd*, which he did alongside B. Michel. He also wrote an obituary for his teacher in *al-Manār* XXIII, 520/30. His brother ʿAlī was born in 1888 and went to al-Azhar at the age of ten. From 1910

onward he studied under Nallino and Santillana at the University of Egypt. In 1910/11, he gave lectures on rhetoric at al-Azhar, which were published in 1912 as *Amālī ʿAlī ʿAbd al-Rāziq fī ʿilm al-bayān wa-taʾrīkhihi.* Towards the end of 1912 he went to London to learn English. In 1913, he started studying economics in Oxford, but this was cut short by the war. From 1915 onward he worked as a judge at the *sharīʿa* court in Alexandria. In his spare time he gave lectures at the school that was run by the mosque there, a subsidiary of al-Azhar. When Mustafa Kemal abolished the caliphate, ʿAlī ʿAbd al-Rāziq opposed its restoraton in his *al-Islām wa-uṣūl al-ḥukm* (Maṭbaʿat Miṣr 1344/1925). Aiming for the complete separation of religion and the state, this bold work caused a storm of indignation, which found its expression in the former Great Mufti Muḥammad Bakhīt's *Ḥaqīqat al-Islām wa-uṣūl al-ḥukm* (Cairo 1343), | in Muḥammad Khiḍr 330
al-Ḥusayn's (*qāḍī* and professor at al-Zaytūna in Tunis) *Naqd Kitāb al-Islām wa-uṣūl al-ḥukm* (1924, Maṭbaʿat al-Salafiyya 1926), and in Muḥammad Rashīd Riḍā's *al-Manār*, volumes 26/8. Not only was the book rejected by the teaching staff at al-Azhar in a ruling (republished in 1344, 1925/6) entitled *Ḥukm hayʾat al-ʿulamāʾ fī Kitāb al-Islām wa-uṣūl al-ḥukm*, but in addition the author himself was declared an infidel and unfit to exercise any spiritual or judicial office by the disciplinary court of *sharīʿa* judges. Things being what they were, no ministry could intervene on his behalf as had been done for Ṭāhā Ḥusayn. Adams 251/3, 259/68, Lammens, *L'Islām* 121/2.

9 Muṣṭafā al-Marāghī

The most important student of Muḥammad ʿAbduh today is Muḥammad Muṣṭafā al-Marāghī, dean of al-Azhar.

When he had completed his studies he became the chief *sharīʿa* judge in the Sudan at the recommendation of Muḥammad ʿAbduh. In 1928 he became dean of al-Azhar for the first time. He tried to thoroughly reform this institution of higher learning on the basis of modern insights,[194] but, in 1930, law no. 49 (*al-Hilāl*, November 1931, 60ff), which he had helped to draft, met with so much resistance in reactionary circles that he felt forced to resign. However, by 1934 he was able to reassume his former responsibilities and implement the planned reforms. In this, he was backed by King Fārūq, at whose wedding he had officiated in his role as imam. Around 1935, he published lectures that he had held at al-Azhar under the title *Fi 'l-lugha*, followed by *Nukhab fī tarjamat al-Qurʾān al-karīm wa-aḥkāmihā* in 1936, and in 1938 by *al-Durūs al-dīniyya* (Maṭbaʿat al-Azhar 1356).

---

194 Cf. Achille Sékaly in *REI* I (1927), 95/116, 465/529, II, 1928, 47/165, 255/337, 401/72.

10 Qāsim Amīn

The teachings of Muḥammad ʿAbduh and his students did their work in silence, only rarely attracting the attention of the masses at large. By contrast, Qāsim Amīn was to be the one who put the issue of women's rights in Egypt on the agenda, triggering a struggle whose happy ending he would not live to see.
331 | Born into a Kurdish family in Cairo in 1865, he was, during his time at al-Azhar, one of Muḥammad ʿAbduh's closest friends. After completing his law studies in France, he intially became *wakīl* of the *nāʾib ʿumūmī* at the mixed court and then counsellor at the court of appeal (*maḥkamat al-istiʾnāf*). When the Duc d'Harcourt disparaged the Egyptian family, speaking with contempt about the wearing of the veil, he responded to this with a pamphlet in French, *Les Égyptiens, réponse à M. le Duc d'Harcourt*, in which he defended the wearing of the veil and, in turn, denounced the European lack of manners. But when circumstances compelled him to read what the Europeans had written on the issue of women's rights, he became convinced that family law in Islam stood indeed in need of reform and that Muslim society would be much enriched if women were granted the right to education and participation in public life. This was the message of his *Taḥrīr al-marʾa* (Cairo 1316/1899 and 1905, Maktabat Ibrāhīm Fāris, transl. O. Rescher, Stuttgart 1928). He answered the many rebuttals of it in his *al-Marʾa al-jadīda* (Maṭbaʿat al-Maʿārif, 1901). He spent the last two years of his life as the vice-chairman of the founding committee of the University of Egypt.[195] He died on 22 April 1908. After his death, some general observations on ethics written by him were published as an appendix to the edition of Ibn Ḥazm's *Mudāwāt al-nufūs* (Maṭbaʿat al-Jamāliyya, 1331/1913). Mayy, *Bāḥithat al-bādiya* 129ff, Ḥusayn Haykal, *Fī awqāt al-farāgh* 96/148, Jirjī Zaydān, *Mashāhīr al-sharq* I, 310/9, *al-Manār* XI, 226/9, *MSOS* XXIX, 243/4, XXXI, 177, 196, *WI* XI, 178/9, Adams 230/9.

11 Al-Nadīm

After the religious and social reformers, we must also briefly mention those who played a leading role in the political development of Egypt, but only the writers among them, as these often contributed directly to the literary upswing. The first to be mentioned here is the 'Tyrteaus' of the ʿArābī (ʿUrābī) movement, ʿAbdallāh Efendi al-Nadīm b. Miṣbāḥ Ibrāhīm al-Idrīsī.
332 | Born in Alexandria in 1261/1834, he belonged to the circle of students around Jamāl al-Dīn al-Afghānī. His blazing rhetoric and passionate poetry fuelled the national excitement that led to the rise of ʿArābī. Although he was a wanted man after the occupation of the country, he succeeded in remaining in

195 For its history, see *Oriente Moderno* VII, 627/31.

hiding. He was only captured in 1891. As punishment, he was simply sent into exile. Having lived in Jaffa for a year, he was allowed to return to Egypt when ʿAbbās II came to power. He then founded the magazine *al-Ustādh*, which had the same goals as *al-ʿUrwa al-wuthqā*. But a year later he was again forced to leave. This time, he went by way of Jaffa to Istanbul. There, he joined Jamāl al-Dīn al-Afghānī and worked as a censor for the government for a time. He died there on 11 October 1896. A collection of his shorter writings, called *Sulāfat al-nadīm fī muntakhabāt al-sayyid Abdallāh Efendi al-Nadīm b. Miṣbāḥ*, was published in two volumes in Cairo (1901, 1914), and his *dīwān*, entitled *Ḥanīn al-nadīm*, in Beirut in 1934.

Jirjī Zaydān, *Mashāhīr al-sharq* II, 94/100, ʿAbbās Maḥmūd al-ʿAqqād, *Shuʿarāʾ Miṣr* 88/97 (who says he has no talent as a poet), Gibb, *BSOS* IV, 755, Adams 221/2, *MSOS* XXXI, 176.

12 Aḥmad Luṭfī Bek

From the leaders of the People's Party (*ḥizb al-umma*) founded by Muḥammad ʿAbduh's friend Ḥasan ʿAbd al-Razzāq around 1906, we mention Aḥmad Luṭfī Bek, founder of *al-Jarīda* newspaper, which was closed down in 1914.

His name was mentioned previously as the translator of Aristotle's *Nicomachean Ethics*, *ʿIlm al-akhlāq* (2 vols, Maṭbaʿat Dār al-Kutub, 1924), for which he based himself on the French translation of Barthélémy St. Hilaire. Later, he became minister of education and now he is Dean of the reorganized University of Egypt; in this capacity he stood up bravely for the freedom of teaching, which was under threat in the case of Ṭāhā Ḥusayn. Cf. Adams, 224.

13 Muṣṭafā Kāmil Pāshā

Feverishly active, including in the field of literature, was the short life of the founder of the National Party (*al-ḥizb al-waṭanī*), Muṣṭafā Kāmil Pāshā.

Born on 14 August 1874 in Cairo as the son of an engineer, he went to the *Madrasat al-ḥuqūq al-Khidīwiyya* there | and finished his legal studies in 1894 333
as *Licencié en droit* in Toulouse. There, he met the French journalist Juliette Adam, who would have a lasting influence on his political development. Back from France, he founded his own party in 1894. Its newspaper, *al-Liwāʾ*, became very influential from 1900 onward. Here, we need not go into his political career up to his untimely death on 10 February 1908 (see M. Meyerhof in *EI* II, 824/5, with a detailed bibliography, and also the short overview in my own *Geschichte der islamischen Völker und Staaten*, 1939, 411).

Sulaymān ʿAlī Fahmī Kāmil (his brother, born in 1870, died 2 January 1926), *Taʾrīkh Muṣṭafā Kāmil Bāshā raʾīs al-Ḥizb al-waṭanī sābiqan fī 34 rabīʿan*, his life and speeches until February 1900 in 9 volumes, C. 1326/8, idem, *Sīrat Muṣṭafā Kāmil fī 34 rabīʿan*, I (until August 1899), C. 1344, Muḥammad Ḥusayn Haykal, *Tarājim Miṣriyya wa-ʿArabiyya*, 139/62, *Abṭāl al-waṭaniyya* (Muṣṭafā Kāmil, Muḥammad Farīd, Saʿd Zaghlūl, Mustafa Kemal, Mahatma Ghandi) *ishtaraka fī taʾlīfihi nukhaba min kuttāb al-ʿaṣr*, Cairo n.d. (*Jāmiʿ* 8). Sarkīs 1754/5, Adams 220, 222ff.

Of his works in Arabic the following were published separately: *Miṣr wal-iḥtilāl al-Inglīzī*, Maṭbaʿat al-Adab 1313; *al-Masʾala al-sharqiyya* ibid. 1898, 1909; *al-Shams al-mushriqa* (on the Russo-Japanese war), Maṭbaʿat al-Liwāʾ 1904; *Difāʿ al-Miṣrī ʿan bilādihi*, ibid. 1324; *Rasāʾil Miṣriyya Faransiyya* (letters to Juliette Adam, with their French originals), C. 1909.

14 Muḥammad Bek Farīd

After Kāmil Pāshā's death, Muḥammad Bek Farīd assumed the leadership of the party, but he was much less energetic.

Until that time, he had been *wakīl al-nāʾib al-ʿumūmī* at the *maḥākim ahliyya*. He founded a new party magazine, called *al-ʿAlam*, joined the Wafd in 1919, and died in Switzerland in the same year (though others say it was in Berlin) when a member of a commission that was party to the negotiations at the peace conference there. He started his literary career in 1890 with *al-Bahja al-Tawfīqiyya fī taʾrīkh muʾassis al-ʿāʾila al-Khidīwiyya*, Būlāq 1308. This work was followed by *Taʾrīkh al-dawla al-ʿaliyya al-ʿUthmāniyya* (up to the Berlin Conference), Maṭbaʿat Muḥammad Muṣṭafā, 1311/1893, 2nd printing Maṭbaʿat al-Taqaddum, 1912, *Taʾrīkh al-Rūmāniyyīn* I, 1318, *Riḥlat Muḥammad Bek Farīd* (1901, to Morocco and Spain, cf. Pérès, L'Espagne in *Publ. de l'Institut d'Études*
334 *Or.* VI, 1937, 88/100, 1902 to Italy and North Africa, 1903 to | Trieste, 1904 to Norway) Alexandria n.d., Maṭbaʿat al-Mawsūʿāt n.d.

See *al-Shawqiyyāt* III, 60/3, Sarkīs 1686, Adams 184, 197, Lord Lloyd, *Egypt since Cromer* I, 78.

15 Saʿd Bāshā Zaghlūl

A master of the spoken word, Saʿd Bāshā Zaghlūl, founder and long-time leader of the Wafd party, can lay claim to a place of honour in the literary history of Egypt.

Son of a peasant and born in Abyāna, in the Mudīriyya Gharbiyya, in 1860, he studied at al-Azhar after finishing at the Qurʾān school in Dasūq. In this period he befriended Muḥammad ʿAbduh. When the latter became editor-in-chief of *al-Waqāʾiʿ al-Miṣriyya* he appointed Zaghlūl as his assistant. In 1883, he started working in the ministry of the interior as *muʿāwin*. After Muḥammad ʿAbduh's involvement in the ʿArābī uprising, Zaghlūl lost his job as his friendship with the former had raised suspicions. He thus started working as a lawyer from 1884 onward. It was only in 1892 that he returned to public service, this time as a counsellor at *maḥkamat al-istiʾnāf*. In 1907 he took charge of the ministry of education—where he had fought, and won, some battles with the British in the past—and then of the ministry of justice. When the cabinet of Muḥammad Saʿīd Pāshā resigned in 1913, he was nominated a member of the legislative council, where his eloquence soon secured him a leading role. When the war ended, the time was ripe for him to rise up as the leader of the masses. On 13 November 1918 he appeared, together with ʿAlī Shaʿrāwī Bāshā and ʿAbd al-ʿAzīz Fahmī Bey, as the *wafd* of the people of Egypt before the high commissioner Sir Wingate. He demanded that they be admitted to the peace talks in their capacity as representatives of the demands of the Egyptian people. His later career, up to his death on 26 August 1927, belongs to the history of the country and need not be retold here (see the overview in my *Geschichte der islamischen Völker und Staaten* 414/9).

His animated career left him no time to be active as a writer. Yet after the solemn pathos of Muṣṭafā Kāmil, his speeches, which he gave in Classical Arabic while systematically neglecting the use of *iʿrāb* and throwing in brief sentences in the Egyptian vernacular, really put the popular address on the map as a separate genre.

ʿAbbās Maḥmūd al-ʿAqqād, *Saʿd Zaghlūl* 1936, cf. p. 253. Muḥammad | Fahmī 335
Ḥāfiẓ, *Taʾrīkh Saʿd Zaghlūl Bāshā*, C. 1927. Muḥammad ʿAbd al-Murshid Dāʾūd, *Taʾrīkh Saʿd Zaghlūl* C. 1926. Aḥmad Luṭfī and Muḥammad al-Juzūlī, *Saʿd Zaghlūl min mahdihi ila ʾl-arbaʿīn fī laḥdihi*, Cairo n.d. Karīm Thābit, *Saʿd Zaghlūl fī ḥayātihi ʾl-khāṣṣa*, C. 1929. Muḥammad Ismāʿīl al-Buḥayrī, *ʿAbarāt al-sharq ʿala ʾl-zaʿīm al-jalīl al-maghfūr lahu Saʿd Bāshā Zaghlūl*, C. 1345. Aḥmad Ḥasanayn al-Qarnī, *Dhikrā Saʿd*, C. 1927.—*Mukhtārāt min ārāʾ wa-aḥādīth Saʿd Zaghlūl* (from 6 December 1918 until 16 August 1923) by Aḥmad Nasīb al-Sukkarī, C. 1923.—*Majmūʿat khuṭab Saʿd Bāshā Zaghlūl al-ḥadītha* by Maḥmūd Fuʾād, Maṭbaʿat al-Muqtaṭaf 1924.—*Kalimāt wa-ḥikam Saʿd Bāshā Zaghlūl* by Maḥmūd Kāmil Fuʾād Efendi, C. 1927.—*Āthār al-zaʿīm Saʿd Zaghlūl fī wizārat al-shaʿb* by Muḥammad Ibrāhīm al-Jazarī, C. 1927.

Chapter 2. Syria

In Egypt, intellectual life was essentially concentrated in Cairo. Here, it could realise its potential, hardly bothered by the British rulers, carried as it was by a flourishing economy and having the local dynasty promoting it as best as it could. In Syria, similar conditions, conducive to a flourishing of the intellectual community, were altogether absent because as long as ʿAbd al-Ḥamīd's despotism weighed down upon the Ottoman Empire, Syria would share the fate of the capital; and, like its Turkish counterpart, Arabic literature too, was very much restrained as a result of overanxious self-censorship.[1] Because of this pressure and due to a weak economy, the most ambitious representatives of the Levantine race, which is well-known for its entrepreneurial spirit, left the country; partly to Egypt, where we have already come across them as leaders and promotors of culture, and partly to the Americas. This is how, as will be de-
336 tailed later, | there arose flourishing areas of Arabic cultural life in the northern and southern parts of the Western Hemisphere, which also worked positively on their land of origin.[2] The revolution of the Young Turks, which the people of Syria, too, had set their hopes on, was a bitter disappointment for the Arabs. Instead of the freedom they had hoped for, all they got was more pressure from the ruling party, which wanted to rally all the citizens around its ideal as if they were Ottomans without exception, and thus suppressed any stirring of an independent Arab spirit almost more severely than ʿAbd al-Ḥamīd had done.

But not even the collapse of the Ottoman Empire brought Syria the intellectual freedom that it had longed for. For instead of the emergence of the greater Arab state they had hoped for, the Arabs saw themselves divided into a number of smaller states, from the Euphrates to the Mediterranean. Ruled by the British and the French, they still hope to be granted their right to self-determination, a delusion that had seduced them into putting a knife in the back of their Turkish overlords.

While in Egypt, the sense of nationhood had developed out of its struggle against British supremacy, in Syria it is up against much greater and manifold types of pressure. At the end of the [First] World War, France saw its centuries-old ambition to take power here come true, and it was easy for her to play off different segments of the population against each other. As well as the Sunnī core of the population, in Lebanon and in the northern coastal region there is

---

1 Delightful samples of this are cited by Sulaymān Bustānī, *ʿIbra wa-dhikrā*, 27ff, for the press, and 40ff, for literature in general.

2 See al-Ab Isḥāq Armala al-Sūryānī, *Baḥth ʿani 'l-Sūryān fī Miṣr*, Beirut 1925; al-Muḥāmī Mīshīl Shiblī, *al-Muhājira al-Lubnāniyya*, n.d. & n.p.

a strong Shīʿī minority that has distinguished itself for centuries by its great intellectual vitality. Although the different denominations | among the Christian 337
population[3] had initially welcomed the foreign domination, they were soon disappointed and therefore ready to support the national opposition of the Muslims. Yet from an intellectual point of view, they remained for a long time under the foreigners' spell. It is the missionary activity of the Americans and the Jesuits in Beirut, especially, that had a decisive influence on the country's intellectual development. The American University, established by Cornelius van Dyck, sowed the seeds of yearning for freedom, this in competition with the Université de St. Joseph, ever since its foundation by the Jesuits in 1869. The latter is primarily focussed on the dissemination of French culture, something that also left its imprint on literature.

But Beirut did not become a centre that dominated the rest. And Damascus, too, was not able to compete with Cairo. Outside of Damascus, there was a flourishing of *udabāʾ* circles and scholars in numerous towns in the provinces, in which the old traditions were continued with greater or lesser success. At the centre of these was most often a family of notables, still very influential in the country. It was only after the foundation of the Academy of Damascus in 1921 that this former capital regained some of its previous importance as a promotor of intellectual life, something which made itself widely felt during the millennial celebrations for al-Mutanabbī in 1935.

1 *Poetry*

(*1. & 2.*) *Forerunners*

1 Before the [First] World War

Before we turn to the developments in poetry that were triggered by the World War and its aftermath, some of the representatives of | the period prior to that, 338
and who could also have found a place in volume II, shall be mentioned.

A *The Lebanon and Beirut*

a Jirjīs al-Lubnānī al-Mārūnī

The lifetime of Jirjīs Faraj al-Hāniʾ al-Lubnānī al-Mārūnī cannot be fixed with any precision. In his *Munājāt al-nafs*, he talks at length about the essence, origin, and destination of the human soul in 1050 *ṭawīl* verses rhyming in *tāʾ*,

---

3 Salīm al-Bustānī, quoted in Yūsuf Ṣufayr, *Majāli 'l-ghurar* (Beirut 1898), 105, points at their incessant jealousy as the main cause of their backwardness.

which he then annotated in a supplement written in prose. Beirut n.d. (see Cairo[2] III, 382).

b Manṣūr al-Hamsh al-Mārūnī

His compatriot Manṣūr al-Hamsh al-Mārūnī al-Lubnānī wrote *al-Maqāma al-Ghazīriyya wal-qāfiya al-ḥamāsiyya maʿa sharḥihimā* (Beirut 1872). He had recited the first of these at a school function in Ghazīr in Lebanon (see Hartmann, *Die arabische Frage*, 78), and the second before the Jesuits in Beirut; see Cairo[2] III, 376, Sarkīs 1898 without date.

c Miṣbāḥ Efendi Ramaḍān

Author of *al-Muwashshaḥāt al-Miṣbāḥiyya*, Beirut 1873, Sarkīs 1749.

d Ḥannā Bek al-Asʿad al-Lubnānī

Abū Ṣaʿb al-Ḥannā (Yūḥannā) b. Asʿad b. Jirjīs, Ḥannā Bek al-Asʿad al-Lubnānī had accompanied Emir Bashīr to Malta and Istanbul in 1840. In 1850, he founded a lithographic printing house in his native country, publishing a number of texts, among them al-Zawzānī's commentary on the *Muʿallaqāt*. In 1860 he became the managing director of the Arab bureau, which was part of the new adminstration that Dāʾūd Pāshā had established in the Lebanon. He would remain in office until his death in 1897. His *Dīwān* (Beirut: Maṭbaʿat al-Yasūʿiyyīn, 1893) contains 777 verses in Arabic and 459 in Turkish. Sarkīs 319, Cheikho, *al-Ādāb al-ʿarabiyya* II, 140/2.

e ʿAṭiyya Jirjī Shāhīn

ʿAṭiyya Jirjī Shāhīn (d. 1912), teacher at the Russian school for woman teachers in Baytjāla, whose juvenile poems, *Nasamāt al-ṣabā fī manẓūmāt al-ṣibā*, were published in Baʿabda in 1904, published a commentary on the *Mukhtaṣar* of Nasīf al-Yāzijī's *Nār al-qirā* (II, 766, iii, 4) and also a translation of Fénélon's *Télémaque, Waqāʾiʿ Tilimāk* (Beirut 1885). A *marthiya* by Iskandar al-Khūrī al-Bitjālī, *Mashāhid al-ḥayāt* 39/42. His son Jirjī published a translation of an American work, *Nahj al-taqaddum*, Beirut: Maṭbʿat al-Amirikān; Hartmann, *Arabic Press* 43, no. 13, Sarkīs 1339, *Jāmiʿ* 497.

f Asʿad Shudūdī

Asʿad Shudūdī was born in 1826 in ʿAliyya in Lebanon. From the foundation of
339 the American University in Beirut | in 1866, he was a teacher of mathematics and physics there. He died in 1906. When Kaiser Wilhelm II visited Palestine, he dedicated a versification of Solomon's aphorisms to him, entitled *Urjūzat*

al-ḥakīm lil-ḥakīm, Beirut 1900. Sarkīs 1104 (based on *al-Muqtaṭaf*, XXXI, 625) also mentions a handbook of physics, *al-ʿArūs al-badīʿa fī ʿilm al-ṭabīʿa*, Beirut 1873.

g Bashīr Efendi Ramaḍān

Bashīr Efendi Ramaḍān tried to support the Arab liberation movement with a collection of poems called *Munājāt al-ḥabīb fī 'l-ghazal wal-nasīb*. He published them anonymously in 1906 at the Maṭbaʿat al-Taqaddum, but they were soon prohibited. After the re-establishment of the constitution he published them again, in his own name, under another title, *Musāmarat al-ḥabīb fī 'l-ghazal wal-nasīb*, Beirut 1909. This was after his publication of his *Badāʾiʿ al-shiʿr fī 'l-ḥamāsa wal-fakhr*, Beirut: Maṭbaʿat al-Adabiyya, 1327.

h The Brothers al-Mallāṭ

Real patriotic poets from before the war were the brothers al-Mallāṭ, Tāmir and Shiblī b. Yūʾākīm b. Manṣūr. Although a Christian, the former, born in Baʿabda in Lebanon in 1856, had studied Islamic law in Beirut, after which he worked as a teacher at the Maronite and then the Jewish school in that city. Later, he became a government official: chief court-stenographer in Kasrouane, judge in Zahleh and the Chouf, and finally chief clerk at the court of appeal of Lebanon. In 1902 he was afflicted with melancholia, dying in Baʿabda in 1914. His younger brother, who worked for a time in the Turkish administration of the *mudīr* of the Lebanon district, published his poems together with his own, much more numerous ones in *Dīwān al-Mallāṭ, yashtamil ʿalā shiʿr al-shaqīqayn al-Lubnāniyyayn Tāmir wa-Shibli 'l-Mallāṭ*, Beirut 1925 (see *al-Mashriq* XX, 634, F.E. Bustānī ibid. XXV, 650, *Jāmiʿ* I, 650). A *Muwashshaḥ al-jamāl wal-kibriyāʾ* (Beirut: al-Maṭbaʿa al-ʿIlmiyya, 1904, see al-Bustānī in *al-Mashriq* XXVI, 623) was recited by Shiblī on 20 March 1904, during the annual meeting of the *Shams al-barr* society in Beirut. A poem on the deposition of ʿAbd al-Ḥamīd is cited by Cheikho in the second appendix to his *al-Ādāb al-ʿarabiyya fī 'l-qarn al-tāsiʿ ʿashsar* II, 187, amidst a selection of political songs on the Turkish revolution, most of which come from Egypt. In *Aḥsan mā katabtu* 120/1, Shiblī published a *qaṣīda* called *Malikat Tadmur*, and a greeting to Mayy in *Mayy fī Sūriyyā wa-Lubnān*, 71/2. He was entirely possessed of the spirit of ancient poetry, from among whose representatives he had a special affinity with ʿAntara. As such, he rudely rejected | any and all attempts at renewal in this art. See the descrip- 340
tions in Ilyās Abū Shabaka, *al-Rusūm* I, 7/11, F.E. Bustānī, *al-Mashriq* XXXI, 137 against Khalīl Ḍāhir, *al-Shiʿr wal-shuʿarāʾ*, Brooklyne, 1931, samples in Rafāʾil Nakhla, *Mukhtārāt*, Beirut 1931, 259/61.

i Amīn Fatḥallāh Ṣabbāgh al-Lubnānī

The art of Amīn Fatḥallāh Ṣabbāgh al-Lubnānī evolves entirely in the style of ancient poetry (which he also tried to revive by writing *takhāmīs* and *tashāṭīr*) in his *Zahrat al-zanbaq li-man ʿashiqa aw sa-yaʿshaq*, Maṭbaʿat Jarīdat Ḥimṣ, 1910, and *Zahrat nisrīn min manẓūmāt al-Amīn* (some of which he had recited during the first Ottoman celebration of the constitution in *Nādi 'l-aḥrār*), Zahleh, Maṭbaʿat al-Muhadhdhib, 1910 (Sarkīs 1191, Cairo[2] III, 180).

k Al-Khūrī Wadīʿ

The publisher of the *Ḥadīqat al-akhbār* in Beirut, al-Khūrī Wadīʿ, published in 1912 a history of the Tripolitanian war in rhyme, titled *Taʾrīkh al-ḥarb al-ʿUthmāniyya al-Īṭāliyya fī Ṭarābulus al-Gharb*, and also a verse translation of Fénélon's *Riwāyat Tilimāk*, something he was inspired to do by Sulaymān al-Bustānī's translation of the *Iliad* (Sarkīs 850).

l Muṣawbaʿ Rashīd Ḥannā al-Lubnānī

Muṣawbaʿ Rashīd Ḥannā al-Lubnānī, who mainly lived in Cairo and Paris, is a typical example of the cosmopolitan Syrian who left the restrictions of his native country, to go out into the world, but who could never take root again anywhere. His first *dīwāns*, *Siḥr al-bayān* (C. 1901) and *al-Nukhaba* (C. 1902), were followed in 1906 by *Tidhkār Rāghib wa-Ṣabrī* (Maṭbaʿat al-Akhbār). The latter *dīwān* is dedicated to Idrīs Bek Efendi Rāghib and to the minister of justice Ismāʿīl Ṣabrī Bāshā (cf. p. 19), whom he also addresses in some of his poems. But he also sings the praises of other social and political leaders, such as Aḥmad Taymūr and Princess Nāzilī, some business tycoons from the provinces and his compatriots Shakīb Arslān and Alexandra de Avierno. But he also wrote an elegy for the Roman Catholic patriarch Buṭrus al-Jurayjirī IV (75) and for the lawyer Niqula Bek Tūmā, read during his memorial service in the House of the Jesuits in Cairo (51). Besides, he maintained good relations with the Jewish community; he besings a charity bazaar organized by Jewish girls in the Hotel Continental (9), a celebration in the Jewish school of Tanta (15) and a Jewish wedding. It is thus perhaps natural that he has no clear emotion for his homeland. In one moment he passionately remembers his Syrian motherland ("You, Syria, are my natural habitat, and that is what a man longs after the most",
341 57,4, "Lebanon, the wind carries me your scent, | and there is nothing more becoming to my body; but the air of safety has a better smell yet, even if I am a product your soil" (88 bottom); in another moment he praises Egypt as his intellectual Fatherland ("How could I leave Egypt, the country where I found my happiness? The most beautiful home of man is the home where he leaves his traces. In Egypt, I left the products of my brain; it is there that I learned

what I did not know before," 88, 8/10). And, of course, he does not have a clear political line of thinking either. At the request of Syrian officials in the Sudan, he sings the praises of Lord Cromer and of Sir Reginald Wingate at the time of his visit (20). In 'Trip to Transvaal' (70) he rallies passionately to the Boer cause while adding a greeting to Saʿd Zaghlūl—who was only at the beginning of his political career—on the occasion of his appointment as minister of education. The poet's language moves along well-trodden tracks and shows little attempt at new creations. His collection of poems *al-Athar* (Cairo: Maṭbaʿat al-Salām, 1910) was followed by another collection, *Ghusn al-naqāʾ* (Maṭbaʿat al-Muqtaṭaf, 1915), which had mostly been written in Paris and which he dedicated to the French minister of foreign affairs Delcassé (Sarkīs 1757).

B *Damascus*

a ʿAbd al-Salām al-Shaṭṭī

ʿAbd al-Salām b. ʿAbd al-Raḥmān b. Muṣṭafā b. Maḥmūd b. Maʿrūf al-Shaṭṭī al-Ḥanbalī al-Dimashqī (b. 1256/1840), whose family hailed from Baghdad, went to Istanbul in 1293/1876, obtained a professorship in Adrianople, then became *imām* of the Ḥanbalīs at the Umayyad mosque and died on 21 (or 11) Muḥarram 1295/26 January 1878. He left a *dīwān* in which he, among other things, versified Bakhraq's *Qiṣṣat al-mawlid*, and which was compiled in 1323/1905 by his relative Muḥammad Jamīl b. ʿUmar b. Muḥammad b. Ḥasan b. ʿUmar b. Maʿrūf al-Shaṭṭī (Sarkīs 1136, where it is mistakely stated that he died in 1307), the father of the author of the *Mukhtaṣar ṭabaqāt al-Ḥanābila* (see II, 448), Damascus n.d. (Sarkīs 1125, Cairo[2] III, 138, Cheikho, *al-Ādāb al-ʿarabiyya* II 76/7).

b Muḥammad Salīm al-Qaṣṣāb

In 1298/1880 Muḥammad Salīm Efendi b. Anīs b. Ḥasan al-Dimashqī al-Qaṣṣāb published his collection of poems *Nashʾat al-ṣibā wa-nasamāt al-ṣabā* (Damascus, Maṭbaʿat al-Jamʿiyya al-Khayriyya), which also contains *takhāmīs*, *tashāṭīr*, and *muwashshaḥāt*.

c Salīm ʿAnḥūrī

Salīm b. Rūfāʾīl b. Jirjīs ʿAnḥūrī al-Dimashqī started | his literary career with a 342
lexical work entitled *Kanz al-nāẓim wa-miṣbāḥ al-hāʾim*, vol. I, Beirut 1878. It was followed by three collections of poems: *Siḥr Hārūt* (Damscus: al-Maṭbaʿa al-Ḥifniyya, 1302/1885), *Badāʾiʿ Hārūt aw shahr fī Bayrūt* (Beirut 1886), *al-Jawhar al-fard wal-shiʿr al-ʿaṣrī*, completed in 1887 (al-Ḥadath 1904). He dedicated a collection of *marāthī* to his brother Ḥannā, titled *al-Mubakkiyāt wa-huwa majmūʿ mā warada manthūran wa-manẓūman fī taʾbīn faqīd al-ʿilm wal-adab al-maghfūr al-marḥūm Ḥannā b. Rūfāʾīl ʿAlī al-mutawaffā fī 13 Ādhār sanat 1890*

fī madīnat Bārīs (Beirut 1890). Born in 1863, Ḥannā had studied in Beirut under Ibrāhīm al-Yāzijī, after which he translated a number of French plays for the theatre company of Jūrj Mīrzā in Damascus (Sarkīs 1380 also mentions the magazines to which he contributed; Cheikho, *al-Mashriq* XXV, 705). He died a student of medicine in Paris in 1890.

d Ṣāliḥ b. Ṭāhā

In 1308/1890, Ṣāliḥ b. Aḥmad b. Muḥammad b. Ṭāhā, born in Dūma around 1860, published his *al-Darārī wal-laʾāl li-madḥ Muḥammad wa-āl* with a *manẓūma* dedicated to ʿAbd al-Ḥamīd II (Cairo[2] III, 99).

e Sulaymān al-Ṣawla

Sulaymān b. Ibrāhīm al-Dimashqī al-Ṣawla was born in Damascus in 1814, studied at al-Azhar and then started working as a government official in Egypt. He accompanied Ibrāhīm Pāshā on his campaign to Syria and worked in his administration in Damascus. He returned to Cairo in 1884, dying there on 14 May 1894. *Dīwān al-Ṣawla*, C. 1312/1894–5 (Cairo[2] III, 136). Cairo[1] ascribes the collection *Mujalli ʾl-ʿibar fī aṭāyib al-ḥikāyāt wal-samar* (Beirut, n.d.) to a certain Sulaymān Qāsim al-Ṣaydāwī; Cheikho II, 144/5, Sarkīs 1217.

C *Aleppo*

a Qāsim al-Bakrajī

In 1293/1876, Qāsim b. Muḥammad al-Bakrajī wrote a *badīʿiyya* entitled *al-ʿIqd al-badīʿ fī madḥ al-nabī al-shafīʿ*, with a commentary called *Ḥilyat al-badīʿ fī madḥ al-nabī al-shafīʿ* (Aleppo: al-Maṭbaʿa al-ʿAzīziyya, 1293).

b Mīkhāʾīl al-Ṣaqqāl

Mīkhāʾīl b. Anṭūn al-Ṣaqqāl was born on Malta in 16 August 1852. In 1854, his father, who had served as an interpreter for the British army in the Crimean war, took him to his native Aleppo. This is where Mīkhāʾīl did all his studies, and where he worked for a time as a teacher before becoming a lawyer. In 1896, he went to Alexandria. Together with Niqolaki and the brothers ʿAzīz and Basīl Simyān, he founded an illustrated magazine for literature and technology there called *al-Ajyāl*, and which he edited together with Yūsuf Shalḥat. However, just a year later he returned to Aleppo. His *al-ʿIbar* (Aleppo: Maṭbaʿat al-Mārūniyya,
343 1911) contains 20 poems in the *basīṭ* metre | in a continuous rhyme in *tu* on the ideals of the revolution of the Young Turks. He first refers to the killing of a Christian family in Antioch in 1909, and calls on the Orientals to rise up from their backwardness, deploring the diversity of religions as an obstacle to every kind of progress. The eighteenth poem is about a pair of lovers who are

happily united after a long separation. In the nineteenth he defends his own prose work, concluding with a lament on the victims of ʿAbd al-Ḥamīd's tyrannical rule. As early as 1907 he had criticised the situation in the empire: *Laṭāʾif al-samar fī sukkān al-zuhara wal-qamar aw al-Ghāya fi ʾl-badāʾa wal-nihāya* (Cairo: Maṭbaʿat al-Najāḥ, Aleppo, Maṭbaʿat al-Mārūniyya, 1911). Although mostly phrased in covert terms, his criticsm was extremely forceful. The book starts with a biography of his father, along with some poems he wrote. He then tells us how his father appeared to him, sixteen years after his death, on 10 August 1901, to tell him about his life on the other side. Initially, he had been banished to the moon for twenty years, like all other sinners, until he was accepted into the land of the blessed on the planet Venus. He then sketches the circumstances there in light of the circumstances here, expounding his social and political ideals. It is characteristic for the political orientation he inherited from his father that he, in the chapter on wars (p. 89ff), condemns the Boer war—during which the Egyptian press was firmly on the side of the rebels—entirely along British lines, as an uprising against the will of God. In the chapter on the educational system he shows himself very pessimistic about the future of the Arabic language, which he says will cease to exist if an academy does not soon undertake to adapt it to the needs of the present age (p. 107ff). Yet he is not at all convincing when he tries to document this in a separate chapter (*Fi ʾl-lugha*, p. 113/4) by citing some *waḥshī*-laden verses and a number of obvious puns based on homonyms. At the same time he likes to embellish his language with outlandish terms whenever possible, which he then has to explain. The only way for him to say something about poetry in the Hereafter is by citing a prose rendering of a poem on love by Fatḥallāh al-Naḥḥās al-Ḥalabī (whose name in the Hereafter is Ṣabr), adding | some poems by his father (154ff). A 344
chapter on the inventions of the inhabitants of Venus is characteristic of the poverty of his imagination in the technical field. In order to avoid any conflict with the teachings of the Church or Islam, the inhabitants of Venus are said to live between 500 and 1000 years, after which they die like the inhabitants of the earth (231ff). He says nothing about the fate of souls after that. Having cited the various demonstrations of God's existence (236ff) and rejecting all superstition, he finally regrets the existence of a variety of religions as an imperfection that he seeks to remedy with his ideal of a world religion. The work is therefore nothing but another imitation of al-Muwayliḥī's *Ḥadīth ʿĪsā b. Hāshim* (see p. 194), even if he does not mention it. Yet it distinguishes itself favorably from others through the boldness of its conception. As a poet, al-Ṣaqqāl is not very talented. Just like his *ʿIbar*, his *Dīwān* I (Aleppo: Maṭbaʿat al-ʿAṣr al-jadīd, 195)—harshly criticized by Khalīl Mardam Bek in *RAAD* V, 564/8—is more like an expression of noble sentiments than a real work of art.

Cheikho II, 120/1, Sarkīs 1215, Hartmann, *Ar. Press* 60, Qusṭakī al-Ḥimṣī, *Udabāʾ Ḥalab* 111/4.

c ʿAbd al-Fattāḥ al-Ṭarābīshī

ʿAbd al-Fattāḥ al-Ṭarābīshī (b. 1277/1860, d. 1331/1912 in Aleppo) wrote his poems in the local dialect but then asked scholars to turn them into classical Arabic. Samples in Rāghib al-Ṭabbākh, *Taʾrīkh Ḥalab* VIII, 563/77, Qusṭakī al-Ḥimṣī, *Udabāʾ Ḥalab* 96/7.

d ʿAbd al-Masīḥ al-Antākī

ʿAbd al-Masīḥ al-Antākī is another Syrian for whom the country had become too oppressive under Turkish dominion. Born the son of a Roman Catholic, he first practiced as a lawyer at the bar of the Turkish courts in Aleppo. As a young man, he founded *al-Shudhūr* magazine in his hometown, but it soon closed its doors again. After that he went to Cairo, where he founded the newspaper *al-ʿUmrān*, which he later turned into a magazine. From an early age and despite his own background, he had a special liking for the Shīʿa. This is clear in his collection of poems *ʿUrf al-khuzām fī maʾāthir al-sāda al-kirām* (Cairo: al-Maṭbaʿa al-Ḥurra, 1902) and his *Qaṣīda ʿAlawiyya*, in which he recounts the life of ʿAlī in more than a thousand verses, and which was published for the first time in his own magazine (see above p. 179f).

345 | In Dhu ʾl-Qaʿda and Dhu ʾl-Ḥijja 1325/December 1907–January 1908 he travelled from Aden to Kuwait and al-Muḥammara, where he established a close relationship with the local emir, Khazʿal. He wrote about this in letters to his magazine in the years 1326/7, and which were later jointly published in his *al-Riyāḍ al-munazzaha bayna ʾl-Kuwayt wal-Muḥammara* (Maṭbaʿat al-ʿArab, n.d.). Besides very vivid descriptions of the circumstances in this volatile area of the Middle East, the book also offers numerous poems exchanged with local *udabāʾ* or recited to local personalities. When passing through Baghdad on his way back from this trip, he was extradited by the local *wālī* Nāẓim Pāshā because he was suspected of anti-Turkish activism. And it is true that he went to Europe several times, in each case to buy weapons and supplies for his patrons. Pérès 427 also mentions an historical novel, *Buṭrus al-Akbar* (Cairo n.d.). He died in Cairo in 1920. Cheikho, *al-Mashriq* XXV, 116, Qusṭākī, *Udabāʾ Ḥalab*, 100/102.

E *Hama*

Abu ʾl-ʿAzm Muḥammad b. Ḥasan b. Aḥmad b. Muḥammad al-Ḥamawī al-Ḥusaynī al-Ḥanafī was born in Hama in Ṣafar 1249/February 1877. *Dīwān al-Ḥamawiyyāt*, C. 1326, Sarkīs 1647, Cairo^2 III 127.

F *Latakia*

Ṣāliḥ Ilyās b. Mūsā b. Simʿān al-Lādhiqī was a Greek Catholic who had been born in Latakia in 1829. In 1875, he tried his luck in Cairo with a poem on the khedive, but returned empty-handed to his town of origin. He died there in 1885. In his lifetime, he published a verse translation of the Psalms, intended for use in the Presbyterian church, entitled *Nahjat al-ḍamīr fī naẓm al-mazāmīr* (Alexandria: al-Maṭbaʿa al-Amirīkāniyya, 1875) as well as a *Khuṭba fī ḥaqīqat al-tahdhīb* (Beirut). His son published his *Dīwān* in Beirut in 1910. Cheikho II, 118/9, Sarkīs 1183, *al-Muqtaṭaf* XXXVII, 1121.

G *Tripoli*

a ʿAbd al-Qādir al-Ṭarābulusī

Like most of his compatriots, ʿAbd al-Qādir al-Ḥusaynī al-Adhamī al-Ṭarābulusī wrote on mystical themes. In 1301/1884, he published his *Irshād al-murīd fi ʾl-ṭarīqa al-Shādhiliyya*, in 1306 *Tarjamat quṭb al-wāsilīn wa-ghawth al-sālikīn al-ʿārif billāh taʿālā sayyid Shams al-Dīn Muḥammad al-Qāwuqjī al-Ḥasanī* (II, 776), Beirut, in 1308 his *badīʿiyya Tarjumān al-ḍamīr fī madḥ al-hādī al-bashīr*, Maṭbaʿat Jarīdat Beirut, 1309, | in 1311 his *Tadhkirat uli ʾl-baṣāʾir fi ʾl-kabāʾir* 346
wal-ṣaghāʾir, Maṭbaʿat al-ʿIlmiyya, and in 1312 in Tripoli his *dīwān, Mawrid al-ṣafāʾ wa-maṣdar al-wafāʾ*, Sarkīs 773. It is genuine dervish poetry, often morphing into outright litanies. He begins by praising God, but then spends the remainder of the *dīwān* on the Prophet, whose *mawlid* he celebrates extensively in a separate song (p. 29/42). On page 51, he celebrates the reconstruction of the al-Tuffāḥi mosque in Tripoli, which was re-consecrated on 21 Dhu ʾl-Qaʿda 1309/18 June 1892 as al-Jāmiʿ al-Ḥamīdī. The *qaṣīda*s are interspersed with a series of *tashṭīr*s, e.g. on verses by Ibn ʿAṭāʾallāh (p. 55) and Ḥasan al-Būrīnī (p. 73). In a postscript, he demonstrates the ʿAlīd origins of his family by citing an inscription of Sultan Arghūn at the gate of the main mosque in Tripoli, and in which the custody of the mosque is entrusted to one of his predecessors.

b Abū ʿAbdallāh al-Shahhāl al-Ṭarābulusī

Abū ʿAbdallāh Maḥmūd al-Shahhāl al-Ṭarābulusī (d. after 1308/1890) left a *dīwān* that was published by his son ʿAbd al-Fattāḥ as *ʿIqd al-laʾāl min naẓm al-Shahhāl* (Tripoli, Maṭbaʿat al-Balāgha). Apart from spiritual songs (*istighāthāt*), the work also contains wordly poems, *madāʾiḥ, tahāniʾ, muwashshaḥāt* and others.

c Taqī al-Dīn al-Rāfiʿī

On 14 Dhu ʾl-Ḥijja 1309/11 July 1892, Taqī al-Dīn ʿAbd al-Ḥamīd b. ʿAbd al-Ghanī b. Aḥmad al-Rāfiʿī al-Fārūqī completed his *dīwān*, entitled *al-Farāʾid al-Rāfiʿiyya fī madḥ al-Ḥadra al-Rifāʿiyya*, which he had written in honour of the Aḥmadiyya sheikh Aḥmad b. ʿAlī b. Yaḥyā al-Rifāʿī and in which he imitated Ṣafī al-Dīn al-Ḥillī's *Urtuqiyyāt* (Cairo: al-Maṭbaʿa al-ʿIlmiyya, 1313). A second *dīwān*, *al-Aflādh al-zabarjadiyya fī madāʾiḥ al-ʿitra al-Ṭāhiriyya al-Aḥmadiyya*, was published in Tripoli in 1906; Sarkīs 923, Cairo² III, 269. Further *qaṣīdas* by him and other poets from Tripoli, as well as a tenso in prose 'Between the Sword and the Pen', are contained in *Jawāhir al-ḥakīm*, Tripoli, 1922 (*Jāmiʿ* I, 193). In his *al-Barāʿim* I, 11/4, ʿUmar Yaḥyā remembers him in a poem that first appeared in *Majallat al-Fatḥ*, in Tripoli.

d ʿAbd al-Qādir al-Adhamī al-Ṭarābulusī

Apart from an account of Ḥanafī *fiqh*, ʿAbd al-Qādir Efendi b. ʿAbd al-Qādir Efendi Ḥusaynī al-Adhamī al-Ṭarābulusī al-Ḥanafī also published *Hadiyyat al-nāsik wa-hidāyat al-sālik fī 'l-masālik* (al-Maṭbaʿa al-ʿIlmiyya, 1312) and a *dīwān* entitled *Ghurar al-iʾtinās wa-durar al-iqtibās* (Alexandria: Maṭbaʿat Jarīdat al-Rafīq, 1313), Sarkīs 1291.

e Muḥammad Rashīd al-Rāfiʿī

Muḥammad Rashīd b. ʿAbd al-Laṭīf b. ʿAbd al-Qādir al-Rāfiʿī wrote a *khamsiyya*
347 on the Prophet and his family, in which | he also extols some of the miracles of ʿAbd al-Qādir al-Jīlānī: *al-Kawākib al-durriyya fī 'l-manāqib al-Qādiriyya* (Tripoli: Maṭbaʿat al-Balāgh, 1312; Cairo² III, 312).

2 Adult Witnesses of the [First] World War

Of the generation that lived through the war and was undoubtedly affected by it, although not enough to let it have a significant effect on their creative output because their ideas were fixed at the time of the events, we mention one person from Aleppo and another from Lebanon.

a *Jirjis Shalḥat*

Al-Khūrifisqūfūs Jirjis b. Yūsuf b. Rāfāʾīl Shalḥat was born in 1856. He began his studies under the Fransiscans in Aleppo and completed them in ʿAyntūra and al-Shurfa, in Lebanon. There, he also learned French and Italian, as well as the Syrian language of the church. After his return he first became privy secretary to his uncle, the patriarch Jirjīs Shalḥat. The latter also ordained him a priest, after which he became chorepiscopos. Having taught in the Syrian municipal school for a time, he founded his own Madrasat al-Taraqqī. For six years he published *Majallat al-warqāʾ*. At the beginning of the war he went to Cairo, returning to his homeland in 1921. His first work in verse, *al-Ṭirāz al-muʿallam fī madḥ al-batūl Maryam* (Beirut 1904), is traditional in form. *Al-Najwa fī 'l-ṣināʿa wal-ʿilm wal-dīn* was published in Beirut in 1903, in abstract in *al-Mashriq* X 981/9, 1021/32, 1094/9, and as an offprint with the title *al-Kawn wal-maʿbad aw al-Funūn al-jamīla wal-kanīsa* (Cairo² III, 312). During the war, he published two collections of poems, *al-Shakwā aw Munājāt al-arwāḥ* (Cairo: Maṭbaʿat Ramsīs, 1915) and *al-Shakwā aw Muḥāwarat al-ḥakīm* (ibid., 1918), in which he addressed himself in particular to the warring powers in order to move them to peace, at the same time praising Maḥmūd Pāshā Shukrī. In his *Qilādat al-dhahab fī Faransā wal-ʿArab* (ibid. 1923), he takes a timid stance on the political situation in Syria under the mandate. But in his *Ḥabk al-darārī al-muraṣṣaʿa bihā ḥabāʾik al-durar* (ibid. 1923), he retreats to neutral territory with *tasmīṭ*s and *tashṭīr*s on religious poetry. Cf. Sarkīs 1139, *Jāmiʿ* I, 618, 690, *al-Mashriq* XXIII, 473.

b Ḥalīm Dammūs

Ḥalīm Dammūs Ibrāhīm, born in Zahleh in Lebanon in 1888, studied in Shurfa, lived for a period in Brazil, during which time he published his *Zubdat al-ārāʾ fī 'l-shiʿr wal-shuʿarāʾ* (Montreal 1910), then returned to Zahleh where he published *Jarīdat al-Muhadhdhib*. In 1911 he published *al-Aghānī al-waṭaniyya*, which are texts to melodies | composed by the editor-in-chief of *Jaridat al-* 348
Mufīd in Beirut. He published his collected poems from the years 1905/19 in his two-volume *dīwān*, taking the year 1908/9 as a dividing line between the two (Damascus 1919; al-Quds: Maṭbaʿat al-Aytām al-Sūriyyīn, 1920). The work is preceded by an introduction on poetry from a European and an Arab viewpoint. He published a second collection of poems, which also includes a series of personal recollections in prose, as *al-Mathālith wal-mathānī* (2 vols., Sidon 1926, 1930; see *Apollo* 592/4, *al-Mashriq* XXXIV, 799). In 1925 he transposed Fr. Coppée's play *Fī sabīl al-tāj* back into a real tragedy (*maʾsāt*), after its earlier transposition into prose by Muṣṭafā al-Manfalūṭī. It was published in Beirut. He published two short stories, *Ḥadīth al-nahr* (*Fatāt al-sharq* IV [1909], 112) and *Adab al-ḥabīb* (*Fatāt al-sharq* V, 315/20). A prizewinning poem called *Qaṣīdat al-muhājir* (1927) was printed in *Aḥsan mā katabtu* 28/9 (and in *al-Majalla al-Sūriyya* III, 1928, 42/3), as was a poem on Shawqī in *Apollo* I, 485/6. A *qaṣīda* for Mayy is included in *Mayy fī Sūriyyā wa fī Lubnān* 141/2. He showed himself a linguist in *Qāmūs al-ʿawāmm* (Damascus: Maṭbaʿat al-Taraqqī, 1923).

3 Sulaymān al-Bustānī

On the border of two eras we find the translator of the *Iliad*, Sulaymān al-Bustānī who, despite all his apparent success, was a tragic figure.

He was born on 22 May 1856 in Bkashtīn, a small village in the Qaḍāʾ al-Shūf, in southern Lebanon. His father, Khaṭṭār al-Bustānī, was a farmer belonging to the Bustānī family that has spread throughout the Lebanon and to which Buṭrus al-Bustāni also belongs. He began his studies in his hometown under the guidance of his uncle, the *maṭrān* ʿAbdallāh al-Bustānī. When he was seven years old his father sent him to Beirut, to al-Madrasa al-Waṭaniyya, founded and led by Buṭrus al-Bustānī, where he studied under Nāṣīf al-Yāzijī and Yūsuf al-Asīr. After finishing school in 1871, he worked for Buṭrus al-Bustānī's bimonthly and bi-weekly magazines *al-Jinān* and *al-Janna*. He also ran the *al-Junayna* newspaper, founded by Salīm al-Bustānī, for a time, but that publication only ran from 1871 to 1875. In those days, he was working on a series of entries for the *Dāʾirat al-maʿārif*. In 1876, the notables of Baṣra, under the chairmanship of Qāsim Bāshā Zuhayr, commissioned him to set up a school and a
349 newspaper. But within a year he went into | the date trade with the Āl Zuhayr family. He then went to Baghdad, where he became a member of the commercial tribunal. In his role as managing director, he reorganised the ʿUmān shipping company founded by Miḍḥat Pāshā so well that it started to make profits again in a very short time. On his extensive travels he got to know Arabia inside out, all the way to the Hadhramaut. The things he saw led to a study of the pariah tribe of the Ṣlīb (see W. Pieper, *MO* XVII, 1923, 1/75), which he published in 1887 in *al-Muqtaṭaf*.

In 1885 he returned to Beirut, where he became chief editor of *Dāʾirat al-maʿārif*, his cousin Salīm having passed away in the previous year. With a team of collaborators the latter had already started preparing a Turkish translation of it, and now it was important to obtain the permission to print this from the ministry of education in Istanbul. He thus went to stay there for three months, obtaining a thorough knowledge of the workings of the Ottoman bureaucracy in the capital. In his *ʿIbra wa-dhikrā* (73ff) he writes about this. Having finally obtained the necessary permission, thanks to the personal intervention of Saʿīd Pāshā, he wanted to start printing in Beirut. But he became so frustrated by the local censor that he angrily left the country to go to Egypt in 1887. There, the khedive, Tawfīq Pāshā, was very positive about the encyclopaedia's lemma on stenography, so much so that he toyed with the idea of introducing Sulaymān's Arabic adaptation of it to Egyptian schools. As such, he wrote an elaborated version of it, *al-Ikhtizāl aw al-istīnughrāfiyya*, but it was only in 1920 that it was finally published in Cairo.

In 1888 he went travelling again, this time to India and Persia, where he stayed for two years, obtaining sound knowledge of Persian literature. After a two-year stay in Baghdad, where he got married and worked on a history of the Arabs that was never finished, he went to Istanbul. In 1893, he was sent to

Chicago to represent the government at the Turkish pavilion at the World's Fair. This is also where he founded a Turkish newspaper called *Šīkāġō Sirkisi*, with the liberal ʿUbaydallāh as its editor-in-chief. But the latter was not to the liking of the Turkish consul there because he did not sufficiently laud the Turkish government.[4] In Istanbul, he wrote | a memorandum on the irrigation 350
of Iraq, which was never implemented by the government. Through the killings of the Armenians in 1896 he became intimately acquainted with the evils of Ḥamīd's despotism, something that reinforced his longtime sympathy for the Young Turks, which he had never brought out into the open until then (see *ʿIbra wa-dhikrā*, 96ff).

In Istanbul, he completed his translation of the *Iliad*, which was published as *Ilyādhat Hūmīrūs muʿarraba naẓman wa-ʿalayhā sharḥ taʾrīkhī adabī* (Cairo: Maṭbaʿat al-Hilāl, 1904). It has a very extensive introduction, in which he first explains who Homer was and what the Homeric question is about, and then sets out the history of its translation. He regretted, from an early age, ever since his acquaintance with Milton's *Paradise Lost* (of which he knew large parts by heart), that Arabic literature could not boast any epic tradition. Then, when he got to know the *Iliad*, he first tried to reproduce individual passages, basing himself on English, French and Italian translations. When he understood that he could not achieve what he wanted to do if he did not know the original, he started taking courses in Greek at the Jesuit university in Beirut.[5] The *Iliad* accompanied him everywhere on his travels, and wherever he went he showed drafts of his translations to the local scholars he knew. In Istanbul, he had the fortune to obtain the advice of the Greek interpreter of the English embassy, Stavridis, and of a teacher at the Greek Chalkī school there, Karolidis. In the summer 1895, he completed his work in the cool surroundings of the Fener Bahçe. He gives detailed explanations of his methodology, e.g. in his reproduction of personal names, whose strange forms he sometimes had to adapt to the phonemics of Arabic. He follows the sense of the text as closely as possible, even if he is sometimes obliged to deviate from the distribution of meaning over the verses. He solved the problem of metre very cleverly. Even if the choice of a single metre, like Firdawsī's *mutaqārib*, would have made his task considerably lighter, it would soon have fatigued his readers. That is why he alternates between the classical metres in the various episodes. Thus, Book I starts in *khafīf*, to switch to *ṭawīl* in verse 68 with the address of Achilles. At

4 Of the history of its foundation, so typical of Turkish bureaucracy under Ḥamīd, he gives a detailed account in his *ʿIbra wa-dhikrā* 76ff.

5 The statement by al-Bustānī in *Mashriq* XXV, 786, that it was only in Cairo that the editor-in-chief of *al-Muqtaṭaf* encouraged him to do this, is, therefore, incorrect.

verse 121 he moves on to *wāfir* and at verse 188 back to *ṭawīl*. The exitement in
351 Achilles' | answer is expressed by *khafīf*. At verse 245ff, the story then switches to *kāmil*. Yet he does not look down upon modern forms of rhyme either, on which he reports in detail on pages 102/6 of the introduction. The introduction concludes with a very concise overview of the history of Arabic literature and poetry based on Arab and European points of view. His translation is accompanied by a very extensive commentary, which aims to introduce the Hellenic world to his readers, who were, for the most part, totally unfamiliar with it. The commentary is accompanied by some well-executed images of ancient monuments. Following the example of European scholars, the work has been made user-friendly by the inclusion of extensive indices and a glossary of difficult terms. While trying to maintain an unadulterated, poetical diction throughout, he does not exaggerate in his use of archaisms.[6] It therefore comes as no surprise that his friends greeted his work with enthusiasm in *al-Mashriq* VII, 1904, 865, 911, 1118, 1138. Yet it did not have the influence on Arabic literature that he had hoped for. In his *Aṭyāf al-rabīʿ* $198_{,15}$, Abū Shādī probably expresses a general feeling among the Arabs when he rejects the translation as "unnatural."

In 1898, al-Bustānī returned to his native Lebanon to quietly work on the *Iliad* and the encyclopaedia and to await developments on the political front. After the restoration of the constitution, he published his *ʿIbra wa-dhikrā, al-dawla al-ʿUthmāniyya qabl al-dustūr wa-baʿdahu* (Cairo: Maṭbaʿat al-Akhbār, October 1908). It is a report, in a very quiet tone, far removed from any kind of heated agitation, on the living circumstances in the empire under the ancient regime. And it is not a partisan text, since on several occasions (e.g. p. 103) he juxtaposes the empire's freedom of religion with the testimony of French nationals concerning the anti-clerical sentiments by which their country is dominated. But time and again he holds the government responsible for the neglect of his country's riches, in each case making proposals for their future exploitation. It is significant that, for him, there is no Arab national sentiment yet, unless he suppresses it on purpose so as not to offend his political friends.
352 | He does not tire of emphasising that, like the Young Turks, he thinks the well-being of the state depends on Christians and Muslims serving in the army side by side and that Turkish should be made obligatory as a national language in all parts of the empire (p. 98 bottom, 200 bottom).

A member of the *al-Ittiḥad wal-taraqqī* party, he was elected as a delegate of Beirut in 1908. He thus moved to Istanbul once again. Due to an intentionally

---

6 And he hardly makes a mistake, like at 225, 6, where he uses *shibīna* as a plural to *shuba* in the sense of 'hero', and which must be a *taṣḥīf* of *thibīna* 'multitudes.'

reserved attitude, he won the trust of the leading circles there, who, in 1910, elected him the vice-chairman of the House of Representatives. They also appointed him leader of the delegation that went to visit the royal courts of Europe to announce Muḥammad Rashād's accession to the throne. Under Saʿīd Ḥalīm Pāshā, he was appointed minister of trade, agriculture, forestry and mining in 1913. In this capacity he succeeded in preventing E. v. Rothschild's purchase of the former royal domains in Ghawr Baysān on behalf of the Zionists, a transaction for which Enver Pāshā had already been won by the prospect of an important provision. He had no sympathy for the latter's foreign policy, and neither for Ṭalʿat's. As such, he retired to Switzerland at the outbreak of the war. There, he fell ill, which necessitated several month's treatment in a sanatorium. This is the period in which he wrote his mournful *al-Dāʾ wal-shafāʾ* (2nd printing, Cairo 1921). At the end of the war he returned once more to Istanbul; even Mustafa Kemal is said to have tried to secure his cooperation. But an eye condition, from which he had suffered since early childhood, forced him to go to Egypt to undergo an operation there. In the spring of 1924 his fellow countrymen invited him to come to the United States, where he received an enthusiastic welcome in New York. But, having gone entirely blind by then, he had to retire from public life, and he died there on 1 June 1925.

Although his compatriots erected a memorial in Beirut in gratitude to him, his works did not find their way to posterity; his literary works did not inspire the younger generation while his political aspirations had been directed to an ideal that had no chance of survival to begin with.

Sarkīs 560, Jirjī Niqūlā Bāz, *Sulaymān al-Bustānī*, Beirut 1925, ʿĪsā Iskander al-Maʿlūf in *Jarīdat al-Istiqlāl* of 6 August 1925, *al-Muqtaṭaf*, August 1925, p. 341/7, Jirjī Zaydān, *al-Hilāl* XVII, 1908, Būlus Ghānim, *Man huwa Sulaymān al-Bustānī* in *Lisān al-ḥāl* V, 3/6 August | 1925, F.E. Bustānī in *al-Mashriq* XXIII, 353
778/91, 824/43, 908/25, a *marthiya* in Ilyās Abū Shabaka, *al-Qīthāra* 82/3, 131/2. I. Kračkovsky, *Sulaymān al-Bustānī*, Ukrainskaja Akademija Nauk, Otd. ottisk iz jubileinogo Sbornika v čest akad. Bagalija, Kiev 1927. Samples in Rafāʾīl Nakhla, *Mukhtārāt* II, Beirut 1931, 184/96.

4 Poets of Damascus

The [First] World War, whose outcome was decided on Syrian soil, and the years of political unrest following it, were not beneficial to the development of poetry. When the treacherous promises of the Entente were made, patriotic sentiments among the Arabs clearly raised to an all-time high. So when, after Fayṣal's kingdom had been transformed into a French mandate, the people's uprising against this injustice was quelled in blood in 1925, this led of course to an outburst of passionate fury in songs. But the years of hardship on the ruins of Syria's capital left no room for a quiet cultivation of the arts. Still, there were some poets, of whom we shall speak below, who tried to carry the flame of Arabic literature forward into better times.

a *Fāris Bek al-Khūrī al-Dimashqī*

Here we mention first two politicians whose intellectual development goes back to the pre-war period, during which they had also been active as writers. The first of these two was Fāris Bek al-Khūrī al-Dimashqī. Born in 1877, he terminated his studies at the American University of Beirut in 1897 with a *licence ès lettres*. He then took up legal practice in Damascus and soon played a leading role in the Arab movement. Early in 1914, he was elected a member of parliament. During the war, in 1916, he became suspected of having had a hand in the uprising of the Arabs of the Hijaz. He was held in custody for a time, but was eventually allowed to return to Damascus in 1918. Under Fayṣal he was chancellor of the exchequer, but when the French arrived in 1920 he had to return to legal practice again. Together with ʿAbd al-Raḥmān Shāhbandar and Iḥsān al-Sharīf, he founded the National Party (*Ḥizb al-waṭan*) on 25 June 1925. On 4 May 1926 he was appointed minister of education in the cabinet of Aḥmad
354 Nāmī Bey | (*Or. Mod.* VI, 283), but on 13 June he was sacked and arrested. He described the major battles in the Russo-Japanese war of 1904/5 in a series of long *qaṣīdas*. These were first published in *al-Muqtabas* and then—with a linguistic commentary and an appendix containing the translation of a letter by Tolstoy to the Tsar dated 1902—as *Waqāʾiʿ al-ḥarb* in Cairo: Maṭbaʿat al-Akhbār, 1906 (Sarkīs 849, Cairo[2] III, 436). A *takhmīs* to a *qaṣīda* by Ibn Zaydūn is reproduced in Kampffmeyer, MSOS 1925, II, 274. His experiences as chancellor of the exchequer and his time as a lecturer at the *Maʿhad al-ḥuqūq al-ʿArabī* served as the basis for his *Mūjiz fī ʿilm al-māliyya* (Damascus: Maṭbaʿat al-Ḥukūma, 1924: *Jāmiʿ* I, 998).

b *ʿAbd al-Raḥmān Shāhbandar*

His friend, the physician ʿAbd al-Raḥmān Shāhbandar, had been minister of foreign affairs in the second Syrian cabinet of national unity and was held prisoner on the island of Arwad by the French. After his release, he played an important political role in Damascus. This not being the place to go into such matters, all we shall say is that it took him abroad a lot, both to Egypt and the Americas. While in prison, he translated an English work, giving it the title *al-Siyāsa al-dawliyya* (Damascus: Maṭbaʿat al-Taraqqī, n.d.; *Jāmiʿ* I, 967), as well as his *Silsilat al-sujūn* (Maṭbaʿat al-Taraqqī, 1343; *Jāmiʿ* I, 280; MSOS XXVIII, 305, XXX, 221).

c *Muḥammad al-Bizm*

Muḥammad b. Maḥmūd b. Muḥammad b. Salīm al-Bizm was born in 1306/1887 in Damascus, where his family had settled from Iraq some two centuries earlier. Having first taken care of his father's factory, he has been a full-time writer since 1913. Until the age of twenty, it would only be by chance if he set eyes on some classical literary work. Indeed, it was not before he visited the Ẓāhiriyya library at the invitation of his friend Khayr al-Dīn al-Zuruklī, that he became interested in the intellectual heritage of the Arabs. From that moment on, he accompanied his friend to listen to the men who were perpetuating this heritage in Damascus at the time: the poet ʿAbd al-Qādir Badrān, the meritorious editor of Ibn ʿAsākir's *Taʾrīkh*, the theologian Jamāl al-Dīn al-Qāsimī (Suppl. II 777) and the philologist Ṣāliḥ al-Tūnisī, who had settled in Damascus. In 1913 he had reached the point where he could give some courses on literature at al-Madrasa al-ʿUthmāniyya, led by Kāmil al-Qaṣṣāb. During the war he had an office job in the Turkish army, | during which time he sang the praise 355
of the Arab freedom movement in a number of songs. But, being obliged to keep them secret, these have been lost. When the French occupied Damascus he was detained for a while on suspicion of political activism. But, after his release, he was able to publish a large number of patriotic poems in the newspapers. Even though these poems have not yet been brought out in collective form, Kampffmeyer reproduces the poet's own selection from them in *MSOS* 1926, II, 176/81. In his poems, his longing for his ancestors' ancient homeland of Iraq often breaks through, nourished by the more fortunate situation that this country was in under the British, allowing it a certain measure of freedom. The violence erupting in Arabia in 1924 on the other hand, filled him with concern, it being impossible for him to foretell its happy ending when he wrote his *Ṣūnu ʾl-Jazīra*. Similarly, he was unable to predict the unhappy fate of ʿAbd al-Karīm, whom he extolls at the end as a defender of Arab freedom.

d *Shafīq Jabrī*

The son of a tradesman and born in 1895 in Damascus, Shafīq Jabrī went to the school of the Lazarists there from 1904 until 1912. He then followed his family, which had meanwhile settled in Jaffa, returning to his hometown in 1917. In 1934, he went to Switzerland and France. He, too, talks admiringly of al-Zuruklī for guiding him down the literary path. His poems, for the most part published in *al-Muqtabas*, seek to add new ideas to an old tradition and extol freedom and the sense of nationhood, as do the poems of al-Bizm. After Ibn Saʿūd's victory over al-Ḥusayn he welcomed the former in Syria as the one "… who has restored unity, uplifted the banner, and carried it with his armies across the lands; who brings the Arabs power and peace, in order that no wolf dare break

into the herd" etc. Being a Christian, he is more at liberty to address certain national issues than his Muslim countrymen. For this same reason, he can also cross the boundaries of religion: "When the regions do not unite in their hour of need, when the sheikh does not reach out to the priest and the metropolitan, when the Gospel of Jesus Christ cannot unite us, then let people have both the Gospel and the Qurʾān; religion is of but a single God, our fatherland is our
356 Kaʿba, let us therefore not let it be brought down by religion. | What is this separation, us being one by origin, sons of ʿAdnān? In Egypt, people work on the foundations of their country, whereas we do everything we can to destroy the foundations of ours. They, the Egyptians, have woken up and wrested themselves from the grasp of the oppressor; in Syria's provinces, however, they are all still asleep as far as I can see", etc. In 1932, *al-Ḥadīth* V, 41/4 featured two poems by him, *al-Ṭifl* and *Iʿādat al-ḥayāt baʿd al-mawt*; in 1936, *al-Ḥadīth* IX, 462/6 featured a *qaṣīda* on al-Mutanabbī. In 1937, he recited a *qaṣīda* in memory of Jamīl Ṣidqī al-Zahāwī in Baghdad; see *al-Ḥadīth* 1937, 303/7. A short story, *ʿAlā Buḥayrat Ṭabariyya*, is printed on pages 11/4 of the same issue. Memories of a trip to Europe were published in *al-Ḥadīth* X (1936), *ʿAlā ṭarīq al-Louvre* 13/6, *Dār al-hudūʾ*, *Rousseau bayna 'l-ḥawr wal-baṭṭ wal-ʿaṣāfīr* 378/83, *Fī Fluransa al-ʿatīqa*, 481/4, *Ilā Rūma* 515/8. For further samples see Kampffmeyer, MSOS 1925, II 256/62. Sāmī al-Kayyālī, publisher of *al-Ḥadīth*, reports a conversation with him in *al-Ḥadīth* V, 1931, 1027.

e *Khalīl Mardam Bek*

Khalīl b. Aḥmad b. ʿUthmān Mardam Bek was born in Damascus in 1313/1895. He was torn away from school when his father died in 1329/1911. It was only later that he could make good on this by means of private teachers. During the war he was detained for a period when he was suspected of political agitation, but then freed on bail. After the retreat of the Turks, the provisional government appointed him secretary in the *dīwān al-rasāʾil al-ʿāmma*. In 1920, under Fayṣal's first cabinet, he was appointed *muʿāwin* to the chairman of the council of ministers, a post that was abolished upon the French occupation. From then on, he lived only by the fruit of his pen. In 1921, he and his friends founded al-Rābiṭa al-adabiyya of which he was the chairman until the French dissolved it and its magazine was closed. In 1923, he was nominated an honorary member of the library association of the ʿUmar mosque in Jerusalem. In 1924, he was appointed honorary director of Arabic studies at the Madrasat al-Jāmiʿa al-Waṭaniyya in Damascus and elected to the Academy of Damascus in 1925. In his poems he cherishes the proud history of the city, and especially its martyrs, such as the volunteers who were the last to venture into battle against the French at Maysalūn, in a *qaṣīda* he recited at a commemorative gathering in May of 1924 (MSOS 1925, II, 266), or the victims of the 'days of terror,' from 18 to 20 October 1920, in the *Dīwān* | *al-thawra* (see below p. 358), 124/5. Like other fellow-sufferers, he eagerly awaited the sound of the first cracks to appear in the ceilings of the states who had conquered them. He thus wrote of the death of the mayor of Cork, T. Mc Swiney, who died as a martyr in a British prison, after a hunger strike of 74 days, on 24 October 1920. Besides the *qaṣīda*, he also cultivated the somewhat more artistic *muwashshaḥ* genre. There is a poetical salute to Mayy by him in *Mayy fī Sūriyā wa-Lubnān* 148/9. Of his prose works, still referred to as unpublished in his autobiography, *Shuʿarāʾ al-Shaʾm fī 'l-qarn al-thālith* was, however, published in Damascus in 1925 (*Jāmiʿ* 677, unfortunately not accessible to me), and a study on ʿAbd al-Ḥamīd al-Kātib in *al-Hilāl* 1937, 530/6. See Mayy, *Bayna 'l-madd wal-jazr* 148, Kampffmeyer, MSOS 1925, II, 262/71. Excerpts in Rafāʾīl Nakhla, *Mukhtārāt* II, Beirut, 1931, 80/3. 357

f *Khayr al-Dīn al-Zuruklī (Zarkalī)*

The friend and inspirer of these poets, the aforementioned Khayr al-Dīn al-Zuruklī (Zarkalī), was mentioned on page 235 in connection with his activities in Egypt. There, he had switched completely to prose-writing, as he must have understood that poetry did not really suit him. Five of his poems were published by Muḥammad Yāsīn ʿArafa in the *Dīwān al-thawra* (Cairo: al-Maṭbaʿa al-ʿArabiyya, 1345/1926, pp. 13, 38, 67, 85, 108): *Bayna 'l-dam wal-nār, Mā bālu Sārāy (Sarrail), Fuʾād, Maṣraʿ al-akramīn, Yā Jīrata 'l-Shaʾm*. His collected poems were published in his *Dīwān* (Cairo, 1343/1925; cf. RAAD V, 205). As was justly observed by al-Jiddāwī (*Naẓarāt al-naqd*, 206), these poems are too much like political editorials. He often bows too willingly to the exigencies of the rhyme. For example, he does not shrink from using the French form 'Dāmās' in *Dīwān al-thawra* 108,5, unless he did this with the intention of ridiculing the people of Beirut who collaborated with the French. That he has great power of expression, no one will deny, even though he might have succeeded better in depicting the horrors of the bombing of Damascus on 13 April had he not given in to the constraints of metre and rhyme. See also the anonymous *Khayr al-Dīn al-Zuruklī shāʿir al-thawra al-ʿArabiyya bi-Dimashq*, n.d., 96pp.

g *Muḥammad al-Shurayqī*

Muḥammad b. Yūsuf al-Shurayqī must be mentioned together with the above Damascenes, even though he only lived for a brief period in the capital, because he played a decisive role in their fate. Born in Latakia in 1314/1896, he went to school in Istanbul, | Beirut, the Lebanon, and Damascus, attended al-Azhar for one year, and then studied at the Madrasat al-ḥuqūq al-ʿUthmāniyya in Damascus. During the war he spoke up for the independence of the Arabs 358 in fiery poems published in the newspapers. This earned him a twelve-year prison sentence, of which he served only three. In 1922, the French government sentenced him to 20 years in prison because of the speech with which he had greeted the American Chr. R. Crane on his vist to Damascus, but he avoided arrest by fleeing to Transjordan. His juvenile poems, *Aghānī 'l-ṣibā, majmū'at qaṣā'id wijdāniyya fī qālab waṣfī riwā'ī, tumaththilu rūḥ al-nāẓim fī madārij al-ḥayāt mundhu 'l-ṭufūla ḥattā ākhir sinī 'l-madrasa* (Maṭba'at al-Hukūma al-'Arabiyya, 1339/1921), show that it was not just political passion that he knew how to put into verse. Samples are cited by Kampffmeyer in *MSOS* 1926, II, 186/193. Besides idylls such as the mother at the cradle (*Ḥawla 'l-mahd*, to be read thus), he also tries his hand at philosophical themes, but, as may be expected, he does not rise beyond some commonplaces. Yet when he complains to Sa'd Zaghlūl about the hardships of the Syrians and the arrogance of the victors, he strikes a more passionate tone (*Nār fī janna*, in *Dīwān al-thawra*, 40/3): "Sarrail, your revenge is reminiscent of Tīmūr; but you, by God, are so much harsher than he! Where is this civilisation whose leaders are supposed to uphold the law?; where are this freedom and this dignity of man? Where is the League of Nations to grant us what is rightfully ours; whose justice should we appeal to in the West? You have now removed the veil from our eyes; henceforth, you cannot fool us with your empty promises!" He now puts all his hopes on Egypt and on Sa'd: "Egypt, you Ka'ba and refuge of the Arabs, you are the sanctum of Syria's hopes; when Sarrail makes her cry in anguish, Sa'd will dry her tears and bring back her smile!" *Miṣr wal-Sha'm* (ibid. 92/4, cited in Kampffmeyer 184/5) are to him "a Fatherland to the sons of Shem, Arab through and through; the Arian cannot hold his ground independently there, even if he tramples its independence for a time" etc.

f *Poets included in the* Dīwān al-thawra

Besides contributions by Iraqi and Egyptian poets (Aḥmad Shawqī, Abū Shādī, Maḥmūd Ramzī Naẓīm), the *Dīwān al-thawra* cited above also contains poems
359 by a number of other, Syrian poets such as Shakīb Arslān, | 'Ādil Arslān, Jirjī Efendi Ṣaydaḥ, Ḥabīb Efendi 'Iwaḍ, 'Alī Efendi Manṣūr, Sālim Efendi Naṣrallāh, Wadī' al-Bustānī, 'Izz al-Dīn Āl 'Alam al-Dīn, and 'Abbās Abū Shaqra. While Rashīd al-Khūrī, from Brazil, could voice his patriotic indignation unreservedly in the sharpest of terms (81/3), other Syrians had to remain anonymous, such as the 'Damascene poet' in his 'French lesson': "They said: 'We come to help you with money and advice. We shall give you a taste of happiness and a sense of achievement, take heavy loads off your shoulders.' But then, when they had achieved their goal and subjugated us all, they taught us a lesson with their unjust rule; a lesson that we will teach our coming generations." A 'great Arab

poet' addresses himself in *al-Thawra al-ʿarabiyya* not only to his compatriots, but also to the Arabs of the Jazīra and Egypt, reminding them of the heroic deeds of people like Ḥasan al-Kharrāṭ while threatening their French overlords with the revenge that was to come. A 'well-known Syrian poet' (50/2) sets his hopes on the Arab banner, even if all he can do is point at the exploits of Ṣalāḥ al-Dīn. Ḥasan Yūsuf extols the heroic death of the sheikh of Ḥajjīra, who defended his village to his last breath (78/9). Al-Shāʿir al-ʿAdnānī and Ibn al-Sāḥil celebrate the martyr Aḥmad Bek Maryūd (87, 116/7), while a 'Syrian poet' (118) calls on the Arabs to revolt.

h *Munīr al-Ḥusāmī al-Dimashqī*

But while the storm of the Arab struggle for freedom was raging, Munīr al-Ḥusāmī al-Dimashqī still found time to sing of love and beauty in his *ʿArsh al-ḥubb wal-jamāl* (Beirut: Maṭbaʿat al-Arz, 1925). In the preface to this work, Amīn al-Rayḥānī introduces this writer to the reader.

i *Aḥmad ʿUbayd*

Here we also mention the bookseller Aḥmad b. Muḥammad Ḥasan b. Yūsuf al-Ḥājj ʿUbayd. Born in 1311/1893, he started his business with his relatives there in 1327/1909. Apart from his *Mashāhīr shuʿarāʾ al-ʿaṣr fi ʾl-aqṭār al-ʿArabiyya al-thalātha* I, *Shuʿarāʾ Miṣr* (Maṭbaʿat al-Taraqqī, 1341/1922), often used by us, he also published a selection from the works of al-Manfalūṭī (p. 195ff), *Kalimāt al-Manfalūṭī* (Maṭbaʿat al-Taraqqī, 1343; *Jāmiʿ* I, 429), an anthology entitled *Ṭarāʾif al-ḥikma, majmūʿa fi ʾl-adab wal-ḥikma wal-amthāl* (Maṭbaʿat al-Raḥmāniyya, 1342) and *Fī sabīl al-akhlāq, qaṣīda ijtimāʿiyya, tumaththilu fiʾa min al-shabāb wa-tadʿū ila ʾl-tamassuk bil-ḥijāb* (Damascus n.d., 1928). In | his autobiography 360
in Kampffmeyer, MSOS 1925, II, 278 he also mentions an unpublished *dīwān*; Kampffmeyer (ibid.) also cites three short poems from *Alifbāʾ*.

k *Aḥmad al-Najafī*

Damascus is also the adoptive city of the Iraqi Shīʿī Aḥmad b. ʿAlī b. Ṣāfī al-Najafī, whose *Dīwān al-amwāj* was recently published there (see *al-Dharīʿa* II, 351, no. 1405) and who also wrote a preface to the *dīwān* of his friend ʿUmar Yaḥyā (see below, 8a).

5 Nuṣayrīs

a *Muḥammad Sulaymān al-Aḥmad*

The Syrian freedom struggle also fuelled the national fervour of the Nuṣayrīs (ʿAlawīs). This is especially clear from the *dīwān* of Muḥammad Sulaymān al-Aḥmad, entitled *Badawī al-jabal* (Sidon: Maṭbaʿat al-ʿIrfān, 1343/1925).

It seems that the poet felt just as much at home in Damascus as in his native region. A number of his creations were first recited at the Academy there, such as his 'Salute to Syria', which he gave to Dr ʿAbd al-Raḥmān Shāhbandar to accompany him on his trip to promote the cause of Syria in Europe and the Americas. But his national sentiment comprises all the Arabs, as is shown by his poem *ʿAlā aṭlāl al-Jazīra* (97/103), which terminates with a strong admonition to the League of Nations. Thus, he voices his reverence for the unfortunate Ḥusayn and his sons on their entry to ʿAmmān, believing himself able to speak in name of his country as well: "I am your poet, in a land where you only have friends.[7] I will speak of you, even at the peril of the executioner's sword. Listen to my words as if they were spoken by your bride, and hear the voice of passion, the voice of burning love. I protected her, this bride, despite their insistence, against other suitors; a virgin, destined for the man descending from the house of the Imam of all the Muslims." Similarly, he complains about the split within the Egyptian Wafd party, while his hatred of the British oppressors inspires him, too, to lament the martyrdom of the mayor of Cork, T. Mc Swiney (see p. 357).
361 Besides politics, the arts are also given their due. He thus extols the spirits of | al-Manfalūṭī and al-Ālūsī in a gathering of the Academy (63/9), in addition to his celebration of the Iraqi Jamīl Ṣidqī al-Zahāwī as the poet who wrote *al-Tāj* (53/9). But if there is one thing he does not tire of, it is expressing his adoration for his lady-friend Mayy of *Apollo* magazine. He improvises in the popular *muwashshaḥ Ughniyat al-Birdawnī* (129/31).[8] He once uses the *radīf* metre in a love song titled *Lā tuḥibbīnī* (157/8). His *Dīwān*, dedicated to the memory of the hero Maysalūn, is prefaced by ʿAfīfa Ṣaʿb, the publisher of *Majallat al-Khidr*, by Muḥammad Kurd ʿAlī, by ʿAbd al-Qādir al-Maghribī, a poem by Khalīl Mardam Bek, and some words by Bishāra al-Khūrī, Jabrān al-Tuwaynī, and by the sister of the poet, Fāṭima Sulaymān, under the pseudonym of Fatāt Ghassān (see also Kampffmeyer, *MSOS* 1926, II, 193,8, with samples).

b *Kāmil Shuʿayb al-ʿĀmilī*

His fellow-ʿAlawī Kāmil Shuʿayb al-ʿĀmilī published the collection *al-Khamsiyyāt fi 'l-nahḍa al-ʿarabiyya*, Sidon 1343/1924. See *al-Mashriq* XXIII, 74, *MSOS* XXVIII, 255, XX, 220.

---

7 In which the metre forces him to an unusual *mā liman wa-illākum fīhi khadhīn* ($172_{,1}$), his language otherwise being quite careful and precise.

8 On the banks of this river in Zahleh in the Lebanon, on which cf. Ilyās Abū Shabaka, *al-Qīthāra* $67_{,10}$.

c *Al-Ḥawmānī*

In the *Dīwān* (Sidon 1927) of al-Ḥawmānī, the fruit of an entire life spent on poetry, politics is the major theme, as it is in his *Nadq al-sāʾis wal-masūs* (Sidon 1928), which contains a series of maxims in the form of *maqṭūʿāt*, in four *bāb*s: 1. *Naqd al-sāʾis*, 2. *Naqd al-masūs*, 3. *Fi ʾl-ijtimāʿ*, 4. *Fi ʾl-waṣāyā.* See *Lughat al-ʿArab* VII, 259, *al-Mashriq* XXV, 875, XXVI, 877, *MSOS*, XXX, 220, XXXI, 213.

d *Muḥammad Najīb Marwa*

Sidon is also the hometown of Muḥammad Najīb Marwa, who published his poems under the title *al-Tuḥfa al-Ṣaydāwiyya* (Sidon: Maṭbaʿat al-ʿIrfān, 1342).

e *ʿAbd al-Raʾūf al-Amīn*

ʿAbd al-Raʾūf al-Amīn published the first volume of his poems, titled *al-ʿAwāṭif al-thāʾira*, under the pen name Fata ʾl-jabal (Sidon: Maṭbaʿat al-ʿIrfān, 1928; see also *RAAD* IX, 320).

6 Poets from the Lebanon

With its French culture and the European manners and customs of its overseas migrants, Beirut had a stronger and more lasting influence in the Lebanon than in the hinterland. | After the war, this led to the amalgamation of Arab national- 362
ism with a global-minded kind of liberalism that sometimes threatened its true character.

a *Nasīb Arslān*

The oldest of these poets was Nasīb Arslān, the elder brother of the famous politician and publicist Shakīb Arslān (cf. § 2). He was born in 1868 in Shwīfāt, in the Qaḍā Shūf in the Lebanon, on the family estate of the princely Druze family of the Arslān, who traced their ancestry all the way to the Lakhmids of al-Ḥīra. His brother and he had been students of Muḥammad ʿAbduh at al-Madrasa al-Sulṭāniyya in Beirut from 1886 onward. He dedicated his entire life to literature, dying in 1934. Shakīb published his *dīwān*, entitled *Rawḍ al-shaqīq fi ʾl-ghazl wal-raqīq*. See *RAAD* XIII, 380/2.

b *Ilyās Fayyāḍ*

The second poet from the Lebanon to be mentioned here is Ilyās Fayyāḍ. Born in 1870, he was also known in politics as a lawmaker and minister. He died in 1930. In 1911, he wrote a play in five acts on the history of Venice, called *Firās al-Bandaqiyya*. His *dīwān* was published in Beirut in 1918. A tale in verse, called *al-Wafāʾ*, is mentioned by Bustānī in *al-Mashriq* XXV, 623. Cf. the description by

Ilyās Abū Shabaka in *al-Rusūm* 34/7, with samples in Rafāʾīl Nakhla, *Mukhtārāt* II (Beirut, 1931), 266/71.

c *Bishāra al-Khūrī*

Bishāra al-Khūrī,[9] who liked to be called al-Akhṭal al-Ṣaghīr, was born in around 1884. In his younger years he published a number of tales in verse, partly inspired by the ancient Arabs, such as in *ʿUmar wa-Nuʿmān* (Beirut n.d.) and *ʿUrwa wa-ʿAfrāʾ* (in Sulaymān Ibrāhīm Ṣādir, *Jawāhir al-adab* [Beirut 1926], 220/5; see al-Bustānī in *al-Mashriq*, XXV, 623), and for another part by contemporary life such as *al-Maslūl* (Beirut n.d.), *Le faux écu* (? Cf. Pérès, no. 521). Later, when he started publishing the magazine *al-Barq*, he almost completely stopped writing poetry, apart from a brilliant *marthiya* for Aḥmad Shawqī in *Apollo* X, 513/6. In 1936, *al-Ḥadīth* published a poem called *Hijrān* on page 351, and in its issue of 1938, page 507, the poem *Khayāl min damr*. See Ilyās Abū Shabaka, *al-Rusūm*, 23/7. Excerpts in Rafāʾīl Nakhla, *Mukhtārāt* II (Beirut 1931), 71/8.

d *Felix Fāris*

The Maronite Felix Efendi b. Ḥabīb Fāris (b. ca. 1886), publisher of *Lisān al-ittiḥād* magazine in Beirut, had the honour of calling himself *Shāʿir Dawlatlū Nāẓim Pāshā Wālī Sūriyā*.

363 | After the restoration of the Ottoman constitution, he and Walī al-Dīn Yegen campaigned for the unification of Muslims and Christians in the spirit of the Young Turks. Because they met with an almost total rejection of this idea among their compatriots, he went to work as a translator for the municipality of Alexandria. He published most of his poems in the magazines that were run by his female Syrian compatriots in Egypt, such as the *muwashshaḥāt al-Ghurūr*, *al-Walāʾ*, and *al-Maghfira* in *Anīs al-jalīs* of July 1903, 1498/1500, September 1566/70, December 1651/7. The versified tale *Ḍāḥiyat al-māl*, about the unhappy marriage between a rich man and an officer's daughter who verbally outclassed her husband, rhyming in a-b in the form of a *mathnawī* in the *raml* metre, was published in *Anīs al-jalīs* of May 1904, 1752/63, *Jarīmat al-shahāma* in ibid., August, 1902/5, *Munājāt al-nafs* in ibid., October 1906, 305, and in another version in *Fatāt al-sharq* of 1909, 57, and *al-Ḥubb wal-mawt* in ibid., 1910/1. While, in his poetry, he often drew atttention to the difficult status of women, that issue is at the very centre of his prose work *Najwā ilā nisāʾ Sūriyā* (Beirut, 1909), in which he urges them openly to stand up for themselves (see *Fatāt*

---

9 Not to be confused with his namesake, the politician; see *al-Rusūm* 80/1.

al-sharq VI, 21/5). After the war, he was happy to acknowledge the modern poetry of his fellow Maronites, even if he himself was no longer able to do any activity in this field. An obituary in verse for his father, the publisher of *Ṣada 'l-sharq* in Cairo, was featured in *Apollo* X, 808/10. See the warm appreciation by Ilyās Abū Shabaka in *al-Rusūm* I, 17–22, and a *marthiya* by Khalīl Shaybūb in *Radio Araba di Bari*, Rome 1939, XVII, vol. II, No. 9, p. 170.

e *Ilyās Abū Shabaka*

The most brilliant representative of this new generation is the Maronite Ilyās Abū Shabaka, who was born in 1904. His first collection of poems was published with the title *al-Qīthāra, wa-hiya al-nubdha al-ūlā min dīwān Ilyās Abī Shabaka* (Beirut: Maktabat Ṣādir, 1926). His earliest poems, from 1920, exhibit a burning amorous passion which, in *Yā layla 'l-ʿumri matā ghaduh?* (124), even breaks the constraints of the metre; he begins in *mutaqārib*, which later on shows up again several times, but then he switches to entirely free verse, even though he retains the rhyme of the *qaṣīda*. An undated poem, *Wa 'l-ʿaynu buḥayratu aḥlām* (128), an answer to a poem by Shiblī Mallāṭ, is structured in a similar way. But in *Daʿīnī amūt*, of 17 October 1920, the *mutaqārib* is applied all along. In later poems, too, love is still a theme. When he, on 15 October 1921, recalls a summer in Mīrūba (125), | there emerges a girl from Kasrawān at the end 364
of the poem, a girl whose beauty eclipses the sparkle of even the meadows and cascades. On 27 October 1923, he laments the death of a lover in a tristich. On 20 February 1923, his recollections of her take the form of a *muwashshaḥ* in free rhyme (90), which is entirely folkloric in tone. On the same day, he speaks of a new love ache (116), although he gives it a humorous preface ("Rufina, come, a glass of wine and fire for my pipe, and then close the door and leave; don't wake up my mother, for I want to stay up working all night"). On 27 February 1923, he writes a tenso between the heart and love in the form of a tristich. On 17 May that same year he uses that same format in a poem on a beautiful fisherwoman (38).

Sentimental in character, his art was inspired by foreign models from early on. On 27 January 1922 he composed a poem (*Mā baʿda muntaṣaf al-layl*, 15/6) in which he pours out his weltschmerz and which he concludes with the following lines: "In my loneliness I spoke to Musset, and in the dark I whispered his magical verses; he was like me, wilted, sinking into his grave much before his time. You, poet of tears, are tears indispensable to an existence whose puddles include the eye?[10] Nature has filled my life with so much pain, that it longs for the burial shroud." On 10 January 1924, he freely (*bi-taṣarruf*) adopted a poem

---

10 I.e. *al-ʿaynu min ghidrānih*, in which the rhyme for once disturbs the meaning.

by A. Musset, calling it *Tadhakkarī* (126/7). But other French authors interest him as well. He translated J. Lemaitre's tale of 'The lunger' into a strophically-structured ballad, held together by an end rhyme in its fifth member. He also made a free adaptation of Lamartine's 'To Laurence' (95/6) and of his poem to a beautiful Bedouin girl that he once saw smoking in a garden (102/3, dated 3 January 1924). On 25 February 1923 he also translated a poem by Marcelline Desbord Valmore (b. 1786), calling it *Lā tuʿṭi 'l-ḥubba* (109).

Alongside all this, the influence of Arabic poetry remains in the background. He only mentions al-Maʿarrī occasionally as someone that he can relate to. With the exception of him, he only associates with his contemporaries. In February and May of 1923, he praised Shafīq Maʿlūf of Damascus in verse (108,
365 110: "Do you think faster | than your pen? Is your prose more striking than your verse? A talent beyond reason, in whose gardens sentiments blossom, must surely stem from God", etc.). He dedicated two letters full of warm admiration to Felix Fāris (103, 129), his fatherly friend who wrote a laudatory afterword to his *Dīwān*. In June and July 1924 he welcomed Khalīl Maṭrān to Jounieh and Zahleh (47, 74). He composed two elegies for Sulaymān al-Bustānī, in June and July of 1925 (82/3, 131/2). At the end of the volume, he counters Aḥmad Shawqī's *qaṣīda* which calls on the people to help the victims of the bombardment of Damascus, such during a meeting in the Ezbekiyya garden in January of 1926, with a *muʿāraḍa* in which he calls on Shawqī to educate the youth of the East in patriotism so such a catastrophe could never happen again.

But his art never bowed to the French nor to his compatriots. His output over the year 1923 shows the great variety of his creations. Besides the aforementioned love songs, there is a humorous poem called 'To my pipe' of 5 February (87/8), 'Elegy for a nightingale' from 23 February (114), the 'Labourers' song' of 21 March (111/2), a salute to al-Rayḥānī and al-Ruṣāfī in a workers' meeting at Zahleh of 20 June ('I am a free man'), three poems about the lawsuit involving Marguérite Fahmī, in which the judge had fallen for the beautiful eyes of the defendant, all from November (26/9), a tale about Mary Magdalene and Jesus on the cross, with an epilogue ('After 20 centuries') in which he complains about the disappearance of Christian love on earth (101/2), the 'Evening song' in free rhyme of 15 August (50/1: "Pray to God, my soul, for the evening has come; take a repose from the agony of thought, for thoughts are terrible; hide your pain for a brief spell in the smile of the beloved, for tomorrow your pains will return, and my instrument [*sic: wa-ālatī*] is near" etc.), the song of mourning addressed to Egypt of 28 August (97/8: "I strove for the summit, but those who envied me sent me home empty-handed … In the valley of the pyramids, dawn welcomes me with a smile, while here, my day does everything to

destroy it" etc.), the idylls of 4 January 'Your goldfinch[11] has died!' | (85/6), 'The 366
prisoner and the run-away goldfinch' of 6 January 1924 (104/6), the 'Lament of the wilted flowers' of 26 January 1923 (107/8), the song to liberty as the beloved of 14 July 1923 (31/2), and the five bitter verses on the disarmament of Kasrawān of 14 October 1923 (85) ("In Kasrawān, there are no more guns, no sword that one could brandish; in Kasrawān, they now just stare, a staring stronger and sharper than is any weapon."

On 28 January 1924 he extols his homeland in free metre (18/20). On 13 April 1924 he writes a lullaby for his daughter Suʿād (65/6). Yet in March he decides to go to Egypt (67/70), even though he knows beforehand that he will always long for his family and for Lebanon. But he feels like a prisoner there, while, in Egypt, freedom beckons. Despite all this, humour breaks through again in the lines about his little sister's tomcat.

But it seems he never went; or else, he must have returned quite soon, for in 1925 we find him in the middle of the political turmoil in his country. On 5 May 1925 he recites his poem 'A worker's awakening' (8/10) to a workers' meeting in Beirut. In it, he still has to fight off the poetasters of the country. Where he was heading is shown by the verses of the victory song (11/12): "I spoke to Christ: 'Cleanse them of their sins with your precious blood'; I said to Qays, Layla's beloved: 'Poetise, and die proud of heart'; I spoke to Lenin: 'Rest in peace, you are a prophet, after so many centuries.' My prayer is silence in his sanctuary, what pain inspires is my faith" etc. He sneers at the clergy, whose assistance in people's final hours is measured by the fee that they are given (13/4), and warns against a conflict between clergy and freemasons that would tear the country apart (44/5). A struggle is, however, not what he is looking for. On 7 November 1925, for instance, he wishes that his quill—which he sees in a vision by his side in his grave—were a plough, crossing fields turning green on its passing, his writing sheets productive lands, moistened by the peasant's front and the early morning dew (133/4).

Over the next few years, the poet immersed himself entirely in translation work: Lamartine's *Jocelyn* of 1836 and *La chute d'un ange* of 1838, he published
| under the titles *Jūsilīn* (Beirut: Maṭbaʿat Ṣādir, 1926) and *Masqat mal'ak aw* 367
Ālihat Lubnān (Beirut: Maṭbaʿat Ṣādir, 1927), respectively. In 1933 he translated Bernardin de St Pierre's *Būlus wa-Firjīnī* (Beirut) and *La chaumière* as *al-Kūkh al-Hindī* (Beirut). He translated Shukrī's French *ʿAntar* in 1926 (Beirut, Maṭbaʿat Quzmā). Copée inspired him to write his play *Majdūlīn*, followed by plays of his own creation in *al-Rawāʾiʿ* and *al-Shāʿir*. Besides a history of Napoleon

11 *Ḥassūn*, cf. *al-Rayḥāniyyāt* I, 7,$_{2}$, III 31,$_{4}$ (pl. *ḥasāsīn*), Barthélemy, *Dict.* 158.

he also published the story *al-ʿUmmāl al-ṣāliḥūn* and a collection of *riwāyāt rūḥiyya* titled *Ṭāqat azhār*.

Commissioned by the literary society *ʿAṣabat al-ʿashara*, he published two series of portraits of leading literary and political personalities of the country, preceded by a foreword by the society's chairman Mīshāl Abū Shalā, entitled *al-Rusūm* (Beirut: Maṭbaʿat al-Maʿraḍ, 1931). His portraits of poets have been, in part, already mentioned, while the remainder will be referred to below. In this first volume, whose sequel, though announced, was apparently never published, politicians are in the majority. Most of these portraits, which are almost all accompanied by photographs, start by considering the physique and facial features of the person involved, and then set down his character and achievements with a minimal amount of strokes. Though not always free from venomenous remarks, the descriptions of his friends are mostly written with an amiable kind of humour. We learn a lot about the literary tendencies of the age, even if there are still many questions that one would like to ask.

His work on Lamartine resulted in a monograph on this poet, entitled *Lāmartīn* (Beirut: Maktabat Ṣādir, 1933). A review of it was published by Ḥasan Kāmil al-Ṣīrafī in *Apollo* 1082/3.

Meanwhile, he published a number of poems in *al-Muqtaṭaf*, such as *Qabl al-zilzāl*, a strophic poem, in vol. 79 (1931), 159/61, *Shamshūn* in vol. 84 (1934), 438/40, and *al-Ghufrān, nashīd min malḥama lahu ʿunwānuhā Ghulawāʾ*, ibid., 554/6. In the appendix to *al-Rusūm*, the latter is announced as being in press and is referred to as a *qaṣīda dhāt sittat anāshīd*. In *Apollo* I, 616/8 he celebrates Aḥmad Shawqī as *shāʿir al-insāniyya*.

In 1938 he published a new collection of poems, entitled *Afāʿī ʾl-Firdaws* (Beirut: al-Makshūf). These are poems from the years 1928–38, and which are all about one and the same subject: his struggle with carnal desire. The oldest poem among these, *al-Ṣalāt al-ḥamrāʾ*, of 21 May 1928, opens and closes with a
368 confession: "Lord, please forgive me, a liar and a sinner, | for starving my soul while feeding transient passions." The poem is composed of six strophes of unequal length. In the penultimate one of these, he compares the world to a vessel, full of moaning and tears where, ever since the days of Cain and Abel, man is led astray by his blindness or by negligence (77/81). In 1929, he extols the snake of seduction (37/8), portrays the ardour in the temple of passions (39/43), and, although the ideal of chastity has never vanished completely from his heart (53), he also knows that the women that he associates with cannot be expected to have a heart (57/8). He thus besings the mistress of his "scarlet passion" as if she were a Roman Messalina (61/3), refusing to let her, with whom he shares his lusts, enter into the sanctuary of his heart (71/3). In 1931, in 'Sodom'

(47/9, first published in *Apollo* I, 775/7), he feels the glow of Lot's daughters still burning his veins. And in the poem *Shamshūn* (see above), the first one in this volume, he objectivates his passion to the point that he can describe it in terms of Samson in Delilah's bonds. But in *al-Daynūna* (85/8) he sees himself once more in Hell, in Satan's power, until a voice, coming from Earth, acquits him. In *al-Qādhūra*, of 1934 (31/3), he has awakened from the spell of lust; as a poet, he sees himself as a man of many guises, whose personality changes completely with each of these, his poetry languishing in lesser company, while in Heaven the angels bemourn him who has chased his soul from its sanctuary, turning it from a temple into a cave of doom. In the last poem, *al-Ṭarḥ*, from 1938, he once more sums up his views on nature; to him, nature is a world of perfect beauty and of nothing but love, even down to lifeless things. "This is God's image; but where is His image to be found in His creatures?"

The poet must have understood that his poems would not immediately appeal to people of his own cultural background. This is why he prefaced them with an exposition on the essence of poetry. In it, he refers—against P. Valéry—to Abbé Brimont, for whom the essence of poetry lies not in its form but in that which inspired it in the first place. Still, he does not go so far in this as Brimont, who even accepts well-sounding but meaningless verses as such. Adopting a
remark by E. Jaloux on the scenic poet from Georgia, Rustaveli, | he expresses 369
concern that nowadays, the orientals have lost the magic of poetry, their literature withering away in a haze of Western colourings, in the same way in which the poisonous swaths of European politics are sapping the life out of them. As such, he wants to bring Arabic poetry back to nature. Yet one may wonder whether this is the right way to do it, even if one admires the maturity of his work.

f *Mīshāl Abū Saḥlā and Khalīl Taqī al-Dīn*

Of the ten people whose portraits were drawn in Ilyās Abū Shabaka's *Rusūm*, we mention, apart from the prosewriters who will be referred to later, two lyricists: Mīshāl Abū Saḥlā and Khalīl Taqī al-Dīn.

The first of the two was born in 1899. The publisher of *al-Jumhūr* magazine in Beirut, he assembled the *ʿAṣabat al-ʿashara* around him. Of his poems, Ilyās is especially admiring of his description of Wādī Ḥamāma and of a long *qaṣīda* called *Ẓulmat al-ʿayn*, which is full of weltschmerz ("Hope in my heart has died; I thus live with desire nor fear; all that I desired has come apart around me, broken to pieces and smashed" etc.). The other, from 1906, is the real driving-force behind this circle. In spite of the boldness of his speech, which often baffles his contemporaries, he is a real lyricist who only follows his heart, as in

Rusūm 50/8: "Satan[12] may fool as many people as he likes, but he won't fool me; I follow my imagination in all I do; even if I love the truth, I'd lose my mind if it were not for my imagination; I construct towering castles, up in the air; it is only there that I want to take refuge and abide." In 1937 he published a collection of short stories, called *ʿAshr qiṣaṣ min ṣamīm al-ḥayāt* (Beirut), the final one of which, *al-Sajīn* (145/63), is an adaption from M. Gorki. See *al-Mashriq* XXXI, 151, Pérès 678.

g *Ṣalāḥ Labkī*

A real lyrical talent is Ṣalāḥ Labkī, who thus far has only published the small collection of poems *Urjūḥat al-qamar* (Beirut: Manshūrāt al-Makshūf, 1938).

The dedication to his friends is without any pretense: "I sang my songs, without there being any relation between me and the God of poetry … Maybe some poor fellow will recite them, someone who has come to like me, without even knowing me, the weepers' brother."

370 | Many of his songs are full of weltschmerz and thoughts of death, but it is difficult to believe that these sentiments are genuine; after all, is this poet not the one who writes so lively about nature in spring, about storms, the peace of an evening, and the stillness of the night? The one who wrote two beautiful poems on his country, free from any political connotations? ("I love you as I love a song, the way I love a dream of peace and bliss; you cause a craving in me like nothing else can do"; and elsewhere: "Whatever state you are in, you are the land of my dreams and fantasies; to live and die for you, it will be my honour"). French culture is, for him, almost as important as Arab culture, as is shown by his poem for Lamartine on the occasion of the 100th anniversary of his trip to Lebanon (66/75). See *al-Ḥadīth* 1938, 399.

h *Poets whose Works were Not Available at the Time of Writing*

Finally, I mention some poets from Beirut and the Lebanon whose works were not accessible to me:

Labīb Efendi al-Riyāshī published *al-Nubūgh*, in Beirut in 1921 (*Jāmiʿ* 483), and in 1924 *al-Jabābira, qaṣāʾid falsafiyya, adabiyya, ijtimāʿiyya* (ibid. 616).

Jirjī al-Ḥajjār, *Dīwān*, Beirut 1922.

ʿAlawān al-Khūrī, *al-Zanābiq al-ʿāṭirāt*, Beirut 1926.

Al-Khūrī Ḥannā Ṭannūs, *Buṣbūṣ al-maʿādī, anīn al-arz*, Jubayl 1928 (cf. *al-Mashriq* XXVI, 793).

Najīb Mashriq al-Muḥāmī, *al-Mashriqiyyāt*, Kharīṣā 1930.

---

12 *Shayṭān*, not in a theological sense, but in the manner of the ancient poets, who ascribed their inspriration to him.

7 Iskandar al-Khūrī al-Bitjālī

Iskandar al-Khūrī al-Bitjālī is truly the poet of Jerusalem and Palestine. Born in 1888 in Bitjālā, where his father al-Khūri Jirīs (sic) Yaʿqūb was a teacher of Arabic at the Russian seminary for girls, he received his education at the Roman Catholic patriarchal school of Beirut, from which he graduated in 1906. He then started his legal studies, which he completed at the Madrasat al-ḥuqūq in Jerusalem. He then started working as a civil servant for al-Maṣlaḥa al-ʿadliyya. In 1913, he published in Jerusalem a collection of essays and some poems that had previously been published in the press with the title *Ḥaqāʾiq wa-ʿibar* (Sarkīs 536). His first *dīwān*, *al-Zafarāt*, was published in Jerusalem in 1919. Then followed a series of literary essays called *al-Dāʾ wal-dawāʾ* (Jerusalem 1921). A second *dīwān*, *Daqqāt al-qalb*, was published in Jerusalem in 1922. The best insight into his work as a poet is provided | by his third collection of 371
poems, *Mashāhīd al-ḥayāh* I, Jerusalem 1927. He is at his best in simple love songs or in a lullaby, like the *dūbayt Ughrūdat al-sarīr* (192/3), in which he can express his sentiments naturally. In 1909, he composed a *marthiya* for the deputy from Jaffa and publisher of the *Majallat al-Aṣmaʿī*, Ḥannā ʿAbdallāh al-ʿĪsī, on behalf of his hometown of Bitjālā. From then on, his poems have accompanied all the major public events in the agitated existence of his country. During the war he was a great supporter of the Entente, which he hoped would bring about the liberation of the Arabs. He even translated an English soldier's song into Arabic (27/32). When the war broke out, he greeted France as a hero of freedom (59/62), repeating the slander of the Entente press (62/74). He turned some tragic events in his native country into narrative verse (74/86, 89/100). He greeted the defeat of the Turks with a triumphant poem in which he offered Syria's thanks to Emir Fayṣal and to Britain as well, because he expected the latter to render the Arabs independent (100/6). He also hailed the security officer of Jerusalem during the occupation, *amīr* Ālāy Jabrāʾīl Ḥaddād Bāshā, as the saviour of Palestine (107/10). His interest focuses primarily on women and what occurs in their lives, as he expects them to contribute significantly to the development of the country. At the same time, however, he publicly criticises some of the female weaknesses, such as their vanity (124/30), while he also complains about the loosening of the bonds of marriage, warning his female compatriots of the bad example set by female Jewish immigrants (134ff). In 1921, he composes an elegy for his brother Niqulā. Niqulā had gone from Bitjālā to a Russian grammar school in St Petersburg, where he had also completed his studies, dying a civil servant in Yekaterinburg on 11 November of that year (166/70). In politics, he went through great disappointments as well. On 1 May 1921, he writes a poem on a flower festival in Jaffa, during which there had been heated confrontations between Arabs and Jews (157/9), while Saʿd's internment

on Gibraltar (164/6) shakes his confidence in Britain's promises. The Treaty of Sèvres heralded the end of a carefree and happy adolescence (162/4). When Balfour visited Palestine, he tells him that his declaration is a betrayal of the
372 Arabs, who now only have | Ibn Saʿūd to set their hopes on (246/8). The way he sees it, the inauguration of the Hebrew University is a blow to all Arabs. As such, he cannot get over the fact that the University of Cairo sent its dean to attend the ceremony, leaving the impression that Egypt had betrayed the Palestinians (248/50). In 1924, al-Nādī al-ʿArabī awarded him the first prize for his *qaṣīda* entitled *Ṣafḥa min taʾrīkhina ʾl-majīd* (203/8), in which he describes the general situation in Palestine and its surrounding countries at the time of the Crusades until their liberation by Ṣalāḥ al-Dīn. Even though he says that he has no hidden agenda, there is a clear parallel with the current situation in the Holy Land. In the same year, he salutes the former ruler of the Hijaz, al-Ḥusayn, when he marches into Amman, saying that his hopes are still set on his house and him as the future saviours of the Arab world. At the instigation of al-Nādī al-ʿArabī, he composed two national anthems for Palestine, *al-Mawt fī ḥubb al-waṭan* and *Bilādī mā uḥaylāhā* (185/91). Of these, the former consists of verse pairs in the *ramal* metre with a continuous rhyme in the second verse, the latter of strophes in *hazaj* of five verses each but in which the metre is not strictly kept at all, with a changing rhyme in the first four lines and a continuous rhyme in the fifth. He does not let himself be discouraged by the catastrophe of Damascus (263/5), calling on his brothers in Syria and the Ḥawrān to stand firm (*Lā namshī warāʾ*) against the French, now of all times, now that France, which once proclaimed human rights, negates these very rights ("Go away and colonise your own country; from now on, we will no longer let ourselves be colonised. Be sure that we shall stand up against injustice, that we don't fear death, and that we shall not move"). Apart from these political poems he also writes simple tales in popular, accessible verse.

He is fond of regarding himself as the guardian of the heritage of the ancients. It is also in such a setting that he subjects two verses by Laylā al-Akhyāliyya to the ancient custom of *taḍmīn* (77, 5,6). Of the modern writers, he celebrates the Iraqi al-Ruṣāfī when the latter visits Jerusalem in July of 1920 (280), and Khalīl Maṭrān on the occasion of a meeting of the Young Men's Christian Association on 25 October 1924 (239/42). And even when he extols Shakespeare on the occasion of a performance of Hamlet in Jerusalem (274/5), his frame of reference is Arab all along.

Apart from the *qaṣīda*, still predominant, he also employs strophic verse
373 on various occasions, as has been mentioned. | In two instances, he employs the rhyme pattern of the *radīf*, clearly to create a burlesque effect (141/3, in a satirical verse on ladies with a walking stick, 145/8, *Ayyuha ʾl-sharqu ʾl-mudhillu ʾl-sayyidāti*).

His language, though classical, avoids the ostentatious use of archaisms; indeed, he even allows for colloquialisms from time to time, such as *karrasa*, 'to consecrate' at $75_{,2}$ (see Dozy; it is true that Abū Shādī, in his *al-Shafaq al-bākī* $228_{,5}$, also condones the use of this term, in his case in prose), and *tamaʿʿana*, 'to observe closely' ($86_{,7}$; see Dozy). In one case, a colloquial *ʿalāmaki tasharīna* ('why are you awake') escapes him (197 bottom), as in a poem in the common vernacular by al-Quss Ḥanāniyya in Cheikho, *al-Ādāb al-ʿarabiyya* ^{1}I, 32, 21 and often in H. Schmidt's *Pal. Volkserzählungen* I, $76_{,3}$, $103_{,17}$, $109_{,4}$, $110_{,8}$ (see *Grundr.* II, 264, § 183b). In one case, he alludes to the common proverb *Mā bayn Ḥānā wa-Mānā ḍāʿat al-ḥāna* ($150_{,6}$), and at 256/8 he even uses it as a theme for a poem. But the only Europeanism he uses is *hilāl al-shahd* for 'honeymoon', at $75_{,5}$.

Excerpts in Rafāʾīl Nakhla, *Mukhtārāt* II, Beirut 1931, 29/30.

8 Aleppo

In Aleppo, this quiet corner gently grazed by the waves of politics, there blossomed a type of poetry that mainly took its inspiration from the French Romantics.

In his *Aṭyāf al-Rabīʿ*, preface 13,7, Abū Shādī calls ʿAlī al-Nāṣir, author of *al-Ẓamaʾ, majmūʿat ashʿār* (Aleppo, 1933) a "Syrian Beaudelaire."

More productive than he is ʿUmar Abū Rīsha, who has published a great number of poems in *al-Ḥadīth* since 1933, such as *al-Kaʾs* VII, 1933, 169/72, *Ḥatta 'l-sarīr* ibid. 327/8, *Mukhāḍiʿ* ibid. 526/7, *ʿAjab al-ʿuyūn* ibid. 632, *al-Faylasūf* ibid. 757, *Ḍajār* ibid. VIII, 1934, 55, *Jināzat al-shabāb* ibid. 390, *Ṭawfān, Opera dhāt faṣl* ibid. 268/81, *Maḥkamat al-shuʿarāʾ* ibid. 145/57, *Shabaḥ al-māḍī* ibid. X, 1936, 384/6, *Dhikrā shāʿir*, recited at the millenarian celebrations of al-Mutanabbī, ibid. 593/6, and *Idṭirāb* ibid. 607. His works were collectively published as *Shiʿr ʿUmar Abī Rīsha*, Aleppo 1936.

9 Hama

Hama is the hometown of ʿUmar Yaḥyā, Shāʿir al-ʿĀṣī, and Badr al-Dīn al-Ḥamīd.

| a *ʿUmar Yaḥyā* 374

Born in Kuwait in 1902, ʿUmar finished his studies at al-Kuliyya al-Ṣalāḥiyya in Jerusalem, after which he became a teacher in his hometown. Together with his friend ʿUthmān al-Ḥawrānī, he was sent to Bahrain to direct two schools at al-Muḥarraq and in Manama.[13] But only a few months had passed before the British administration suspected them of nationalist leanings. They had

13 Unfortunately the date of this assignment is given by neither his biographer nor himself in his *Dīwān*.

to leave the country within 24 hours, returning to their hometown by way of India, Basra, Baghdad and Damascus. ʿUmar Yaḥyā became the director of the Dār al-ʿilm there, and was later transferred to Antioch as a teacher of Arabic literature.

His poems, of which the first two—dating from 1925—were written on the occasion of a tribute to Aḥmad Zakī Pāshā at his school and in honour of the editorial board of *al-Kashshāf* at a reception in Homs (15/21), were initially published in newspapers and magazines across Syria, such as *al-Ḥadīth*. They were then published collectively as *al-Baraʿim*, and dedicated to the memory of Shawqī and Ḥāfiẓ (Aleppo: al-Maṭbaʿa al-ʿIlmiyya, 1354/1936). They embrace the entire horizon of Arabic poetry and avoid all affectation of modernity, as is rightly observed in the preface (4) by his friend Aḥmad Ṣafī al-Najafī. The poems dedicated to the author's hometown make the *dīwān* something special: 'The Citadel of Hama' (1/3), 'At the Orontes River' (3/4), *Anīn al-nāʿūra* (92/3), and 'An Hour on the Banks of the Orontes' (179). The poet is right in avowing that he owes his best inspiration to nature (*Naẓra fi 'l-ṭabīʿa* 52/4, *Shāʿir al-ṭabīʿa* 165/6). He never refers to his personal life in his poems. This is also true of his poems about his trip to Bahrain, preceded (103) by two farewell poems for his friends Badr al-Dīn al-Ḥamīd and Ibrāhīm al-ʿAẓm, who also wrote a foreword to the *dīwān*. In Bahrain he founded a *nādī adabī*, which he inaugurated with a *qaṣīda*. In India and Baghdad he was constantly exacerbated at the impotence of the Orient. Even if love poems are not entirely absent from his *dīwān*, they lack the personal note, moving along well-trodden tracks instead. In the pref-
375 ace (31), his friend Muḥammad ʿAbd al-Raḥmān ʿAdī | is right to emphasise that this is precisely his weakest point.

In contrast, he is fond of writing about events from the history of Islam. He resuscitated the memory of the Hijra in Hama twice, once in 1352 (50) and another time in 1353 (72). When he imagines what Boabdil must have thought when he left Granada (44) he merely follows the example of his predecessors. But when he waxes lyrical on the sad situation of his country and other Arab states, he is all the more personal. He dedicates a moving lament to the martyrs of Hama (68/70); for one of these, Dr Ṣāliḥ Qambāz, he even writes a *marthiya* (47/50). He extols the martyrs of Damascus (22) and Palestine (32) with a similar kind of emotion, while lamenting Fayṣal's untimely death (78/81) as tragedy for the Arab world as a whole.

His art is entirely based on that of the ancients. He thus does not hesitate to start his lament on Fayṣal's death with a verse by Ibn Zaydūn and to insert another one elsewhere in the poem. The poem for the millennial celebrations of al-Mutanabbī (199/208) is an attempt to copy his style from beginning to end. But, even for his friend Muḥammad ʿAbd al-Raḥmān ʿAdī, his use of *gharīb* is just too much here (preface 25). His elegies on the contemporary poets ʿAbd al-Ḥamīd al-Rāfiʿī (cf. p. 346 c), Ḥāfiẓ Ibrāhīm and Shawqī (11, 139, 199) are all written in the same style. Even when greeting the Danish archeologist Ingolt on his visit to Hama, he moves entirely in the universe of the ancients.

At the same time, however, he does have a rather good knowledge of foreign literature. He recites a poem on Lamartine in Beirut (10/1), and on page 58 translates a poem by an unidentified French poet called 'A Hope Lost.' Knowing Persian, he also tried his hand at the translation, or rather, adaptation, of the *Rubāʿiyyāt* (151/4). In the preface to the *dīwān* (29), Muḥammad ʿAbd al-Raḥmān ʿAdī also mentions translations from Turkish, but without source reference.

b *Badr al-Dīn al-Ḥamīd*

In 1929, his friend and compatriot Badr al-Dīn al-Ḥamīd (b. 1901), who had written a farewell poem for him when he left Bahrain, published his *dīwān* in Cairo with a foreword by Shafīq Jabrī.

| 10 Folk Poetry 376

Apart from poetry as an art form, folk poetry in the local dialect also flourished in Syria, especially in the Lebanon. At first burlesque comments on the news of the day, they slowly tried to treat their subjects more seriously as time went on. On this kind of poetry, there is the excellent study by Jean Lecerf, written on the basis of active knowledge of this tradition, entitled *Littérature dialectale et renaissance arabe moderne*, Extrait du Bulletin d'Études Orientales de l'Institut Français de Damas, vols. II, III. From this work we only mention some poets, namely those whose works may later turn out to have been decisive for the development of this kind of literature.

a. The folk poet al-Quss Ḥanāniyya still belongs to the previous period. His *Qiṣṣat al-burghūth*, in strophes of four verses each with a rhyme in the fourth verse throughout the poem, is mentioned in Cheikho's *al-Ādāb al-ʿarabiyya fī 'l-qarn al-tāsiʿ ʿashar* I, 324.

b. One of the oldest folk poets was Shahwān b. Yūsuf Ilyās Bū Shihāb of Baʿabda, who died in 1898 at the age of 70. Because, later in life, he had adopted the Bedouin way of life, he was also called al-Badawī. His *Kawkab al-shihāb fī Manẓūmāt Abī Shihāb* (*Dīwān nawābigh al-ʿatābā* IV) (Kfar Shīmā, Maṭbaʿat al-Rashīdiyya) also contains a biography and poems by Yūsuf Saʿd Ḥātim; excerpts in *Kitāb al-khawāṭir al-shiʿriyya aw al-Manẓūmāt al-zajaliyya* (Kfar Shīma 1916, 21/60) (Lecerf 170).

c. Luṭfallāh Naṣr al-Bakāsīnī of Bakāsīn, north of Jizzīn, whose *Dīwān intiqādāt ʿala ʾl-sittāt wal-khawājāt* (Beirut: al-Maṭbaʿa al-Waṭaniyya, n.d.) (*Jāmiʿ* I, 633) contains *zajal* poems in the common vernacular; similar are his *Qaṣīdat al-jamāʿa fī malbūs al-khalāʿa*, n.d. (after 1920), and his *Qaṣīdat ḥalq al-shaʿr al-shālīsh* (Beirut, n.d.), while his *al-Dīwān al-shahīr fi ʾl-suʾālāt wal-ḥazāzīr* (n.p., n.d.) and the corresponding *al-Dīwān al-ʿāl fī ḥall al-ḥazāzīr* (n.p., n.d.) are both inspired by the classical tradition (Lecerf 158).

d. Karam Najīb Najm, publisher of the *Firʿawn* newspaper in Beirut,
377 published his *Bāqat zahr* | *min al-ḥaqla, majmūʿ qaṣāʾid wa-aghānī dārija Lubnāniyya wa-Sūriyya wa-Miṣriyya* in 1933 in Beirut; see Kampffmeyer, MSOS XXXVI, 1933, 147/53, Lecerf 165, and a *Qāmūs al-ʿāmma bi-Miṣr wa-Sūriyyā maʿa majmaʿ amthāl al-ʿawāmm*, in Beirut in 1931.

e. Nakhla Rashīd Bey, of Bārūk near Dayr al-Qamar, who first worked in public administration and then became a politician and who lives presently in Beirut, has been proclaimed *amīr al-zajjālīn* by his artistic friends, with whom he publishes the weekly *al-Zajal al-Lubnānī* since March 1933. It is said that he wrote around 12,000 verses in the local dialect (Lecerf 166). He also published *Muḥsin al-Hazzānī,*[14] *zajal ʿāmmī shāʿirī*, Beirut n.d.

f. Ṭanyūs Jirjīs al-Biskintāwī, of Biskintā in Kasrawān, in the foothills of Jabal Ṣannīn, wrote most of his poems in the style of the poets of Jabal ʿĀmil (see Lecerf, 44/6). His poems were published in anonymous collections, in *al-Badāʾiʿ wal-laṭāʾif* (*Dīwān nawābigh al-ʿatābā* III), the majority of which is by him, as well as in dialogues with other poets, such as *al-Durar al-ʿawālī* (ibid. II), a dialogue with Ḥannā al-Maqdisī, impersonating a married man and a bachelor, *Mukhtārāt al-ʿatābā* (ibid. V), a poetical epistolary exchange with Dāʾūd Badr al-Maʿlūf, *Nūr al-Aʿlām* 39/40, on king Ḥusayn, Foch and Allenby (Lecerf 172/3).

g. Yūsuf Yazbak al-Khūrī, of al-Ḥadath, *al-Khaṭarāt al-shahīra wal-intiqādāt al-khaṭīra* I, (Beirut: al-Maṭbaʿa al-Lubnāniyya, 1922), II (Maṭbaʿat al-Minbar, n.d.), III (Maṭbaʿat al-Arz, 1924); *Qaṣīdat al-ḥarb*, n.p. and n.d., Lecerf 173.

h. Ilyā Abū Ḍāhir, *Faẓāʾiʿ al-Atrāk wal-Almān fī Sūriyā wa-Lubnān, zajal* in the local dialect, al-Maṭbaʿa al-Yūsufiyya, 1921 (*Jāmiʿ* 687, not in Lecerf).

i. A handwritten *dīwān* by Salīm al-Jazāʾirī is mentioned in Lawrence, *Seven Pillars* 232.

k. Here we must also mention the most famous Bedouin poet of Transjordan, Nimr b. ʿAdwān of the Qarīdī family, who died in al-ʿAjūz in 1238/1822. His poems, and most of all those on his wife Waḍḥāʾ, are still much loved among

14 A poet from ʿAnīza in Qasīm, cf. Wetzstein, ZDMG XXII, 133, A. Musil, *Arabia Petraea* II, 235, where we read al-Hazzali instead of ʿAnīza.

the Bedouins and have been recorded by various scholars, such as Wallin, *ZDMG* VI, 190/218, A. Socin, *Dīwān aus Centralarabien*, Leipzig 1900/1, III, 32, H.H. Spoer, *ZDMG* LXVI, 189/203, | *JAOS* XLIII, 177/205, together with E. N. 378
Ḥaddād, *ZS* VII, 29/62, 274/94 (to be continued). A *rithāʾ* on Waḍḥāʾ by Būlus Salmān is contained in *al-Mashriq* XVIII, 505. His biography, *Qiṣṣat al-amīr Nimr b. ʿAdwān*, written by Ṣāliḥ al-Khaṭīb (Maṭbaʿat Sālim, n.d.), is very inaccurate and more a type of romance (Lecerf 167).

l. Other Bedouin poets of Transjordan are mentioned in Būlus Salmān, *al-Shiʿr al-ʿarabī fī sharqī al-Urdunn* in *al-Mashriq* XVII, 263/305, 332/42, 496/510; he mentions *qaṣīdas* by Abu 'l-Kabāʾir, *Fī madḥ ʿawdat al-Tāyih min ʿArab al-Ḥuwayṭā* from 1909, ibid. 496/506, and the *Qaṣīda madḥiyya* by Sālim al-Marʿī of the Khaywāt, 500/5. Other Bedouin poets are mentioned in A. Musil, *Arabia Petraea* III, 235; individual poems, mostly anonymous, are mentioned on pages 236/53.

2 *Narrative and Debating Prose (Novels, Short Stories, and Essays)*

1 Forerunners

In Syria, too, the *adab* genre continued to be cultivated, even though it was just for amusement, without any claim to artistic innovation. Let us begin by citing some of these works which could also have been mentioned in the previous volume.

a. The *Riwāyat al-shābb al-jāhil al-sikkīr* (Beirut 1868) by Ṭannūs al-Ḥurr is a moralising tale of a popular kind.

b. Based on an *adab* work entitled *Tasliyat al-khawāṭir bil-laṭāʾif wal-nawādir* (Beirut 1864), Yūsuf al-Ṣaffūr published a handbook on letter-writing called *Tarjumān al-mukātaba* (Beirut 1869).

c. The *Durar al-nafāʾis fī jamāl al-ʿarāʾis* (Cairo 1882; Sarkīs 551, 1044) is an *adab* work that was written jointly by Ilyās Efendi Samāḥa and Dr. Anṭūn Efendi Barakāt al-Dimashqī.

d. In Syria, the European art of storytelling was introduced by two Armenian Catholics, Yūsuf b. Ilyān al-Dimashqī and Nakhla Ṣāliḥ. The former was born in Damascus in 1856 but lived, from 1860, in Beirut. He was a civil servant and director at the Ottoman Bank for 35 years, working in various places in the Levant. In 1912, he moved to Cairo where he founded his famous bookshop, | which published his *Muʿjam al-maṭbūʿāt al-ʿarabiyya wal-muʿarraba* 379
(Cairo 1928/1346), continued in the *Jāmiʿ al-taṣānīf al-ḥadītha*, I and II. From the French works that he mentions in his *Muʿjam* 1022/3, he published an abbreviated Arabic version of a tale by an anonymous author, adding some geographical information on northern Europe, and called *ʿĀṣin wa-shijʿān* (Beirut: Imprimerie Catholique, 1874).

[e.] Nakhla Ṣāliḥ published an account of his trip to Egypt and Syria in 1874, calling it *al-Dalīl al-amīn lil-siyāḥa al-bahiyya fī 'l-aqṭār al-muqaddasa al-Shāmiyya* (Būlāq 1291), and of his trip to Europe in *al-Kanz al-mukhabbaʾ lil-siyāḥa fī Urubbā* (lith. Cairo 1876). He also translated a work by H. Brugsch as *al-Durra al-ḥaqīqiyya al-bahiyya aw Khurūj al-Isrāʾiliyyīn min Miṣr wal-āthārāt al-Miṣriyya* (Cairo n.d.) and a French short story of unknown authorship into the Syrian dialect, naming it *al-Daryāq fī aḥwāl al-ʿushshāq* (Beirut 1875; Pérès 372, Sarkīs 1189). In 1884, Adīb al-Dimashqī translated *La belle parisienne* by Countess Dash (see Suppl. II, 759), while Sāmī Quṣayrī translated E. Sue's *Mathilde* in 1885 (Beirut; Pérès 336). In 1887, Shākir Shuqayr al-Butlānī adapted X. de Maistre's *La jeune sibérienne* into something oriental in his *Hind al-Ghassāniyya* (Beirut 1887; Pérès 657).

f. Nasīb Manṣūr al-Mashʿalānī wrote a work on the language of flowers, called *Mukhābarāt al-ḥubb al-sirriyya wa-rasāʾil al-mamlaka al-nabātiyya*, Beirut 1889. In 1908 he translated Dumas-père's and A.W. Schlegel's *Le capitaine Richard* as *al-Qāʾidān* (Cairo 1321; Pérès 235, 1907) and Mühlbeck's historical novel *Muḥammad ʿAlī* (Cairo: Maṭbaʿat al-Hilāl; Sarkīs 1748).

g. Muḥammad b. Muḥammad al-Mubārak al-Jazāʾirī was an Algerian who had gone to Damascus in the retinue of ʿAbd al-Qādir and whose *marthiya* on the latter was mentioned earlier in Suppl. II 887. In 1313/1895, he published a description of his adoptive country in Beirut, entitled *Bahjat al-rāʾiḥ wal-ghādī fī aḥāsin maḥāsin al-wādī*. Before then, he had published a few *maqāma*s and tensos, *Abhā maqāma fī 'l-mufākhara bayna 'l-ghurba wal-iqāma* (Damacus 1286), *al-Maqāma al-laghziyya* (Damascus 1300), *Gharīb al-anbāʾ fī munāẓarat al-arḍ wal-samāʾ* (Damacus 1302), *Nadrat al-bahār fī muḥāwarat al-layl wal-nahār* (Beirut 1308), and a work on stylistics called *Maʿārij al-irtiqāʾ ilā samāʾ al-inshāʾ* (Damascus n.d.; Sarkīs 695).

2 ʿAbd al-Raḥmān al-Kawākibī

The first true champion of resistance against the despotism of ʿAbd al-Ḥamīd,
380 after some meek efforts by | Jabrāʾīl al-Dallāl (Supp. II, 761), was his compatriot ʿAbd al-Raḥmān al-Kawākibī of Aleppo, who was banished in punishment for his boldness.

His family, proud of their blood relationship with the Safavids of Ardabil, had been residents of Aleppo for four generations. One of his ancestors had founded al-Madrasa al-Kawākibiyya there. It was also there that ʿAbd al-Raḥmān (b. 1265/1849) received his education following his father Aḥmad's departure for Damascus, where he had been appointed professor at the Umayyad mosque. Apart from his studies of Arabic and Turkish, he also spent time on mathematics and physics. He then joined the editorial staff of the government newspaper *al-Furāt* in Aleppo and later founded his own newspaper, *al-Shahbāʾ*. As a journalist and civil servant in various posts, his transconfessional patriotism and outspoken commitment to political liberalism made him suspicious to various actors in the government. It was only by fleeing that he could avoid arrest, but all his possessions were seized by the government and lost. He first went to Egypt and, after extensive travels in Africa and Asia, he returned to Cairo, dying there in 1320/1903. He only dared to sign his major work, *Ṭabāʾiʿ al-istibdād wa-maṣāriʿ al-istiʿbād* (Cairo: Maṭbaʿat al-Tawfīq, n.d.; samples in Ode-Vasilieva, 13/7), with al-Raḥḥāla K. He then developed his own political ideas in *Umm al-qurā* in the form of protocols of a fictitious meeting of an Islamic reform party in Mecca in the year 1316/1898. The first edition (Maṭbaʿat al-Taqaddum, n.d.) also contains his biography, which was omitted from the second, entitled *Sijill mudhākarāt jamʿiyyat Umm al-qurā aw muʾtamar al-nahḍa al-Islāmiyya*. Both works were banned in Turkey, of course, where they nevertheless helped prepare the revolution of the Young Turks. Sulaymān Muḥammad Rāghib al-Ṭabbākh, *Iʿlām al-nubalāʾ* VII, 507, Sarkīs 1574/6, Cheikho, *al-Mashriq* XXIII, 383, Kračkovsky, preface to Ode Vasilieva, German, *MSOS* XXXI, 186.

3 Nakhla Qalfāṭ

Nakhla b. Jirjīs Qalfāṭ, his intellectual comrade, paid an even higher price for his loyalty to his ideas, even if he expressed them with much greater caution in his literary works.

| Born in 1851 in Beirut, he had studied under Iskandar Āghā Abkāriyūs, after 381
which he went to study law. He began in quite an innocent and old-fashioned way with a booklet on the language of flowers, *Qurʿat al-athmār fī kashf al-iḍmār* (Beirut 1880). He then translated Dumas-père's *The Count of Monte Cristo* as *Qiṣṣat al-Kunt* (Beirut 1883).[15] Together with Qadrī Yaḥyā Bek, he translated Ḥusayn Pāshā Fahmī's Turkish (Istanbul 1300) *Ḥuqūq al-duwal* (Beirut 1884). He then adapted two Persian legends in *Qiṣṣat Fayrūz Shāh* (Beirut 1885/6) and *Qiṣṣat Bahrām Shāh Ardashīr* (Beirut n.d.). He also wrote a novel himself, calling it *Ḍarar al-ḍarratayn* (Cairo n.d.). In 1887/8 he published his four-volume *Taʾrīkh Rūsiyyā*. He then founded the magazine *Silsilat al-fukāhāt fī aṭāyib al-riwāyāt*, in which he also engaged in political satire. As such, the magazine was banned in its fourth season, and Qalfāṭ himself was banished to Konya. Not long before that, he had published his *Taʾrīkh mulūk al-Muslimīn mundhu shurūq al-risāla al-nabawiyya ila ʾl-jīl al-ḥāḍir* (Istanbul 1308/1891). Only after two years and with great financial sacrifice was he able to obtain his release. In 1893, he went to Cairo, where he tried without success to resuscitate his

15 Pérès, no. 213, only mentions a translation of this novel by Bishāra Shadīd, Cairo 1288.

magazine. He then returned to Beirut, where he opened a bookshop. Suspected of selling banned books, such as those by al-Kawākibī, he was detained for a whole year in 1904, dying soon after his release on 13 October 1905. Al-Ṭarrāzī, *Ta'rīkh al-ṣiḥāfa al-ʿarabiyya* II, 63, Sarkīs 1520, Cheikho, *al-Mashriq* XXIII, 761.

4 Prose under the Ottomans

Under the pressure of ʿAbd al-Ḥamīd's government, several writers tried to exercise their profession in literary domains of a less sensitive character. Yet even under the regime of the Young Turks, literature could not freely develop in Syria.

a *Mīkha'īl ʿAwrā*

The family of Mīkhā'īl b. Jirjīs b. Mīkhā'īl ʿAwrā came from Sidon and had moved to Acre at the time of Aḥmad al-Jazzār Pāshā. It was there that he was born in 1855. He then followed his family to Beirut, where he studied Arabic literature under Nāṣif al-Yāzijī and *fiqh* under Yūsuf al-Asīr.

382 | In 1887 he went to Paris. When his attempt at a career in business there failed, he founded the *Jarīdat al-ḥuqūq*. But when this initiative, too, failed, he went to Cairo, where he started working as a civil servant in the translation bureau. His second attempt at rendering himself independent, this time with the *Majallat al-ḥaḍāra*, was soon frustrated by the ʿArābī uprising. He returned to Beirut, where he founded the *Jarīdat al-Bayān*. He also wrote a historical novel called *Muntaha 'l-ʿajab fī akalat al-dhahab* (Beirut: Maṭbaʿat al-Bayān, 1302/1885), while translating the Syriac story of Sindbān as *ʿAjā'ib al-bakht fī qiṣṣat al-aḥad ʿashar wazīran wa-ibn al-malik Ādarakht* (Cairo 1886). He died in Naples in 1906 while on holiday. Al-Ṭarrāzī, *Ta'rīkh al-ṣiḥāfa al-ʿArabiyya* II, 304, Sarkīs 1391/2.

b *Muḥyi 'l-Dīn b. Ibrāhīm al-ʿAṭṭār*

Published his *Bulūgh al-arab fī ma 'āthir al-ʿarab* in 1304/1886 (ʿAbiyya-Lubnān: Maṭbaʿat al-Ṣafā', 1319; Sarkīs 1338).

c *Najīb Mīkhā'īl Gharghūr*

Najīb Mīkhā'īl Gharghūr wrote several novels on women: *Hilāna* (Beirut 1885), *ʿIfrīt al-niswān* (Alexandria 1886), and *al-Qātila* in his magazine *Ḥadīqat al-adab* (Alexandria 1888; Sarkīs 1407, according to Pérès 468, Beirut).

d *Ibrāhīm Bek al-Aswad*

Ibrāhīm Bek al-Aswad, head of the educational system in the *mutaṣarrifliq* Lubnān and publisher of the *Jarīdat Lubnān*, gave an account of Kaiser Wilhelm II's visit to the Orient, with special regard being given to the poems that had been written on that occasion, in his *al-Riḥla al-Imbarāṭūriyya fī 'l-mamālīk al-ʿUthmāniyya* (Baʿabda 1898). On local history he wrote *Dhakhāʾir Lubnān* (Baʿabda 1896) and *Tanwīr al-adhhān fī taʾrīkh Lubnān* (Beirut 1925) (*Jāmiʿ* I, 85). Two shorter works are mentioned in Sarkīs 448.

e *Muḥammad Amīn al-Sukkarī*

The former head clerk of the *mudīr* of Tripoli, Muḥammad Amīn al-Ṣūfī al-Sukkārī al-Ṭarābulusī tried to do something similar in his *Samīr al-layālī*, which offers a description of the Ottoman Empire through consideration of the general geography, with a number of literary and historical essays. 1st printing in one volume, Ṭarābulus al-Shām 1317, 2nd printing in two volumes, ibid. 1327.

f *Fāʾiz Khalīl Hammām and other Historical Novelists*

Historical novels of a conventional character were written by Fāʾiz Khalīl Hammām in his *Abū Samrāʾ aw al-baṭal al-Lubnānī* (Beirut 1905; Sarkīs 1434) and by the Jesuit Rabbāṭ Anṭūn with his *al-Rashīd wal-Barāmika* (Beirut 1910). The Ottoman revolution provided the material for the historical novels *Arwāḥ* | *al-arwāḥ* (Damascus 1909; Pérès 436) by Nasīm al-ʿĀzār, *Sajīn al-ẓulm* (Zahlé 383 n.d.) of Muḥammad b. Maʿlūf, and *Ghādat Buṣrā* (ʿAliyya Lubnān 1911) of Amīr Nāṣir al-Dīn, who had already published two earlier novels, *al-Amīr ʿĀmir al-Kinānī* and *Ḥasarāt al-muḥibbīn* (Pérès 582/4).

g *Shākir Bek al-Khūrī*

Dr Shākir Bek al-Khūrī al-Lubnānī, a graduate of the Qaṣr al-ʿAynī medical school in Cairo, worked as a teacher in ophthalmology at the university of the Jesuits in Beirut, dying there in 1913. As well as some publications on medicine, he wrote two works of personal recollections, *Mudhakkirāt* (Beirut 1905) and *Majmaʿ al-masarrāt* (Beirut 1908; Cairo[2] III, 326 has a mistaken "Cairo"), in a thick dialect, together with many letters and poems accompanied by biographies of their authors (Sarkīs 848).

h *Najīb al-Lādhaqānī*

Published his memoirs, like al-Khūrī, giving them the title *al-Durr al-nadīd min al-ʿahdayn al-qadīm wal-jadīd* (2 vols. Beirut, 1911).

i *Amīn al-Khūrī al-Lubnānī*

Amīn al-Khūrī al-Lubnānī, of Bkāsīn in the Lebanon, was born in 1885. He studied medicine in the Qaṣr al-ʿAynī medical school, then worked as a doctor for the government in the Sudan, before opening a practice in al-Manṣūra, in Lower Egypt, and finally returned to his native country, where he died in 1919. Apart from a work on popular medicine, the *Rayḥānat al-nufūs fī 'ntikhāb al-ʿarūs* (Alexandria n.d.) and two other works mentioned in Sarkīs 845 (following al-Zuruklī's *al-Aʿlam*) but which cannot be further identified, he wrote an *adab* work called *Firdaws al-surūr bishtirāḥ al-ṣudūr* (Beirut n.d.).

k *Amīn Efendi al-Ghurayyib*

The publisher of the *Jarīdat al-Ḥāris* in Beirut, Amīn Efendi al-Ghurayyib, published, as well as the linguistic study *Asmāʾ al-banāt* (Beirut 1911), a collection of historico-literary articles from his magazine *Akhbār wa-afkār* (Beirut 1912), an *adab* work called *Ashwāk ward* in three volumes (Beirut 1912/14), and a book on contemporary royalty, *Fī zawāya ʾl-quṣūr* (Beirut 1913) (Sarkīs 1408).

l *Ṭāhir b. Ṣāliḥ b. Mawhūb al-Waghlīsī*

While, elsewhere, one could see at least the beginnings of a renewal in literature, Ṭāhir b. Ṣāliḥ b. Aḥmad b. Mawhūb al-Waghlīsī al-Jazāʾirī adhered strictly to the traditions of a time-honoured scientific practise. He was born in 1268/1851 in Damascus, where his father had travelled as a member of the retinue of Emir ʿAbd al-Qādir in 1263/1847 and had become *muftī* of the Algerians there. A member of the retinue of Emir ʿAbd al-Qādir, he was promoted to the position of *muftī* of the Algerians there. After he had learned Turkish, Ṭāhir started working for the *wālī* of Damascus, joining al-Jamʿiyya al-Khayriyya in the city, which had been founded on 5 February 1894.

384 | He is especially credited with the reorganisation of al-Ẓāhiriyya library and founding the Khālidiyya library in Jerusalem. Following a trip to Europe, he went to Cairo in 1910, where he worked in the libraries of Aḥmad Taymūr and Aḥmad Zakī. He fled to Cairo again when the war broke out. When he returned to Damascus in 1918 he was appointed director of the Ẓāhiriyya, and died on 16 Rabīʿ II 1338/8 January 1920. As well as a collection of stories on the prophets that he translated from Turkish (*Munyat al-adhkiyāʾ fī qiṣaṣ al-anbiyāʾ*, Damascus 1299) and a work on the technical terminology of the science of Tradition (*Tawjīh al-naẓar ilā uṣūl ʿilm al-athar*, Cairo 1320), his printed works, listed in Sarkīs 689/91 (with *Ashhar al-amthāl*, Cairo 1338), encompass all domains of classical *adab* and textbooks on mathematics, as well as popular anatomy in his *al-Fawāʾid al-jisām fī maʿrifat khawāṣṣ al-ajsām* (Damascus 1300). Sulaymān Muḥammad Saʿīd al-Bānī, *Tanwīr al-baṣāʾir bi-sīrat al-shaykh Ṭāhir*, Damascus 1920 (*Jāmiʿ* 86), ʿĪsā Iskandar Maʿlūf in *al-Mashriq* XVIII, 144/8, ibid. XXIV, 861/2, cf. Suppl. II 777,$_{17}$.

m Muḥammad Efendi ʿIzz al-Dīn ʿArabī Kātibī al-Ṣayyādī al-Shāfiʿī's *al-Rawḍa al-bahiyya fī faḍāʾil Dimashq al-maḥmiyya* (Damascus 1330) was written along similar lines (Sarkīs 1681).

n *Aḥmad Fawzī al-Sāʿātī*

Their compatriot Aḥmad Fawzī al-Sāʿātī, on the other hand, used the achievements of modern science as a tool for apologetics in his *Mishkāt al-ʿulūm wal-barāhīn fī ibṭāl adillat al-māddiyyīn* (Damascus 1328).

5 Prose After the [First] World War

Since the [First] World War there has undeniably been a certain upswing in prose literature, even if there is, as yet, no boom such as there is in Egypt. Before we get to the two main representatives of this new blossoming, some of their predecessors will be briefly mentioned:

(*a–x*) *Forerunners*

a *Yūsuf Ṣufayr*

The bookseller Yūsuf Ṣufayr, of Beirut, dedicated himself to a reverential cultivation of various literary traditions. His *Majāli ʾl-ghurar li-kuttāb al-qarn al-tāsiʿ ʿashar* (Baʿabda: al-Maṭbaʿa al-ʿUthmāniyya, 1898, 1904) offers samples from the pens of almost every known nineteenth-century Syrian author. A similar collection, *Nafathāt al-kuttāb fī ʿahd al-nahḍa al-ʿarabiyya al-ākhira* (*min sanat 1800 ila ʾl-ʿahd al-ḥāḍir*), *majmūʿ* | *200 maqāla adabiyya*, was pub- 385
lished in Beirut in 1926. An anthology of the older *adab* genre is his *al-Durr al-muntakhab min kutub al-adab* (2 vols, Beirut 1908/9). He championed the education of girls in his *Taraqqi ʾl-ʿāʾilāt fī tarbiyat al-banāt* (Beirut 1910). In his *Jaghrāfiyyat Lubnān al-Kabīr wa-ḥukūmat Sūriyyā wa-Filasṭīn* (Beirut 1924; cf. *RAAD* V, 41) he describes the changed conditions in his country as a result of the World War. *Tarjumān al-afkār* (Beirut: Maṭbaʿat Quzmā, 1926) contains a collection of his love letters (Sarkīs 1215, *Jāmiʿ* II, 114). See al-Ṭarrāzī, *Taʾrīkh al-ṣiḥāfa al-ʿArabaiyya* I, 41, *al-Hilāl* VII, 63.

b *Muṣṭafā al-Ghalāʾīnī*

Of a similar type is the work of Muṣṭafā b. Muḥammad Salīm al-Ghalāʾīnī, publisher of the *Majallat al-Nibrās* and teacher of Arabic at al-Maktab al-Sulṭānī and al-Kulliyya al-ʿUthmāniyya in Beirut. He published a number of schoolbooks, listed in Sarkīs 1419 (see Suppl. I, 36,$_3$), a short biography of the Prophet, *Lubāb al-khiyār fī sīrat al-mukhtār* (Beirut 1328, Cairo 1924), and a *dīwān* (Haifa: al-Maṭbaʿa al-ʿAbbāsiyya, 1925; see *Jāmiʿ* I, 644, *al-Mashriq* XXIV, 396), *Naẓarāt fi ʾl-adab* (Beirut,1927) and his view on the issue of women's rights in his *Naẓarāt fī ʾl-sufūr wal-ḥijāb* (Beirut 1928).

c *ʿĪsā Iskandar Maʿlūf*

The literary activity of ʿĪsā Iskandar Maʿlūf was extremely diverse, even if he had predilection for the history of dynasties in the Lebanon. Born in Kfar ʿUqab,

in the Lebanon, in 1869, he made a living as a teacher in Zahlé. It was there that he founded *Majallat al-āthār* in 1911, which, though temporarily closed during the war, has flourished again thereafter. Maʿlūf is a member of the academies of Damascus and Cairo. Two of his articles, *al-Iqtiṣād* and *Ḥayāt al-bilād*, first published in *Jarīdat Lubnān*, were reprinted in Yūsuf Ṣufayr, *Majāli 'l-ghurar*, 160/70. His *Lamḥa fī 'l-kitāba* (Baʿabda 1895) was followed by his *Lamḥa fī 'l-shiʿr wal-ʿaṣr* (Baʿabda 1898). He entered his true domain with a 749-page history of his own family, entitled *Dawāni 'l-quṭūf fī sīrat Bani 'l-Maʿlūf* (Baʿabda 1907/8), which also deals with other Syrian families. In *al-Akhbār al-marwiyya fī ta'rīkh al-usar al-sharqiyya* (Damascus 1924), he delved into the histories of these fam-
386 ilies in greater detail.[16] The regional history of his country is the subject of | his *al-Biqāʿ al-Lubnāniyya* (Beirut 1913), *Ta'rīkh al-amīr Bashīr al-Shihābī al-kabīr al-maʿrūf bil-Malṭī* (Beirut 1914), and of his *Ṣināʿāt Dimashq al-qadīma wal-ḥadītha* (1922). In 1923, he published a brief history of medicine, entitled *Ta'rīkh al-ṭibb ʿinda 'l-umam al-qadīma wal-ḥadītha* (Damascus). In 1926 he published *Qaṣr āl al-ʿAẓm bi-Dimashq* (Beirut) and *Makhṭūṭāt al-khizāna al-Maʿlūfiyya fī 'l-Jāmiʿa al-Amirīkiyya*. He also wrote *qaṣīda*s in his younger years, two of which were published in *Fatāt al-sharq* II, 341/2 and 395/7. RAAD published many of his articles, from its first volume onward. In the *Majallat Majmaʿ al-lugha al-ʿarabīya al-malikī* I (Cairo, 1935), 350/68, he published the study *Fi 'l-lahja al-ʿarabiyya al-ʿāmma*, followed by *al-Lahja al-ʿāmmiyya fī Lubnān wa-Sūriyya* in volume IV (1939), 294/315. Of the many works that remain unpublished, Lecerf (*Lit. dialectale* 32f) mentions *Nayl al-mutamannā fī fann al-muʿannā*, which is about a special type of popular poetry from Lebanon. For his sons Shafīq Fawzī and Riyāḍ, see Chapter 3, 13. Sarkīs 1765, MSOS, XXX, 214.

d *Jirjī Niqūlā Bāz*

Jirjī Niqūlā Bāz, publisher of the *Majallat al-ḥasnā'* magazine in Beirut, was a very firm supporter of the education of women. Born around 1881,[17] the Jamʿiyyat Shams al-barr awarded him a prize for his *Āfāt al-madaniyya al-ḥāḍira* in 1902, of which 355 copies were bought by *al-Muqtaṭaf* magazine for distribution among its subscribers. In this same year, he wrote *al-Insān ibn al-tarbiya*—a work entirely based on Europen sources—but it was only in 1907 (n.d.) that it was published in Beirut through a subsidy of the aforementioned

16 A supplement thereto was published by ʿAbdallāh al-Najjār (*mudīr maʿārif* of Jabal al-Durūz) in his *Banū Maʿrūf fī Jabal Ḥawrān* (Damascus: al-Maṭbaʿa al-Ḥadītha, 1924; *Jāmiʿ* I, 1181, RAAD V, 48/9, which has a mistaken Maʿlūf).

17 See *al-Insān ibn al-tarbiya*, 5; Sarkīs' claim that his translation *al-Rawḍa al-badīʿa fī ta'rīkh al-ṭabīʿa* was published in Beirut in 1881 is, therefore, untenable.

society. His *Āthār al-tahdhīb* (Beirut 1912) contains a collection of speeches and poems read by him at the Jamʿiyyat tahdhīb al-fatāt al-Sūriyya. Of a second collection, *al-Nisāʾiyyāt*, a second printing was published in Cairo in 1919. In 1907, he published a biography of L. Proctor, *Ṣadā maʾāthir Lūʾīza P.* (Beirut), and in 1914 *Ilyās Ṭarrād, āluhu, sīratuhu, maʾāthiruhu* (see above pages 262, 352). He discussed the issue of women's rights again in *Iklīl Ghār* (Beirut n.d.) (*Jāmiʿ* 516) and in his collected speeches *Ḥusn al-tadhkār* (Beirut 1926) (*Jāmiʿ* 537). A talk entitled *Taqaddum al-Yābān* was published in Beirut in 1922.

e *Ṭanyūs Abū Nāḍir, Ilyās Niqūlā Ẓāhir, and Jamīl al-Baḥrī*

Pure entertaiment, with no literary pretense, was offered by the stories in Dr. Ṭanyūs Efendi Abū Nāḍir's *al-Ṭabīb al-ṭarīd* (Beirut 1922; *Jāmiʿ* II, 223, Pérès 416), | Ilyās Niqūlā Ẓāhir's *al-Ḥubb al-ḥalāl* and *Ghādat Berlīn* (Beirut 1920) (Pérès 387
694), and Jamīl al-Baḥrī's *al-Waṭan al-maḥbūb* (Haifa 1923) (Pérès 437). The last of these writers, who also published *Majallat al-Zahrāʾ* in Haifa, also adapted several European detective novels, as well as writing a history of his hometown of Haifa, *Taʾrīkh Ḥayfāʾ* (Haifa 1922; *Jāmiʿ* I, 51) (see p. 416, 6).

f *ʿAbd al-Ḥasīb Efendi*

ʿAbd al-Ḥasīb Efendi al-Shaykh Saʿīd, publisher of *Jarīdat al-hadaf* in Hama, published a collection of essays entitled *al-Khawāṭir* (Damascus, 1921) (*Jāmiʿ*, 540).

g *Abū Ghanīma*

In Egypt, the short story had been a flourishing genre for some time. The first person to try his hand at it in Syria was Muḥammad Ṣubḥī Abū Ghanīma, with the publication of *Aghāni 'l-layl, majmūʿat qiṣaṣ ijtimāʿiyya akhlāqiyya adabiyya* I (Damascus: Maṭbaʿat al-Taraqqī, 1922/1340). In *Anā wal-shiʿr*, he tells the reader that he had felt his calling as a poet from his early childhood onward and that he also had followed the advice of his teacher on how to attain this goal step by step, until the day on which the sight of yet another victim of social injustice provided him with the final element of his trade: a compassionate, weeping heart. This is also the tone of most of the stories by this apparently rather young author, which still lack the graphic sense of reality that is so typical of a writer like Maḥmūd Taymūr. In *Lā tabkī* (73/9), he tells us how one of his friends tries to get him out of his melancholic mood, but also understands when Abū Ghanīma tells him about a scene at the Umayyad mosque where a solemn service of a group of pilgrims was rudely disturbed by a parish clerk who had started sweeping up. He is at his best when he writes about moods, such as the vision he had had when visiting the ruins of a Roman theatre at

Gerasa (*Waqfa ʿalā ṭalal* 56/63), and in his adaptation of the myth of Zeus and the poet (*Ayna kunta* 50/5); in this case, his role is given to the Orient, which goes empty-handed when the assets of the world are divided because it had wasted its time on the creation of a multitude of religions instead of serving God and Truth. I know of no sequel to these sketches, which do not seem to have had any significant impact.

h *Najīb Efendi Naṣṣār*

In his *Fī dhimmat al-ʿarab* (Haifa 1922), Najīb Efendi Naṣṣār tried to bring the era of al-Nuʿmān al-Mundhir to life for his readers, in the style of Jirjī Zaydān.

i *Ḥannā Khabbāz*

In *Ḥawl al-kura al-arḍiyya* vol. 1 (2nd printing Santiago 1922), Ḥannā Khabbāz,
388 director of al-Kulliyya al-Waṭaniyya in Homs, | gives an account of his trip around the world. A second volume, *Laṭāʾif akhbārī fī matāḥif asfārī*, was published in Homs in 1923, and a third volume, *al-Burj al-qadīm aw Khabāyā akhbārī fī zawāyā asfārī*, was published in that same place and year (*Jāmiʿ* I, 107, 1106, Pérès 481); see also p. 215, n.

k *Wajīh Efendi Bayḍūn and ʿĪsā Mīkhāʾīl Sābā*

Collections of literary essays were published by Wajīh Efendi Bayḍūn in his *al-ʿIbar* (Damascus 1924; *Jāmiʿ* I, 557) and by ʿĪsā Mīkhāʾīl Sābā in his *Waḥy al-ghāb*, which also contains poems (Beirut: Maṭbaʿat al-Qāmūs, 1925). In the previous year, the latter had also published an anthology, *Jawāhir al-maḥfūẓāt* (Beirut: al-Maṭbaʿa al-ʿIlmiyya).

i *Rafīq al-ʿAẓm*

The literary output of Rafīq Bek b. Maḥmūd al-ʿAẓm was extremely varied. Born in 1282/1865, he belonged to the distinguished Āl al-ʿAẓm family of Damascus. A *dīwān* written earlier by his father was never published. He devoted himself to literature from an early age, never thinking of making a career as a civil servant or in the clergy. During the reign of ʿAbd al-Ḥamīd, he joined the Young Turks. In 1310/1892, he avoided the state's political countermeasures by emigrating to Egypt, where he associated with Muḥammad ʿAbduh and his followers. But all this time he remained faithful to the Young Turks, for whom he edited the Arabic section of their party magazine, *al-Shūrā al-ʿUthmāniyya*, even when the Arab liberation movement turned against the politics of the al-Ittiḥād wal-taraqqī Party. When Fayṣal was proclaimed king in Damascus, he returned to his homeland, but due to ill-health he was forced to turn down an offer of a

ministerial post. He died on 11 Dhu ʾl-Ḥijja 1343/4 July 1925. His first work, *al-Bayān fi ʾl-tamaddun wa-asbāb al-ʿumrān*, was published by ʿAbd al-Hādī Najāʾ al-Abyārī (II, 741) (Cairo 1304). In *Risāla fī bayān kayfiyyat intishār al-adyān* (Cairo n.d.) he defended Islam against the criticism of its being a religion of the sword. In 1317, he published *al-Durūs al-ḥikmiyya lil-nāshiʾa al-Islāmiyya*, and in 1318 *Tanbīh al-afhām ilā maṭālib al-ḥayāt al-ijtimāʿiyya fi ʾl-Islām*. In 1903, he began working on a large biographical lexicon, entitled *Ashhar mashāhīr al-Islām fi ʾl-ḥarb wal-siyāsa*, of which 4 volumes were published in 1903 (Maṭbaʿat al-Mawsūʿāt; 2nd edition 1908, Maṭbaʿat al-Hindiyya). In 1325/1907 he returned to apologetics with *al-Jāmiʿa al-Islāmiyya wa-Ūrūbā*. In 1326/1908, he was co-editor of the Arabic version of the Turkish report on the Ottoman | mission— 389
headed by Ṣādiq Pāshā al-Muʾayyad al-ʿAẓm—to the Negus of Abyssinia, the *Riḥlat al-Ḥabasha* (Cairo, Maṭbaʿat Jarīdat al-Iqbāl). After his death, his brother ʿUthmān Bek published his collected shorter writings as *Majmūʿat āthār Rafīq Bek al-ʿAẓm* (Maṭbaʿat al-Manār, 1344; *Jāmiʿ* I, 446). See Sarkīs 1342, after *al-Zahrāʾ* II, 224, *RAAD* V, 561/4.

k *Al-Khūrī Mārūn Ghuṣn*

Al-Khūrī Mārūn Ghuṣn started his literary career with a study on how to battle misogamy among the youth in *al-Ziwāj, al-sibāqāt al-ʿashara* (Beirut: al-Maṭbaʿa al-Kāthīlīkiyya, 1924). This was followed by a collection of short stories, lectures, anecdotes and poems entitled *Durūs wa-muṭālaʿa* (Beirut, 1925; *Jāmiʿ* I, 350), and a linguistic study called *al-Lugha al-ʿāmmiyya, ḥayāt al-lughāt wa-mawtuhā* (Beirut: Maṭbaʿat al-Yasūʿiyyīn, 1925) that was severely criticised by Cheikho in *al-Mashriq* XXIII, 161/71. *Al-Baraka baʿd al-laʿna* and *Difāʿ al-ibn ʿan sharaf abīh* are both modern stories, published in Beirut in 1927 (Pérès, 479/80). He tried his hand at the theatre with his translation from the French of the play *al-Shaykh al-hāʾil aw inqādh al-amīr* (Beirut: Maṭbaʿat Jidʿūn, n.d.; *Jāmiʿ* II, 221) and with the opera *Riwāyat al-malakayn, maghnāt dhāt 3 fuṣūl* (music by Wadīʿ Ṣabrā) (Beirut: al-Maṭbaʿa al-Kāthūlīkiyya, 1927; *Jāmiʿ* II, 217). In *Fī metlo hal-ektāb* (Beirut 1925), he used the local dialect (Lecerf, *Lit. dial.* 21, n.).

l *Aḥmad al-Dimashqī*

Author of *Jamīl wa-Fāʾiza aw Jihād al-ḥubb walwājib* (Beirut, 1925) (Péres 421).

m *Khurfisqufūs Yūsuf Rabbānī*

Author of *al-Kūnt wal-markīz wal-dūk al-muḥtālīn wal-ʿimyān al-shaḥḥādīn* (Harissa, 1926) (*Jāmiʿ* II, 228).

n *Fuʾād Afrām al-Bustānī*

Fuʾād Afrām al-Bustānī, a professor of Arabic literature at the Université St. Joseph whose studies on the history of Arabic poetry were published in *al-Mashriq* and in the first volume of the serial work *al-Rawāʾiʿ*, often cited in volume I, was also a storyteller. He began in 1926 with a collection of short stories from the history of the Lebanon (*Jāmiʿ* I, 1139) entitled *ʿAlā ʿahd al-amīr*. There then followed *Li-mādhā* in 1930, first published in *al-Mashriq* XXVI and XXVII (Pérès 440/1), *Amān al-Lubnānī*, ibid. XXVIII, 56/9, a translation of P. Bourget's *Résurrection*, ibid. 292/3043, 79/84, *Baṣṣāra barrāja bil-ṣūf al-bakht*, ibid. XXIX 56/65, and *Kathrat al-jalaba*, ibid. 298/301.

o *Tawfīq Ḥasan al-Sharnūbī and Other Writers on Literature and Sociology*

Works on literature and sociology were published by Tawfīq Ḥasan al-
390 Sharnūbī, *al-Ḥayāt fī Lubnān* | (Beirut: al-Maṭbaʿa al-Adabiyya, 1927) (*Jāmiʿ* II, 42), by al-Khūrī Buṭrus al-Bustānī, *al-Sanābil* (Beirut: Maṭbaʿat Ṣādir, 1927), and by Salīm al-Jundī together with Muḥammad al-Dāʾūdī, *ʿUddat al-adab* (3 vols, Damascus, 1345 (*Jāmiʿ* II, 141).

p *Yūsuf Ghaṣūb*

In his *Akhlāq wa-mashāhid* (Beirut n.d.) (*Jāmiʿ* I, 511), Yūsuf Ghaṣūb began with images of life in the Orient and in Syria in particular. In 1928, he published a *dīwān* called *al-Qafaṣ al-mahjūr*. Even if the influence of A. de Musset and Khalīl Maṭrān is undeniable, the work is original in many ways. Cf. F.E. Bustānī in *al-Mashriq* XXVI, 375/82.

q *Muṣṭafā al-Arnāʾūt*

In his long-winded historical novels, Muṣṭafā al-Arnāʾūt tried to give literary expression to the life of the ancient Arabs. In *Sayyid Quraysh* he depicted the Arabs of ancient times (2nd printing Damascus 1350/1931 in 3 volumes, with a foreword by Khalīl Maṭrān and Munīr al-ʿIjlānī), the spread of Islam in *ʿUmar b. al-Khaṭṭāb* (4 vols, Damascus 1932) (Pérès 430/1), and the conquest of Spain in *Ṭāriq b. Ziyād* (*al-Ḥadīth* 1931/2011).

r *Iskandar al-Riyāshī*

Iskandar al-Riyāshī translated the historical novel *Le roman d'émir Saif*, by André Devens, under the title *Sayf al-Dawla* (Beirut 1349/1929). He then started writing romantic novels himself, entitled *Ahl al-gharām* (Beirut 1933) and *Iṣābat al-gharām* (Beirut 1935) (Pérès 208, 603/4).

s *Ḥārith Nakht and Muḥammad al-Najjār*

Historical novels were written by Ḥārith Nakht, *Hind al-Barmakiyya* (Beirut 1356/1936) (Pérès 578), and by Muḥammad al-Najjār, *Fī quṣūr Dimashq*, 31 stories with a preface by Munīr al-ʿIjlānī (Damascus 1937) (Pérès 576).

t *Tawfīq Ḥasan al-Sharṭūni and Tawfīq Yūsuf ʿAwwād*

Stories from modern life were written by Tawfīq Ḥasan Nāḍir al-Sharṭūni (see p. 234, and also *al-Ḥakīm wa-Salmā*, Beirut 1933, see Pérès 636/7) and Tawfīq Yūsuf ʿAwwād, *al-Ṣabī al-aʿraj wa-qiṣaṣ ukhrā* (Beirut 1936; see *al-Mashriq* xxxv, 150) and *Qamīṣ al-ṣūf wa-qiṣaṣ ukhrā* (Beirut 1938; Pérès 435). In 1930, the latter had published an article on popular poetry in *al-Mashriq* xxviii, 436/43, 501/8 (see Lecerf, *Lit. dial.* 32). His second collection of short stories shows that he is a man of great talent. These seven tales encompass the entire universe of human sentiments, from the tenderest motherly love in *Qamīṣ al-ṣūf* to the aversion of a father for his newborn daughter, still widespread in the Orient, culminating in *Tūhā* in the murder of the unwelcome infant; and from the act of despair by the tormented residents of a home for the blind | against their 391
director at the moment when he receives a medal for "service" in some celebration, to the satire on the showing-off of an American who, on his return to his hometown, dazzles everyone for a brief period with his purported riches, until he vanishes, steeped in debts; from the feelings of a fallen woman who craves for the illusion of genuine love, if only just once, to the derailment of a socialist who, once a hard labourer and happy family man, having been led astray by the misguided ideas of his comrades, degenerates into a miserable proletarian and then, due to his mistaken ideas about justice, into a common thief. The story about the war at the end, dedicated to Mīkhāʾīl Nuʿayma, stands apart; *Mīthāq al-mawt* is an impressive tale about the effects of the imagination on a superstitious soldier who expects to die any time but with whom death only catches up when his car arrrives at the front door of his home after the war has ended. The author knows very well how to catch the attention of the reader immediately and to draw out the suspense right to the end. The language is classical but free of affectation, and is only rarely mingled with phrases in the Syrian vernacular.

u *Karam Malḥam Karam*

Karam Malḥam Karam (b. 1904), publisher of the *Majallat Alf layla wa-layla* and *al-ʿĀṣifa*, is one of the most productive storytellers in Syria. By 1931, he had 200 short stories available in print, although most of these were translated and adapted from French. He thus continues the work of Ṭanyūs ʿAbduh. The story

Ṣarkhat al-alam (Beirut, Alf layla wa-layla) is a story that, by his own statement in the preface, is based on a personal experience and thus written from the heart. It is the story of the unhappy love of a girl who has an affair with an unworthy party behind her parents' back and wants to elope with him, before a relative of hers tells her that her lover is already married and a father. From then on, the idea of love just makes her sick, until she meets a young man who tells his adventures in the first person. It is through him that she starts to have confidence in love again. The two entertain hopes of a happy union until the girl's father tells her that he has promised her in marriage to someone else.
392 Since her mother convinced her that there was no use | in trying to resist her father's decision, she takes a slowly-working poison when she meets her lover for the last time, a poison to which she succumbs in his arms two days later. The sentimental theme goes well with the style, the whole thing just brimming with emotion, in classical Arabic of the purest kind without the slightest affectation. Pérès also mentions *Riwāyat al-maṣdūr*, Cairo 1937 (no. 542); *al-Ḥadīth* 1937, 541/2 mentions four village tales that are not free from exaggeration and are entitled *Ashbāḥ al-qarya*. See Ilyās Abū Shabaka, *al-Rusūm* I, 43/6.

v *Sāmī al-Kayyālī*

In 1935, Sāmī al-Kayyālī of Aleppo, the meritorious publisher of *al-Ḥadīth*, the leading literary magazine of Syria which has so often been gratefully made use of, went on a trip to Europe with his friend and poet from Damascus, Shafīq Jabrī (cf. p. 355), and which took them, over the course of a month, to Paris, London, and Italy. He gives an account of it in his *Shahr fī Ūrūbā* (Cairo: al-Maṭbaʿa al-ʿAṣriyya, 1935), to which his travelling companion wrote a preface. Even though the book does not claim that it provides its readership with any new insights into Western civilization, apart from being a good read, it is often very informative about the opinions that orientals have of Europe. His descriptions are dominated by the City of Lights, which is quite natural as it was there that they spent half their time while travelling. His images of Paris are captivating, never omitting to correct received opinions on the city's way of life. Like most orientals, he is at first overwhelmed by the contrast with life in London. There, he feels at the centre of world politics, happy to see that, in Britain at least, the Arab Question predominates. In Geneva, he marvels at the palace of the League of Nations, so out of touch with the practical aims of the organisation. In Italy, he is much impressed by the Renaissance culture of Venice and Florence and by life's pulse in modern Rome, where he understands the historical importance of Mussolini. At the end, and summarising his European impressions, his most vivid memory is of the contrast between the pace of life in Europe's major cities and the quiet peace of the town where he was born. What

he hopes for is that these two temperaments can be reconciled in | friendly 393
competition, to the future benefit of mankind.

w *Muḥammad Isʿāf al-Nashāshībī*

For an Arab, Jerusalem, where the struggle for Palestine's future was at its fiercest, was hardly a place for quiet intellectual labour. In this period, the only one to work there, promoting the ideals of Arabic literature, was Muḥammad Isʿāf al-Nashāshībī, who came from a family of notables famous for its party activism. His first publication, *Kalima mūjiza fī siyar al-ʿilm*, appeared in 1921 (Jerusalem 1340) (*Jāmiʿ* 431). Next year, he published a textbook for the primary and secondary schools of Palestine which he had been commissioned to write by the ministry of education, entitled *Majmūʿa fi ʾl-akhlāq wal-kalām* (Cairo 1341). An *adab* work, *al-Bustān*, with a commentary, was published in Cairo (al-Maṭbaʿa al-Salafiyya n.d.). On 17 March 1924, he gave a lecture at the American University of Beirut entitled *Qalb ʿArabī wa-ʿaql Ūrūbī*, which was published in Jerusalem in 1342. The ideas developed therein, close to those of Jamāl al-Dīn al-Afghānī, received the full approbation Abū Shādī, as can be seen in his poem *al-ʿAṣabiyya al-ṭāʾisha*, in his *al-Shafaq al-bākī* 351/2. A member of the Academy in Damascus, he gave a talk at the *Dār Jamʿiyyat al-rābiṭa al-sharqiyya* in Cairo entitled *Kalima fī ʾl-lugha al-ʿarabiyya*. An augmented version of this talk, originally given on 1 Dhu ʾl-Qaʿda 1343/24 May 1924, was published in Jerusalem (Maṭbaʿat Bayt al-Maqdis) in 1925. The talk is about the—in his view—deplorable state of the Arabic language at the time, which he seeks to remedy in various ways. Basically, he believes that the solution lies in a return to the strictests form of classical Arabic. But he does not realise that the language of the poets of old cannot satisfy the needs of the present, and that its continuation into medieval Muslim culture was not uniform enough to provide us with binding standards. Yet he is absolutely right to emphasise that a complete breach with the past would mean the end of Arab intellectual culture. Incidentally, he does not limit himself to Arabic sources in support of his statements, but instead tries, whenever possible, to refer to European experts as well. His conclusion is that it is the task of modern Arabic literature to resuscitate the language of the Qurʾān. In his lecture, he followed this idea, though it is so overloaded with outlandish expressions that he felt obliged to provide it with a lengthy lexical
commentary. | The appendix includes many approving comments on his talk 394
from the Cairene press and a short speech by Khalīl Maṭrān, made during that same gathering, in which the latter declares that he agrees entirely with the speaker. In his *al-Shafaq al-bākī* (331), Abū Shādī also thanked him for this lecture. In his *al-Baṭal al-khālid Ṣalāḥ al-Dīn wal-shāʿir al-khālid Aḥmad Shawqī*, al-Nashāshībī voiced the gratefulness of the Arabic-speaking world towards

this prince of poets. And, in his latest work, *al-Islām al-ṣaḥīḥ, baḥth wa-taḥqīq* (Jerusalem 1354/1935), he talks about the problems of modernism.

x *Ḥannā al-Khūrī al-Fighālī*

In Egypt, the local dialect was at first only rarely used in prose literature.[18] And in Syria, too, few writers were inspired by it, in contrast to the popular folk song, which was widely used. From among these writers we first mention Ḥannā al-Khūrī al-Fighālī of Wādī Shaḥrūr, a brother of Michael Fighālī, the famous scholar who described the dialects of Lebanon. While their brother ʿAbduh was studying medicine in France, Ḥannā would write to him from home in the local dialect. Later, these letters were published by ʿAbduh and his brother Michael in their Textes de Wadi Chahrour, *JA* 1927, 59/88. The publisher of the satirical weekly *al-Dabbūr*, he also wrote the *Raṣāʾil Shmūnī akhlāqiyya adabiyya bi-lugha ʿāmmiyya Sūriyya* (Beirut n.d.). They are fictional letters to her mother by a village girl named Shmūnī, in which she describes her life in Beirut with all the innocence of her age (see the samples in Lecerf, 133/41).

6 Amīr Shakīb Arslān

The first of the two great Syrian post-war prose writers is Amīr Shakīb Arslān, the brother of Nasīb (see p. 362 a).

He was born on the family estate of Shwīfāt, in the Qaḍāʾ Shūf in the Lebanon, on 15 December 1869. From 1886 onward he went with his brother Nasīb to al-Madrasa al-Sulṭāniyya in Beirut, where they studied under Muḥammad
395 ʿAbduh. | When his father passed away in 1887, he succeeded him as *mudīr* of the Shwīfāt district. But he left his post after just two years, preferring to travel to Istanbul, Paris and London to complete his studies. Back in Lebanon in 1893, he started working as a political correspondent for *al-Ahrām*, *al-Muʾayyad* and other Egyptian and Syrian publications. In 1902 he became a civil servant again, succeeding his uncle Amīr Muṣṭafā Arslān as *qāʾim maqām* of the Qaḍāʾ Shūf. But when he fell out with the governor of the Lebanon, Muẓaffar Pāshā, he was removed from office by the latter. And even though Muẓaffar Pāshā's successor Yūsuf Franco Pāshā reinstated him in office, he was not able to assert himself in it for more than two and a half years. When the Italo-Turkish war broke out, he and some of his followers participated in the fighting for eight

---

18 In connection with page 237, we also mention (following Lecerf, *Lit. dial.* 130) the collections *Mudhakkarāt al-futuwwā* by Abu ʾl-Ḥājj (Cairo 1929/30), *Mudhakkarāt nashshāl* by ʿAbd al-ʿAzīz al-Nuṣṣ (Cairo 1930), and the *Mukhtārāt al-shabāb* with the anonymous *al-Sayyid wa-marʾatuhu fī Miṣr* (Cairo 1925) and *al-Sayyid wa-marʾatuhu fī Bārīz* (Cairo 1926).

months, during which time they were based at Enver Pāshā's military camp in Barqa. During the Balkan war he was a representative for Tripoli in Istanbul. The Egyptian Red Crescent also commissioned him to take care of the Muslim refugees from Adrianople and Salonika.[19] In 1912, he became a member of parliament for the Ḥawrān, defending the policies of the Young Turks for five consecutive years and warning the Arabs against one-sided initiatives. During the war he and 150 other soldiers participated in the failed raid on the Suez Canal. After that, he was the commander of an army corps of 12,000 Druze. When Jamāl Pāshā once more took action against the Arabs, he went to Istanbul to lodge a complaint. In 1917, he went to Germany for the first time, where he witnessed the collapse of the empire in Berlin. From then on, he lived alternately in Geneva—where he represented the Syro-Palestinian delegation in the League of Nations—and Berlin. In 1925 in Paris, he had high-level talks with the high commissioner de Jouvenel on the situation in Syria. But next year, the government of Poincaré rejected his draft treaty regulating the changed relations between France and Syria. In 1927, he attended the Syrian national congress in Detroit, after which he travelled through the United States for five months. In 1929 he made the pilgrimage, during which time he tried to mediate between his host Ibn Saʿūd and Emir Yaḥyā of Yemen in a bid to solve their conflict over ʿAsīr. He succeeded in getting Ibn Saʿūd and King Fayṣal of Iraq to sign an agreement. In 1930, he and Iḥsān Bek al-Jābirī founded | the magazine 396
La Nation Arabe, published in Geneva. It was not until 1937 that he could return to his native country. In Damascus, he became head of the Académie Arabe in 1939 (see *Or. Mod.* 1939, 218).

Shakīb Arslān started his literary career in 1887 as a poet with the *dīwān al-Bākūra* (Beirut). In later times too, he has often used the rigid, stylised patterns of the classics to defend his political and cultural ideals. Muḥammad Rashīd Riḍā (see p. 321) compiled a collection of his poems, calling it a *Dīwān* (Cairo 1354/1935). A specialist of the Arabic language, Arslān edited *al-Mukhtār min rasāʾil Abī Isḥāq al-Ṣābī*, with a commentary (Baʿabda 1898; see Suppl. I, 153), Ibn al-Muqaffaʿs *al-Durra al-yatīma* (Cairo 1910; see Suppl. I, 236), and the anonymous *Maḥāsin al-masāʿī fī manāqib al-Awzāʿī* (see Suppl. I, 308, 1a). In 1937 he started working on his critical edition of Ibn Khaldūn's universal history (see Suppl. II, 343). He published countless magazine articles, of which G. Widmer translated a part from *al-Muqtaṭaf* in *WI* XIX (1937), 13/31, entitled *Der Aufstieg des Orients in der Gegenwart*.[20] As well as all these articles, the

19 See his account in Stoddard's *Ḥāḍir al-ʿālam al-Islāmī* I, 114/5.

20 Another sample, entitled *Ḥaqīqat al-shiʿr*, is cited in al-Manfalūṭī, *Mukhtārāt* 114/8.

first publication in which he set out his views on the political situation in the Orient is his very elaborate and digression-laden commentary on *Ḥāḍir al-ʿālam al-Islāmī*, ʿAjjaj Nuwayhiḍ's translation of Lothrop Stoddard's *The New World of Islam* (2nd ed. 2 vols, London 1922) (Cairo: al-Maṭbaʿa al-Salafiyya, 1343; 2nd augmented ed. 1352). In the same year, he translated Chateaubriand's *Les aventures des derniers Abencerages*, with an elaborate appendix on the final days of Arab rule in Spain, entitled *Ākhir Banī Sarrāj wa-yalīhi khulāṣat taʾrīkh al-Andalus ilā suqūṭ Gharnāṭa* (Cairo: Maṭbaʿat al-Manār, 1343/1925). He also translated J.J. Brousson's *Anatole France en pantouffles*, together with Nic. Ségur's *Conversations avec Anatole France ou les mélancolies de l'intelligence*, with obituaries from the French press, entitled *Anātūl Farāns fī mabādhilihi, taʾlīf J.J.B. maʿa khulāṣat Kitāb Muḥādathāt maʿa Anāṭūl Farāns li N.S. wa-zubdat mā qālathu ʾl-jarāʾid al-Faransiyya fī Faransā yawm wafātihi* (Cairo: al-Maṭbaʿa al-ʿAṣriyya, n.d. [1925]) (see Kampffmeyer, *MSOS* XXIX, 1926, 256, Muḥammad Kurd ʿAlī, *RAAD* VI, 329/32). In the preface to Muhammad Aḥmad al-Ghamrāwī's *al-Naqd al-taḥlīlī li-kitāb fi ʾl-adab al-Jāhilī* (Cairo 1347/1929), translated by Widmer in *WI*, XIX, 32/93, he joined the debate around the authenticity of ancient Arabic poetry that had been triggered by Ṭāhā Ḥusayn.

397 | Meanwhile, and much to the regret of his friends, Amīr was wasting his energy in the media. Nevertheless, he still found time to join the debate on what constitutes acceptable linguistic practice, carried on at the Academy of Damascus, such in his *Muṭālaʿāt lughawiyya* in *RAAD* IX, 1918, 1579, while also discussing historical matters in his *al-Naqd al-taʾrīkhī wa-ʿurūbat āl Maʿrūf* in *RAAD* XI, 449/69. It was only in 1930 that his friend Muḥammad Rashīd Riḍā was able to make him embark upon a larger project. The imam of the maharaja of the Samba on Borneo, Muḥammad Basyūnī ʿImrān, had asked the publisher of *al-Manār* magazine for a detailed answer to his question of why Islam is so backward today. When Amīr returned from his trip to Spain, Riḍā obtained from him the promise that he would answer this question, which resulted in his *Li-mādhā taʾakhkhara ʾl-Muslimūn wa-limādhā taqaddama ghayruhum* (Cairo: Maṭbaʿat al-Manār, 1349; 2nd ed. 1351). In this, he sharply criticises his fellow-Muslims and does not hesitate to ascribe their backwardness to lack of religious zeal and lukewarm patriotism. He compares this with the sacrifices made by the peoples of Europe during the [First] World War, in comparison with the achievements of the Muslims in the Italo-Turkish war and their economic haggling over Palestine. Indeed, he does not even shrink from accusing leading Moroccans, such as the vizir al-Muqrī and the mufti of Fes, of facilitating the missionary activities of the Christians among the Berbers. To progress, neither Islam, nor Christianity or the Shinto religion of Japan form an obstacle; it is just the mental sluggishness of many of a religion's adherents that delays

progress. He proudly points out the heyday of Islamic culture in the Middle Ages, for the downturn of which Islam carries just as little responsibility as Christianity for the downturn of Hellenic culture. Only the sciences, which the Qurʾān repeats time and again we should foster, can lead to the advancement of Islam.

On 22 April 1931 he finished his account of his pilgrimage in Lausanne, which was published as *al-Irtisāmāt al-liṭāf fī khāṭir al-ḥājj ilā aqdas maṭāf wa-hiya ʾl-riḥla al-Ḥijāziyya li-amīr al-bayān wa-nādirat al-zamān al-Amīr Shakīb Arslān*, with a commentary by Muḥammad Rashīd Riḍā, Cairo: Maṭbaʿat al-Manār, 1350. The work is radically different from earlier such accounts, the one by Ḥusayn Haykal included, | in that the religious aspect of it is only alluded 398
to in passing, such as his remark that it was precisely because of its barren suroundings and its heat, only bearable to the locals, that Mecca was chosen by God as His site of worship so that, by bearing all these sufferings, the merit of his servants would only be increased. For the rest, he is very brief about the commencement of his journey, his relations with Ibn Saʿūd, an illness in Mecca and his relocation to Taif. Then follows a series of colourful digressions, which make up the remainder of the book. For instance, he defends the Muṭawwifūn of Mecca and the Muzawwirūn of Medina (71ff) against the accusation of extortion of the pilgrims. On the other hand, he takes great interest in the condition that the country is in as a result of Ibn Saʿūd's administration, extolling its benefits time and again. At every opportunity, he makes proposals to improve on it by revitalising agriculture or by reintroducing the mining industry. Following Moritz, he then lists all the reports on the mines of Arabia as they are found in the ancient geographers. In two places he refers to modern research on the geology of Arabia (113ff, 237ff), while on pages 117ff he tries to identify the Laplace principle in the Qurʾān. In between, there are countless historical digressions, such as one on the markets of Arabia, where, talking about ʿUkāẓ on pages 119ff, he rails once more against Ṭahā Ḥusayn's attacks on the authenticity of ancient poetry, and on Ibn ʿAbbās and his tomb in Taif (143/59). The history of the conquest of Taif (192ff) provides him with an occasion to champion the use of modern war machinery such as tanks. The result is a work with two faces: on the one hand it is very modern, while on the other, it is full of reminiscenses about *adab* and *taʾrīkh* in the style of old.

His trip to Spain occasioned him to delve deeply into the sources of the history of the Arabs in al-Andalus. The first result of these studies was his *Taʾrīkh ghazawāt al-ʿArab fī Fransā wa-Swīserā wa-Iṭālyā wa-jazāʾir al-baḥr al-mutawassiṭ*, Cairo: Maṭbaʿat Dār al-Iḥyāʾ al-ʿArabī, 1352. Further contributions on the history of Spain were published in his *al-Ḥulal al-sundusiyya fī ʾl-akhbār wal-āthār al-Andalusiyya*, Cairo 1936, 2 vols, which will reportedly be

followed by two further studies. In October 1937, in a lecture at the Academy of Damascus, he brought up the subject of the rising of the Orient once more,
399 after his initial discussion of it in *al-Muqtaṭaf* magazine, in 1927. | Even if he repeats himself literally in places, he also updates and improves upon it on many points. The lecture was published in *Jarīdat al-Jazīra* and then in the form of an offprint entitled *al-Nahḍa al-ʿArabiyya fi ʾl-ʿaṣr al-ḥāḍir* (Cairo: Maṭbaʿat Dār al-Nashr, n.d.). Widmer mentions a study on Shawqī as being in press (1937) and a study on Rashīd Riḍā as being in preparation. In *RAAD* XIII, 383, al-Maghribī also mentions a planned book on Bolshevism and another one on his trip to Berlin during the war.

See v. Oppenheim, *Vom Mittelmeer zum pers. Golf* I, 116, *Die Beduinen* I, 17, G. Widmer, *WI* XIX, 1937, 1/93 (with a portrait).

7 Amīn al-Rayḥānī

The person who did the most to open the Orient to the spirit of Western civilisation was Amīn al-Rayḥānī (Rihani).

Coming from a Christian home, he was born in Qaryat al-Furayka, near Beirut, in 1876. When he was twelve years old he emigrated with his family to the United States. Having tried his luck as an actor for a while, he soon turned to journalism. Due to the fact that an Arabic book written by him—he gives no title—had met with disapproval among the Syrians of New York,[21] he just wrote in English for a time, but soon started writing in his native tongue again. After eighteen years in the United States he returned to his homeland, where he settled again in al-Furayka. But his restless mind made him return to the United States once again. After the war he returned to his homeland once more, but could not settle down. It was at that time that he converted to Islam (see *al-Mashriq* XXI, 1923, 478). Soon after, he embarked on his first trip among the royal courts of the Arabs, together with Muḥammad Kurd ʿAlī and Konstantin Yannī, who at the time was putting together an air force for King Ḥusayn.

In his homeland, his debut as a writer was with the play *al-Sujanāʾ aw ʿAbd*
400 *al-Ḥamīd fī Atīnī*, | which had its premiere in 1909 at the New Stage in Beirut but was never printed (*al-Rayḥ.* II, 92). In 1910 he published his first book, *al-Rayḥāniyyāt, wa-hiya majmūʿat maqālāt wa-khuṭab wa-shiʿr manthūr* (2 vols), which established his name among a larger audience. It is a collection of essays that had, in part, been written in the United States. He still has remarkable control of literary Arabic, even though he puts no great weight on grammatical

21 Perhaps it was one of the two works mentioned in Sarkīs, 958/59, *al-Thawra al-Faransāwiyya* (inspired by T. Carlyle; New York, 1903) or *al-Muḥālafa al-thulāthiyya fi ʾl-mamlaka al-ḥayawāniyya wal-mukārī wal-kāhin* (New York, 1903).

purity, letting colloquialisms slip in without giving it a second thought. In one instance he ridicules the *waḥshiyya* in ancient poetry in a very ingenious way, which was in the opening lines of a talk that he gave in Sidon in 1910 (II, 66/82, "On the value of life"), following a request to come up with something unusual.

In *Wādi 'l-Furayka aw al-ʿawd ila 'l-ṭabīʿa* (*al-Rayḥāniyyāt* I, 5/20) he lavishes praise on the beauty of his reclaimed homeland. In its forests, he finds the inner peace he had lost in the clamour of America's big cities. But the thought of the bustling life of New York City 'On Brooklyn bridge', 'On the roofs of New York', 56/67) still fills him with a hidden yearning. He does not close his eyes to the social damage caused by this New World, the bloodsucking methods of capitalism, child labour, and the poverty among the miners. But his main concern are his compatriots, whom he wants to help disengage themselves from the stifling limitations of their traditional way of life. He therefore does not shrink from criticising the clergy, still so dominant among them. In a New Year's sermon, addressed to people of all religions and social classes (I 51/5), he endorses one universal human morality, in one case invoking a maxim from the *ḥadīth*. His whip lashes out more fiercely in a sermon by Jesus on an imaginary visit to the modern world. Indeed, he does not hesitate to propose a new type of prayer to replace the Lord's Prayer, desecrated by wrongful practices (I, 46/7). He does not tire of preaching tolerance (*al-tasāhul*). In the same way in which he had done this on 9 February 1900, in a lecture to the Maronite youth of New York (II, 112/40), he campaigns against a belief in the Devil who, according to a verdict by an English court, had seduced the British citizen Lynch into fighting against his Motherland in the ranks of the Boers (107/110). Yet he certainly does not want to uncritically accept the ideology of the French | Revolution and 401
its forerunners. He translates Carlyle's sharp criticism (I, 191/206) and uncovers the human weaknesses of Voltaire (I, 160/5)—whom he compares to Abū Nuwās—and Rousseau (160/73). On the other hand, he praises W. Garrison, the champion of the abolition of slavery (174/8), and Tolstoy, whom he juxtaposes with Morgan as the dreamt-of successor to Christ (179/85). In his inner life, Muslim culture does not play a significant role at first. He is right to criticise two verses by al-Mutanabbī, extravagant in their praise (I, 137/41), and to contrast him with the Spanish poet Ibn Sahl, a real poet of nature (186/90).

It seems that this gifted journalist soon acquired renown and influence among his compatriots. The second volume contains a series of lectures that he had given in Beirut and other cities, in meetings of the Shams al-barr Society, the first of which dates from 19 March 1908. One of these lectures ('Here, there, and yonder') gave such a sharp analysis of the situation at home and in the United States that the people who had invited him dared not let him give this talk in the final year of ʿAbd al-Ḥamīd's reign. His praise of freedom and progress was, therefore, all the more wholehearted after the victory of the constitution. But in order for political freedom to fully unfold, intellectual liberation was of the essence. He praises Beirut as the intellectual capital of the Lebanon (101/4) which, in the new empire, increasingly tried to link up with Western culture. They even dared stage Shakespeare's *Hamlet* there, and he gave a speech right before the curtain went up (83/91). Of course, he does not ignore the dangers of partisanship among his compatriots, sparking conflict every time that confessional rivalries were at stake. He also tried to influence intellectual life in Brazil, criticising two works by Jamīl Bek Maʿlūf that had been published in São Paolo, one a translation of Fuʾād Pāshā's political testament and the other a work on the New Turkey and human rights.

His attempts at free verse, in imitation of W. Whitman (see above p. 90) at the end of the second volume, are purely literary. Its strophic, rhyming prose
402 is an unmistakable echo of ancient Arabic literary prose, | indeed (at times) of the Qurʾān itself. This is especially clear in the first two pieces, 'Revolution' and 'Sandstorm', while the others are truly lyrical pieces: 'Heal me, mistress of the valley,' 'Rose twig,' and the poems on the birth and death of his sister's son Fuʾād (b. 27 April 1908, d. 20 November 1908).

In the long run, his country was too small for his ego; when the second volume of the *Rayḥāniyyāt* went to press, he was already in London.

The third volume (Beirut: Maṭbaʿat Yūsuf Ṣādir, 1923) opens with an account of his trip to Spain, *Nūr al-Andalus* (325), the date of which he does not mention and which is not included in Pérès's *L'Espagne*, the author in those days not having converted to Islam yet. He describes spring in Seville and Granada, the air filled with the sounds of partying day and night. To escape this, he takes off to Cordova, where a tourist guide puts him up in the house of an uncle of his, in a quiet part of town. The enchanted house still shows traces of Arab decorations and, on a stone inserted in a wall, he identifies the letters *r-sh-d*. Not much is needed for him to imagine that this was the house of the great philospher Ibn Rushd, or else the stone was hauled there from his tomb in some derelict graveyard. Then, when he goes to sleep, the philosopher himself appears to him and tells him about the fate of the Arabs of Spain for which they, always quarrelling, like all the other Arabs, only have themselves to blame. Ibn Rushd then gives him an order to warn the Arabs to finally pick up the signs of the age and to bury all tribal and religious hatred because the road to progress lies open. In *Taʾrīkh Sūriyā* (26/8), he talks about the inscriptions along the borders of the Nahr al-kalb and which contain the history of Syria in a nutshell. Because of their history, Syria's cedar trees are more important to him than the Sequoias of California; in the grotto of Afqa he traces old Semitic religions. In a short article, *al-Shiʿr wal-shuʿarāʾ* (34/7), he tells us that, of all the Arab poets, he can only regard the poetry of ʿUmar b. Fāriḍ and al-Maʿarrī as genuine. In *Bilādī* (44/51) he describes his inner contradictions as a patriot, being American and Lebanese at one and the same time. This piece was published earlier as 'My own country' in *The Path of Vision*.

| In 'Church and mosque' he juxtaposes the peace and uniform human dig- 403
nity that one finds in a mosque with the pretentiousness with which people had decorated a church in Newport, Rhode Island. In a study on what makes a language a living language (60–76), inspired by an article by Jabr Ḍūmat in *al-Hilāl* magazine, he speaks out in favour of the modernisation of written Arabic, something which could easily be achieved by an academy—whose foundation he insists on (71 bottom, 78,$_1$)—without violating the spirit of it. On a similar note, he also believes that it is possible to select the treasures from the tangled mass of al-Maʿarrī's *Luzūmiyyāt* and publish them in about 1,000 verses all. In this way, this work would be rendered truly accessible to the modern reader. In March of 1911, while in the United States, he juxtaposes revolutionary movements with the ideal of mental growth, which in the Orient, should, first of all, lead to economic change, on which true intellectual freedom could then be based. The future (86/91) is said to belong to autonomous nation states that would put an end to the injustices of large colonial empires, in an atmosphere of mutual respect. An English book dating from 1720 prompts him to tell his readers about Hypatia as a warning against the dangers of fanaticism (97/102). When he compares Augustine and al-Ghazzālī (109/18) he feels obliged to point out, with due recognition of the depth of their mysticism and the greatness of their religious personalities, that they were limited by the level of knowledge in the natural sciences of their times and that one cannot use them as authorities to confirm the findings of modern science, in the way in which Muslim scholars have tried to do with the Qurʾān. When he introduces his friend Nāṣir al-Dīn al-Baghdādī to his readers (119/36),[22] he introduces them to a Muslim reformer who is a Wahhābī when it comes down to religion and a Khārijī when it comes down to politics; he lets him criticise his articles on the expected revolution, concluding that, in the Orient too, economic hardship will determine the political balance of power (117/36). In *Abarshiyyat al-Furayka* (141/46) he ridi-
cules the religious bigotry of his compatriots and in 'Peace on earth' | (141/155) 404
the disinformation campaigns of the Entente during the [First] World War. His obituaries of the philosopher Shiblī Shumayyil (see p. 212) and the philanthropist G.D. Sursuq (156/63) are affectionate. In two lectures, one of which he gave in Zahleh (*al-Tarqīʿ fī 'l-ʿamal* 164/72) and the other, on 17 May 1913, in Beirut

22 First in *al-Murāqib al-agharr* V, 1126, which was then reprinted in Muḥammad al-Ḥusayn, *al-Murājaʿāt al-Rayḥāniyya* 1, 15/29.

(*Rūḥ al-thawra*), he sets out his political ideals once more, telling his compatriots that they should not expect too much of the reforms which the Young Turks were introducing in their country, these reforms being nothing but the mending of an old garment with new cloth. In a lecture at the American University of Beirut in 1912 (*al-Akhlāq* 193/232), he developes several theories to explain the national character, reiterating that, while there was undeniably an intellectual upsurge in the Orient, so far it had not borne any fruit; and that no fruit could be expected before people decided that all these ideals that they apparently subscribed to also needed to be put into practice.

The fourth volume starts with a prayer (*Najwā*), written in Riyadh (in the Najd) on 1 December 1923. A description of the seaside in Alexandria is followed by a hymn on New York dated December 1910 and a translation of W. Whitman's 'To him that was Crucified' in free verse. It is also in free verse that he writes in March of 1913 in al-Furayka to celebrate Khalīl Maṭrān (34/7), on the occasion of a ceremony in his honour in Cairo. He also uses this same format in his hymns on the Orient, composed on 14 February 1922 in Cairo; on Egypt, recited at the foot of the pyramids during a cerenomy in honour of Aḥmad Zakī Pāshā; on the rulers of Iraq, signed Baghdad, 14 September 1922; in *Rafīqatī* (i.e. freedom), signed Baghdad, 18 September 1922; in *al-ʿAwd ila ʾl-wādī*, signed Beirut, 17 May 1923; in *Arākī ya bilādī bi-ʿaynayn*, written as a welcome to P. Pinot when he came to Syria; and, finally, also in *Nafḥa min luʾluʾ*, in memory of a lady friend who was drowned in the Amazon river.

The collection of essays is opened by *al-Ṣalīb aw yawm fī Bayrūt*, which is a description of Lebanon's capital after the suppression of the freedom movement by Jamāl Pāshā.[23] In it he recounts how, after wandering through the
405 town in a vain search for the houses of his former friends, he | stumbles upon a square full of gallows and a mother hanging from a cross, crying over her lost sons; a symbol of the town, abandoned to its misery while its sons rip each other to pieces in party struggles over in America, Paris, and Egypt. In a relief effort, he launched several calls for help to his compatriots in America, one on 25 January 1915 in New York, and another on 1 August 1916, also in New York. In it, he recommended that they fast in solidarity with their starving compatriots back home, putting his money where his mouth was by fasting himself for two consecutive days. He then describes the effects of hunger on his own body so as to convince the Syrians of America of the kind of distress that Syria the country is in. Even during this charity campaign, he finds himself up against the partisanship of the Syrians of America, who would

23 See G. Antonius, *The Arab Awakening*, 203.

rather see their charity just benefit the village from which they came (*al-Taʿmīm wal-takhṣīṣ*, IV, 116/21).

The section "The war and afterwards" opens with an essay entitled "Third class," in which he relates his encounters with French soldiers during the war in France. While they travelled together, one of these told him of a volunteer from the Lebanon who wanted to take revenge for the suffering of his family by getting himself a human head from the enemy trenches but who, on his way back from there, was hit by a bullet and died. In an article called *al-Ḥaqq wal-quwwa* (signed Paris, 12 January 1917) (139/43), he explains the ideology behind the Entente, which he still believed was there to protect the Arabs, unable to anticipate the terrible fate that would await them at the end of the war. In *Lā ḥayāta illā bil-ḥurriyya wa-lā ḥurriyya illā bil-sayf*, which was the title of an address to the Syrians of New York, he tried to get them to participate in the struggle for the liberation of their homeland from the yoke of the Turks; in it, he repeats the many beautiful promises that had been made by the French (144/58). In the printed version, he then has to point out in three timid footnotes that the prospects with which they had lured the Syrians had not materialized. In his imaginary '1950,' he first describes the breakdown of the world order established by the Treaty of Versailles and the League of Nations—still celebrating Wilson as the saviour of humanity who had been cheated of his success by his allies—and then predicts that the outbreak of | a war be- 406
tween the United States and Britain will be prevented by the workers' masses, who will subsequently establish a truly social system of global government, cleansed of the delusions of Bolshevism. In his 'Travelling companions and fellow congress-goers' he describes his talks with H.G. Wells, in Washington and while crossing the Atlantic, and which turned mainly around the future of the Orient. In the same manner in which America left China (supposedly) alone, both as a power and in terms of how it was going to develop internally, in Asia Minor too, the rise of the Arabs must come from within by adopting a modern atitude to technology; England should grant the Egyptians absolute freedom except for the protection of the Suez Canal, in which all nations are stakeholders.

The section 'Syria and Lebanon' is opened by two strongly-worded appeals—one of them signed New York, 10 October 1907—to those coming from the same region as he to waive their parochial interests and desist from counting on the allegedly disinterested help of the French. Instead, they should enter the struggle as volunteers, but with the aim of founding a united Syria. Around that same period, *al-Mirʾāt* magazine brought a *qaṣīda* entitled *Zahra min uqḥuwān*, by Abū Māḍī (chapter 3, 1.6), and an article called 'Syria at the crossroads,' by Zaydān the Younger. Al-Rayḥānī had to speak out against these two because the pessimistic renunciation of the poet was just as dangerous as the political indifference of the scholar; for it would not be enough to reject party politics if the Syrians would not be able at the same time to force themselves into an effective sort of patriotism.

Under the title *al-Taṭawwur wal-istiqlāl* he once more states his political credo: "First of all, I am a Syrian, then Lebanese, and after that, a Maronite. As a Syrian, I subscribe to the national, political and geograpical unity of Syria etc." He calls for a decentralized constitution with complete separation between religion and state. In answer to the partisans of the French in Lebanon, who refer to the supposedly historical tradition of the Crusades and the time of the Mardaites, he rightly points out that, in those days, the problems were religious rather than national. At the end, he lists his demands for the political configuration of Syria once more in 20 points.

The first two volumes of *al-Rayḥāniyyāt* caused quite a sensation in the
407 Muslim world, as may be inferred from | *al-Murājaʿāt al-Rayḥāniyya*, which constitute volumes I and II of *al-Muṭālaʿāt wal-murājaʿāt wal-nuqūd wal-rudūd*, 1331/1913 (vol. I Beirut: al-Maṭbaʿa al-Ahliyya, vol. II Sidon: Maṭbaʿat al-ʿIrfān) by Muḥammad al-Ḥusayn Āl Kāshif al-Ghiṭāʾ al-Najafī (see Suppl. II, 802, 48), which M. Hartmann reports on in *WI* II, 287ff. It might be added that, while Āl Kāshif al-Ghiṭāʾ was mainly interested in al-Rayḥānī's opinion on his own *al-Dīn wal-Islām*, an opinion for which he had asked himself, he also comments on many of al-Rayḥānī's statements on Islam from the *Rayḥāniyyāt*, defending his own book against assertions by Father Anastase al-Karmalī in *Lughat al-ʿArab*. At the end, he reproduces the pieces by al-Rayḥānī that were mentioned on page 403, above. In the second volume he only talks about al-Rayḥānī in the introduction, citing two letters by him from New York, dated 21 September and 19 October 1913, and a critique by al-Khūrī Ilyā al-Ḥamātī (*al-Funūn* [New York], vol. 1, issue 7) of al-Rayḥānī's article on his friend Nāṣir al-Dīn, in each case accompanied by al-Najafī's counter-criticism. The major part of the volume is taken up with a detailed criticism of Jirjī Zaydān's *Taʾrīkh ādāb al-lugha al-ʿarabiyya* and a rebuttal of its attacks on the Shīʿa.[24]

During the war al-Rayḥānī wrote a number of novels. While these provide additional proof of his brilliant eloquence, they were not in keeping with his true talents, as he himself must also have understood later on. The first one of these novels is *Riwāyat khārij al-ḥarīm*, New York: Ṭabʿ Shirkat al-Funūn, 1915, 2nd printing Cairo 1922 (see Pérès 597), Beirut 1923 (*Jāmiʿ* II, 125), published by Dr. Shakhāshīrī, Cairo n.d. (see *MSOS*, 1925, 298/9), 1922 (? Pérès, 597) under the

---

24 A very hateful critique of *al-Rayḥāniyyāt* was published by Cheikho in *al-Mashriq* XXII, 623/9.

title *Jahān*, Beirut: Maṭbaʿat al-Ṣādir, n.d. It is the story of a young Turkish lady, Jahān, the daughter of a pasha, who is filled with enthusiasm for the women's liberation movement, who translates Nietzsche's *Also sprach Zarathustra* into Turkish and who works as a journalist for the realisation of her ideals. As a nurse she meets the German commander, General von Wallenstein, a widower, in an army hospital in Istanbul, and to her he is the incorporation of Nietzsche's "blonde Bestie." They fall in love and the general is even ready to convert to Islam for his beloved. But Jahān's cousin believes he has the right to her hand already. | As such, the general sends the latter from his post in the 408
War Office to the front. But before he has even left, Jahān's brother, the pasha's youngest son, is killed by a bullet from the gun of a German officer wanting to protect his retreating troops against him. On the very same day, the general goes to the father and offers him the Iron Cross for his son; but, having already been informed about the circumstances of his death, the father turns it down. Then the pasha comes under suspicion of being in connivance with the Ittiḥād Party's enemies in Paris and is arrested. After an angry exchange of words with the general, Jahān's nephew wants to assassinate him. In an effort to save both her father and the nephew, Jahān surrenders to the general, only to learn that her father has killed himself and her nephew has been shot. At this point Jahān and her faithful servant flee to Konya, where her father had always wanted to retire with her. This is where she writes her book *A Nation Born* and gives birth to a fair-haired boy as well. This is clearly a love story that was written in support of the Entente. The character of the general is quite unrealistic, while Turkish ladies will have great difficulty in recognising their ideal of a female leader in her.[25]

The novel *Zanbaqat al-ghawr* (New York: Ṭabʿ Shirkat al-Funūn, 1917) was written with much more imagination. It is the history of a village girl who is the unlawful child of a monk. When the latter neglects his duties towards her, another monk takes care of her. Because she is unhappy in the convent, the monk takes her to live with one of his cousins. There, she is seduced and then abandoned by the cousin's son. Then, when she is imprisoned on suspicion of having taken part in the murder of another guest in that same house, her protector comes and secures her release. Together they go and live in a village near Tiberias where they wait for her to give birth. Right after being born, the baby is abducted for reasons that remain unclear. Because their efforts to find the baby remain without success, she accepts the offer of a French lady to come

25 The title page of *Zanbaqat al-ghawr* also mentions a *Kitāb Khālid* (*The book of Khalid*, New York: Dodd, Mead & Co., 1911). According to Kračkovsky it is a kind of psychological novel-poem dedicated to the subject of self-education (*MO* XXI, 203).

409 along with her | to Paris to work there as her son's tutor of Arabic, but omits to tell this to her protector. In Paris, she has an affair with a wealthy Syrian whom she had met while crossing the Mediterranean by boat. When the lady that she worked for wants to send her to Egypt, she sells her boat ticket and tries to fend for herself, seeking her fortune as a dancer. But having no training as a dancer whatsoever, no theatre will hire her. She then sells her last piece of jewelry and goes to Cairo after all. There, the owners of a casino much admire her natural and civilised way of dancing. In this nightclub she then celebrates one triumph after another for an entire season. Among the throngs of admirers there is also the Syrian from Paris but she turns him down, just as she turns down a poet whose *qaṣīda*s she had adapted for dancing. During a trip to Syria, one of the owners of the casino—who had tried to seduce her in vain—finds out her background. In order to rid himself of her, he tells all to the aforementioned poet, who soon informs the press. Assailed by her creditors, she has to leave her beautiful home and take refuge in some miserable neighbourhood. There, she is tracked down by a preacher who had, until then, railed against her dancing from the pulpit, and he brings her old protector to her, who had come down to Cairo looking for her. Now, it turns out that the preacher is none other than the monk who had seduced her mother so many years before and who had changed his name. The two men take care of her, convincing her to relocate to Tiberias because her son, now four years old, has, meanwhile, also resurfaced. His father, who is now a settled man in Haifa, is willing to marry her, and it is not long before her first protector joins them in holy matrimony. But the beginning of tuberculosis does not allow her to come live with her husband. After regaining her health in an institution in the Lebanon, she and her father decide to return to Europe with her son. This novel was written with great imagination; its characters, however, remain vague and unclear. It is, for instance, not clear what motivated her protector, and the same goes for the man who seduced her and who later became her husband. On the other hand, the author gives a humorous description of the goings-on in the Syrian convents and of the life in the house of a high-placed civil servant in Nazareth. His
410 descriptions of life in Paris and | Cairo, on the other hand, are more schematic and apparently based on what he had read in other novels rather than on his own experience. Yet there can be no doubt that the novel has an important place in modern narrative literature and that al-Rayḥānī, had he given himself more time to develop this branch of literature, would surely have advanced it in an important way.[26]

---

26 I. Kračkovsky published selected samples from his writings as an adolescent in *A. R. Izbannije proizwedenije*, St. Petersburg 1917. Muḥammad Saʿīd al-Yūsuf mentions in RAAD 1, 254 also *al-Mukārī wal-kāhin*, *al-Thawra al-Ifransiyya* (see 399 n.), *al-Tasāhul*

While, in the preface to *Mulūk al-ʿArab*, he confesses that in America he had little opportunity to read Arabic literature,[27] towards the end of the war he fell under the spell of Abu ʾl-ʿAlāʾ al-Maʿarrī. This led to his English *A Chant of Mystics and other Poems*, New York 1921 (see Mīkhāʾīl Nuʿayma, *al-Ghirbāl* 161/7: *al-Risāla fī ʿālam al-shiʿr*).

But this, too, was just one phase in a life which, from then on, was dedicated to Arab nationalism. In this context, he wanted to get to know Arabia and King Ḥusayn of the Hijaz, who at the time was still considered to be the rightful incarnation of the people's national aspirations. Having spoken to his old friend Konstantin Yannī, who had started working for al-Ḥusayn, he left New York in early 1922, arriving in Jedda on 25 February. From the Hijaz he went to Yemen and, following the coastline, to Laḥaj. From there he went to pay his respects to King Saʿūd and then, passing through Bahrain, to King Fayṣal in Iraq. With his diplomatic skills, he succeeded in gaining admittance to all the princes of Arabia, collecting invaluable information on the lands that they ruled. All this he wrote down in his two-volume *Mulūk al-ʿArab, riḥla fi ʾl-bilād al-ʿarabiyya tashtamil ʿalā muqaddima wa-thamāniyat aqsām, muzayyana bil-kharāʾiṭ wal-rusūm* (Beirut: al-Maṭbaʿa al-ʿIlmiyya li-Yūsuf Ṣādir, 1929, 2nd printing). It is an extremely fascinating work, written in a style that is perhaps even more careless in its use of Europeanisms than *al-Rayḥāniyyāt* had been. | The material that he collected on this trip he then used in a further 411
three works in English, skilfully adapted to the Anglo-Saxon taste, with many new observations, but often copying whole passages literally from the earlier Arabic work. This led to the following texts: *Maker of Modern Arabia* (Boston 1928), *Ibn Saʿoud of Arabia, his People and his Land* (London 1928), *Around the Coasts of Arabia* (London 1930), *Arabian Peak and Desert, Travels in al-Yaman* (London 1930).

From then on, he believed he could best serve his patriotic ideals by working as an historian. Muḥammad Kurd ʿAlī's detailed history of Syria, *Khiṭaṭ al-Shaʾm*, provided him with an opportunity to summarise his own views on the history of his country. He gave it the significant title *al-Nakabāt aw khulāṣat taʾrīkh Sūriyya mundhu ʾl-ʿahd al-awwal baʿda ʾl-ṭūfān ilā ʿahd al-jumhūriyya bi-Lubnān* (Beirut: al-Maṭbaʿa al-ʿIlmiyya li-Yūsuf Ṣādir, 1928). But he does not spend much time on the history of early antiquity in Syria. Usually, he links passages from the Bible to the findings of modern science in a rather arbitrary manner, leading, on the whole, to a distorted image. It is not before the Roman-Hellenic period that his account comes to life; but still, it lacks the elements

---

al-dīnī and the the English *Allouzoumiat, The Quatrains of Abu el-ula, The Path of Vision, Ali ibn abi Taleb, The descent of Bolshevism.*

27 He lists the books that he had read in his youth in *al-Hilāl* xxxv, 399.

that could have thrown light on Syria's cultural position in the general context of its time. It is only when he gets to the Arab conquest that history really has his interest. Lammens (*al-Mashriq* XXI, 621/6) is right to criticise al-Rayḥānī's negative judgement of the Umayyads, the more so since the Syrians of the time, including the Christians, were all of the opinion that they had made the country prosper in many respects. The Ḥamdānids, too, he judges extremely harshly, but perhaps that was just to counterbalance the current view, which overestimates the importance of their patronage. While one can accept his moderate picture of the sufferings of the country under the Turks and the Mongols, his image of the Ottoman period is surely much too negative; the only thing that he can talk about are the excesses of this or that local governor. He quickly passes over modern history with some conventional phrases, contenting himself with a reference to the "blessings" of the colonisation by France, *al-umm al-ḥanūn*. Instead of all this, he could have rendered real service to future historians by exploiting his own intimate knowledge of the situ-
412 ation in the country | to describe it in greater detail (see Muḥammad Kurd ʿAlī, *RAAD* VIII, 442/3).

All the more meritorious is his *Taʾrīkh Najd al-ḥadīth wa-mulḥaqātihi wa-huwa yashtamil ʿalā nubdhāt thalāth fī nawāḥī Najd wa-Muḥammad b. ʿAbd al-Wahhāb wal-Wahhābiyya wa-āl Saʿūd mundhu nashʾatihim ilā ḥīni ʾstīlāʾ Muḥammad b. al-Rashīd ʿalā Najd wa-sīrat ʿAbd al-ʿAzīz b. ʿAbd al-Raḥmān Fayṣal āl Saʿūd malik al-Ḥijāz wa-Najd wa-mulḥaqātihimā* (Beirut: al-Maṭbaʿa al-ʿIlmiyya li-Yūsuf Ṣādir, 1928). After his first trip, Amīn al-Rayḥānī went to Arabia for a second time in 1925, witnessing the conquest of the Hijaz while in Jedda. Once again he was given full admission to the king, who told him many things from his personal life while granting him access to key documents. For the earlier period his sources were ʿUthmān b. ʿAbdallāh b. Bishr's *ʿUnwān al-majd*[28] (see Suppl. II, 531), Ḥusayn b. Ghannām al-Ḥanbalī's (d. 1225/1810, see Suppl. II, 532, 5) *Rawḍat al-afkār* in an Indian edition, and the handwritten history of the Ḥanbalīs of Shaykh Ibrāhīm b. Ṣāliḥ b. ʿĪsā in Ushayqir. He has done well to draw an exciting picture of the most important period in the history of Arabia since the Prophet's passing, even in his description of the smallest tribal feuds. He tries to do justice even to his hero's enemies, although he makes no real effort to try and understand what motivated the policies of the Young Turks. And his description of the unfortunate King Ḥusayn is not fair either, explaining his fiscal policies as motivated by personal greed while, actually, they were meant to finance his high political ambitions. Earlier, in his English works, he had made no secret of his admiration for the person who has

28 Which he mistakenly cites as the *ʿUluww al-majd* in I, 4.

shaped modern Arabia. In this Arabic work, it now finds its fullest expression without ever degenerating into the panegyrical representations of the past. The book is especially valuable because it cites many personal observations by the ruler, whose eloquence as a true Arab was recorded in writing as he spoke; also, there are the many documents that are cited in the text and in the Appendix. | Needless to say, this work is a valuable source for the topography 413
and ethnography of Arabia. The theme being truly Arab, the author being also much more at home in the phraseology of genuine Arabic than in his younger years, Europeanisms only rarely sneak in.[29]

His *Fayṣal al-awwal* (Beirut: Maṭbaʿat Ṣādir, 1934) is of the same quality. The book is based on his personal acquaintance with the former ruler and in the first chapters he tries to give a rigidly objective appreciation of the founder of modern Iraq. His description of the conspiracies of the powers of the Entente is of uncompromising frankness; disappointing the son of Ḥusayn—who had nonetheless contributed in several ways to their victory—first heavily in Syria, Britain then saw in him the ideal instrument to implement its imperialist designs for Iraq. The book is not written in the dry style of a chronicle, but seasoned throughout with well-executed descriptions of the leading figures, both on the Arab and on the British side. In this he truly follows the example of Gertrude Bell, whose fervent patriotism and genuine love for the Arabs served the interests of both sides.

On page 88, he gives a brilliant description of Britain's situation after the war, some amusing gossip included. His description of the king, whose doings and character (*manāqib*) are treated in separate chapters, is one of a sweet old *sayyid* who does not owe his success to some kind of misplaced recklessness, but rather to his *ḥilm*, which eventually also won him the hearts of his adversaries. In order to put Fayṣal's achievements in their proper context, the last chapter recounts an imaginary meeting between him and Hārūn al-Rashīd at an exhibition in Baghdad, during which the caliph cannot help but express his fullest appreciation for his successor. The book terminates with a letter to the ruler in the Hereafter and a hymn in free verse on him, titled *al-Naṣr al-ʿArabī*; this hymn was read at the *arbaʿīn* ceremonies in commemoration of him in Jerusalem and Damascus and published for the first time in *al-Muqtaṭaf* 87, 380ff. | On pages 83 bottom and 143 n. he promises 414
a supplementary volume on Iraq and its inhabitants, which thus far remains unpublished.

29 Like *fa-ghadā kullu wāḥidin min zuʿamāʾihi ʿAbda Ḥamīdin rahīban*, "… and thus each of his companions turned into a terrible ʿAbd al-Ḥamīd," 165, 5.

In his *al-Taṭarruf wal-iṣlāḥ* (Beirut 1929) he develops some general ideas on politics and the party system. In his *Antumu 'l-shu'arā'* (Beirut 1933; 92 pp.) he gives his opinion on the purpose of poetry in modern Arab life, taking issue with the lachrymose sentimentality that still dominates so much of it. In a joint answer, entitled *Ajal naḥnu 'l-shuʿarāʾ* (Beirut 1933; see *al-Mashriq* XXXI, 937/40), Aḥmad Aḥmad Muʿawwaḍ, Ṭanyūs Niʿma and Samīr Muʿawwaḍ opposed al-Rayḥānī's views.

From the many articles that he wrote for magazines etc., we can only mention the most important ones, such as *Baʿḍ umarāʾ al-ʿArab* in *al-Hilāl* 35, 1926, 73/7, *Fatḥ al-Ḥasā* ibid. 178/82, *al-Saʿāda wa-arkānuha 'l -arbaʿa* ibid. 36, 57/60 and in *Aḥsan mā katabtu*, 117/9, *Kayfa taṣluḥ al-umma* in *al-Muqtaṭaf* 72, 1928, 266/72, 432/7, *Fī rabīʿ al-ya's* ibid. 84, 66/5, *al-Shudhūdh fi 'l-mīzān al-shamsī* ibid. 89, 1936, 145/7, *Mā huwa 'l-dhawq, al-Ḥadīth*, 1933, 642ff, *al-Zaʿfarān wa-shaqāʾiq al-Nuʿmān*, ibid., 1936, 5/10.

Tawfīq al-Rāfiq, *Amīn al-Rayḥānī nāshir falsafat al-sharq fī bilād al-gharb*, Cairo n.d.; idem, *Mukhtārāt al-Rayḥānī* (a biography which also contains the speeches held in his honour at a ceremony in Cairo as well as samples from his works), Cairo 1922. Rafāʾīl Buṭṭī, *Amīn al-Rayḥānī fi 'l-ʿIrāq*, Baghdad 1923, Isʿāf al-Nashāshībī, *al-Lugha al-ʿarabiyya wal-ustādh al-Rayḥānī*, Cairo 1928; Kračkovsky *MO* XXI, 201/6.

8 Female Authors

Of the women of Syria and the Lebanon too, the intellectually most active ones went to work in Egypt, like Zaynab Fawwāz and Mayy. So, here, we mention the few female authors who remained at home.

a. *Maryam Naḥḥās Nawfal bint Jabrāʾīl Naṣrallāh Naḥḥās* was born on 6 January 1856 in Beirut, married Nasīm Nawfal on 14 November 1872, and died in April 1888 while travelling to Naples. She wrote *Maʿraḍ al-ḥasnāʾ fī tarājim shahīrāt al-nisāʾ* (see p. 176). Begun in 1873, it was printed at the expense of one of the wives of Khedive Ismāʿīl in 1879. See *Fatāt al-sharq* II, 81/2.

415 b. *Hannā Kasbānī Kūrānī* was born on 1 February 1870 in Kfarshīmā, | in the Lebanon. She was a teacher at the American school for girls in Tripoli. Early in 1892, she left for America to participate in a conference of the Syrian women's organisations in Chicago. She remained in America for three years, after which she returned to her native country, suffering from tuberculosis. She died on 6 May 1898 in Kfarshīmā. She wrote several novels, such as *Zuqāq al-miqlāt, Fāris wa-ḥimāruhu, Risāla fī 'l-akhlāq wal-ʿādāt, al-Ḥaṭṭāb wa-kalbuhu Bārūd*, see Jirjī Niqula Bāz in *Fatāt al-sharq* II, 362/6.

c. *Labība bint Mīkhāʾīl b. Jirjis Ṣuwāyā* was born in Tripoli in 1876 and died during the war in Homs. She published an historical novel on the Turkish revolution entitled *Ḥasnāʾ Salānīk* (Beirut n.d.) (ʿAbdallāh Ḥabīb Nawfal, *Tarājim ʿulamāʾ Ṭarābulus* 1929, 232/4).

d. *Farīda ʿAṭiyya* used the downfall of ʿAbd al-Ḥamīd to write her historical novel *Bayna ʾl-ʿarshayn* (Ṭarābulus al-Shām 1912).

e. In Damascus, *Mārī ʿAjamī* founded the *Majallat al-ʿArūs* magazine; on the occasion of her silver jubilee Jirjī Niqula Bāz (see p. 386) wrote her biography, entitled *Mārī ʿAjamī* (Beirut: Maṭbaʿat Ṣādir, n.d.). Bāz also collected the works of Salmā Ṣāʾigh (see Khayrallah, *La Syrie* 112/3, Kračkovsky, MSOS 1928, 197) in *Nasamāt Salmā Ṣāʾigh* (Beirut 1923).

f. *Alice Abkāryūs* wrote a manual for the girlscout unions, which was translated by Jabrāʾīl Jabbūr as *al-Murshidāt* (Beirut 1925) (see *al-Jāmiʿ* I, 589, RAAD V, 343/4).

g. *Naẓīra Zayn al-Dīn* stood up for the liberation of women in her *al-Sufūr wal-ḥijāb* (Beirut 1928) (see RAAD VIII, 501/8) and in *al-Fatāt wal-shuyūkh, naẓarāt fi ʾl-sufūr* (Beirut 1929).

h. In *al-Khaṭarāt* (n.p., n.d.) (1931), *Wadād al-Sakākīnī* published a series of texts on literature, modern culture, the issue of women's rights, etc. (see RAAD XII, 382). Many of her pieces were also published in *al-Ḥadīth* in Aleppo.

3 *Drama*

Even though Syria was the first country in which modern Arab theatre made its appearance, it was seen earlier that it was only in Egypt that it really developed into an independent artform. Even though the Jesuit university in Beirut offered the possibility of staging drama as part of the curriculum, | as do Jesuit 416
schools in Europe, this did not result in the kind of drama that could survive on its own. And in other cities there were even fewer possibilities. As such, people with a talent for acting were forced to try their luck abroad. So, all we can do is mention a series of plays that were printed in bookform and published in Syria in the last few decades.

Cf. F.E. Bustānī, *al-Mashriq* XXV, 623ff.

1. An example of a Jesuit play for students, of which several were also published in *al-Mashriq*, is *Anṭūn Rabbāṭ al-Yasūʿī*'s *al-Rashīd wal-Barāmika*, Beirut 1910 (see Bustānī, loc. cit.).

2. *Mīshal al-Ḥāʾik* had tried to resuscitate the popular novel with his *Ḥasnāʾ al-Ḥijāz, ḥawādithuhā wa-aḥwāl al-ʿArab qabla ʾl-Islām*, in 18 *juzʾ* (Beirut n.d.). His *Baṭal Lubnān, Yaḥyā Bek Karam, riwāya tamthīliyya dhāt khamsat fuṣūl* (Beirut 1922) is the first patriotic play.

3. *Al-Khūrī Yūḥannā Ṭūbī Ṭannūs* dramatised myths from pre-Islamic times in his *al-Nuʿmān malik al-Ḥīra fī Banī Shaybān, riwāya dhāt arbaʿat fuṣūl*, Beirut 1924 (*al-Jāmiʿ* I, 1166; see *al-Mashriq* XXXIII, 315), *al-ʿAmrāni, Dāḥis wal-Ghabrāʾ*, and *Kulayb wal-Muhalhil*.

4. In *Lawla ʾl-muḥāmī, riwāya tamthīliyya*, Beirut 1924 (see *al-Mashriq* XXXIII, 236), *Saʿīd Efendi Taqī al-Dīn* used a subject from the history of the [First] World War.

5. In *Fatāt al-Nāṣira, riwāya tamthīliyya fī arbaʿat fuṣūl*, Beirut 1925 (see *Jāmiʿ* I, 1147, *al-Mashriq* XXXIII, 55), *al-Khūrī Būlus al-Bustānī* turned the story of the birth of Jesus up the death of Herod into a play. ʿAbdallāh al-Bustānī, a teacher of Arabic at the patriarchal school in Beirut (Sarkīs 560), adapted Shakespeare's *Julius Caesar* in verse as *Maqtal Herodes li-waladayhi* and an episode from the history of England in *Riwāyat al-wardatayn*.

6. Having written a brief *Taʾrīkh Ḥayfāʾ*, Haifa n.d. (1922, cf. *Jāmiʿ* I, 51 Muhammad Kurd ʿAlī in *RAAD* II, 136/8), and after translating a work on the Bahai (*ʿAbd
417 al-Bahāʾ wal-diyāna al-Bahāʾiyya*, Haifa 1921, | *Jāmiʿ* I, 281), the bookseller and publisher of the *Majallat al-Zahrāʾ Jamīl al-Baḥrī* (see p. 387) of Haifa tried to introduce the theatre into his city. He wrote, among other things, *al-Khāʾin, maʾsāh adabiyya tamthīliyya fī thalāthat fūṣūl*, Haifa n.d. (*Jāmiʿ* I, 1118), *al-Waṭan al-maḥbūb*, Cairo 1923, *Qātil akhīhi*, Cairo 1923, *Fī sabīl al-sharaf, maʾsāh dhāt khamsat fuṣūl*, Haifa 1926 (said to be the eighth of his plays; see *al-Mashriq* XXIV, 714), *Sajīn al-qaṣr, qātil akhīhi*, Haifa 1927. He returned to historiography once more with his biography of the metropolitan of Acre, Haifa, Nazareth and Galilee, *Ghrīghūryūs al-Ḥajjār*, Haifa 1927 (*Jāmiʿ* II, 69).

7. *Asmā al-Ṭūbī* describes the downfall of the Tsar and his family in her play *Riwāyat maṣraʿ qayṣar Rūsiyya wa-ʿāʾilatihi, maʾsāh taʾrīkhiyya adabiyya dhāt khamsat fuṣūl*, Acre: al-Maṭbaʿa al-Waṭaniyya, 1925 (*Jāmiʿ* II, 216).

8. In his play *al-ʿAfw ʿinda ʾl-maqdara aw al-Maʾmūn wa-ʿammuhu Ibrāhīm b. al-Mahdī, riwāya tamthīliyya dhāt arbaʿat fuṣūl* (Dayr al-Mukhalliṣ, 1928), *al-Khūrī Niqūlā Ḥannā*, a monk and teacher of Arabic at Dayr al-Mukhalliṣ, recounts an episode from the history of the ʿAbbāsids.

9. While Syrian and Lebanese playwrights had thus far limited themselves to concrete historical themes, *Wadīʿ Abū Fāḍil*, who had published a *Dalīl Lubnān* in 1909 (Sarkīs 1911) and a novel in 1927 (*Riwāyat al-mutawālī al-ṣāliḥ, qiṣṣa adabiyya taʾrīkhiyya*, Cairo n.d., *Jāmiʿ* II, 215), undertook to express the patriotic ambitions of his compatriots in a mythologico-symbolic play entitled *Riwāyat Tammūz wa-Baʿla, riwāya shiʿriyya tamthīliyya waṭaniyya* (Cairo: Maṭbaʿat Wadīʿ Abī Fāḍil, n.d. [1937]). In the same way in which Egyptians today delight in their country's great cultural heritage from antiquity, Wadīʿ's compatriots often consoled themselves for their present hardships with the long-gone glory of Phoenicia, even drawing hope from it for the future, living as they did in the same geographical area and claiming its inhabitants as their ancestors. As such, Wadīʿ used the Tammūz legend, although he changed it completely. In his representation of the legend, Tammūz is the king of Byblos (Jubayl), with whom his childhood playmate Baʿla, the daughter of the former king of Sidon, is in love. Even if their love is reciprocal, Tammūz generously gives her up because her cousin Baʿlūn, | current ruler of Sidon, was already courting her. But 418
the latter, distrusting this generosity, tells one of the notables of the city, when Tammūz goes hunting, to make sure that a wild boar cross his path. But, while the rumour is spreading that Tammūz was killed by the animal and Baʿlūn believes he has attained his goal, it turns out that, in fact, it was Tammūz who had killed the boar. After a brief outburst of despair, Baʿlūn makes a complete turnaround and generously decides to give up Baʿla to Tammūz. At the same time, he also bestows the rulership of Sidon upon him, thereby bringing about the unification of the country, which people had long been hoping for. This verse-play in changing metres, poor in dramatic force, seems to be too abstract to be able to arouse the kind of patriotic feelings among the audience that its author must have hoped for, if ever it was put on stage.

10. Even more abstract is the latest Syrian play to have come to my notice, which is *Aḥmad Maky*'s[30] *Laylat al-qadr* (Beirut: Manshūrāt al-Makshūf, 1937). Even if the book were not dedicated to a lady in Montpellier, where he must have done his studies, it is impossible not to notice the influence of French symbolism. Apart from the play mentioned in the title, the book contains two further symbolic plays, *al-ʿĀṣifa* and *al-Sarāb*. The first carries a motto from the Qurʾān, the other two from the Gospel of Luke and from the Psalms. The hero of the first piece, an ascetic (*nāsik*), falls, after a prolonged struggle, for the charms of the spectre of a young girl who romances him upon the instruction of three houris who have accompanied her down to earth. When he finally declares his love to her she disappears, "… just like the truth escapes the scientist at the moment

30 This is how he transliterates his name himself.

when he thinks he has grasped it …" 'The storm' kills a pair of lovers hiding in a cave from their pursuers. Before they die, they go through all imaginable stages of hope and despair which, for the author, are stages in their religious development. In *Sarāb*, a mirage lures a desert caravan into believing that a freshwater stream is awaiting them in the distance, an event that is witnessed by two wayfarers who accompany the scene with their songs. People leave the caravan in
419 small groups, trying to reach their destination on their own; | a father with his children, a mother with her little baby, a pair of lovers, a knight and an injured man with whose blood he quenches his thirst, and three men, two of whom lose their way quarreling over nothing while the third one follows them blindly. When the caravan believes it has reached its destination, an old man tells them that the stream has dried up long ago, like happiness, which man is always striving for in vain. It is, of course, a platitude with which the young poet lets the choir conclude the penultimate scene that takes place between the three men: "1. Do they always get lost like this?[31]—2. By God! If I could, I would grab their tongues and tear them out![32]—1. The painful thing is that they are followed by a third man who takes no step without them. By God, that's terrible!—2. But there are many like him; it's always the blind followers who pay the price.—1. My God, why do people not let themselves be guided by their own insight, instead of waiting for others to tell them what to do?—2. God has given man plenty of faculties, but many are all too willing to give up their rights to others, much to their disadvantage.—1. Do you mean to say that man should address himself directly to God for help, without intermediary?—2. Is that not better, when the intermediaries are like these two idiots?—1. I don't know; let's move on." It seems that the author never thought of his plays' being brought to stage. Their rude symbolism is mitigated somewhat by their cultivated language and fascinating dialogues. Their natural rhythm is also present in the single lyrical piece that he wrote, a herdsman's song, which needs no metre. I was unable to establish whether the collection of tales *al-Armala al-majnūna* announced on the cover has been published or not.

11. a. A young author writing under the pseudonym *al-Muqannaʿ* participated in the contest for a play symbolising the Syrian nation with a short play called *Abu 'l-ʿAlāʾ al-Maʿarrī, masraḥiyya fī faṣlayn*; *al-Ḥadīth* XI, 1931, 678/693. b. Yūsuf Saʿāda's play *Ibnat al-arz* is only known to me from an announcement in Beirut's *al-Makshūf*.

---

31 Correcting *yuẓillāni* to *yaḍillāni*.

32 Read: *wa-antaziʿuhā*.

| 4 *Historiography (general), Literary Criticism, and Local History* 420

(*1.–13.*) *Historiography*

Owing to the fact that, until recently, Syria had no history of its own, there was no patriotic feeling that could have motivated the writing of history. Humiliated in their self-pride by constant occupation, the intellectuals sought refuge in those few historical moments whose memory could alleviate their emotional distress. This is why, in the nineteenth century, a rather widespread historiographical interest developed among both Muslims and Christians, in the Lebanon in particular, with people writing mostly about local history, while, as far as the Muslims were concerned, these writings still copied the time-proven scheme of the history of cities through recording the lives of their most prominent inhabitants. The most important representatives of these groups will now be briefly mentioned.

1 Yūsuf Dibs

The metropolitan Yūsuf Dibs was born in Kafar Zaynā near Tripoli in 1833. He was ordained a priest in 1872 and later made bishop of Beirut. In this latter capacity he not only gave the Maronites a new great church in the image of the Maria Maggiore in Rome but also created a new educational centre in the form of the Madrasat al-ḥikma, inaugurated in 1875. As well as a series of theological works, he also wrote a detailed *Taʾrīkh Sūriyya*, from the time of Creation until his own days (8 vols, Beirut: Maṭbaʿat al-ʿUmūmiyya, 1893/1902). A summary of it, *al-Mūjiz fī Taʾrīkh Sūriyya*, was published in two volumes, ibid. 1907. His *al-Jāmiʿ al-mufaṣṣal fī taʾrīkh al-Mawārina al-muʾaṣṣal* (Beirut 1907) is dedicated to the history of his own sect. He passed away on 4 October 1907. See Cheikho, *al-Mashriq* XXIII, 72, *Fatāt al-sharq* II, 142/5, Sarkīs 864.

2 Jirjī Yannī al-Ṭarābulusī

The founder of the *Majallat al-mabāḥith* of Tripoli, Jirjī Yannī al-Ṭarābulusī, made his debut as a writer with a history of Syria that was actually a series of local histories, entitled *Taʾrīkh Sūriyya* (up to 1878) (Beirut: Maṭbaʿat al-Adabiyya, 1881). In the following years, | he introduced his compatriots, 421
through translations, to the latest findings of European scholarship in the field of cultural history. The first work of his choice was an English book by B.L. Symonds, which he translated as *ʿAjāʾib al-baḥr wa-maḥāṣiluhu ʾl-tijāriyya* (Beirut: Maṭbaʿat al-Amirīkān, 1891). In 1909, he translated Seignobos' *Histoire de la civilisation moderne* as *Taʾrīkh al-tamaddun al-ḥadīth* (Maṭbaʿat al-Hilāl). His history of the Franco-German war, initially published in *Majallat al-Jinān*,

was published in one volume, entitled *Taʾrīkh ḥarb Firansā wa-Almānyā* (Cairo 1911), by Yūsuf Efendi Tūmā al-Bustānī (Sarkīs, 1954).

3 Ṣādiq Pāshā al-ʿAẓm

The memoirs of Ṣādiq Pāshā al-ʿAẓm find their inspiration in the happenings of an eventful military and diplomatic career. Born into a distinguished family (see above p. 386) in Damascus, he first studied with the Jesuits in Beirut, but then opted for a military career. When he was an officer of the general staff in Sofia, he was made a special envoy to Menelik of Abyssinia. He wrote an account of this mission in Turkish, which his cousin Jamīl Bek al-ʿAẓm (see 14.e below) translated into Arabic. Together with his cousin Rafīq Bek al-ʿAẓm (see p. 388), he founded *Jarīdat al-Shūrā al-ʿUthmāniyya* in Istanbul. When this newspaper was banned from publication not long after, he had to flee to Egypt, where he started teaching at al-Madrasa al-Tawfīqiyya. After the victory of the movement of the Young Turks he could return to Istanbul, dying there on 12 October 1910. In *al-Mashriq* XXIV, 291/2, Cheikho also mentions a study on warfare entitled *Taʾrīkh difāʿ Plewna.*

4 Rashīd Duʿbūl al-Baʿabdawī, Ṣāliḥ al-Madhūn al-Yāfī and Adīb Efendi Luḥūd

Two brief histories of the Ottoman Empire were published before the [First] World War, *Mūjiz taʾrīkh al-salāṭīn al-ʿUthmāniyyīn* by Rashīd Duʿbūl al-Baʿabdawī (Cairo 1912)[33] and *Mulakhkhaṣ al-taʾrīkh al-ʿUthmānī* by Ṣāliḥ al-Madhūn al-Yāfī (Damascus 1333), as well as a history of the Arabs by Adīb Efendi Luḥūd, titled *Nayl al-arab fī taʾrīkh al-ʿArab* (ʿAmshiyya, Lebanon 1914).

5 Aḥmad b. Ibrāhīm al-Ṣābūnī and Aḥmad ʿĀrif al-Zayn

To this same period belong two local histories, one of Hama, *Taʾrīkh Ḥamāt* (Hama 1322) by Aḥmad b. Ibrāhīm al-Ṣābūnī, who later (1928) published the political study *al-Dawla al-Islāmiyya aw māḍī al-sharq wa-ḥāḍiruhu*, and the other of Sidon, by the Shīʿite Aḥmad ʿĀrif al-Zayn, publisher of the *dīwān* of
422 Ibn Ṭabāṭabā | and of the *Wasāṭa* of al-Jurjānī, entitled *Taʾrīkh Ṣaydāʾ, yaḥtawī taʾrīkhahā wa-sāʾir shuʾūnihā mundhu ʿumrānihā ila ʾl-waqt al-ḥāḍir* (Sidon 1913).

6 Rūḥī Bek al-Khālidī

Rūḥī Bek al-Khālidī wrote a history of the Oriental question. Born into this famous Jerusalem family in 1864, he studied there and in Beirut, Istanbul and Paris. He acted as the Turkish consul to Bordeaux, was elected a member of the

33 Listed in Sarkīs, 400 as bound in one volume, together with the work of a Syro-American, probably just by accident.

Turkish parliament for Jerusalem in 1908, and died on 20 June 1913 in Istanbul. He published *al-Muqaddima fī 'l-mas'ala al-sharqiyya mundhu nash'atihā ila 'l-waqt al-ḥāḍir* in Jerusalem in 1917 (Maṭbaʿat Madrasat al-aytām al-Islāmiyya) (see Cheikho, *al-Mashriq* XXIV, 292). In Bordeaux (n.d.) he published *ʿIlm al-adab ʿinda 'l-Firanj wal-ʿArab*. His *Ta'rīkh al-inqilāb al-ʿUthmānī, al-ʿĀlam al-Islāmī* and *Riḥla ila 'l-Andalus* were never published.

7 ʿAbd al-Razzāq Bayṭār

ʿAbd al-Razzāq Bayṭār (b. 1837, d. early 1918 in Damascus) wrote a history of the nineteenth century titled *Ḥilyat al-bashar fī ta'rīkh al-qarn al-tāsiʿ ʿashar* (see Cheikho, *al-Mashriq* XXIV, 295).

8 Ḥusayn Kāẓim Bek and Umayl al-Ḥabashī

During the [First] World War, Ḥusayn Kāẓim Bek was commissioned by the Turkish authorities to compile a description and history of the Lebanon, a task that he carried out with a team of people including Anṭūn al-Ṣāliḥānī, L. Cheikho, Salīm Efendi al-Aṣfar, and Ibrāhīm Bek al-Aswad, among others. Issued as *Ta'rīkh Lubnān, mabāḥith ʿilmiyya wajtimāʿiyya, al-sana al-ūlā* (Beirut 1918), its publication was stopped when the empire dissolved (see ʿĪsā Iskandar Maʿlūf, *RAAD* III, 28/30). Umayl Efendi Yūsuf al-Ḥabashī wrote a history of the Lebanon during the war,[34] entitled *Jihād Lubnān wajtihāduhu*, Beirut 1920 (*Jāmiʿ* II, 37).

9 Memoirs of the Druze Revolt: Muḥammad Saʿīd al-ʿĀṣ and Others

The suffering of Syria during the uprising of the Druzes and the battles that followed it were described in three works (see Kampffmeyer, *MSOS*, 1931, II, 165/9) by one of its heroes, the commander of the northern front Muḥammad Saʿīd al-ʿĀṣ (b. 1899/90): *Ṣafḥa min al-ayyām al-ḥamrā', istishhād al-amīr ʿIzz al-Dīn wal-maʿārik al-ākhira* (n.d., n.p., 131 pp.), *Ṣafḥa min al-ayyām al-ḥamrā'* 1925/7 (*Kitāb yabḥath ʿani 'l-thawra al-Sūriyya wa-taṭawwurātihā*, 1929) (ʿAmmān, al-Maṭbaʿa al-Waṭaniyya, n.d., 184 pp.), and *Ṣafḥa min al-ayyām al-ḥamrā'* 1925/7, | April 1930 (n.d., n.p., 209 pp.). It seems that they have their basis in the entries 423
of a type of journal that was, however, never systematised so that many questions, especially of chronology, remain unanswered. This is compensated by the first-hand, lively depiction of events, which are often elucidated by vivid descriptions of the locations where they took place; the author does this in a type of prose that is sometimes plainly poetic, even if he did not spend much time on the narrative's form. Abu 'l-Faḍl al-Walīd recorded his memories of

---

34 An Arabic translation of the memoirs of Jamāl Pāshā by ʿAlī Aḥmad Shukrī, entitled *Mudhakkirāt Jamāl Pāshā*, was published in Cairo in 1923 (cf. *RAAD* III, 285).

these days in his *Aḥādīth al-majd wal-wajd*, Qurnat al-Ḥamrāʾ, al-Matn, 1929 (see RAAD IX, 447). Other accounts are given in Sūrī Kātib's *Thawrat al-Durūz wa-ḥawādith Sūriyya* (Cairo 1925) and in Ḥannā Abū Rashīd's (publisher of *Majallat al-Qāmūs al-ʿāmm* in Beirut) *Jabal al-Durūz* (Cairo 1925) (*Jāmiʿ* I, 8).

10 Taysīr Ẓabyān et al.

Due to the [First] World War, there was also a renewed interest in universal history in Syria, satisfied by works such as *Zubdat al-taʾrīkh al-ʿāmm* I (1922), by Taysīr Ẓabyān, teacher at the madrasas of Transjordan (*Jāmiʿ* I, 137), and *Mukhtaṣar al-taʾrīkh al-ʿāmm* by Muḥammad Efendi ʿĀrif al-Tawʾam (Damascus 1929) (*Jāmiʿ* II, 83). Limited to the history of Islam were ʿAbd al-Bāsiṭ al-Fakhūrī's *Tuḥfat al-anām, Mukhtaṣar taʾrīkh al-Islām* (Beirut 1920), Rizqallāh Maqaryus al-Ṣidqī's (secretary of a trading house) *Taʾrīkh duwal al-Islām* (Maṭbaʿat al-Hilāl, 1343, 1923) (*Jāmiʿ* I, 52), and ʿAbd al-Ḥaqq Manṣūr's *Mabādiʾ al-Islām* (Beirut 1349/1930).[35]

11 Amīn Khalīfa et al.

Amīn Khalīfa wrote a history of pre-Islamic Syria, *Taʾrīkh Sūriyya qabl al-fatḥ al-Islāmī* (Beirut 1930) (RAAD XI, 120); Jūrj Marʿī Ḥaddād wrote a history of the Arab conquest of Syria, *Fatḥ al-ʿArab al-Shaʾm* (Beirut 1933) (RAAD XI, 767); Mīkhāʾīl Barīk al-Khūrī wrote a general history of Syria, *Taʾrīkh al-Shaʾm* (Harissa 1930); al-Amīr ʿAlī ʿAbd al-ʿAzīz al-Ḥasanī wrote an economic history, *Taʾrīkh Sūriyya al-iqtiṣādī* (Damascus 1342/1923) (*Jāmiʿ* I, 268). Isḥāq Armala
424 al-Suryānī al-Qudsī described the Crusades in *al-Ḥurūb al-Ṣalībiyya* | *fī ʾl-āthār al-Suryāniyya* (Beirut 1929). Other works by him are mentioned in *Jāmiʿ* I, 298, II, 77. Al-Khūrī Būlus wrote a counterpart to his work on the Syrians and the Arabs mentioned earlier (p. 336, n. 1), entitled *al-Sūriyyūn fī Miṣr*, I, *ʿAhd al-Mamālīk* (Cairo 1928) (cf. also Muḥammad Kurd ʿAlī, *al-Hijra ilā Miṣr* in *al-Qadīm wal-ḥadīth* 251/7). Sulaymān Abū ʿIzz al-Dīn deals with an episode from modern history in his *Ibrāhīm Bāshā fī Sūriyya* (Beirut 1929). An inventory of sources for the history of Syria under Muḥammad ʿAlī was prepared by Dr. Asad Rustum, teacher of history at the American University of Beirut, entitled *al-Uṣūl al-ʿarabiyya li-taʾrīkh Sūriyya fī ʿahd Muḥammad ʿAlī Bāshā*, I (*al-Awrāq al-siyāsiyya li-sanat* 1247 AH) (Beirut: al-Maṭbaʿa al-Amīrkiyya [see RAAD X, 185]); before then, he had published an anonymous work of history, entitled

---

35 The theory—introduced in Europe by H. Grimme—according to which Muḥammad was a social reformer in his early days, was taken up again by Professor al-Sayyid Bendelī Jawzī of Baku, who tried to work it out along Marxist lines in his *Min taʾrīkh al-ḥarakāt al-fikriyya fī ʾl-Islām* I, *al-Ḥaraka al-ijtimāʿiyya* (Jerusalem: Maṭbaʿat Bayt al-Maqdis, 1928) (cf. RAAD IX, 125).

Ibrāhīm Bāshā al-Miṣrī ḥurūbuhu fī Sūriyyā wal-Anaḍūl (Cairo: al-Maṭbaʿa al-Sūriyya, n.d. [1927]).

12 Anīs Zakariyyāʾ al-Naṣūlī

Having learned the methods of European historiography while a student at the American University of Beirut, Anīs Zakariyyāʾ al-Naṣūlī applied them in his work on Umayyad history, *Muʿāwiya b. Sufyān*, Beirut: Maṭbaʿat Ṭabbāra, 1924 (*Jāmiʿ* I, 228). After his appointment as a teacher of history at the École Normale of Baghdad he published *al-Dawla al-Umawiyya fī Qurṭuba*, Baghdad 1925 (see Muḥammad Kurd ʿAlī in *RAAD* VI, 236/9) and *al-Dawla al-Umawiyya fī 'l-Shaʾm*, Baghdad 1926 (see Salīm ʿAnḥūrī in *RAAD* VII, 554/7). His glorification of the Umayyads triggered the jealousy of local scholars who succeeded in organising a mass demonstration against him, meaning the government saw no other option than to fire him (see *Or. Mod.* XIII, 596/604). He then returned to his homeland where he dedicated himself to modern history, publishing *al-Nahḍa al-ʿArabiyya fī 'l-qarn al-tāsiʿ ʿashar*, n.d. & n.p. (*Jāmiʿ* I, 256) and *Asbāb al-nahḍa al-ʿArabiyya fī 'l-qarn al-tāsiʿ ʿashar*, Beirut, Maṭbaʿat Ṭabbāra (see *Jāmiʿ* I, 295, Cheikho, *al-Mashriq* XXIV, 794, Muḥammad Kurd ʿAlī in *RAAD* VI, 381/2).

13 Muḥammad Jamīl Bahum and Muʿammar Riḍā Kaḥḥāla

Muḥammad Jamīl Bahum and Muʿammar Riḍā Kaḥḥāla introduced their fellow-countrymen to historico-philosophical ideas, once again under European influence. The former wrote *Falsafat al-taʾrīkh al-ʿUthmānī*, Beirut 1925, Maṭbaʿat Ṣādir (*Jāmiʿ* I, 174, *RAAD* V, 153), a history of the issue of women's rights called *al-Marʾa fī 'l-tamaddun al-ḥadīth*, Beirut, Maṭbaʿat al-Salām, 1345/1927 (*Jāmiʿ* II, 189), and a history of the governments under the French and British mandates, called *al-Intidābāt fī 'l-ʿIrāq wa-Sūriyya* Sidon 1929 (cf. *RAAD* XI, 637); the latter wrote *al-ʿĀlam al-Islāmī wal-ʿArab* | *qabla 'l-Islām, al-baʿtha al-Muḥammadiyya,* 425
khulāṣa wa-falsafa fī taʾrīkh al-ʿālam al-Islāmī, Damascus 1933.

(*14a.–15.*) *Literary Criticism*

14a Anīs al-Khūrī al-Maqdisī

While countless schoolbooks on the history of Arabic literature were published in Egypt, the introduction of such works in Syria was initially very slow. Anīs al-Khūrī al-Maqdisī, teacher at the American University of Beirut, translated Dr W. Vandyk's English entry for the official history of Lebanon of no. 8, above, into Arabic as *Ḥayawānāt Lubnān* (*RAAD* III, 29). He then started with his colleague Aḥmad Dāy on a natural history, the *Mamālīk al-ṭabīʿa*, of which only the first volume, on animals, was published in Beirut in 1923 (*Jāmiʿ* I, 1087). The next year he published an abstract of Jirjī Zaydān's history of literature, entitled *Taʾrīkh ādāb al-lugha al-ʿarabiyya* I at Maṭbaʿat al-Hilāl, followed by a more independent work that gave more space to political history, called *al-Duwal al-ʿArabiyya wa-ādābuhā* (Beirut: Maṭbaʿat al-Amīrkān, 1924). In 1925, he translated poems by Tennyson from English, entitled *al-Dhikrā* (Beirut: Maṭbaʿat al-Amīrkān, 1925). Meanwhile, he had further intensified his readings in classical Arabic literature, on whose halcyon days he wrote *Umarāʾ al-shiʿr al-ʿarabī fi ʾl-ʿaṣr al-ʿAbbāsī* (Beirut 1932), which offers a decent description of its general outlines but does not do justice to the individual poets (see Shafīq Jabrī in *RAAD* XII, 376). He supplemented this with a history of prose called *Taṭawwur al-asālīb al-nathriyya* (Beirut 1935). His portrait of al-Mutanabbī was published in *al-Ḥadīth* 1935, 486/96.

14b ʿUmar Aḥmad Farrūkh

ʿUmar Aḥmad Farrūkh[36] wrote on similar things. Muṣṭafā Fatḥallāh, owner of the Maktabat al-Kashshāf in Beirut, had the idea of publishing a series of monographs on the history of literature called Silsilat al-Kashshāf al-adabiyya, the first volume of which was ʿUmar Farrūkh's *Abū Nuwās, shāʿir Hārūn al-Rashīd wa-Muḥammad al-Amīn*, I. *Dirāsa wa-naqd*, II. *Mukhtār min shiʿrihi* (Beirut 1351/1932–3). After a critical biography of the poet, in which he took the wise decision not to lose himself in a description of the age, the author gives a detailed appreciation of his art, which is, however, still dependent on
426 the classical standards of what makes good Arabic poetry. | Then, in 1353/1935, there followed *Abū Tammām, shāʿir al-khalīfa Muḥammad al-Muʿtaṣim billāh*. This work gives more room to discussion of historical events, which is only right since these had more influence on the art of Abū Tammām than on that of Abū Nuwās. Just like Ṭāhā Ḥusayn, the author is inclined to overestimate the influence of Greek culture on Abū Tammām's way of thinking, without trying to furnish any proof for this. At the end of his studies he went to Erlangen, Germany, where he obtained his doctor's degree with a dissertation called *Das Bild des Frühislāms in der arabischen Dichtung von der Hiǧra bis zum Tode ʿUmars*, Leipzig 1937.

14c Shafīq Jabri and Khalīl Mardam Bek

The Damascene poets Shafīq Jabrī and Khalīl Mardam Bek (see above, p. 355/6) had a more lasting influence on literary studies in Arabic. Without giving up their artistic production, both turned to research in their more productive

---

36 In his dissertation, XI, he mentions as his first publication a school-opera, *Noah's Ark*, from 1932.

years. The former developed first of all, in RAAD, soon after its foundation, the underpinnings of a literary aesthetics and criticism (*Ḥanīn ila 'l-awṭān* I, 263/9, *al-Adab, ufquhu, fiʿluhu, ghāyatuhu*, ibid. X 93/7, *Thaqāfatu 'l-dhawq*, ibid. 98/102, *Tamāzuj al-thaqāfāt*, ibid. 103/7, *Taʾrīkh al-adab*, ibid. 153/9, *Naqd al-muʾarrakhāt al-adabiyya, aṭwār al-naqd*, 160/72), and then, in volumes X–XII, applied these methods to two profound studies on the poetry of al-Mutanabbī and the literary production of Jāḥiẓ that belong to the very best that has ever been written on Arabic literature. In between, he also published an essay on A. France (RAAD VII, 145/59). The latter of the two aforementioned poets began his historico-literary career with a subtle study, entitled *Shuʿarāʾ al-Shaʾm fi 'l-qarn al-thālith* (see Suppl. I, 134), which was first published in RAAD V and then in a separate printing in Damascus in 1925. Later, he became interested in Jāḥiẓ (RAAD X, 636) and his predecessor ʿAbd al-Ḥamīd al-Kātib (ibid. XIV, 395/401), as well as in the Umayyad poets Walīd b. Yazīd (ibid. XV, 1/33) and ʿAdī b. Riqāʿ (ibid. 340/51, 450/5). In his *Silsilat aʾimmat al-adab* (Damascus, Maktabat ʿArafa) he published, in 1930, on Ibn al-Muqaffaʿ, on Ibn al-ʿAmīd in 1931, and in 1939 on al-Farazdaq.

14d Jabr Ḍūmaṭ and Qusṭakī Bek al-Ḥimṣī

Despite efforts to lend a new spirit to literary studies in Arabic, old-fashioned literary criticism was still maintained. A representative of the latter at the American University of Beirut was Jabr Ḍūmaṭ, born in Qaryat Burj Ṣāfīṭā, north of Tripoli, on 14 September 1859. He celebrated his 50-year jubilee as a teacher in February 1927 (see Abū Shādī, *al-Shafaq al-bākī*, 1016, with a facsimile of his handwriting, | ibid. 1043/4), dying on 19 January 1930 (see RAAD 427
V, 492/7). Apart from some smaller philological works (cf. Sarkīs 683, together with a strange article on Hittites and Arameans in RAAD IV, 544/50), he wrote: *Khawāṭir fi 'l-lugha* (Beirut: al-Maṭbaʿa al-Adabiyya, 1886), in which he was the first to try and explain the development of the Arabic language on the basis of Hebrew and Syriac, with which it is related; *al-Khawāṭir al-ḥisān bil-maʿānī wal-bayān* (Cairo: Maṭbaʿat al-Hilāl, 1896; Beirut, 1930); and *Falsafat al-lugha al-ʿarabiyya wa-taṭawwuruhā* (Cairo, 1929). For a list of his articles covering the years 1888/1928, see RAAD IX, 441/2. In his last work, *Sifr al-takwīn, baḥth naẓarī, falsafī, tashrīḥī li-bayān man huwa kātib hādha 'l-sifr etc.* (Beirut: Maṭbaʿat Quzmā), he tried to prove that Joseph, the son of Jacob, is the author of the Book of Genesis (see Kampffmeyer, MSOS, 1930, 199/202, with a detailed biography).

Qusṭakī Bek al-Ḥimṣī, who was a poet in his younger years (*al-Bulbul al-maʿshūq* in *Fatāt al-sharq* VI, 260/3), followed a similar path in his *Manhal al-wurrād fī ʿilm al-intiqād* (3 vols, Beirut, 1907/35; see RAAD IV, 37). His *Udabāʾ*

Ḥalab dhawu 'l-athar fī 'l-qarn al-tāsiʿ ʿashar (Aleppo: al-Maṭbaʿa al-Mārūniyya, 1925) was often used in this book. Inspired by the work of Asín Palacios, he made the far-fetched claim, in his *al-Muwāzana bayna 'l-Ulʿūba al-ilāhiyya wa-Risālat al-ghufrān aw bayna Abi 'l-ʿAlāʾ al-Maʿarrī wa-Dante shāʿir al-Ṭalyān* (in *RAAD* VII und VIII), that Dante not only had borrowed from al-Maʿarrī, but also that he had distorted his visions and rendered them obscene (see also *al-Ḥadīth*, IX, 1935, 562/7).

14e Jamīl Bek al-ʿAẓm

Jamīl Bek al-ʿAẓm worked entirely in the style of ancient literature. Born into this famous Turko-Arab family in Istanbul in 1290/1873, he was just five years old when his father took him back with him to their native soil. He studied at the university and was a civil servant for a time. He died in Damascus on 26 Jumādā II 1353/15 October 1933. Of his various writings that are listed by ʿĪsā Iskandar al-Maʿlūf in *RAAD* XIV, 556/8, only the following were published in print, besides his translation of his cousin Ṣādiq Pāshā's report of his diplomatic mission, mentioned on page 421, above: *Tafrīj al-shidda fī tashṭīr al-Burda* (lith. Istanbul 1895/1313), *Tarjamat ʿUthmān Bāshā al-Ghāzī* in *al-Maʿlūmāt* magazine (Istanbul 1315/1897), and his historico-literary study (often used by us) *ʿUqūd al-Jawhar fī tarājim man lahum khamsūna taṣnīfan fa-miʾa fa-akthar*
428 I, | (Beirut: al-Maṭbaʿa al-Ahliyya, 1326), which he wrote when he was *muḥāsib al-maʿārif* in Beirut.

14f Edwār Murqus

A representative of the Arabic language and literature in a dangerous, faraway place, we also mention the linguist Edwār Murqus, even though his works are not properly historical. Teaching Arabic literature at the madrasa of Latakia, he had started out as a poet. The first collection of his writings, *al-Ghurar aḥsan mā qālahu*, was published in Beirut in 1905. A *qaṣīda* on the downfall of ʿAbd al-Ḥamīd is mentioned in Cheikho II, 185. In 1933 he published a didactic poem on social ethics, entitled *al-Faḍīla al-mulaththama* (see *RAAD* XIII, 411). That year also saw the publication of his *Dīwān* and two textbooks on style and poetics, *Kāfil al-inshāʾ* and *Kāfil al-bayān wal-shiʿr* (ibid. XIV, 79).

14g L. Cheikho

Here we must also mention Father L. Cheikho (Shaykhū) S.J. (d. 1928), who promoted Arabic philology through many valuable editions. His *al-Ādāb al-ʿarabiyya fī 'l-qarn al-tāsiʿ ʿashar* I (1800/70), Beirut 1908, II (1870/1900), Beirut 1910, 2nd edit. Beirut 1924, and continued in *al-Ādāb al-ʿarabiyya fī 'l-rubʿ al-awwal min al-qarn al-ʿishrīn* in *al-Mashriq* XXXIII/V, opened the door for modern literary studies in Arabic in which he was followed by friar

F.E. Bustānī S.J. in his *Rawāʾiʿ* (see Muḥammad Kurd ʿAlī in *RAAD* VIII, 231/5, *al-Mashriq* XXVI, 1/5).

14h Qusṭākī Ilyās ʿAṭṭāra al-Ḥalabī

In his *Taʾrīkh al-ṣuḥuf al-Miṣriyya* (Alexandria: Maṭbaʿat al-Taqaddum, n.d.), and also in his *Takwīn al-ṣuḥuf fi ʾl-ʿālam* (Cairo 1926), Qusṭākī Ilyās ʿAṭṭāra al-Ḥalabī imitated Ph. de Ṭarrāzī's *Taʾrīkh al-ṣiḥāfa al-ʿarabiyya*.

15 Muṣṭafā Farrūkh

Alongside all these founders of cultural historiography, should also be mentioned the first Arab artist to be able to record his feelings in a literary manner and provide them with historical underpinnings: the painter Muṣṭafā Farrūkh. Born in Beirut in 1905, his talent for painting soon created a sensation, with his teacher Muḥammad Surūr encouraging him in this. In 1924/7, he studied in Rome, and in 1930, in Paris. From there he undertook a trip to Spain which he described—on his return to in Paris in 1931—in his *Riḥla ilā bilād al-majd al-mafqūd* (Beirut 1352/1933). In the book, packed with lyrical descriptions, the author is never superficial; on the contrary, rather than just describe the art of Spain that interests him most, | he also portrays the country and its people 429
with the sharp eye of a painter, although it is always the long-lost glory of his race that he is after. Cf. Pérès, *L'Espagne vue par les voyageurs mus.*, 161/71.

(*16a.–18.*) *Local History*

After the war, the writing of local histories too, was still continued by many.

16a Jūrj Yuzbek et al.

The lawyer Jūrj Yuzbek published an overview of the history of Beirut in his *Bayrūt fi ʾl-taʾrīkh*, Beirut 1925 (*Jāmiʿ* I, 40). Al-Khūrī Isṭīfān al-Bishʿalānī wrote a richly-illustrated history of the Lebanon, supported by countless charters, in his *Lubnān wa-Yūsuf Bek Karam*, Beirut 1925 (*Jāmiʿ* I, 188). The contemporary history of the country is described by Būlus Masʿad in his *Lubnān wa-Sūriyya qabla ʾl-intidāb wa-baʿdahu*, Cairo 1929 (sharply criticised by Muṣṭafā al-Shihābī in *RAAD* X, 254).

16b Ṣāliḥ al-Burghūthī et al.

Together, Ṣāliḥ al-Burghūthī and Khalīl Tūtaḥ[37] wrote a history of Palestine, *Taʾrīkh Filasṭīn*, Jerusalem 1923 (*Jāmiʿ* I, 59, *RAAD* V, 103), while al-Quss Asʿad

37 In Columbia (NY) he also wrote a *Jaghrāfiyyat Filasṭīn*, together with Ḥabīb al-Khūrī (Jerusalem 1923; see *RAAD* IV, 87), and in cooperation with H. Vitelis he published

Manṣūr wrote a history of Nazareth from its beginnings until the present, *Ta'rīkh al-Nāṣira*, Maṭbaʿat al-Hilāl 1924 (ibid., 70, *RAAD* V, 101).

16c Muḥammad Adīb al-Ḥiṣnī et al.

In his *Muntakhabāt al-tawārīkh li-Dimashq* (ibid., 1346/1927), Muḥammad Adīb ʿAbdallāh al-Ṭarābulusī al-Ḥiṣnī al-Dimashqī offers a number of selected sources on the history of Damascus. A history of Damascus under Ibrāhīm Pāshā by an anonymous contemporary, identified by ʿĪsā Iskandar Maʿlūf (*RAAD* II, 228/32) as ʿAbdallāh Nawfal al-Ṭarābulusī (b. 1797 in Tripoli, d. 1866 in Lebanon), was published by Qusṭanṭīn Bāshā al-Mukhalliṣī (b. 1870, see Sarkīs 1512) as *Mudhakkirāt ta'rīkhiyya ʿan ta'rīkh Dimashq* (Harissa: Maṭbaʿat al-Qaddīs Būlus, 1925; *Jāmiʿ* I, 209).

16d Mīkhā'īl Mūsā Allūf al-Baʿlabakkī

Mīkhā'īl Mūsā Allūf al-Baʿlabakkī published a history of Baalbek entitled *Taʾrīkh Baʿlabakk* (4th printing, Beirut 1926; *Jāmiʿ* II, 20).

16e ʿAbdallāh Ḥabīb Namal and Salīm Sarkīs

As for Tripoli, ʿAbdallāh Ḥabīb Namal published his *Kitāb tarājim ʿulamā' Ṭarābulus al-fayḥā' wa-udabā'ihā* (Tripoli: Maṭbaʿat al-Ḥaḍarāt, 1929; see *RAAD* IX, 39), while Salīm Sarkīs (see p. 228, with Jirjī Niqūlā Bāz, S. S. Beirut 1924, see *al-Mashriq* XXIV, 397) published a history of a family of notables, collected
430 from *Majallat Sarkīs*, and entitled *al-Umarā'* | *āl Luṭfallāh* (Cairo n.d. [1911?]; see *al-Jāmiʿ* I, 287).

16f Muḥammad Amīn Ghālib al-Ṭawīl

Muḥammad Amīn Ghālib al-Ṭawīl, a judge at the Court of Appeal in Latakia, wrote a history of the ʿAlawites, titled *Taʾrīkh al-ʿAlawiyyīn* (Latakia: Maṭbaʿat al-Taraqqī, 1343; *Jāmiʿ* I, 266, Muḥammad Kurd ʿAlī in *RAAD* V, 570/6).

16g Al-Khūrī Būlus Qar'allī et al.

As for Aleppo, al-Khūrī Būlus Qar'allī published the memoirs of the Maronite bishop Būlus Arūtīn covering the years 1798/1850, giving it the title *Ahamm ḥawādith Ḥalab fi 'l-niṣf al-awwal min al-qarn al-tāsiʿ ʿashar*, first in *al-Majalla al-Sūriyya*, and then as a separate publication, Aleppo 1917. Kāmil b. Ḥusayn

---

Palestine, A Decade of Development, in the Annals of the American Ac. of Pol. and Soc. Sciences, 1932; *Or. Mod.* XIV, 615.

b. Muṣṭafā al-Bābī (b. 1832, d. 1933) al-Ḥalabī al-Ghazzī[38] wrote a history of Aleppo with special consideration of the biographies of its most distinguished inhabitants, entitled *Nahr al-dhahab fī taʾrīkh Ḥalab*, I, II (Aleppo 1342/5; see *RAAD* IV, 526/8, V, 240), while Muḥammad Rāghib al-Ṭabbākh published the painstakingly thorough *Iʿlām al-nubalāʾ bi-taʾrīkh Ḥalab al-Shahbāʾ*, 7 vols, Aleppo 1341/5, and in a shortened version, *al-Anwār al-jaliyya bi-mukhtaṣar al-athbāt al-Ḥalabiyya*, ibid. 1351.

16h Salmān Būlus

The archimandrite Salmān Būlus, privy secretary to the Roman Catholic patriarch, published his experiences, together with extensive material on the geography and ethnology of the country, in *Khamsat aʿwām fī sharqiyy al-Urdunn*, Beirut 1929 (a special issue of *al-Mashriq*), see *RAAD* X, 254.

17 Muḥammad Kurd ʿAlī

Muḥammad Kurd ʿAlī made a very successful transition from the lower regions of petty journalism to the highest levels of academic research.

The son of a Kurdish father and a Circassian mother, Kurd ʿAlī was born in Damascus in 1876. After his studies—on which Ṭāhir al-Jazāʾirī left a definitive imprint; see his warm obituary of him in *RAAD* VIII, 577/96, 666/79—he began a career in journalism. In 1315/1897–98, he became chief editor of the weekly magazine *al-Shaʾm*, occupying this post for three consecutive years. He was then hired by *al-Muqtaṭaf* and, in 1901, he became the director of *al-Rāʾid al-Miṣrī* newspaper for a period of ten months. Back in Damascus, his political orientation came under suspicion. As such, he moved back to Cairo in 1324/1906–7. There, he founded *al-Muqtabas* magazine, | assumed the post of director of 431 *al-Ẓāhir* newspaper, while also joining the editorial board of *al-Muʾayyad*. After the Turkish revolution he returned to Damascus, expanding his *al-Muqtabas* magazine with a daily newspaper with the same title. In 1908 he published an anthology of classical prose as *Rasāʾil al-bulaghāʾ* (Maṭbaʿat al-Ẓāhir 1326, 2nd printing Maṭbaʿat Muṣṭafā al-Bābī al-Ḥalabī, 1331/1913). In Ramaḍān 1327/ Autumn 1909, one of his articles caused the displeasure of the Wālī of Syria. His newspaper being banned, the printing-house under lock and key, and he himself threatened with immediate arrest, Kurd ʿAlī made a rapid escape via Lebanon and Egypt to Paris, where he immersed himself in the study of French literature for a full three months. Acquitted, he returned by way of Vienna and

38 In *RAAD* VII, 385/95 he published an article on the dialect of his native city entitled *al-Hujna fī lahjat Ḥalab*, and an autobiographical note in idem, VIII, 493/4. An obituary by Sāmī al-Kayyāl was published in *al-Ḥadīth*, 1933, 151/2.

Istanbul to Damascus, where he took up his regular work at the newspaper again. In 1912 he was again indicted; while his brother Aḥmad—who signed as the responsible editor—and his assistant Shaykh Ibrāhīm al-Uskūbī were arrested and hauled off to Istanbul, Kurd ʿAlī succeeded in escaping to Egypt by slipping into a caravan that happened to be going there. Six months later he was able to resume his activities in Damascus again. In his magazine he had published a series of articles on the history of the city that were such a success, that he had the plan of turning them—following the example of al-Maqrīzī's *Khiṭaṭ*—into a comprehensive history of the country. But because the available sources were not sufficient to carry out such a scheme, he decided in 1913 to travel to Europe to supplement them with information gathered from European libraries. His expectations in this regard were confirmed by the collection of Prince Caetani in Rome in particular.

Just before the outbreak of the war his newspaper was banned once again. However, during the war he had to publish it again on the order of Aḥmad Jamāl Pāshā, although later he had to limit his activities to the publication of the *al-Sharq* newspaper, mouthpiece of the Turko-German alliance. On the order of the supreme commander, Kurd ʿAlī, Muḥammad Bāqir Ḥusayn al-Ḥabbāl, ʿAbd al-Basīṭ al-Ḥabbāl, and ʿAbd al-Basīṭ al-Unsī all went on a 'scientific' mission to Istanbul and Čanaq Qalʿa, a mission on which he reported in his *al-Baʿtha al-ʿilmiyya ilā dār al-khilāfa al-Islāmiyya*, Damascus n.d. On the order of the commander he also wrote a book on Enver's propaganda tour to Medina entitled *al-Riḥla al-Enweriyya ila 'l-aṣqāʿ al-Ḥijāziyya wal-Shaʾmiyya*, Beirut: al-
432 Maṭbaʿa al-ʿIlmiyya, 1334/1916. After Jamāl's dismissal | he went to Istanbul, returning to Damascus three months after its fall. The military commander there made him head of educational affairs, enabling him to create the Arab Academy, established on 8 June 1919. When the French took control of Syria, they confirmed him in his office on 7 September 1920. On their order, he took ten young people to France to study there. When he had completed this mission, he made a tour of western Europe, including Spain and Germany. After his return he was soon in trouble with the French, who misused his name in their struggle with the nationalists. As such, he quit his job in the ministry and only returned to it on 15 February 1928. All this we read in his autobiography, to which we can add that when he became a member of the Royal Academy of Egypt, he moved to Cairo in 1937. In 1341/1923 he published a first impression of his trip to Spain—brought out earlier in *RAAD* 11, 129ff—entitled *Ghābir al-Andalus wa-ḥāḍiruhā* (Cairo: al-Maṭbaʿa al-Raḥmāniyya; see Pérès, *L'Espagne* 122). But his stay in that country was not long enough to live up to the goal that he had set for himself in that book. He is almost exclusively interested in Arab monuments, every one of which causes an outpouring of patriotic sentiment.

Apart from Ṣāʿid al-Andalusī's *Ṭabaqāt al-umam* and al-Maqqarī's *Nafḥ al-ṭīb*, he also draws on A. Marvaud's *L'Espagne au XXe siècle* and Alfred Fouillé's *Esquisse psychologique des peuples européens*, from whom he gets most of his data on modern Spain and on whom he completely depends for his account of Portugal, which he never visited. That first travelogue was also published in his collected impressions of Europe, entitled *Gharāʾib al-gharb* (2 vols, Cairo: al-Maṭbaʿa al-Raḥmāniyya 1341/1923, 2nd printing). This latter work begins quite dramatically with the story of his flight from Damascus and continues with an account of Lebanon and its inhabitants, including a separate chapter on their tendency to go abroad. The first entry in that journal is focussed on Paris, which he, like most orientals, considers his second home. There is not much about Istanbul; on pages 154/77 he reproduces a lecture on education in Europe that he gave in *al-Muntada 'l-ʿArabī* there. Another lecture, *Ḥayātunā wal-ḥayāt al-Ūrūbiyya*, likewise delivered in Istanbul, on 20 February 1914, concludes his | journal's second entry in volume I, pp. 319/330. This second entry 433
contains much detail on Italy, with an extensive account of the rise of nationalism there on pages 210/50. But he also talks engagingly about the women of Europe (184/8) and dancing there (207/10). The other part of that entry is about Switzerland, whose institutions he admires as much as its nature, and about Hungary and Greece. The account of his third trip, during which he also visited Spain, is again mostly about France, and then Belgium and Holland. At the end of his trip he also visits Germany, which, even at the time of its deepest humiliation, leaves the same strong impression on him as it did on Ḥusayn Haykal. As he knows no German he is, besides his own impressions, mostly dependent on foreign sources, as was the case for Spain. Apart from Fouillé's *Esquisse*, he mostly uses J. Huret's *Berlin*, R. Cruchet's *Les universités allemandes au XXe siècle*, and H. Lichtenberger's *L'Allemagne moderne*; he also uses Madame de Staël in several instances. In his account of Germany's economic potential he uses Helfferich's work on the material welfare of the German people (translated into Arabic by Felix Fāris, Aleppo 1916), while additionally translating Huret's impressive description of a country estate in Silesia.

In 1343/1925 he published a collection of articles that had earlier been printed in newspapers and magazines, entitled *al-Qadīm wal-ḥadīth* (Cairo: al-Maṭbaʿa al-Raḥmāniyya; see Salīm ʿAnhūrī, *RAAD* V, 242/5). The book's title is not just taken from the article from the fourth issue of *al-Muqtabas*, with which it opens; indeed, its whole aim is to deliver its readers a strong image of their own proud history, a history that they are, often, only too ready to forget, impressed as they are by the achievements of modern civilisation. He thus talks about the Shuʿūbiyya and the Muʿtazilīs, about Sayf al-Dawla and Ṣalāḥ al-Dīn, about the Wahhābīs and Muṣṭafā Kāmil, about the Arab city and the

way it was organised, and about the eloquence of the Arabs, comparing it with the eloquence of the Europeans in which he cites from two French authors. At the same time, he also emphasises the value of European languages, for the learning of which he recommends the methods of the Berlitz schools. On three occasions (p. 208ff, 219ff, 224ff) he tries to penetrate the essence of European music in its comparison to that of the Orient. But other, more practical sub-
434 jects, too, have his interest, such as the issue of emigration | (p. 243ff) or the problems of alcoholism (p. 273).[39]

The president of the Arab Academy, he took an active part in its daily operations. His many publications in *RAAD* deal with the history of Islam, of Syria in particular, and of French literature, and in one instance also of the poetry of A. Frances (*Majālis A. Fr.*, RAAD X, 32ff, 393ff). Meanwhile, he also published *his opus maior, Khiṭaṭ al-Sha'm* (6 vols, Damascus 1343/8). It has much more to offer than its title gives reason to expect. After a brief geographical introduction, it gives an account of the history of Syria from ancient times until the Treaty of Ankara of 1921; the work is supplemented by a number of studies on cultural history, which contain much rare material. A forerunner of these was his *al-Ḥukūma al-Miṣriyya fi 'l-Sha'm*, published in Cairo in 1343. Once the *Khiṭaṭ* was finished, Kurd ʿAlī applied himself once more to literary and cultural-historical research with the publication of his *al-Islām wal-ḥaḍāra al-ʿArabiyya* (2 vols, Cairo 1936)[40] and *Umarāʾ al-bayān* (Cairo 1937).

Autobiography at the end of the 6th volume of the *Khiṭaṭ*, up to the year 1928. Ismāʿīl ʿAbd al-Ḥamīd in *al-Udabāʾ al-khams* (Cairo: Maṭbaʿat al-Saʿāda, 1925, no. 2), Kampffmeyer, *MSOS* XXX, 206/16.

18 ʿUmar Abu 'l-Naṣr

The extraordinarily prolific author ʿUmar Abu 'l-Naṣr also writes about literary and historical subjects, although lately his interest has been mostly focussed on historiography.

He began in 1926/7 with the history of Syria: *Sūriyya wa-Lubnān fi 'l-qarn al-tāsiʿ ʿashar*, Beirut 1926, and *Sūriyya wa-Lubnān ḥattā awwal al-qarn al-tāsiʿ ʿashar*, ibid. 1927 (see *al-Mashriq* XXIV, 698/704). In his *Ḥasan, qiṣṣa sharqiyya* (*al-Ḥadīth* 1931, p. 589/95), on the other hand, he is a storyteller, and in his

39 As a matter of curiosity it may be noted that on page $287_{,10}$ he refers to alcohol as *al-alkuḥūl*.

40 Which was even translated into Chinese by the Egyptian mission to China, as was Ḥusayn Haykal's *Ḥayāt Muḥammad* and Muḥammad Rashīd Riḍā's *al-Waḥy al-Muḥammadī*, on which see *Or. Mod.* 1936, 598.

Fī dawlat al-adab wal-bayān (Beirut 1932), a literary critic. Since then, his numerous monographs have been devoted almost | exclusively to historiography: 435
Muḥammad al-nabī al-ʿArabī, Fāṭima bint Muhammad, Khulafāʾ Muḥammad, Abū Bakr al-Ṣiddīq, ʿUmar b. al-Khaṭṭāb, ʿUthmān b. ʿAffān, ʿAlī b. Abī Ṭālib in 2 volumes, *Muʿāwiya b. Abī Sufyān, Yazīd b. Muʿāwiya, Hārūn al-Rashīd* (translated from French), *al-ʿIrāq al-jadīd, Fayṣal malik al-ʿIrāq* (translated from English), *Sayyid al-Jazīra al-ʿArabiyya b. Saʿūd*, Beirut 1935. He also translated Hitler's *Mein Kampf* as *Kifāḥ Hitlir*, followed by a pamphlet entitled *Hitler al-murʿib aw Būlīsat al-siyāsī al-mukhīf*.

5 *Reformist Theologians*

In the twentieth century, too, representatives of the various *madhab*s produced quite a number of writings in the traditional theological vein. Even though we cannot list them all, there are two people who need to be referred to here briefly as they represent the reformist movement of Syria, something in which they base themselves on the ideas of Jamāl al-Dīn al-Afghānī and Muḥammad ʿAbduh.

In the years 1906/14, ʿAbd al-Qādir al-Maghribī published a series of articles on religious and social issues in the spirit of Muḥammad ʿAbduh in the Egyptian press. These articles, in which he demonstrated the need to reform Islam, were published jointly as *al-Bayān fi ʾl-dīn wal-ijtimāʿ wal-adab wal-taʾrīkh* (Cairo: Maṭbaʿat al-Salafiyya, 1343), *al-Akhlāq wal-wājibāt fi ʾl-tarbiya al-akhlāqīya wal-ijtimāʿiyya* (ibid., 1344), vol. 2. *al-Bayyināt fi ʾl-dīn wal-ijtimāʿ wal-adab wal-taʾrīkh* (ibid. 1344; with a biography of the author by the publisher of *al-Manār*, see *al-Jāmiʿ* I, 743, II, 165/360, Ph. Hitti, JAOS XLVII, 78/9, Adams, *Islam and Modernism* 247). Afterwards, he became increasingly interested in literary and historical work. This is shown by his joint publication of three lectures (Beirut: Maṭbaʿat Quzmā, 1929/1347): *Muḥammad wal-marʾa, Muḥākamat wazīrayn fī amrayn khaṭīrayn, Ibn Khaldūn fi ʾl-madrasa al-ʿĀdiliyya*. In the first lecture, he speaks out firmly against the issue of women's rights, even though his language is gentle in the extreme, seeking to show his female readers that it was in fact the Prophet who was the first to recognise their true dignity as human beings.
| According to him, the veil, their lower rank in matters of inheritance and 436
as a witness in court, indeed, even polygamy, were only introduced in their own best interest. The two other lectures deal, in a brilliant and novel style, with two interesting periods in the history of Islam. Even though he published a warm and grateful biography of his teacher in theology, Badr al-Dīn al-Ḥasanī (b. 1850, d. 1935), in RAAD XIII, 297/9 and 351/8, all the other articles that he, one of its most productive contributors, wrote for that magazine, are

only about literary history and philology in the purest sense; among them, his emendations to the edition of al-Nuwayrī's *Nihāyat al-arab* in *RAAD* v/xiv deserve special mention.

On page 384, we mentioned Aḥmad Fawzī al-Sāʿātī who, in 1910, had tried to reconcile Islamic theology with European science. Later, his theological opinions became ever more orthodox. As did the Salafiyya of Cairo, he tried resolve the struggle between the *madhāhib*, which become more intense due to the increasing power of the Wahhābīs. He did this in his *al-Inṣāf fī daʿwat al-Wahhābiyya wa-khuṣūmihim li-rafʿ al-ikhtilāf* (Damascus 1340), as did Muḥassin al-Amīn al-Ḥusaynī's *Kashf al-irtiyāb fī atbāʿ Muḥammad b. ʿAbd al-Wahhāb, yataḍamman taʾrīkh al-Wahhābiyya etc.* (Damascus 1346),[41] while he defended Islam against Christianity in his *Kanz al-barāhīn* (Damascus 1343; see *al-Mashriq* xxiii, 554). Before then, he had set forth his conservative views in *al-Burhān fī iʿjāz al-Qurʾān* (Damascus 1924).

Lately, Mājid al-Mālikī is a very successful protagonist of the ideals of Arab unity and progress.

---

41 Other works by him are mentioned in Sarkīs 1622, *Jāmiʿ al-taṣ.* i, 745/811, 822/3, 846, together with *al-Siḥr al-ḥalāl fī 'l-mufākhara bayna 'l-ʿilm wal-māl*, Damascus 1330.

Chapter 3. The Syrians in the Americas

Mīrzā ʿAbd al-Raḥīm al-Ilāhī al-Tabrīzī, *al-Islām fī Amīrkā*, C. 1311.

Muḥammad Kurd ʿAlī, *al-Hijra min Lubnān, Gharāʾib al-gharb* I, 26/34, *al-Hijra, al-Qadīm wal-ḥadīth*, 242/51.

| Fuʾād Ḥaddād (Buenos Aires), *al-ʿArab wal-ʿArabiyya fī ʾl-ʿālam al-jadīd*, 437
RAAD VI, 143/4.

Mūsā Kurayyim, *al-Barāzīliyyūn wal-Sūriyyūn, al-lugha al-Burtūqāliyya wal-ʿArabiyya*, *RAAD* VIII, 45/57.

Sulaymān Saʿīd, *al-Muhājara*, *RAAD* XI, 752/61.

Tawfīq al-Rāfiʿī, *Mā warāʾ al-biḥār aw al-nubūgh al-ʿArabī fī ʾl-ʿālam al-jadīd*, n.d. & n.p. (Cairo: Maṭbaʿat al-Hilāl, *Jāmiʿ* I, 193).

Muḥyi ʾl-Dīn Riḍā, *Balāghat al-ʿArab fī ʾl-qarn al-ʿishrīn*, C. 1924.

I. Kratschkovsky, Die Literatur der arabischen Emigranten in Amerika, *MO* XXI (1927), 193/213.[1]

From time immemorial, the entrepreneurial spirit of the Near-Eastern race had flooded the countries of the Mediterranean with Jews and Syrians. In the nineteenth century, and under the strain of Turkish rule, this same spirit made many Lebanese Syrians cross the Atlantic. While the intellectual elite had gone to Egypt in search of a place where they could exercise their profession in freedom, the hordes of mostly Lebanese who went to the Americas made their fortunes mainly in trade; and in their wake came the writers, ready to fill their intellectual needs.

As early as 1660/83, there was a priest from Mosul, Ilyās b. Ḥannā, who lived in America and who described the wonders of the New World to his countrymen back home (see vol. II, 508). In 1848, the Syrians al-Khūrī Flavianus al-Kafūrī and Nāṣif al-Shudūdī went to North America to appeal to the charity of the people there on behalf of their fellow-Christians in need; and in 1874 the *maṭrān* Basilius Ḥajjār went to South America with this very same purpose. But it was the World Exhibition of 1876 in Philadelphia that really marked the beginning of a major flow of immigrants. In that city, some business people
| from Bethlehem had made a fortune with wood inlay products. The riches 438
that they brought back home incited others to go as well and so, by the 1890s,

1 In his *Mashāhid Ūrūbā wa-Amīrkā* (Cairo: Maṭbaʿat al-Muqtaṭaf, 1900), Edwār Bek Ilyās gives a description of the capitals of Europe that must surely be interesting for his oriental readership, but it is only at the end (460/502) that he tells us about a brief visit to the United States at the time of the World Exhibition of 1876, although he does not refer to the Arab immigrants there.

5000 emigrants departed each year, a number that had swollen to 20,000 per year by the early twentieth century. At the outbreak of the [First] World War, a quarter of the population of Syria had left for America, and in some regions the number of emigrants was a high as 40%. But, like the Italians, they remained in close contact with their country of origin, investing their savings there and preferring it as a place to find wives, much to the irritation of Syrian women in America who had adopted the American way of life (*al-Rustumiyyāt* 143/4).

Even though there are no precise statistics on the number of Syrians in the Americas, the figure probably lies around 600,000. They did not only go to the United States, but also to South America, preferably Brazil, whose climate they liked and with whose inhabitants they mixed more easily and enduringly than in the United States. In Brazil, their energetic activity soon bore its fruits; the Yāfith company of São Paulo gained a major stake in the textile industry while in agriculture, too, the Syrians found their place. In the years 1910/28 they founded a number of coffee plantations, which, together, hold over 3 million trees. But in Argentina and Uruguay, and in Mexico and Middle America too, the Syrian communities prosper.

Even if many of these orientals tried to adapt themselves to the intellectual climate of their new surroundings, most of them stubbornly kept to their native tongue and traditions; and, remaining true to their own religion as well, the Patriarchate of Antioch has so far been able to establish no less than four eparchies in South America. The first Arabic newspaper of the
439 Americas was *Kawkab Amīrkā*,[2] founded in 1891 in New York. | This publication was soon followed by Mīkhāʾīl Rustum's *al-Muhājir* and Nasīb ʿArīḍa's *al-Funūn* magazine (which closed its doors in 1919), and then, in 1911, by ʿAbd al-Masīḥ Ḥaddā's *al-Sāʾiḥ*, Maḥbūb al-Khūrī al-Shartūnī's *al-Rafīq*, Ilyās Abū Māḍī's *al-Samīr*, and also *al-Hudā*, *al-Naṣr*, *Mirʾāt al-gharb* and others. In Brazil, Qayṣar al-Maʿlūf founded the *Jarīdat Barāzīl* in 1898. São Paulo saw the publication of *Majallat al-sharq*, Shukrī Efendi al-Khūrī's humorous magazine *al-Aṣmaʿī* and its continuation *Abu ʾl-hawl* and *Fatā Lubnān*, as well as *al-Mufīd* newspaper and a magazine with the same name, both published by Tawfīq Efendi Daʿūn. In Buenos Aires there is *al-Rāʾid al-mumtāz*, Jūrjī Ṣuwāyā's *al-Iṣlāḥ* and Mūsā Yūsuf ʿAzīza's *al-Jarīda al-Sūriyya al-Lubnāniyya*, and in Rio de Janeiro *Majallat al-Ṣawāb*.[3] This is how a strong intelligentsia could be

---

2 This is the most common form of the name as it is also used by Ilyās Qunṣul, for instance, in his *ʿAlā madhbaḥ al-waṭaniyya* 38,$_7$, and in a verse, next to Amrīka, ibid. 56,$_7$.

3 On the influence of the Syro-American press on the development of nationalist ideology in the Middle East, see also E. Jung, *La révolte arabe* II, 192.

developed amongst the Syrians. In São Paulo, which counted 80,000 Syrians in a 1922 census, there lived at the time 15 Syrian doctors and 5 Syrian lawyers.

As material wealth increased, so too did the demand for a literary ouput at a higher intellectual level. The first to meet this demand were the journalists. However, it was not long before ambitious traders and industrialists also took up the pen, and there was even a group of writers in New York who organised themselves with the name *al-Rābiṭa al-qalamiyya*[4] and in São Paulo as the *Ḥaflat al-Maʿarrī*. Because they could | openly criticise the situation in their 440
country of origin, ahead of the re-establishment of the Ottoman constitution and the freedom—if limited—that this would imply for Syria, their writings were much in demand there. But their new artistic ideals too, appealed to a large audience back home. The literature of the Syrians of the Americas thus had a strong influence in the East even though it diminished somewhat after the war.

1 *Poetry*

Majmūʿat al-Rābiṭa al-qalamiyya, New York n.d. (1921, *Jāmiʿ* I, 448, *MSOS* XXX, 218).

Al-Sāʾiḥ al-mumtāz, special literary issues of *al-Sāʾiḥ*, New York 1925, 1927 (*MSOS* XXX, 218).

Ph. Ḥittī, *Amīrkā fī naẓm sharqī*, C. 1924.

Khalīl Ḍāhir, *al-Shiʿr wal-shuʿarāʾ*, Brooklyn 1931 (see F.E. Bustānī, *al-Mashriq* XXXI, 222ff.).

(*1.–10.*) *Poets in North America*

1 Mīkhāʾīl Efendi Asʿad Rustum al-Shuwayrī

Mīkhāʾīl Efendi Asʿad Rustum al-Shuwayrī, founder of the *al-Muhājir* newspaper of New York, was also the one who printed the first Arabic book in the United States, a *dīwān* entitled *al-Gharīb fi ʾl-gharb* (New York 1895/1910), which is a versified account of his passage to the United States; a second volume was published in 1913, also in New York (Sarkīs 931, 1162, a portrait in *al-Rustumiyyāt* 109).

2 Asʿad Muḥammad Rustum

He was succeeded by his son Asʿad Muḥammad Rustum. Born in Baalbek in 1875, the latter is a practising Protestant. Not only did he continue his father's

4 Portraits of its members Ilyās ʿAṭāʾallāh, Rashīd Ayyūb, Nadra Ḥaddād, Wadīʿ Bāḥūṭ, Nasīb ʿArīḍa, W. Katesflis(?), Jabrān Khalīl Jabrān, Mikhāʾīl Nuʿayma, ʿAbd al-Masīḥ Ḥaddād, Ilyā Abū Māḍī were published at the end of Jabrān's *al-Badāʾiʿ wal-ṭarāʾif*.

newspaper with great success, but he also made such a fortune in the carpet business that, besides his estate in New Jersey, he could also buy the Duḥdūḥ fortress on the Marḥātā mountain, expand it and rename it Burj Rustum. His *Dīwān* was published in Beirut in 1908. Since then, he has published countless
441 poems and essays in many different newspapers and magazines, | samples of which may be found in *al-Rustumiyyāt* and in *Taḥiyyat al-shaʿb li-shāʿir al-shaʿb Asʿad Rustum ṣāḥib Dīwān Rustum wal-raʾīs al-sābiq li-taḥrīr Jarīdat al-Muhājir; Compliment of the Syrian People to their Eminent Poet, Orator and Former Chief Editor of the "Emigrant"*; New York: The Eagle Press, 1919.

His poetry is mostly humorous, although entertainment often switches to bitter scorn in the early days when he denounced his people's enemies, the Turks (13/6, 65/8), and especially ʿAbd al-Ḥamīd (114) and Jamāl Pāshā (17/9). Yet he also mocks the members of the city council of Beirut who study the sanitary systems of various European cities on expensive tours abroad but remain unable to root out common typhoid fever in their communities back home (39/44, dated 1910), while the Lebanese party leaders, too (75/6), are the victim of his scorn, usually couched in rude, popular language. Likewise, he does not spare the Americanised women among the Syro-Lebanese (51). His sense of humour is also apparent in essays like 'Uncle Sam and the emigrants' (77/83), in which he caricatures the Germans, the French, the Irish and the Italians to finally extol the business sense of his compatriots; and he uses the same kind of wittiness to describe a marital row between Victoria and Albert (124/5). But when talking about more serious things, too, as in his poem on the restoration of the Ottoman constitution (145) or on freedom in the USA (147), his sense of humour never leaves him.

He still feels connected to the poetry of his homeland. This is clear from his praise of Ḥāfiẓ Ibrāhīm in a poem that was recited on his behalf by Dr. Ibrāhīm al-Shudīnī in a gathering in honour of the former, organised by Salīm Sarkīs, in which he emphasised Ibrāhīm's merit in his support for the Syrians (126/7). Once, when the *Majallat Sarkīs* organised a competition around the question: "What would I do if I were Rockefeller?", he answered, out of competition, with a poem (150/1) that closed with the following words: "I would give a million to each of Shaykh Ibrāhīm and Zaydān and erect a monument in the most
442 beautiful street for the translator of the *Iliad* al-Bustānī. | I would throw out Shawqī and replace him by Rustum, the noble cavalier. This is what I would do in Egypt, if I were Rockefeller, the American."

He had perfect command of the English language, to the point that he was able to write satirical poems in the same way he did in his mother tongue (110/3). As such, he could permit himself the farce, while visiting an American university, of reciting an Arabic *qaṣīda* in which English words would determine the rhyme (93/4).

Even though he had such complete control of classical Arabic that he once delivered a speech to students of the American University of Beirut that was entirely in rhyming prose (90/3), he prefers to season his poems with phrases taken from the common vernacular (like *laysa fīhā dūmarī*, 'there is no one there', 145 bottom, cf. Feghali, *Syntaxe* 324), indeed, even with Americanisms such as *tukūt*, 'tickets' 7,$_{15}$, or *farmashiyya*, 'pharmacy' 51,$_{12}$, 81,$_{15}$.

See Saʿd Mikhāʾīl, *Ādāb al-aṣr fī shuʿarāʾ al-Shām wal-ʿIrāq wa-Miṣr* (Cairo: Maṭbaʿat al-ʿUmrān, n.d.), 79/84.

3 Amīn Ẓāhir Khayrallāh

Al-Bustānī's translation of the *Iliad* which, though much admired, left no trace in the literature of the Orient, was imitated in America by Amīn Ẓāhir Khayrallāh, who tried give a Homeric account of the Great Fire of San Francisco of 1906 in his *Kalimat shāʿir fī waṣf khaṭb nādir* (New York 1906; see F.E. Bustānī in *al-Mashriq* XXV, 322, 633, Kratschovsky, *MO* XXI, 197).

In his *al-Arḍ wal-samāʾ* (Beirut 1909), he then tried to apply the same style to ethical and historical themes. In his *Durūs al-ḥayāt al-insāniyya* (Beirut 1909), a collection of stories mixed with poetry, he describes family life among the Syrians of New York (Sarkīs 476). His *al-Bayān al-ṣurāḥ ʿan nadhr Yaftāḥ* (Damascus 1913) deals with biblical lore.

4 Ilyās Manṣūr al-Farrān al-Lubnānī and Mitrī Jirjīs Kafurī

While Asʿad Rustum used the common vernacular only to create stylistic effects, Ilyās Manṣūr[5] al-Farrān al-Lubnānī of Shuwayfāt | used the dialect 443
throughout. He did this in his *dīwān* called *Salwa 'l-humūm* (New York: Jarīdat Mirʾāt al-gharb, 1912),[6] which not only contains satirical pieces, but also extols the Syrian clergy and contains some elegies.

On the other hand, in his *Tāj al-ʿatāba* (New York n.d.; *Jāmiʿ* I, 316) Mitrī Jirjīs Kafurī limited himself, again, to the form in which the dialect was originally used, the *zajal*.

Lecerf, *Lit. dial.* 160, also mentions al-Farrān's *Kitāb al-samar fī awqāt al-sahar* (Baʿabda: Maṭbaʿa ʿUthmānīya, 1899), *Jannāz al-bīʿ wal-shirāʾ fī Tukumān Amīrkā* (*ʿĀl al-ʿĀl* V), and some short pieces.

---

5 As such in Cairo^2 III, 188, Lecerf "Naṣīf."

6 As such in Cairo, loc. cit., Lecerf "n.d. M. 1913."

5 Maḥbūb al-Khūrī al-Shartūnī

In New York, Maḥbūb al-Khūrī al-Shartūnī (d. 27 June 1931), an admirer and imitator of Aḥmad Shawqī, represented the classical tradition.

He published many *qaṣīdas* and *muqaṭṭaʿāt* in *al-Hudā* magazine and then in *al-Rafīq*, which he founded, a *dīwān* (New York n.d., 2nd printing 1937), as well as many articles on literary criticism. See Amīn al-Ḍāhir in al-Bustānī, *al-Mashriq* XXXI, 222ff).

6 Ilyā Abū Māḍī

Ilyā Abū Māḍī is an important lyricist whose stylised language is in the same league as that of Aḥmad Shawqī and Khalīl Maṭrān. His first *dīwān* was published in New York in 1919, followed by *al-Jadāwil*, Maṭbaʿat Mirʾāt al-Gharb 1927.

Even though much influenced by the French Romantics, Abū Māḍī also took inspiration from the work of W. Whitman. He struggles with the many impressions that assail him, unable to answer all the questions that they raise. His *dīwān* terminates with five poems of four strophes each, in every case ending with a *lastu adrī*, like the first: "I came, I don't know whence, but I came all the
444 same; I see a road in front of me, and | I walk; I must always wander, like it or not; how did I come? How did I know where to go? I have no idea!" One moment he believes he has found the answer to the meaning of existence in the immortality and omnipresence of the human soul: "Then a voice answered me from the dark, saying: 'You're wrong, you do not hear the north wind but the souls of the dead, looking for a place to settle in but finding nothing … They are in the drinks that we drink, in the food we that eat, in the air that we breathe, in the words that we speak, and in the deeds that we do. Whoever divides life into a 'here' and a 'yonder' is utterly wrong" (20/1 'The North Wind'). At another time, he feels suspended in time as on an ocean wave, in storm and quiet alike (49,$_{10}$). Yet he does not always struggle with problems of this magnitude; he is also able to share his wisdom in the form of a tale, as in 'The frog and the stars' (12) or 'The foolish fig tree' (28). He also joyfully participates in the literary life of his country of origin, be it by congratulating *al-Muqtaṭaf* on its fiftieth anniversary (81/5) or through an elegy on Sulaymān al-Bustānī (86/8).

Besides the *qaṣīda*, he also uses the *muwashshaḥ* (33, 45, 52, 79) with equal dexterity. In one of these strophic poems (*al-Ashbāh al-thalātha*), he blows up its metre to impose a free metre in the style of W. Whitman.

As well as in the *diwān*, he also published numerous other poems in various magazines like *al-Samīr* in New York, *al-Muqtaṭaf* 76, 405/6, 1937, 48 (*Anā wabnī*), 82, 1933, 192/4 (*al-Damʿa al-kharsāʾ*), ibid. 316/8 (*al-Shāʿir wal-sulṭān al-jāʾir*), *al-Ḥadīth* II, 1928, 64 (*Barridī yā suḥub*), *Zahra min uqḥuwān* in *al-Mirʾāt* (see p. 439) etc.

See Ilyās Abū Shabaka, *Abū Māḍī al-shāʿir, al-Muqtaṭaf*, 1932, 305/9, Yūsuf Baʿīnī, ibid. 1936, 287/91, Bishr Fāris in *al-Ahrām* of 3 May 1934, Amīn Ḍāhir in al-Bustānī, *al-Mashriq* XXXI, 225ff.

7 Nasīb ʿArīḍa

The torn emotions of the uprooted migrant manifest themselves even more strongly in the *diwān* of Nasīb ʿArīḍa, *al-Arwāḥ al-ḥāʾira*, New York n.d.

Born in Nazareth, the poet went to New York in 1905, where he founded *al-Funūn* magazine, which ceased production in 1919. In America, his poetry, initially full of nostalgia, | has become increasingly dominated by the pointless- 445 ness of life in general ("No difference whether you take good advice or not, my soul, the future will always be like the past." "Why do winds blow over mountain tops that do not need them while refusing their coolness to deserts where caravans are starving?" "I have a long way to go, me alone; is there no comrade, no guide, no weapon, not even a friend's prayer? Have mercy on him who treks through the desert, without a canteen, mocked by one fata morgana after the other."). Only rarely does he rise above this enduring pessimism, in moments of mystical desire ("The castles of the imagination are shining up high in the skies; come on, sister of my soul, you have lingered there for too long … I see you do not know me any more; has all beauty left me then? Yes, my nature has changed since I came down to this wretched earth, trading my splendour for this bag of bones. Come on, sister of my soul, I'm disgusted with the human kind."). Even rarer are the occasions when he sees a glimmer of hope ("Soul, go foreward on this rugged path, for life is short; go on, if you really want to, you will realise your dreams and catch the rays, before they're gone; go on, go on"); further samples may be found in *Mukhtārāt Rafāʾīl Nakhla*, 229/33. See also the detailed analysis in Mīkhāʾīl Nuʿayma, *al-Ghirbāl*, 128/44; cf. F.E. Bustānī in *al-Mashriq* XXV, 677. I had no access to his four-act play, *Riwāyat al-shāʿir ʿAbd al-Salām b. Raghbān*, New York 1933.

8 Niʿma al-Ḥājj

Even if he was not a member of it, Niʿma al-Ḥājj was close to al-Rābiṭa al-qalamiyya.

Ilyā Abū Māḍī wrote a preface to his *dīwān, al-Juzʾ al-awwal* (New York: Maṭbaʿat al-Tijāriyya al-Sūriyya al-Amīrkiyya, n.d.). Niʿma al-Ḥājj feels called as a poet, but is not always able to live up to it ("The muses turned their backs on me, each time that Mercury seduced me again" 15,$_1$). Just like his colleagues, he has distanced himself from its traditional forms (*ʿAlā mafriq al-ṭarīq*, p. 47);

instead of caravans, he is excited by trains (p. 87). From the classics, the only poet of importance to him is Abu ʾl-ʿAlāʾ al-Maʿarrī ("You have been sleeping
446 for the past thousand years, | but your voice still reverberates in today's poetic gatherings", 108,$_{10}$). Of his contemporaries, he is only interested in Jabrān Khalīl Jabrān, whose *Damʿa wabtisāma* he salutes on pages 131/2, in the *Ayyūbiyyāt* of Rashīd Ayyūb, in the *dīwān* of Ilyā Abū Māḍī, and in the *Ḥikāyāt al-mahjar* of ʿAbd al-Masīḥ Ḥaddād (136/8). Yet he does not depend on them. Singing of his love of life and his intense feelings for nature, the melody of his drinking- and friendship songs (73, 148) is very much his own, as is that of a hunting song (112) and a series of Spring- and Autumn songs, such as *Jāʾa faṣl al-rabīʿ* (105/7, in a jubilant free metre, composed of quatrains with an artful, intertwined rhyme) and the *Rabīʿiyya* (140/1) in short quatrains in a free metre, with each of the quatrains having three lines that rhyme with each other while the fourth line rhymes with the last line of all the others, throughout the poem. Even though he sometimes sings of love, more often he complains of his advancing age. While completely acclimatised to the New World, as can be seen in his 'Salute to New York' (61), he has not forgotten his country of origin (16, *Dhikra ʾl-waṭan*). During the war, he worries about it time and again. Even though, on New Year's Eve 1914/5 (p. 91/4), he bewails the miseries of the world at large, he regards his homeland as being under some particular kind of threat. He still hopes that it will be saved by the Entente, which is why he juxtaposes the brave country of Serbia with the lethargy in his native land. Yet he cannot give up hope that, for the Arabs, too, one day freedom will come (27/9), if only it will remember its glorious past and its people will unite, rather than setting their hopes now on Britain, and then on France or Uncle Sam (65/6). All this does not prevent him from composing a war song for the American army (22/4: "Hail to the warriors! The troops of Uncle Sam are like falcons, the heroes of a just cause") or from turning the British marching song 'The song of Tipperary' into a very free quatrain in the *radīf* metre (180/1).

In the same way that his themes are far removed from the classics, he also attaches great value to an artful development of form. As well as the *qaṣīda*, he likes the *muwashshaḥ*, for which he created new possibilities through a varied application of the *radīf* metre.

447 | 9 Rashīd Ayyūb

Much more mature is the art of Rashīd Ayyūb, who pours the mellow wisdom of his advancing age into pleasant-sounding songs.

Born in 1875 in Biskintā, northeast of Beirut, he was still young when he went to France for study. He remained there for a long time, then moved to New York where he joined *al-Rābiṭa al-qalamiyya*. His first *dīwān*, *al-Ayyūbiyyāt*, was published there but is undated. He later included some of its poems in his *Aghāni 'l-darwīsh* (New York: al-Maṭbaʿa al-Sūriyya al-Amīrkiyya, n.d. [1928]), some of which had been published previously in *Majmūʿat al-Rābiṭa al-qalamiyya* p. 65, 75, 97, 186, 212, 277, 290, 306, in *al-Sāʾiḥ al-mumtāz*, 1925, p. 42/4, 1927, 34/6, and in Muḥyi 'l-Dīn Riḍā, *Balāghat al-ʿArab fi 'l-qarn al-ʿishrīn* 267/74. Mīkhāʾīl Nuʿayma wrote a preface to this second collection of poems and rightly called Ayyūb a great artist. In a poem in free verse, called 'The Poet' (86/9, 269/71 in Muḥyi 'l-Dīn Riḍā, with some variants), Ayyūb describes his ideals as follows: "It is not the metre that makes a poet, nor the rhyme; rather, it is a heart ready to sacrifice itself in love; a heart that sees beauty and wisdom in the humility of a soul, and which embraces all humans alike with the same kind of brotherly love." He describes himself as a dervish (93/5, in M.R. 271/3) who, after long wanderings, has sunk to his knees by the roadside, not despairing but imploring hope to return: "Life of my soul, lantern of my thoughts, my everything." At times, when hardship weighs down heavily upon him or when a longing for a youth lost forever takes him, yet again, in its clutches, he seeks refuge in a shining fortress (14/9), high in the sky, the combined product of revelation and fantasy, convinced that, when one day his heart forever ceases to beat, it will be there that all his dreams come true, in the soul's eternal abode, in the gardens of the Hereafter. Even so, besides such mellow wisdom that comes with age, his poems occasionally resound with youthful passion ("I, too, once carried love's banner afield, loved the nights, whichever way they turned out to be, took a glass of sparkling wine from the hand of the cup-bearer, then raised it, in a toast to you" etc. p. 25/6) and, most of all, with an acute sense of nature's beauty, often triggering a painful longing for the faraway country where he was born.

| In the same way in which his pleasant-sounding, unaffected language car- 448
ries his emotions in all their forms, his poems too, are of many kinds. Besides free verse, of which he is a true master, he likes all types of strophic poems, at one point even trying something new when, in *Dhikrā Lubnān*, he inverts the *radīf* by beginning each line with a rhymeword of three syllables (36/8).

See Muḥyi 'l-Dīn Riḍā in *al-Muqtaṭaf*, 1929, 103/5 (also ibid. 1928, 402, which contains a sample from the *Aghānī*) and the detailed review by Kampffmeyer, *MSOS*, 1929, 179/93, with sample poems.

10 Three Inaccessible *dīwāns*

The *dīwāns* of Wadīʿ Rashīd al-Khūrī, entitled *Nidāʾ al-ghāb* (New York), of Sulaymān Salāma (New York 1929), and of Colonel Masʿūd Samāḥa (New York 1938) were not accessible to me.

(11.–13.) *Poets in South America: Brazil*

11 Beginnings: Qayṣar Bek Maʿlūf et al.

Arabic poetry made its way to Brazil later than to the United States. It was only in 1905 that the first *dīwān* was published, in São Paulo by Qayṣar Bek Maʿlūf, the owner-publisher of *Jarīdat al-Barāzīl* (see p. 439, Sarkīs 1767), and called *Tadhkār al-muhājir*. Then, in 1915, there followed *al-Gharbiyyāt* (São Paulo, al-Maṭbaʿa al-Fanniyya) by Ilyās ʿAbdallāh Ṭuʿma al-Lubnānī, who was born in al-Ḥamrāʾ in the Lebanon and who founded the newspaper *Jarīdat al-Ḥamrāʾ* in 1913. Twenty-one years old at the time, the poet sings of love and homesickness, as well as of his memories from his travels to the United States, Brazil, Egypt, Paris, and Granada (Sarkīs, Cairo^2 III, 264). Adīb al-Khūrī al-Shartūnī published a *dīwān* in Rio de Janeiro (n.d.) (*Jāmiʿ* I, 631), while in São Paulo Ilyās Farḥāt published his *Rubāʿiyyāt* (ibid., 659), which Ḥasan Kāmīl al-Ṣīrafī counts as modern in Abū Shādī's *Aṭyāf al-rabīʿ* 122,$_9$.

A poem by Qayṣar, dedicated to his nephew Fawzī (no. 13), and the latter's response are reproduced in Kampffmeyer, MSOS XXXI, 158/60, from *al-Āthār* 1928, 419/22.

449 |
12 Rashīd Salīm al-Khūrī

The 'Brazilian School' of poetry owes its fame primarily to its founder Rashīd Salīm al-Khūrī, who wrote under the alias al-Qarawī.

His first *dīwān*, *al-Rashīdiyyāt*, was published in São Paulo in 1917 and his second, *al-Qarawiyyāt*, in 1922 in that same place. While in his first *dīwān* he was clearly still prejudiced by the artificialitites of classical poetry, his art unfolds itself in all its glory in the second. Like many others, he, too, had very strong feelings for his homeland. This is not only evident from his poems, full of longing for the Lebanon (see *al-Mashriq* XXV, 679), but also from his passionate battle-cry during the Syrian uprising of 1925 and reproduced in *Dīwān al-thawra*, 81/3. After *Ḥiḍn al-umm*, one of the most beautiful narrative poems to exist in the Arabic language, he went back to unadulterated lyricism in *al-Aʿāṣīr* (São Paulo: Maṭbaʿat al-Sharq, n.d. [1933]). In this collection he also included some poems that had earlier been published in *al-Qarawiyyāt*, such as *Hadhayān al-shāʿir* (46/7), *Hunā wa-hunāka* (66/9), and *Suqūṭ Urūshalīm wa-Arīḥā* (108),[7] although the latter was downsized from 50 to a mere 17 lines. Even if there is more wisdom in *al-Qarawiyyāt* when compared to his first *dīwān*, still the overall mood is one of pessimism, so much so that he even has a word of comfort

7 Characteristically, Mīkhāʾīl Nuʿayma (*al-Ghirbāl*, 160) considers just one line of this poem everlasting.

for a cow: "You complain about the cold, harsh winter; what should I then say in the company of men? Just sleep on the snow, which is nothing compared to an insensitive heart. Lucky you, when rain pours down on you, for raindrops are still no tears." In his recent poems, and due to the political developments in the Middle East, this general mood of pessimism is overshadowed by religious conflict, which for him is reason to reject the teachings of Christianity: "If you want to banish injustice, strike out with the sword of Muḥammad and stay away from Jesus. 'Loveth one another,' we preached to the wolf, but this did not save a single sheep … You were angry when pigeons were sold, so where is your anger now, when your own people are bartered away?! Don't you want to reveal another Gospel, one that preaches pride rather than humility? Beware us | of 450
the yoke (*nīr*) if you can, rather than of the fire (*nār*) of Hell" etc. (27/8). But, being a Christian, he can also write a poem at the end of which he urges all religions to stand united, such as on the occasion of the ʿĪd al-Fiṭr of al-Jamʿiyya al-khayriyya al-Islāmiyya of São Paulo in 1933: "I celebrate this feast, as a poet, with verses first spoken by the great Prophet; but I long for a feast involving all the people, in celebration of its liberation from the stranger's yoke; for a flag, woven by ʿĪsā and Muḥammad, jointly; a flag, in whose shadow Āmina and Maria will join hands. Give me a feast in which the Arabs stand united as a people, and then sacrifice me, in fulfilment of Brahma's teachings. Sectarianism shattered our unity and caused us to fight like cat and dog. For this reason I welcome the unbelief that unifies, and to Hell with Hell!" (p. 111). The ups and downs of his native country are still very important to him, which is why he writes a poem on the celebration of the "independence" of Lebanon (50/3), which he thinks is a travesty ("Woe to the proud mountain that sinks its head in deference to the conqueror and his power … woe to Beirut, showcase of the passions of the conquering soldiers and of the shame of its daughters" 52), why he pillories the Balfour Declaration (72/84: "If you were half the decent fellow that you claim to be, mister Balfour, you would not have spent on charity from the pockets of other people" 72,5), and why he turns against the Jewish poet Reʾūbēn for vilifying the Arabs in a Palestinian newspaper (80, bottom). Only once is he personal, in *Ṣayḥat al-jihād* (96), when he breaks up with Maud, his British lover, whose family had ruined their relationship with their arrogant behaviour ("I cannot love you, as long as my native country is at war").

See F.E. Bustānī, *al-Mashriq* XXV, 623, Mīkhāʾīl Nuʿayma, *al-Ghirbāl*, 155/60 (*al-Qarawiyyāt*). A poem, *al-Rabīʿ al-akhīr* of March 1932 was published in *al-Muqtaṭaf* 80, 1932, 543/5.

13 Fawzi Maʿlūf

As well as al-Qarawī, Brazil owes its fame in Arabic literature primarily to Fawzi Maʿlūf.

The son of ʿĪsā Iskandar al-Maʿlūf (see p. 385), Fawzī was born in Zahleh on 21 January 1899. There, in the region where his family has been held in high esteem since times immemorial, he spent a happy childhood amidst his siblings, four brothers and two sisters. When he was still quite young his father intro-
451 duced him to | Arabic literature, while his years at the Catholic Collège Oriental in his hometown (1909/13) also gave him access to the great representatives of French literature. During the war he worked for his uncle Qayṣar, supplying the Turkish army with flour at Murayjāt, near Zahleh. At that time, he met Felix Fāris (see p. 362). After the war he went with his father to Damascus, where he became secretary to the dean of the Faculty of Medicine, Dr Riḍā Saʿīd. Having few prospects in his native country, he departed for Brazil on 17 September 1921. There, in the city of São Paulo, his uncle Jirjīs Maʿlūf and his brothers ran an important silk business. At their request, Fawzī opened a branch office in Rio de Janeiro. In November 1922, he founded al-Muntadā al-Zaḥlī with some of his Lebanese acquaintances there, wishing to cultivate his taste for literature in their midst. But on 7 January 1930 death snatched him away from his succesful business and from poetry, which he had always consistently combined.

From an early age and while still in Lebanon, Fawzī had tried his hand at poetry, mostly in insignificant personal effusions that only show his agility as a poet, and also in connection with political issues of the day, even if politics never interested him very much. In those days he also wrote some unpublished stories and a play, called *Ibn Ḥāmid, suqūṭ Gharnāṭa*, the subject-matter of which he had borrowed from Florian's novel *Gonzalve de Cordove*, which he himself had translated before writing the play. The play was brought to stage twice in Zahleh and also, after the war, in Damascus and Brazil, but was never published in print. Even though the characters of the play remained quite flat and left much to be desired in terms of their psychological makeup, the success that it had did prove that he knew what kind of theatre would impress the public. In Rio de Janeiro, he initially had very little leisure time. In the poem *ʿAlā shawāṭiʾ al-Rio* he describes the charms of his adoptive country; a *muwashshaḥ*, *Bāqat al-zahr*, is a messenger of love; in *Amāni ʾl-muhājir* he champions—as did Rashīd al-Khūrī—the unity of the Arab people, whose religious fragmentation is very prominent among the people of the diaspora; in *Maqtal al-sirdār* he takes a stance on recent political developments in Egypt while also mourning the deaths of al-Manfalūṭī and Sulaymān al-Bustānī. His ride in an aeroplane in May of 1926 and the feelings that accompanied it triggered his most beautiful poetic creation ever. Initially, he just praised the air-
452 plane: "Heavenly bird, fly away, carried by the wind; and | carry me with you, over the earth; in my body, I fly to where my soul once lived, body-less." This

was the fourth strophe and the centerpiece of a poem in 14 strophes (*anāshīd*) that he published in the *al-Jāliya* newspaper, giving it the title *Shāʿir fī ṭayyāra*, and later published separately in São Paulo in 1926 (*Jāmiʿ* II, 136). He revised the first 11 strophes, renaming it *ʿAlā bisāṭ al-rīḥ*, but illness and then death prevented him from fully completing the job. This revised version was first published in his father's *al-Āthār* of October 1927, and then in São Paulo (Maṭbaʿat al-Funūn, 1929; republished in *al-Fawāʾid*, Beirut 1932, no. 9/11), prefaced by his friend, the Spanish poet Fr. Villaespesa (d. 1936), who was crazy about Arab culture and who dreamed of creating a commonwealth of the Mediterranean peoples, and who later made a Spanish translation of it called "En la Alcatifa de los Vientos" (n.p. & n.d.). The poem was also translated into Portuguese by Venturelli Sobrinho as "No Tapete do Vento" (Rio de Janeiro n.d.). The first song takes the poet up in the ether, the eternal homeland of his soul; he praises its beauty in the second song. In the third song he juxtaposes this to the slave, who is bound to the earth. The fourth song, dedicated to the aeroplane, is followed by a fifth in which there is an angry encounter with the eagles, which are appeased by the poet telling them that he only wanted to get away from the sufferings on the earth. These he then depicts in the sixth song (*Ramz al-alam*: "Look, there he goes; in pain with every move; in haste, propelled by his craving for nothingness"). The seventh and eighth songs take the poet up to the stars, with which he enters into a conversation. In the ninth song he comes to the realm of ghosts, where he is enveloped by incomprehensible melodies, which his poetry reflects with an accomplished kind of musicality, but without any logic in the images which it conveys. From these incomprehensible sound sequences, the voice of a lone ghost detaches itself in the tenth song to confront humanity, in sound Christian manner, with its depravity. In the eleventh song this is continued by another ghost, who condemns progress because man always misuses it, immediately calling the much longed-for aeroplane the instrument of a killer. In the twelfth song, the poet's soul confronts his accusers, explaining that he is on earth against his will, wearing the same kind of clothes as do his brothers. The thirteenth song is one of ecstatic delight in communicating with his soul and, when he finally has to return to earth in
the fourteenth song, | he is comforted by his pen, which has accompanied him 453
throughout his life, a faithful companion in his struggle for truth and justice. The whole poem was composed in the *khafīf* metre, its strophes carrying alternate rhymes, with the first two verses, which have an independent inner rhyme, in each case interrupted by two four-syllable phrases, with the rhyme a-b-a-b. Abū Shādī acclaimed the first version of this poem in *al-Muqtaṭaf* 75, 533/40, while the second version was hailed by Maḥmūd Abu 'l-Wafā' in ibid.

78 (1931) 374/6, by Ṭāhā Ḥusayn in *Ḍād* 131 and in *Wādī* of 18 July 1933, and by F.E. Bustānī in *al-Mashriq* XXIX, 1931, 557/8 (see also Kampffmeyer, *MSOS*, 1931, 158/65).[8] He answered critics who had condemned his pessimism with another strophic poem, *Shuʿlat al-ʿadhāb*, of which songs 4 to 6 have the same rhyme, but which he was unable to complete due to his untimely death (samples from 1. *Laghz al-wujūd* and 2. *Fī Haykal al-dhikrā* in Kampffmeyer, op. cit., 161/2). He is one of those people who are always puzzled by the mystery of existence ("How did we come into this world, whence? To what kind of world shall we go one day? Shall we be resuscitated at the end of times and if so, on what sort of earth? How can I uncover my tomorrow and understand my past, not even knowing how my day shall be, today?! Before we were born, we were already alive, but this was in our ancestors, who all passed away, like we will, one day. When we are gone, we shall live on in our sons, in a form which we hand down from generation to generation"). But he cannot understand the sense of a life in which every bit of joy comes with bitter tears. If the poet had lived long enough to finish his poem, he may still have found some comforting answer, but his long illness prevented him from doing so.

His two brothers are also poets in their own right. Shafīq, who was born in Zahleh on 31 May 1905 (see p. 364) but who went to live in Brazil in 1926, where he is a business associate of his brothers Fawzī and Iskandar, published *al-Aḥlām, qaṣīda khayāliyya ijtimāʿiyya muzayyana bil-rusūm*, Beirut 1926 (*Jāmiʿ* II, 136 mistakenly qualifies it as a *qiṣṣa*; see *RAAD* VI, 478/80), a poem entitled *ʿAbqar*, São Paulo, *Majallat al-Sharq*, and *Fī kharāʾib Baʿlabakk*, which was pub-
454 lished | in *Apollo* I, 170/1, *Ibn Nāyī* in Kampffmeyer, *MSOS* XXXI, 157. The other brother, Riyāḍ, remained in Zahleh and published *al-Awtār al-muqaṭṭaʿāt* in Cairo, Maṭbaʿat Elias. Works by their cousin, Jamīl Bek Maʿlūf, were mentioned above, on page 410.

There is a *marthiya* by Abū Shādī in *al-Muqtaṭaf* 76, 317, *Dhikrā Fawzī al-Maʿlūf*, Beirut 1932 (with many poems, prose pieces and critical essays by Villaespesas and Arab poets). Faïez J. Aoun, *F.M. et son œuvre*, Paris 1939 (with an extensive bibliography, in which the only thing missing is Shafīq Jabrī's announcement of the *Dhikrā* in *RAAD* XI, 774).

8 Characteristically, his father ʿĪsā Iskandar had pointed out a degree of similarity with a verse by al-Ḥijārī in *al-Ḍād* of August 1926, which, for him, was reason to change it in the second edition of the poem (Aoun 105).

(14.–15.) *Poets in South America: Argentina*

14 Jurjī Ṣuwāyā

Dr Jurjī Ṣuwāyā, publisher of *Jarīdat al-Iṣlāḥ* in Buenos Aires, was also a poet. His *dīwān*, entitled *Hams al-shāʿir*, was published in Buenos Aires in 1929. As he states, as well as poems based on personal experience, it also contains other poems that he only considered worthy of publication because of their form, their content being rather trivial. In *RAAD* IX, 767/8, al-Maghribī makes special mention of a poem inspired by a Spanish piece of Elias Anṭūn, which seeks to prove that Arabic is the source of all languages.[9]

15 Elias Konsol

The youngest of the South American poets is Elias Konsol (Qunṣul), who published four *dīwān*s in Buenos Aires in 1931: *al-Sihām, al-Aslāk al-shāʾiʿa* (Alambres de púa), *al-ʿAbarāt al-multahiba* (Lagrimas ardientes), and *ʿAlā madhbaḥ al-waṭaniyya* (En el altar de la patria).

Born in Yabrūd, in Lebanon, in 1901, he went to Argentina at an early age but was often overcome by intense pangs of homesickness (*ʿAb.* 29). He thus condems the sea (ibid., 49/52) for keeping him from returning. Such feelings are amplified by a love-affair with an unhappy ending that caused him to lose himself sometimes in an other-worldly pessimism. In a poem dedicated to al-Qarawī, called "God and | the Poet," he indicts the Lord Himself: "Don't You 455
see, Lord, what injustice You inflicted upon him, creating him from the ether, compressing the aroma of violets to generate his soul, and then blowing magic into him, the moment that he was conceived? ... How often did he not call upon You in his loneliness, empty his heart to You, while You would not listen? You did not care about his weeping, which shook the hearts of others and made them cry" (56/7). He dedicated two impressive *marthiyas* to the memory of Fawzī and Jabrān Khalīl Jabrān (60/5). While the *qaṣīda* still has pride of place in *al-ʿAbarāt al-multahiba*—even though he also tries his hand at some strophic forms and, in one case (23/5), even imitates a sonnet—*al-Aslāk al-shāʾiʿa* only contains quatrains from the years 1928/9. And while he still talks about his personal sufferings occasionally, these have given way to nationalistic sentiments. In poem no. 19, he complains about the enslavement of his native country; in no. 32 about its being torn apart by religious strife, making him declare, in poem no. 45: "If you ask me about my religion, well, I'm a Christian, a Muslim, a Buddhist and a Jew." In poem no. 41, he ridicules his compatriots for merely adopting the superficial aspects of Western civilization

9 *Al-Masātīr, dīwān al-Shaykh Ḥannā Asʿad Zakharyā al-Lubnānī al-shāʿir al-Balamī* was published in Belem, near Rio de Janeiro, in 1929.

without taking any interest in the sciences on which it is based. And, in poem no. 43, a bullfight just makes him sick. He understands that his people can only uplift themselves if they are willing to fight, which is why he ridicules the Kellogg-Briand Pact in poem no. 31. The quatrains at the end are followed by a counterpiece (*muʿāraḍa*) to al-Qarawī's *qaṣīda Tashbīḥāt al-ḥubb*, in strophes that are composed of five hemistichs each, all in the *wāfir* metre. Of these, the first four rhyme with each other while the fifth has a rhyme that is maintained throughout the poem.

ʿAlā madhbaḥ al-waṭaniyya is entirely dedicated to his native country and its heroes, with a preface written by Mūsā Yūsuf ʿAzīma, the publisher of *al-Jarīda al-Sūriyya al-Lubnāniyya*; it was published on 21 June 1931. The phrase at the beginning admonishes the Arabs to unite. The partition of Syria, which the French are very much in favour of (19/20), outrages him, calling the Lebanese member of parliament a "traitor" (26/8: "Do not blame the 'compassionate mother,' as you call her, for she saw how, tamely, you let yourself be chained" etc.). Again he complains about the barriers thrown up by religion, preventing his people from uniting ("When my religion is an obstacle to the liberation of my country, then goodbye to religion and its rules," 32 bottom). Apart from
456 the freedom fighters killed in battle, he also salutes those in | whom he has placed his hopes for the future of the country, such as Shakīb Arslān, the "lion of Lausanne" (38,$_5$), such in a *qaṣīda* that he recited in the Nilo theatre on 31 January 1930 (31/41). In spite of his young age, he is very self-assured: "As I have a lot of enemies, people spread rumours about me, about crimes that I am told I have committed;[10] but I am merely a sweetly singing nightingale, which is why people like me and my songs. There is magic in them, even if I am just a lone moon on life's horizon. Yabrūd will one day proudly claim my poems, for in them, I am erecting a monument to it, a structure whose glory is unequalled" (23/4). See Shafīq Jabrī in *RAAD* XII, 379.

2 *Prose*

1 Sulaymān Sarkīs

The older generation of Syro-American journalists, most of whom had emigrated at a relatively advanced age, had a style of writing which had already matured when they arrrived in their adoptive homeland, and which they then also applied in their attempts to write narrative prose. The novel *al-Qulūb al-muttaḥida fi 'l-mamālīk al-muttaḥida*, by Sulaymān Sarkīs, distinguishes itself from the rest—in the view of Kratschkovsky in *MO* XXI, 197—by being the only

10 Interlocked because of the rhyme, producing: *arājīfa min jarrāʾihā bittu kal-jānī.*

work that takes its inspiration from real-life events, even if it has no particular literary merit.

2 ʿAfīfa Karam

Characteristically, it was not long before a woman let herself be heard among the Syro-Arab journalists of America: ʿAfīfa Karam, daughter of Yūsuf b. Mīkhāʾīl Ṣāliḥ Karam, of ʿAmīshat in Lebanon, who was born in 1887 and worked in New York from 1908.

Fatāt al-sharq II, 121/2. An article entitled *al-Marʾa al-Sūriyya al-muhājira* was published, ibid., 283/9; a collection of essays entitled *Badīʿa wa-fuʾād* was published in New York, n.d.

| 3 Jabrān Khalīl Jabrān 457

As well as Amīn al-Rayḥānī (p. 399), Arabic literature in America owes its greatness primarily to the works of the artist of many talents, Jabrān[11] Khalīl Jabrān.

Born on 6 January 1883 in Bsharrī, in the Wādī Qādīsā in Lebanon, he went to school in Beirut. In 1895, he went, by way of Egypt and Paris, with his family to Boston, where he remained for some time. He once returned for four years to Beirut here he studied at the Madrasat al-ḥikma (see p. 420), mostly Arabic language and culture. In 1903 he returned with his mother to Boston, where he wrote his first Arabic books. In the years 1908–12 he lived in Paris, where he was a student of Rodin, who had a very high opinion of him, calling him the William Blake of the twentieth century. He next moved to New York, where he became the head of al-Rābiṭa al-qalamiyya, devoting himself to literature and painting. Several of his paintings were consecrated in Paris and at exhibitions in America, where he died on 10 April 1931. He was buried in his native country.

He started his literary career with stories that he published collectively in two volumes, *ʿArāʾis al-murūj* (Beirut 1910, with a postscript by Amīn Ghurayyib; Maṭbaʿat al-Hilāl, n.d., 1341/1923) and *al-Arwāḥ al-mutamarrida* (reprint Aleppo: Maṭbaʿat al-Maʿārif, n.d., C. 1920). A short novel, *al-Ajniḥa al-mutakassira*, in which he eternalised an adolescent's love story involving a girl named Salām Karāma, was published separately in New York in 1912 (its preface, *Tadhkārāt al-mawt*, was also published in *al-Badāʾiʿ wal-ṭarāʾif*, 42/3). Still situated in his native country, brilliantly written and free from any rhetoric, these stories are completely imaginary, their only purpose being to serve as a vehicle for the author's own ideas. On the one hand, he preaches the eternity of love, as in *Ramād al-ajyāl wal-nār al-khālida*, the first story of *ʿArāʾis al-murūj*,

---

11 Also Jibrān and Jubrān.

in which he lets the love of a priest of Astarte from Baalbek, a love for a woman who died in 116 BC, be reborn after 2000 years in the person of an Arab shepherd living among the ruins of this ancient town; but when the story moves to
458 the present, he takes no interest in creating characters | that look even remotely like the people of Lebanon today. And when, in *Maḍjaʿ al-ʿarūs*,[12] the third story of *al-Ajniḥa al-mutakassira*, he tells the story of an ill-omened wedding from the end of the nineteenth century in a village in northern Lebanon, purportedly from the mouth of an old woman, the female hero does not become, despite her tragic fate, a real person of flesh and blood, but instead, only acts as a female prosecutor who condemns the lack of freedom for the female sex. The same goes for her sister from the big city, *Warda al-Hāniʾ*,[13] who flees from the house of a rich but unloved husband into the arms of a poor lover, and for *Martā al-Bāniya*,[14] the victim of an unscrupulous lover. The 'puppetness' of his characters is even more conspicuous in two stories about people fighting the domineering attitude and greed of the clergy and the monks, *Yuḥannā al-majnūn* in *ʿArāʾis al-murūj*, *Fī ʿālam al-ruʾyā* 48/58, *al-Badāʾiʿ wal-ṭarāʾif* 182/8, and *Khalīl al-Kāfir* in *al-Arwāḥ al-mutamarrida*. Instead of learning about the background to their conflict with the clerics who are protected by the state, the reader is misguided by the endless angry rants of the protagonists. And in all this, the author does not once ask if a Lebanese village shaykh would let the accused hold such lengthy monologues, worthy of some militant socialist activist. In spite of all this, the language of these stories is free from the constraints of tradition,[15] full of daring trains of thought, so typical of his later works, and rich in imagery, which sometimes lead him to make strange comparisons.[16]

---

12 First published in *Fatāt al-sharq* II, 232/40, reprinted in *Mamlakat al-khayāl*.

13 Reprinted in *Fī ʿālam al-ruʾyā* 26/47.

14 Reprinted in *Fī ʿālam al-ruʾyā* 144/9.

15 Even if, on the whole, his diction is that of classical Arabic, he uses dialectal words, such as *lihāt* 'sigh', from the root *l-h-th, bakkala* 'to cross (the arms)', in *ʿArāʾis* $58_{,8}$ *kardasa* 'to heap up', in *Damʿa wabt.* $186_{,9}$, *mushaqlab* 'disorderly', *ʿAwāṣif* $135_{,6}$ *jāniḥ* 'wing' ibid. $140_{,10}$, *murashshaḥ* 'having a cold' ibid. $188_{,9}$, and others. Whether it was he himself who put the common *tasāʿah*, 'embraces him' in *ʿAwāṣif* $55_{,4}$ (*Grundr.* I, 598 in the middle) is anyone's guess.

16 For instance: "The fragance of myrh and incense filled the air, enveloping the image of the goddess as in a tender shroud, similar to the shroud of hope that envelops the heart of man", *ʿArāʾis al-murūj* $4_{,5}$; or "She was sitting by a spring whose waters wrestled free from the fetters of the earth, like images from the fantasy of the poet", ibid. $26_{,1}$.

| But in this first period[17] he must have understood that narrative prose was 459
not really his thing and that he was much better as a poet. He still wrote a number of stories that later also appeared in books, in addition to the aforementioned collections of stories. But these stories only serve as a vehicle for the symbolic representation of his inner self, caught between two cultures, too big for his land of origin and dissatisfied with the ambivalence of the West. At times, this makes him give in to a kind of pessimism that is more pronounced than that of any of his contemporaries, Amīn al-Rayḥānī included. This pessimism is nowhere more poignant than in *Ḥaffār al-qubūr*, published in *al-ʿAwāṣif* [2] 5/14 and in *al-Badāʾiʿ wal-ṭarāʾif* 131/5. In it, he sees himself in a ramshackle and crumbling world, in which the only thing he can do is to start cleaning it up. This theme is continued in *Ṣafḥa maṭwiyya min dafātir Ḥaffār al-qubūr* in *Fī ʿālam al-ruʾyā* 20/2. At a time when he felt that he had already outgrown them—as can be read in the foreword—the Maṭbaʿat al-Atlantīk brought out a collective edition of his prose pieces from this period, entitled *Damʿa wabtisāma*, with a preface by Nasīb ʿArīḍa (New York 1914). There are still some stories in it, such as *Rujūʿ al-ḥabīb* (192/200), situated in Lebanon in the eighteenth century.[18] But despite the high quality of his epic prose, the return of the dead warrior is, for him, just a symbol for the all-powerfulness of love. The remaining stories are completely disconnected from reality and only differ in form from the essays that well up from within his seething soul. On his birthday, in Paris in 1908 (162/72),[19] he looks back in despair upon his life of 25 years when, in fact, one would expect him to feel happy, a student of Rodin and highly regarded as an artist by his teacher. But even after breaking with the past (*Madīnat al-māḍī*, 123/4), the only thing he sees before him (*Naẓra ila ʾl-ātī*, 100/3) is the unattainable ideal of a future in which humanity, liberated
from all needs | and desires, enters the kingdom of beauty. He would like to 460
make his poet-friends commit themselves to it (*Shuʿarāʾ al-mahjar* 94/6), but for the time being he can only reproach them for being caught up in the kingdom of matter. Many of these pieces, some of which he even calls *munājāt*, are very lyrical and hardly different from the penultimate part, entitled *Aghānī*, in which waves, rain, beauty, happiness, flowers and finally, man too, are all made to sing, just as the poet himself besings the wind on pages 187/92. In *Ṣawt al-shāʿir*, at the end, he confesses to his longing for his beautiful native

17 To which probably also belong a book on music and several pieces in *Majallat al-funūn*, such as *Laylā al-ʿarūs*, all of which which were not accessible to me.

18 Reprinted in *Fī ʿālam al-ruʾyā* 5/9 and *Munājāt al-arwāḥ* 1ff.

19 Reprinted in *al-Badāʾiʿ wal-ṭarāʾif* 26/30.

country and its unhappy people but, at the same time, he also feels an aversion from it because social injustice there is still widespread. This is why he embraces the humanitarian ideal that roams the earth, an apparition of the divine which is still not recognised as such and only disparaged. This is also why he is only a spectator of the fate befalling his country. His affinity with what happened in Egypt is described in a love scene between an houri from the Nile and the mountain god of the Lebanon, surrounded by seraphim (*al-Liqāʾ* 125/8). In other places, too, he likes to invoke characters from oriental or classical mythology,[20] as in his reference to Helena and Cleopatra on page 216. Even if he uses a maxim from the Qurʾān sometimes, the work contains many more references to the Bible. Besides, he also likes to borrow from Indian tradition. Only once does it show that he lives in the Anglo-Saxon world, when, on pages 38/40, instead of Keats' self-chosen epitaph "Here lies One whose Name was writ in Water", he proposes "… whose Name was writ with Fiery Letters in the Skies."

He published another collection of prose pieces with the title *al-ʿAwāṣif* (Cairo: Maṭbaʿat al-Hilāl, 1923, 2nd printing). This collection opens with the story *Ḥaffār al-qubūr*, referred to earlier. In *ʿArāʾis al-murūj* he resuscitates a pair of lovers from ancient Baalbek among Arabs living on its ruins today; in *al-Shāʿir al-Baʿlabakkī* (204/13)[21] he hails Khalīl Maṭrān as the resurrection of
461 a court poet | of a prince of that city, where an Indian sage had preached the doctrine of transmigration in 112 BC. The story *al-Shayṭān* (159/80)[22] has epic force and is a blistering testimony to his hatred of the clergy. In it, a priest finds a badly-wounded man by the side of the road. When, hearing his supplications, he finally decides to tend to him, he learns that it is the Devil, who had fallen into the hands of some angels and been badly injured by them. Hearing this, the priest turns away from him immediately, whereupon the Devil reminds him that without him, he would be out of a job and so they'd better cooperate. What Jabrān thinks of Christianity is clear from his Good Friday meditation, called 'Jesus at the cross' (25/30). But there is also the unassuming story of an unhappy love entitled *al-Samm fi 'l-dasm* (214/22).[23] In *al-Sarjīn al-mufaḍḍal*

20 Apart from Baʿlīm, regarded as singular in *ʿAwāṣif* 189$_{,13}$, we also find, on page 190$_{,3}$, Ahriman and Siva (Çiva).

21 Initially in *Majallat Sarkīs* in Cairo of 13 April 1913, on the occasion of a celebration in honour of the poet at the University of Egypt, and then reprinted in *al-Badāʾiʿ wal-ṭarāʾif* 37/41, *Fī ʿālam al-ruʾyā* 106/13.

22 *Fī ʿālam al-ruʾyā* 124/43, *Munājāt al-arwāḥ* 141ff.

23 *Al-Badāʾiʿ wal-ṭarāʾif* 81/4, *Mun. al-arwāḥ* 146ff.

(86/95) he needs only a few bold strokes to depict some of the members of Beirut's lazy upper class. Then there is also *Falsafat al-manṭiq aw maʿrifat al-dhāt* (130/4), which contains the portrait of a self-satisfied artist in the style of Hogarth. In the dramatic piece *al-Ṣalbān* (181/203)[24] he defends the freedom of the artist against the claims of a snobbish upper class. Where the famine in Syria caused by the war moved Amīn al-Rayḥānī to action (see p. 405), Jabrān only writes a passionate complaint (*Fī ẓalām al-layl*, 97/100). His pessimism is most visible in the story *al-ʿĀṣifa* (136/58),[25] whose main character has retired to lead the existence of a hermit in a deserted convent so as not to be constantly confronted by the world's stupidity and injustice; similarly, fate had brought Jabrān himself to distant places where it would be madness to lead such a monastic life. In his *al-Mukhaddirāt wal-mabādiʿ* (75/81)[26] he turns against his critics who had denounced his pessimism and regarded his writings thus far, notably his *al-Ajniḥa al-mutakassira*, as an assault on the sanctity of matrimony. | But painkillers such as the foundation of a *Jamʿiyya iṣlāḥiyya* 462
cannot undo the damage done to the Orient; with the exception of the sharp knife of a surgeon, like the one he himself is using, it will all be to no avail (see Mīkhāʾīl Nuʿayma, *al-Ghirbāl* 217/41).

At the end of this period in which he expressed his ideas in epic form, even though his work always had a strong lyrical element to it as well, he cast them once more in metrical form in *al-Mawākib, naẓarāt shāʿir wa-muṣawwir fi 'l-ayyām wal-layālī* (with an introduction by Naṣīb ʿArīḍa, published by Niqūlā ʿArīḍa, Cairo, Maṭbaʿat al-Muqtaṭaf, 1923, 2nd printing).[27] It is a long strophic poem with changing rhyme, which begins with a single voice reciting the outcome of a sceptical/pessimistic view on life in a sedate kind of verse in the *basīṭ* metre; there then follows a response in the form of a welcoming kind of optimism towards life in mildly exhilarating verses in *khafīf*, concluded at regular intervals by two lines with the same beginning: "The soul's goal lies within the soul itself; there is no outer sign nor image that could disclose it. One person claims that the soul, once it reaches the summit of perfection, simply

24 Reprinted in *al-Badāʾiʿ wal-ṭarāʾif* 171/81.

25 *Al-Badāʾiʿ wal-ṭarāʾif* 136/42.

26 *Al-Badāʾiʿ wal-ṭarāʾif* 101/6, *Munājāt al-arwāḥ* no. 4.

27 Reprinted in *Mamlakat al-khayāl* and in Muḥammad Muḥammad ʿAbd al-Majīd, *al-Kawākib wal-Mawākib wal-Durar, al-Manfalūṭī, Walī al-Dīn Yegen J. Kh.. J.* Cairo, Maṭbaʿat ʿAṭiyya n.d., 51/64.

disappears and that that is the end of the story;[28] as if the soul is a piece of fruit that is shed by a tree once it is ripe, at the first rustling of the wind. Another person says: when bodies sleep, there is no slumber in the soul nor watchfulness; it is like a reflection in the water which, when it gets turbid, disappears without leaving a trace. They are all wrong. There are no atoms in the body and neither do they perish in the soul. Whenever the north wind upsets the hem of a thinking soul, the east wind comes to straighten it out again. When in the forest, I saw no distinction between body and soul. The air is something moving and humidity stagnant water. Flowers incline themselves under a light breeze heavy with their fragrance, their luster frozen. The shadows of poplars are poplars which only dozed off because they though that night had fallen. Hand me
463 the flute and sing, for a song is body | and soul. The sound of the flute outlives the evening and the morning drink." (p. 26/7).

No matter whether one agrees with the author of the preface in hearing the voices of two men, one young and one old, or just the swings of the mood in the soul of a poet, as does Mayy in *al-Ṣaḥāʾif* 71/87, in *al-Hilāl* of July 1919, the fact remains that he is already starting to break away from the path he had followed thus far. To him, making sense of life can no longer lie in a simple rejection of it as he had done before, and neither can it lie in a revolt against its laws; in this work, he starts off down the road that will inevitably lead him to recognise a higher order. The volume is adorned with symbolic drawings that are not meant to illustrate his ideas, but rather to reflect them artistically with the help of other means.

It seems that ʿAbbās Maḥmūd al-ʿAqqād did not completely understand the meaning of his work when he says—in *al-Ahālī* of May 1919 (*al-Fuṣūl*, 45/9)—that he feels reminded of ʿUmar Khayyām, venting petty criticisms at his language; and *al-Mashriq* XXII, 75 could only find damning words for it.

But the author must have realised that his writings so far had missed the desired effect on his fellow countrymen, even if the beauty of his language was widely recognised. In *The Madman* (New York 1919) and *The Forerunner* (New York 1920), translated into Arabic as *al-Majnūn* (by the archimandrite Anṭūniyūs Bashīr, Cairo, al-Maṭbaʿa al-ʿAsriyya, 2nd printing) and *al-Sābiq* (by the same, ibid., Maṭbaʿat al-Hilāl [*Jāmiʿ* I 378]), he developes his ideas in the English language and in a new style. He now breaks completely with narrative prose and the essay, only using the parable in free verse and the fable to express his ideas. The first book carries the motto: "They think I'm crazy because I do not sell my days for money, while I, for my part, think they're nuts to think

28 While such a turn of the phrase may sound worn to us, in Arabic, *wantaha 'l-khabar* does not produce the same associations.

that money could purchase my days" (*Ramal wa-Zubad* 56,$_{5}$). In his madness he finds his freedom by isolating himself, escaping from those who vainly try to grasp what makes him tick. One more time, he meets the gravedigger from the writings of his youth (p. 47); and he too, cannot help but conclude that he finds himself on the outside of society because, unlike them, he buries their dead—meaning the deceased parts of what society is made up of—with a smile instead of a tear. He criticises the foolishness of man in his description of two wise men (79), one religious | and the other an atheist, who struggle 464
with each other to the point that they change places, or of the two immigrants (22/4), the oldest of whom just quarrels for the sake of quarreling. He also likes to illustrate man's weakness by drawing comparisons with the animal world, such as the fox and the two prisoners, the man suffering from a cataract and the lion in a cage, and the three ants on the nose of a sleeping man. One of his parables, 'Renewed appetite' (2), was praised in Abū Shādī's *al-Shafaq al-bākī*, 1213, as a paragon of trenchant prose.

In *The Forerunner* (*al-Sābiq*),[29] Jabrān prefers the fable over the allegory in free verse. But there are some treasures here, such as the story by which the book that carries its title begins. In it, the author presents himself as the torch-bearer of an endless chain of developments, in which mankind is forever carried upwards, an eternal beneficiary of the past. 'The dying man and the kite' competes with the previous story in the beauty of its prose. In it, the kite circles high over the head of a man in his death throes, ready to plunge down onto his corpse, while he, unable to escape his fate, calls out to it. In the story 'From the deepest of my heart' the author sets out his new philosophy on life, in which he sees "victory in defeat." The fable of the lamb and its mother, who tells it to pray to God to restore peace between two eagles fighting over them, their future kill, symbolises "the war and the small peoples" over whom the major powers are in conflict—purportedly because they want to protect them—in a much more vivid manner than a long discourse could ever have achieved. 'The four frogs', floating on a log while arguing over the cause of their movement until three of them throw off the fourth because he wants to summarise their opinions in some abstract formula, symbolise the eternal struggle between man and his spiritual leaders, who only want to improve his understanding of things. And the fable of the white sheet of paper that wants to remain empty so as not to lose its purity, symbolises the stupidity which refuses to learn. 'The scholar and the poet'[30] appear as a snake which rejoices in the treasures of the insides of the earth, and a bird (*ḥassūn*), high in the skies, which the former | would like 465

29 The preface was reprinted in *Mamlakat al-khayāl* no. 13.

30 Reprinted in *Mamlakat al-khayāl* no. 10.

to drag downwards, while the latter, soaring in the realm of the mind, praises the beauty of the skies and the expanse of its horizons. Even if some of the subtleties of the English original were lost in the Arabic translations of the two works just mentioned, it was only in such a form that the goal with which they were written was fully realised, there being nothing that they could offer to the English reader (see Mīkhā'īl Nuʿayma, *al-Ghirbāl* 168/75).

In 1923, Yūsuf Tūnā al-Bustānī published a selection of Jabrān's writings up to then, entitled *al-Badā'iʿ wal-ṭarā'if, maqālāt wa-manẓūmāt ḥadītha wa-rusūm khayāliyya li-Jabrān Khalīl Jabrān*, Cairo: Maṭbaʿat Yūsuf Kawwī. While *al-Majnūn* already contained some symbolic drawings by him, we now get to know his pictorial art through a series of idealised portraits of Arab poets such as al-Mutanabbī, al-Khansā', Abu 'l-ʿAlā' al-Maʿarrī, Dīk al-jinn, al-Muʿtamid, and ʿUmar b. al-Fāriḍ, and of philosophers like Ibn Khaldūn, Ibn Sīnā and al-Ghazzālī.[31] Apart from pieces already known, some of which were also mentioned earlier, this collection contains a number of articles that were thus far only accessible through the press. Among these are *Lakum Lubnānukum wa-lī Lubnānī* (62/7) and *Anā fī ʿālam al-ru'yā* (65/72) in which he, sharply condemning the materialism and superficiality of his compatriots, presents his own idealised image of his native country, of which he also makes a drawing based on the image of his mother. In *al-Istiqlāl wal-ṭarbūsh* (70/1) he ridicules their habit of sticking to their customs, even when abroad. In this volume he also tries for the first time to pay homage to some of the voices of Islamic culture, such as Ibn Sīnā, whose *Qaṣīdat al-nafs* he admires the most, al-Ghazzālī (115/8), and ʿUmar b. al-Fāriḍ (129), while Jirji Zaydān, too, is not forgotten. In his *Mustaqbal al-lugha al-ʿarabiyya* (121/8)[32] he rightly points out that Arabic can only impose itself as a universal language if those who write in it would have something to say to the world. For the common vernacular, one would need a great poet
466 like Dante to open literature's gates to it; | until then, the literary language only stands to gain from a lively interchange with the common language, not looking down on enriching itself with its vocabulary just as he had done himself (see above, p. 458,4). This volume also contains a reprint from the *Majmūʿat al-rābiṭa al-qalamiyya* in the form of the short play *Iram dhāt al-ʿimād* (189/20) (see *al-Mashriq* XXX, 651ff.). It relates how a Christian poet from Beirut and a Persian dervish meet a local woman called Āmina al-ʿAlawiyya in a small forest near the village of al-Harmal in the year 1883. Once upon a time, while on pilgrimage with her father, this Āmina had discovered the legendary capital

---

31 Other drawings by him, which had already been published separately in New York in 1919, were printed in *al-Muqtaṭaf* 78 (1930), issue 5.

32 Inspired by a survey by *al-Hilāl*, reprinted in *Mamlakat al-khayāl* no. 64.

of the kings of South Arabia in the Rubʿ al-Khālī desert. Asked about its wonders, she describes the city as a symbol of the God-filled universe in which the mystic must seek to dissolve. At the end, there are also some poems in the less pliable forms of the *qaṣīda* and the *muwashshaḥ*, whereas he mostly prefers free verse. In an appendix, Mīkhā'īl Nuʿayma interprets a symbolic drawing by him in a *muwashshaḥ*: *Law tudrik al-ashwāk sirr al-wurūd*. The Jesuits of Beirut regarded Jabrān's philosophy of life, of which his art was a vehicle, as extremely dangerous, which is clear from the very hateful criticism of this work in *al-Mashriq* XXI 487/92, 910/19, XXX, 658/60.

Another selection from his essays, for the most part published earlier in one of the aforementioned collections, but more in particular aphorisms from his earlier writings, were published—with the support of Yūsuf Tūmā al-Bustānī publishers—by the translator of his English works, the archimandrite Antonius Bashīr, and given the title *Kalimāt Jabrān Khalīl Jabrān*, Cairo: al-Maṭbaʿa al-ʿArabiyya, n.d. His 'Jesus at the cross' (see page 461) is preceeded by a similar 'Jesus as a child' (118); these are the germs of a later work. The aphorisms are living proof that his public found his flashes of sudden insight more important than the question of whether his compositions were structurally complete, just like the ancient critics judged a *qaṣīda* only on the merits of its individual verses.

An arbitrary mish-mash of selected writings entitled *Fī ʿālam al-ruʾyā* was published by Muḥammad Muḥammad ʿAbd al-Majīd, Cairo: Maṭbaʿat Muḥammad ʿAṭiyya, n.d. Besides stories already known from other collections, this volume only contains the piece *al-Malik al-sājin*, a figure of speech to denote the lion's cage in the New York Zoo (p. 100/3), but for which no source is given. Another | selection, *Fī ʿālam al-adab, al-kitāba wal-shiʿr, maqālāt fi 'l-ʿilm* 467 *wal-adab wal-falsafa wal-ijtimāʿ*, was published by Muḥammad Muḥammad Zakī al-Dīn, Cairo: Maṭbaʿat al-Maḥrūsa, 1924.

In his writings so far, Jabrān Khalīl Jabrāb often touched upon religious issues, looking for answers outside the familiar areas of religious dogma. Having reached the summit of his creative powers, he took up the subject again, and in September of 1923 he published his English book *The Prophet*, which was reprinted ten times between then and 1926, and translated into 10 European languages as well as Hindustani and Japanese Again it was the archimandrite Antonius Bashīr who made the Arabic translation, titled *al-Nabī*, which was published in Cairo at Yūsuf Tūmā al-Bustānī publishers in 1926 (with a lecture by Rabbi Frankel of Detroit as an epilogue). Jabrān talks about a prophet by the name of Muṣṭafā, who spent twelve years in the land of Orflīs (Orplid) where he had obtained the respect and the love of its people. When he waits for the ship that is to take him back to his native land, the people throng around him

to say goodbye. At the request of some of them he sets out his doctrine once more, for a final time, emphasising what matters most in it. He thus preaches in short, well-polished sentences on love, marriage, and children, but also on charity, food and drink, labour, joy and sorrow as well as all other aspects of human existence, up to death. It is a deeply religious work. When a priest approaches the prophet with the request to also talk about religion now, he answers (93) "Have I spoken this day of aught else? Is not religion all deeds and all reflection, and that which is neither deed nor reflection, but a wonder and a surprise ever springing in the soul, even while the hands hew the stone or tend the loom? Who can separate his faith from his actions, or his belief from his occupations? Who can spread his hours before him, saying, "This for God and this for myself; "This for my soul and this other for my body"? All your hours are wings that beat through space from self to self. He who wears his morality but as his best garment were better naked. The wind and the sun will tear no holes
468 in his skin. And he who defines his conduct by ethics | imprisons his song-bird in a cage. The freest song comes not through bars and wires. And he to whom worshipping is a window, to open but also to shut, has not yet visited the house of his soul whose windows are from dawn to dawn." The prophet concludes his farewell speech with the proverb (John 16.16): "A little while, and ye shall not see me: and again, a little while, and ye shall see me", adding: "and another woman shall bear me." Of course, the Jesuits of Beirut could only reject a work of this kind (*al-Mashriq* XXIV, 633, 680ff.), in the same way in which they had condemned *al-Mawākib* before (ibid. XXII, 75), while Abū Shādī for his part showered it with the highest praise in *al-Ashiʿʿa*, 132.

In the booklet *Sands and foam*—translated by the same Antonius Bashīr as *al-Ramal wa-zubad* (Cairo: Yūsuf Tūmā al-Bustānī, al-Maṭbaʿa al-Raḥmāniyya, 1927)—Jabrān Khalīl Jabrān incorporates the reincarnation of this prophet. The work, which is also adorned with a series of symbolic pictures, opens with the 'Song of the *sāqiya*'—a facsimile in the poet's own hand included—in free verse, in each case bordered by two strophes in the *ramal* metre, in answer to the question about the meaning of life and death. The poet walks on the beach, picking up the symbols of his thoughts as he goes along, turning them into finely-polished aphorisms. Even though he confesses to being an agnostic ("I am ignorant of absolute truth. But I am humble before my ignorance and therein lies my honour and my reward" 24 bottom; "A truth is to be known always, to be uttered sometimes" 28,$_{5}$; "We shall never understand one another unless we reduce the language to seven words," 41,$_{8}$), he is proudly aware of his responsibility ("Only an idiot and a genius break man-made laws; and they are the nearest to the heart of God" 48,$_{6}$), proclaiming—as before—a religion of love and justice, free of any dogma whatsoever: "I too am visited by angels

and devils, but I get rid of them. When it is an angel I pray an old prayer, and he is bored; when it is a devil I commit an old sin, | and he passes me by" 45; 469
"He who can put his finger upon that which divides good from evil is he who can touch the very hem of the garment of God" 46,$_{6}$; "There is neither religion nor science beyond beauty" 35,7; "Inspiration will always sing, inspiration will never explain" 62,$_{6}$; "There lies a green field between the scholar and the poet; should the scholar cross it, he becomes a wise man; should the poet cross it, he becomes a prophet" 68,$_{7}$. As in his earlier works, he sometimes presents his ideas in the form of a fable (43 bottom, 66,$_{2}$) or an allegory (69). At the end (85), the truths of Christianity once more well up in his soul. Even if sometimes haunted by doubts ("Was the love of Judas' mother less than the love of Mary for Jesus?"), he still proclaims: "Crucified One, you are crucified upon my heart; and the nails that pierce your hands pierce the walls of my heart. And tomorrow when a stranger passes by this Golgotha he will not know that two bled here. He will deem it the blood of one man."

What he merely hints at here, he fully actualises in *Yasūʿ b. al-insān, aqwāluhu wa-afʿāluhu kamā akhbarahā wa-dawwanaha 'lladhīna ʿarafūhu*, translated from the English by Aḥmad Bashīr, C. 1932. In a series of 77 loosely-connected scenes, he renders the life and times of the Saviour accessible to the modern reader. First of all there is James, son of Zebedee, who talks about the Kingdom of Jesus in the world to come. Then the author talks about Hannah, Mary's mother, and the birth of Jesus. The impact of the herald of divine love on womenkind is illustrated through various female personalities. Mary Magdalene herself describes her first encounter with the Redeemer as a real love scene, permeated by a hidden, carnal glow. A certain Joan, the wife of someone named Ḥāfiẓ Herod (?), Salome, Rachel, another Mary and a woman from Jubayl (Byblos) who bemourns Jesus' death in a way comparable to the mourning for Tammuz, all have the same kind of experience. Citing three of his parables, ʿAssāf, a preacher from Sidon, illustrates the verbal power of Jesus. He juxtaposes him, the Prince of the Physicians, with the symbol of the healing practices on earth in the person of a Greek pharmacist-cum-philosopher. From the wedding in Cana, the author takes the reader to Damascus, where a Persian philosopher is preaching about old and new gods. A young priest from
Capernaum | sees Jesus the magician, while the rich Levi only knows him as 470
the simple fisherman from Nazareth; the aged Uriah, who came from the same place as he, declares that Jesus had always been regarded as a stranger where he came from. Cleopas al-Batrūnī crosses his path as a representative of the law while Sābā al-Anṭākī talks about Shāʾūl al-Ṭarasūsī as the man who distorted Jesus' sermon by resuscitating the law; Malākhī, an astronomer from Babel, tries to shed light on the miracles of Jesus by using the insights of modern

psychology, only skipping the resurrection of the dead. "When you can tell me what death is, then I will tell you what life is." In whatever light the Redeemer appears in this work, in each case the poet is actually talking about his own views on the religion of love and salvation, in the same way in which he did in his earlier writings, summarising it once more at the end with the poem *Rajul min Lubnān ba'da 19 qarnan*. But in spite of the beauty of the language and the poetry, there is no denying that the form of this book hardly suited its purpose. It is quite understandable that the Jesuits of Beirut had to condemn it from beginning to end (see Amīn Khālid, *al-Mashriq* XXXI, 108/15, 197/202, 278/82).

In the same year, *Ālihat al-arḍ* was also published, translated from the English by Antonius Bashīr (Cairo: al-Maṭba'a al-'Aṣriyya, 1932) but whose printing he did not live to see, the work indeed seeming to miss his final touch. It is an antiphony involving three nameless gods who, born on earth, decide about life and death, somewhere high up in the mountains. They quarrel about the laws that the life which they are about to create will be subjected to. The first wants to rule over life like a real tyrant ("But my self love is limitless and without measure. I would rise beyond my earth-bound mortality and throne me upon the heavens. My arms wood girdle space and encompass the spheres. I would take the starry way for a bow, And the comets for arrows, and with the infinite would I conquer the infinite" p. 10). The second wants to govern life like an enlightened despot ("I would ... raise man from secret darkness ... and yet [to] confine his days and his nights to their immutable resemblance ... to give him gladness that he may sing before us, and sorrow that he may call unto us ... Man is born to bondage, and in
471 bondage is his honour | and his reward." p. 7/8). Finally, the third god, who so far just made some remarks in the margin of the dispute between the other two, sings the praises of love as the only rule in life ("But love shall stay, and his finger-marks shall not be erased. The blessed forge burns, the sparks rise, and each spark is a sun. Better it is for us, and wiser, to seek a shadowed nook and sleep in our earth divinity, and let love, human and frail, command the coming day" p. 39). Thus, his last poem reflects the same harmony that we see throughout his life (see Aḥmad Khālid, *al-Mashriq* XXXI, 230/6).

As well as the anthologies mentioned earlier, the year 1927 saw the publication of *Mamlakat al-khayāl* by 'Uthmān Shākir (Cairo: Maṭba'at al-Nahḍa), *Munājāt arwāḥ* (Maṭba'at al-Shabāb), and *Mā warā' al-ḥayāh* (Cairo n.d.).

See Barbara Young, *A Study of Kahlil* (sic) *Gibran, this Man from Lebanon*, privately printed, New York: Syrian-American Press, 1931. Mayy, *J. Kh. J. yaṣifu nafsahu bi-yadihi fī rasā'ilihi, al-Ḥadīth*, 1931, 363/6, idem in *al-Muqtaṭaf* 74, 1929, 9/13, Sāmī al-Kayyālī, *J. Kh. J.* in *al-Ḥadīth* 1931, 461/6, Ma'rūf al-Arna'ūṭ, *J. Kh. J.* ibid., 336/8, Amīn Khālid, *Muḥāwalāt fī dars J. Kh. J.* Beirut 1933 (a special issue of *al-Mashriq* xxx), Ph. Hitti, *Maqām J. Kh. J. fī 'l-adab al-ʿarabī, al-Muqtaṭaf* 74, 1929, 299/300, Amīn al-Rayḥānī, *Dhikrā J. Kh. J.*, Beirut 1931 (see *al-Muqtaṭaf* 79, 198/203). Mīkhāʾīl Nuʿayma, *J. Kh. J. ḥayātuhu, mawtuhu, adabuhu, fannuhu*, Beirut:, Maṭbaʿat Lisān al-ḥāl, 1934, (see *al-Hilāl*, November 1934, 81/6). Felix Fāris (cf. p. 362), *Risālat al-minbar ila 'l-sharq al-ʿarabī, majmūʿat khuṭab rannāna wa-abḥāth wa-qaṣāʾid tarmī ilā taʿzīr al-rābiṭa al-ʿArabiyya wa-iqāmat ḥaḍāratihā wa-iṣlāḥ usratihā wa-fuṣūl falsafat J. Kh. J. wa-ḥayātihi wa-radd li-kitāb al-ustādh Nuʿayma*, Beirut n.d. (350 ss.). T. Khemiri and G. Kampffmeyer, *Leaders* 17/9.—Ḥabīb Masʿūd, *J. ḥayyan wa-mayyitan, majmūʿa tashtamil ʿalā mukhtārāt min kitābāt J. wa-rusūmihi wa-mā qīla fīhi*, São Paolo 1933.—*Manẓūmāt J. Kh. J.* Prose Poems transl. by Andrew Gribb, New York 1935.

4 Mīkhāʾīl Nuʿayma

Mīkhāʾīl Nuʿayma[33] steered the prose of the Syrians of America from the lofty heights of Jabrān Khalīl Jabrān | back to the solid ground of the here-and-now. 472

Born in Biskintā on 22 November 1889, he went to the Russian teachers' college of Nazareth starting from 1902. He was then enrolled in the seminary of Poltava (Ukraine) where he devoted himself to the study of Russian literature and of Tolstoy in particular. In 1909 he participated in a students' strike—very common in those days—and was subsequently banned from the seminary for a period of time; but in the spring of 1911 he was nevertheless allowed to pass his final examination. Back in his native country he wanted to go to Paris to continue his studies, but then accepted the invitation of his brother to come to the United States, where the latter had been living for the last eleven years. In December of 1911 he arrived in Walla Walla in the state of Washington, enrolling at the University of Washington in 1912 and obtaining an A.B and an LL.B in 1916. He then settled in New York where he became a member of al-Rābiṭa al-qalamiyya and made a living by working for N. ʿArīda's magazine *al-Funūn*. After the magazine had fallen victim to the war, he started working for the Russian Commission for the Purchase of Ammunition, where he remained until February 1918. In May of that same year he joined the American army and together with a number of other American students he went on a scholarship to the university of Rennes in France. In July of 1919 he returned to America, where he went back to his previous occupation as a journalist, mainly for ʿAbd al-Masīḥ al-Ḥaddād's *al-Sāʾiḥ*. It was not long before he started to publish essays

33 This he how he spells his name explicitly on the title page of *al-Ghirbāl*; in English he called himself Naimy with the colloquial *nisba* Nʿaymī. Because of a misunderstanding over this, this then changed to Naʿīma in Kampffmeyer and strangely also in Kračkovsky and Lecerf, *Lit. dial.* 83.

and poems in the English language.[34] In 1932 he returned to his native country, where he was soon celebrated as a poet and appreciated as a public speaker.

His first publication in Arabic is the play *al-Ābāʾ wal-banūn, riwāya tamthīliyya dhāt arbaʿat fuṣūl* (New York: Ṭabʿ Shirkat al-Funūn, 1917). In the
473 preface he talks | about the history of the Arabic theatre, which he justly qualifies as quite unsatisfactory until then. According to him, one of the greatest obstacles in the way of a national theatre was the problem of the language, which had also been the cause of Muḥammad ʿUthmān Jalāl's failure in Egypt. He went a middle road by letting the educated in his plays talk in Classical Arabic, and women and children in the common vernacular. This is indeed a good way of marking out the characters. It remains unclear how the public reacted, if this piece was ever brought to stage. The story treats of the agony of young girls who are going to be married off against their will, a subject that had been brought to stage several times before. In this play too, there is a daughter from "a good house" whose mother wants to marry her off to some unloved and unworthy member of her own class who is only after her dowry. The mother being a widow, the title is not entirely appropriate. The atmosphere in the thoroughly middle class household in which Zayna, the female hero of the story, an older brother of hers (immersed in weltschmerz and always planning some literary scheme) and also a younger one (playful and buddies with the suitor favored by the mother) all live in the mother's care, is described very well. Then a friend of the older brother appears onto the scene, like a knight in shining armour, a poor teacher at that, together with his sister, also a teacher, who just keeps him company the time of the holidays. Fearing the influence of this friend, the suitor wants to let some hired thugs finish him off, such with the consent of the younger brother. But the assassination attempt is a failure and when the teacher has brought himself to safety in his house, Zayna comes to see him in order to warn him. This is how the male protagonist discovers that the love which he had felt for her all along is reciprocal. When the mother wants to bring her back by force, the girl falls victim to some ailment. The sister of the teacher saves her life through her selfless care and devotion. Now that the suitor has been unmasked as an imposter, the mother finally consents to the girl's marriage to the male hero. The piece does have some dramatic climaxes, such as the nightly scene in the house of the teacher, but the dialogues which are meant to give substance to the characters are for the most part still too long.

---

34 This according to his autobiography in a letter written in English, published by I. Kračkovsky in *WI* XIII, 104/10.

It was not before 1923 that Nuʿayma published something else, a book this time, titled *al-Ghirbāl, majmūʿat maqālāt naqdiyya*, Cairo, al-Maṭbaʿa al-ʿAṣriyya. ʿAbbās Maḥmūd al-ʿAqqād | wrote a foreword to it in which he de- 474
clares to agree with the author's views while at the same time regretting his careless use of the language, so common among the average Americans. The book opens with an essay on the tasks of literary criticism, which should not only be defined negatively, but also contribute to literature's development by fixing new objectives. His literary ideals are set out in the prefaces to the *Majmūʿat al-rābiṭa al-qalamiyya* of 1921 (*Miḥwār al-adab*, reprinted in *Aḥsan mā katabtu* 84/6) and to his play *al-Ābāʾ wal-banūn*. In *al-Ḥabāʾib*, the poetasters, whose *qaṣīda*s fill the newspapers and the magazines, get the full load of his sarcasm. When an American asks him to mention the name of the greatest Arab poet alive, he is ashamed to say he does not know. In *al-Maqāyīs al-adabiyya* he observes that in Arabic literature too, there have always been perennial and universal aesthetic criteria—conformity with the intellectual needs of the time, truth, beauty, and the music of the language—but that these criteria are no longer applied by the professionals. To the question, asked so often, also in the poems of his friend Jabrān, regarding the nature of poetry, his only answer is "If you don't feel it right away, you're never going to find it." He ridicules the never-ending petty criticisms of the linguists as mere *naqīq al-dafādiʿ*, barring modern poets as they do from any and all deviation from the traditional phraseology, criticizing someone like Jabrān because instead of *istaḥamma* ('to bathe') he used in one case a fifth form *taḥammama*. Metre and rhyme should no longer be the sole criteria for distinguishing the poetic from the unpoetic. The existing lack of ideas must be remedied by taking one's inspiration from Western literature (*falnutarjim*!). These basic rules of literary criticism he then applies to individual works, first of all to *al-Arwāḥ al-ḥāʾira* by his friend N. ʿArīḍa, then to Aḥmad Shawqī's much-praised song on Spain (*al-Durra al-Shawqiyya*) whose hollow phrases he merciless exposes, to *al-Qarawiyyāt*, to Aḥmad al-Rayḥānī's English translations from mystical poetry, to Jabrān's *Forerunner* and *al-ʿAwāṣif*, to Mayy's translation of | W. Müller's 'Deutscher 475
Liebe' and to her lecture titled *Ghāyat al-ḥayāh*, to Muḥammad al-Shurayqī's (see p. 357/8) *Aghāni 'l-ṣibā*, to the *Dīwān al-nubūgh* by Labīb al-Riyāshī (p. 370) and which he exposes as empty materialist blabber, to Khalīl Maṭrān's translation of Shakespeare's *Merchant of Venice*, and finally also to the *Dīwān* and *al-Fuṣūl* of ʿAbbās Maḥmūd al-ʿAqqād.

In 1936, his *al-Marāḥil, siyāḥat fī ẓawāhir al-ḥayāt wa-bawāṭinihā* (Beirut 1932, not acessible to me) and his obituary for Jabrān Khalīl Jabrān were followed by *Zād al-maʿād, majmūʿat khuṭab fi 'l-nās wal-ḥayāh* (Cairo, Maṭbaʿat al-Muqtaṭaf wal-Muqaṭṭam). They are lectures held during the years 1930/5 in his hometown of Biskintā, in Beirut and in other cities all over Lebanon, in Jerusalem, in one case in the Friends Schools in Ramallah, Palestine, in Damascus, Homs, Tripoli and in Ṣāfīṭā in ʿAlawī territory. Many of these lectures were first translated from English. They treat of all the cultural issues that were hotly debated among his compatriots: the place of religion in the lives of young people, the issue of women's rights, the weakness of literature, etc. He does not shrink from rejecting as "broken trumpets" (17/23) the church's doctrine of reward and punishment by God the Creator and the belief in progress, freedom and equality for all of mankind. At the same time, he warns his compatriots against the temptations of the country where the Dollar reigns supreme, praising the merits of their native country, despite its being backward in many respects.

His latest work, *Kān mā kān* (Manshūrāt al-Makshūf, Beirut, Maṭbaʿat al-Ittiḥād 1937) is a collection of six stories published in the years 1914/19. The first of these, 'The cuckoo clock' (1915), was inspired by the life of Lebanese emigrants abroad. In a small villlage in the Lebanon, where a young peasant is preparing himself to get married, one of its former inhabitants returns from America. The locals are full of admiration for his wealth, his cuckoo clock causing a real sensation. The clock enchants the peasant's prospective wife to such an extent that one day, she runs off with the American. The peasant now lets himself no longer be restrained by his parents and emigrates as well. During the war he acquires great wealth in America, where he marries a woman who loves his money but loathes his backwardness. She ridicules him especially be-
476 cause of a cuckoo clock which he had | bought from his first savings and from which he will not separate. One day, when the couple visits a posh restaurant in the company of an American, an admirer of the woman, the man runs into his former fiancée who now has to wait on him. When she comes to visit him at his home, the following day, the man's wife, who is just leaving the house in the company of her lover, pushes her aside. In her fall, she draws an elderly Syrian lady servant of the household with her, who dies of her injuries on the spot. In that very same moment, the cuckoo clock strikes the hour, reminding the man of his entire wasted life. After all this he returns to his native country where he settles in some village under the assumed name of Mr Thompson. There, his goodness earns him the love of and respect of the peasants. Much better are the next two stories, 'New Year' (1914) and 'The woman who would not give birth' (1915). The main theme in both stories is a peasant's wish for a son and heir. In the first story, a 'shaykh' hopes—after the six daughters that his wife bore him already—to finally welcome a son and heir. But when she gives birth to another daughter on New Year's eve, her husband buries the child immediately in the stable. Now the whole village pities him because his long-awaited heir

turned out to be still-born. The second story is about a woman who remained childless for ten years. Wishing to give her husband the heir that he has been waiting for so long, she gives herself to another man. Even if this hope finally-come-true gains her the love of her husband and his mother, she cannot live with the fact that she betrayed him. Thus, before the child is born and exactly on their wedding day, she lets herself be killed by her husband's hand, telling him that the cause of their childlessness was not she, but he. With its subtle descriptions of the psychology of its characters and its colourful descriptions of life in the countryside, this is the jewel of this volume. In contrast, 'The treasure', about a superstitious person who learns the hard way that amulets don't work, 'Saʿādat al-Bek', about some seedy Lebanese village aristocrat who is still respected by his compatriots in New York, and the tale from the war called 'Shorty' (1919) are none of them convincing. Between these short stories there is the dramatic piece *Jamʿiyyat al-mawtā* (1917) about a meeting of the victims | 477
of the famine in Syria led by ʿAzrāʾīl, and during which a merchant from Brazil who had spent some dollars on their behalf, a poet who had collected money for them in Egypt by writing a *qaṣīda*, a journalist who had donated advertising space, and a politician who had established relief foundations on their behalf in Paris are all thrown out for being without merit.

Another story, *Huwa 'l-ḥubb qīla lanā kūnī fa-kunnā*, was published in *al-Hilāl* 43 8/16. In *al-Ḥadīth* 1929, 430/2, there is a poem called *al-Nahr al-mutajammid*, which to him symbolizes his own heart ("You, stream, frozen, like my heart, with this difference that one day, you will thaw up; not so my heart"). Three *qaṣīda*s were published in *al-Muqtaṭaf* 94, 363/4.

See Kāẓim al-Dāghistānī, *al-Ṭabīʿa al-insāniyya fī adab Mīkhāʾīl Nuʿayma, al-Hilāl*, 1933, 238/42, *MSOS* XXVIII, 255, XXX, 219, XXXI, 168, 183, 193. Khemiri and Kampffmeyer, *Leaders* 30.

5 ʿAbd al-Masīḥ Ḥaddād et al.

Of the prose writers in North America we also mention 1. ʿAbd al-Masīḥ al-Ḥaddād, the publisher of *al-Sāʾiḥ* magazine, 2. Ilyās Efendi ʿĀzār al-Khūrī, 3. Salīm Efendi Yūsuf al-Khāzin, and 4. Salīm ʿAbbās Ḥamdān al-Lubnānī.

1. His *Ḥikāyāt al-mahjar* (New York 1921) contains lively scenes from the lives of the Syrian emigrants (for a sample see Ode-Vasilieva, 158/62).—2. A story, *al-Niyyāt min al-dāʾim fī wādi 'l-tāʾim*, was published in New York, *Jarīdat Mirʾāt al-Gharb*, n.d.—3. Living in Old Ortshire in the state of Maine, this author published *Mudhakkirāt Kleopatra* in the same periodical (reprinted in *Fatāt al-sharq* II, 55/60, 101/6).—4. Lives in Detroit in Michigan and published a collection of essays called *al-Ḥamdāniyyāt* n.p. & n.d. (*Jāmiʿ* I, 344).

6 Shukrī al-Khūrī

In São Paolo (Brazil), where he had emigrated as a young man and founded the humorous magazines *al-Aṣmaʿī* and *Abu ʾl-Hawl*, Shukrī al-Khūrī tried to pre-
478 serve the bond between his | compatriots and their native country by reviving their recollection of those who had remained behind by means of witty stories in the Lebanese vernacular.

His best-known story is *al-Tuḥfa al-ʿāmmiyyā fī qiṣṣat Finyānūs*, initially published incomplete in *Majallat al-Ṣawāb* in Rio de Janeiro, São Paolo 1902; printed together with an English translation by Frank E. Nurse, *The Pitiful Pilgrimage of Phinyanus*, Diss. Heidelberg, n.d. (1908); réédité avec l'autographe de l'auteur par le P.E. Ley, suivi d'un lexique de mots rares, illustré par M. Farrūḫ (see p. 428), Impr. Cath. 1932; selected passages in D.V. Semenov, *Chrestomatia razgovornogo Arab. jazyka* (Siriskoje narečne), Leningrad 1929, 24/39 (with an ending that is not in Nurse concerning F.'s will and notes on the leading Syrian businesses of Brazil); trans. E. Littmann, *F. die Abenteuer eines amerikanischen Syrers*, Tübingen 1932. Even though the author uses the dialogue as the format for his story, the one who tells it is merely incited to continue his account by questions that he is asked while talking. He talks about his return to his native country, after his arrival in Alexandria. In humorous scenes he relates his adventures, the festive reception by family and friends, his illness in the wake of it, the old women's attempts to heal him, his failed search for a bride, the house that he built and the lawsuit that his neighbours filed against him and which provided him with first-hand knowledge of the Turkish legal system. Before the revolution, the story was banned in Syria because he had criticised the corrupt practises of Turkish officials. A second story was adapted by Em. Mattson: *Ṭūlit il-ʿumr*, texte ar. vulg. transcrit et traduit avec introduction, notes et commentaire, *MO* VI, 81/117, 206/31, VIII, 16/57 following the edition *Ṭūlit al-ʿumr fī ḥadīth Abī Yūsuf wa-Nimr*, New York: Maṭbaʿat al-Hudā, 1904. This work is of a more serious character. It is an account of three nightly conversations between Yūsuf and Nimr on the sad conditions that Lebanon is in. A third book, *Murūr fī arḍ al-hanāʾ wa-nabaʾ min ʿālam al-baqāʾ* (New York 1905) is more literary in
479 style, like the one that he used in his *Abu ʾl-Hawl* magazine. | Even if European researchers regard his writings as valuable literary monuments, they left no imprint whatsoever on the literature of his compatriots because, even in the diaspora, the classical language remained the common standard throughout. See Kračkovsky, *MO* XXXI, 1927, 209/13.

7 Yūsuf Saʿd Naṣr

In the short story *al-Ḥaqq yaʿlū* by Yūsuf Saʿd Naṣr (São Paolo 1922; *ṭabʿa thāniya munaqqaḥa muʿallaq ʿalayhā ḥawāshī*, ibid. 1923), we get an altogether different picture of life among the emigrants.

Written in the first person, the story is about someone re-migrating from Brazil, shortly before the war, to start working as a typesetter in Cairo, and how, little by little, he starts suffering from paranoia and megalomania. Soon after having been hired he falls out with his boss, which feeds his delusion that he is being persecuted for political reasons. At the beginning, he thinks that he is only under suspicion because he is friends with a Jesuit priest; but then he starts to doubt the latter's honesty as well, imagining as he does that he wants to set him up in a marriage. At the same time, he considers himself a victim of the Freemasons, becoming ever-more convinced that British foreign policy in Egypt turns mainly on him. A real troublemaker, he even manages to penetrate to Kitchener himself. Back in São Paolo, he feels threatened by the spiritualist powers of his enemies, among them King George himself. For this reason he flees to New York and then Beirut, where he is overtaken by the outbreak of the war. In the end, he recovers his inner peace in the house of a Jesuit priest in the Alsace. A naïve reader might mistake this psycho-pathological study for a thriller. While its language has literary pretences, it is actually less grammatical than any other work in Arabic coming out of the Americas.

8 Ilyā al-Khūrī Abū Rizq et al.

Ilyā al-Khūrī Abū Rizq describes the lives of the Syrians of Brazil in his *al-Fāʾih fī bayḍāʾ al-ḥayāh* (Cairo: Yūsuf Tūmā al-Bustānī, 1928), while Dr Khalīl Saʿādat Bek's *Qayṣar wa-Kleopatra* (São Paolo 1927) is a lengthy historal novel. The publisher of the | newspaper and magazine *al-Mufīd*, Tawfīq Efendi Daʿūn, pub- 480
lished a collection of his articles as *Mukhtārāt al-jadīd*, São Paolo n.d. (1925).

Chapter 4. Iraq[1]

This Muslim country, whose independence existed initially just on paper and which one would therefore have expected to be a cradle of nationalist ideology, had no capacity for such a thing. Just like Syria, Iraq is a religiously-divided country. Even if Christianity did not play a prominent role there the way it does in Syria, the rift between Sunnīs and Shīʿa was so much the deeper. Like elsewhere, civil movements could only be expected to do well in the cities. But apart from the Sunnīs of Baghdad and the Shīʿa of Najaf and Karbala, there was no intellectual life worth mentioning. And even in modern times, the latter are still entirely under the influence of the medieval tradition, which is why their authors were mentioned previously in Supplement II, pages 792ff, including those who are still active today. Similarly, the intellectual movements of Egypt and Syria linking up to Western culture did not have much of an impact on the Sunnīs of Iraq either, even if the government tried to reform the education system based on the example of those two countries.[2]

481 | Intellectual life in Iraq still being very much in a state of fermentation, the bookselling trade is not much developed either. It is, therefore, not easy to obtain an even remotely complete idea of the book production of that country. If this is true for local scholars,[3] it is all the more so for people working from Europe.

1 *Poetry*

Riḍā wa-Ẓāhir wa-Zayn (see p. 421a), *al-ʿIrāqiyyāt, al-Juzʾ al-awwal wa-huwa mukhtār min shiʿr ʿasharat shuʿarāʾ min mashāhīr shuʿarāʾ al-ʿIrāq*, Sidon: Maṭbaʿat al-ʿIrfān, 1331.

Rafāʾīl Buṭṭī, *al-Adab al-ʿaṣrī fi ʾl-ʿIrāq al-ʿArabī, Qism al-manẓūm, Juzʾ* I and II, Cairo: al-Maṭbaʿa al-Salafiyya, 1341/2 1923 (was to be continued); see A. Schaade, *OLZ*, 1926, columns 865/72.

---

1 Significantly abbreviated.

2 See ʿAjjan al-Hadid, Le développement de l'éducation nationale en Iraq, *REI* VI, 1932, 231/67 and the official reports mentioned in Ph.W. Ireland, *ʿIraq*, 481/2.

3 "I am surely not mistaken in claiming that today there is no printing house in Iraq which keeps a complete list of all its prints and publications; and I do certainly not exaggerate if I claim that not even the government of Iraq itself has a complete listing of all the books, newspapers and articles that are and have been published there," see al-Sayyid ʿAbd al-Razzāq al-Ḥasanī, *Taʾrīkh al-ṣiḥāfa al-ʿIrāqiyya* vol. I (Maṭbaʿat al-Gharī), p. 7.

Muḥammad Mahdī al-Jawāhirī, *Ḥalbat al-adab, hiya nubdha min dīwān al-Musābaqāt tajmaʿ ʿiddat qaṣāʾid mukhtāra lahu jārā bihā ʿiddat shuʿarāʾ kibār maʿa tarājimihim wa-maqāla fī ʾl-tawshīḥ*, Baghdad: Maṭbaʿat Dār al-salām, 1341.

Saʿd Mikhāʾīl, *Ādāb al-ʿaṣr fī shuʿarāʾ al-Shaʾm wal-ʿIrāq wa-Miṣr*, Cairo: Maṭbaʿat al-ʿUmrān, n.d.

1 Najaf and Karbala

Among the Shīʿa of Najaf and Karbala poetry is still written entirely in the style of the classics. Two of these poets, Jaʿfar al-Ḥillī and Ibrāhīm al-Ṭabāṭabāʾī, who took the ʿAbbāsid poets as their model, have already been mentioned in Supplement II, 796/7. Here we just mention some of their predecessors and contemporaries.

| a *Ḥaydar b. Sulaymān al-Ḥillī* 482

In his own time, Ḥaydar b. Sulaymān b. Dāʾūd b. Ḥaydar al-Ḥillī (Ḥillāwī) was the most outstanding poet of Iraq. He was born in Shaʿbān 1246/January 1831 and died in Rabīʿ II 1304/January 1887. He is famous as *Shāʿir ahl al-bayt al-kirām* because he wrote many *marthiya*s on the leaders of Shīʿism; still, he also practised a very elegant variant of the love song. *Dīwān al-durr al-yatīm*, Bombay 1312.[4] Samples in *al-ʿIrāqiyyāt* 95/119. Besides this, he also wrote an *adab* work called *al-ʿIqd al-mufaṣṣal, athar adabī, lughawī, intiqādī, taʾrīkhī* in 2 volumes, Baghdad: Maṭbaʿat al-Shābandar, 1331 (see Cairo[2] III, 254, Sarkīs 788).

b *Al-Sayyid Muḥammad Saʿīd al-Najafī*

Al-Sayyid Muḥammad Saʿīd b. al-Sayyid Maḥmūd Ḥubūbī al-Najafī, born around 1850, died in Shaʿbān 1333/June 1915 in Najaf. His *Dīwān* was published in 1331 by ʿAbdallāh al-Jawharī, Beirut: Matbaʿat al-Ahliyya; samples in *al-ʿIrāqiyyāt* 9/73.

c *Muḥammad b. Ṭāhir al-Samāwī*

Muḥammad b. Ṭāhir al-Samāwī wrote entirely in the style of the classics. Born in al-Samāwa on the Euphrates east of Kufa in 1293/1876, he became a member of the Anjuman al-wilāya in Baghdad in 1904. After the British occupation he retired to Najaf where he became a *qāḍī*. His poetry is entirely dedicated to the glorification of the Prophet and the ʿAlids. He collected his poems in two *dīwān*s: *Shajarat al-riyāḍ fī madḥ al-nabī al-fayyāḍ* (Baghdad: Maṭbaʿat al-Adab, 1330; this is according to Buṭṭī; Cairo[2] III, 190 has a mistaken "Cairo")

---

4 Based on information taken from the catalogue of ʿĀṣaf, the work was mistakenly mentioned in Supplement II, p. 859.

and *Thamarat al-shajara fī madḥ al-ʿitra al-muṭahhara*, ibid. 1331. His historical writings were mentioned in Supplement II, 804, no. 65. See R. Buṭṭī, II, 151/63.

d *Muḥammad Ḥasan Abu ʾl-Maḥāsin*

Where Egypt and Syria had long since seen a development of nationalist poetry, among the Shīʿa it was Muḥammad Ḥasan Abu ʾl-Maḥāsin who was the first to practice it. Born in Karbala in 1293/1876, he continued to live there after his studies, making a living as a scholar. Later he actively participated in various political movements and events in Iraq, notably in the revolt against the British of the year 1920, such in his capacity as a deputy for Karbala and as the chairman of the interim government. He laid his political creed down in a *qaṣīda* called *Yuʿīdu taʾrīkhu ʾl-ʿulā nafsahu*; R. Buṭṭi, *al-Adab al-ʿaṣrī* II, 131/50.

e *Muḥammad Riḍā al-Shabībī*

Muḥammad Riḍā b. Muḥammad Jawād al-Shabībī worked in the same vein.
483 | Born on 6 Ramaḍān 1306/6 June 1890 in Najaf, he continued to live there after his studies, working as a professional writer. Enjoying the confidence of his compatriots, they made him their representative at the Peace Conference. As such, he first went to Mecca, arriving there on 6 Dhu ʾl-Ḥijja 1337/11 September 1919 with the aim of contacting King Ḥusayn. From there he went to Damascus to study the Arab question, also taking time to visit his co-religionists in Sidon in 1338/1920. When he learned of the uprising in Iraq he returned there instantly. After the revolt had failed, he remained for a while in the capital and then returned to Najaf. The inspired, patriotic tone of his early poems[5] gradually gave way to an increasingly dry kind of didacticism, even if he still glorifies the rising of the Orient (*Dīwān al-thawra* 44/6), and then to a form of outright, worn-out resignation like in *Lāmiyyat al-ʿArab al-kubrā*, which he sent from Baghdad to the Arab Academy in Damascus in 1926 (*RAAD* VI, 551/4). See R. Buṭṭī, *al-Adab al-ʿaṣrī* I, 113/28, Saʿd Mīkhāʾīl, *Adab al-ʿaṣr* 251/5, Muḥammad Mahdī al-Jawāhirī, *Ḥalbat al-adab* 25/43.

2 Baghdad

a *Jamīl Ṣidqī al-Zahāwī*

Of the poets of Baghdad, first place goes to their senior member who died two years ago, Jamīl Ṣidqī al-Zahāwī, even though he himself would have preferred to be remembered as a thinker.

---

5 Like the *qaṣīda Shakwā wa-ʿitāb* in al-Sayyid ʿAbd al-Razzāq al-Ḥasanī, *Taʾrīkh al-thawra al-ʿIrāqiyya*, Sidon 1935, 15/6.

He was born in Baghdad on 30 Dhu ʾl-Ḥijja 1279/18 June 1863, the son of the *muftī* of that city, Muḥammad Fayḍī al-Zahāwī,[6] a Kurd who was a relative of the prince of Sulaymāniyya, the Bābān, and a woman from an upscale Kurdish family. After his studies he became a member of the Majlis al-maʿārif, then director of the state printing mill, Arabic-language editor at the state newspaper *al-Zawrāʾ*, and a member of the Court of Appeal. During his first stay in Istanbul, where he had been summoned by the sultan in 1896, ʿAbd al-Ḥamīd suspected him of being a liberal because of some of his poems and articles published previously in the Egyptian press. | In order to get him away from the capital he was 484
sent to Yemen as a member of the Commission for Reforms, but he returned after eleven months. Raising suspicions against himself for a second time by his relations with the Young Turks, he was arrested and shipped off to Baghdad under guard, where he was granted a stipend of 15 Turkish pounds. After the restoration of the constitution he returned to Istanbul where he became a professor of Islamic philosophy at al-Jāmiʿa al-Mülkiyye and of Arabic literature at the Dār al-funūn. Being unable to adapt to the local climate, he returned to Baghdad in October 1909, where he assumed a professorship at the local lawschool.[7] An article by him on the issue of women's rights, published in *al-Muʾayyad*, caused so much local indignation that the *wālī* Nāẓim Pāshā had to remove him from his post. But later his successor, Jamāl Pāshā, re-appointed him again. He participated frequently in the sessions of the Ottoman parliament, first as a deputy for the Muntafiq and then for Baghdad. After the defeat of the Turks in Iraq he was going to be arrested by the British, but was released because he carried a press card of *al-Muqaṭṭam*; meanwhile, his comrades were deported to India. Afterwards, he succeeded in gaining the trust of the British, who then appointed him member of the Majlis al-maʿārif and Head of the Bureau for the Arabic translation of the Ottoman civil code. When, during the October unrest of 1920, High Commissioner Sir Arnold Wilson asked the freely chosen deputies of the people and some of the notables of Baghdad to give him their opinion, al-Zahāwī endorsed their demand for complete independence; and again he was spared while others were shipped off to the island of Hinjām. After the revolt had been put down he was made a member of committee that prepared a constitutional meeting of the national parliament and for which he edited the statutes. He greeted King Fayṣal with a *qaṣīda* when he

6 His grandfather was given this name upon his return to Sulaymāniyya after a stay of several years in Zahāw(b), in Kirmanshāh in Persia.

7 On his way back on board of one of the vessels of Messageries Maritimes, somewhere between Istanbul and Beirut, he made the acquaintance of M. Lidbarski, on which see *Das Johannesbuch der Mandäer* ii, 40.

485 acceded to the throne on 23 September 1921; but people jealous of him | succeeded in throwing suspicions on him so that he lost all his offices. When King Fayṣal then offered him the position of Poet Laureate, he refused. After all this, he decided to go and work on his health in Lebanon and Egypt. But the upheavals in Syria prevented him from going there until Autumn, by which time a fractured leg bound him to the sickbed for a period of five months. At this time he wrote his *Rubāʿiyyāt*. After a stay of five months in Cairo, he returned home. The king then appointed him as a member of the Senate, but after four years he retired from public life. From that time onward, he commented on events in Iraq on a weekly basis in *qaṣīda*s published in *al-Siyāsa al-uṣbūʿiyya*. The criticism that he vented in these were so sharp that the administration of Ismāʿīl Ṣidqī Pāshā was finally forced to move against him. A *qaṣīda* called *Thawra fi ʾl-jaḥīm*, published in *al-Duhūr* magazine in Beirut in 1931, caused the displeasure of the reactionaries; in one of his sermons a cleric accused him of heresy, which almost led to riots. From that time he fell silent, until his death on 23 February 1936.

From early childhood he had been interested in the natural sciences, but knowing no foreign languages he depended on Arabic magazines, notably *al-Muqtaṭaf*. As such, he never obtained the kind of knowledge with which to guide his curious mind. In 1897 he published his ideas on natural philosophy in his *Kitāb al-kāʾināt* (Cairo: Maṭbaʿat al-Muqtaṭaf; see Maḥmūd al-ʿAqqād, *Sāʿāt bayna ʾl-kutub* 196). In 1910 he published another work, this time on gravity, concerning which he had developed his own, entirely imaginary theory, entitled *al-Jādhibiyya wa-taʿlīluhā* (Baghdad). As has already been mentioned, he often came under fire from reactionary circles, but only once did he take up his pen to defend himself. On his first return from Istanbul, a Wahhābī leader set the *wālī* of Baghdad, ʿAbd al-Wahhāb Bāshā al-Albānī, against him because al-Zahāwī supposedly not only undermined the government, but religion as well. He defended himself against this accusation in *al-Fajr al-ṣādiq fi ʾl-radd ʿalā munkiri ʾl-tawassul wal-karāmāt wal-khawāriq* (Maṭbaʿat al-Wāʿiẓ 1323/1905). Still, this defence of the cult of saints and the belief in miracles seems inconsistent with the person that he elsewhere professes to be.

486 | Al-Zahāwī discovered early in life that his real field was poetry. The poems that he wrote as an adolescent were partly published in the press under different aliases while for another part they were transmitted orally. It was only in 1909, after the restoration of the constitution, that he could publish a selection of these poems, entitled *al-Kalim al-manẓūm* (vol. 1, Beirut, al-Maṭbaʿa al-ahliyya), from which a further selection was published in *al-Lubāb* (see below). The poems from his adolescence clearly show his talent as a lyricist. He also tried his hand at narrative poetry such as ʻThe war widow,ʼ 56/62, reprinted in

his *Dīwān* 82/6, and others. His *shiʿr mursal* contains poetic apothegms of a single line, stringed together without a rhyme (171/5). A selection from these is contained in *Dīwān* 31/2, shorter in *Lubāb* 2. At times, his interest in the natural sciences has a disturbing effect on his narrative poetry, for instance when he degrades his muse to the level of barren didacticism in his diatribes against the Milky Way on pages 51/3, a shortened form of which was included under the title *Ḍimnu 'l-majarra* in his *Dīwān* pages 22/3, and in other places as well.

In 1922, during the bleakest period in his life when, in conflict with his homeland, he wanted to leave to Egypt but was withheld from doing so by unrest in Syria and then also by personal health issues, he emptied his soul into quatrains, like ʿUmar al-Khayyām. These quatrians were published as the *Rubāʿiyyāt* (Beirut 1924). He included a selection of these in a separate section of his *Dīwān* called *al-Khaṭarāt*, and another selection in *al-Lubāb* 117/94 (of which samples in translation are cited in Widmer 37/41).

Most of the works that were mentioned as being in preparation in 1923 in Buṭṭī I, 13/5 were never published. Instead, he published his *Dīwān al-Zahāwī* with an introduction entitled *Nazʿatī fī 'l-shiʿr* in 1924/1343 (Cairo: al-Maṭbaʿa al-Saʿdiyya). Originally, the work was to be called *al-Mukhtār min Dīwān al-Zahāwī* and contained—as he himself states—more than a third but less than half of his production thus far (see the note by Salīm al-Jiddī in *RAAD* V, 117/21). The *Dīwān* reprints a large part of the poems that were published earlier in *Kalim al-manẓūm*, but of many there are just some verses, while several *qaṣīda*s were split up into different sections.

At the instigation of King Fayṣal, who wanted his country to have a theatre as well, he wrote the play *Riwāyat Laylā wa-Samīr, Leila et Samir* (on the second title page Sumeir), *drame ottoman constitutionel,* | Baghdad: Maṭbaʿat al- 487
Aytām lil-ābāʾ al-Kirmiliyyīn al-mursalīn, 1927, also in *Lughat al-ʿArab* V, 1928, 577/608. This piece, which reads like a series of scenes taken from some third-rate novel, has no drama in it whatsoever, while its main characters too, are entirely colourless.

In 1928 he published a translation of 130 *rubāʿiyyāt* in *Rubāʿiyyāt ʿUmar al-Khayyām* (Baghdad). In the same year, he published a selection of his own poems, *al-Lubāb* (Baghdad, Maṭbaʿat al-Furāt), mentioned several times before in this lemma and the source of Widmer's translations. The collection is, for the most part, ordered chronologically. It has a preface in which the author gives a detailed account of his artistic objectives and which was translated in Kampffmeyer, *MSOS* XXXI, 1928, 2, 207 and reprinted in Widmer 14ff.

Having outlined his views on classical poetry once more in his *Qaṣīda ʿalā aṭlāl al-shiʿr al-Jāhilī* (1931) published in *RAAD* XI, 712/4 and *al-Awshāl* 145/6, he published a larger composition—completed on 21 October 1929—titled

Thawra fi 'l-jaḥīm, first in *al-Duhūr* magazine, vol. 1, Beirut 1931, 641/69, and then again in *al-Awshāl* 293/317, and which was translated in Widmer, 50/79. Inspired by al-Maʿarrī's *Risālat al-ghufrān*, it is the account in monorhyme, in the first person, of the adventures of someone dead in Hell, where the inmates rise up against their torturers and then launch an assault on Heaven.

He published his fifth and last *dīwān* on 20 September 1934, entitled *al-Awshāl*, Maṭbaʿat Baghdād. It contains a mish-mash of poems from the years 1928/34. The poems of his elder years, which he wanted to publish in a collection entitled *al-Thumāla*, were never published, and neither was his *Nazaghāt al-shayṭān*, a collection of his sharpest criticisms of religion, which he was reluctant to publish. In the appendix to Abū Shādī's *Zaynab* (Cairo 1924), p. 44/8, Ḥasan Ṣāliḥ al-Jiddāwī cites a piece called *Tawallud al-ghināʾ wal-shiʿr*.

Autobiography *RAAD* VIII, 292/8, which must be supplemented by the obituary by Ṭāhā al-Rāwī in ibid. XIV, 248/55. R. Buṭṭī, *al-Adab al-ʿaṣrī fi 'l-ʿIrāq al-ʿArabī* I, 1/66, ʿAbbās Maḥmūd al-ʿAqqād, *Sāʿāt bayna 'l-kutub* 195/200. Aḥmad Muḥammad ʿAyshī in *al-Muqtaṭaf* 90, 1937, 55/7, Maḥmūd al-Sayyid, *al-Zahāwī al-faylasūf*, in *al-Ḥadīth* X, 1936, 45/50, Sāmī al-Kayyālī, *Dhikra 'l-Zahāwī*, ibid. XI, 1937, 265/8, *al-Zahāwī al-mufakkir wa-nazaʿātuhu 'l-tajdīdiyya*,
488 | ibid. 308/16.—*Ḥaflat takrīm al-shāʿir al-faylasūf al-kabīr Jamīl al-Zahāwī allatī aqāmahā lahu udabāʾ al-ʿIrāq*, Baghdad 1923. Sulaymān b. Saḥmān al-Najdī (see chapter V), *al-Ḍiyāʾ al-shāriq fī radd shubuhāt al-māriq wa-huwa radd ʿalā Jamīl Ṣidqī al-Zahāwī*, Cairo 1344 (307 pp.). —G. Widmer, Der ʿirāqische Dichter Jamīl Ṣidqī al-Zahāwī aus Baghdād, *WI* XVII, 1/79.

b *Maʿrūf al-Ruṣāfī*

Besides al-Zahāwī, there is his somewhat younger contemporary Maʿrūf al-Ruṣāfī, less productive but with a clearer head, the renewer of poetry in Iraq.

He was born in Kirkuk in 1292/1875, the son of a Kurdish father. Having taught at a primary school for a time, he went to teach Arabic literature at al-Madrasa al-iʿdādiyya al-rasmiyya. His first literary work was a translation of Nāmyq Kemāl's *Riwāyat al-ruʾyā*, Baghdad 1909. In those days his *qaṣīda*s on liberal ideology were so widespread that the editor-in-chief of *al-Iqdām* invited him to come to Istanbul to take charge of a planned Arabic edition of this magazine. It was there that he witnessed the revolution of the Young Turks and from there that he went to visit Thessalonica. The plan for the realisation of that for which he had been invited to Istanbul being a failure, he had no other option than to return home. On his way back, in Beirut, he sold the manuscript of his poems to the booktrader Muḥammad Jamāl, who had them printed in 1910 (see Cheikho, *al-Ruṣāfiyyāt wal-Rayḥāniyyāt, Mashriq* XIII, 1910, 379/92). Just one month after his arrival in Baghdad, he was called back to Istanbul to

work as a teacher of Arabic at al-Medrese al-Mülkīye al-ʿalīye and as editor-in-chief of a magazine called *Sabīl al-irshād*, which the deputy for the Viyalet of Aidin, ʿUbaydallāh, was going to publish. He taught there for a year, and also at the seminar for preachers of the Ministry of Awqāf, publishing his collected lectures there as *Nafḥ al-ṭīb fī 'l-khiṭāba wal-khaṭīb*, Istanbul 1915. For his students, he also wrote a work on Arabic loan-words in Turkish, *Dafʿ al-hujna fī 'rtiḍākh al-lukna*, Istanbul 1331/1913. He was also a member of the Ottoman parliament as a deputy for the Muntafiq. After the [First] World War he initially went to Syria in the hope of being able to serve the Arab government there. | However, in 1921 the Iraqi government appointed him head of the transla- 489
tion bureau of the ministry of education. Meanwhile, he also gave lectures on Arabic literature for the teachers of Baghdad, which were published in two volumes as *Muḥāḍarāt al-adab al-ʿarabī*, Baghdad 1922.

Muḥyi 'l-Dīn al-Khayyāṭ organised a second edition of his *Dīwān*, now with a philological commentary by Muṣṭafā al-Ghalāyīnī, entitled *Dīwān al-Ruṣāfī* I, Cairo: al-Maktaba al-Ahliyya, 1343/1925. See R. Buṭṭī, I, 67/96, Saʿd Mikhāʾīl, *Adab al-ʿaṣr*, 268/73, Amīn al-Ḍāhir in al-Bustānī, *Mashriq* XXXI, 134/5.

c *Muḥammad b. ʿAlī al-Kāẓimī*

Muḥammad b. ʿAlī al-Kāẓimī, who moved to Egypt for political reasons, also belongs to the previous generation.

Born in Baghdad on 15 Shaʿbān 1282/14 January 1865, he joined Jamāl al-Dīn al-Afghānī when the latter, expelled from Persia, passed through the city. Having thus rendered himself suspicious to the government, he left for Cairo where he joined the entourage of Muḥammad ʿAbduh. He championed their ideas in a famous ʿayniyya, at the end of which he confronts Hanoteaux and his attacks on Islam. See R. Buṭṭī, I, 97/112, *al-ʿIrāqiyyāt* 179/98. A selection of his poems was published with the title *Muʿallaqāt al-Kāẓimī*, Cairo: al-Maṭbaʿa al-ʿArabiyya, 1924.

d *Muḥammad Mahdī al-Baṣīr al-Baghdādī*

The blind Muḥammad Mahdī al-Baṣīr al-Baghdādī campaigned for the freedom of the Arabs, both as a singer and activist and as an historian.

Born in al-Ḥilla in 1313/1895, he went to Baghdad in 1920 where he stirred up resistance to the British with speeches and songs. Thus, he was arrested and sent to Hanjām, along with the other nationalists.

His smaller poems, which mostly consist of 1/7 verses, were first published with the title *Dīwān al-shadharāt*, Baghdad 1340. That same year, he published a selection from his poems and essays entitled *al-Mukhtaṣar*, ibid. A history of the Iraqi question in two volumes, called *Taʾrīkh al-qaḍiyya al-ʿIrāqiyya* (up to the year 1922), was published in Baghdad in 1342/1923 (see Ph.W. Ireland, *ʿIrāq* 487). In 1343, he published an historical novel called *Dawlat al-bukhalāʾ* (Baghdad).

490 | e *Muḥammad b. Yaḥyā al-Hāshimī*

Muḥammad b. Yaḥyā b. ʿAbd al-Qādir al-Hāshimī was one of the voices of modern education in Iraq.

Born in Baghdad in 1898 and descendant of ʿAlawān al-Ḥamawī (Suppl. II, 461), he moved to Cairo in 1913. But he did not like the teaching method at al-Azhar, even though he graduated from it in 1917. His studies at the University of Egypt were interrupted by the turmoil of the war. He then went to Damascus, and returned to his homeland in 1920. After his arrival there, he started working as a civil servant, and then became a teacher at the Baghdad Lawschool. He also founded *Majallat al-Yaqīn* there, which only lasted for three years.[8]

His first *dīwān* was published in Damascus in 1918. In Cairo he also published the *Dīwān b. al-Dumayma al-Khathʿamī*,[9] Maṭbaʿat al-Manār 1918, with a commentary (see *al-Mashriq* 1920, 489). See R. Buṭṭi II, 17/50.

f *Nasīm Mallūl*

Al-Zahāwī's first attempt at drama was imitated in 1928 by Nasīm Mallūl, director of the Ṣāliḥ Sāsūn Dāniyāl School in al-Ḥilla.

The *Riwāyat shahāmat al-ʿArab aw al-Samawʾal wa-Imraʾ al-Qays, riwāya tamthīliyya taʾrīkhiyya shiʿriyya waqaʿat ḥawādithuhā qabla ẓuhūr al-Islām, dhāt thamāniyat fuṣūl*, Baghdad: Maṭbaʿat Dār al-salām, 1349/1928, was written as an homage to the founder of the school, a member of a famous Jewish family of bankers from Baghdad.

g *ʿAbd al-Ḥamīd al-Rāḍī*

ʿAbd al-Ḥamīd al-Rāḍī boldly tried to cast the history of the Arab liberation struggle into dramatic form.

His *Thawrat al-ʿArab al-kubrā, masraḥiyya shiʿriyya*, Baghdad: Maṭbaʿat al-Jazīra, 1355/1936, tries to bring this vast subject under control by dividing it into three *fuṣūl*, each of which subdivides into a number of *manāẓir*. The piece is situated in al-Ḥusayn's palace in Mecca, on the battlefields of the Arabs, in
491 Damascus, at the Versailles Peace Conference, | and closes with the death of

8 See *Taʾrīkh al-ṣiḥāfa al-ʿIrāqiyya* I, 27, no. 10.

9 See *Ag.*^{2} XV, 144/51, Ibn Qutayba *Poesis* 458/9, MSS in Istanbul ʿĀšir, 950, *MSOS* XIV, 12, *MFO*, V, 515, Cairo^{2} III, 107, see van Arendonk *EI*, II, 397, Rescher, *Abriss* I, 172.

al-Ḥusayn in Amman. It is a typical book-drama, totally unsuitable to being brought to the stage, if only because of its many characters, fifty of whom are introduced by their full names. The whole thing is in verse, mostly in *ṭawīl, kāmil, hazaj* and *khafīf*, and bears testimony to an extraordinary control of the language, whose imagery is only rarely commonplace.

h *Nuʿmān Thābit ʿAbd al-Laṭīf*

The latest product of Iraqi poetry known to me is the *Dīwān* of Nuʿmān Thābit ʿAbd al-Laṭīf, an officer who died when he was still quite young.

Born in Baghdad in 1907, he was promoted to the rank of lieutenant in 1927, joining the general staff in 1936. He died on 12 June 1937 in a confrontation with rebels in al-Zarījiyya, in the Qaḍāʾ al-Samāwa.

His friends ʿAbd al-Sattār al-Qurghūlī and Ibrāhīm Adham al-Zahāwī collected and published his poems, giving them the title *Shaqāʾiq al-Nuʿmān, dīwān al-shahīd raʾīs al-rukn al-ustādh Nuʿmān Thābit ʿAbd al-Laṭīf*, Baghdad 1357/1938. The *dīwān* contains *qaṣīdas*, *muwashshaḥāt*, and *maqṭūʿāt*. It opens with three *qaṣīdas* in homage to King Fayṣal, dated 1934, and a *marthiya* on his death.

2 **Prose**

1 Storytelling

In Iraq, the art of storytelling is still in its infancy, moving slowly towards independence, away from its (mostly) Egyptian models.

a *Yūsuf Efendi Hurmuz and Anwar Shāʾūl*

After Yūsuf Efendi Hurmuz's publication of a collection of seven tales called *al-Ḍuʿafāʾ* (Basra: al-Maṭbaʿa al-Waṭaniyya, 1927), Anwar Shāʾūl followed in the footsteps of Maḥmūd Taymūr with his *al-Ḥaṣād al-awwal, 31 qiṣṣa ʿIrāqiyya* (Baghdad: al-Maṭbaʿa al-Khayriyya, 1930).

His stories are all much shorter than those of Taymūr. Mostly, there is only one plot while the story's characters are little developed. The images, which he takes from daily life, | are, for the most part, the same as those in Egypt. The 492
book's language is extremely cultivated, not even once using the local dialect in any of its dialogues. It is only in *Ibnat al-rāʿī* (no. 23) that he quotes a popular song in dialect in order to seize the atmosphere of the countryside.

In the book, the author announces *al-Ḥasād al-thānī, majmūʿat qiṣaṣ Ifranjiyya li-ashhar qiṣasiyyi ʾl-ʿālam* as being in preparation, while in 1936 he published his translation of *Arbaʿ qiṣaṣ ṣiḥḥiyya* (see *al-Ḥadīth* x, 373), on the order of the *Maṣlaḥat al-ṣiḥḥa al-ʿāmma*.

b *Maḥmūd Aḥmad al-Sayyid al-Baghdādī*

The art of Maḥmūd Aḥmad al-Sayyid al-Baghdādī is more Islamic than western. He translated some stories from Turkish, which he published in *al-Ḥadīth*. The same magazine also published an essay on the works of Saʿdī, III, 1929, 421/5. After the publication of several short stories, such as *Jalāl khālid* and *al-Ṭalāʾiʿ*, he published a collective volume called *Fī sāʿ min al-zaman* in 1936. While Anwar Shāʾūl tried to portray an image of the half-educated townsfolk of Baghdad, al-Sayyid al-Baghdādī draws on the primitive passions of the common people, on which see Wadād al-Sakākīnī in *al-Ḥadīth* X, 304/7 and her reply ibid. 461/4.

c *Muḥammad ʿAlī al-ʿĀmilī*

Muḥammad ʿAlī Sharaf al-Dīn al-Mūsawī al-ʿĀmilī adapted the period immediately before the advent of Islam into an historical novel entitled *Shaykh al-Abṭaḥ aw Abū Ṭālib, kitāb taʾrīkhī falsafī ʿilmī*, Baghdad 1349.

2 Popular Science

a *Sulaymān Ghazāla*

The deputy for Basra in the Iraqi parliament, Dr Sulaymān Ghazāla, rendered outstanding service in the dissemination of modern insights from sociology and philosophy in Iraq.

His collective works are called *al-Waḍʿiyya fī ʾl-ḥikma al-khuluqiyya* and
comprise the following titles: 1. *al-Ḥayāh al-ijtimāʿiyya*, Baghdad: Maṭbaʿat Dār
al-salām, 1342.—2. *Minhāj al-ʿāʾila*, ibid. 1344.—3. *Khulāṣat arkān al-iqtiṣād al-*
siyāsī wa-taʿalluquhu bi-ʿilmay al-adab wal-ḥuqūq, ibid. 1345.—4. *al-Ḥurriyya*
falsafiyyan wa-naẓaran ila ʾl-ḥayāh al-ijtimāʿiyya, ibid. 1342.—5. *al-ʿIshq al-*
ṭāhir; al-Qaṣīda al-firdawsiyya fī ʾl-ḥubb al-ṭāhir al-muqaddas aw al-ʿafāf, ibid.
493 1344.—6. *Khiṭāb al-iʿtimād ʿala ʾl-nafs fī | ʾl-kifāḥ lil-ḥayāh*, ibid. 1345.—7. *al-*
Hawā, ibid. 1344.—8. *al-Ḥubb al-basharī*, ibid. 1344.—9. *Khulāṣat al-adab al-*
riyāḍī al-ʿamalī, ibid. 1345.—10. *al-Iqtiṣād al-siyāsī* I, ibid. 1346.—11. *al-Adab*
al-naẓarī al-ʿumūmī, 1346.—12. *al-Mushkilāt al-adabiyya*, ibid. 1346 (see *al-*
Mashriq XXIV, 716, XXV, 715, XXVI, 23). Later he also published, among other
things, *al-Ḥaqq wal-ʿadāla, riwāya manẓūma*, Baghdad 1929.

b *Mīkhāʾīl Yūsuf Taysī*

Mīkhāʾīl Yūsuf Taysī wrote a popularising work on psychology entitled *Māhiyyat al-nafs wa-rābiṭatuhā bil-jasad*, Baghdad 1922, and also *Naqadāt kannās al-shawāriʿ*, in 3 volumes, ibid. 1922 (*Jāmiʿ* II, 184, 196).

c *Muḥammad Efendi al-Mawṣilī*

Kayfa tajid al-saʿāda, Baghdad n.d. (*Jāmiʿ* I, 572).

d *ʿAṭāʾ Efendi Amīn*
An official at the court of King Fayṣal, he is the author of *al-Salām al-duwalī al-ʿāmm wa-jahd al-ʿālam fī taḥqīqihi*, Baghdad n.d. (*Jāmiʿ* I, 140).

e *Ṭāhā al-Hāshimī*
Nahḍat al-Yābān wa-ta ʾthīr rūḥ al-umma fi ʾl-nahḍa, Baghdad 1925 (*Jāmiʿ* I, 258, 1191).

f *Makkī Jamīl*
ʿAlāmāt al-madaniyya, Baghdad 1923.

g *Muḥammad ʿAbd al-Ḥusayn al-Kāẓimī*
Al-Maʿārif fi ʾl-ʿIrāq ʿalā ʿahd aliḥtilāl, Baghdad 1923 (according to Ph. W. Ireland, *ʿIrāq* 487, Muḥammad ʿĪd al-Ḥusayn).

3 Philology
In Baghdad, the most important authors in philology were two Christians:

a *Rafāʾīl Buṭṭī*
Rafāʾīl Buṭṭī, whom we have already come across as the author of the literary historical overview *al-Adab al-ʿaṣrī* (see p. 481), was the publisher of *Majallat al-Ḥurriyya* in Baghdad. Earlier, he had published an anthology of poetics called *Siḥr al-shiʿr*, Cairo 1922 (cf. p. 414). Influenced by al-Rayḥānī and Jabrān Khalīl Jabrān, he also published *al-Rabīʿiyyāt* in *Majallat al-Ḥurriyya* in 1925. These are poems in free rhyme in celebration of, among other things, the birth of Christ (*Ila ʾl-ṭifl al-ʿaẓīm*) on Christmas Eve of the year 1920, and of his crucifixion (*Ṣalībuka wa-ṣalībunā, Yasūʿ wal-insāniyya*) on Good Friday of the year 1921, but also of the birth of the Prophet (*al-Rasūl al-ʿarabī*) in 1341/1922.

b *Anastase Marie de St. Élie al-Kirmilī*
Purely literary-historical was the work of the Carmelite Anastase Marie de St. Élie al-Kirmilī.[10]

| Born in Baghdad in 1866, where his father had emigrated from Lebanon in 494
1850, he joined his order in 1888. Apart from a number of theological works, we also owe him a collection of valuable text editions. In 1911, he wrote a history of Baghdad from the Mongol conquest until the year 1495, titled *al-Fawz bil-murād fī taʾrīkh Baghdād*, Baghdad: Maṭbaʿat al-Riyāḍ, 1329. Following a

10 This is the explicit vocalisation of his *nisba* in the title of his most recent work.

suggestion by the British Head of Educational Affairs, Major H.E. Bowman, he wrote a *Khulāṣat taʾrīkh ʿIrāq* from its beginnings until the present times, Basra: Maṭbaʿat al-ḥukūma, 1919 (see Sarkīs 481). But, since then, he has focussed exclusively on lexical research, publishing in many magazines, notably *Lughat al-ʿArab*, founded by his own order in 1917, but also in *RAAD*, *al-Mashriq* and, recently, in publications of the Academy of Egypt. In these publications he often speaks out on the issue of the modernisation of the written language.[11] A collection of some of these articles was published as *Aghlāṭ al-lughawiyyīn al-aqdamīn*, Baghdad 1933. While he had always taken an interest in the etymology of foreign loanwords in Arabic, recently his research into the root-forms of the Arabic lexicon—always a tricky subject—led him to the thesis, already voiced by Jurjī Zaydān (see p. 187), that all Arabic roots can be traced back to onomatopoeia. In his *Nushūʾ al-lugha al-ʿarabiyya wa-numuwwuhā waktihāluhā* (Cairo: al-Maṭbaʿa al-ʿAṣriyya, 1938) he entangles himself, unrestrained by any sort of linguistic methodology, in untenable fantasies, completely forgetting to write the history of the Arabic language promised in the title of this work, which would have been so welcome and for which he was so well prepared through his research.

4 Historiography

For many years, historiography kept moving along the traditional tracks of local history and biographies; European methods in reporting and the study of source material have started to have an impact only recently.

a *Ḥusayn b. Aḥmad al-Burūqī al-Najafī, et al.*

The following works are entirely in the style of tradtional *taʾrīkh* works: *Taʾrīkh*
495 *al-Kūfa* by Ḥusayn b. Aḥmad al-Burūqī al-Najafī (d. 1332/1914), | published by Muhammad Ṣādiq Āl Baḥr al-ʿulūm, 2 vols, Najaf 1356, Ṣadr al-Dīn al-Ṣadr, *Mukhtaṣar taʾrīkh al-Islām*, Baghdad 1330, Sulaymān al-Dahrī al-Baghdādī, *Tuḥfat al-alibbāʾ fī taʾrīkh al-Aḥsāʾ*, ibid. 1331, *al-Tuḥfa al-saniyya fi ʾl-mashāyikh al-Sanūsiyya* by ʿAlī b. Jamīl al-Mawṣilī, Mosul 1331, and *ʿAlām al-ʿIrāq, sīrat al-imām al-Ālūsī al-kabīr wa-tarājim al-Ālūsiyyā*, Cairo 1345 (see Suppl. II, 785ff) by Muhammad Bahjat al-Atharī al-ʿIrāqī, *al-Anwār al-ʿAlawiyya fī aḥwāl amīr al-muʾminīn wa-faḍāʾilihi wa-manāqibihi wa-ghazawātihi* by Aḥmad ʿAbdallāh al-Ṣādiq Jaʿfar, Najaf 1343, *Dhakhīrat al-dārayn fīmā yataʿallaq bil-sayyid al-Ḥusayn*, ibid. 1345, by ʿAbd al-Majīd Muḥammad Riḍā al-Ḥāʾirī, *Taʾrīkh*

11 See *al-Muṣṭalaḥāt al-ʿilmiyya wal-ṭibbiyya wa-naqd Muʿjam Sharaf, raddan ʿala ʾl-abīl al-Kirmilī lil-Dr. Muḥammad Sharaf*, Cairo 1929.

al-Mawṣil by al-Quss Sulaymān Ṣā'igh, I, Cairo: al-Maṭbaʿa al-Salafīya, 1342, 1923 (*Jāmiʿ* I, 69), II, Beirut 1928.

b *Āl al-Muṣīb al-ʿUmarī*

In his *Ta'rīkh muqaddarāt al-ʿIrāq al-siyāsiyya* (3 vols, Baghdad: Maṭbaʿat al-Fallāḥ, 1921/2), Āl al-Muṣīb Muḥammad Ṭāhir al-ʿUmarī attempted to give an account of the contemporary history of Iraq against the background of world politics and the Arab movement.

c *Adīb al-Taqī al-Baghdādī*

Adīb al-Taqī al-Baghdādī, who had translated a pedagogical work from Turkish in 1337, calling it *Manāhij al-tarbiya wal-taʿlīm*, published a small collection of Muslim biographies with the title *Siyar al-ta'rīkh al-Islāmī*, Damascus: Maṭbaʿat al-Taraqqī, 1340/1921, and a universal history from antiquity until the present day entitled *al-Ta'rīkh al-ʿāmm*, I, Damascus 1341, II, Sidon: Maṭbaʿat al-ʿIrfān, 1342, for which he relied heavily on Turkish sources (see Muḥammad Kurd ʿAlī, *RAAD* III, 349/52).

d *Kāẓim al-Dujaylī*

Kāẓim al-Dujaylī (born in Jumādā I 1301/March 1884 in the village of Dujayl), a poet in his leisure time, is a cultural historical researcher in Baghdad with wide interests.

Magazines have, so far, only published samples of his historical work, such as *Ta'rīkh Karbalā'* in *Lughat al-ʿArab, Sāmarrā' qadīman waḥadīthan* ibid., *al-Āthār al-ʿIrāqiyya* ibid., *al-Sufun al-ʿIrāqiyya* ibid., *Ta'rīkh al-Kāẓimiyya* in *Mir'āt al-ʿIrāq*; cf. R. Buṭṭī I, 187/222.

e *Yūsuf Rizqallāh Ghanīma*

Yūsuf Rizqallāh Ghanīma's interest was also entirely focussed on cultural history.

| Following lectures held in al-Maʿhad al-ʿilmī in Baghdad, he published his 496
Tijārat al-ʿIrāq qadīman wa-ḥadīthan in 1922, Baghdad: Maṭbaʿat al-ʿIrāq, 1341 (see Muḥammad Kurd ʿAlī, *RAAD* III, 186). In 1924, there followed the books *Ta'rīkh mudun al-ʿIrāq* and *Nuzhat al-mushtāq fī ta'rīkh Yahūd al-ʿIrāq*, ibid. (*Jamiʿ* I, 248). A copiously illustrated work, *al-Ḥīra al-madīna wal-mamlaka al-ʿArabiyya* was published in Baghdad: Maṭbaʿat Dhunkūr al-Ḥadītha, 1936 (see *RAAD* XIV, 312).

f *Ra'ūf Bek al-Jadarjī*

The director of the Law-School of Iraq, Ra'ūf Bek al-Jadarjī, wrote *al-Ta'rīkh al-siyāsī*, published by Rashīd al-Ḥāshimī, Baghdad: Maṭba'at al-Furāt, 1924 (*Jāmi'* I, 53).

g *Al-Sayyid 'Abd al-'Azīz al-Rashīd*

Al-Sayyid 'Abd al-'Azīz al-Rashīd wrote a very detailed history of Kuwait, *Ta'rīkh al-Kuwayt*, 2 vols, Baghdad: al-Maṭba'a al-'Aṣriyya, 1344/1926 (see Muḥammad Kurd 'Alī, *RAAD* VI, 624).

h *'Alī Ẓarīf al-A'ẓamī al-Baghdādi*

'Alī Ẓarīf al-A'ẓamī al-Baghdādi wrote *Ta'rīkh mulūk al-Ḥīra*, Baghdad: al-Maṭba'a al-Salafiyya, 1338/1920, *Mukhtaṣar ta'rīkh Baghdād al-qadīm wal-ḥadīth aw Baghdād fī 4000 sana*, Baghdad: Maṭba'at al-Furāt, 1344/1926 (*Jāmi'* I, 68, 200), 1346/1927, *Ta'rīkh al-duwal al-Fārisiyya bil-'Irāq*, ibid. 1346/1927, and *Ta'rīkh al-dawla al-Yūnānīya bil-'Irāq*, ibid.

i *Muḥammad Ṣādiq al-Ḥusaynī*

'Umrān Baghdād, Baghdad 1348.

k *Muḥammad Ṣāliḥ Abu 'l-Barakāt*

Muḥammad Ṣāliḥ Āl al-Suhrawardī Abu 'l-Barakāt, *Lubb al-albāb, ta'rīkh wa-adab yaḍummu tarājim 'ulamā' wa-udabā' al-'Irāq*, Baghdad 1932, *al-Ajwiba al-Suhrawardiyya* on revelation, punishment in the grave etc., ibid. 1927.

l *Al-Sayyid 'Abd al-Razzāq al-Najafī*

Al-Sayyid 'Abd al-Razzāq al-Ḥasanī al-Najafī tried to work entirely according to the standards of European scholarship.

His *Riḥla fī 'l-'Irāq*, Baghdad 1343, was followed by a collection of Iraqi folk songs entitled *al-Aghānī al-sha'biyya fī shu'ūb al-aghniya wa-tafāṣīl al-ash'ār bi-lisān al-Ḥasaka*, ibid. 1348 (see II, 805,$_{71}$ and *RAAD* IX, 640), by *Mūjiz ta'rīkh al-buldān al-'Irāqiyya* 1930, by *Ta'rīkh al-wizārāt al-'Irāqiyya*, Sidon 1933, 2 vols, Baghdad 1935,[12] and by his magnum opus *Ta'rīkh al-thawra al-'Irāqiyya*, Sidon: Maṭba'at al-'Irfān, 1935/1353. In the latter work he also used the British High
497 Commander Sir Aylmer Haldane's *The Insurrection in Mesopotamia*, 1922, | and in addition disclosed many valuable documents. Finally, he also published *Ta'rīkh al-ṣiḥāfa al-'Irāqiyya*, I, Najaf: Maṭba'at al-Ghariyy, 1353/1935.

---

12 In Ph.W. Ireland's *'Irāq*, 486, there is a mistaken 'Abd al-Rāzī, and his magnum opus is not mentioned.

n *ʿAbbās al-ʿAzzāwī*

Not entirely at the same level but still very useful as sourcebooks are the following works by al-Muḥāmī ʿAbbās al-ʿAzzāwī: *Taʾrīkh al-ʿIrāq bayna ʾkhtilālayn*, I, *Ḥukūmat al-Mughūl*, II, *Ḥukūmat al-Jalāʾiriyya, min sanat 739/1338 ilā sanat 814/1411*, Maṭbaʿat Baghdād al-ḥadītha, 1353/1935, 1354/1936 and his *Taʾrīkh al-Yazīdiyya wa-aṣl ʿaqīdatihim*, Maṭbaʿat Baghdād 1354/1935. It was the research of G. Furlani, published in *Lughat al-ʿArab* IX, 3, which inspired him to write his second work. Contrary to Furlani but with Michelangelo Guidi, he adheres to the—correct—view that the Yazīdiyya do not owe their name to some Persian sect, but rather to the Ghulāt Yazīd who, contrary to the Ghulāt al-Shīʿa, elevated the gratitude of the Syrians towards the house of Umayya to the point of a divine kind of worship of that individual from among its members whom their enemies hated most. He substantiates this view by extensive use of the available sources, adding some extremely valuable information on the modern history of the Yazīdīs and their present situation, including the last campaign by the government to suppress a revolt in Sinjar in October 1935.

o *ʿAbd al-Sattār al-Qurghūlī*

The poet ʿAbd al-Sattār al-Qurghūlī wrote a work on the conqueror of Iraq, entitled *al-Muthannā b. al-Ḥāritha al-Shaybānī*, published as no. 3 in the catalogue of Maktabat al-Muthannā, Baghdad 1355/1936.

p *ʿMuʾallif Fāḍilʾ*

An anonymous author, writing under the pen-name Muʾallif Fāḍil, published a work on British colonial policy in Asia Minor with special consideration of Iraq, titled *ʿAlā ṭarīq al-Hind*, Baghdad 1936 (370 pp.); see *al-Ḥadīth* X, 373.

Chapter 5. Arabia

Muḥammad Surūr al-Ṣabbān, *Adab al-Ḥijāz,* Cairo 1345 (samples from the works of 17 poets and writers, Ibrāhīm al-ʿAzzāwī and other poets from the Hijaz); see Ḥusayn Haykal, *Fī manzil al-waḥy* 161/2, and Khayr al-Dīn Zuruklī, *Mā raʾaytu wa-mā samiʿtu* 120ff.

498 | Qustandī Bek b. Dāʾūd, *Dīwān b. Dāʾūd, shāʿir Āl al-Saʿūd*, Cairo 1931.

Omar el-Bedavi (born in 1887, has lived in Riyadh since 1925). *La tribù distrutta, romanzo, trad. di Paolo Giudici*, Rome-Milan 1933.

Ḥāfiẓ Wahba (special envoy of Ibn Saʿūd to London), *Jazīrat al-ʿArab fi 'l-qarn al-ʿishrīn*, Cairo 1354/1935.

Sulaymān b. Saḥmān al-Najdī (see p. 488), *Tatimmat taʾrīkh Najd*, as an appendix to Ālūsī, *Taʾrīkh Najd*, Cairo 1347.

——, *al-Hadiyya al-saniyya wal-tuḥfa al-Wahhābiyya al-Najdiyya*, Cairo: Maṭbaʿat al-Manār, 1342.

——, *Irshād al-ṭālib ilā ahamm al-maṭālib wa-minhāj ahl al-ḥaqq wal-ithbāt fī muṣṭalaḥ ahl al-jahl etc.*, Cairo 1340.

Bā Salāma, *Ḥayāt sayyid al-ʿArab*, Mecca-Jeddah, 1349–53/1930–5.

Fuʾād Hamza, *al-Buldān al-ʿArabiyya al-Saʿūdiyya*, Mecca: Maṭbaʿat Umm al-qurā, 1933.

——, *Qalb Jazīrat al-ʿArab*, Cairo 1933.

Khazʿal Khān, amīr al-Muḥammara, *al-Durar al-ḥisān fī manẓūmāt wa-madāʾiḥ mawlānā ... sumuww al-shaykh Khazʿal Khān* (collected by ʿAbd al-Masīḥ al-Anṭākī, see p. 179, 344). Cairo: Maṭbaʿat al-ʿArab, 1326.—*al-Riyāḍ al-Khazʿaliyya fi 'l-siyāsa al-insāniyya*, Maṭbaʿa Hindiyya 1321.

Ṣāliḥ al-Ḥāmid al-ʿAlawī al-Ḥaḍramī, *Dīwān*, Cairo 1936 (cf. *Apollo* I, 698).

Chapter 6. The Maghreb

Muḥammad al-Hādī al-Zāhirī, *Shuʿarāʾ al-Jazāʾir fi ʾl-ʿaṣr al-ḥāḍir*, Tunis 1926, see *RAAD* XII, 125.

Zayn al-ʿĀbidīn al-Sanūsī, *al-Adab al-Tūnisī fi ʾl-qarn al-rābiʿ ʿashar* I, *Qism al-naẓm*, Tunis: Maṭbaʿat al-ʿArab, 1346/1927.

Muḥammad al-Nayfir, *ʿUnwān al-arīb ʿammā nashaʾa bil-mamlaka al-Tūnisiyya min ʿālim wa-adīb*, 2 vols, Tunis 1932.

| Maḥmūd Kabādu, *Dīwān*, collected by Maḥmūd al-Sanūsī, 2 vols, Tunis 499 1295.

Muḥammad al-Shādhilī Khaznadār, *Ḥayāt al-shiʿr wa-aṭwāruhu*, Tunis 1338.

Abu ʾl-Qāsim al-Shābī (see Zayn al-ʿĀbidīn, 209/54, Saʿd Mīkhaʾīl, *Samīr al-udabāʾ* 119/21, the Index to *Apollo*), *al-Khayāl al-shiʿrī inda ʾl-ʿArab*, Tunis 1933, see *Apollo* I, 833/5, 1172/5.

Saʿīd Abū Bakr al-Tūnisī, *al-Saʿīdiyyāt* I, *Dīwān*, Tunis 1928.

ʿAbd al-Salām b. ʿUthmān b. ʿIzz al-Dīn b. ʿAbd al-Salām al-Fītūrī al-Ṭarābulusī, *al-Ishārāt li-baʿḍ mā bi Ṭarābulus al-Gharb min al-mazārāt*, Ṭarābulus al-Gharb 1921.

Aḥmad b. al-Ḍayyāf al-Tūnisī, *al-ʿIqd al-awwal min Kitāb itḥāf ahl al-zamān bi-akhbār mulūk Tūnis wa-ʿahd al-amān*, Tunis 1319.

Al-Sayyid Aḥmad Tawfīq al-Madanī, *Kitāb al-Jazāʾir*, al-Maṭbaʿa al-ʿArabiyya fi ʾl-Jazāʾir, 1350 (see *RAAD* XII, 312).

ʿAbd al-Raḥmān b. Zaydān, *Itḥāf aʿlām al-nās bi-jamāl akhbār ḥāḍirat Miknās*, Rabat 1930/1.

Addenda & Corrigenda

Supplement Volume 1

5. Bankipore XIX, I. Principles of Jurisprudence 1931, II. Inheritance Law 1933, XX. Philology 1936, XXI. Encyclopaedia, Logic, Philosophy, Dialectics 1936, XXII. Science 1937, XXIII. Poetry and Elegant Prose 1939.

n. 1. Harry N. Howard, Preliminary Materials for a Survey of the Libraries and Archives of Istanbul, JAOS 1939, 227/46.

7. Esc., *Les mss. arab. de l'Escurial d'après les notes de H. Derenbourg; revues, mises à jour et complétées par le Dr Renaud*, II.2, Médecine et Histoire Naturelle, II.3, Sciences exactes et sciences occultes, Paris 1939 (I have not seen this publication yet).

8. Halle, H. Wehr, *Verzeichnis der ar. Hadss. in der Bibliothek der* DMG, AKM XXV.3, Leipzig 1940.

Ind. Off., III. Fiqh by Reuben Levy, London 1937, A.J. Arberry, Handlist of Islamic Mss. acquired by the India Office Library 1936/8, JRAS 1939, 353/96.

9. W. Heffening, Die islamischen Hdss. der Universitätsbibliothek Löwen (fonds Lefort, série B und C) mit einer besonderen Würdigung der Mudauwanahdss. des IV, VI, X, XI, Jahrh., *Muséon*, vol. L, 1937, 85/100.

Patna, Or. Library: V.C.S. O'Connor, *An Eastern Library with Two Catalogues of its Persian and Arabic Mss. compiled by Khan Sahib Abdulmuqtadir and Abdulhamid*, 1920.

10. M.A. Simsar, *Oriental Mss. of the John Fr. Lewis Collection of the Free Library of Philadelphia*, Philadelphia 1937.

Ph.K. Hitti, Nabih Amin Faris, Buṭrus ʿAbd-al-Malik, *Descriptive Catalogue of the Garrett Collection of Arabic Mss. in the Princeton University Library*, Princeton 1938 (Butrus Abdalmalik, *A Critical Study of the Barudi Mss. in the Princ. Un.-Libr.*, Diss. Princeton 1935).

13. Line 16, read: ʿAbd al-ʿAzīz al-Bishrī.

18. n. 1., read: Bauer, *Volksleben* etc.

 | DOI:10.1163/9789004369795_003

24. n. 4. E. Bräunlich, Versuch einer literargeschichtlichen Betrachtungsweise altarabischer Poesien, *Isl.* XXIV, 201/69; G. von Grünebaum, *Die Wirklichkeitsweite der früharabischen Dichtung*, Beihefte zur *WZKM* 3, Vienna 1937.

32. n. 2. *Naqd kitāb* Fi 'l-shiʿr al-Jāhilī *li-Muḥammad Khiḍr Ḥusayn, aḥad ʿulamāʾ al-Azhar*, Cairo n.d.

35. 2. F.L. Bernstein, Des Ibn Kaisān Kommentar zur Muʿallaḳa des Imruʾ ulḳais, *ZA* 29, 1/79.—3. Bank. XXIII, 1, 2504.

40. Comment. 2. Bank. XXIII, 70, 2564.—3. Ibid. 71, 2565, Ḥūr Laylā 367.

Line 17. Damascus 1348.

4a. al-Tabrīzī, *Sharḥ al-Ḥamāsa*, MS commenced on 5 Dhu 'l-Ḥijja 507 AH, Ind. Off. 4631, *JRAS* 1939, 395, MS dated 578 AH, Bank. XXIII, 72, 2566.

Yūsuf b. Qizoghlū (I, 589), *Muqtaḍa 'l-siyāsa fī sharḥ nukat al-Ḥamāsa*, Istanbul, Un. R. 3180, *ZS* III, 252.

47. 3. Krenkow has informed me that the British Museum possesses an old copy of the *dīwān*.

1192 | 48. 4. Yūsuf Efendi, *al-Maʿānī al-badīʿa fī shiʿr Zuhayr b. Rabīʿa*, Beirut 1300.

5. Read: Abū Qābūs, i.e. Nuʿmān III; poem no. 8, in which al-Zibriqān is mentioned, is by Khālid b. ʿArqama (see *Orientalia* VII, 344).

50. Line 17. Another copy of MS Lālelī is preserved in Ind. Off. 4574, and probably also in the library of Ismāʿīl Pāshā (no. 3); al-Tabrīzī has wrongly been credited with a commentary, see *JRAS* 1939, 366.—*Mukhtaṣar Sharḥ qaṣīdat* I (the *muʿallaqa*) by al-Sijāʿī (Suppl. II, 445) Brill–H. 3 = Garr. 3, Alex. Adab 157.—Salīm al-Jundī (Suppl. III, 390) *Imraʾ al-Qays*, Damascus 1936.

54. *Dīwān al-Shanfarā*, in *al-Ṭarāʾif al-adabiyya*, Cairo 1937.—For the commentary by Muḥammad b. Qāsim b. Zākūr al-Maghribī see also Alex. Adab 135, 5 (*Tafrīj al-kurab ʿan qulūb ahl al-arab fī maʿrifat Lāmiyyat al-ʿArab*).

57. 14. *Dīwān al-Afwah*, in *al-Ṭarāʾif al-adabiyya*, C. 1937.

64. Nabia Abbott, *The Rise of North-Ar. Script and its Kuranic Development with a Full Description of the Kuranic MSS in the Or. Institute of the University of Chicago*, Un. of Chic. Or. Publ. L, 1939.—G. Richter, *Der Sprachstil des Korans, aus dem Nachlass hsg. von O. Spies*, Leipzig 1940.—A. Fischer, Der Wert der vorhandenen Qoranübersetzungen von Sura 111, *BSAW* 89, 2, Leipzig 1937.—Text in Latin script, Istanbul-Ankara 1932.—*Der K. ar. und deutsch mit Erklärung von Maulana Sadruddin*, Berlin, Verlag der Mosl. Revue, 1939.—J. Naish, *The Wisdom of the Q. Engl. Transl.* London 1937.—R. Bell, *The Q. Transl. with a Critical Rearrangement of the Surahs* I, Edinburgh 1937.—Ali Muhammad, *Introduction to the Study of the Holy Q.*, Lahore 1938.—Sia Talat, *Die Seelenlehre des Korans mit bes. Berücksichtigung der Terminologie*, Diss. Halle 1929.—Samana Abdalhamid, *Notes on the Cosmological Ideas in al-Q.*, Lund 1938 (Lunds Un. Årsskr. N.F. Hist. Notes and Papers no. 13).—A. Jeffery, *The Foreign Vocabulary of the Q.* (Gaekwar of Baruda Or. Series) 1938.

68. Bahāʾullāh Khan M., *Vom Einfluss des Qorʾāns auf die arab. Dichtung, eine Untersuchung über die dichterischen Werke von Ḥ. b. Ṯ. Kaʿb b. Mālik und ʿAl. b. Rawāḥa*, Leipzig 1938.—*Dīwān*, Teh. Sip. II 585/6.

Ibid., *Qaṣīda rāʾiyya fī madḥ al-anṣār li-Kaʿb b. Zuhayr*, Alex. Adab 128.

69. Commentaries: 29. *Fatḥ al-jawād* by al-Jamal (Suppl. II, 480), Alex. Adab 140.—30. ʿAbdallāh b. Fakhr al-Dīn b. Yaḥyā al-Ḥusaynī al-Mawṣilī, Alex. Fun. 187, 6.—*Takhmīs* by Jamāl al-Dīn Muḥammad b. ʿAbd al-Ghaffār, Alex. Adab 140.

70. 7. *Dīwān*, with a commentary by Ibn al-Sikkīt, Bank. XXIII 2,$_{2504v}$.

74. Line 7, *Anwār al-ʿuqūl min ashʿār waṣiyy al-rasūl*, Bank. XXIII 6, 2517.

Line 15, read 513/1119, collected by Quṭb al-Dīn Abu ʾl-Ḥasan Muḥammad b. al-Ḥusayn b. Ḥasan al-Bayhaqī al-Nīsābūrī al-Kaidarī, composed in 576/1180, according to *Dharīʿa* II, 43/4, no. 1697.—*Takhmīs al-Qaṣīda al-Zaynabiyya* by ʿAlī b. Manṣūr b. Najm al-ʿAzzīmī, Alex. Adab 23.

75. 2. Anon., *Tafsīr baʿḍ asmāʾ Allāh al-Suryāniyya allatī waradat fi ʾl-Qaṣīda al-Juljulātiyya*, Qawala I, 225.

3. Teh. Sip. II 73, versified Persian transl. by ʿĀdil Teh. Sip. II 68/72.—*Ghurar al-ḥikam* al-Āmidī (to be read thus) Teh. Sip. II 76—78. *Nathr al-laʾāliʾ*, ibid. 102/7 (where the author is said to be Abū ʿAlī Ṭabarsī, Suppl. I 708, 3). *Alf kalima min*

1193 *kalām* | *amīr al-muʾminīn ʿAlī b. Abī Ṭālib mujarrada min Sharḥ Ibn Abī Ḥadīd ʿalā Nahj al-balāgha*, Beirut 1329.

5. *Naṣīḥat al-imām ʿAlī li-Mālik b. al-Ḥārith fī umūr al-ḥukūma wa-riʿāyat al-Muslimīn*, AS 2908.

77. Raʾīf Khūrī, *Wa-hal yakhfa ʾl-qamar* (on the life of ʿUmar b. Abī Rabīʿa), Beirut 1938.

79. 4. F. Gabrieli, *RSO* XVII, 40/71, 133/72, *Contributi alla interpretatione di Jamīl*, ibid. XVIII (1938), 1/26, 173/98, *ZDMG* 93, 163/8.

84. *al-Takmila li-shiʿr al-Akhṭal ʿan nuskhat Ṭihrān al-khaṭṭiyya ikhtārahā wa-ṣaḥḥaḥahā wa-ʿallaqa ḥawāshiyahā al-ab Anṭūn Ṣālḥānī al-Yasūʿī*, Beirut 1938.

85. Khalīl Bek Mardam, *al-Farazdaq* (Silsilat aʾimmat al-adab), Damascus 1939. Turkish commentary on a *qaṣīda* by Naẓmīzāde, Bešīr Āġā 542 (*MFO* V, 535).

89. Dhū ʾl-Rumma, *Dīwān*, Teh. Sip. II, 598/600, *Sharḥ dīwān Dhī ʾl-Rumma* by ʿAbdallāh b. Aḥmad b. Yaḥyā b. al-Mufaḍḍal b. Ibrāhīm, in the library of Yāsīn b. Bāshayān al-ʿAbbāsī in Baṣra (Ritter).

90. 2. Line 4, instead of al-Bahyuti, read: *Bahjat al-Atharī, Dīwān* ed. ʿAbd al-ʿAzīz al-Maymanī in *al-Ṭarāʾif al-adabiyya*, 55/71.

93. 1. e. Hudba b. Khashram, the *rāwī* of Ḥuṭayʾa and a member of the Banū ʿUdhra, was, under al-Muʿāwiya, involved in all kinds of disputes which eventually landed him in jail and even caused his death, *Agh.* XXI^{2}, 169/77, Ibn Qut. *Shiʿr* 434/8, Rückert, *Hamāsa* no. 152, 334, G. Dugat, *JA* 1855, 360ff, Rescher, *Abriss* II, 301.

2. *Qaṣīdat al-ʿarūs* in *al-Ṭarāʾif al-adabiyya* 102/4.

97. aa. J.H. Harley, Abu Nuhaila, a Postclassical Arabic Poet, *JRASB*, Letters III, 1937, p. 55—70.—*Dīwān b. Abī Dumayna*, see Suppl. III, 490.

99. 17. P. Hahn, *Surāqa b. Mirdās, ein schiitischer Dichter aus der Zeit des 2. Bürgerkrieges*, Diss. Erlangen, Göttingen 1938.

101. 1b. *Qiṣaṣ al-anbiyāʾ*, Alex. Taʾrīkh 98.

103. 3. *al-Amālī al-Idrīsiyya*, Alex. Taṣawwuf 33, *Risāla fi ʾl-takālīf*, ibid. Funūn mutanawwiʿa 164, 9.

106. 6. *Dīwān al-nujūm*, additionally Dam. Z. 85, 12.

Chapter 2. ʿUthmān Shukrī, *Mulūk al-shiʿr fi ʾl-dawla al-ʿAbbāsiyya*, C. 1927.

110. Ḥusayn Manṣūr, *Bashshār b. Burd bayna ʾl-jidd wal-mujūn*, C. 1930, F. Gabrieli, Appunti su B. b. B., *BSOS* 1938, 151/63.

113. 4. J.H. Harley, Marwān b. Abī Ḥafṣa, a Postclassical Poet, *JRASB*, Letters III, 1937, p. 71/90.

117. al-Qaddūr b. Jibrīl (envoy of the sultan of Morocco in Paris), *Abou Nuwas*, Paris 1931.—*Dīwān* in the recension of Ḥamza al-Iṣbahānī, Istanbul, Un. R 843, *ZS* III, 253.

118. O. Rescher, *Beiträge zur arab. Poesie, II, Diwan des Muslim b. al-Walīd*, German transl., Stuttgart 1938.

121. 9b. Under ʿAlī b. Hishām, Khālid b. Yazīd al-Kātib Abū ʾl-Haytham of Baghdad worked as a civil servant in Qom for the organisation that was in charge of the payment of pensions (*kuttāb al-iʿṭāʾ*). Al-Faḍl b. Marwān introduced him to al-Muʿtaṣim (r. 218–27/833–42) prior to the construction of Samarra; towards the end of his life and after a series of ill-fated love affairs, he totally lost his mind: Agh. XXI 44/54,[2] 31/8, *Dīwān* Dam. ʿUm. 91, 12 (see Suppl. II. 900, 35, Kr.).

| 125. 14. Ṭāhā Ḥusayn, *Min ḥadīth al-shiʿr wal-nathr*, 227/68. 1194

127. 15. Idem, ibid., 188/226.—Abu ʾl-ʿAlāʾ al-Maʿarrī, *ʿAbath al-walīd, sharḥ Dīwān al-Buḥturī*, Damascus 1936.

129. Ṭāhā Ḥusayn, op.cit., 269/312.

130. *The Ṭabaqāt al-shuʿarāʾ al-muḥdathīn of Ibn al-Muʿtazz*, reproduced in facs. from a MS dated 1285 H, 1869 AD, with an introduction, notes and variants by A. Eghbal, E.J.W. Gibb Memorial Series, N.S. London 1939.

131. Muḥammad Sayyid al-Kīlānī, *al-Sharīf al-Raḍī, shiʿruhu, taʾrīkh ḥayātihi*, C. 1939. Zakī Mubārak, *ʿAbqariyyat al-Sharīf al-Raḍī*, C. 1939.

132, 9. *Dīwān* Teh. S. 70 II, 601, *al-Ḥijāziyyāt* Dam. Z. 85, 5, 2.

133. 2. Instead of 'uncle' read 'cousin' (Kr.).

136. Ṭāhā Ḥusayn, *Min ḥadīth al-shiʿr wal-nathr*, 152/8.—*Akhbār Abī Tammām, taʾlīf Abī Bakr Muḥammad b. Yaḥyā al-Ṣūlī wa-bi-awwalihi Risālat al-Ṣūlī ilā Muzāḥim b. Fātik fī taʾlīf akhbār Abī Tammām wa-shiʿrihi* ed. Khalīl Maḥmūd ʿAsākir, Muḥammad ʿAbduh Gharām, Naẓīr al-Islām al-Hindī, C. 1356/1937. Translation of the *Risāla* in Naẓīr al-Islam, *Die Akhbār von Abū Tammām von al-Ṣūlī*, Diss. Breslau 1940.—Mulḥam Ibrāhīm al-Aswad, *Badr al-tamām fī sharḥ dīwān Abī Tammām* Beirut 1934. *Dīwān* Teh. Sip. II 552/4.

141. ʿAbd al-Qādir al-Mubārak, *Ḥayāt al-Mutanabbī*, *RAAD*, XIV 286/93, Ibrāhīm ʿAbd al-Qādir al-Māzinī, *Abu ʾl-Ṭayyib al-Mutanabbī*, in *Ḥaṣād al-hashīm*, 199/244.

142. 1. Anonymous abstract Bank. XXIII 15, 2513—3. Qaw. II 216, Taymūr Majm. 199.—5. Bank. XXIII 17, 2514.—5a. *Sharḥ dīwān al-Mutanabbī* by Murhaf b. Usāma b. Munqidh, d. 613/1216, Paris 3106, see M. Jawād, *REI*, 1938, p. 285.—8. C. 1936/9, 4 vols.—Paris 3105 instead by Abū ʿAbdallāh Ḥusayn b. Ibrāhīm al-Irbilī al-Kūrānī, d. 656/1258, see M. Jawād loc. cit.

144. *Dīwān*, Bank. XXIII 1825/5, in the recension of Khālawayh Asʿad Ef. 2603, see *MFO* Beirut V, 534.

147. 3. *Dīwān*, Bank. XXIII 19,25/6.—7. Dīwān, ibid., 21,2517.

150. 1. *Khuṭab*, additionally Garrett 1907, Ist. Um. 5575 (*ZS* III, 249).

2. *al-Makārim wal-mafākhir, sharaḥahu* ʿIzzat al-ʿAṭṭār, C. 1938.

152. 3. *Maqāmāt* additionally Ist. Un. R. 800 (*ZS* III, 249), Alex. Adab 134, 1, Teh. Sip. II 85/90.

153. f. Suter 125; see III, 297.

157. Muḥammad Asʿad Ṭalas, *Taʾrīkh al-naḥw*, *RAAD* XIV, 69/73, 227/31, 271/6.

158. 2. al-Jazarī, *Ṭab.* I, 288/92 (Kr.).

159. *Tafsīr ḥurūf al-lugha al-hijāʾiyya*, Alex. Fun. mut. 96, 2—*al-Nuqaṭ wal-shakl* AS 4456 (*Dharīʿa* I, 39, 184).—*Wujūh al-naṣb*, which others claim was written by Abū ʿAbdallāh Muḥammad b. Shuqayr, Ṣāḥib al-Mubarrad, Qawala II, 118—He is also credited with a *Kitāb al-imāma*, which was then perfected by Abū ʾl-Fatḥ Muḥammad b. Jaʿfar al-Marāghī (d. 371/981), *Dhariʿa* II, 425, no. 292. Commentary by al-Sīrāfī, read: Selīm Āghā 1158, and additionally Faiẕ. 1983.

160. *Sharḥ ʿuyūn Kitāb Sībawayhi* by Abū Naṣr Hārūn b. Mūsā (d. 401/1010 in Córdova), *Br. Mus. Quart.* X, 31.

162. 2 is the well-known work by Pseudo-Ibn ʿArabī (Ritter).

4. *Majāz al-Qurʾān*, in the estate of the late Ismāʿīl Efendi, director of the ʿUmūmiyya in Istanbul (Rescher, *Abriss* II, 135).

| 166. 13, 4. See I. Lichtenstädter, *JRAS* 1939, 1/28. 1195

14, 1. *Kitāb al-ajnās* ed. ʿA. ʿArshī, Rampur, State Libr. Publ. Series 2, Bombay 1938.

167. 15. Ibn al-Jazarī, *Ṭab.* I, 320/1.

168. 18, 1. An anonymous commentary, in the estate of the late Ismāʿīl Efendi (Rescher II, 150n).

169. 18, 3. C. 1936, 24 pp.—4a. (see vol. I, 108) Mubarrad's Epistle on Poetry and Prose, ed. G. v. Grünebaum, *Orientalia* X 372/82.

170. 22. (see p. 942) *Iʿrāb al-Qurʾān wa-maʿānīhi*, ʿUm. 247, part I, NO,$_{15}$ 220 (Rescher II, 155).

172. 25, I, 1. Garrett 11, Alex. Fun. mut. 1462, Wehbi Ef. 916, library of Yāsīn b. Bāshayān al-ʿAbbāsī in Basra (Ritter).—2. Garrett 20.—6. Alex. Adab 140.—11. Berl. 7558,$_7$, Garrett 21/2.—*Takhmīs* by Ibn Mollā Jirjis, Alex. Adab 23.—Abu ʾl-Qāsim Muḥammad al-Gharnāṭī, *Rafʿ al-ḥujub al-mastūra fī maḥāsin al-Maqṣūra*, C. 1344.

173. 25, I, 11. Berl. 7558,$_{7}$, Garr. 21/2, Bank. XXIII, 10,$_{2511}$. Glosses by Aḥmad Efendi al-Madanī, d. 1135/1722 (Mur. I, 148), ibid. C. 1347—XI. Garrett 251.—XVII. al-*Akhbār al-manthūra*, folios from *juz*ʾ IV—VI, Jer. Khāl. (*Dharīʿa* I, 311, no. 1612).

174. 26a. Abū Yūsuf Yaʿqūb b. Safīn al-Fasawī, *Kitāb al-maʿrifa wal-taʾrīkh, riwāyat Abī Muḥammad ʿAbdallāh b. Jaʿfar b. Durustawayh al-naḥwī samāʿ min al-shaykh Abī ʾl-Ḥusayn Muḥammad b. Ḥusayn al-Qaṭṭān*, Revan Köšk 1554 (parts 10–17), Asʿad Ef. (parts 18–29), see Cl. Cahen, *REI* 1937, SA 4.

1. Additionally Lālelī 3331, AS 4451 (*ZDMG* 64, 490/6), Qilič ʿA.P. 930 (Rescher II, 165)

176. 29, 8. *Iʿrāb al-Qurʾān*, Cairo (*Dharīʿa* II, 235, no. 934).—9. *Maqāṣid dhawi ʾl-albāb fi ʾl-ʿamal bil-asṭurlāb* Qawala II, 282 (?).—10. *al-Awwaliyyāt fi ʾl-naḥw*, MS in al-Khizāna al-Gharawiyya and signed by his sister's son, *Dharīʿa* II, 489, no. 1888.—11. *al-Masāʾil al-Shīrāziyyāt*, Rāġib 1379.

177. Line 1. Instead of Abū ʿUbayda, read Abū ʿUbayd, see Yāqūt, *Irshād* II, 396 no. 145, probably identical with 146, *Fihrist* 108 (to be supplemented on the basis of *Irshād* II, 396,$_{9}$), see Peñuela on Ibn al-Munāṣif, *Die Goldene*, p. 23 n. 5.

180. 7. *Iṣlāḥ al-manṭiq*, old MS Alex. Lugha 3, Lālelī 3534/6, ʿĀṭif 2712. 1. *Jawāmiʿ Iṣlāḥ al-manṭiq*, Hyderabad 1354/1935 (see *ZDMG*, 90, 201), 2. Also by Abu ʾl-Ḥasan Zayd b. Rifāʿa b. Masʿūd al-Kātib, *Kitāb al-amthāl*, Hyderabad 1351.

181. 8. (*Nukhaba min*) Kitāb al-ikhtiyārayn, *ikhtiyār al-Mufaḍḍal al-Ḍabbī wa-ʿAbd al-Malik b. Qurayb al-Aṣmaʿī min ashʿār fuṣaḥāʾ al-ʿArab fi ʾl-Jāhiliyya wal-Islām mimmā ruwiya ʿan mashāyikh ahl al-lugha al-mawthūq bi-riwayātihim* (MS in Ind. Off.), ed. with an Engl. transl. Dr. Syed Muazzam Hussain, The Univ. of Dacca 1938.—*Ancient Musical Instruments as Described by al-Mufaḍḍal b. Salama in the Unique Istanbul MS of the* Kitāb al-malāhī, *in the Handwriting of Yāqūt al-Mustaʿṣimī AD 1298*, text in facs. and transl. by J. Robson including notes on the instruments by H.G. Farmer (Coll. of Or. Writers on Music IV), 1939.

183. 11, a. See p. 328/9.

13. See al-Rājkūtī, *RAAD* IX, 601/16.

| 185. 2. See Cl. Cahen, *REI* 1936 (1938) SA 2.—5. Ed. Muḥammad al-Saqqāʾ, 1196
C. 1350/1932.—7. Teh. Sip. II, 4.—8. C. 1355/1936.

186. 11. b. C. 1355, 2 vols.

187. 2. Suter no. 60.

189. 5, 4. Instead by a certain Yaḥyā al-Washshāʾ, additionally Berl. 4024/5, Br. Mus. 913, 1, BDMG 54/5.—5. Additionally Berl. 3351 (which has Ibrāhīm b. Aḥmad al-Washshāʾ).

190. 9, 1b. See Jeffery, *Islca* = *AKM*, XXIII, b. 130/55.—8. *Ishtiqāq al-shuhūr wal-ayyām, Dharīʿa* II, 101, 395.—9. A work on the art of reading the Qurʾān, Murād Mollā 84, Ritter, *Isl.* XVII, 249, Rescher, *Abriss* II, 305.

9a. *Kitāb al-muthannā*, in the estate of ʿIzz al-Dīn al-Tanūkhī, who will publish it in *al-Majalla* (letter by Krenkow dated 25 January 1937), see *RAAD*, XV, 313.

191. 9b, 4. See Krenkow, *Islca* IV, 272/82.

192. 1. ʿĀšir 817 (*MFO* V, 508), Dāmād Ibr. P. 1068 (ibid. 528), ʿĀṭif Ef. 2476 (ibid. 492).—2. ʿĀṭif Ef. 2588 (*MFO* V, 493), Rāġib 1316, NO 4545/7 (*ZDMG* 64, 208).—7. A very old copy in Medina, Bergsträsser—Pretzl, *Gesch. des Qorʾāntextes* 228, n. 2.

193. 11, 1. With the title *Taṣḥīḥāt* (sic) *al-muḥaddithīn fī gharīb al-Qurʾān*, in the margin of al-Suyūṭī's *Talkhīṣ al-Nihāya*, C. 1322 (see Qawala I, 105).—4. is by Abū Hilāl (11a); see Rescher, *Abriss* II, 211.

194. 11a, 8. Read: Ḥakīm Oġlū; abstract by Kamāl al-Dīn ʿAbd al-Raḥmān b. Muḥammad b. Ibrāhīm al-ʿAtāʾiqī al-Ḥillī, autograph in al-Khizāna al-Gharawiyya, together with *al-Shuhda fī sharḥ al-Muʿarrab* and *al-Zubda*, comnposed in 788/1386, *Dharīʿa* II, 481, no. 1889.

195. 2. *Diwān al-adab* (to be read thus), Teh. Sip. II 180/5, Yeni 1084, l. Bešīr Āġā 121.

196. 3, 1 b. Garr. 261, Teh. Sip. II, 166—c. See Barthold, *12 Vorl. über die Gesch. der Türken Mittelasiens*, deutsch von Th. Menzel, Berlin 1935 p. 194/5, Teh. Sip. II. 200/4.—d. Additionally Garr. 262/4, Qawala II, 8.

197. 4. *Tahdhīb al-lugha*, Teh. Sip. II 166/73, anon. *Mukhtaṣar* ibid. 280/2.—2. Read: *al-Zāhir*.

198. 5, 6. With the title *Akhṣar sīrat sayyid al-Bashar*, Hamb. Or. Sem. 14, 10 (M. Krause).—12. Teh. Sip. II 285/93, see al-Maghribī, *RAAD* XI, 65/71, excerpts ibid. 352/5.

199. 6, 9. *al-Ibāna fī madhhab ahl al-ʿadl bi-ḥujaj min al-Qurʾān wal-ʿaql*, MSS in Samarra and Najaf, Dharīʿa I, 56, no. 288.

200. 8c. See GAL first ed., vol. I, 127. 13, with Yāqūt, *Irshād* IV, 208.—*ʿUmdat al-kātib* (*kuttāb*), following Qudāma b. Jaʿfar, Cairo III, 258.

201. 1a. Read: ʿAlī b. al-Ḥasan—2, 3 C. 1938.

202. 2a. See Ch. D. Matthews, *JAOS* 58, 615/37.—4, 1. *al-Tanbīh* see *RAAD* VI, 269/73.—*Fahāris Simṭ al-laʾālī*, C. 1937/1356.

3. b. Qāsim b. Thābit b. Ḥazm al-Saraqusṭī, a traditionist and student of al-Nasāʾī and al-Bazzār and also a philologist, was the first to bring Khalīl's *Kitāb al-ʿayn* to Spain. He died in Zaragoza in 302/914. Al-Ḍabbī (BAH III) 434, Ibn al-Faraḍī (ibid. VII) 293, Abū Bakr b. Khayr (ibid. IX) 191/4, Yāqūt, *Irshād* VI, 154 (undated), al-Suyūṭī, *Bughya* 376/7, Flügel, *Gr.* 200/1, Rescher, *Abriss* II, 238, al-*Dalāʾil fī l-ḥadīth* (*gharīb al-ḥadīth*) vol. II, Dam. Z. 62, 41.

1197 | 206. 3, 1. Ed. Muḥammad al-Saqqāʾ al-Abyārī, Aḥmad Sabtī, C. 1936, and also by Muḥammad Muḥyi ʾl-Dīn ʿAbd al-Ḥamīd ibid. 1937, in 4 vols.

209. 6, 2. Geschichte des Propheten und der ersten Khalifen, Fātiḥ 4210, see Cl. Cahen, *REI* 1938 (1936) SA 2.

211. 6. *Taʾrīkh Bukhārā*, Persian transl. by Abū Naṣr Aḥmad b. Muḥammad b. Naṣr al-Qubāwī, ed. Riḍawī, Tehran n.d. (128pp).

212. 1, 1. *Mukhtaṣar* Rāġib 999 (based on a copy in the handwriting of Yāqūt).—3. See Nyberg in *ΔΡΑΓΜΑ M.P. Nilsson*, Uppsala 1939, p. 346/66, R. Klinke-Rosenberger, *Das Götzenbuch der I. al-K.*, transl. with an introd. and a comm., Leipzig 1941.

1 a. *al-Jamhara* additionally *Br. Mus. Quart.* VI, 79.

213. 2b. See Muḥammad Kurd ʿAlī, *RAAD* VII, 5/27.

216. 3, 2. VI B, ed. M. Schlössinger, Jerusalem 1938.—*II Califfo Moawiya I, secondo il* Kitāb ansāb al-ashrāf, *tradotto e annotato da O. Pinto e G. Levi della Vida*, Rome 1938.

217. 4, 1. Istanbul MSS in Cl. Cahen, *REI* 1939 (1936) SA 3. I. Guidi, Sommario degli annali di Tabari per gli anni 65–99/684/5–710, *Rend. Lincei* VI, 1925, 352–407.

219. 3 and 4 see ad p. 136.—8. *Dīwān* ed. ʿAbd al-ʿAzīz al-Maymanī in *al-Ṭarāʾif al-adabiyya*, C. 1937, p. 118/94.

220. 5b, 1. New edition by Muṣṭafā al-ʿAqqād, Ibrāhīm al-Abyārī and ʿAbd al-Ḥāfiẓ, C. 1939.

6, 1. C. 1938. On the anonymous *Jumān fī mukhtaṣar Akhbār al-zamān* see Muḥammad Kurd Ali, *RAAD* III, 239/42.—3. See Cl. Cahen, *REI* 1938 (1936) SA 4, a fragment in Esc.^{2} 280, 2, Antuña, *al-Andalus* III, 1935, 447/9 (contra Derenbourg); C. 1347.—4. Ed. ʿAbdallāh Ismāʿīl al-Ṣāwī, C. 1357/1938.

221. 6, 5. *Dharīʿa* I, 110, 536.

222. 7, 6. *Kitāb afʿal*, Qawala II, 210.

8. See Cl. Cahen, *REI* 1939 (1936) SA 4.

223. 1a, see al-Ṣūlī, *Ashʿār awlād al-khulafāʾ* 17/49.

225. 1d, 1. MSS in Dār al-kutub in Tehran and in the collection of Sayyid Aḥmad al-Ṣafī al-Najafī, see al-Tanūkhī, *RAAD* XV, 335/9.

1e, 1. Ed. H.G. Farmer in *The Music in the* Kitāb al-Aghānī, London 1940.

1f. See Cahen, loc. cit., SA 3.

226. 1. On Faiẓ. 1561 see Holter in *Jahrb. des Kunsthist. Inst. Vienna* N. F. 11, 1937, p. 38.

2, 2. As *al-Hadāyā wal-tuḥaf*, Topkapu 2618c (*RSO* IV, 723).

228. 2. See Cahen, loc. cit., 3.

229. 3. Suter 78, Becker, *Beitr. z. Gesch. Äg.* II, 151/3.—5. Būhār 353, Bank. XXII, $108,_{2474}$.—6. *Fi 'l-nisab wal-tanāsub*, Algiers 1446, 2, Cairo 1 V, 198.—7. *De arcubus similibus*, Bodl. I, 941.—8. On the *ṣaḥīfa* at any latitude, ibid. (Kračk.).

230. 4a. Bank. XV, 1070, Brill—H.[2] 264, Garr. 759 (which has ʿAmr b. al-ʿĀṣ b. Yūsuf al-Kindī).

231. 1. *Makārim al-akhlāq*, see Abū Bakr b. Khayr, Index 290.—2. The chronicle by his son ʿĪsā is the main source of Ibn Ḥayyān's *al-Muqtabis* until the year 361 AH, see ed. Antuña XVII.

1198 | 233. Chapter 5. Muḥammad Kurd ʿAlī, *Umarāʾ al-bayān*, C. 1937.

235. II, 1. Instead by Aḥmad b. ʿAbdallāh b. al-Muqaffaʿ, see P. Kraus, *RSO* XIV, 1934, 1/20.

241. 2. Ed. ʿAbd al-Salām Muḥammad Hārūn, vol. 1, C. 1938.

242. 3. *Kitāb al-bukhalāʾ*, with a commentary by al-ʿAwāmirī Bek and Muṣṭafā al-Jārim Bek, C. 1938 (Maṭbaʿat wizārat al-maʿārif).

243. 18. Transl. O. Rescher, *Or. Misz.* I (Constantinople 1925), 107/70.—19. Transl. O. Rescher, *Or. Misz.* II (Constantinople 1926), 146/86.—46a (see Suppl. I, 946) instead by Yaḥyā b. ʿAdī, see *RAAD* IV, 561, V, 39, A. Périer, *Yaḥyā ben ʿAdī*, Paris 1920, p. 108.

244. 54. *al-Tabaṣṣur fi 'l-tijāra*, ed. Ḥasan Ḥusnī ʿAbd al-Wahhāb, Damascus, Maṭbaʿat al-Majmaʿ al-ʿilmī, see *RAAD* XII, 321/55.

246. 90. From which the description of the Umayyad Mosque in Yāqūt, *GW* II, 593ff.—Some fragments in Mosul 100, 24, see *Lughat al-ʿArab* IX, 174/81.

247. Line 8, 5. Maybe the work of a Christian, see H. Baneth in *Magnes Annivers. Vol.*, Jerusalem 1938, 24ff.

2a. Aḥmad b. Abī 'l-Sarḥ al-Kātib (*Fihrist* 128) wrote, in 274/887: *Kitāb al-ʿilm, Rasāʾil, Kitāb rumūz*, Rāġib 1463, f. 100/6, ed. S.M. Ḥusayn, *RAAD* XI, 642/55.

3. 3. Together with Majd al-Dīn al-Ṭūsī al-Ghazālī, *Bawāriq al-ilmāʿ* (see p. 756, 6, 4), ed. with introduction, transl. and notes by J. Robson, Or. Transl. Fund, N.S. XXXIV, London 1938.

250. 8. Read: Abū ʿUmar (ʿAmr) Aḥmad b. Muḥammad.

251. *al-ʿIqd*, see Cl. Cahen, *REI* 1938 (1936) SA 3.

253. 1. Additionally Alex. Mawāʿiẓ 29, print. C. 1938, see F. Gabrieli, Il valore letterario e storico del *Faraj baʿd al-shidda* di T. *RSO* XIX, 1940, 16/44.—2. Edition and study by L. Pauly, Bonner Or. St. H. 23, Stuttgart 1939.

254. 11. The identification with the author mentioned in al-Bākharzī, *Dumya* $6_{,10}$, is uncertain because both the edition and MS Welīeddīn f. 41b, and elsewhere, have the reading 'Muṭarriz' (Rescher, *Abriss* II 299).

12. Bank. XXIII, $114_{,2603}$.

257. ε. *Kitāb al-fitan*, abstract by Naṣr b. ʿAbd al-Munʿim al-Tanūkhī al-Ḥanafī, Dam. Z. 82, 62.

259. ρ. See p. 691. 1.

259 τ. Ibn al-Khaṭīb, *Taʾrīkh Baghdād* XIV, 177, al-Samʿānī, *Ansāb* 525a, 567b, *Lib. Cl.* II, 5, no. 17, Abu 'l-Maḥāsin I, 699/700 (ed. Cairo II, 270/4), *Ann. Musl.* II, 186, 191.

260. J. Fück, Beiträge zur Überlieferungsgeschichte von Bukhārī's Traditionssammlung, *ZDMG* 92, 60/87.

261. Line 35, read: *JRAS* 1936.

263. 18. *Sharḥ ʿiddat aḥādīth Ṣaḥīḥ al-Bukhārī* by Muḥammad al-Safīrī (d. 956/1549, GAL II, 99) additionally Alex. Ḥadīth 31.—42. *al-Iʿlām bi-sharḥ aḥādīth sayyid al-anām* (on the *Bāb al-ṣawm*) by Ismāʿīl al-Jarrāḥī, Brill-H.[2] 693, Garr. 1355 (MS dated 915/1510).

264, 8. *Fatḥ al-mubdī*, additionally Qawala I, 103.—Line 19. 10. *Bahjat al-nufūs, sharḥ Mukhtaṣar Ṣaḥīḥ al-Bukhārī* by Ibn Abī Ḥamza, 4 vols., C. 1349/54.—Line 26. ʿAbdallāh b. Sālim al-Baṣrī, d. 1134/1721 (II, 521), Garr. 1354.—Line 28,

1199 | 9. *Asāmī ruwāt Ṣaḥīḥ al-Bukhārī* by Ḥasan b. Ḥasan Ṣūfīzāde, d. 1279/1862, Istanbul 1282.—10. *Taḥrīr ʿalā Kitāb al-ʿilm min* Ṣaḥīḥ *al-Bukhārī* by Muḥammad al-Najjār, *mufti l-diyār al-Tūnisiyya*, Tunis 1325.—11. Commentary by al-Qāriʾ al-Harawī, II, 543.—111a. In the library of Yāsīn Bāshayān al-ʿAbbāsī in Basra (Ritter)—111b. Arranged chronologically, purchased in Hyderabad in 1937 (Krenkow, 25 October 1937).

266. 9. Qawala I, 117, Alex. Ḥad. 24.—Line 36, 8. *Rijāl* Ṣaḥīḥ *al-imām Muslim* by Abū Bakr Aḥmad b. ʿAlī b. Manjawayh al-Iṣfahānī (d. 428/1037), Alex. Taʾr. 70, Muṣṭ. Ḥad. 10 (MS dated 664 AH).

268. I, 3. Additionally Makr. 12.—II, 2. Additionally Alex. Ḥad. 6.—3. Ibid. 54, Qawala I, 101, Garr. 631.—5. BDMG 14, Garr. 632, Qaw. I, 113.—(I.?) 10. *Tuḥfat al-aḥwadhī bi-sharḥ* Jāmiʿ *al-Tirmidhī* by ʿAbd al-Raḥmān al-Mārkfūrī, 4 vols., Delhi 1346/53.

269. 6. C. 1306.—8. Alex. Ḥad. 9.—Line 26. *al-Shiyam*, with the commentary *Ḥulal al-iṣṭifāʾ*, Alex. Ḥad. 21.—*Ṣalāt al-shamāʾil wa-kanz al-ḥaṣāʾil* by Muḥammad b. Khalīl al-Ḥākim p. 270. c. 2. C. 1308., Alex. Faw. 12.

274. (275?) 13a. Abū Bakr Muḥammad b. ʿUmar al-Warrāq, d. 390/1000 (or, according to others, in 396/1005), known as a weak traditionist, wrote the *Kitāb al-ʿālim wal-mutaʿallim*, transmitted in 396 AH by Abū Naṣr b. Abī ʾl-Ḥusayn Muḥammad b. Muḥammad al-Ṣrmnjī (Ibn al-Khaṭīb, *Taʾrīkh Baghdād* III, 35/6, al-Samʿānī, *Ansāb*, 580r).

275. 13, 9. *Risāla fi ʾl-ghunya ʿani ʾl-kalām wa-ahlihi* is cited by Ibn Tamiyya in *Majm. ras. al-kubrā* I, 439, penultimate line and following.

277. 13 (16 ?), 4. Alex. Ḥad. 63.—5. Anon. Persian table of contents in Bursa, see V.A. Hamdani, *JRAS* 1938, 561.

17. *Sharḥ mushkil al-ḥ.*, Alex. Ḥad. 32.—*Ibn Fūrak, Bayān mushkil al-aḥādīth*, Auswahl nach den Hdss. in Leipzig, Leiden, London und dem Vat. von R. Köbert, Analecta Or. 22, Rom. Pont. Inst. Bibl. 1941.

278. d. Also Dam. Um. 25, no. 362.—e. See Suppl. II, 932.

279. f. Instead of "al-Ḥasan" read "al-Ḥusayn."

285. I (II?), 5. By Abū 'l-Muntahā Aḥmad b. Muḥammad al-Maghnīsawī, additionally BDMG 32, Garr. 666/8, Alex. Tawḥīd 23, Mawāʿiẓ 35. 3, Fun. mut. 76, 156,2, 149,9.—Anon. *Mukhtaṣar al-ḥikma al-nabawiyya* Alex. Tawḥ. 43.

286. V, 7. Alex. Ḥad. 16, Qilič ʿA. 273/4.

287. Line 2, additionally Qawala I, 107, with the title *Tanwīr al-sanad fī īḍāḥ rumūz al-musnad*.—VI. Qawala I, 213, 270.—*al-Jawāhir al-munīfa* Garr. 1769, Alex. Mawāʿiẓ 25—VII. Alex. Fun. 156, 8.—VIII. Alex. Fun. 156, 7.—XII. Heid. *ZDMG* 91, 386, no. 327, 1.—XVI. *Naṣāʾiḥ*, with the commentary *Zubdat al-Naṣāʾiḥ* by ʿUthmān b. Muṣṭafā, completed in 1059/1649, Alex. Maw. 36, Fun. mut. 102, 5.—XVII. *al-Ḍawābiṭ al-thalātha*, with the commentary *al-Wuṣūl ila 'l-kanz al-akbar wa-ilā mā huwa anfaʿ min al-kibrīt al-aḥmar*, Garr. 2120, 3.

288. 2, 1. Ind. Off. 1511. Of the commentary *Fiqh al-mulūk* (see page 950) additionally Medina, *ZDMG* 90, 115.

289. I, 5. Part of an anonymous commentary, Ind. Off. 1422.—II, 2. Alex. Fiqh Ḥan. 33.—IV. C. 1356.—4. With the title *Jāmiʿ al-Ṣadr al-Shahīd*, Alex. Fiqh Ḥan. 17.

290. IV, 9. Alex. Fiqh Ḥan. 11.—12. (11.?)Commentary by ʿUthmān b. Muṣṭafā, completed in 1159/1746, Br. Mus. Suppl. 252.—V. Ind. Off. 1512 (in the recension of ʿUmar b. ʿAbd al-ʿAzīz b. Māza), lith. also Delhi 1291 (Āṣaf. 1080).—a. Garr. 1672/3, Alex. Fiqh Ḥan. 32.

| 291. V, c. Alex. Fiqh Ḥan. 32.—IX. A commentary, Alex. Fun. mut. 115, 2.— 1200
X. C. 1938.

292. 5. Alex. Fiqh Ḥan. 4.

5a. 2. Qawala I, 186, 340, Alex. Fiqh Ḥan. 54.—3. *Asīr al-malāḥida fi 'l-alfāẓ al-mukaffira* Alex. Fiqh Ḥan. 6, Fun. mut. 194, 10.

6. 2. Qawala I, 304.—a. Ind. Off. 1514, Garr. 1669, Āṣaf. 1088, Alex. Fiqh Ḥan. 31.—3. Alex. Fiqh Ḥan. 23, Ind. Off. 1696 (abstract?).

293. 71 (7?), 2. Qawala 153.

294. 7. Garr. 2127, 1, Alex. Tawḥ. 25, 30 (*Bayān al-sunna wal-jamāʿa*).—d. Shujāʿ al-Dīn Hibatallāh b. Aḥmad b. al-Muʿallā al-Turkistānī (671–733/1272–1333), Garr. 1543.—e. Anon. Goth. 665 = Ind. Off. 4569, see *JRAS* 1939, 359.

8. 1. Qawala I, 274.

295. 10, 1. Garr. 2127,2.—2. *Risāla fī bayān anna ʾl-īmān juzʾ min al-ʿamal*, in *Majmūʿa*, Istanbul 1288 (Qawala I, 186).

12. 1. Ind. Off. 1516/9, Garr. 1674/5, Alex. Fiqh Ḥan. 62, Qaw. I, 392/3.

296. 4. Alex. Fiqh Ḥan. 21.—6. Ibid. 24.—7. Ibid. 51—8a. Qaw. I, 319 (which has *al-Jawhara al-munīra*).—9. Ind. Off. 1521/2 (which has al-Kādūrī).—12. Qaw. I, 386.—15. *al-Yanābīʿ fī maʿrifat al-uṣūl wal-tafārīʿ* see p. 951, additionally Dam. ʿUm. 57, 21, Alex. Fiqh Ḥan. 73.—16. *al-Fawāʾid al-badriyya* by Ḥamīd al-Dīn ʿAlī b. Muḥammad b. ʿAlī al-Ḍarīr al-Rīshī al-Bukhārī (d. 667/1268 see below ad p. 644), Qaw. I, 381.—*Mushkilāt al-Q.*, by the author himself (?), Alex. Fun. mut. 87, 1.—17. Anon. *Fātiḥ al-Q.*, Ind. Off. 1520.—*Taṣḥīḥ al-Q.*, Alex. Fiqh Ḥan. 13.

297. 1, I. Garr. 1338.

298. 5. Qaw. I, 107, Alex. Ḥad. 12.—6. Qaw. I, 132.

299. 11. See p. 475.

11. al-Mahdī d. 558/1163.

13. *Risāla ilā Hārūn al-Rashīd wa-Yaḥyā al-Barmakī*, Būlāq 1311.

2a. Line 28, 1. 6 or 7. Rajab 280.—Yāqūt, *GW* I, 348.

300. *al-Mudawwana*, 4 fragments from a MS on vellum Louvain, *Muséon* I, 86f.—(301?) 4. *al-Tafrīʿ*, based on Alex. Fiqh Māl. 15.

301. 5, 1. Entitled *al-Taqyīd*, Alex. Fiqh Māl. 6, 10,—ibid. 10.

302. 5, b. Ibid. 6, 10.—c. Glosses by ʿAlī b. Aḥmad b. Makram al-ʿAdawī al-Sūdī al-Manāfisī, Makr. 23.—Line 13, *Tafassur etc.*, Alex. Fiqh Māl. 9 entitled *Tanwīr etc.*—12. Ibid. 13.—13. *Murshid al-mubtadiʾīn* by Saʿīd b. al-Ḥusayn b. Muḥammad al-Ḥumaydī, ibid. 18.—*Tahdhīb al-M. wal-Mukhtaliṭa*, Alex Fiqh Māl. 16.

304. Line 27, L.J. Graf, *Al-Shāfiʿīs verhandeling van de „wortelen" van den fiqh*, Diss. Leiden, Amsterdam 1935.—*al-Tamhīd fī uṣūl al-fiqh*, Ind. Off. 1428.

305. Line 18, *Munājāt al-Shāfiʿī*, Heid. ZDMG 91, 387, b.

307. 6a. See Brockelmann in *Mélanges de géographie et d'orientalisme, offerts à M.E.F. Gautier*, Paris 1938, G. v. Grünebaum, *Arabica* I, Roma 1937, 41/64.—*Fatāwī* additionally Cairo[2] I, 527 (where the name of the author is identical with the one given in Sulaim. 675).—*Jawāmiʿ al-kalim fi 'l-ḥadīth min al-mawāʿiẓ wal-ḥikam* Selīm Āġā 481, Alex. Fun. mut. 66, 4.

| 6. b. Al-Ḥasan b. Ḥarb al-Ḥassūnī composed around 400/1010, on the order 1201
of the vizier Abū 'l-Ḥasan Aḥmad b. Muḥammad al-Suhaylī, al-*Suhayl fi 'l-madhhab al-Shāfiʿī wal-Ḥanafī* (ḤKh III, 637, no. 7300) *fi 'l-furūʿ al-Shāfiʿiyya*, Alex. Fiqh Shāf. 24.

7. *Taḥrīr etc.* Alex. Fiqh Shāf. 18, glosses by al-Ujhūrī ibid. 42, by al-Qalyūbī ibid. 19, by al-Madābighī ibid. 20.

310. 2, 1. *Ghāyat al-maqṣad fī zawāʾid al-Musnad* by Nūr al-Dīn Abū 'l-Ḥasan ʿAlī b. Abī Bakr b. Sulaymān al-Haytamī (II, 82), Alex. Ḥad. 37.—7. Qawala I, 184.

311. c, 3. *Kitāb al-sunna* is cited by Ibn Taymiyya, *Majm. Ras. al-kubrā* I, 410, 1.

f. *al-Khalʿ wa-ibṭāl al-ḥīla* in Muḥammad Ḥāmid al-Faqqī, *Min dafāʾin al-kunūz*, C. 1349, no. 1 (which has Abū ʿAbdallāh b. Baṭṭa).

313. Line 19, Muḥammad Muḥsin, nazīl Sāmarrā, al-Shahīr bil-shaykh Āghā Bozorg al-Ṭihrānī, *al-Dharīʿa ilā taṣānīf al-Shīʿa* I, Najaf 1355, II, ibid. 1356.

314. 1, 3. See Jeffery, RSO 16 (1937) 249/89.

316. III, 10. Hamb. Or. Sem. 132, 2.—17. Ibid. 137, 1.

318. 9, 4. *Amālī* print. Ṣanʿāʾ 1355 (Rossi, *Or. Mod.* XVIII, 572)

(318. Chapter 7, 5. ?) 2. 1. The oldest book of the Shīʿa was, according to Ibn al-Nadīm, *Fihr.* 219, 14, the *Kitāb al-ʿadl* of Sulaym b. Qays al-Hilālī, who fled from al-Ḥajjāj to Abān b. Abī ʿAyyāsh to whom he transmitted it, with divergent *isnāds*, *Dhariʿa* II, 152/9. no. 590.

2. 1. The *Fiqh Riḍā* (print. Tehran 1274, together with the *Muqnaʿa* of Mufīd [p. 322]), which owed its popularity to a large extent to Majlisī (II 572 ff), is also preserved in Teh. Sip. I, 491/4.

319. 2a. Abū Muḥammad al-Faḍl b. Shādhān b. al-Khalīl al-Nīsābūrī ṣāḥib al-imām al-Riḍā, d. 260/874, al-Ṭūsī, *al-Fihrist*, ed. M. Ṣādiq āl Baḥr al-ʿUlūm, 124, *Manhaj al-maqāl* 260, *al-Īḍāḥ fī 'l-radd ʿalā sāʾir al-firaq* MSS in Iraq, *Dharīʿa* II, 490, no. 1946, see Suppl. II, 1014, 14.

320. 7, 1. Garr. 1608/9, Alex. Firaq 10.

9. 1. See *Dharīʿa* II, 28, 112.—2. *al-Ādāb wa-makārim al-akhlāq*, MS in the collection of ʿAbd al-Ḥusayn b. Qāsim al-Ḥillī al-Najafī, ibid. I, 12, 54.

321. 10, 2. *Dharīʿa* II, 315, no. 1251.

322. 10, 20. *Ṣifāt al-Shīʿa, Lughat al-ʿArab* VII (1929), 223.—21. *al-Ikhtiṣāṣ*, in the collection of Amīn al-wāʿiẓīn Ibrāhīm b. Muḥammad ʿAlī in Iṣfahān, *Dharīʿa* I, 358, no. 1889.

323. 12, 13. *al-Iʿlām fīmā wāfaqat al-Imāmiyya ʿalayhi min al-aḥkām*, an introduction to *Awāʾil al-maqālāt* (no. 19), composed at the request of al-Sharīf al-Murtaḍā, in numerous copies, *Dharīʿa* II, 237, no. 944.—14. *al-Ishrāf fī ʿilm farāʾiḍ al-Islām* ibid. II, 106, 901.—15. *Aḥkām al-nisāʾ*, in the collection of ʿAbd al-Ḥusayn al-Ḥillī al-Najafī, ibid. I, 302, no. 1578.—16. *al-Asʾila al-Sarawiyya*, asked by al-Sayyid al-Fāḍil al-Sharīf in Sariyya, MSS in the collections of Hādī Āl Kāshif al-Ghiṭāʾ in Najaf and of Rājā Muḥammad Mahdī in Faizabad, ibid. II 183, no. 330.—17. *Uṣūl al-fiqh*, which al-Kārajakī included in the *Kanz al-fawāʾid*, ibid. II, 209, no. 814.—18. *al-Ifṣāḥ fī 'l-imāma* in countless copies in Iraq, ibid. II, 258/9, no. 1051.—19. *Awāʾil al-maqālāt fī 'l-madhāhib al-mukhtārāt* ibid. II, 472, no. 1844.

325. 7, 12. *al-Ikhtiṣāṣ*, an abstract of the work with the same title by ʿAlī b. al-Ḥusayn b. Aḥmad b. ʿImrān, a contemporary of al-Shaykh al-Ṣadūq, Mashh. (not catalogued) Tehran, Sipāhsalār (likewise not catalogued), *Dharīʿa* I, 358 no. 1888/90.

1202 | 327. 9. 2 (328 bottom, M. b. Muqsim?) See page 183, 11a. Some lines further on, read Shanabūdh, Bergstr. P. 110ff, 183ff.

330. b. La Qaṣīda fi 'l-tajwīd attribuita a Mūsā b. ʿUbaydallāh b. Khāqān nota di P. Boneschi, *R. Acc. dei Lincei, Rend. cl. Sc. mor. stor. e. fil.* ser. VI, vol. XIV, fs. 1/2, 1938, *RSO* XVIII, 258/67.

d. 3. *Tuḥfat al-anām fi 'l-tajwīd*, Āṣaf. I, 296, 57.

331. 1. *Tafsīr*, Qawala I, 45 (*Riwāyat al-Kalbī ʿan Abī Ṣāliḥ ʿan Ibn ʿAbbās*).

334. 3e. Ibn al-Jazarī, *Ṭab.* II, 119/31.—3ee. His student Abū Ḥafṣ ʿUmar b. ʿAlī b. Manṣūr wrote the *Kitāb ʿadad āy al-Qurʾān*, Berl. Ms. or. qu. 1386 (Bergstr.—Pretzl, *Gesch. d. Qorʾāntextes* 238, n. 4).

335. 3g. Aḥkām al-Qurʾān, C. 1347, 3 vols.

3k. Read: Zamanīn, Nallino, *Rend. Linc.* ser. VI, vol. VII, 324.

311. (misplaced?) Muḥammad b. ʿAlī b. Aḥmad Abū Bakr al-Adfuwī al-Miṣrī al-Muqriʾ al-Naḥwī, a student of al-Naḥḥās, d. 22. Rabīʿ I, 388/25 March 998 in Cairo aged 88 (Suyūṭī, *Ṭab. al-muf.* 113), wrote *al-Istiftāʾ fī ʿulūm al-dīn* in 120 vols (ḤKh I, 273, 616, II, 353,2216), Selīm Āġā 6314/6.

342. (?) His *Kitāb naqd ʿUthmān b. Saʿīd ʿala 'l-kādhib al-ʿanīd fī-ma 'ftarā ʿala 'llāh fi 'l-tamhīd* is cited by Ibn Taymiyya in *Majm. ras. al-kubrā* I, 426,12.

345. ρ. L. Rost, Die *Risālat al-Kindī*, eine missionsapologetische Schrift, in *Allg. Missionszeitschr.* 50 (1923) 134/44; new edition announced by Rabbath, *MFB* XIV, f 3, p. 43/5.

2. 1. Abū Bakr Muḥammad etc. *Kitāb al-tawḥīd* etc., additionally Alex. Tawḥ. 144, 2, print. C. 1937.

346. 3, 7. *al-Ibāna fī uṣūl al-diyāna: The Elucidation of Islam's foundation*, transl. with introd. and notes by Walter C. Klein, Am. Or. Series vol. 19, New Haven 1940.—8. *Kitāb al-tawḥīd*, Alex. Fun. mut. 154,3.

4. 2. Additionally Qawala I, 43.

347. 6, 2. Alex. Fiqh Ḥan. 23.—4. Commentary by Abū Ḥafṣ ʿUmar al-Nasafī (I, 758), *Br. Mus. Quart.* IV, 8.

348. 6, 5. Qaw. I, 396/7, Alex. Fiqh Ḥan. 66, commentaries: a. Alex. Fiqh Ḥan. 13.—b. Ibid. 15, 55, Qaw. I, 314.—f. Ḥasan b. Ḥusayn al-Ṭūlūnī (II, 39), Alex. Fiqh. ḥan. 34.—g. Anon., Garr. 1890.—8. Garr. 920, 2133, 1.—9. Ibid. 1889, Alex. Mawāʿiẓ 11.—15. *Taʾsīs al-fiqh*, Alex. Fiqh Ḥan. 10.

7a. *al-Tanbīh etc.*, see Strothmann, *Isl. Culture* XII, 6/16.

349. 8, 9. *Kitāb al-ibāna* is cited by Ibn Taymiyya in *Majm. ras. al-kubrā* I, 452, 9.

351, aa. (?) ʿAbdallāh b. al-Mubārak (d. 180/796, but see p. 334, 3b), *Kitāb al-raqāʾiq*, Alex. Mawāʿiẓ 18.

352. Abdelhalim Mahmoud, *Al-Moḥāsibī, un mystique musulman religieux et moraliste*, Paris 1940.—2. Copy from a Cairo MS in Ind. Off. 4598, *JRAS* 1939, 378.—3. Ed. A.J. Arberry, C. 1937.

353. 1e, 19. As *Risālat al-Mustarshidīn* in Alex. Fun. mut. 100,13.—21. *Risāla fi 'l-taṣawwuf*, ibid. Taṣ. 35, 11.

2a. On the apocryphal *Masāʾil al-ruhbān* (copy Ind. Off. 4585, *JRAS* 1939, 373) see Arberry, *JRAS* 1938, 89/91. An anonymous *Manāqib* or *Waṣāyā* is preserved in Alex. Taʾr. 116.

354. 2b. Ed. and transl. from the Istanbul Unicum by A.J. Arberry, London 1937 (Isl. Research Assoc. Ser. 6).

1203 | 355. Line 15. Copy Ind. Off. 4597, *JRAS* 1939, 375, ed. H.K. Ghazanfar, Allahabad, *Univ. Studies* XI (1935) 263/97, XIII (1937) 226/54.

(4. ?) 1. Anon. comment. on *al-Masāʾil al-rūḥāniyya* contained in it, Alex. Taṣ. 40, 3.

356. 5, 11. The MS Leipz. 212 contains, under the incorrect title *al-Durr al-maknūn etc.*, a number of separate treatises, among which no. 5 and 8, see Arberry, *RSO* XVIII, 1940, p. 315/27.—12. Qawala I, 158, comment. *Mirqāt al-wuṣūl* by Muṣṭafā al-Dimashqī, completed in 1313, in *Majmūʿa*, Istanbul 1313.

357. 5, 34. *al-Masāʾil al-maknūna* Alex. Fun. mut. 145, 1.—35. *Radd ʿala 'l-Muʿaṭṭila*, ibid. 2.

5a. al-ʿAṭṭār, *Tadhkirat al-awliyāʾ* II, 265/8.

358. 6d. Read: b. al-Aʿrābī.

359. 7b, 2. A fragment from it in Walzer, *JRAS* 1939, 407.

360. 9, 1. Published in the margin of al-Ghazzālī's *Iḥyāʾ*, Istanbul 1321.

361. 9a, 3. A treatise on Divine Wisdom, which is said to reveal itself in the Old Testament, in the person of Muḥammad, and in Nature, Paris 824, 2 (which has al-Zandabūstī).—10. 1. On the *Tahdhīb al-asrār*, see A.J. Arberry, Khargushi's Manual of Sufism, *BSOS* 1938, 345/9.

362. 11, 2. Additionally Qaw. II, 239, ed. Pedersen, fs. 1. Paris 1938.—8. Additionally Alex. Maw. 3.—17. *Muqaddima fi 'l-taṣawwuf*, Alex. Taṣ. 46.

363. 1. *Euclidis elementa etc.* cont. Junge, Raeder, Thompson, Copenhagen 1932; on which Klamroth, *ZDMG* 35, 265/81.

364. 2, 1. Additionally Garr. 779/80, ʿĀšir 1002 (Ritter, *RSO* XVI, 212), Mosul $55_{,134}$.

3. Read: ʿAbd al-Masīḥ b.ʿAbdallāh b. Nāʿima.

365. Line 6. Additionally AS $2457_{,11}$ (*Islca* IV, 528), adaptation by Abū 'l-Khayr Taqī al-Dīn al-Fārisī, Mashh. I, $14_{,14}$, in the collection of ʿAlī Akbar al-Khwānsārī, *Dharīʿa* I, 120, 577.

365. 4. 1a. Berl. 5387, delete Serāi and Asʿad.—b. Berl. 6357.—f. Paris $2544_{,10}$.—g. Serāi $3505_{,3}$.—h. and k. Garr. 2006, 22.—f., h. and k. in three recensions: α AS 2633, β Serāi 3475, Asʿad $2025_{,1}$, γ Serāi $3505_{,5}$ AS 2635, 2637/8, Asʿad $2015_{,3}$.

366. 4., 2 f. Upps. 321.—i. Serāi $3464_{,6}$.—k. Ibid. 7.—l. According to Krause by al-Ṭūsī.

367. Suter 44.—4. *Le livre des questions sur l'oeil de Ḥūnayn b. I.sḥāq, publié par P. Sbath et M. Meyerhof*, Mém. de l'Inst. d'Egypte, Cairo 1938.

368. 5, I, 19. *al-Mudkhal al-kabīr ilā ʿilm al-rūḥāniyyāt*, Alex. Ḥurūf 16.—II, 2–4 by his son Isḥāq.—2. Additionally Upps. 321, Copenhagen 63, no. 81,

Fātiḥ 3439,$_1$—4. Is based on an earlier transl., see Krause, *M. Sphärica* 20/3.—5c. Additionally Alex. Ṭibb 12.

369. 5, II, 6, h. Not by Ḥunayn, see Bergsträsser, *Ḥunayn b. Isḥāq und seine Schule*, Leiden 1913, 54/9.—i. Additionally Garr. 1075,$_6$.—k. Additionally Garr. 1075,$_1$.—l. Ibid. 7 (*ilā Ṭūtharūn* = Teuthras).—m. Ibid. 8.—n. Ibid. 9.—q. *Kitāb al-buḥrān*, together with *Ayyām al-buḥrān*, ibid. 1075,$_2$.—r. *Aṣnāf al-ḥummayāt* ibid. 3.—s. *Ḥīlat al-bur'* ibid. 4.—t. *Tadbīr al-aṣiḥḥā'* ibid. 5.—8. Apollonius (?) *Fī ta'thīr al-rūḥāniyyāt* Alex. Ḥurūf 16.

1204 369. 6. Suter 39.—1. a. Based on a translation by Ḥunayn, Bergstr. | 76.—b. *Hermeneutica*, ed. Pollak, AKM XIII, 1.—3. Probably a commentary on Archimedes, *On Conoids and Spheroids*, abstract Fātiḥ 3414,$_3$.—6. Ptolemy's *Almagest*, revised by Thābit b. Qurra, Paris 2482, Esc. 915, see O.J. Tallgren, *Rev. fil.hisp.* XV (1938), 57.—7. *Jawāmiʿ kitāb Jālīnūs*, Qaw. II, 287 (see p. 368, 5, I, 17).

370. 7a. Suter 98.—3. Junge and Thompson, *The Commentary of Pappus on Book X of Euclid's* Elementa, Cambridge 1930 (ed. Woepcke, Paris 1855, n.p. & n.d.), transl. Suter, Abh. z. Gesch. der Nat. u. Math. IV, Erlangen 1922. See Bergsträsser *Isl.* XXI, 195/222, Junge, Das Fragm. der lat. Übers. von P.s Cmt. zum 10. B. des E. *QS* III, 1/17.—4. A treatise on geometry in Latin translation, Paris 9335, see Steinschneider, *Üb.* p. 532, § 329.

371. Goffredo Quadri, *La filosofia degli Arabi nel suo fiore I, delle origini fino ad Averroe*, II *Il Pensiero di Averroe*, Florence 1939.

372. 2, III, 3, H. Ritter and R. Walzer, *Studi sul Kindi II, Uno scritto morale inedito di al-K.* (*Themistios περὶ ἀλυπίας*), Mem. R. Acc. Lincei ser. VI, vol. VIII, 1, Rome 1938.

374. 2, V, 10 Bank. XXII 32,$_{2438}$.—VII, 3. *Muntasikh al-mūsīqī fī ta'līf al-naghm wa-ṣanʿat al-ʿūd* Berl. 5531, Farmer, *Sources*, 20.—4 *Kitāb al-ʿiẓam fī ta'līf al-luḥūn*, Br. Mus. Or. 2361, f. 165v, ibid.—5. *Risāla fī tarkīb al-naghm al-dālla ʿalā ṭabāʾiʿ al-ashkhāṣ al-ʿaliyya*, Berl. 5530, ibid.

375. 3. Suter 63.—*Adab al-nafs min kalām sayyid al-ʿArab wal-ʿAjam* (ḤKh no. 344), Alex. Mawāʿiẓ 4 (anon.?).

376. *Rasāʾil al-Fārābī, Maqāla fī aghrāḍ mā baʿd al-ṭabīʿa*, Hyderabad 1349. *Tajrīd risālat al-daʿāwi ʾl-qalbiyya*, ibid. 1349, *Masāʾil mutafarriqa*, ibid. 1344, *Ithbāt al-mufāraqāt*, ibid. 1345, *Fī faḍīlat al-ʿulūm wal-ṣināʿāt*, ibid. 1340, *al-Tanbīh fī sabīl al-saʿāda*, ibid. 1346, *al-Taʿlīqāt*, ibid. 1346, *Taḥṣīl al-saʿāda*, ibid. 1345.—E. 4. *Mukhtaṣar kitāb al-mudun*, Serāi 3483, 2 (Krause).—*Ibṭāl aḥkām al-nujūm* in a *majmūʿa* in the handwriting of Maḥmūd al-Nayrizī, executed between 903/19, in the collection of Sayyid Naṣrallāh al-Taqawī in Tehran, *Dharīʿa* I, 66, no. 326.—7. Entitled *Kitāb al-mūsīqī al-kabīr*, photograph of a MS from Istanbul in Cairo, *Nashra*, 22.—9. Additionally Rāġib 876. A.J. Arberry, Fārābī's *Canons of Poetry, Risāla fī qawānīn al-shiʿr*, *RSO* XVII, 266ff.

377. 4, D, 4, *Risāla fi ʾl-ʿAql*, texte arabe intégral en partie inédit (ms. de Stamboul) établi par M. Bouyges (Bibl. Ar. Scholast.), Beirut 1938.—17. *Kayfa yastawi ʾlladhīna yaʿlamūna walladhīna lā yaʿlamūna* Hyderabad, 1341.—E, 2. Aligarh 79$_{,18}$.

378. 4a. 1. *Mukhtaṣar*, Bašīr Āġā 494, Murād Mollā 1408, Köpr. 903 (*Islca* IV, 534/8).

381. Aldo Mieli, *La Science Arabe et son rôle dans l'évolution scientifique mondial avec quelques additions de* H.P.J. Renaud, M. Meyerhof, J. Ruska, Leiden 1938.

382. 1, 7. Bank. XXII, 76 XXIV, delete "with … etc.", see ad p. 862$_{,20,2}$.

2. Šerefeddin, *Mešāhīri mühendisīn i Arabden B. M.*, Istanbul 1321. 1 = 2, see Kohl ad 4.

383. 2, 8. *Kitāb al-daraj fī ṭabāʾiʿ al-burūj*, NO 2800, IIa, Pet. Inst. 119$_{,3}$.—9. *Aḥkām al-daraj lil-mawālīd*, Br. Mus. Suppl. 501, Garr. 968. |—10. *Darajāt al-kawākib*, 1205
Bank. XXII, 110, 2476.—1b. With the title *Fī uṣūl al-handasa*, Bank. XXII, 79, 2968, XXIX.

384. 2, a. Original version NO 2958, 1, on the recension by al-Ṭūsī see Krause, *QSB* III, 499/500.—b. Additionally Bank. 28, 2519 (wrong in *Tadhk. Naw.* 152).—3. Original version, AS 2671$_{,6}$.—7b. Also Br. Mus. 426$_{,11}$ (only the Arabic version remains).

385. 6a. *Kitāb fi ʾl-shakl al-mulaqqab bil-qaṭṭāʿ*, AS 4832,3, Serāi 3464,6.—b. *Kitāb fi ʾl-nisba al-muʾallafa* Paris 2457$_{,15}$, Serāi 3464, 1.—11. Read: *wa-ṣurʿatihā*,

see O. Schirmer, Studien zur Astronomie der Araber *SB Erl.* 58/9, 33/88.—29. P. Lucky, Thābit b. Qurras Buch über die ebenen Sonnenuhren, *Qu. u. St. z. Gesch. der Math. Astron. u. Phys.* IV (1937), 95–148.

386. 3, 2, B, 35 = B, 6.—38. *Tashīl al-Mijisṭī*, AS 4832, 10.

5. Suter 113 (see idem, *Vierteljahrsschr. der Nat. Ges. Zürich* 63, 1918, p. 214).—1. Read: Bank. XXII, 78, 2468$_{,\mathrm{XXVII}}$.—2. Bank. XXII, 62$_{,2468\mathrm{III}}$, see A. Taymūr, *RAAD* III, 364.—3. Read: *fī rasm al-quṭūʿ al-thalātha*, Bank. XXII, 63$_{,2468,\mathrm{IV}}$.—4. Read: *fī waṣf al-maʿāni ʾllati ʾstakhrajahā*, ibid. 61$_{,2468,\mathrm{II}}$.—5. Read: ibid. 63$_{,2468,\mathrm{V}}$.—6. Read: *ḥarakāt*, ibid. 77$_{,2468,\mathrm{XVI}}$.—7. *Kitāb Arshīmīdīs*, ibid. 78$_{,2468,\mathrm{XXVIII}}$.—10. *al-Risāla fī uṣūl al-raṣad* (author?), ibid. 60$_{,2468,\mathrm{I}}$.—Line 9: Instead of 'grandson' read 'nephew'.

387. 6b, 2. Berl. 5927.—6. *al-Faṣl fī takhṭīṭ al-ṣalāt al-zamāniyya fī kulli qubba aw fī qubba yustaʿmal lahā*, Bank. XX, 80$_{,2468,\mathrm{XXX}}$.—(6e see p. 1092).—6f Contemporary of al-Bīrūni, see Schoy, *Die trigonometr. Lehren der Ar.* 30.

6e. Contemporary of al-Bīrūnī, who refers to an observation by him from the year 378/988 (*Taḥdīd nihāyat al-amākin* 91 calls him "Abū ʿAlī", see *al-Qānūn al-Masʿūdī* VII, 6, Welīeddīn 1739, Krause).

6g. "Abu ʾl-Ḥusayn" in *Jawāmiʿ qawānīn ʿilm al-hayʾa*, *QSB* III, 511, fol. 42a. A treatise whose content remains to be determined is in Paris 4821.

388. Line 3. 358 is the dating of the manuscript, see Bergsträsser, *Isl.* XXI, 197/8, Suter, Ausmessung der Parabel, *SB Erl.* 48, 66/7.—10. ʿĀšir etc. = 29.

389. 7, 27. = 22.—32. An unnamed treatise in Paris 4821.—33. *al-Risāla fī ʾl-shakl al-qaṭṭāʿ*, Bank. XXV, 90$_{,2468,\mathrm{XL}}$.

7a. Suter 131.

8. 1. Sbath 111, comm. by Abū ʿAbdallāh al-Ḥusayn b. Aḥmad al-Shaqqāq in Serāi 3155,2, see *QSB* III, 516.

390. 8, 3. Bank. XXII, 84$_{,2468,\mathrm{XXXII}}$.—9. *Mukhtaṣar fī ʾl-ḥisāb wal-misāḥa*, Alex. Fun. mut. 82,4.—6. *ʿIlal ḥisāb al-jabr wal-muqābala*, Uri 986, see *RSO* XIV, 249/64.

8a. 2. *Sharḥ Uqlīdis*, Bank XXII, 25$_{,2430}$.

8b. See ad II, 1024$_{,75}$

10. 1. Maybe Paris 4946$_{,2}$.

11. 3. Transl. by Schirmer, *Studien zur Astronomie der Araber*.

391. 12 = 6g? (Krause).—2. Transl. by Kohl, Zur Gesch. der Dreiteilung des Winkels = *SB Erl.* 54/5 (1926) 186/9, maybe = 3.—4. A treatise on the fact that the sum of two uneven square numbers cannot itself be a square number, Paris 2457$_{,49}$.

391. 1a. Yāqūt, *Irshād* VI, 268, Suter l, 4.

392. Line. 1. R.F. Gunsberg, *Chaucer and Mesahalla on the Astrolab*, Oxford 1922.

1e. The book of Dorotheus, Berl. Oct. 2663, Yeni 784.—8. *al-Ikhtiyārāt* Alex. Ḥurūf 12.

393. 2, 1. = 4, see *Hesp.* XV 88$_{,5b}$.—7. *al-Jadāwil* with emendations by 1206
Muḥammad b. Muḥammad b. al-ʿAṭṭār (II 158,9), Bank. XXII, 98$_{,2469\mathrm{VI}}$.

2a. His original name was Bīzist b. Fīrūzān, while his Arabic name was given to him by al-Maʾmūn, *Ibn Isfandiyār*, transl. by Browne, 87.

4. 1. = 3. Nallino in Suter, 208/9.

394. 4a. Instead of *al-Mughnī*, read: *al-Muqniʿ*.

5. 2. With the title *Aḥkām al-mawālīd*, Alex. Ḥurūf 12, 1.—4. *Kitāb al-masāʾil fī aḥkām al-nujūm*, ibid. Ḥisāb 52.

395. 6, 2. Yeni 1193$_{,6}$ contains the brief introduction, see *QS* III, 450ff.—20. *Aḥkām al-qirānāt*, Persian transl. in the library of Muḥammad ʿAlī al-Khwānsārī al-Najafī, *Dharīʿa* I, 301$_{,1570}$.

396. 6b, 7. With the title *Kitāb al-nujūm*, Beirut 199, no. 400 (*MFO* VII, 275), *al-Aḥkām fī taḥwīlāt al-nujūm*, Alex. Ḥurūf 16.—10. *al-Qirānāt wal-ittiṣālāt fī ʾl-burūj al-ithnaʿ ashar*, ibid.

397. 7a. Jamāl al-Dīn al-Qāsim b. Maḥfūẓ, Suter 490.—2 Additionally Br. Mus, Or. 5734,$_2$ (DL 39).

9. 1. Additionally Alex. Ḥisāb 50.—2. Additionally Bank. XXII 111,$_{2477}$, Sarāi 3498, Qawala II, 281 and entitled *Aṣl ṣināʿāt al-aḥkām al-falakiyya* in Alex. Ḥurūf 7.

398. 9, line 1. Read: Asʿad 2004.—4. Additionally Paris 4731.—7. *al-Maqāla fī ʾl-abʿād wal-ajrām* Bank. XXII, 64,$_{2468,VI}$.

10. Suter 174.

11. Ibid. 138.—1. Additionally Fātiḥ 3422, Serāi 2493 dated 525 AH, see Holter, *Jahrb. Des Kunsthist. Inst. Vienna* N.F. 11. 1937, 36. AS 2642^2 is an abstract of a lost work on the astrolabe in 1760 capita (Krause).

399. 11a, 1. Alex. Ḥurūf 19, Bank. XXII, 111,$_{2478}$.

12. 9. Bank. XXII, $_{2648,XXXIV}$.—10. Read: Paris 4821.

400. 12, 21. *Kitāb al-mafrūḍāt*, AS 4830,$_6$ (Krause).—22. *Fī mā zāda min al-ashkāl fī amr al-maqāla al-thāniya* (of Euclid), Bank. XXII, 85,$_{XXXV}$.

13. 6. *al-Risāla fī iqāmat al-burhān ʿala ʾl-dāʾir min al-falak min qaws al-nahār wartifāʿ niṣf al-nahār wartifāʿ al-waqt*, Bank. XXII, 65,$_{2468VII}$.—8. *Qānūn juzʾ al-taʾlīf li-Uqlīdīs*, Rāmpūr I, 417,576.

401. 15. 1. Alex. Ḥisāb 43, see V. Stegemann, *Beitr. zur Gesch. der Astrologie* (Studien zur Gesch. u. Kultur der Antike u. des MA, hsg. v. F. Bilabel u. A. Grohmann) Reihe D, vol. 2, Heidelberg 1935, idem, Astrologische Zarathustra-Fragmente bei Abū ʾl-Ḥasan ʿAlī b. Abi ʾl-Rijāl, *Orient.* VI, 317/36.—2. Garr. 972, with the title *Sharḥ al-dalāla al-kulliyya ʿani ʾl-ḥarakāt al-falakiyya*.

13. b. 3. *Kitāb fī kayfiyyat tasṭīḥ al-kura ʿalā saṭḥ al-asṭurlāb*, Bank. XXII, 90,$_{2468XXXIX}$.

402. Line 2. Additionally Alex. Ḥisāb 60, 1 (with the wrong date).

Chapter 15. I. Kračkovsky, Arabskie geografii putešestvenniki, *Izv. gos. geogr. občestva*, 1937, 738/65.

404, 2. *Kitāb al-lahw wal-malāhī*, in the collection of Ḥabīb Efendi Zayyāt in Alexandria, *Hilāl* XXVIII, 214, see Farmer, *Sources*, 33.

405. 2b. Excerpts from the cosmography in Paris 2186, in Seippel, *Rerum norm. fontes arabici* 28, no. XXIV, V. Minorsky, The Khazars and the Turks in the *Ākām al-marjān*, BSOS 1938, 141/50.

3. 1. Baghdad 1938.—*Les Pays*, tr. G. Wiet, Cairo 1937 (Textes et traductions d'auteurs orientaux I).

| 406. 7. *The Journey of Ibn al-F. to the Volga River, Arab. Text reproduced from the* 1207
Ms. al-Meshhed with Transl. Introd. and Notes in Russian by I. Kratshkovsky, 1939. Togan Zeki Validi, *Ibn F. s Reisebericht*, AKM XXIV, 1940. A. Vasiliev, Hārūn b. Yaḥyā and his description of Constantinople, in *Seminarium Kondakovianum*, Recueil d'Études V, 1932, 149/63, G. Ostrogorsky, Zum Reisebericht des H. b. Y., ibid. 251/7, (who fixes the account in the year 912).

407. 8, 3. Ṭāhā Ḥusayn, *Min ḥadīth al-shiʿr wal-nathr*, 125ff upholds the authenticity of the work, characterizing it as an imitation of Aristotle's *Rhetoric*.

9. See J. Marquart, *Ostas. u. Osteurop. Streifzüge* 160/206, 466/73.

10. See ibid. 74/95, A. v. Rohr-Sauer, Des *Abū Dulaf Bericht über seine Reise nach Turkestan, China und Indien, neu übers u. erklärt*, Bonner Or. St. 26, Stuttgart 1939.

408. *Opus geographicum auctore Ibn Hauḳal secundum textum et imagines codicis constantinopolitani conservatii in Bibliotheca Antiqui Palatii no. 3346 cui titulus est "Liber imagines terrae"*, ed. J.H. Kramers (Bibl. Geogr. II, 1), Leiden 1938.

409. 12. Instead of 'vol. 9', read: vol. 8, see Garr. 748, vol. 8, 10 Paris 6056/7. See *The Antiquities of South Arabia*, being a translation from the Arabic with linguistic, geographic, and historic notes of the eighth book of al-Hamdāni's *al-Iklīl*, reconstructed from al-Karmali's edition and a ms. in the Garrett collection, Princeton University Library, by Nabih Amin Faris, London 1938 (Princ. Or. Texts III).

From vol. 8, *Risāla fī maʿārif al-ghālib wal-maghlūb wal-ṭālib wal-maṭlūb* by Aristotle, Alex. Ḥurūf 4.—2. Additionally ʿAlī Emīrī 2687/8.

411. 14. Excerpts in *RAAD* IX, 490/7.

416. 2. With the title *Murshid*, Alex. Adab 158.

3. 9. Additionally Alex. Ḥikma 16.—12. *Kitāb jawāhir al-ṭīb al-mufrada, Traité sur les substances simples aromatiques par J. B. M. publié par P. Sbath*, Extr. Bull. del' Inst. d'Inst. d' Égypte XIX (1936/7). Another copy in Garr. 2154,$_2$.

417. 7. See P. Guigues, Les noms arabes dans Serapion, *Liber de simplici medicina*, essai d'illustration et d'identification de médicaments usités au M.A., *JAS* 1905, ser. 10, vol. 5, 473/546, vol. 6, 49/112.

419. 9, 1. Garr. 2160,$_1$, see M. Meyerhof, The early clinical observations of Rhazes, *Isis* 1935, 320/72. *Abu Bekri Muhammedis filii Zachariae Rhagensis (Razis) opera philosophica fragmentaque quae supersunt*, collegit ed. P. Kraus (Univ. Fouad I, Lit. Fac. Publ. XXII)m Cairo 1939.—7. Additionally Garr. 1076.—9. Two different books with this same title, Qawala II, 287.

420. 9, 14. Additionally Alex. Ṭibb 32.

422. 14, 2. *Quwa 'l-adwiya al-mufrada*, composed in 353/964, Br. Mus. Or. 11, 615, see Fulton, *Br. Mus. Qu.* XI, 81.

423. 19. 1. Garr. 1077/8, Suppl. 1. *Die Augenheilkunde des ʿAli Abbas X. Jahrh. zum erstenmal ins Deutsche übers. v. Xenophon Gretschischeff*, Diss. Berlin 1900. Jul. Wiberg, The anatomy of the brain in the works of Galen and Ali Abbas, a comparative hist. anat. study, *Janus, Arch. internat. pour l'hist. de la méd.* XIX Leiden 1914, 17/32, 84/114, idem, *Hjaerneanatomien hos Galen og Ali ʿAbbās, en sammenlignende historiskanatomisk Studie*, Copenhagen 1913.

1208 | 424. 22, 3. *al-Jazzar, Liber fiduciae de simplicibus medicinis* (*Kitab etc lat.*) *in der Übersetzung des Stephanus de Saragossa, übertr. aus der Hds. München, Cod. lat. 253 von L. Volger* (Texte u. Unters. Zur Gesch. der Naturw. Heft 26), Diss. Berlin, Würzburg 1941.

425. 26, 1. See *RAAD* VII, 374/80.

426. 28, 6. *Kitāb al-Misāḥa* is cited in Ibn Isfandiyār, 77.

427. J. Ruska, The History of the Jabir Problem, *Isl. Cult.* XI, 303/12.—*Mukhtār Rasāʾil Jābir b. Ḥayyān*, ed. P. Kraus, C. 1354.

429. 1, 86. *al-Khawāṣṣ al-kabīr* or *al-Maqālāt al-kubrā*, Alex. Kīm. 5.

2. Line 7. Read: Atrefius, see Levi della Vida in *Speculum* XIII, 80/5.

430. 3, 1. *Mukhtaṣar* by ʿAlī b. Ḥasan b. Muḥammad al-Ḥusaynī al-ʿIrāqī (Paris 2942), composed in 883/1478 in Cairo, Bank. XXII 152$_{,2500}$.

431. 4, 1. Alex. Kīm. 6.—2. Ibid., Ḥurūf. 15.—Instead of "in Spanish translation known etc." read "whose Latin translation, which was made in Spain, is known etc."

432. 4, 7. Not a translation but an emendation, Ar. AS 2671$_{,3}$, Latin transl. by Heiberg, *Ptol. Opera* II, 227/58, see J. Drecker, *Isis* IX (1927), 255/78.—12. Alex. Kīm. 127.

6. Excerpts in al-Majrīṭī's *Ghāyat al-ḥakīm*, 106ff, see Ruska, Griech. Planetendarstellungen, *SBHeid.* 1919, 3, Ritter in *Stamb. Mitt.* fasc. 3, S. 3.

433. 8. al-Qādirī, Bank. XXII, 403$_{,2502}$.

436. 2, 1. Alex. Fun. mut. 134$_{,1}$.—4. Read: *Fi 'l-ṣadāqa wal-ṣadīq*, see ZDMG 66, 526.—10. 6. Additionally Ǧārullāh 1647 (Rescher, *Abriss* II, 252).

439. Line 3. Asad Talas, *L'enseignement chez les Arabes, la madrasa Nizamiya et son histoire*, Paris 1939.

1. Read: Garr. 35, Qawala II, 194.

440. b. Ind. Off. 4564, *JRAS* 1939, 35, Bank. XXIII, 27$_{,2521}$, print. C. 1305, 1309. Abstract by al-Damīrī, Bank. XXIII, 29$_{,2522}$.—f. Garr. 36, Bank. XXIII, 30$_{,2523}$, print. also 1309.—h. With the title *Īḍāḥ al-mubham*, Garr. 37.—p. Ayyūb b. Mūsā al-Kaffawī (II, 673), Mosul 49, 44, 31, 121,2.—q. *Tuḥfat al-rāʾī li-Lāmiyyat al-Ṭughrāʾī* by Muḥammad ʿAlī Efendi al-Munyāwī (a teacher at al-Madrasa al-Tawfīqiyya, d. 1335/1916), Būlāq 1311, 1313, 1324 (Sarkis 1683).—*Takhmīs: Ītilāf al-maʿānī wal-mabānī bi-mujārāt al-Ṭughrāʾī, Abī Firās wal-Ḥamdānī lil-Jambīhī*, Būlāq 1318 (Sarkis 715).—3a. *Jāmiʿ al-asrār*, Br. Mus. Or. 8229 f 182b/96b + 1b/30a(?).—b. *Tarākīb al-anwār*, ibid. 161b/182a, Cairo Ṭab. 345.—c. *Ḥaqāʾiq al-istishhād*, Cairo Ṭab. 170, Taymūr Majm. 2, 11.—d. *Kitāb al-Asrār*, Cairo Ṭab. 169 (= 9?).—e. *Risāla fi 'l-Ṭabāʾiʿ*, ibid. 345.—f. Alchemistic poems, ibid. 176, 731, Taymūr, Ṭab. 74 (*Orientalia* VIII, 285).—4. = 8. = 9.? Levi della Vida, *Speculum* XIII, 80/4.

442. 4. Teh. Sip. II, 546/8. O. Rescher, *Beitr. zur ar. Poesie*, I, *Aus dem Dīwān des Sibṭ b. al-Taʿāwīdhī, ed. Margoliouth*, Stuttgart 1937.

443. 7, 1. C. 1305.

444. 11, 1. Alex. Adab 133, 4, Qawala II, 22.—2. Garr. 58/9, Alex. Adab 23, C. 1311.—*Sharḥ wa-takhmīs al-Qaṣīda al-witriyya* by Muḥammad b. ʿAbd al-Wāḥid al-Naẓīfī al-Sūsī al-Marrākushī, C. 1331.

445 1, 1. Garr. 26.—2. Garr. 2126,$_{3}$. Commentary a. *al-Hidāya lil-mustafīdīn wal-dirāya lil-mustafīḍīn* additionally Garr. 27, Qaw. II, 200, Alex. Adab 141 (which has Aḥmad b. Muḥammad).

1209 | 446. 3, 1. *Ikhtiyār al-bikr min al-thayyib*, al-Akhsīkatī (d. after 520/1126, see Yāqūt, *GW* I, 162) *Dharīʿa* I, 364, no. 1910.—4. Anonymous commentary, Qaw. II, 201.

447. 5, 1. Garr. 725, Alex. Adab 144, Bank. XXIII 143,$_{2635}$, C. 1936.

6. *Dīwān*, print. Beirut 1327 (Sarkis). 1. Bank. XXIII 25,$_{2520}$.

448. 6, 2. Garr. 34.

9. BDMG 106.

452. Qazwīnī, *Kosmographie* 172, 181. see II, 194, 262.—Ḥusayn Futūḥ, *ʿAqīdat Abī ʾl-ʿAlāʾ*, 1910.—ʿAbd al-Raḥīm b. Aḥmad, *Notice biographique et bibliographique concernante l'illustre poète philosophe Abu ʾl-ʿAlāʾ al-Maʿarrī*, C. 1897.—1. Garr. 29, BDMG 104, Bank. XXIII, 23,$_{2518}$.

453. 1, 1, d. Qaw. II, 204. f. Ibid. II, 190.—2. Garr. 28.—3b. Garr. 2191.—d. Ed. Kāmil Kīlānī, C. 1938.—al Arnawṭī (III, 390), *Firdaws al-Maʿarrī*, Beirut 1333/1915.—8. Ed. Maḥmūd Ḥasan Zanātī, C. 1356/1938 (incomplete).—9. Ed. Muḥammad ʿAlī al-Madanī, Damascus 1355/1936 (*RAAD* XIV 5/11).—12. = 9.

455. 2a. Muḥammad b. Muḥammad al-Wāʿiẓī, d. 509/1115, *Qaṣīda mīmiyya fī makārim al-akhlāq*, Berl. 8088,$_{5}$, Heid. *ZDMG* 91, 388.

456. 6. *Dīwān*, ed. Anīs E. Khūrī, Beirut 1938.

457. 8. *Iʿlām etc.*, Berl. 7029/30, attributed to Ibn Mālik, see Suyūṭī, *Muzhir* II, 145, Naṣr al-Hūrīnī, *al-Maṭāliʿ al-Naṣriyya fi ʾl-maṭābiʿ al-Miṣriyya*, C. 1304, p. 88, Muḥammad b. Cheneb, *RAAD* VIII, 692.

9a = $727_{,14}$.

10. 2. see Muḥammad Jawad, *REI* 1938, 287 (dated 659/1260).

458. 15. *Dīwān*, C. 1298, Beirut 1310.

16. Muḥammad al-Qāḍī, *Durrat al-ḥijāl* II, $476_{,321}$.

459. 1. *Dīwān*, Bank. XXIII, $24_{,2519}$.

460. Line 1. Bank. XXIII, $30_{,2524}$.

462. 6. BDMG 107, C. 1313.

7. c. Alex. Adab 98.

8. BDMG 108, Qaw. II, 192. Teh. Sip II, 550/2.

463. 8, 3. Garr. 50, Mosul 140,5, 123,38, 172,11, 229,26, Bank. XXIII $34_{,2528}$.—4. *Rashf al-sirr al-ghāmiḍ*, Alex. Adab 114, Mosul 189,12.—7. Anon., Mosul 49,40, C. 1313 (*Hesp.* III, 122,1014).

464. c. Qaw. II, 210.—g. *al-Madad al-fāʾiḍ wal-kashf al-ʿāriḍ* by ʿAlawān b. ʿAlī b. ʿAṭiyya (II, 333) additionally Qāw. II, 214, Alex. Adab 157.—k. Mosul 175, 70.—n. ʿAllāma al-Ṭībī, Alex. Adab 135, 2.—4. i. Read: ʿAbd al-Tawwāb, Garr. 53.—l. Additionally Vienna 1941, see II, 310.—o. Ismāʿīl b. Aḥmad al-Anqirawī (II, 662), Halet 221, 1.—5a. Additionally Garr. 52.—b. *al-Fatḥ al-Makkī al-fāʾiḍ*, Alex. Adab 135,1.

465. 10. A commentary by al-Qayṣarī, Mosul $263_{,8,1}$.

466. 12. *Dīwān*, Ind. Off. 4633, *JRAS* 1939, 396.—Muṣṭafā ʿAbd al-Rāziq, *al-Bahāʾ Zuhayr, baḥth*, C. n.d.

467. 16. I, 1. Alex. Adab 135,3 Qaw. II, 201.—5. Qaw. II, 186, Alex. Adab 10, *Talkhīṣ* ibid. 26. Abstract from the *Ṭīb al-ḥabīb* of Muḥammad b. Marzūq al-Tilimsānī, d. 781/1379, by Muḥammad b. ʿAbdallāh b. Maḥmūd, Bank. XXIII, $38_{,2533}$.

468. 7. Garr. 67.—8. Khālid al-Azharī, d. 905/1499, Bank. XXIII, 41,$_{2536}$.—
8a. Jalāl al-Dīn Abū Ṭāhir Aḥmad al-Khujandī, d. 802/1400, Garr. 66.—
9. Alex. Adab 84.—9a. *Washy al-Burda* by Zayn al-Dīn Ṭāhir b. Ḥasan al-Ḥalabī,
1210 d. 807/1404 (Suppl. II, 90), Alex. Adab 186.—9b. *Ḥāshiya* by | Muḥammad b.
Bahādur al-Zarkashī (Suppl. II, 108), Bank XXIII, 39,$_{2534}$.—9c. Aḥmad b. Shams
al-Dīn al-Dawlatābādī, d. 849/1445 (Suppl. II, 309), ibid. 40,$_{2535}$.—14. Qaw. II,
197, Alex. Adab 83.—15. *Mashāriq al-anwār al-muḍīʾa*, Garr. 68, Alex. Adab
160.—16. *al-Zubda al-rāʾiqa*, Alex. Adab 76.—17. Ibid. 82.—18. Ibid. 83, Fun.
mut. 176,$_{1}$.—23. Alex. Adab 141.—31. Ibid. 42 (which has al-Karrārī).—31a. *al-Durra al-farīda* by Muḥammad al-Shāfiʿī al-ʿInānī (d. 1098/1687), ibid. 42.—43. *ʿAṣīdat al-shahda*, ibid. 100, Qaw. II, 205, Istanbul 1292, 1298, 1317, 1320, Būlāq 1291.—57. Muḥammad b. Saʿd al-Ālānī, MS dated 1169, Alex. Adab 83.—58. *al-Barq al-lamīḥ* by ʿAbd al-Ḥaqq b. Yūsuf al-Ḥajjājī, ibid. 18.—59. *ʿUmda* by Ismāʿīl b. ʿUthmān b. Abī Bakr Niyāzī (to be read thus, see Suppl. II, 657, g), Qaw. II, 206.—60. Turkish by Saʿdallāh al-Ḥulwānī ibid. I, 247.—*Khātima taʾrīkhiyya* by Muḥammad b. al-ʿArabī Qaṣṣār, composed in 1310/1892, Alex. Fun. mut. 94/5.—*Takhmīs*: 1. Garr. 2126,$_{1}$.

470. ff. Shams al-Dīn Muḥammad al-Fayyūmī, 8th cent., Būlāq 1287, Alex. Adab 130.—gg. ʿUmar al-Qaṣabī al-Yaqḍī, MS dated 899/1493, Garr. 71.—hh. Muḥammad b. Ibrāhīm, d. after 984/1576, ibid. 70.—ii. ʿUshrī Ismāʿīl b. Darwīsh b. Muṣṭafā ʿUthmān b. ʿIwaḍ b. ʿAwīḍa al-Subkī al-Khuṣūṣī, composed in 1038/1628, Alex. Adab 22.—kk. *al-Aflāk al-dawriyya* by ʿIzz al-Dīn Muḥammad b. ʿAbdallāh al-ʿAlawī al-Yamanī, ibid. 128.—ll. *Anīs al-waḥda* by ʿAbbās Efendi Fawzī Dāghistānī, Istanbul 1300.—*Tasbīʿ*: d. Alex. Adab 130.—ibid. e. Fun. mut. 88,$_{3}$.—kk. Jawīshān Wazīr Miṣr Amīr ʿUthmān Bāb al-Rūmī, ibid. Adab 25.—*Tashṭīr*: d. Garr. 72 (which has Ḥalāwa, just like Cairo^{2} III, 63).—q. ʿAlī Efendi al-Sayyid in *Muʿāraḍāt al-Burda* by Ḥasan al-ʿĀmilī, C. 1306.—r. *Takhmīs ṭayy al-Burda wa-talkhīṣ nashr al-warda*, on the *Burda* and the *tashṭīr* of ʿUmar b. ʿAbbās al-Qafṣī al-Maghribī al-Qaṣabī by Muḥammad b. Aḥmad b. Abi ʾl-ʿĪd al-Mālikī, Alex. Adab 23.—Muḥammad b. Muḥammad b. ʿAbd al-Wāḥid b. ʿAbd al-Raḥīm al-Tamīmī, *Risāla fī khawāṣṣ al-Kawākib al-durriyya*, Qaw. I, 236.

II. Garr. 74, Alex. Fun. 175,$_{2}$, C. 1310.

471. II, 3. Alex. Adab 169, Qaw. 219/20., Bank. XXIII 42,$_{2537/8}$. Glosses by Sālim al-Ḥifnī, Alex. Adab 14, Qaw. II, 188.—4. Alex. Adab 90.—6. Makr. 32 (which has al-Suʿūdī).—13. Qaw. II, 212—15. Alex. Adab 90.—17. *Zubdat al-qirā* by ʿUthmān b. ʿAlī al-Kallīsī al-ʿUryūnī, d. 1168/1755, Qaw. II, 195.—18. *Taqrīrāt* by

Muḥammad ʿArafa al-Dasūqī (Suppl. II, 737), Alex. Adab 137.—19. Anon. glosses, Bank. XXII, $44_{,2539}$.—*Takhmīs* 5, C. 1309.

472. V. Heid. *ZDMG* 91, 386, Alex. Fun. $147_{,13}$, $175_{,3}$, $182_{,2}$, Qaw. II, 209.—3. Alex. Adab 141.—*Takhmīs* by al-Ziyādī, ibid. Fun. 173,6.—VII. Commentary by al-Būrīnī, ibid. Adab 90.—IX. 1. C. 1313.

F. 1. Garr. 189, Bank. XXIII, $73_{,2567/8}$.

473. 4, 2. Garr. 30.

474. 6. Additionally Alex. Fun. $176_{,4}$, $187_{,3}$, Qaw. II, 220.—Comm. a. Qaw. II, 188.—b. *al-Fatḥ mufarrij al-karab*, Alex. Fun. $173_{,11}$, $174_{,8}$, $176_{,3}$, $177_{,1}$, $189_{,1}$.—e. Būlāq 1300.—*Takhmīs* a. Alex. Fun. $187_{,2}$.—h. ʿUmar al-Qawsī al-Qurashī, Br. H^2. 1148 = Garr. 2002,9.—6. 1. Alex. Adab 73, 89.

475. *Recueil etc.* read: Ghernata; also with the Arabic title *Majmūʿ al-aghānī wal-alḥān min kalām al-Andalus dīwān al-awwal* (sic, Colin). Alcocer Martinez R., *La corporación de los poetas en la España musulmana*, Ceuta 1940 (Publ. dél Inst. General Franco para la investigación Hisp. ar. Ser. 6, No. 3).

| 477. Menendez Pidal, Poesia arabe e poesia europea, *Bull. Hispanique* 40, 1211
p. 337–423, Bordeaux Feret et fils, see R. Hartmann, *OLZ* 1941, 40/4.

479. 2b. Read: Shuhayd.

480. 7. *Dīwān*, Cairo^2 III, 119.

8. Commentary a. Garr. 583, Alex. Adab 117.

481. 9. *Dīwān*, Teh. Sip. II, 548/50.

482. 11. R. Nykl, Biographische Fragmente über Ibn Quzmān, *Islam* XXV (1938), 101/13. *Ibn Quzmān*, édition critique partielle et provisoire (ch. X, XIX, LXXXIV. LXXXXVII, XC) par O. J. Tuulio, Helsinki 1941 (Studia or. ed. Soc. Or. Fenn. IX, 2).

13, 2. a. With the title *Safīnat al-saʿāda li-ahl al-ḍiʿf wal-najāda*, C. 1320.

483. 13, 7. *Dīwān al-wasāʾil al-mutaqabbala* with a *takhmīs* by Muḥammad b. al-Mahīb and an explanation of particular expressions by a scholar from

Timbuktu, C. 1322, together with *al-Ṣāfināt al-jiyād* by Yūsuf al-Nabhānī (Suppl. II, 763).

14. 1. *Hesp.* XII, 113,979.

15. Massignon, *EI* IV, 423. *Dīwān* not in *muwashshaḥ*, but only *qaṣīdas* and *zajals* in a Spanish dialect (Colin), additionally Garr. 79, Br. Mus. Or. 9254, library of Shaykh Mubārak in Damascus.—2. Alex. Tawḥīd 35.—3. Fun. $152_{,26}$.

484. 15, 8. *al-Maqālīd al-wujūdiyya wal-dāʾira al-qidamiyya*, cabalistic, Taymūr, Taṣawwuf 149.

16a. *Dīwān* additionally Berl. 8084/5.

17. Born 604/1207 in Malaga, d. 699/1300 in Fez, Ibn al-Qāḍī, *Durrat al-ḥijāl* II, 323/7.

485. 1b. Aḥmad al-Iskandarī, *RAAD* XI, 513/22, 577/92, 656/69, Muṣṭafā Jawād, *Mazāliq b. Zaydūn al-lughawiyya*, *Apollo* I, 1002/7.—1. Comm. a. Qaw. II, 196.—2. Print. "Baghdad" read "Wilāyat Sūriyya" (Alex. Adab 27). Comm. b. Bank. XXIII $110_{,2599,2600}$.

486. 3, 3. Paris 4434, see M. Jawad, *REI* 1938, 286.—On his Persian *Ḥadāʾiq al-siḥr fī daqāʾiq al-shiʿr* there is the Arabic commentary *Rawḍat al-daqāʾiq* by Maḥmūd Adham, d. after 899/1494, Garr. 499.

487. Line 29. *al-Istidrākāt* by ḤKh I, 447, VI, 61 (cited in Suyūṭī, *Bughya*, although he does not mention the work in question on p. 30), Br. H.[2] 134, Garr. 200 wrongly credits Muwaffaq al-Dīn ʿAbd al-Laṭīf al-Baghdādī with the work.—Comm. 1. See Suppl. II, 910, 52.—1a Garr. 2151, 1.—3. Alex. Adab 16, Teh. Sip. II, 39, 17, Bank. XXIII, $94_{,2585}$.—6. 1. ʿAbd al-Munʿim, Teh. Sip. 398, Bank. XXIII, $95_{,2586,7}$.

488. I, 9a. Alex. Adab 163.—17. Makr. 57, Bank. XXIII, $98_{,2589,90}$.—18. Leid. 418, Vienna 375, Bank. XXIII, $97_{,2588}$, where he is said to be author of the work mentioned in Suppl. I, 620. 6, 1 d.—19. See Suppl. II, 910,52.—21. Muḥammad b. Ismāʿīl al-Murādābādī, d. 1253/1837 in Lucknow, Bank. XXIII, $99_{,25/91}$.—22. Anon. ibid. $95_{,2584}$.

VI. Alex. Lugha 11, Fun. mut. 76,22, Qaw. II, 3, Teh. Sip. II, 1942.

VII. BDMG 67a, Garr. 324, Qaw. II, 97.

VIII. 3. Hamb. Or. Sem. 66, 72, 130, Alex. Naḥw 5.—4. *Kashf al-niqāb*, Hamb. Or. Sem. 59, 131, 134.—10. *Nafḥat al-ādāb*, see Alex. Naḥw 64.—12. Aḥmad b. Ḥusayn b. Raslān al-Ramlī (II, 113), BDMG 83.

489. 5a. Read: al-Mukhalliṣī.

490. 5dd. al-Qāḍī al-Rashīd Abu 'l-Ḥusayn Aḥmad b. ʿAlī b. al-Zubayr al-Ghassānī | al-Uswānī, d. 563/1168, *al-Maqāma al-Ḥaṣībiyya*, with a self- 1212
commentary, Alex. Adab 142, 163.

491. 1b, 3. See Suppl. II, 1015, 24.

492. 2. Alex. Lugha 33.

3a. See *RAAD* V, 233, VII, 36/43, 66/73, 114/21, 160/7, 315/22, 460/4, 497/505, 536/44.

4. 2. *Takmilat Iṣlāḥ mā taghlaṭu bihi 'l-ʿāmma*, ed. al-Tanūkhī, Maṭbūʿāt al-Majmaʿ al-ʿilmī al-ʿArabī, no. 7, Damascus 1936 (see *RAAD* XIV, 164/266).

493. 6, 3. *Br. Mus. Quart.* VIII, 15 (wrongly said to be a unique copy).

7. Read: Muḥammad b. ʿAlī b. ʿAbdallāh.

8. Tadhkirat b. Ḥamdūn, Istanbul Un. R. 1014, ʿUm. 5363 (*ZS* III, 248), a fragment in Esc.[2] 280 (contra Derenbourg 171/2, see Antuña, *al-Andalus* III, 1935, 447/9).

8a Read: ʿAbdallāh b. Aḥmad.

495. 10, 1. BDMG 76 (see Kautzsch, *ZDMG* 28, 331ff), Garr. 335.

496. 12. *Muṣannaf Abi 'l-Baqāʾ al-ʿUkbarī*, see ad II, 421.—12. b. Abū ʿAbdallāh Badr al-Dīn b. Rustam b. Anūsharwān b. Ṣāliḥ b. Badr al-Amīr, 6th (?) cent., *Shifāʾ al-qulūb wa-rāḥat al-makrūb fī ḥarakat al-insān wa-sukūnihi*, Istanbul Un. R. 803, *ZS* III, 253.

497. 14. Read: b. Abi 'l-Ḥadīd.

16. I. BDMG 66,1, Garr. 396/7, Qaw. II, 25/6, Teh. Sip. II, 312/3. Comm. 1. BDMG 82, Garr. 398/405, Qaw. II, 34/6, Teh. Sip. II, 344/6.

498. I. g. = l.—k. Anon. Garr. 401/2.—1. Qara Dede, d. 973/1565, *ShD* VIII, 374, *al-ʿIqd al-manẓūm*, in the margin of Ibn Khall. 1299, II, 286/90, 1310, II, 164/7, ḤKh IV, 209,5 (which has Dede Jankī), Teh. Sip. II, 317/20, Qaw. II, 28, (which has Khalīfa Jūnkī).—n. ʿIzz al-Dīn Abu ʾl-Faḍāʾil Ibrāhīm b. ʿAbd al-Wahhāb b. ʿImād al-Dīn b. Ibrāhīm al-Zanjānī, Qaw. II, 28.—2a. Istanbul 1280, 1292, 1301, 1318.—3. al-Qāriʾ al-Harawī, *al-Fatḥ al-rabbānī*, C. 1289.—7. C. 1312 (Alex. Adab 6).

500, 2. Das Kap. X aus al-Thaʿālibis *Laṭāʾif al-maʿārif* über die Eigentümlichkeiten der Städte und Länder, transl. O. Rescher, *Or. Misz.* I, 194/228.—3. Garr. 516.—4. Qaw. II, 5, C. 1345, ed. Muṣṭafā al-Saqqāʾ, Ibrāhīm al-Abyārī and ʿAbd al-Ḥāfiẓ Shalabī, C. 1357/1938.

501. 10. BDMG 103.—13. From which: Zahlensprüche in der ar. Lit., in O. Rescher, *Or. Misz.* II, 38/99.—17. Bank. XXIII, 88,$_{2580,1}$.

503. 5. 1. Garr. 391/4, 2121,$_{2}$, 2124,$_{1}$, Alex. Naḥw 34,$_{2}$, Fun. 142,$_{5}$, Qaw. II, 60, 103, Teh. Sip. II, 387/8.

504. 3. Garr. 315/6, Alex. Fun. 175,$_{2}$.—4. Garr. 318/9.—34. Ibid. 321/3.—34. *Miʾa kāmila* by Ḥājjī Bābā b. Ḥājjī Ibrāhīm b. Ḥājjī ʿAbd al-Karīm b. ʿUthmān al-Ṭūsī (Ṭūsiyawī II, 312), Alex. Naḥw 33.—35. *Hadiyyat al-ṣibyān*, grammat. analysis by Muṣṭafā b. ʿAlī al-Awralawī (d. 1100/1688), Gotha 196, 4a, Paris 4212, Garr. 317.—II. Teh. Sip. II, 314/6.—V. Muḥammad al-Ḥanafī al-Ḥalabī, d. 1342/1923 (al-Ṭabbākh, *Taʾr. Ḥalab* VIII, 681).—IX. *al-Mukhtār min dawāwīn al-Mutanabbī wal-Buḥturī wa-Abī Tammām* in *al-Ṭarāʾif al-adabiyya*, p. 195/305.

505. 7, 1. Teh. Sip. II, 282/5.—8. *Dustūr al-lugha*, Teh. Sip. II, 176/80.

1213 | 506. 9, 1. BDMG 116 (fragm.).—2. Alex. Adab 27, Qaw. I, 82 (fragm.).

10. 2. Alex. Lugha 13.

507. 10b. Abū Ḥafṣ ʿUmar b. ʿUthmān al-Jawzī, the teacher of al-Samʿānī (*Ansāb* 137b), was a poet and a scholar, d. 505/1111 in Marw, *al-Wāfī fi ʾl-ʿarūḍ wal-qawāfī*, Ind. Off. 4618, *JRAS* 1939, 385.

11. 1. Istanbul Um. 5574, R. 255 (ZS III, 249).

12. 1. Ṭāsköprīzāde, *Miftāḥ* II, 409/10, warns against the study of the *Kashshāf*, so popular in his time.

508. Glosses 4. Aḥmad b. al-Ḥasan al-Jārabardī (II, 193) additionally Qaw. I, 56.—8. Ibid. I, 57.

509. 17. Teh. Sip. II, 457/9.

510. II, 2a. Garr. 327, Teh. Sip. II, 382/4.—5. *al-Īḍāḥ*, Alex. Naḥw 4.—III. 1. Alex. Naḥw 21, Qaw. II, 89, Teh. Sip. II, 343/4.—2. Alex. Naḥw 14, Garr. 332/3.

511. III, 8. ʿAlī b. ʿAbdallāh b. Aḥmad b. Zayn al-ʿArab, composed in 736/1336, Alex. Fun. $96_{,1}$.—9. Anon. Garr. 334.—V. Garr. 497/8.—VI. N.N. Poppe, *Mongolskij slovar, Muqaddimat al-adab* I/II, Ak. Nauk SSSR. Trudy Inst. Vostok. XIV, Moscow-Leningrad 1938.—IX. Baghdad 1938.—XII. Mosul $144_{,62,7}$.

512. XIV. Read: Mosul 229,37.—XV. Qaw. II, 211.—XVI. Bank. XXIII $115_{,2614/5}$, 2. Garr. 727, Alex. Adab 73.—7. *Mukhtār bi-anwār Rabīʿ al-abrār* by Aḥmad b. ʿAbd al-ʿAzīz b. Muḥammad b. al-ʿAjamī al-Shāfiʿī, 8th cent., Berl. 8354, Bank. XXIII $117_{,2616}$ (anon. Ḥkh III, 345).—8. Anon. *Nafaḥāt asḥār Rabīʿ al-abrār*, Bank. XXIII $118_{,2617}$.—XVII. Teh. Sip. II, 11–14—a. Alex. Adab 134,2, Fun. 117, 17, Teh. Sip. II, 8–11. Garr. 204.—b. Comm. by. Muḥammad Mīrzā Yūsuf Khān Iʿtiṣām al-Mulk, completed in 1319.—XXVI. *Risāla fi ʾl-majāz wal-istiʿāra* (?), Teh. Sip. II, 414/5.

513, 14b. See p. 557, 4.

514, 15. I. Garr. 337/9, 2105, 2121,1, Qaw. II, 120/1.—1. BDMG 81,6, Garr. 340/5, 2105, Ind. Off. 4567, *JRAS* 1939, 358, Qaw. II, 92/3, 98/9, Teh. Sip. II, 372/3.—2. Garr. 349/50, Alex. Naḥw 3, Qaw. II, 60.—5. Garr. 352, Qaw. II, 86.—10. BDMG 81a.

515. 15. I, 19. Glosses thereon called *al-Ḥamdiyya* by Aḥmad b. ʿImād al-Ḥanafī, Alex. Naḥw 14.—21. Glosses by Yaʿqūb b. ʿAlī al-Burūsawī, Qaw. II, 90, Alex. Naḥw 25.—24. *Nūr al-miṣbāḥ* by Yūsuf b. ʿAbd al-Malik b. Bakhshāyish Qara Sinān, d. after 868/1464, Garr. 351.—25. *al-Iṣlāḥ fī sharḥ Sharḥ dībājat al-Miṣbāḥ* by Muḥammad b. Yūsuf Qarabīrī, Alex. Naḥw 35.—26. Anon. *Iʿrāb dībājat al-Miṣbāḥ*, Berl. 6545/6, Br. Mus. $486_{,11}$, Suppl. $934_{,iii}$, $935_{,i}$, Garr. 354,18, *al-Ifṣāḥ*

Qaw. II, 61, on the *Dībāja* Garr. 347, *Risāla li-abyāt al-Ḍaw' wal-Iṣbāḥ wal-Iftitāḥ wa-Mishkāt al-Miṣbāḥ* Garr. 348.—III. Garr. 1447, Alex. Lugha 32.

515. 16. On his death see Bartold, 12 *Vorles*, 197.—1. BDMG 93, Qaw. II, 175.—Comm. 1b *Miftāḥ al-Miftāḥ*, Garr. 518.—2. Teh. Sip. II, 429/32, Qaw. II, 159.—5. Ibid. 171/2, Alex. Bal. 14, Garr. 522.—Glosses c. Garr. 523.

516. d. Qaw. II, 158.—g. *Ifāḍat al-fattāḥ*, see Suppl. II, 635.—h. Qaw. II, 141.—1. *al-Miṣbāḥ*, Alex. Bal. 24.—2.*Taghyīr al-Miṣbāḥ*, ibid. 4., Qaw. II, 136, Ind. Off. 4584*JRAS* 1939, 373.—1. *Talkhīṣ al-Miṣbāḥ*, BDMG 94, Garr.

1214 | 519. A. BDMG 95a, 96, Garr. 524/8, Qaw. II, 172/4, Makr. 56, Teh. Sip. II 420/3.—Glosses a. Alex. Bal. 9, Qaw. II, 145/6, Teh. Sip. II, 413/4; anon. supergl. Qaw. II, 149.

517. Line 3. Supergl. by Abu 'l-Qāsim b. Abī Bakr al-Laythī al-Samarqandī (Suppl. II 259), completed in 875/1470 and dedicated to Mīr ʿAlīshīr Nawāʾī, Teh. Sip. II, 410/1, Istanbul 1307 (see II, 260v).—aa. Qāḍīzāde al-Rūmī, d. 815/1412, II, 297, Garr. 529.—b. Qaw. II, 146.—d. Ibid. 141, BDMG 97.—e. BDMG 98, lith. Istanbul 1307.—f. Qaw. II, 151, Alex. Bal. 9, Teh. Sip. II 402/4. 9; from it, the *Tajrīd* by Maḥmūd b. al-Sayyid Ayyūb, completed in 1292/1875, Istanbul 1292 (Qaw. II, 135).—ff. Alex. Bal. 9.—g. Qaw. II, 147/9.—m. Alex. Bal. 22, 25.—n. Qaw. II, 147.—o. Ibid. 152, and read "1096," Teh. Sip. II, 426/7 (which has *kitāb* Muḥammad b. Muʿīn al-Dīn Muḥammad Fadshakūʾī Fasāʾī Mīrzā Kamālā).

518. x. A. b. ʿAbd al-Awwal al-Qazwīnī, written for Sultan Sulaymān, Qaw. II, 182.—y. A certain Zāde (not Qāḍīzāde aa, maybe *Bughya* 248, 17?), MS dated 902, ibid. 144.—z. Anon., ibid. 147.—B. Qaw. II, 168/7, Teh. Sip. II, 406/9.—Glosses a. Teh. Sip. II, 406/9.—β Alex. Bal. 6, Teh. Sip. II, 411/13.—δ Ḥāmid b. Burhān b. Abī Dharr al-Ghifārī (see ad 850), Teh. Sip. 405/6.—b. Garr. 546, Qaw. II, Teh. Sip. II, 416/20 142, Makr. 17.—d. Alex. Bal. 10.—f. Qaw. II, 135, Makr. 8.—k. Qaw. II, 134/4, Makr. 19.

519. x. Superglosses on al-Khayālī's glosses by ʿAbd al-Ḥalīm al-ʿAlāʾī, Qaw. II, 149.—y. al-Jarbī, MS dated 1137, Alex. Bal. 8.—5. Qaw. II, 133/4.—6. Ibid. 175, Teh. Sip. II, 424/6.—Abstracts: 2. Alex. Bal. 26.—4. On which glosses, *Khulāṣat al-maʿānī*, by Ḥasan b. ʿUthmān b. Ḥusayn b. Mazyad b. ʿAbd al-Wahhāb al-Muftī, 2nd half of the 10th cent., Qaw. II, 154.—5. *al-Masālik fi 'l-maʿānī wal-bayān* by Nūr al-Dīn Ḥamza b. Ṭurghūd, composed in 962–70/1555–62 in Constantinople, ibid. 171.

520. 19, I. Alex. Naḥw 32.—Comm. 5. ibid. 24, Teh. Sip. II, 369/71.—6. Alex. Naḥw 24.—20. Masʿūd b. Maḥmūd wrote, in 662/1264, *Mukhtār min al-ashʿār*, an anthology from later poets, Qaw. II, 215.—3. 1aa ʿAlī b. Ṭāhir b. Jaʿfar Abu ʾl-Ḥasan al-Sulamī al-Naḥwī, born in 431/1039, gave lectures at the central mosque of Damascus and died on 21 Rabīʿ I 500/20 November 1106 (Suyūṭī, *Bughya* 339, following Ibn ʿAsākir), *Kitāb al-jihād*, Dam. Z. 30$_{,20}$, 36$_{,60}$, *juzʾ* 9, 2, 8, 18.

521. 1, 1. Alex. Adab 187.

522. I. BDMG 77, Garr. 403, Alex. Naḥw 5.—II. Qaw. II, 95, C. 1938 (Dār al-kutub).—Comm. 1. Heid. A, 388, *ZDMG* 91, 391, Garr. 406/7, Alex. Naḥw 20, Pers. transl. Teh. Sip. II, 335/7.—b. See Ibn al-Qāḍī, *Durrat al-ḥijāl* II, 398, no. 1121.—e. BDMG 91.

523. II, 3. Teh. Sip. II, 306/8.—b. Qaw. II, 66, 80, Makr. 10, Teh. Sip. II 309/12.—6. Alex. Naḥw 17.—7. Qaw. II, 89, Teh. Sip. II, 333.

524. 10. Garr. 415, Alex. Naḥw 21, Qaw. II, 88.—12. Alex. Naḥw 42, Qaw. II, 125.—Glosses a. Makr. 21.—b. Alex. Naḥw 40.—c. Ibid. 8, Qaw. II, 125.—g. ʿUllaysh, Makr. 24.—h. *Zawāhir al-kawākib* by Abū ʿAbdallāh Muḥammad b. ʿAlī b. Saʿīd al-Tūnisī al-Mālikī, d. 1199/1785, Tunis 1298.—14. Qaw. II, 69, Teh. Sip. II, 313/45.—15. Qaw. II, 63, Makr. 7.—15a. *Nukat* by al-Suyūṭī, Alex. Naḥw 44.

| 525. 15. Teh. Sip. II, 337/41.—15 e. Composed in 1223/1808, ibid. II, 329.— 1215
f. Anon. comm. on the *shawāhid*, ibid. 384/5.—27. Garr. 418.—42. Teh. Sip. II, 341/2 (which has Tūsirkānī).—46. Muḥammad b. Masʿūd al-Ṭurunbāṭī, composed in 1206, Alex. Naḥw 10.—*al-Wafiyya fi ʾkhtiṣār al-Alfiyya* see II, 195$_{,263q}$—*al-Muʿāraḍa ʿalā Alfiyyat Ibn Mālik*, also known as *al-Iḥmirār*, by al-Mukhtār b. Būn al-Shinqīṭī, Rabat 262, 13, C. 1327.

526. III. BDMG 78, Alex. Adab 8.—6. *al-Sharḥ al-ṣaghīr*, Alex. Adab 7.—IX. Instead of "al-Kanatī" read "al-Kuntī", see II, 895.—XIII. See ad p. 457.

528. 1, 4. *Khulāṣat al-siyar*, Alex. Taʾr. 63.

529. 1, I. Alex. Naḥw 41.

1a. Abū ʿAlī al-Ḥasan b. Jaʿfar al-Naḥwī al-Iskandarī, ca. 517/1123 (Suyūṭī, *Bughya* 218), *Thamarat al-ṣināʿa*, Alex. Naḥw 8.

530. 6, 1a (see Suyūṭī, *Bughya* 131). *al-Kifāya*, with the supercommentary *al-Nihāya*, Garr. 359.—aa. *al-Ghurra al-makhfiyya*, by the same, Alex. Naḥw 26.

532. 5. Qaw. II, 95, Teh. Sip. II, 361/3, Istanbul 1305, 1310. Abstract from the *Khizānat al-adab* by the same author, Qaw. II, 199.—*Takhrīj*, Qaw. II, 104.—7. Alex. Naḥw 43, on which *Sharḥ abyāt al-Muwashshaḥ* by ʿĪsā b. Aḥmad al-Shirwānī, Garr. 381.—8b. BDMG 70, Garr. 361/5, Qaw. II, 130/1, Teh. Sip. II, 363/6.—Glosses α Alex. Naḥw 13.—ε ibid. 26.—ι anon. Garr. 368/9.—9. Aḥmad b. ʿAlī b. Maḥmūd al-Ghujduwānī, MS dated 720, ibid. 30.

533. 11a. Berl. 6884, Paris 4054, Garr. 370, Cairo[1] IV, 73, 88, Qaw. II, 95.—13. Qaw. II, 109/13, Teh. Sip. II, 323/4, 357/60. Anon. Pers. trans. ibid. 353.—Glosses a. Qaw. II, 74, Istanbul 1272, 1279, 1306, 1309, 1312.—a. Ibid. 73, Istanbul 1256, 1302, 1308.—e. Qaw. II, 78, Istanbul 1266, 1274, 1277, 1287, 1292, 1318, 1320, 1325.—f. Qaw. II, 75, 93, Teh. Sip. II, 320/2, Istanbul 1256, 1281, 1306, 1309, 1313, 1320.—Superglosses by Ḥasan Efendi Istanbul 1277, by Mūsāzāde Garr. 379, *al-ʿIqd al-nāmī* by Muḥammad Raḥmī b. al-Ḥājj Aḥmad al-Akīnī Istanbul 1312 (Qaw. II, 99).

534. u. Istanbul 1307 (Qaw. II, 79).—x. Teh. Sip. II, 324/7.—kk. Mollā Aḥmad Abiwārdī, Mashh. III, 8, Teh. Sip. II, 327/8.

535. 47. Istanbul 1262.—49. Read "Gīpāʾī," Teh. Sip. II, 366/8.—53. *al-Fawāʾid al-shāfiya ʿalā iʿrāb al-Kāfiya* by Ḥusayn b. Aḥmad Zaynīzāde, completed in 1167/1754, Qaw. II, 106/9, Istanbul 1200, 1233, 1235, 1257, 1260, 1267, 1278/9, 1281, 1287, 1301, 1306, 1313, 1320.—54. a. al-Iṣfahandī (l. al-Iṣfahbadhī?), Istanbul 1284, Qaw. II, 96.—55. On the *khuṭba*, by Maqṣūd Efendi, Qaw. II, 77.—56. Turkish by Sūdī, Garr. 384.—57. Anon. *al-Ifṣāḥ* ibid. 382.

536. 2. Teh. Sip. II, 350/2.—3. Qaw. II, 38.—4. BDMG 73, Garr. 391, Alex. Adab 7, 12, Qaw. II, 37, Teh. Sip. II, 348/50.—Glosses: a. BDMG 74.—b. Alex. Adab 12—d. *al-Durar al-kāmila*, ibid. Qaw. II, 28.—5. Garr. 392/3, Alex. Adab 12, Qaw. II, 39, Istanbul 1319, 1320.—6. Qaw. II, 44.—7. Garr. 394, Alex. Adab 12, Qaw. II, 52.—14. Teh. Sip. II, 352.

537. Versification 3. al-Germiyānī, d. 1016/1607. Commentary *al-Fawāʾid al-jamīla* Qaw. II, 45.—VIII, 2, BDMG 42, Asʿad $3804_{,2}$ (*Uṣūl al-fiqh*, 42 fols., Krause).—Commentary 1a. Damādzāde 685, Fez Qar. 1380.—3. Louvain Mus. L 98, Ind. Off. 1478/9, Alex. Fun. 77,4, Qaw. I, 286, Bank. XIX, 1545/7.

| 538. a. Garr. 1629, Qaw. I, 282, C. 1217.—b. Ind. Off. 1480/5, 1873, Garr. 2170,$_{2}$, 1216
Qaw. I, 282, Bank. XIX, 52.—Supergl. δ Qaw. I, 284.—ε Muḥammad Yaʿqūb b. ʿAlī al-Banbānī, d. after 1081/1670, Ind. Off. 1871.—η al-Sīwāsī (Ismāʿīl b. Sinān?), Alex. Fun. 99,$_{2}$.—ϑ Ḥasan al-Harawī, C. 1317.—e. Ind. Off. 1869, Bank. XIX, 1549.—f. See II, 562.—8. Yaḥyā b. Mūsā al-Rahūnī, a professor at the Manṣūriyya and the Khānqāh al-Shaykhūniyya in Cairo, d. 774/1372 or 755, Ibn al-Qāḍī, *Durrat al-ḥijāl* II, 490, no. 1424.—12. Read: *Rafʿ al-ḥājib*.—21. ʿAbd al-ʿAzīz b. Muḥammad al-Ṭūsī, d. 706/1306 in Damascus, Alex. Uṣūl 14.—23. ʿAbd al-Qādir b. ʿAbd al-Hādī, Dam. ʿUm. 57, 1.—24. Bahrām Fez, Qar. 1008/13.—25. al-Bisāṭī, ibid. 1014/7—VIII. Alex. Fiqh Māl. 7.—Commentary 2. See II, 226, 1, 4.

540. 1. Muḥammad al-Ḥilyāwī, *Ibn Rashīq, raʾyuhu fī ʾl-shiʿr wal-shāʿir*, in *Apollo* I, 1161/7.—1. *al-ʿUdda fī ʾkhtiṣār al-ʿUmda* by Abū ʿAmr ʿUthmān b. ʿAlī al-Anṣārī al-Khazrajī al-Ṣaqalī al-Naḥwī (Suyūṭī, *Bughya* 393, with no date), Alex. Adab 98.

541. 3, 1. *al-Mudkhal*, Esc. *Madkhal*.—Read: al-Māzarī and al-Kattānī (Colin).

4. BDMG 67a, Garr. 271, Alex. Fun. 188,$_{9}$.

542. 1, 2. Vol. 18, Garr. 266.—4. An *urjūza*, ed. Ḥabīb b. Zayyāt, *al-Mashriq* XXXVI, 181/91.—2. 2. Qaw. II, 190.

544. 9. Garr. 560, Alex. Fun. 175,$_{3}$, Qaw. I, 180/1.—Comm. 1. *Fatḥ al-nuqūd*, Garr. 501/2, Alex. ʿArūḍ 2, Fun. 64,$_{2}$, 69,$_{5}$, 187,$_{2}$, print. in *Majmūʿa*, Istanbul 1308, Turkish transl. by ʿIṣām al-Dīn Ibrāhīm b. Muḥammad b. ʿArabshāh al-Isfarāʾinī (II, 571), print. in *Majmūʿa*, Istanbul n.d. (Qaw. II, 179).

545. 11. Alex. ʿArūḍ 4, Fun. 64,$_{2}$, Qaw. II, 179/80.—Comm. 2. Alex. ʿArūḍ 1.—3. Ibid. 2, Qaw. II, 182.—5. Alex. Fun. 68,$_{1}$.—8. *Fatḥ rabb al-bariyya*, Alex. ʿArūḍ 2, Fun. 65,$_{5}$, 131,$_{13}$.

546. 11, 15. Alex. Fun. 79,$_{1}$.—28. Muḥibb al-Dīn al-Baṣrī, Alex. ʿArūḍ 4.—II. *Mukhtaṣar fī ʿilal al-aʿārīḍ wa-ḍurūb khāṣṣa*, ibid.—12. Read: Abū ʿAbdallāh Muḥammad b. ʿAbdallāh.

547. 1. *al-Kitāb al-Yamīnī*, Qaw. II, 250.

548. 1, 2. Qaw. II, 242.

1b. Abū Isḥāq Ibrāhīm al-Isfarāʾinī died on the day of ʿĀshūrāʾ 418/21 February 1027; *Nūr al-ʿayn* (II 842) together with *Qurrat al-ʿayn fī ʿahd āthār al-Ḥusayn* by Abū ʿAbdallāh ʿAbdallāh b. Muḥammad, C. 1279, 1298 (Alex. Taʾr. 113).—2. 1. Garr. 587.

549. 2, 4. Teh. Sip. II, 504/9.

551. 4, 10. Alex. Mawāʿiẓ 7.

8. 1. See E. Strausz, WZKM 45, 19/202; contra Björkman, *Beitr.* 82ff (ad II, 318), see R. Hartmann, ZDMG 70, 500, Strausz, op. cit., 202.

553. 11, 9. *al-Badīʿ fī naqḍ al-shiʿr*, Alex. Adab 17.

1. Abu ʾl-ʿAlāʾ Muḥammad b. ʿAlī b. Ḥassūl Ṣafī al-Ḥaḍratayn was born in Hamadan and grew up in Rayy, where he was in charge of the *dīwān al-rasāʾil* and, later, also for Masʿūd of Ghazna. He died in 450/1058. *Tatimmat al-Yatīma* I, 107, *Dumyat al-qaṣr* 90 (which a mistaken Ḥassūn).—*Risāla fī tafḍīl al-Atrāk etc.*, ed. ʿAbbās ʿAzzāwī, *Belleten* IV, 4/5, Ankara 1940, p. 1/51, Turkish transl. Šerefeddin Yaltkaya, ibid. 235/66.

555. 3. *Zubdat al-tawārīkh*, see Houtsma, *Acta Or.* III, 145.

4b. Muḥammad b. al-Ḥusayn al-Ḥasanī al-Miṣrī wrote, in 659/1260: *al-Tuḥfa*,
1217 which is the introduction to | a lengthy work on the genealogies of the Arab tribes with a view to launching a propaganda campaign against the ʿAbbāsids in Cairo, dedicated to the Ḥafṣid Abū ʿAbdallāh Muḥammad b. Abī Zakariyyāʾ (647–75/1249–76); see M. Jawad, REI, 1938, 286.

6. 1. Vol. 2 (592/635 AH), Molla Čelebi 119 (Ritter).

556. 2. Chwolson, *Ssabier* I, 604, 606.—2. An edition of the *Akhbār al-Qarāmiṭa* from it is being prepared by B. Lewis (*Or.* VIII, 285).

557. 2b. Abu ʾl-Ḥasan Muḥammad b. Hilāl b. al-Ṣābī (ḤKh II, 656/7), *Kitāb al-Hafawāt*, Top Kapu 2631,$_{2}$ (RSO IV, 725), see II, 922.—c. Ghars al-Niʿma Abū Ḥusayn Hilāl b. al-Ḥasan al-Ṣābī, *Rusūm dār al-khilāfa*, MS in al-Azhar, see al-ʿAzzāwī in *Belleten* IV, 17n.—4. RAAD II, 193ff, Mīrzā Muḥammad Qazwīnī, *Bīst Maqāla* II, Tehran 1313, p. 78ff.

558. 6b, 1. See p. 565, 2d.—3. Garr. 242, Vienna 414 (*Lubb al-lubāb wa-nuzhat al-aḥbāb al-majmūʿ min kulli kitāb*).

560. 9, 1. Read: al-Sharafī, see II, 550.—3. With the title *Maḥāsin al-azhār fī manāqib al-ʿitra al-aṭhār*, Hamb. Or. Sem. $38_{,2}$.

9a. Abu ʾl-Barakāt Mubārak b. Abī Bakr b. Shiʿār (?) al-Mawṣilī, d. 654/1256, ḤKh IV, 236, *ʿUqūd al-jumān fī farāʾid shuʿarāʾ hādha ʾl-zamān* (*al-mudhayyal ʿalā Kiāb muʿjam al-shuʿarāʾ li-Muḥammad b. ʿImrān al-Marzubānī*) vol. I, Hamza Asʿad 2323 (refers to his *Tuḥfat al-wuzarāʾ* in the introduction), Ritter.

9b. During the reign of the caliph al-Nāṣir billāh (575–622/1180–1225), Abū Naṣr Sahl b. ʿAbdallāh al-Bukhārī al-Nassāba wrote *Ansāb āl Abī Ṭālib*, in the library of al-Ḥasan Ṣadr al-Dīn, *Dharīʿa* II, 377, no. 1517.

563. ʿAlī Riḍā in *RAAD* III, 129/36, 161/8, 260/7—The part that is missing in the section on Muḥammad was added in vol. V, 231/477.

565. 1, 15. *al-Jāmiʿ li-akhlāq al-rāwī wa-ādāb al-sāmiʿ*, MS dated 500, in 10 vols., Alex. Muṣṭ. Ḥad. 8.

2. al-Kattānī, *Fihris* II, 373, *al-Lubāb*, C. 1358. 3. 1. The earliest version Br. Mus. Add. 2524, Cambr. 169, a second version, edited 10 years later, Paris 2133 (M. Jawad).

566. 3, 1. A part of which is in Paris 2087 (M. Jawad, *REI* 1938, 285).

567. Abstracts: a. Abū Shāma, additionally Paris 2137 (M. Jawad, *REI* 1938, 285).—g. Abu ʾl-Fatḥ al-Khaṭīb, Garr. 584.

3a. Anon., Une chronique syriaque du VI/XII s. (a. 490/593), *Bustān al-jāmiʿ* (Oxf. Hunt. 142, Serāi 2959), publié par Cl. Cahen, *Bull. Inst. franç. de Damas* VII/VIII, 1937/8, 113/58.

568. 1. *Bughyat al-ṭālib* etc. Serāi A. III, 2925 (8 vols.), Faiẓ. 1404 (1 vol.), see A. Hamdani, *JRAS* 1938, 562, other MSS in Istanbul in Cahen, *REI* 1936, SA, no. IV.

569. 9. *Mukhtaṣar bulūgh al-āmāl mimmā ḥawa ʾl-kamāl min qaṣāʾid mukhammasāt*, Alex. Adab 123.—10. *al-Inṣāf wal-taḥarrī fī dafʿ al-ẓulm wal-tajarrī ʿan Abī ʾl-ʿAlāʾ al-Maʿarrī*, see *RAAD* II, 266/44.

573. 2, a. Attributed to al-Suyūṭī with the title *Risāla fīmā warada fī Qarāqūsh*, Qaw. II, 236.—5. *Aʿlām al-naṣr*, see Kračkowsky, CR Ac. Leningrad 1928, 1/7.

1218 | 2b. Abu ʾl-Rabīʿ Sulaymān b. Yakhlaf al-Mazālī (see vol. I, 336) died 1078 in Warghlān; *Kitāb al-Siyar*, included by Aṭfiyash (II, 893) in his *ʿUqbā*, Tunis 1320; see Lewicki, *REI* 1934, 59ff.

577. 3, 5. Bank. XXIII, 101,$_{2592}$.

578. 2. Died 28 Rabīʿ I, 460/6 February 1068.—2. Vol. 2. On the government of al-Ḥakam II, in Constantine, Sidi Hammouda 339 (see Codera, Manoscritto de Aben Haiyan en la biblioteca de los herederos de Cidi Hammouda en Constantine, *Bol. RAH* XIII, 53ff). *Ibn Ḥayyān, al-Muḳtabis*, tome troisième: *Chronique du règne du calife Umaiyade ʿAbdallāh à Cordoue*, Texte ar. publié pour la première fois d'après le Ms. de la Bodl. avec une introduction par le P. Melchor M. Antuña, Paris 1937 (Textes Ar. rel. à l'histoire de l'Occident Musulman III), see Brockelmann, *OLZ*, 1941, 168/71.

2a. Lévi-Provençal, Les Mémoires de Abdallah, dernier Ziride de Grenade (460–83/1173–90), *al-Andalus* III 233/344, IV 29/142 (1935/6).

3. 3. Comm. *Ifṣāḥ*, Qaw. I, 423.

579. 4, 1. Qaw. II, 209.

579. 5. MSS. vols. I—III. See Lévi-Provençal, *Hesp.* XVII, 19f, vol. IV in Morocco, Allouche ibid. XXVI, 92/3, one MS in Leningrad, Kračkovsky, ibid. III, 89/96.

580. 8, 1. b. al-Zubayr, *Ṣilat al-ṣila*, ed. E. Lévi-Provençal, Paris, 1938.—10. al-Kattānī, *Fihris* I, 99.

584. Line 1. On *Jāwīdhān khirad* see al-Rājkūtī, *RAAD* IX, 129/9, 193/202.

3. 1. Dāmādzāde 1410 (Cl. Cahen, *REI* 1936, SA 4).—4. Garr. 240, 1370, Alex. Ḥad. 34, 49, with the title *Risāla tashtamil ʿalā alf kalima min al-ḥikam al-nabawiyya wa-kathīr min al-waṣāyā wal-mawāʿiẓ*, Alex. Adab 134,1.

586. 5, 3a. *Nuzl al-sāʾirīn*, Alex. Ḥad. 67.

5a. al-Tanūkhī al-Ḥalabī, b. 482/1089, d. 556/1161, see Cl. Cahen, *REI* 1936 SA 4/. *Taʾrīkh*, La chronique abrégée d'Al. ʿAẓīmī, *JA* 1938, 355/448.

5b. b. Ibn Bābā, see Yāqūt, *Irshād* I, 230 (b. Lāwa?), Yeni 234 is an autograph, see V.A. Hamdani, *JRAS* 1938, 562.

588. 11, 2. Alex. Taʾr. 40.

589. 13. al-Kattānī, *Fihris* 451—5, *Sharḥ al-Ḥamāsa* Istanbul Un. R. 3180 (*ZS* III, 252).—6. *al-Aḥādīth al-Mustaʿṣimiyyāt al-thamāniyyāt*, al-Kattānī, *Fihris* I, 145.

590. 15. See *Revue de l'Orient Chrétien* 28, 390/405.

591. 17, 3. *Mukhtaṣar fī ʿilm al-nafs al-insāniyya*, in part different from the *Maqāla mukhtaṣara fi ʾl-nafs al-badaniyya* in *Onze traités philos.*, Beirut 1918, 76/102.

592. 1, 1. Garr. 728, 765

2. 3. Garr. 1255.

593. 1a. See II, 1010, 132.

1b. Read: Ṭāhir b. Muḥammad b. Naṣr al-Marwazī, Garr. 182.

595. 4, 2. *Urjūza fī naẓāʾir al-Qurʾān*, Alex. Fun. 200,2.

5. 1. AS 4043, NO 3944/6, Walīaddīn 2602, Alex. Adab 152, Bank. XXIII, 110,$_{2608}$.—7. Bank. XXIII, 121,$_{2609,2610}$.

597. 8, 1. *Nuzhat al-albāb etc.*, written by someone from the Maghreb for the sultan of Morocco Ismāʿīl al-Thamīn (1083–1139/1672–1727), Bank. XXIII, 123,$_{2611}$.

| 598. 11. Read: *Rawḥ.* 1219

602. Read: Muḥammad b. ʿAlī, and d. 449/1057.—3. *al-Istibṣār fi ʾl-naṣṣ ʿala ʾl-aʾimma al-aṭhār*, print. Najaf 1346 with the title *al-Istinṣār*, see Dharīʿa II, 16,$_{44}$, 34,$_{132a}$. and p. 969 ad 602. 2, 3.

602. 2b. Abū Ḥafṣ ʿUmar b. ʿAlī b. Aḥmad al-Zanjānī al-Dāraquṭnī al-Baghdādī studied in Damascus and settled in Baghdad where he died in Jumādā I 459/March-April 1064. Subkī, *Ṭab.* IV, 8. *al-Muʿtamad min al-manqūl fīmā ūḥiya ila ʾl-rasūl*, ḤKh V, 623,$_{12303}$, Alex. Ḥad. 61 (but see II, 212, 3a).

4. 1. On which *Takmilat al-Ikmāl* by Muḥammad b. ʿAbd al-Ghanī b. Abī Bakr b. Nuqṭa al-Baghdādī (see 609,16), Garr. 1448.

6. Additionally Garr. 2168,$_{1}$, Alex. Ḥad. 5. Comm. ibid. 30 (which has al-Daylamī).

603. 8, 2. Alex. Fun. 95,$_{9}$.—9. Ibid. Ḥad. 10.

604. 10d. Muḥyi ʾl-Dīn Muḥammad b. ʿAbdallāh b. al-ʿArabī, d. 543/1148, *Ḥikam al-nabī*, Alex. Ḥad. 21.

10e. Saʿd al-Dīn al-Ḥusayn b. Muḥammad b. Abī Tammām al-Takrītī wrote *Sīrat al-nabī*, reading it to his son in the year 546/1151, ʿUmūm. 748 (Ritter).

605. 13a. Aḥmad b. Maḥmūd b. Saʿīd al-Ghaznawī, d. 593/1197, wrote *Rawḍat al-shihāb fī bayān maʿāni ʾl-alfāẓ al-nabawiyya wal-ādāb al-sharʿiyya*, from which *Muntaqā*, Alex. Ḥad. 64.

14. 1. Hamb. Or. Sem. 58, Garr. 1377/9, Alex. Ḥad. 35, Qaw. I, 137, 424.—Comm. a. Garr. 1390, Alex. Ḥad. 4.

606. 1. a. ʿAbdallāh ʿAlī b. Ibrāhīm b. Dāʾūd al-ʿAṭṭār al-Shāfiʿī, d. 724/1324, Garr. 1391.—3. *al-Tahdhīb* Garr. 686, Alex. Taʾr. 101, Muṣṭ. Ḥad. 13, *Tahdhīb al-Tahdhīb* Garr. 687.

607. 14a. Alex. Ḥad. 33, Dam. Z. 49,$_{15}$ (which has al-Qaṣrī).

608. I. Garr. 1381/3, Alex. Ḥad. 13.—2. Print. Ind. 1301.—4. Garr. 1414, Alex. Ḥad. 16, Qaw. I, 112.—Note (= Engl. 627, note 2) see II, 923,$_{23}$.

609. II. Teh. Sip. II, 292/302, *al-Durr al-nathīr*, Garr. 1384, print. in *Majmūʿa* C. 1322 (Qaw. I, 102).

610. 18, 1. Alex. Ḥad. 7, Mawāʿiẓ 6.—19. 1. Alex. Ḥad. 63.

611. *Muqaddima fī ʿulūm al-ḥadīth*, Bombay 1938.—Abstract a. Alex. Fun. 63,$_{2}$.—Comm. α ibid. Muṣṭ. Ḥad. 6, Qaw. I, 89.—c. C. 1937.—e. Garr. 1452, 1467, Alex. Muṣṭ. Ḥad. 14/6, Fun. 103,$_{2}$, 110,$_{2}$, Qaw. I, 95/6, Cmt. β Qaw. I, 94, Alex. Muṣṭ. Ḥad. 16.

612. η Alex. Muṣṭ. Ḥad. 15.—ν *Saqt al-durar* by ʿAbdallāh b. Ḥusayn al-ʿAdawī al-Mālikī, completed in 1309, C. 1323.—Versif.: a. Alex. Muṣṭ. Ḥad. 18.—c. Comm.

α print. Bombay n.d.—β Alex. Fun. $64_{,3}$.—Glosses by Sulṭān al-Mazzāḥī, see II, 452.—h. Manṣūr Sibṭ al-Nāṣir al-Ṭablāwī (d. 1014/1605, cf. II, 443), Alex. Fun. $198_{,5}$.—Abstract *al-Shadha 'l-fayyāḥ min ʿulūm Ibn al-Ṣalāḥ* by Burhān Ibrāhīm b. Mūsā al-Abnāsī (II, 228), Alex. Musṭ. Ḥad. 10.

613. 20. 1. *al-Mukhtār al-mudhayyal bihi ʿalā taʾrīkh b. al-Najjār* by Abu 'l-Maʿālī Muḥammad b. Rāfiʿ b. Salām (II, 30); from which *Muntakhab al-Mukhtār* by Taqī al-Dīn al-Fāsī (II, 220), ed. ʿAbbās al-ʿAzzāwī, Baghdad 1357/1938 (Maṭbaʿat al-ahālī).—21. 1. Istanbul, *ZS* III, 83, Alex. Ḥad. 60. Qaw. I. 151.

614. Comm.: Alex. Ḥad. 19.—b. Ibid. 9.—c. Ibid. 45, Qaw. I, 147/8. | —d. 1220
Muḥammad b. ʿAṭāʾallāh al-Harawī, d. 829/1426, see al-Sakhāwī, *Ḍawʾ* VIII, 151/5, al-Shawkānī II, 201/8.—Abstracts: e. Aḥmad b. Muṣṭafā b. Faḍlallāh al-Ḥamawī, around 1148/1735, Garr. 2071,3.—2. Qaw. I, 156, Alex. Ḥad. 24, $174_{,6}$, different from *al-Durr al-multaqaṭ fī tabyīn al-ghalaṭ*, Alex. Fun. $95_{,10}$, $162_{,6}$, 1747, and from the *Risāla fī 'l-ḥadīth al-mawḍūʿ fī faḍāʾil al-qirāʾa sūra sūra*, ibid. $95_{,11}$.

615. 11. See *RAAD* V, 524/5.—21. *Risāla fī 'l-aḥādīth al-wārida fī ṣadr al-tafsīr fī faḍl al-Qurʾān wa-ghayrihā*, Qaw. I, 118.

21b. See II, $930_{,5,3}$, Garr. 1425, MS dated 706/1306.

23. 2. C. 1356/1937.—6. Alex. Taʾr. 7.—8. Jerus. Khālid.

616. 24, 14. *Ghazāt sabʿ ḥuṣūn* AS 3307.—15. *Islām al-Ṭufayl b. ʿĀmir al-Dawsī*, C. 1322 (Alex. Qiṣ. 7).

617. 1, 1. Vol. 1—8. C. 1938.—Abstract a. Alex. Mawāʿiẓ 3.

618. 4, 1. Louvain L. 97, Garr. 1371.

619. 4, 5. Alex. Ḥad. 16.

5. 3. Delete: see p. 343 (Heffening).

620. 6, 1. Ind. Off. 4580, *JRAS* 1939, 370, Qaw. I, 152, with *Madkhal* by the author himself, Qaw. I, 94.—Comm.: c. Alex. Ḥad. 32.—d. Ibid. 63, Qaw. I, 153.—h. Alex. Ḥad. 32 (MS dated 858 AH).

621. r. Abū ʿAbdallāh Ismāʿīl b. Muḥammad b. Ismāʿil b. ʿAbd al-Malik b. ʿUmar al-Fuqqāʿī al-Ashraf, early 8th cent., Alex. Ḥad. 32.—Comm.: a. Qaw. I, 144, on which a *Muqaddima* in Alex. Fun. 100,$_2$.—d. BDMG 13, Qaw. I, 149.

622. 4 BDMG 8/9, Garr. 1262/4, Qaw. I, 80.

624. 8d. See II, 994,$_{54}$.

9. See al-Kattānī, *Fihris* II, 339/42.—2. Ibid. II, 61.—2a. Read: al-Lūbūdī, II, 85,$_{23}$.—11. *Arbaʿūna ḥadīthan fī ḥaqq al-fuqarāʾ*, collected by his student ʿĪsā b. Ḥasan al-Silafī, Alex. Ḥad. 48.—12. Correspondence with Zamakhsharī, Garr. 2066,3.

625. 12a. See [1] I, 181, II, 937,$_{79}$.

14. al-Kattānī, *Fihris* II, 58.—*al-Jawāhir*, Alex. Mawāʿiẓ 14.

626. Line 11. *Riwāyat*, ʿĀṣim b. Aḥmad b. ʿAbd al-ʿAzīz al-Anṣārī, Alex. Fun. 98,$_3$.

1. 3. See II, 943, 130.

627. 4, 1. Qaw. I, 105.—Abstracts: c. see II, 764, 12, read: 1329.—4. Alex. Taʾr. 52.

628. 7. al-Kattānī, *Fihris* II, 97: *Nuzhat al-nāẓir*.

629. 1, 7. Printed together with Ibn al-Muqaffaʿ's *al-Adab al-kabīr* with the title *Jawāhir al-ḥukamāʾ*, C. 1907.—16. *al-Istidhkār etc.* see I, 297.—17. *al-Taqāṣud fi ʾl-ḥadīth al-nabawī* Cairo[2] I, 98.

3. al-Kattānī, *Fihris* II, 254.

630. 5. ʿAbd al-Ḥayy al-Kattānī, *Fihris* II, 183/9.—1. Qaw. II, 135/5.

631. d. Makr. 55, see II, 935,$_{55}$.—f. Qaw. I, 128/9.—1. Ibid. 157, Istanbul 1317.

632. a. Alex. Ḥad. 54, lith. C. 1276.—2. Qaw. I, 150.—5. *Br. Mus. Quart.* X, 134.

633. 6, 1. Alex. Fun. 143, 1.

8. b. On which *Khātima*, Alex. Ḥad. 22.

634. 10, 2. Alex. Ḥad. 4.—c. al-Qaṭṭān al-Fāsī, whose *Masāʾil al-muṭāraḥāt* are preserved in Ind. Off. 1777.

| 10a. Abu ʾl-Qāsim Muḥammad b. ʿAbd al-Wāḥid b. Ibrāhīm al-Ghāfiqī 1221
al-Mallāḥī, from the village of al-Mallāḥ near Granada, b. 549/1154, d. 619/1222, see al-Kattānī, *Fihris* 252; *Lamaḥāt al-anwār wa-nafaḥāt al-azhār fī thawāb qāriʾ al-Qurʾān* Fez, Qar. 263 = (?) *Lamaḥāt al-anwār wa-nafaḥāt al-azhār fī faḍāʾil al-Qurʾān al-ʿaẓīm*, ḤKh V, 329,$_{11163}$, see also II, 981,$_{27}$.

12. al-Kattānī, *Fihris* I, 367.—1. Alex. Taʾr. 4.

635. 16, 1. Alex. Muṣṭ. Ḥad. 15, Fun. 198,$_8$. Comm. 1. Alex. Muṣṭ. Ḥad. 16, Fun. 123,$_5$, 145,$_2$, 188,$_1$.—3. Alex. Muṣṭ. Ḥad. 14, Fun. 123,$_4$.—14. Read: al-Bībānī.—15. Muḥammad b. Muḥammad b. al-Amīr, d. 1232/1817, Alex. Muṣṭ. Ḥad. 11.

636. 1. Garr. 2129 (*Jumal al-aḥkām*), Alex. Fiqh Ḥan. 4.—2. *al-Rawḍa*, ibid. 29.

637. 2a. Alex. Fiqh Ḥan. 69.

4. 1. Ind. Off. 1423/5, Garr. 1677, Qaw. I, 273.—c. Qaw. I, 293, Istanbul 1307.—d. Qaw. I, 275.

638. 4, 1. k. Anon., Ind. Off. 1426/7.

5. 2. Ind. Off. 1523.

639. 6a. Muḥammad b. Ibrāhīm b. Anūsh (?) al-Ḥaṣīrī, d. in Bukhārā 500/1106, ʿAbd al-Qādir b. Abi ʾl-Wafāʾ, *Jawāhir* II, 3, *Ḥāwi ʾl-Ḥaṣīrī*, Alex. Fiqh Ḥan. 22 (see 653. 36, 3).

8. 1. Alex. Fiqh Ḥan. 23.—2. Ibid. 51.

640. 10, 1. Ind. Off. 1429 (?); Berl. 4372 is rather by al-Ḥusāmī, see Ind. Off. 1438.—5. Garr. 1687.—9. Qaw. I, 316.

11. 2. Abstract, *Zād al-gharīb al-ḍāʾiʿ min Badāʾiʿ al-ṣanāʾiʿ* by Muḥammad al-Bardīnī al-Ḥusaynī al-Ḥanafī, with a *taqrīẓ* of the ʿAbbāsid caliph al-Mutawakkil dated 925/1519, RAAD IX, 308.—4. *Mīzān al-uṣūl fī natāʾij al-ʿuqūl*, Garr. 1626.

641. 12, 2. Garr. 1688/90, Alex. Fiqh Ḥan. 24.

13a. *Jawāhir al-fatāwī*, written in 577/1181, Qaw. I, 318.

14. 1. Garr. 1691, Alex. Fiqh Ḥan. 61.—3. Mosul $64_{,225}$, Alex. Fiqh Ḥan. 72 (attributed to Burhān al-Dīn Maḥmūd b. Aḥmad al-Bukhārī, d. 616/1219).

16. *Ṭarīqat al-khilāf bayna 'l-a'imma*, Qaw. I, 368.

642. 18, 1. Alex. Fiqh Ḥan. 60.

19. I. Garr. 1693/5, Alex. Taṣawwuf 22, Qaw. I, 248, Mosul $63_{,193}$, $156_{,81}$, $175_{,74/5}$, $232_{,98}$.—1. Alex. Taṣ. 45, Mawāʿiẓ 44, Qaw. I, 264, Garr. 1696, Ind. Off. 1524.

643. Line 2. Print. Istanbul additionally 1306.—6. (see p. 970) Ind. Off. 1525.

20. 1. Anon. *Ḥāshiya*, Ind. Off. 1714.—4. See II, 991, 15.

22. See Heffening, *EI*, Erg. 115/6.

644. 23, 1. Ind. Off. 1643/8, Alex. Fiqh Ḥan. 42, Qaw. I, 378.

24. Anon. biography, Garr. 2102,2.—I. Ind. Off. 1538/48, Garr. 1697, Qaw. I, 406/7, Mosul $159_{,144}$.—1. Garr. 1698/1700.—Supercomm.: 1b. Ḥamīd al-Dīn ʿAlī b. Muḥammad al-Ḍarīr al-Bukhārī, d. 666/1268 (Ibn Quṭl. 136), Ind. Off. 1549. 4. Alex. Fiqh Ḥan. 70.

645. 8. Garr. 1746/8, Alex. Fiqh Ḥan. 38, Qaw. I, 371.—Glosses: a. Qaw. I, 321.—10. Ind. Off. 1650/1, Qaw. I, 380, Bank. XIX, 1643/9, As. Soc. Beng. 1904, p. 17.—1a. Alex. Fiqh Ḥan. 33 (*Kitāb al-ḥajj*).

646. Line 1. Read: al-Ḥamawī.—33. Garr. 1701.—43. Anon., Garr. 1702.—
1222 44. *Ḥāshiya ʿalā Kitāb al-karāhiya wal-waṣāyā* by Sinān Efendi, d. | 965/1557 in Istanbul, Alex. Fiqh Ḥan. 21.—45. *Risāla fī tafsīr baʿḍ masā'il al-H. min Kitāb al-rahn* by Walī b. Yūsuf al-ʿImādī, written in 988/1580, Qaw. I, 342.—46. *Risāla fi 'l-ghaṣb min Kitāb al-h.* by Ḥinālīzāde, ibid. 348.—Versific. read: "al-Hāmilī" (II, 240); Comm. read: "*Sirāj al-ẓalām wa-badr al-tamām*", additionally Alex. Fiqh Ḥan. 30, 67.—*Wiqāya*, Garr. 1680/2, Ind. Off. 1559/61, Qaw. I, 408.—Comm. a. BDMG 35/6, Ind. Off. 1577/91, Qaw. I, 362/3, Rāmpūr 304/9, Bank. XIX, 1654/7.—Glosses: β Ind. Off. 1592/3, Alex. Fiqh Ḥan. 20/6, Qaw. I, 335, Mosul $62_{,178}$, $96_{,70}$ (see II, 301).

647. γγ (= p?) Ibrāhīm b. Muḥammad ʿIṣām al-Dīn al-Isfarāʾinī, d. 944/1537 (cf. II, 410), Ind. Off. 1594, Alex. Fiqh Ḥan. 20, Qaw. I, 324, Āṣaf. 1082.—ε Alex. Fiqh Ḥan. 21.—κ Garr. 1684.—bbb. ʿIzz al-Dīn Muḥammad b. ʿAbd al-Laṭīf b. ʿAbd al-ʿAzīz al-Malak, around 820/1417, Qaw. I, 367.—c. Ind. Off. 1595/6, Garr. 1749, Alex. Fiqh Ḥan. 8, Qaw. I, 306/7.—i. Alex. Fiqh Ḥan. 36.

648. r. Qaw. I, 315 (which has *tawfīq*), Alex. Fiqh Ḥan. 15.—s. Mollā Ilyās Efendi, Alex. Fiqh Ḥan. 36.—t. *Risāla fī baʿḍ mabāḥith min Kitāb al-w.* by Khwājazāde, composed in 1045/1635, Qaw. I, 339.—u. *Risāla fī sharḥ baʿḍ al-mawāḍiʿ min al-W.* by ʿAlāʾ al-Dīn al-Isbījābī, ibid. 346.—*al-Nuqāya*, Ind. Off. 1561/8, Garr. 1683, Qaw. I, 405.—Comm. c. Alex. Fiqh Ḥan. 35, Qaw. I, 366.—e. Ind. Off. 1573, Alex. Fiqh Ḥan. 36, Bank. XIX, 1668/70; idem, *al-Ajwiba al-rāḍiya al-murḍiya ʿani ʾl-asʾila al-Rāziyya al-muzriya* (on Fakhr al-Dīn's *Risāla fi ʾl-ṭaʿn ʿalā madhhab al-imām Abī Ḥanīfa*), Qaw. I, 159.—f. Ind. Off. 1569/75, Alex. Fiqh Ḥan. 35, Bank. XIX, 1671.—g. Ind. Off. 1552/3, Bank. XIX, 1672, Alex. Fiqh Ḥan. 16.—i. Ind. Off. 1572.—k. Ibid. 1574/5, print. Delhi 1314/5.—n. Anon. Ind. Off. 1576.—o. *al-Ḥawāshī wal-nikāt wal-fawāʾid al-muḥarrarāt ʿalā Mukhtaṣar al-maʿānī*, Mosul 115,136.

649. Comm. *al-Fawāʾid etc.*, Alex. Fiqh Ḥan. 45.—II. Ibid. 61, Qaw. I, 391 (anon.?).—III. Alex. Fiqh Ḥan. 11.

25. 1. Garr. 1894, Alex. Fiqh Ḥan. 66, Mosul 160,$_{182}$.—Comm. a. Alex. Fiqh Ḥan. 37.—c. Ibid. 71.—2. Ibid. 22, Berl. Qu. 1600.

650. 26, I. Heid. *ZDMG* 91, 384, Ind. Off. 1741/7, Alex. Fun. 174,10, Qaw. I, 429.—Comm. 2. Alex. Far. 11, Qaw. I, 431, *al-Minhāj al-muntakhab min al-Ḍawʾ* Alex. Far. 17.—5. Qaw. I, 429/30, Alex. Far. 10,15, Ind. Off. 1748/54, Garr. 1872/3.—Glosses: a. Garr. 2073,$_1$.—d. Muḥammad b. Ḥamza al-Fanārī (II, 233) or an independent commentary(?), Paris 864.—e. Muḥammad b. Muṣṭafā al Kūrānī al-Wānī, composed in 992/1584, Alex. Far, 6, 15.—f. Aḥmad b. ʿAbd al-Awwal al-Qazwīnī, d. 966/1559, ibid. 16.—g. Badr al-Dīn, Mosul 81,28.

651. 7. Alex. Far. 10, 15, Qaw. I, 430.—(*Sharḥ Taṣḥīḥ Mukhtaṣar al-S. li-Kamālpāshā*, Alex. Far. 8).—22. Alex. Far. 7.—24. With the title *Jāmiʿ al-durar*, Alex. Far. 5.—25. Ḥaydar b. Muḥammad b. Ibrāhīm al-Ḥalabī (al-Harawī, d. 830/1427?), Alex. Far. 10.—26. Anon. *al-Jadīd*, Alex. Far. 13.—*Urjūza fi ʾl-farāʾiḍ* ʿAbd al-Muḥsin al-Qayṣarī, ḤKh IV, 408,$_{8997}$, Paris 1266,$_7$.—III. See ad 765, IV.—27. Ind. Off. 1671.

652, 27a. See II, 949,16.

28. 1. Garr. 2076,3, Alex. Taṣ. 16, Mosul 72,20.

30. Qaw. I, 377.

1223 | 653. 35, 1. Alex. Fiqh Ḥan. 16, Qaw. I, 315.—2. Ind. Off. 1649/50, Mosul 97, 83.

36. 5. Garr. 1686 (*fī 'l-fawāʾid*), see ad 639, 6a.—37. Alex. Fiqh Ḥan. 68.

654. 40. al-Ḥusāmī, Berl. 4372 (mistakenly attributed to Ibn Māza, see ad 640), Ind. Off. 1430/3, Garr. 1705, Alex. Fun. 103$_{,3}$.—Comm. 2. Ind. Off. 1434/6.—3. Alex. Uṣūl 5.—7. Qaw. I, 291.—9. Read: al-Banbānī, d. after 1081/1670, written in Kabul, Ind. Off. 1437. 12. Anon. Ind. Off. 1438.

655. 42, 1. Comm. *Tuḥfat al-ḥarīṣ* by ʿAlāʾ al-Dīn Muḥammad b. Balābān al-Fārisī, d. 739/1338 in Cairo, Alex. Fiqh Ḥan. 11.—42a. 1. Garr. 1766.—43. 1. Ibid. 1692.

656. Line 4. Garr. 2151, Alex. Fiqh Ḥan. 13 (*tartīb*).

44. 1. Ind. Off. 1651, Alex. Fiqh Ḥan. 46.—3. Alex. Fiqh Ḥan. 22, Qaw. I, 327.

45. Ind. Off. 1652/3, Garr. 1707/8, Mosul 219$_{,138}$.

657. 47, 1. Ind. Off. 1527, Garr. 1709/12, Qilič ʿA. 393, Alex. Fiqh Ḥan. 5, 61, Bank. XIX, 1684, a.—Comm. a. Garr. 1713.—c. Anon. ibid. 1714.—2. *al-Fawāʾid al-mushtamila ʿala 'l-Mukhtaṣar wal-Muqaddima*, with anon. comm., Alex. Fiqh Ḥan. 33.

48. *Shudhūr al-dhahab* V, 419.—1. Garr. 1715, Alex. Uṣūl 20.—Comm. a. Read: "al-Qāʾānī".—b. Garr. 1716, Qaw. I, 286.—c. Alex. Uṣūl 11.

48a. See p. 641, 13a.

48. b. Mosul 182$_{,197}$, d. II, 951$_{,34}$.

658. 49. 1. Garr. 1678/9, Qaw. I, 390, Mosul 98$_{,89}$, 167$_{,45}$.—Comm. a. Alex. Fiqh Ḥan. 34.—c. Ind. Off. 4579, *JRAS* 1939, 370, v. 28. Muḥ. 832/21, 7, 1438 (see II, 315), Alex. Fiqh Ḥan. 34, Qaw. I, 354.—2. b. al-Iṣfahānī, d. 749/1348, DK IV, 327, Ind. Off. 1460 (*maʿānī* instead of *masāʾil*).

659. 50, 1. Garr. 1717, Alex. Fiqh Ḥan. 12, Fun. $159_{,1}$, Qaw. 1, 311.—Comm. e. anon. Garr. 1713.—6. Garr. 1904.—10. *Muʿāni ʾl-Maʿānī*, Alex. Adab 161.

52. Hamb. Or. Sem. 22, Ind. Off. 1654/66, Garr. 1750/1, Qaw. I, 402, Mosul $97_{,91}$, $114_{,209/110}$, $133_{,196}$, $146_{,106}$.—Comm. 1. *Ḥilyat al-mujallī*, Ind. Off. 1668, Qaw. I, 327.—2a. Ind. Off. 1667, Garr. 1752, Alex. Fiqh Ḥan. $55_{,6}$, 62, Qaw. I, 373, Bank. XIX, 1690.

660. 2b. Garr. 1759, Alex. Fiqh Ḥan. 34, Qaw. I, 356/60, Mosul $181_{,21}$, lith. Lahore 1889., on which the anon. *Masāʾil Munyat al-muṣallī*, Garr. 1754. *Ḥilyat al-nājī*, completed in 1241/1825, Qaw. I, 328, printings also Istanbul 1251, 1308, 1322.

53. See II, $950_{,28}$, $958_{,111}$.

1. 1. Comm. *Rawḍat al-mustabīn* by Dāʾūd b. ʿAlī al-Shādhilī, Fez, Qar. 823.

664. 5. Comm. see II, 251, 1018.—6b. Fez, Qar. I, 812/5, 819 (see II, 963,51).

665. 9, 1. Alex. Fiqh Māl. 4.

666. 9, 12. *al-Munjiyāt wal-mūbiqāt fī ʾl-adʿiya*, Alex. Fiqh Māl. 16.

10. 2. d. Alex. Far. 8.

12. Abū Yaḥyā b. Jamāʿa al-Tūnisī, 7/14 cent. *Masāʾil fī ʾl-buyūʿ*, with a commentary by Abu ʾl-ʿAbbās Aḥmad b. Qāsim al-Judhāmī al-Fāsī al-Qabbāb, Leid. 1824.

667. 2a, 3. *Mawqif al-imām wal-maʾmūm*, Alex. Fiqh shāf. 38,2.

668. 4, 1. H.A.R. Gibb, al-Māwardī's Theory of the Khilafat, *Isl. Cult.* XI, 291/302.—8. Qaw. I, 217.—10. On an independent work entitled *al-Rutba fī ṭalab al-ḥisba* preserved in a MS in Istanbul, essentially the same as *Maʿālim* | *al-qurba* (see Z. II, 210 [*sic*, = 1254 ad Suppl. 2, 101. 7a?]) and the *Nihāyat* 1224 *al-rutba* (I, 832), and composed in Egypt or Syria, see Gaudefroy Demombynes, *JAS* 230, 452/4.—12. Garr. 1258, in the library of Yāsīn Bāshayān al-ʿAbbāsī in Basra (Ritter).

669. 5. Alex. Fun. $170_{,4}$.

9. I. Ind. Off. 1775.—Yaḥyā al-Yamānī, Subkī,*Ṭab.* IV, 324, *ShDh* IV, 185.—*Iḥtirāz al-Muhadhdhab* by Ibn Abī 'l-Haytham ʿUbaydallāh b. Yaḥyā al-Ṣanʿī, d. 550/1158, ḤKh, VI, 275, Ind. Off. 1776.

670. 9. II, 5. Adaptation entitled *Tashīl al-hidāya* by Aḥmad b. Lu'lu' b. al-Najīb Shihāb al-Dīn Abu 'l-ʿAbbās, d. 769/1368, Garr. 1782.—13. Abu 'l-ʿAbbās Aḥmad al-Zuhrī, composed in 784/1382, Alex. Fiqh Shāf. 25.—VI. print. together with *Ṭabaqāt al-Shāfiʿiyya* by Ibn Hidāyatallāh al-Ḥusaynī, d. 1014/1605, Baghdad 1356.—X. *al-Ishāra ilā madhhab ahl al-ḥaqq*, Alex. Tawḥīd 30,2 (= V ?).

671. 10. Read: al-Khabrī.—1. BDMG 43.

12. Hamb. Or. Sem. 128.—2. Alex. Fun. 170,$_1$, Makr. 45.

672. 2. Glosses: 1. *Qurrat al-ʿayn* additionally Alex. Uṣūl 17.—2. Aḥmad b. Salāma al-Qalyūbī, d. 1069/1658, Alex. Uṣūl 9, 18.—3. Aḥmad b. Muḥammad al-Dimyāṭī al-Shāfiʿī, C. 1303.—3. Alex. Uṣūl 12, Fun. 170,$_2$.—4. Ibid. Uṣūl 18.—6. Ibid. Fun. 114,$_1$.—11. *Zubdat al-mukhtaṣarāt* (see p. 971) by Sharaf al-Dīn Yūnus al-ʿAyṭāwī, ibid. 174,14.—III. Ibid. Fiqh Shāf. 44.—IV. Ibid. Uṣūl 20.—V. Ed. and transl. J.D. Luciani, Paris 1938.—Abstract, *al-ʿAqīda al-Salālajiyya*, by Abū ʿAmr ʿUthmān b. ʿAbd al-Raḥmān al-Salālajī, ḤKh IV, 243, Garr. 1559, see 768,19b.—VI. BDMG 16.

673. XII. Cited as *al-Risāla al-Zayniyya* in Ibn Taymiyya, *Majm. ras. al-kubrā* I, 464,9.—XVIII. *Ghiyāth al-umam fī 'ltiyāth al-ẓulam*, Alex. Ta'r. 92.

674. 16, 2. Alex. Far. 3, anon. comm. *al-Mawāhib al-saniyya*, ibid. 17.

17, 4. *Kitāb al-uṣūl*, also called *Kitāb al-khamsīn* because he completed it when he was 50 years old, ḤKh V, 81, by a certain al-Shāshī of whom it is not certain if he is identical with al-Qaffāl, Ind. Off. 1439/40, Bank. XIX, 1, 1501, Āṣaf. 881, Rāmpūr 2, Calc. Madr. 17, print. Lucknow 1210, 1279, Delhi 1303, comment. a. by Ilāhdād (?), born 923/1517 or 932/1525, Ind. Off. 1441/3, Bank. XIX, 1, 1494, Calc. Madr. 18, print. Delhi 1293, 1302.—b. *Maʿdin al-uṣūl* by Ṣafiallāh al-Nuṣayrī, Ind. Off. 1444.

675. 18, 1. AS 1839/42, Šehīd ʿA. 1209 (F. Meier, *Isl.* 24, 6), Zanjān, *Lughat al-ʿArab* VI, 1928, 94.

18a. Quṭb al-Dīn Masʿūd b. Muḥammad al-Nīsābūrī, d. 578/1182; al-Hādī, Alex. Fiqh Shāf. 45.

20. *Bughyat al-bāḥith etc.* additionally Alex. Fun. $92_{,1}$, $146_{,5}$, $149_{,6}$, C. 1310.—Comm. 2. Alex. Far. 9.—3. Heid. *ZDMG* 91, 384, Garr. $2111_{,1}$, Alex. Far. 9, 15.

676. Glosses a. Makr. 89.—4. Alex. Fun. $142_{,2}$.—Glosses c. Ibid. Far. 6.—e. Ḥasan al-Khiḍrī al-Dimyāṭī, Būlāq 1293.—11. Alex. Fun. 82, 3.—14. Ibid. 7.—16. *Fatḥ aqfāl al-mabāḥith* by ʿAbdallāh al-Sarmīnī al-Shāfiʿī or, according to others, by Yūsuf al-Ḥalabī, ibid. 12.—17. Anon. *Taʿlīq*, Ind. Off. 1740.—II. *Nuzhat al-mushtāq fī ʿulamāʾ al-ʿIrāq*, Medina, *ZDMG* 90, 119 (which has Abu ʾl-Barakāt).—21. *Ṭabaqāt etc.*, Alex. Taʾr. 85.

677. 3. Hamb. Or. Sem. 62, 4, Garr. 1785.—4. Makr. 5.—4b. Alex. Fiqh Shāf. 14.—4f. Ibrāhīm b. ʿAbd al-Raḥmān al-Bilbaysī, completed in 1179/1765, Alex. Fiqh Shāf. 16.—4g. *Taqrīr al-jumal* by Sulaymān al-Jamal, d. 1204/1789, ibid. 19.—4h. Ibrāhīm b. ʿAṭāʾ al-Marhūnī, d. 1073/1662, ibid. 20.—12. *Tuḥfat al-abrār*
| *fī ḥall alfāẓ Ghāyat al-ikhtiṣār* by Abu ʾl-ʿAbbās al-Bulqīnī al-Shāfiʿī, ibid. 7.— 1225
13. Anon. on the preface, Garr. 1788.

678. 25, 1. *al-Ījāz mukhtaṣar al-Muḥarrar* by Tāj al-Dīn Maḥmūd b. Muḥammad al-Kirmānī al-Shāṭibī, d. 807/1414, Alex. Fiqh Shāf. 7.—2. Alex. Taʾr. 47.—26. 4. Garr. 828.

679. I, 2. Ind. Off. 1767.—3. Ibid. 1768, Alex. Fiqh Shāf. 14.—9. Ind. Off. 1769. 12. *Bayān al-fatāwī* by ʿUthmān b. Aḥmad al-Kūhī al-Kīlūnī, Ind. Off. 1770.—Abstract *Irshād etc.*, Hamb. Or. Sem. 54, Alex. Fiqh Shāf. 3.—Comm. 3. Alex. Fiqh Shāf. 24.—5. Alex. Fiqh Shāf. 3.—6. *al-Masāʾil al-mufīda al-ṣarīḥa fī ʿibārāt al-Irshād al-ṣaḥīḥa* by Taqī al-Dīn ʿUmar al-Fatā b. Muʿaybid al-ʿAbdalī al-Zabīdī, who is probably not the vizier by that name who died 781/1379 as stated in the catalogue, but rather the *faqīh* who died in 887/1482 (al-Shawkānī I, 513), ibid. 40.—Versif. *al-Bahja al-marḍiyya*, additionally Garr. 83, lith. C. 1311.

680. 29. b. Tāj al-Dīn Abu ʾl-Qāsim ʿAbd al-Raḥīm b. Muḥammad b. Yūnus al-Mawṣilī, b. 598/1201 in Mosul, fled from the Mongols to Baghdad, dying as *qāḍī* of the eastern part of that city in 671/1272 (Subkī, *Ṭab.* V, 72), *al-Taʿjīz, mukhtaṣar al-Wajīz* (I, 753, 50), with the commentary *al-Taṭrīz*, Alex. Fiqh Shāf. 12.

30. Heffening, *Isl.* XXIV, 131/50.—I. BDMG 44, Ambr. B. 106 (*RSO* IV, 1040), Mosul $160_{,184}$, $182_{,118}$, $200_{,211,\ 212}$. Self-commentary Alex. Fiqh Shāf. $38_{,2}$.—3. Ibid. 3.—5. *al-Furūq*, ibid. 32/3.—8. *Tuḥfat al-muḥtāj*, ibid. 10.—10a. Ibid. 28.—b. Ibid. 5.—d. Ibid. 28.

681. 19. Hamb. Or. Sem. 52, Alex. Fiqh Shāf. 11.—Glosses: a. Ibid. 18.—20. Ibid. 44.

682. 30. Read: *Ḥatm.*—31. Anon. Garr. 1793/7.—32. *Jawāmiʿ al-fikar fī tartīb masāʾil al-Minhāj al-mukhtaṣar* by ʿAlī b. ʿUthmān b. ʿUmar b. Ṣāliḥ al-Ṣayrafī, d. 844/1440, Garr. 1798—2a. α. Alex. Fiqh Shāf. 16.—δ ibid. 15.—θ ʿAlī b. Yaḥyā al-Ziyādī al-Miṣrī, d. 1024/1615, ibid. 17.—ʿAbd al-Barr b. ʿAbdallāh al-Ujhūrī, 11th cent., ibid. 15.—II. Mosul $36_{,187}$.—VI. = (?) *Ḍawābiṭ al-fuṣūl*, Ind. Off. 1771.—IX. Alex. Fun. $175_{,1}$, Qaw. I, 99.

683. Comm. 1. Alex. Ḥad. 29.—6. 3b. 16.—2a. Najm al-Dīn Sulaymān b. ʿAbd al-Qawī al-Ṭūkhī (read: al-Ṭawfī) al-Ḥanbalī (cf. II, 133), ibid. 29.—8a. Ibid. 30.—11. Ibid. Fun. 177,3, Makr. 49. Qaw. I, 140, Mosul 232,90. Glosses by Aḥmad al-Madābighī, Makr. 25.—12. Qaw. I, 148/9.—16. Ibid. I, 141, C. 1307, 1318.—19. Read: al-Ḥayāt, II, 522.

684. 34. Mosul $102_{,56,11,6}$.—36. Muʿīn b. Ṣafī, Garr. 1437.—X. Alex. Mawāʿiẓ 20, Mosul $165_{,7}$.—XIII. Glosses by Ibn Ḥajar al-Haytamī, Ind. Off. 1772, anon., completed in 938/1531, Alex. Fiqh Shāf. 17, anon. comm. ibid. 25.—XIV. Vat. 958, Alex. Lugha 10, Qaw. II, 231.—Abstracts: b. Vat. 958.

685. XVII. Alex. Fun. $63_{,1}$, $87_{,1}$, $162_{,11}$, Mosul $100_{,28,12}$.—XIX. Garr. 1949/50, Alex. Ḥad. 21, Mosul $72_{,16,17}$.—Comm. b. read: Muḥammad ʿAlī b. Muḥammad ʿAllān (II, 533 see ad II 233).—Abstracts: b. Mosul 106,30, 110.—XXII. Mosul $128_{,109,8}$.

686. XXVI. Garr. 1803, Mosul $38_{,219,3}$.—XXVII. Mosul $200_{,209}$.—XXXIV. *Ruʾūs al-masāʾil*, Alex. Fiqh Shāf. 39,1.

1226 | 4, 1. 3. Asʿad 543 (see p. 557, 2a).—8. *Ibṭāl al-taʾwīl* is cited in Ibn Taymiyya, *Majm. al-ras. al-kubrā* I, 445,1.

687. 1b. al-Samʿānī, *Ansāb* 486 v, 6. *al-Tahdhīb fi ʾl-farāʾiḍ* Munich 338.

2.4. A single volume, Paris 787, M. Jawad following Massignon, *REI* 1938, 285.

688. 2b. 2. Alex. Fiqh Shāf. 5.

3. 1. Abstract supercommentary, *al-Rawḍ al-murbiʿ*, Alex. Fiqh Ḥanb. 4.—*Muntaha ʾl-irādāt*, ibid. 7, *RAAD* XII, 631.—Commentary by Bahūtī, *Irshād uli ʾl-nuhā li-daqāʾiq al-Muntahā*, ibid. 3.

689. 4. Commentary abstract by al-Ṭawfī, Alex. Uṣūl 19.—6. With the title *Risāla fi 'l-waswās wal-muwaswis*, Alex. Tawḥīd 43,16.—7. Ibid. Mawāʿiẓ 31.—25. *ʿUmdat al-aḥkām*, ḤKh IV, $254_{,8299}$, on which a commentary entitled *al-Mudda* by Bahāʾ al-Dīn al-Maqdisī, Alex. Fiqh Ḥanb. 4.—26. *al-Tabyīn fī ansāb al-ṣaḥāba al-Qurashiyyīn*, ʿĀšir I, 593, ʿA. Emīrī ʿArabī 2413.

690. 5. Read: Ḍiyāʾ al-Dīn Muḥammad.

6. 2. Comm. by Sharaf al-Dīn ʿAbd al-Muʾmin, written in 905/1499, Garr. 1846.—3. Alex. Ḥad. 65.

692. 5. Ibrāhīm b. Qays Abū Isḥāq b. Sayf al-Nuqqād al-Ḥaḍramī, ca 520/1126, *Diwān*, C. n.d.

6. Sayf b. Nāṣir al-Ḥarūṣī, *Jāmiʿ arkān al-Islām*, C. 1346.

5. 1. Read: 384/7 November 994.

695. 16. Read: *al-ghināʾ*.—17. On which a *Naqd* by Ibn Taymiyya, printed after *Maḥāsin al-Islām wa-sarāʾir al-Islām* by Abū ʿAbdallāh al-Bukhārī, C. 1357.

696. 26. Read: 353/964. Brockelmann in *Mélanges de géographie et d'orientalisme offerts a. M. E. T. Gautier*, Paris 1938.

699. 1d. *al-Arbaʿūn al-Saylaqiyya*, Ambr. A, 29, 4, 72, B, 12, 4. Comm. by Yaḥyā b. Hamza, *al-Anwār al-muḍīʾa*, ibid. D, 454, anon. B, $74_{,xxxi}$, $23_{,iii}$.—2a. 1. Adapted by Abu 'l-Ḥasan ʿAlī b. Aḥmad b. Abī Ḥurayṣa, Hamb. Or. Sem. 18 (dated 1136 AH).—5a. 1. d. 573/1177 (*RS* II, 166).

700. 5a, 5. *al-Naqd ʿalā ṣāḥib Majmūʿ al-muḥīṭ fīmā khālafa fīhi 'l-Zaydiyya min bāb al-imāma*, Alex. Fun. $132_{,1}$—6. *Masāʾil al-ijmāʿ*, Ambr. C 56, IV (*RSO* VII, 69).—7. *Durrat al-ghawwāṣ etc.*, Alex. Adab $129_{,16}$.

701. 8, 1. b. Hamb. Or. Sem. 20.—c. Ibid. 76.

702. 11, 1. Hamb. Or. Sem. 122.—Comm. a. Ambr. D 445.—c. Hamb. Or. Sem. 19, 19 B, 74, 129.

703. 12c. *Anwār al-yaqīn etc.* library of ʿAlī Āl Kāshif al-Ghiṭāʾ, *Dharīʿa* II, $448_{,1740}$.

704. B. Dwight M. Donaldson, *The Shiite Religion, a History of Islam in Persia and Irak*, London 1933.—1aa. ʿAbd al-Wāḥid b. Muḥammad b. ʿAbd al-Wāḥid al-Tamīmī al-Āmidī, d. 436/1144, *Rawḍāt al-jannāt* 464.—*Jawāhir al-kalām fi ʾl-ḥikam wal-iḥkām min kalām* (ḤKh *qiṣṣat*) *sayyid al-anām*, ḤKh II, 646,$_{4294}$, ^{2}I 616 (undated), abstract *Nafāʾis al-jawāhir* by Qudratallāh al-Murīdī al-Ādharī, written in 937/1530, Alex. Fun. 68,$_{8}$.

1a. *Ijāza* regarding his works for Abu ʾl-Ḥasan Muḥammad b. Muḥammad al-Buṣrawī, dated 417/1026, at the beginning of a *majmūʿa* of his *rasāʾil* and *masāʾil* in Mashhad, *Dharīʿa* I, 216,1132.—i. Part 2. Mosul 36,$_{186}$, as *Majālis al-Sharīf al-Mūsawī*, ibid. 66,$_{261}$.

705. 5. See Massignon, *Salman Pak* (Publ. de La Soc. des Études Iran. no. 7, Tours 1934) 9, Garr. 238/9, NO 4361, Teh. Sip. II, 113/59 (where 66 commentaries are
1227 listed).—Comm. by Abu ʾl-Ḥadīd al-Madāʾinī, Teh. Sip. II, | 48/9, Bank. XXIII, 85,$_{2576/7}$.—b. Teh Sip. II, 49/54, Bank. XXIII, 87,$_{2578/9}$.—f. al-Kāshānī, d. 988, according to the chronogram in the *Rawḍa* (Heffening), Teh. Sip. II, 17.

706. i. *Minhāj al-barāʿa* by Ḥabiballāh al-Mujtahid al-ʿAlawī al-Mūsawī, lith. Tehran 1350/1, 6 vols.—k. Arab. *Ḥadāʾiq al-ḥaqāʾiq* by ʿAlāʾ al-Dīn b. Muḥammad al-Amīr Shāh Abū Turāb Muḥammad ʿAlī al-Ḥasanī Gulistānī, d. 1100/1689, Teh. Sip. II, 60/3.—1 Pers. by Muḥammad Ṣāliḥ Rawghanī, 11th cent. ibid. 63/8.—Pers. trans. (*sharḥ*) by Mīr Muḥammad Mahdī, Imām-i Jumʿa in Tehran, 1185–1263/1771–1847, Teh. Sip. II, 55/7, by Muḥammad Bāqir Lāhijī Nawwāb, composed in 1225–6/1810–1, Teh. Sip. II, 17/9, print. Tehran 1317, by ʿIzz al-Dīn Āmulī, Teh. Sip. II, 57/60.—*Mukhtaṣar al-Shahrastānī min Minhāj al-barāʿa*, Sidon, ʿIrfān 1352; *Anwār al-faṣāḥa wa-asrār al-balāgha* by Niẓām al-Dīn ʿAlī b. al-Ḥasan b. Niẓām al-Dīn al-Gīlānī, *Dharīʿa* II, 436,$_{1701}$.—7. *Lughat al-Arab* VI, 512, 2.—8. See *Dharīʿa* 260,$_{1455}$.—10. Questions by Abū ʿAbdallāh Muḥammad b. ʿAbd al-Malik al-Tabbān, d. 27 Dhu ʾl-Qaʿda 419/18 December 1028, *Dharīʿa* II, 78,$_{310}$.—13. Mashh. V, 38,$_{128}$.—21. *Aḥkām ahl al-ākhira*, printed in *Kalimāt al-muḥaqqiqīn, Dharīʿa* I, 295,$_{1542}$.—22.*Tanzīh al-anbiyāʾ*, Najaf 1352.—23. *al-Asʾila al-Sallāriyya* by Abū Yaḥyā Ḥamza Sālār b. ʿAbd al-ʿAzīz al-Daylamī, d. 463/1071, in Mashh., *Dharīʿa* II, 83,$_{331}$.—24. *al-Asʾila al-Rassiyyā al-ūlā wal-thāniya*, asked by Abu ʾl-Ḥusayn al-Muḥsin b. Muḥammad b. al-Naṣr al-Ḥusaynī al-Rassī and answered in 429/1038, MS in possession of Muḥammad Muḥsin, ibid. 82,$_{327/8}$.—25. *Risāla fī jawāb masāʾil kathīra, Lughat al-ʿArab* VI, 514,$_{18}$.—26. *al-Masāʾil al-Ramliyya, Ṭarābulusiyya, al-Radd ʿala ʾl-munajjimīn, Ajwibat al-masāʾil al-wārida ʿalayhi min al-Rayy*, MS in Birjand, ibid. 515.

2. According to Shahrāshūb no. 742, he died in 458/1066 in Najaf.

707. 2. Garr. 1610, Ind. Off. 1782, Birjand, *Lughat al-ʿArab* VI, 512.—Abstract *al-Istibṣar* in Birjand, *Lughat al-ʿArab* VI, 512, comm. and gloss. see *Dharīʿa* II, 1416,$_{43}$.—7. *Fihrist al-rijāl*, rédigé par Muḥammad Ṣādiq Baḥr al-ʿUlūm, Najaf 1356/1937.—8. In the edition wrongly attributed to his son Abū ʿAbdallāh al-Ḥasan (*Dharīʿa* II, 309,$_{1236}$), divided into *majālis*, ibid. 313,$_{1488}$.—9. = 1a.—10. Mashh. IV, 62, 188.—11. *Nihāyat al-aḥkām fi ʾl-fiqh*, Ind. Off. 1781, Garr. 1779.—12. Ibid. 1259.—14. *Thalāthīn masʾala ʿalā madhhab al-Shīʿa*, Taymūr ʿAqāʾid 237.—15. *al-Iqtiṣād al-hādī ilā ṭarīq al-rashād*, MSS in Najaf and Yazd, *Dharīʿa* II, 269,$_{1089}$.—16. *Iṣṭilāḥāt al-mutakallimīn* with a commentary by Muḥammad Saʿīd b. Muḥammad Mufīd al-Qummī, ca. 1099/1688, library of Rājā Muḥammad Mahdī in Faizabad, ibid. II, 123,$_{495}$.—17. *al-Ījāz fi ʾl-farāʾiḍ*, MS in Najaf ibid. II, 486,$_{1985}$.—18. *al-Tamhīd fi ʾl-uṣūl*, Mashh. I, 23, 54.

708. 2b. *Rawḍat al-wāʿiẓīn*, in Mashh. IV, 40,$_{24}$ ascribed to a certain Abū ʿAbdallāh Muḥammad b. al-Ḥasan b. ʿAlī al-Ḥāfiẓ al-Wāʿiẓ al-Nīsābūrī al-Fārisī.—3. 1. Garr. 272, Tehran 1275, 1314. Cf. Jeffery in Bergstr.-Pretzl, *Gesch. des Qorantextes* 246.

709. 2. Mosul 94,27 (corrupted to al-Ṭurṭūshī, and similarly in ḤKh II, 638,$_{4248}$, ^{2}I, 611, to al-Ṭarasūsī).—3. Printings: Persia 1268, 1300, Najaf 1354 (*Dharīʿa* I, 283,$_{1472}$).—7. See ad 707.—9. *al-Ādāb al-dīniyya lil-khizāna al-Muʿīniyya*, library of Ḥasan Ṣadr al-Dīn; from this work his son Ḥasan distilled his *Makārim al-akhlāq*, *Dharīʿa* I, 18, no. 89.

| 3b. 2. Kentūrī 3261, Rāmpūr I, 109, 337. 1228

710. 3d. 1. Written as a counterpart to *Arbaʿūn ḥadīthan ʿani ʾl-arbaʿīn fī faḍāʾil amīr al-muʾminīn* by Abū Saʿīd Muḥammad b. Aḥmad b. Ḥusayn al-Ḥuzāʿī Ṣāḥib Rawḍat al-Zahrāʾ al-Shaikh al-Mufīd, *Dharīʿa* I, 432,$_{2201}$, MSS ibid. 433,$_{2202}$.—2. Printed in the last volume of the *Biḥār al-anwār*.

3e. His nephew Muḥyi ʾl-Dīn al-Ḥāmid Muḥammad b. ʿAbdallāh b. ʿAlī b. Zuhra al-Ḥusaynī, d. ca. 655/1257, wrote *Arbaʿūna ḥadīthan*, MSS in various libraries in Iraq, *Dharīʿa* I, 426,2181.—His student Sadīd al-Dīn Abu ʾl-Faḍl Shādhān b. Jabrāʾīl b. Ismāʿīl b. Abī Ṭālib al-Qummī nazīl al-Madīna (*Amal al-āmil* 477,$_{13}$, 476) wrote: 1. *al-Faḍāʾil wal-manāqib*, Tabriz 1304.—2. In 558/1163, *Izāḥat al-ʿilla fī maʿrifat al-qibla min sāʾir al-aqālīm*, which al-Ḥurr al-ʿĀmilī and others attribute to Faḍl b. Shādhān (see ad 319), *Dharīʿa* I, 517,$_{2572}$.

3g. *Sarāʾir al-ḥāwī*, Alex. Firaq 11.

711. 3i. *Tabṣirat al-ʿawāmm*, Mashh. I, 24,57. Read: al-Tanukābunī.

4. 1. Ind. Off. 1783/5, Alex. Firaq 7.

712. a. BDMG 45, a *ḥāshiya* on a. by his grandson Muḥammad b. Ḥasan b. Zayn al-Dīn al-ʿĀmilī, 11/17th cent., Ind. Off. 1789.—h. al-Radhtī, d. 1260/1884.—1. Read: al-Aʿsam, *Dharīʿa* II, 497,$_{1951}$, where other MSS are listed.—p. A *ḥāshiya* by ʿAlī b. Muḥammad b. Ḥasan al-ʿĀmilī (d. 1103/1691, *Rawḍāt al-jannāt* 44), Ind. Off. 1788, Āṣaf. 1180, according Bank. XIX, 2 134, by ʿAlī b. ʿAlī b. ʿAbd al-ʿĀlī al-Karakī, d. 940/1533.—Abstract a. Ind. Off. 1786/7, Alex. Firaq 17, with comm. (*al-sharḥ al-kabīr* g) by al-Ṭabāṭabāʾī, Tehran n.d.—7. *Irshād al-adhān*, Br. Mus. Or. 8335/6 (*Quart.* VIII, 286).

713. 4a. Asʿad b. Ibrāhīm b. Ḥasan b. ʿAlī b. ʿAlī al-Ḥillī wrote, in 610/1213, *al-Arbaʿūna ḥadīthan*, in private collections in Najaf and Tehran, *Dharīʿa* I, 410,2131.

714. 13. ʿAlī b. Muḥammad al-Laythī al-Wāsiṭī, 6th or 7th cent., *ʿUyūn al-ḥikam wal-mawāʿiẓ wa-dhakhīrat al-muttaʿiẓ wal-wāʿiẓ*, inspired by the sayings of ʿAlī, Teh. Sip. II, 74/6 (cited in Muḥammad Bāqir, *Biḥār al-anwār* XVII, 136).—1a. *al-Hidāyatu ʾl-Amīriyy*, being an Epistle of the Tenth Fatimid Caliph M. Amir bi-aḥkām allāh (d. 534/1131) and an Appendix, *Īqāʿ ṣawāʿiq al-irghām*, ed. with an introd. and notes by Asaf A.A. Fyzee (Isl. Res. assoc. Series 7), Bombay 1938.

716. M. Sprengling, The Berlin Druze Lexicon, *AJSL* 1939, 388/414.

717. 5. BDMG 127/8, Garr. 1612/9.

718. 1b. Against Nöldeke's pronunciation of "Makī", also adopted in Bergsträsser-Pretzl, *Gesch. Des Qorantextes* passim, speaks the diminutive "Mukayk", Yāqūt, *Irshād* VII, 177,8, Ibn Khall. II, 160,7, which points rather to "Makkī".

719. Line 1. Read: Qaw. I, 19,$_{9,15}$.—8. *Risāla fī ḥukm ka-lā wa-bilā wa-naʿam wal-waqf ʿalayhā wal-ibtidāʾ bihā*, ibid. I, 17, 92b.—2. 1. Comm. a. *al-Durr al-nathīr wal-ʿadhb al-namīr* by Abū Muḥammad ʿAbd al-Wāḥid b. Muḥammad al-Bāhilī, d. 705/1305, Taymūr 235.—b. Ibn al-Jazarī (d. 633/1429), Bergstr.-Pretzl, *Gesch. des Qorantextes* 219, n. 4.—3. Qaw. I, 33/4.

720. 2, 8. *al-Waqf al-tāmm*, Qaw. I, 28/9.—16. Ibid. I, 8, 9, 48.—22. *al-Tarjama*, ibid. I, 27.—23. *Zawāʾid*, 26 verses on the spelling of the Qurʾān, Paris 610, 3, *rajaz* on the pronunciation of the letters of the alphabet ibid. 4, see de Sacy, *Not. et Extr.* VIII, 352.—53. 3. Istanbul Un. R. 259, ZS III, 249.—
| Pretzl, *Gesch. d. Q.* III, 229 mistakenly attributes his *al-Iqnāʿ fi ʾl-qirāʾāt* 1229
al-shādhdha (Yāqūt VI, 427, 1, *fī iḥdā ʿashra qirāʾa*) to the otherwise unknown Abū ʿAlī al-Ḥasan b. ʿAlī b. Ibrāhīm al-Hudhalī al-Miṣrī (Spitaler, letter of 23 September 1938).

722. 4g. *al-Kāfī fi ʾl-qirāʾāt al-sabʿ*, Makr. 51.

5. 1. *Sūq al-ʿarūs*, Makr. 30.—4. *Kitāb fahm al-Qurʾān*, Alex. Fun. 144,3.

723. 6c. 1. Makr. 8 (which has ʿAbd al-Raḥmān b. ʿĀshiq b. Khalaf b. Abī Bakr b. Abī Saʿīd), Garr. 2094,1.

8. *al-Miṣbāḥ al-zāhir* see *Rend. d. Linc.* 1938, 86, n. l.

724. 10, 1. Garr. 1193, comm. ibid. 1194.—7. *Kitāb al-wuqūf*, Qaw. I, 29.—11d. Ibn al-Jazarī, *Ṭab.* I, no. 945.

11. In his *Qurrat ʿayn al-qurrāʾ fi ʾl-qirāʾāt*, Esc. 1337, his second-generation student Abū Isḥāq Ibrāhīm b. Muḥammad b. ʿAlī al-Qawwāsī al-Marandī cites al-ʿAṭṭār's *Ghāyat al-ikhtiṣār*, transmitting his teachings through a certain Yūsuf b. Mūsā al-Ḥaqqī al-Marandī (Pretzl, *Gesch. Des Qorantextes* 229).

725. 12. Bergsträsser-Pretzl, *Gesch. d. Qorantextes* 220ff.—Line 10. Garr. 701 with the title *Minḥa min minaḥ al-Fatḥ al-Mawāhibī tunbiʾ ʿan lamḥa min sīrat Abi ʾl-Qāsim al-Shāṭibī*.—I. Makr. 26, Teh. II, 30, lith. C. 1286.—Comm.: 2. BDMG 10, Fātiḥ Waqf Ibr. 51, Jārullāh 15.—3a. lith. Peshawar 1279.—4. al-Lūrqī, whose *Qaṣīda fī riḥlatihi fī ṭalab al-Qurʾān wa-qirāʾatihi waʿtimād riwāyatihi* is preserved in Dam. Z. 82,1.—5. Print. C. 1349.—9. Makr. 34, *Hesp.* XII 1931, 119,1007.

726. 12. Qaw. I, 19.—23. Ibid. I, 21.—27. Read: al-Dabbāʿ, *Isl.* XXI, 133.—31. Muḥammad b. Muṣṭafā al-Qūṣī Qūjawī Shaykhzāde, d. 950/1543, ibid. 21.—II. 1. Ibid. I, 36.—5. Qaw. I, 9.—8. Anon. *Taysīr al-ʿAqīla*, ibid. I, 10.—9. Anon. *Sharḥ al-Rāʾiyya*, Garr. 1206.—V. Read: *Nāẓimat*, Garr. 1195.

12a. 2. See II, 982,36.

728. 14, 8. Comm. *al-Iqtiṣād*, Alex. Fun. 134,$_7$ 190,$_1$, ^{2}I, 466.

730. 4, 1. Makr. 4.

732. 7, 2. Qaw. I, 43.—10. 2. Makr. 2.

734. 12, 2. Alex. Taʾr. 8.—12. 1. *Taqshīr*, ḤKh II, 391.

735. 15. Read: ʿAlī b. Aḥmad—*Ibdāʾ al-khafāʾ fī sharḥ asmāʾ al-Muṣṭafā*, Qaw. I, 215 (see II, 935,$_{57}$).

736. 21, 2. Garr. 1253/4.

737. 23, 2. Qaw. I, 224, Alex. Mawāʿiẓ 10.—6. *Br. Mus. Quart.* X, 34.

24. 1. Read: *al-mutadhakkir*.

738. 27. Ibn al-Qāḍī, *Durrat al-ḥijāl* II, 348, no. 969, follows al-Ṣafadī in placing his death in 785/1383 (in Tabriz), while according to al-Subkī (*min al-ṭabaqa al-ṣughrā lil-Suyūṭī!*) it was in 791.—4. Qaw. I, 62.

739. 11. Qaw. I, 57, Alex. Fun. 95,$_1$.—10. Qaw. I, 60.—12. Qaw. I, 59/60.—19. Ibid. I, 58 (read: d. 986).

740. 30. Qaw. I, 58.—31. Ibid. I, 72.

741. 83. Ismāʿīl b. Muḥammad b. Muṣṭafā al-Qūnawī al-Ḥanafī, d. 1195/1781, Qaw. I, 12.—Abstract, anon. al-ʿImādī, Philadelphia no. 23.—Critique *al-Itḥāf etc.* Alex. Fun. 95, 2 (where the author is Muḥammad b. Yūsuf al-Shāmī, the work being based on the glosses of his teacher al-Suyūṭī).—II. Alex. Uṣūl 21.—Comm. 21 Ind. Off. 1477, Āṣaf 98 (?), Bank. XIX, 1562.—3. Alex. Uṣūl 22, Qaw. I, 301.

1230 | 742. IV. Qaw. II, 119.—Comm. b. ibid. II, 61/2, Alex. Naḥw 3.—VI. BDMG 17, Garr. 1487/8, Qaw. I, 204.—Comm. 1. Alex. Tawḥīd 21, Qaw. I, 195. Glosses by Muḥammad b. ʿUmar al-Khalafī, Qaw. I, 168.—2. Alex. Tawḥ. 44/5, Makr. 56, Qaw. I, 210/1.

743. With the title *Sharḥ awāʾil al-ṭawāliʿ fi ʾl-ḥikma*, Rāġib 1457,$_{13}$, print. C. 1323.—b. Alex. Tawḥ. 14.—7. Qaw. I, 212 (*Nihāyat al-afkār*).—XIV. *Taʿrīfāt al-ʿulūm*, Alex. Fun. 79,7.

744. 3a. Abū Saʿīd b. Abī Saʿīd al-Mutawallī al-Shāfiʿī, d. 478/1085, *al-Mughnī fī uṣūl al-dīn ʿalā ṭarīqat Abi ʾl-Ḥasan al-Ashʿarī*, Alex. Tawḥīd 30.

5. Tāšköprīzāde, *Miftāḥ* II, 119/210.—Note 1. For 'weaver' read: 'spinner'. The original form of his name is also alluded to by the verses written by him: *ghazaltu lahum ghazlan daqīqan fa-lam ajid + li-ghazliya nassājan fa-kassartu mighzalī*, which are cited without source reference in al-Rayḥānī, *al-Rayḥāniyyāt* III, 110, 13/4.

745. M. Umaruddin, An exposition of al-Ghazzalis view on the problem of the freedom of the will, *Muslim Univ. Journal* III, 1, 1936, 31/51.

746. 1. Alex. Fun. $152_{,29}$, Qaw. I, 55, Mosul $156_{,16}$.—*al-Jawāhir al-ghawālī lil-imām al-Gh.*, C. 1924.—1b. *Anwār al-asrār wa-hiya risāl fī tafsīr qawlihī taʿālā sūra* $2._{21}$ *wa-mā fī maʿnāhu fi ʾl-ḥadīth*, Alex. Fun. $126_{,5}$—3. Alex. Fun. 164. See Kraus, Abstr. Isl., *REI* 1936.—5. Garr. 1891, Alex. Taṣ. $35_{,9}$.—6. Alex. Fun. $75_{,2}$, Mawāʿiẓ $40_{,2}$, Mosul 263,8 (to be read thus).—9. Qaw. I, 160.—13. Mosul 75,1 (*Fayṣal al-tafriqa bayna ʾl-Islām wal-zandaqa*) transl. H.J. Runge, Kiel 1938.—16. Garr. 2167,2.—23g. *Risāla fi ʾl-mawt*, Alex. Fun. 65,1.—23h. *Sharḥ ʿalā qawl ḥujjat al-Islām al-Ghazzālī laysa fi ʾl-imkān abdaʾ etc.* by Muḥammad al-Nashshārī, Qaw. I, 200.

748. 24. *Jawāhir al-ḥ.*, origen y testo por A. J. Casas y Manrique, Uppsala 1937, a pseudepigraphon, basically the same as the *Tuḥfat al-safara*, 796, 26.—25. Garr. 1477/8, Istanbul 1321, C. 1334.—H. Wehr, *Al-G.'s Buch vom Gottvertrauen*, das 35. Buch der *I. al-ʿu.* (Islamische Ethik IV), Halle/S. 1940.—H.H. Dingemans, *Al-Gh.'s Boek der Liefde*, Diss. Leiden 1938.—Abstracts: 1. Garr. 1482.—2. Alex. Taṣ. 43, Mawāʿiẓ 49.—7. Read: *Isʿād al-umma* (*Jāmiʿ* 82).

749. 21. *Mawʿiẓat al-muʾminīn min* Iḥyāʾ ʿulūm al-dīn, by Muḥammad Jamāl al-Dīn al-Qāsimī al-Dimashqī, d. 1332/1914, C. 1331.—26. Garr. 921, Alex. Mawāʿiẓ $40_{,1}$.

750. 30. Qaw. I, 223, Alex. Mawāʿiẓ 48, on the basis of the Persian original by Jalālī Humāʾī, Tehran, Majlis 1315/7 and on the MSS in Istanbul, see F. Meier, *ZDMG* 93, 395/406.—31. Alex. Mawāʿiẓ 23.—32. Qaw. I, 234, Alex. Mawāʿiẓ 35, Fun. 194,8.—Comm. d. Muḥammad b. Yūsuf al-Ḥalabī al-Sāqirī, *Minḥat al-samāʿ*, Garr. 784.—e. Abū Saʿīd Muḥammad b. Muḥammad b. Muṣṭafā al-Khādimī, 12th cent., Qaw. I, 245.—f. ʿAbd al-Raḥmān b. Aḥmad ʿUmar Baṣīrī, ibid.—32a. Also in the margin of Ibn Miskawayh, *Tahdhīb al-akhlāq*, C. 1322.

751. 34a. Alex. Fun. 52,$_{30}$, Qaw. I, 262.—34c. Garr. 1892, Mosul 176,$_{81}$.—38. BDMG 19, Garr. 2068, Qaw. I, 267, Mosul 124,$_{52}$, 155,$_{66}$, 192,$_{33}$, C. 1351 (with *Bidāyat al-hidāya* in the margin).

1231 752. 40. Transl. by M. Smith, *JRAS* 1938, 177/200, 353/74.—42. | Qaw. I, 259.—43. Source of the *Kitāb al-dalāʾil wal-iʿtibār*, see ad 247,5 and Baneth, op. cit., 23ff.—47. Alex. Taṣ. 35,$_{8}$.—47x. Alex. Fun. 90,$_{20}$.—47gg. *Khulāṣat al-taṣānīf fi ʾl-taṣawwuf*, C. 1327.—47hh. *Aṣnāf al-maghrūrīn*, Taymūr, Akhlāq 164.—47ii. *Mawāʿiẓ al-Gh.*, Garr. 1544.—47kk. *Jawāhir al-fākhira* (?), Heid. 337 (*ZDMG* 91, 389).—48. Ind. Off. 1766.—Part IV, Ambr. *RSO* III, 277.

753. 50. Anon. comm., Alex. Fiqh Shāf. 26.—Abstract with the traditions *al-Talkhīṣ al-kabīr*, Alex. Ḥad. 11.—c. Glosses by Jalāl al-Dīn Muḥammad b. ʿAbd al-Raḥmān al-Bakrī al-Ṣiddīqī (d. 891/1486, al-Sakhāwī, *al-Ḍawʾ al-lāmiʿ* VII, 284/6), Alex. Fiqh Shāf. 17.—Abstracts: e. *Rawḍ al-ṭālib*, see II, 254/5.

754. 51. 1. Mosul 64,$_{216}$.—53h. *Risāla arsalahā ila ʾl-sulṭān Muḥammad b. Malikshāh*, C. 1325.

755. 57. Alex. Tawḥīd 45.—58. Alex. Fun. 87,$_{1}$, 151,$_{9}$ (with the title *al-ʿIlq al-maḍnūn etc.*), Taymūr Majm. 1,$_{12}$.—59. Alex. Fun. 64,$_{1}$.—61. Anon. abstract, Qaw. I, 265.—64g. *Maʿārij al-quds fī madārij maʿrifat al-nafs*, C. 1927.—67. With the title *al-Sirr al-maṣūn wal-durr al-maknūn*, Alex. Faw. 24,$_{1}$. Comm. *Mustawjibat al-maḥāmid*, by Muḥammad b. ʿUthmān al-Anṣārī, Paris 2670/1.

756. 72. Persian letter to the son of Niẓām al-Mulk, Ḍiyāʾ al-Mulk, ed. Dhabīḥullāh Ṣafā in *Mihr* (Tehran) vol. 6, no. 5, 363/7, see F. Meier, *ZDMG* 93, 406ff.—8, 1. Garr. 2003/19, Alex. Tawḥīd 6, Fun. 160,$_{1}$, Qaw. I, 162, Mosul 158,$_{128}$, Un. Egypt 11900, 15008.—4. Cairo, *Nashra* 6, Ambr. B. 75ix (*RSO* IV, 1030), ed. J. Robson, *Tracts on Listening to Music*, together with Ibn Abi ʾl-Dunyā's, *Dhamm al-malāhī*, Or. Transl. Fund XXXIV, London 1938.—6. Taymūr, ʿAqāʾid 252.

757. 7, 1. = 4. Garr. 1545 (*Muʿtaqad fī uṣūl al-dīn*), Heid. *ZDMG* 91, 402,5, Alex. Tawḥīd 5, Fun. 80,$_{2}$, 86,$_{3}$.—Comm. 2. Alex. Tawḥ. 6.—3. Baghdad, Makt. al-awqāf 2746, see al-ʿAzzāwī, *Taʾrīkh al-Yazīdiyya*, 20 n.

758. 8. al-Kattānī, *Fihris* II, 382.—1. *al-Ḥadāʾiq* see M. Asín Palacios, Ibn al-Sid de Badayoz y su libro de los circos, *Andalus* IV, 45/54.—7. See idem in *al-Andalus* III, 345/89 (text of a *masʾala*, ibid. 380/3).—12. *Risāla fi ruʾūs masāʾil*

al-falsafa, AS 2415,2 (Krause).—11. Garr. 1545, 2100,$_1$, Alex. Tawḥīd 31, Qaw. I, 204/5.—Comm. 1. Heid. A. 359,1, *ZDMG* 91, 391, Garr. 1546/9, 2147,$_2$, 2155,$_2$, Alex. Tawḥīd 22, 31,$_2$, Qaw. I, 197/210.—Glosses: b. Garr. 1550, Alex. Tawḥīd 11. Qaw. I, 169/72, Makr. 18.—α Garr. 1551, Qaw. I, 179.—β Qaw. I, 173/5. Supergl. by Muḥammad b. al-Ḥājj al-Manlā Rasūl b. Muḥammad b. Muḥammad b. al-Rasūl, d. 1264/1848, Istanbul 1303.—γ Qaw. I, 179, Istanbul 1227.

760. Φ Qaw. I, 178.—ω Aḥmad Rushdī b. ʿUthmān al-Qūnawī Bakjajīzāde, Qaw. I, 165.—αα ʿAlī b. Ṣāliḥ b. Ismāʿīl al-Ayyūbī, Istanbul 1306.—ββ Shujāʿ al-Dīn, Qaw. I, 176.—γγ ʿAbdallāh b. Ḥasan al-Uskudārī al-Anṣārī al-Kāngārī, 13th cent., Būlāq 1244 (Qaw. I, 179).—δδ al-Mawjānī, Istanbul 1327 (Qaw. I, 182).—εε On the *Dībāja* by Muḥammad Amīn b. Taqī al-Dīn Abū Ḥāmid Aḥmad b. ʿImād al-Dīn b. Muḥammad b. Ismāʿīl al-Mawṣilī, Qaw. I, 182.—h. Alex. Tawḥīd 26, Makr. 49.—m. Istanbul 1292/3, 1316.—q. Garr. 1554 (MS dated 845 AH).—y. Istanbul 1276 (Qaw. I, 177).

761. gg. al-Bājūrī, Alex. Tawḥīd 9.—Versif.: c. *Naẓm iḍāʾat al-dujunna* | *fi ʿtiqād* 1232
ahl al-sunna by Aḥmad al-Maqqarī, see II, 408, 10.—II. Ind. Off. 1779, Garr. 1623/4, Alex. Fiqh Ḥan. 67, Bank. XIX, 1609.—Comm.: 1. *Ḥaṣr al-masāʾil wa-qaṣr al-dalāʾil*, Alex. Fiqh Ḥan. 22.—2. Ibid.—5. Ibid. 64.—Note 1. *Miʿyār al-ṭarīqa*, Vienna 1901, 2.

762. VI. Garr. 1625, Alex. Lugha 14.—VIII. Alex. Taʾr. 179,$_2$.—XIII. *Risāla fi ʾl-firaq al-Islāmiyya*, with the anon. comm. *Jāmiʿ ikhtilāf al-madhhab li-kashf al-maqāṣid wal-maʾārib*, Qaw. I, 165.—XIV. *Taṭwīl al-asfār ltaḥṣīl al-akhbār*, see al-Kattānī, *Fihris* I, 215.

12. 1. Garr. 1605/6, Alex. Fun. 95,$_8$.

763. 12. 3. See *ZDMG* 1935, 131ff.

13. 2. *al-Durra al-bahiyya fī ḥall alfāẓ al-Qurṭubiyya* by Muḥammad b. Yaḥyā b. Khalīl al-Tataʾī, Makr. 27.

764. 15, I, Alex. Tawḥīd 40, Fun. 195,$_1$, Qaw. I, 161.—Comm.: 1. Garr. 2003,$_{21}$, 2127,$_3$, Alex. Tawḥīd 47.—2. *Nafīs al-riyāḍ*, Alex. Tawḥīd 46, Qaw. I, 212.—3. Alex. Tawḥīd 16.—6. Garr. 1555/7, 2100,$_2$, Alex. Tawḥīd 24, Fun. 86,$_1$, 102,$_2$, 109,$_5$, Qaw. I, 202/3.—Mosul 44,$_{59}$.

765. 17. Mosul 36,$_{175,8}$, 244,$_{322}$.—30. Ibn Kamālpāshā, Alex. Tawḥīd 23.—iv. *al-Fatāwā al-Sirājiyya*, completed in 569/1173, Ind. Off. 1640,$_{2}$, Būhār II, 168, see p. 651, III mistakenly attributed to al-Sajāwandī.

767. Anon. *Manāqib al-shaykh ʿIzz al-Dīn al-Sulamī*, Garr. 2083,$_{3}$.—2b. Alex. Fiqh Shāf. 33.—25. Istanbul 1311, see II, 923.

768. 35. C. 1317.

19a. Instead of ʿAlī read ʿAbd.

21a. A collection of his writings from the years 670/9, among which *al-Lamʿa al-Juwayniyya fī ʾl-ḥikma al-ʿilmiyya wal-ʿamaliyya* for al-Ṣāḥib Shams al-Dīn Muḥammad b. al-Ṣāḥib Bahāʾ al-Dīn Muḥammad al-Juwaynī, together with selections (*iltiqāṭ*) from al-Bīrūnī's *al-Āthār al-bāqiyya*, the *Shamsiyya* of Qazwīnī, the *Qānūn al-Masʿūdī* of al-Bīrūnī and the *Kitāb al-hayʾa* of Muʾayyad al-Dīn al-ʿArūḍī (read: "al-ʿUrḍī" p. 869), is preserved in al-Khizāna al-Gharawiyya: *Dharīʿa* II, 286, 1157/60.—Abstract from the year 817, c. ibid. 1161.

769. 21a, 6. *Risāla fī abadiyyat al-nafs*, Rāġib 1482 (Deft. p. 151, penult. ff).—9. Ibid. (p. 151 ult.).

22. 1. Alex. Firaq 8.

771. 1. Heid. ZDMG 91, 383,$_{7}$, Alex. Fun. 96,$_{3}$, Qaw. I, 240.

772. 4. *Mukhtaṣar al-taḥiyya, sharḥ asmāʾ Allāh al-ḥusnā*, Alex. Taṣawwuf 21.—8. Garr. 2117,$_{2}$.—12. Garr. 1261.—19. *Kanz al-yawāqīt*, see *Br. Mus. Quart.* VI, 97.—20. *al-Takhbīr fī ʿilm al-tadhkīr*, Alex. Mawāʿiẓ 40,1.—21. *al-Uṣūl fī naḥw arbāb al-qulūb mustanbaṭa min naḥw arbāb al-ghuyūb*, ibid. Taṣawwuf 6.

1g. 2. *al-Maqāmāt wal-ādāb*, Alex. Taṣawwuf 46.

774. I. Garr. 2117,$_{3}$.

775. 2, IX. *Anwār al-taḥqīq bil-muntakhab min kalimāt Khwāja Harawī*, selection by ʿAlī b. Ṭayfūr al-Bisṭāmī, in the library of ʿImād al-Fihrisī al-Ṭihrānī in Mashhad, *Dharīʿa* II, 421,1664.—3. Pines, *Orientalia* VII, 1938, 331ff.—3a. See II, 1000,$_{37}$.

776. 6. Read: ʿArīf (Colin).—1. Alex. Fun. 173,$_7$, with the title *Majālis al-mujālis*, Alex. Mawāʿiẓ 37,3, see Horten, *Islca* = *AKM* XXIII 6, 1/17. 7. 1. Garr. 674.—2. *Ṭabaqāt al-awliyāʾ*, apparently completed in 762, Alex. Taʾr. 84.—7a. See II, 1010,137.

| 777. 8. *Akhbār ʿAdī b. Musāfir from the Kitāb al-Habashī fī tarājim al-Ṣūfiyya etc.* 1233
Makr. 51.—9. According to Evliyā (?), he came from the village of Gīl in the *liwāʾ* of Kirkuk, see al-ʿAzzāwī on Ibn Ḥassūl, 31, n.—Margoliouth, Contributions to the Biography of ʿAbd al-Qādir of Jilan, *JRAS* 1907, 267/310.—Muḥammad ʿAlī ʿAynī, *Aq. Guilani, un grand saint dans l'islam*, en collaboration avec F. J. Simore-Munir, Paris 1938 (Les grandes figures de l'Orient VI).

778. 18. See II, 884,$_{45}$, 869,$_{39}$.—21. *ʿIqd jawāhir al-maʿānī fī manāqib al-shaykh ʿAbd al-Qādir al-Jīlānī*, Alex. Taṣawwuf 43, see II, 999,$_{30}$.

779. 36. Alex. Faw. 16.—37. Print. Tunis 1325 in *Majmūʿa*.—47. *Nuzhat etc.*, Garr. 40 (which has Muḥammad Ṣadaqa b. Muḥammad b. Muḥammad).—53. *al-Risāla al-Ghawthiyya*, Alex. Taṣ. 43,5.—54. *Ḥizb al-wasīla*, with the commentary *al-Mawāhib al-jalīla* by Muḥammad al-Amīn al-Kīlānī, completed in 1273/1856, in *Majmūʿa* (see 37), no. 3.—55. *Taʿālīq ʿalā tisʿ ṣalawāt ukhrā*, ibid. 2.—56. *Qaṣāʾid min kalām al-Quṭb al-Jīlānī maʿa qaṣāʾid wa-amdāḥ qīlat fīhi min baʿḍ murīdīhi*, ibid. 4.—57. *Wird al-bāz al-ashhab*, Alex. Faw. 24,$_7$.—58. *al-Qaṣīda al-khamriyya*, Bank. XXIII, 31,$_{525}$, Rāmpūr I, 154, Āṣaf. 1248, comm. by Abu 'l-Faraḥ Muḥammad Fāḍil al-Dīn, and Indian scholar of the 12th century, Bank. XXIII, 32,$_{2526}$.

780. 11. Ritter, *Isl.* XXV, 31ff.—1. Alex. Fun. 87,$_3$.

13. 1. Alex. Taṣ. 36,$_2$.—2. *al-Bustān al-maʿrūf bi-shams al-qulūb*, ibid. 1.—3. *Maḥajjat al-saʿāda*, ibid. 3.—4. *ʿAyn al-ḥaqīqa*, ibid. 4.

781. 13a. *Kitāb al-barākīn* (?), Alex. Taṣ. 28.

14. Qazwīnī, *Kosm.* 383.—H. Corbin, *S. d'Alep (+ 1191) fondateur de la doctrine illuminative (Ichrāqī)*, publ. de la Soc. d'Études Iran. no. 16, Paris 1939.—Excerpts from his writings in A. v. Kremer, *Gesch. der herrschenden Ideen des Isl.* 92ff.

782. 1. Taymūr, Ḥikma 94.—Comm. a. Alex. Fun. 131,$_9$.—2. Taymūr Ḥikma 119/20, 130 (physics and metaphysics) together with 3, Zanjān, *Lughat al-ʿArab*

VI, 93.—Comm. b. Br. Mus. 7728, Taymūr, Ḥikma 92 (only part 2).—4. Alex. Ḥikma 20.—5. Comm.. a. Alex. Fals. 15, Taymūr, Ḥikma 15/6, Rāġib 1478,$_{2,3}$.—b. With *Ishrāq Ḥ. al-n. ʿan ẓulumāt Shawākil al-ghurūr*, MS in the collection of the author of the *Dharīʿa* II, 103,$_{404}$.

783. 14. Taymūr, Ḥikma 189.—17. *Le familier des amants*, trad. franç. avec introd. par H. Corbin, *Recherches philosophiques* II (1932/3) 371/423.—21. In *Three Treatises* ed. and transl. by O. Spies and S.K. Khettas, Stuttgart 1935, French transl. *Deux épîtres mystiques de S.*, par H. Corbin, Épître de la modulation de Simourg et Épître de la Langue des fourmis (22) in *Revue Hermes* 3, s. III, 1939.—28. Gotha 914,5, d. ḤKh V, 209,$_{10720}$.—29. See Gunzburg, *Les mss. ar. de l'Inst. d. l. or de St. Pétersbourg*, 1891, no. 230 (Corbin, p. 46).

784. 14b. Abu 'l-Qāsim ʿAbd al-Raḥmān b. Abi 'l-Ḥajjāj al-Naḥwī, completed in 599/1202, *Shams al-qulūb*, Alex. Taṣ 22.

15. Cmt. 1. b. Heid. *ZDMG* 91, 382, Alex. Fun. 90,15.—2. Gotha 1128.

785. 10. Ibn Bāʿasham, Alex. Taṣ. 41,$_{3}$—13. Ibid. Fun. 145,$_{1}$.

786. 19, 5. *Mirʾāt al-maʿānī etc.*, Alex. Fun. 151,$_{10}$.

787. 20, 3. With the title *Aqrab al-ṭuruq*, Alex. Fun. 173,$_{9}$.—4. Ibid. 86,$_{4}$, 151,$_{13}$ (*fī ṭarīq Allāh*).—12. Garr. 2076,$_{2}$.

20 a. Read: Khabrī.

21. Last line read Wāzzān (Colin).

1234 | 788. 21. *Ṣalawāt*, Qaw. I, 249.—Comm. 1. Alex. Faw. 19.—2. Read: *al-rāfiʿāt.*—4. Alex. Faw. 29 *al-Nafaḥāt al-Qudsiyya.*—5. Ibid. 4.

789. Ritter, *Isl.* XXV, 36ff.—1. Garr. 1573, Qaw. I, 254.—Pers. transl. Yeni II, 179 (Defter Maḥmūd al-Qāshānī).

790. Line 3, read: 16.—26. Comm. Alex. Taṣ. 16, Qaw. I, 229.

791. al-Kattānī, *Fihris* I, 233/5.—Muḥammad Rajab Ḥilmī (a descendant), *al-Burhān al-azhar fī manāqib al-shaykh al-akbar*, C. 1326.—A.E. Afifi, *The Mystical Philosophy of M. b. al-A.*, Cambridge 1939.

792. 11. Qaw. I, 255.—12. Ibid. I, 255.—Comm. aa. *Miftāḥ F. al-ḥ*, a self-commentary, Alex. Adab 132,2.

793. h. Qaw. I, 247 (attributed to Muṣṭafā b. Sulaymān Bālīzāde, d. 960/1553).—k. BDMG 22, print. C. 1304.

794. ee. Aḥmad b. Aḥmad b. Rumḥ al-Zabīdī, completed in 992/1584, ibid. 31.—Abstracts: c. Read: 1058.—14. Comm. a. completed in 954/1547, Alex. Taṣ. 51.—e. Anon., *al-Aghrab min al-ʿujāla*, ibid. 35,7.—15. Ibid. 41,2.

795. 18. *Br. Mus. Quart.* VI, 55, Alex. Taṣ. 11.—21. Garr. $1574_{,2}$ (*yumnaḥ*), Alex. Taṣ. 78.—22. *Risālat al-khalwa, Risālat al-anwār*, ibid. 37.—25. Ibid. 34,4, Fun. $151_{,20}$.

796. 26. See Asín Palacios, *Psicologia* 79, *Isl. crist.* 271/99, according to ḤKh II, 228 by Jalāl al-Dīn Aḥmad al-Bisṭāmī, but in fact by Qiwām al-Dīn Muḥammad al-Bisṭāmī (a student of Aṣīl al-Dīn al-Balyānī, cf. II, 287), Alex. Fun. $68_{,3}$, which has Ibn ʿAbd al-Ḥamīd, Tunis, Zayt. III, 164, 1581,2, which has Ibn Ḥāmid, see the preface to A.J. Casas y Manrique, see p. 1230 ad p. 748.—27. Alex. Taṣ. 33,6.—42. *al-Ḥikma al-ilhāmiyya fī ʾl-radd ʿala ʾl-falāsifa* (I, 444), Leid. 1514/5 = Taymūr, Ḥikma 85.

797. 50. Alex. Taṣ. 12.

798. 77. *Miftāḥ al-jafr al-jāmiʿ* additionally Br. Mus. Or. 10887, with the title *al-Jafr al-jāmiʿ* in Alex. Ḥurūf 9.—86. Alex. Taṣ. 10.—94. Ibid. $33_{,1}$.—108. Ibid. Fun. $151_{,17}$. 112. Ibid. Taṣ. 34,3 (?).—113. Ibid. Fun. $151_{,14}$.

799. 122b. *al-Ṣalāt al-Fayḍiyya*, Qaw. I, 249.—124. Alex. Taṣ. 15, 42,2, Fun. 151,4.—126. Ibid. Ḥurūf 5. Comment. a. Garr. 2103,2, Alex. Ḥurūf 8.—b. Garr. 2103,3, Alex. Ḥurūf 5.—e. Garr. 2103,1, *Zuhūr al-bustān* in Alex. Ḥurūf 4.—f. *al-Dāʾira al-kubrā* by Muṣṭafā Efendi b. Suhrāb, ibid. 12.—130. Berl. 8365/8 (*Musāmarāt al-a. wa-muḥ.*).—126a. See ad II, 173, $1039_{,19}$.—131. BDMG 109 with comm.

800. 132, Garr. 54/5.

801. Lines 13—25 before line 1. 173. Garr. 947.

802. 216. Köpr. II, 163.—218. *al-Durr al-aʿlā*, Qaw. I, 234.—219. ʿAlawān b. ʿAlī b. ʿAṭiyya al-Ḥamawī, *Kashf al-kāʾināt fī qawl Muḥyi ʾl-Dīn "kunnā ḥurūfan ʿāliyāt"*,

a *manẓūma* on verses by Muḥammd al-Sīlīnī al-Maghribī, Makr. 52.—220. *al-Zahr al-fā'iḥ fī satr al-ʿuyūb wal-qabā'iḥ*, Alex. Mawāʿiẓ 21.—221. *al-Dhakhā'ir wal-iʿlān*, Fez Qar. 1446,1.—222. *Muẓhirāt ʿarā'is al-mukhabba'āt bil-lisān al-ʿArabī*, with a comm. by Aḥmad al-Jauwharī al-Khālidī d. 1187/1773, Garr. 847.—223. *Risāla fī taḥqīq wujūb al-wājib li-dhātihi*, Alex. Fun. 149,$_{6}$.—224. *Risāla fi 'l-ṭarīq*, ibid. 15.—225. *Risāla fī sirr al-ḥurūf*, ibid. 16 (= 180 ?).—226. *Naghamāt al-aflāk* or *al-Sirr al-maktūm*, ibid. 19.—227. *Mawlid al-nabī*, Alex. Ta'r. 16.—228.
1235 *Risāla fi 'l-taṣawwuf*, Alex. Taṣ. 17.—229. | *al-Durar*, ibid. 33,2.—230. *Risālat jawāb li-baʿḍ ikhwānihi*, ibid.. 3.—231. An answer to two questions by al-Ḥakīm al-Tirmidhī, ibid. 7.—A defense against *al-Radd al-matīn ʿani 'l-shaykh Muḥyi 'l-Dīn* by Ibrāhīm al-Madanī, written in 1093/1682, Alex. Tāṣ. 42,$_{4}$.

25c. Ismāʿīl al-Tinnīsī, a student of Ibn ʿArabī, *Tuḥfat al-tadbīr li-ahl al-tabṣīr* Alex. Kīm. 10.

804. 29. Instead of Aḥmad, read: ʿAlī (*EI* IV, 246/7). Read: Ghumāra instead of Ghamāra, and Zaghwān instead of Zafrān (Colin).—a. Garr. 719.—b. Read: Ẓafir, see II, 1009.

805. 5. Comm. a. Alex. Fun. 172,$_{3}$. h. Garr. 1946 (*Kawkab al-fajr*).—6. Comm. c. Alex. Faw. 20.—d. *Fatḥ al-qadīr* by al-Ḥasan b. ʿAlī al-Manṭawī (to be read thus), additionally Heid. *ZDMG* 91, 387, Alex. Faw. 13.—8. Qaw. I, 229.

806. 29, 29. *al-Risāla al-Ḥawḍiyya*, with a commentary by ʿAbdallāh b. Ḥusayn al-Ḥasanī al-Sharīf, Alex. Tawḥīd 28.—30. *al-Takallī wal-tabaṣṣur ʿalā mā qaḍāhu 'llāh min aḥkām ahl al-tajabbur wal-takabbur*, Alex. Mawāʿiẓ 38,$_{1}$.—31. *Duʿā'*, Ind. Off. 4576, *JRAS* 1939, 307.

31. Biography by al-Khazrajī (ed. Muḥammad Asʿad), cf. I, 160/2.—1. MS in collection Kračkovsky, more detailed than the others.—5. Vat. V. 1184,$_{1}$.—6. *Kitāb al-tawḥīd*, Garr. 1897.

807. 31, b. Badīʿ al-Zamān Furūzān, *Mawlānā Jalāl al-Dīn*, Tehran 1316/1936.—*Mevlanin mektublari*, ed. M. T. Nafiz Uzluk, with Turkish transl. by A.R. Akyürük, Istanbul 1356/1937 (Anadolu Selcüklerin gününde Mevlevi bitikleri II).

31d. Abū Muḥammad ʿAbdallāh b. Muḥammad al ʿArshī al-Marjānī, a *faqīh* and Sufi, went to Egypt where he became famous for his preaching. When in Tunis, he became involved in a dispute with the *fuqahā'* there, resulting in his being sentenced to death for unbelief in 609/1272; al-Shaʿrānī, *al-Ṭabaqāt al-kubrā* I, 172. *Al-Futūḥāt al-rabbāniyya fi 'l-mawālīd al-Marjāniyya*, ḤKh IV, 380$_{,8903}$, Dam. Z. 59$_{,124,2}$.

31. e. Muḥammad b. Bahā' al-Dīn, d. 672/1273, *Sharḥ asmā' Allāh al-ḥusnā*, Alex. Faw. 10.

32. 1. Alex. Taṣawwuf 33$_{,5}$, Qaw. I, 38.—6. Qaw. I, 268.—9. Alex. Taṣ. 46.

808. 23. *Kashf asrār jawāhir al-ḥikam al-mustakhraja al-mūratha min jawāmiʿ al-kalim*, Qaw. I, 144.—29. *Risāla Jafriyya*, Alex. Ḥurūf 10.

33. 1. Aḥmad b. ʿAlī, *Bayān aḥkām al-farā'iḍ fī ʿilm al-mīrāth*, Garr. 1871 (Princ. 278, only Aḥmad al-Badawī).

34. 1. MS Kračkovsky, Alex. Adab 114, Mawāʿiẓ 32.—1. *al-Asad wal-ghawwāṣ* additionally Bank. XXIII 144$_{,2636}$.

809. 34, 3. Print. titled *al-Qawl al-nafīs fī taflīs Iblīs*, additionally C. 1874.

810. 38, 1. Read:"*al-Qaṣīda al-dāliyya.*

811. 39, 1. Ind. Off. 1731.—8. Alex. Faw. 28.—17. Garr. 1575.—26. *Majlis fi 'stiqbāl shahr Ramaḍān*, Alex. Fun. 147$_{,14}$.—27. *Muthallathāt lughawiyya*, Berl. 7081/2, Garr. 272, Alex. Lugha 25.

40. 4. Alex. Fun. 90$_{,14}$, 151$_{,12}$.—5. Read: al-Bānī.—11. *Risāla fi 'l-taṣawwuf*, Alex. Fun. 150,8.

812. 40d. Ṣadr al-Milla wal-Dīn Abu 'l-Maʿālī al-Muẓaffar b. Muḥammad al-Muẓaffar al-Bāghanawī al-Shīrāzī, *al-Marmūzāt al-ʿishrūn*, MS dated 714 AH, Alex. Mawāʿiẓ 43.

| 813. Būlus Musʿid, *Ibn Sīnā faylasūf*, Beirut 1937.—Shalībā Jamil, *Ibn Sīnā. Dars,* 1236
taḥlīl, muntakhabāt, Damascus 1937.—A.M. Goichon, *La distinction de l'essence et de l'existence d'après Ibn Sīnā*, Paris 1938.—Idem, *Lexique de la langue philosophique d'Ibn Sīnā*, ibid. 1938.—*Majmūʿ rasā'il al-Shaykh al-Ra'īs*, Hyderabad 1354/1925 (*Risāla fi 'l-fiʿl wal-infiʿāl, Risāla fī sirr al-qadar, Risāla fi 'l-saʿāda, fī dhikr asbāb al-raʿd, al-Risāla al-ʿarshiyya, fi 'l-tawḥīd, Risāla fi 'l-ḥathth ʿala 'l-dhikr, Risāla fi 'l-mūsīqī*).—3. Mosul 75$_{,88,7}$, with 4, 5, Mashh. II, 31$_{,104}$.—5a. Mosul 183$_{,16,2}$.

814. 9b. In Ergin no. 62 with the title of 9a and without MS AS.—9e. Spurious (in the index of Ergin, Ṣadr al-Dīn al-Qūnawī is mentioned as the author).—13. MSS in Najaf and Tehran, *Dharīʿa* II, $48,_{195}$.—14b = 63.

815. 17. Taymūr, Ḥikma 102.—18. Mosul $189,_{16}$.—b. Garr. 861.—*Fann-i samāʿ-i ṭabīʿī az Kitāb al-shifāʾ* transl. Muḥammad ʿAlī Furūghī, Tehran 1316/1937. Abstract: a. *al-Najāh* ed. Muḥyi ʾl-Dīn Ṣabrī al-Kurdī, Cairo, Maṭbaʿat al-Saʿāda 1939.

816. 20. Sarāi A III, $3248,_{1}$ (Ritter, *Isl.* 24, 265nl), Qaw. II, 380.—*Ḥall mushkilāt al-Ishārāt*, Garr. 806.

817. 20h. Abstract in a *majmūʿa*, al-Khizāna al-Gharawiyya, *Dharīʿa* II, $97,_{382}$.—n. *Sharḥ masāʾil ʿawīṣa fī ʾl-Ishārāt* by Zayn al-Dīn Ṣadaqa, Carullah 1503.—21. Zanjān, *Lughat al-ʿArab* VI, 94.—21. b. *Taʿlīqāt ʿalā Uthūlūjiyya*, Taymūr, Ḥikma 102.—23. a. *al-Mūjiz*, Ergin 195, omits AS 4849, f. 88/109a (Krause).—23. b. Ergin 176 = 68rrr.—24. Alex. Fun. $100,_{8}$.—25. 1. *Lughat al-ʿArab* VI, 94.—27a. In *Tisʿ rasāʾil*, C. 1326, p. 158ff, adaptation of a translation of Ḥunayn by Isḥāq.

818. 29. Univ. Egypt. 1176.—32c. Faiẓ. $2144,_{1}$.—35. Comm. h. Wehbī 1340.—q. Shams al-Dīn al-Samarqandī, Heid. ZDMG 91, 389, A $336,_{90}$ = Berl. 5353 by Abu ʾl-Baqāʾ al-Aḥmadī.

819. 38. Qaw. II, 385.—42. *Risālat al-maʿād*, Taymūr, Ḥikma 10,5.—42 b. Zanjān, *Lughat al-ʿArab* VI, 93.—45. AS $4849,_{25}$ (134b/5a).—54. C. 1352.

820. 58. Mashh. II, $31,_{105}$.—63 = 14b.—68c. Taymūr, Ḥikma 10,2.—68g = (?) *Risāla fī khaṭaʾ man qāla inna shayʾan wāḥidan jawhar wa-ʿaraḍ maʿan*, Zanjān, *Lughat al-ʿArab* VI, 93.

821. 68g. In *Majmūʿa*, Hyderabad 1354, no. 6.—68nn. Mosul $180_{159,2}$.

822. 68ccc. (a letter of Abū Saʿīd to Ibn Sīnā, Alex. Fun. $126,_{11}$).—68zzz. *Risāla fī ʾl-khuṭab wal-jumaʿāt*, *Lughat al-ʿArab* VI, 93.—68aaaa. *Risāla fī īḍāḥ barāhīn thalāth masāʾil*, ibid.—68bbbb. (= 10?) *Ithbāt al-nubuwwa wa-taʾwīl mā fī kalimāt al-anbiyāʾ min al-rumūz*, in a *majmūʿa* in the library of Hādī Āl Kāshif al-Ghiṭāʾ, *Dharīʿa* I, $100,_{492}$.—68cccc. (= 14?) *Risāla fī ʾl-ziyāra*, Taymūr, Ḥikma 10,2.—71. = 72. (Krause).—74. AS 2739, $4853,_{4}$, print. in *Jāmiʿ al-badāʾiʿ*,

C. 1355/1917, p. 119/51.—79i. = k. = Ergin 92.—79m. Bank. XXII, 136,$_{2499}$, BII, *Epistula ad regem Hasan de re recta*, see Ruska, *Isis* XXI, 1, (1934) 14, n. 5.—79o. Read: "Rāmpūr II, 687,$_{27}$".—79r. *Mukhtaṣar Uqlīdis*, Fātiḥ 3211, Erg. 165.—79s. *Mukhtaṣar Kitāb al-arithmāṭīqī*, Emīr 2850, Ergin 116.—80. Mosul 273,$_{63,1}$.—81. Leningrad, As. Mus. (Kr.).—Comm. c. = Sharaf al-Dīn Mūsā b. Ibrāhīm al-Mutaṭabbib, the author of *al-Nukat al-wafiyyāt fī aḥkām al-ḥummayāt*, Garr. 1115,31, additionally Alex. Ṭibb 15.

824. Line 6. Read: Mashh. XVI, 30, 86/90. M. Meyerhof, D. Joannides, *La* | *gyné-* 1237
cologie et obstétrique chez Avicenne et leurs rapports avec celles des Grecs, Cairo 1938.—Comm. b. Mosul 217,$_{99}$.—d. *Sharḥ muqaddimat al-Qānūn*, *RAAD* XII, 320.

825. Line 1. Read: "23,$_{70}$".—Abstracts: a. Garr. 1084/6, Alex. Ṭibb 49, Qaw. II, 290, Mosul 192,$_{22}$, 237,$_{78}$.—Comm.: aa. Garr. 1087, Alex. Ṭibb 46.—dd. Garr. 1089/90, Mosul 270,$_{24}$.—ee. Garr. 1088, Alex. Ṭibb 15.—gg. al-Amshāṭī, d. 902/1496, II, 169.

826. b, Alex. Ṭibb 34.—c. *al-Asbāb wal-ʿalāmāt*, Alex. Ṭibb 4.—γ *al-Īmāqī* by Kamāl al-Dīn ʿAlī b. Muḥammad b. Ibrāhīm b. Muḥammad b. Yūsufbal-ʿAtāʾiqī al-Ḥillī, composed in 754/5, in *al-Khizāna al-Gharawiyya*, *Dharīʿa* II, 509,$_{2000}$.

827. 83. Ünver A. Süheyl, *Hindibā risalesi Buharali b. S.* (Istanbul Ün. Tib Tar. Enst. 7) 1937, see 95r.—86. MSS in various private collections, *Dharīʿa* I, 403,2099. Beginning printed in *al-ʿIrfān*, Sidon, Rabīʿ I 1345. *Maqāla fi ʾl-adwiya al-qalbiyya*, Qaw. II, 290.—92. *Urjūza fi ʾl-mujarrabāt min al-aḥkām al-nujūmiyya wal-qawāʿid al-ṭibbiyya*, in the library of Niʿmat al-Ṭarīḥī, *Dharīʿa* I, 495,$_{2438}$.—95c. In Ergin, read: AS 4853,$_{10}$ (Krause).—95r. = 83 (Kāshānī = *Hindibāʾ*, Krause).

828. V, 108. *Khulāṣat al-taʿbīr*, Garr. 930.—109. *Risāla fi ʾl-ruʾyā wal-infiʿālāt wal-afʿāl*, Taymūr, Ḥikma 37 = (?) *al-Afʿāl-wal-infiʿālāt fi ʾl-muʿjiza wal-siḥr wal-nayranjāt* in a *majmūʿa* of his *rasāʾil* in Mashhad, *Dharīʿa* II, 260,$_{1056}$.

829. 4. *al-Kāfī fi ʾl-mūsīqī*, Br. Mus. Or. 236, f. 220/36r; see Farmer, *Sources* 42, and see II, 1036,6.

830. 8, 1. M. Asín Palacios, Avenpace botanico, *Andalus* V, 255/99 (based on a treatise in Berl. 5060, Bodl. Poc. 206, p. 266/78, *Hādhā kalām al-Wazīr Abī Bakr fi ʾl-nabāt*, 279/99), on the *Kitāb al-nafs* see Farmer, *Sources* 44.—3. *Min al-maqāla al-ūlā min Tadbīr al-mutawaḥḥid*, Taymūr, Akhlāq 290; *Die Abh. des a. Bekr b.*

al-Ṣāʾigh vom Verhalten des Einsiedlers, T. al-m., nach Mōšē Narb.'s Auszug hsg. v. D. Herzog, Beitr. z. Philos. des MAs, Heft I, Berlin 1896, E. Rosenthal, Politische Gedanken bei I. B., *MGWJ*, 1937, 153/68, 185/6.

8a. al-Qazwīnī, *Kosm.* 259.—1. Read: al-Naṣīriyya.

831. 9. S. Pines, Études sur Awḥad al-zamān Abu 'l-Barakāt al-Baghdādī, in *REJ*, N.S. IV (CIV), 194ff.

10a. Abu 'l-ʿAbbās al-Faḍl b. Muḥammad al-Lawkarī, a contemporary of ʿUmar al-Khayyām, *Tatimmat Ṣiwān al-ḥikma* 120, 204. *Bayān al-ḥaqq wa-zamān al-ṣidq*, natural philosophy in 5 capita following Aristotle's *Physics*, based on the commentary by Ibn Sīnā, Paris 5900.

11. 1. Mistakenly attributed to Ibn Sīnā in Taymūr, Ḥikma 19.—2. With the title *Mirqāt al-zulfā wal-mashrab al-aṣfā*, Taymūr, Taṣawwuf 149, f. 323/400.

832. Line 11. On García Gómez see Kračkovsky, *Literis* IV (1927), 28/33.

12. al-Mubashshir, 13. Line 4, read: "1193".—1. Istanbul Un. H, 4196, *ZS* III, 253, C. 1326.—2. Br. Mus. 9221, 9588, Top Kapu 2479 (*RSO* IV, 727, which has al-Ḥarrānī), see Gaudefroy Demombynes, *JA* 230, 453.

833. 13. 3. Alex. Ṭibb 7, $41_{,1}$.

834. Goffredo Quadri, *La filosofia degl Arabi nel suo fiore*, II, *Il pensiero filosofico di Averroe*, Florence 1939.—L. Strauss, *Philosophie und Gesetz*, Berlin 1935, 69ff.

1238 835. B. Fr. Rosenthal, A.'s Middle Cmt. on Aristoteles' *Analytica* | *Priora et Posteriora*, *Bull. John Rylands Libr. Manchester* 21 (1937), 479/83 (on Mingana 374).—6. Photograph: *Quitab el Culiat*, Publicaciones del Inst. General Franco, sect. 1a. Mss. árabes, Larache 1939.

836. Line 6. *Mā baʿd al-ṭabīʿa min talkhīṣāt b. Rushd*, Taymūr, Ḥikma 117, 3.—Line 10. Read: 1919.—8. *Averroes Tafsīr ma baʿd al-ṭabīʿa*, ed. M. Bouyges, Bibl. Ar. Schol. V, 1, 2, Beirut 1938.—18. MS dated 539 AH, so not Ibn Rushd (Krause).—21. *Kashf ʿan manāhij al-adilla*, Taymūr, Ḥikma 129.

837. 17. Comm. 2. Qaw. I, 241/2, Istanbul 1273, 1289, 1306, 1319 (with 6 in the margin).—8. Qaw. I, 244 (which has al-Faqī).

838. 21. I, 1. Comm. 1. Read: al-ʿAjīsī, II 240 [*sic*, but see Suppl. 2, 357, 3c].—5. *Hesp.* XVIII 94, 18e.—*Naẓm al-Jumal* by Muḥammad b. ʿAbd al-Jabbār (?), ibid. 94, 18d.

839. 22, 7. Read: *manāqib āl al-rasūl.*

23. I. Qaw. II, 388.

840. 3. Garr. 830. Glosses by ʿAbd al-Wahhāb al-Astarābādī, see ad II, 258$_{,6a}$.—5. Ibid. 829, 2155$_{,1}$ Ambr. B. 77$_{,i}$, 82 (RSO IV, 103c, 35), Qaw. I, 386/7.—Glosses: a. Alex. Fals. 7.—c. Garr. 2130/1, Qaw. II, 383/4, Supergl. by al-Kaffawī ibid. 382/3.—f. Read: *Ghāyat al-hidāya*, and al-ʿAlamī.—7. Alex. Fals. 15, Aligarh 78$_{,5}$, 79$_{,3}$, 8/51.

841. λ on the *qism ṭabīʿī* and *ilāhī* by Aḥmadzāde b. Maḥmūd al-Khirziyānī (Harawī), Alex. Fals. 15, Qaw. II, 387 (9. Subḥānallāh 78$_{,5}$). II Hamb. Or. Sem. 105, 1, Alex. Manṭiq 23$_{,2}$, Fun. 120$_{,4}$, 129$_{,5}$, 142$_{,3}$, 187$_{,2}$, Qaw. II, 317/21, *Hesp.* XVIII, 1934, 90, 8h.—Comm.: 1. Ambr. A. 88 (RSO III, 591), Alex. Manṭiq 15, 22/3, 25$_{,4}$, 28$_{,4}$, Fun. 172$_{,2}$, 187$_{,4}$.—Garr. 807, 2081$_{,3}$, 2141$_{,1}$, 2152$_{,1}$, 2156,1.—Glosses: a. Garr. 808, Alex. Manṭiq 7, 29$_{,2}$, Qaw. II, 331.

842. d. Garr. 2081$_{,4}$, 2152$_{,2}$, Alex. Manṭiq 11, 28$_{,5}$, Qaw. II, 330/1.—g. Alex. Manṭiq 15 (classified as a commentary).—l. Read: Ibn Yūsuf.—p. Alex. Manṭiq 15.—s. al-Shirwānī, ibid.—t. Yaḥyā al-Ruhawī al-Ḥanafī, ibid. Fun. 96$_{,1}$.—2. Alex. Manṭiq 18, 24, 28$_{,1}$, Fun. 177$_{,2}$.—Glosses a. Alex. Manṭiq 11, 24$_{,2}$, 28$_{,2}$, 31, Qaw. II, 344/8.—Supergl. β Qara Khalīl al-Tīrawī, 12th cent., Istanbul 1242, 1275, 1307 (Qaw. II, 328).—γ al-Ḥāfiẓ b. ʿAlī al-ʿImādī, Qaw. II, 342.—d. Garr. 813, 2149, 2, Alex. Manṭiq 24, 31$_{,2}$, Qaw. II, 379.—g. Aḥmad b. ʿAbdallāh Shawqī, completed in 1093/1682, Istanbul 1302, Qaw. II, 338.—h. Abū Muḥammad ʿAbdallāh b. Ḥasan al-Kāngārī al-Anṣārī al-Uskudārī, Istanbul 1279, Qaw. II, 348.—i. Maḥmūd Efendi Amīn Shahrī, Qaw. II, 349.—k. Muḥammad al-Fawzī b. al-Ḥājj Aḥmad Yārān Kamawī Adranawī (see 843, 11a), *Khulāṣat al-mīzān*, Istanbul 1288, 1301.—5. Hamb. Or. Sem. 105$_{,2}$, 119, Garr. 817, *Hesp.* XVIII, 92, 11e, Alex. Manṭiq 20$_{,5}$, 22$_{,2}$, 25$_{,1,5}$, 32$_{,5}$, Fun. 87$_{,2}$.

843. Glosses, instead of a., read: d., Alex. Manṭiq 8.—g. *Kashf al-lithām* by Muḥammad b. ʿAbdallāh al-Kharashī, d. 1101/1689, additionally Alex. Manṭiq 8.—Muḥammad al-Bahūtī, ibid. 19.—h. Aḥmad b. Muḥammad b. ʿAlī al- Ghunaymī al-Anṣārī, d. 1044/1634, Qaw. II, 342.—i. Muḥammad b. Ibrāhīm al-Dalajī, Alex. Manṭiq 22, 1, Makr. 19.—k. ʿAlī b. Khiḍr b. Aḥmad al-ʿUmrūsī al-Mālikī, Makr. 24.—

11. Garr. 825/6. Glosses by ʿUthmān b. Nuʿmān al-Anjustawī, ca. 1279/1862, Qaw. II, 329.—16. Qaw. II, 355/7; glosses on the *Dībāja* by Ibrāhīm b. al-Yalwajī, Qaw. II, 352/3.—24. Read: Zākhir, and Suwayr.—28. *Tuḥfat al-Rushdī*, Istanbul 1279, Qaw. II, 326.—32. Nūr al-Dīn ʿAlī al-Ujhūrī, d. 1066/1656, Alex. Manṭiq
1239 15.—33. *Dharīʿat al-imtiḥān* | by Aḥmad al-Ṣidqī b. ʿAlī Burūsawī, Istanbul 1300 (Qaw. II, 357).—34. Ismāʿīl b. Muṣṭafā Maḥmūd al-Kalanbawī, Qaw. II, 360.—35. ʿAlī b. Ḥusayn al-Ḥanafī, Istanbul 1310 (Qaw. II, 361).—36. *Mīr Īsāghūjī*, comm. by Muḥammad Faḍl al-Ḥaqq al-Rāmghūrī, Ind. 1309 (in ed. C. 1321 attributed to al-Jurjānī).—VI. Heid. TA 385, *ZDMG* 91, 395.

844. 24. Read: "Ibn Dāra" (Colin).—On his suicide out of his desire to become one with God, see Massignon, *Eranos-Jahrb.* 1937, 37.—8. *Risāla fī asrār al-kawākib wal-daraj wal-burūj wa-khawāṣṣihā*, Alex. Ḥurūf 12.—9. *al-Maqālīd al-wujūdiyya*, ibid. Ḥikma 27.—10. *Adwār al-mansūb*, library of Taymūr, Farmer, *Sources* 47.—11. *ʿAwāṣim al-qawāṣim*, A. Taymūr, Taṣawwuf 318.—12. *al-Yad*, ibid. Ḥurūf 221.—13. *Kitāb al-naṣīḥa wa-hiya al-Risāla al-nūriyya*.—14. *Kitāb al-alwāḥ*.—15. *al-Risāla al-faqīriyya*.—16. *al-Risāla al-riḍwāniyya* .—17. *Kitāb al-qawsayn* .—18. *Kitāb al-iḥāṭa*.—19. *Kitāb al-daraj* and other treatises, most of them without a title, see *Orientalia* VIII, 286.

845. 25b. Abu 'l-Ḥasan b. Abī Dharr wrote, after Bar Hebraeus and mainly as a reflection of his philosophy, the *Kitāb al-saʿāda wal-isʿād*; see Muḥammad Kurd ʿAli, *RAAD* IX, 553/73.

26. I. Alex. Fun. 142, 4, Qaw. II, 367/8.—Comm.: 1. Garr. $2157_{,2}$, Alex. Fun. $148_{,2}$, Makr. 9.—Glosses: a. Alex. Manṭiq $29_{,3}$, Fun. 1201, Qaw. II, 335.—Supergl. α Alex. Manṭiq 10, Qaw. II, 343.—β Qaw. II, 334/5.

846. δ Qaw. II, 341/2.—ε Rāġib $1478_{,11}$, Qaw. II, 339.—ν Qaw. II, 339, Supergl. by Muḥammad b. Ḥasan Kharpūtī Dallālzāde, Istanbul 1275, ibid. II, 332.—aa. On the *Qism al-taṣdīqāt* by Khalīl b. Muḥammad al-Riḍawī, completed in 759/1358, ibid. II, 333.—n. *Taqrīr ʿalā dībājat T. al-q.* by Shukrī b. Ṭāhir al-Brshtnawī, Istanbul 1310 (Qaw. II, 327).—3. Qaw. II, 365.—4. Ḥusayn b. Muʿīn al-Dīn al Maybudī, d. ca. 890/1485, Garr. 844, Qaw. II, 365.

847. 17. Mīrzājān, d. 994/1586, Garr. $2065_{,1}$, 2137,2.—25. Muḥammad Nūrī al-Ṣūfiyawī, ca. 1295/1878, Qaw. II, 364.—26. Muṣṭafā b. Yūsuf al-Fāshilī al-Mūstārī, ca. 1101/1689, ibid. 365.—27. *Mīzān al-intiẓām* by Aḥmad al-Ṣidqī al-Burūsawī, Istanbul 1303, 1327, 1337 (with 4 in the margin), Qaw. II, 377/8.—On *Mīzān*

al-manṭiq see II, 625.—II. Taymūr, Ḥikma 97, Un. Eg. 11654, 11788.—Comm.: 1a Garr. 2065$_{,2}$, 2137$_{,1}$, Qaw. II, 386.

848. II, 3. *Īḍāḥ al-maqāṣid min ḥikmat ʿayn al-qawāʿid* by Āyatallāh al-ʿAllāma al-Ḥillī (II, 208, 29) additionally Hālet, Baghdad, al-Maktaba al-Mīrghaniyya, *Dharīʿa* II, 501$_{,1961}$.—X. *Baḥth al-fawāʾid, Br. Mus. Quart.* X, 133.

27, I. 2. Garr. 848, Alex. Manṭiq 23$_{,2}$, Qaw. II, 373/6.—Glosses: a. *Tanwīr al-maṭāliʿ wa-tabṣīr al-maṭāliʿ* or *al-Ḥāshiya al-jadīda*, Garr. 847, Alex. Manṭiq 8, Qaw. II, 338.—Supergl. α Qaw. II. 350.—β Rāġib 1478,9.—δ Qaw. II, 352.

849. 27, ο Qāḍīzāde al-Rūmī, Qaw. II, 343, 358.—π ʿAlī al-Astarābādī, ibid. II, 329.—ρ Ḥusayn al-Muḥtasib, ibid. II, 351.—σ v. Dāʾūd al-Shirwānī, Alex. Manṭiq 23.—5. See 2a. additionally Teh. II, 116.—*Mukhtaṣar al-Yāniyawī* II, 666, 5.—VI. *Laṭāʾif al-ḥikma* Mashh. I, 71$_{,230}$.

29. I. Garr. 868, 2118$_{,3}$, Alex. Fun. 127$_{,5}$, Rāmpūr I, 675$_{,12}$.—Comm. 2. Heid. *ZDMG* 91, 385, 319, Garr. 869, 2112, Alex. Ādāb al-b. 7,3, 8,3, 10,1, Qaw. II, 306/7.—Gl. a. Heid. *ZDMG* 91, 385$_{,319,2}$, Alex. Ādāb 10$_{,2}$.—β Garr. 2139,1, Qaw. | II, 296.— 1240
b. Qaw. II, 297.—c. Garr. 2139$_{,2}$, Qaw. II, 297.—f. Alex. Ādāb al-b. 7$_{,2}$, 8, 9$_{,2}$, Qaw. II, 299.—Supergl. α ibid. 6$_{,1}$, Fun. 148$_{,1}$, Qaw. II, 297.

850. I, 2, i. Muḥammad b. al-Ḥājj Ḥāmid al-Kaffawī, Qaw. II, 300.—k. Ḥāmid b. Burhān b. Abī Dharr al-Ghifārī (see ad p. 518), Qaw. II, 296.—l. ʿAbd al-Raḥīm Shāh Shirwānī, Qaw. II, 298.—m. Qara Khalīl b. Ḥasan Tīrawī, ibid.—4. Qaw. II, 314.—8. Alex. Ādāb al-b. 6, 8$_{,1}$.—Glosses by Aḥmad b. Yūnus al-Khalīfi al-Shāfiʿī (d. 1209/1794), ibid. 3; al-Kīlānī, ibid. 5.—10. Instead of Khayr, read: Ḥusayn, Garr. 2147$_{,1}$.—11. Ulugh Beg Muḥammad b. Shāh Rukh, d. 853/1449 (II, 289), Alex. Ādāb al-b. 9.—II. With comm. Alex. Manṭiq 16.—III. Fātiḥ 3385$_{,2}$, 5330, Rāġib 919$_{,4}$, Asʿad 3797$_{,3}$, Yeni 1176$_{,17}$, *Hesp.* XVIII, 91$_{,91}$.—Comm. a. Garr. 1058/9, 2159, Alex. Ḥisāb 30, Fun. 106$_{,3}$, *Hesp.* XVIII, 91$_{,9}$, 93$_{,13a}$. Glosses: γ Garr. 1060, Cairo 1 V, 195.—8. Muḥammad b. Ḥusayn al-ʿAṭṭār (II, 158,9), Bank. XXII, 107$_{,2477}$, II.—IV. Alex. Fals. 16 (*Ṣaḥāʾif fī ʾl-kalām*).—Comm. Garr. 1485.—VI. = (?) *Risāla fī kalimat al-tawḥīd*, Alex. Fun. 88$_{,39}$. *Bayān madhhab ahl al-sunna*, Garr. 1558.—VII. Read: 3586,1.

851. 30, 1. Ind. Off. 4613, *JRAS* 1939, 383, Asʿad 3804$_{,5}$ (ca. 665 AH, Krause).—*Mukhtaṣar Rawḍat al-afrāḥ*, Istanbul ʿUm. 5573 (*ZS* III, 243).—36. Muḥammad b. Sālim b. Wāṣil Jamāl al-Dīn al-Ḥamawī, ca. 697/1297, teacher of Abu ʾl-Fidāʾ

(see 838. 21. I, 1a., *Annales* V, 144ff), *Tajrīd al-aghānī min al-mathālith wal-mathānī*, Br. Mus. 571, AS 1400, Farmer, *Sources* 49.

852. 2. Additionally Berl. Oct. 2970,$_{13}$.—7. Alex. Ḥisāb 42.—19. Berl. 2970,$_{11}$.—22. Ibid. Oct. 2970.—24. Ibid. 16.

853. 25. Ibid. 6.—30. Berl. Oct. 3548,1.—32. Ibid. 15.—33. Ibid. 7.—33b. Ibid. 8.—34. Rāmpūr I, 412,$_{20}$, see Hirschberg, *Die ar. Lehrb. der Augenheilkunde* 111. *Tanqīḥ al-manāẓir*, Bank. XXII, 47,$_{2455}$.—38. Bank. XXII, 84,$_{2648}$ XXXIII.—39. Berl. Oct. 2970,$_{17}$.—41. Ibid. 10.

854. 44. Berl. Oct. 2970,$_{9}$.—45. Ibid. 5.—46. Ibid. 4.—51. *Maqāla fī kayfiyyat al-taraṣṣud*, Alex. Ḥisāb 42.—52. *Maqāla fī māʾiyyat al-athar alladhī fī wajh al-qamar*, ibid.—53. *Maqāla fi ʾl-tanbīh ʿalā mawāḍiʿ al-ghalaṭ fī kayfiyyat al-raṣad*, ibid. 61.

1b. See ad 400.

2. C. Schoy, *Isis* 1925, 5/8.—Read: *min jihat aḍlāʿihi.*

855. Ghulam Ḥusayn Muṣāḥib, *Jabr umuqābala i Khayyām*, Tehran 1317/1938.—2. Anon. Paris 4946,$_{4}$.—4. Berl. 2362, 2570.

857. 4c, 12. Two geometrical problems, Leid. 1006.

4d. With the title *Kitāb al-ḥisāb fi ʾl-jabr wal-muqābala*, Garr. 1045.

858. I, 4a. Alex. Ḥisāb 24, Fun. 128,$_{2}$.—Glosses: Alex. Ḥisāb 23 (which has Muḥammad al-Ḥanafī, *Fawāʾid ʿawāʾid jabriyya*), Makram 17.—9. Alex. Ḥisāb 22, Bank. XXXII, 22,$_{2427}$, Berl. 5964.—III. *Tanqīḥ al-afkār fi ʾl-ʿilm bi-rusūm al-ghubār*, Alex. Ḥisāb 6.

859, 9aa. Abū Ḥāmid Aḥmad b. Muḥammad b. Abī Ṭālib al-Malaṭī al-Khāṭirī wrote, before 609/1212, *Bayān al-ḥikma*, geometry after Euclid, Ptolemy, and Archimedes, Garr. 1057, see II, 1019.

860. 9e. Bank. XXII, 1,$_{2413}$, where the date of composition of the work is placed at 505 AH, but on a very weak basis. It was written after his *ʿUmdat al-rāʾiḍ* and *al-Ḥāwī.*

9f. Abu ʾl-Majd | b. ʿAṭiyya b. al-Majd al-Kātib, before 639/1241 (date of the MS), 1241
on multiplication, division etc., Br. Mus. 426,$_{21}$ (Suter 498).

10. 5. *al-Tuffāḥa fī aʿmāl al-misāḥa,* Rabat 507,$_{23}$ print. in *Majmūʿa* C. 1310 (Qaw. II, 266).

12a. Shams al-Dīn Muḥammad b. Rabīʿ al-Zarkashī al-Muhandis, *Kulliyyāt al-ḥisāb,* MS dated 677 AH with an *ijāza* by the author dated 684, Alex. Ḥisāb 4.

861. 2, 2. Bank. XXII, 74, xxl.—3. Bank. XXII, 67,$_{2468}$, x.—4. Read: *al-Taqsīm fī zīj Ḥabash al-Ḥāsib* (p. 393), Bank. XXII, 66, $_{2468}$, viii.—5. Ibid. 67, ix,—7. Read: *fī dawāʾir al-sumūt fi ʾl-asṭurlāb,* ibid. 69, xii.—9. Ibid. 70, xiv.—10. Ibid. 70, xiv.—11. Ibid. 71, xvi.—12. Ibid. 72, xvii.—13. Ibid. 72, xviii.—14. Ibid. 71, xix.—15. Instead of *huwa,* read: *mawwahahu,* ibid. 73, xx.—16. Ibid. 74, xxii.—16a. *al-Risāla fī ṣanʿat al-asṭurlāb bil-ṭarīq al-ṣināʿī* for Abī ʿAbdallāh Muḥammad b. ʿAlī al-Maʾmūnī, ibid. 69, xiii.

862. 2a. Ibn al-Qifṭī, 181.

2b. cf. 887. 7a.

2c. Abu ʾl-Ḥasan ʿAlī b. Muḥammad b. Bāmshād al-Qāʾinī, a contemporary of al-Bīrūnī, wrote: 1. *al-Maqāla fi ʾstikhrāj sāʿāt mā bayna ṭulūʿ al-fajr wal-shams kullu yawm min ayyām al-sana li-madīnat Qāʾin,* Bank. XXII, 75,$_{2463}$, xxiii.—2. *al-Maqāla fi ʾstikhrāj taʾrīkh al-Yahūd,* ibid. 76, xxv.—3. On the name see Renaud, *Hesp.* 1937, 1, n. 6.—See Archeion, *Archivo di storia della scienzia* XIV, 1932, 392/412.—Don Profeit Tibbon, *Tractat de l'Assafea d'Azarquiel* (Bibl. hebraica-catalana IV), Barcelona 1933.—3a. Under Nāṣir al-Dawla lived his brother Abū Saʿd al-Faḍl b. Jarīr, Cat. Beirut 1924, 76, no. 268.

863. 3a. Cheikho, Cat. 75/6, 267, Graf, *Christl.-Arab. Literatur* 51/2, *Theol. Quartalschrift* 95 (1913), 183.

864. 4b. According to Suter, 496 it was originally in Persian, AS 2602,3.

4bb. Abu ʾl-Qāsim ʿAlī b. Yūsuf al-Balkhī wrote, under the *atabeg* of Mosul Zayn al-Dīn ʿAlī, *al-Madkhal ilā aḥkām al-nujūm,* Bank. XXII, 112,$_{2479}$, 117,$_{2483,i}$.

4c. Read: Ibn al-Kammād (Colin).

865. 5, 1. Garr. 974, 2104$_{,3}$, ʿĀšir Ḥafīd 203$_{,1}$, Mosul 235$_{,137}$, Bank. XXII, 33$_{,2439}$. Comm. 1a. Alex. Ḥisāb 39/41, Bank. XXII, 34$_{,2440/1}$, lith. Persia 1286.—Glosses: a. Qaw. II, 270.—b. Ibid. 269$_{,3}$, Bank. XXII, 36$_{,2442/2}$.—g. Sinān Pāshā b. Yūsuf b. Khiḍr, d. 891/1486 (II, 327), Qaw. II, 270.—2. Garr. 2104$_{,2}$, Alex. Ḥisāb 39, Qaw. II, 272, Jārullāh 1496.—10. Jalāl al-Dīn al-ʿUbaydī, Faiẕ. 1334$_{,2}$ (copied in 751/1350 when the author was still alive).—11. *al-Ifāda al-khaṭīra etc.* II, 857$_{,5}$.

866. 6b. al-Bitrawjī (Suyūṭī, *Lubb*: Bitrawshī).

6d. Al-Muẓaffar b. ʿAlī b. al-Muẓaffar al-Qāsim wrote, before 639/1241 (the date of the MS), *al-Mukhtaṣar fī 'l-qirānāt*, Br. Mus. 426,9 (Suter).

8. al-Kawwāsh.

867. 8, 3. Alex. Ḥisāb 61.—7. *Taysīr al-maṭālib fī tasyīr al-kawākib*, Alex. Ḥisāb 47.

9a. Krause, *Stamb. Hdss.* 495.

868. 12, 2. Bank. XXII, 53$_{,2462}$.—13. Mashh. XVIII, 3, 5, Teh. II, 200$_{,2}$.—23. *al-Durr al-thamīn fī 'l-ḥukm ʿalā taḥāwīl al-sinīn*, Alex. Ḥurūf 14.—24. *al-Arbaʿ maqālāt fī 'l-nujūm*, in the library of al-Muḥaddith al-ʿImād al-Fihrisī in Mashhad, *Dharīʿa* I, 408$_{,2124}$.

869. Renaud, Les Ibn Bāṣō, *Hesp.*, 1939, 1/12.

870. 17. See ad 768, 21a.

18. 1. To be deleted, as may be inferred from a comparison with the quotations in al-Ṭūsī's treatise on transversal lines (Krause).

1242 | 872. M. Krause, Al-Bīrūnī, ein iranischer Forscher im MA, *Islam* 26, 1/15.—Muḥammad Yaḥyā al-Hāshimī, Naẓariyyāt al-iqtiṣād ʿinda 'l-Bīrūnī, *RAAD* XV, 456/65.—2. According to Sachau, completed in India between 30 April and 30 September 1030.—9. *RAAD* V, 247, ed. Jalāl Humār, Tehran 1940.

873. 4. C. Schoy, Originalstudien aus al-Bīrūnīs *al-Qānūn al-Masʿūdī, Isis* 1923, 51/74.—7. Bank. XXII, 92$_{,2468,XLII}$.

874. 8. Bank. XXII, 88$_{,2468,XXX/II}$.—11. A fragment in Taymūr, Ṭabīʿa 953, ed. F. Krenkow Hyderabad 1355. *Die Einleitung zu al-B. s Steinbuch*, mit Erläuterungen

übers. v. Taqīaddīn al-Hilālī, Leipzig 1941 (Sammlung or. Arb. 7).—12. Read: *Mashriq* IX, 1905, 19.—15. Read: *Taḥdīd nihāyāt al-amākin li-taṣḥīḥ etc.*, see Zakī Validi Togan, Bīrūnī's Picture of the World, in *Mem. Arch. Survey of India*, no. 43.—17. Bank. XXII, $85_{2468,\mathrm{XXXVI}}$.—19. Ibid. 89_{XXXVIII}.—26. Épître de B. *Fi ʾl-khalāṣ min al-irtibāk.*

875. 27. *Birunlu Ebn Rayhan kitabus saidala fittib mukkaddimesi, türceye ceviren Yaltkaya Šerefeddin*, Istanbul 1937 (lst. Un. Tib Tar. Enst. no. 9).—2. Read: ʿAbdallāh b. ʿAbd al-ʿAzīz.

876. 2, 2. MS in Morocco, see Minorsky, *BSOS* IX (1937), 149, n. 1.—A. Kunik i V. Rosen vol. II, St. Petersburg 1903.

2a. = 567, 1a. Read: Makkī.

877. 4, 1. Leningrad, Public Library, see Miller and Tallgren; Shumen in Bulgaria, *Petermanns Mitt.* 1933, no. 11/2. 304 (Kračkovsky).—W. Hoenerbach, *Deutschland und seine Nebenländer nach der Geographie des Idrisi*, Stuttgart 1938 (Bonner or. St. 21).

880. 10, 1. a. lith. Tehran 1315—3. New edition in 20 volumes, C. 1936/8; see Bergsträsser, *ZDMG* 65, 799ff.

881. 11, 17. *Fi ʿilm mā baʿd al-ṭabīʿa*, Taymūr, Ḥikma 117,2.

882. 12, 1. C. 1933.—3. Lith. Tehran 1310.

883. 13. BDMG 58, Bodl. Marsh 333, anon. see Amedroz, *JRAS* 1902, 801, Cl. Cahen, La Djezira au milieu du XIIIe s. d'après Izzaddin b. S. *REI* I, 109/28, Ledit, *Mashriq* 33 (1935), 161/223, *Cent. Amari* II, 152ff.

15. Read: *Taʾrīkh al-mustabṣir* (Paris 6021, composed by a certain Ibn Muḥammad b. Masʿūd b. Aḥmad b. Aḥmad b. al-Mujāwir al-Baghdādī al-Nīsābūrī, around 626/1229; see Muḥammad Jawad, *REI* 1938, 286).

884. 1. See Cat. Beirut 22/3.

1a. 1. Leningrad, see Kračkovsky, *RAAD* IV, 285, 318.

885. 1b. Abū Bakr Ḥāmid b. Samḥūn, 11th cent. in Cordoba, *al-Adwiya al-mufrada*, Br. Mus. Or. 11, 614, o.s. Fulton, *Br. Mus. Quart.* XI, 8.

885. 2. See V. Rosen, *Auszüge aus Yaḥyā al-Anṭākī*, St. Petersburg 1883, 38/52. G. Graf, die Eucharistielehre des b. B., *Oriens Christ.* III, 13, 1938, 44/70.

3. 2. Garr. 1065.

886. 3a. See Kračkovsky, *RAAD* IV, 285, 318.

4. 2. Earlier in Esc., see N. Morata, *al-Andalus* II, 1934, 273.—16. Bank. XXII, 109,$_{2475}$.

887. 5, 1. Alex. Ṭibb 22.—2. Garr. 1097.

6. See p. 826, c.

7a. = 862,$_{26}$.

888. 8, 2. Qaw. II, 290.

8a. In ca. 484/1091, al-Ḥusayn b. Abī Thaʿlab b. al-Mubārak al-Ṭabīb wrote *al-Munqidh min al-halaka etc.* for al-Mufaḍḍal b. al-Mubārak, a minister of Sayyid Ḥurra who played a central role in Ṣanʿāʾ after the death of the Ṣulayḥid
1243 al-Mukarram Aḥmad in 473–84/1080–91, | Garr. 1098, further MSS II, 169, 1b.

9. 1. Garr. 1101, Alex, Ṭibb. 46.—3. *al-Ḥudūd wal-furūq*, MS from the lifetime of the author, Alex. Fals. 8.—7. *al-Mujadwal fi ʾl-ṭibb*, Mosul 259,1.

10.$_{8}$. II 1032,50.

889. 14. Suter 272.—2. Mosul 259,$_{1}$.

890. 15. al-Bayhaqī, *Tatimmat Ṣiwān al-ḥikma* 111.—2. Persian abstract, *al-Aʿrāḍ al-ṭibbiyya wal-mabāḥith al-ʿAlāʾiyya* for the vizier of Khwārizmshāh ʿAlāʾ al-Dīn Tukush, Majd al-Dīn al-Bukhārī, Mashh. XVII, 1, 1, 2, in al-Kāẓimiyya, *Dharīʿa* II, 251,$_{1009}$.

16. Suter 288.

17. 1. Br. Mus. Or. 9128.

891. 18, 2. Aqrābādhīn, Br. Mus. Or. 8293 (525 AH).—3. *Quwa ʾl-adwiya*, ibid. 8294.

893. 24a, 10. Teh. Sip. II, 247/50.—11. *Qawāfī*, an Arabic-Persian dictionary, ibid. 250/1.

894. 25, 2, Rāmpūr I, 403,200, see II, 962,44.—13. Garr. 1070.—6. See II, 1031,42 and the Addenda thereto; Rabbinowitz, *Traité*, 2nd ed., Paris 1935.

895. 26a. ʿAlāʾ al-Dīn Abū ʿAbdallāh Muḥammad b. Aḥmad (Dam. Abū Muḥammad Aḥmad) al-Ilbīrī wrote, before 612/1215 (the date of the MS), *al-Natāʾij al-ʿaqliyya fī ʾl-wuṣūl ila ʾl-manāhij al-falsafiyya wal-qawānīn al-ṭibbiyya*, Paris 2961, Dam. Z. 88,32,2, copy Beirut 335.

28.1. Mosul 237,164.—Comm. a. Madr. Fāḍiliyya, *Dharīʿa* II, 12,36.—3. Additionally Madrasat Fāḍil Khān in Mashhad, *Dharīʿa* II, 179,658 (*Uṣūl al-tarākīb*).

896. 6. Madrasat Fāḍil Khān, *Dharīʿa* II, 217,848.—7. Mosul 237,175,2.—13. *Kitāb fi ʾl-ṭibb*, ibid. 33,148 (dated 594 AH).—14. *Maqāla fī kayfiyyat tarkīb ṭabaqāt al-ʿayn*, ibid. 269,14,10.—30. *Sharḥ Taqdimāt al-maʿrifa* (by Hippocrates), compiled by his student Badr al-Dīn al-Muẓaffar b. Qāḍī Baʿlabakk, Alex. Ṭibb 22.

897. 33, 2. Mosul 58,42.—Abstracts: c. Read: Muḥammad b. Manẓūr.—*Risāla fī tadāwi ʾl-sumūm*, Qaw. II, 288.

898. 34b. = Anon. *al-Lamḥa al-ʿafīfa fi ʾl-asbāb wal-ʿalāmāt*, Mosul 93,152,15 (Krause); on the comm. see II, 93,22.

899. 36, line 4. Read: ʿAjlūn.

900. 37, 14. An orthodox imitation rather than a polemical tract.

38. Ibn Abī Uṣaybiʿa II, 266/7, Meyerhof, *QSt. Gesch. Med. u. Nat.* IV, 47.—1. a. Alex. Fun. 89,2.—Anon. abstract Garr. 1120.—2. *al-Bāhir fi ʾl-jawāhir*, see Ritter, *Istanb. Mitt.* III, 8,8.

901. 39. See II, 236.

902. 1b. Muḥammad b. Ḥasan b. Ibrāhīm al-Khāzin Abū Bakr wrote, in 421/1030 in the Jazīra, the *Kitāb al-ṭīb*, Garr. 2154,1.

1. c, 1. See H. Bauerreis, *Zur Gesch. des spezifischen Gewichts im Altertum und im MA*, Erlangen 1914.

903. 2. On Serāi 3472 see Holter, *Jahrb. des kunsthist. Inst.*, Vienna 1937, p. 37.—2a. See Minorsky, *CRAc. Inscr.* 1937, 317/24.

3. Shakīb Arslān, *RAAD* XI, 436/40.

904. 5, 1. Istanbul MSS in Ritter, *Istanb. Mitt.* III, 4 no. 6, Alex. Kīm. 3.—4. Alex. Ṭibb 41,$_{3}$.

905. 1a. Anon., Berl. 2890 (591 AH).

3. 2. Dam. Z. 86,$_{22}$.

907. 1. Read: Rāġib 919,3, NO 3653/4 (photograph Cairo, *Nashra* 2), anon.
1244 | comm. Br. Mus. Or. 2361, f. 68/153, transl. Erlanger, *La musique ar.* III, Paris 1938, Farmer, *Sources* 56, attributed to al-Jurjānī.—5. *Dā'irat al-buḥūr wal-awzān*, in a *Majmū'a*, photograph Cairo, *Nashra* 10.—6. *Sharḥ dā'irat al-ʿaql al-awwal* (*al-rāst*), ibid. 17

2. See II, 1036,$_{9}$.

2a. II, 1035,$_{3}$, in Farmer, *Sources*, dated to around 1228.

908. 2. Ibn Arfaʿ ra's (on the name see Hartmann, *Muw.* 26f) al-Shudhūrī al-Gharnāṭī.—1. *Dīwān*, Alex, Kīm. 7, Taymūr, Ṭabīʿa 70/1, 110, Cairo Ṭabīʿa 731.—Comm. by ʿAbdallāh al-Umawī, Alex. Kīm. 7.—6. Abū ʿAbdallāh al-Sīmāwī, Taymūr, Ṭab. 72.—*Takhmīs* by Ḥasan b. Aḥmad al-Iṣfahānī al-Jalāl al-Naqqād, composed in 810/1408 in Mashhad ʿAlī, BDMG 65.—3. *al-Ṭibb al-rūḥānī bil-Qor'ān al-raḥmānī*, Paris 2643.—4. *al-Jihāt fī ʿilm al-tawajjuhāt fī sharḥ qaṣīdat Thābit b. Sinān*, Garr. 41.

909. 3, 1. Alex. Kīm. 13, Cairo Ṭab. 455/6, Bank. XXII,$_{130,\ 2493/5}$.—3. Garr. 936/7, Cairo Ṭab. 419, 426, Bank, XXII,$_{159,\ 2501}$.—*Ṣifat al-ʿamal bil-ramal*, Alex. Ḥurūf 6.

3a. 2. Alex. Ḥurūf 5.

910. 4. 5 MSS in Istanbul in Rescher, *ZS* III, 247/8.

5. Ibn al-Munāṣif, *Takmila, Bibl. Ar. Hisp.* V. no. 962, Aḥmad Bābā, *Nayl* 229, 3.—2. = *al-Mudhhaba*, classified in Ahlwardt, Berl. 5370 as a work on

physiognomy—which is why it was included in this chapter although the author was actually a *faqīh*—while in fact it is a *qaṣīda* of philological content, similar to the one published by Ahlwardt in the Appendix to his *Sammlungen alter arab. Dichter* I; see *"Die Goldene" des Ibn al-Munāṣif*, ein Beitrag zur medizinisch-arab. Lexikographie und zur Geschichte der spanisch-arabischen Literatur im Zeitalter der Almohaden, von J.M. Peñuela, S.J. (Scripta Pontificii Instituti Biblici) Rome 1941.

6. 1. *Risāla fī faḍā'il al-basmala* additionally Garr. 2173,1, *Bayān faḍl al-b.* Garr. 2009,18.—2. See II, 1010,$_{136}$.—3. Alex. Ḥurūf 5, 15.—7. Read: *kushūfāt.*

911. 15. *al-Uṣūl wal-ḍawābiṭ* additionally Alex. Ḥurūf 8.—24. Ibid., Taṣ. 34,$_1$.—34. *Sharḥ taṣarrufāt al-waqf wa-huwa ism allāh al-aʿẓam min al-āyāt al-Qur'āniyya*, Qaw. I, 243.—35. *Silk al-jawāhir wal-maʿānī wal-muqtabas min al-sabʿ al-mathānī*, Alex. Mawāʿiẓ 23.

912. 1. Additionally *Br. Mus. Quart.* VI, 55, other MSS in *Dhariʿa* I, 343,$_{1365}$.—7. See *Dhariʿa* II, 264,1078.—9. Composed after *al-Anwār al-bāhira fi 'ntiṣār al-ʿitra al-ṭāhira*, dated 660, and before the *Kitāb al-taḥsīn*, his final work, *Dharīʿa* II, 418,1656.

913. 7, 19. *Asrār al-ṣalāt wa-anwār al-daʿawāt aw Mukhtār al-daʿawāt wa-asrār al-ṣalāt*, fragm. in a *majmūʿa* in the library of Ḥasan Ṣadr al-Dīn al-Kāẓimī, *Dharīʿa* II, 49,199.

913. 8, 1. Qaw. II, 354.—4. Read: *al-Muʿlam.*

914. 1. *al-Mufīd* is attributed to al-Khwārizmī in Cambr. 1081 and Garr. 181.

2. Read: 1164.

2a. Abū. ʿAbdallāh Muḥammad b. Ismāʿīl b. al-Baqqāl, professor at the Niẓāmiyya, d. 588/1192, *al-Muqtaraḥ*, Paris 4639; see M. Jawad, *REI* 1938, 286.

5. al-Kattānī, *Fihris* I, 226, 8.

915. Anon. *Sīrat b. al-Jawzī*, Garr. 2198.—1. *Mukhtaṣar*, Teh. Sip. II, 81/5.—2. On Dam. ʿUm. 84,$_2$ see *RAAD* XI, 119.—6. In the library of Yāsīn Bāshayān al-ʿAbbāsī in Basra (Ritter).

916. 10h. *Irshād al-murīdīn fī ḥikāyāt al-ṣāliḥīn*, ḤKh, I, 252, ^{2}I 67, Garr. 677.—11. Read: Ḥasan al-Ḥabbās.—14. Alex. Taʾr. 133.

1245 | 918. 27, i. *Kashf mushkil ḥadīth al-ṣaḥīḥayn* Garr. 1450.—38. With title title *Kashf talbīs Iblīs*, Heid. ZDMG 91, 382, Alex. Mawāʿiẓ 32, see W. Braune, Publ. Inst. Un. di Napoli, *Annali* I, 1940, 305/3.

919. 43. *Br. Mus. Quart.* XIII, 3, 90.—44. *Mukhtaṣar al-m.*, Ambr. A 1605, xiii (*RSO* III, 905).—53. Br. Mus. Or. 9249.—56. Ad p. 512 (Garr. 204).—57. Istanbul Un., *ZS* III, 248.—66. *al-Laṭāʾif* additionally Alex. Mawāʿiẓ 34.—67. Ibid. 39.—68. *Baḥr al-dumūʿ* ibid. 7.—73. Ibid. 18, anon. abstract ibid. 37,$_1$.—75. *Mukhtaṣar T. al-gh.* Jārullāh 2108,2.—75. d. Alex. Mawāʿiẓ 35.

920. 75, 1. Garr. 1896.—75, r. *Luṭf al-mawāʿiẓ*, Alex. Maw. 34, 39,$_2$.—75, s. *Dīwān khuṭab*, ibid. 37,$_3$.—75, t. *al-Nūr fī faḍāʾil al-ayyām wal-shuhūr*, ibid. 49.—75, u. *Anwār al-jalīs*, Garr. 1895.—75, v. *Risāla fī kayd al-shayṭān li-nafsihī qabla kaydihī li-Ādam maʿa sharḥ al-firaq al-muḍilla*, Alex. Fun. 136,$_1$.—76. Garr. 1102.—79. Garr. 586.

921. Ibn Quṭlūbughā 93, read: F. Gabrieli, *Isis*, 1925, 9/13.—1. Alex. Taʾr. 95.—3. Paris 790, Ind. Off. 1445, Cairo^{1} II, 263.—b. Asʿad 3804,$_1$.—5. Glosses: a. Āqā Bihbihānī, d. 1200/1793, Teh. Sip. I, 564.—b. ʿAlāʾ al-Dīn Ḥusayn b. Mīrzā Rafīʿ al-Dīn Muḥammad b. Amīr Shujāʿ al-Dīn Maḥmūd Ḥusayn al-Āmulī al-Iṣfahānī, d. 1064/1654, ibid. 567/9.—c. *Hidāyat al-mustarshidīn* by Muḥammad Taqī al-Dīn b. ʿAbd al-Raḥīm, d. 1248/1832 (*Rawḍāt al-j.* I, 131), ibid. 570/2.—d. Mollā Mīrzā Shirwānī Muḥammad b. Ḥasan, d. 1098/1686, ibid. 574/6.—Comm. e. *Aṣl al-uṣūl* by Rafīʿ b. Rafīʿ al-Jīlānī, ca. 1233/1818, author of *al-Madārik*, print. 1268 with *Muqaddamaʾi Kashf al-madārik* in the margin, *Dharīʿa* II, 168, 261.—f. Muḥammad b. Ibrāhīm al-Ḥusaynī al-Ḥasanī, Alex. Uṣūl 8.

922. 6. Qaw. I, 81—read: al-Qamūlī.—9. Garr. 1486, Hyderabad 1353/1934. anon. comm. Mashh. I, 21,41.—14. Alex. Fun. 43, 67,$_{11}$, C. 1355.

923. 18. With the comm. *Ghāyāt al-āyāt* by Maḥmūd al-Urmawī, d. 672/1273, Alex. Manṭiq 17.—20e. *al-Arbaʿūn fī uṣūl al-dīn*, Qaw. I, 160.—20f. *Wird*, ibid. I, 269.—21. Br. Mus. Or. 9004, anon. abstract Alex. Ḥikma 26.—22. Taymūr, ʿAq. 268.—25. *Iʿtiqādāt firaq al-Islām wal-mushrikīn*, Taymūr, ʿAq. 178, ed. al-Nashshār, C. 1938.—27b. *Munāẓarāt al-ʿallāma F. ar-R. fī hijratihi ilā Samarqand thumma jihāt al-Hind*, see P. Kraus, *Bull. Inst. Eg.* XIX, 1937, 187/214, *Isl. Culture* XII (1938), 131/53.—27 Read: *Risāla fi ʾl-nafs*, Alex. Fun. 155,$_5$.

924. 29. Garr. 933, Br. Mus. Or. 9147, Bank. XXII, 113,$_{2480/1}$, demonstrably written by Rāzī through a self-quotation in *al-Mulakhkhaṣ*, see Šerefeddin in Ritter, *Isl.* XXIV, 285, n. 2.—30. Berl. Oct. 2488.—30b. *Risāla fī nafy al-ḥayyiz wal-jiha*, Mashh. II, 31,$_{110}$.—30c. *Risāla dar ḥaqīqat-i marg va aḥwāl-i rūḥ*, ibid. II, 31,109.—32. Qaw. II, 178, Alex. Balāgha 26.—33. NO 3760, Farmer, *Sources*, 45.—35. Br. Mus. Or. 9510, see Y. Mourad, *La physiognomie arabe et le* Kitāb al-firāsa *de F. ar-R.*, Paris 1939.

925. A redaction of his middle works, Berl. Or. Qu. 1867.—1. Comm. b. by Abu
'l-Ḥasan b. Aḥmad al-Sharīf al Qā'inī from the time of Ṭahmāsp (1524/76), in the
libraries of Muḥammad al-Ṭihrānī, Muḥammad ʿAlī al-Urdubādī in Najaf, and
Jaʿfar Sulṭān al-Umarā' in Tehran, *Dharīʿa* I, 439,$_{2214}$, Pers. transl. with a comm.
by Abu 'l-Ḥasan in the library of Muḥammad ʿAlī Khwānsārī, ibid. 2213.—c. ʿAlī
b. al-Ḥusayn al-Karakī, d. 940/1533, in the library of Rājā Muḥammad | Mahdī 1246
Ṣāḥib in Faizabad, ibid. I, 446,$_{2243}$.—2. *Tajrīd al-kalām* Birjand *Lughat al-ʿArab*
VI, 513.

926. Comm. b. *Lughat al-ʿArab* VI, 514,5.—Glosses: α Alex. Tawḥīd 10, Garr. 865/6, 2248,$_{1}$.—c. *al-Umūr al-ʿāmma* Birjand *Lughat al-ʿArab* VI, 514,8.—Glosses: β *al-Ṭabaqāt al-Jalāliyya*, Qaw. II, 368.—δ Alex. Tawḥīd 32.

927. εε Alex. Tawḥīd 33,3—ηη ibid. 24.—3. Ind. Off. 4589,$_{1}$, *JRAS* 1939, 375.—3d. Delete: by Shaykh al-Ṭā'ifa, I 706.—3f. *Muqaddimat al-kalām*, Br. Mus. Or. 10968.—3g. *Aqall mā yajibu 'l-iʿtiqād bihi*, MSS in Karbala, *Dharīʿa* II, 226,$_{888}$, 274,$_{1108}$ b.—4. Comm. b. by al-Miqdād b. ʿAbdallāh b. al-Ḥusyan al-Suyūrī al-Ḥillī, d. 826/1423, *Dharīʿa* II, 423,$_{1670}$.—III. Glosses by al-Astarābādī, ad (see II, 258,6a).

928. 17. Rāġib 1482, Fātiḥ 5380,$_{3}$, Najaf Dharīʿa I, 86,407, print. with comm. by Abū ʿAbdallāh al-Zanjānī, 1341 (*Jāmiʿ* 909).

a8. Garr. 797 (*Sharḥ Risālat ithbāt al-ʿaql*).—22a. *Āghāz u anjām*, Pers. eschatology, library of Naṣrallāh al-Taqawī in Tehran, *Dharīʿa* I, 36,173.—22e. Fātiḥ 5380,$_{1}$.—22k. Library of al-Ḥusayniyya, *Dharīʿa* II, 83,$_{329}$.—22m. Mashh. I, 86,$_{267}$.

929. 22r. *Ithbāt al-wājib*, library of Meḥmed Pāshā in Istanbul, Persian abstract by Muḥammad ʿAlī Khwānsārī, *Dharīʿa* I, 108,$_{525}$.—22s. *Aqsām al-ḥikma*, Rāġib ibid. II, 272,$_{1098}$.—22t. *Asās al-iqtibās fī 'l-manṭiq*, Pers. Mashhad II, 1, 2, Teh. II, 595,1, Najaf ibid. II, 5,9.—22u. *As'ilat al-Sayyid Rukn al-Dīn Abi 'l-Faḍā'il*

al-Ḥasan b. Muḥammad b. Sharafshāh al-ʿAlawī al-Astarābādī, b. 718/1318 in Mosul, Rāġib, library of al-Ḥusayniyya in Najaf, and al-Khizāna al-Gharawiyya ibid. II, 83,329.—22v. *Risālat al-nufūs al-ʿaraḍiyya*, AS 2623,$_{4}$, Asʿad 3748,$_{5}$—22w. *Risālat al-ʿaql al-kullī*, with anon. comm., Asʿad 3748,$_{14}$.—23. Garr. 1054, Mashh. XVII, 12,$_{33/4}$, Bank. XXII 28,$_{24312}$, comm. by Hāshim additionally ibid. 29,$_{24,33/4}$, Persian transl. Zanjān, *Lughat al-ʿArab* VI, 95, comm. by Mawlawī Muḥammad Barakāt, 13th cent. AH, Bank. XXII 30,$_{2435,6}$.—23a. *Taḥrīr uṣūl al-handasa wal-ḥisāb*, different from 23, Alex. Ḥisāb 28.—24. Garr. 1055.—25. Mashh. XVII, 13,35, Teh. II, 207,$_{1}$.—29. Mashh. XVII, 11,$_{70}$.—30. Ibid. 27,82.

930. 32. Zanjān, *Lughat al-ʿArab* VI, 96.—34. Paris 2467,$_{20}$, Mashh. XVII, 11,$_{32}$.—36. Paris 2467,$_{1}$ (anon.).—36c. = e.—36d. Teh. II, 155, 205,$_{1}$, 207,$_{2}$, 208,$_{4}$, 209,$_{8}$.—36f. Appendix to 25.—38. Library of al-Qāsim al-Khwānsārī al-Mūsawī, *Dharīʿa* II, 399,$_{1601}$.—38a. = 55c., Fātiḥ 5380,$_{10}$, Asʿad 3738,$_{9}$.—39. Bank. XXII, 37,$_{2444/6}$. Comm. b. Alex. Ḥisāb 37, Qaw. II, 269, glosses by Qāḍīzāde al-Rūmī, Berl. 5657.

931., 40. Pers. Mashh. XVII, 31,$_{33}$.—Comm. a. Read: al-Ḥimādhī.—b. Garr. 2106,$_{1}$, Bank. XXII 38,$_{2447/8}$.—c. Alex. Ḥisāb 39, Makr. 33.—Bank. XXII, 40,$_{2449/50}$. d. Bank. XXII, 41,$_{2451}$.—45. Pers. comm. AS 2696.—Comm. *ʿIqd al-amālī* by Shihāb al-Dīn al-Ḥalabī, see ad II, 485,$_{69}$.—47. = *Istikhrāj al-taqāwīm* Ḥamīd, *Dharīʿa* II, 20,$_{66}$. Comm. a. Anon., dedicated to Sultan Sayf al-Dīn, 678,$_{69}$/1279$_{90}$, Berl. 5679, Br. Mus. 394/5, Bank. XXII, 114,$_{2482}$.—b. Ḥasan b. Muḥammad Niẓām al-Nīsābūrī, Leid. 1176, AS 2664.—c. Muḥammad b. Muḥammad al-Kāshgharī Zanjān, *Lughat al-ʿArab* VI, 95.

932. 48. Comm. a. Zanjān, *Lughat al-ʿArab* VI, 95.—c. To be deleted.—d. Mashh. XVIII, 38,$_{16}$.—54. d. Mashh. XVII, 8,$_{23}$.—56a. Read: "*Hidāyat al-baṣar*", Aligarh Subḥānallāh 79.

1247 | 933. 57. Berl. Oct. 3071 (supposedly written in 995 AH!), Ritter in Ruska, *Istanb. Mitt.* 1935, p. 4, no. 7.—58 *Jawāhirnāme*, Berl. or. Oct. 3184.—59. *Risāla fī ʿilm al-mūsīqī*, Paris 2466 (not from the Persian *Kanz al-tuḥaf*, contra Sarton, *Intr.* II, 1009), Farmer, *Sources*, 47.

937. 60, 4. Read: al-Sijāʿī.

63. Read: Rivlin, Jerusalem 1934.

64. 1701. *Or. Mod.* 1928, 592.—Read: Fracassi, Ali.

938. 79. Read: Beirut 1934.

939. 101, lcc read: al-Ḥummara.—*Zap.* XVII, 0147/9.

940. 122. See ad II, 791.

946. Line 1: see II 1032,$_{2}$.

952. 319, line 33. *Firaq al-Shīʿa* Najaf 1936.

322. 14. Ind. Off. 4632, *JRAS* 1939, 395.

956. 371, 16. An 18th-century Arabic translation of a Latin commentary on the Arabic *Physics*, written in 1648 by the Macedonian monk Jo Kuttunius, who was active in Padua; see *Forsch. u. Fortschr.* 1934, 392/3.

957. 373, III. See R. Walzer, Un frammento nuovo di Aristotele in *St. Ital. di Fil. Cl.* no. XIV, 1937, 125/37.—I, Guidi and Walzer, Introduction to Aristotle, II, Ritter and Walzer, *On sadness*, Mem. Acc. Lincei 1938. III, Metaphysics ed. M. Guidi.

958. 378, 5. See 888,$_{10}$, 1032.

963. Line 4. Contra Gildemeister, Levi della Vida *Speculum* XIII, 81, n.

964. 504. Read: "al-Qadārī", see Kračkovsky, *Mél. Gautier* 289.

969. 602. See ad p. 698.

970. 643. 6, Ind. Off. 1525.

Supplement Volume 2

1. 1b. Read: Sirāj al-Dīn. Alex. Adab 63.

2. 6. Ibn al-Qāḍī, *Durrat al-ḥijāl* II, 428,$_{220}$.

3. 9. *ʿUmdat al-sālik wa-ʿuddat al-nāsik*, Alex. Fun. 126, 2 (only Ibn al-Naqīb).

11. *Dīwān* with poems from the years 770–971/1368–94, Bank. XXIII, 49,$_{2544}$ (which has Raḍī al-Dīn).

4. 13, 1. I, 454,2.

14. 2. *al-Qaṭr al-Nubātī*, Alex. Adab.—4. Anon., *Mukhtaṣar Sūq al-raqīq*, Bank. XXIII, 47,$_{2543}$.—6. Alex. Adab 128,$_{11}$.

5. 14 = 684, 6a.

15b. In 767/1365, Ḥusayn b. Muḥammad b. ʿAlī al-Musawwadī completed *al-Mawāhib al-qadariyya fī madḥ khayr al-bariyya*, together with another *qaṣīda*, Alex. Fun. 133, 6,7.

6. 17, 7. Alex. Mawāʿiẓ 13.

18. 1. Alex. Fun. 94,$_{7}$.—13. = 921,$_{73}$.

7. 19b. ʿAlī b. ʿĪsā b. Maḥmūd Mahdī al-Fihrī al-Busuṭī, d. 786/1384, *Zahrat al-ādāb wa-tuḥfat uli ʾl-albāb*, completed in 764, Alex. Adab 76.

23. See p. 16, 5a.

9. 1. *Taqdīm Abī Bakr*, Bank. XXIII, 51,$_{2547}$. Comm. *al-ʿIqd al-badīʿ fī fann al-badīʿ* by Būlus ʿAwwād, Beirut 1881.—4. Garr. 98, Alex. Fun. 198,$_{1}$.—10. Alex. Adab
1248 29.—23. *Rashf al-manhalayn, takhmīs* on a | *qaṣīda* by Abu ʾl-Ḥasan b. ʿAlī b. Muḥammad b. Maḥmūd b. ʿAbd al-Qādir al-Gīlānī, juxtaposed with an earlier *takhmīs* by Badr al-Dīn b. al-Ṣāḥib, Br.-H.^{2} 25 (imprecise), Garr. 97.

11. 27. al-Kattānī, *Fihris* II, 274.—1. Garr. 105, Bank. XXIII, 54,$_{2549}$.

29. *al-Fawāʾid al-laṭīfa etc.* additionally Alex. Adab 137.

12. 31, 2. Garr. 213, Bank. XXIII, 78,$_{2572}$, NO 2916.—4. *Jannat al-wildān etc.*, 3 *Kunnāsh al-jawārī*, 7 *Qalāʾid al-naḥw etc.* C. 1326 (Alex. Adab 130/1).—11. *Nadīm al-kaʾīb wa-ḥabīb al-ḥabīb, dīwān* and anthology, Daḥdāḥ 243.

32a. Muḥammad b. ʿUmar al-Miṣrī al-Makkī, a poet from the Mamlūk period, *Dīwān, Br. Mus. Quart.* VI, 97.

13. 34. Delete: *Tasliyat al-khawāṭir etc.*, see p. 758.

34a. Probably the same as 382,$_{26}$ and 413,$_{26}$.

38. Read: ʿAlī b. Muḥammad b. ʿAbdallāh.

41. Read: al-Ghūrī.

14. 1. *Marāḥ*, BDMG 66a, Garr. 422/5, Qaw. II, 47/9, Teh. Sip. II, 393/4.—Comm. 1. Garr. 429/30, Alex. Taṣr. 8, Qaw. II, 41/3, glosses by Dāʾūd al-Ashkashī (?) Alex. Taṣr. 4.—3. *al-Falāḥ*, Qaw. II, 45.—4. Garr. 426/8, Alex. Adab 8, Teh. Sip. II, 371/2.—8. Garr. 431 (anon).—10. *Fatḥ al-fattāḥ*, Alex. Adab 10.

15. 3, 1. ʿAbdulqayyūm, *Fahāris Lisān al-ʿArab*, I, *Asmāʾ al-shuʿarāʾ*, Lahore 1938.

3b. Muḥammad al-Ṣalghūrī (p. 924,94) b. 631/1233, d. 713/1313, Suyūṭī, *Bughya*, 106.—3. *Qaṣīda fī qawāʿid lisān al-Turk*, cited by Suyūṭī.

3c. Nāṣir al-Dīn Abu ʾl-Faḍl Shāfiʿ b. Nūr al-Dīn Abi ʾl-Ḥasan ʿAlī b. ʿImād al-Dīn Abi ʾl-Faḍl ʿAbbās al-Kinānī, b. 649/1251, d. 730/1330, *al-Raʾy al-ṣāʾib fī ithbāt mā lā budda minhu lil-kātib*, Garr. 2195.

16. 5, 2. c. Alex. Naḥw 2.

5a. See p. 7, 23.

5b. Muḥammad b. Aḥmad b. Sulaymān b. Yaʿqūb b. ʿAlī b. Salāma b. ʿAsākir b. Ḥusayn b. Ṣakhr b. Muḥammad al-Anṣārī al-Khazrajī wrote, in 760/1359 in Damascus: *Unmūdhaj murāsalāt*, Garr. 2996.

6. 1. Alex. Naḥw 8.

7. 1. BDMG 67b, Garr. 450/2, Philadelphia 31, Alex. Fun. 110,4, Sbath 200, Mosul 39,$_{241}$, 44,$_{50/1}$, 107,$_{96}$, 148,$_{132}$, 163,$_{243}$, 224,$_{207}$, 244,$_{323/4}$ Teh. Sip. II, 356/7.

17. 1. Comm. Alex. Naḥw 35,4, 39, Makr. 54.—Glosses: α Alex. Naḥw 12.—β Read: ʿAlī b. ʿAbd al-Qādir al-Nabtītī—ε Read: " Jerusalem 1320" (Alex. Naḥw 12).—η Yūsuf al-Mālikī al-Fayshī, d. 1061/1651, Vat. V. 830,7, Alex. Naḥw 12.—b. Print. C. 1323, on which a *taqrīr* by Sayyid al-Sharmīnī al-Sharqāwī, completed in 1272,

Alex. Naḥw 7.—ζ ʿUthmān b. Makkī al-Zabīdī, C. 1324.—η Anon. Mosul $79_{,12}$, $186_{,293}$.—t. *Murqiṣ al-akhyār*, Makr. 55.—u. *Hadiyyat al-arīb li-aṣdaq ḥabīb* by Abū ʿAbdallāh Muḥammad b. ʿĀshūr al-Ṭāhīr Naqīb al-Ashrāf bi-Tūnis, d. 1284/1867, C. 1296.—2. BDMG 80, Garr. 445/6, Qaw. II, 121, Makr. 87, Mosul $70_{,260}$, $148_{,135}$, $164_{,261}$, $224_{,215}$, Teh. Sip. II, 394/7.—(glosses by Muḥammad al-Amīr, Makr. 15).—a. Teh. Sip. II, 375/8.

18. aa. Another commentary by the same, Garr. 448.—b. Mosul $40_{,254}$, Teh. Sip. II, 380/2, Istanbul 1305.—c. Qaw. II, 91, Teh. Sip. II, 385/6, C. 1324.—*Muntakhab*, Teh. Sip. II, 398/9.—o. *Muntahā amal al-arīb* (*adīb*) by Aḥmad b. Muḥammad b. ʿAlī b. al-Mollā, d. 990/1582 or 973/1564, Qaw. II, 124, Teh. Sip. II, 379/80.—p. *Ighnāʾ al-adīb* by Muḥammad Mahdī b. ʿAlī Asghar Qazwīnī (ca. 1120/1708), Teh. Sip. II, 373/5.—Abstracts: c. Alex. Naḥw 39.—3. Hamb.
1249 Or. Sem. 120, Garr. 455, Alex. Fun. $171_{,60}$, Sbath 916, Qaw. II, | 59, Mosul $241_{,24591}$.—1. Teh. Sip. I, 15 = II, 310.—Comm.: a. Garr. 457.—b. Ibid. 458, Hamb. Or. Sem. $75_{,1}$, Alex. Naḥw 30, 43, Qaw. II, 125, Makr. 60, Mosul $241_{,2458}$, Teh. Sip. II, 332.

19. Glosses by Muḥammad b. ʿAbd al-Raḥmān al-Ḥamawī, completed in 1031/1622, Alex. Naḥw 11.—d. Ibid. 14.—f. Alex. Fun. $96_{,3}$.—n. Alex. Naḥw 13.—Anon. Sbath 747.—Versific.: k. *al-Ṣila wal-ʿāʾid li-naẓm al-qawāʿid* by Muḥammad b. Sālim b. Wiṣāl, Ambr. A. 43, iv (*RSO* III, 275).—1. *Minaḥ al-wahhāb fī qawāʿid al-iʿrāb* by Yūsuf al-Shahīd al-Barnāwī, comm. *Muwaṣṣil al-ṭullāb* by Muḥammad b. Muḥammad ʿUllaysh al-Mālikī (p. 738), Makr. 60.—4. BDMG 79, Alex. Naḥw 45, Fun. $142_{,6}$, Mosul $147_{,138}$, $189_{,10,11}$. Self-commentary, Makr. 39.—b. Hamb. Or. Sem. $49_{,2}$.—20. g. *Sharḥ al-ṣudūr bi-sharḥ zawāʾid al-shudhūr* by al-Birmāwī, Alex. Naḥw 36, Qaw. II, 92.—n. Alex. Naḥw 11.—p. *al-Durr al-manṭūr ʿalā Sharḥ al-ṣudūr* by Muḥammad Manṣūr al-Yāfī al-Ḥanafī, completed in 1237, Alex. Naḥw 16.—q. Anon., Sbath 183, 195, Mosul $224_{,206}$.—5. Alex. Fun. $188_{,3}$—6. Ibid. $133_{,10}$.—25. *Risāla fī iʿrāb faḍlan wa-lughatan waṣṭilāḥāt wa-khilāfan wa-hālumma jarran*, Qaw. II, 86.—26. *Risāla fī tawjīh al-naṣb*, ibid. 188,5.

21. 10, 1. Alex. Fun. $88_{,4}$.

11. See p.336,6.

14. 6. Autograph dated 795/1393, Mosul 278,59,3.

22. 15. *al-Kāfī*, Garr. 506/7, Alex ʿArūḍ 3, 4, Fun. 128,$_1$. Comm. 2. Alex. ʿArūḍ 6.—4b. Makr. 55.—6. Alex. ʿArūḍ 3.—*Mawāhib al-kāfī ʿala ʾl-tibr al-ṣāfī fī naẓm al-Kāfī etc.* by Ibrāhīm b. Muḥammad al-Ṣūfī al-Wādī al-Muṣʿabī al-Shabāṭī al-Sharīf, Tunis 1323.

16. 1. BDMG 84/5.

23. 16. c. Alex. Naḥw. 10.—f. Aḥmad b. Salāma al-Qāsim, Alex. Naḥw 9, Makr. 32 (Aḥmad al-Miṣrī?).—l. *al-Farāʾid wal-ʿuqūd fī ḥall alfāẓ sharḥ al-A.* by Nūr al-Dīn ʿAlī b. Ibrāhīm al-Ḥalabī al-Qāhirī al-Shāfiʿī, d. 1044/1634, Alex. Naḥw 27.—m. Muḥammad Qush b. Yūsuf b. Ibrāhīm al-Gharqī, d. 1232/1817, Alex. Naḥw 34.—n. Muḥammad b. Saʿd ʿAyyād(?), completed in 1253/1837, ibid. 20, see 201, 3.—18. See 916, 18.—2. Berl. 7170/1, Garr. 510 (*Dafʿ*).

25. 5. Read: "Un. Eg. 11049".—3. Sarāi A III, 3104.—5. Delete: "AS 2167", see *Türk. Macm.* III, 172.—6. Vol. 2. Sarāi A III, 88, *Türk. Macm.* III, 182 (Ritter).

6. 1. Alex. Taʾr. 65.

26. 1. Read: "Ibrāhīm b. Aḥmad".

27. 2, 1. Alex. Taʾr. 83, print. C. 1914.—3. Cairo, *Nashra* 4, abstract *Tashnīf al-asmāʿ bi-aḥkām al-samāʿ* by Abū Ḥāmid al-Maqdisī, Alex. Fun. 160,2.

28. 1. Vol. 13/4, Garr. 682. Indices additionally ibid. XXIV, 551/615.—5. See Muḥammad Kurd ʿAlī, *RAAD* V, 445/56.—8. Bank. XXIII, 46,$_{2542}$.—9. *RAAD* XII, 405, XIV, 38/40.—12. Heid. *ZDMG* 91, 308.

29. 25. Read: Rosen and Kračkovsky, *Zap. Koll. Vost.* I, 1925, 291/304.

30. 4. See ad I, 613.

7. *Muntakhab min Kitāb al-kawākib al-muḍīʾa fī ʾl-dhayl ʿalā Taʾrīkh Ibn Ḥ. al-N.*, Alex. Taʾr. 115.

31. 7a, 1. Dam. Z. 77,$_{25}$.

9. al-Kattānī, *Fihris* II, 335/8.

32. 7. Alex. Ḥad. $55_{,2}$, 64, Mosul $195_{,30}$.—Abstracts a = b Heid. ZDMG 91, 381, Garr. 1499.—Abstract *Aḥādīth etc.* Alex. Ḥad. 59.—12. Ibid. 54,1, Faw. 15 (Indian print.); instead of *al-maʿāni*, read: *al-manīʿ*.—15. Alex. Ta'r. 44, Qaw. II, 231, print. C. 1937.

33. 37. *al-Iṣṭifā' fī asmā' al-Muṣṭafā*, Qaw. II, 227.

1250 | 34. 2. See Kahle, *Mél. Maspéro* III, 1935, 141/54.

35. Line 4. Köpr. 1047 by Shams al-Dīn Muḥammad b. Ibrāhīm al-Jazarī.

4. Ṭabbākh, *Ta'rīkh Ḥalab* V, 66/71.—2. Alex. Ta'r. 56.—4. Ibid. 16.—6. Bank. XXIII, $104_{,2594}$, Istanbul 1302.—12. *Qaṣīda tā'iyya*, Alex. Adab 129 = Ṭabbākh 69/70.

36. 7, 1. Garr. 595.—History of the Copts from the *Khiṭaṭ*, *al-Qawl al-ibrīzī lil-ʿAllāma al-Maqrīzī* by Mīnā Efendi, C. 1898.

37. Line 1. C. 1939.—8a. Ed. M. Ṣādiq ʿAbdallāh, Najaf 1356.—o. C. 1937.—r. Alex. Fun. $99_{,6}$.

38. 8. See I, 574.

9. *Takhmīs qaṣīdat b. Zurayq*, Heid. ZDMG 91, 388.

39. 10, 1. Garr. 596.—2. Ibid. 597.

40. 10, 7. Abstract by ʿAlī b. Muḥammad al-Ḥalabī, Daḥdāḥ 45.—9. Read: *Zap.* XXI, 1912, 16/22.

10b. MSS in Istanbul in Tauer, *Arch. Or.* VI, 99.

10c. It was probably Qāḍī Shams al-Dīn Muḥammad b. Maḥmūd al-Ḥalabī b. Ajā, b. 820/1417 in Aleppo, d. 881/1476 (al-Sakhāwī, *Ḍaw'* X, 43, no. 146), who wrote the *Riḥlat al-amīr Yashbak* (murdered in Ruhā[Edessa/Urfa] in 885/1480, during the campaign against Shāhsiwār, see p. 78, 5a); see A. Taymūr, RAAD V, 316/33.

11. 1. *al-Durr al-muntakhab* see J. Sauvaget, *Les perles choisies d'Ibn Chihna*, Mém. de l'Inst. fr. de Damas I, Ḥ. Zayyāt, *Mashriq* 32 (1934), 504/9.

41. 12. Instead of ca., read: d. (al-Sakhāwī, *Ḍawʾ* v, 738).

42. 15. See Ṣāliḥ b. Yaḥyā, ed. Cheikho, 1927, 230/2.

43. 1, 3. Garr. 2194.—4. Alex. Adab 15.

2. 1. Vol. VII (the years 400/89), Faiẓ. 1459.—n. 1. Strausz, *WZKM* 43, 1936, p. 194.

44. 2a. Alex. Taʾr. 67.

3. 2. *Aqālīm al-buldān wa-taqwīmuhā*, Mosul 28,86.

45. 3a. Köpr. 1047.

4. al-Kattānī, *Fihris* I, 312/4.—1. Until 744, Mosul 233,224.—*Dhayl* by his son Aḥmad to his father's *dhayl* to the *ʿIbar* covering the years 762/86, Alex. Taʾr. 70.—*Mulakhkhaṣ taʾrīkh al-Islām* by Muḥammad b. Muḥammad al-Jazarī al-Shāfiʿī, d. 833/1429, completed in 798, Alex. Taʾr. 132.

46. Line 3. *al-ʿIbar*, Alex. Taʾr. 86.—3. Qaw. I, 87, II, 227.—a. Alex. Muṣṭ. al-Haḍ. 14.

47. 16. C. 1332.—34. *al-Nāfiʿ bi-maʿrifat al-kabāʾir ijmāʿan wa-tafṣīlan*, Heid. *ZDMG* 91, 385.—35. *al-Kāshif fī asmāʾ al-rijāl*, Alex. Taʾr. 101, Muṣṭ. al-Ḥad. 13.—36. *al-Muhadhdhab al-mukhtaṣar asānīd al-Sunan al-kubrā*, Cairo² I, 153.—37. *Risāla fī ʾl-adʿiya al-ḥadīthiyya* (from the *Silāḥ al-muʾmin* by Muḥammad al-Miṣrī al-Gharnāṭī, d. 745/1344), Alex. Fun. 150_{12}.—38. *Kitāb fī maʿrifat al-anghām*, Paris 2480, Bodl. Marsh 82, Ous. 106, Cairo f. 340, 342, see Farmer, *Sources* 53.—4a. Qaw. II, 228.

48. 5, 2. Abstract of 1, Alex. Taʾr. 3, anon. abstract ibid. 15.—9. *al-Sīra al-sariyya fī manāqib khayr al-bariyya* (= 6 ?), Alex. Taʾr. 8.

6. 1. Vol. 6, Garr. 589.—2. Fragm. ibid. 681.

49. 8. 1. Vols. I—VII, C. 1348/51.—2. C. 1937, 4 vols.—10. Ed. Zurayk, part II Beirut 1938 (*Bull.* IX, 245/596).—10a. Ibrāhīm b. Muḥammad b. Aydamur al-ʿAlāʾī.

50. 10a, 2. Sarāi A III, 2303 (until 813 AH, Ritter).—3. On which the *Fihrist al-asmāʾ wal-aʿlām* by Muḥammad al-Biblāwī and ʿAlī Efendi Subḥī, Būlāq 1314.

13. 4. Garr. 694.—9. *Sanad*, ibid. 1465.

1251 | 51. 14, 1. MSS in Istanbul in ʿĀdile ʿĀbidīn, *Istanbul Ün. Tarih Semineri Dergisi* II (Istanbul 1938), 150ff.—20. *Majmūʿ al-bustān al-nūrī li-ḥaḍrat mawlāna ʾl-sulṭān al-Ghūrī*, 14 treatises of varied content, AS 4793 (Ritter).

53. 17, 9. Delete.—11. *al-Majmaʿ al-mufattan* (read: *mufannan*?) *bil-muʿjam al-muʿanwan*, on the lives of scholars, princes, etc., in alphabetical order, Alex. Taʾr. 107.

§ 4. Muḥammad Jād al-Mawlā Bek, Muḥammad al-Baghawī, Muḥammad Abu ʾl-Faḍl Ibrāhīm, *Qiṣaṣ al-ʿArab* I, C. 1939.

54. 2, 1. d. Anon., Alex. Adab 133/4.—2. Read: *Mabāhij*.—7b. See p.387,37b.

55. 2a. Br.-H.^{2}, 152 = Garr. 222, not = Br. Mus. Suppl. 1147, and different from *Safīnat al-bulaghāʾ* Mosul 49,$_{34}$, fragm.

9. Alex. Adab 158.

56. 10, I, BDMG 117, Garr. 210/1, Qaw. II, 215, Ḥamīd. 1293/4, Bank. XXIII, 74,$_{2569/70}$, Rāmpūr 616.—11. Kračkovsky, *EI*, Erg. 181/2.—1. Teh. Sip. II, 500/2.—Garr. 10, Bank. XXIII, 76,$_{2571}$.

57. 11, 16. Bank. XXIII, 107,$_{2596}$.—21. *Kitāb fī ḥukm ḥarf al-muḍāraʿa*, Alex. Fun. 188,6.—22. *al-Ṭirāz al-muwashshā fi ʾl-inshāʾ*, Teh. Sip. II, 72/7.

58. 17. See p. 909,41.—20. *Khayr al-aḥlām* in *maqāma* form, written in 895, Istanbul. Un. H. 7168 (*ZS* III, 252).

62. Ḥasan al-Zayyāt, *Alf layla taʾrīkh ḥayātihā*, *RAAD* XII, 129/42, 204/15, 282/91. D.B. Macdonald, A bibliographical and literary study of the first appearance of the Arabian Nights in Europe, *The Lit. Quart.* II, 2, Oct. 1932, 387/420. A. Abel, *Les enseignements des Mille et une nuits*, Brussels 1939.

63. *Tawaddud al-jāriya*, ed. M. Brugsch, Heidelberg 1924.—*The Thousand and One Nights*, new revised completed and unabridged transl. from the French of Dr. J. Mardrus by E.P. Mathois, 4 vols, London 1937ff.—Danish transl. by Oestrup, Copenhagen 1937/8. Russian by Salier I–VIII, Leningrad 1929/36 (see idem, *Izv. Ak. Nauk* 1928, 185/6, 299/300, MSS in Leningrad).—Persian transl. by

ʿAbd al-Laṭīf Tabrīzī (on the order of Prince Bahman of Azarbaijan, a grandson of Fatḥ ʿAlī), Tehran 1315.

64. B. Heller, *Der ar. Antarroman* was never published (see preface to *Die Bedeutung etc.*).—2. *Taghrībat Banī Hilāl*, Damascus 1922, *Qiṣṣat Banī Hilāl*, ibid. 1927.—4. Garr. 730, where the author is said to be Muḥyi ʾl-Dīn Abu ʾl-Faḍl ʿAlbdallāh b. ʿAbd al-Ẓāhir b. Najda al-Ḥizāmī al-Miṣrī.

65. 8. BDMG 120.—9. Read: Muʿādh.

66. *Naẓm al-jumān fī amthāl Luqmān* by ʿAbdallāh Efendi Furayj, C. 1311.

1. 2. Alex. Ḥad. 6, self-commentary Qaw. I, 126; on Ibn al-Munayyir, see Ibn al-Qāḍī, *Durrat al-ḥijāl* II, 389, al-Kattānī, *Fihris* II, 313.—2. al-Kattānī, *Fihris* I, 107.

67. 3, 4. Alex. Bal. 3.

68. 5. al-Kattānī, *Fihris* II, 117/8.—8. Garr. 1457.

70. 7. Ibn al-Qāḍī, *Durrat al-ḥijāl* II, 369, no. 1032, al-Kattānī, *Fihris* II, 197/9.—2. Garr. 643, Alex. Taʾr. 17. Fun. 103,$_3$, 158,$_1$.—Comm.: aa. Self-commentary *Fatḥ al-mughīth*, Garr. 1461, Alex, Muṣṭ. Ḥad. 13.—b. | Alex. Taʾr. 12.—g. Muḥammad 1252
b. Aḥmad al-Sakhāwī, d. 902/1496, Alex. Taʾr. 11.—h. *Fatḥ al-bāqī* by Zakariyyāʾ al-Anṣārī, d. 926/1520, Garr. 1462/4, Alex. Muṣṭ. Ḥad. 12.—i. *al-Badr al-munīr* by Muḥammad al-Rashīdī al-Burullusī al-Awsī al-Anṣārī, composed in 1102/1690, Alex. Taʾr. 5.—6. Garr. 1519/20, Qaw. I, 256, on the printings see Alex. Fun. 135.—7. In the margin of the *Tafsīr* by ʿAbd al-ʿAzīz b. Aḥmad al-Dīrīnī, C. 1310.—16. See al-Kattānī, *Fihris* II, 249.—19. Alex. Fun. 170,$_5$.

71. 8. 3. Alex. Lugha 9.

9. al-Kattānī, *Fihris* II, 435/6.—4. Garr. 1851.—14. Ibid. 1218.

72. 11. al-Kattānī, *Fihris* I, 158.

13. Ibid. I, 236/50.

73. 3. *Taqrīb al-tahdhīb*, Alex. Muṣṭ. Ḥad. 7, Mosul 54,101.—13. *al-Mashyakha al-bāsima lil-Qabbābī* (i.e. Zayn al-Dīn Abū Zayd ʿAbd al-Raḥmān b. ʿUmar

al-Lakhmī al-Miṣrī al-Maqdisī) *wa-Fāṭima (bint) Ṣalāḥ al-Dīn b. al-Fatḥ*, al-Kattānī, *Fihris* II, 59.—19. Alex. Ḥad. 8, Fun. $133_{,11}$.

74. 19. b. Print. India 1311.—e. *Ifhām al-afhām min Sharḥ Bulūgh al-marām* by Yūsuf b. Muḥammad b. Yaḥyā al-Baṭṭāḥ al-Zabīdī, ca. 1243/1827, in the library of Aḥmad b. Ismāʿīl al-Barzanjī in Medina, see al-Kattānī, *Fihris* II, 458.—20a. Alex. Fun. 18.—b. Ibid. $85_{,2}$.—24. Ibid. $20_{,3}$.—34. Istanbul 1315.—39. Glosses by Muḥammad b. ʿUbāda al-Barrī al-ʿAdawī al-Mālikī, Makr. 22.

75. 46. Read: Mosul $47_{,11}$.—57a. *al-Amālī al-Ḥalabiyya*, Alex. Ḥad. 7.—64. Garr. 1466, Alex. Ḥad. $55_{,1}$.—66. Garr. 1405, attributed to al-Haytamī.

76. 79. See p. 529, al-Haytamī.—80. Mosul $52_{,80}$, attributed to al-Haytamī.—84. Garr. 2076,1.—91. *al-Imtāʿ bil-arbaʿīn al-mutabāyina b-sharḥ al-samāʿ*, Alex. Ḥad. 7.—92. *al-Fatāwī al-ḥadīthiyya*, Qaw. I, 138.—93. *al-Durr al-manẓūm ʿani ʾl-Muʿashsharāt*, Alex. Ḥad. 23 (?).—94. *Risāla tataʿallaq bi-baʿḍ asʾila fī aḥwāl al-mayyit*, Alex. Mawāʿiẓ 17.—95. *Khulāṣat mā rawāhu ʾl-wāʿūn fī ʾl-akhbār al-wārida fī ʾl-ṭāʿūn*, continued up to 1053/1643 by Muḥammad al-Ḥimṣī b. al-ʿAtīq al-Shāfiʿī, who died in 1088/1677 in Egypt, Alex. Fun. $85_{,1}$, Ḥad. 22 (autograph).

13a. al-Kattānī, *Fihris* II, 451.

B. 2. *Taḥqīq al-awlā min ahl al-rifq al-aʿlā* Qaw. I, 223.

77. 3, 1. Alex. Taʾr. 11, Makr. 47, C. 1356, 2 vols.—Abstracts: a. Garr. 641, Alex. Taʾr. 18.—*Naẓm ʿuyūn al-athar* by Muḥammad b. Yūsuf (?), Alex. Taʾr. 17.—9. In the library of Yāsīn b. Bāshayān al-ʿAbbāsī in Basra (Ritter).

3d. Shams al-Dīn Muḥammad b. Nāṣir al-Dīn al-Dimashqī, d. 742/1341, *Jāmiʿ al-āthār fī mawlid al-mukhtār*, ḤKh II, $499_{,3559}$, ^{2}I, 533, in 3 vols., Dam. Z. $74_{,42}$.

78. 4, 6. Garr. 663 (author ʿAlī al-ʿAmrīṭī).

5a. Murdered in Ruhā (Edessa/Urfa) in Ramaḍān 885/November 1481, see p. $46_{,10c}$, *Shajara* Alex. Taʾr. 117.

5b. In 868, Muḥammad b. Ärkmäs (-mish ?) al-Ḥanafī al-Ṭawīl al-Yashbakī copied al-Ḥamdānī's *Tadhkira* in Cairo and also wrote *al-Durr al-thamīn fīmā warada fī ummahāt al-muʾminīn*, Fez, library of the sultan, al-Kattānī, *Fihris* I, 441, n. 1.

7. al-Kattānī, *Fihris* II, 318/20.—1. Garr. 650, Alex. Ḥad. 65, Makr. 60.

79. d. Qaw. I, 128.—4. Ibid. I, 29.—13. *Zahr al-riyāḍ wa-shifāʾ al-qulūb al-mirāḍ*, Alex. Mawāʿiẓ 20.

C. 1. b. al-Qāḍī, *Durrat al-ḥijāl* II, 396,1115, al-Kattānī, *Fihris* I, 304/6.

80. 2a, 4. Instead of *al-imām*, read: *al-ilmām*.

| 81. 4. Alex. Taʾr. 43. Ed. H. Kofler, *Islca* = *AKM* XXIII, 6, 18/129.—6. Garr. 787.— 1253
8. Mosul 103$_{,57}$.—4. Additionally Mosul 94$_{,21}$.

82. 8, 1. Mosul 145$_{,57}$, C. 1356; abstract *ʿIqd al-marjān* Alex. Fun. 155$_{,4}$.—Abstract by Ibrāhīm b. ʿUmar al-Shirbīnī al-Shāfiʿī Khaṭīb Ḥalab, composed in 850/1446, in the library of Muḥammad ʿAlī Hibat al-Dīn al-Shahrastānī, and *Unmūdhaj maḥāsin al-wasāʾil* by Abū Muḥammad al-Ḥasan b. Abi ʾl-Ḥasan al-Hādī al-Mūsawī al-ʿĀmilī al-Kāẓimī, d. 1334/1935, written in 1334, *Dharīʿa* II, 408$_{,1630}$ (where the author's name is given as Badr al-Dīn Muḥammad b. ʿAbdallāh al-Subkī, d. 747).

11. 1. Garr. 1393.

83. 12, 1. Leningrad, collection Smogorzewski, Bank. XXIII, 106$_{,2595}$.—b. Read: "*al-adhwāq*".—2. See p. 100, 35a.

13. 2. Alex. Fun. 99$_{,3}$.—7. *Risāla fī dhabb man tāb*, ibid. 2.

85. 22. al-Kattānī, *Fihris* II, 314/6.

86. 1a. 1. Garr. 1630, Cairo^2 IV, 163.

87. 4. 1. Alex. Fiqh Ḥan. 7, Mosul 146$_{,91}$.—2. Alex. Fiqh Ḥan. 26.—6. *ʿUmdat al-ḥukkām*, ḤKh IV, 258, Ind. Off. 1878 (?).

88. 6, 2. Alex. Fiqh Ḥan. 13, Qaw. I, 312.—7. Alex. Fun. 68$_{,9}$, Faw. 25$_{,12}$, Qaw. I, 186.—Comm. by al-Qāriʾ al-Harawī, Alex. Fun. 99$_{,1}$.

89. 8. 1. BDMG 37, Garr. 1736/7, ʿUm. 2454, Alex. Fiqh Ḥan. 18, Qaw. I, 319.

9. 1. Read: DK III, Ind. Off. 1875.—2. Alex. Fiqh Ḥan. 41, rearranged as *al-Fawākih al-Ṭūriyya fī ʾl-ḥawādith al-Miṣriyya* by Muḥammad b. Ḥusayn al-Ṭūrī al-Ḥanafī al-Qadīmī, ibid. 44.

9a. See p. 958,$_{105}$.

9b. Muḥyi ʾl-Dīn ʿAbd al-Qādir b. Muḥammad al-Ḥanafī b. al-Miṣrī, d. 775/1373, *al-Anwār al-sāṭiʿa fī aḥkām al-jumla al-jāmiʿa*, Qaw. I, 306.

10a. 1. Alex. Taʾr. 57.—Abstract *Intikhāb* ibid. 132(?).—4. *al-Mukhtaṣar fī ʿilm al-athar*, Alex. Muṣṭ. Ḥad. 21.

90. 12, 12. Alex. Fun. 66,$_{3}$.—13. Read: I, 538,14.

17. 1. Comm. a. Qaw. I, 287.

91. 17, 1. b. Cairo I^2, 338.—d. *Tanqīḥ al-muʿtabar* by al-Qāriʾ al-Harawī, Lālelī 763, Cairo I^2, 382.—e. *Jawāhir al-afkār* by Manṣūr b. Abi ʾl-Khayrr al-Bilbaysī al-Ḥanafī, Qaw. I, 279.

18. Mosul 37,$_{199}$, answers to questions ibid. 112,$_{80,\ 2}$.—19. Qaw. I, 396.

92. 19a, I. Ind. Off. 1461, Būlāq 1316/7.—Comm., *al-Taqrīr*, Qaw. I, 275.—2b. *Fatḥ al-qadīr lil-ʿājiz al-faqīr*, on which *Natāʾij*, Qaw. I, 403.—3. b. Alex. Tawḥīd 43, Qaw. I, 209.

93. 21. al-Kattānī, *Fihris* II, 321.

21a. Sarī al-Dīn b. al-Shiḥna al-Ḥanafī, ca. 880/1475, *al-Kalām fī tanfīdh mā thabata bil-shahāda ʿala ʾl-khaṭṭ*, Garr. 1731.

22. 3. Paris 3025/6, Garr. 1110, but see ḤKh V, 329,$_{1168}$.

94. 25. Alex. Fun. 99,$_{4}$.

27. 1. Garr. 1733, Alex. Fiqh Ḥan. 26.—6. See p. 88.

27a. See p. 1021,$_{43}$.

28. 1. Alex. Fiqh Ḥan. 68.

95. 30. See p. 920,75a.

B. 1. 1. Garr. 1507, print. Alexandria 1291. 2. Printed edition and Mosul 236$_{,155,5b}$, al-Ḥājj al-Tilimsānī al-Maghribī, *al-Azhār fi 'qtiṣār Shumūsh al-anwār*—5. *Bulūgh al-qaṣd wal-munā fī khawāṣṣ asmā' Allāh al-ḥusnā* or *Khawāṣṣ al-Dimyāṭī*, see addendum to 361, n.

97. 1. Makr. 55.—Comm. a. Alex. Fiqh Māl. 11.—d. Ibid. 5.—dd. Ibid. 14. With glosses by ʿAbd al-Raḥmān al-Ujhūrī, d. 957/1550, see ggg.—f. Makr. 14.—ff. al-Suyūṭī, see ad p. 191.

98. m. Makr. 37.—β Ibid. 48. See al-Kattānī, *Fihris* I, 162.—n. | *al-Mawāhib* 1254
al-jalīla, ibid. 59.—o. Ibid. 35.—α Ibid. 23.—s. Ibid. 36. Glosses by al-Dasūqī, ibid. 19.

99. oo. *Iklīl* by Muḥammad b. Muḥammad al-Sunbāwī al-Amīr, Makr. 5.—pp. *Mawāhib al-jalīl* by Aḥmad b. Sulaymān al-Jīzī al-Shādhilī, Alex. Fiqh Māl. 20.—*al-Muqaddima, mulakhkhaṣ Mukhtaṣar al-shaykh Khalīl* by ʿAlī b. Khiḍr b. Aḥmad al-ʿAmrūsī, d. 1173/1759, ibid. 11.—2. Ibid. 16.

100. 2, 2. Read: 1285.

4, 4. Additionally Dam. Z. 42,25.

101. 5. Read: Makkī.

5a. Muḥammad b. Muḥammad b. Muḥammad Fakhr al-Dīn al-Ṣaqalī, a student of Quṭb al-Dīn al-Sunbāṭī, *qāḍī* in Cairo, d. 15 Dhu 'l-Qaʿda 727/3 December 1327, Subkī, *Ṭab.* VI, 31, *Sirāj al-maʿrifa fi 'l-tanbīh ʿalā nakth al-mutaṣawwifa*, Dam. Z. 36$_{,101,2}$.

6. Read: Najm al-Dīn ʿAbd al-Raḥīm.—3. Aḥmad b. ʿUmar ʿUthmān b. Qarā, whose al-*Rawḍ al-bāsim fi 'l-takannī bi-Abi 'l-Qāsim* is preserved in Dam. Z. 38$_{,127,1}$, an abstract of *al-Durr al-naẓīm fī faḍl bismillāh al-raḥmān al-raḥīm*, ibid. 73$_{,37}$, and an abstract from *al-Masālik bil-manāsik* by Abū Manṣūr al-Kirmāstī, ibid. 38$_{,127,3}$.

7. Ibn al-Qāḍī, *Durrat al-ḥijāl* II, 427,1216.—4. *Risāla jāmiʿa li-zubdat ʿaqāʾid ahl al-sunna wal-jamāʿa*, Garr. $2091_{,1}$.

7a. Read: Ibn al-Ukhuwwa.—1. *Maʿālim al-qurba fī aḥkām al-ḥisba* ed. by R. Levy, Gibb Mem. NS XII, London 1938 (additionally Bodl. II, 96, no. 315, Āṣaf. II, $456_{,181}$), see A.S. Khālidī in *al-Thaqāfa* I (Cairo 1939) no. 7, 47/8, Gaudefroy Demombynes, *JAs.* 230, 454.—2. *al-Mukhabbaʾ wal-raghba fī aḥkām al-ḥisba*, Tunis, Zayt. IV, $432_{,2906}$.

102. 9. Ibn al-Qāḍī, *Durrat al-ḥijāl* II, 466, al-Kattānī, *Fihris* II, 369/71.

103. 10. 2 vols., C. 1356.—17. Bank. XXIII, $46_{,2541}$.—27. Garr. $2003_{,24}$.—33 = (?) *al-Sayf al-ṣaqīl fi ʾl-radd ʿalā Ibn Zafīl* (i.e. the *Nūniyya* by Ibn Qayyim al-Jawziyya), C. 1937.

104. 47. Instead of AS, read: Āṣaf.—*al-Masāʾil al-Ḥalabiyya wa-ajwibatuhā*, Alex. Fiqh Shāf. 40.—50. *Fatwā fī qawl al-nabī kullu mawlūd yūlad ʿala ʾl-fiṭra*, ibid. Fun. $67_{,15}$, $95_{,4}$.—51. *Risāla fi ʾl-farq bayna ṣarīḥ al-maṣdar wa-an al-fiʿl*, ibid. 95,3.—12. Ibn al-Qāḍī, *Durrat al-ḥijāl* II, 347/8.

105. al-Kattānī, *Fihris* II, 372.—1. Alex. Uṣūl 7, Tawḥīd $42_{,4}$.—Comm. c. Alex. Uṣūl 10, Qaw. I, 288, Makr. 41/2.—Glosses: α Garr. 1812, Alex. Uṣūl 9, Mosul $24_{,25}$, $93_{,8}$, $238_{,194}$ (see p. $944_{,147}$); his *Sharḥ al-Irshād* is preserved in Mosul $132_{,187,3}$.—γ Qaw. I, 273.—δ Makr. 16.

106. h. al-Ṣabbān, d. 1206/1791, Garr. 1815.—i. Ḥasan b. Muḥammad al-ʿAṭṭār, d. 1250/1834, C. 1316.—Versif. a. Alex. Uṣūl 11, Dam. Z. $48_{,61}$.—6. Alex. Fiqh Shāf. 5.—7. Garr. 923, Leningrad, Un. 847, 7670/1.—9. *Manāqib al-imām Abī Bakr b. Qawwām*, Garr. 688.

107. 21. 2 vols., C. 1356/1937.—24. *Awḍaḥ al-masālik ila ʾl-manāsik*, Dam. ʿUm. 47, 278/81.

15. Ibn al-Qāḍī, *Durrat al-ḥijāl* II, $376_{,1133}$.—1. With the title *Tamhīd al-wuṣūl ilā maqām istikhrāj al-furūʿ min qawāʿid al-uṣūl*, Alex. Fiqh Shāf. $40_{,1}$.—2. Ibid. $40_{,2}$.—4. Ibid. 41.—6. Ibid. 28.—19. *al-Kalimāt al-muhimma*, *Br. Mus. Quart.* X, 134.

16. 1. Qilič ʿA. 375, Qaw. I, 415.

108. 16, 2. Paris 2093.

18. 9. *Zahr al-ʿarīsh fī aḥkām al-ḥashīsh*, Alex. Fun. 154,1, Qaw. I, 419.—22. *Risāla fī kalimat al-tawḥīd*, Alex. Fun. 87/8.

109. 19, 1. *Ādāb al-qaḍāʾ*, Alex. Fiqh Shāf. 3.

| 110. 21, 22. *al-Ishārāt ilā mā waqaʿa fi ʾl-Minhāj* (I, 681) *min al-asmāʾ wal-amākin* 1255
wal-lughāt, Alex. Fiqh Shāf. 5.

21a. Ibn al-Qāḍī, *Durrat al-ḥijāl* II, 415$_{,1176}$.

22. 4. Alex. Fun. 77$_{,1}$.—a. Ibid. 2.—b. Ibid. Fiqh Shāf. 39$_{,2}$.

111. 22. 4. e. *Fatḥ al-mubīn* by Aḥmad b. Khalīl al-Subkī al-Shāfiʿī, d. 1032/1623, Alex. Fiqh Shāf. 31.—f. Aḥmad al-Azharī al-Tarmānīnī, 1281/1864, copied in the author's lifetime, ibid. 26.—7. Read: *al-awānī*.—12. Alex. Fun. 157$_{,8}$.—15. Garr. 92/3, Alex. Fun. 116.—17. Alex. Fiqh Shāf. 26.—27. *Urjūza fī ṭabaqāt al-anbiyāʾ*, Alex. Fun. 98$_{,1}$.—28. *Majmūʿ fī aḥkām al-najāsāt wa-anwāʿihā*, Alex. Fiqh Shāf. 38$_{,1}$.—29. *Risāla fī Nīl Miṣr wa-ahrāmihā*, Alex. Fun. 77$_{,3}$, Taʾr. 112.—30. *Fī manbaʿ al-Nīl*, composed in 780, ibid. Fun. 77$_{,4}$.

22a. See p. 967$_{,6}$.

112. 23, 12. See Dam. Z. 88$_{,44}$.—13. *Zawāl al-taraḥ* see I, 635.

24. 1. Comm. Garr. 1826, Alex. Fiqh Shāf. 28.—2. Comm. a. *Isʿāf al-qāṣid li-tafhīm masāʾil al-Sh. al-Z.* by Abu ʾl-Ḥasan ʿAlī b. Muḥammad b. Muḥammad al-Maḥallī al-Shāfiʿī, Alex. Fiqh Shāf. 4.—b. *al-Futūḥāt al-Aḥmadiyya*, Garr. 1827 (mistakenly identified as glosses on the *ʿUmdat al-rābiḥ*, I), Alex. Fiqh Shāf. 16$_{,32}$.—d. *Tadhkirat al-ʿābid* by Shihāb al-Dīn Aḥmad b. Muḥammad b. ʿAbd al-Salām, d. 931/1524, ibid. 11.

25. 6. Alex. Mawāʿiẓ 30$_{,1}$, 39$_{,2}$.—10. *al-Asbāb al-muhlikāt wal-ishārāt al-wāḍiḥāt fī manāqib al-muʾminīn wal-muʾmināt wa-mā la-hum min al karāmāt wal-ʿalāmāt*, Qaw. I, 217, II, 226.

113. 27, 1. Alex. Uṣūl 21; on which glosses by Abū ʿAbdallāh Muḥammad b. Aḥmad b. ʿAbdallāh, Ind. Off. 1487.

28. See p. 1027$_{,3}$.

29. 1. f. Būlāq 1291, in the margin of a β.

114. 29c. Aḥmad b. Yūsuf al-Sharjī, d. 862/1458, *al-Ṭirāz al-mudhahhab li-aḥkām al-madhhab*, ḤKh IV, 156,$_{7945}$, Mosul 199,$_{17,19}$.

115. 32, 2. Instead of *min al-*, read: *bil-*.—Garr. 1828.—4. *al-Jawhar al-fard fīmā yukhālif fīhi 'l-ḥurr al-ʿabd*, Alex. Fun. 121,$_{8}$.

33. See p. 932,$_{23}$.—*Bishārat al-maḥbūb bi-ghufrān al-dhunūb*, Dam. Z. 53,$_{87}$.

35b. Taqī al-Dīn Abū Bakr b. Walī al-Dīn b. Qāḍī ʿAjlūn al-Shāfiʿī, d. 876/1471, *Iʿlām al-nabīh bi-mā zāda ʿala 'l-Minhāj min al-Ḥāwī wal-Bahja wal-Tanbīh*, Alex. Fiqh Shāf. 5.

36. Garr. 2092,1.

117. 41. al-Kattānī, *Fihris* II, 81/2.—1. Alex. Fun. 88,$_{1}$.—2. Ibid. Mawāʿiẓ 9.—11. Ibid. Fun. 167,$_{23}$.

44. 4. *Br. Mus. Quart.* VI, 97 (dated 888 AH).

45. al-Kattānī, *Fihris* I, 344.

118. 3. Qaw. I, 74.—4. *Fatḥ al-jalīl etc.* Makr. 47.—7a. Alex. Fun. 40.—Glosses by ʿAlī b. Aḥmad b. Mukarram, Makr. 22.—c. *Khayr al-kalām* by ʿAlī al-Ḥalabī, Qaw. II, 255.—d. Anon. ibid. 257.—14. *al-Iʿlām wal-ihtimām etc.*, Alex. Fiqh Shāf. 6.—15. Ibid. Fun. 150,$_{15}$.—18. *al-Adwāʾ al-bahiyya*, ibid. 166,$_{4}$.—42. Following the *Ādāb al-qaḍāʾ* of al-Ghazzī (p. 109,19), Garr. 1818.—45. *Nubdha fī bayān al-alfāẓ al-muṣṭalaḥ ʿalayhā ʿinda 'l-uṣūliyyīn*, Qaw. I, 300, *Qurrat ʿuyūn*, Garr. 1964.—53. *al-Daqāʾiq al-muḥkama*, Alex. Fun. 174,$_{20}$, 190,$_{2}$.—54. *Taḥrīr tanqīḥ al-lubāb*, comm. *Tuḥfat al-ṭullāb*, glosses by Ḥabīb b. Aḥmad b. ʿAbdallāh al-Madābighī, Makr. 25.—50. *Tuḥfat al-rāghibīn fī bayān amr al-ṭawāʿīn*, Alex. Fun. 144,$_{1}$.

119. 3. al-Kattānī, *Fihris* I, 199/202.

1256 120. H. Laoust, *Essai sur les doctrines sociales et politiques d'Ibn* | *T.* Cairo, IFAO (in press).—ʿAbdallāh b. Muḥammad b. ʿAbd al-Hādī, *al-ʿUqūd al-durriyya min manāqib Shaykh al-Islām Ibn Taymiyya*, C. 1938 (518 pp., with an inventory of his works on p. 38ff.).—5a. *al-Muntaqā min akhbār al-Muṣṭafā*, 2 vols., C. 1933.—11. In *Majmūʿa*, India 1296.—13a. *Muqaddima fī uṣūl al-tafsīr*, Damascus

1936.—13b. *Risāla fi 'l-Qur'ān wa-mā waqa'a fīhi min al-nizā' hal huwa qadīm am muḥdath*, Qaw. I, 189.—13c. *Risāla fīmā waqa'a fi 'l-Qur'ān bayna 'l-'ulamā' hal huwa makhlūq aw ghayr makhlūq wa-bayān al-ḥaqq fī dhālika wa-mā dalla 'alayhi 'l-kitāb wal-sunna wal-ijmā'*, Qaw. I, 67.—13d. *Tafsīr qawlihi ta'ālā wa-kallama 'llāhu Mūsā taklīman* (p. $4_{,162}$), in *Majmū'a*, India 1296.

121. 24b. *Taḥwīl mukhtalaf al-ḥadīth fi 'l-radd 'alā ahl al-ḥadīth wal-jam' bayna 'l-akhbār allati 'dda'aw 'alayka 'l-tanāquḍ wal-ikhtilāf*, C. n.d.—25. *Sharḥ al-'aqīda al-Iṣfahāniyya* by Muḥammad b. Maḥmūd Shams al-Dīn al-Iṣfahānī (d. 688/1289), C. 1329.—29. Qaw. I, 206.

122. 43. Read: "Dam. Z. $36_{99,15}$".—48. Read: "35,99".

123. 75. Read: "Dam. Z. $82_{,2,4}$".—81. See M.A. Guidi, *RSO* XIII, 394/403.—84a. *al-Radd 'ala 'l-Ikhnā'* (the Mālikī *qāḍī* of Damascus), in the margin of the *Kitāb al-Istiyāh = al-Radd 'ala 'l-Bakrī*, C. 1346, Laoust, loc. cit.

124. 93. See *Isl. Culture* I, 1927, p. 91.—102a. *Qā'ida fī ziyārat bayt al-Maqdis*, ed. Ch. D. Matthews, *JAOS* 56, 1/21.—109. *al-Ijtimā' wal-firāq fī masā'il al-aymān wal-ṭalāq*, Dam. Z. 35, 99, 8.—*Risāla fi 'l-ijtimā' wal-iftirāq fi 'l-ḥilf bil-ṭalāq*, C. 1934, see H. Laoust, Une *riṣāla* d'Ibn Taymiyya sur le serment de répudiation. *Bull. d'Et. Or. de l'Inst. franç. de Damas*, VII/VIII, 1937/8, 215/36.—114. Mosul $62_{,181}$ = *al-Siyāsa al-shar'iyya fī aḥkām al-sulṭān 'ala 'l-ra'iyya* (anon.), ibid. 157,107.

125. 131. C. 1318.—140a. *al-Masā'il wal-ajwiba*, Alex. Fiqh Ḥanb. 7.—140b. *Faṣl mujtahidīn hal kullu mujtahid muṣīb etc.*, Dam. Z. $36_{,99,12}$.—140. c. *Kalām 'alā mas'alat al-shiṭranj*, ibid. 86, 2, 3a. *Faṣl fī anwā' al-istiftāḥ fi 'l-ṣalāt*, ibid. b.—*Jawāb 'an su'āl ulqiya 'alayhi 'ani 'l-qiyām ba'd al-adhān al-awwal yawm al-jum'a*, ibid. c. and elsewhere—141. Delete: "Mosul $62_{,181}$".

126. 7. Alex. Mawā'iẓ 26.—8. Print. in *Rasā'il Munīriyya*, 4 vols., Damascus n.d.—12. Vol. 2 *Br. Mus. Quart.* XI, 184, vol. 3. Alex. Fun. $133_{,15}$.

127. 14. Garr. 1905.—15. Ed. Maḥmūd Ḥasan Rabī', C. 1939.—23. Br. Mus. Or. 8090, 9259. See F. Cooke in *The Moslem World* 1937, SA 1/18, print. C. 1938, abstract by Ismā'īl b. Muḥammad b. Bardis entitled *As'ila 'adīda wa-ajwiba mufīda etc.* Heid., *ZDMG* 91, 381 (mistakenly said to be new).—31. C. 1323.

128. 40. Br. Mus. Or. 9219.—47. C. 1344.

4b. 6. *al-Muḥarram fi 'l-ḥadīth*, Cairo^{2} I, 144.

129. 6, 3. *Aḥwāl al-qubūr*, Alex. Mawāʿiẓ 6.—5. Alex. Mawāʿiẓ 34, C. 1924.

130. 13. Alex. Fun. 160, 6.—17. *Faḍāʾil al-Shām*, Alex. Taʾr. 108.—18. *Mashyakha* see al-Kattānī, *Fihris* II, 60.

7a. 3. Garr. 1844.

8. 1. *al-Mibrad* (al-Kattānī, *Fihris* II, 453), see p. 947,$_{81}$.

131. 48. *Wuqūʿ al-balāʾ wal-bukhl wal-bukhalāʾ*, Dam. Z. 81,$_{46}$.—49. *Maḥḍ al-khalāṣ fī manāqib Saʿd b. Abī Waqqāṣ*, ibid. 83,$_{78}$.—50. *al-Mashyakha al-wusṭā*,
1257 ibid. 84,$_{86,2}$.—51. *Sayr al-ḥāthth ilā ʿilm al-ṭalāq al-thalāth* ibid. 35,$_{99,2}$.— | 52. *Wafāt al-nabī*, ibid. 6.—53. *al-Arbaʿūn al-mukhtāra min ḥadīth b. Abī ʿUmar* (Shams al-Dīn al-Ḥanbalī), Garr. 2123,2.—54. *al-ʿAshara al-mukhtāra*, ibid. 3.

E. 1. Read: al-Shahīd al-Awwal, 792.—RAAD IX, 273/6.

132. Glosses: b. see p. 450, on which *ḥawāshī* by himself, in light of notes by Khalīfa Sulṭān (g) to the commentary by his grandfather, Ind. Off. 1836, another *ḥāshiya* ibid. 1837 and a *taʿlīq* ibid. 1839.—i. Read: *al-Tuḥfa al-Gharawiyya*, see p. 498.—k. Shaykh Jaʿfar, who was *qāḍī* of Isfahan in the 12th/18th century, Ind. Off. 1838, Bank. XIX, 2, 1922.—l. *al-Anwār al-Gharawiyya*, in 10 vols., by Muḥammad al-Jawād b. Taqī b. Muḥammad Mollā Kuttāb al-Aḥmadī al-Bayānī al-Najafī, d. after 1267/1851, MSS *Dharīʿa* II, 435,$_{1700}$.—3. Comm. by Ḥusayn al-Khwansārī, (p. 412) Teh. Sip. I, p. 445.—4. Ind. Off. 1804/6; 31 commentaries on it are listed in *Dharīʿa* II, 296/7.—Supplement thereto *Bayān al-mutaḥābbāt fi 'l-ṣalāt* Ind. Off. 1807.—8. *al-Asʾila al-Miqdādiyya*, asked by Abū ʿAbdallāh Miqdād b. ʿAbdallāh b. Muḥammad b. Ḥusayn b. Muḥammad al-Suyūrī al-Ḥillī al-Asadī, d. 826/1423 (p. 209) in *Majmūʿat rasāʾil Aḥmad b. Fahd al-Ḥillī* in Mashhed, *Dharīʿa* II, 92, 265.

133. 2a. His student, Ḥasan b. Sulaymān b. Khālid al-Ḥillī, wrote *Ithbāt al-rajīʿa*, library of Rājā Fayḍābādī no. 3, Madrasat Fāḍil Khān in Mashhhed, *Dharīʿa* I, 91,$_{439}$.—2. *Mukhtaṣar al-Baṣāʾir* ibid.—3. See p. 898,$_{7}$.—4. RAAD IX, 341.—3. *Nūr ḥadaq al-badīʿ* Qaw. II, 178.

134. 2, 14. *Ibṭāl al-ḥiyal* is cited by Ibn Ḥajar, DK, I, 153,$_{15}$.

2a. 5c. Garr. 1213/4.

135. 2a. 17. *Khulāṣat al-abḥāth fī sharḥ Nahj al-damātha, naẓm al-qirā'āt al-thalāth* Garr. 1210.—20. Qaw. I, 13.—25. *Diwan* C. 1324.

4. Read: "Qaw. I, 78/9, Makr. 53".

136. al-Kattānī, *Fihris* I, 108.—2. C. 1926.—14. 1. *Ḥirz al-amānī* (I, 725).—21. *Hidāyat al-naḥw*, anon. glosses *Dirāyat al-Hidāya*, India n.d. (Alex. Naḥw 16).

137. 7, 8. *Bayān maʿānī mushkil al-badīʿ* see I, 658.

8. 3. Garr. 1292.

139. 20, 1. 1. Qaw. I, 7.

22. See p. 42,11.

141. 25. 52. *Lawāmiʿ al-anwār fi 'l-taṣawwuf* (according to others by Sirāj al-Dīn ʿUmar al-Hindī, d. 773/1371) Alex. Fun. 159,4.

142. 27, 2. Read: al-Qaṭr, Garr. 1226.—3. Ibid. 1225.—4. Additionally Istanbul, Un. Riza P. 1142 (Pretzl on al-Dānī, *Taysīr Muq*. S.ṭ.)

§ 8. 2. Read: Sighnāq in Central Asia, see Barthold, *Turkestan*, Index.

144. 4f. Abū Firās ʿUbaydallāh b. Shibl b. Abī Firās b. Jamīl wrote, on 17 Rajab 725/30 June 1325, *al-Radd ʿala 'l-Rāfiḍa wal-Yazīdiyya* Köpr. *Majmūʿa* 1617, see ʿAbbās al-ʿAzzāwī, *Ta'rīkh al-Yazīdiyya* 81ff. M. Šerefeddīn Yazidiler, *Dār al-funun Ilah. Fak. Mecm.* 1926, p. 1135, M. Guidi, *Atti del XIX congr. d. or.* 560.

4g. Raslān b. Sībawayh b. ʿAbdallāh al-Dimashqī, a contemporary of Taqī al-Dīn al-Subkī, d. 771/1369, *Risāla fi 'l-Tawḥīd*, comm. by Ḥasan b. Mūsā al-Bānī al-Kurdī al-Dimashqī, d. 1118/1735 in Damascus, Alex. Tawḥīd 21.

145. § 9. 2. 9. Additionally Alex. Faw. 20, Makr. 13.

146. 12. Garr. 2003,$_{17}$, Alex. Adab 134,$_{2}$, Mawāʿiẓ 36,$_{1}$, published in *Saʿādat al-dārayn* together with *al-Manẓūma al-Mawṣiliyya al-ʿUthmāniyya fī* | *asmā'* 1258
al-suwar al-Qur'āniyya, C. (?) 1318 (Sarkīs 1791).—Comm. a. Qaw. I, 254/5.—

b. Alex. Taṣ. 20.—t. *Īqāẓ al-himam* by Aḥmad b. Muḥammad b. ʿAjība al-Ḥusaynī al-Maghribī, composed in 1211/1796, in *Majmūʿa*, C. 1324.—13. Alex. Taṣ. $35_{,10}$, $41_{,1}$.—15. Makr. 53.

147. 20. *Uns al-ʿarūs*, Alex. Taṣ. 7.—21. *Waṣiyyat shuhbat al-samāʿ*, with the commentary *Kashf al-qināʿ* by ʿAlī b. Muḥammad al-Miṣrī, 10th cent. Alex. Taṣ. 29.—3. Garr. 683/4, Alex. Taʾr. 23, Makr. 7.

148. 6, 6. Makr. 45.—11. *Ḥizb al-fatḥ*, Alex. Taṣ. 35, 13.—7. *Ḥayāt al-qulūb*, Alex. Taṣ. 16.

149. 11, 1. Additionally Garr. 87, 94, Alex. Adab 132, Bank XXIII, $30_{,2545}$.—10. *al-Tāʾiyya al-kubrā*, Alex. Adab 132.—11. *al-ʿUrūsh*, ibid. Taṣ. 24.

11a. ʿAbdallāh Makhdūm al-Malik wrote, in 809/1406 in Jerusalem: *Kashf al-ghumma ʿan baṣāʾir al-aʾimma*, Alex. Mawāʿiẓ 32.

12a. Bank. XXIII, $51_{,2546}$.

150. 15a, 8. *al-Ḥukm al-maḍbūṭ fī taḥrīm fiʿl qawm Lūṭ*, Alex. Fun. 159,1.

151. 22. Abu ʾl-Fatḥ Muḥammad b. Badr al-Dīn Muḥammad b. ʿAlī b. Ṣāliḥ b. Abi ʾl-Wafāʾ al-ʿAwfī al-Iskandarī (ḤKh IV, 356). 3. *al-Ḥujja al-rājiḥa*, Dam. ʿUm. $68_{,125}$.

23. See A. Schmidt, *al-Shaʿrānī*, 1924, Index.

24. Ibn ʿAbdallāh b. Muḥammad b. Maḥmūd Raḍī al-Dīn Khaṭīb Qaḍāʾ wrote, in 845/1441: *Kitāb al-khuṭab*, Br-H.[2] 1133, Garr. 1914.

152. 29b. Ibrāhīm b. Ḥasan b. ʿAlī b. Isḥāq al-Faraḍī, d. 880/1475, *Minhāj al-mudhakkirīn wa-miʿrāj al-muḥaḍḍirīn*, Alex. Maw. 46.

32c. = p. 359, 3c, $1006_{,92}$, al-Shaʿrānī, *Ṭab.* 62, al-Nabhānī, *Karāmāt al-awliyāʾ* I, 170.—1. Leid. 2285, Garr. 1583, print. Damascus 1309, see E. Jabra Jurji, *Illumination in Islamic Mysticism*, (Princeton Oriental Texts IV), Princeton 1938, on which C. Brockelmann, *Or.* IX, 1940 p. 176/9.—4. AS 4296,11, Fātiḥ 2620,2, Cairo *Nashra* 21 with *Qarʿ etc.*, see Farmer, *Sources* 58.

153. 35, 1. *Risālat al-ikhwān etc.* additionally Alex. Fun. $80_{,1}$.—2. Garr. 1917.—3. *al-Risāla al-Maymūniyya fī tawḥīd al-Jurrūmiyya*, ibid. 2.

37. M. Demirdāš. 1. Alex. Fun. $150_{,9}$.

§ 10. 1. Alex. Ḥisāb 18.—Comm. d. Ibid. 4.—Abbreviation. a. Comm. β Garr. 2145, entitled *Nuzhat al-albāb fī taʿrīf al-ḥisāb* Alex. Ḥisāb $15_{,1}$.—ζ *al-Nubha* by Muḥammad b. Fakhr al-Dīn b. Qays al-ʿUrḍī, Bodl. I, $966_{,5}$ (Suter 505).—η Aḥmad b. Muḥammad b. Muḥammad al-Ghazzī Shihāb al-Dīn, d. 983/1575, Garr. 1042.—ϑ *Tuḥfat al-ṭullāb* by Abu ʾl-Faḍl Muḥammad b. Aḥmad b. Ayyūb al-Shāfiʿī Imām al-Naḥḥāsiyya, BMS 752 (MS dated 889/80). Anon. comm. on a versification, Garr. $2084_{,4}$.—2. Garr. 1035/6, $2113_{,3}$, $2145_{,1}$, Lālelī $2723_{,9}$.—Comm. a. Alex. Ḥisāb 11, $15_{,2}$, Fun. $142_{,4}$, $186_{,1}$.—b. Aḥmad b. Mūsā b. ʿAbd al-Ghaffār, Garr. 1038.—3a. See ḤKh VI, 95, Alex. Ḥisāb 24 (which has *al-Musriʿ* just like Berl. 5991, Bank. XXII, $23_{,2428}$), abbreviated from *al-Mumtiʿ* Makr. 58 (as in Bank., loc. cit., where this information is wrongly doubted).

155. Line 5. Instead of 3, read: c. Garr. 1049, Alex. Ḥisāb 23, Bank. XXII, $24_{,2429}$.—4. Garr. 1876.—Comm. *al-Fuṣūl*, ibid. 1877, Alex. Far. 11.—5. Alex. Far. 4.—6. Comm. a. Self-commentary, Garr. 1825.—7. Alex. Ḥisāb 19, abstract *al-Wasīla* in Garr. 1034, Alex. Ḥisāb 16, 20, Lālelī $2723_{,9}$.—*Ḥāshiya* by Muḥammad b. Muḥammad b. Bakr al-Azharī al-Bilbaysī, Cairo[1] II, 180.—8. Alex. Far. 16, Ḥisāb $15_{,2}$.—19. *al-Shubbāk fī aʿmāl al-munāsakhāt*, Alex. Far. 8.—20. *Ghāyat* | *al-sūl fī ʾl-iqrār bil-dayn al-majhūl*, Alex. Ḥisāb 22.—21. *Manẓūma fī ʾl-jabr* 1259
wal-muqābala, Alex. Fun. $82_{,9}$.—2. See p. 379, § 9. 2. 1. *Rafʿ al-ishkāl* additionally Alex. Ḥisāb 30.—2. *Marāsim al-intisāb* see p. 379, Jārullāh $1509_{,1}$ dated 774 AH.—3. *Kayfiyyat al-ittifāq fī tarkīb al-awfāq* Jārullāh $1581_{,3}$ (Krause).—See Sánchez Pérez, *Biografías de los matemáticos que florescieron en España*, Madrid 1922, p. 142.

156. 3. *Ḥāwi ʾl-lubāb*, of which a fragment is cited in Carra de Vaux, *Bibl. Math.* 13 (1899), p. 35 (Suter 502).

4. Muḥammad b. ʿAbdallāh b. ʿAyyāsh (Suter 495).

5. = 1018,13.

§ 11. 1. Aḥmad b. Abī Bakr b. ʿAlī (AS 2762, which belonged to him at a certain point in time; in the year 714/1314 he copied AS 1719, see Krause, *Stamb. Hdss.* 506). Suter 508, see p.327, 4.—3. *Risāla fī ʾl-jayb al-mujannaḥ*, Cairo[1] V 274.—4. *Masāʾil handasiyya*, ibid. 205.—5. *al-ʿAmal bi-rafʿ al-muqanṭarāt*, Berl. 5859.

2. Muḥammad b. Samʿūn al-Muwaqqit, d. 737/1336.—3. *Kanz al-ṭullāb fī ʾl-ʿamal bil-asṭurlāb*, Paris 2524,₃.—4. *al-Uṣūl al-thāmira fī ʾl-ʿamal bi-rubʿ al-musātara*, Qaw. I, 275.

3. See Schmalzl, *Zur Gesch. des Quadranten* p. 33/7. 86.—3. Alex. Ḥisāb 49.—8. *Kashf al-rayb*, Serāi 3483,$_{18}$.

157. 4. See Sánchez Pérez, *Los matemáticos en la Biblioteca del Escorial*, Madrid 1929, p. 8.—1. *al-Zīj al-jadīd*, Garr. 973, comm. see ad p. 160,$_{13}$. 485, 6a.—3. Qaw. II, 277.

5. 4. Mosul 179,$_{129}$.

5a. 1. Garr. 2141,$_{1}$.

158. 1. *Imām awqāt al-ṣalāt* at the Umayyad mosque, *Talkhīṣ* additionally Paris 2547,$_{12}$ (untitled).—3. *Risāla fī ʾl-rubʿ al-musattar bi-arḍ Dimashq*, ibid. 8.

8. 1. Alex. Ḥisāb 52.—b. Read: Muḥammad b. Aḥmad al-Khaḍarī, d. 1288, see Alex. Ḥisāb 51.

9. 1. Bank. XXII, 97,$_{2469\ IV}$, composed in 874/1469, comm. *al-Riyy wal-ishbāʿ* by al-Urmayūnī Berl. 573, Cairo[1] V, 260, 310.—5. *al-Risāla fī ʿurūḍ al-bilād wa-aṭwālihā*, Bank. XXII, 94,$_{2469}$.—6. *al-Fuṣūl fī maʿrifat al-mawqiʿ wa-niṣf al-quṭr wa-buʿd al-markaz lil-muqanṭarāt*, ibid. 95,$_{III}$.—7. *Dhayl al-musāfir* (10, 11), ibid. 97, $_{V}$.—8. *Risāla fī maʿrifat mawāḍiʿ arkān al-Kaʿba min al-jihāt al-arbaʿ*, ibid. 10,$_{XIII}$.—9. *Risāla fī ʾl-asṭurlāb*, composed in 874, ibid. XIV.

159. 10, 8. Manual for its use also in Esc. 956, 3. Cairo[1] V, 282.—20. *Ibrāz laṭāʾif al-ghawāmiḍ* additionally Alex. Far. 3. Fun. 82,1.—21. *al-Muftakarāt al-ḥisābiyya* with the commentary of Nūr al-Dīn ʿAlī al-Faraḍī, composed in 868 AH, Esc. 948,$_{3}$.—26. Read: Bodl. I, 1023,$_{3}$.—28. *al-Fuṣūl al-ʿashara* with the commentary *Ghāyat al-sūl* by Yūnus b. ʿAbd al-Qādir b. Aḥmad al-Rashīdī, Alex. Ḥisāb 60,$_{3}$.—29. *Bahjat al-albāb fī ʿilm al-aṣṭurlāb*, ibid. 44.—30. *Manẓūma fī maʿrifat ikhrāj al-qibla*, with the commentary by al-ʿAṭṭār (p. 9), Bank. XXII, 100,$_{2469,XII}$.

160. 13. Abu ʾl-ʿAbbās Aḥmad b. Burhān al-Dīn Ibrāhīm b. Khalīl b. Aḥmad al-Ḥalabī Shams al-Dīn, d. 859/1455.—2. *Nuzhat al-nāẓir fī taṣḥīḥ uṣūl Ibn al-Shāṭir* (157,4), Bank. XXII, 56,$_{2465}$.—3. *ʿIqd al-amālī* see ad p. 485, 6a.

15. 4. Read: *al-naẓar*.—5. Lālelī 2726,$_5$, AS 2626, comm. *al-Mufaṣṣal fī 'l-ʿamal bi-dāʾirat al-muʿaddil* by Muḥammad b. Abi 'l-Fatḥ al-Ṣūfī, 9th cent., Alex. Ḥisāb 53.

16. 1. Additionally Cairo[1] V, 228, 272.

161. 1, 2. Heid. ZDMG 91, 384 (*Aḥkām al-firāsa*), Qaw. II, 291, Alex. Fun. 53.

2. 1. Alex. Taʾr. 111, 116, Jaghr. 5, see C.D. Matthews, *JPOS* 1935, 284/93, text 51–87.—4. *Manṭiq*, Garr. 819.

162. 3a. ʿAbdallāh b. Hishām, d. 761/1360, *Taḥṣīl al-uns li-zāʾir al-Quds*, Alex. Taʾr. 108.

6. *al-Kawākib etc.* Būlāq 1325.

7. *Muthīr al-gharām* | *etc.* Garr. 590, Alex. Taʾr. 107. 1260

8. *Kharīdat al-ʿajāʾib*, Garr. 767/70, 21122, Alex. Jaghr. 20.

10a. al-Sakhāwī, *Ḍawʾ* X, 226/9 (on his family), Wiet in *Mél. Basset* I, 1923, p. 311 (Heffening).

11. 5. As. Mus. Leningrad A. 327.

13. b. 810/1407.

164. 13, 1. Garr. 598, Alex. Taʾr. 5.—2. *Jawāhir al-ʿuqūd wa-muʿīn al-quḍāt wal-muwaqqiʿīn wal-shuhūd*, Garr. 1824, Alex. Fiqh Shāf. 14.

§ 13. 1. *Badhl etc.*, see Oestrup, *Orient. Höflichkeit*, Leipzig 1929, 68/9.

165. 2, 1. Vol. 2. Garr. 209. See H. Lammens, La Chine d'après al-Calc., *al-Mashriq* IV, 406/11, 446/61, O. Spies, *An Arab account of India in the 14th Century*, Stuttgart 1936 (Bonner Or. St. 14).—2. Baghdad 1332 (see Sarkis).

3. 2. Maqarr b. Rashīd in al-Sakhāwī III, 17 Baqar (Heffening).

4b. Muḥammad b. Aḥmad al-Ṣaydāwī, *al-Kiyāsa fī aḥkām al-siyāsa* (MS dated 884 AH) Jer. Khāl. 49,1.

4c. Nūraddīn ʿAlī b. Abi ʾl-Fatḥ wrote, before 947/1540 (the date of the MS): *Manhaj al-ṣawāb fī qubḥ istiktāb ahl al-kitāb*, Qaw. I, 267.

6. 1. Additionally Garr. 752, see ʿAbbās al-ʿAzzāwī, *Taʾrīkh al-ʿIrāq bayna ʾl-iḥtilālayn*, passim.

166. § 14. 2a. Baktūt, a general under Baybars, d. 711/1311, *Kitāb fī ʿilm al-furūsiyya*, from which *Fawāʾid jalīla fī maʿrifat al-dawābb allatī lā taṣluḥ lil-qany wa-lā lil-jihād waʿādātihā*, Garr. 2083,4.

2b. al-Ḥusayn b. Muḥammad al-Ḥusaynī (= 986, 34?) wrote, in 729/1329: *Idrāk al-sūl fī musābaqat al-khuyūl*, on the horses of Sultan al-Nāṣir, Garr. 1066.

167. 4. *Kitāb fi ʾl-jihād wal-furūsiyya wa-funūn al-ādāb al-ḥarbiyya* additionally Alex. Fun. ḥarb. 78.

5. 3. Alex. Fun. ḥarb. 76, Leningrad 762 (following Pet. Ros. 213, see Kračkovsky, *Tantāwī* 108, no. 19).—5. *al-Aḥkām al-mulūkiyya wal-ḍawābiṭ al-nāmūsiyya fī fann al-qitāl fi ʾl-baḥr*, collection A. Taymūr, see J. Zaydān, *Taʾr. al-adab* III, 254/5, *al-Muqtaṭaf*, May 1932, p. 88).

168. 6b, 3. *al-Lumaʿ fi ʾl-ḥawādith wal-bidaʿ* Berl. Qu. 1681, Cairo ²I, 351, ḤKh V, 332,11180.

6c. See *RSO* IV, 723.

6e. Ḥusayn b. ʿAbd al-Raḥmān b. Muḥammad b. ʿAbdallāh al-Yūnānī, *al-Qaṣīda al-Yūnāniyya fi ʾl-ramy ʿani ʾl-qaws* Alex. Fun. ḥarb. 81 (MS dated 942 AH).

6f. Yūsuf al-Ḥāṣibānī, *Sirāj al-layl fī surūj al-khayl*, Beirut 1066.

169. 1b. See ad I, 888.

1c. *al-Nāṣirī* or *Kāmil al-ṣināʿatayn al-bayṭara wal-zardaqa*, Alex. Ṭibb 36.

3.5. Ed. P. Anastase Marie de St. Élie, C. 1939. *al-Durr al-naẓīm*, fragm. in Hebrew characters, Gottheil, *JQR* XXIII, 1932, 176/80, not identified as such, see Farmer, *Sources* 52.

170. 4. See M. Meyerhof, *The History of Trachoma Treatment*, C. 1936, p. 46/7.

4b. Additionally Mashh. XVI, 6,$_{20}$.

171. § 16. 1. I, 1. BDMG 61, Garr. 1067, Mashh. XVI, 12,$_{38/9}$, see J. de Somogyi, Biblical Figures in al-Damīrī's *Ḥayāt al-ḥayawān, Jub. Vol. Mahler*, Budapest, 1937, 263/99.—2. BDMG 62 (?), anon. *Mukhtaṣar* Alex. Fun. 201.

§ 16a. Music. 1. Muḥammad b. Muḥammad al-Ṣabbāḥ, 14th cent., see p. 1036, 7.

2. Abu 'l-Ḥasan Muḥammad b. Ḥasan b. al-Ṭaḥḥān, 14th cent. 1. *Ḥāwi 'l-funūn wa-salwat al-maḥzūn*, Cairo, Fun. jam. 539 (*Nashra* 71). See Farmer, *Studies in Or. Musical Instr.*, Glasgow 1939, *Sources* 55.

3. Muḥammad b. ʿAbd al-Ḥamīd al-Lādhiqī, d. 849/1445. 1. *al-Risāla al-fatḥiyya fi 'l-mūsīqī*, Br. Mus. Or. 6629, Cairo, Fun. jam. 364 (*Nashra* 71), Farmer, *Sources* 57.—2. *Zayn al-alḥān fī ʿilm ta'līf al-awzān* ibid.

| 172. 2. See J. Holmyard, *Iraq* IV, 47/53.—1. Additionally NO, 3618, Bank. XXII 131, 1261
2496/8.—3. Cairo Ṭab. 318, 413.—7. *Natā'ij al-fikar* additionally Alex. Kīm. 12,$_{1}$.—8. Cairo, Ṭab. 566, NO 3620, Bank. XXII, 133,$_{24991}$.—10. Cairo, Ṭab. 417.—Published as *Kanz al-ikhtiṣāṣ*, Bombay 1891 (composed in Damascus ca. 743 AH).—16. Taymūr, Ṭab. 95.—21. *Ghāyat al-surūr*, composed in 741 AH, C. 1881.

4. *Zahr etc.* Alex. Bal. 12.

173. 9, 1. Garr. 841.—3. *Sharḥ bayt min manẓūmat Kashf al-rān li-Ibn ʿArabī*, Garr. 942.

§ 18. 1. 1. Corrections by al-Maghribī, *RAAD* vols V, VII, IX, X, see Kračkovsky, *EI* III, 1045ff.

174. 2. I, 3. Heid. *ZDMG* 91, 389, Garr. 81, 2903,$_{23}$, Qaw. II, 222.—Comm. a. Garr. 82, 1810, Alex. Mawāʿiẓ 26, Fun. 127,$_{1}$.

175. 5d. *al-Kalām ʿalā mi'at ghulām* Serāi 2373,1, (*RSO* IV, 705), Alex. Adab 32,2.—6. See ad I, 525.—IV. 9. *Bahjat al-ḥāwī*, with the commentary *al-Ghurar al-bahiyya* by Zakariyyā' b. Muḥammad al-Anṣārī, d. 926/1520 (see p. 117), Alex. Fiqh Shāf. 29.—V. 13. Garr. 938/9, commentary entitled *al-Minaḥ al-il.* Alex. Mawāʿiẓ 45.

3. 1. Alex. Ta'r. 125, Fez, Qar. 1324 (*al-Masālik wal-mamālik*).

176. 3. 3. *al-Shatawiyyāt*, Istanbul Un. R. 3014 (*ZS* III, 249).

177. 5, 7. Alex. Tawḥīd 38, 41. Comm. by al-Sharīf Aḥmad al-Ḥamawī, ibid. 41.—11. Qaw. II, 176, Teh. Sip. II, 432/4 in *Majmūʿ al-mutūn*, C. 1340 p. 363/9.—12. Abstract by Zayn al-Dīn b. Aḥmad b. ʿAlī b. al-Ḥusayn b. ʿAlī al-Shuʿaybī, from the abstract by Ibn al-Manlā (Muḥammad b. Aḥmad al-Ḥaṣkafī?), Alex. Taʾr. 122.

178. 6, 3. Garr. 1224, Dāmādzāde 309.—22. Alex. Ḥad. 6.

7. al-Kattānī, *Fihris* II, 353/6 (who mentions on p. 359 a list from the year 904 AH that he had seen in Egypt and contained 538 titles).—Biography *Bahjat al-ʿābidīn* by his student ʿAbd al-Qādir b. Muḥammad b. Aḥmad al-Shādhilī (ḤKh IV, 64, *ShDh* VIII 53, GAL II, 137,8), which also uses al-Suyūṭī's lost autobiography *al-Taḥadduth bi-niʿmat allāh*, Ind. Off. 4574,2 (*JRAS* 1939, 366).—Anon. *Fihrist muʾallafāt al-Suyūṭī wa-sīrat Ibn al-Jawzī*, Garr. 2198.

179. *Majmūʿa* of 20 works, Garr. 2004, of 43 works, Mosul 240,$_{230}$.—1. Mosul 27,$_{60}$, 230,$_{60}$.—4. Read: *Mufḥamāt*, Qaw. I, 82.—6. Hamb. Or. Sem. 11, Garr. 1295/6, Mosul 65,$_{235}$, 125,$_{63/4}$, 193,$_{45}$.

180. 6. d. Qaw, I, 75, Abstract *Tuḥfat al-Mukhtār wa-hiya Talkhīṣ ḥāshiyat al-Jamal ʿalā Tafsīr al-Jalālayn min taʾlīf shaykh al-Islām al-asbaq Mukhtār Bek Ḥafīd Qūja Yūsuf Pāshā*, Ṭarābulus al-Gharb 1317 (Spies).—8. Alex. Bal. 16, Fun. 130,$_{2}$—10. Qaw. II, 243.—15. Ibid. II, 233.—20. Ibid. I, 183.—21a. Ibid. I, 29.—21. l. *al-Nadāda fī taḥqīq wa-ḥall al-istiʿāda*, Qaw, I, 84.—21. m. *Risāla fī tafsīr qawlihi* sura 78,$_{6}$, Qaw I, 64, II, 271.—21. n. *Risāla fī tafsīr qawlihi* sura 75,$_{2}$, ibid. I. 64.—21. o. *Risāla fī tafsīr qawlihi* sura 48,$_{2}$ ibid. 65.—21. p. *Risāla fī tafsīr qawlihi* sura 20,$_{123}$, ibid. 66.—21. q. *Risāla fī tafsīr qawlihi* sura 74,$_{3}$ ibid.—21. r. *al-Maʿānī al-daqīqa fī idrāk al-ḥaqīqa* on sura 2,$_{29}$, ibid. I, 81.—26. Alex. Muṣṭ. ḥad. 19.—28. *Ikhtiṣār*, Qaw. I, 98.—29. Alex. Ḥad. 22.—*Unmudhaj al-labīb*, Alex. Ḥad. 7, Fun. 166,$_{3}$, Mosul 240,$_{230}$, *Mukhtaṣar* by ʿAbd al-Wahhāb al-Shaʿrānī, Alex. Taʾr. 14. Versif. b. Garr. 648/9, Alex. Ḥad. 44.—d. *Fatḥ al-gharīb bi-sharḥ Mawāhib al-mujīb fī khaṣāʾiṣ al-ḥabīb*, commentary on an *Urjūza* on al-Suyūṭī's *Khaṣ*. by Abu 'l-Najīb Aḥmad b. ʿAlī al-ʿAdawī al-Manīnī, d. 1172/1758, Alex. Ḥad. 38.—30. Garr. 1503/4, Alex. Ḥad. 31, Mawāʿiẓ 36,$_{5}$.

1262 | 182. 30. Abstracts: a. Alex. Mawāʿiẓ 8, Fun. 183,$_{1}$, Qaw. I, 162.—30a. Read: *Thimār al-tankīb*, see p. 861,$_{45}$.—31. Garr. 1502, Alex. Mawāʿiẓ 7, Fun. 65,$_{3}$.—32. Alex.

Maw. 36, Fun. $130_{,1}$.—32a. *Fā'ida bil-wiqāya min al-ṭā'ūn*, Alex. Fun. 130,4.—33. Alex. Taṣ. $41_{,3}$.—35. Qaw. I, 102.—37. Ibid. I, 120.

183. 43. Qaw. I, 164.—44. Alex. Ta'r. 193, Fun. $83_{,1}$ (*Risāla fī wāliday al-nabī*), $83_{,2}$ (b. attributed to Kamālpāshā), $164_{,1}$, $166_{,1}$, Dam. Z. 38, $125_{,31}$.—46. Alex. Ta'r. 113.—51. Alex. Ḥad. 19, Maw. 38 (*Fī irsāl al-nabī ila 'l-malā'ika*).—52. Qaw. II, 232.—53. Alex. Fun. $85_{,1}$.—54. Qaw. II, 226.—56. Qaw. I, 112 (*Jamʿ al-jawāmiʿ*), Alex. Ḥad. 16, Moṣul $28_{,91}$, $231_{,77/8}$.—*al-Jāmiʿ al-ṣaghīr*, Qaw. I, 111, C. 1321.—*Ziyādāt*, Alex. Ḥad. 26, Qaw, I, 121.

184. 36a. Garr. 1398, Alex. Ḥad. 43.—d. C. 1324, abstract *Sharḥ duʿā' al-J. al-ṣ.* Garr. 1399.—e. Alex. Ḥad. 40, Qaw. I, 142, print. 6 vols C. 1938.—n. Amīr al-Ḥājj Aḥmad Katkhudā Ṣāliḥ Musṭaḥfiẓān, Qaw, I, 139.—Abstracts: k. Self-commentary *Fatḥ al-sattār wa-kashf al-asrār*, Alex. Ḥad. 37.—o. ʿAbd al-Laṭīf b. Qaḍībalbān, composed in 1050/1640, Alex. Ḥad. 58.

185. 59. Dam. Z. $38_{,123,13}$, Mosul $31_{,116}$ (with the title of no. 61).—61. *al-Durr al-munaẓẓam fī 'l-ism al-aʿẓam*, Alex. Fun. $78_{,11}$, Qaw. I, 232.—66. Hamb. Or. Sem. $15_{,1}$, Alex. Fun. $41_{,3}$. Abstracts b. Qaw. II, 271, p. 273.—66a. *Risāla fī khalq al-arḍ wa-miqdārihā bil-nisba lil-shams*, Qaw. II, 271.—66b. *Risāla tataʿallaq bil-shams wa-ilā ayna tadhhab baʿda ghurūbihā*, ibid. 276.—66c. *Risāla fī kusūf al-shams wa-asbābihi*, ibid. 278.—66d. *Risāla fī 'l-kalām ʿala 'l-shams wal-qamar*, ibid. 68, Alex. Maw. 19 (*faḍā'il*), $41_{,1}$.—70. Alex. Fun. $76_{,3}$.—72. Garr. $2003_{,13}$, Qaw. I, 143, 207.—4. Qaw. I, 120.—76. Ibid. I, 216.—77. Ibid. I, 143, 257.—81. Alex. Fun. $134_{,6}$.—82. Ibid. Maw. $36_{,2}$.—84. Qaw. I, 413.

186. 85. Alex. Fun. 130,4.—86. Ibid. $85_{,10}$, $133_{,1}$, $155_{,3}$, Faw. 7, Qaw. I, 115.—77. Qaw. I, 97, 225, Dam. Z. $61_{,153,5}$.—93. Qaw. I, 9.—94. Ibid. I, 184.—100. Garr. $2003_{,12}$.—101. Alex. Fun. $120_{,6}$.—103. *al-Ḥaẓẓ al-wāfir*, Qaw. I, 415.—104. Ibid. I, 422.—105. Qaw. I, 63, *Muqaddima fī 'l-basmala* Makr. 58.—111. Qaw. II, 240.—112. Garr. 1852.—114. Ibid. 1523, Alex. Fun. $121_{,2}$, $133_{,2}$, Mosul $240_{,230}$.—117. Qaw. I, 146.—118. Ibid. I, 418.—119. Ibid. I, 161.

187. 121. Alex. Fun. $85_{,6}$, $163_{,15}$, $177_{,4}$, Qaw. I, 160.—122. Alex. Fun. $59_{,1}$, $164_{,2}$, Qaw. I, 411 (*Iltiqāṭ*).—123. Alex. Fun. $67_{,18}$, Qaw. I, 164.—124. Ibid. I, 257.—126. Ibid. I, 203.—127. Garr. 1522, Alex. Fun. $164_{,8}$, Qaw. I, 209.—129. Garr. $2093_{,3}$, Alex. Fun. $134_{,1}$, Qaw. I, 159.—130. Alex. Mawāʿiẓ $36_{,3}$, Mosul $25_{,9,3}$, $199_{,196,3}$, comm. a. Garr. 1505, Alex. Maw. $36_{,4}$.—38, Makr. 48.—132. Qaw. I, 189.—133. Alex. Maw. 9.—135. BDMG 46, Heid. *ZDMG* 91, $384_{,317,3}$, Alex. Ḥad. 41, Fun. 100, $160_{,2}$, $174_{,9}$.—138. Qaw. II, 229.

188. 142. Alex. Fun. 199,$_2$, Qaw. I, 222.—161. Read: *al-Faḍl al-ʿamīm*.—164. See al-Kattānī, *Fihris* II, 95/7, from which *al-Nādiriyyāt min al-ʿushāriyyāt*, Qaw. I, 156.—169c. BDMG 46, Alex. Fiqh Shāf. 21; no. 271 is a *risāla* taken from it, see
1263 Qaw. I. 265, 421.—169 e. C. 1351.—169 i. *al-nabawī*, | in Garr. 2041,$_3$ *al-sinnawr*.—169 j. *al-Bahja al-saniyya fī 'l-asmāʾ al-nabawiyya* Alex. Ḥad. 8.—169 k. In Qaw. I, 413 described as an abstract of no. 157 by ʿAlī al-Muttaqī (see p. 518).

189. 169 n. Qaw. I, 97, II, 225.—169 o. Qaw. I, 411.—169 v. Muḥammad Raḍī al-Dīn's *al-Risāla al-bahiyya* is instead an imitation of the *Anwār al-saʿāda fī ṭabaqāt al-shahāda*, on the ranks of martyrdom (cf. *Asbāb al-shahāda*, Paris 659,$_2$).—169 gg, Ibid. I, 420.—169 rr. Ibid. I, 101 (which has *aʿdhab al-mafāʿil*).—169 yy. See 164.

190. 169 fff. Alex. Fun. 177,$_2$.—169 cccc. *Risāla fi 'l-tafḍīl bayna 'l-mashriq wal-maghrib wa-bayna 'l-arḍ wal-samāʾ*, Qaw. I, 236.—169 dddd. *Risāla fī faḍl al-tawsiʿa ʿala 'l-ʿiyāl yawm al-ʿĀshūrāʾ*, ibid. 238.—169 eeee. *Risāla fī lubs al-khirqa wa-talqīn al-dhikr wal-ṣuḥba*, ibid.—169 ffff. *Risāla fi 'l-aḥādīth al-wārida fī ithm man ightaṣaba shayʾan min al-arḍ wa-ṭarīq al-Muslimīn*, ibid. I, 416.—169 gggg. *Risāla fī aḥkām al-libās wa-hayʾat ʿimāmat al-nabī wa-mā kāna taḥta ʿimāmatihi*, ibid.—169 hhhh. *Risāla fī bayān jawāz iṭlāq al-ukht ʿala 'l-zawja wa-bayān al-sabab alladhī ḥamala sayyidanā Ibrāhīm al-Khalīl ʿalā qawlihi fī zawjatihi innahā ukhtī*, ibid. 417.—169 iiii. *Risāla fī 'l-jinn wa-mā yataʿallaq bihā min al-aḥkām*, ibid.—166 kkkk. *Risāla fī dhamm al-qaḍāʾ wa-taqallud al-aḥkām wa-mā warada fī dhālika min al-aḥādīth wal-akhbār*, ibid.—169 llll. *Jiyād al-musalsalāt*, library of Aḥmad Taymūr, Ḥad. 941, see al-Kattānī, *Fihris* II, 360, see 169 nnn, 245$_y$.—169 mmmm. *Bayān al-ṭālib bi-īmān Abī Ṭālib*, Qaw. I, 162.—169 oooo. *Risāla fī aṭfāl al-mushrikīn*, Qaw. I, 185.—169 pppp. *Risāla fī ḥukm idkhāl al-muʾminīn al-ʿāṣīn al-nār li-yaʿrifū qadr al-janna*, ibid. 188.—169 rrrr. *Risāla fī ḥawādith ayyām al-dajjāl wa-miqdār ayyāmihi wa-layālīhi wa-mawāqītihā*, ibid.—169 ssss. *Risāla fī sharḥ qawl al-nabī libnihi Ibrāhīm "Law ʿāsha Ibrāhīmu la-kāna ṣiddīqan nabiyyā"*, ibid. 119.—169 tttt. *Risāla fi 'l-kalām ʿalā qawl al-nabī "Sa-yakūnu rajul min Quraysh etc."*, ibid.—169 uuuu. *Risāla fī maʿnā qawlihi "al-ṣabī alladhī lahu ab yamsaḥu raʾsahu ilā khalf wal-yatīmu yamsaḥu raʾsahū ilā quddām"*, ibid.—169 xxxx. *Risāla fī khalq al-ṣuwar baʿda khalq al-samāwāt wal-arḍ*, ibid. 188.—169 yyyy. *Risāla fī sīmāʾ al-malāʾika*, Qaw. I, 418.—169 zzzz. *Bāb al-ḥadīth*, Makr. 6.—170. Ed. Muḥammad Ḥāmid al-Faqqī, C. 1356/1938.—178. Qaw. II, 221.

191. 178 n. *Fatāwā uṣūliyya dīniyya*, Dam. Z. 38,$_{126,21}$.—178 o. *Sharḥ Mukhtaṣar Khalīl, ḥabs* in the Riwāq Sayyidinā ʿUthmān in Madīna, al-Kattānī, *Fihris* II,

359.—178 p. *Risāla fī ṣalāt al-ḍuḥā*, Qaw. I, 418, Alex. Fun. 85,$_{4}$.—178q. *Risāla fī faḍl al-dhikr baʿd al-ṣalawāt al-khams*, Qaw. I, 237, 418.—178 r. *Risāla fī tashbīk al-aṣābiʿ fi ʾl-masjid wa-ghayrihi*, ibid. 417.—178 s. *Risāla fī bayān hal yuktafā bil-fiqh ʿani ʾl-taṣawwuf*, ibid. I, 235.—181. Ibid. I, 412.—185. Alex. Fun. 85,$_{5}$.—186. *Basṭ al-kaff*, Qaw. I, 413.—187. Alex. Fun. 85,$_{8}$, Qaw. I, 266, 421. *Mukhtaṣar* entitled *al-Tanqīḥ fī mashrūʿiyyat al-tasbīḥ*, ibid. 226, 441.—190. Alex. Fun. 85,$_{3}$.—191. Qaw. II, 223.—193. Ibid. I, 412.—195. Alex. Fiqh Shāf. 37,$_{2}$.—196. Alex. Fun. 66,$_{7}$.—197. Qaw. I, 165.—200. Qaw. I, 268.—200a. *Iʿmāl al-fikr fī tafḍīl al-dhikr* or *Faḍl al-dhikr ʿala ʾl-ṣadaqa*, Dam. Z. 126,$_{11}$, Qaw. I, 218.—201. Alex. Fun. 167,$_{12}$, Qaw. I, 226.—202. Alex. Fun. 121,$_{3}$, 130,$_{3}$.—203. Qaw. I, 414 (*al-Ḥadīth al-khātim*).

192. 204. Alex. Taʾr. 57.—207. Alex. Adab 141, Qaw. II, 257. | —209. Read: 1264
Nawāḍir.—209b. Read: *al-ḥashafa*.—212. Paris 3039,$_{16}$, Garr. 1111.—213. Qaw. I, 102.—215. Alex. Adab 141.—216. Qaw. II, 185.—220. Ibid. II, 215.—222. Ibid. I, 419.—224. Alex. Fun. 120,2.—225. Qaw. I, 421.—226. Ibid. I, 420, II, 245.—227. *Risāla fī lubs al-sarāwīl*, ibid. II, 235.—238. Ibid. I, 414.—230. Ibid. I, 411.—232. Ibid. 420, Alex. Maw. 41,$_{2}$.

193. 242. Qaw. II, 223.—244. Garr. 1959.—245a. *Qaṭʿ al-mujādala*, Alex. Fun. 110,$_{3}$.—245 x. See *RAAD* IX, 638, 8.—245 aa. *Ghāyat al-raghba fī ādāb al-ṣuḥba*, Garr. 2007,$_{8}$, Alex. Maw. 27.—245 bb. *Taʿrīf al-fiʾa bi-ajwibat al-asʾila al-miʾa*, Alex. Fun. 85,$_{4}$.—245 cc. *al-Zarārī fī abnāʾ al-sarārī*, Qaw. II, 236.—245dd. *Aqwāl al-ʿulamāʾ fi ʾl-ism al-aʿẓam*, Alex. Fun. 85,$_{9}$.—245ee. *Urjūza fī suʾūl al-malʾakayn fi ʾl-qabr*, Alex. Fun. 1551.—245ff. *al-Asʾila al-wazīriyya wa-ajwibatuhā*, ibid. 134,$_{1}$.—245gg. *al-Ajwiba al-zakiyya ʿani ʾl-alghāz al-Subkiyya*, ibid. 2.—245hh. *al-Muʿtalī fī taʿaddud al-walī*, ibid. 166,5.—247. Alex. Naḥw 28, comm. a. Garr. 463.

194. 250. Teh. Sip. II, 346/8.—259. BDMG 87, Mosul 183,$_{238}$.—260. Many excerpts in J.M. Peñuela, *Die Goldene des Ibn al-Munāṣif*, Rome 1941.—262. Alex. Fun. 120,$_{3}$, anon. Taymūr, Majm. 201 (*Or.* VIII, 285).—263. BDMG 88 (fragm.), Alex. Naḥw 2, Mosul 198,$_{2}$.—263e. Alex. Fun. 134,$_{3}$, 177,$_{1}$.

195. 264. C. 1934.—266. Qaw. I, 231.—267. Ibid. I, 81, 263,—268. Garr. 1133, 2096,$_{1}$.—a. Alex. Fun. 5.—269. *ʿUqūd al-jumān*, Alex. Fun. 198,$_{7}$, Mosul 162,$_{224}$.—270. Alex. Bal. 5.—271. A *risāla* from *al-Ḥāwī lil-fatāwī*, Qaw. I, 265, 421, Alex. Fun. 76,$_{2}$.—273. Alex. Fun. 83,$_{3}$.—274a. Alex. Fun. 67,$_{19}$, Dam. Z. 38,$_{126,32}$.—274f. *Risāla fi ʾl-qawl bil-ḥulūl wal-ittiḥād wa-buṭlānihi*, Alex. Fun. 67,$_{17}$.

196. 278. *Ta'rīkh al-khulafā'*, additionally Garr. 602/3, Mosul $209_{,30}$.—282. Garr. 601, Alex. Fun. $285_{,2}$ (*Bulbul al-rawḍa*).—284. See al-Kattānī, *Fihris* II, 29.—285. Qaw. I, $415_{,1}$, II, 29.—286. Heid. ZDMG 91, 383, Alex. Fun. $85_{,1}$.—288. Qaw. II, 189.

197. 290 Read: *al-muḥattam*.—290a. Alex. Ta'r. 50.—291. Ibid. Fun. $127_{,1}$.—292. Garr. 215, Qaw. II, 192.—296 See Rescher, *Orient. Miszellen* II, 129/45.—297. Print. Damascus 1350.—302. Mosul $42_{,4}$, 50, 61.—302a. *al-Maqāma al-wardiyya* additionally Qaw. II, 219.—302g. *al-Maqāma al-tuffāḥiyya*, Qaw. II, 217.—302h. *al-Maqāma al-dhahabiyya al-zumurrudhiyya*, ibid. 218.—302i. *al-Maqāma al-miskiyya*, ibid.—302k. *al-Maqāma al-fustuqiyya*, ibid.—302l. *Maqāma fī waṣf al-nisā'*, ibid.—302m. *al-Maqāma al-lāzawardiyya fī mawt al-dhurriyya*, Alex. Maw. $36_{,3}$.—304. Alex. Fun. $85_{,7}$.

198. 309. Qaw. II, 221.—311. Mosul $106_{,90,5}$.—313. Garr. 107, 567, Qaw. II, 277.—327. Qaw. I, 219, Istanbul 1311.—334. *al-Shihāb al-thāqib fī dhamm al-khalīl wal-ṣāḥib*, Alex. Fun. $191_{,2}$.

199. 1. Bank. XXIII $102_{,2503}$.

3. RAAD XII, 243/9, 292/8, Ibn al-Qāḍī, *Durrat al-ḥijāl* II, 372,342.—1. Garr. 84.—2. Ibid. $85_{,16}$ (which has *imtidāḥ*), C. 1322.—3. Alex. Adab 87, Qaw. II, 177, Bank. XXIII $45_{,2540}$.—7. Garr. 565, $2146_{,1}$.

200. 3,22. *Tasmīṭ Miftāḥ al-tawba ilā ahl Ṭība* with the commentary *al-Badīʿ fī aṣnāf al-badīʿ* by al-Ḥasan b. ʿAlī b. Ṣāliḥ al-ʿAdawī al-Bukurī, 9th cent. (see I,
1265 462,7), | Alex. Adab 98.—23. *Tasmīṭ* on an *urjūza* by Mudrik b. ʿAlī al-Shaybānī (I, 438) on a Christian boy, Heid. ZDMG 91, 388.—24. *Fā'ida fī tawallud al-anghām baʿḍihā ʿan baʿḍ wa-tartībihā ʿala 'l-burūj*, photograph Cairo, *Nashra* 19, Farmer, *Sources* 53.—4. Died in 856 (?), al-Sakhāwī, *al-Tibr al-masbūk fī dhayl al-Sulūk*, Būlāq 1896, 399/400.—1. Ed. al-Shalfūn.—3. *al-Qaṣīda al-jalīla min naẓm al-Khalīl* 1. The life of the Prophet, 2. An eulogy of his father al-Ashraf and his grandfather al-ʿĀdil, 3. Sermons, 4. On love, 5. *Muwashshaḥāt* and *zajals*, 6. Varia, Berl. 7898, Garr. 646.—§ 2. 1a. Berl. 6832, Mosul $169_{,8,3}$, comm. by Ibn ʿAbd al-Ghanī, Garr. 442, anon. Alex. Naḥw 23.

201. 2, 2. Comm. by Dā'ūd b. Sulaymān Abu 'l-Jūd al-Burhānī, d. 863/1459, Alex. Ta'r. 11.—3. See p. 23, 20.

202. 3a. al-Kattānī, *Fihris* II, 275, Muḥammad Iqbāl in *Isl. Culture* XI, 516/22.

203. In the footnote, read: Ibn al-ʿArīf.

204. 5. Suyūṭī, *Bughya* 423.—5. See p. 926,$_{119}$.—8. *al-Fawāʾid al-Surramarriyya min al-Mashyakha al-Badriyya*, see al-Kattānī, *Fihris* II, 284.

§ 5. *Khizānat al-muftīn* additionally Ind. Off. 1598/1600.

205. 5, 4. *Taqwīm al-adhhān fī ʿilm al-mīzān*, Alex. Manṭiq 5.

206. E. 1, 3. Ind. Off. 1794/6.—*Dharīʿa* I, 511/2 lists 38 commentaries.

207. 3. k. *al-Iqtiṣād* by ʿAbd al-Nabī b. Saʿd al-Jazāʾirī, d. 1021/1612, *Dharīʿa* II, 268,$_{1088}$.—4. Ind. Off. 1798/1800, comm. a. ibid. 1801, other MSS *Dharīʿa* II, 496,1950.—d. Ind. Off. 1802/3.—5. *Dharīʿa* I, 291,$_{10}$.—*Nahj al-taʿṭīl* or *Ibṭāl Nahj al-bāṭil*.—8. Comm. *al-Īḍāḥ wal-tabyīn* by Kamāl al-Dīn ʿAbd al-Raḥmān b. Ibrāhīm b. Muḥammad b. Yūsuf b. al-ʿAtāʾiqī al-Ḥillī, completed in 787/1385, together with *al-Risāla al-mukammila* or *Zubdat Risālat al-ʿilm*, about questions asked by Kamāl al-Dīn Miʾtham al-Nāṣir lil-Dīn al-Ṭūsī, autograph in al-Khizāna al-Gharawiyya, *Dharīʿa* II, 502,$_{1965}$.

208. 10a. Ind. Off. 1502.—c. Jamāl al-Dīn ʿAbdallāh al-Ḥusaynī al-Jurjānī, Ind. Off. 1501.—11. Autograph dated 721/1321, Br. Mus. Or. 8328.—18. *Dharīʿa* II, 444,$_{1725}$.—19. Ind. Off. 1791/2.—21. Written in 2 vols. in 709 and 712 in Dīnawar for his son Fakhr al-Muḥaqqiqīn (p. 209, 2) who re-arranged it 754; of the second 1000 only a small amount is extant, *Dharīʿa* II, 298,$_{1199}$.—23. Comm. *Irshād al-ṭālibīn* by al-Miqdād (p. 209, 4), completed in 792/1390, MSS *Dharīʿa* I, 515,$_{1520}$.—25. Ind. Off. 1793, print. Tehran 1329.—27. See ad p. 209.—28. *Istiqṣāʾ al-naẓar* or *Istiqṣāʾ al-baḥth wal-naẓar*, MSS *Dharīʿa* II, 31,$_{122}$.—30. Other MSS ibid. II, 498,$_{1954}$.—29. See ad I, 847.

209. 34. Berl. 4427, Ind. Off. 1500, Alex. Uṣūl 18,$_{1}$, anon. comm. ibid. 2.—37. Ind. Off. 1790, lith. Persia 1324/1906.—39. Autograph in al-Khizāna al-Gharawiyya, *Dharīʿa* II, 45,$_{175}$.—40. *Wājib al-iʿtiqād fī ʾl-uṣūl wal-furūʿ* with the commentary *al-Iʿtimād* by al-Miqdād (no. 4), print. in *Majmūʿat kalimāt al-muḥaqqiqīn*, Persia 1315.—41. *Masāʾil Muhannā b. Sinān b. ʿAbd al-Wahhāb al-Ḥusaynī*, who travelled from Medina to Baghdad to ask him some questions, composed in 719/1319, published in 803/1401 (Kantūrī 2887), Ind. Off. 1797.—42. *al-Arbaʿūn masʾala fī uṣūl al-dīn*, in the library of Sayyid Rājā Muḥammad in Faizabad, *Dharīʿa* I, 435,$_{2205}$.—43. *Ithbāt al-rajʿa*, Madrasat Fāḍil Khān in Mashhad, ibid. I, 92,$_{442}$.—44. *Ādāb al-baḥth*, in a *majmūʿa* in the library of Muḥammad ʿAlī

al-Khwānsārī al-Najafī, *Dharīʿa* I, 13,$_{60}$.—*al-Abḥāth al-mufīda fī taḥṣīl al-ʿaqīda*, with the commentary of Nāṣir b. Ibrāhīm al-Buwayhī, d. 853/1449, and of Hādī
1266 al-Sabzawārī in al-Khizāna | al-Riḍawiyya, *Dharīʿa* I, 63,$_{310}$.

2. 4. *Irshād al-mustarshidīn wa-hidāyat al-ṭālibīn fī uṣūl al-dīn*, MSS in Najaf and Tabriz, *Dharīʿa* I, 521,$_{2599}$.

3. 2. *al-Asʾila al-Āmuliyya*, composed in 759/1358 in Ḥilla, questions asked of Fakhr al-Muḥaqqiqīn (no. 2), copy with ʿAbd al-Ḥusayn al-Ṭihrānī in Karbala, *Dharīʿa* II, 72,$_{190}$.

3a. Rukn al-Dīn Muḥammad b. ʿAlī al-Jurjānī al-Gharawī wrote, in 728/1328 in al-Gharī: *al-Abḥāth fī taqwīm al-ḥadīth*, arguments against the Zaydīs by Twelver Shīʿīs, copy with al-Ḥājj Muḥammad Sulṭān al-Mutakallimīn in Tehran, *Dharīʿa* I, 63,$_{308}$.

3b. Raḍī al-Dīn Rajab b. Muḥammad b. Rajab al-Ḥāfiẓ al-Birsī al-Ḥillī wrote, in 773/1371, *Mashāriq al-anwār* and, in 811/1408, *Mashāriq al-amān; Kitāb al-alfayn fī waṣf sādat al-kawnayn*, MS in al-Maktaba al-Ḥusayniyya, *Dharīʿa* II, 299,$_{1200}$

3c. Bahāʾ al-Dīn ʿAlī b. Ghiyāth al-Dīn ʿAbd al-Karīm b. ʿAbd al-Ḥamīd al-Ḥusaynī al-Nīlī al-Najafī wrote: 1. Between 772 and 777/1370 and 1375, *al-Anwār al-ilāhiyya fī ʾl-ḥikma al-sharʿiyya*, preserved in al-Khizāna al-Sharīfa al-Gharawiyya, *Dharīʿa* II, 415/8.—2. *al-Inṣāf fī ʾl-radd ʿalā ṣāḥib al-Kashshāf*, ibid. 397,$_{1594}$.

3d. Abū ʿAbdallāh Shams al-Dīn Muḥammad b. Jamāl al-Dīn Makkī b. Muḥammad b. Ḥāmid b. Aḥmad al-Nabaṭī al-ʿĀmilī al-Jazāʾirī, who was killed in 786/1384: 1. *Arbaʿūna ḥadīthan fī ʾl-ʿibādāt*, MSS *Dharīʿa* I, 427,$_{2185}$, printed together with *Ghaybat al-Nuʿmānī*, Persia 1318.—2. *al-Arbaʿūn masʾala fī ʾl-kalām*, with the title al-*Masāʾil al-arbaʿīniyya* included in *Mukhtaṣar Taʾrīkh al-Shīʿa* by Aḥmad ʿĀrif al-Zayn al-ʿĀmilī, print. in Sidon, ibid. 436,$_{2206}$.

4. Died on 26 Jumādā II 826/7 June 1423 (*Dharīʿa* II, 92,$_{365}$).—7. *al-Adʿiya al-thalāthūna*, in the library of Muḥammad ʿAlī Sabzawārī in Kāẓimiyya, *Dharīʿa* II, 396,$_{2058}$.

210. 5, 11. Ind. Off. 1873.—13. *al-Mūjiz al-ḥāwī li-taḥrīr al-fatāwī* (Kantūrī 3212), Ind. Off. 1808, comm. by (?) Mufliḥ b. Ḥusayn al-Ṣammīrī, a contemporary of ʿAlī b. ʿAbd al-ʿĀlī al-Karakī, d. 944/1537, Kantūrī 2000, ibid. 1809.

5a. His student ʿAbd al-Ṣamad b. Fayyāḍ al-Asadī al-Ḥillī wrote the *Kifāyat al-ṭālibīn*, Mashh. V, 102,$_{328}$.

7. Yūsuf al-Wāsiṭī, i.e. Yūsuf b. Makhzūm al-Aʿwar al-Maqṣūdī, ca. 700/1300, *Dharīʿa* II, 419,$_{1657}$.

8. Aḥmad b. Muḥammad b. ʿAbdallāh b. ʿAlī b. Muḥammad b. Subayʿ b. Rifāʿa al-Baḥrānī al-Subaʿī composed in 853/1449 *al-Anwār al-ʿAlawiyya fī sharḥ al-Risāla al-alfiyya* for a friend in India, MS in Najaf *Dharīʿa* II, 434,$_{1698}$.

9. Muḥammad b. Zayn al-Dīn ʿAlī b. Ḥusām al-Dīn Ibrāhīm b. Abī Jumhūr al-Aḥsāʾī, ca. 901/1495, *al-Aqṭāb al-fiqhiyya wal-waẓāʾif al-dīniyya ʿalā madhhab al-Imāmiyya*, MSS in Najaf and Tehran, *Dharīʿa* II, 273,$_{1106}$.

10. See ad p. 660, § 8, 3b.

211. 2. *ʿUmdat al-qurrāʾ wa-ʿiddat al-iqrāʾ* (see p. 981, 19), Garr. 1253, 4.

212. 4, 1. Heid. *ZDMG* 91, 393, Garr. 1215, Qaw. I, 26.—8. Garr. 1216/7.

5. Read: Mashh. III, Ind. Off. 1810.

215.—§ 9. 1, 1. Garr. 2106,$_{3}$.—Comm. a. Köpr. I, 941,$_{1}$, Qaw. II, 261, Bank. XXII, 11,$_{2417}$.—b. ʿUm. 4528 (Krause, *Stamb. Hdss.* 518).—3. See p. 1027,$_{7}$.

2. 1. AS 3752,$_{2}$, Alex. Ḥisāb 5.

216. Line 3. *Khulāṣat al-fikar*, Alex. Ḥisāb 10.—2. Alex. Far. 11, comm. ibid. 3. Makr. 3.—7. Garr. 2006,$_{11}$, Alex. Ḥisāb 51, Qaw. II, 276.—7. Comm. g. Makr. 36.—h. *al-Shams al-muḍīʾa* by Yūsuf b. Muḥammad al-Masdī al-Mālikī al-Maḥallī (p. 1025, 83,$_{2}$), Alex. Ḥisāb 53.—8. Alex. Ḥisāb 53,$_{4}$, *Kifāyat al-qunūʿ etc.* Garr. 2006,$_{7}$, Alex. Ḥisāb 55, 61, Fun. 65,$_{6}$, Qaw. II, 281.—11. Alex. Ḥisāb 48.

| 217. 14. Garr. 2006,$_{15}$, Alex. Fun. 65,$_{10}$, Ḥisāb 59.—16. Comm. by Aḥmad b. 1267
Aḥmad al-Sunbāṭī, Alex. Ḥisāb 60,$_{1}$.—28. Garr. 1960 (ad 484,$_{3}$?).

3. Kamāl al-Dīn ʿAbd al-Raḥmān b. Muḥammad b. Ibrāhīm b. Muḥammad b. Yūsuf b. al-ʿAtāʾiqī al-Ḥillī, a student of ʿAllāma al-Ḥillī (p. 206) and of Nāṣir al-Dīn ʿAlī b. Muḥammad al-Kāshānī, d. 755/1354, wrote: 1. *al-Irshād fī maʿrifat maqādīr al-abʿād fi ʾl-handasa*, together with many other works in autograph

from the period 732/88, preserved in al-Khizāna al-Gharawiyya, *Dharīʿa* I, 510,2507.—2. See ad p. 207.

218. 21, 1. Comm. Makram 3.—Abstracts: a. Garr. 985.

219. § 12. 1. *Majmaʿ al-manāfiʿ al-badaniyya*, Alex. Ṭibb. 40.

221. 4. *Taḥqīq al-nuṣra*, Alex. Taʾr. 47, Dam. RAAD XII, 319, biogr. note Ind. Off. 4576 (JRAS 1939, 368).

5. 1. Qaw. II, 240; a *dhayl* titled *al-Kamīn* is mentioned by his grandson Muḥammad b. ʿAbd al-ʿAzīz, see p. 538.

222. 5, 5. Garr. 594.—10. *Muntakhab al-mukhtār* see I, 613.

223. 9, 4. Qaw. II, 232.—6. Abstract *Talkhīṣ al-iḥrāʾ*, Alex. Fiqh Shāf. 36, 37,2, Fun. 120,1.

224. 21. Alex. Uṣūl 13.

225. 1b. See I, 604.—5. *Bughyat al-ṭālib al-fāliḥ min mashyakhat Qāḍī Ṭāba Abi ʾl-Fatḥ Ṣāliḥ*, Alex. Muṣṭ. al-Ḥad. 5, Taʿr. 21.

226. 4, 1. Alex. Taʾr. 5.—Comm. ibid. 10.

B. 1. 2. Read: *al-Dībāj al-mudhahhab*, Garr. 690.—3. ibid. 1835.

227. § 4a. Qurʾān. 1. Zayn al-Dīn ʿAbd al-Raḥmān b. Shihāb al-Dīn Aḥmad b. Yūsuf b. ʿAlī b. ʿAyyāsh al-Makkī, b. 772/1370, d. 853/1449 (*Naẓm al-ʿiqyān*, 123), *Ghāyat al-maṭlūb fī qirāʾat Abī Jaʿfar wa-Khalaf wa-Yaʿqūb*, Garr. 1222.

2. Muʿīn al-Dīn Muḥammad b. ʿAbd al-Raḥmān b. Muḥammad b. ʿAbdallāh b. Muḥamnmad b. ʿAbdallāh al-Ījī al-Ṣafawī, d.. 902/1496, *Jāmiʿ al-bayān fī tafsīr al-Qurʾān*, completed in 870/1465 near the Kaʿba, print. in *Majmūʿa*, India 1296.

§ 5. 1a. 2. Read: *Shams al-īmān*.

228. 12. Javan transl. see S.W.S. Drewer and R.Mg.A. Poerbatjaraka, *De mirakelen van Abdalkadir Djilani*, Bandoeng 1938 (Bibl. Javan. 9).—13. c. Yaʿqūb b. Sayyid ʿAlī al-Burūsawī, d. 930/1524 in Egypt, Qaw. II, 246.—15. Berl. 5826, Garr.

767.—16. *al-Durr al-naẓīm fī manāfiʿ āyāt al-Qurʾān al-ʿaẓīm* (author?), Alex. Faw. 8.—23. *Manẓūma ṭibbiyya*, Alex. Ṭibb 49.—24. *Baḥth al-samāʿ*, Berl. 5509, Farmer, *Sources* 53.

229. 2, 1. BDMG 27, Qaw. I, 240, C. 1321.

5. Read: ʿAlī b. Muḥammad b. Aḥmad.

230. 8, 2. Garr. 695$_{,6}$, Alex. Taʾr. 120.

§ 6. 2. Anon. comm. Alex. Ḥisāb 11.

231. 1, 3a. *Urjūza* on shipping lanes, As. Mus. Leningrad B. 992. f. 83/105, see Kračkovsky, *Nachr. der Geogr. Ges. in Leningrad*, 1937, no. 5, p. 758/60 with facs.

232. 1c, 3. Alex. Adab 186.

233. 6. Read: b. Shājir.

9. Towards the end of the 10th century, Sulaymān b. ʿĀmir b. Rāshil b. Abi ʾl-Ḥaqīr al-Ṭarawī al-ʿAqarī collected the anthology *Nūr al-azhār al-muntakhab min funūn al-ashʿār*, Bank. XXIII, 78$_{,2573}$.

234. 4, 5. Read: ʿĀṣim Efendi, d. 1235/1819 (Heffening).—d. Read: ʿAlī b. Ghānim.

235. k. BDMG 92 (?), Garr. 283.—o. *al-Jumūʿ wal-maṣādir* (missing in the *Q.*) by Muḥammad Yaḥyā b. al-Shāfiʿī al-Qazwīnī (ca. 1112/1703), Teh. Sip. II, 316/7.—4. Alex. Adab 32.—5. = (?) *al-Muthallath*, Garr. 284.

| 236. 2a. Isḥāq b. Jarīr al-Ṣanʿānī, the teacher of al-Janadī (no. 3), *Taʾrīkh Ṣanʿāʾ* 1268
al-Yaman, Alex. Taʾr. 35.

3. A section from *al-Sulūk* entitled *al-Qarāmiṭa fi ʾl-Yaman* is text no. 3 in a *majmūʿa*, Alexandria 1899.

237. 5a. See p. 251, 5.

238. 5h. Read: al-Hamdānī; see I, 555, 7.

6. 1. Alex. Taʾr. 89.—2. *The Pearlstrings*, by Redhouse.

239. 8. ʿUmar b. Zayd al-Dawʿanī, *al-Durr al-nafīs fī manāqib al-imām Idrīs*, Alex. Taʾr. 66.

240. 10, 1. Alex. Taʾr. 29.

§ 4, A. 1 See ad I, 646, II, 250.

241. 3. During the reign of the Rasūlid al-Malik al-Mujāhid Sayf al-Dīn ʿAlī b. Dāʾūd (721–64/1321–62), Jamāl al-Dīn Muḥammad b. Aḥmad b. Sufyān al-Ghassānī al-Shāfiʿī wrote *Maʿdin al-fiqh wal-fatwā wa-ʿumdat ahl al-tadrīs wal-taqwā*, Hamb. Or. Sem. 69.

242. 2, 12. *al-Anwār al-muḍīʾa* abstract Hamb. Or. Sem. 117.

244. 4, 11. *Manẓūma fī uṣūl al-dīn*, with the anon. comm. al-*Irshād al-hādī ilā Manẓūmat al-Sayyid al-Hādī*, Hamb. Or. Sem. 133.

4c. Jamāl al-Dīn Abū ʿAbdallāh al-Hādī b. Ibrāhīm b. ʿAlī al-Murtaḍā b. al-Hādī b. Rasūlallāh, b. before 765/1363, d. 15 Muḥarram 840/13 April 1446, converted to Sunnism, which he defended in his *al-Qawāsim fi ʾl-dhabb ʿan sunnat Abi ʾl-Qāsim*, and wrote *al-Abyāt al-Ṣūfiyya*, on which his brother Muḥammad b. Ibrāhīm wrote the commentary *al-Tuḥfa al-ṣafiyya*, Bank. XXIII, $53_{,2548}$.

6. I. Alex. Firaq 3.

245. I, 10. On the *muqaddima* by Yaḥyā b. Muḥammad b. Ḥasan b. Ḥumayd al-Mughrānī, Br. Mus. Suppl. 1216. i.—16. *al-Ghayth al-midrār* by Jamāl al-Dīn ʿAbd al-Raḥmān b. Hādī b. Muḥammad Samāja al-Ithnayʿasharī, MS dated 1075/1664, Rāmpūr I, $220_{,347/50}$.

246. III, lines 4ff belong to II.—On n. 1 see Kračkovsky in *Mélanges Gautier* 294.

247. 8a, 3. Read: *Qanṭarat al-uṣūl.*

8c. 7. *al-Masāʾil al-mukhtāra min Kitāb al-yāqūt al-muʿaẓẓam al-mufawwaq baʿd ʿiqyān al-ḥikam*, Cairo^2 VI, 212.

9. See p. 360, 5b.

248. 10, 1. *Nubadh shāfiya wāfiya*, Hamb. Or. Sem. 3.

11. 5. a. Read: b. Fand.

250. 1. See ad 240.

251. 5. See 237. 5.

6. Aḥmad b. Aḥmad b. ʿAbd al-Laṭīf al-Zabidī al-Yamanī, d. 898/1492, *Risāla fī miʾat fāʾida li-baʿḍ al-āyāt al-Qurʾāniyya*, with the title *al-Fawāʾid wal-ṣilāt wal-ʿawāʾid*, Alex. Fun. 186,$_{4}$.

§ 6. 1, 1. Alex. Mawāʿiẓ 7, Makram 6.—3. *al-Tadhkira bi-mā ilayhi ʾl-masīr*, Makr. 10.—4. *ʿUmdat al-ṭālib fi ʾl-iʿtiqād al-wājib*, ibid. 47.

252. *Kitāb al-Raḥma*, Garr. 1109, 2169,1 (which has al-Ṣubunrī), Alex. Fun. 146,$_{2}$.

254. 2, 4. *Nuzhat al-aḥbāb fī gharāʾib al-ittifāq wa-nawādir dhawi ʾl-albāb*, ḤKh VI, 230, Garr. 725.—5. al-*Jawāb al-shāfī fi ʾl-radd ʿala ʾl-mubtadiʿ al-jāfī*, against the Yazīdīs, Dam Z. 77,$_{50}$; 2, see p. 999, 28.

§ 10. 1, 8. Alex. Fun. 187, Garr. 99, 2146 (where the commentary is entitled *al-Jumānāt al-badīʿa fī madḥ aʿlām al-sharīʿa* and the poem as *al-Ḥimāyāt al-badīʿiyya*), Cairo^{2} I, 214 (where the commentary is entitled *al-Farīda al-jāmiʿa lil-maʿāni ʾl-rāʾiʿa*).—10. = *Mukhtaṣar al-Rawḍa* I, 753.

255. 10. Garr. 1868/9, Alex. Fiqh Shāf. 4.—12. Alex. Adab 140.—14. See 8.

| 256. 5, 1. Garr. 1135, Alex. Adab 8. 1269

257. 6. See p. 856,$_{30}$.

§ 2. 2, 1a. Garr. 443/4, 2105,1.

258. 2a, 1. a. See p. 926,$_{113}$.

3. Anon. Pers. comm., Teh. Sip. II, 187/9.

3a. Comm. by Aḥmad b. ʿAlī b. Muḥammad al-Sijistānī, Pet. AM Buch. 884.

6. Garr. 285.

6a. ʿAbd al-Wahhāb b. ʿAlī al-Ḥusaynī al-Astarābādī wrote, in 879/1474, *al-Unmūdhaj fī ʿulūm al-balāgha min al-maʿānī wal-bayān wal-badīʿ* or also *Mūjiz al-bayān*, Teh. Sip. II, 415/6, autograph in a *majmūʿa*, in which we also find, among other works, the *Sharḥ al-Fuṣūl al-Nāṣiriyya* (I, 927, III, 4) and the *Ḥāshiya ʿalā sharḥ Mīrak ʿala ʾl-Hidāya al-Athīriyya* (I, 839), preserved in the library of Muḥammad Bāqir, the grandson of Muḥammad Kāẓim al-Yazdī al-Ṭabāṭabāʾī, *Dharīʿa*, II, 402,$_{1617}$.

259. I. BDMG 95b, Hamb. Or. Sem. 75, Garr. 901, Qaw. II, 156/7.—1. To be deleted, see I, 849.—1a. Qaw. II, 160/1.—Glosses a. ibid. 143, Alex. Bal. 4, 20, Fun. 111,$_6$, anon. supergl. Qaw. II, 150.—c. Qaw. II, 145, Teh. Sip. II, 409/10 (identified as glosses on b.).—g. Alex. Fun. 11,$_7$—w. Alex. Bal. 22.—x. Aḥmad Efendi al-Ḥalabī, Garr. 561.—y. Muḥammad b. Ismāʿīl al-Nafrāwī al-Mālikī, completed in 1183/1769, Alex. Bal. 22.—3. Alex. Bal. 14, Qaw. II, 164.

260. 4. Alex. Bal. 13, 20 (*kabīr*), Qaw. II, 160.—Glosses: a (on the *ṣaghīr*), Garr. 574, Alex. Bal. 19,$_2$, 23,$_1$, 25, Fun. 108,$_5$, Makr. 61.—b. Alex. Bal. 21, Fun. 128/9.—On which *taqrīrāt* by Aḥmad al-Ujhūrī, d. 1276/1859, Alex. Bal. 4, Muḥammad al-Shabīnī (?) ibid.—d. Alex. Bal. 8.—h. on which *taqrīr* by al-Sharshīmī al-Sharqāwī, Alex. Bal. 4.—6. Ibid. 2, Fun. 108,$_4$.—9. Alex. Bal. 17.—14. To be deleted, see ad I, 849.—12. *al-Ḥāshiya al-jadīda ʿalā ʿIṣām al-farīda* by Aḥmad Khalīl al-Fawzī b. Muṣṭafā al-Ghilbāwī al-Qusṭanṭīnī, completed in 1282, Istanbul 1282, 1306 (Qaw. II, 141/2).—15. Garr. 905, Qaw. II, 160.—18. Aḥmad b. ʿUmar al-Qāhirī al-Asqāṭī, d. 1159/1746, Alex. Bal. 7.—24. *al-Mawāhib al-ṣamadiyya li-kashf lithām al-S.* by Ṭāhir b. Masʿūd khalīfat Imām al-Jāmiʿ al-Zaytūniyya, Tunis 1298.—25. Anon., Teh. Sip. II, 423/4.

261. 9. Teh. Sip. II, 251/3

10. *Nihāyat al-bahja*, with a self-commentary, Qaw. II, 97.

§ 3. 3. A contemporary of *Fakhr al-Muḥaqqiqīn* (p. 239, 2), *Rawḍāt al-jannāt* 177/8, *Dharīʿa* I, 517,$_{2537}$.

262. 3a. Shams al-Dīn Muḥammad b. Yūsuf al-Zarandī, d. 750/1349, *Bughyat al-murtāḥ fī ṭalab al-arbāḥ fī nuṣḥ al-salāṭīn wal-wulāt al-muslimīn wal-ḥukkām min al-rāghibīn fi ʾl-falāḥ*, Alex. Mawāʿiẓ 8 (40 traditions with a commentary, ḤKh II, 60,$_{1885}$).

5a. See p. 991,15.

263. 1. *DK* II, 247 (d. 701!). I. Garr. 1631/2, Ind. Off. 312, 1447/8, Qaw. I, 298, Bank. XIX, 2, 1502/3.—Comm. 1. Ind. Off. 314, 1449, 4572 (*JRAS* 1939, 364), Qaw. I, 293.—2b. Alex. Uṣūl 7, Qaw. I, 278.—3. Qaw. I, 274.—Garr. 1633/6, Qaw. I, 288/9.—Glosses: a. Alex. Uṣūl 8, Qaw. I, 281.—b. BDMG 39.

264. 4e. *Natāʾij al-afkār* by Muṣṭafā b. Muḥammad ʿAzmīzāde, Alex. Uṣūl 21.—6. Qaw. I, 291.—8. *Mishkāt al-anwār*, Garr. 1637.—11. Glosses, *Nasamāt al-asḥār*, Alex. Uṣūl 21.—13. Abstract 1. On which a comm., Ind. Off. 1450/3.—Anon. glosses, Ind. Off. 1454, Pers. ibid. 1455.—14. Ind. Off. 1456/9, print. Calcutta 1818, Lucknow 1266, Kanpur 1882 etc.

265. II. Ind. Off. 1610, Alex. Fiqh Ḥan. 47, 72.—III. Ind. Off. 1611/22, Garr.
1719/20, Alex. Fiqh Ḥan. 48, Qaw. I, 384/5.—Comm.: 1. | Ind. Off. 1623/5, Qaw. I, 1270
309, Mosul $226,_{20}$.—Glosses by Karīmallāh b. Luṭfallāh al-Fārūqī al-Dihlawī,
d. 1291/1874 (*ʿUlamāʾi Hind* 172), Ind. Off. 1627.

266. 3. Ind. Off. 1628/30, Qaw. I, 353, Makram 29.—4. Read: d. 860, Alex. Fiqh Ḥan. 53.—6. Garr. 1721, Qaw. I, 366.—c. Ibn Abi ʾl-Suʿūd, Qaw. I, 380/1, Makr. 48.—6a. *Sharḥ al-kanz* by Ibrāhīm b. Muḥammad al-Ḥalabī, d. 956/1546 (see p. 642, 7), Mosul $239,_{202}$.—7. Ind. Off. 1631/6, Qaw. I, 307/8.—8. Ind. Off. 1637/8, Alex. Fiqh Ḥan. 70; on which a *takmila, al-Baḥr al-rāʾiq*, Qaw. I, 313.

267. 23. al-Samarqandī, author of *Fatāwa ʾl-Kāfūriyya*, 8th cent., additionally Ind. Off. 1626, AS Beng. Ashraf Ali 19.—34. *Kashf al-ḥaqāʾiq*, by Bakr Abū Isḥāq (?), Alex. Fiqh Ḥan. 48.—35. Anon., Ind. Off. 1639, Mosul $198,_{162}$.

268. XI. Garr. $2091,_{3}$ = (?) *ʿUmdat al-muwaḥḥidīn fī uṣūl al-dīn*, Alex. Fun. $190,_{1}$.—XVI. *al-Mustaṣfā*, see I, 655, bottom line—XVII. *Faḍāʾil al-aʿmāl*, ḤKh IV, 446a, Br. H^{2}. 254 (mistakenly attributed to the Nasafī who is mentioned in vol. I, p. 374), Garr. 922.

3. Berl. Oct. 3187, Garr. 1644, Alex. Fiqh Ḥan. 39.—Comm. c. *Sharḥ al-funūn* by ʿAbd al-Bāsiṭ b. Khalīl b. al-Wazīr al-Ḥanafī (p. 52, 17), Alex. Fiqh Ḥan. 30.

269. 5a, 1. Ind. Off. 1672/5, Qaw. I, 329.—Comm. d. Garr. 1958, *Mukhtaṣar* Qaw. I, 393.—k. With the title *al-Aʿlā al-shamsī al-thānī*, composed in 1296/1879, Ind. 1302.—l. Ibn Kamālpāshā, Gotha 936, Ind. Off. 1676.—m. Anon., Ind. Off. 1677/80.

5b. Muḥammad b. Maḥmūd b. Aḥmad, *Dustūr al-quḍāh*, Ind. Off. 1045, vii, 1601/2, Garr. 1645.

270. 7a. See p. 282, 3c.

7c. Muḥammad b. ʿAbd al-Rashīd, *Jawāhir al-f.*, Alex. Fiqh Ḥan. 18 (composed in 557/1162!).

271. 3. Ind. Off. 1773.

272. 2, 2. Garr. 693.

4. 8. *Asrār al-ḥajj*, composed in 901/1495, *Dharīʿa* II, 43,$_{170}$.

273. 1. b. Also *Taʾrīkh al-Ghāzānī, Taʾrīkh Čingizkhān*, composed in 702/1302 at the request of Sultan Maḥmūd Ghāzān.

2a. Suter 395.—1. Garr. 1291, Qaw. I, 73.—2. Comm. by al-Birjandī, Bank. XXII, 9,$_{2414}$, by Abū Isḥāq b. ʿAbdallāh composed in 963/1556, ibid. 10,2416.—3. Completed in 704/1304.—4. Completed in 711/1311.—6. Pers. comm. on the *Zīj Ilkhānī*, AS 2696. See I, 931.—7. *Sharḥ Sī Faṣl* (ibid.), Leid. 1178, AS 2664.

274. 3, 1. *Tafsīr*, Cairo^2 I, 40.

6. Autobiography *Ṭabaqāt* 3433, see Bergsträsser-Pretzl, *Gesch. des Qorʾāntextes* 225ff.—1. Garr. 1219, Qaw. I, 35.—Abstracts: n. *Mukhtaṣar al-nashr*, by the author himself, Garr. 1219a, Qaw. I, 30.—c. Garr. 1253, 1, Qaw. I, 22/3.

275. Comm. b. Qaw. I, 21.—f. Ibid. I, 6.—g. *Taḥrīr al-ṭuruq wal-riwāyāt min ṭarīq T. al-n.*, by the same, ibid. 8.—4. Garr. 2067,$_{1}$, Qaw. I, 15, comm. by his son Abū Bakr Aḥmad, ibid. I, 20.—b. Makr. 47.—8. Garr. 1220/1, 1253,$_{3}$, Alex. Fun. 146,$_{2}$, 195,$_{19}$, Qaw. I, 32/3.

276. Cmt. a. completed in Ram. 876/Feb. 1472, Qaw. I, 13, 22.—e. Hamb. Or. Sem. 15,2, Garr. 1231/2, Qaw. I, 15, 22, Makr. 27.—Gl. β. al-Naḥrāwī, Garr. 1245.—f. Qaw. I, 22.—11. A pretty useless abstract, *Tarājim rijāl Kitāb al-nashr min naqalat al-qirāʾāt al-ʿashr* by al-Sayyid Muḥammad ʿĀrif al-Ḥifẓī b. al-Sayyid Ibrāhīm, autograph dated 1202, Berl. Ms. or. Oct. 2192 (Bergstr.-Pretzl, *Gesch. des Qorʾāntextes* 159, n.4).

| 277. 13. Comm. *al-Ghāya* by Shams al-Dīn Abu 'l-Khayr Muḥammad al-Sakhāwī 1271
al-Shāfiʿī, d. 902/1496, Alex. Ḥad. 36.—18. Garr. 645.—19. Ibid. 1955, Alex. Ḥad. 20.—Comm. a. Alex. Ḥad. 64.—b. Ibid. 20, Qaw. I, 115.—e. Deceased 1116/1704, Alex. Ḥad. 31.—Abstracts: a. Ind. Off. 4591 (*JRAS* 1939, 375), Garr. 1956/7.—aa. *Muntakhab*, of unknown authorship, Alex. Ḥad. 55,3.

278. 29. *al-Zawāʾid al-mufīda fī ridf al-qaṣīda, manẓūma fī shawādhdh al-qirāʾāt*, Alex. Fun. 165,$_{14}$, Qaw. I, 26.—30. *Mukhtaṣar al-Naṣīḥa bil-adilla al-ṣaḥīḥa*, Alex. Maw. 42.—31. *Risāla fī arbaʿīna suʾlan min al-masāʾil al-mushkila wal-jawāb ʿanhā*, Alex. Fun. 167,$_{26}$.

279. Line 2. Read: al-Dūrī.

§ 7. 3, 5. Several small treatises, Taymūr, Ḥikma 55.—6. *Risālat ithbāt al-bāriʾ wa-ṣifātihi*, Alex. Fun. 88,$_{7}$.

280. 1b, 1. Alex. Taṣ. 33,$_{1}$, see II, 990.

281. 17. Garr. 1936 (which has al-Sijistānī).

282. 3. See Gordlewski in *Festschr. Oldenburg*, Leningrad 1934, 174/69.

3b. al-*Risāla al-Makkiyya*, Alex. Taṣ. 18 (copied in 755 when he was still alive).

283. 3c, 8. *Taḥqīq al-arkān al-arbaʿa*, Garr. 2003,4 (see p. 270, 7a).

4. 4. 1. BDMG 20, Garr. 1579.

284. 5. Alex. Fun. 135/6, 151,$_{19}$.—*Ḥaqīqat al-yaqīn etc.*, Alex. Taṣ. 32.—12. Ibid. 30, 32, Fun. 136,$_{3}$, 152,$_{28}$.—19. Comm. Alex. Taṣ. 39, 40, Fun. 90,$_{3}$—*Takhmīs* by Abu 'l-Fatḥ Sirḥān al-Samarjī al-Sharnūbī al-Dimyāṭī, *Manẓūm qalāʾid al-durr al-nafīs*, Alex. Taṣ. 39.—28. *Sabab al-asbāb wal-kanz li-man ayqana wastajāb*, Alex. Fun. 152,$_{24}$.

285. 4b. Alex. Mawāʿiẓ 20.—5. 1. Ibid. 50.

286. 2. Comm. by Mollā Ibrāhīm b. Ḥaydar al-Kurdī b. al-Ḥusaynābādī (?), Alex. Fun. 96,$_{2}$.—*Risāla fī bayān kalimat sal-shahāda*, Alex. Tawḥīd 18.—30. *Risāla fī taḥqīq madhhab al-Ṣūfiyya wal-mutakallimīn wal-ḥukamāʾ fi 'l-wujūd*, ibid. Ḥikma 24,$_{1}$.

10. Read: see 996,$_{3}$.

287. 1. II. Alex. Fun. 156,$_{4}$, Qaw, II, 293.—Comm: 1. Alex. Fun. 107,$_{7}$, 156,$_{6}$, Qaw. II, 301/2, Makram 25.—Garr. 889/91, Alex. Fun. 106,$_{5}$, 156,$_{52}$, Qaw. II, 312/3.

288. Supergl. δ Muḥammad b. al-Ḥājj Ḥamīd al-Kaffawī, Qaw. II, 300.—ε Ismāʿīl b. Muṣṭafā b. Maḥmūd al-Kalanbawī Shaykhzāde, ibid.—d. Makram 17.—1. al-Dalajī, Makram 20.—3. Alex. Fun. 107,$_{6}$.—13. Ghiyāth al-Dīn Manṣūr b. Ṣadr al-Dīn al-Dashtakī al-Shīrāzī (p. 593), MSS in Najaf and with Muḥammad Muḥsin in Samarra, *Dharīʿa* I, 14,$_{64}$.—III. Garr. 872/3, Alex. Waḍʿ 2, Ādāb al-b. 7,$_{3}$, 11,$_{2}$.—Comm: 1. Garr. 874, Alex. Ādāb al-b. 11, Qaw. II, 308.—2. Garr. 875/8.—3. Garr. 883, Qaw. II, 16/8, Makr. 37.—Glosses: b. Garr. 882, Alex. Waḍʿ 3, Makr. 19, print. Istanbul 1275, 1320.—c. Alex. Waḍʿ 2.

289. 3. f. Supergl. α Ḥāfiẓ Sayyid Efendi, Istanbul 1259, 1267, 1272, 1285, 1305 (Qaw. II, 11/2).—β Mīr Abu ʾl-Baqāʾ, ibid. 13.—5. Alex. Waḍʿ 3, Ādāb al-b. 9, 2, 115, Fun. 172,$_{3}$, Qaw. II, 16, 309.—Glosses: f. Qaw. II, 13.—g. Ḥāfiẓ Sayyid Efendi, print. Istanbul Qaw. II, 12.—h. Ḥasan b. Muḥammad al-ʿAṭṭār, d. 1250/1834, Alex. Waḍʿ 2.—11. Garr. 889/91, Alex. Ādāb al-b. 6,$_{1}$, 7,$_{1}$. 8,$_{1}$, 9,$_{3}$, 11,$_{2}$.—Glosses: a. Aḥmad Shāh, Qaw. II, 297.—b. Yūsuf al-Ḥifnī al-Shāfiʿī, d. 1178/1764, Alex. Ādāb al-b. 3.—c. Muḥammad al-Dalajī, ibid.—d. Mīr Abu ʾl-Fatḥ Muḥammad Tāj al-
1272 Din al-Saʿīdī, d. | 956/1549, Alex. Ādāb al-b. 5, 7,$_{3}$, on which superglosses by ʿAbd al-Raḥmān, ibid. 4.—e. Ḥasan b. Muḥammad al-ʿAṭṭār, d. 1250/1834, ibid. 4.—f. Anon., ibid. 7.—18. Murshid b. Imām al-Shīrāzī, Qaw. II, 308.—19. Aḥmad al-Janadī, ibid.—20. ʿAbd al-ʿAlī b. ʿAlī b. Ḥusayn al-Birjandī, d. 911/1505, ibid. 309.—21. Anon., ibid.—22. Glosses on an unidentified commentary by Muḥammad al-Ṣabbān, d. 1206/1791, Alex. Ādāb al-b. 4, 7,$_{2}$.—Versif. d. Muḥammad b. ʿAlī al-Ḥamawī al-Ḥanafī, completed in 969/1561, Alex. Fun. 198,$_{4}$.

290. IV. 1a. Garr. 1492/5, Qaw. I, 195.—c = (?) Masʿūd b. Aḥmad al-Shirwānī, Qaw. I, 176.—8. Qaw. I, 169.

291. V. *Sharḥ al-Risāla al-ʿAḍudiyya fī ʾl-akhlāq*, comm. by Mufaḍḍal b. Muḥammad b. ʿAbd al-Raḥīm, d. 1124/1713 in Allahabad, Manch. 426.—VI. Comm. *Silk al-niẓām* by Ibrāhīm al-Ḥalabī al-Ḥanafī, Qaw. I, 191.—VII, 1. Garr. 1560, Qaw. I, 196/7, Mosul 130,$_{139}$, 158,$_{137}$, 169,$_{19}$, C. 1322.—Glosses: aa. Qaw. I, 168.

292. Line 1. Instead of al-Shihābawī, read: al-Sihālawī.—kk. Ḥakīmshāh Muḥammad b. Mubārak al-Qazwīnī, d. ca. 902/1496, Alex. Tawḥīd 14.—11. Muḥammad al-Ḥifnī, d. 1181/1767, ibid. Fun. 110,$_{2}$.

293. XIII *al-ʿAḍudiyya fi ʾl-istiʿārāt*, Alex. Fun. 189,$_{13}$.—XIV. *al-Maqāla al-muqarrara fī taḥqīq al-kalām al-nafsī*, with a commentary by Ibn Kamālpāshā, Alex. Fun. 152,$_{3}$.

294. 2, 12. Alex. Fals. 11.

295. 4, 4. Fragm. Mashh. XVIII, 33,102.—5. = 9. = 12.—15. *Sharḥ i āla i raṣad*, Leid. V, 237,$_{12}$.

6. 6. *Fi ʾl-hāla wa-qaws quzaḥ* Zanjān *Lughat al-ʿArab* VI, 1928, 93/6.—7. Comm. on the writings of Ibn al-Haytham, see Krause, *Stamb. Hdss.* 508.

295. 5, 1. Būhār 31, Bank. XXII, 13,$_{2418/9}$.—7. Krause, *Stamb. Hdss.* 17/8.

296. 1. Köpr. I, 951, AS 2757.—5. *Īḍāḥ al-maqāṣid*, see p. 215, § 9, 1.—6. *Risāla fī burhān al-masʾalatayn*, ʿĀṭif 1714,$_{21}$, Berl. Oct. 2978,$_{2}$ (Samarqand 817) on two geometrical problems.—7. Translation of ʿIzz al-Dīn al-Zanjānī's *Fī maʿrifat al-waqt al-tāmm*, Zanjān, *Lughat al-ʿArab* VI, 94.—8. *Mukhtaṣar al-Ṣalāḥī*, Jārullāh 1506, Kemānkeš 321, Serāi 3131, 1, Vat. Barb. 31, comm. *al-ʿImādiyya* by Shams al-Dīn Muḥammad al-Khaṭībī (ḤKh V, 449,$_{11612}$), Serāi 3133,$_{2}$, Vat. Barb. 31,$_{2}$.

296. 1, 1. Bank. XXII, 42,$_{2452/3}$.—2. 2. ibid. 46,$_{2454}$.

297. 22 = 30, completed in Shaʿbān 681/November 1282, Zanjān *Lughat al-ʿArab* VI, 32/6.—31. Persian metaphysics, *juzʾ* 2, Aligarh 3, other *juzʾ*s ibid. 10, 2.

1. b. 3. *al-Zīj al-muḥaqqaq al-Sulṭānī ilā raṣad al-Ilkhānī*, dedicated to Ilkhān Bahādur Khān, see Krause, *Stamb. Hdss.* 518/9 (which has Muḥammad b. ʿAlī Shams al-Munajjim al-Wābiknawī, see ḤKh III, 566, which has Muḥammad b. Yamlī?).—7.*Maʿrifati asṭurlābi shimālī*, Serāi 3327,$_{4}$ (dated 703 AH)

1d. Abū Bakr al-Hamdānī, a Sufi and astrologer, composed in the 8th(?) century: 1. *al-Mudkhal*.—2. *al-Masāʾil*, Bank. XXII, 118,$_{2485,IV,\ V}$.

2. Mūsā b. Muḥammad b. Maḥmūd Qāḍizāde al-Rūmī, d. 815/1412, Suter 430, *Nachtr.* 178.—5. *Ḥāshiya ʿalā Sharḥ Taḥrīr al-Mijisṭī* (see p. 273, 2a, 3), Būhār II, 373.

298. 3, 1. AS 2693, Pertew P. 376, Faiẕ. 1346, Rāġib 920, Ya. Ef. | 246, Ḥamīd. 844, 1273
ʿĀšir Reʾīs 1571, ʿĀšir Ḥafīd 195, Welīaddīn 2284,3, Yeni 783, Bešīr Āġā 427, ʿĀṭif

1705, NO 2932, Serāi Rēvan Kōšk 1714, Jārullāh 1478, Es'ad 993, Alex. Ḥurūf 14 (Faṣl 4), Qaw. II, 279.—*Tashīl Zīj Ulughbeg* by Shams al-Dīn Muḥammad b. Abi 'l-Fatḥ al-Miṣrī al-Ṣūfī, 9th cent., Alex. Ḥisāb 45, with the title *Taqwīm al-kawākib al-sab'a* ibid. 46.

5. Aḥmad b. Mūsā al-Bisṭāmī wrote, in 869/1464: *Risāla fī 'l-raṣad*, Bank. XXII, $99_{,24691X}$.

299. 1d. See p. $1029_{,31}$.

1f. Abu 'l-Faḍl al-Ḥusayn b. Ibrāhīm al-Mutaṭabbib at-Tiflīsī, *Majmū'at al-rasā'il al-ṭibbiyya* (9 in all), MS dated 738/9 AH, Garr. 1108.

300. § 16. 4. Najīb al-Dīn al-Iṣfahānī (when?), *Uṣūl al-malḥama*, print. 1306, *Dharī'a* II, $212_{,826}$.

§ 17. 1. 1. From which is taken the *Risāla fī 'l-jabr wal-qadar*, Alex. Fiqh Ḥan. 59, 6.—2. Comm. a. Alex. Uṣūl 6, Qaw. I, 277, Ind. Off. 1463/6, Mosul $93_{,7}$, $121_{,4}$, $167_{,38}$, $208_{,19}$, $226_{,17}$.

301. 1, 2b. Ind. Off. 1467/72, Garr. 1642/3, 1722, Qaw. I, 276, $Mosul_{61}$, $162_{,121}$, $203_{,197}$, $121_{,241}$, 253, published with *tawḍīḥ*, Kazan 1311, with *tawḍīḥ* and *tanqīḥ*, Lucknow 1281.—Glosses αα Ind. Off. 1473.—γ ibid. 1474, Qaw. I, 284, print. Istanbul 1284.—ρ = Φ, Φ = Ḥafīd al-Taftazānī (p. 309, 5), Ind. Off. 1476, Bank. XIX, $1_{,1523}$. χ Aḥmad b. 'Abdallāh al-Qarīmī, d. 850/1446, Alex. Uṣūl 7.—c. al-Dawwānī, Mosul 226, 256.—e. See I, 646.—f. Qaw. I, 257.—g. Anon. *Kulliyyāt tanqīḥ al-uṣūl*, Qaw. I, 294.—4. *Ḥāshiyat al-uṣūl wa-ghāshiyat al-fuṣūl* on the four *muqaddimāt* by al-Nāfi' Aḥmad b. Muḥammad b. Isḥāq Qāzābādī, Qaw. I, 280.—9. *al-Wishāḥ fī ḍabṭ ma'āqid al-Miftāḥ* (I, 515), on which the commentary *Ḥall al-wishāḥ* by 'Abd al-Raḥmān b. Abī Bakr b. Muḥammad al-'Aynī, d. 893/1488, ḤKh VI, 443, Garr. 533.—10. *Fī 'ilm al-ṣarf*, Mosul $107_{,22}$, $138_{,76}$.—2. According to *ShDh* he died 797, but according to *ḤS* III, 3, 87, he died in 791.

302. 1. Alex. Fun. $107_{,8}$.—Comm. c. Qaw. II, 362/3, Alex. Manṭiq 17 (*Sharḥ qism al-manṭiq*).—Glosses: α Qaw. II, 351/2, Garr. 851, $2080_{,1}$.—γγ Qaw. II, 348.—Note. 1. *al-Burhān fī 'l-manṭiq*, Istanbul 1221 (Qaw. II, 361), *Risālat al-ādāb*, ibid. II, 314.

303. δ Qaw. II, 332/3.—e. Ibid. II, 367, Garr. 852 (delete: Princ. 123 = Garr. 855, anon.).—f. Qaw. II, 326, Makr. 10.—Glosses: α Qaw. II, 341.—δ Print. Istanbul 1264, 1272, 1279, 1288, 1304, among others (Qaw. II, 322/5).

304. ff. ʿAlī b. Aḥmad al-Qusṭanṭīnī, 11th cent. Qaw. I, 193.—gg. *Khulāṣat al-bayān etc.* by Muḥammad b. ʿAbd al-Ḥalīm al-Laknawī (p. 856$_{,33}$), Delhi 1327 (Qaw. II, 354).—hh. *Takhrīj aḥādīth Sharḥ al-ʿaqāʾid lil-T.* by al-Suyūṭī, Alex. Fun. 155$_{,2}$.—ii. *Sharḥ naẓm muwajjahāt Kitāb al-tahdhīb*, with the commentary by Manṣūr al-Manūfī al-Azharī, completed in 1090/1679, Alex. Manṭiq 17.—kk. *Sharḥ qism al-kalām* by Burhān al-Dīn Lār Muḥammad al-Ḥusaynī al-Pattanī al-Hindī, completed in 1015/1616, Indian printing 1312.—II. *Tuḥfat al-labīb* on the *qism al-kalām* by Ḥāfiẓ b. ʿAlī al-ʿImādī, Qaw. I, 163. Anon. glosses, *al-Ḥawāshī wal-nukat wal-fawāʾid al-muḥarrarāt ʿalā Mukhtaṣar al-maʿānī*, Mosul 115$_{,236}$.—10. Garr. 2150$_{,1}$, Qaw. I, 201, Makr. 57.—22. *Dalālāt* (?), Alex. Manṭiq 13.

305. Line 2. Instead of Tājū, read: Tājān, biogr. see ʿAbd al-Qādir Sarfarāz, Cat. Bombay 78, Suter 424.—2. Garr. 1578, Qaw. 1/2, Mosul 25$_{,48}$, 235$_{,141}$.—7. Alex. Fun. 86$_{,11}$.—Comm. a. Read: ʿAbd al-Bāqī.

306. 37 = 21 (?).—45. *Dalāʾil al-iʿjāz*, Qaw. II, 155.—46. *Risāla fī ʿadam kawn afʿāl Allāh (subḥānahu wa-taʿālā) muʿallala bil-aghrāḍ*, Alex. Fun. | 86,9.— 1274
46. *Risāla fī taḥqīq al-wāqiʿ wa-nafs al-amr wal-farq baynahu wa-bayna ʾl-khārij*, Qaw. II, 385.

306. 2.—4. *Thabt*, Alex. Fun. 88$_{,5}$.—1. Other MSS in *Dharīʿa* II, 406/7, 1627.

307. 7. Alex. Fun. 86$_{,7}$.—10. Alex. Fun. 64$_{,3}$.—11. Alex. Tawḥīd 35, Qaw. I, 184, III, 379, Mosul 96$_{,59}$, 109$_{,133,1}$, Najaf in *Dharīʿa* I, 106/752. Comm. c. Alex. Tawḥīd 35, Qaw. I, 201$_{,82}$.—n. Anon., Mosul 158$_{,131}$.—12. *Dharīʿa* I, 107$_{,522}$.—Comm. b. ibid. 109$_{,530}$.—e. Maḥmūd b. Muḥammad b. Maḥmūd al-Nayrizī, a student of Ṣadr al-Dīn al-Dashtakī, composed in 921/1515, MSS in Iraq and Mashhad in *Dharīʿa* I, 103/4$_{,509}$, 108$_{,537}$.—15. Garr. 1500/1, 2005$_{,3}$, Alex. Fun. 152$_{,8}$, Mosul 104$_{,73,24}$.

308. 16. Taymūr, Majāmīʿ 7, print. in *Majmūʿat kalimāt al-muḥaqqiqīn* 1315, *Dharīʿa* II, 260.—17. Garr. 795, Mosul 105$_{,8}$, 180$_{,154}$.—20. Alex. Taṣ. 42$_{,6}$, Fun. 126$_{,2}$, Taymūr, Ḥikma 45.—Comm.: a. Garr. 2005$_{,1}$.—Glosses by Ilyās, ibid. 1611.—28. Garr. 214.—31. = (?) *Risāla fi ʾl-ʿaqāʾid wa-ṣifāt Allāh*, Alex. Fun. 88$_{,6}$.

309. 71. *Sharḥ Minhāj al-wuṣūl* I, 742$_{,9}$.—72. *Risāla fi ʾl-nafs* and *Risāla fi ʾl-ʿawālim al-thalātha*, Taymūr, Ḥikma 44.—73. *Sharḥ ʿalā qawl al-Shaykh*

al-akbar, Alex. Fun. 126,3.—74. *Ishtikākāt al-ḥurūf wa-ṭabāʾiʿuhā wa-aʿdāduhā wa-mā yataʿallaq bi-aʿdād al-ḥurūf min al-masāʾil al-mawsūma bi-ariṭmāthīqī*, in the library of Hādī Āl Kāshif al-Ghiṭāʾ, *Dharīʿa* II, 33,129.

4a. Ḥasan al-Yazīdī, *Risāla fī ādāb al-baḥth*, Alex. Fun. 152,7.

5. Deceased in 916, thus in *ḤS* III, 4, 343, 916, ḤKh, II, 406, and see 906.—1. Qaw. II, 258.—9. *al-Talwīḥ*, see p. 301.

§ 1. 1. Read: Aḥmad b. Shams al-Dīn b. ʿUmar.

310. § 3. 1b. Muḥammad b. Ḥājjī b. Muḥammad al-Samarqandī wrote, for Khwājā Kāfūr, the governor of Ẓafarābād under Fīrūz Shāh (? Ṭughluq 752–99/1351–97): 1. *al-Fatāwā al-Kāfūriyya*, Ind. Off. 1670.—2. *Maʿdin al-ḥaqāʾiq*, p. 266.—4. *Khizānat al-riwāyāt*, Ind. Off. 1603/4.

§ 4. 1. Read: ʿAlī b. Aḥmad.

311. Line 1. Qaw. I, 44.

§ 5. 1. Read: Dam. Z. 67,119.

1a. See p. 985,19.—8. As. Mus. 1381.—10. Dresd. 152, see Steinschneider, *AKM* VI, 3, 182,5.

312. § 1. 2. Garr. 281.

313. § 2. 1. Alex. Taʾr. 13.

1a. Ismāʿīl b. Muḥammad Sharīf, *mudarris* in Āqsarāy, wrote, in 756/1335: *Tadhkirat al-ʿibar wal-āthār fī baḥth al-umam wal-anṣār*, MS in Konya, see *ZDMG* 95, 367.

314. 3. *ShN*, Rescher 26. 1. Alex. Fiqh Ḥan. 64 (where it is wrongly stated that it was written in 879 for Sultan Muḥammad Fātiḥ).

315. 5, 1. Qaw. I, 317.—Glosses by al-Ramlī, *al-Laʾālīʾ al-durriyya fī ʾl-fawāʾid al-Khayriyya*, Alex. Fiqh Ḥan. 48, Qaw. I, 320, 385, 392, *Nūr al-ʿayn etc.* Ind. Off. 1692, Alex. Fiqh Ḥan. 71.

5a. 1. 6. Alex. Ṭibb 44, Qaw. I, 395.

6a. 9. *al-Durr al-naẓīm* cf. p. 630, 2a.

316. 7. Instead of Sarāsh, read: Sarāy.—1. Alex. Fiqh Ḥan. 18, Qaw. I, 318; glosses by Najm al-Dīn b. Khayr al-Dīn al-Ramlī, Qaw. I, 325.—Abstract by al-Qāriʾ al-Harawī, Alex. Fiqh Ḥan. 24.—6. *Adab al-qaḍāʾ*, Alex. Fiqh Ḥan. 5 (only al-Kardarī).—7. *Mukhtaṣar fī bayān taʿrīfāt al-aḥkām*, Garr. 1665.—8. See p. 91/2.

2. This is 9. Qaw. I, 316.

317. 10, 1. Garr. 1728/30, Qaw. I, 331/3, 371.—Comm.: d. Garr. | 1763, Qaw. I, 1275
372/3.—f. Qaw. I, 321.—g. *Kashf rumūz Ghurar al-aḥkām etc.* by ʿAbd al-Ḥalīm b. Pīr Qadam b. Naṣūḥ b. Mūsā b. Muṣṭafā. ʿAbd al-Karīm b. Ḥamza, completed in 1060/1650, Qaw. I, 383.—h. Minqārīzāde, d. 1088/1677, Garr. 2162,$_1$.—i. *Risāla fī iṣlāḥ al-ghalaṭāt al-wāqiʿa fi Kitāb d. al-aḥkām*, by Ibrāhīm b. Muḥammad al-Ḥalabī, Qaw. I, 338.—k. *Risāla fī baʿḍ maʾākhikh ʿalā D. al-a.* by ʿUmar Muḥyi ʾl-Dīn, a *qāḍī* in Edirne, ibid. 339.—2. Garr. 1648/9, Alex. Uṣūl 19, Qaw. I, 295/7, print. Istanbul 1217, 1272, 1273, 1282, 1310, 1321.—Glosses b. Garr. 1650, Qaw. I, 283, Istanbul 1317.—e. See p. 973,$_{12}$.—g. Qaw. I, 281.—i. *Taqrīr al-mirqāt*, Istanbul 1297, 1311.—l. Muḥammad b. Walī b. Rasūl al-Qarashahrī al-Izmīrī, Istanbul 1275, 1285, 1317.

318. 11, 2. Istanbul 1285.—3. *Hadiyyat al-muhtadīn fi ʾl-masāʾil al-fiqhiyya wal-tawḥīdiyya*, Qaw. I, 407.

319. 12. 1. Garr. 1734/5.—2. Alex. Fiqh Ḥan. 42.—3. *Targhīb al-labīb*, Qaw. I, 312 (which has "d. 983"?).

§ 4. 3. *ShN* Rescher 17.—1. Garr. 1293; this formed the basis for a compendium on Shīʿī *fiqh*, written at the request of Miqdād (see p. 209, 4) and entitled *Maʿārij al-masʾūl wa-madārij al-maʾmūl*, Ind. Off. 1810.—3. See p. 974,$_{20}$.—4. *Sharḥ al-Sirājiyya* I, 379.—4. *Farāʾiḍ*, with the commentary by ʿAbd al-Ḥalīm al-Sukkarī, d. ca. 900, Alex. Far. 16.

3a. Read: al-Kūyabānī (Yāqūt, GW IV, 316)—Garr. 1244.

3b. Read: al-Falakābādī (Spitaler).

320. 4, 2. Qaw. I, 72.

321. § 5. 1, 1. Alex. Tawḥīd 41, print. in *Majmūʿa*, Istanbul 1318.—Comm.: aa. Qaw. I, 193.—Glosses: θ Istanbul 1318.—e. Muḥammad b. al-Ḥājj Ḥasan Ḥāfiẓ al-Kabīr, Qaw. I, 200.—f. Ḥāfiẓ al-Dīn Muḥammad Amīn b. Taqī al-Dīn Abī Ḥāmid Aḥmad b. ʿImād al-Dīn Muḥammad b. Ismāʿil al-Mawṣilī, completed on 2 Ramaḍān 1215/29 January 1800, ibid. 202.

322. 3, 1. Garr. 799.

5. 2. Garr. 1732, Alex. Uṣūl 22, Fun. 64,$_{5}$.

323. 1, 4. Garr. 588.—8 = (?) *Taḥqīq māʾ al-ḥayāt wa-kashf astār al-ẓulumāt*, about al-Khidr, Garr. 731, Taymūr, Majm. 8.—10. MS in a private library in Mashhad, *Dharīʿa* II, 7, 18.

4. 1. Alex. Taṣ. 11.

324. 5, 22. Köpr. II, 166, Bank. XXII, 125,$_{2486}$.—35. *Manāhij al-aʿlām fī manāhij al-aqlām* Alex. Adab 167.—36. *Lumʿat al-ishrāq fī maʿrifat ṣanʿat al-awfāq*, Alex. Ḥurūf 8 (only al-Bisṭāmī).—37. *al-Risāla al-waḍʿiyya* (?), Alex. Fun. 152,$_{9}$.

325. 6, 1. With a self-commentary, Qaw. I, 124/5, 243 (*Sharḥ al-arbaʿīn ḥ. al-nabawyya wal-Qudsiyya*).—5. *al-Ḥiṣn al-akbar, sharḥ qawlihi ṣlʿm fīmā yarwīhi ʿan rabbihi ʿazza wa-jalla: lā ilāha illa ʾllāhu ḥiṣnī fa-man dakhala ḥiṣnī amina min ʿadhābī* (also attributed to al-Ghazzālī), Qaw. I, 115, 229.—6. *Anwār al-qulūb li-ṭalab ruʾyat al-maḥbūb*, ibid. I, 219.—7. *Risāla fī ḥaqīqat al-adhkār*, ibid. 236.—8. *al-Mawʿiẓa al-ḥasana*, ibid. 267.—9. *Asrār al-wuḍūʾ*, ibid. 304.—

8. See p. 641,3a.

326. § 7. 1. Alex. Ṭibb 30.

2. 1. Garr. Suppl. 2.

327. § 7. 3. Qaw. II, 288.

§ 7a. 2. Suter 455.—1. *Mūḍiḥ al-awqāt etc.*, Garr. 2006,$_{14}$.—2. *Mīzān al-kawākib*, AS 2710.

3. Read: 891/1486.

4. See p. 156,$_1$.

328. § 8. 3, 1. See p. 1041,$_{37}$.

§ 9. 1b, 2. Alex. Fun. 151,$_1$, Qaw. | I, 51.—3. Qaw. I, 292, on which the *Baḥth fī 'l-nāsikh wal-mansūkh min tafsīr al-Fātiḥa*, Alex. Fun. 153,10. 1276

329. 12. Alex. Fun. 69,$_6$ (attributed to his son Muḥammad Shāh and completed in 824/1421).

3. 6. To be deleted, see ad p. 632, 9, b.

330. 2. Comm. a. Garr. 990.—4. ibid. 460.—5. Comm. by ʿAbd al-Raḥīm for Sultan Selīm, print. Istanbul (?), Alex. Adab 7.

5. Mollā Luṭfī Maqtūl, I. Garr. 1130/1.—10. *Risāla fī taḍʿīf al-madhbaḥ*, texte ar. publié par Şerefeddīn Yaltkaya, trad. franç. et introduction par Abdulhak Adnan et H. Corbin (Études Orient. publ. par l'Institut franç. d'arch. de Stamboul sous la direction de M.A. Gabriel), Paris 1940.

331. 1b. Read: 711/1311.

3. *Dīwān*, Garr. 105, print. Damascus 1874, Beirut 1875, read: al-Shaqīfātī.—*Madāʾiḥ nabawiyya*, Alex. Adab 157.

332, 5. al-Wahrānī died on 9 Shaʿbān 866/9 May 1462 (al-Ḥifnāwī, *Taʿrīf al-salaf* II, 7/11); comm. by al-Qalaʿī, see p. 362,7, and by Abū Zakariyyāʾ Yaḥyā al-Madyūnī, Algiers 497,4.

333. 6. BDMG 68 c, 86, Garr. 434.—Glosses e. Alex. Naḥw 28.—d. ibid. 17.—e. C. 1320.—g. Completed in 1223/1818, Alex. Naḥw 32.—n. Makr. 48.—p. Read: Muḥammad b. Muḥammad al-Amīr.—q. Yūsuf b. Muḥammad b. Yūsuf al-Qurashī al-Maḥallī al-Aḥmadī, MS dated 1190 AH, Alex. Naḥw 29.—15. I.e. Abu 'l-Ḥasan ʿAlī b. Nāṣir al-Dīn Muḥammad b. Muḥammad b. Muḥammad b. Khalaf b. Jibrīl al-Manūfī al-Miṣrī, Makr. 31, Alex. Naḥw 34.

334. 35. Alex. Naḥw 2.—41. ibid. 20.—51. ibid. 17.—58. *Iʿrāb al-Ā.* by Najm al-Dīn al-Faraḍī, MS dated 1121 AH, Alex. Naḥw 34,2.—59. *al-Durra al-saniyya* by Muḥammad b. ʿAballāh al-Khirashī al-Mālikī, d. 1101/1689, Alex. Naḥw 17.—60. *al-Durra al-Ṣabbāghiyya* by Muḥammad b. Muḥammad b. ʿAlī al-Ṣabbāgh,

Garr. 438.—61. *Iḍā'at al-badr al-jaliyya ʿalā alfāẓ al-Ā.* by Muḥammad Abu 'l-Khayr al-Khaṭīb(?), Alex. Naḥw 2.—62. *Kanz al-ʿarabiyya fī ḥall alfāẓ al-Ā.* by Muḥamnmad b. Mubārak al-Mkudsī(?), ibid. 32.—63. Mystical commentary by Ismāʿīl al-Bībīdī, ibid. 20.

335. 2. Alex. Adab 135,6.—5. *Miftāḥ al-masā'il al-naḥwiyya ʿalā naẓm al-Ā.* by al-Shaykh al-Rasmūkī, composed in 1264/1847, ibid. Fun. 80, 3.

336. 7. 1. c. read: al-Zayyātī.

357. 1a. MS in the collection of A. Bels, see *La religion musulmane en Berbérie* I, Paris 1938, 344, n. 3.

338. 3, 10. Alex. Fiqh Māl. 17.—12. *al-Majālis al-Miknāsiyya*, Fez, Qar. 1120.

339. B. 2. 1. Read: *REI* 1934, 59/78.—3. *Sard al-ḥujja ʿalā ahl al-ghafla*, Alexandria 1309.

343. Line 2. Read: *RAAD* XI, 421/32, 461/71.—*al-ʿIbar* vol. I, Garr. 593.

344. § 4, 1. Sanchez Pérez, *Biogr.* 117.—2. Alex. Mawāʿiẓ 22, 33.—2. *al-Tuḥfa al-ẓarīfa bil-asrār al-sharīfa* Fez, Qar. 1494.

345. 1a. Read: b. Rāshid.

346. 1a, 1. *Lubāb* Alex. Fiqh Māl. 14.—2. *al-Martaba al-ʿulyā fī taʿbīr al-ru'yā* ibid. Fun. 202.

3c. Abu 'l-Rūḥ ʿĪsā b. Abī Masʿūd b. Manṣūr al-Naklātī al-Ḥimyarī al-Zawāwī, d. 774/1372, *Manāqib al-imām Mālik*, Alex. Ta'r. 133, Cairo^2 V, 366 (see p. $961,_{33}$).

3d. ʿAlī b. Masʿūd al-Khuzāʿī, d. 789/1387, *Takhrīj al-dalālāt al-samiyya ʿalā mā*
1277 *kāna fī ʿahd rasūl Allāh | min al-ḥiraf wal-ṣanāʾiʿ wal-ʿamālāt al-sharʿiyya*, Berl. Oct. 2871, see Massignon, Enquêtes sur les corporations musulmanes d'artisans et de commerçants du Maroc d'après les réponses à la circulaire résidentielle du 15 octobre 1923, *RMM* 1924, p. 242.

348. 10, 3. *Le livre des magistratures*, texte arabe publié et trad. par H. Brunot et Gaudefroy Demombynes, Collect. de textes arabes publiée par l'Institut des Hautes Études Maroc. VII, Rabat 1937.

349. § 5a. 1a. Shihāb al-Dīn Aḥmad al-Suʿūdī al-Shammākhī, 8th cent., *al-Farīda al-aḥadiyya fī tajrīd al-shajara an-nabawiyya*, Alex. Taʾr. 12.

§ 6. 1, 2. Alex. Fun. 146$_{,9}$.

350. 3, 1. Garr. 274.

351. 5, 5. *Riyāḍ al-ṣāliḥīn wa-tuḥfat al-sunniyyīn* Alex. Mawāʿiẓ 20.

6. 1. *al-Fawāʾid al-jamīla* Alex. Faw. 14.

§ 7. 2, 1. Commn. Garr. 924.

352. Garr. 1521, 2167$_{,1}$, C. 1904.

3b. Alex. Faw. 17, see p. 359, 3b.

4. I. Alex. Fun. 77$_{,3}$, 147$_{,9}$.

353. I, Glosses: g. *al-Tuḥfa al-sundusiyya* by Dāʾūd b. Sulaymān al-Raḥmānī, completed in 1065/1655, Alex. Tawḥīd 6, Makr. 46.—h. Muḥammad b. Qāsim Jassūs al-Fāsī, 12th cent., Alex. Tawḥīd 11.—II. Garr. 1499, 2003$_{,18}$.—Comm. a. Alex. Tawḥīd 19, Makr. 38.—d. Makr. 18/9, C. 1314.—e. *Taqrīr* by Muḥammad al-Anbābī, d. 1313/1895, Alex. Tawḥīd 8, by Sayyid al-Sharqāwī al-Sharshīmī, ibid.

354. 2. Alex. Tawḥīd 20.—7. ibid. Fun. 85$_{,2}$, Makr. 44, BDMG 31c.—Glosses: b. Makr. 20.—c. Alex. Tawḥīd 11, Makr. 18.—d. Alex. Tawḥīd 45, *Talkhīṣ* by Muṣṭafā al-Saqqāʾ al-Maḥallī, ibid. 38.—f. ʿ Alī b. Aḥmad b. Makram al-Saʿīdī al-ʿAdawī al-Mansafīsī, d. 1189/1775, ibid. 31, Makr. 32.—g. Muḥammad b. ʿUbāda al-Barrī al-ʿAdawī al-Mālikī, Makr. 22.—i. *al-Aqāʾid al-mufīda* by ʿAlī b. Muḥammad b. Qāsim al-Sharanqāshī al-Khaṭīb, completed in 1145/1732, Alex. Tawḥīd 5.

355. 37. Abū Muḥammad Manṣūr b. Abi ʾl-Qāsim b. Naṣr al-Saʿīdī al-Thawrī, Alex. Tawḥīd 41 (whose *ʿAqīda* is preserved in ibid. 3).—38. Muḥammad b. Manṣūr al-Hudhudī, ibid. Fun. 1$_{,1}$, 108$_{,3}$.—39. Aḥmad al-Dardīr, ibid. 11$_{,8}$.—40. *Tawkīd al-ʿaqd fīmā akhadha ʿalayna ʾllāhu min al-ʿahd* by Yaḥyā b. Muḥammad Abu ʾl-Barakāt al-Shāwī al-Jazāʾirī, ibid. Tawḥīd 8.—Versif.: 6. Sīdī ʿAbdallāh b. Hamza, *Hesperis* XVIII, 97, 27, 9.—II A. Comm. by Aḥmad b. ʿAbd al-Fattāḥ al-Mollawī al-Shāfiʿī, d. 1181/1767, Alex. Tawḥīd 21.—Abū Muḥammad

b. Muḥammad al-Harrājī al-Darʿī, d. 1006/1597 in Fez, ibid. 38.—III. Alex. Tawḥīd 21.—Glosses e. Ibrāhīm al-Andalusī, ibid. 12.—VI. Alex. Tawḥīd 38.—Comm. a. ibid. 29, 42, Garr. 1500.—e. *al-Anwār al-bahiyya* by ʿAbd al-Ghanī al-Nābulusī, Alex. Fun. 90,$_{11}$.—VIII. Garr. 820, Alex. Tawḥīd 38, Manṭiq 31.—Comm. 1. Garr. 857, Alex. Manṭiq 31,$_{2}$, 35.

356. 8. *Lawāmiʿ al-naẓar* by Muḥammad b. Yaʿqūb al-Miknāsī al-Mālikī, Makr. 54.—10. ʿAṭiyya, Alex. Manṭiq 12.—XXVII. Read: *"al-maʿidatu etc."*, with the title *Tafsīr mā taḍammanathu kalimāt khayr al-bariyya min ghāmiḍ asrār al-ṣināʿa sharḥ* (sic) *al-ṭibbiyya*, Alex. Ḥad. 47,$_{1}$.

357. 5. al-Manẓūma etc., Alex. Fun. 147,$_{11}$.—Comm. 1. Qaw. 194.—2. Abbreviation by Abū Hurayra ʿAbd al-Salām b. ʿAbd al-Raḥmān b. ʿUthmān b. Nabhān al-Ṣaffūrī al-Shāfiʿī, Alex. Tawḥīd 20.

§ 8. 1a. Read: al-ʿAbdarī, see p. 95 B, 1.

1b. ʿUmar b. ʿAlī al-Jazāʾirī. 1. *Ibtisām al-ʿarūs*.—2. *Qamʿ al-nufūs min kalām Ibn*
1278 *ʿArūs*, Gotha 2362, Frank 427, different from Gotha 2363, *Dīwān*, lith. | C. 1880.

1c. Muḥammad b. Abi ʾl-Qāsim al-Ḥimyarī b. al-Ṣabbāgh, beginning 8th cent., *Durrat al-asrār wa-tuḥfat al-abrār fī manāqib Sayyidī Abi ʾl-Ḥasan al-Shādhilī*, Tunis 1304.

358. 2. See p. 1042,$_{54}$.—2. 2. Dahdāh 17.—6. Garr. 1953.

2a. Read: al-Hawārī.

3. 2. *al-Īmāʾ ʿalā ʿilm al-asmāʾ*, completed in 880/1475, Alex. Faw. 5.

359. 3a. Comm. 2. *al-Ishārāt al-saniyya fī baʿḍ maʿāni ʾl-Mabāḥith al-aṣliyya* by Muḥammad b. ʿAlī al-Andalusī al-Shāṭibī, d. 963/1556, Alex. Tasawwuf 5.

3b. See p. 352,$_{3}$.

3c = p. 152, 32a.

4. 1. Qaw. I, 233.

360. 4a. 1a. Qaw. I, 263, Makr. 56.—3 = 13. Alex. Faw. 28.—14. ʿAbdallāh al-Ḥamdūnī al-Ḥamawī al-Azharī, composed in 1142/1729, *Munawwir al-sarīrāt* Alex. 10, 29.—15. *al-Minaḥ al-ilāhiyya* by Sulaymān b. ʿUmar al-Jamal, d. 1204/1789, ibid. 29.—16. Anon., Hamb. Or. Sem. 16.—17. Glosses by Abū ʿAbdallāh Muḥammad al-Ṣaghīr al-Suhaylī, MS dated 1174, Alex. Faw. 7.

5b. = 247,9.

361. 7. Alex. Mawāʿiẓ 41,2, 49.—9. Ibid. Faw. 28.—10 = *Safīnat al-najāʾ li-man ila ʾllāh iltajaʾ* Alex. Faw. 21.—Comm. c. Alex. Faw. 4, 19, 20.—d. *al-Lawāqiḥ al-Qudsiyya* by Aḥmad b. Muḥammad b. ʿAjība al-Ḥasanī, completed in 1196/1782, ibid. 19, in *Majmūʿa* C. 1324.—e. *al-Anwār al-Qudsiyya wal-asrār al-unsiyya* by Muṣṭafā b. Kamāl al-Dīn al-Bakrī, d. 1162/1749, ibid. 4/5, print. Būlāq(?) n.d.—f. *Fatḥ al-ṣifāt al-saniyya* by ʿAlī al-Suṭūḥī al-Baysūsī, 12th cent., ibid. Fun. 91,2.—11. *al-Durra al-muntakhaba fi ʾl-adwiya al-mujarraba* additionally Garr. 1126, Alex. Ṭibb 17.—Note. 1. Comm. *Bulūgh al-qaṣd wal-munā fī khawāṣṣ asmāʾ Allāh al-ḥusnā* by al-Fāsī additionally Alex. Faw. 51, where Muḥammad al-Dimyāṭī's death year is mistakenly given as 924, Berl. 3757.

362. 6b. Muḥammad b. ʿAlī b. Muḥammad al-Khamīnī al-Ṣiqillī al-Shuṭaybī, 9th cent., *Miftāḥ al-janna al-mutawaqqif ʿalā ʾl-kitāb wal-sunna*, Alex. Faw. 27.

9a. Attributed to Aḥmad b. Yūsuf al-Rāshidī (see p. 1001, 43; persecuted by the Banū Zayān, he first went to Bijāya and then to the Orient. On his return he joined the Turks, dying in 931/1524) is: Les Dictons attribués à Sidi A. b. Y. ed. R. Basset, *JA* s. VIII, vol. 16, p. 203ff.

363. § 9. 1. Tlemcen, *RAAD* XI (1931), 97/101.—4

§ 10. P.J. Renaud, Ibn al-Bannāʾ al-Marrakochi sufi et mathématicien du XIII/XIV s. J. C., *Hespéris* XXV (1938), 13/42, idem *Isis* 27, 216/8, Sánchez Pérez, *Biogr.* 51.—1. Bodl. I, 1001, *al-Jabr wal-muqābala*, Cairo[1] V, 213.

364. aa. Garr. 1032a.—c. 1. Paris 2463.—d. Alex. Ḥisāb (author Abu ʾl-Ḥasan ʿAlī b. Muḥammad b. ʿAbdallāh al-Tādilī).—h. Aḥmad al-Majdī, Br. Mus. 417.—5. Bodl. I, 873,2. Esc. 904,1.—14. Cairo[1] V, 314,3.—15. *Muwashshaḥ kāfī lil-mutaṭallib*, Ambr. 246.—16. *Mudkhil fī tasyīr wa-maṭāriḥ al-shuʿāʿāt*, Berl. Oct. 2592,9.—17. *Fī ʿamal al-ṭilasm*, ibid. 11.

§ 11. 1. See Colin and Renaud in *Hespéris* XXV (1938), 94/6.

2. See W.H. Morley, *Description of an Arabic Quadrant*, London 1860, P. Schmalzl, *Zur Gesch. des Quadranten* (1929), p. 37/8.—3. *Risāla fī thumn al-dāʾira*, composed in 746, Cairo^{1} v, 288.—4. *Risāla fī rubʿ al-musātara*, ibid. 251.

365. 3, 1 a. Garr. 986/7.

366. Line 26. Muḥammad Fatḥallāh al-Baylūnī al-Ḥalabī, d. 1042/1632, whose *Khulāṣat mā yaḥṣil ʿalayhi ʾl-sāʿūn fī adwiyat dafʿ al-wabaʾ wal-ṭāʿūn* is in Alex. Fun. $89_{,3}$.

1279 | 367. 1a. 1. BDMG 64, not identical with the *Kitāb ḥifẓ al-ṣiḥḥa* and *al-Ṭibb al-sharīf*, see Griffini, *Cent. Amari* II, 487/9.

§ 13a. Music. Muḥammad b. Ibrāhīm al-Shalākhī wrote, around 701/1301, for the Merinid sultan Abū Yaʿqūb b. Abī Yaḥyā b. ʿAbd al-Ḥayy: *al-Imtāʿ wal-intifāʿ*, on music, Madr. 603 (dated 701 AH), see Farmer, *Studies in Arabic Musical Instruments* II, London 1939, 21/35, *Sources* 49.

§ 14. 1, 1. *Kāfi ʾl-wāfī*, Alex. Kīm. 9.—3. *Tuḥfat man ṣabar ʿalā taṭhīr arkān al-ḥajar*, ibid.—4. *Kitāb fī ʿilm al-raml*, Berl. Qu. 1734 (which has Ibn Makhfūf), Mosul $236_{,153}$.—With the title *Kanz al-asrār al-khafiyya fī aḥkām al-zāʾiraja al-ramliyya*, Bank. XXII, $126_{,2457}$.

368. 1, 1. Rāmpūr I, 581.

369. § 1, 2, 3. Read: *Taḥṣīl gharaḍ etc.*

372. 8. *Khaṭrat al-ṭayf etc.*, from which comes the account of the trip of Prince Abu ʾl-Ḥajjāj to the eastern districts of Granada, in Müller, op. cit., I, 14/41.

373. 19. Read: *al-Wuṣūl*.—26. *Manẓūma fi ʾl-ṭabāʾiʿ wal-ṭubūʿ wal-uṣūl* (also attributed to ʿAbd al-Wāḥid al-Wansharīshī), Cairo, *Nashra* 27, Madr. 334, f. 15/9, see Farmer, *Collection of Oriental Writers on Music* I, Glasgow 1939, *Sources* 54.

5. Alex. Taʾr. 56.

375. 3, 1a. Alex. Fiqh Māl. 10.—2. Ibid. Adab 35.

376. 4, 2. d. *Tuḥfat al-ḥukkām* by Muḥammad b. ʿAbd al-Salām al-Bannānī, composed in 1129/1717, Alex. Fiqh Māl. 15.—e. *Tuḥfat al-ḥukkām fī masāʾil al-daʿāwī*

wal-aḥkām by Abū ʿAbdallāh Muḥammad b. al-Ṭālib al-Murrī al-Fāsī al-Tāʾūdī, d. 1207/1792, ibid. 9, as *Taʿlīq* ibid. 15.—f. Anon., ibid. 12.

§ 5. 1. I, 733.

377. 1a, 2. (§ 8, 1a) Alex. Ḥad. 49,2.—Comm. *Lubb al-azhār* by Abu ʾl-Ḥasan ʿAlī b. Muḥammad b. ʿAlī al-Qurashī al-Basṭī al-Qalaṣādī, d. 891/1486 in Bāja, 3b. 44.

378. 3. *Zahr al-kimām etc.*, Alex. Taʾr. 75.

§ 8. 1. See Sánchez Pérez, *Biogr.* 109.

1a. Read: ʿAlī.—1. Alex. Ḥisāb 4.

379. 1a, 2. Garr. 1039, Alex. Ḥisāb 17.—4. Alex. Taʾr. 4.

§ 8a. Medicine. Abū ʿAbdallāh Muḥammad b. ʿAlī al-Lakhmī al-Shaqūrī (from Segura) wrote, on the occasion of the plague of the year 749/1348: 1. *Taḥqīq al-nabaʾ ʿan amr al-wabaʾ*, abstract *al-Naṣīḥa*, Esc.[2] 1785,7.—2. *Tuḥfat al-mutawassil wa-rāḥat al-mutaʾammil*, Algiers 1774.—3. *Mujarrabāt fī ʾl-ṭibb*, Leid. 1367,3 Madr. 270, *Hespéris* XII, 127.

§ 9. 2. See p. 155,2.

3. Abū ʿAbdallāh Muḥammad b. ʿAbd al-Munʿim al-Ḥimyarī wrote, around 800/1397, *al-Rawḍ al-miʿṭār fī khabar al-aqṭār*, which was adapted by one of his descendants around 900/1494 in Jedda (ḤKh III, 490,6596/7) while the original was used by al-Qalqashandī and al-Maqrīzī; from this comes E. Lévi-Provençal, *La péninsule iberique au moyen-âge*, Leiden 1938 (Publ. du Fonds de Goeje 12).

§ 10. 5. Read: "C. 1303, 1318".

381. Heyworth-Dunne, Arabic literature in Egypt in the 18th century with special reference to poetry and poets, BSOS IX (1938) 675/90 (mainly based on al-Jabartī).

1. 1. Garr. 109, C. 1304.

2. 1. In Baghdad, *al-Muqtaṭaf*, Febr. 1928, p. 201/4.

382. 2b. See p. $13_{,34a}$, $413_{,2b}$.

2d. ʿAlāʾ al-Dīn b. Mulayk al-Ḥamawī, d. 917/1513, *al-Nafaḥāt al-adabiyya min al-riyāḍ al-Ḥamawiyya*, Beirut 1312.

4. 1. *Rawḍat al-ʿushshāq etc.* additionally NO 1782, Bank. XXIII, $55_{,2550}$.

383. 5b. Read: b. al-Bakkāʾ and *Ghawāni ʾl-ashwāq*.

7. 1. Print. Būlāq 1313, in which it is no. 2.

1280 | 384. 9, 1. Cairo n.d.

10b. *al-Inʿām fī maʿrifat al-anghām*, photograph of a MS in Paris, Cairo, *Nashra* 411, Alex. Adab 77.

386. 30. See p. 630,3, Garr. 121, Bank XXIII, $58_{,2552}$.

33. al-Ṭabbākh, *Taʾrīkh Ḥalab* VI, 362/73, *Dīwān* Garr. 123, print. Beirut 1872, 1326.

33b. Muḥammad b. Zayn al-ʿĀbidīn al-Bakrī al-Ṣiddīqī al-Miṣrī, d. 1087/1676, *Dīwān* with many *muwashshaḥāt*, Alex. Adab 52.

387. 35, 5. Comm. by ʿUthmān al-ʿUryānī, d. 1168/1754, Garr. 128.

37b. See p. $54_{,7b}$.

388. 37f. Naṣr al-Khalwatī al-Jalwatī al-Dimashqī, *Dīwān*, MS dated 1101 AH, Alex. Adab 142.

41. 2. Garr. 158 (where the author is ʿAbdī Bishr al-Khāl).

43 = 494, 4.

49. *BSOS* IX, 681.

49a. *al-Durr etc.* C. 1346.

389. 53a, 7. *Naẓm al-laʾāliʾ bil-baḥr al-shimālī, dīwān*, Aleppo 1895.—8. *Bulūgh al-arab fī ʿilm al-badīʿ fī lughat al-ʿArab*, Alex. Bal. 3.—9. *Mukhtaṣar al-ʿarūḍ wal-qawāfī*, ibid. ʿArūḍ 5.

391. 62. *BSOS* IX, 681.—1. Garr. 129, 130, Leningrad, Un. Or. 858, Qaw. II, 207.—4. C. 1282.—9. BDMG 67c.—15. Garr. 151 (which has al-Bakhātī).

63. Read: in 1172, or according to others in 1189.—4. With a commentary, attributed to his son, Alex. Taṣ. 14.

392. 4. Garr. 1968/9, Qaw. I, 246, print. C. 1281.—5. Qaw. I, 139.—7. *al-Qawl al-sadīd fī 'ttiṣāl al-asānīd*, Qaw. II, 93.

66. 11. *Risāla fī 'l fasd wal-ḥijāma*, Alex. Ṭibb 20.—12. *Sharḥ al-Risāla al-sharṭiyya*, see ad 487.

67. *BSOS* IX, 683. 1. Garr. 133 (which has *al-muntaẓam*).

393. 67. 7. Garr. 1857.

67a. 1. Commentary on the *adab* verses of al-Mardāwī.

67c. Ismāʿīl b. Tāj al-Dīn b. Aḥmad al-Maḥāsinī al-Ḥanafī al-Dimashqī, b. 1139/1726 in Damascus, d. 1187/1773 (al-Murādī II, 162), *Dīwān*, *RAAD* IV, 506/8.

67c. ʿAbdallāh b. Yūsuf b. ʿAbdallāh al-Yūsufī al-Ḥalabī, d. 1194/1780 (= 1018, 10?), *Mawārid al-sālik li-aṣḥāb al-masālik*, Būlāq 1308, Alex. Adab 131.

69b. 1. a. 2. *Nuzhat al-ʿuqūl fī maʿālim Ṭāhā al-rasūl*, C. 1319.

67c. Read: 69b.

69c. Qāsim b. ʿAṭāʾallāh al-Miṣrī, d. 1204/1789, poet in the popular genre, *BSOS* IX, 685.

69d. Muḥammad Mujāhid Abu 'l-Najāʾ al-Ṣaghīr, d, after 1205/1790, *Majmūʿat ashʿār fī madḥ sayyidī Aḥmad al-Badawī*, Garr. 137.

69e. Badrī al-ʿAwdī, d. 1214/1799, *al-Sawāniḥ al-anwariyya*, Cairo, Adab 1419.

§ 2. 1, 5. *ʿĀlam al-malāḥa*, print. Damascus 1299.

394. 1, 6. Garr. 1585.

9. See p. 402, 8. 11.

8a. 1. Excerpts in Kračkovsky, *Izvestija* AK. *Nauk*, 1926, 279/99, other works ibid. 286/7, 293/5.

395. 9a. See p. 429,16.

396. 10, 1. See Jirjī Zaydān, *Ta'rīkh al-adab* IV, 126.—4. Read: *al-nadd.*—7. Garr. 218.

397. 14, 4. AM Buch. 456.

16. al-Ṭabbākh, *Ta'rīkh Ḥalab* VI, 535.—2. *Badīʿiyya*, with the commentary *Ḥilyat al-badīʿ fī madḥ al-nabī al-shafīʿ*, Aleppo 1293.

398. 18, 9. Alex. Ta'r. 18.

399. 18, 18. Garr. 712.—22. ibid. 1858.

18a. Born in 1161/1747, died in 1211/1796, while others say he died in 1221/1806. *al-Kifāya*, Berl. 6794, Garr. 479, print. Istanbul 1289.

19. 3. *al-Kāfiya al-shāfiya*, Alex. ʿArūḍ 2, Qaw. II, 184, C. 1310.—4. Comm. by al-Sanbāwī, Garr. 1313.—6. Alex. Ta'r. 3, C. 1317 in the margin of Abu 'l-Ḥasan al-ʿAdawī al-Ḥamzāwī, *Mashāriq al-anwār*; basis for the *Risāla laṭīfa fī sīrat al-nabī* of ʿAlī al-Manshalīlī, Garr. 662.

1281 | 400. 12. C. 1310.—13. Alex. Adab 11.—14. Makr. 28.—16. *Naẓm asmā' ahl al-Badr*, with the commentary *Rawḍat al-ṭālibīn li-asmā' al-ṣaḥāba al-Badriyyīn* by Muṣṭafā b. Muḥammad b. ʿAbd al-Khāliq al-Bannānī, composed in 1232/1817, Alex. Faw. 9.

20. 8. *Urjūzat ḍabṭ al-masā'il al-mustathnāt min qāʿidat kull ṣalāt baṭalat ʿala 'l-ma'mūm bi-lā ishtibāh*, with a comm. Alex. Fiqh Māl. 9.

§ 3. 3. Aḥmad b. Muḥammad b. Yūsuf al-Khālidī, d. 1034/1624, *Ta'rīkh al-amīr Fakhr al-Dīn al-Maʿnī* Garr. 606, see P. Paolo Carali, Fakhraddīn II al-Mani in Toscana, Sicilia, Napoli e la sua visita a Malta 1613/8, *Annali R. Inst. Or. Napoli* VII, 4, 1937.

4a. Aḥmad b. Muḥammad b. Aḥmad b. ʿUthmān wrote, in 1157/1744: *Manāqib al-shaykh ʿAbdallāh al-Yūnīnī* (d. 617/1221) Garr. 711.

401. 3, 12. *Khulāṣat al-fawāʾid fī naẓm al-ʿaqāʾid*, Alex. Fun. 98, 1.

402. 7, 5. See p. 997, 23.

8. 11. *ʿIqd al-niẓām bi-ʿaqd al-kalām*, Alex. Mawāʿiẓ 27.—12. *Itqān mā yaḥsun min al-akhbār al-dāʾira ʿala ʾl-alsun*, ibid. Ḥad. 1 (see p. 394. 1, 9).

9. 3. *Ṭarīq al-hudā wa-muzīḥ al-radā*, Alex. Mawāiʿẓ 26.

403. 12, 1. Garr. 710.—3. Alex. Adab 179.

404. 14, 3. Garr. 1234.

12c. ʿAbd al-Qādir b. ʿAbdallāh al-ʿAbdalānī al-Kurdī, Nazīl Dimashq, d. 1178/1764, *Tuḥfat al-kirām fī dhikr baʿḍ al-khalāʾiq al-ʿiẓām*, Alex. Taʾr. 47.

405. 17. See p. 813, 4g.—1. 2. *Fihrist* I/III by Muḥammad al-Biblāwī, Būlāq 1314.

406. 2. 1. Alex. Taʾr. 97.

408. 1. vol. 1. Garr. 608/9.—3. Alex. Taʾr. 17.—4. Qaw. I, 141.—5. *Nayl al-marām al-mughtabaṭ etc.*, Alex. Ḥurūf 17.—8a. Alex. Adab 105.—d. *al-Anwār al-qamariyya* by Abu Bakr ʿAbd al-Wahhāb b. Muḥammad Amīn al-Zarʿī, d. ca. 1236/1821, Garr. 140.—10. Hamb. Or. Sem. 14,5, Garr. 2003,1, Alex. Tawḥīd 38.—15. *al-Jumān min mukhtaṣar akhbār al-zamān*, Le Livre des Perles recueillies de l'abrégé de l'histoire des siècles, tr. S. de Sacy, *Not. et Extr.* 1788.

409. 8, 1. *al-Tuḥfa al-bahiyya*, see H. Jansky, MOG II, 173.

14. Ibn al-Qilaʿī, *Les exploits des chefs, poème historique des croisades libanaises 1075/1450*, publié pour la première fois et annoté par P. Carali, *La Revue Patriarcale*, 1935/7, 96 pp.

410. 1, 2. *Tuḥfat al-mulūk wal-raghāʾib etc.*, Alex. Jaghr. 5.

3. 2. Alex. Mawāʿiẓ 14.

4. 2. Read: *fī wafq*, Garr. 944.

412. 2, 1. Abstract by Abu ʾl-ʿAbbās Aḥmad Čalabī al-Qaramānī al-Dimashqī (no. 4), d. 19 Shawwāl 1019/5 January 1611, Alex. Taʾr. 8.

4. 2. Read: al-Rawḍ, Arabic transl. of *Sīrat al-Sulṭān Ibrāhīm b. Adham* by Darwīsh Ḥasan al-Rūmī, Dam Z. $39_{,30,2}$.

5. 6. *Tuḥfat al-ẓurafāʾ bi-dhikr al-mulūk wal-khulafāʾ*, Alex. Taʾr. 119,1.—2. *al-Futūḥāt al-ʿUthmāniyya lil-diyār al-Miṣriyya*, ibid. 2.—7 = (?) 433, 19. *Sharḥ ḥadīth fī faḍl al-Rūm*, Garr. 61.

413. 2b. See 13, 34a, 382, 2b.

414. 13a. Read: "1101" = 637, 9b, see Kračkovsky, *al-Andalus* III, 92.

415. § 5. 1, 9. Alex. Ḥad. 7.

1b. ʿAbd al-Qādir b. Muḥammad b. Aḥmad al-Shādhilī al-Mālikī al-Muʾadhdhin, ca. 920/1514, *Radd al-ʿuqūl al-ṭāʾisha ilā maʿrifat ma ʾkhtaṣṣat bihi Khadīja wa-ʿĀʾisha*, Garr. (see p. 932, 19).

2. 1. Makr. 30, with the title *Rabīʿ al-atqiyāʾ fī dhikr faḍāʾil sayyid al-aṣfiyāʾ* Garr. 651.

1282 | 416. 2, 6. Köpr. 1289, AS 4034, Paris $4236_{,2}$ (see Index).

4. 3. Garr. 1974.—6. *Muzīl al-ʿanāʾ fī sharḥ asmāʾ allāh al-ḥusnā*, on a poem by Shaḥḥādha b. ʿAlī al-ʿIrāqī, ibid. 1308.

5. 1. Alex. Ḥad. $47_{,1}$.

6. a. 1. See p. $394_{,9}$ and ad 407, 8, 12.

417. 9, 1. Makr. 56, lith. Istanbul 1285.—6. Hyderabad 1323.—8. Garr. 1113.—13. Alex. Taʾr. 104, Makr. 53.—23. Garr. 707.—24. Ibid. 708 (*al-Futūḥāt al-Makkiyya*).—30. Taymūr, Ṭab. 59.—35. *Sharḥ asmāʾ Allāh al-ḥusnā wa-khawāṣṣihā*, Alex. Faw 10.—36. *Fatḥ al-qadīr al-khabīr bi-sharḥ Taysīr al-Taḥrīr*, see ad p. 442, 10a. 3.

418. 9a. Garr. $2002_{,6}$.

10. 1. Qaw. II, 228.—Abstracts a. Read: *Khulāṣat al-āthār*.—2. Alex. Taṣ. 50.

419. 10e, see p. 1008, 121.

11. 2. Makr. 1.—8. Br. Mus. 9118.

12. 6. *Risāla fī sharḥ qawlihi*, on sura $42{,}_{49}$, Qaw. I, 65.—13. Comm. a. Alex. Muṣṭalaḥ Ḥad. 12.—g. ibid. 11, 18.—i. ʿAbdallāh Suwaydān al-Damlijī (p. 736 § 5, 1), ibid. 15.—k. Ḥasan al-Jiddāwī, completed in 1288/1871, ibid. 18.

13a. Shihāb al-Dīn Abū ʿAbdallāh al-Bābilī al-Qāhirī, d. 1077/1666, *Muntakhab al-asānīd fī waṣl al-muṣannafāt wal-ajzāʾ wal-masānīd*, collected by his student ʿĪsā b. Muḥammad al-Maghribī al-Jazāʾirī al-Thaʿālibī, d. 1080/1669, Alex. Muṣṭ. Ḥad. 17.

420. 17b. Qaw. I, 233.

17d. See p. 487, 6b, $945{,}_{162}$.

17e. Muḥammad b. Yūsuf Abū Shāma al-Dimashqī, d. 1101/1689.—1. *Muzīl al-labs ʿan ḥadīth radd al-shams*, Alex. Fun. 166_{6}, *Ajwibat al-asʾila al-wāridāt ʿani ʾl-azwāj wal-banīn wal-banāt* ibid. 16.

421. 19c. ʿAlī b. Yaḥyā b. Aḥmad b. ʿAlī b. Qāsim al-Kaysalānī al-Qādirī al-Ḥamawī, d. 1113/1701 in Hama, *Naẓm al-durar fī ḥilyat khayr al-bashar*, with the commentary *Bulūgh al-bughya fī sharḥ Manẓūmat al-ḥilya*, Alex. Taʾr. 5.

19d. Ibrāhīm b. Muḥammad b. Kamāl al-Dīn b. Ḥamza al-Ḥusaynī al-Ḥanafī al-Dimashqī, d. 1120/1708 (Muḥ. II, 10/5, Mur. II, 120, Sarkīs 88), *al-Bayān wal-taʿrīf fī asbāb wurūd al-ḥadīth al-sharīf* (from the *Muṣannaf* of Abu ʾl-Baqāʾ al-ʿUkbarī, with additions), 2 vols., Aleppo 1329/30 (see p. 223, line 4).

422. 22b, 5. *RAAD* IX, 638, 7 (which has *al-musaddala*).—9. *al-Kalim al-jawāmiʿ fī bayān masʾalat al-Uṣūlī li-Jamʿ al-jawāmiʿ*, Alex. Uṣūl 17.

23. Read: al-ʿAjlūnī.—2. *ʿIqd al-jawhar al-thamīn fī arb. ḥad.*, BDMG 15, Alexandria 1301.—6. Alex. Muṣṭ. Ḥad. 9.—10. *al-Farāʾid wal-darārī fī tarjamat al-imām al-Bukhārī*, Alex. Taʾr. 114.—11. *Shadha ʾl-rawḍ al-badīʿ al-mudrik fī ziyārat al-sayyida Zaynab wa-sayyidī Mudrik*, ibid.

423. 25b. Read: al-Nafzāwī.—Names of the warriors at Badr, Sbath 1165.

27. 2. Alex. Faw. 10, Būlāq 1294.

27b. Nūr al-Dīn ʿAlī al-Mīqātī bi-Umawī Ḥalab, d. 1192/1778, *Mawlid al-nabī*, Alex. Ḥad. 47.

28. 3. *Nuzhat al-ṭullāb fīmā yataʿallaq bil-basmala min fann al-iʿrāb*, Alex. Fun. $97_{,1}$.

424. 32a. Karam al-Dīn ʿAbd al-Karīm b. Aḥmad b. Nūḥ al-Ṭarābulusī wrote, in 1206/1791: *Fatḥ al-muʿīn ʿala ʾl-durr al-thamīn fī naẓm asmāʾ al-Badriyyīn*, Qaw. II, 242.

§ 6. 1. Badr al-Dīn Abu ʾl-Yusr. 1. Garr. 1736, entitled *Fī adab al-qaḍāʾ*, ibid. $2129_{,2}$ (= 2).—3. *Risāla fī ḥukm al-māʾ al-mustaʿmal*, ibid. 1737.

2. 1. Garr. 1738.

425. 2a. al-Qarāfī Nūr al-Dīn, Āṣaf I, $644_{,346,2}$.

3. 1. Ind. Off. 1605/7, Garr. 1742/3, Alex. Fiqh Ḥan. 56, Qaw. I, 415.—Comm. c. 1. Aḥmad b. Muḥammad (see ad 471, 38a), Ind. Off. 1608/9, Alex. Fiqh Ḥan. 39,
1283 Qaw. I, 372.—g. Alex. | Fiqh Ḥan. 14, Qaw. I, 314.—i. Alex. Fiqh Ḥan. 14, 56.—
m. Zīrakzāde, d. 1010/1601, Qaw. I, 355.

426. n. Alex. Fiqh Ḥan. 29.—o. Qaw. I, 404, Istanbul 1920 (sic, but read "1290").—p. *Taḥqīq al-bāhir* by Muḥammad Hibatallāh b. Muḥammad b. Yaḥyā al-Tājī, first half of the 10th cent., Qaw. I, 311.—q. Muḥammad b. Walī al-Rasūl Qarashahrī Nazīl Īzmīr, Qaw. I, 355.—2a. Garr. 1755.—b. Qaw. I, 337, Istanbul 1290.—c. *Tartīb F. Z.*, Alex. Fiqh Ḥan. 13, 59.—4. Ibid. 33, Algiers 552, Comm. by al-Sīwāsī, Garr. 1933, $2037_{,5}$.—7. Alex. Fiqh Ḥan. 57.—8. Qaw. I, 348.—9. Alex. Fiqh Ḥan. 57.—12. a. Qaw. I, 344.—14. Qaw. I, 345.—15. Ibid. 348.—16. Alex. Fiqh Ḥan. $59_{,8}$, Qaw. I, 310.—17. Qaw. I, 347.—18. Ibid. 339.—24. Ind. Off. 1462, Qaw. I, 300.—25. Qaw. I, 343.—27. Ibid. 344, Alex. Fiqh Ḥan. 28.—36. Qaw. I, 343.—37. Ibid. 340.

427. 38. Qaw. I, 341.—50. *Risāla fī sharḥ waqf al-sulṭān al-Ghūrī fī shaykh al-Ghūriyya*, ibid. 346.—51. *Risāla fī sharḥ Kitāb waqf Khāʾir Bek al-Nāṣiri*, ibid.

346.—52. *al-Wusūl ilā qawāʿid al-uṣūl*, ibid. 301.—53. *al-Khabar al-bāqī fī jawāz al-wuḍūʾ min al-fasāqī*, ibid. 329.—54. *Risāla fi ʾl-afʿāl allatī tufʿal fi ʾl-ṣalāt etc.*, ibid. 339.—55. *Risāla fī bayān al-iqṭāʿāt*, ibid. 340.—56. *Risāla fi ʾl-safīna idhā ghariqat etc.*, ibid. 345.—57. *Risāla fi ʾstiʿdāl al-waqt*, ibid. 338.—58. *Risāla fi ʾl-istiṣḥāb*, ibid.

4. Read: Muḥammad b. ʿAbdallāh (= 5?) 1. Alex. Fiqh Ḥan. 65, attributed to no. 5.

4a. Ind. Off. 1693/5, Garr. 1775, MS Massignon (see Gaudefroy Demombynes, *JA* 230, 451), Leningrad, Un. Or. 260 (Kračkovsky, *Bibl. Vost.* 24, 1934, 101/2), Alex. Fiqh Ḥan. 70, Fun. 186, Qaw. I, 404, Taymūr, *RAAD* XII, 57.

5. 1. Ind. Off. 1687, Garr. 1756, Alex. Fiqh Ḥan. 14.

428. Comm. a. Garr. 1757, Alex. Fiqh Ḥan. 67.—b. Ind. Off. 1688, 4571 (*JRAS* 1939, 364), Garr. 1758/9, Alex. Fiqh Ḥan. 24, Qaw. I, 329/31, abbreviation of his *Khazāʾin al-asrār etc.* or *al-Taḥrīr ʿala ʾl-Tanwīr*, Alex. Fun. 107,4.—Glosses: β Garr. 1760.—ε Read: *Radd al-muḥtār*, Qaw. I, 323, *Qurrat al-ʿuyūn* C. 1307.—η Qaw. I, 323.—ν *Lawāʾiḥ al-anwār ʿalā M. al-gh.* by Khayr al-Dīn al-Ramlī, Qaw. I, 386.—Φ *Natāʾij al-afkār ʿalā M. al-gh.* by Najm al-Dīn b. Khayr al-Dīn al-Ramlī, ibid. 403.—ϰ Aḥmad b. Muḥammad al-Ṭahṭāwī, d. 1230/1815, Ind. Off. 1715/6, Bank. XIX, 2, 50.

429. 4. Alex. Fiqh Ḥan. 64, *Tuḥfat al-aqrān*, ibid. 9.—6. Alex. Fiqh Ḥan. 49, 55, Qaw. I, 375.—12. *Fayḍ al-mustafīḍ fī masāʾil al-tafwīḍ*, Alex. Fiqh Ḥan. 45, Qaw. I, 381.

6. 1. Read: *al-shamʿa*, Alex. Fun. 173,1.—3. Ibid. Lugha 5.—4. *Risāla badīʿa al-mutaʿalliqa bi-bayān naqḍ al-qisma etc.*, Garr. 2002,3.—7. *al-Nasama al-nafsiyya*, with a comm., Makr. 43.

7. 2. Garr. 2002,10.

7b. Sharaf al-Dīn ʿUmar b. Luṭf al-Maqdisī, d. 1003/1594, *Risālat irsāl al-ghamāma bi-mā ḥalla min al-ẓalāma*, Alex. Fun. 178,2.

430. 9, 2. *Majmaʿ al-fatāwī*, Garr. 1761, Alex. Fiqh Ḥan. 41.

9a. *Ṣūrat suʾāl wa-jawābih*, composed in 1045/1635, Qaw. I, 365.

10b. Aḥmad b. Muḥammad Makkī al-Ḥamawī al-Ḥusaynī wrote, in 1056/1646: *Naẓm al-ḍawābiṭ al-fiqhiyya*, Alex. Fiqh Ḥan. 54.

12. 4. Alex. Fiqh Ḥan. 71, 128$_{,4}$ Qaw. I, 515.—Comm. a. Garr. 1764, Alex. Fiqh Ḥan. 7.—Abstract *Marāqi 'l-falāḥ*, Qaw. I, 394.—Comm. by al-Kumākhī, *Sullam al-falāḥ*, composed in 1160/1747, Alex. Fiqh Ḥan. 31.

431. 6. *al-Rasā'il etc.*, Alex. Fiqh Ḥan. 67, 21.—8. Ibid. 162$_{,3}$ Fun. 162$_{,3}$.—11. Garr. 1765.—13. Alex. Fiqh Ḥan. 185$_{,3}$.

1284 | 432. 13, 4. Alex. Fiqh Ḥan. 164,4.—15. *Risāla fī man adraka rak'a fi 'l-ẓuhr aw ghayrihi*, ibid. Fun. 67$_{,10}$.

15. Garr. 1766.

16. 1. Garr. 1667/8, Qaw. I, 376/7.—2. Alex. Fun. 68$_{,2}$.—6. *Risāla fī jawāb 'an su'āl*, Ya. Ef. Qaw. I, 337.—7. *Mas'alat al-inṣāf fī 'adam al-farq bayna mas'alatay al-Subkī wal-Khaṣṣāf*, ibid. 395.

16a. 'Alī Efendi b. al-Shaykh 'Uthmān al-Ḥanafī al-Khalwatī al-Ḍarīr 'Nāẓim al-Durar al-mutriba' wrote, in 1069/1658 in Ṭarābulus al-Shām: *al-Ḥūr al-'īn, urjūza fi 'l-madhhab*, Alex. Fiqh Ḥan. 23.

433. 17a. Amīn al-Dīn Muḥammad b. 'Alī b. 'Abd al-'Āl al-Ḥanafī, *Fatāwī*, MS dated 1095, Qaw. I, 374.

18. 6. *Manẓūmat al-Kawākibī*, C. 1317, Alex. Fiqh Ḥan. 67.—7. *Risāla fī ḥayāt* (sic) *ṣl'm fī qabrihi*, ibid. Ta'r. 113.—8. *Risāla fī tafsīr qawlihi*, on sura 23$_{,53}$, ibid. Fun. 155$_{,4}$.

18b. Aḥmad b. Muḥammad al-Kawākibī, Mufti 'l-Ḥanafiyya bi-Ḥalab, d. 1137/1724 (Ṭabbākh, *Ta'rīkh Ḥalab* IX, 465, which has Abu 'l-Su'ūd b. Aḥmad b. Muḥammad), *Fatāwī*, Alex. Fiqh Ḥan. 43.

19. 1. Garr. 1530, print. in *Majmū'a* C. 1319 (Alex. Fun. 83$_{,3}$).—18. *Ḥusn al-ibtihāj bi-ru'yat al-nabī rabbahu bi-'ayni baṣarihi laylata 'l-mi'rāj wal-isrā'*, Alex. Fun. 83$_{,5}$.—19. *Qurrat al-'uyūn bi-numūdhaj al-funūn* or *Natījat al-anẓār wa-sawāniḥ al-afkār*, Garr. 2002$_{,25}$.—20. *al-'Uqūd al-ḥisān fī qawā'id madhhab al-Nu'mān*, a *manẓūma* with the commentary *Farā'id al-lu'lu' wal-marjān*, Qaw. I, 381.—21. *Ghamz al-'uyūn*, cf. p. 425, 3, 1c.

434, 21a, 1. Garr. 1770.

21b. 2. See I, 646,$_{35}$.

23b. See p. 937,$_{75}$.

23c. Muḥammad b. Muḥammad b. Maḥmūd al-Ḥanafī al-Azharī, d. after 1173/1759, *Risālatāni fī irth dhawi 'l-arḥām*, Garr. 1850.

24a. Read: Aḥmad b. Muḥammad.

24b. Muḥammad b. Ibrāhīm b. Muḥammad al-Shahīr bil-Shaykh Muḥammad al-Fallāḥ wrote, in 1151/1738 in Aleppo: *Risāla fī ṣuwar masāʾil al-riḍāʿ ʿala 'l-madhāhib al-arbaʿa*, Alex. Fiqh Ḥan. 28.

435. 1, 3a. On this was written *al-Ifāḍāt al-ilāhiyya li-ḥall al-Zurqānī ʿala 'l-ʿIzziyya* by Muḥammad b. ʿAbd al-Rabbih b. ʿAlī al-ʿAzīzī al-Shilbī al-Mālikī b. al-Sitt, Makr. 4.—b. Ibid. 50.

2b. 1a. Alex. Fiqh Māl. 7.—α Cairo 1287 (Makr. 22).

2c. Sālim al-Sanhūrī al-Mālikī, d. 1015/1606, *Faḍāʾil layl al-niṣf min Shaʿbān*, Alex. Mawāʿiẓ 29.

436. 3, 4 Garr. 1836 (*al-muntashira*).

5. 1. Garr. 1565, Alex. Fun. 147,$_{10}$, Qaw. I, 166.—a. Alex. Tawḥīd 47, Qaw. I, 212.—Glosses by his son ʿAbd al-Salām, *Hadiyyat al-murīd*, Alex. Tawḥīd 3, 14, 40.—b. β BDMG 31b, Hamb. Or. Sem. 62.

437. αα Makr. 23.—γγ ibid. 15.—ζζ Alex. Tawḥīd 26.—ηη. Aḥmad b. Muḥammad al-Ṣāwī al-Mālikī, d. 1241/1825, ibid. 12.—g. *al-Manhaj al-ḥamīd* by Muḥammd b. ʿAbd al-Raḥīm b. Ibrāhīm al-Ḥanafī, ibid. 46.—h. *al-Manhaj al-sadīd* by Muḥammad al-Ḥanīfī, d. 1342/1923, print. al-Ṭabbākh, *Taʾr. Ḥalab* VIII, 681.—3. Alex. Mawāʿiẓ 41, Fun. 157,$_{2}$.

7. 2. Garr. 665, print. Cairo 1314.—21. *Muqaddima fī faḍāʾil yawm ʿĀshūrāʾ*, Alex. Fun. 216.

438. 8, 3. *Ḥusn al-ṣanīʿ, sharḥ Badīʿiyyat al-Ziftāwī* (p. 385, 25), Paris 4420,$_{2}$, Garr. 569.

9. 1. Alex. Adab 36.—2. Garr. 1837.—4. Garr. 1507.

10a. ʿAbd al-Qādir b. ʿAbd al-Hādī al-ʿUmarī, d. 1100/1688. 1. *Khulāṣat al-tawḥīd lil-mustafīd wal-mufīd*, Garr. 2165.—2. *Sharḥ Muntaha ʾl-suʾūl*, N. I, 538.

439. 14, 4. Alex. Fiqh Māl. 15.

15. Muḥammad b. Sulaymān al-Kaffūrī al-Mālikī wrote, in 1170/1756, *Fatāwī*, Alex. Fiqh Māl. 12.

1285 | 440. 1a. Muḥammad b. al-Qāsim b. Muḥammad Ṣāliḥ, d. 918.

1b. ʿAbd al-Bāsiṭ b. Muḥammad b. Aḥmad b. Muḥammad b. ʿAbd al-Raḥmān b. ʿUmar b. Raslān b. Naṣr b. Ṣāliḥ b. ʿAbd al-Khāliq al-Bulqīnī al-Shāfiʿī, born in Dhu ʾl-Qaʿda 870/June 1466 (*Ḍawʾ* IV, 28/9). wrote, in Muḥarram 899/October 1493: *al-Wafāʾ bi-sharḥ al-Iṣṭifāʾ*, on his *qaṣīda* named *al-Iṣṭifāʾ min asmāʾ al-Muṣṭafā* (400 names). autograph Ind. Off. 4630 (*JRAS* 1939, 394).

3. 2. a. Alex. Fun. 114,$_{2}$.—7. Read: 897.

4. 3. *Risāla fi ʾl-zakāt*, Alex. Fawāʾid 24.

441. 5, 2. Garr. 1301.—11. Ibid. 1920, which has *al-shafiyya*.

10. 9. *al-Ḥawāshī wal-nikāt wal-fawāʾid al-muḥarrarāt*, Qaw. II, 155.—10. *Ḥāshiya ʿalā sharḥ al-Alfiyya* I, 522.

442. 10a, 3. Comm. *Fatḥ al-raʾūf al-khabīr* by ʿAbd al-Raʾūf al-Munāwī, d. 1031/1622, Alex. Fiqh Shāf. 30.

11. 1. Alex. Muṣṭ. ḥad. 10.—3. Garr. 1870.

13, 5. *Risāla fī qawāʿid al-īmān*, Alex. Fun. 114,$_{5}$.—6. *Ghāyat al-marām*, see p. 440.

443. 14b. 4. Qaw. II, 176.—Muḥammad Abū Naṣr al-Ṭ., *Risāla fi ʾl-taqsīm etc.*, Garr. 856, 1353, Cairo[1] VII, 567.

14c. Abū Bakr b. Hidāyatallāh al-Ḥusaynī al-Muṣannif al-Kūrānī al-Kindī, d. 1014/1604 (Muḥ. I, 110, Sāmī, *Qāmūs al-aʿlām* 691), *Ṭabaqāt al-Shāfiʿiyya*, Baghdad 1356.

15a. 3. *Risāla fī ṣalāt al-ẓuhr baʿd al-jāmiʿa*, Alex. Fiqh Shāf. 36,$_{5}$.

15b. Muḥammad b. ʿUmar b. ʿAbd al-Wahhāb al-ʿUrḍī al-Ḥalabī, a Muftī in Aleppo and a poet who died in Ṣafar 1071/October 1660, *Risāla fī faskh al-ṭalāq wa-ilghāʾihi*, Alex. Fiqh Shāf. 36,$_{6}$.

444. 18, 2. Alex. Fun. 171,$_{3}$.

19. *Kitāb al-Mīthāq etc.*, RAAD IX, 638, 4.

19a. 2. Garr. 1841.—Ibid. 657.—6. Ibid. 1881.—8. With the title *al-Bahiyya al-Wardiyya*.—14. With the title *Kanz al-inʿām fī faḍāʾil shahr al-ṣiyām*, Alex. Ḥad. 59,$_{3}$.

19b. Jamāl al-Dīn Abū ʿUmar Maḥmūd b. Muḥammad b. ʿAlī al-Qādirī al-Shaykhūnī al-Shāfiʿī, d. 1119/1707.—1. *Birr wāliday khayr al-waraʾ*, Alex. Fun. 122,1—2. *Najāt al-qāriʾ min faḍl al-bāriʾ*, ibid. Faw. 18.—3. see p. 940,$_{104}$.

445. 20, 8. *Iẓhār al-surūr bi-mawlid al-nabī al-masrūr*, Alex. Taʾr. 3.

21. 2. Alex. Fiqh Shāf. 29, Fun. 174,$_{12}$.—3. Ibid. Fiqh Shāf. 36,$_{4}$.—4. Qaw. II, 289; see Becker, *Islamst.* II, 103.—5. *Manāsik al-ḥajj*, ibid. 39,$_{4}$.—6. *Risāla fī farāʾiḍ al-ḥajj wa-shurūṭihi wa-ādābihi*, ibid. 2.

22. 1. Alex. Taʾr. 14, 35.—6. *al-Ifṣāḥ fī ʿaqd al-nikāḥ etc.*, ibid. Fiqh Shāf. 6.—7. *Muntaha ʾl-irādāt bi-jadwal al-munāsakhāt*, ibid. 15, see p. 155.

23. 2. Alex. Fiqh Shāf. 36,$_{1}$, 37,$_{1}$ (*Risāla fī buṭlān etc.*).—4. Ibid. 36,$_{2}$.—10. *Risāla fī taqlīd al-furūʿ*, ibid. 37,$_{2}$.

446. 7. Garr. 800, Alex. Fiqh Shāf. 7.—Glosses by Muḥammad b. Muḥammad al-ʿAṭṭār, d. 1250/1835, Garr. 803.—14. Glosses by Muḥammad Mujāhid Abu ʾl-Najāʾ, Alex. Fun. 129,$_{4}$.—31. *Mukhtaṣar Sharḥ qaṣīdat Imraʾ al-Qays* see Addenda et corrigenda I, 50.—32. *Sharḥ dīwān al-Samawʾal* I, 937 (to be read thus).—33. *Risāla fī ithbāt karāmāt al-awliyāʾ* in *Majmūʿa*, Būlāq 1319.—34. *Hidāyat uli*

ʾl-baṣāʾir wal-abṣār fī maʿrifat ajzāʾ al-layl wal-nahār, Alex. Ḥisāb 63.—35. *Fatḥ al-mālik fīmā yataʿallaq bi-qawl al-nās wa-huwa ka-dhālik*, Alex. Ṣarf 11,$_{2}$.—36. *Manẓūma fi ʾl-ʿarūḍ*, with glosses by Muḥammad b. Muḥammad al-Amīr, Alex. ʿArūḍ 3.

447. D. 1, 1. Alex. Fiqh Ḥanb. 5.

448. 3a, 6. *Dalīl al-ṭālib li-nayl al-maṭālib*, Alex Fiqh Ḥanb. 4.

3b. Muḥammad Abu ʾl-Mawāhib Mufti ʾl-Ḥanābila bi-Dimashq, 11th cent., *Mashyakha*, Alex. Fun. 122,$_{4}$.

5. 3. Read: Ibn Ḥamdān.—5. Extract from 1. Garr. 1849.

1286 | 5a. Ibrāhīm b. Bakr al-Danābī al-ʿAwfī al-Dimashqī, d. 1094/1683 in Cairo, *al-Rawḍ al-murbiʿ fī manāsik al-ḥajj*, with the commentary *Bughyat al-mutatabbiʿ*, Alex. Fiqh Ḥanb. 3.

449. 8, 2. Alex. Tawḥīd 29, self-commentary *Lawāmiʿ al-anwār al-bahiyya wa-sawāṭiʿ al-asrār al-athariyya*, C. 1324.

8b. His contemporary ʿAbdallāh b. ʿAwda b. ʿĪsā b. Salāma b. al-Ḥājj ʿUbayd al-Qudūmī al-Nābulusī al-Ḥanbalī, Khādim al-ʿIlm bil-Ḥaram al-Nabawī, wrote *al-Riḥla al-Ḥijāziyya wal-riyāḍ al-unsiyya fi ʾl-ḥawādith wal-masāʾil al-ʿilmiyya*, Nablus 1324 (Sarkīs 1498).

E. 1. RAAD IX, 344/6.—1. Ind. Off. 1813.—13. al-Sammākī, see *Dharīʿa* II, 86,$_{38}$.—14 = (?) *Risāla fi ʾl-ḥajj*, Ind. Off. 1812.—17. Ibid. II, 267,$_{1087}$.

450. 1, 26. *Ādāb al-ṣalāt*, *Dharīʿa* I, 22,107.—27. *al-Masʾala al-Māziḥiyya* by Aḥmad al-ʿĀmilī al-Māziḥī, ibid. II, 91,$_{261}$.—28. *al-Īmān wal-islām wa-bayān ḥaqāʾiqihimā wa-ajzāʾihimā wa-shurūṭihimā*, print. 1305, ibid. II, 514,$_{2019b}$.

2. RAAD IX. 347. 1. Ind. Off. 1503/4, Alex. Uṣūl 20.—Comm. b. Ind. Off. 1506, Rāmpūr 48.—g. Read: Muḥammad Ṣāliḥ Aḥmad (p. 578), Ind. Off. 1505.—6. *Zubdat al-uṣūl*, see p. 597,$_{7}$.—*al-Asʾila al-Madaniyya* by Muḥammad b. Juwaybir al-Madanī (*Amal al-āmil* 499), in a private library in Mashhad, *Dharīʿa* II, 91,$_{363}$.

2a. His grandson Muḥammad b. Muḥammad b. al-Ḥasan b. Qāsim al-Ḥusaynī al-ʿAynātī al-ʿĀmilī al-Jazīnī wrote *al-Ithnāʿashariyya fī ʾl-mawāʿiẓ al-ʿadadiyya*, Pers. print. 1322, *Dharīʿa* I, 119,$_{576}$.

3a. Deceased in 1103/1691, *Rawḍāt al-jannāt* 411.

3b. Abū Jaʿfar Muḥammad b. Abī Manṣūr al-Ḥasan (no. 2) b. Zayn al-Dīn al-ʿĀmilī al-Shaʾmī, d. 1030/1621 in Mecca, *Istiqṣād al-iʿtibār fī sharḥ al-Istibṣār* (I, 707), in a private library in Najaf, *Dharīʿa* II, 30,120.

451. 4. Read: al-Jabaʿī.

6. Instead of b. Ḥaydar, read: b. Jāndār al-Biqāʿī, d. 1076/1665 (Muḥ. II, 90/4, Ibn Maʿṣūm, *Sulāfat al-ʿaṣr* 355), *Hidāyat al-barara*, Bank. XIX, 2,$_{1585}$.—2. *Shawāhid al-Miftāḥ*, Suppl. I, 517, t.

7. Muḥammad ʿAlī b. Ḥaydar al-Mūsawī al-ʿĀmilī al-Makkī, b. 1071/1660, d. 1139/1726, *Īnās sulṭān al-muʾminīn* (i.e. Shāh Ḥusayn) *biqtibās ʿulūm al-dīn min al-nibrās al-mūjiz al-mubīn fī tafsīr al-āyāt al-Qurʾāniyya allatī hiya fī ʾl-aḥkām al-aṣliyya wal-farʿiyya wa-āyāt al-aḥkām*, MS in Isfahan, *Dharīʿa* I, 41,$_{93}$, II, 517,$_{2034}$.

452. 3a. see p. 524, 1.

5, 1. Abstract from *Baḥr al-maʿānī wa-kanz al-sabʿ al-mathānī*, Qaw. I, 11,$_{98}$.—2. Ibid. I, 139,$_{34}$.—6. *Kayfiyyat istikhrāj al-taqwīm*, Berl. 5778, Gotha 1430, AS 2690, Suter 514.

453. 7a, 3. Qaw. I, 16.—4. *Risāla fī bayān al-awjuh allatī bayna ʾl-suwar lil-qurrāʾ al-ʿashara min ṭarīq al-Durra li-Ibn al-Jazarī*, ibid. 17.

8. 3. Garr. 1316, Cairo^{1} I, 151/2.

9. 1. Alex. Taʾr. 112.—4. *Mablagh al-amānī fīmā ṣanaʿahu Ibn al-Jazarī min Ḥirz al-amānī wa-wajh al-tahānī lil-Shāṭibī*, Qaw. I, 30.

10a. 1. See p. 979,$_{9}$.

10b. ʿAbd al-Raḥmān b. ʿAbd al-Ḥalīm al-Marʿashī, middle of the 11th cent., *Risāla fī tafsīr qawlihi*, on sura 4,$_{51}$, Qaw. I, 64.

10c. Muḥammad b. Ḥamdān al-Qurashī wrote, in 1011/1603, *Tafsīr baʿḍ al-āyāt*, Garr. 1306.

454. 12, 2. Alex. Fun. 146$_{,1}$, 178$_{,2}$.

14. 1. Garr. 1235, Qaw. I, 5.—11. *Riyāḍ al-nayyirayn fī ʿamal al-kusūfayn*, Garr. 1003.

14c. Abu ʾl-Ḥasan Muṣṭafā b. Ḥasan b. Yaʿqūb al-Islāmbulī wrote, in 1144/1731, *Murshid al-ṭalaba fī maʿrifat ṭuruq al-Ṭayyiba*, Qaw. I, 31.

455. 15a. Garr. 1236.

1287 16. 4. Qaw. I, 18$_{,70}$.—16a. 2. Garr. | 1239.—3. Ibid. 1238.

19. 7, Alex. Taʾr. 14, 1, on which glosses by Muḥammad b. ʿAlī al-Shanawānī, d. 1233/1818, ibid. 2.

456. 23, 3. Garr. 1860, Alex. Fun. 13.—7. *al-Zahr al-fāʾiq fī mawlid ashraf al-khalāʾiq*, Garr. 660 (see p. 935$_{,52}$).

23a. *Qurrat al-ʿayn fī maʿrifat al-qullatayn*, Garr. App. 5.

23b. 1. Sulaymān b. Ḥasan al-Jumzūrī, *Tuḥfat al-aṭfāl*, composed in 1198/1784, the most popular textbook on *tajwīd* (Bergstr.-Pretzl, 234), C. 1310 (Qaw. I, 8, see p. 983, 4, Sarkīs 708, 810$_{,2,3}$).

25. 3. *Ashrāṭ al-sāʿa*, Garr. 1509.

§ 8. 1. Read: *man ḥarrafa.*

3. Muṭahhar b. ʿAbd al-Raḥmān b. ʿAlī b. Ismāʿīl b. ʿArab Qāḍī wrote, in 988/1581, *Mushtamil al-aqāwīl fi ʾl-radd ʿala ʾl-Rawāfiḍ wa-ʿaqāʾidihim*, Berl. 2135 (which has Ibn ʿAbd al-Salām), Garr. 1525.

1b. Ibrāhīm b. Aḥmad b. ʿAlī al-Ḥalabī, d. 956/1549, *al-Lumʿa fi ʾl-qaḍāʾ wal-qadar*, Alex. Tawḥīd 29.

457. 4a. Nūr al-Dīn ʿAlī al-Ḥalabī, d. 1044/1634, *Taʿrīf ahl al-islām wal-īmān bi-anna Muḥammadan ṣlʿm lā yakhlū minhu makān wa-lā zamān*, Alex. Fun. 19.

458. 10. Deceased in 1069/1659 (Muḥ. III, 385, see I, 307 bottom).—1. In *Majmūʿa*, Būlāq 1319.

10a. Deceased in 1078/1667 (Muḥ. II, 285), Garr. 1529.

10c. Ibrāhīm al-Ghamrī al-Khaṭīb al-Shāfiʿī wrote, in 1092/1681, *Risāla fi ʾl-firaq al-Islāmiyya*, Alex. Fun. 33.

459. 15b, 1. *Kitāb al-baḥth etc.*, see A. Schmidt, *Zap. Koll. Vost.* V, 791/900, MS Kračkovsky ibid. 774/9.—2. *al-Ajwiba al-jaliyya li-daḥḍ al-daʿawāt al-Naṣrāniyya*, MS Kračkovsky ibid. 780/97.

17. Read: al-Bulaydī.—2. Garr. 801/2, Alex. Manṭiq 20,$_{4}$, Fun. 97,$_{2}$, on which glosses by Muḥamad ʿArafa al-Dasūqī, d. 1230/1815, abbreviated from the *Taqyīdāt* of Muḥammad al-Dimyāṭī, Alex. Fals. 5.

18. 4. Garr. 1531.—6. ibid. 1440.

460. 18, 16. *Munqidh al-ʿabīd, ʿaqīda* with a commentary by his son Muḥammad, *Laṭāʾif al-tawḥīd*, composed in 1192/1778, Alex. Tawḥīd 29.

20. *Manẓūma*, on which glosses by Ibrāhīm b. Muḥammad al-Jārim al-Rashīdī, d. 1265/1849, Alex. Tawḥīd 10.

§ 9. 1a. Read: Aḥmad b. Aḥmad b. Muḥammad.

461. 2, 1. *Jawharat al-ghawwāṣ etc.*, Qaw. II, 255 (which has al-Muhājirī).

3. 6. Alex. Mawāʿiẓ 15.—11. Ibid. Fun. 188,$_{2}$.—Abstract, ibid. Fiqh Shāf. 12, Fiqh Ḥan. 62.—14. Ibid. Mawāʿiẓ 48.—27. *ʿArāʾis al-ghurar*, ibid. Fun. 160,2.—28. *Qaṣīda nūniyya fi ʾl-ādāb al-sharʿiyya*, ibid. Taṣ. 37.—29. *Risāla fi ʾl-waswasa*, ibid. Faw. 24,5.—30. *Urjūza fi ʾl-mīqāt*, ibid. Fun. 118,$_{1}$.—31. *Khulāṣat Rawḍat al-abṣār wa-lubāb sharḥ Ghāyat al-ikhtiṣār fi ʾl-qirāʾāt*, ibid. 118/9.—32. *Nathr al-durar fī farsh al-ḥurūf fi ʾl-qirāʾāt*, ibid. 119,$_{3}$.—33. *Mukhtaṣar min Khulāṣat Sīrat sayyid al-bashar*, ibid. 141,$_{2}$.

462. 5, 24. Garr. 1918.—25. *Tafsīr wāḍiḥ al-majāz*, ḤKh VI, 416,$_{14149}$, Sul. 144.—26. *Kifāyat al-muḥsin fī waṣf al-muʾmin*, Qaw. I, 145, 208.—27. *Bushrā kull karīm bi-thawāb al-malik al-karīm*, ibid. I, 102 (40 trad.).—28. *Tuḥfat al-kirām fī faḍāʾil iṭʿām al-ṭaʿām*, ibid. 103.

6. 1. Alex. Taṣ. 11.

7. 6. Farmer, *Sources* 60.

463. 9, 1. Garr. 703.

11. 2. Dam. Z. 84$_{,88}$ (which has Muḥammad al-Rukhkhajī al-Ḥanbalī al-Shaybānī).

11. 4. Alex. Ta'r. 112, Mawāʿiẓ 38$_{,2}$.—5. Garr. 1586.—8. RAAD IX, 638$_{,2}$.

1288 464. 12, 10. RAAD IX, 638$_{,3}$.—14. *Kīmiyyāʾ al-saʿāda fī ibṭāl kīmiyyat* | *al-ʿāda*, A. Ṭaymūr, Ṭab. 75.—15. *Ghāyat al-taʿarruf fī ʿilmay al-uṣūl wal-taṣawwuf*, with the commentary *Baḥr al-anwār al-muḥīṭ*, composed in 968/1560, Alex. Taṣ. 8.—16. *al-Ajwiba al-muskita ʿan masāʾil al-samāʿ al-mubhita*, Cairo, *Nash*. 1.

13a. I.e. ʿAlī al-Khawwāṣ al-Burullusī, d. 939/1532, while others say 961/1554 (*ShDh* VIII, 233, 330, al-Shaʿrānī, *Ṭab*. II, 130ff, al-Nabhānī II, 193, Heffening).

14. M. Smith, al-Shaʿrānī the Mystic, *The Moslem World* XXIX, 240/7.—1. Alex. Fun. 149$_{,7}$.—2. Ibid. Taṣ. 51.—4. Garr. 1591, Alex. Fun. 54.

465. 5. *al-Fatḥ al-mubīn fī jumla min asrār al-dīn*, Alex. Fun. 174$_{,16}$.—12. Ibid. Mawāʿiẓ 12, C. 1318.—15. Garr. 1587.—16. Ibid. 1588/9, Alex. Taṣ. 8.

466. 22. Alex. Fun. 161$_{,5}$.—23. Ibid. Taṣ. 15.—27. Ibid. Ḥad. 8.—30. Ibid. Mawāʿiẓ 14.—33. Garr. 1590.—43. Makr. 54.

467. 45. Garr. 474.—60. Alex. Fun. 174$_{,18}$.—65. *Asʾila*, ibid. 174$_{,15}$.—66. *Wird al-aqṭāb*, ibid. 161$_{,6}$.—67. *Mīzān al-qāṣirīn wa-hiya risāla fī ḥāl baʿḍ al-mutaṣawwifa mimman yaddaʿūn al-wilāya*, ibid. 127$_{,2}$.

16. 3a. Garr. 654.—Abstract by al-Madābighī, Alex. Ḥad. 47$_{,2}$.—4. Garr. 2177, 1. Alex. Ḥad. 47$_{,8}$.

468. 4a. Read: Naṣr, composed in 1243/1827, Alex. Fun. 93$_{,2}$.—b. Ibid. Ḥad. 47$_{,3}$, Makr. 18.—c. *Taqrīrāt* by al-Ujhūrī, d. 1210/1795, Alex. Ḥad. 11.—e. Aḥmad al-Qalyūbī, d. 1069/1658 (see p. 492 ult.), Garr. 656, 664.—7. Alex. Fun. 134$_{,2}$.—9. Ibid. 167$_{,20}$, with the title *al-Imtinān fi ʾl-kalām ʿalā awāʾil sūrat al-dukhān* Garr. 2177$_{,2}$.—10. Hamb. Or. Sem. 14$_{,7}$.—22. *Risāla fi ʾl-kalām ʿalā Khiḍr*, Alex. Fun. 120$_{,5}$, 166$_{,2}$.—23. *Risāla fi ʾl-islām wal-īmān*, ibid. 121$_{,1}$.

17a. Garr. 1926, Alex. Mawāʿiẓ 20 (completed in 904!).

469. 18, 1. Garr. 1564.—2. Alex. Taṣ. 26.—3. Ibid. Taʾr. 103 20.—4. Garr. 110, C. 1880.

22. 2. Read: *al-juyūb*.

22a. Aḥmad Bābā b. Iqqīt, d. 1036/1626, *al-Manhaj al-mubīn fī sharḥ ḥadīth awliyāʾ Allāh al-muttaqīn*, Alex. Fun. 160,$_4$.

22b. Aḥmad b. ʿUmar al-ʿUlwānī al-Ḥammāmī al-Ḥamawī, d. 1017/1608, *Aʿdhab al-mashārib fi l-sulūk wal-manāqib*, Alex. Taṣ. 6.

22c. ʿAbd al-ʿAzīz al-Sīwāsī completed, in 1011/1602 in the Umayyad mosque in Damascus, *al-Qaṣīda al-nūniyya* with an anonymous commentary, *Jilāʾ ʿuyūn al-ʿarāʾis al-mukhaddara fī ḥujub al-ghayb al-mastūr etc.*, Alex. Taṣ. 14.

470. 27a. Alex. Taʾr. 56.

471. 30a, 3. Alex. Faw. 18,$_2$, Fun. 144,$_2$, 158,$_5$.

38. *Sharḥ al-basmala wal-ḥamdala*, Alex. Fun. 100,$_5$ (*Nukat wa-fawāʾid ʿala ʾl-b. wal-ḥ. min khuṭbat Sharḥ al-Minhāj*), on which the commentary *al-Ṭawāliʿ al-munīra* by Abū Bakr b. Ismāʿīl al-Shanawānī, d. 1026/1617 (p. 394, 8), ibid. 6.

472. 40, 1. Garr. 1593/5, Alex. Taṣ. 19,$_2$, Manṭiq 20,$_2$.—3. *Muntakhab al-Sirājiyya wa-sharḥ al-sayyid ʿalayhā*, Alex. Fun. 161,$_1$.—4. *Risāla fī ʾl-ridda wa-aḥkāmihā*, ibid. 1603.—5. *al-Taḥqīq fī ʾl-radd ʿala ʾl-zindīq*, ibid. Taṣ. 33,$_4$.—6. *Majālis*, ibid. Mawāʿiẓ 34.—7. *al-Ṭarīq al-wāḍiḥ ʿalā ʿaqīdat al-salaf al-ṣāliḥ*, ibid. Fun. 67,$_{20}$.

47. See below, p. 664,$_{19}$.

47a. Alex. Faw. 14.

47b. ʿAlī al-Ḥalabī al-Nūrbakhtī wrote, in 1118/1706, *Jāmiʿ al-asmāʾ wal-adʿiya wa-hāmiʿ al-āthār wal-athniya*, Alex. Faw. 6.

473. 49. A inventory of 209 of his works by his grandson Muṣṭafā, BDMG 23.—5. Alex. 42, Fun. Taṣ. 90,$_{13}$ = 92.—8. Ibid. Taṣ. 42,$_1$.—19. Ibid. 12.—22. Ibid. Fun. 90,18.—28a. Ibid. 42,$_1$, 161,$_7$.

1289 | 474. 32. Garr. 1856, Alex. Fun. 157,$_{6}$, Fiqh Ḥan. 37.—33. Cairo *Nash.* 4, Alex. Fun. 135,$_{1}$.—34. Read: *al-mumaḥḥaṣa.*—35. Garr. 1771.—36. (sic) *Jawāhir al-nuṣūṣ etc.*, Garr. 1596.—38. Alex. Fun. 90,$_{21}$.—40. Alex. Fun. 90,$_{16}$.—41. Ibid. 17.—42. Ibid. 90, 8.—43. Ibid. 9.—44. Read: 'Dam. Z. 52, 49,$_{3}$', Alex. Fun. 90,$_{19}$ (*Rafʿ etc.*).—59. Read: *Nuqūd al-ṣurar.*—66. Garr. 1410.—68. *al-Fatḥ al-rabbānī wal-fayḍ al-raḥmānī*, Alex. Taṣ. 24, Fun. 90,$_{4}$.

475. 71. BDMG 59.—72. Garr. 758.—75. Alex. Adab 57, Qaw. II, 193, Mosul 151,$_{12}$, Būlāq 1270.—78. 90, 91. Read: 'Dam. 52, 49, 4, 6'.—92. = 5. Mosul 143,$_{35,6}$.—93. Alex. Taṣ. 42,$_{9}$, Fun. 152,$_{23}$, Bank. X, 578.—97. Alex. Fun. 162,$_{4}$.—109. Alex. Fun. 90,$_{6}$.—112. Read: *al-khān*, see I^{1}, 452, ^{2}811.

476. 117. On which *Kashf al-mukhaddarāt fī khabar al-muʿashsharāt* by ʿAlī al-Qādirī b. ʿAbd al-Wahhāb b. al-Ḥājj ʿAlī al-Jaʿfarī, composed in 1163/1750, Mosul 26,$_{54}$.—121. Alex. Fun. 10,$_{5}$.—122. Read: *wa-rafʿ*.—146. *Fatḥ al-ʿayn wa-kashf al-ghayn ʿani 'l-farq bayna 'l-basmalatayn*, Alex. Fun. 152,$_{25}$.—147. *al-Aḥkām al-mulakhkhaṣa fī ḥukm kayy al-ḥimmaṣa* (cf. 34), ibid. 162,$_{2}$.—148. *Miftāḥ al-futūḥ fī mishkāt al-jinn wa-zujājat al-nafs wa-miṣbāḥ al-rūḥ*, ibid. 151,$_{5}$.—147. *Khamrat Bābil wa-ghināʾ al-balābil*, ibid. Adab 40.—148. *Wujūd al-ḥaqq wa-khiṭāb al-shuhūd al-ṣidq*, ibid. Taṣ. 51.—149. *Nūr al-afʾida, sharḥ al-Murshida fī 'l-iʿtiqād* by al-Layth al-Samarqandī, ibid. Fun. 90/1.—150. *Risāla fī thubūt al-qadamayn fī suʾāl al-malʾakayn*, ibid. Fun. 90,$_{2}$.—151. *al-Kawkab al-mutalaʾli*, see I, 752,$_{47x}$.—152. *Manẓūma fī asmāʾ Allāh al-ḥusnā*, Alex. Fun. 98, 2. 3.—153. *Manẓūma fi 'l-istighfār*, ibid. 4.—154. *Manẓūma yāʾiyya*, ibid. Faw. 25,$_{11}$.—155. *Qaṣīda* with the comm. by Muḥammad Hilāl b. ʿUmar al-Rāmhamdānī, ibid. Taṣ. 21.—156. *Izālat al-khafāʾ ʿan ḥilyat al-Muṣṭafā*, ibid. Fun. 90,$_{7}$.—157. *Bidāyat al-murīd wa-nihāyat al-saʿīd*, ibid. 10.—158. *Adʿiya wa-ṣalawāt mukhtalifa*, Dam. Z. 58, 4.—49a. Garr. 1312.—49c. ʿAbd al-Qādir b. Muṣṭafā al-Ṣaffūrī al-Dimashqī, d. 1081/1670, *Nuzhat al-nufūs*, Alex. Maw. 48.

477. 51, 2. Comm. Alex. Taṣ. 15.—7. Ibid. 39,2.—10. *al-Asrār al-Qudsiyya etc.* ibid. 23.—11. Ibid. Faw. 17.—13. Comm. *Irshād al-murīdīn fī maʿrifat kalām al-ʿārifīn* by Abū Jaʿfar al-Shubrāwī al-Shāfiʿī, completed in 1270, Būlāq 1292.—14. Alex. Faw. 16, 25,$_{6}$, comm. *al-Lamḥ al-qudsī* Faw. 16, *al-Lamḥ al-nadsī*, abstract from comm. a. additionally Hamb. Or. Sem. 14,$_{11}$.—16. C. 1310.—18. Alex. Faw. 19.—38. Garr. 2166,$_{2}$, Alex. Taṣ. 32.

478. 63. *al-Ḥawāshi 'l-rāfiʿāt al-ghawāshī ʿalā baʿḍ kalimāt al-waṣiyya dhāt al-sirr al-fāshī*, Alex Taṣ. 39, 1.

52a. Muḥammad b ʿAbdallāh al-Dimashqī al-Ḥanbalī wrote, in 1155/1742: 1. *ʿArūs al-jalwa fī faḍl iʿtikāf al-khalwa*, Alex. Fun. 158,$_{2}$.—2. *al-Shamʿa al-muḍīʾa fī sayr ṭarīq al-Ṣūfiyya*, ibid. 3.—3. *Khirqat al-dāliyya fi ʾl-kiswa al-Khalwatiyya*, ibid. 4.

54. Ḥusayn b. Ṭuʿma b. Muhammad al-Baytimānī, d. 1175/1761.—7. *al-Hidāya wal-tawfīq fī ādāb sulūk al-ṭarīq*, Alex. Fun. 148, 1.

54a. ʿAbd al-Karīm al-Sharābātī, d. 1178/1764. 1. *Adʿiya mubāraka fi ʾl-asfār al-ṣāliḥa*, Alex. Fun. 122,$_{6}$.—2. *Sanad ijāza li ṣalāt sayyidī ʿAbd al-Salām al-Mashīshī*, ibid. 7.—3. *Ṣalawāt Muḥyi ʾl-Dīn b. al-ʿArabī*, ibid. 8.—4. *al-Ḥadīth al-musalsal*, ibid. 9.—5. *Ijāza ḥadīthiyya* | ibid. 10. 1290

56a. Muḥammad b. Muḥammad b. al-Ṭayyib al-Tāfilātī al-Maghribī, *muftī* of the Ḥanafīs in Jerusalem, d. 1191/1777.—1. *al-Dawr al-aʿlā*, with the commentary *al-Dawr al-aghlā*, Alex. Faw. 7.—2. *Ḥusn al-istiqṣāʾ limā ṣaḥḥa wa-thabata fi ʾl-Masjid al-Aqṣā*, ibid. Taʾr. 111.8.

479. 58, 15. Cairo, *Nashra* 7.—18. *Risāla fi ʾl-waḍʿ*, with the commentary *Tashnīf al-samʿ bi-baʿḍ laṭāʾif al-waḍʿ* by ʿAbd al-Raḥmān al-Ujhūrī, Alex. Waḍʿ 3.

59. 1. Alex. Taṣ. 11.—4. *al-ʿĀdāt al-saniyya al-Ḥifniyya wal-afʿāl al-sharīfa al-ʿaliyya li-murīd sulūk al-ṭarīqa al-Khalwatiyya*, ibid. 40,$_{1}$.—5. *Sharḥ al-basmala*, ibid. 20.

480. 60, 1a. Glosses by ʿAbd al-Muʿṭī b. Aḥmad b. ʿAbd al-Karīm b. Aḥmad b. Muḥammad al-ʿAdawī al-Mālikī, Cairo, Makr. 24,$_{1}$.—*Manāqib al-Ṣāwī*, C. 1310 (Makr. 20).—7. Alex. Bal. 13, Fun. 108,$_{3}$, Makr. 9, glosses by al-Ṣāwī, ibid. 35, Alex. Bal. 6.—Glosses by Ḥijāzī b. ʿAbd al-Muṭṭalib al-ʿAdawī al-Mālikī, Makr. 16.—8a. Alex. Taʾr. 6.—e. *Ishrāq maṣābīḥ al-anwār*, by Aḥmad b. Muḥammad b. Naṣr al-Salāwī, composed in 1235/1819, Alex. Fun. 93, 1.—f. *al-Rawḍ al-naḍīr* by ʿAlī b. ʿAbd a-Ḥaqq al-Ḥajjājī al-Qūṣī al-Mālikī, Alex. Taʾr. 8.—9. Cairo, Makr. 32.—Glosses by al-Ṣāwī, ibid. 7.—Commentary by ʿUllaysh, C. 1285 (Makr. 61).—14. Garr. 1471.—20. *Risālat al-majāz wal-tashbīh wal-kināya*, Alex. Bal. 23.

61. 9. *al-Futūḥāt al-ilāhiyya*, see ad p. 180.—10. *Fatḥ al-jawād*, see ad I, 69.

481. 2, 1. *Taḥṣīn al-manāzil etc.* A. Taymūr, Ṭab. 93.

3a. Garr. 1967.

482. 5, 11. *al-Laʾālīʾ al-manthūra ʿalā naẓm al-muwajjahāt*, Alex. Tawḥīd $37_{,1}$.—11. *Sharḥ al-ṣudūr bil-ṣalāt wal-salām ʿala ʾl-nāṣir al-manṣūr*, ibid. Faw. 21.

6. Khālid b. Muḥammad al-Khuḍarī al-Shāfiʿī al-Rashīdī, d. 1186/1772. *al-Durar al-yatīma etc.*, completed in 1159/1746, Alex. Fun. 30.

§ 11. 4. *al-Risāla al-Ḥusayniyya*, Garr. 914, print. in *Majmūʿa*, Istanbul (Qaw. II, 302).—Comm. a. Garr. 916.—b. Ibid. $2099_{,1}$.—c. Aḥmad b. Muḥammad Yägän al-Marʿashī ʿAbd al-Raḥīm Pāshā, ibid. 915.—f. Muḥammad b. Muṣṭafā Āqkirmānī, ca. 1150/1737, Qaw. II, 295.—g. Muḥammad Ṣādiq b. ʿAbd al-Raḥīm Arzanjānī Muftīzāde, ibid. 301.

6. Manṣūr al-Manūfī al-Shāfiʿī completed, in 1090/1679: *Manẓūmat al-muwajjahāt fī ʾl-manṭiq*, with a commentary, Alex. Fun. 128 u.

483. § 13. 2. Comm. by al-Maḥallī, Alex. Ḥisāb 11/2, Rāmpūr I, 418, 87.—2. *Mukhtaṣar fī ḥisāb al-jumal*, Alex. Ḥisāb 17.

6. Garr. 783 A, see p. 741, 1a.

484. 3a. ʿAbdallāh b. Muḥammad b. Muḥammad b. Abī Bakr al-Tīzīnī, *muwaqqit* of the Umayyad Mosque in Damascus, Suter 450.—2. *ʿAmal al-muqanṭarāt*, Berl. 5803, Gotha 1421, Paris $2547_{,21}$, Cairo[1] V, 308.—3. *Fī ʿilm al-waqt*, Berl. 5804.—4. *Fī ʿamal al-rubʿ al-mujayyab*, Paris $2847_{,22}$, Cairo[1] V, 315.—5. *Risālat al-rubʿ al-kāmil*, Bodl. I, $967_{,9}$.—6. Sine tables for the year 896/1491, Bodl. I, $1035_{,2}$.—7. *Risāla mukhtaṣara fī ʿamal bi-rubʿ al-dāʾira etc.*, Paris $2547_{,9}$.—8. *Risāla fī ʿamal al-ṣafīḥa al-Zarqāliyya*, ibid. 10.—9. Tables for the eras of the Arabs, the Greeks, and the Copts, Bodl. I, $1039_{,1}$.

6. J.H. Mordtmann, Das Observatorium des Taqiaddin zu Pera, *Islam* 13 (1923), p. 82/96.—4. Read: ʿAsʿad 2022, 2055ʾ.—8. Carullah 1454.—10. Treatise on the calculation of oblique triangles, Yeni 797, 2.—11. *Fī ʿamal āla tursam biha ʾl-kawākib ʿalā saṭḥin mustawin*, ibid. 3.—12. *Tarjamat al-aṭibbāʾ*, Bešīr (Sül.) $658_{,2}$.—13. *Tashīl al-zīj al-Aʿshārī al-Shahānshāhiyya*, composed in 988/1580 for Sultan Murād III, Bank. XXII, $58_{,2466}$.—14. 15. See p. 665, 3.

1291 | 485. 6a. Yūsuf b. Aḥmad b. Ibrāhīm al-Nābulusī wrote, in 998/1589, *al-Misk al-ʿāṭir fī ḥall Zīj Ibn al-Shāṭir*, using Shihāb al-Dīn al-Ḥalabī's commentary on the *Zīj Ilkhānī*, the *ʿIqd al-amālī*, and his abstract of the *Zīj Ibn al-Shāṭir*, Bank. XXII, $54_{,2464}$.

7. 5. Garr. 996.

8. For Ṣādiq, read: Ṣiddīq, Suter 193, 475.—2. *Bughyat al-ṭullāb fi ʾl-ʿamal bil-asṭurlāb*, Paris 4580, 4.

9a. al-Ṭaḥḥān, Suter 511.—1. See *RAAD* VIII, 765, IX, 378.—2. Garr. 1018, Cairo[1] V, 319.—5. *Sharḥ Kashf al-qināʿ*, see p. $158_{,9}$.

9b. Suter 459.

486. 10b, 3 Cairo[1] V, 292.

15. 3. Garr. 1001 (which has *Risāla ʿalā faḍl al-dāʾir*).

487. 16b. See p. 420, 17d.

16c. ʿAlī b. Faḍlallāh al-Marʿashī wrote, in 1131/1719: 1. *Risāla fī rubʿ al-muqanṭar fi ʾl-mīqāt*, Alex. Fun. $101_{,10}$.—2. *Sullam al-samāʾ wal-āfāq fi ʾl-rubʿ al-mujayyab*, composed in 1140/1728, ibid. $101_{,11}$.

18. 7. *al-Zīj al-mufīd ʿalā uṣūl al-raṣad al-jadīd* (after Ulugh Beg), Garr. 1004.

21. 1. Garr. 1006.—2. Ibid. 1005, Alex. Ḥisāb $56_{,3}$, Qaw. II, 277.

22. 6. Garr. 1864.—9. Alex. Fiqh Ḥan. 7, Fun. $135_{,5}$, Makr. 5.—10. Instead a *ḥāshiya* to the commentary by al-Ḥifnī, d. 1178/1764, Garr. 478.—13. Ibid. 1007.—16. Ibid. 1882.—17. *Risāla fī dāʾirat al-muʿaddil*, Alex. Ḥisāb 49.

488. 3, 3. See *RAAD* XI, 318.

4. 1. Alex. Fun. $143_{,1}$.—2. Ibid. 2.

489. 7. Garr. 753/5, Alex. Taʾr. 44.

9. Muḥammad b. Nāṣir al-Dīn al-Sawāʾī al-Shafūnī al-Khaṭīb, ca. 1054/1644.—2. *Bahjat al-aḥbāb fī faḍāʾil wa-karāmāt al-shaykh Abī Bakr b. Qawwām*, Alex. Naḥw $34_{,3}$, see $1008_{,113}$.

10. 3. *Qūt al-arwāḥ fī aḥkām al-samāʿ al-mubāḥ*, autograph, Cairo, *Nashra* 21, see Farmer, *Sources* 64.

490. 11b. Aḥmad b. Ṣāliḥ b. Manṣūr al-Ṭarābulusī, *muftī* in Damietta and *naqīb al-ashrāf* in Cairo, d. 1159/1746 (Mur. II, 69, A. Taymūr, *RAAD* VII, 226, excerpts from the *Tuḥfat al-adab* of al-Maghribī, ibid. 346/58, 549/53).

13. Garr. 232.

15. 3. *Dīwān*, Br. Mus. 1088 (which has Ibn Luqayma).

491. 3, 1. Read: Mashh. XVI, $7_{,21}$.

492. 4. Cairo Ṭibb 30, see Meyerhof, *al-Andalus* III, 38.

5. 1. Alex. Ṭibb 44.—5. *al-Hidāya min al-ḍalāla etc.* Garr. $2096_{,2}$, Alex. Ḥisāb 64.—12. *al-Farāʾid al-gharāʾib al-ḥisān fī faḍāʾil laylat niṣf min Shaʿbān* Alex. Ḥad. $57_{,1}$.—17. Garr. 7236.—20. Alex. Ḥad. 40 (see 468, e).

493. 21. Garr. 756.—23. *Risāla fī faḍāʾil Makka wal-Madīna wal-bayt al-ḥarām al-muqaddas min taʾrīkhihā*, Alex. Taʾr. 71.

§ 19. 1a, 1. *Bahjat al-muḥaddith fī aḥkām jumla min al-ḥawādith*, Alex. Ḥisāb 44.—8. Comm. *Kashf al-ghumūḍ*, Berl. 7139, Garr. 572.

2. 2. Alex. Ḥurūf 8.

494. § 20. 1. Four *rasāʾil*, Alex. Fun. 83.

495. 34. Instead of *al-ḥawṭa*, read: *al-Ghawṭa*, see Muḥammad Kurd ʿAlī, *RAAD* V, 216/22.—43. *ʿArf al-zaharāt fī tafsīr al-kalimāt al-ṭayyibāt*, Garr. 702.—44. *Qayd al-sharīd min akhbār Yazīd*, Cairo² V, 300.

2. 11. Alex. Taʾr. 65, read: Abū Dharr.—14. Ibid. Fun. $177_{,1}$.

496. 19. Alex. Fun. $126_{,7}$.—23. Read: *al-Manthūr*.—25. See p. 1021, 48.—30. *Kuḥl al-ʿuyūn al-nujl fī ḥall masʾalat al-kuḥl* (*fi ʾl-naḥw*), Alex. Fun. $177_{,2}$.

4. 1. *Fatḥ al-ḥayy al-qayyūm*, Alex. Adab 9.

5. 4. Garr. 1527.—14. *Taḥqīq al-burhān fī shaʾn al-dukhān*, Qaw. I, 424.—15. Bank. XXIII, $112_{,2601}$.—17. Garr. 772, Alex. Mawāʿiẓ 8.—18. Garr. 607, Alex. Taʾr. 42.

| 497. 19. See p. 939, 99, 2.—23. Garr. 1847.—28. Ibid. 1848, Alex. Ta'r. 3.—33. 1292
Qalā'id al-marjān fī 'l-nāsikh wal-mansūkh min al-Qur'ān, MS Damascus, RAAD IX, 638,$_{1}$.—34. *Taḥqīq al-rajaḥān bi-ṣawm yawm al-shakk min Ramaḍān*, ibid. 6.—35. *Munyat al-muḥibbīn wa-bughyat al-ʿāshiqīn*, Alex. Adab 170.

498. 8. 1. Qaw. II, 250.—5. Alex. Fun. 65, Adab 59, Qaw. II, 250, 304/5.—Comm. b. Garr. 919, Qaw. II, 309/10.—c. Qaw. II, 295.—g. Ḥasan b. Muṣṭafā al-Islāmbulī Nāzīkzāde, Qaw. II, 310.—h. Ḥasan b. Muḥammad al-ʿAṭṭār, d. 1250/1834, Alex. Adab 4.—6. Garr. 918, Alex. Adab 3, 10, Fun. 100,$_{1}$, 106,$_{4}$, Qaw. II, 294, glosses by the author entitled *Taḥrīr al-taqrīr*, Alex. Adab 10.—8. *Fī ḥukm* (*aḥkām*) *al-taghannī* (*al-ghināʾ wal-mūsīqī*), Alex. Fun. 64,$_{2}$, 101,$_{7}$, Fiqh Ḥan. 27.—15. Garr. 1237.—16. Alex. Fun. 67,$_{6}$.—22. *al-Farā'iḍ al-Fāḍiliyya fī ʿilm al-munāẓara lil-Risāla al-Ḥusayniyya*, Alex. Fun. 97,$_{1}$.—23. *Risāla fī 'l-ḍād al-muʿjama*, ibid. Lugha 13.—24. *Risālat al-tanzīhāt*, ibid. Tawḥīd 17.

9. *al-Laṭā'if al-nūriyya*, Garr. 2201.—1. Ibid. 1331.—4. Alex. Fun. 55.—7. Ibid. Tawḥīd 28.—10. Garr. 945.—14. Alex. Fun. 93,$_{2}$.—25. Ibid. Ṭibb. 36.—30. *Risāla fī ḥall al-rumūz al-jafriyya*, ibid. Ḥurūf 9.—31. *al-Ḥadhāqa fī anwāʿ al-ʿalāqa*, a précis on rhetoric, Garr. 571.

§ 1. 1b. Jaʿfar b. Muḥammad al-Khaṭṭī al-ʿAbdī, d. 1028/1619, *Dīwān*, see RAAD VIII, 38/44, 84/90, 160/6.

3. *Dīwān*, Garr. 122, Alexandria 1290.

4. Garr. 125, see p. 388, 434.

500. 6. See p. 910, 58.

7. See p. 784, 1.

501. 5a. Read: *ifḥām*, Mosul 508,$_{2}$ (at the end).

6. 1. Alex. Ta'r. 136.—6. 1. See R. Frank, Scheich ʿAdī, *Türk. Bibl.* XIV, 95.

502. § 4. 2, 1. Alex. Fiqh Ḥan. 46, 58, 67, Garr. 1762 (*Risāla fī taʿāruḍ al-bayyināt*).

503. C. 2. 17. *Aḥkām al-Nawāṣib*, in the library of Mahdī ʿAbdallāh al-Sayyid Ḥaydar al-Kāẓimī, *Dharīʿa* I, 302,$_{1580}$.—18. *Fiqh al-athariyyīn*, Āṣaf. II, 1182,$_{24}$.

2a. Nāṣir al-Dīn Ḥusayn b. Mufliḥ (who wrote the *Jawāhir al-kalimāt fi ʾl-ʿuqūd wal-iʿtiqādāt* in 870/1466) b. al-Ḥasan b. Rāshid (Rashīd) b. Ṣalāḥ al-Ṣaymarī, d. 1 Ramaḍān 933/1 June 1527 in Salīmābād in Bahrain, *al-Īqāẓāt fi ʾl-ʿuqūd wal-īqāʿāt*, in Mashhad, *Dharīʿa* II, 508,$_{1989}$.

2.b. Muḥammad b. al-Faraj al-Ḥimyarī al-Najafī wrote, in 1052/1642, *Abwāb al-jinān al-mushtamil ʿalā rasāʾil thamān*, in the library of ʿAbd al-Ḥusayn al-Ṭihrānī, d. 1226/1869 in Karbala, *Dharīʿa* I, 77,$_{372}$.

2c. Qāsim b. Muḥammad b. Jawād al Kāẓimī al-Najafī b. al-Wandī, d. 1100/1689, *Istibṣār al-akhbār*, MS in Najaf, *Dharīʿa* II, 17, 46.

2d. Sulaymān b. ʿAbdallāh b. ʿAlī b. al-Ḥusayn b. Aḥmad b. Yūsuf b. ʿAmmār al-Māḥūzī al-Baḥrānī, a student of al-Majlisī (p. 572), d. 1121/1709. 1. *al-Iḥbāṭ wal-takfīr* in *Majmūʿat al-rasāʾil*, in the library of Muḥammad ʿAlī Khwānsārī in Najaf, *Dharīʿa* I, 280,$_{1468}$.—2. *Madārij al-yaqīn fī sharḥ al-arbaʿīn fi ʾl-imāma*, dedicated to Shāh Ḥusayn, in the library of Aḥmad Ṣāliḥ ʿAbdallāh al-Ṭaʿʿān al-Baḥrānī, ibid. 418,$_{2157}$.

2e. Abu ʾl-Riyāḍ Ibrāhīm b. ʿAlī b. Ḥasan al-Bilādī al-Baḥrānī completed, in 1150/1737, *Naẓm jamʿ al-riyāḍ* and *al-Iqtibās wal-taḍmīn min kitāb Allāh al-mubīn fī ithbāt ʿaqāʾid al-dīn* (*manẓūma fī uṣūl al-dīn*), MS in Kāẓimiyya, *Dharīʿa* II, 266,$_{1084}$.

2f. His student Abū Muḥammad ʿAbdallāh b. Muḥammad b. al-Ḥusayn b. Muḥammad al-Shuwaykī al-Khaṭṭī wrote *al-Iqtibās wal-taḍmīn li-miʾa āya min al-Qurʾān al-mubīn fī ithbāt ʿaqāʾid al-dīn wa-tabkīt al-mukhālifīn*, autograph in the library of Hādī Āl Kāshif al-Ghiṭāʾ in Najaf, *Dharīʿa* II, 267,$_{1085}$.

1293 | 505. 6. *Qiṣaṣ al-ʿulamāʾ* no. 27, Browne, *Lit. Hist.* IV, 410 (which has an incorrect "d. 1240").—2. *al-Durra fī ʾl-fiqh*, Mashh. V, 59,$_{194}$. A commentary by his grand-cousin Mīrzā Maḥmūd Birūjirdī, *al-Mawāhib al-saniyya*, Tehran, 1280, 1288.—3. *Urjūza fī faḍāʾil al-rummān*, in 47 verses, print. at the end of *al-Mawāhib al-saniyya*, *Dharīʿa* I, 488,$_{2415}$.

10. Read: Teh. Sip. I, 502.—*Bughyat al-ṭālib*, comm. *Munyat al-rāghib* by his son Mūsā, Teh. Sip. I, 548/9.

11. 1. For *wujūb*, read: *wujūh*, Tehran 1317.

506. 1c. For al-Kakāʾī, read: al-Katkānī.—6. *Tanbīh al-arīb fī takhrīj al-tahādhīb*, abstract *Intikhāb al-jayyid min Tanbīh al-sayyid* by Ḥusayn b. Muḥammad b. ʿAlī b. Khalaf b. Ibrāhīm b. Ḍayfallāh al-Baḥrānī al-Damistānī, completed in 1173/1759, MS in Najaf, *Dharīʿa* II, 358,$_{1445}$.—6. *al-Inṣāf fī 'l-naṣṣ ʿala 'l-aʾimma al-ashrāf min āl ʿAbd al-Manāf* or *al-Nuṣūṣ*, 308 traditions, completed in 1097/1686, in al-Maktaba al-Ḥusayniyya in Najaf, ibid. 398,$_{1596}$.—7. *Īḍāḥ al-mustarshidīn fī bayān tarājim al-rājiʿīn ilā wilāyat amīr al-muʾminīn*, ibid. 499,$_{1956}$.

2. See p. 980,$_{18}$.

507. 6. See p. 785,$_{5}$.

508. § 7a. Philosophy. Aḥmad b. Muḥammad, *muftī* of Baghdad, wrote, in 1199/1785, for the vizier Sulaymān: *Ajwibat al-asʾila al-Hindiyya*, Alex. Fals. 4.

§ 8. 2, 5. See A. Schmidt, in *Festschr. für Bartold*, Tashkent 1927, p. 73/107.—8. *Talkhīṣ al-munāẓara bayna ʿulamāʾ al-sunna wal-Shīʿa*, see *RAAD* V, 179/86.

509. 1, 3. *Takhmīs*, Alex. Adab 128.

3. 8. *al-Araj al-miskī wal-taʾrīkh al-Makkī*, MS in Mecca, see Zuruklī, *Mā raʾaytu wa-mā samiʿtu*, C. 1923, 68.—9. *Rafʿ al-ishtibāk ʿan tanāwul al-tunbāk*, Ind. Off. 1861.

510. 5, 3. Garr. 115.

7. 1. Garr. 117, C. 1290.

511. 8. 2. Garr. 220.—14. Ibid. 138/9.

15. 1. Ibid. 131.

16. Ibid. 132 (d. 1181/1767).

16a. ʿAlī Ṣadr al-Dīn al-Madanī b. Aḥmad Niẓām al-Dīn al-Ḥusaynī, d. 1123/1711, *Anwār al-rabīʿ fī anwāʿ al-badīʿ*, a comm. on his *Badīʿiyya*, Indian printing n.d., Alex. Adab. 14.

512. 17a. See p. 905,$_{1}$.

514. 1, 2. *Naẓm al-qawāʿid*, with the comm. *al-Bayān al-musāʿid* by Muḥammad b. ʿAlī b. ʿAllān, d. 1037/1627, Qaw. II, 64.

2. 2. *Risāla fī misāḥat al-Kaʿba wal-masjid al-ḥarām*, completed in 943/1536, Alex. Fiqh Ḥan. 52.

515. 3, 2. Alex. Taʾr. 20.—10. *al-Kanz al-musammā fī ʿilm al-muʿammā*, Alex. Adab 117.

6a. See p. 645,$_{18a}$.

516. 10, 6. *Risāla fī taḥrīm al-dukhān*, Alex. Fun. 157,3.

517. 12, 1. Comm. a. Jaʿfar b. Ismāʿīl al-Barzanjī, *muftī* of the Shāfiʿīs in Medina, completed in 1279/1862, Alex. Taʾr. 13.—e. Read: *ʿalīm*, Garr. 661.—h. Aḥmad Jamāl al-Dīn al-Tūnisī, whose *al-Nashr al-ʿāṭir bi-mawlid al-shaykh ʿAbd al-Qādir* (*al-Jīlānī*) is preserved in Tunis 1321.

518. 12, 3. Alex. Fun. 147,$_{2}$.

§ 4. 1, 1. Garr. 1524.

519. 1, 4. Garr. 1925.

2. Garr. 604.

520. 3. See p. 572, 3a.—1. Lith. Tehran 1262.

4. 4. *Sadd al-ādhān etc.*, additionally Alex. Ṭibb 41.

5. 4. *Masālik al-abrār ilā aḥādīth al-nabī al-mukhtār*, Alex. Fun. 1233.—6. Alex. Muṣṭ. Ḥad. 53,$_{2}$, Fun. 123,$_{2}$.

521. 23. Alex. Fun. 167,$_{24}$.—27. Ibid. 110,$_{1}$.—38. *al-Jawāb al-muḥiqq fīmā huwa*
1294 *ʾl-ḥaqq*, Alex. Tawḥīd 42,$_{3}$.—39. *Risāla fī tafsīr qawlihi*, | on sura 2,$_{180}$, Alex. Fun. 163,2.—40. *Nashr al-zahr fi ʾl-dhikr bil-jahr*, Ind. Off. 1859.—41. *Itḥāf al-munīb* (?) *al-ruwāh fī faḍl al-jahr bi-dhikr Allāh*, ibid. 1860.—42. *Inbāh al-anbāh fī iʿrāb lā ilāha illa ʾllāh*, Alex. Naḥw 4.

5a. See p. 936,$_{14}$, Garr. 1470, Alex. Fun. 122,$_{5}$.

522. 6, 3. Garr. 2069$_{,1}$.—7. al-*Fawāʾid al-jalīla fī musalsalāt Muḥammad b. Aḥmad ʿAqīla*, Alex. Ḥad. 39.

523. 7, 1. Garr. 1412.

524. 1. See p. 452, 3a. Garr. 927, Alex. Fiqh Ḥan. 10, Taṣ. 10, Qaw. I, 223.

2. Alex. Uṣūl 14.

525. 2c. Read: al-Bayāḍī, see p. 647, 27.

3. Garr. 2097$_{,2}$, Alex. Fiqh Ḥan. 55, 72, Qaw. I, 408.

5. A refutation of the Wahhābīs, Manch. 92c.

526. 2, 7. *Hidāyat al-sālik al-muḥtāj ilā bayān afʿāl al-muʿtamir wal-ḥājj*, Alex. Fiqh Māl. 16.—8. *Irshād al-sālik al-muḥtāj*, ibid. see p. 537,11.

527. 1. *Manāqib b. Ḥajar al-Haythamī*, by his student Abū Bakr b. Muḥammad b. ʿAbdallāh b. Bā ʿAmr, Alex. Fun. 118$_{,1}$.—2. Garr. 789, 2013$_{,2}$, Mosul 195$_{,85,4}$.—3. Alex. Fiqh Shāf. 6, Mosul 230$_{,63}$, As. Mus. Rosen 24.—4. Mosul 127$_{,106}$, 235$_{,147}$, print. also C. 1307.—*Tanbīh al-ghabī* by Aḥmad b. ʿAbdallāh al-Nāshirī, Garr. 2078$_{,3}$. For Ibrāhīm al-ʿUbaydī see p. 939$_{,99}$.—*al-Biḥār al-muḥriqa*, Alex. Taʾr. 90.—5. Mosul 196$_{,99}$.

528. 10. Garr. 1963, Alex. Ḥad. 23, Qaw. I, 232, Dam. Z. 60, 134$_{,1}$.—19. Alex. Fiqh Shāf. 22.—23. Ind. Off. 1853, Alex. Fun. 155$_{,3}$. Dam. Z. 60, 134$_{,2}$.—26. Mosul 111$_{,107/8}$, 238$_{,200}$; on Bā Faḍl al-Ḥaḍramī see p. 555, 1c.—Glosses: read: al-Tirmīsī. Muḥammad b. Sulaymān al-Kurdī al-Madanī, d. 1194/1780 (Sarkīs 1555), Garr. 1929, Rāmpūr I, 229$_{,409}$, print. C. 1284, whose *Fatḥ al-qadīr bikhtiṣār al-mutaʿalliqāt bil-ajīr* is preserved in Rāmpūr I, 232, 426 (but which has: Maḥmūd), *Fatāwī* C. 1307.—27/8, Mosul 100$_{,232}$, 102$_{,56,2}$, 239$_{,208}$.—29. Glosses by ʿAbdallāh b. ʿAlī Suwaydān al-Damlījī, Alex. Taʾr. 6.—30. Garr. 653.—31. Glosses by Muḥammad b. ʿUbāda al-Ṣaʿīdī al-ʿAdawī, d. 1193/1779, Alex. Ḥad. 57$_{,2}$.—32. = 50. Alex. Tawḥīd 30, Mosul 230$_{,62}$.

529. 38. See p. 76$_{,79}$.—44. With the title *al-Wafāʾ fī bayān baʿḍ ḥuqūq al-Muṣṭafā*.—48. Garr. 1919, Dam. Z. 53$_{,95/6}$.—55. = 6.—57. Hamb. Or. Sem. 63.—58. *Talkhīṣ al-Iḥrāʾ*, see p. 223.—59. *Sharḥ dībājat al-Minhāj*, Mosul 103$_{,56,5}$.—60. *Sharḥ al-ʿUbāb* (p. 75$_{,74}$), ibid. 106$_{,88,1}$.—61. *Tashnīf al-asmāʿ bi-ḥukm*

al-samāʿ, ibid. 145,$_{66,7}$.—62. *Jawāb fi ʾl-taʾrīkh li-suʾāl warada min al-Yaman*, ibid. 166,$_{28,2}$.—63. *Fatḥ al-jawād, sharḥ al-Irshād*, Hamb. Or. Sem. 21.—64. *al-Manhal al-ʿadhb fī iṣlāḥ mā wahiya min al-Kaʿba*, Alex. Taʾr. 134.—65. *al-Īḍāḥ wal-bayān fī laylat niṣf min Shaʿbān*, ibid. Fun. 66,$_{1}$.

2. 1. Ind. Off. 4573,$_{2}$.—6. *Ḥuṣūl al-munā bi-uṣūl al-ghanā*, ibid. 4573,$_{1}$ (*JRAS* 1939, 365).

3. 2. Garr. 1508, Alex. Mawāʿiẓ 4, Mosul 126,$_{86}$.

530. 8. Garr. 1526.—11. Autograph dated 1093/1682, Lālelī 4744.

531. Comm. c. *Fatḥ al-majīd* by ʿAbd al-Raḥmān b. Ḥasan Qaṣīla, C. 1347.—2. Alex. Fun. 123,2.

532. 4a. His grandson ʿAbd al-Raḥmān b. Ḥasan b. Shaykh al-Islām Muḥammad b. ʿAbd al-Wahhāb, d. 1285/1868, *Kitāb al-īmān wa-rasāʾil wa-fatāwī*, and Ḥamīd b. Naṣr b. Muʿtamar's *rasāʾil* and three *rasāʾil* by ʿAbdallāh b. ʿAbd al-Raḥmān b.
1295 Aḥmad b. Buṭayn, d. | 1282/1865, in *Majmūʿat rasāʾil wa-fatāwī fī masāʾil muhimma li-ʿulamāʾ Najd al-aʿlayn*, C. 1349.—

5. Deceased in 1275/1810, *Rawḍat al-afkār*, Indian printing cited in al-Rayḥānī, *Taʾrīkh Najd* 1.

534. 2, 16. *Rafʿ al-ilbās bi-bayān ishtirāk maʿāni ʾl-Fātiḥa wa-sūrat al-Nās*, Qaw. I, 68.

§ 8. 1, 1. *Waṣiyyat al-muntaẓar gharīb al-waṭan*, Dam. Z. 60, 130, 1 (which only has "Ibn ʿArrāq").—3. Read: *Nashr al-laṭāʾif*, Alex. Taʾr. 142, MS in Mecca, Zuruklī, *Aḥsan mā raʾaytu wa-samiʿtu*, 99.

4. 5. Garr. 114, by Muḥammad b. Muḥammad b. ʿAlī al-Bakrī al-Ṣiddīqī Abu ʾl-Mawāhib, d. 1037/1627.

535. 6, 12. *al-Kanz al-asnā fi ʾl-ṣalāt wal-salām ʿala ʾl-dhāt al-Aḥmadiyya al-Muḥammadiyya al-ḥusnā*, Dam. Z. 53,$_{70}$ (which only has: Aḥmad al-Anṣārī).

7a. Aḥmad b. Muḥammad al-Qurashī al-Ḥasanī completed, in 1152/1739: *Futūḥ al-lahaj bi-sharḥ manẓūmatihī Tafrīj al-faraj*, Alex. Faw. 13.

7b. ʿAbd al-Jabbār b. Ḥasan al-Barzanjī, ca. 1163/1750, *Aḥsan al-ṣalāt wa-akmal al-taḥiyyāt ʿalā ashraf al-bariyyāt*, Garr. 2171,$_{1}$.

8. 4. = (?) *al-Nafaḥāt al-ilāhiyya fī kayfiyyat al-sulūk fi 'l-ṭarīqa al-Muḥammadiyya*, Alex. Taṣ. 50.—5. *Wird al-shaykh al-Sammān*, Garr. 2082$_{,3}$.

536. 1, 1. Garr. 1040.

3. Read: *Taḥrīr al-kalām*.

4. 19 works, ibid. 2008.

537. 1, 1. Alex. Ḥisāb 56$_{,2}$.—11. See p. 526.

538. 2, 1. Garr. 2077$_{,1}$.

§ 12. 1, 4. *Tuḥfat al-laṭā'if fī faḍā'il al-Ḥibr b. ʿAbbās wa-Wajj wal-Ṭā'if*, from the library of Aḥmad Taymūr, is mentioned in Shakīb Arslān's *al-Irtisāmāt al-liṭāf*, 131$_{,15}$ (with the death year of his father).

2. 2. Garr. 219.

539. 2, 3. Qaw. I, 52.—3a. Ibid. I, 235.—3b. *Risāla fī tafsīr qawlihi* (sura 7$_{,29}$) *wa-bayān mā qālahu fī tafsīrihi Niẓām al-Dīn Yaʿqūb al-Karkhī*, ibid. 67.—4. Alex. Fun. 88$_{,2}$.

540. 10. As *al-Mawḍūʿāt fī muṣṭalaḥ al-ḥadīth* in Alex. Fun. 77$_{,5}$, 116$_{,1}$.—11. Alex. Ḥad. 54$_{,2}$, Qaw. I, 155, C. 1289.—12. Qaw. I, 118$_{,237}$.—20. BDMG 30c.—34. Alex. Fun. 66$_{,6}$.—37. Ibid. 97$_{,2}$.—47. Ind. Off. 1733.—49. Alex. Fun. 66$_{,4}$.

541. 51. Hamb. Or. Sem. 8, Garr. 1965.—Comm. b. Garr. 1966, Alex. Faw. 15.—c. Muḥammad al-Nābulusī al-Maqdisī al-Azharī, composed in 1160/1747, Qaw. I, 244.—d. *al-Durr al-munaẓẓam* by Muḥammad al-Madanī, composed in 1274/1857, ibid. 32.—69. Alex. Ta'r. 7.—78. Ibid. Fun. 97.—82. Cairo, *Nashr*. 20.—85. Alex. Mawāiʿẓ 10.

542. 97. Istanbul 1307.—98. Alex. Taṣ. 45.

543. 161. *Risāla fī laylat al-niṣf min Shaʿbān*, Alex. Fun. 178$_{,1}$—162. *Risāla fi 'l-radd ʿalā man taʿaqqabahu fī risālatihi fī mas'alat al-ishāra bil-masbaḥa fi 'l-ṣalāt*, ibid. 2.—163. *Risāla fī mas'alat al-ishāra bil-masbaḥa fi 'l-ṣalāt*, ibid. 3.—164. *Risāla fī qawlihī ṣʿlm inna 'l-qawma yabʿathu 'llāhu ʿalayhimu 'l-ʿadhāb etc.*,

ibid. 4.—165. *Risāla fī 'l-taṣawwuf* contra Ibn ʿArabī, ibid. Fun. 95,$_{14}$.—166. *Risāla fī tabʿīd al-ʿulamāʾ ʿan abwāb al-umarāʾ wal-wuzarāʾ*, ibid. 101,$_{9}$.—167. *Risāla fī taḥqīq anna 'l-kabāʾir mukaffira aw ghayr mukaffira*, ibid. 163,$_{1}$.—168. *Risāla fī waḍʿ al-yad ʿala 'l-ṣadr fī 'l-ṭawāf*, Rāmpūr 100, Ind. Off. 1854.—169. *Risāla fī Ḥukm iqtidāʾ al-Ḥanafiyya bil-Shāfiʿiyya*, Alex. Fiqh Ḥan. 28.—170. *Risāla fī*
1296 *kalimat al-jalāla*, ibid. Fun. 67,$_{14}$.—171. *Risāla* | *fī qawlihi*, on sura 2,$_{206}$, ibid. 13.—172. *Risāla fī 'l-ʿaṣā wa-mā warada fī ḥaqqihā*, Garr. 2088,$_{4}$.

3. 2. Garr. 1051.—3. *Miʿrāj al-albāb ilā ʿilm al-ḥisāb*, Bank. XXII, 21,$_{2426}$.

See p. 1039,$_{23}$.

§ 1. 1a. See Rihani, *Arabian Peak and Desert* 208.

3. Garr. 216.

544. 7a. 1. Garr. 124.

7 b. Garr. 119 (Nazīlī), Badīʿiyya ibid. 120.

545. 11d. See p. 968,12.

547. 19. Poems in Landb. Br. 352 (which has a mistaken Qānī).

20. See p. 817, 2a. a Ḥumaynī in transliteration in E. Rossi, *L'Arabo parlato a Ṣanʿā*, Rome 1939, p. 131.

548. § 2. 1. See p. 917,$_{29}$.

5. See p. 918,$_{35}$.

549. 1, 1. Garr. 625, Makr. 7, on which *Dhayl al-faḍl al-mazīd*, ibid. 50.—8. C. 1345.

550. 6, 1. Garr. 618, Alex. Taʾr. 72.

552. 12. Read: ʿAlī Amīrī Ef. 2207.

553. 3. Khālid b. Ḥusayn al-Ḥaḍramawtī ca. 1100/1688, *Fatḥ Allāh al-karīm etc.* additionally Qaw. I, 206.

4. See p. 529$_{,3}$.

3a. In 1095/1684, al-Sayyid Muḥammad b. Muḥammad al-Saqqāf al-Bāʿalawī wrote the *manẓūma Durrat al-ṣafāʾ li-ukhuwwat al-wafāʾ fī īmān abaway al-Muṣṭafā*, Alex. Fun. 122$_{,2}$.

555. 1a, 2. Garr. 2070$_{,2}$.—12. *Naẓm qiṣṣat al-mawlid*, see III, 341, Ba.

1b. 5. *al-Qawl al-mūjiz*, with a commentary, Berl. 4912, Ambr. B 35, ii.

2b. ʿAbdallāh b. Muḥammad b. Qushayr al-Ḥaḍramī, 10th cent., *Aḥkām al-ḥayḍ wal-nafās wal-istiḥādha*, Alex. Fiqh Shāf. 35$_{,1}$, glosses by Aḥmad b. al-Ḥajar al-Haythamī, d. 947/1540, ibid. 2.

556. 4. See p. 902$_{,54}$.—9. Garr. 164.

5. See p. 983$_{,1}$.

557. 1b, 3. a. Comm. *Shifāʾ jahl al-sāʾil ʿammā taḥammalahu ʾl-Kāfil* by ʿAlī b. Ṣāliḥ b. ʿAlī b. Muḥammad al-Ṭabarī, print. Ṣanʿāʾ n.d., see E. Rossi, *Or. Mod.* XVIII, 571, *al-Kāshif li-dhawi ʾl-ʿuqūl ʿan wujūh masāʾil al-Kāfil* by Aḥmad b. Muḥammad b. Luqmān b. Aḥmad b. Shams al-Dīn b. al-imām al-Mahdī bi-dīn Allāh Aḥmad b. Yaḥyā b. al-Murtaḍā, 11th cent., Sanʿāʾ 1347, ibid. 502.—5. Alex. Adab 129,15.

2. 8. *Tanqīḥ al-fawāʾid wa-taqyīd al-shawāriḍ fī tabyīn al-maqāṣid wa-taṣḥīḥ al-ʿaqāʾid*, Garr. 2078$_{,1}$.

558. 4b. See p. 967$_{,3}$.

559. 5. 1. Hamb. Or. Sem. 44, 82.

6. 2. *Ādāb al-ʿulamāʾ wal-mutaʿallimīn*, Ṣanʿāʾ 1344, see Rossi, OM XVIII, 571.

6d. ʿAlī b. Sulaymān Shams al-Īmān completed, in 1052/1642, *Ḥayāt al-aḥrār wa-ḥibā al-aḥbār*, Alex. Firaq 5.

560. Line 1, read: Ambr. N.F. 312, v.

562. 13, 6. *Risāla fī tafsīr qawlihi*, on sura 71$_{,14}$, Alex. Fun. 125$_{,23}$.

14. 3. *Ibānat al-ṣawāb fī maʿnā iqtiṣāṣ al-jammāʾ min al-qarnāʾ yawm al-ḥisāb*, Alex. Fun. 125,$_{25}$.—4. *Risāla fi ʾl-waḥy*, ibid. 28.—5. *Rasāʾil*, ibid. 29.—6. *Baḥth fī ḥadīth iftirāq al-umma*, dated 1133, ibid. 22.—7. *Rafʿ al-iltibās ʿan tanāzuʿ al-waṣiyy wal-ʿAbbās*, ibid. 124,$_{7}$.

563. C. l. see p. 608, 1, I, 403.

564. § 6, 1a. See p. 455.

3. Muḥammad b. al-Ḥusayn b. Amīr al-Muʾminīn al-Manṣūr bi-llāh al-Qāsim b. Muḥammad b. ʿAlī, 11th cent., *Muntaha ʾl-marām fī sharḥ āyāt aḥkām*, Ṣanʿāʾ 1342, see Rossi, *OM* XVIII, 571.

§ 7. 1. 2. Garr. 2078,$_{2}$.

3. See p. 967,9.

1297 | 565. 2. Muḥ. I, 496.—1. *al-Dīwān al-muwashshaḥ*, Bank. XXIII, 57,$_{2551}$.

3. 4. *Ghurrat al-bayān ʿan ʿumr al-zamān* or *al-ʿArḍ al-kāfī lil-ʿirḍ al-shāfī*, Qaw. I, 206, on which *Kashf al-ghubār ʿani ʾl-ishārāt fīmā baqiya min ʿumr hādha ʾl-zamān* by ʿAbd al-Raḥmān b. Aḥmad, ibid. 208.

566. 4, 1. Bank. XXIII, 62,$_{2557}$.—10. Read: Aḥmad b. Abī Bakr.—12b. Garr. 1599.

6. 2. *Sahm al-saʿāda fī iṣābat al-ḍamīr ʿalā wafq al-irāda*, Alex. Ḥurūf 13.

567. § 10.—1. *Sahm al-ghayb etc.*, Garr. 943, Hamb. Or. Sem. 111.

568. 2. Darwīsh b. Jumʿa al-Maḥrūqī, *Kitāb al-dalāʾil wal-wasāʾil*, C. 1320.

7. Read: Ḥamīd, see p. 823.

569. 11. See p. 823,$_{2}$, see Hedwig Klein, *Kap. 33. der anonymen ar. Chronik* Kashf al-ghumma li-akhbār al-umma, Hamburg 1938.

13. Abū Sulaymān Muḥammad b. ʿĀmir b. Rashīd al-Maʿwalī wrote an Arabic chronicle about Oman and Zanzibar, but not before 1154/1742; see M. Guillain, *Documents sur l'histoire la géographie et le commerce de l'Afrique orientale* I, Paris 1856, I, 514/5, H. Klein, op. cit., p. 3.

570. 1. See p. 383,$_{5b}$. Read: *Ghawānī.*

4. 1. On which the commentary *Safīnat al-ʿilm*, completed in 1131/1719, Bank. XXIII, 108,$_{2597}$.

571. *al-Tuḥfa al-Nāṣiriyya*, written on the order of Shāh Nāṣir al-Dīn (1848/96), so ad p. 841.

§ 1b. 1, 1. Qaw. II, 99, Alex. Naḥw 43, Fun. 42.

572. 4. See p. 598,$_{4}$.

§ 2. 1a. Jamāl al-Dīn ʿAṭāʾallāh b. Faḍlallāh al-Ḥusaynī al-Fārisī al-Dashtakī al-Harawī, *Ṣāḥib Rawḍat al-aḥbāb*, a contemporary of Shāh Ismāʿīl (d. 930/1524), wrote *al-Arb. ḥad. min aḥādīth sayyid al-mursalīn fī manāqib amīr al-muʾminīn*, in the library of ʿAbd al-Ḥusayn in Mashhad, *Dharīʿa* I, 422,$_{2170}$.

1b. ʿAbdallāh b. Mahdī b. Saʿīd al-Tustarī al-Khurāsānī was burned at the stake by the Uzbeks; this happened in the main square of Bukhara in 997/1589 after the Uzbeks had captured Mashhad. *Arb. ḥad.* in the library of ʿAbd al-Ḥusayn al-Ḥajjī in Karbala, *Dharīʿa* I, 420,$_{2167}$.

3d. Fayḍallāh b. ʿAbd al-Qāhir al-Ḥusaynī al-Tafrīshī, d. 1020/1161, *Arb. ḥad. fī aḥwāl al-nuṣṣāb wal-mukhālifīn*, print. together with *Nathr al-laʾālī*, *Dharīʿa* I, 424,$_{2174}$.

3a. See p. 520, 3.

573. Line 2. *Ḥadīqat al-muttaqīn* additionally Teh. II, 42, abstract *Rawḍat al-muttaqīn* (Kentūrī 1599), Ind. Off. 1831/2, Browne, *Lit. Hist.* IV, 409.

574. 6, 12. *al-Arb. ḥad. fī ʾl-uṣūl wal-furūʿ wal-khuṭab wal-mawāʿiẓ wa-mā yaḥtāj ilayhi ʾl-nās fī umūr dīnihim*, *Dharīʿa* I, 412,$_{2135}$.—17. *Ādāb ṣalāt al-layl*, Pers. Najaf, in the library of Muḥammad Riḍā b. Yaḥyā al-Tabrīzī, *Dharīʿa* I, 22,$_{110}$.—18. *al-Asʾila al-Khalīliyya*, asked by Khalīl b. al-Ghāzī al-Qazwīnī, d. 1089/1678, in the library of ʿAlī al-Khiyābānī in Tabriz, ibid. II, 82,$_{324}$.—19. *al-Asʾila al-Hindiyya*, asked by his brother ʿAbdallāh from India, in the library of Abu ʾl-Qāsim al-Mūsawī al-Riyāḍī in Najaf, ibid. II, 94,$_{372}$.

7a. Muḥammad Ṭāhir b. Ḥusayn al-Shīrāzī al-Najafī al-Qummī, *Shaykh al-Islām* and *Imām al-Jumʿa* in Qom, d. 1089/1678, *al-Arb. ḥad. wa-dalīlan fī imāmat al-aʾimma al-ṭāhirīn*, in the library of Muḥammad ʿAlī al-Khwānsārī in Najaf, *Dharīʿa* I, 419$_{,2162}$.

7b. In 1124/1712, ʿAlī b. Ḥusayn b. Muḥyi ʾl-Dīn b. ʿAbd al-Laṭīf al-Jāmiʿī completed his *Tawqīf al-masāʾil* and also wrote an *Arb. ḥad.*, with a commentary, which is in the library of Mahdī ʿImād al-Fihrisī in Mashhad, *Dharīʿa* I, 422$_{,2170}$.

575. 3a. Ind. Off. 1811, As. Soc. Beng. 15.—12. To be deleted.—13. Read: *Siyagh*.—
1298 14. See *Dharīʿa* I, 293$_{,1529}$.—16. *Ithbāt al-rajʿa*, in the library of Rājā | Fayḍābādī in *Majmūʿat fiqh* 4, ibid. I, 93$_{,447}$.—17. *al-Asʾila al-Ṣaymariyya* by Ḥusayn b. Mufliḥ al-Ṣaymarī, d. 933/1527, in the library of al-Mujaddid al-Shīrāzī, ibid. 89$_{,302}$.—18. *al-Ishrāf ʿalā siyādat al-ashrāf*, in the library of Muḥammad al-Samāwī, ibid. 101$_{,398}$.—19. *al-Irth*, in the library of Ḥasan Saʿd al-Dīn al-Kāẓimī and of Rājā Muḥammad Mahdī in Faizabad, ibid. I, 466$_{,2243}$.—20. *Sharḥ al-Farāʾiḍ al-Naṣīriyya*, see I, 925.

1aa. His student Ḥusayn b. ʿAlī b. Ḥusayn b. Abī Sarwāl al-ʿUwālī al-Ḥajarī al-Baḥrānī wrote *al-Aʿlām al-jaliyya fī sharḥ al-Alfiyya al-Shahīdiyya*, autograph in Mashhad, completed in 950/1543, *Dharīʿa* II, 238$_{,947}$.

1c. *al-Fatāwi ʾl-Amīniyya* additionally Ind. Off. 1684 (which has: al-Ḥanafī).

1cc. Muḥammad b. Aḥmad al-Fārisī al-Khafarī, d. 957/1550, *Ithbāt al-wājib taʿālā*, Mashh. I, 13, $_{17,8}$ (which has: d. 1015, see p. 588), *Dharīʿa* I, 106$_{,520}$.—2. *Ithbāt al-hayūlī*, in Madrasat Fāḍil Khān in Mashhad, ibid. I, 112$_{,542}$.

1ccc. Aḥmad b. al-Mawlā Aḥmad al-Qāʾinī, a student of ʿAbd al-ʿĀlī b. al-Muḥaqqiq al-Karakī, wrote: *Ithbāt al-wājib taʿālā ʿalā shaʾnihi ʾl-ʿazīz*, in the libraries of Shaykh Hādī Kāshif al-Ghiṭāʾ and Shaykh ʿAlī Kāshif al-Ghiṭāʾ, *Dharīʿa* I, 102$_{,503}$.

1d. ʿAbd al-Ṣamad (d. 935/1528), *Arb. ḥad. fī manāqib al-aʾimma al-ṭāhirīn* in *al-Tuḥfa al-saniyya al-Ṣafawiyya*, in the library of Qāsim b. Ḥasan Muḥyi ʾl-Dīn Jāmiʿī Najafī, *Dharīʿa* I, 419$_{,2165}$.

576. 1d, 2. Persian MSS *Dharīʿa* I, 414$_{,2146}$.—8. *al-Asʾila al-Shadqamiyya*, asked by Badr al-Dīn al-Ḥasan b. ʿAlī b. al-Ḥasan b. ʿAlī b. Shadqam al-Madanī, d. ca. 1010/1601 in India, Mashhad, *Dharīʿa* II, 87$_{,344}$.—9. *al-Dirāya fī ʿilm al-hidāya*, print. together with the *Dirāya* of *Bahwat al-Milla wal-Dīn Muḥammad al-ʿĀmilī al-Bahāʾī*, Tehran 1306.

1ff. Muḥammad Amīn Ḥāfiẓzāde, a descendant of Muḥammad al-Bāqir, *Mufīd al-uṣūl fī taḥqīq al-ḥuṣūl*, Alex. Uṣūl 120.

1gg. Muḥammad b. ʿAlī b. al-Ḥasan al-ʿĀmilī, *Ṣāḥib al-Madārik*, d. 1009/1600, *al-Asʾila al-Shadqamiyya* (see 1d, 8), in the library of Sayyid Āqā al-Tustarī, *Dharīʿa* II, 88,346.

1. i. See *Dharīʿa* II, 230,906.

1k. Yūsuf Kawsaj.

577. 1. l. See p. 590,4.—*al-Fawāʾid etc.*, Ind. Off. 1507.

1. o. Was appointed vizier in 1033/1624 by ʿAbbās I, deposed by Ṣafī, but restored to office by ʿAbbās II.—2. *Unmūdhaj al-ʿulūm, Dharīʿa* II, 405,1623.

578. 2, 23. *ʿUmdat al-iʿtimād fī kayfiyyat al-ijtihād*, composed in 1080/1669 during a visit to Kabul, Ind. Off. 1677.

2a. See p. 450,2.

2b. *Rawḍāt al-jannāt* 116/8.—1. Persian transl. *Hidāyat al-aʿlām* by Muḥammad ʿAlī al-Ardakānī, written on the order of Shāhzāde Muḥammad Walī, Teh. II, 52.

2d. Al-Muʾmin b. Dūst Muḥammad al-Ḥusaynī al-Astarābādhī, d. 1080/1669 as a martyr in Mecca, *Ithbāt al-rajʿa wa-ẓuhūr al-ḥujja wal-akhbār al-maʾthūra fīhā ʿan āl al-ʿiṣma*, completed in 1069 in Mecca, MSS in Tehran and in the libraries of the Rājā of Faizabad and Hasan Ṣadr al-Dīn, *Dharīʿa* I, 94,456.—2. *Tatmīm al-Amal* by ʿAbd al-Nabī al-Qazwīnī, an *ijāza* for it, *Dharīʿa* I, 256,1350.

579. 4. Ind. Off. 1843/4, As. Soc. Beng. acq. 1903/7, no. 1089; on which *al-Ishārāt ilā mā takarrara min al-wasāʾil min al-iḥālāt* by ʿAbd al-Ṣāḥib b. Ḥasan al-Ṣaghīr b. al-Faqīh Ṣāḥib al-Jawāhir, d. 1352/1933 in Najaf, print. Najaf 1356, *Dharīʿa* II, 95,377.—10. *al-Durr al-maslūk fī akhbār al-anbiyāʾ wal-awṣiyāʾ wal-khulafāʾ wal-mulūk*, following Ibn al-Shiḥna's *Rawḍ al-manāẓir*, Teh. II, 545.—11. *al-Īqāẓ min al-hajʿa bil-burhān ʿala ʾl-rajʿa*, in many MSS, *Dharīʿa* II, 506,1985.

3b. *Arb. ḥad. fī ʾl-maʿārif*, with a commentary, *Dharīʿa* I, 407,2156; *al-Arbaʿīniyyāt li-kashf al-anwār al-Qudsiyyāt* ibid. I, 436,2209.

1299 | 580. 5, 1. *Dharīʿa* II, 261,$_{1063}$.—13. Ibid. II, 507,$_{1957}$.—17. *al-Iʿḍālāt al-ʿawīṣāt*, print. together with 4, 1317, ibid. II, 237,$_{942}$.

5. See p. 996,9.

581. 6, 2. *al-Aḥādīth al-nāfiʿa*, in a *majmūʿa* in the Madr. Sipāhsālār in Tehran, *Dharīʿa* I, 280,$_{1465}$.

6a. Ṣafī al-Dīn ʿAlī b. Ḥusayn b. ʿAlī al-Kāshifī al-Sabzawārī wrote, during the reign of Shāh Tahmāsp (930–84/1524–76), *Anīs al-ʿārifīn fī ʾl-mawāʿiẓ wal-naṣāʾiḥ wa-tafsīr baʿḍ al-āyāt wa-sharḥ baʿḍ al-akhbār etc.*, MS in the collection of Muḥammad ʿAlī al-Khwānsārī, *Dharīʿa* II, 461,$_{1788}$.

6b. Muḥammad b. ʿAbd al-Karīm al-Ṭabāṭabāʾī al-Iṣfahānī (*al-mawlid*) al-Burūjirdī (*al-maskin*), grandfather of Āyat Allāh Baḥr al-ʿUlūm, wrote *Ithbāt al-ʿiṣma lil-aʾimma al-ṭāhirīn min āyat* 2,$_{118}$, in the library of Muḥammad ʿAlī Khwānsārī in Najaf, *Dharīʿa* I, 97,$_{468}$.

6c. ʿAlī b. Muḥyi ʾl-Dīn al-Jāmiʿī al-ʿĀmilī, d. after 1035/1626 in Tūn, in Persia, *al-Irth*, in the library of Muḥsin al-Amīn al-ʿĀmilī, *Dharīʿa* I, 446,$_{2244}$.

6d. Jamāl al-Dīn Abū Manṣūr al-Ḥasan b. Zayn al-Dīn, *Ṣāḥib Maʿālim al-Dīn*, d. 1011/1602, *al-Ithnāʿashariyya fī ʾl-ṣalāt*, completed in 989/1581, in the libraries of Muḥammad Shīr and al-Ḥasan al-Ṣadr, *Dharīʿa* I, 116,$_{561}$.

6e. Rafīʿ al-Dīn Muḥammad b. Ḥaydar Mīrzā Rāfiʿī al-Nāʾīnī, d. 1080/1669, *Aqsām al-tashkīk wa-ḥaqīqatuhu*, print. in the margin of the *Sharḥ al-Hidāya*, 1313, *Dharīʿa* II, 271,$_{1094}$.

6f. Muḥammad al-Jīlānī Mollā Shamsā, a contemporary of al-Muḥaqqiq Āqā Ḥusayn al-Khwānsārī, d. 1098/1687, *Majmūʿat rasāʾil*, among which *Ithbāt al-wājib taʿālā* from his *al-Ḥikma al-mutaʿāliya* and a fragment (in Persian) from his *Kitāb al-taḥqīqāt fī aḥwāl al-mawjūdāt*, *R. ʿilm al-wājib*, *R. ḥudūth al-ʿālam* in the collection of ʿAbdallāh al-Burhān al-Sabzawārī, *Dharīʿa* I, 105,$_{513/4}$.—*Sharḥ Ḥikmat al-ʿayn* I, 848.

6g. Muḥammad b. al-Ḥasan al-Muḥaqqiq al-Shirwānī, d. 1098/1687, *Ithbāt al-wājib taʿālā*, Mashhad (not in the catalogue) and in the library of Muḥammad ʿAlī Khwānsārī, *Dharīʿa* I, 107, 523.

6h. Ḥaydar ʿAlī b. Muḥammad b. Ḥasan al-Shirwānī, a nephew of Muḥammad Bāqir Majlisī, d. after 1098/1686. 1. *Manāqib ahl al-bayt*, Būhār II, 210.—2. A short *risāla* on matters to do with prayer, Ind. Off. 1840.—3. On the length of a journey which admits of the abbreviation of one's prayers, ibid. 1841.—4. On the necessity of *al-ṣalāt ʿala ʾl-nabī*, ibid. 1842.—5. *Istinbāṭ al-aḥkām fī ʿaṣr ghaybat al-imām*, in a *majmūʿa* in the libraries of al-Ḥājj al-Sayyid ʿAlī al-Īrwānī in Tabriz and of Sayyid Muḥammad Aḥmad al-Sabzawārī, *Dharīʿa* II, 34,$_{130}$.

7a. Āqā Jamāl al-Dīn Muḥammad b. Āqā Ḥusayn b. Jamāl al-Dīn al-Khwānsārī al-Iṣfahānī, d. 1125/1713, *Ikhtiyārāt al-ayyām wal-saʿd wal-naḥs minhā wa-min al-layālī wal-sāʿāt*, composed for Shāh Sulaymān (d. 1105/1694), in a *majmūʿa* in the library of Ḥasan Ṣadr al-Dīn al-Kāẓimī, *Dharīʿa* I, 367,$_{1919}$.

7b. ʿAlī b. Muḥammad Ḥusayn al-Zanjānī, killed in 1136/1724, *Urjūza fi ʾl-kalām*, versification of *al-Bāb al-Ḥādī ʿashar*, in the library of the *Shaykh al-Islām* in Zanjan, *Dharīʿa* I, 494,$_{2433}$.

7c. Muḥammad Ashraf al-Qāʾinī al-Qazwīnī, d. 1136/1724 in Qazvin, *Ithbāt al-badʾa*, in the library of ʿAlī Muḥammad Najafābādī, d. 1332/1914, *Dharīʿa* I, 85,$_{206}$.

7c. Quṭb al-Dīn Muḥammad al-Dhahabī al-Shīrāzī, d. 1130/1718 in Qazvin, *Urjūza fi ʾl-ʿawāmil al-naḥwiyya*, in 320 verses with lots of digressions, the commentary by ʿAbd al-Amīr b. ʿAbdallāh al-Baṣrī, d. 1346/1927, *Nuzhat al-ṭālib*, part I, print. 1344 (where the author is said to be Jalāl al-Dīn al-Tibrīzī).—2. *Urjūza fī sharḥ al-ḥadīth*, together with *Naẓm al-laʾālīʾ fi ʾl-ṣarf*, in the library of Hādī al-Khurāsānī al-Ḥāʾirī, and together with *Mufriḥ al-awlād fi ʾl-ʿawāmil* by Mīrzā Abu ʾl-Ḥasan Khān and a Persian *Manẓūma fī uṣūl al-dīn* in *Dharīʿa* I, 486,$_{2414}$, and *Urjūza fi ʾl-fiqh wal-uṣūlayn wal-mawāzīn al-sharʿiyya*, ibid. 490,$_{2423}$—

7d. Khalīl b. Muḥammad Zamān al-Qazwīnī | wrote, in 1148/1735, *Ithbāt ḥudūth* 1300
al-irāda wa-ithbāt azaliyyatihā wa-annahumā min ṣifāt al-fiʿl lā min ṣifāt al-dhāt, in the library of Muḥammad Nāṣir al-Ḥusaynī al-Ṭihrānī, *Dharīʿa* I, 88,$_{424}$.

7e. Muḥammad b. al-Ḥājj Muḥammad Zamān b. al-Ḥusayn b. Muḥammad Riḍā b. Ḥusām al-Dīn al-Kāshānī (*mawlidan*) al-Iṣfahānī (*maskinan*) al-Najafī (*madfanan*) wrote, in 1163/1750, *al-Ithnāʿashariyya fi ʾl-qibla*, in the library of Muḥammad Sulṭān al-Mutakallimīn in Tehran, *Dharīʿa* I, 118,$_{593}$.

7f. In 1180/1766, during a sea voyage, Muḥammad b. Muḥammad Shāh Muḥammad al-Iṣṭahbahānī al-Shīrāzī wrote *Ithbāt ʿālam al-mithāl*, in the library of Ḥasan Ṣadr al-Dīn, *Rawḍat al-ʿĀrifīn*, a commentary on *al-Ṣaḥīfa al-kāmila* (I, 76), ibid. *Dharīʿa* I, 96,$_{465}$.

582. 5. See p. 828, 988, *Kashf al-āyāt* additionally Mosul 102,$_{47}$.

6. 2. Print. in *Majmūʿa min al-manẓūmāt al-mukhtaṣara*, Tabriz 1300, *Dharīʿa* I, 496,$_{2444}$.

583. § 5. 3. Alex. Mawāʿiẓ 21.

4. 2. Garr. 473.

584. 5, 2. Abstract *al-Aṣfā* in the margin of one of its printings, MS in the library of Ḥasan Ṣadr al-Dīn, *Dharīʿa* II, 124,$_{496}$.—3. Actually a commentary on his *Muʿtamad al-shīʿa*, Ind. Off. 1833.—5. Ind. Off. 1834.—8. Abstract *Anwār al-ḥikma* in numerous MSS, *Dharīʿa* II, 425,$_{1674}$.

585. 17. *Dharīʿa* II, 178,$_{656}$, MSS in Najaf and Tehran, ibid. II, 211,$_{824}$.—18. Teh. Sip. II, 388/9.—28. In *Majmūʿat rasāʾilihi*, 1311, *Dharīʿa* II, 398,$_{1595}$.—33. *Risāla fī shakkiyyāt al-ṣalāt*, Ind. Off. 1836.—34. *Ahamm mā yuʿmal fī ʾl-yawm wal-nahār wal-usbūʿ wal-sana*, two MSS in *Dharīʿa* II, 485,$_{1902a}$.

586. 8. Read: al-Tanukābunī.—2. *Ithbāt al-ṣāniʿ al-qadīm bil-burhān al-qāṭiʿ al-qawīm*, in the library of Muḥammad ʿAlī Khwānsārī, *Dharīʿa* I, 96,$_{463}$.

6. 1. *Dharīʿa* II, 446,$_{1729}$.—9. *Zahr al-rabīʿ* (anthology), Bank. XXIII, 131,$_{2617/8}$ (which has Muḥammad b. ʿAbdallāh b. Muḥammad).

10. 5. *Dharīʿa* II, 424,$_{1671}$.

587. § 6, 1a. See p. 1015,$_{22}$.

1d. See p. 1014,$_{15}$.

589. 37. *Iksīr al-ʿārifīn fī maʿrifat ṭarīq al-ḥaqq al-yaqīn*, completed in 1031/1622, in *Majmūʿat rasāʾilihi*, Tehran 1313, *Dharīʿa* II, 279,$_{1133}$.—38. *al-Asʾila al-Jīlāniyya*, asked by his student ʿAlam al-Dīn Muḥammad al-Jīlānī, print. with no. 27, ibid. II, 81,$_{321}$.—39. *al-Asʾila al-Naṣīriyya*, questions by Naṣīr al-Dīn al-Ṭūsī addressed

to Shams al-Dīn al-Khusrawshāhī, who did not answer them, print. after no. 27 and after the *Sharḥ al-Hidāya*, ibid. II, 93$_{,368}$.

590. 4. See p. 577, 1l.—3. Ind. Off. 1507.

591. 1, 5. Garr. 997 (which has *Risāla fī maʿrifat awqāt al-ghurūb*).—6. ibid. 1307.

1a. 5. Autograph dated 929, NO 2932.—14. A Persian work on the astrolabe, Arabic transl. *al-Risāla al-muʿarraba*, Br. Mus. Suppl. 760,3, Bank. XXII, 54$_{,2463}$.

3. See p. 1024$_{,72}$, Bank. XXII, 15$_{,2420}$.

592. 1, 1. Berl. Oct. 2081, Garr. 1122/3, Mashhad XVI, 5$_{,17/8}$.

1a. Zayn al-Dīn ʿAlī ʿArab wrote, for Shāh Ismāʿīl I (907–30/1501–24) who had named him *shaykh al-Islām* in Herat 928/1522, *Ādāb al-nikāḥ*, print. Tehran, *Dharīʿa* I, 33$_{,161}$.

2. See p. 1030,30.

4. 2. Pers. *al-Afyūniyya*, Mashhad XVI, 2$_{,15}$.—3. *R. i bīkhi čīnī*, ibid. 20$_{,61}$.

5. 2. *al-Adwiya al-qalbiyya*, Mashhad XVI, 2$_{,15}$.

6. Read: al-Tanukābunī, *Tuḥfat al-muʾminīn*, Mashhad XVI, 7$_{,22,4}$.

593. § 11. 1. His father Muḥammad Ṣadr al-Ḥaqīqa Shadr al-ʿUlamāʾ wal-Ḥukamāʾ b. Mīr Ghiyāth al-Dīn Manṣūr b. Ṣadr al-Dīn Muḥammad, b. 2 Shaʿbān 828/20 June | 1425 and killed by Turkmens on 12 Ramaḍān 903/5 May 1498, 1301
wrote: *Ithbāt al-wājib taʿālā*, copies in Najaf and Tehran, library of Naṣrallāh al-Taqawī, *Dharīʿa* I, 108$_{,526}$.—10. Garr. 1299.—11. Ibid. 1300 (or *Ḥujjat al-kalām li-īḍāḥ maḥajjat al-Islām*.—16. Bank. XXII, 104$_{,2471,\text{iii}}$ (with a mistaken: al-Ṣufayr).—17. Library of Muḥammad ʿAlī al-Khwānsārī, *Dharīʿa* I, 378$_{,1967}$.—24. *al-Risāla al-zakiyya fi ʾl-tawfīq bayna ʾl-sharīʿa wal-ḥikma*, A. Taymūr, Ḥikma 111.

594. 1b. Abstract, *Asāmi ʾl-ʿulūm waṣṭilāḥātuhā*, in the library of Muḥammad Ṣadr al-Dīn in Kāẓimayn, *Dharīʿa* II, 9$_{,23}$.

1c. His student Fakhr al-Dīn Muḥammad b. Ḥusayn al-Ḥusaynī, *Ādāb al-munāẓara*, 2 MSS in Mashhad, *Dharīʿa* I, 321$_{,55}$.

595. 4. Read: al-Jabāʾī, *RAAD* IX, 348.—1. Alex. Ḥad. 31, *Dharīʿa* I, 425$_{,2180}$.—2. Pers. *Ādābi ʿAbbāsī*, in the library of al-Ḥājj ʿImād, ibid. I, 24/5$_{,127}$.—6. Hamb. Or. Sem. 123, Garr. 998/9, Alex. Fun. 65$_{,1}$, Bank. XXII, 48$_{,2457}$.—Comm. d. Bank. XXII, 104$_{,2472i}$.—g. ʿIṣmatallāh b. Aʿẓam b. ʿAbd al-Rasūl al-Sahāranpūrī, 11th cent., Bank. XXII, 49$_{,2458}$, 102$_{,2470i}$, 103$_{,2471i}$.—h. Muḥammad Rashīd al-Dīn, 11th cent., ibid. 50$_{,2459}$.—7. Bank. XXII, 102$_{,2470ii}$.—Comm. *Sawāniḥ al-qarīḥa* by Muḥammad ʿAlī Fakhr al-Dīn al-Ḥusaynī al-Mawṣilī, Alex. Ḥisāb 53$_{,1}$.—8. Garr. 1043/4, 2086$_{,1}$, Alex. Ḥisāb 8, 56, Fun. 65$_{,15}$, 99$_{,3}$, Bank. XXII, 16$_{,2421/2}$.

596. 8. Comm. b. Bank. XXII, 18$_{,2424}$.—c. Garr. 2086$_{,2}$.—d. Bank. XXII, 105$_{,2472ii}$.—e. ibid. 18$_{,2423}$, Rāmpūr 49.—f. Garr. 2086.—h. Ind. Off. 762 (*G.* II, 415, c) continued by Muḥammad Ashraf b. Ḥabīballāh al-Ḥasanī al-Ḥusaynī al-Ṭabāṭabāʾī, Bank. XXII, 20$_{,2425}$.—n. During the reign of M. IV (1058–99/1648–87), Alex. Ḥisāb 16, Garr. 2086$_{,2}$ (which has ʿAbd al-Raḥīm), 2087, 2138$_{,1}$.—9. Teh. Sip. II, 389/90. Comm. a. The large one, *al-Ḥadāʾiq al-nadiyya*, ibid. 353/4, the small one, *al-Farāʾid al-bahiyya*, ibid. 354/5.—d. Muḥammad b. ʿAbd al-Ghanī ʿAbd al-ʿAẓīm al-Ḥasanī, 12th cent., ibid. 355.—11. Bank. XXIII, 127$_{,2612/4}$, anon. abstract ibid. 2615.

597. 17. Ind. Off. 1510, Pers. print. 1302.—Comm. h. Ind. Off. 1824/6.—Versif. Alex. Uṣūl 12.—18. Read: Būhār 186, Ind. Off. 1814/7, Madr. al-Fāḍiliyya in Mashhad, *Dharīʿa* I, 113$_{,547}$.—19. Library of Ṣadr al-Dīn in Mashhad, *Dharīʿa* I, 117$_{,565}$.—43. *al-Ithnaiʿashariyya fī manāsik al-ḥajj*, Ind. Off. 1822/3, *Dharīʿa* I, 115$_{,558}$.—44. *al-Ithnaiʿashariyyāt al-khams fī ʾl-ṭahāra wal-ṣalāt wal-zakāt wal-ṣawm wal-ḥajj*, Mashhad V, 21, *Dharīʿa* I, 113$_{,547}$.—45. al-*Ithnaiʿashariyya fī wājibāt al-ṣalāt al-yawmiyya*, comm. 1092/1681, Ind. Off. 1818/21, *Dharīʿa* I, 117$_{,563}$ = (?) *al-Ithn. al-ṣalātiyya*, on which the commentary *al-Anwār al-bahiyya* by Nūr al-Dīn ʿAlī b. ʿAlī b. Ḥasan al-Mūsawī al-ʿĀmilī, d. 1067/1657, in the library of Qāsim b. Ḥasan Āl Muḥyi ʾl-Dīn al-Jāmiʿī in Najaf, *Dharīʿa* II, 421$_{,662}$.—46. *al-Ithn. fī ʾl-khums wal-zakāt*, Ind. Off. 1827/8, *Dharīʿa* I, 116$_{,563}$.—47. *Ithbāt al-anwār al-ilāhiyya*, Rāġib 1460, *Dharīʿa* I, 85$_{,405}$.—48. *Risāla fī masʾalat al-jabr wal-ikhtiyār* Rāġib 1460, c.—49. *Risāla fī maʿna ʾl-ḥadīth al-Qudsī* ibid. 1460, a.—*Risāla fī ādāb al-tawḥīd*, ibid. b.—51. *Risāla fī taḍārīs al-arḍ*, Alex. Ḥisāb 39$_{,2}$.—52. *Urjūza fī taʾrīkh al-maʿṣūmīn al-arbaʿata ʿashar*, *Dharīʿa* I, 465$_{,2325}$.—52. *al-Asʾila al-tafsīriyya*, ibid. II, 79$_{,312}$.—53. *al-Asʾila al-Jazariyya*, ibid. II, 80$_{,321}$.—54. *al-Asʾila al-Shadqamiyya* by Zayn al-Dīn Aḥmad b. Badr al-Dīn Ḥasan b.

Aḥmad b. Shadqam, in the library of Sayyid Sulaymān Āqā al-Tustarī, ibid. II, $87_{,345}$.

| 598. 4. See p. 572, 4.—2. *al-Hadiyya, sharḥ al-Wajīz fī 'l-farā'iḍ* (anon.), Ind. Off. 1758/61. 1302

600. 6, 1. Read: *Shamāmat.*—2. Composed in 1193/6, Garr. 136, Bank. XXIII, $147_{,2641}$, print. Hyderabad.

602. 1, 1. Garr. 1406/7.—2. Read *ḥukm* and *umm*, Dam. Z. $73_{,36,1}$.—2. *Qaṭʿ al-jidāl bi-taḥqīq mas'alat al-istibdāl*, ibid. 2.

2a. Ghawthallāh b. Khaṭīr al-Dīn al-Hindī, d. 970/1562.—1. *al-Akhbār wal-anbā' bi-shaʿā'ir dhawi 'l-qurbā*, Garr. 2009,1.—2. *al-Asmā' al-Suhrawardiyya wal-duʿā' bihā*, ibid. 6.

603. 5, 14. *Asānīd*, Alex. Fun. $123_{,6}$.

604. 1a. Ind. Off. 1704, Calc. Madr. 306.

2. See p.$964_{,10}$.—3. Ind. Off. 1706/10.—*Majmaʿ al-barakāt*, ibid. 1701/2.

2a. ʿIṣmatallāh b. Zayn b. ʿAbd al-Rasūl al-Sahāranpūrī, d. 1039/1629 (Loth 759, *Tadhk. ʿUlamā' Hind* 140), *Bayān al-amr bil-maʿrūf wal-nahy ʿani 'l-munkar*, Ind. Off. 1697.—2. On the unlawfulness of music and singing, ibid. 1855.—3. *Sharh Tashrīḥ al-aflāk* see ad p. 595.

605. 5. *Tadhk. ʿUl. Hind.* 6.—*Ḥasab al-muftī*, Ind. Off. 1703 (which has Abu 'l-Ghāzī ʿUbaydallāh al-Shaybānī, 940–6/1533–9).

11. Ind. Off. 1689/91.

606. 13. Ind. Off. 1701 (during the reign of Awrangzīb).

13a. Ḍiyā' al-Dīn Yūsuf b. Qāsim al-Astarābādhī completed, in 1098/1687 in Awrangābād, a short treatise on the times of the daily prayers, Ind. Off. 1845.

13b. Muḥammad ʿĪsā Sindhī Burhānpūrī wrote, in 1137/1725, *Risāla fi 'khtilāf ḥurmat al-samāʿ wal-ghinā'*, Ind. Off. 1856.

13c. Sirāj al-Dīn ʿAlī Khān Akbarābādī, d. 1169/1756 (*Tadhk. ʿUl. Hind* 7), *Jāmiʿ al-taʿzīrāt min kutub al-thiqāt*, Ind. Off. 1718, Rāmpūr 181,$_{118}$.

13d. *Badr al-Hāshimī al-Qurāshī* wrote, at the instigation of his teacher Muḥammad Jān Ṣiddīq, *Mukhkh al-uṣūl*, Ind. Off. 1498.

14. See p. 976,$_{46}$.

18. See p. 910,$_{55}$.

607. § 5a. 1, 2. Read: *al-Ṣawārim al-muḥriqa.*

1a. Shāh Ṭāhir b. Raḍī al-Dīn al-Ismāʿīlī al-Ḥusaynī al-Kāshānī, who died in 952/1545 after having converted Niẓāmshāh b. Aḥmad Shāh of the Deccan to Shīʿism, wrote: *Unmūdhaj al-ʿulūm*, in the library of the Rājā of Faizabad, *Dharīʿa* II, 406,$_{1624}$.

608. 1, 4. C. 1326, *Dharīʿa* I, 290,$_{1521}$.—6. Read: *masḥ.*

6. Al-Fāḍil al-Hindī Bahāʾ al-Dīn Muḥammad b. Tāj al-Dīn Ḥasan al-Iṣfahānī, d. 1195/1781, *Iḥālat al-naẓar fi ʾl-qaḍāʾ wal-qadar*, in the library of Muḥammad Riḍā Kāshif al-Ghiṭāʾ in Najaf, *Dharīʿa* I, 280,$_{1466}$.

§ 5b. 1. See p. 563,$_{1}$.

615. 3, 8. Alex. Fun. 135,$_{2}$.—11. Ibid. 135,$_{4}$.

617. 1c. Alex. Taṣawwuf 41.—2. *al-Tuḥfa etc.*, Alex. Taṣ. 42,$_{8}$, 49, Fun. 88,$_{8}$, 135,$_{1}$, 150,$_{10}$, 151,$_{8}$.

618. 4, 1. Alex. Taṣ. 46.

619. 11. See: Les entretiens de Lahore (entre le prince imperial Dāra Šikuh et l'ascète hindou Babāhāl Dās, en 1653) par Cl. Huart et L. Massignon, *JA*, 1926, 285/334.

12a. ʿAbd al-Raḥmān b. Jalāl al-Dīn b. ʿAbd al-Karīm al-Hindī ca. 1100/1688, *Risāla Ṣūfiyya* (on the terminology of the Naqshbandiyya), Garr. 1592.

623. III, Ind. Off. 1489/93; instead of Aymara, read: Aligarh.

624. 3, 4. Ind. Off. 1494.—6. = (?) Mawlānā Muḥammad Ḥasan, ibid. 1496.—11. Anon., ibid. 1495, 1497.

5. 1. See p. 952$_{,51}$.

625. 8. Read: EI I, 607.—2. Read: p. 624.—5. *Risāla fī bayān al-ḥadīth*, | Rāmpūr 1303
I, 126.—6. *al-Risāla al-saniyya*, ibid. 342.—7. *Risāla fī waḥdat al-wujūd*, ibid. 343$_{,328}$.

11. See I, 847$_{,24}$.—*Badīʿ al-mīzān*, with glosses by Jalāl b. Nāṣir Čannabī, ca. 1019/1610, in abstract Kanpur.

12. Muḥammad Faḍl al-Imām, *al-Mirqāt al-mīzāniyya*, on which a Persian comm. by ʿAlī Ḥasan Bhōpālī, *Hadiyye'i Shāhjahāniyye*, Kanpur 1296.

626. 4b. ʿAbdallāh al-Aʿlam wrote, in 1028/1619 for Muḥammad Qulī Quṭbshāh, *al-Farīda fi 'l-ṭibb* and *al-Iṣṭilāḥāt al-ṭibbiyya*, in the library of Muḥammad Majd al-Dīn al-Shīrāzī, *Dharīʿa* II, 122$_{,2192}$.

627. § 9b. Astrology. Ashraf Sharīf al-Ḥusaynī b. al-Sharīf dedicated to Sultan ʿAlī ʿĀdilshāh (965–87/1557–79) of Bījāpūr: *Najm al-ʿulūm*, Bank. XXII, 115$_{,2483}$.

§ 10. 1. *Rawḍāt al-jannāt* 412.—2. Garr. 511.

628. 4. Teh. Sip. II, 401/2.—Garr. 570, Indian printing 1304 (?). *Anwār al-badīʿ*, Bank. XXIII, 59$_{,2553/6}$.—7. Teh. Sip. II, 204/9.

§ 11. 1. See p. 954$_{,66}$.

629. 8, 3. *Kitāb al-ṣalāt*, Garr. 1975.

630. 5. Read: ʿĀrif. 1. Garr. 580.—2. Ibid. 223.—3. Ibid. 578.

§ 1a. 3. Muṣṭafā b. Muḥammad al-Burūsawī Khusrawzāde, d. 998/1590.—2. *Majmaʿ al-ʿibārāt ʿalā afṣaḥ al-lughāt*, Alex. Lugha 26.

3b. Instead of al-Shamsī, read: al-Shimnī (?).

631. 5b. Read: al-ʿAyshī; Garr. 563.—2. *Rūḥ al-shurūḥ*, see p. 657.

632. 8. Garr. 476, Alex. Naḥw 41.

9a. Muṣṭafā al-Qīral-Shahrī (! from Qyrshahr) al-Marʿashī, d. after 1138/1725, *Majmūʿa*, Garr. 225.

9b. Maḥmūd al-Anṭākī, Sayyid Ḥāfiẓ, see p. $329_{,3,6}$.

633. 1a. ʿAlī b. Muḥammad al-Laḥmī al-Ishbīlī al-Maghribī wrote, in 923/1517, *al-Durr al-muṣān fī sīrat al-Muẓaffar Selīm Khan*, Serāi Baghdād Köšk 197.

4. 2. Autograph dated 965, Garr. 704/5.—4. Garr. 1136.—*Madīnat al-ʿulūm*, Br. Mus. Or. 9242.

634. 13. Garr. 907/10, 2099,3, Alex. Fun. $120_{,2}$. Self-commentary, Garr. 911/2, glosses by Khalīl b. Ḥasan al-Sīrawī, Garr. 913, by Aḥmad b. ʿUmar b. Muḥammad, ʿAlī Alex. Fun. $79_{,2}$.—20. Garr. 572.—25. *Risāla fī ʾl-waḍʿ*, Br. H.[2] $448_{,7}$.

635. 5, 1. Transl. Rescher, Stuttgart 1934 (which has ʿAlī Mynyq).—2. Read: *Ifāḍāt al-fattāḥ*.

636. 1. *Kešf al-zunun Birinci Cilt, Katip Čelebi*, Istanbul Maarif Matbaasi 1941 (ed. Šerefettin Yaltkaya ile Kilisli Rifat Bilge).

637. 9a, 1. 1. Barthold, *Iran* 1927, 52.

9b. = 414, 13a, see Kračkovsky, *al-Andalus* III (1935), 92.

638. First paragraph, delete: "Is he etc.".

§ 3. 2. See p. $910_{,49}$.

639. 7. Garr. 226 (wrong).

7a. Muḥammad b. Mustaqīm, professor at the Madrasa Sayyid Ḥasan Pāshā in Istanbul, d. 30 Muḥarram 1164/29 December 1750, *al-Khaṭṭ al-mustaqīm fī ʾl-ṭarīq al-mustaqīm* (collection of anecdotes), Bank. XXIII, $134_{,2620}$ (for his son Sulaymān, see I, 286).

8. Garr. 1929.

640. 3, 2. *Risāla fī 'l-siyāsa al-sharʿiyya*, Alex. Fun. 162,$_{5}$, Fiqh Ḥan. 31.

641. 3, 2. Alex. Fiqh Ḥan. 61.

3a. See p. 325,$_{8}$, Garr. 1774, Alex. Fiqh Ḥan. 65.

3b. *Tafsīr*, Berl. Qu. 1591.

642. 7, 1. BDMG 38, Ind. Off. 1705, Garr. 1739/40, Mosul in many copies.

643. f. Alex. Fiqh Ḥan. 25.—k. Garr. 1741.—o. Read: Ismāʿīl Efendi al-Sīwāsī. |— r. *Sabk al-anhur ʿalā farāʾiḍ Multaqa 'l-abḥur* by ʿAlāʾ al-Dīn b. Nāṣir 1304
al-Dīn al-Ṭarābulusī al-Dimashqī al-Ḥanafī, completed in 999/1582, Alex. Fun. 107,$_{5}$.—4. Alex. Fiqh Ḥan. 40, 61, Fun. 97,$_{6}$.—11. *Naẓm sīrat al-nabī wa-sharḥuhu*, Garr. 652.—12. *Risāla fī tawjīh al-tashbīh*, Alex. Fun. 64.

644. 9. Alex. Fiqh Ḥan. 41.

10. 1. Garr. 706, 1. Vat. 1460,2.—8. *al-Risāla al-qalamiyya*, Garr. 214,$_{4}$.—10. With the title *Risāla fī dawarān al-Ṣūfiyya wa-raqṣihim* in Alex. Fun. 172,1.

646. 19. See p. 945,$_{163}$.

22. *Muftī* of Wardār, *Tartīb zībā* additionally Mosul 183,$_{221}$, 293,$_{2}$.

23. 1. Mosul 147,$_{115,2}$.—4. Read: Mosul 160, 177,$_{2}$.

23a. ʿAṭāʾallāh al-Qāḍī Nawʿīzāde, d. 1044/1634, *al-Qawl al-ḥasan fī jawāb al-qawl li-man* (!) *fī 'l-qaḍāʾ wal-fatwā*, Alex. Fiqh Ḥan. 46.

647. 26a, 1. Garr. 2097,$_{1}$.—2. Ibid. 2002,$_{11}$.—3. Ibid. 13.

27. See p. 525, 2c.—Read: Mosul 239.—a. Alex. Tawḥīd 4.

28. 1. BDMG 40.

648. 29. Additionally Mosul 131,$_{17}$, 181,$_{154}$, Alex. Fun. 36.

32. 53 *rasāʾil* in Alex. Fun. 295/7,$_{21/74}$.

649. 67. *Fatwā fī bay‘ al-dukhān*, Alex. Fun. $157_{,11}$.

32c. Aḥmad b. Ḥusayn b. Aḥmad al-Kirīdī wrote, in 1118/1707, *Risāla fiqhiyya*, Garr. 1863.

32d. ‘Aṭā’allāh Efendi, Shaykh al-Islām, d. 1127/1715, *Qiṭa‘ mukhtāra min fatāwī*, Alex. Fiqh Ḥan. 46.

32e. Ṣan‘allāh b. ‘Alī al-Ḥanafī, Qāḍī fī Qusṭanṭīniyya, wrote, in 1130/1718: *Marāṣid al-khitām*, Alex. Fiqh Ḥan. 62.

650. 3, 3. BDMG 110.

651. 4, 1. *ShN* II, 81. 1. Garr. 1302/4, Mosul $64_{,228}$, $125_{,59}$, $210_{,51}$, on which anon. *Kalām ḥawl Tafsīr Abi ’l-Su‘ūd*, ibid. 119, $296_{,4}$.—10. Comm. Mosul $164_{,3,2}$.—18. Alex. Fun. 78.—20. *Risāla fī waqf al-manqūl wal-nuqūd*, Garr. $2085_{,2}$ Alex. Fun. $101_{,1}$; against this is *Risāla fī ibṭāl waqf al-nuqūd* by al-Mawlā Muḥyi ’l-Dīn Muḥammad b. Ilyās Jāwīzāde, d. 954/1547, Alex. Fun. $101_{,2}$.—21. *Fatwā fī taḥlīl qatl al-Yazīdiyya*, translated from the Turkish on the order of Sultan Süleymān, Mosul $264_{,9}$.

652. 6b. Ḥasan b. Umm Sinān Imāmzāde, d. 1088/1677, *al-Majālis al-Sināniyya al-kabīra*, on individual passages from the Qur’ān, ḤKh VI, $627_{,14933}$, Qaw. I, 260/1, abstract ibid. 261, Istanbul 1260, 1288 (Sarkīs 1054).

653. 9, 2. Turkish transl. Rieu, Turk. Mss. $237_{,xxii}$.—11. *Wāridāt kubrā* in the library of Wafā’, *Osm. Mü’ell.* I, 31.—12. 1. see p. 948,5.—6. *al-Anwār al-asmā’iyya fī sharḥ al-asmā’ al-nabawiyya*, Alex. Ta’r. 4.

654. 1. Alex. Mawā‘iẓ 14.—3. 7 *rasā’il* in Alex. Fun. 194.—1. Alex. Fun. $78_{,9}$, Fiqh Ḥan. 56.—2. Garr. $2088_{,2}$, Alex. Fun. $78_{,7}$, comm. by Aḥmad al-Rūmī, d. ca. 1040/1630, Garr. $2046_{,3}$, $2088_{,1}$.—5. Garr. 1924, Alex. Fun. $78_{,1}$, Mawā‘iẓ 13, Mosul $129_{,125}$, abstract ibid. $76_{,83,2}$.—a. Alex. Taṣ. 78/9.—8. Alex. Fun. $119_{,2}$.

655. Garr. $2085_{,3}$, Alex. Fiqh Ḥan. 56, 65, Fun. $78_{,12}$, $164_{,3}$.—c. Āṣaf. II, $1106_{,15}$ (corrupted).—d. Read: al-Erzerūmī, Rāġib 527.—10. Anon., comm. Mosul $174_{,48}$.—11. Alex. Fiqh Ḥan. 54.—Comm. by Isḥāq b. Ḥasan al-Zanjānī, Alex. Fiqh Ḥan. 54.—12. Garr. 1880, Alex. Fun. $78_{,2}$.—15. BDMG 28.—b. Garr. 1922/3.—c. Abstract *al-‘Urwa al-Wuthqā al-Ṣamadiyya* by Aḥmad b. Aḥmad al-Salāwī al-Mālikī al-Shādhilī al-Aḥmadī al-Shāwī, Alex. Taṣ. 24.—k. Alex. Taṣ. 48.

| 656. 16. Garr. 2029,$_{2}$, 2176,$_{1}$, Alex. Fun. 66,$_{5}$, 78,$_{8}$.—17. Glosses by Aṭālīzāde, 1305
Garr. 385, Istanbul 1260, 1270.—20. BDMG 69d, Garr. 468, Alex. Mawāʿiẓ 33.—Comm. a. Garr. 469/70.

657. c. Garr. 471.—3. Ibid. 472.—21. Alex. Naḥw 33.—Comm. b. Garr. 466/7.—c. Ibid. 464/5.—d. α Alex. Naḥw 35,1, Istanbul 1298.—e. Additionally Mosul 1148,$_{134}$ on which glosses by Mollā Ḥāmid al-Sūsī, ibid. 2; *al-kabīr*, ibid. 137,$_{274,75}$.—h. Muḥammad Khāliṣ, d. after 1229/1814, Garr. 481.—i. Güzelḥiṣārī, Alex. Naḥw 378.—25. Garr. 305/6, Alex. Fun. 175,$_{1}$.—25. b. BDMG 90, see page 631,5b.

658. 25, f. Garr. 307.—h. *al-Maṭlūb* by Shihāb al-Dīn Aḥmad b. Muḥammad b. al-Mughriṭ, d. 912/1507, Gotha 205,$_{1}$, Paris 4189, Bodl. II, 418,$_{2}$, Garr. 308.—i. *al-Shukriyya*, by Ibn al-ʿImād, Garr. 310.—k. Anon., *Ḍiyāʾ al-qulūb wa-tanwīr al-Maqṣūd*, ibid. 308.—36. Alex. Fun. 194,$_{14}$.—42. *Risāla fi ʾl-naḥw*, Mosul 40,$_{250,2}$.—43. *Ādāb al-baḥth*, comm. by al-Marʿashī Sāčaqlīzāde, d. 1150/1737, Alex. Ādāb 11,$_{6}$.—44. *Risāla fī ḥall masʾala fi ʾl-waqf*, Alex. Fun. 95,$_{12}$.—45. *Risāla fī tafḍīl al-ghanī al-shākir ʿala ʾl-faqīr al-ṣābir*, ibid. 102,$_{1}$.—46. *Risāla fī dam al-ḥayḍ wa-aḥkāmih*, ibid. 78,$_{6}$.

7. 1. Additionally Mosul 262,5.

659. 9. a. See p. 303,$_{9}$.

9d. Alex. Fun. 67,$_{9}$.

660. 1b. See p. 644, 9b. 2. *Taḍlīl al-taʾwīl*, print. see Brussali M. Ṭāhir, *ʿOM.*, loc. cit.

3b. Read: Raḍī al-Dīn Rajab b. Muḥammad b. Rajab al-Ḥāfiẓ al-Birsī, belongs to p. 210.

661. 3b, 1. Composed in 773/1371.—3. *Mashāriq al-amān*, composed in 811/1408.—4. *Kitāb al-alfayn fī waṣf sādat al-kawnayn*, MS in al-Madrasa al-Ḥusayniyya, *Dharīʿa* II, 299,$_{1200}$.

4. ʿAbd al-Ḥakīm (Ḥalīm) b. Muḥammad al-Ḥanafī Akhīzāde, as a poet with the *nom de plume* ʿḤalīmīʾ, d. 1013/1605, Brussali, *ʿOM*, I, 228.—2. *Hadiyyat al-mahdiyyīn* (*fi ʾl-fiqh*), Garr. 1651.—3. *Rasāʾil*, Vat. V, 1395.

6\. 13. *Dīwān Hudāʾī,* Mosul 42,13.

6a. Read: *ʿOM* I, 23.

662\. 7, 1. Garr. 1506, Mosul 165$_{,15}$.

8a. ʿAlī al-Jisr al-Kutāhī al-Germiyānī al-Qaraḥiṣārī wrote, in 1074/1664, *al-Minhāj al-Muḥammadi al-Aḥmadī,* Garr. 1928.

10\. Read: 1041/1639.

10a. In BDMG 21, with the title *Ghunyat al-s.*, a comm. on a prayer called *Wird al-sattār,* Berl. 3795$_{,21}$, Brussali, *ʿOM* I, 97 (with a mistaken: d. ca. 1000).

663\. 15, 2. Read: *al-Wasīla.*

664\. 16, 2. Garr. 1597.—4. *Mukhtaṣar* by ʿUllaysh (see p. 735), print. C. n.d., comm. a. *Tuḥfat al-basmala* by Aḥmad b. Ḥasan al-Qaramānī, d. 1190/1776, MS Ḥamīd.—b. *Risālat al-b.* by Muḥammad ʿAlī Qaramānī Arzanjānī (during the reign of ʿAbdul Ḥamīd I), ibid. see p. 738$_{,4,7}$.—11. *Muqaddima fi ʾl-manṭiq,* Alex. Fun. 100$_{,3}$.—12. *Asʾila ʿuriḍat ʿalā Abī Saʿīd al-Khadīmī ajāba ʿanhā Muḥammad Ḥayāt al-Sindī al-Madanī,* d. 1163/1750 (p. 522, 6a), ibid. 1014.

19\. Muḥammad b. Yūsuf al-Ḥalabī al-Nahālī al-Ruhāwī, d. 1185/1771 in Istanbul, 1. *al-Sirr al-ilāhī al-munajjī min waswasat al-lāhī,* composed in 1144/1731, NO 2416 (see G II, 344, 15).—2. A treatise on the depravity of Sufism in his days, composed in 1116/1704, Paris 4591$_{,3}$.—3. *Jāmiʿ al-jawāhir wal-laʾāliʾ,* see I, 765$_{,22}$.—4. *Bayān mā ḥawāhu taʾrīkh al-Waṣṣāf min al-tarākīb al-ʿarabiyya,* Cairo^2 III, 40 (the same?).—5. *Minḥat al-ṣamad,* see I, 750, 32d (the same?).

§ 9. 1 b. Muḥammad b. al-Ḥājj Ḥumayd al-Kaffawī, *Risālat al-ādāb,* Alex. Ādāb 11, comm. by ʿUmar b. Ḥusayn al-Qaraḥiṣārī al-Sharqī, ibid. 2.

1306 | 665. § 10. 1. Brussali, *ʿOM* III, 298/9, Suter 457.—7. *Risālat al-jayb al-jāmiʿa,* Garr. 2006$_{,20}$.

2\. 1. Alex. Fun. 65$_{,8}$.—5. Ibid. 7.

2a. ʿUthmān al-Muhtadī al-Tarjumān bi-Qalʿat Bulghār, d. after 960/1553, *Hadiyyat al-Muhtadī fī ʿilm al-hayʾa wal-misāḥa wa-ramy al-khumbara* (to be read thus) *wa-ḥafr al-lughm,* Garr. 1056.

3. Taqī al-Dīn Muḥammad b. Mollā Maʿrūf b. Aḥmad al-Rāṣid, b. 927/1521, d. 993/1585 in Istanbul, see p. 484,$_{6}$.

666. § 11, 1. Brussali, *ʿOM* III, 239. 1. Garr. 1112, Alex. Ṭibb 20.

2. *ʿOM* III, 224 (which has "d. 1080"). 1. AS 3682, Mosul 33,$_{144}$, 129,$_{118}$, 270,$_{29}$, according to Abdulhakk Adnan, *La Science chez les Turcs ottomans*, Paris 1939, 96ff, different from *al-Ghāya fī 'l-ṭibb*, Berl. 6315.

667. 2, 4. *Aqrābādhīn*, Mosul 299,$_{1}$.

3. Brussali, *ʿOM* III, 232. 2. *Khulāṣat al-ṭibb*, Turkish in Rāġib 945.

§ 12. See Khalīl Mardam Bek, *RAAD* IV, 57/9.—1. Cairo, *Nashra* 12.—2. *Zayn al-iḥsān fī ʿilm taʾlīf al-awzān*, NO 3655.

§ 13. 3. *Bulūgh al-amal fī taḥqīq daʿwa 'l-mushtari 'l-ḥabal*, Garr. 2002,$_{14}$ (see p. 976,$_{43}$).

§ 14. 2, 2. Taymūr, Ṭab. 68,$_{1}$.

668. 2, 12. Taymūr, Ṭab. 68,4.—13. See p. 1034,7.

§ 15. 2. *Rasāʾil* additionally Lālelī 2433 (*ZDMG* 66, 256), Mosul 117,$_{212}$ (9 *rasāʾil*), Alex. Fun. 169/70, 153/4,$_{7}$ (41 *rasāʾil*), 165,$_{1}$, 176,$_{8/12}$.

669. 6. Ind. Off. 4607 (*JRAS*, 1939, 381).—8a. Mosul 104,$_{73,7}$.—9c. *Tafsīr āyat* 6,$_{159}$, Alex. Fun. 152,$_{5}$.—27. Read: Mosul 296,$_{7}$.—32. Alex. Fun. 152,$_{4}$.—35. Mosul 28,$_{33}$, 296,$_{13}$.—36. Ibid. 296,$_{18}$.—38. Br. Mus. Or. 9574, 15, Alex. Fun. 86,$_{4}$ (*Risāla fī taḥqīq al-z.*), ibid. 161,$_{4}$ (*Maqāla fī taʿrīb lafẓ al-z.*). Read: Cl. Huart, Les zindiqs etc.

670. 42/3. Mosul 130,$_{39,2}$.—53. Read: *al-istikhlāf.*—63. Alex. Fun. 86,$_{12}$.—67. Ibid. 86,$_{5}$, Mosul 37,$_{194}$.—75. Mosul 296,$_{11}$.—76. Alex. Fun. 86,$_{10}$.—80. Mosul 296,$_{20}$.

671. 83. Mosul 104,$_{73,3}$.—88. Alex. Fun. 152,$_{2}$.—95. Read: *al-saʿy*, Mosul 296,$_{14}$, Alex. Fun. 69,$_{2}$, 86,$_{2}$.—99. Ibid. 165.—106. Ibid. 69,$_{3}$.—109. Mosul 104,$_{73,4}$.—113. With the title *al-Risāla al-tawsīʿiyya*, Garr. 2114,$_{3}$.

672. 118. Mosul $297_{,55}$.—124. Alex. Fun. $164_{,8}$, $67_{,3}$.—126. Mosul $297_{,46}$.—127. With the title *al-Risāla al-Ṭūriyya* or *Bayān maʿāni ʾl-rūḥ wal-qalb wal-ʿaql*, Garr. $2005_{,6}$.—151. As a *Ḥāshiya*, Mosul $197_{,28}$, $296_{,21}$ (*Taʿlīqāt ʿalā Kitāb al-ṭahāra min al-Hidāya*).

673. 164. Garr. 906.—171. *Ṣafwat al-manqūlāt fī shurūṭ al-ṣalāt*, Alex. Fiqh Ḥan. $57_{,1}$.—172. *Risāla fī anna ʾl-shuhadāʾ aḥyāʾ fi ʾl-dunyā*, Garr. $2122_{,2}$.—173. *Risāla tataʿallaq bil-ḍamāʾir*, Mosul $296_{,5}$.—174. *Risālat al-tamthīl*, ibid $296_{,17}$.—175. *Risāla fī ʿilm al-nafs*, ibid. $104_{,73,1}$.—176. *Risāla fī ʿilm al-maʿānī*, ibid. $104_{,73,2}$.—177. *Risāla fi ʾl-madhhab*, Alex. Fiqh Ḥan. 58.—178. *Shubbāk wa-fawāʾid fī ʿilm al-farāʾiḍ*, ibid. Fun. $131_{,16}$.—179. *Sharḥ al-Maqāla al-muqarrara*, see ad p. 292.

5. Brussalī, *ʿOM* II, 23. 1. Alex. Fur.. 50.

674. 6. Brussalī, *ʿOM* I, 230.

7. 4. *Tawjīh al-basmala*, Garr. 477.—5. *Risāla fī ḥukm al-siwāk*, Alex. Fun. $59_{,2}$.—6. *Sharḥ al-tasmiya* (*basmala*), ibid. 4.—7. *Risāla fī iʿrāb Kitāb al-ṭahāra*, ibid. $60_{,30}$.

675. 1, 1. Alexandria 1291 (Alex. Adab 140).

677. See p. 699, 5.

§ 3. 2. Anon. *Ghazawāt*, Algiers 1934.

681. 2h. al-Fāsī al-ʿĀrif.

1307 | 682. 3, 1. Alex. Taʾr. 141.

683. Muḥammad b. Aḥmad al-Ḥalfāwī, *Urjūza*, additionally Paris 5113.

684. 6a. See p. $933_{,31}$.—1. Alex. Taʾr. 66.

8. Alex. Adab 81.

686. 12b. See p. $706_{,1}$, I, 623, 788, 805.

690. 1. See $909_{,42}$.

4. 1. Alex. Adab 21.—4. *Khuṭab*, Fez, Qar. 1538.

691. 1a. Berl. 3930, Garr. 1961/2, Dam. Z. $61_{,143}$, *Mukhtaṣar* Alex. Fawāʾid 26.

1c. See p. $939_{,102}$.—6. *Risāla fi ʾl-ḥaqīqa al-Ṣūfiyya al-nabawiyya wal-dhikr wal-sabḥa*, Alex. Fun. $122_{,3}$.

2. 1. *Ṣilat al-khalaf etc.*, Garr. 2199.—2. With the title *Bahjat al-ṭullāb fi ʾl-asṭurlāb*, with the commentary by Muḥammad b. Qāsim al-Mawṣilī al-ʿAbdalī, composed in Damascus in 1113/1701, Mosul $103_{,66,1}$ (which has "al-Yardanī").

3a. Muḥammad b. ʿAbd al-Raḥmān b. ʿAbd al-Qādir al-Fāsī, *al-Minan al-bādiya fi ʾl-asānīd al-ʿāliya wal-musalsalāt al-rāsiya wal-ṭuruq al-hādiya al-kāfiya, thabt* following his teacher ʿAbd al-Qādir b. ʿAlī al-Fāsī, d. 1091/1680, Alex. Muṣṭ. ḥad. 22.

692. 5. Garr. 1411, Alex. Ḥad. 38.

693. 1a, 2. Read: Colin.

694. 2a. See p. $978_{,65}$.

695. 4, 4. See p. $1038_{,6}$.—19. Partial ed. and transl. H.G. Farmer, Coll. of Or. Writers on Music, *An old Moorish Lute Tutor*, Glasgow 1933 (*Sources* 64).

698. 3, 1. Read: Bank. XVIII, C. 1341 (Bergstraesser-Pretzl, *Gesch. d. Q. textes* 129, n. 1).

699. 4. See p. $677_{,2}$.

§ 8. 2, 1. a. Alex. Fun. 17.

700. 1, i. *Manhal al-māʾ al-maʿīn* by Muḥammad b. Muḥammad b. Badr al-Dīn, Alex. Fiqh Māl. 19.

2a. See p. $939_{,8}$.

701. § 9. 1b. Read: b. Khajjū.

702. 2a. See p. $707_{,10}$, $961_{,28}$.

704. 5. See p. 958.—2. Read: *Radd al-tashdīd.*

5a. Abū ʿAbdallāh Muḥammad b. Muḥammad b. al-Faqīh b. al-ʿAṭiyya al-Sharīf al-Ḥasanī wrote, in 1127/1715, *Shams al-qulūb wa-ṭarīqat al-wujūb fī maʿrifat ʿallām al-ghuyūb*, autograph in a Maghribi hand in Alex. Taṣ. 22.

5b. Muḥammad b. ʿAlī al-Sanūsī al-Khaṭṭābī al-Ḥasanī al-Idrīsī, 12th cent., *al-Musalsal al-muʿayyan fī ʾl-ṭarāʾiq al-arbaʿīn*, Alex. Taṣ. 19.

705. 1. al-Akhḍarī deceased in 953/1546 (see Nallino, *Or. Mod.* I, 570).—1a. Garr. 821, Alex. Manṭiq 15, 25,$_3$, 31,$_4$.—Glosses: γ Alex. Manṭiq 20.—b. Alex. Fun. 110,$_5$.—e. Garr. 822, Alex. Manṭiq 9, 25,$_2$.—Glosses: α Alex. Manṭiq 9.—f. Garr. 823, Alex. Manṭiq 21,$_4$, 25,$_2$, Fun. 108,$_2$.—g. al-Quwaysinī, d. 1255/1839, Alex. Manṭiq 15, 16, 21, Fun. 128,$_3$, print. C. 1314.

706, k. See p. 686, 12b, Garr. 824 (which has: Muḥammad b. Bannān al-Muḥsinī al-Zarfānī al-Fāsī), Alex. Manṭiq 15.—Glosses by al-ʿAṭṭār, Alex. Manṭiq 10.—s. Saʿīd Qaddūra al-Maghribī al-Mālikī, Alex. Manṭiq 15.—2. See *JA* 1854, II, 438, 61.—4. Garr. 1041.

707. 1c. See p. 702, 2a.

2. 1. Garr. 1002, Alex. Ḥisāb 16/7, Comm. a. α Alex. Fun. 142, 159,$_7$, read: al-Warzīzī.

708. 3a, 5. *Urjūza fī ʾl-asṭurlāb* with the commentary by Muḥammad b. ʿAbd al-Salām al-Qabbānī, Alex. Ḥisāb 50.

709. 6, 2. Br. Mus. Or. 7007, in *Majmūʿ al-aghānī wal-alḥān min kalām al-Anda-*
1308 *lus, jamʿ wa-tartīb* Nathan Edmond Yāfīl, Algiers 1904, see Farmer, | *MO* 1906, p. 215, *An Old Moorish Lute Tutor*, Glasgow 1931, 23/4, *Sources* 60, A. Chottin, *Corpus de musique marocaine*, Paris 1931, I, S. VIII.

710. 1a. *L. A. De la descripción de Africa y de las cosas notables que en ella se encuentran* vol. I, Ceuta 1940 (Publ. del Inst. General Franco para la investigación hispan.-ar. Serie VI, 5).

711. 3, 1. *Br. Mus. Quart.* XIII, 3, 90.

712. 4a. *El viaje del Visir para la liberación de los cautivos, texto árabe y versión esp. por Alfredo Bustani*, Tangier 1940 (Publ. del Inst. General Franco para la

investigación hisp.-ar. Serie II, 11), see H. Pérès, *L'Espagne vue par les voyageurs musulmans*, Paris 1938, 5–17.

714. 6. *al-Shuqrūniyya*, Tunis 1323, see *Annales de l'Inst. d'Ét. or.*, Algiers 1937, III, 90/9.

9. Abū Muḥammad ʿAbd al-Wāḥid b. Aḥmad al-Wansharīshī wrote untitled *ṭawīl* verses on music, Madr. 334, f. 15/19, see Farmer, Coll. of Or. Writers on Music, Glasgow 1933.

§ 14. 1. Read: Abū Ḥafṣ ʿUmar.—2. Completed in 1057, Paris $2568_{,12}$, Alex. Ḥurūf $17_{,8}$.

715. 2, 1. Bank. XXII, $118_{,2485,ii}$ (where he is said to be a student of Shaykh Multānī [d. 660/1361], but that does not sit well with no. 2, which is why al-Shaykh al-ʿĀrif al-Multānī of Delhi mentioned here must be someone else).

§ 11.1. Read: al-Takrūrī.

719. H.A.R. Gibb, Studies in contemporary arabic literature, *BSOS* IV, 745/60.

720. 1. b. *Dīwān*, Asʿad Ef. 2631 (*MFO* V, 534).

1. c, 5. Transl. Rescher, *Orient. Miszellen*, I (Istanbul 1925), 229/32, after the appendix to al-Suyūṭī's *maqāmas*, lith. C. 1275, p. 91ff.

721. 4a, 1. Read: al-Safatī, see p. 898.

722. 6. See al-ʿAqqād, *Shuʿarāʾ Miṣr* 78/86.

723. 8a. *Dīwān*, ed. Anīs E. Khūrī al-Maqdisī, Beirut, Americ. Press, 1938.

8b. Instead of "a poetical description of Egypt", read: "a description of Egypt in prose".

8d. 7. C. 1886.—8. *Rashf al-mudām fī 'l-jinās al-tāmm*, C. 1894.

724. 9. ʿAqqād, *Shuʿarāʾ Miṣr* 150/4, ʿAbd al-Fattāḥ, *Hilāl* XXXV, 401/8.

725. 1 Deceased 16 January 1898. ʿAqqād, *Shuʿarāʾ Miṣr* 112/8.

727. 7. Read: Husayn b. Aḥmad.

728. 8c. ʿAqqād, *Shuʿarāʾ Miṣr* 22/9, Saʿd Mīkhāʾīl, *Ādāb al-ʿaṣr* 133/9, Shakīb Arslān in *Radio Araba di Bari* III, 102/6.

730. 3, 2. Garr. 615.

731. 4, 2. Garr. 613.

6. J. Heyworth Dunne, *BSOS* 1938, 961/7.

732. 13. C. 1290.

733. 8. 12. Read: ʿAlam al-Dīn.

734. 9c, 4. See Pérès, *L'Espagne*, 89/100.

736. 3a, 3. Read: *Ḥazanbal, Zalkūna.*

§ 5. 1, 7. *Sharḥ al-ʿAqīda al-mashhūra allatī tuqraʾ baʿd al-asmāʾ al-ḥusnā*, Garr. 1970.—8. *Sharḥ al-Ṣalāt*, ibid. 1971.—9. *Risāla tataʿallaq bil-basmala wal-ḥamdala wal-shukr wal-madḥ*, Br.-H.^{2} 1129.—10. *al-Kawākib al-nayyira fī aqsām al-mutaḥayyira*, Garr. 2208.

737. § 6, 1. Read: Muḥammad b. Aḥmad.—8. *Manāsik al-ḥajj*, Garr. 1859.

738. 2, 1. Comm. by al-Zaynabī, Garr. 1839.—2. Comm. b. by Muḥammad
1309 b. | Ramaḍān b. Manṣūr b. Muḥammad al-Marzūqī al-Makkī, *al-Fawāʾid al-Marzūqiyya*, Alex. Fiqh Māl. 16.—9. Alex. Fiqh Māl. 15.

4. 7. Alex. Fun. 100$_{,2}$.

739. B. 1. See p. 923, 88a.

741. 1a. See p. 483$_{,6}$.

742. 3, 12. Alex. Bal. 5.

4. See below, ad p. 862.

744. § 7, 1. Jabartī III, 166.—2. Garr. 1861.—9. ibid. 2178.—13. *al-Durr al-naẓīm fī taḥqīq kalām al-qadīm*, Alex. Fun. 17,$_5$.—14. *Itḥāf al-laṭīf bi-ṣiḥḥat al-nadhr lil-mūsir wal-sharīf*, ibid. 6.—15. *Itḥāf al-aḥibbāʾ bi-jawāb ʿan masʾalat al-ḍabba*, ibid. 7.—16. *Bulūgh al-arab bi-masʾalat al-qaṣab*, ibid. 8—17. *Ḥilyat dhawi ʾl-afhām bi-taḥqīq dalālāt al-ʿām*, ibid. 9.—18. *al-Qawl al-muwaffī fī taḥqīq al-shukr al-ʿurfī*, ibid. 10.

746. 7. See p. 884,$_{31}$.

750. 5, 4. Garr. 485.

Chapter 2. J.T. Reinaud, De l'état de la littérature chez les populations chrétiennes de la Syrie, *JA* s. V, vol. 9 (1857), 465/89.

752. 2a, 4. Garr. 142.—6. *Majmūʿat al-manẓūmāt*, mostly in praise of Emir Bashīr Shihāb al-Dīn, d. 1850, Garr. 143.—7. *Murāsalāt*, ibid. 144.—8. Two *qaṣīdas*, ibid. 145.

2b. 3. A poem on the conversion of a Jewish banker, *RAAD* IX, 648/50.

754. 2, i. *Riwāya muḍḥika mulaḥḥana dhāt khamsat fuṣūl*, São Paolo 1914.

755. 5. Instead of 1786, read: 1875.

756. 6, 6. Read: *Ghābat al-ḥaqq wa mashhad al-aḥwāl etc*, Alexandria 1298.—7. Instead of "his daughter," read: "his sister".

7, 1. Read: *Dīwān al-marʾa al-gharība*.

757. 9, 7. Dam. ʿUm. 91,$_{31}$.—8. ibid. 30.

759. 14. Ṣadīq Shaybūb in *Radio Arabe di Bari* III, 106/8.

760. 16, 2. *Farāʾid al-laʾāl fī majmaʿ al-amthāl*, see p. 506, 10.

762. 19. Cheikho II, 139.

20. Saʿd Mīkhāʾīl, *Ādāb al-ʿaṣr* 278/83, *Ḥilm al-mulūk* C. 1910.

764. 5a. *Ṭayyibat al-gharrāʾ fī madḥ sayyid al-anbiyāʾ*, Beirut 1314.—10. Read: *al-Ṣāfināt*.—12. *bi-itḥāf aḥādīth*, C. 1329.

765. 1. Saʿd Mikhāʾīl, *Ādāb al-ʿaṣr*, 274/7.

766. 9. Beirut 1872, 1881, 1889.—13. By his son Ibrāhīm.

767. 2, 9. *Rasāʾil al-Yāzijī wa-dīwānuhu ʾl-taʾrīkhī, ʿuniya bi-nashrihi* Yaḥyā Tūmā al-Bustānī.

2d. 1. See N. Barbour, *BSOS* VIII, 175.

768. 3, 14. By Fuʾād Afram al-Bustānī—15. *Khuṭba fī ādāb al-ʿArab*, Beirut n.d. (Alex. Adab 39).

770. 3, 1. Born ca. 1760. 1. Garr. 624, C. 1900, Beirut 1933.

771. 6. Insteas of Ubayya, read: Abeih.

5a. Al-Khūrī Ḥanāniyya al-Munayyir wrote: *al-Durr al-marṣūf fī ḥawādith Jabal Ṣūf*, from the fall of Maʿn until the rise of the Shihābs, 1109–1222/1697–1807, Garr. 626a.

9. Deceased in 1928, *RAAD* VI, 370/2, Lecerf, *Littérature dialectale et renaissance arabe* 168.

772. 9. *Nawādir fukāhāt*, the fables of Lafontaine, Damascus 1913.

11. Instead of Ḥāsibya, read: Ḥasbayya.

773. 3. 32 treatises, Alex. Fun. 167/9.—14. Read: *al-raqūd*, Alex. Fun. 162$_{,1}$.—24. Alex. Muṣṭ. al-Ḥad. 12.

774. 7. Read: 1279.—2. Abstract, *al-Awrāq al-Qudsiyya fī manāqib al-sāda al-Naqshbandiyya* by Muḥammad Muḥammad Nāsī al-Ruhawī, C. 1344.

1310 | 775. 9, 18. See p. 739.—23. A fatwa on the mass killings of Christians of 1860, BDMG 47.—24. A *Risālat al-burhān ʿalā baqāʾ mulk Banī ʿUthmān ilā ākhir al-zamān* is mentioned in Shakīb Arslān, *al-Irtisāmāt*, 149$_{,8}$.

776. 10. ʿAbd al-Qādir al-Adhamī al-Ṭarābulusī, *Tarjamat al-Qāwuqjī*, Beirut 1306.—12. *Tuḥfat al-mulūk fi ʾl-siyāsa wal-salām*, Alex. Taṣ. 11.

13. 4. In *Majmūʿa*, C. 1324.—4a. *Nuzhat al-fikr fī manāqib mawlāna ʾl-ʿārif billāh taʿālā quṭb zamānihi wa-ghawth awānihī Muḥammad al-Jasr*, Beirut 1306.

777. Line 1. al-Buḥayrī, d. 25 December 1920, see Cheiko, *al-Mashriq* XXIV, 862.

15. See *al-Mashriq* XVIII, 1036, p. 975,37.—1. C. 1331.

778. 18. See M. Hartmann, *Die arab. Frage* 555, n. 2.

§ 5. 1a. Muḥammad b. al-Ḥusayn al-ʿAṭṭār wrote, in 1212/1797, *Risāla fī ʿilm al-ḥisāb wal-miyāh al-jāriya fī madīnat Dimashq*, Bank. XXII, 106,257,i.

779. 4. Instead of Barshīma, read: Rasmaya.—Farmer, *EI*, Erg. 173/4.—10. *al-Risāla al-Shihābiyya fi ʾl-mūsīqī al-ṣināʿiyya*, Cairo *Nashra* 11.

780. § 2. A manuscript copy of his *Kitāb umm al-ʿibar* in the estate of the late Ismāʿīl Ef., as mentioned in Rescher, *Orient. Miszellen* II, 38/40, *Aqāwīl al-Yazīdiyya*.

781. 2. See p. 1028,10.

5. 1. See Siouffi, *JA* s. VIII, vol. 5, 1885, p. 81/5.

782. 5, 8. *Gharāʾib al-athar*, Alex. Taʾr. 91.

7a. ʿAbd al-Raḥmān al-ʿUmarī al-Mawṣilī wrote, in 1246/1830, *Majmūʿa taʾrīkhiyya*, autograph in the collection of ʿAbbās al-ʿAzzāwī al-Baghdādī, see *Taʾrīkh al-Yazīdiyyīn*, p. 60.

8. See M. Hartmann, *WI* III (1915), 147, n 1. *EI*, II, 73.—2. C. 1326.

783. 11, 5. *Bustān al-ikhwān wa-mawrid al-ẓamʾān*, Mosul 87,6.

12. 2. Read: *li-tāʾiyyat*.

12a. Muḥammad b. Muṣṭafā al-Ghulāmī, *Shamāmat al-ʿanbar wal-zahr al-muʿanbar*, biographies of 50 famous contemporaries from Mosul and Aleppo, Mosul 291$_{,2}$.

784. Mollā ʿUthmān al-Mawlawī b. al-Ḥājj ʿAbdallāh al-Mawṣilī.—1. *al-Abkār al-ḥisān fī madḥ sayyid al-akwān*, C. 1313.—2. *Saʿādat al-dārayn, majmūʿa taḥtawī ʿala ʾl-Manẓūma al-Mawṣiliyya al-ʿUthmāniyya fī asmāʾ al-suwar al Qurʾāniyya thumma matn al-Ḥikam li-Ibn ʿAṭāʾallāh al-Sikandarī*, C. (or Istanbul) 1318, Sarkīs 1791.—3. *Takhmīs al-Hadiyya al-Ḥamīdiyya*, see I, 472, IX.

§ 4, 2. See p. 904$_{,64}$.

2a. ʿAbd al-Raḥmān al-Saftī al-Sharqāwī wrote, in Baghdad, in the mid-13th century, *Talāqi ʾl-arab fī marāqi ʾl-adab, dīwān*, collected by Muḥammad ʿAyyād, d. 1288/1871, and dedicated to the grandson of Ismāʿīl Pāshā Aḥmad ʿĀrif Bey Ḥikmat, Bank. XXIII, 64$_{,2560}$.

785. 5a. Ibrāhīm al-Rāwī al-Rifāʿī, *mudarris* at the Jāmiʿ al-Sulṭān ʿAlī, *al-Awrāq al-Baghdādiyya fi ʾl-radd ʿala ʾl-Wahhābiyya*, Beirut 1245.

786. A.D. Mordtmann, *Anatolien*, ed. Babinger, p. 569, n. 197.

787. 7, 17. *Fawāʾid fī ʿilm al-Qurʾān*, Berl. 1428.

788. 9. *RAAD* IV, 1924, 481/2, L. Massignon, *RMM* LVII, 1924, 244/6.

791. 1, 4. Bombay 1306.—8. *Dīwān*, Bank. XXIII, 66$_{,2561}$.—*al-Ṣārim al-qirḍāb*, a rebuttal of a *qaṣīda* by Diʿbil (I, 121) against the first two caliphs, ibid. 67$_{,2562}$, Rāmpūr 604$_{,243}$, see ad Suppl. I, 940 on vol. I, 122.

792. 4. *Mashriq*, XXIV, 296.—*Dīwān*, Beirut 1331.

794. 9, 4. *Sharḥ al-Khuṭba al-Tathgiyya* (sic, which ʿAlī had supposedly pronounced in a village between Medina and Kufa), completed in 1235/1819, Bank. XXIII, 109$_{,2598}$.

1311 | 795. 16a. Ṣāliḥ b. Sayyid Mahdī b. Riḍā al-Ḥusaynī al-Qazwīnī, d. 1297/1880 in Najaf, Aḥsan al-wadīʿa II, 65.—*Dīwān: al-Durar al-Gharawiyya*, Teh. Sip. II, 920/1.

800. 36, 6. *Qaṭarāt min yarāʿ Baḥr al-ʿulūm yaḥtawī ʿala ʾl-waqf wal-riḍāʿ etc.*, Baghdad 1331.

38a. Muḥammad Kāẓim al-Ṭabāṭabāʾī, al-*ʿUrwa al-wuthqā fīmā ta-ummu bihi ʾl-balwā*, Baghdad 1330.

802. 51a. Muḥammad Jaʿfar al-Naqdī, a Shīʿī *qāḍī* in Baghdad. 1. *Mawāhib al-wāhib fī faḍāʾil Abī Ṭālib*, Najaf 1341.—2. *Minan al-raḥmān*, ibid. 1344 (*Jāmiʿ* 84,$_{5}$).

804. 65. Read: *Anṣār*, see III 179, 190.

805. 71. Read: *al-shaʿbiyya.*

806. 78a. Muḥammad ʿAlī al-Urmahādī, *al-Radd ʿala ʾl-Wahhābiyya*, Najaf 1345.

78b. ʿAbd al-Azīz b. Aḥmad al-Rāshid al-Baddāḥ al-Kuwaytī, *Taḥdhīr al-Muslimīn ʿan ittibāʿ ghayr sabīl al-muʾminīn* (against the Wahhābīs), Baghdad 1329.

807. 83, 8. Read: *ʿan-mawāniʿ.*—10. See Browne, *Lit. Hist.* IV, 434.—13. *Mā huwa Nahj al-balāgha*, Sidon, Maṭbaʿat ʿIrfān 1352.

85a. Muḥammad al-Najafī, *Ālāʾ al-raḥmān fī tafsīr al-Qurʾān*, Sidon 1933.

Note 1, 1. See p. 969,1.

808. 1b. Ṣāliḥ b. Muḥammad b. Nūḥ al-ʿUmarī al-Fullānī al-Madanī, d. 1218/1803, *Qaṭf al-thamar fī rafʿ asānīd al-muṣannafāt fī ʾl-funūn wal-athar*, Alex. Fun. 123,$_{7}$.

813. 4g, 1. See p. 405,17.

815. 12. See p. 934,$_{42}$

13. 3. Read: *Nabsh.*

816. 17. Rāshid b. ʿAlī al-Ḥanbalī, *Muthīr al-waja fī maʿrifat ansāb mulūk Najd*, is cited in Rīḥānī, *Taʾrīkh Najd al-ḥadīth* 63.

817. 1e. See p. 915.$_{8}$.

2a. See p. 547,$_{20}$.

2b. ʿAbd al-Raḥmān b. Sulaymān al-Ahdal, d. 1250/1835, 1. *Jamʿ al-aḥādīth fī ʾl-baḥth ʿalā dhikr Allāh*, Alex. Fun. 124,4.—2. *Talqīḥ al-afhām fī waṣāyā khayr al-anām*, ibid. 5.—3. *al-Risāla al-jalīla ilā ikhwānī fī mutābaʿat al-nabī*, ibid. 6.—4. *Ithḥāf al-fikra bi-ḥukm ahl al-faṭra*, ibid. 8.—5. *Arb. ḥad. fī faḍl lā ilāha illa ʾllāh*, ibid. 9.—6. *Jawāb ʿan suʾāl*, ibid. 11.—7. *Fatwā fī ʾl-banādiq al-maʿrūfa*, ibid. 125,$_{26}$.—8. *Masāʾil min al-shaykh Aḥmad b. ʿAbd al-Qādir al-ʿUjaylī al-Shāfiʿī*, ibid. 27.

818. 4, 1. In the collection of Rathjen, now in Jerusalem.

819. 15. Alex. Fun. 124,$_{6}$.—25. *Lumaʿ fī ʾl-iʿtidād bi-ʿiddat al-rakʿa min al-jumʿa*, ibid. 14.—26. *Risāla fī sabab tasmiyat al-ʿallāma al-Ṭabarānī li-maʿājimihi ʾl-thalātha* (see I, 279), ibid. 18.—27. *Muntakhab min Wabl al-ghamām ʿalā Shifāʾ al-uwām*, ibid. 125,$_{21}$.

821. 15, 5. *Kanz al-najāt fī ʿilm al-awqāt*, Hamb. Or. Sem. 77.

822. 26. ʿAbd al-ʿĀlī Saʿd al-Dīn b. Hibatallāh al-Hindī al-Yamanī al-Anṣārī, *Simṭ jawāhir farīd al-nuhūr al-muwāzin qalāʾid al-nuḥūr*, in the fashion of the *Urtuqiyyāt* of Ṣafī al-Dīn al-Ḥillī, ordered by rhyme letter, starting with a poem on the Prophet, Indian printing 1291.

27. Ḥasan Bashīr b. Faḍl Bashīr al-ʿAlawī al-Ḥusaynī, al-Ḥijāzī, imam of Ẓafār, *Ṣidq al-khayr fī khawārij al-qarn al-thānī ʿashar*, Latakia n.d.

28. Ḥusayn b. Aḥmad al-ʿArshī, *Bulūgh al-marām fī sharḥ Misk al-khitām fī man tawallā mulk al-Yaman min malik wa-imām*, ed. P. Anastase Marie de St. Élie (Ouvrage complété jusqu'à 1939 et enrichi de notes lexicographiques), C. 1939.

823. 1. See p. 568,$_{7}$.

2. See p. 569,$_{11}$.

1312 3a. Muḥammad al-Sayyid al-Dahiyānī | wrote, in 1305/1887 in Oman, *Tuḥfat al-rashād ilā bayān al-iʿtiqād*, Hamb. Or. Sem. 79.

824. 2. See p. 504, 5.

3a. Muḥammad ʿAlī b. Mīrzā ʿAbd al-Ḥusayn b. Muḥammad ʿAlī Raqqī Ṭabasī Khurāsānī Nūr ʿAlīshāh, d. 1212/1797 in Mosul, *Jannat al-wiṣāl*, a Sufi work, Teh. Sip II, 489/92, where his Persian writings are also listed (according to E.G. Browne, *Lit. Hist. of Persia* IV, 420, he was killed during the 1806 persecution of the Sufis).

826. 10. Deceased in 1242.—2. Completed in 1228.—3. Read: Mashh. V.—6. See Kentūrī 3144.

827. 18. Deceased in 1286/1869. 3. *al-Risāla al-Sulṭāniyya fī ithbāt al-nubuwwa wal-imāma wal-wilāya*, Persian, written in 1274, lith. Bombay 1277 (Mashh. I, print. 10/31).

828. 24. See p. 582.

834. 56a. Mīrzā Muḥammad b. ʿAlī b. Muḥammad b. Ṣādiq al-Shīrāzī, *Miʿyār al-lugha*, Pers. print.1314 (Cairo^2 IV, b. 6).

836. 69, 3. Read: *Risāla fī ṣiyagh.*

837. 77, 10. d. Read: *Risāla fī ṣiyagh.*

841. 3. See p. 607, § 5a, 1.

842. 8. See ad I, 548.

19. 2. *al-Mawāʿiẓ al-ʿadadiyya*, autograph(?) dated 1127, Alex. Mawāʿiẓ 32.

843. 27. Read: *Iljām.*

32. See p. 796, 22,2.

848. Line 24, read: Salīm Qubʿayn.

850. 5. Kundanlāl Ashkī b. Manūnlāl Falsafī b. Rāymuhan Singh ʿĀṣī b. Rāylūkrāj M. Shāhī b. Rāynandlām ʿĀlamgīrī b. Rāykhatildās Shāhjahānī wrote: 1. In 1237/1822, in Delhi, aged 24: *al-Qusṭās*, on astronomy, Bank. XXII, 51,$_{2461}$.—*Muntakhab al-tawārīkh* (Bank. *Handlist of printed books*, no. 1340).

851. Line 9. Read: Puna.

6a. His student Awḥad al-Dīn al-Bilghrāmī wrote *al-Abjad al-masbūk fī qiṣṣat badr dhāt al-jamāl wa-sayf al-mulūk*, Bank. XXIII, 151,$_{2642}$.

852. 7, 2. *al-Murāsalāt al-Sābāṭiyya*, Bank. XXIII, 113,2602.

856. 30. See p. 257,6.

857. 9. Additionally Ind. 1295.

859. See p. 988,$_{55}$.

39. To be deleted.

862. ʿAbd al-Malik b. ʿAbd al-Wahhāb al-Fattanī al-Makkī al-Madanī (G. II, 488, 4) wrote: *1. al-Maṭālib al-ḥisān*, on dogmatics, with glosses entitled *Mawāhib al-raḥmān*, Būlāq 1304, C. 1305.—2. *Khulāṣat al-farāʾiḍ* (versification of the *Sirājiyya* I, 650), with the commentary *al-Sharḥ al-muqarrib*, C. 1292/3, 1305.—3. *Natījat al-ādāb, manẓūma* with the commentary *Kamāl al-muḥāḍara fī ādāb al-baḥth wal-munāẓara*, C. 1306.—4. *ʿIqd al-laʾālī fī ʿilm al-waḍʿ*, ibid. 1306.

866. 2, 1. Garr. 1011.

867. 5. See 944,$_{152}$.

5a. Shabīb Bek. b. ʿAlī Bek al-Asʿad al-ʿĀmilī al-Wāʾilī wrote: 1. *al-ʿIqd al-munaḍḍad, dīwān*, Istanbul 1309.—2. *al-Qaṣīda al-bāʾiyya fī madḥ khayr al-bariyya* (with the appendix *al-Qaṣīda al-sīniyya fī madḥ al-ḥaḍra al-saniyya al-sulṭāniyya al-musammāh Masarrat al-nufūs bil-julūs al-maʾnūs*), ibid. 1323 (Sarkīs 1103).

868. 6, 3. See Kračkovsky, *al-Maʿarrī* 26.

1313 | 869. Line 5. Walī al-Dīn Yegen, *al-Maʿlūm wal-majhūl* I, 90, 104. ʿAbdallāh Nadīm al-Idrīsī, d. 1314/1896, *al-Masāmīr, riwāyat al-sharīf Abī Hāshim ʿani ʾl-shaykh Madyan al-Qāsim al-shahīr al-ʿĀrif billāh* (a description of Abu ʾl-Hudā), C. n.d. (Alex. Adab. 159).—17. Alexandria 1892.—39. Read: ch. 13, 45.

871. 3. Muḥammad b. Muḥammad Ramzī, read: Murād, d. 5 October 1934 in Tschugatschak in Dzungaria, see Z.V. Togan, *Ibn Faḍlāns Reisebericht* IX, n. 3.—

4. Letters from Shāmil, see Garcin de Tassy, *JA*, s. V, vol. 15 (1860), 271, Kračkovsky, *Zap. Inst. Vost.* II (1933), 9/20, *Hist. Archiv* (Russ.) II, 1938, G. Tsereteli *Zap. Inst. Vost.* V, 1935, 97/116, *Acts of the first session of Arabists* (Russ.), Leningrad 1937, 93/112.

878. 17. Read: 1169/1755.

879. Lévi-Provençal, *EI* IV, 1300/1.

880. 17, 1. See *RAAD* XI, 631/3.

19. 9. *Risāla fi 'l-radd ʿala 'l-Būlāqī*, on the Jews, Garr. 575.

881. 20. Read: maʿālim al-riwāya.

22. See p. $903_{,58}$.

883. 9. *Naẓm sayr al-sulūk fi 'l-ṭaraqqī ilā ḥaḍrat malik al-mulūk*, composed in 1247, Alex. Taṣ 40,4.

884. 30, 3. Alex. Taṣ. 47.

31. See p. $746_{,7}$.

887. Line 1. Read: 1835.

888. 46, 2. *Shahīrāt al-Tūnisiyyāt*, Tunis 1934.

889. 49. 4. *Naẓm muṣṭalaḥ al-ḥadīth*, Fez 1323.

891. 54, 3. Damascus 1342.—9. *Nayl al-munā wal-su'ūl bi-dhikr miʿrāj al-nabī al-mukhtār al-rasūl*, Damascus 1332/1924.

55. 6. *Inārat al-aghwār wal-anjād* (against the claim that Muḥammad was the son of a slave woman), Tunis, Maṭbaʿat al-Nahḍa 1928 (*RAAD* IX, 127).

892. 57a. Muḥammad al-Ḥujjawī al-Thaʿālibī, professor at the al-Qarawiyyīn in Fez and minister of education for a period of time, *al-Fikr al-sāmī*, vols. I–IV, see *RAAD* IX, 506, XII, 603.

893. f. To be deleted, see *G.* II, 409.

g. Read: Aṭfiyash.—9. *al-Tuḥfa wal-tuʾam fī ʿilm al-farāʾiḍ*, Tunis 1344.—10. *al-Uqbā*, Tunis 1321.

895. 5. Muḥammad b. al-Mukhtār Abū Zayn al-ʿĀbidīn wrote, in 1207/1792, *al-Qurā al-shāfiya min nafḥ al-Kāfiya*, Alex. Taṣ. 13.

897. 1a. ʿAbdallāh al-ʿAyṭāwī al-Ṣāliḥī al-Dimashqī, *al-Sabʿiyyāt al-adabiyya*, Cairo² III, 111.

898. 5b. al-Ṣafatī, see p. 721, 4a. Madr. 152 (Derenbourg, *Homenaye a Fr. Codera*, Zaragoza 1904, p. 90), Leningrad, Un. 892.

10 Read: *al-Buhlūl.*

899. 15. See I, 802, 25a.

15a. Aḥmad b. Nāfiʿ al-Dunaysarī al-Hudhalī, *Qaṣīda fī madḥ al-rasūl*, Dam. Z. $31_{,28,10}$.

21. a. ʿAlī b. Durayhim al-Mawṣilī, *Qaṣīda*, Dam. Z. $86_{,23,1}$.

22. See p. $471_{,35}$.

23a. ʿAlī b. Muḥammad al-Brzī al-Andalusī Abu ʾl-Ḥasan, *al-Qaṣāʾid al-muʿashshara*, alphabetically arranged, verses begin and end with the same letter, Dam. Z. $85_{,5.2}$.

900. 30a. Ibn Jibrīl al-Muqriʾ al-Miṣrī, *Manāʾiḥ al-ʿuqūl fī madāʾiḥ al-rasūl*, Dam. Z. $31_{,28,19}$.

32. Abu ʾl-Ḥasan b. Muḥammad b. ʿAlī, MS dated 994.

34. Garr. 147 (which has al-Ṣāfūrī).

35. Khālid al-Kātib, see ad I, 121, 9b.

901. See p. 941, 11b.

902. 54. See p. 556, 4.

| 903. 57, 1. ḤKh VI, 179$_{,13129}$. 1314

58. See p. 881$_{,22}$.

63. See p. 962$_{,39}$.

66. See p. 2, 2a.

904. 75. Read: al-Sābūrī.

77. See p. 784$_{,2}$.

78. Garr. 416, MS dated 1003.

905. 1. See p. 539$_{,4}$.

3. Read: b. Abi ʾl-ʿAbd, Garr. 227, Paris 3476$_{,2}$.

906. 5. MS Gotha dated 1170.

11. Read: ʿAbd al-Muʿīn, see *G* II, 285$_{,6}$.

907. 15. See p. 438$_{,9}$.

16. Read: al-Satīwī.

17. Read: b. al-Ḥusayn.

18. See p. 100$_{,35}$.

23. Read: b. Qarabughā.

24a. ʿAlī b. al-Mufarrij al-Ṣaqalī al-Qāḍī Abu ʾl-Ḥasan, *al-Ḥikāyāt wal-akhbār al-ḥisān*, Dam. Z. 31$_{,28,7}$.

908. 30. See p. 566, 3a.

30a. Dawqala b. al-ʿAbd al-Manbijī, *al-Qaṣīda al-Taymiyya*, Dam. Z. 34$_{,79,1}$.

33. Read: *Amālī Ibn al-Ḥaṣīn.*

909. 37, 2. *al-Tanzīl wa-tartībuhu*, Dam. Z. $31_{,26}$ (which has: Ḥasan).

37a. Ḥusayn b. Aḥmad al-Astarābādhī, *Minnat al-adab*, Dam. Z, $29_{,9,2}$.

40. See p. $248_{,11}$.

41. See p. $58_{,17a}$, Garr. 734/5.

42. See p. $690_{,1}$.

43. Additionally $59_{,129,2}$.

919. 48. See p. $638_{,2}$.

52. See I, $488_{,19}$.

54a. Muḥammad b. ʿAlī al-Ḥaymī Abū Ṭālib, *Nuzhat al-malik fī waṣf al-kalb wal-mukallabīn*, Dam. Z. $79_{,16}$.

54b. Muḥammad b. ʿAlī b. Ṣakhr al-Baṣrī al-Qāḍī Abu ʾl-Ḥasan, *al-Ḥikāyāt wal-akhbār wal-nawādir wal-ashʿār*, Dam. Z. $32_{,38,1}$.

57. See p. $606_{,18}$.

58. See p. $500_{,6}$.

911. 64. Deceased in 1815, see J. Zaydān, *Taʾrīkh al-adab* IV, 232/3 (Kr.).

912. 70. Garr. 1935 (which has al-Shahāwī al-Barhāmī).

71. Garr. 229.

76a. Muḥammad b. Sulayman al-Rabaʿī Abū Bakr, *Akhbār wa-ḥikāyāt*, Dam. Z. $34_{,17,4}$.

913. 83, 2. *Taḥrīm nikāḥ al-mutʿa*, Dam. Z. $32_{,40,1}$.

914. 94a. al-Sulṭān Aḥmad Khādim al-Kaʿba al-Musharrafa, *Tuḥfat al-aṣḥāb*, Dam. Z. $85_{,51}$.

96. See p. 448, 6, ii.

102. Persian poet, see Cl. Huart, *EI* IV, 1066.

915. 3a. Delete: (-).

4a. Abū Muḥammad ʿAbdallāh b. al-Ḥasan b. ʿAlī b. ʿUthmān b. Dāʾūd b. Abī Mūsā al-Maṣmūdī al-Mushtarāʾī, d. after 778/1377, *al-Ḥulwāniyya fī ʿilm al-ʿarabiyya*, Garr. $2153_{,2}$.

8. See p. $817_{,1}$e.

917. Garr. 514/5, Gotha $376_{,1}$.

22. See p. $457_{,4,10}$.

25. *al-Taḥqīqāt al-bābniyya* (*sic*) *ʿala ʾl-qawāʿid al-burhāniyya*, Dam. Z. $69_{,167,1}$.

25a. Aḥmad al-Kabshī al-Khaḍīrī (Khuḍayrī?) al-Ṭūlūnī, *al-Nubdha al-muqarriba fī tashīl qawāʿid al-naḥw lil-ṭalaba*, Garr. 484.

28. See p. $548_{,1}$.

918. 35. See p. $548_{,5}$.

39. Read: b. Faḍlallāh, see p. $1014_{,12}$.

920. 58a. Read: *al-majāz*.

921. 64. Read: al-Āsī, see I, 435, *RAAD* VII, 523.

68a. Maḥmūd b. ʿUmar b. Muḥammad b. Manṣūr al-Qāḍī al-Zanjī al-Sanjarī al-ʿArabī al-Shaybānī, *Muhadhdhib al-asmāʾ*, Arabic-Persian dictionary, Teh. Sip. II, 294/7 (with uncertain conjectures on the identity of the author).

73. See p. $6_{,13}$.

922. 75a, 1. Garr. 1934, 2193 (attributed to Muḥammad b. ʿUmar al-Rāzī).

82. See I, 217, 557.

923. 84. See I, 492.

88a. See p. 739,$_{1}$.

89. See p. 994,$_{48}$.

92. See I, 608, n. 1.

924. 94. See ad p. 15.

99. Muḥammad al-Ṣiddīqī Shams al-Dīn, *al-Jawāhir al-muḍīʾa fī tajnīs iḍāfat al-jāzim lil-mashīʾa*, Dam. Z. 52,$_{48,4}$.

102. al-Juwaynī, d. 683/1284, Garr. 439, 441, 2116.

1315 925. 103. Damascus, RAAD IX, 638,$_{5}$.—*Kashf al-ḍawʾ ʿan maʿnā* | *law* ibid.

109. Comm., Dam. Z. 68,$_{149}$.

110. See I, 860,14.

926. 113. See I, 498, II, 258.

119. See p. 204,$_{5}$, Dam. Z,99,$_{1}$.

121. Yūsuf b. Muḥammad Abū ʿAbdallāh.

927. 3. Read: Ḥaṣīr.

3a. ʿAbdallāh b. Muḥammad b. Nufayl al-Ḥarrānī Abū Jaʿfar, *Kitāb al-maghāzī*, Dam. Z. 36,$_{110,2}$.

928. 10. See p. 230,$_{8}$.

14. His *Riḥla* is cited in Ibn Ḥajar, DK I, 153,$_{10}$.

929. 20a. Ḥusayn b. Qāsim b. Jaʿfar al-Kawkabī Abū ʿAbd al-Raḥmān, *Akhbār, juzʾ* 9 Dam. Z. 36,$_{110,1}$.

26. Read: *al-malāḥim*, and b. ʿAbd al-Munʿim.

27. 2. *al-Farīda al-wardiyya fī takhmīs al-Duraydiyya* (I, 173), Mosul 42,$_{19}$, autograph dated 1232.—A collection of *qaṣīdas* dated 1271, ibid. 274,$_{49}$.

28a. ʿUbaydallāh b. Muḥammad al-Saqaṭī, *Faḍāʾil Muḥammad b. Abī Sufyān*, Dam. Z. 31,$_{25,2}$.

930. 32. See I, 587,$_{8}$a.

3. See ad I, 615. MS dated 706/1306, Garr. 1425.

4. Autograph dated 1004/1596, Garr. 605.

931. 8. See I, 347,$_{5,2}$.

14. See p. 521,$_{5}$a.

932. 18. See p. 109,$_{20}$.

19. See Suppl. ad p. 415.

21. Read: al-Tamīmī, see I, 278,$_{19}$e.

22. See p. 115,$_{33}$.

23. 1. Read: *wa-bughyat.*

933. 29a. ʿAfīf b. Muḥammad al-Khaṭīb Abu ʾl-Ḥusayn, *al-Manẓūm wal-manthūr*, traditions in verse and in prose, Dam. Z. 34,$_{81}$.

31. See p. 684,$_{6}$a.

32a. See I, 611, e.

33. See p. 497/8.

35. See I, $691_{,1}$, d.

37. Garr. 1303.

934. 39a. Aḥmad al-Bulqīnī, *Sharḥ al-ṣalāt ʿala ʾl-nabī*, Dam. Z. $37_{,125,4}$.

42. See p. $815_{,12}$.

44a. Aḥmad al-Makkī, *Kitāb al-farāʾiḍ*, Dam. Z. 41,18,1.

46a. Aḥmad b. Muḥammad b. al-Ḥajjāj al-Marwazī, *Akhbār al-shuyūkh wa-akhlāqihim*, Dam. Z. $37_{,119,2}$.

48a. Aḥmad b. Muḥammad al-Yashkurī Abu ʾl-ʿAbbās, *al-Yashkuriyyāt*, Dam. Z. $29_{,11}$.

935. 50. See p. 745/6, introduction to AMK 917/8.

51. See p. 560,7b.

52. See p. $456_{,23}$.

53a. Aḥmad b. Shujāʿ Abū Manʿa, *al-Sirr al-samāwī li-tafḥīm ahl al-daʿāwī*, Dam. Z. $74_{,43,2}$.

57. Read: al-Ḥirālī, see I, $735_{,15}$.

936. 60. Autograph dated 978, Alex. Muṣṭ. Ḥad. 6.

61. Garr. 721.

60a. ʿAlī b. Ḥasan b. Hibatallāh al-Shāfiʿī Abu l-Qāsim, *Arb. ḥad. fi ʾl-ḥaththʿala ʾl-jihād*, Dam. Z. $63_{,54,2}$.

66. See I, 608, I, 4.

66a. Abū Bakr al-Marwazī, *Kitāb al-waraʿ*, Dam. Z. $59_{,129,11}$.

68. See p. $261_{,9}$.

68a. Jaʿfar b. Muḥammad b. al-Ḥasan al-Mustafād a. Bekr, *Dalāʾil al-nubuwwa*, Dam. Z. 73,27,1.

937. 75. See p. $434_{,23}$b.

76. Additionally Dam. Z. $51_{,21,6}$.

78. Additionally Alex. Taʾr. 18 (which has: al-Bakhshī, d. 1190/1776).

79. See I, $625_{,12}$a.

938. 84a. Ḥusayn b. Bukayr al-Ḥāfiẓ, *Faḍāʾil man ismuhu Aḥmad wa-Muḥammad*, Dam. Z. $50_{,20,3}$.

87. Read: *al-riwāya*, see I, 905.

89. *Kitāb al-fiqh*, MS dated 960/1553, Garr. 1840.

91. Ibrāhīm b. Muḥammad, d. 1265/1849, see ad p. 460.

939. 93. Read: al-Isfarāʾinī.

96. Garr. 658 (autograph dated 1138/1726).

98. See p. $185_{,66}$b.

69. See p. 527.

102. See p. $691_{,1}$c.

940. 104. See ad p. 444.

111. See p. 692, 5.

941. 1. Vat. V. $938_{,7}$, Barb. $129_{,2}$.

116. See p. $901_{,45}$.

942. 128. Garr. 1443/4.

943. 135. See I, 626$_{,1,3}$.

137. *al-Mawāʿiẓ wal-ḥikam*, Garr. 241 (which has: al-Khāzī).

140. See *G.* I, 356$_{,10}$.

944. 146. al-Baʿlī, Dam. Z. 80$_{,60}$ (autograph).

147. See p. 105, 1, a, α.

152. See p. 867$_{,65}$.

154. See p. 421$_{,22}$a.

1316 | 945, 160. See *G* I, 372$_{,4}$.

161. See p. 416$_{,2,2}$.

163. See p. 515$_{,6}$a, 645$_{,18}$a.

946. 168a. *Dalāʾil al-nubuwwa*, Garr. 1534.

171. See I, 278.

947. 179. See p. 557$_{,3}$.

180. See I, 266$_{,1}$.

181. See p. 130$_{,8}$.

948. 2. See p. 524$_{,3}$.

5. See p. 653$_{,12}$.

949. 15. Read: Ashraf al-Dīn.

16. See I, 652$_{,27}$a.

950. 23. See Muḥ. III, 161.

24a. ʿAlī b. ʿAlāʾ al-Dīn b. al-ʿIzz al-Ḥanafī, *Tanbīh ʿalā mā fī kalām al-shaykh Akmal al-Dīn* (see p. 89) *min al-ishkāl fī risāla allafahā lil-intiṣār li-madhhab Abī Ḥanīfa*, Dam. Z. 32$_{,39,2}$.

28. See I, 660, II, 958$_{,111}$.

951. 33. Shaykh Yabanbuwā (?), *Anwār wa-naṣīḥa*, Gotha 2104.

34. See p. 657$_{,48}$b.

38. According to ḤKh, loc. cit., quoted in *al-Fatāwī al-Tātārkhāniyya* (see p. 643,4), so before 752.

952. 46. Muḥammad b. ʿAbd al-Raḥīm b. Ibrāhīm, his grandson, whose *Qilādat al-ʿiqyān* is preserved in Mosul 246$_{,356,3}$, together with an anonymous commentary entitled *Silk al-bayān*.

51. See p. 624$_{,5}$.

953. 52. Read: "ḤKh IV, 366$_{,8811}$".

954. 66. See p. 628$_{,1}$.

956. 85. See p. 1017$_{,36}$.

88. Garr. 1773.

957. 100. Ca. 1279, see ad I, 843.

958. 105. See p. 89$_{,1}$a.

108. Garr. 2097$_{,3}$ (which has: Muḥammad b. Ṭāhir and *Niʿmat al-qadīr fīmā yaḥill lil-rajul min al-ḥarīr*).

109. Garr. 1540.

111. See I, 660, II, 950$_{,28}$.

B. 1. See p. 704$_{,5}$, read: *al-tashdīd*.

959. 8. See p. $700_{,2b}$.

11. See p. $438_{,9}$.

12. See p. 468. I. a. composed in 1243, $480_{,7e}$.

960. 14. See I, 843, II, $791_{,1}$, *Risāla fī faḍāʾil al-niṣf min Shaʿbān*, Alex. Fun. 33.

24. See I, $661_{,1c}$.

961. 28. See $702_{,2a}$.

32. MS dated 909.

33. See ad p. 346.

962.37. See *G* II, $266_{,37}$ (?).

38. See $865_{,5}$.

39. Garr. 1855 (which has: Aḥmad b. Naṣr al-Darʿi, see p. $903_{,63}$?).

40. See $696_{,9}$.

44. See I, $893_{,25}$.

963. 50. See $1041_{,45}$.

51. = b. Shās I, $664_{,6b}$.

53. See I, $663_{,4a}$.

964. 3. See *G* II, 403/4.

4. 2. Garr. 1404 (ca. 940/1533).

8. Garr. 18, 32.

10. See p. $604_{,2}$.

965. 19. Garr. 1833, see p. $971,_{21a}$.

21. See p. $441,_{6}$.

966. 2a. Badr al-Dīn b. ʿAbd al-Ghanī al-Ḥanbalī al-Maqdisī, *Tadhkira mukhtaṣara fī uṣūl al-fiqh ʿalā madhhab Aḥmad b. Ḥanbal* Dam. Z. 35,92.

5. See ad p. 944.

967. 3. See p. $558,_{4b}$.

6. See p. $111,_{22b}$.

8. See I, 607, $_{14d}$.

9. See 564, § 7. 11, 3.

968. 12. See p. $545,_{11d}$.

13. See p. $560,_{8a}$.

16. Read: al-Nāẓirī, see I, 702, 11,5.

969. 1. See p. 807 n.

3. See p. $843,_{31}$.

5. See p. $971,_{25}$.

9. See p. $209,_{1}$, at the end.

970. See p. 775, 9, 16.

971. 21a. See p. $965,_{19}$.

25. See I, $713,_{7}$, II, $969,_{5}$.

27. See p. $843,_{30}$.

972. 4, 1. Garr. $2002,_{4}$.

5. Read: ʿAbdallāh b. ʿUmar, see *G.* I, 274.

7a. ʿAbdallāh b. al-Walīd al-Baghdādī Muwaffaq al-Dīn Abū Manṣūr, *al-Ḥirz wal-manʿa fī bayān amr al-hudā wal-mutʿa*, Dam. Z. 45$_{,37,2}$.

1317 | 973. 8. Read: b. Yūsuf, Mosul 101$_{,38,7}$.

12. See p. 317$_{,2}$c.

12a. Ibn ʿAbd al-Salām, *al-ʿImād fī mawārīth al-ʿibād*, Dam. Z. 41$_{,20}$.

16. See ad 314.

974. 20. See p. 319$_{,3,3}$.

975. 34. = Aḥmad b. ʿAbdallāh al-Fayḍī al-Mawṣilī Abu ʾl-Barakāt. 1. Composed in 1330.—2. Mosul, 299$_{,16}$ (anonymous)

37. See p. 777$_{,15}$.

37b. Jamāl al-Dīn b. Ziyād al-Waḍḍāḥī al-Shaʿrabī al-Yamanī, *al-Miṣbāḥ al-munīr wal-murshid lil-ʿābir fi ʾl-masīr fīmā yataʿallaq bil-ḥajj fi ʾl-muʾajjir wal-ajīr*, Garr. 1652.

39. See I, 724$_{,11d}$, II, 981$_{,2d}$.

976. 43. See p. 667, § 13.

46. See p. 606$_{,14}$.

49a. Mubārak b. ʿAbd al-Ḥaqq b. Nūr, *Tuḥfat al-fuqahāʾ*, Garr. 1655.

60. Garr. 1772 (Ḥanafī).

978. 64. Muḥammad b. al-Waḍḍāḥ al-Qurṭubī al-Andalusī, d. 1289/1902 (? Abū Bakr b. Khayr, *Bibl. Ar. Hisp.* IX, 150, 255, 274, Ibn al-Faraḍī, ibid. VII, 70, no date).—1. Garr. 2070$_{,1}$.—2. *Kitāb al-bidaʿ wal-nahy ʿanhā*, ed. Muḥammad Duhmān, Damascus 1349, *RAAD* XI, 127.

65. See p. 694$_{,2a}$.

66. See I, 320$_{,7}$.

70. See p. 995$_{,55}$.

72a. Abū Ṭāhir al-Samarqandī, *ʿUyūn al-madhāhib fī khilāfāt al-amṣār*, Garr. 1654.

73. See p. 557$_{,2}$.

979. 5. Garr. 1222, see ad II, 227.—7. Garr. 1243.—9. See p. 453$_{,10a}$.

980. 18. See p. 506.—2. With a self-commentary entitled *Sirāj al-adhhān bi-tajwīd al-Qurʾān.*

981. 19. See p. 211$_{,2}$.

20. See I, 724$_{,11d}$.

22. See *G* II, 202$_{,8k}$.

27. See ad I, 634.

28. a. Muḥammad b. Ayyūb b. al-Ḍurays Abū ʿAbdallāh, *Faḍāʾil al-Qūrʾān wamā nazala min al-Qūrʾān bi-Makka wamā nazala bil-Madīna*, Dam. Z. 34$_{,78,1}$.

982. 36. See I, 727$_{,12a}$.

39. The *nisba* "al-Yāmī" is also carried by the traditionalist Zubayd, *Khulāṣa* 11$_{,3}$, *TA* VIII, 196$_{,26}$ (Spitaler).

983. 42. See p. 456$_{,23b}$, with addendum.

B. 1. See p. 556$_{,5}$.

2. Read: *al-shaffāf.*

5. Garr. 2173$_{,2}$.

984. 6. See S. to 455.

12a. Aḥmad al-Ḥanafī al-Ḥuṣūlī, *Rawḍat al-ʿāshiqīn wa-zahrat al-ṭālibīn*, Paris 4537, Garr. 1242 (MS dated 1075/1662).

14. See p. 142$_{,28}$.

985. 17. See I, 263$_{,39}$.

19. See p. 311$_{,1a}$.

20. See I, 741$_{,67}$.

21. See p. 250, § 5. 1.

986. 30a. Al-Ḥasan b. Muḥammad b. Ḥabīb Abu ʾl-Qāsim, *al-Tanzīl wa-tartībuhu*, Dam. Z. 31$_{,26}$.

33. See *G* I, 373.

34. See ad p. 166.

35. See p. 241.$_{1c}$.

987. 39. See *G* II, 326.

43a. Muḥammad Muḥammad b. Aḥmad al-Jahmī al-Waṣṣābī, *al-Ḍawʾ al-munīr al-lāʾiḥ fī iʿrāb wa-taʾrīkh al-fawātiḥ*, Garr. 1317.

988. 48. Garr. 1292, see p. 137$_{,8,3}$.

49. See p. 582,5.

55. See I, 270, c. 2, 859$_{,38}$.

989. 63, 2. *al-Jawhara fī ʿilm al-ʿarūḍ*, Mosul 211$_{,60,2}$.

5. See p. 399$_{,18a}$.

990. 9. See p. 280$_{,1b}$.

10a. See I, 806$_{,31}$.

11. See p. 459$_{,18,2}$.

12. Garr. 1568.

14, 1. See p. 814$_{,36}$.

991. 15. See I, 643$_{,20}$, II,262$_{,5a}$.

17a. Amīrak Abū Muḥammad, *al-Tadhkira fī aḥkām al-maʿlūmāt wa-awṣāfihā*, Dam. Z. 48$_{,64}$.

23. 1. Gotha 866$_{,1}$.

992. 23a. See p. 1003$_{,70}$.

27. Read: al-Jūrādī, MS dated 896.

31b. | Mamkubars b. Yalanqilič b. Najm al-Dīn al-Imām al-Nāṣirī, *al-Nūr* 1318
al-lāmiʿ wal-burhān al-sāṭiʿ, Dam. Z. 45$_{,31}$.

993. 35a. Muḥammad b. Aḥmad b. al-Muḥibb al-Maqdisī al-Ḥanbalī, *Ṣifāt rabb al-ʿālamīn*, Dam. Z. 33$_{,57}$.

994. 46a. Muḥammad al-Wafāʾī Abu ʾl-Maʿālī al-Shāfiʿī, *Wāḍiḥ al-dalīl wal-burhān fi ʾl-radd ʿala ʾl-qāʾil bi-khalq al-Qurʾān*, Dam. Z. 29$_{,8,6}$.

48. Read: b. Sumaiṭ, Garr. 1567, see p. 923$_{,89}$.

51a. Najjārzāde, *muftī* of Adana, *al-Risāla al-sharīfa al-tartībiyya*, Garr. 2091$_{,2}$.

54. See I, 624$_{,8d}$.

995. 55. See p. 978$_{,70}$.

59. Read: Taqī al-Dīn.

9. 2. see p. 1037$_{,1}$.

996. 3. See p. 286$_{,10}$.

4. See p. 520,$_{5}$.

6. See p. 722,$_{7b}$.

9. See p. 580,$_{5}$.

997. 13b. ʿAbd al-Majīd Shaykhī, *Risālat mawāʿiẓ*, Dam. Z. 84,$_{105}$.

998. 23. See p. 402,$_{7}$.

999. 27. Read: al-naḍīr.

28. See p. 254,$_{2}$.

30. 2. Additionally Alex. Taṣ. 43.

1000. 35. See p. 907,$_{8}$.

35a. See p. 83,$_{12}$.

37. See I, 775,$_{3a}$.

38a. Aḥmad b. Muḥammad al-Harawī Abū Saʿd, al-*Arbaʿūn fī shuyūkh al-Ṣūfiyya*, Dam. Z. 59,$_{121}$.

41. Garr. 1927 (which has: al-ʿUsālī, d. 1048/1639).

1001. 43. See ad p. 362.

45. Additionally Gotha 1158,$_{2}$.

49. Read: al-Ghīshī.

1002. 53. Read: *sīrat khayr al-khalāʾiq*.

1003. 66. Jalāl al-Dīn Khalwatī, *Murshid al-sālikīn wa-munqidh al-hālikīn*, Berl. 3777 (wrongly attributed to al-Ghazzālī), Ind. Off. 4575 (*JRAS* 1939, 367).

70. See p. 992,$_{23a}$.

1004. 77. Maybe = Ṣalāḥ al-Dīn Khalīl b. Muḥammad al-Aqfahsī, who is called *ṣāḥib*, i.e. his contemporary, in al-Damīrī, *Ḥayāt al-ḥayawān* I, 89,5 (Spitaler).

80. Read: C. 1323.

81. Read: (*al-dār wal-mawlid*).

1005. 82a. Ismāʿīl al-Ghazzī al-ʿĀmirī, *Ḥuṣūl al-uns fī 'ntiqāl ḥaḍrat al-quds* (*tarjamat al-Shaykh Khālid al-Naqshbandī*), Dam. 79,92.

83. Read: Jizduwānī.

91. See p. 372,13.

1006. 92. See ad p. 152,32a.

94. See p. 153, bottom.

95. See ad p. 469.

101. See I, 913,11.

1007. 108. See p. 470,29.

112. a. Muḥammad b. Muḥammad b. Muḥammad al-Nasafī al-Maʿrūf bi-Muḥammad al-Amīn al-Ḥulwī al-Kubrawī al-Bulghārī, *Kanz al-abrār*, MS dated 791, Garr. 1937.

1008. 113. See p. 489,9.

115a. Muḥammad al-Saʿdī Shams al-Dīn, *al-Risāla al-Muḥammadiyya fī 'l-radd ʿala 'l-sāda al-Saʿdiyya*, Garr. 1601 (MS dated 1224).

118a. Muḥammad b. Ṭāhir b. al-Ḥusayn, *Maslak qarīb li-kull sālik munīb*, Garr. 1973.

119. For his ancestor, see p. 375,3a.

1009. 123, 3. Read: 1310.

124. See I, 785, line 13.

125. Read: *taḥṣīn* and *ilā*.

125a. Muḥyi ʾl-Dīn b. Abī Bakr al-Ḥanafī, *Tadhkirat al-dhākirīn*, Dam. Z. $51_{,39,2}$.

127. Read: al-Rankusī, autograph dated 1175/1762.

131. See I, 756, 773.

1010. 132. See I, $593_{,1a}$.

135aa. ʿUmar b. ʿĀṣ al-Tulawī (?), *Risālat maqāmāt al-ṭarīqa al-Naqshbandiyya*, BDMG. 24.

135ab. ʿUthmān al-Abharī Abū ʿUmar, *Risāla fi ʾl-fuqr wal-fuqarāʾ*, Dam. Z. $51_{,35,2}$.

135d. Saʿīd b. Muḥammad al-ʿUdhrī b. al-Raqqām, *Nūr al-yaqīn wa-ishārat ahl al-tamkīn*, Dam. Z. $60_{,131,2}$.

136. See I, 910.

137. See I, $776_{,a}$.

1319 | 1011. 141a. Read: al-Jaʿfarī, see p. $809_{,1c}$.

143. See I, $785_{,19}$.

1012. 148. Muḥammad b. Ṭāhir, Garr. 973.

155. al-Kurdī read: lil-awliyāʾ, composed in 1211/1797, Mosul $86_{,3}$.

1013. 2. Garr. 1539.

3. See I, $838_{,21}$, I, c.

1014. 7a. Shihāb al-Dīn Aḥmad b. al-Jundī, *Kitāb al-ḥudūd*, Berl. 5377, f. 149/56.

12. Grandson of $498_{,8}$, *Tuḥfat al-aḥbāb* additionally Alex. Fun. $97_{,2}$ (supposedly written in 1138); *Risāla fī rubʿ al-muqanṭar fi ʾl-mīqāt*, ibid. $101_{,10}$ (composed in

1131); *Sullam al-sawāʾ wal-āfāq fi ʾl-rubʿ al-mujayyab* (composed in 1148), ibid. 101,$_{11}$, see I, 753, penult., II, 918,$_{39}$.

14. See ad I, 319.

15. See p. 587,$_{1d}$, $_{2}$. *Ithbāt al-wājib*, Garr. 804.

17. Garr. 217, Berl. 8709,$_{2}$.

1015. 20. See I, 286.

22. See I, 743, II, 587,$_{1a}$, 966,$_{5}$,$_{33}$.

24. See I, 159, 491.

1016. 29. = I, 521,$_{1}$ (?).

1017. 36. See p. 956,$_{85}$.

36a. ʿUthmān b. Muṣṭafā al-Ṭarasūsī (= *G* I, 519 ad 171, 20?), *Risāla istidlāliyya*, Garr. 805.

37a. Shams al-Dīn al-Tustarī, *Makārim al-akhlāq wal-siyāsa*, Cairo I, 363, no. 994, 1353 (Bishr Fāris, *Mabāḥith ʿarabiyya* 33,$_{9n}$).

5. Garr. 1015.

1018. 10. See ad 393.

13. See p. 156,$_{5}$.

14. See I, 494, line 5.

16. See I, 664.

1019. 24. al-Khāṭirī, Garr. 1057.

24a. Aḥmad b. Nāʾib Ḥusayn b. Muḥammad al-Awsī al-Anṣārī, *al-Barāhīn al-wāḍiḥa al-jaliyya ilā thubūt sayr al-aflāk wa-sukūn al-kura al-arḍiyya*, Garr. 1018.

27a. Ḥaydar b. ʿAbd al-Raḥmān al-Ḥusaynī al-Jazarī, *Nuzhat al-ṭullāb fī ʿilm al-asṭurlāb*, Berl. 5807, Garr. 1014.

1020. 28. Muḥyi ʾl-Dīn al-ʿAwfī, *Sharḥ Lamḥ al-ḥifẓ fī ḥisāb ʿuqūd al-aṣābiʿ*, ed. M. Bahjat, *RAAD* V, 701/9.

28a. ʿAlī b. ʿAbdallāh al-Ṭūsī Nūr al-Dīn, *Miftāḥ al-asrār fī ʿilm al-falak al-dawwār*, Garr. 1016.

36a. Abū ʿAbdallāh Ḥasan b. Muḥammad b. Ḥamla al-Baghdādī, *Risāla fi ʾl-maqādīr al-mushtarika wal-mutabāyina*, Bank. XXII,$_{2648,xxxi}$.

1021. 43. See 94,$_{27a}$.

44. See p. 244/5.

46. Additionally AS 2732, 1/41.

47. See p. 538,$_{2,3}$.

49. See E. Wiedemann, Über Bestimmung der spezifischen Gewichte, *SB Ph. med. Soz. Erlangen* 38 (1906), 166/70.

1023. 64, 1. Additionally Berl. 5765/6, Garr. 1012.—2. Read: Tuwaynī, Garr. 2158.

1024. 70a. Muḥammad Sharābī al-Idkāwī, al-*Fawāʾid al-muhimmāt fī maṭāliʿ al-awqāt*, with the commentary *al-Ghāyāt*, Garr. 2077,$_{1}$.

75. = (?) Naṣr b. ʿAbdallāh, author of the *Risāla fī anna ʾl-ashkāl kullahā min al-dāʾira*, who had written a work on the same subject for Sultan al-Manṣūr ʿAḍud al-Dawla (369–72/979–82), Bank. XXII, 91,$_{2468}$xlii.

79. Before 664/1266, which is the date of the Berlin MS.—2. *al-Hidāya wal-tabyīn fi ʾl-ḥikma al-ṭabīʿiyya.*—3. *Risāla fi ādāb al-baḥth.*—4. A work on arithmetic, AS 4382, ii, 34, see Ritter, *Arch. Orientálny* IV, 1932, 370.

1025. 80. See I, 400.

82. See p. 296,$_{9}$.

82a. Yūsuf al-Aṣamm, *Risāla fī ʿilm al-ḥisāb*, Dam. Z. 41$_{18, 2}$.

1026. 2. Garr. 774.

3. See I, 405$_{2b}$.

4. Garr. 773 (which is hardly an abstract from al-Mufīdī's *Majālis*).

4a. Muḥammad al-ʿAlawī al-Ḥusaynī, *Faḍl al-Kūfa wa-faḍl ahlihā*, Dam. Z. 35$_{93}$.

1027. 3. See p. 113$_{28}$.

6. Garr. 1114.

7. Read: al-Khawwām, see p. | 215$_{1}$ (?). 1320

8a. ʿAbd al-Raḥmān b. Abī Ṣādiq Abū l-Qāsim, *Awfar al-shurūḥ li-Fuṣūl Ibbuqrāṭ*, Dam. Z. 87,27,2.

1028. 9, 1. Garr. 1116.—5. *al-Shuhda fī takmīl muqaddimat al-Zubda*, ibid. 1117.

16. See p. 781$_{2}$.

1029. 21. See p. 299.

1030. 31. = Najīb al-Dīn al-Samarqandī, I, 895/6, MS dated 594.

34. See p. 366$_{1}$.

35. Garr. 1121a (Darwīsh Muḥammad).

38. See I, 826, g.

1031. 42, 1. Mosul 237$_{175}$, Taymūr, Ṭibb 450, AS 363 (see Ritter and Ruska, *Istanb. Mitt.* 3), see ad 894.

49a. al-Ṣūrī, *al-Kāfī fī ṭibb al-ʿayn*, Dam. Z. 87$_{18,2}$.

1032. 50. See I, 888$_{10}$.

14. 2. See I, 945 ad 239 (?).

4. See p. $693_{,1e}$.

1033. 7. Read: b. Sāʿid, see p. 169.

1034. 5. Read: Gotha 1254.

7. See p. $667_{,2}$.

13. Read: b. Masʿūd.

1035. 3. See ad I, 907, Farmer, *Sources* 46.

1036. 6. See I, 829.

7. 14th cent. Bodl. Ouseley 102, f. 1/11 s. Farmer, *Sources* 54.

9. See p. $907_{,2}$.

1037. 7. Read: *al-rimāya bil-nushshāb*, Gotha $1337_{,1}$.

1. See $995_{,1}$.

2. See p. 367.

1038. 6, 2. See p. $694_{,5}$.

13. See I, 909 bottom.

1039. 19. See I, 799, 26c, 1. Ḥurūf $14_{,1}$.

24. Read: "b. Sha'mī", see p. $543_{,3}$.

24a. Ibrāhīm b. Muḥammad b. Kasbāy al-ʿImādī, *Fawāʾid manẓūma*, Dam. Z. $86_{,23,4}$.

1041. 37. See p. $328_{,1}$.

45. See p. $963_{,50}$.

1042. 47. Bank. XXII, 128,$_{2491}$ (which has: al-Ḥanbalī, ca. 1144).

54. See p. 358.

1043. 8. See p. 519.

1044. 10. Garr. 926. 11. See p. 162,$_{sa}$.

Supplement Volume 3

18. ʿAqqād, *Shuʿarāʾ Miṣr* 120/48, *Adab wa-taʾrīkh* 7/110, Ṭāhir al-Ṭannāḥī, *Hilāl* 39 (1930), 47/80, *Marāthi ʾl-shuʿarāʾ ʿalā M. P. S. al-B. jamaʿahā* Khalīl al-Maṭrān, C. 1322, Saʿd Mīkhāʾīl, *Ādāb ʿal-aṣr* 216/24, ʿIzzaddīn Ṣāliḥ, *Shuʿarāʾ al-jīl al-ʿishrīn B. S. al-B.*, Alexandria 1329.

20. ʿAbd al-Laṭīf al-Ṣayrafī, *Dīwān ʿAbd al-ʿAzīz Ṣabrī* (his son), C. 1335/1908, see Cheikho, *Mashriq* 23, 307; *Dīwān*, ed. Aḥmad al-Zayn, C. 1938. ʿAqqād, *Shuʿarāʾ Miṣr* 22/9, Saʿd Mīkhāʾīl, *Ādāb al-ʿaṣr* 73/8, Mayy, *Ṣaḥāʾif* 116/21.

24. Bottom, read: H.A.R. Gibb.

25. Instead of *Dall wa-Taymān*, Alex. Qis. 57 lists: *Lādiyās* (so) *aw ākhir al-Farāʿina*, C. 1898.

41. Line 20. Instead of ʿAbdallāh, read: Aḥmad.

48. Various *maqāmas* and *qaṣīdas* in *al-Zahrāʾ* I/III, ʿAqqād, *Shuʿarāʾ Miṣr* 156/88, Saʿd Mīkhāʾīl, *Ādāb al-ʿaṣr* 7/22; Line 29, read: Ph. Boiti, idem, *Poème historique sur les événements importants de la vallée du Nil composé par A. Chauki et trad.*, Cairo 1895.

| 56. Saʿd Mīkhāʾīl, *Ādāb al-ʿaṣr* 283/90. 1321

68. n., line 24. Instead of Schlier, read: Shulayr, Mons Solarius in Andalusia, Yāqūt III, 316, Pérès, *Les voyages ... And.* 232.

70. O. Coterini, Peu de mots sur le diwan de H. M. I., *Transact. 13th Congr. of Or.* London 1904, 312/3. Saʾd Mīkhāʾīl, *Ādāb al-ʿaṣr* 232/40.

71. 11. Instead of Roi, read: Leroi.

73. 4. Instead of Mait, read: Mīt.

76. *Raʾy fī ʾl-ḥaḍāra al-jīliyya, Hilāl* 35 (1926) 33/6, Saʿd Mīkhāʾīl, *Ādāb al-ʿaṣr* 263/7.

77. 25. Read: Dārīn.

78. 27. Read: *Musājalāt.*

79. 7. Saʿd Mīkhāʾīl, *Ādāb al-ʿaṣr* 57/64.—8. Ibid. 65/72.

80. 9. Ibid. 50/6.—10. Ibid. 127/31.

82. 12. Ibid. 225/31.

84. k. Cheikho, *Mashriq* XXIV, 2/42.

85. r. 3. *Ḥabāʾil al-shayṭān*, Alexandria 1334.

86. Khalīl Maṭrān, born in 1871 in Baalbek, went to Egypt in 1873 where he founded *al-Majalla al-Miṣriyya* and *al-Jawāb* in 1899.

95. Saʿd Mīkhāʾīl, *Ādāb al-ʿaṣr* 147/52. Various *qaṣīdas, Zahrāʾ* I/III, C. 1343/5. Mīkhāʾīl Nuʿayma, *Ghirbāl* 195/205. *Bāʾiʿat al-azhār, Hilāl* 35 (1926), 22. Molière ibid. 37 (1928) 17/9. *Fī waṣf Muʿāwiya*, ibid. 23. *Inna min al-bayān la-siḥran, ḥikāyat shāʿir*, ibid. 39 (1930) 277/81. *Hind*, ibid. 189. *al-Umm*, ibid. 40, 516/8. *Rūwād al-nahḍa al-ʿarabiyya al-ḥadītha*, ibid. 42 (1922) 919/24. *Bint shaykh al-qabīla, al-Muqtaṭaf* 80 (1932) 23/4. *Al-Lugha al-ʿarabiyya, dhakhāʾiruha ʾl-adabiyya qadīman wa-ḥadīthan*, ibid. 77, 317/25. *al-Fallāḥ*, from the French by Yūsuf Bek Naḥḥās (*Jāmiʿ* 56).

101. A juvenile work, *ʿIbrat al-taʾrīkh*, C. 1330/1912 in Alex. Qiṣ. 40, final.

117. 8. *al-ʿĀṣifa*, first in *al-Muqtaṭaf* 75/6, 1929/30. Aḥmad Muḥarram, *Aḥmad Zakī Abū Shādī, shiʿruhu fī dīwān al-Shuʿla*, C. 1933.

124. *Miṣriyyāt*, selection by Ḥasan Ṣāliḥ al-Jiddāwī, Maṭbaʿat al-Salafiyya (*Jāmiʿ* 699).

128. Various *qaṣīdas* in *al-Zahrā'* I/III, C. 1343/5.

129. *Sirr al-khayāl, Hilāl* 42, 188/92.

130. Sa'd Mīkhā'īl, *Ādāb al-'aṣr* 187/92.

131. 21. *al-Ash'āl, dīwān*, C. 1932.

144. *al-Ṣayḥa, Hilāl* 35 (1926) 20ff.

147. Mīkhā'īl Nu'ayma, *Ghirbāl* 206/16.

151. Idem, ibid. 242/9.

154. Line 22. On 'Abdallāh Nadīm, see Aḥmad Taymūr, *Hilāl* 41, 116/7.

156. 15. Maṭba'at Ḥijāzī, C. 1936.

160. Line 7. Read: *Qabḍ al-rīḥ*.

165. 31. *al-Alḥān al-ḍā'i'a*, 2nd print. Alexandria 1939.

168. Line 21. Read: *Khaybat*, line 24 read: *al-Kharīf*.

175. Line 18. *al-Zaynabiyya*, C. 1331.—23. Read: *aw ghādat*.—c. *al-Mar'a al-raḥīma, qiṣṣa masraḥiyya*, C. 1939, see *Radio Araba di Bari* II, 1939, 193: *Khāṭira*.

180. 40. *Shu'arā' al-Sūdān*, before 1926, Kračk.

189. I, 3 To be deleted.

190. 22 and 24 additionally 1922.—*Riḥlat Jirjī Zaydān ilā Ūrūbā*, C. 1912 (*Jāmi'* 130).

| 192. n. 2. Read Malwa instead of Melfa. 1322

193. 4 from below, read: al-Sha'b.—n. read: *al-Munāẓir*.

194. 5. *Marāthī* (*Jāmi'* 39).—'Abdallāh Ḥabīb Nawfal, *Tarājim 'ulamā' Ṭarābulus* 227/30.—2. Ḥadīth 'Īsā b. Hishām 2nd print. 1330 (al-Maṭba'a al-Azhariyya).

195. 26. Read: *Ayna 'l-insān.*—Adams 211.

202. 7. *Amsi wal-yawm* from *Majallat al-bayān* in *Dīwān al-adab aw abdaʿ mā katabahu udabāʾ al-Gharb wal-ʿArab,* Maṭbaʿat al-Taqaddum n.d. 4/9.—Saʿd Mīkhāʾīl, *Ādāb al-ʿaṣr* 250/62.

211. 9. Adams 250/1.

212. 10. *Miṣr al-Islāmiyya wa-taʾrīkh al-khiṭaṭ al-Miṣriyya,* C., Maṭbaʿat Dār al-Kawkab al-munīr, 1931, see *RAAD* V, 580.

213. 11a. *al-Rayḥāniyyāt* III, 156/70.

214. Line 10. Read: *Muqaddimat.*

215. 11b. See *Mél. de l'Inst. Franç. de Damas* 39, 57. 11c. Instead of father, read: uncle, see *RAAD* VIII, 59/60, *Amīr Lubnān,* translated from the French by Asʿad Efendi Dāqir.

217. 22. Read: *Asāṭīn.*

220. 30. Read: *Mahzalat.*

226. 15. Read: *al-zarqāʾ.*

227. 1887. Read: Bustros.

228. Line 1. Read: Muʿtamid, 1899. Read: Muḥammad Ayyūb.—1900. Ibrāhīm Zaydān, read: (a brother of Jirjī Zaydān).

229. Line 12. Read: *ʿAdhrāʾ.*—On *Asrār al-thawra al-rūsiyya,* see Kračkovsky, *Hist. Roman* 85.

230. 1910. On Niqula Rizqallāh, see Cheikho, *Mashriq* XXIV, 299; *al-Riwāyāt al-jadīda,* 7 vols, C. 1910

1911. ʿAbd al-Muʿṭī Marʿī wa-Muḥammad ʿAbd al-Muṭṭalib, *al-Riwāyāt al-ʿarabiyya,* C. 1329.

1912. Iskandar Shaffūn, *al-Sabāyā*.

1917. ʿAbd al-Rashād al-Raḥḥāla, *Aḍghāth aḥlām*, essays, Alexandria.

1918. Tawfīq Muṣṭafā Fahmī Efendi, *Ḥayāt baʾīs*, C.

232. 1927. Naṣr Ḥannāʾ Efendi, *Bayna Miṣr wal-Ḥijāz*, C. Delete: ʿAbdallāh al-ʿAlawī b. al-Ḥaddād, see II, 288, 49a.

233. 1937. Read: Muḥammad ʿAwḍ Muḥammad (the translator of Goethe's *Faust* and of *Hermann und Dorothea*).

234. 1940. Maḥmūd Kāmil al-Muḥāmī, *al-Rabīʿ al-āthim, Ḥayāt al-ẓalām*, see *Radio Araba di Bari* III, 140/1.

16. Read: *Shiḥāta*.

236. 19. Read: ʿAḥmad al-Hilbāwī.

237. 20. See Lecerf, op. cit., 130.

241. Line 4. *Warāʾ al-biḥār*, an account of a trip through Greece, Turkey, Romania, Hungary, and to Vienna, C. 1936.

Line 5. Read: Paxton.

243. Line. 26. Russian transl. by Sallier, Leningrad 1935, ibid. read: Morik Brin.

Line. 30. Read: Dhuhnī.

Line 35. Read: Jean Giraudoux.

247. Line 14. Sample in *al-Ḥadīth* 1938, 498/501, review ibid. 490/7.

248. 26. Read: Ḥamāda (Bishr Fāris).

250. Ismāʿīl Adham, *Tawfīq Ḥakīm, al-fannān al-ḥāʾir*, Aleppo 1939.

251. Line 5. See Kampffmeyer, *MSOS* XXXII, 1929, 218.

1323 | 255. Line 13. Instead of Beirut, read: Cairo; autobiograpy, transl. Fr. Gabrieli, *Or. Mod.* XIX, 505/15.

256. Line 12. Meanwhile published in Beirut, 1939.

258. Line 10. Kračkowsky, foreword to the translation of Qāsim Amīn, *Tahrīr al-mar'a*, St. Petersburg 1912, XIV.

260. al-*Musāwāh* see Shakīb Arslān, *RAAD* IV, 531/44.

262. Line 33. Lecerf, Tradition nationale et culture moderne dans l'oeuvre de Maiy, *Bull. de l'Inst. franç. de Damas*, 1932, II, 1, 202/9. R. Nakhla, *al-Muqtaṭaf* I, 1930, 143/55, VI, 47/50. L. Massignon, *RMM* 62, 1925, 230. R. Strothmann, *Die kopt. Kirche* 76, P. Kraus, *EI* Suppl. 23.

Last line: Ibnat al-Shāṭi', i.e. 'Ā'isha 'Abd al-Raḥmān.

264. Line 25. *Radio Araba di Bari* II, 1939, 196.

§ 3. Lecerf. l'influence des spectacles sur l'évolution linguistique des dialectes modernes du Levant, *Atti del III. Congr. Intern. dei Linguisti*, Florence 1935, p. 181/6.

265 On Abū Naḍḍāra, Kračkovsky, *Vost.* IV, 1924, 165/8, Arabic in *al-Ikhā'*, I, 1924, 150/6.

268. Line 18, on Najīb see Kračkovsky, *Hist. Roman* 64/5.

276. b. Ibrāhīm Ramzī, b. 1884, *al-Ḥākim bi-amrillāh*, C. 1915, *al-Badawiyya*, C. 1922, see Sa'd Mīkhā'īl, *Ādāb al-'aṣr* 23/8.

c. Read: Aḥmad Khayrī.

282. Line 18. Read: Bonola.

290. al-Ayyām, 3rd print. C. 1939, transl. Kračkovsky, Leningrad 1934.

292. Line 25. On Nasīm, see Sa'd Mīkhā'īl, *Ādāb al-'aṣr* 50/9.

297. Line 33. Read: Ibn al-'Amīd.

301. *Min al-adab al-tamthīlī al-yūnānī* (transl. from *Elektra, Aias, Antigone, Oedipus Rex*), C. 1939.—*Maʿa Abi ʾl-ʿAlāʾ fī sijnihi*, ibid. 1939.

302. 3. *al-Akhlāq ʿinda ʾl-Ghazzālī*, see Snouck-Hurgronje, *Verspr. Geschriften* VI, Leiden 1927, 206/29.

305. 4. Aḥmad Ḍayf, *Muqaddima li-dirāsat balāghat al-ʿArab*, C. Maṭbaʿat al-Sufūr, 1921, adaptation of his French dissertation, *Essai sur le lyrisme et la critique littéraire chez les Arabes*, Paris 1917.—ʿAbd al-Raḥmān Badawī, *al-Turāth al-Yūnānī fi ʾl-ḥaḍāra al-Islāmiyya*, R. Maṭbaʿat al-Nahḍa al-Miṣriyya, 1940.

309. 1924, ʿUmar Ṭusun, on whose *Kalimāt fī sabīl Miṣr*, C. 1928, see *RAAD* IX, 123.

310. 1929. ʿAbd al-Ḥamīd al-ʿAjātī wa-Riyāḍ Jundī, *Taʾrīkh al-fann al-jamīl min ʿaṣr al-nahḍa ila ʾl-waqt al-ḥāḍir*, C.

1933. Read: Amīn Muḥammad Saʿīd, idem *al-Dawla al-ʿarabiyya al-muttaḥida*, C. 1938.

1940. ʿAbd al-Qādir Ḥamza Pāshā. *ʿAlā hāmish taʾrīkh Miṣr al-qadīm* and Selīm Ḥasan Pāshā Ismāʿīl, *Miṣr al-qadīm*, C.

312. 27. Riyāḍ.

321. 2. C. C. Adams, M. Abduh and the Transvaal Fetwa, *Macdonald Presentation Volume*, p. 13/39.

323. 3. Muḥammad Bahjat al-Bīṭār, *RAAD* XV, 365/74, 474/80.

326. 7. Tanṭāwī Jawharī died on 12 January 1940.

329. 7. Collected works in *Nahḍat al-umma wa-ḥayātuhā*.

331. 10. *Taḥrīr al-marʾa* Russian transl. I. Kračkovsky, St. Petersburg 1912 (Mir Islama). *Kalimāt li Q.B.A.* Cairo, Maṭbaʿat al-Jarīda, 1908.

336. n. Muḥammad Kurd ʿAlī, *al-Hijra ilā Miṣr, Min al-qadīm wal-ḥadīth* p. 251/7.

1324 | 338. e Read: Shāhīn ʿAṭiyya".

f. Read ʿAleih instead of ʿAliyya.

340. h. Saʿd Mīkhāʾīl, *Ādāb al-ʿaṣr* 159/66.

341. c. b. 1850, d. 10 July 1933 (*EI* I, 371).

342. c. *ʿUkāẓ fī shuʾūm al-ʿArab*, MS Upps. no. 205, *Āyāt al-ʿaṣr, dīwān*, C. 1905.

C. a. Delete, see II, 397.

344. d. See Kračkovsky, *Hist. Roman* 75/6.

346. c. Saʿd Mīkhāʾīl, *Ādāb al-ʿaṣr* 193/200.

347. a. Read: Shulḥut and al-Sharfa.

348. 2. Saʿd Mīkhāʾīl, *Ādāb al-ʿaṣr* 137/46, with the sample "Love in the Language of the Crafts", 138/45.

352. Bottom *RAAD* V, 249/52, Kračkovsky, *Hermes* (Russ.) 1909, 34/42.

354. b. Murdered in Damascus in 1940.

356. Individual articles by him also in *RAAD*, I, 248, 263, II, 32, 64, VII, 145/59, X, 93/103, 103/4, 153ff, 160/5, 217/22, 223/9, 27, 33/46, 385/402, 449/60, 526/35, 498/9, XI, 156, 201/3, 265, 367/83, XII, 760/73.

357. 3. Individual articles in *RAAD* V, 293/308, 349/64, 405/27 (*Shuʿarāʾ al-Shaʾm fi ʾl-qarn al-thālith*), XIV, 395/401 (*ʿAbd al-Ḥamīd al-Kātib*), XV, 15/33 (*al-Walīd b. Yazīd*), 340/51, 450/6 (*ʿAdī b. ar-Riqāʿ*). Review of his bookj on Jāḥiẓ, ibid. X, 636.

358. e. Mīkhāʾīl Nuʿayma, *al-Ghirbāl* 187/90.

361. 5f. Muḥammad Nājī al-Ṭarābulusī, *Dīwān al-waṭaniyyāt*, C. 1929, see *RAAD* IX, 639.

362. c. Saʿd Mīkhāʾīl, *Ādāb al-ʿaṣr* 97/103.

370. Labīb Efendi al-Riyāshī, *al-Nubūgh*, see Mīkhāʾil Nuʿayma, *al-Ghirbāl* 191/4.

7. Read: al-Batjālī.

375. 12. On Dr. Ṣāliḥ Qambāz see *RAAD* VII, 74/7.

378. § 2. a. *Riwāyat al-shābb etc.*, abstract in Semenov, *Chrest.* 19/23, s. ibid. 7/18.

379. Line 19. Read: al-Batlūnī.

26. Read: Louise Mühlbach.

380. 2. Kāmil al-Ghazzī in *al-Ḥadīth* 1929, 405/20.

382. b. Instead of ʿAbiya, read: ʿAleih, see *al-Mashriq* XXIII, 159.

383 Line 3. Read: ʿAleih.

384. l. See *RAAD* VIII, 576/96, 666/79.

389. k. See Kračkovsky, *Zap. koll. vost.* III (1928), 186/911.

n. Read: *bi-shūf al-bakht*.

390. q. *Firdaws al-Maʿarrī*, Beirut 1333/1915.

397. See Kračkovsky, *Izv. Ak. Nauk*, 1931, 617/8.

399. Line 8. *al-Sayyid Rashīd Riḍā aw ikhāʾ arbaʿīn sana*, Damascus, Maṭbaʿat b. Zaydūn, 1356/1937 (834 pp.).

Line 10. Riposto di Sh. A. a. dichiarazioni del Mufti di Beirut favorevoli a la democrazia (from *Waḥdat al-Maghrib*, Tiṭwān vols. of 31 May 7 June 1940) tr. E. Rossi, *Or. Mod.* XX (1940) 376/80. 7. That he should have converted to Islam is, according to Kračkovsky, a malicious invention of *al-Mashriq*.

n. 1. This was an address held in New York on 3 February 1900, *al-Tasāhul al-dīnī*, print. Philadelphia, Maṭbaʿat al-Hudā, 1901 (Kračkovsky).

403. Line 6. Read: Dūmiṭ.

| 414. 7. Saʿd Mīkhāʾīl, *Ādāb al-ʿaṣr* 91/5. 1325

419. Last line, instead of son, read: ich.

422. Line 14. *ʿIlm al-adab etc.* under the pen name of al-Maqdisī, Cairo, Maṭbaʿat al-Hilāl 1904, cover page 1909, see *al-Hilāl* 1912, 375/7 (Kračkovsky).

423. 11. Instead of Mīkhāʾīl Barīk, read: Burayk (Brēk), who belongs to the 18th cent., see Cheikho, *Cat. de mss. des auteurs chrétiens depuis l'islam*, Beirut 1924, no. 201 (Kračkovsky).

426. 4 lines from below, read: Dūmiṭ.

429. 9. Read: Yazbek al-Bashʿalānī.

e. Instead of Namal, read: Nawfal.

Footnote. *The Contribution of the Arab to Education* (Teachers College, Columbia Univ. Contribution to Education, no. 231), New York 1926 (Kračkovsky).

431. i. Works of Emīr ʿAbdallāh of Transjordan: *Jawāb* al-sāʾil ʿani ʾl-khayl al-aṣāʾil, print. in ʿAmmān.—*Man anā* (history and essence of Arabhood), ibid.—*al-Amālī al-siyāsiyya* in print, see *Or. Mod.* XXI, 1941, 98.

439. Line 13, delete: *al-mumtāz*.

Footnote: Instead of W. Katesflis, read: W. Katseflis (from an Arab family of Tripoli, Kračkovsky).

445. 7. See I, 137, 3, more precisely *Qiṣṣat Dīk al-jinn al-Ḥimṣī, ḥikāyat gharām shāʿir ʿarabī qadīm* in *Majmūʿat al-Rābiṭa al-qalamiyya*, New York 1921, 105/40 (Kračk.).

448. 10. *Nidāʾ al-ghāb, al-juzʾ al-thānī*, New York, al-Maṭbʿa al-tijāriyya 1928 (Kračk.).

490. f. Read: Saḥāmat.

496. l. Ḥimāda (?) Saʿīd, *al-Niẓām al-iqtiṣādī fī ʾl-ʿIrāq*, Beirut 1938.

498. Line t. See R. Paret, H. W. s Arabienbuch, *WI* XXII, 67/101.

499. Line 10. Read: al-Ṭītūrī, see II, 683.

517. a. Line 6. Addenda I, 264.

b. Line 12: Wāfī al-Fayyūmī, S II, 724.

522. a. Line 14, read: 446.

533. b. Line 11. Aḥmad b. Ḥusayn b. Muḥammad al-ʿAjamī, Addenda I, 512.

542. a. Line from below, read: G. II, 219, Suppl. Addenda II, 160.

551. a. Line 35. Read: Suppl. II, 309, Addenda I, 69, 468.

558. a. Line 20. Read: Taqī al-Dīn.

b. Line 18. Addenda I, 511.

565. b. bottom, ʿAlī b. Muḥammad al-Laythī al-Wāsiṭī, Suppl. Addenda I, 714.

588. a. Line 22.—Dimyāṭī Nūr al-Dīn, Suppl. II, 362.

602. a. Line 24. Ibn Hiffān, Suppl. I, 117.

605. b. Line 37. Ibn Abī Dharr al-Ghifārī, Suppl. Addenda I, 518, 850.

623. a. Line 17. Read: al-Zanjānī.

646. a. Line 14. Read: 291.

730. a. Line 7. Najīramī Ibrāhīm b. ʿAbdallāh, Suppl. I, 201.

743. b. Line 5. 1. Suppl. Addenda I, 202.

755. Sijāʿī Aḥmad b. Muḥammad, Suppl. I, 445.

761. b. Line 24, Addenda II, 578.

769. a. Line 28. Ibn al-Taʿāwīthī see Sibṭ.

789. b. Line. 6.—*ʿābir fi ʾl-anṣār wal-muhājir*, Suppl. II, 746, *ʿābir sabīl* Suppl. III, 147.

800. b. Line 9. *alfiyyat b. Muʿṭī*, Suppl. I, 530.

1326 | 817. b. Line 16. Suppl. I, 597.

829. a. Line 26. Suppl. Addenda II, 95, 361.

831. b. Line 4. Suppl. Addenda I, 202.

949. a. Line 18. Suppl. II, 14.

986. a. Line 19. *al-misk al-ʿāṭir*, Suppl. Addenda II, 485.

1025. a. Line 9 from below: S I, 276.

b. Line 27. *nūr*, Suppl. I, 427.

1028. a. Line 7. *nuzhat al-awzān*, Suppl. II, 715.

1029. a. Line 32. *nuzhat al-afkār fī maʿrifat al-nabāt wal-ashjār*, Suppl. II, 171.

1046. a. Line 4. *rashḥ al-sirr al-ghāmiḍ*, Suppl. Addenda I, 463

1047. a. Line 30. *rawḍ al-nasīm wal-durr al-yatīm*, G II, 301, Suppl. 412 (to be read thus).

Abbreviations

Introduction

Perhaps the most challenging feature of GAL is Brockelmann's use of abbreviations, which are often hard to understand. This was noted previously by Richard S. Cooper in his "How to use GAL", in *MELA Notes* 3/October 1974, p. 19, and also by J.J. Witkam in his "Brockelmann's *Geschichte* revisited", in vol. 1, p. xv of the 1996 reprint of GAL's second edition. As problems of understanding may unduly prevent the reader from consulting valuable sources, it was decided to draw up a list of the majority of the abbreviations used in GAL's second edition, as a kind of appendix to the English translation. If an abbreviation is not among those listed here, this is because one or more of the following considerations apply:

- the abbreviation is judged to be understandable to the average reader
- in the Indices, there is only one author or work that fits the (partial) description
- the abbreviation can be explained by what comes just before or just after the reference concerned (either in the same lemma or on the same page) or by consulting the bibliography that is often given at the beginning of a section or chapter
- the abbreviation refers to the second or next work by the same author whose name was not repeated after the first citation, e.g. 'Massignon, *Passion* 428, *Textes* 155'
- the abbreviation refers to a subdivision of a manuscript collection and is mentioned after just one citation of the main collection and a first subdivision, e.g. 'Alex. Taʾr. 101, Muṣṭ. Ḥad. 13'

In the below list of abbreviations used in GAL, the reader will find both straightforward abbreviations, like *Islca* (*Islamica*, a journal), and 'shorthand' references, such as 'al-ʿAskarī, *Amthāl*' for 'Abū Hilāl al-ʿAskarī, *Jamharat al-amthāl*', or 'Alex.' for manuscripts in Alexandria, Egypt, that are described in publications by, among others, Aḥmad Abū ʿAlī and I. Kratchkovsky. At the beginning of an entry the definite article (i.e. 'Al-') in names and book titles has been retained, e.g. 'Al-Marzubānī'. In general, abbreviations should be looked up the way they are written in the book, e.g. "A. Amīrī', the way it is found in GAL, and not under "Alī' or 'Amīrī'. Variants are given between round brackets: '(…)', and elements that are sometimes—but not consistently—included between square brackets: '[…]'; when we are dealing with a variant within a variant, then round brackets are used again, as, for example:

 | DOI:10.1163/9789004369795_004

- *Al-Khiṭaṭ al-jad*[*īda*] (*al-Khiṭ. al-jadīda, Khiṭ jad.*)
- Al-Shawkānī [, (*al-*)*Badr*]

When variants are listed between round brackets, the author's name is represented by an En-dash if it is identical to the name cited at the beginning of the entry, while there is no comma between the En-dash and the title cited along with it. When the author's abbreviated name is cited in isolation it will be listed among the variants of the original entry; if the author's name is cited in another way, this other citation will be recorded, for example:

- Al-Hujwīrī, [transl.] Nicholson (Hujwīrī *Kashf* Nich.)
- Massignon, *Rec. de textes* (– *Textes* [*inéd.*], Mass. *T.*)

At times including all these aspects in one concise statement can be confusing, for if we abbreviate

- Ibn Bashkuwāl, *al-Ṣila* (Ibn Bashk[uwāl])

to

- Ibn Bashk[uwāl] [, *al-Ṣila*],

this is consistent with the stated methodology, but is difficult to interpret. As such, entries like these were deliberately not compressed.

As a rule, text editions are not mentioned unless an edition is mentioned in a place other than the lemma in which one would expect to find it (which is only rarely the case), or if an abbreviation refers to an edition:

- A. al-ʿAlamī, *Anīs*—Muḥammad b. al-Ṭayyib al-Sharīf al-ʿAlamī, *al-Anīs al-muṭrib fī man laqiyahu muʾallifuhu min udabāʾ al-Maghrib*.
- ʿAbd al-Qādir al-Baghdādī, *Khiz.*—ʿAbd al-Qādir b. ʿUmar al-Baghdādī, *Khizānat al-adab wa-lubb lubāb lisān al-ʿArab* (mostly just '*Khiz.*' or '*Khizāna*'), 4 vols. Būlāq, 1299 (also mentioned: Cairo 1344 and Cairo 1930–).
- Abu 'l-ʿAlāʾ, *Letters*—Abu 'l-ʿAlāʾ al-Maʿarrī, *Rasāʾil*, ed. & transl. D.S. Margoliouth, *Letters of Abu 'l-ʿAlāʾ of Maʿarrat al-Nuʿmān*, Oxford: Clarendon Press, 1898.

In the explanations of the abbreviations, the names of authors are cited in the same way as they are in the Indices, which is often not exactly the way in which their names are given in the lemma devoted to them. One example is A. ʿAlamī, mentioned above, who in the Index of Names is cited as Muḥammad b. al-Ṭayyib al-Sharīf al-ʿAlamī, while in vol. 2, p. 539, no. 9 he is listed as Abū ʿAbdallāh Muḥammad b. al-Ṭayyib al-Sharīf al-ʿAlamī. So it seems that the letter 'A.' in 'A. al-ʿAlamī' does not refer to 'Aḥmad' as we would have reason to expect (see GAL[2], Suppl. I, XVII) but rather to 'Abū'. And even in the case of well-known authors, the name by which they are cited in the indices is often not the name by which they are commonly known; one example of this is Jalāl al-Dīn al-Suyūṭī, who is listed twice: once as al-Suyūṭī ʿAbd al-Raḥmān b. Abī Bakr b. Muḥammad, and again as ʿAbd al-Raḥmān b. Abī Bakr al-Suyūṭī.

First and later editions are often referred to by numbers in superscript, e.g. *Agh.*[1], *Agh.*[2], which stand for the first and second editions of Abu 'l-Faraj al-Iṣfahānī's *Kitāb al-aghānī*. Superscript is also used to refer to earlier and later catalogues of some manuscript collection, such as Leid.[1] and Leid.[2]

References to modern printed publications usually contain publication data, even if it was not always possible to identify the publisher, as in:

- Abdulhakk Adnān, *Science*—Abdulhakk Adnān, *La science chez les Turcs Ottomans*. Paris: Maisonneuve, 1939.
- Basset, *Khazrajiyya*—R. Basset, *La Khazradjiyah* : traité de métrique arabe. Algiers: Fontana, 1902.
- Abulghazi Romanzoff—N. Romanzoff (ed.), *Abulghazi Shajaraʾi Türkī*. Kazan, 1825.

In cases where Brockelmann's bibliographical information is lacking or insufficient, its improvement falls outside the scope of this list of abbreviations, although occasional additions have been made, especially with regard to modern works other than text editions. In connection with oriental manuscripts in the libraries of Cambridge, for instance, Brockelmann refers to an article by E.H. Palmer as: Ar. etc. Mss. in the Kings College, *JRAS*, NS III, 105ff (see Supplement 1, p. 6). In fact, the correct title of the article is: "Catalogue of the Oriental Manuscripts in the Library of King's College". But since the reference to *JRAS* NS III, 105ff does lead the reader to the correct publication, the corrected title of this publication was not included in the present list. However, in connection with the successor to the first catalogue of the Dār al-Kutub in Cairo, GAL gives the following reference (Supplement 1, 6):

- Cairo[2]—*Fihrist al-kutub al-ʿarabiyya al-mawjūda bi-Dār al-Kutub al-Miṣriyya li-ghāyat shahr Septembir* 1925 II–VI, Cairo 1345/1926–1348/1934, I.[3] ibid.

This is a complicated entry. The title as given is not entirely correct; the actual title has '*bil-Dār*' instead of '*bi-Dār al-Kutub al-Miṣriyya*'. Moreover, this precise title, ending in '*li-ghāyat shahr Septembir* 1925', is not a blanket title but only covers volume 2, while the titles of volumes 3–6 are slightly different (as is that of volume 1). In fact, this is a serial publication that was published by Dār al-Kutub in 9 volumes in 10 tomes. The first six volumes (1924–33) have the blanket title *Fihris al-kutub al-ʿarabiyya al-mawjūda bil-Dār* (in each case followed by further information on the contents of the volume concerned, something which also applies to volumes 7, 8 and 9.1–2), the main title of the other volumes being: vol. 7 (1938) *Fihris bil-kutub al-ʿarabiyya allatī waradat ʿala 'l-dār*; vol. 8 (1942) *Fihris al-kutub al-ʿarabiyya allatī waradat lil-dār*; and vol. 9.1 (1959) and 9.2 (1963) *Fihris al-kutub al-ʿarabiyya allati 'qtanathā Dār al-kutub* (volume 9 only contains printed works). Also, at the end of the above entry in GAL we read: 'I.[3] ibid.'. This seems to refer to a third—undated—printing, in Cairo, of the first volume, not included in the first part; however, such a printing could not be found in any major library around the world and it seems that it is never referred to again in GAL either. In view of all this, I decided to replace Brockelmann's somewhat sketchy data with more detailed information, based on a personal inspection of the physical documents:

- Cairo[2]—*Fihris al-kutub al-ʿarabiyya al-mawjūda bil-Dār*, 9 vols. in 10 tomes. Cairo: Dār al-Kutub al-Miṣriyya, 1924–63 (1342–83 AH); title varies: vol. 7 *Fihris bil-kutub al-ʿarabiyya allatī waradat ʿala 'l-dār*, vol. 8 *Fihris al-kutub al-ʿarabiyya allatī waradat lil-dār*, vol. 9.1–2 *Fihris al-kutub al-ʿarabiyya allati 'qtanathā Dār al-kutub*. Brockelmann only mentions volumes 2–6 (Supplement I, 6). Yet he also refers to volume 1, e.g. in Supplement 2, p. 6: 'Cairo[2] I, 284', and to vol. 7, e.g. in volume 1, p. 569: 'Cairo [2]VII, 201'.

Abbreviations of the titles of journals or scholarly series are generally not included as these are, for the most part, known to the average reader or can be easily understood, if necessary with the help of, for instance, the list of journal abbreviations of H. Daiber's *Bibliography of Islamic Philosophy* vol. 1 (Leiden: Brill, 1999), pp xxxv ff. If difficulties persist, information may also be found in S.M. Schwertner (ed.), *International Glossary of Abbreviations for Theology and Related Subjects*, 2nd edition Berlin & New York: Walter de Gruyter, 1992 (IATG[2] = Internationales Abkürzungsverzeichnis für Theologie und Grenzgebiete). Some abbreviations, less obvious to the average specialist of Arabic and Islamic studies or absent from one or both of the reference works just mentioned, have been included, as, for example:

- BBA—*Sitzungsberichte der Königlich Preussischen Akademie der Wissenschaften zu Berlin* (N.B. Daiber & IATG²: *Berliner byzantinischen Arbeiten*).
- FFC—Folklore Fellows' Communications, a series of monographs and articles published under the auspices of the Finnish Academy of Science and Letters (not in Daiber).
- *KCs.A.*—*Kőrösi Csoma Archivum* (in neither Daiber nor IATG²).

The abbreviations of some institutions were included as well, such as:

- BDMG—Bibliothek der Deutschen Morgenländische Gesellschaft, Halle.
- Moskau Lazarew-Inst.—The Lazarev Institute in Moscow was established in 1815. After various name changes and being left without students, it was dissolved in the 1930s and its library transferred to the Lenin State Library in Moscow, now the Russian State Library, for which see Roper II, 676, Rossiĭskaya Gosudarstvennaya Biblioteka.

Abbreviations of manuscript collections are followed by information on catalogues, if furnished by Brockelmann himself (see volume 1, 4–6, vol. 2, 591–92, Supplement 1, 4–11, 972–74, and Supplement 3.1, 407). If no catalogue is mentioned, in each case GAL either gives a reference to a book or journal article from which Brockelmann culled his information, or not. If such information is provided, the abbreviation in question will not be recorded in the below list of abbreviations. Instead, abbreviations like these—with or without source information—will be followed by a more general reference to the relevant entry in G. Roper (ed.), *World Survey of Islamic Manuscripts* (4 vols. London: Al-Furqan Foundation, 1992–1994), if such an entry exists. This is because there are about 150 manuscript libraries or collections from around the world, many of which are private, mentioned in GAL but which are not included in Roper, vol. IV, 431ff, 'Index of titles of collections vols. I–IV', something which will be recorded in the below list as well. Still, some of these collections might be identified if one were to consult some of the publications listed in the section 'Union Catalogues' mentioned at the beginning of the relevant country file in Roper (e.g. the libraries and collections mentioned in A. al-Ma'mūn Suhrawardy, Notes on important Arabic and Persian MSS. found in various libraries in India, in *Journal & Proceedings of the Asiatic Society of Bengal*, New Series, vol. xiii [1917], lxxvii–cxxxix, referred to in Roper, vol. I, 397). Nevertheless, many, if not most, of these collections are mentioned in Muḥammad Muḥsin's *al-Dharīʿa ilā taṣānīf al-Shīʿa* (26 vols, Najaf, 1355–1406 AH). There is an index of names to this work, prepared by ʿAlī Naqī Munzavī, *Fihris-i aʿlām-i al-Dharīʿa ilā taṣānīf al-Shīʿa*, 3 vols. Tehran: Intishārāt-i Dānishgāh-i Tihrān, 1377 HSh, but an inventory of libraries and collections is still lacking. So what is needed is a detailed survey of the libraries, collections, and collectors mentioned in *al-Dharīʿa*; for without a thorough knowledge of these it will often be impossible to locate and consult important manuscript resources. It should be added here that the many unidentified collections and collectors from *al-Dharīʿa* referred to in GAL are only from *al-Dharīʿa*'s first two volumes, which since the 1930s has grown into a work of massive proportions, comprising 26 hefty tomes. It is therefore very much to be hoped that a survey of the type just mentioned will soon be prepared by our colleague-researchers in Iran and/or Iraq.

In connection with Iran, a very important 45-volume inventory (45,000 pages!) of all the Arabic and Persian manuscripts in Iran was published a few years ago, which is why it is not listed in Roper: M. Darāyatī (ed.), *Fihristigān-i nuskhahā-yi khaṭṭi-yi Īrān*, 45 vols, Tehran: Sāzimān-i asnād ō kitābkhāna-yi Milli-yi Jumhūri-yi Islāmi-yi Īrān, 1390–94. Finally, in the Appendix at the end of this Introduction, the reader will find a brief list of publications cited in GAL in connection with manuscripts from Istanbul and Cairo (mostly) and for which otherwise no library catalogue was mentioned.

No effort was made to provide the reader with complete bibliographical information on manuscript collections up to the present day, indeed, not even up to the time that the second edition of GAL was completed in the 1930s and '40s. For instance, in the case of the Bāyezīd library in Istanbul (see below, 'Bāyezīd'), circumstantial evidence made it clear that Brockelmann must have used the *defter* of the Veliyüddin collection which was published in 1304 (1887) and an article by O. Rescher in *ZDMG* 64 (1910). But even if, at the time, there was another catalogue available (*Kütüphane-i Umumî Defteri*, Istanbul 1300 [1883]), as there is no indication that Brockelmann used this work, it was not included in the present list.

Sometimes Brockelmann refers to a title in shortened form, e.g. 'al-Jāḥiẓ, *al-Bayān*', for 'al-Jāḥiẓ, *Kitāb al-bayān wal-tabyīn*', mentioned for the first time in full in the lemma on Jāḥiẓ, in vol. 1, p. 137. Abbreviations like this, where the name of a unique author (there is only one Jāḥiẓ) is followed by a shortened title whose full version can be easily retrieved, were not included in the present list. And even when there is only the title of a work, without an author, no further information is provided if this is the only such title in the Indices, as in the case of the *Hidāyat al-abrār* (vol. 2, 373) by al-Karakī. A similar principle is followed if an author is only referred to by name when this name has only one occurrence in the Indices, except in case he wrote multiple works. An example of this is the abbreviation 'Ibn Qut.' which, if cited alone, stands for

Ibn Qutayba's *Kitāb al-shiʿr wal-shuʿarāʾ* in the edition of M.J. de Goeje; for even if Ibn Qutayba's name is unique, yet he authored a number of works.

It may also happen that an abbreviated book title has too many occurrences in the Index of Works referred to for the reader to quickly identify the proper reference, such as '*Jamhara*' in vol. 1, 19, or '*Jamhara*' in vol. 1, 99. The former refers to Abū Zayd al-Qurashī's *Jamharat ashʿār al-ʿArab*, the latter to Ibn Durayd Muḥammad b. al-Ḥasan, *al-Jamhara fī 'l-lugha*. Since there are about 10 titles starting with *Jamhara* in the Indices, it was decided to include them both under '*Jamhara*' in the present list. Also, in cases where an author is mentioned without a book title and there being either different authors with the same name or one author with more than one work to his name, both author and title will be included in our list.

GAL is at times inconsistent and confusing. Take the reference 'al-Jumaḥī, *Ṭab.*' in vol. 1, p. 50, last paragraph. The Index of Names will yield nothing under 'al-Jumaḥī', while the Index of Works will yield an endless list of works whose title starts with '*Ṭabaqāt*.' I then ran a search on 'al-Jumaḥī, *Ṭab.*' which yielded 'al-Jumaḥī, *Ṭabaqāt al-shuʿarāʾ*' in vol. 1, p. 34, at the end of the page. There being only one [*Kitāb*] *ṭabaqāt al-shuʿarāʾ* listed in the Index of Works, I was then directed to Supplement 1, p. 160 no. 12a, where Hell's German title of the edition, *Die Klassen der Dichter*, clearly is a literal rendering of the Arabic *Ṭabaqāt al-shuʿarāʾ*. At the same time, I learned that al-Jumaḥī's full name was Abū ʿAbdallāh b. Sallām al-Jumaḥī. Yet this name turned out to be absent from the Index of Names. I then ran another search on just *Ṭabaqāt al-shuʿarāʾ*, without searching for the author. This brought me to Supplement 1, p. 39, where the author is referred to as 'Muḥammad b. Sallām al-Jumaḥī'. This name turned out to be included in the Index of Names, with a reference, among other places, to p. 165 of the first edition, which in the English edition is Supplement 1, p. 160, no. 12a mentioned earlier. So, strangely, the indexed name of the author turned out to be 'Muḥammad b. Sallām al-Jumaḥī', while in the lemma devoted to him his name is given as 'Abū ʿAbdallāh b. Sallām al-Jumaḥī'.

With regard to shortened titles of publications other than those written by the people whom GAL is primarily about, the problem is that there is often no logical place where one could look for their full versions, the way we could, for instance, in the case of 'al-Jāḥiẓ, *al-Bayān*', mentioned earlier. It was therefore decided to include some, but not all, abbreviations of this kind in the present list. When titles are abbreviated but understandable to the average reader, no further information will be provided. 'Weil, *Gesch. d. Chal.*', for example, clearly stands for [G.] Weil, *Geschichte der Chalifen*; and 'Ahlwardt, *The Divans*' obviously refers to 'W. Ahlwardt, *The Divans of the Six Ancient Arabic Poets*';

similarly '*Abh. zur arab. Philologie*' refers to '*Abhandlungen zur arabischen Philologie*.' Also, references like 'de Slane, *JA* s. III, vol. 9, p. 66ff' (*History*, vol. 1, 81) were deemed clear enough as they are, since we have the name of an author, the title of a magazine, a (series- and) volume number, and a page reference. And in cases where the reference is just to the issue of a magazine, with a page reference but without an author, this was also judged to be sufficient in light of GAL's immediate purpose of providing useful information. And even when there is just a name it is sometimes still possible to identify the precise reference when other clues are provided, as in the case of 'Stapleton' in vol. 1, 243 n. 1, where the addition '(see Suppl.)' is enough to find the necessary information. In this and similar cases, the abbreviation will not be included in our list. But the information provided in vol. 1, page 7, note 3 is confusing: "See A. Müller, *Der Islam* I, 470". Is the reference here to the first (1910) issue of the journal *Der Islam*? The answer is no; that issue only has only 396 pages. Rather, the reference is to the first volume of A. Müller, *Der Islam im Morgen- und Abendland*, 2 vols, Berlin: G. Grote'sche Verlagsbuchhandlung, 1885–1887. So, in this case, the reference to *Der Islam* is not unequivocal, which is why 'Müller, *Der Islam*' was included in our list, and likewise in comparable cases.

A few explanations grew into larger bibliographical notes, such as those on 'Ibn Taghr[īb]. (Juynboll) etc.', 'Kraus (Kr.)', and 'Vat.'. I wrote these simply to save the reader the considerable amount of time that it took me to understand what these abbreviations referred to.

Finally, whenever one of the abbreviations explained below is followed by a (volume and) page reference that does not yield the expected information, this does not mean that the explanation of the abbreviation in question is wrong; rather, in such cases, it is the reference in GAL that is more likely to be mistaken, while it is also possible that the reader consulted a different edition than the one Brockelmann refers to.

Appendix

Selected Publications on Manuscripts in Turkey and Egypt Cited in GAL[1]

Cahen, C., Les chroniques arabes concernant la Syrie, l'Égypte et la Mésopotamie de la conquête arabe à la conquête ottomane dans les bibliothèques d'Istanbul, in *REI* 10 (1936), 333–358.

Edhem [Karatay], F. and I.V. Stchoukine, *Les manuscrits orientaux illustrés de la Bibliothèque de l'Université de Stamboul*. Istanbul, 1934.

Krause, M., Stambuler Handschriften islamischer Mathematiker, *Quellen und Studien zur Geschichte der Mathematik, Astronomie und Physik*, Abt. B. 3 (1936), 437–532.

Rescher, O., Kütübḫāné-i-Feizīyé (in der Nähe der Fātiḥ-Moschee) und ʿĀšir Efendi I. II. III. (Nachtrag), in *ZDMG* 68 (1914), 377–91.

Rescher, O., Über arabische Manuscripte der Lâlelî-Moschee (nebst einigen anderen, noch unbeschriebenen arabischen Codices), in *MO* 7 (1913), 97–136.

Rescher, O., Mitteilungen aus Stambuler Bibliotheken, *ZDMG* 64, 195–217, 489–528.

Rescher, O., Mitteilungen aus Stambuler Bibliotheken, *Mélanges de la faculté orientale* de l'Université Saint Joseph [*MFO*] 5 (1912), 489–540.

Rescher, O., Arabische Handschriften der Köprülü Bibliothek, *MSOS* 14 (1911), 163–198.

Rescher, O., Weitere arabische Handschriften der Köprülü Bibliothek, nebst anderen der Jeni Ǧâmiʿ und Nûrî ʿoṯmânîye, in *MSOS* 15 (1912), 1–29.

Rescher, O., Arabische Handschriften des Top Kapú Seraj (Privatbibliothek des Sultans), in *RSO* 4 (1911), 695–733.

Rescher, O., Über arabische Handschriften der Aja Sofia, in *WKZM* 26 (1912), 63–95.

Rescher, O., Über einige arabische Handschriften der Hamidie-Bibliothek, in *ZA* 27 (1912), 147–158.

Rescher, O., Neuerwerbungen der Universitätsbibliothek von Constantinopel, in *ZS* 3 (1924), 247–53.

Ritter, H., Ayasofya Kütūphânesinde tefsir ilmine âit Arapça yazmalar, *Türkiyat Mecmuası*, 7–8 (1945), 1–93.

---

1 This short bibliography is limited to publications which deal specifically with manuscripts, excluding works of a more general character which only mention some manuscript in passing. As such, this list may be regarded as a supplement to Brockelmann's own listing of manuscript resources on Turkey and Egypt in volumes 1, 2 and Supplement 1. Finally, there are also cases where Brockelmann relied on handwritten notes which Hellmut Ritter would send him from Istanbul (and probably also on notes by Kraus sent to him from Cairo, for which see Abbreviations s.v.).

Ritter, H., Schriften Ja'qūb ibn Isḥāq al-Kindī's in Stambuler Bibliotheken, in *Archiv Orientální* 4 (1932), 363–72.

Ritter, H., Philologika I: Zur Überlieferung des Fihrist, in *Der Islam* 17 (1928), 15–23.

Ritter, H., Philologika II: Über einige Koran und Ḥadīṯ betreffende Handschriften hauptsächlich Stambuler Bibliotheken, in *Der Islam* 17 (1928), 249–57.

Ritter, H., Philologika III: Muhammedanische Häresiographen, in *Der Islam* 18 (1929), 35–55.

Ritter, H., Philologika IV: Die Stambuler Handschriften des Ḥiljat al-aulijā' des Abū Nu'aim, in *Der Islam* 18 (1929), 55–9.

Ritter, H., Philologika V: Die Lücken in Ibn Sa'd V. (gest. 230 h. EI s.v.), in *Der Islam* 18 (1929), 196–99.

Ritter, H., Philologika VI: Ibn al-Ǧawzīs Bericht über Ibn ar-Rēwendī, in *Der Islam* 19 (1931), 1–17.

Ritter, H., Philologika VII: Arabische und persische Schriften über die profane und die mystische Liebe, in *Der Islam* 21 (1933), 84–109.

Ritter, H., Philologika VIII: Anṣārī Herewī—Senā'ī Ġaznewī, in *Der Islam* 22 (1935), 89–105.

Ritter, H., Philologika IX: Die vier Surawardī, in *Der Islam* 24 (1937), 270–86.

Ritter, H., Philologika IX: Die vier Suhrawardī (Fortsetzung und Schluss), in *Der Islam* 25 (1939), 35–86.

Ritter, H. & R. Walzer, *Arabische Übersetzungen griechisher Ärzte in Stambuler Bibliotheken*. Berlin: Verlag der Akademie der Wissenschaften, 1934. Offprint from *Sitzungsberichte der Preussischen Akademie der Wissenschaften*, Phil.-Hist. Klasse vol. 26 (1934).

Schacht, J., Von den Bibliotheken in Stambul und Umgegend, in ZS vol. 5 (1927) 288–94, vol. 8 (1930) 120–21.

Schacht, J., Idem, *Aus den Bibliotheken von Konstantinopel und Kairo*. Abhandlungen der Preußischen Akademie der Wissenschaften, Philosophisch-Historische Klasse, 1928 no. 8. 75 pp. Berlin, 1928.

Schacht, J., Idem, *Aus Kairiner Bibliotheken*. Abhandlungen der Preußischen Akademie der Wissenschaften, Philosophisch-Historische Klasse, 1929 no. 6. 36 pp. Berlin, 1930.

Schacht, J., Idem, *Aus orientalischen Bibliotheken* (III). Abhandlungen der Preußischen Akademie der Wissenschaften, Philosophisch-Historische Klasse, 1931 no. 1. 57 pp. Berlin, 1931.

Schacht, J., Von den Bibliotheken in Stambul und Umgegend, in ZS 5 (1927), 288–94.

Weisweiler, M., *Istanbuler Handschriftenstudien zur arabischen Traditionsliteratur*. Bibliotheca Islamica vol. 10. Istanbul: Druckerei Universum, 1937.

Abbreviations

In this list of abbreviations, no distinction is made between 's' and 'ṣ', 'd' and 'ḍ', 't' and 'ṭ', 'h' and 'ḥ', and 'z' and 'ẓ' in establishing alphabetical order, while the letters 'ẖ' and 'š' are regarded as if they were 'h' or 's'. *ʿAyn* and *hamza*, on the other hand, were not considered.

A. al-ʿAlamī, *Anīs*—Muḥammad b. al-Ṭayyib al-Sharīf al-ʿAlamī, *al-Anīs al-muṭrib fī man laqiyahu muʾallifuhu min udabāʾ al-Maghrib*.

ʿA. Amīrī—See ʿAlī Emīrī.

A. Bābā—See Aḥmad Bābā.

ʿAbbās al-ʿAzzāwī al-Baghdādī (collection of, no place)—Not in Roper.

ʿAbbās Iqbāl, *Khand. N.* (ʿAbbās Iqbāl, Iqbāl)—ʿAbbās Iqbāl, *Khāndāni Nawbakhtī, Les Naubakht, leur biographie, leurs oeuvres politiques, littéraires et intellectuelles*. Tehran, 1311/1933

Abel—See L. Abel.

ʿAbd al-ʿAzīz al-Maymanī (collection of, no place)—Not in Roper.

ʿAbd al-ʿAzīz Mayman, *Iqlīd*—Muḥammad ʿAbd al-ʿAzīz Mayman, Iqlīd al-Khizāna *or Index of Titles of Works Referred to or Quoted by ʿAbd al-Qādir al-Baghdādī in the* Khizānat al-Adab. Lahore: The University of the Panjab, 1927.

ʿAbd al-Ḥamīd (library of, Istanbul)—Not in Roper (= Roper III 349, Hamidiye ?).

ʿAbd al-Ḥayy (library of, Lucknow)—See Firengi Maḥall, 2.

ʿAbd al-Ḥayy al-Kattānī (library of, no place)—Roper II 306, Kattānī Library (Fez).

ʿAbd al-Ḥayy al-Kattānī, *Fihris*—See al-Kattānī, *Fihris*.

ʿAbd al-Ḥayy, *Nuzha*—Al-Laknāwī Muḥammad ʿAbd al-Ḥayy, *Nuzhat al-khawāṭir wa-bahjat al-masāmiʿ wal-nawāẓir*, vol. II, *ʿUlamāʾ al-Hind fi ʾl-qarn al-thāmin*. Hyderabad, 1350.

ʿAbd al-Ḥusayn (library of, Mashhad)—Not in Roper.

ʿAbd al-Ḥusayn al-Ḥājjī (library of, Karbala)—Roper II 32, ʿAbd al-Ḥusayn Āl Ṭuʿma Library ?

ʿAbd al-Ḥusayn [b. al-Qāsim] al-Ḥillī al-Najafī (library of, no place)—Not in Roper.

ʿAbd al-Ḥusayn al-Ṭihrānī (collection of, Karbala)—Not in Roper; = previous entry ?

ʿAbdallāh al-Burhān al-Sabzawārī (collection of, no place)—Not in Roper.

ʿAbdallāh Gannūn [al-Ḥusaynī/al-Ḥasanī], *al-Nubūgh al-maghribī* (ʿAbdallāh Gannūn [*al-*]*Nubūgh*, ʿAbdallāh Gannūn)—ʿAbdallāh Gannūn al-Ḥasanī, *al-Nubūgh al-maghribī fi ʾl-adab al-ʿarabī*. 2 vols. Tetouan: al-Maṭbaʿa al-Mahdiyya, 1357 (1938).

ʿAbdallāh Sakhāwat al-Ḥusayn (library, Lucknow)—Not in Roper, see *JRASB* 1917, lxxxii, no. (10), Mawlavī Sakhāwat Ḥusayn Library, Nakhkhās.

ʿAbd al-Qādir al-Baghdādī, *Khiz.*—ʿAbd al-Qādir b. ʿUmar al-Baghdādī, *Khizānat al-adab wa-lubb lubāb lisān al-ʿArab* (mostly just '*Khiz.*' or '*Khizāna*'). 4 vols. Būlāq, 1299 (also mentioned: Cairo 1344 and Cairo 1930–).

ʿAbd al-Qādir b. Abi 'l-Wafāʾ, [*al-*]*Jaw*[*āhir*] (ʿAbd al-Qādir b. Abi 'l-Wafaʾ)—ʿAbd al-Qādir b. Abi 'l-Wafāʾ al-Qurashī, *al-Jawāhir al-muḍīʾa fī ṭabaqāt al-Ḥanafiyya*.

ʿAbd al-Qādir b. Abi 'l-Wafāʾ, *Khiz. al-adab*—See: ʿAbd al-Qādir al-Baghdādī, *Khiz*.

ʿAbd al-Qādir b. al-Wafāʾ—Read: ʿAbd al-Qādir b. Abi 'l-Wafāʾ.

ʿAbd al-Raḥmān b. Khaldūn, *ʿIbar*—See Ibn Khaldūn, *al-ʿIbar*.

ʿAbd al-Wahhāb Ḥusnī (collection of, Tunis)—Roper II 259, ʿAbd al-Wahhāb Ḥasan Ḥusnī.

Abdülhak Adnān Adîvar, *Ilim* (Abdülhak Adnan, *Ilim*)—Abdülhak Adnān Adîvar, *Osmanlı Türklerinde İlim*. Istanbul: Maarif Matbaası, 1943.

Abdulhakk Adnān, *Science*—Abdulhakk Adnān, *La science chez les Turcs Ottomans*. Paris: Maisonneuve, 1939.

A. Bels (collection of, no place)—Not in Roper.

Aberystwyth—Not as such in Roper, but see ibid. vol. III, 437–38.

Abh.—Abhandlung(en).

Abh. der Kgl. Ges. d. Wiss. [*zu Göttingen*]—*Abhandlungen der königlichen Gesellschaft der Wissenschaften zu Göttingen.*

Abh. f. d. K. d. Morg.—*Abhandlungen für die Kunde des Morgenlandes.*

Abh. G.G.W (*Abh.GW*)—*See Abh. der Kgl. Ges. d. Wiss.*

Abjad al-ʿulūm—Muḥammad Ṣiddīq Khān al-Qannawjī, *Abjad al-ʿulūm*.

Abjadiyyat al-ʿulūm—This is a misprint, see previous entry.

Abkarius—It is not clear to what printing of what work by I. Abkarius this reference in Supplement 1, p. 165 refers. There are several works by him, listed in vol. 2, p. 573–74, and Supplement 1, p. 38.

Abstr. Isl.—*Abstracta Islamica.*

Abt.—Abteilung.

Abū ʿAbdallāh al-Iṣfahānī (library of, Najaf)—Not in Roper.

Abū Bakr b. Khayr, *Index libr.*—Al-Ishbīlī Muḥammad b. Khayr: *Index librorum de diversis scientiarum ordinibus quos a magistris didicit Abu Bequer Ben Khair*: ad fidem codicis Escurialensis arabice nunc primum ediderunt indicibus additis Franciscus Codera ... et J. Ribera Tarrago. 2 vols. Bibliotheca Arabico Hispana, IX–X. Zaragoza: Comas, 1894–95.

Abu Hilāl—Abu Hilāl al-ʿAskarī.

Abū Isḥāq Ibrāhīm al-Ṣarfandī, n.p.—'n.p.' is a misrendering of the abbreviation 's.l.' in the German text, which does not mean 'sine loco' here (i.e. 'no place'), but rather 'so zu lesen' = 'to be read thus'. Brockelmann based his spelling of the *nisba* al-Ṣarfandī on al-Samʿānī's *Kitāb al-ansāb*, p. 351.

Abu 'l-ʿAlāʾ, *Letters*—Abu 'l-ʿAlāʾ al-Maʿarrī, *Rasāʾil*, ed. & transl. D.S. Margoliouth, *Letters of Abu 'l-ʿAlāʾ of Maʿarrat al-Nuʿmān*. Oxford: Clarendon Press, 1898.

Abu 'l-ʿArab Muḥammad b. Aḥmad b. Tamīm, transl. M. b. Cheneb—See al-Khushanī *Ṭab.*, vol. 2.

Abu 'l-F. [, *Ann.*] (Abulf. [*Ann.*])—Abu 'l-Fidāʾ Ismāʿīl b. ʿAlī b. Maḥmūd al-Ayyūbī: *Abulfedae Annales Muslemici* / opera et studiis Io. Iacobi Reiskii, sumtibus atque auspiciis Petri Friderici Svhmii. 5 vols. Copenhagen: Thiele, 1789–94.

Abu 'l-Fidāʾ [, *Taʾr(īkh)*]—Abu 'l-Fidāʾ Ismāʿīl b. ʿAlī b. Maḥmūd al-Ayyūbī, *Mukhtaṣar taʾrīkh al-bashar*.

Abulghazi Romanzoff—N. Romanzoff (ed.), *Abulghazi Shajara 'i Türkī*. Kazan, 1825.

Abu 'l-Jaʿd (library of, Tādla [Morocco])—Not in Roper.

Abu 'l-Qāsim al-Iṣfahānī (library of, Najaf)—Not in Roper (= next entry ?).

Abu 'l-Qāsim al-Mūsawī al-Riyāḍī (library of, Najaf)—Not in Roper (= previous entry ?).

Abu Nuʿaym, *Ḥilya*—Abū Nuʿaym Aḥmad b. ʿAbdallāh b. Isḥāq al-Iṣfahānī, *Kitāb ḥilyat al-awliyāʾ wa-ṭabaqāt al-aṣfiyāʾ*, also known as *Ḥilyat al-abrār*.

Abū Yaʿlā—See Ibn Abī Yaʿlā.

Abū Zayd, *Muṣannaf* (mentioned in Suppl. I, 501)—In GAL no such work is listed under the name of Abū Zayd. So maybe the reference is rather to Abū ʿUbayda Maʿmar b. al-Muthannā's *Kitāb al-muṣannaf* (in Suppl. I, 157–58, the two are also mentioned one after the other [nos. 9 and 10,] which may have brought about the confusion).

Ac.—Accademia.

Act. Or.—*Acta Orientalia*, ediderunt societates orientales Batava, Danica, Norvegica; see also *Arch. Or.*

Adams—Ch. C. Adams, *Islam and Modernism in Egypt*: a study of the modern reform movement inaugurated by Muḥammad ʿAbduh. London: Oxford University Press, 1933, 2nd ed. 1936.

Adnan Adivar, *Ilim* (Adnan *Ilim*, Adnan)—See Abdülhak Adnān Adîvar.

Aeg. Bibl.—See Cairo[1] and Cairo[2].

ʿA. Emiri [Ef.]—See ʿA[lī] Emīrī.

A.F. Ellis (collection of, London)—Not in Roper.

Afrānī (Afr.)—See al-Ifrānī.

Afyūn Gedik P.—Roper III 292, Gedik Ahmet Paşa İl Halk Kütüphanesi (Afyon).

Äg.—Ägypten(-s).

Agh. (*Aghānī*)—Abu 'l-Faraj al-Iṣfahānī ʿAlī b. Ḥusayn, *Kitāb al-aghānī*.

Aghṣān al-arbaʿa—Walī Allāh Lakhnawī Firangī Maḥallī, *al-Aghṣān al-arbaʿa lil-shajara al-ṭayyiba*. Lucknow, 1881. Persian.

A. Gonzales Palencia—See Palencia.

Ahli Islam Libr. Madras—Not in Roper. Now called Muhammadan Public Library, Triplicane Chennai (http://www.muhammadanpubliclibrary.com, accessed 2 January 2018).

Ahlw. (Ahlwardt)—See Berl. and also below.

Ahlwardt, *Abu nowas* (Ahlw.)—W. Ahlwardt, *Diwan des Abu nowas* I, *Die Weinlieder*, Greifswald: Koch, 1861.

Ahlwardt, *App.*—Idem, *The Divans of the Six Ancient Arabic Poets* (London: Trübner & Co., 1870), the Appendix or the Supplement to the latter.

Ahlwardt, *Bemerkungen* (Ahlwardt)—Idem, *Bemerkungen über die Echtheit der alten Arabischen Gedichte*, Greifswald: Bamberg, 1872.

Ahlwardt, *Samml.*—Idem, *Sammlungen alter arabischen Dichter*. 3 vols. Berlin: Reuther–Reichard, 1902–3.

A[ḥmad] Bābā, *Nayl* [*al-ibt.*]—Aḥmad b. Aḥmad b. Aḥmad Bābā al-Takrūrī al-Timbuktī, *Nayl al-ibtihāj bi-taṭrīz al-Dībāj*.

Aḥmad b. Ismāʿīl al-Barzanjī (library of, Medina)—Not in Roper.

Aḥmad b. Rabban al-Ṭabarī—See al-Ṭabarī.

Aḥmad Ṣāliḥ ʿAbdallāh al-Ṭaʿʿān al-Baḥrānī (library of, no place)—Not in Roper.

Aḥmad Shādī—Aḥmad Zakī Abū Shādī.

Aḥmad ʿUbayd, *Mashāhīr* [*shuʿarāʾ al-ʿaṣr*]—Aḥmad ʿUbayd, *Mashāhīr shuʿarāʾ al-ʿaṣr fī aqṭārihā al-ʿArabiyya al-thalātha: Miṣr, Sūriya, wal-ʿIrāq*, vol. 1: *Shuʿarāʾ Miṣr*. Damascus: al-Maktaba al-ʿArabiyya fī Dimashq, 1341 (1922).

Aḥsan mā katabtu—*Aḥsan mā katabtu*. Cairo: Idārat al-Hilāl, 1934.

Aḥsan al-athar—See Muḥammad Ṣāliḥ al-Kāẓimī, *Aḥsan al-athar*.

a.k.a.—also known as.

Akbar al-Khwānsārī (collection of, no place)—Not in Roper. *Al-Dharīʿa* I, $120_{,577}$ has ʿAlī Akbar al-Khwānsārī.

Akhbār—May refer to: a) L. Massignon and P. Kraus (eds.), *Akhbār al-Ḥallāj* / Texte ancien relatif à la prédication et au supplice du grand mystique musulman. Paris: Larose, 1936: b) Ibn Manẓūr al-Miṣrī, *Akhbār Abī Nuwās: taʾrīkhuhu, nawādiruhu, shiʿruhu, buḥūthuhu*, ed. Muḥammad ʿAbd al-Rasūl Ibrāhīm. Cairo: Maṭbaʿat al-Iʿtimād, 1924.

Ak. Nauk SSSR, Trudy Inst. Vostokoved.—*Akademija Nauk SSSR, Trudy Instituta Vostokovedenija.*

Al-Ādāb—See Cheikho.

Al-ʿAlamī, *Anīs al-muṭrib*—See A. al-ʿAlamī.

Al-Ālūsī, *Jalāʾ al-ʿaynayn*—ʿAbd al-Bāqī b. Maḥmūd al-Ālūsī, *Jilāʾ al-ʿaynayn fī muḥākamat al-Aḥmadayn*.

Al-Anbārī—See Ibn al-Anbārī.

Al-Anbārī, *Nuzha*—See Ibn al-Anbārī.

Al-Ashʿarī, *Maqālāt*—ʿAlī b. Ismāʿīl al-Ashʿarī, *Maqālāt al-Islāmiyyīn wakhtilāf al-muṣallīn*.

Al-ʿĀṣim ad Imr.—This is a reference to the commentary on the *muʿallaqa* of Imraʾ al-Qays by Abū Bakr ʿĀṣim b. Ayyūb al-Baṭalyawsī.

Al-ʿAskarī, *Amthāl*—Abū Hilāl al-ʿAskarī, *Jamharat al-amthāl*.

Al-ʿAskarī, *Dīw. al-m.*—Idem, *Dīwān al-maʿānī*.

Al-ʿAskarī, *Ṣin.*—Idem, *Kitāb al-ṣināʿatayn al-kitāba wal-shiʿr*, also called *al-Mukhtaṣar fī ṣināʿatay al-naẓm wal-nathr*.

Al-ʿAynī (ʿAynī)—Abu ʾl-Thanāʾ b. Aḥmad b. Mūsā al-ʿAynī, *al-Maqāṣid al-naḥwiyya fī sharḥ Shawāhid shurūḥ al-Alfiyya*.

Al-ʿAynī, *ʿUqūd al-zamān*—Idem, *ʿIqd al-jumān fī taʾrīkh ahl al-zamān* ?

Al-Azhar—See Azhar.

Al-Azharī MO 1920—K.V. Zetterstéen, Aus dem *Tahḏīb al-luġa* al-Azhari's, in: *Le Monde Oriental* xiv (1920), 1–106.

Al-Baghdādī, *Kitāb al-Farq* (– *[al-]Farq*)—Al-Baghdādī ʿAbd al-Qāhir b. Ṭāhir, *al-Farq bayna ʾl-firaq*.

Al-Bakrī, GW—Abū ʿUbayd al-Bakrī ʿAbdallāh b. ʿAbd al-ʿAzīz, *Muʿjam ma ʾstaʿjama*.

Al-Bashīr, *Yawāqīt*—See Muḥammad al-Bashīr, *al-Yawāqīt*.

Al-Bayhaqī, *Tatimma*—Al-Bayhaqī ʿAlī b. Abi ʾl-Qāsim Zayd, *Tatimmat Ṣiwān al-ḥikma*.

Al-Ḍabbī—Al-Ḍabbī Aḥmad b. Yaḥyā b. Aḥmad b. ʿAmīra, *Kitāb bughyat al-multamis fī taʾrīkh rijāl ahl al-Andalus*.

Al-Damīrī—See Damīrī.

Al-Ḍawʾ—See al-Sakhāwī, *al-Ḍawʾ etc.*

Al-Dhahabī—In isolation in Supplement 1 this refers to Muḥammad b. Aḥmad b. ʿUthmān al-Dhahabī (a.k.a. Shams al-Dīn al-Dhahabī), *Tadhkirat al-ḥuffāẓ*, the Hayderabad edition.

Al-Dhahabī, *Biogr.*, ed. Fischer—A. Fischer (ed.), *Biographien von Gewährsmännern des Ibn Isḥâq, haupsächlich aus aḏ-Ḏahabî.* Aus berliner und gothaer Handschriften herausgegeben. Leiden: Brill, 1890.

Al-Dhahabī, *Ḥuff[āẓ]*—See Al-Dhahabī, *Tadhkira*.

Al-Dhahabī in Grünert VII, n. 1—M. Grünert (ed.), *Ibn Kutaiba's* Adab al-kâtib (Leiden: Brill, 1900), vii, note 1. There, the reference is to Muḥammad b. Aḥmad b. ʿUthmān al-Dhahabī, *Mīzān al-iʿtidāl fī tarajim al-rijāl*.

Al-Dhahabī, *[al-]Mīzān*—Muḥammad b. Aḥmad b. ʿUthmān al-Dhahabī , *Mīzān al-iʿtidāl fī tarajim al-rijāl*.

Al-Dhahabī, *Lisān al-mīzān*—Refers to an abstract of the previous title by al-Dhahabī, by Ibn Ḥajar al-ʿAsqalānī: *Lisān al-Mīzān*.

Al-Dhahabī, *Ṭab. al-ḥuff.*—See al-Suyūṭī, *Ḥuff.*

Al-Dhahabī, *Ṭab. al-qurrāʾ*—Muḥammad b. Aḥmad b. ʿUthmān al-Dhahabī, *Ṭabaqāt al-qurrāʾ al-mashhūrīn*.

Al-Dhahabī, *Tadhkira* (*Tadhk. al-ḥuff., Tadhk., Ḥuffāẓ, Ḥuff.*)—Idem, *Tadhkirat al-ḥuffāẓ*.

Al-Dhahabī, *Tajrīd*—Idem, *al-Iṣāba fī tajrīd asmāʾ al-Ṣaḥāba.*

Al-Dhahabī, *Taʾr. al-ḥuffāẓ*—See idem, *Tadhkira.*

Al-Dhahabī, *Taʾrīkh*—Idem, *Taʾrīkh al-Islām.*

Al-Dharīʿa—Muḥammad Muḥsin (Āghā Bozorg Ṭihrānī), *al-Dharīʿa ilā taṣānīf al-Shīʿa*, vols. 1–2. Najaf: Maṭbaʿat al-Gharī, 1355–56.

Al-Dimashqī, *Dhayl Ṭab. al-ḥuff.*—See next entry.

Al-Dimashqī, *Dhayl Tadhk. al-ḥuff.*—Abu ʾl-Maḥāsin al-Ḥusaynī al-Dimashqī, *al-Tanbīh wal-īqāẓ fī dhayl Tadhkirat al-ḥuffāẓ* (in Supplement 2, p 51 where this title is mentioned, his name is given as Abu ʾl-Maḥāsin Muḥammad b. ʿAlī al-Ḥusaynī al-Dimashqī).

Aleppo Aḥmadiyya (Aleppo Madr. Nūr Aḥm., Aleppo Madr. Aḥm[adiyya])—Roper III 192, al-Madrasa al-Aḥmadiyya.

Alex. (mostly adding the abbreviated title of a sub-collection, like: 'Fiqh Ḥan.', 'Fiqh Ḥanb.', 'Fiqh Shāf.', 'Fiqh Māl.', 'Adab', 'Fun.', 'Ḥad.', 'Taṣ.' and others, in some cases referring to several collections at the same time, e.g. 'Alex. Fiqh Ḥan. 6, Fun. 1, 194,10' [*History* 1, 156, 5a])—Aḥmad Abū ʿAlī, *Fihris al-maktaba al-baladiyya fī ʾl-Iskandariyya*, 6 vols. Alexandria, 1926–9; I. Krachkovskiĭ, Arabskie rukopisi Gorodskoĭ Biblioteki v Aleksandrii i Dīvān ʿOmara al-Makhkhāra, in *Zapiski Vostochnago Otdéleniya Imperatorskago Obshchestva* 22 (1913–14), 1–30. For a variant title of the journal, see: *Zap. Vost. Otd.*

Alexandria, municipal library—See previous entry, first reference.

Al-Fakhrī, ed. Der.—H. Derenbourg (ed.), *Al-Fakhri: histoire du Khalifat et du Vizirat depuis leurs origines jusqu'à la chute du Khalifat ʿAbasside de Bagdâdh (632–1258) … avec des prolégomènes sur les principes du gouvernement, par Ibn aṭ-Ṭiḳṭaḳâ*; nouv. éd. du texte arabe. Paris: Bouillon, 1895.

Al-Faraḍī—See Ibn al-Faraḍī.

Al-Faw. al-bah[iyya]—*Al-Fawāʾid al-bahiyya fī tarājim al-Ḥanafiyya.*

Alger—See Algiers.

Al-Ghazzālī, *[al-]Munqidh*—Abū Ḥāmid al-Ghazzālī, *al-Munqidh min al-ḍalāl.*

Al-Ghazzālī, *Iḥyāʾ*—Idem, *Iḥyāʾ ʿulūm al-dīn.*

Al-Ghuzūlī, *Maṭāliʿ [al-budūr]*—Al-Bahāʾī ʿAlī b. ʿAbdallāh al-Ghuzūlī, *Maṭāliʿ al-budūr fī manāzil al-surūr.*

Algiers (Algiers Fagn., Alger)—E. Fagnan, *Catalogue général des mss. des bibliothèques publiques de France, Départements, Tome XVIII, Alger*, Paris: Plon, Nourrit et Cie, 1893.

Algiers Gr. M[osquée]—M. Ben Cheneb, *Catalogue des mss. conservés dans les principales bibliothèques algériennes, Grande Mosquée d'Alger*, Algiers: Jourdan, 1909.

Al-Ḥafnāwī, *Taʿrīf al-khalaf*—See Al-Ḥifnāwī, *Taʿrīf al-khalaf.*

Al-Ḥājj al-Sayyid ʿAlī al-Īrwānī (library of, Tabriz)—Not in Roper.

Al-Ḥājj ʿImād (library of, no place)—Not in Roper.

Al-Ḥājj Muḥammad Sulṭān al-Mutakallimīn (collection of, Tehran)—Not in Roper.

Al-Ḥalabī, *Sīra*—Al-Ḥalabī ʿAlī b. Ibrāhīm Nūr al-Dīn, *al-Sīra al-Ḥalabiyya.*

Al-Ḥarīrī, *Durra*—Abu ʾl-Qāsim b. ʿAlī al-Ḥarīrī, *Kitāb durrat al-ghawwāṣ fī awhām al-khawāṣṣ.*

Al-Ḥasan al-Ṣadr (library of, no place)—See next entry?

Al-Ḥasan Ṣadr al-Dīn (library of, no place)—Not in Roper. See also Ḥasan Ṣadr al-Dīn and Ḥasan al-Ṣadr.

Al-Ḥifnāwī, *Taʿrīf al-khalaf*—Abu ʾl-Qāsim Muḥammad al-Ḥifnāwī b. al-Shaykh b. Abi ʾl-Qāsim al-Daysī b. Sīdī Ibrāhīm al-Ghūl, *Taʿrīf al-khalaf bi-rijāl al-salaf.* 2 vols. Algiers: Fontana, 1906.

Al-Hujwīrī, [transl.] Nicholson (Hujwīrī *Kashf* Nich.)—R.A. Nicholson (transl.), *The* Kashf al-maḥjúb, *the Oldest Persian Treatise on Sufism by ʿAlí b. ʿUthmán al-Jullábí al-Hujwírí.* 'E.W.J. Gibb Memorial' vol. 17. Leiden and London: Brill and Luzac & Co., 1911.

Al-Hujwīrī, *Kashf al-maḥjūb* [Nich.]—Ibn ʿUthmān al-Hujwīrī, *Kashf al-maḥjūb*. This is a Persian treatise, which why this author did not receive a separate lemma, was not mentioned in GAL's Index of Names, and also why the title of this work was excluded from the Index of Works. The work is different from the two works by the same title that are mentioned in GAL's Index of Works. For the reference to Nicholson see previous entry.

Al-Hujwīrī, *Shuk.*—Idem, *Kashf* [*al-maḥjūb*]?

Al-Ḥumaydī, *Jadhwa*—Al-Ḥumaydī Muḥammad b. Abī Naṣr Futūḥ, *Kitāb jadhwat al-muqtabis fī dhikr wulāt al-Andalus wa-asmāʾ ruwāt al-ḥadīth wa-ahl al-fiqh wal-adab wa-dhawi ʾl-nabāha wal-shiʿr.*

Al-Ḥusayniyya (library, Najaf)—Not in Roper.

ʿAlī Akbar al-Khwānsārī (library of, no place)—Not in Roper.

Alī Akbar al-Kirmānī (library of, Mashhad)—Not in Roper.

ʿAlī al-Khiyābānī (library of, Tabriz)—Not in Roper.

ʿAlī Āl Kāshif al-Ghiṭāʾ—See ʿAlī Kāshif al-Ghiṭāʾ

ʿAlī al-Qaṭīfī (library of, Karbala)—Not in Roper.

ʿAlī Amīrī Ef.—See second next entry.

ʿAlī b. Sahl b. Rabban [al-Ṭabarī]—See al-Ṭabarī.

ʿA[lī] Emīrī (Emir?)—Roper III 342, Ali Emirî Efendi.

ʿAlī al-Qaṭīfī (library of, Karbala)—Not in Roper.

Aligarh—Sayyid Kāmil Ḥusayn, *Fihrist nusakh qalamī* (*ʿArabī, Fārsī wa-Urdu*), Moslem University ʿA., Aligarh 1930.

Aligarh Ṣubḥānallāh—See Roper I 425, Janab Subhanullah Khan.

ʿAlī Kāshif al-Ghiṭāʾ (library of, Najaf)—Roper II 39, Shaykh ʿAlī Kāshif al-Ghiṭāʾ.

ʿAlī Muḥammad Najafābādī (library of, Najaf)—Not in Roper.

Al-ʿIqd—See Ibn ʿAbd Rabbih.

Al-ʿIrāqiyyāt—A. Riḍā & Z. Ẓāhir, *al-ʿIrāqiyyāt wa-huwa mukhtār min shiʿr ʿashara shuʿarāʾ min mashāhīr shuʿarāʾ al-ʿIrāq*, vol. 1. Sidon, 1331/1912–13.

ʿAlī Šehīd P[āshā]—See Šehīd ʿA.

Al-Iṣfahānī, *Kharīda*—Al-Kātib al-Iṣfahānī Muḥammad b. Muḥammad Ḥamīd, *Kharīdat al-qaṣr wa-jarīdat ahl al-ʿaṣr.*

Al-Ishbīlī, *Fihrist*—Al-Ishbīlī Muḥammad b. Khayr, *Fihrist mā rawāhu ʿan shuyūkhihi min al-dawāwīn al-muṣannafa fī ḍurūb al-ʿilm wa-anwāʿ al-maʿārif.*

Al-Jabartī—Al-Jabartī ʿAbd al-Raḥmān b. Ḥasan, *ʿAjāʾib al-āthār fī ʾl-tarājim wal-akhbār.*

Al-Jāḥiẓ, *R.*—O. Rescher, *Excerpte und Übersetzungen aus den Schriften des Philologen und Dogmatikers Jāḥiẓ aus Baṣra (150–250 H) nebst noch unveröffentlichten Originaltexten.* Stuttgart, 1931–.

Al-Jahshiyārī [, *Kitāb al-wuzarāʾ*]—Muḥammad b. ʿAbdūs al-Jahshiyārī, *Kitāb al-wuzarāʾ wal-kuttāb.*

Al-Jazarī—See Ibn al-Jazarī.

Al-Jumaḥī, *Ṭab. al-sh[uʿarāʾ]* (—*Ṭab.*)—Muḥammad b. Sallām al-Jumaḥī, *Kitāb ṭabaqāt al-shuʿarāʾ.*

Al-Jurjānī, *Asrār*—ʿAbd al-Qāhir b. ʿAbd al-Raḥmān al-Jurjānī, *Asrār al-balāgha fī ʾl-maʿānī wal-bayān.*

Al-Jurj(g)ānī, *Kin[āyāt]*—Al-Jurjānī Aḥmad b. Muḥammad, *Kitāb kināyāt al-udabāʾ wa-ishārāt al-bulaghāʾ.*

Al-Jurjānī, *[al-]Wasāṭa*—ʿAlī b. ʿAbd al-ʿAzīz al-Jurjānī, *Kitāb al-wasāṭa bayna ʾl-Mutanabbī wa-khuṣūmihi.*

Al-Juzūlī—See al-Ghuzūlī.

Al-Kantūrī (al-Kentūrī)—Al-Kantūrī, *Kashf al-ḥujub wal-astār ʿan asmāʾ al-kutub wal-asfār* / or *The Bibliography of Shīʿa Literature*, ed. Muḥammad Hidāyat Ḥusayn. Bibliotheca Indica no. 203. Calcutta, 1912–14.

Al-Kardarī, *Manāqib*—Al-Kardarī Muḥammad b. Muḥammad b. al-Bazzāzī, *Manāqib Abī Ḥanīfa.*

Al-Kashshī, *Maʿrifat akhbār al-rijāl* (al-Kashshī *Rijāl*)—Abū ʿAmr Aḥmad b. ʿUmar b. ʿAbd al-ʿAzīz al-Kashshī, *al-Kitāb al-mustaṭāb al-musammā bi-Maʿrifat akhbār al-rijāl.* Bombay, 1317.

Al-Kattānī, *Ṣafwat al-anfās*—A mistake, see next entry.

Al-Kattānī, *Salwa[t]*—Al-Kattānī Muḥammad b. Jaʿfar, *Salwat al-anfās wa-muḥādathat al-akyās mimman uqbira min al-ʿulamāʾ wal-ṣulaḥāʾ bi-Fās* (*Salwat al-anfus* is a misprint).

Al-Kattānī, *Fihris*—Al-Kattānī Muḥammad b. [*sic*] ʿAbd al-Ḥayy, *Fihris al-fahāris wal-athbāt wa-nujūm al-maʿājim wal-mashyakhāt wal-musalsalāt.*

Al-Khafājī, *Rayḥ[āna]*—Al-Khafājī Aḥmad b. Muḥammad, *Rayḥānat al-alibbāʾ wa-nuzhat al-ḥayāt al-dunyā.*

Al-Khalājī, *Rayḥ.*—See previous entry.

Al-Khalīl Nawfal, *Ṭar. al-tar.*—Al-Ḥabīb Nawfal, *Tarājim ʿulamāʾ Ṭarāblus wa-udabāʾihā.* Tripoli: Maṭbaʿat al-Ḥaḍāra, 1929.

Al-Khaṭīb, *Ta'r. Baghdād* (– *Ta'r. B[aghd]*., al-Khaṭīb)—Al-Khaṭīb al-Baghdādī Aḥmad b. ʿAlī, *Ta'rīkh Baghdād*.

Al-Khayyāṭ—Al-Khayyāṭ ʿAbd al-Raḥīm b. Muḥammad b. ʿUthmān, *Kitāb al-intiṣār wal-radd ʿalā Ibn al-Rāwandī al-mulḥid mā qaṣada bihi min al-kadhib ʿala 'l-Muslimīn wal-ṭaʿn ʿalayhim*.

Al-Khazrajī, *al-ʿUqūd al-lu'l[u'iyya]*—Al-Khazrajī ʿAlī b. al-Ḥasan, *al-ʿUqūd al-lu'lu'iyya fī akhbār al-dawla al-Rasūliyya*.

Al-Khiṭaṭ al-jad[īda] (*al-Khiṭ. al-jadīda, Khiṭ jad.*)—ʿAlī Mubārak, *al-Khiṭaṭ al-Tawfīqiyya al-jadīda li-Miṣr al-Qāhira wa-mudunihā al-qadīma wal-shahīra*. 20 vols. Būlāq, 1306.

Al-Khizāna al-Gharawiyya—Roper II 45, Khizānat al-Rawḍa al-Ḥaydariyya, also known as al-Khizāna al-Gharawiyya (Najaf).

Al-Khizāna al-Riḍawiyya—Roper I 481, Āstān-i Raẕavī Library (Mashhad).

Al-Khizāna al-Sharīfa al-Gharawiyya—See al-Khizāna al-Gharawiyya.

Al-Khushanī, *Ṭab.* (al-Khushanī transl. Ben Cheneb)—Mohammed Ben Cheneb (ed. & transl.), *Classes des savants de l'Ifrīqīya* / par Abu 'l-ʿArab Moḥammed ben Aḥmed ben Tamīm et Moḥammed ben al-Ḥāriṯ ben Asad al-Ḫošanī. 2 vols. Paris: Leroux 1915 (vol. 1, Arab. text) & Algiers: Carbonel 1920 (vol. 2, Fr. transl.).

Al-Khushanī, ed. Ribera—Muḥammad b. al-Ḥārith al-Khushanī, *Kitāb al-quḍāt bi-Qurṭuba*, ed. & transl. J. Ribera, *Historia de los jueces de Córdoba*. Madrid: Ibérica, 1914.

Al-Khwānsārī Library (Najaf)—Not in Roper (= Muḥammad ʿAlī [al-]Khwānsārī [al-Najafī] library/ collection, Najaf?).

Al-Kindī, ed. Guest—Rh. Guest, *The Governors and Judges of Egypt / or* Kitāb al-umarā' (al-wulāh) wa-kitāb al-Quḍāh *of al-Kindī*. E.J.W. Gibb Memorial Series XIX. Leiden–Brill & London–Luzac, 1912. See also next entry.

Al-Kindī, *Kitāb al-wulāt*—Muḥammad b. Yūsuf al-Kindī, *Tasmiyat wulāt Miṣr*. See also previous entry.

Al-Kutubī, *Fawāt*–Al-Kutubī Muḥammad b. Shākīr, *Fawāt al-wafayāt*.

Al-Lubāb—See Ibn al-Athīr, [*al-*]*Lubāb*.

Al-Maʿārif—See *Maʿārif*.

Al-Madrasa al-Fāḍiliyya (in Mashhad)—Not in Roper. But see M. Darāyatī (ed.), *Fihristigān-i nuskhehā-yi khaṭṭi-yi Īrān* (45 vols. Tehran: Sāzimān-i asnād ō kitābkhāna-yi Milli-yi Jumhūri-yi Islāmi-yi Īrān, 1390–94), vol. 1, lxxxvi.

Al-Madrasa al-Ḥusayniyya—See: Al-Maktaba al-Ḥusayniyya.

Al-Maḥmūdiyya—Roper III 26, Maḥmūdīya Library (Medina).

Al-Maktaba al-Ḥalwiyya (Aleppo)—Not in Roper.

Al-Maktaba al-Ḥusayniyya (in Najaf)—Not in Roper.

Al-Maktaba al-Marjāniyya (Baghdad)—Not in Roper.

Al-Maktaba al-Mawlawiyya (Aleppo)—Roper III 192, al-Maktaba al-Khusrawiyya wal-Mawlawiyya.

Al-Maktaba al-Mīrghaniyya (Baghdad)—Not in Roper.

Al-Maktaba al-Nāṣiriyya (no place)—Not in Roper.

Al-Maktaba al-Sindiyya—See Makt. Sindiyya.

Al-Makt. al-ʿAlawiyya (no place)—Roper IV 177, Alawi Bohra Library (Baroda, India)?

Al-Manfalūṭī, *Mukhtārāt*—Al-Manfalūṭī Muṣṭafā Luṭfī, *Mukhtarāt al-Manfalūṭī*.

Al-Maqdisī, *Kitāb al-kamāl*—ʿAbd al-Ghanī b. ʿAbd al-Waḥīd b. Surūr al-Jammaʿīlī, *Kitāb al-kamāl fī maʿrifat (asmāʾ) al-rijāl*.

Al-Maqqarī (Maqqarī, Maqq.)—Al-Maqqarī ʿAlī b. Muḥammad, *Nafḥ al-ṭīb min ghuṣn al-Andalus al-raṭīb wa-dhikr wazīrihā Lisān al-Dīn al-Khaṭīb*.

Al-Marṣafī, *Wasīla*—Al-Marṣafī Ḥusayn b. Aḥmad, *Kitāb al-wasīla al-adabiyya ila ʾl-ʿulūm al-ʿarabiyya*. 2 vols. Cairo: Maṭbaʿat al-Madāris al-Malakiyya, 1292–96 (1875–79).

Al-Marzubānī, [*al-*]*Muʿjam*—Muḥammad b. ʿImrān al-Marzubānī, *Muʿjam al-shuʿarāʾ*.

Al-Marzubānī, [*al-*]*Muwashshaḥ* (—[*al-*]*Muw.*, al-Marzubānī)—Idem, *al-Muwashshaḥ fī maʾākhidh al-ʿulamāʾ ʿala ʾl-shuʿarāʾ*.

Al-Masʿūdī, *Murūj* (al-Masʿūdī)—Al-Masʿūdī ʿAlī b. al-Ḥusayn, *Murūj al-dhahab wa-maʿādin al-jawāhir*.

Al-Masʿūdī, *Tanbīh*—Idem, *Kitāb al-tanbīh wal-ishrāf*.

Al-Maydānī, *Amthāl* ([al-]Maydānī, Mayd.)—Al-Maydānī Aḥmad b. Muḥammad b. Aḥmad, *Majmaʿ al-amthāl*.

Al-Misk al-adhfar—Al-Ālūsī Maḥmūd Shukrī, *al-Misk al-adhfar, tarājim ʿulamāʾ Baghdād fi ʾl-qarn al-thānī ʿashar wal-thālith ʿashar*. Baghdad 1348/1935.

Al-Mubarrad—Al-Mubarrad Muḥammad b. Yazīd al-Azdī, *al-Kāmil*.

Al-Mufaḍḍal, *al-Fākhir*—Al-Mufaḍḍal b. Salāma al-Ḍabbī, *Kitāb al-fākhir* (*fi ʾl-amthāl*).

Al-Muḥaddith al-ʿImād al-Fihrisī (library of, Mashhad)—Not in Roper; see also Mahdī ʿImād al-Fihrisī and ʿImād al-Fihrisī.

Al-Mujaddid al-Shīrāzī (library of, no place)—Not in Roper.

Al-Muqaddasī—Al-Muqaddasī Muḥammad b. Aḥmad b. Abī Bakr, *Aḥsan al-taqāsīm fī maʿrifat al-aqālīm*.

Al-Murtaḍā—May refer to al-Murtaḍā *Itḥāf* or to al-Murtaḍā *al-Muʿtazila*.

Al-Murtaḍā, *al-Muʿtazila* (al-Murtaḍā)—See Ibn al-Murtaḍā.

Al-Murtaḍā, *Itḥāf* (al-Murtaḍā)—See Murtaḍā.

Al-Murtaḍā, *TA*—Al-Zabīdī Muḥammad Murtaḍā, *Tāj al-ʿarūs, sharḥ al-Qāmūs*.

Al-Mushtabih—Al-Dhahabī Muḥammad b. Aḥmad b. ʿUthmān, *Kitāb al-mushtabih fī asmāʾ al-rijāl*.

Al-Muʾtalif—Al-Ḥasan b. Bishr al-Āmidī, *Kitāb al-muʾtalif wal-mukhtalif min asmāʾ al-shuʿarāʾ wa-alqābihim*.

Al-Nabhānī, *Karāmāt al-awliyāʾ*—Al-Nabhānī Yūsuf b. Ismāʿīl, *Jāmiʿ karāmāt al-awliyāʾ*.

Al-Nadwī, *Tadhk. al-nawādir*—Hāshim al-Nadwī, *Tadhkirat al-nawādir min al-makhṭūṭāt al-ʿArabiyya*. Hyderabad, 1350.

Al-Nāfiʿ—Al-Laknawī Muḥammad ʿAbd al-Ḥayy, *al-Nāfiʿ al-kabīr li-man yuṭāliʿ al-Jāmiʿ al-ṣaghīr.*

Al-Najjāshī—Read: al-Najāshī.

Al-Nāṣirī, *al-Istiqṣāʾ*—Al-Salāwī Aḥmad b. Khālid, *Kitāb al-istiqṣāʾ li-akhbār duwal al-Maghrib al-aqṣā.*

Al-Nathr al-fannī—See Zakī Mubārak, *al-Nathr al-fannī.*

[Al-]Nawawī (Naw.)—See next entry.

Al-Nawawī, *Biogr. Dict.* (– *Tahdhīb*, – W., [al-]Nawawī, Naw.)—Yaḥyā b. Sharaf al-Nawawī, *Tahdhīb al-asmāʾ wal-lughāt.* The edition referred to is the one by Wüstenfeld (2 vols.).

Al-Nawawī, comm. on al-Shīrāzī's *Tanbīh*—Idem, *Taṣḥīḥ al-Tanbīh* (i.e. the *Kitāb al-tanbīh fi ʾl-fiqh* by al-Fīrūzābādī Ibrāhīm b. ʿAlī b. Yūsuf al-Shīrāzī).

Al-Nawawī, *Tahdhīb*—See al-Nawawī, *Biogr. Dict.*

Al-Nawawī, *W.*—See al-Nawawī, *Biogr. Dict.*

Al-Nawbakhtī—Al-Nawbakhtī, *Firaq al-Shīʿa.*

Al-Nuwayrī, *al-Nihāya*—See next entry.

Al-Nuwayrī, *Nihāya*[*t al-arab*] (– *Nih. al-ar.*, [al-]Nuwayrī)—Al-Nuwayrī Aḥmad b. ʿAbd al-Wahhāb, *Nihāyat al-arab fī funūn al-adab.*

ʿAlq.—ʿAlqama.

Al-Qab[*a*]*s al-ḥāwī*—Al-Shammāʿ ʿUmar b. Aḥmad b. ʿAlī, *al-Qabs al-ḥāwī li-ghurr al-Ḍawʾ al-lāmiʿ.*

Al-Qāḍī, *Am.*—See al-Qālī, *Am.*

Al-Qādirī, NM—Muḥammad al-Ṭayyib b. ʿAbd al-Salām al-Qādirī, a.k.a. Muḥammad b. al-Ṭayyib al-Qādirī, *Nashr al-mathānī li-ahl al-qarn al-ḥādī ʿashar wal-thānī.* 2 vols. in one tome. Lith. Fez, 1310.

Al-Qalānisī—Ibn al-Qalānisī Ḥamza b. Asad, *Dhayl Taʾrīkh Dimashq.*

Al-Qālī [, *Am.*]—Ismāʿīl b. al-Qāsim al-Qālī, *al-Amālī.*

Al-Qalqashandī, *Ṣubḥ.*—Al-Qalqashandī Aḥmad b. ʿAlī b. ʿAbdallāh, *Ṣubḥ al-aʿshā fī ṣināʿat al-inshāʾ.*

Al-Qāsim al-Khwānsārī al-Mūsawī (library of, no place)—Not in Roper.

Al-Qazwīnī, *Kosm*[*ographie*] (– *Kosmol., sic*)—*Das Steinbuch aus der Kosmographie des Z. b. M. b. M. al-K. übers. u. mit Anm. versehn v.* J. Ruska, *Beilage zum Jahresber. der prov. Oberrealschule zu Heidelberg*, Kirchhain N/L, 1896.

Al-Qazwīnī (W.)—Refers to F. Wüstenfeld's (Göttingen, 1848) edition of al-Qazwīnī Zakariyyāʾ b. Muḥammad b. Maḥmūd, *ʿAjāʾib al-makhlūqāt wa-āthār al-bilād.*

Al-Qifṭī, *Anbāh al-ruwāt*—Al-Qifṭī ʿAlī b. Yūsuf b. Ibrāhīm, *Inbāʾ al-ruwāh ʿalā anbāʾ al-nuḥāh.*

Al-Qummī, *Tafsīr*—Al-Qummī ʿAlī b. Ibrāhīm b. Hāshim, *Tafsīr al-Qurʾān.*

Al-Rawāʾiʿ—Title of a series of literary studies by Fuʾād Afrām al-Bustānī.

Al-Ṣafadī, *al-Wāfī* (al-Ṣafadī)—Ṣalāḥ al-Dīn al-Ṣafadī Khalīl b. Aybak, *al-Wāfī bil-wafayāt*.

Al-Ṣafadī, *Ghayth*—Idem, *al-Ghayth al-musajjam*, also known as *Ghayth al-adab alladhi 'nsajam*.

Al-Ṣafadī, *Wafā'*—This is a mistake in GAL; the reference is in fact to the second previous entry.

Al-Ṣaḥartī[, *Adab al-ṭabī'a*]—Muṣṭafā ʿAbd al-Laṭīf al-Ṣaḥartī, *Adab al-ṭabīʿa*. Cairo: Maṭbaʿat al-Taʿāwun, 1937.

Al-Sakhāwī, *al-Ḍaw'* [*al-lāmiʿ*]—Al-Sakhāwī Muḥammad b. ʿAbd al-Raḥmān b. Muḥammad, *al-Ḍaw' al-lāmiʿ fī aʿyān al-qarn al-tāsiʿ*.

Al-Sakhāwī, *Iʿlān* [*al-tawbīkh*]—Idem, *al-Iʿlān bil-tawbīkh li-man dhamma ahl al-ta'rīkh*.

Al-Sakhāwī, *al-Tibr al-masbūk*—Idem, *al-Tibr al-masbūk* [*fī dhayl al-Sulūk*].

Al-Samʿānī, *Ansāb*—Al-Samʿānī ʿAbd al-Karīm b. Muḥammad b. Manṣūr, *Kitāb al-ansāb*.

Al-Sandūbī (collection of, no place)—Not in Roper.

Al-Ṣarfandī—See Abū Isḥāq Ibrāhīm al-Ṣarfandī.

Al-Sarrāj, *al-Lumaʿ*—Al-Sarrāj ʿAbdallāh b. ʿAlī b. Muḥammad, *Kitāb al-lumaʿ fi 'l-taṣawwuf*.

Al-Sarrāj, *Maṣāriʿ*—Al-Sarrāj Jaʿfar b. Aḥmad b. al-Ḥusayn al-Qāri' al-Baghdādī, *Maṣāriʿ al-ʿushshāq*.

Al-Shahrastānī (Shahrast.)—Al-Shahrastānī Muḥammad b. ʿAbd al-Karīm, *Kitāb al-milal wal-niḥal*.

Al-Shammākhī[, *Siyar*]—Al-Shammākhī Aḥmad b. Abī ʿUthmān Saʿīd, *Kitāb al-siyar*.

Al-Shaq. al-Nuʿm.—See *ShN*.

Al-Shaʿrānī, *Ṭab.*—Al-Shaʿrānī ʿAbd al-Wahhāb b. Aḥmad b. ʿAlī, *Lawāqiḥ al-anwār fī ṭabaqāt* (*al-sādat*) *al-akhyār*.

Al-Sharīshī on al-Ḥarīrī—Al-Sharīshī Aḥmad b. ʿAbd al-Munʿim, *Sharḥ Maqāmāt al-Ḥarīrī*.

Al-Shawkānī [, (*al-*)*Badr*]—Al-Shawkānī Muḥammad b. ʿAlī b. Muḥammad, *al-Badr al-ṭāliʿ bi-maḥāsin man baʿd al-qarn al-sābiʿ*.

Al-Shawkānī, *Mulḥaq*—See previous entry, Appendix to vol. 2 of the edition mentioned there.

Al-Siʿāya—Al-Laknawī Muḥammad ʿAbd al-Ḥayy, *al-Siʿāya, ḥāshiya ʿalā Sharḥ al-Nuqāya*.

Al-Subkī, *Ṭab.* [*al-Shāf.*] (Subkī *Ṭab.*, [al-]Subkī *Ṭ.*, [al-]Subkī)—Al-Subkī ʿAbd al-Wahhāb b. ʿAlī Tāj al-Dīn, *Ṭabaqāt al-Shāfiʿiyya*.

Al-Ṣūlī, *Awrāq*—Al-Ṣūlī Muḥammad b. Yaḥyā, *al-Awrāq fī akhbār āl al-ʿAbbās wa-ashʿārihim* (= *Kitāb al-awrāq*).

Al-Suyūṭī, *al-Jāmiʿ al-ṣaghīr*—Al-Suyūṭī ʿAbd al-Raḥmān b. Abī Bakr b. Muḥammad, *al-Jāmiʿ al-ṣaghīr min ḥadīth al-bashīr al-nadhīr* (see vol. 2, p. 159, no. 56, the abbreviation).

Al-Suyūṭī, *al-Shāfī*—There is no work by al-Suyūṭī that has *al-Shāfī* in its title. The reference (Suppl. 1, 307) is in fact to his *Sharḥ al-ṣudūr fī sharḥ ḥāl al-mawtā wal-qubūr* (see vol. 2, p. 157, no. 30). The catalogues (see e.g. Berl. 2665) seem to have '*bi-sharḥ*' rather than Brockelmann's '*fī sharḥ*'.

Al-Suyūṭī, *Bughya* (– *B.*)—Idem, *Bughyat al-wuʿāt* (see vol. 2, p. 171, no. 277 * *Ṭabaqāt al-naḥwiyyīn wal-lughawiyyīn*, c. *al-sughrā*).

Al-Suyūṭī, *Dhayl* [*Ṭab. al-ḥuff.*] (– *Dhayl Ṭab.*)—Idem, *Dhayl Ṭabaqāt al-ḥuffāẓ*. This work is not mentioned in the lemmas on al-Suyūṭī in vol. 2 or Suppl. 2; it only referred to in passing in Suppl. 2, p. 51, lines 3–4.

Al-Suyūṭī, *Fajr al-thamd etc.*—Idem, *Fajr al-thamd fī iʿrāb akmal al-ḥamd* (see vol. 2, p. 170, no. 257).

Al-Suyūṭī, *Ḥuff.*—Idem, *Ṭabaqāt al-ḥuffāz* (see vol. 2, p. 171, no. 275).

Al-Suyūṭī, *Ḥusn al-muḥ*[*āḍ*]. (– *Ḥusn.*)—Idem, *Ḥusn al-muḥāḍara fī akhbār Miṣr wal-Qāhira* (see vol. 2, p. 171, no. 279).

Al-Suyūṭī, *Interp*[*r*]. (– *De interpret. Kor.*, – *Int.*)—A. Meursinge (ed.), *Specimen e litteris orientalibus, exhibens Sojutii liber de interpretibus Korani.* Leiden: Luchtmans, 1839 (see vol. 2, p. 171, no. 276: *Ṭabaqāt al-mufassirīn*).

Al-Suyūṭī, *Itqān*—Idem, *al-Itqān fī ʿulūm al-Qurʾān* (text divided into *nawʿ*s or sections) (see vol. 2, p. 155, no. 1).

Al-Suyūṭī, *Lubb*—Idem, *Lubb al-lubāb fī taḥrīr al-ansāb* (see vol. 2, p. 157, no. 27).

Al-Suyūṭī, *Mufass.*—See idem, *Interpr.*

Al-Suyūṭī, *Mughnī*—Among al-Suyūṭī's works, no so title is listed; so maybe the reference is rather to his *Sharḥ shawāhid al-Mughnī* (see vol. 2, p. 169, no. 249), also known as the *Fatḥ al-qarīb, sharḥ shawāhid Mughni 'l-Labīb* (see Supplement 2, p. 202, no. 2630).

Al-Suyūṭī, *Muḥāḍarāt*—Idem, *al-Muḥāḍarāt wal-muḥāwarāt* (see vol. 2, p. 172, no. 294 *).

Al-Suyūṭī, *Muzhir*—Idem, *al-Muzhir fī ʿulūm al-lugha* (see vol. 2, p. 170, no. 258 *).

Al-Suyūṭī, *Naẓm*—Ph. K. Hitti (ed.), *As-Suyuti's Who's who in the Fifteenth Century*: Nazm ul-ʿIqyân fi Aʿyân-il-Aʿyân. New York: Syrian-American Press, 1927.

Al-Suyūṭī, *ShshM*—Idem, *Sharḥ shawāhid al-Mughnī* (see vol. 2, p. 169, no. 249).

Al-Suyūṭī, *Ṭab.*—May refer to his *Ḥuff.*, *Tab. al-mufass.*, or *Bughya.*

Al-Suyūṭī, *Ṭab. al-mufass.*—See idem, *Interpr.*

Al-Suyūṭī, *Tadrīb* [*al-rāwī*]—Idem, *Tadrīb al-rāwī fī sharḥ Taqrīb al-Nawāwī* (see vol. 2, p. 157, no. 24).

Al-Suyūṭī, *Taʾrīkh al-khulafāʾ*—Idem, *Taʾrīkh al-khulafāʾ* (see vol. 2, p. 171, no. 278, the abstract).

Al-Suyūṭī, *Tazyīn al-mamālik*—Idem, *Tazyīn al-mamālik fī manāqib sayyidina 'l-imām Mālik* (see Supplement 2, p. 204, no. 290a).

Al-Ṭabarī, *Firdaws al-ḥikma*—ʿAlī b. Sahl Rabban al-Ṭabarī, *Firdaws al-ḥikma.*

Al-Ṭabbākh, *Taʾrīkh Ḥalab*—Muḥammad Ghārib al-Ṭabbākh, *Iʿlām al-nubalāʾ bi-taʾrīkh Ḥalab al-Shahbāʾ*. 7 vols. Aleppo, 1341–45.

Al-Tabrīzī on *Ḥam.*—Yaḥyā b. ʿAlī al-Tabrīzī, *Sharḥ al-Ḥamāsa.*

Al-Taʿl. al-san. (*Taʿl. san.*)—Al-Laknawī Muḥammad ʿAbd al-Ḥayy, *al-Taʿlīqāt al-saniyya ʿala ʾl-Fawāʾid al-bahiyya fī tarājim al-Ḥanafiyya.*

Al-Tanūkhī [, *al-Faraj*]—Al-Tanūkhī al-Muḥassin b. ʿAlī, *Kitāb al-faraj baʿd al-shidda.*

Al-Taqāwī (library of, Tehran)—See Sayyid Naṣrallāh al-Taqawī.

Al-Ṭarāʾif al-adabiyya—ʿAbd al-ʿAzīz al-Maymanī, *al-Ṭarāʾif al-adabiyya.* Cairo: Lajnat al-Taʾlīf wal-Tarjama wal-Nashr, 1937.

Al-Thaʿālibī, *Histoire des rois de Perse* (– *Hist. d. rois de Perse*)—Al-Ḥusayn b. Muḥammad al-Marghānī al-Thaʿālibī, *Ghurar al-siyar* or *al-Ghurar fī siyar al-mulūk wa-akhbārihim*, extract in H. Zotenberg (ed. & transl.), *Ghurar akhbār mulūk al-Furs wa-siyarihim.* Histoire des rois des Perses par Aboû Manṣoûr ʿAbd al-Malik Ibn Muḥammad Ibn Ismāʿīl al-Thaʿālibī. Paris: Imprimerie Nationale, 1900.

Al-Thaʿālibī, *Kin.*—Thaʿālibī ʿAbd al-Malik b. Muḥammad, *al-Kināya wal-taʿrīḍ.*

Al-Thaʿālibī, *Man ghāba*—Idem, *Man ghāba ʿanhu ʾl-muṭrib.*

Al-Thaʿālibī, *Tatimma*—Idem, *Tatimmat al-Yatīma.*

Al-Thaʿālibī, *Yatīma*—Idem, *Yatīmat al-dahr fī maḥāsin ahl al-ʿaṣr.*

Al-Ṭihrānī (library of, Najaf)—Not in Roper (= Muḥammad al-Ṭihrānī, library of ?).

Altona—Hamb. ? Not in Roper.

Altosm. anon. Chr.—F. Giese (ed. & transl.), *Die altosmanische anonyme Chroniken.* 2 vols. Breslau: self-edition, 1922 (ed.) & Leipzig: Brockhaus, 1925 (transl.); see also idem, Einleitung zu meiner Textausgabe der altosmanische anonymen Chroniken tewārīḫ-i āl-i ʿos̱mān, in *Mitteilungen zur osmanischen Geschichte*, vol. 1 (1922), 49–75.

Al-Tuḥfa al-bahiyya, Istanbul 1302—*Al-Tuḥfa al-bahiyya wal-ṭurfa al-shahiyya.* Istanbul: Maṭbaʿat al-Jawāʾib, 1302. Anonymous compilation of 17 classical texts.

Al-Ṭuraf al-adabiyya—Muḥammad Amīn al-Khānjī, *al-Ṭuraf al-adabiyya li-ṭullāb al-ʿulūm al-ʿarabiyya.* Cairo: Maṭbaʿat al-Saʿāda, 1325. This collection of classical texts was apparently followed by other volumes with the same title, whose bibliographical details could not be verified.

Al-Ṭuraf al-ʿarabiyya—See previous entry.

Al-Ṭurṭūshī, *Sirāj*—Al-Ṭurṭushī Muḥammad b. al-Walīd b. Abī Randaqa, *Sirāj al-mulūk.*

Al-Ṭūsī (Ṭūsī¹, Ṭūsī List, Tusy List, Ṭūsy, Tusy)—A. Sprenger, Mawlawy ʿAbd al-Ḥaqq and Mawlawy Gholam Qadir (eds.), *Tusy's List of Shy'ah books and ʿAlam Al-Hoda's Notes on Shy'ah biography.* Calcutta: Baptist Mission Press, 1854 (Al-Ṭūsī = Al-Ṭūsī Shaykh al-Ṭāʾifa Muḥammad b. al-Ḥasan).

Al-Ṭūsī²—See Al-Ṭūsī, *Fihrist* ².

Al-Ṭūsī, *Fihrist*² (al-Ṭūsī *Fihr.*², al-Ṭūsī²; if preceded by ʻal-Ṭūsīʼ or ʻṬūsī¹ʼ and a number, sometimes just ʻ²ʼ followed by a number., e.g. in vol. 1, 173: ʻAl-Ṭūsī, no. 561, ²695ʼ; vol. 1, 178: ʻTūṣī¹ no. 451, ²370)—Muḥammad Ṣādiq Āl Baḥr al-ʿUlūm (ed.), *al-Fihrist* /

ta'līf Shaykh al-Ṭā'ifa Abū Ja'far Muḥammad b. al-Ḥasan al-Ṭūsī al-mutawaffā sanat 460. Najaf: al-Maktaba al-Riḍawiyya, 1937/1356 (Al-Ṭūsī = Al-Ṭūsī Shaykh al-Ṭā'ifa Muḥammad b. al-Ḥasan).

Al-Ṭūsī on Labīd—This is ʿAlī b. ʿAbdallāh al-Ṭūsī's recension of the *dīwān* of Labīd: Yūsuf Ḍiyā' al-Dīn al-Khālidī (ed.), *Dīwān Labīd al-ʿĀmirī riwāyat aṭ-Ṭūsī = Der Diwan des Lebîd*. Vienna: Gerold, 1297/1880.

Al-ʿUtbī—Muḥammad b. ʿAbd al-Jabbār al-ʿUtbī, *al-Kitāb al-yamīnī*.

Al-Yaʿqūbī, ed. Houtsma—M. Th. Houtsma (ed.), *Ibn Wadhih qui dicitur al-Jaʿqūbī Historiae*. 2 vols., Leiden: Brill, 1883.

Al-Zabīdī, *Itḥāf*—Murtaḍā al-Zabīdī, *Itḥāf al-sāda al-muttaqīn*.

Al-Zarkalī—See al-Ziriklī.

Al-Ziriklī (Ziriklī, [al-]Zuruklī, al-Zarkalī), *Aʿlām*—Khayr al-Dīn Maḥmūd al-Ziriklī, *al-Aʿlām : qāmūs tarājim li-ashhar al-rijāl wal-nisā' min al-ʿArab wal-mustaʿribīn fi 'l-Jāhiliyya wal-Islām wal-ʿaṣr al-ḥāḍir*. 3 vols. Cairo: al-Maṭbaʿa al-ʿArabiyya, 1345–47 (1927–28).

Al-Zub.—Al-Zubaydī Muḥammad b. al-Ḥasan, *Ṭabaqāt al-naḥwiyyīn* (*al-lughawiyyīn*).

Al-Zuruklī—See al-Ziriklī.

Amālī—Al-Qālī Ismāʿīl b. al-Qāsim, *Amālī*.

Amar—Read: Amari.

Amari, *Altri framm.*—M. Amari, Altri frammenti arabi relativi alla storia d'Italia, in: *Atti della Reale Accademia dei Lincei. Classe di Scienze morali, storiche e filologiche*, s. IV, 6 (1889), pp. 5–31.

Amari, *Bibl. Ar.-Sic.*—May refer to one of the following two publications: a) M. Amari, *Biblioteca Arabo-Sicula* : ossia raccolta di testi Arabici che toccano la geografia, la storia, le biografie e la bibliografia della Sicilia. Leipzig: Brockhaus, 1857. Arabic text; b) M. Amari, *Biblioteca Arabo-Sicula* : versione Italiana. Turin & Rome: Loescher, 1880. Italian translation of the texts presented in a).

Amari, *Storia*—M. Amari, *Storia dei Musulmani di Sicilia*. 3 vols. in 4 tomes. Florence: Le Monnier, 1854–72.

Ambr. A, B, C, D, E, or F (Ambr. N.F. A, B. etc., sometimes just Ambros. N.F. or Ambros.)—Subdivisions of the Nuovo Fondo of the Biblioteca Ambrosiana. For a description of the Oriental manuscripts of the Nuovo Fondo, see E. Griffini, Catalogo dei manoscritti arabi di Nuovo Fondo della biblioteca Ambrosiana di Milano, in *Rivista degli Studi Orientali*, vols. 3 (1910) 253–78, 571–94, 901–21; 4 (1911) 87–106, 1021–48; 6 (1913) 1283–1316; 7 (1916) 51–130, (1917) 565–628; 8 (1919) 241–367. These articles were also published together in one volume as *Catalogo dei manoscritti arabi di Nuovo Fondo della biblioteca Ambrosiana di Milano* vol. 1, Codici 1–475. Estratto dalla *Rivista degli Studi Orientali* vol. III–VIII. Roma, 1920; idem, Die jüngste ambrosianische Sammlung arabischer Handschriften, in ZDMG 69, 63–88.

Ambr. Hammer Cat.—J. von Hammer-Purgstall, Catalogo dei Codici arabi, persiani e turchi della Biblioteca Ambrosiana, in *Biblioteca Italiana o sia Giornale di letteratura, scienze ed arti* 94 (1839) 22–49 (1), 322–48 (2).

Ambr. N.F.—Biblioteca Ambrosiana, Nuovo Fondo. See Ambr. A, B. etc.

Ambros.—E. Griffini, *I manoscritti sudarabici di Milano*. Estratto della "Rivista degli Studi Orientali" vol. II e III (con I tavola). Roma: Casa Editrice Italiana, 1910; see also above, Ambr. A, B, C, D, E, or F.

A. Mez, *Ren.*—See Mez, *Ren.*

ʿAm. Ḥu. P.—See Amuča Ḥü.

Amīn al-Wāʿiẓīn Ibrāhīm b. Muḥammad ʿAlī al-Iṣfahānī (library of, Isfahan)—Not in Roper.

AMK—See Pet. AMK.

AM Leningrad B—See Pet. A.M. Buch.

Amsterdam—See Inst. Reg. Belg.

Amuča Ḥü. (ʿAmūja Ḥu. [P.], ʿAm. Ḥu. P.)—Roper III 348, Amcazâde Hüseyin Paşa.

A. Müller, *Der Islam* (– *Islam*)—A. Müller, *Der Islam im Morgen- und Abendland*, 2 vols., Berlin: G. Grote'sche Verlagsbuchhandlung, 1885–1887.

Anb.—See Ibn al-Anbārī.

Angel.—Biblioteca Angelica. Apart from Cat., see also Roper II 102, Biblioteca Angelica.

Angora, Diyānet işlerī Riyāsetī—Roper III 300, Ankara Diyanet İşleri Başkanlığı Kütüphanesi.

Anm.—Anmerkung ('note').

Ann. f. Nord. Oldk. (*Annaler for Nord. Oldk.*)—*Annaler for Nordisk Oldkyndighet.*

Ann. Musl.—See Abu 'l-F., *Ann.*

Anth. sent.—H.A. Schultens, *Anthologia sententiarum arabicarum cum scholiis Zamachsjarii.*, Leiden: Le Mair, 1772.

Antuña, *al-Muqtabis*—M.M. Antuña, *al-Muktabis, tome troisième : Chronique du règne du calife Umaiyade ʿAbd Allāh à Cordoue*. Paris: Geuthner, 1937.

Apollo—Of this literary journal, only 25 issues were published between September 1932 and December 1934. Page numbers run on continuously from the first to the last issue.

ʿAq.—ʿAbd al-Qādir b. Abi 'l-Wafāʾ.

Āqā Āyatallāh al-Mujaddid al-Shīrāzī (library of)—See al-Mujaddid al-Shīrāzī.

Āqā Khalīlallāh (collection of, Madras)—Not in Roper.

Āqā Muḥammad ʿAlī (collection of, Hyderabad)—Not in Roper.

ʿAqīlat al-ḍamān (*ʿAqīlat al-ḍimān*)—Yaḥyā b. al-Ḥusayn b. al-Muʾayyad billāh, *ʿAqīlat al-daman, al-mukhtaṣar min Anbāʾ al-zaman fī akhbār al-Yaman.*

Āqsarāy—Roper III 294, Akşehir Halk Kütüphanesi ?

Ar.–Arabic, arabe, arabisch(..).

Arch. f. Rel.—*Archiv für Religionswissenschaft*

Arch. Or.—*Archiv Orientální.*

Argent.—Argentina (= Strasbourg).

ʿArīb—*Ṭabarī continuatus / Arīb ; quem edidit, indicibus et glossario instruxit* M.J. de Goeje. Leiden: Brill, 1897. ʿArīb = al-ʿArīb b. Saʿd al-Qurṭubī (Index has 'S.', which is usually 'Sulaymān').

ʿĀrif Ḥikmat—Roper III 26, ʿĀrif Ḥikmat Library.

Arm. Mus. (Army Museum)—Army Museum, Istanbul (= Askêri Müze ?). Not in Roper.

Arnold, *Chr. Ar.*—F.A. Arnold, *Chrestomathie arabica*. Halle: Pfeffer, 1853.

AS—*Defteri Kutubkhana-yi Aya Sofia*, Istanbul 1304.

Asʿad Ef. (Asʿad, Esʿad, Esad)—*Defteri Kutubkhana-yi Asʿad Ef.* Istanbul n.d.

Āṣaf. (Āṣāf.)—*Fihrist-i kutub-i ʿArabī, Fārsī va Urdū makkhzūna-i Kutubkhāna-i Āṣafiyya-i Sarkār-i ʿĀlī.* 3 vols. Hyderabad: Kutub Khāna-i Āsafiya-i Sarkār-i ʿĀlī, 1332–1347/1914–1928.

ʿĀshiqpāshāzāde ed. Giese—F. Giese (ed.), *Die altosmanische Chronik des ʿĀšīkpašazāde.* Leipzig: Harrassowitz, 1929.

ʿĀshiqpāshāzāde G.—See previous entry.

ʿĀshiqpāshāzāde St.—Probably in reference to ʿAlī Bey's edition of ʿĀshiqpāshāzāde's *Tawārīkh-i āl-i ʿUthmān*, which was published in Istanbul in 1332 AH.

Ashraf ʿA.—See As. Soc. Beng.

Asin—See Granada.

Āsitāna, Jawāʾib—See Istanbul Jawāʾib.

ʿĀšir Ef. [Mur.] (ʿĀšir)—Roper III 348, ʿÂşir Efendi.

ʿĀšir Ḥafīd—Not in Roper. In volume 1, 546 Ḥafīd seems to refer to a sub-collection of ʿĀšir. See also volume 2, 239 where we find ʿĀšir Reʾīs, which is not listed as such in Roper either (see also Supplement I, 248: Reʾīs Muṣṭafā).

ʿĀšir Reʾīs [Muṣṭafā]—See previous entry.

ʿAskarī, *Amth*[*āl*]—See al-ʿAskarī, *Amthāl.*

ʿAskarī, *Ṣin.*—See ibid., *Ṣin.*

Askeri Müze—See Arm. Mus.

Aṣm[*aʿiyyāt*]—Al-Aṣmaʿī ʿAbd al-Malik b. Qurayb, *al-Aṣmaʿiyyāt.*

ASB, Govt. Coll.—See As. Soc. Beng., second catalogue.

As. Mus. II, 161—In Supplement 1, 217, 5c, reference is made to "German As. Mus. II 161". This is a literal translation of "… deutsch As. Mus. II, 161, …" in GAL, Supplement I, 220. This mysterious reference is the result of Brockelman's misreading of Wüstenfeld, *Die Geschichtschreiber der Araber und ihre Werke*, 85 # 541, at the end: "… die Flucht und Ermordung Yazdegirds in d. Asiatische Magazin, Bd. 2. S. 161." So the reference is in fact to *Asiatisches Magazin* [verfasst von einer Gesellschaft von Gelehrten, herausgegeben von Julius Klaproth], vol. 2 (Weimar: Verlag des Landes, Industrie, Comptoirs, 1802), 161.

As. Mus. (Kr.)—Probably the same as Pet. AMK.

As. Mus. Rosen—See Pet. AM.

Assemani *BO*—J.S. Assemani, *Bibliotheca Orientalis Clementino-Vaticana: in qua manuscriptos codices Syriacos, Arabicos, Persicos, Turcicos, Hebraicos, Samaritanos, Armenicos, Aethiopicos, Graecos, Aegyptiacos, Ibericos, & Malabaricos, … recensuit, digessit & genuina scripta à spuriis secrevit, addita singulorum auctorum vita*. 3 vols. in 4 tomes. Rome: Sacra Congregatio de Propaganda Fide, 1719–28.

As. Soc.—W. Jones, *Author-Catalogue of the Hyderabad Collection of Manuscripts and printed Books*. Calcutta 1913.

As. Soc. Beng.—Shams ul-ʿulamā Mīrzā Ashraf ʿAlī, *Catalogue of the Arabic Books and Manuscripts in the Library of the Asiatic Society of Bengal*, Calcutta: Baptist Mission Press, 1899–1904; H. Husain and E.D. Ross, *List of Arabic and Persian Manuscripts Acquired on Behalf of the Government of India by the Asiatic Society of Bengal during 1903–7*. Calcutta, 1908.

As. Soc. Beng. Pers.—See previous entry, second publication.

As. Soc. Calcutta—See As. Soc. Beng.

As. Soc. Gov. Coll.—See As. Soc. Beng., second catalogue.

A. Taymūr P. (A[ḥmad] Taymūr, Taymūr, Taymūr Pāshā, Bibl. A. Taymūr), often specifying the subcollection, e.g. 'Ḥikma', 'Taʾrīkh' etc.—ʿĪsā Iskandar al-Maʿlūf, *Khazāʾin al-kutub al-ʿarabiyya 2: Min nafāʾis al-khizāna al-Taymūriyya*, in *RAAD* vol. 3, 337–44, 360–6; Muḥammad Kurd ʿAlī, *al-Khizāna al-Taymūriyya wa-fihrist makhṭūṭātihā*, in *al-Muqtabas* 7 (1912), 437–58.

Āthār al-uwal—ʿAbd al-Bārī, *Āthār al-uwal min ʿulamāʾ Firangī Maḥall*. N.p & n.d.

ʿĀṭif Ef. (ʿĀṭif)—*Defteri Kutubkhana-yi ʿĀṭif Efendi*, Istanbul 1310.

ʿAtīq Ef.—Not in Roper. Misprint for ʿĀṭif Ef.?

ʿAṭṭār, *Tadhkirat al-awliyāʾ* (– *Tadhk. al-awl.*, – *Tadhk.*, – *Awliyāʾ*)—Ghawth al-Hindī Muḥammad b. Khaṭīr al-Din, *Tadhkirat al-awliyāʾ*, as edited in: R.E. Nicholson and Mīrzā Muḥammad b. ʿAbd al-Wahhāb al-Qazwīnī (eds), *The Tadhkiratu ʾl-awliyá* ("Memoirs of the saints") *of Muḥammad bin Ibráhím Farídu'ddín ʿAṭṭár*. 2 vols. London, Luzac & Leiden, Brill: 1905–07.

Aumer—See Munich.

Ausf.—Ausführung (explanation).

Ausland—*Das Ausland.*

A. v. Kremer—See von Kremer and v. Kremer.

ʿAwfī, *Lubāb al-albāb*—E.G. Browne & Mīrzā Muḥammad ʿAbd al-Wahhāb al-Qazwīnī (eds.), *The Lubábu ʾl-albáb of Muḥammed ʿAwfi*. 2 vols. London: Luzac & Leiden: Brill, 1903–06. Persian.

ʿAwfī, *Lubb al-lubāb*—See previous entry.

Awlād Ibrāhīm Pāshā (library of, Alexandria)—Not in Roper (descendants of Shaykh Ibrāhīm Pāshā of Roper I 207, 'Shaykh Ibrāhīm Pāshā Mosque'?).

Awqāf Museum Library—Now Turkish and Islamic Arts Museum; see Roper III 364, Türk ve İslam Eserleri Müzesi Yazma Eserler Kütüphanesi.

ʿAynī—See al-ʿAynī.

Ayyūb—Roper III 348, Eyüp Câmii Hz. Hâlid.

Azhar—See J. Schacht, *Aus den Bibliotheken von Konstantinopel und Kairo* (Schacht I) and idem, *Aus Kairiner Bibliotheken* (Schacht II). At the time at which GAL was written—first and second edition—there was no published catalogue of the Azhar libraries available.

Azharī *MO* 1920—See al-Azharī *MO* 1920,

B.—Beirut.

Bāb—'chapter'.

Bābar, *Mem.* Ed. Beveridge—A.S. Beveridge, *The Bábar-náma, being the autobiography of the Emperor Bábar, the founder of the Moghul dynasty in India, written in Chaghatáy Turkish.* Leiden: Brill, 1905.

Babinger, *GO* (Babinger *Gesch.* [*d. Osm.*], Babinger)—F. Babinger, *Die Geschichtsschreiber der Osmanen und ihre Werke.* Mit einem Anhang: Osmanische Zeitrechnungen, von Joachim Mayr. Leipzig: Harassowitz, 1927.

Babinger, *Stamb. Buchw.*—Idem, *Stambuler Buchwesen im 18. Jahrhundert.* Leipzig: Deutscher Verein für Buchwesen und Schrifttum, 1919.

Babk.—See Bank.

Badāʾūnī, *Muntakhab al-tawārīkh*—ʿAbd al-Qādir b. Mulūk Shāh Badāʾūnī, *Muntakhab al-tawārīkh* (ed. W.N. Lees & Munshi Ahmad Ali). 3 vols. Calcutta: Published under the superintendence of the Asiatic Society of Bengal at the College Press, 1865–69 (Persian).

Badr—See al-Shawkānī, first entry.

Baghdad Kiöshk (Baghdād Köshk)—Roper III 360, Bağdat Köşkü.

Baghdad, Makt. al-Awqāf—See Makt. al-Awqāf.

Baghdād, Marjāna Library—See al-Maktaba al-Marjāniyya.

Baghdādī, *Farq*—See al-Baghdādī.

Baghdadly Ismāʿīl Pāshā (library of, Makriköy)—Not in Roper (no longer extant, see Rescher, *Abriss* I, 55 n. 1). See also Ismāʿīl Pāshā Baghdādī.

BAH—Bibliotheca Arabico Hispana.

BAH III—See al-Ḍabbī.

BAH VII—See Ibn al-Faraḍī.

BAH IX—See Abū Bakr b. Khayr.

Bahāʾ al-Dīn Zuhayr—Bahāʾ al-Dīn al-Muhallabī Zuhayr.

Baḫčiserāi—Roper III 415, Bakhchisaraĭ/Bahchisaray.

Bank. (Bankipore, Patna)—Mawlawī ʿAbd al-Ḥamīd, *Fihrist-i dasti-yi kutub-i qalami-yi lāybiriri-yi ... Khudā Bakhsh Khān musammā bi-Miftāḥ al-kunūz al-khafiyya.* 2 vols.

Patna etc.: Sādiqpūr, 1918–22 (vol. 3 by Sayyid Athar Shīr was published in 1965); *Catalogue of the Arabic and Persian Manuscripts in the Oriental Public Library at Bankipore*. Patna: Govt. Print. Bihar, 1908–, 43 volumes to date; from vol. 27 (1961) onward: *Catalogue of the Arabic and Persian manuscripts in the Khuda Bakhsh Oriental Public Library at Patna*. In his bibliographical listings in Supplement 1, 4–5 and 972, and Supplement 3, 1191, Brockelmann only refers to vols. IV, V, VII, IX, X, XII, XIII, XIV, XV, XVIII, XIX.1–2, XX, XXI, XXII, and XXIII. But it is clear that he also used some of the other volumes, like vol. III, page 252, referred to in *History*, Supplement 2, 624. See also Patna.

Bank Hdl.—See previous entry, Mawlawī ʿAbd al-Ḥamīd, *Fihrist-i dasti-yi etc.*

Barbour—N. Barbour, The Arabic theatre in Egypt, in *BSAOS* VIII (1935), 173/87, 991/1012.

Barnāmaj 1354 (*Barnāmaj*)—*Barnāmaj li-ṭabʿ al-kutub*. Hyderabad, 1354.

Barhebreus—See next entry.

Barhebraeus, *Chr.* Bedjan—See idem, *Chron. Syr.*

Barhebraeus, *Chr*[*on*]. *eccl.*—J.B. Abbeloos and T.J. Lamy (eds.), *Gregorii Barhebraei Chronicon ecclesiasticum*. 3 vols. Leuven: Peeters, 1872–77.

Barhebraeus, *Chr*[*on*]. *Syr.*—P. Bedjan (ed.), *Gregorii Barhebræi Chronicon Syriacum*. Paris, 1890.

Barhebraeus, *Hist. dyn.*—*Historia compendiosa dynastiarum authore Gregorio Abul-Pharajio, Malatiensi medico, historiam complectens universalem, a mundo condito, usque ad tempora authoris, res orientalium accuratissime describens / Arabice edita Latine versa ab* Edvardo Pocockio. Oxford: Davis, 1663.

Barhebraeus, *Hist. eccl.*—A contamination of his *Hist. dyn.* and *Chron. eccl.*, referring to the latter?

Barhebraeus, *Mukhtaṣar* (*Mukht.*)—Abu ʾl-Faraj Ibn al-ʿIbrī (Barhebraeus), *Mukhtaṣar al-duwal.*

Barthélémy, *Dict.*—A. Barthélémy, *Dictionnaire arabe-français. Dialectes de Syrie: Alep, Damas, Liban, Jérusalem*. Paris: Geuthner, 1935.

Barthold, *Iran* II–V. (W.) Barthold, *Tadhkira-yi jughrāfiyā-yi tarīkhī-yi Īrān* (English title: *Historico-geographical Survey of Iran* / transl. from Russian into Persian by H. Serdadver). Tehran: Chāpkhāni-yi Ittiḥādiye, 1308 (1930). The addition 'II' must refer to the fact that it is a translation of the original from 1903.

Barthold (Bartold), *Turkestan* (*Turkest.*)—Idem, *Turkestan down to the Mongol Invasion*, London: Luzac & Co., 1928, 2nd ed.

Barthold, *Zwölf Vorlesungen*—W. Barthold, Theodor Menzel and Hans Heinrich Schaeder, *Zwölf Vorlesungen über die Geschichte der Türken Mittelasiens*. From *Die Welt des Islams*, Beiband zu Band 14–17 (1932–35), Berlin: Deutsche Gesellschaft für Islamkunde, 1935.

Bārūdī [Library]—ʿĪsā Iskandar al-Maʿlūf, *Min nafāʾis al-khizāna al-Bārūdiyya al-kubrā fī Bayrūt*, in RAAD 5 (1925), 32–4, 133–36, 187–90, 223–25; 420 manuscripts from the collection of Murād Bey Bārūdī are now part of the Garret Collection in Princeton University Library, on which see Princ. Garr., Introduction, iii.

Basle [Stadtbibliothek]—Brockelmann received information on the manuscripts in the Stadtbibliothek in Basle from Fritz Meier (See vol. 2, 624).

BASS—*Beiträge zur Assyriologie und semitischen Sprachwissenschaft.*

Basset (collection of, Leiden)—Roper II 373.

Basset, Hamel—See Zaouiyah d'El Hamel.

Basset, *Khazrajiyya*—R. Basset, *La Khazradjiyah*: traité de métrique arabe. Algiers: Fontana, 1902.

Basset, *Rech.* [*bibl.*]—See next entry.

Basset, *Sources* (– *Rech.* [*bibl.*])—R. Basset, *Recherches bibliographiques sur les sources de la Salouat el-Anfas*, Algiers: Fontana, 1905.

Bat.—See Ludg. Bat. and Batavia (Friedrich & van den Berg).

Batavia (Bat.)—R. Friedrich and L.W.C. van den Berg, *Codicum arabicorum in Bibliotheca Societatis Artium quae Bataviae floret asservatorum* catalogus. Batavia: Bruining en Wijt & The Hague: Nijhoff, 1873; Ph. S. van Ronkel, *Supplement to the Catalogue of the Arabic Manuscripts Preserved in the Museum of the Batavia Society of Arts and Sciences*. Batavia: Albrecht & The Hague: Nijhoff, 1913.

Bat. Mal.—Probably: Ph.S. van Ronkel, *Catalogus der Maleische handschriften in het museum van het Bataviaasch Genootschap van Kunsten en Wetenschappen*. Batavia: Albrecht & The Hague: Nijhoff, 1909.

Bat. Suppl.—See Batavia, Ph. S. Ronkel.

Bat. v. Ronkel—See Batavia and Bat. Mal.

Bāyezīd (Welieddīn, Bāy., Bāyazīd)—Brockelmann gives the following reference: '*Deft. K.B.*, Istanbul 1304'. But looking at Roper, vol. 3 it seems there never was a *defter* with that title. What Roper cites (vol. 3, 329) as published in the year 1304 is: *Defter-i Kütüphane-i Veliyüddin*, Istanbul 1304 (1883). The collection Veliyüddin Efendi is one of the many special collections of Bayezit Devlet Kütüphanesi (Roper, ibid.).

Bayhaqī, Schw.—Al-Bayhaqī Ibrāhīm b. Muḥammad, *Kitāb al-maḥāsin wal-masāwī*, ed. F. Schwally, Giessen: Ricker, 1902 (reprint Cairo, 1906).

Bayhaqī, *Tatimma*—See al-Bayhaqī.

Bayt Marʿī Bāshā al-Mallāḥ (private collection, Aleppo)—Not in Roper.

Bayt Sulṭān (private collection, Aleppo)—Not in Roper.

BBA—*Sitzungsberichte der Königlich Preussischen Akademie der Wissenschaften zu Berlin.*

BDMG—Bibliothek der Deutschen Morgenländische Gesellschaft, Halle.

Beale, *Dict. of Or. Biogr.*—Th.W. Beale, *The Oriental Biographical Dictionary*. Calcutta: Baptist Mission Press, 1881.

Becker [*Papp. Schott-Reinhardt*]—C.H. Becker, *Papyri Schott-Reinhardt*, vol. 1. Heidelberg: Winter, 1906.

Becker, *Beitr.* [*z. Gesch. Äg.*]—Idem, *Beiträge zur Geschichte Ägyptens unter dem Islam*. 2 vols. Strasbourg: Trübner, 1902–03.

Beirut—L. Cheikho, Catalogue raisonné des mss. ar. la Bibliothèque orientale de l'Université de St. Joseph, in *MFOB*, VI, VII, VIII, X, XI, XIV; *Makhṭūṭāt al-khizāna al-Maʿlūfiyya fi'l-jāmiʿa al-Amīrikiyya* (Khizānat ʿĪsā Iskandar Maʿlūf). Beirut: al-Maktaba al-Adabiyya, 1926.

Beitr.—Beiträge.

Beitr.—In connection with [E.] Wiedemann, this refers to a series of publications with the blanket title *Beiträge zur Geschichte der Naturwissenschaften*, which were published in *Sitzungsberichte der physikalisch-medizinischen Sozietät zu Erlangen* (*SBPhMS Erl.*, also referred to in GAL as in *SBPMS*).

Ben ʿĀshūr (collection of, Tunis)—Not in Roper.

Ben Cheneb, *Idjāza*—See Muḥammad (M.) b. Cheneb, *Idjāza*.

Beninsammlung—J. Marquart, *Die Benin-Sammlung des Reichsmuseums für Völkerkunde in Leiden: beschrieben und mit ausführlichen Prolegomena zur Geschichte der Handelswege und Völkerbewegungen in Nordafrika*. Leiden: Brill, 1913.

Ber.—See Berl.

Bergstr[ässer]—This abbreviation may refer to two related publications: a) G. Bergsträsser, *Ḥunain ibn Isḥāq und seine Schule: sprach- und literargeschichtliche Untersuchungen zu den arabischen Hippokrates- und Galen-Übersetzungen*. Leiden: Brill, 1913; or b) Idem, *Ḥunain ibn Isḥāq über die syrischen und arabischen Galen-Übersetzungen*. Abhandlungen für die Kunde des Morgenlandes 17.2. Leipzig: Brockhaus, 1925.

Bergsträsser, *Einl.*—G. Bergsträsser, *Einführung in die semitischen Sprachen; Sprachproben und grammatische Skizzen*. Munich: Hueber, 1928.

Bergstr[ässer], *Gesch. des Qorʾāns* III (– *Gesch. al-Q.* III, – *Gesch.* III, – *Gesch. des Qorantextes* [*Qorʾāntextes*], – *Gesch. d. Qorantext.*, – *Gesch. d. Q.*)—See Nöldeke, *Gesch. des Qorans*.

Bergstr.-Pretzl, *Gesch. d. Q.* (Bergsträsser-Pretzl *Gesch. des Qurʾāntextes*, Bergstr.-Pretzl *Gesch. des Qorʾānt.*, Bergsträsser and Pretzl *Gesch. d. Qor.* III, Bergstr.-Pretzl III,)—See Nöldeke, *Gesch. des Qorans*.

Berl. (Berl. Ahlw., Ahlw., Cat. Berl.)—W. Ahlwardt, *Verzeichnis der arabischen Handschriften der Königlichen Bibliothek zu Berlin*. 10 vols. Berlin: Schade (vol. 1) and Asher & Co. (vols. 2–10), 1887–99.

Berl. 4⁰—See Berl. Ms. or. quart.

Berl. acc. mss. or.—Refers to a MS that was not included in Ahlwardt's catalogue and may be looked up in *Standortverzeichnis der orientalischen Handschriften der preußischen Staatsbibliothek*, 3 vols. This is a handwritten source, for which see: Datenbank der orientalischen Handschriften der Staatsbibliothek zu Berlin, which may be found on the library's website.

Berl. Brill M. (Berl. Br. M.)—see Daḥdāḥ.

Berl. Burch.—See Burch.-Fischer.

Berl. cod. sim. (Berl. ms. sim. or., Berl. sim., cod. sim.)—Hs. or. sim., this signature refers to photographical reproductions of oriental manuscripts in what is now the Staatsbibliothek zu Berlin (earlier: Königliche Bibliothek).

Berl. Fol.—See Berl. Ms. or. fol.

Berl. Mf.—See Berl. Ms. or. fol.

Berl. Mq—See Berl. Ms. or. quart.

Berl. Ms. or. fol. (Berl. Fol., Berl. Mf.)—Manuscripts in folio of the old collection of the Royal Library in Berlin (also referred to as the *manuscripta orientalia Berolinensia*), referred to in Ahlwardt's catalogue as 'Mf. (= Mss Or. Folio)'. For correspondences between the old numbering and the numbering of Ahlwardt's catalogue, see the catalogue, vol. 10, 12–14. Manuscripts in folio from no. 1322 onwards are not included in Ahlwardt's catalogue, but in *Standortverzeichnis der orientalischen Handschriften der preußischen Staatsbibliothek*, vol. 1: *Orientalische Handschriften in folio*, 3. This is a handwritten source, for which see: Datenbank der orientalischen Handschriften der Staatsbibliothek zu Berlin, which may be found on the library's website.

Berl. Ms. or. oct.—Manuscripts in octavo of the old collection of the Royal Library in Berlin (also referred to as the *manuscripta orientalia Berolinensia*), referred to in Ahlwardt's catalogue as 'Mo. (= Mss Or. Octavo)'. For correspondences between the old numbering and the numbering of Ahlwardt's catalogue, see the catalogue, vol. 10, 21–23. Manuscripts in octavo from no. 404 onwards are not included in Ahlwardt's catalogue, but in *Standortverzeichnis der orientalischen Handschriften der preußischen Staatsbibliothek* vol. 3: *Orientalische Handschriften in octavo*, 2. This is a handwritten source, for which see: Datenbank der orientalischen Handschriften der Staatsbibliothek zu Berlin, which may be found on the library's website.

Berl. Ms. or. quart. (Berl. Ms. or. qu, Berl. or. qu., Berl. qu., Berl. Mq, Berl. 4^0)—Manuscripts in quarto of the old collection of the Royal Library in Berlin (also referred to as the *manuscripta orientalia Berolinensia*), referred to in Ahlwardt's catalogue as 'Mq. (= Mss Or. Quarto)'. For correspondences between the old numbering and the numbering of Ahlwardt's catalogue, see the catalogue, vol. 10, 15–21. Manuscripts in quarto from no. 765 onwards are not included in Ahlwardt's catalogue, but in *Standortverzeichnis der orientalischen Handschriften der preußischen Staatsbibliothek* vol. 2: *Orientalische Handschriften in quarto*, 2. This is a handwritten source, for which see: Datenbank der orientalischen Handschriften der Staatsbibliothek zu Berlin, which may be found on the library's website.

Berl. Ms. sim.—See Berl. cod. sim.

Berl. or. qu.—See Berl. Ms. or. quart.

Berl. Pers.—W. Pertsch, *Die Handschriften-Verzeichnisse der Könichlichen Bibliothek zu Berlin, vierter Band, Verzeichnis der persischen Handschriften*. Berlin: Asher, 1888.

Berl. qu.—See Berl. Ms. or. quart.

Berl. sim.—See Berl. cod. sim.

Berl. Spr. (Spr.)—Berlin Sprenger. For a concordance between the numbers of the Sprenger collection and those of Ahlwardt's catalogue, see W. Ahlwardt, *Verzeichnis der arabischen Handschriften der Königlichen Bibliothek zu Berlin* vol. 10, 47–59 (see above: 'Berl.').

Berl. Wetzst.—Berlin Wetzstein. For a concordance between the numbers of the Wetzstein collection and those of Ahlwardt's catalogue, see W. Ahlwardt, *Verzeichnis der arabischen Handschriften der Königlichen Bibliothek zu Berlin* vol. 10, 25–47 (see above: 'Berl.').

Berth.-H.—M. Berthelot, *La chimie au moyen âge* III, *L'alchimie arabe*, avec la collaboration de M.O. Houdas. Paris: Imprimerie Nationale, 1893.

Bešīr Āġā—*Defteri Kutubkhana-yi Bešīr Āġā*, Istanbul n.d.

Bešīr Āġā Ayyūb—Roper III 348, Beşir Ağa Eyüp.

Bešīr (Sül.)—See Bešīr Āġā.

Bezzenbergers Beitr.—*Beiträge zur Kunde der indogermanischen Sprachen*, herausgegeben von A. Bezzenberger.

Bezold—C. Bezold (ed.), *Orientalische Studien Theodor Nöldeke zum siebzigsten Geburtstag (2 März 1906) gewidmet von Freunden und Schülern*. 2 vols. Gieszen: Töpelmann, 1906.

BG—Bibliotheca Geographorum Arabicorum.

Bibl. Ac. Scient. [Leiden]—See de Jong.

Bibl. ar.-hisp. IX—See Abū Bakr b. Khayr.

Bibl. A. Taymūr—See A. Taymūr P.

Bibl. Dahdāh—See Daḥdāḥ.

Bibl. DMG—See BDMG.

Bibl. Geogr. Ar.—See BG.

Bibl. Gregor. IV—See Pet. Libr. Grig. IV.

Bibl. Isl.—Bibliotheca Islamica.

Bibl. Ital.—See Hammer, *Lettere*.

Bibl. Math.—Bibliotheca Mathematica.

Bibl. R. Dahdah—See: Daḥdāḥ.

Bibl. Vost.—*Bibliografija Vostoka*. Leningrad.

Biogr. Univ.—*Biographie universelle, ancienne et moderne*.

Björkman, *Beitr.*—W. Björkman, *Beiträge zur Geschichte der Staatskanzlei im islamischen Ägypten*. Hamburg: Friederichsen, 1928.

Bland (collection of, Randall's Park [Surrey, UK])—Not in Roper.

B.M. Daḥdaḥ—See Berl. Brill M.

B. Moritz (collection of, no place)—Not in Roper.

BMS—See Br. Mus. Suppl.

BO—J. Th. Zenker, *Bibliotheca orientalis, Manuel de bibliographie orientale*, 2 vols., Leipzig 1846, 1861.

Bodl.—*Bibliothecae Bodleianae codicum manuscriptorum orientalium Catalogus*, pars I a J. Uri, Oxford: Clarendon Press, 1787; pars II, vol. I, ab Alex. Nicoll, Oxford: Clarendon Press, 1821; pars II, vol. II ab E.B. Pusey, Oxford: Clarendon Press, 1835. See also: H.G. Farmer, Arabic musical manuscripts in the Bodleian Library, *JRAS* 1925, 639–54.

Bodl. A[rab].—Bodleian Arabic.

Bodl. d'Orv.—Jacques Philippe d'Orville collection in the Bodleian Library. Not mentioned in Roper.

Bodl. Éthé—*Catalogue of the Persian, Turkish, Hindûstani, and Pushtû manuscripts in the Bodleian Library*: I. The Persian manuscripts / begun by Ed Sachau, contin., compl. and ed. by Hermann Ethé. Oxford: Clarendon Press, 1889; II: Turkish, Hindûstânî, Pushtû and additional Persian manuscripts / by Hermann Ethé. Oxford: Clarendon Press, 1930.

Bodl. H.—Bodleian Hebrew, see next entry.

Bodl. Hebr.—Avr. b. Y. Neubauer (Noyboyer) and A.E. Cowley, *Catalogue of the Hebrew manuscripts in the Bodleian Library and in the College libraries of Oxford, incl. mss. in other languages, which are written with Hebrew characters, or relating to the Hebrew language or literature, and a few Samaritan mss.* 2 vols. in 3 tomes. Oxford: Clarendon Press, 1886–1906.

Bodl. I, Turc.—See Steinschneider in *ZDMG* 8 (1854), 378–79.

Bodl. Marsh—Refers to the Narcissus Marsh collection of oriental manuscripts in the Bodleian Library.

Bodl. Mich.—Refers to the Heimann Joseph Michael collection of Hebrew manuscripts in the Bodleian Library.

Bodl. Neub. (Bodl. Nb.)—See Bodl. Hebr.

Bodl. Nic[oll]—See Bodl., pars II, vol. I.

Bodl. Ouseley (Bodl. Ous.)—W. Ouseley, *Catalogue of Several Hundred Manuscript Works in Various Oriental Languages, Collected by Sir William Ouseley LL. D. &c.* London: Valpy, 1831.

Bodl. Pers.—See Bodl. Éthé, I.

Bodl. Poc.—Refers to the Pococke Collection in the Bodleian Library.

Bodl. Sp. 401/3—See Bodl. Éthé, I, column (Germ. 'Spalte') 401–03.

Bodl. Uri—See Bodl.

Bold.—See Bodl.

Bollet. ital. degli studii or. (*Bollet. ital.*)—*Bollettino italiano degli studii orientali.*

Bol.-Mars. (Bol.)—V. Rosen, *Remarques sur les mss. or. de la collection Marsigli à Bologne, suivies de la liste complète des mss. ar. de la même coll.* (*Atti d. R. Acc. dei Lincei Ser.* 5, Vol. XIII. Rome: Imprimerie de l'Académie Royale des Lyncei, 1885).

Bol. RAH—*Boletín de la Real Academia de la Historia.*

Bombay—A. Rehatsek, *Catalogue raisonné of the Arabic, Hindustani, Persian and Turkish Manuscipts of the Molla Firuz Library*. Bombay Byculla: The Education Society's Press, 1873.

Bombay Un.—*A descriptive Catalogue of the Arabic, Persian and Urdu Manuscripts in the Library of the University of Bombay by Khān Bahādur Shaikh ʿAbdu 'l-Ḳādir-e-Sarfarāz*. Bombay: Qayyimah Press, 1935.

Bonn—J. Gildemeister, *Catalogus librorum manu scriptorum in Bibliotheca Academica Bonnensi*. 7 vols. Bonn: Georg, 1864–76.

Bonon.—See Bol.-Mars.

BOS—*BSOS*.

Boustani, *Enc.* I—Buṭrus al-Bustānī, *Dāʾirat al-maʿārif, wa-huwa qāmūs ʿāmm li-kulli fann wa-maṭlab* (French subtitle: *Encyclopédie arabe*), vol. 1. Beirut, 1876.

Bräu on Geyer *al-Ṭayālisī*—*Die* Mukāṯarat *von aṭ-Ṭayālisī*, herausgegeben von R. Geyer, mit einer Beilage: *Die alte Einteilung der arabischen Dichter und das ʿAmr-Buch des Ibn al-Jarrāḥ*, von H.H. Bräu. Vienna: Hölder-Pichler-Tempsky, 1927.

Breslau St.—C. Brockelmann, *Verzeichnis der arabischen, persischen, türkischen und hebräischen Handschriften der Stadtbibliothek zu Breslau*. Breslau: Marcus, 1900.

Bresl[au] Un.—G. Richter, *Verzeichnis der orientalischen Handschriften der Staats- und Universitätsbibliothek Breslau*. Leipzig: Harrassowitz, 1933.

Br.-Fischer, *Chrest.*—See Fischer, *Chrest.*

Br. H.—See Brill–H.

Brill, *Cat. pér.*—Brill, *Catalogue périodique*, 8 parts, Leiden: Brill, 1883–91.

Brill–H[outsma] (Br. H.)—M.Th. Houtsma, *Catalogue d'une collection de mss. arabes et turcs appartenant à la maison E. J. Brill à Leide*. Leiden: Brill, 1886; 2nd enhanced edition Leiden: Brill, 1889 (in a different order and augemented by 403 nos., now in the Garrett Collection in Princeton USA).

Brill M. (B.M. Daḥdaḥ)—See Berl. Brill M.

Br. M. S.—See Br. Mus. Suppl.

Br. Mus. (Rieu Cat.)—W. Cureton and C. Rieu, *Catalogus codicum manuscriptorum orientalium qui in Museo Britannico asservantur*, Pars Secunda, *Codices Arabicos* amplectens, 1 volume in 3 tomes, London: Impensis Curatorum Musei Brittanici, 1846–71 [tome 1, pages 1–180, 1846; tome 2, pages 181–352, 1852; tome 3, pages 353–882, 1871].

Br. Mus. Add.—Additional Manuscripts, acquired after the Foundation Collections. Indexed in Br. Mus. and Br. Mus. DL.

Br. Mus. Add. 2524 (vol. 1, 349, bottom page)—This reference to a copy of al-Wāsiṭī's *Dhayl Ta'rīkh Baghdād* could not be located in P. Stocks & C.F. Baker, *Subject-Guide to the Arabic Manuscripts in the British Library*. London: The British Library, 2001.

Br. Mus. DL—A.G. Ellis and Edward Edwards, *A Descriptive List of the Arabic Manuscripts Acquired by the Trustees of the British Museum since 1894*, London: British Museum, 1912.

Br. Mus. Or.—Oriental manuscripts acquired after the establishment of an independent Oriental book department in the British Museum (now British Library). Indexed in Br. Mus. DL.

Br. Mus. *Or. Stud. Browne*—See *Or. Stud. Browne*.

Br. Mus. Pers.—Ch. Rieu, *Catalogue of the Persian Manuscripts in the British Museum*. 3 vols. London: British Museum, 1879–83.

Br. Mus. Pers. Suppl.—Ch. Rieu, *Supplement to the Catalogue of the Persian manuscripts in the British Museum*. London: British Museum, 1895.

Br. Mus. Suppl. (BMS, Rieu Suppl., Br. M[us]. S., Br. Suppl.)—Ch. Rieu, *Supplement to the Catalogue of the Arabic Manuscripts in the British Museum*. London: British Museum, 1894.

Br. Mus. Suppl. Ol.—At *History* 1, 567, 'Br. Mus. Suppl. 8 Ol. 2 2/2' is mistake of the typesetter, the actual reference being to Br. Mus. Suppl. 801,$_2$ and 802.

Br. Mus. Turk.—Ch. Rieu, *Catalogue of the Turkish Manuscripts in the British Museum*. London: British Museum, 1888.

Brockelmann, *Arab. Gramm.*—K. (C.) Brockelmann, [*Arabische Grammatik*] *A. Socin's Arabische Grammatik : Paradigmen, Literatur, Übungsstücke und Glossar* / bearbeitet von Karl Brockelmann, 5. Verbesserte Auflage, Berlin: Reuther u. Reichard et al., 1904, many reprints.

Browne, followed by Roman number—See Browne, *Lit. Hist.*

Browne (Cat. Browne, Browne Cat., Browne C.)—E.G. Browne and Reynold A. Nicholson, *A Descriptive Catalogue of the Oriental Mss Belonging to the Late E.G. Browne*, Cambridge: Cambridge University Press, 1932.

Browne, *Lit. Hist.*—E.G. Browne, *A literary History of Persia*. 4 vols. Cambridge: Cambridge University Press, 1928.

Browne, *Med.*—Idem, *Arabian Medicine, being the Fitzpatrick Lectures delivered at the College of Physicians in November 1919 and November 1920*. Cambridge: Cambridge University Press, 1921.

Browne, *Materials*—Idem, Browne, *Materials for the Study of the Babi Religion*. Cambridge: Cambridge University Press, 1918.

Br. Suppl.—See Br. Mus. Suppl.

Brūsalī (Brusali)—See Brussali.

Brussa, Baghd. Ism. P.—There is no such library or collection in Bursa. In fact, the reference is to the private collection of Baġdādly Ismāʿīl Pasha in Makriköy, a district of Istanbul, as stated in *ZDMG* 68, 62ff.

Brussali (Brūsalī, Brusali) [M. Ṭāhir], *ʿOthm. Müʾell.* (*ʿOM*) [in many variants]—Meḥmed Ṭāhir Bursalı, *ʿOs̱mānlı müʾellifleri*. 3 vols. Istanbul: Maṭbaʿa-i ʿĀmireh, 1333–43.

BSOS—Bulletin of the School of African and Oriental Studies (BSAOS).

BSPhL—Beiträge zur semitischen Philologie und Linguistik.

Buch.—See Pet. A.M. Buch.

Budapest, Ung. Nationalmuseum (Goldziher)—A. Szilágyi (ed.), *Catalogus codicum Bibliothecae Universitatis R. Scientiarum Budapestinensis* (Budapest, 1881), 102–04 ("Codices Arabici", by I. Goldziher).

Būhār—M. Hidayat Husain, *Catalogue raisonné of the Būhār Library*, vol. II *Catalogue of the Arabic Manuscripts in the Būhār Library*, Calcutta: Imperial Library, 1923.

Bughya—Al-Suyūṭī, *Bughyat al-wuʿāh*.

Bull. de Corr. Afr.—Bulletin de Correspondance Africaine.

Burch.-Fischer (Fischer-Burch., Burch.)—*Arabische und persische Handschriften aus dem Besitz des verstorbenen Reisenden Dr. Burchardt, mit Vorwort von Geh. Rat Prof. Dr. A. Fischer, Leipzig* (*Arabian and Persian Manuscripts from the Property of the Late Dr Burchardt, with a Foreword by Prof. A. Fischer, Leipzig*), Leipzig: Fock, 1921. This is a sales catalogue containing descriptions of 32 Arabic and 7 Persian manuscripts which were acquired by the Deutscher Staatsbibliothek in 1921.

Bursa—O. Rescher, Notizen über einige arabischen Handschriften aus Brussaer Bibliotheken; nebst Manuskripten der Selīm Aġá (Skutari) etc., ZDMG 68, 47–63; K. Süssheim, Aus anatolischen Bibliotheken, *Beiträge zur Kunde des Orients*, VII (1909), 77–88.

Bursa Bābā Ef.—Not in Roper.

Bursa H[Ḫ]araccizade (Bursa Ḫarāğz. Medr.)—Roper III 309, (Bursa) Haraççıoğlu.

Bursa Ḥü. Čelebī (– Ḥü. Č., – Ḥu. Č., – Ḥu. Celebi, Ḥu. Č[elebī])—Roper III 309, (Bursa) Ḥüseyin Çelebi.

Bursa Orkh[an]—Roper III 309, (Bursa) Orhan.

Bursa Ulu [Ula] Cami [C., Jāmiʿ]—Roper III 309, Ulucami.

Bust. [*al-m*(*uḥ*).]—See next entry.

Bustān al-muḥaddithīn (*Bustān al-muḥ*[*add*]., *Bust. al-m*[*uḥ*.], *Bust.*)—Shāh ʿAbd al-ʿAzīz b. Shāh Waliyyallāh al-Dihlawī, *Bustān al-muḥaddithīn*, lith. Lahore, n.d.

Bustānī Cat.—See Cat. Boustany.

Buṭṭī—See R. Buṭṭī.

B.V.S.A.W. (SBSGW)—*Berichte über die Verhandlungen der sächsichen Akademie der Wissenschaften zu Leipzig*. Philologisch-historische Classe.

C.—Cairo.

Caetani—G. Gabrieli, *La Fondazione Caetani per gli studii musulmani* (Roma: Reale Accademia Nazionale dei Lincei, 1926), 22–42.

Caetani, *Ann*[*ali*]—L. Caetani, *Annali dell'Islām*. 11 vols. Milan: Hoepli, 1905–26.

Čahār Maqāla—Abu ʾl-Ḥasan Niẓām al-Dīn (or Najm-al-Dīn) Aḥmad b. ʿUmar b. ʿAlī Niẓāmī ʿArūḍī Samarqandī, *Čahār Maqāla* (Persian).

Cahen, *REI* 1938 (1936) SA, 4—C. Cahen, Les chroniques arabes concernant la Syrie, l'Égypte et la Mésopotamie de la conquête arabe à la conquête ottomane dans les bibliothèques d'Istanbul, in *REI* 10 (1936), 333–358. The addition SA means that the reference is to the offprint of this article (Paris: Geuthner, 1936), page 4.

Cairo¹ (Cairo)—*Fihrist al-kutub al-ʿarabiyya al-maḥfūẓa bil-kutubkhāna al-Khidīwiyya al-Miṣriyya al-kāʾina bi-Sarāy Darb al-Jamāmīz bi-Miṣr al-maḥrūsa*, 7 vols. in 8 parts, Cairo 1301–03; vol. 1, 2nd ed. 1310 (1893).

Cairo²—*Fihris al-kutub al-ʿarabiyya al-mawjūda bil-Dār*, 9 vols. in 10 tomes. Cairo: Dār al-Kutub al-Miṣriyya, 1342–63; title varies: vol. 7 *Fihris bil-kutub al-ʿarabiyya allatī waradat ʿala ʾl-dār*, vol. 8 *Fihris al-kutub al-ʿarabiyya allatī waradat lil-dār*, vol. 9.1–2 *Fihris al-kutub al-ʿarabiyya allati ʾqtanathā Dār al-kutub*. Brockelmann only mentions volumes 2–6 (Supplement I, 6). Yet he also refers to volume 1, e.g. in Supplement 2, p. 9: 'Cairo² I, 284', and to vol. 7, e.g. in volume 1, p. 569: 'Cairo ²VII, 201'.

Cairo² App.—Refers to the Appendices (sg. *mulḥaq*, pl. *malāḥiq*) of Cairo². Sometimes the ² in superscript (e.g. ²I) was omitted.

Cairo f.j.—Cairo¹, *funūn jamīla*.

Cairo Makram (Makr., Mukr.)—*Fihrist maktabat Makram*. Cairo: Dār al-Kutub, 1351/1933. This is a sub-collection in the Dār al-Kutub in Cairo.

Cairo Mukr.—See previous entry.

Cairo Muṣṭafā P.—Roper I 212, Muṣṭafā Fāḍil?

Cairo *Nashra* (*Nashara, Nash.*)—See *Nashra*.

Cairo, Qawala—See Qawala.

Cairo Ṭab. (vol. 2, 149)—Cairo¹ or Cairo², section on natural sciences.

Cairo, TK—A. Taymūr ?

Calc.—See Calc[utta].

Calc. As. Soc. [Ashraf ʿA.]—See As. Soc. Beng.

Calc. Fort Will.—See Calc[utta].

Calc. Madr. (Calcutta Medr.)—Kamaluddin Ahmad and Abdul Muqtadir, *Catalogue of the Arabic and Persian Manuscripts in the Library of the Calcutta Madrasah*, with an introduction by E. Denison Ross, Calcutta: The Bengal Secretariat Book Depot, 1905.

Calc[utta]—May refer to 'As. Soc. Beng.', 'Būhār', or to 'A. Ẓuhūr ʿAlī, *Fihrist-i kutub-i qalamī wa maṭbūʿ-i kitābkhāna-i Asiatic Society … maʿa kutub-i College Fort William yaʿni madrasa-i ingrīzī-yi shahr-i Calcutta ki ba naql wa taḥwīl dar īn kitābkhāna rasīda*. Calcutta, 1837. This last publication is referred to but not listed in GAL (e.g. vol. 1, 237 [English] last line).

Calcutta Medr.—See Calc. Madr.

Cambr. (Cambr. Palmer)—E.H. Palmer, *Descriptive Catalogue of the Arabic, Persian and Turkish Manuscripts in the Library of Trinity College*, Cambridge 1870; idem, *Catalogue of the Oriental manuscripts in the Library of King's College*. London: Royal Asiatic Society, 1867 (repr. in *JRAS* NS 3 [1868], 105–31).

Cambr. Br.—See Cambr. Suppl. Handl.

Cambr. Burckh.—See Cambr. Preston.

Cambr. Handl.—E.G. Browne, *A Handlist of the Muhammadan Manuscripts of Cambridge*, Cambridge: Cambridge University Press, 1900.

Cambr. Kings Coll.—See Cambr., second publication.

Cambr. Prest[on] (Cambr. Pr., Cambr. Burckh.)—Th. Preston, *Catalogus Bibliothecae Burckhardtianae cum appendice librorum aliorum orientalium in bibliotheca academiae Cantabrigiensis asservatorum*. Cambridge: Cambridge University Prtess, 1853.

Cambr. Suppl. [Handl.] (Cambr. Br.)—E.G. Browne *A Supplementary Handlist of the Muhammadan Manuscripts Preserved in the Libraries of the University and Colleges of Cambridge*, Cambridge: Cambridge University Press, 1922.

Cantor [*Vorl.*]—M. Cantor, *Vorlesungen über Geschichte der Mathematik*, vol. I (Leipzig: Teubner, 1880), 593–700.

Carullah—See Ǧārullāh.

Casiri—See Escur.[1]

Caskel, loc. cit.—W. Caskel, W. Caskel, Aijām al-ʿArab, Studien zur altarabischen Epik, in *Islamica* 3.5 (1930), 1–99. So "loc. cit." (a.a.O. in German) is in fact "op. cit."

Cat.—See Cat. Ital.

Cat. Berl.—See Berl.

Cat. Beyrouth (Cat. Beirut)—See Beirut.

Cat. Bombay Un.—See Bombay Un.

Cat. Boustany (Cat. Bustany)—Yūsuf Tūmā al-Bustānī, *Catalogue [général?] de la Librairie al-Arab*, Cairo. This is a serial publication which is almost impossible to find.

Cat. Browne—See Browne.

Cat. Būhār—See Būhār.

Cat. Curzon—Most likely a sales catalogue of Curzon Press (now Routledge).

Cat. Hamb.—See Hamb.

Cat. Harrassowitz—See Harrassowitz.

Cat. Haupt—See Haupt.

Cat. Hiersemann—Sales catalogue of Hiersemann publishers in Leipzig.

Cat. Ital.—I. Guidi et al., *Cataloghi dei codici orientali di alcune biblioteche d'Italia*, 5 fsc. Florence: Le Monnier (fasc. 1–3, and 4?), Stabilimento Tipografico Fiorentino (fasc. 5), 1878–1892.

Cat. Lugd.—See Leiden, Leiden[1], or Leiden[2], depending on further data provided by Brockelmann.

Cat. Munshī Nawalkeshor—Refers to a sales catalogue of the oldest publishing house in Asia today, that of Munshi Newal Kishore, established in Lucknow in India in 1858.

Cat. Paris—See Paris.

Cat. Sarkis—See Sarkīs, 1).

Cat. Strassburg—See Stras[s]burg, Spitta.

Cat. Syr.—See Sachau.

Cat. U. Hoepli—This must be a sales catalogue of U[lrico] Hoepli Publishers in Milan.

Cat. Vienna—See Vienna.

Caussin—Refers to an unspecified work by A.P. Caussin de Perceval which I was unable to identify.

Caussin de Perceval I, II, III—A.P. Caussin de Perceval, *Essai sur l'histoire des Arabes avant l'Islamisme, pendant l'époque de Mahomet, et jusqu'à la réduction de toutes les tribus sous la loi musulmane.* 3 vols. Paris: Didot, 1847–48.

Cavalla Ef. Cat. no. 1973, see P. Kraus, *Abstracta Isl.* V, *REI* 1936 (vol. 1, 470)—The only reference I can find in *REI* 1936, is to 'Cavalla Veliyeddin efendi Kütüphanés' MS no. 1075 (p. A 331), this in connection with an edition (in *Ilahiyat* [Istanbul Oct. 1928] pp. 46–58) of a Turkish abstract of al-Ghazzālī's *al-Qānūn fi 'l-taʾwīl,* and not to a copy of his *ʿAqīda*. Moreover, this edition is *not* mentioned in connection with Ghazzālī's *al-Qānūn al-kullī fi 'l-taʾwīl* (vol. 1, p. 470, no. 21) where would have every reason to expect it.

Čelebi ʿAl. Ef. (Čel. ʿAl. [Ef.])—Roper III 348, Čelebi Abdullah.

Cent. Amari (*Cent. d. nasc. Amari*)—*Centenario della nascita di Michele Amari.* Scritti di filologia e storia araba, di geografia, storia, diritto della Sicilia medievale. Studi bizantini egiudaici relativi all'Italia meridionale nel medio evo. Documenti sulle relazioni fra gli stati italiani ed il levante. 2 vols. Palermo: Stabilimento Tipografico Virzì, 1910.

Chanykow (Chanikov)—See Pet. Chanykow.

Chardin, *Voyage*—C. Ferrand (ed.), *Voyage de Monsieur le Chevalier Chardin en Perse, et autres lieux de l'Orient.* 10 vols. Paris: Mazuel, 1723 (this being the only edition with a volume VI, or so it seems).

Chauvin, *Bibl.* (Chauvin)—V. Chauvin, *Bibliographie des ouvrages arabes ou relatifs aux Arabes, publiés dans l'Europe chrétienne de 1810 à 1885.* 12 vols. Liège: Vaillant-Carmanne, 1892–1922.

Cheikho—In Supplement 2, 746ff, this refers to: L. Cheikho, *al-Ādāb al-ʿArabiyya fi 'l-qarn al-tāsiʿ ʿashar* (French title: *La litérature arabe au 19e siècle*). 2 vols. Beirut: Maṭbaʿat al-ābāʾ al-Yasūʿiyyīn (Imprimerie Catholique), 1908–10, 2nd revised and augmented edition, Beirut: al-Maṭbaʿa al-Kāthūlīkiyya lil-Ābāʾ al-Yasūʿiyyīn, 1924–26.

Cheikho, *Cat. Beyrouth*—See Beirut.

Cheikho, *Chrest.* [*ar.*]—A. Durand and L. Cheikho, *Elementa grammaticae arabicae, cum chrestomathia, lexico, variisque notis*. 2 vols. Beirut: Typographia Patrum Societatis Jesu, 1896–7; 2nd ed. Beirut: Typographia Patrum Societatis Jesu, 1910–11.

Cheikho, *Poètes ar. chrét.* (– *Les poètes chrét.*)—L. Cheikho, *Les poètes arabes chrétiens après l'Islam* (*Kitāb shuʿarāʾ al-Naṣrāniyya baʿd al-Islām*). Reprint of a series of articles that had earlier been published in *al-Mashriq*. 4 fascicles. Beirut: Imprimerie Catholique, 1924–27.

Cheikho, *Shuʿarāʾ Naṣr.*—Idem, *Kitāb shuʿarāʾ al-Naṣrāniyya*. In 6 fascicles. Beirut: Maṭbaʿat al-ābāʾ al-mursalīn al-Yasūʿiyyīn, 1890.

Cheikho & Durand, *Chrest.*—See Cheikho, *Chrest* [*ar.*].

Chosrew P.—*Defteri Kutubkhana-yi Khusraw Pasha*, Istanbul n.d.

Chrest.—Chrestomathie.

Chr[*ist*]. *Vost.*—Unresolved.

Chwolsohn, *Ssabier* (Chwolsohn)—D. Chwolsohn, *Die Ssabier und der Ssabismus*. 2 vols. St. Petersburg: Buchdruckerei der Kaiserlichen Akademie der Wissenschaften, 1856.

CIA—*Matériaux pour un Corpus Inscriptionum Arabicarum.*

Cidi Hammouda—See Roper IV 16–17, where this collection—which is no longer extant—is (partly) described in publications by de Slane, Cherbonneau, Codera, and Fagnan (all 19th cent.).

Coburg—See Gotha.

Codazzi—Angela Codazzi, Compendio geografico Arabo di Ishaq b. al-Husayn, in *Rend. della R. Accad. Naz. dei Lincei, Cl. di scienze mor.* etc., serie VI, vol. V (Rome, 1929), 373–463.

cod. Amsterd.—See de Jong.

Codera, *Missión*—F. Codera y Zaidín, *Misión histórica en la Argelia y Túnez*: trabajos leídos ante la Real Academia de la Historia en virtud de una misión histórica en la Argelia y Túnez. Madrid: Fortanet, 1892.

cod. sim.—See Berl. cod. sim.

cod. Wetzst.—The collection Wetzstein is one of the sub collections in the department of Oriental manuscripts of the State Library in Berlin. For a concordance between the shelf numbers of the collection Wetzstein and Flügel's numbering, see Berl. vol. 10, 25–47.

Colin—In Supplement 2 and 3, just the name 'Colin' is cited in several places, without any further details. Unresolved.

Coll.—Collection de textes inédits relatifs à la mystique musulmane.

Coll. Landb.—See Landb.

Comm. *Naq.*—See *Naqāʾid* ed. Bevan, vol. 3.

Constantinople—See Istanbul.

Copenhagen (in one case 'Hayn.' [for 'Havn.']—F. Mehren, *Codices Orientales Bibliothecae Regiae Hafniensis, Pars altera codices Hebraicos et Arabicos continens*. Copenhagen: Schulz, 1851.

Čorlulu ['A.] P.—Roper III 348, Çorlulu Ali Paşa.

Corpus—See Griffini, *Corp. jur.*

CR *Ac. Inscr.*—*Comptes Rendus des Séances de l'Académie des Inscriptions et Belles-Lettres.*

CR *Ac. Leningrad*—*Comptes Rendus de l'Academie des Sciences de Russie* (Doklady Rossiyskoi Akademii Nauk), Leningrad.

C. van Arendonk—See Van Arendonk.

Daḥdāḥ (Daḥdaḥ, Dahdah)—M.Y. Bîtâr, *Catalogue de manuscrits précieux et livres rares arabes composant la bibliothèque de M. le Cte Rochaid Dahdah*. Paris: Meynial, 1912.

Dām[ād] Ibr. (Dām. I.)—*Defteri Kutubkhana-yi Dāmād Ibrāhīm Pāshā*. Istanbul, 1312.

Dāmādzāde (Dāmādzāde M. Murād, Dāmādz., Murād Mollā)—*Defteri Kutubkhana-yi Dāmādzāde Qāḍīʿasker M. Murād*. Istanbul, 1311. See also Murād Mollā.

Damascus (Dam. Z.)—Ḥabīb Zayyāt, *Khazāʾin al-kutub fī Dimashq wa-ḍawāḥīhā*. Cairo: Maṭbaʿat al-Maʿārif, 1902.

Damīrī (al-Damīrī, *Ḥay.* [*al-ḥay.*])—Al-Damīrī Muḥammad b. Mūsā, *Ḥayāt al-ḥayawān*.

Dam. ʿUm. (Dam. Ẓāh.)—*Shāmi sherīfde Malik Ẓāhir Qubbesi nām mahallede teʾsīs u gushād olunan Kütübhāneʾi ʿUmūmīnin ḥāwī olduju bil-jümle kütüb u resāʾilin miqdār weʾenwāʿini mübeiyin defterdir* (*Hādhā sijill jalīl yataḍamman taʿlīmāt al-Maktaba al-ʿUmūmiyya fī Dimashq maʿa asmāʾ al-kutub al-mawjūda bi-hā*). Damascus: Maṭbaʿat al-Jamʿiyya al-Khayriyya, 1299 (1882).

Dam. Z.—See Damascus.

Dam. Ẓāh.—See Dam. ʿUm.

Darbār-i Akbarī—Muḥammad Ḥusayn Āzād, *Darbār-i Akbarī* (Urdu). Lahore: Maṭbaʿ-i Rafāh-i ʿĀmm 1898, Āzād Buk Dipo 1910.

Dathīna—See Landberg Dathīna.

Ḍawʾ—See al-Sakhāwī, *al-Ḍawʾ etc.*

Dawlatshāh—Amīr Dawlatshāh Samarqandī, *Tadhkiraʾi shuʿarāʾ* (Persian).

de Gayangos—P. de Gayangos, *History of the Mohammedan Dynasties in Spain*. 2 vols. London: Hughes, 1840.

De Goeje-Stift.—Stichting De Goeje.

de Jong (*Bibl. Ac. Scient.*)—P. de Jong, *Catalogus codicum orientalium bibliothecae academiae regiae scientiarum*. Leiden, 1862.

Delambre—[J.B.J.] Delambre, *Histoire de l'astronomie du moyen âge*. Paris: Courcier, 1819.

Denkschr. phil.-hist. Cl. WA—*Denkschriften der Kaiserlichen Akademie der Wissenschaften, philosopisch-historische Classe*. Vienna (Wien).

Derenb.—See Escur.[2]

Derenbourg, *Not. cr.*—See Madr. Der.

de Rossi—See Hebr. de Rossi.

de Rossi, Cod. Ar.—See Hebr. de Rossi, vol. 3, 162ff, Codices Arabici.

de Sacy, *Abdollatiph* (de Sacy)—M. le Baron Silvestre de Sacy, *al-Ifāda wal-iʿtibār fī 'l-umūr al-mushāhada wal-ḥawādith al-muʿāyana bi-arḍ Miṣr = Relation de l'Égypte par Abd-Allatif, médecin arabe de Baghdad*; suivie de divers extraits d'écrivains orientaux, et d'un état des provinces et des villages de l'Égypte dans le XIV. siècle / le tout trad. [de l'arabe] et enrichi de notes historiques et critiques. Paris: Imprimerie Impériale, 1810.

de Sacy, *Anth. gramm.* (– *Anth. gr.*)—Idem, *Anthologie grammaticale arabe*. Paris: Imprimerie Royale, 1829.

de Sacy, *Chrest.* [*ar.*]—Idem, *Chrestomathie arabe, ou extraits de divers écrivains arabes, tant en prose qu'en vers, avec une traduction française et des notes, a l'usage des élèves de l'école royale et spéciale des langues orientales vivantes*. 3 vols. 2nd ed. Paris: Imprimerie Royale, 1826–27.

de Sacy, *Druzes*—Idem, *Exposé de la religion des Druzes* : tiré des livres religieux de cette secte et précédé d'une introduction et de la vie du khalife Hakem-biamr-Allah. 2 vols. Paris: Imprimerie Royale, 1838.

de Sacy, *Exposé*—See previous entry.

de Slane—See Paris.

de Slane, *Biogr. Dict.*—See Ibn Khall., de Slane.

de Slane, *Hist. d. Berbères*—M. Le Baron de Slane, *Histoire des Berbères et des dynasties musulmanes de l'Afrique septentrionale, par Ibn-Khaldoun*, traduite de l'arabe par M. Le Baron de Slane. 4 vols. Algiers: Imprimerie du Gouvernement, 1852–56.

de Slane, Ibn Khall.—See Ibn Khall., de Slane.

de Slane, Tr.—See Ibn Khall., de Slane.

Dharīʿa—See *al-Dharīʿa*.

Dhayl al-Shaq. al-Nuʿm.—*Dhayl al-Shaqāʾiq al-Nuʿmāniyya*, no such title is mentioned in GAL, but see vol. 2, p. 496 (560/425), no. 2, 'Continuations'.

Dhayl al-Tadhk.—There is no such title in GAL, but see al-Suyūṭī, *Dhayl Ṭab. al-ḥuff.* and al-Dimashiqī, *Dhayl Tadhk. al-ḥuff.*

Dhikra 'l-shāʿirayn (*Dhikrā*)—Aḥmad ʿUbayd (ed.), *Dhikra 'l-shāʿirayn Shāʿir al-Nīl wa-Amīr al-shuʿarāʾ dirāsāt wa-marāthin wa-muqāranāt mudabbaja bi-yarāʿ aʾimmat al-bayān wa-aʿlām al-kalām fī 'l-bilād al-ʿArabiyya*. Damascus: al-Maktaba al-ʿArabiyya, 1351 (1932–33).

Die Chroniken—F. Wüstenfeld, *Die Chroniken der Stadt Mekka*, 4 vols. Leipzig: Brockhaus, 1857–61.

Diet.—In connection with al-Mutanabbī: F. Dieterici, *Mutanabii Carmina cum commentario Wâḥidii* (Ar. *Dīwān Abi 'l-Ṭayyib al-Mutanabbī wa fī athnāʾi matnihi Sharḥ al-Imām al-ʿAllāma al-Wāḥidī*). Berlin: Mittler, 1861.

Dieterici—F. Dieterici, *al-Fārābī's philosophische Abhandlungen*. Leiden: Brill, 1890.

Di Matteo, *Taḥrīf*—I. Di Matteo, Il "*taḥrīf*" od alterazione della bibbia secondo i Musulmani, in *Bessarione* 26 (1922), 64–111, 223–60.

Dīw.—*Dīwān.*

Dīwān al-Māḥī—*Dīwān Muḥammad Muṣṭafā al-Māḥī*. Cairo, 1934.

Djelfa—R. Basset, Les manuscrits arabes du Bach-Agha de Djelfa, in *Bulletin de Correspondance Africaine* 1884, 363–75.

DK—Ibn Ḥajar al-ʿAsqalānī, *Kitāb al-durar al-kāmina fī aʿyān al-miʾa al-thāmina*.

DL—See Br. Mus. DL.

d'Ohsson, *Allgemeine Schilderung des Osman. Reiches*—See Muradjea d'Ohsson.

Dokl. [Ak. Nauk]—*Dokladij Akademii Nauk SSSR*.

Dorn—See Pet. A.M. Dorn.

Dorpat *Jahrb.*—Most likely: *Acta et commentationes Imp. Universitatis Jurievensis* (*olim Dorpatensis*) (1893–1917) or *Acta et commentationes Universitatis Tartuensis* (*Dorpatensis*) (1921–40).

Dozy (Suppl. 3, 9 note)—R.P.A. Dozy, *Supplément aux dictionnaires arabes*. 2 vols. Leiden: Brill, 1881.

Dozy, *Abb[ad]*—See idem, *Script. ar. loci de Abbad.*

Dozy, *[al-]Bayān*—Idem, *Histoire de l'Afrique et de l'Espagne intitulée* al-Bayano 'l-Mogrib *par Ibn Adhárí (de Maroc)*. 2 vols. Leiden: Brill, 1848–51.

Dozy, Cat. I, 240–60—See Leid.[1], pp. 240–60.

Dozy, *Ibn Badroun*—Idem, *Commentaire historique sur le poème d'Ibn-Abdoun / par Ibn-Badroun*. Leiden: Luchtmans, 1846.

Dozy, *Hist.*—Idem, *Histoire des musulmans d'Espagne jusqu'à la conquête de l'Andalousie par les Almoravides (711–1110)*. 4 vols. Leiden: Brill, 1861.

Dozy, *Loci de Abbadidis*—See idem, *Script. etc.*

Dozy, *Not.*—Idem, *Notices sur quelques manuscrits arabes*. Leiden: Brill, 1847–51.

Dozy, *Recherches* (*Rech.*)—Idem, *Recherches sur l'histoire politique et littéraire de l'Espagne pendant le moyen-âge*. Leiden: Brill, 1849; 2nd ed., 2 vols. Leiden: Brill, 1860; 3rd ed., 2 vols. Paris: Maisonneuve & Leiden: Brill, 1881.

Dozy, *Scr[ipt]. ar. loci de Abbad.* (Dozy *Abbad.*, Dozy *Loci de Abbadidis*)—Idem, *Scriptorum arabum loci de Abbadidis*. 3 vols. Leiden: Luchtmans, 1846–63.

Dresd.—H.L. Fleischer, *Catalogus codicum manuscriptorum orientalium in Bibliothecae Regiae Dresdensis*. Leipzig: Vogel, 1831.

Dukas—Probably refers to an edition or translation of Doukas the historian's *History of Byzantium*, as published—among others—in J.P. Migne's *Patrologia Graeca* series, vol. 157 (Paris, 1866), 743–1166: *Ducae Michaelis Ducae Nepotis Historia Byzantina etc.* The reference in GAL is not to this edition, but to another, unmentioned, edition or translation.

Dupont and Coppolani, *Confr. mus.*—O. Dupont and X. Coppolani, *Les confrèreries religieuses musulmanes*. Algiers: Jourdan, 1897.

Durand and Cheikho, *Chrest.*—See Cheikho, *Chrest.* [*ar.*]

Dustūr al-iʿlām (*Dustūr al-aʿlām*)—Muḥammad b. ʿUmar b. Muḥammad b. ʿAzm al-Khaṭīb al-Wazīrī, *Dustūr al-iʿlām bi-maʿārif al-aʿlām.*

Düyümlī—Probably: Roper III 348, Düğümlü Baba.

E. Algiersmissen—Read: E. Algermissen.

Eccl. [*of the*] *Abbas. Cal.* (*Eccl.*)—H.F. Amedroz and D.S. Margoliouth (ed. & transl.), *The Eclipse of the Abbasid Caliphate*. 7 vols. Oxford: Blackwell, 1920–21.

Edinb.—Ashraful Hakk, H. Éthé, and E.R. Robertson, *Descriptive Catalogue of the Arabic and Persian Manuscripts in Edinburgh University Library*, Edinburgh: Austin & Sons, 1925.

Egypt. [Nat.] Libr.—See Cairo[1] and Cairo[2], with J. Schacht, *Aus den Bibliotheken von Konstantinopel und Kairo* and idem, *Aus Kairiner Bibliotheken*, cited below as 'Schacht I' and 'Schacht II'.

EI—M.Th. Houtsma (ed.), *Enzyklopädie des Islam*, 4 vols. + vol. 5 Ergänzungsband (Erg., add., Suppl.), Leiden: Brill, 1918–38.

EI Erg. (EI add., EI Suppl.)—Supplementary volume to the *Enzyklopädie des Islam*. See previous entry.

Eichhorns Repert.—Joh. Gfr Eichhorn, *Repertorium für biblische und morgenländische Literatur*. 18 vols. Leipzig: Weidemann, 1777–86.

El-Bekrī, trad. de Slane—Mac Guckin de Slane (transl.), *Description de l'Afrique septentrionale par El-Bekri*. Paris: Imprimerie Impériale, 1859 (2nd ed. Algiers: Jourdan, 1913).

Ellis—A.G. Ellis, *Catalogue of Arabic Books in the British Museum*. 3 vols. London: British Museum, 1894 (vol. 1), 1901 (vol. 2), 1935 (vol. 3, Indexes by A.S. Fulton, with the slightly different title: *Catalogue of Arabic Printed Books in the British Museum*).

Emir—ʿAlī Emīrī ?

Enderūn—Not in Roper.

Eph. Or.—*Ephemerides Orientales.*

Erfurt, Ampl.—Bibliotheca Amploniana, Erfurt (Germany).

Erg., following EI—Ergänzungsband (i.e. Supplement).

Erg[in]—O. Ergin, Ibni Sina bibliografyası, in *Büyük Türk Filozof ve Tib Üstadı İbni Sina.* Şasiyeti ve eserleri hakkında tetkikler. Türk Tarih Kurumu Yayınları, VII, 1.Istanbul: Muallim Ahmet Halit Kitap Evi, 1937 (last fascicle).

Erlangen—Roper I 334, Universitätsbibliothek Erlangen.

Esʿad (Esad)—See Asʿad Ef.

Esʿad Efendi Medr.—Roper III 348, Esad Efendi Medresesi.

E. Sarkis, Cat.—See Sarkīs, 1).

Escur.[1] (Esc.[1])—M. Casiri, *Bibliotheca Arabico-Hispana Escurialensis opera*. 2 vols. Madrid: Perez de Soto, 1760–70.

Escur.[2] (Esc.[2])—H. Derenbourg, *Les manuscrits arabes de l'Escurial*, vol. I, Paris: Leroux, 1884, vol. II.1, Paris: Leroux, 1903, vol. III (décrits d'après les notes de Hartwig Derenbourg, revues et mises à jour par by E. Lévi-Provençal), Paris: Geuthner, 1928. Cf. N. Morala, Un cátalogo de los fondos árabes primitivos de El Escorial, in *al-Andalus* II (1934), 87–181; *Les Manuscrits arabes de l'Escurial décrits d'après les notes de H. Derenbourg*, revues, mises à jour et complétées par H.P.J. Renaud, vols. II.2 and II.3. Paris: Geuthner, 1941 (II.3 not seen by Brockelmann, who in vol. 2, p. 591 lists these two fascicles as having been published in 1939).

Eshrefz[āde] (Bursa)—Not in Roper.

Esmā Khān (Esmāḫān)—Not in Roper. Maybe the College of Esmakhan is meant, mentioned in Evliya Celebi's *Siyâhatnâme*, for which see J. v. Hammer, *Narrative of Travels in Europe, Asia, and Africa in the Seventeenth Century by Evliyá Efendí* (London: Oriental Translation Fund, 1834), 172. On the website www.yazmalar.gov.tr (accessed 12/15/2017), 'Esmihan Sultan' is mentioned among the collections of the Süleymaniye Kütüphanesi. See also G. Gabrieli, *Manuale di Bibliografia Musulmana* I (Rome, 1916), 202, which mentions a catalogue for the 'Ismīkhān sulṭān' collection (*defter* no. 30 of the late 19th cent. 40–volume series of catalogues of the libraries of Istanbul), and J. Schacht, Von den Bibliotheken in Stambul und Umgegend (*ZS* 5/1927), p. 292 no. 65: Esmāḫān Sulṭān (associated/identical with Šehīd Meḥmed Paša).

Éthé, Bodl.—See Bodl. Éthé.

Éthé, Ind. Off.—See Ind. Off. Ethé.

Études relig. phil. et lit.—*Études religieuses, philosophiques, historiques et littéraires* / par des Pères de la Compagnie de Jésus. Paris: Douniol, 1872–1896.

Euting—J. Euting, *Katalog der Kaiserlichen Universitäts- und Landesbibliothek in Strassburg, Arabische Literatur*. Strasburg 1877.

Evliyā', *Siyāḥatn.* II (Evliyā' II)—See Evliyā, *Siyāḥatnāme* I, II.

Evliyā I—See Evliyā, *Siyāḥatnāme* I, II.

Evliyā, *Siyāḥatnāme* I, II—Ewliyā Čelebi, *Seyāḥatnāme*, vols. 1 and 2. Istanbul: Iqdām, 1314. Turkish.

Ewliyā' (Evliyā')—See previous entry.

Fāḍil A.[P.]—See Fāẓil A.

Fagnan, *Cat.*—See Algiers.

Faiẓ. (Faiz., Faiẓ., Faiẓullāh, Faiḍ.)—Roper III 342, Feyzullah Efendi.

Faqīr Muḥammad, *Hidāyat al-Ḥanafiyya*—See *Ḥad. al-Ḥan.*

Farmer, Coll. of Or. Writers on Music, Glasgow 1933—G.H. Farmer, *An old Moorish Lute Tutor*. Glasgow: The Civic Press, 1933.

Farmer [, *Sources*]—Idem, *The sources of Arabian music : an annotated bibliography of Arabic manuscripts which deal with the theory, practice, and history of Arabian music.* Bearsden: Farmer, 1940.

Fātiḥ—*Defteri Kutubkhana-yi Fātiḥ Jāmiʿ*. Istanbul n.d.

Fātiḥ Waqf Ibr. (Waqf Ibr.)—The Waqf Ibrāhīm collection of the Fātiḥ library (now part of the Süleymaniye Library, see Roper III, 348, Fâtih) does not seem to have a separate catalogue and is not mentioned as such in Roper. In some cases (e.g. *History* I, 176) Brockelmann refers to Ritter as his source; it is therefore not to be excluded that all his information on Fātiḥ Waqf Ibr. was taken from notes sent to him by Ritter.

Faw. [*al-*]*bah.*—See *al-Faw. al-bah.*

Fawāt—Al-Kutubī Muḥammad b. Shākir, *Fawāt al-wafayāt.*

Fāẕil A. (Fāḍil A.[P.])—See Köpr. Fāḍil A.P.

FFC—Folklore Fellows' Communications, a series of monographs and articles published under the auspices of the Finnish Academy of Science and Letters.

Feiẓ[īye] (Feiẓiyye)—Not in Roper.

Ferīdun, *Munshaʾāt*—Aḥmed Ferīdūn Bey, *Munshaʾāt al-salāṭīn.* 2 vols. Istanbul: Dār al-Ṭibāʿa al-ʿĀmira, 1274–75.

Festschr. Kahle—W. Heffening, W. Kirfel, P. Kahle (eds.), *Studien zur Geschichte und Kultur des Nahen und Fernen Ostens.* Paul Kahle zum 60. Geburtstag überreicht von Freunden und Schülern aus dem Kreise des Orientalischen Seminars der Universität Bonn. Leiden: Brill, 1935.

Festschr. Littmann—R. Paret (ed.), *Orientalistische Studien* : Enno Littmann zu seinem 60. Geburtstag am 16. September 1935 überreicht von Schülern aus seiner Bonner und Tübinger Zeit. Leiden: Brill, 1935.

Festschr. Oppenheim—*Aus fünf Jahrtausenden morgenländischer Kultur*: Festschrift Max Freiherrn von Oppenheim zum 70. Geburtstage gewidmet von Freunden und Mitarbeitern. Berlin, 1933.

Fez—See Fez Qar.

Fez B.—R. Basset, *Les manuscrits arabes de deux bibliothèques de Fās*, Algiers: Fontana, 1883 (offprint from *Bulletin de Correspondance Africaine*, vol. 1 (1882), 366–93.

Fez [Qar.]—A. Bel, *Catalogue des livres arabes de la Bibliothèque de la Mosquée d' el-Qaraouiyine à Fes*, Fez: Imprimerie Municipale, 1918.

Fih[*r*(*ist*)]—Ibn al-Nadīm Muḥammad b. Isḥāq, *Kitāb al-Fihrist, herausgegeben von G. Flügel, nach dessen Tode besorgt von* J. Rödiger *und* A. Müller. 2 vols., Leipzig: Vogel, 1871–2.

Fihris—See al-Kattānī.

Fihrist al-Riḍawiyya—See Mashh.

Fir.—Olga Pinto, Manoscritti arabi delle biblioteche governative di Firenze non ancora catalogati, in *La Bibliofilia* XXXVII (1935), 234–46; see also Flor.

Firangi Mahall Muḥammad ʿAlī Būrī Library—See next entry, no. (1).

Firengi Maḥall—Firangī Maḥall (Lucknow). Not in Roper, see *JRASB* 1917, lxxx, nos. (1) Mawlavī ʿAbd al-Bārī Library, and (2) Mawlavī ʿAbd al-Ḥayy Library.).

Firishta—Muḥammad Qāsim Hindū Shāh Astarābādī (Firishta), *Gulshan-i Ibrāhīmī* (or its second recension called *Taʾrīkh-i Nawras-nāma*, both Persian). GAL just has 'Firishta', without a title, and this only in one place.

Fir. Mar.—Fir. 236–37, Biblioteca Marucelliana.

Fir. Naz. (Flor. Naz.)—Fir. 237–38, Biblioteca Nazionale Centrale.

Fir. Ricc. (Flor. Ricc.)—Fir. 238, Biblioteca Riccardiana.

Fir. Un.—Fir. 237, Biblioteca della Facoltà di Lettere della Reale Università.

Fischer-Burch.—See Burch.-Fischer.

Fischer, *Chrest.*—A. Fischer, *R. Brünnows Arabische Chrestomathie aus Prosaschriftstellern*: zweite Auflage, völlig neu bearbeitet und herausgegeben. Berlin etc.: Reuther & Reichard, 1913 (3rd ed. 1924, 4th ed. 1928).

Fischer, *Festschr.*, Browne—A. Fischer, Die *masʾala zunbūrīja*, in: *Or. Stud. Browne*, 150–56.

F. Kern—See Kern.

Fleischer, *Kl. Schr.*—H.L. Fleischer, *Kleinere Schriften*, 3 vols. in 5 tomes, Leipzig: Hirzel, 1885–88.

Flor. (Fir., Fir. Ricc.)—Olga Pinto, Manoscritti arabi delle biblioteche governative di Firenze non ancora catalogati, in *La Bibliofilia* XXXVII (1935), 234–46. See also Fir. Ricc.

Flor. Ass. (Flor. Laur., Flor. Med., Flor. Pal.[-Med.])—S. E. Assemani, *Bibliothecae Mediceae Laurentianae et Palatinae codicum mss. or. catalogus*, Florence 1742. See also Roper II 78, Biblioteca Mediceo-Laurenziana.

Flor. Laur.—See Flor. Ass.

Flor. M.—See Flor. Med.

Flor. Med.—See Flor. Ass.

Flor. Naz.—See Fir. Naz.

Flor. Pal.—See Flor. Ass.

Flor. Pal.-Med.—See Flor. Ass.

Flor. Ricc.—See Fir. Ricc.

Flr. Naz—See Flor. Naz.

Flügel—May refer to Flügel *Ḥanaf.* or Flügel, *Die grammat. Schulen*. In one case (*History* 1, 243 n. 1) the reference is to Vienna (below s.v.) vol. 2, 570, referred to in Pet. Ros. (below s.v.) [1877] 130 as 'Flügel W H II 570'.

Flügel, *Cl[assen]*—See Flügel, *Ḥanaf.*

Flügel, *Def.*—G. Flügel, *Definitiones viri meritissimi Sejjid Scherif Ali Ben Mohammed Dschordschani*. Leipzig: Vogel, 1845.

Flügel, *Die grammat. Schulen* (– *Gr. Sch[ulen]*, – *Gr[amm].*, Flügel)—Idem, *Die grammatischen Schulen der Araber*. Leipzig: Brockhaus, 1862.

Flügel, *Gr*[*amm*].—See idem, *Die grammat. Schulen.*

Flügel, *Gr. Sch*[*ulen*]—See idem, *Die grammat. Schulen.*

Flügel, *Ḥanaf.* (– *Classen der Ḥanaf.*, – *Cl*[*assen*], Flügel)—Idem, *Die Classen der ḥanefitischen Rechtsgelehrten*, in *Abhandlungen der Königliche Sächsische Gesellschaft der Wissenschaften* VIII, ph.-hist. Klasse III (Leipzig: Hirzel, 1861), 267–358.

Fort William—See Calc[utta].

Fournel, *Les Berbères*—H. Fournel, *Les Berbers: Étude sur la conquête de l'Afrique par les Arabes d'après les textes arabes imprimés*. 2 vols. Paris, 1875–81.

Fragm. hist. ar. (*Fragm. hist.*) [ed. de Goeje]—*Fragmenta historicorum Arabicorum : et quidem pars tertia operis Kitábo 'l-Oyun wa 'l-hadáïk fi akhbári 'l-hakáïk, et pars sexta operis Tadjáribo 'l-Omami / auctore Ibn Maskowaih ; quae cum indicibus et glossario edidit* M.J. de Goeje *et* P. de Jong. 2 vols. Leiden, Brill, 1869–71. Note: volume 2 without the cooperation of de Jong.

Franck—*Catalogue d' une belle collection de manuscrits et livres arabes, dont la vente aura lieu le 20 Juin 1860 dans la librairie A. Franck*, Paris: Franck, 1860 (only cited following Pertsch).

Frank—Read: Franck.

Frengi Maḥall—Firangi Maḥall (Lucknow).

Freytag, *Ar. Prov.*—G.W. Freytag, *Arabum proverbia*. 3 vols. Bonn: A. Marcus, 1838–43.

Freytag, *Versk.*—Idem, *Darstellung der arabischen Verskunst*: mit sechs Anhängen. Bonn: Cnobloch, 1830.

Fried.—K. Friederici, *Bibliotheca orientalis oder vollständige Liste aller 1876–83 in Deutschland, Frankreich, England und den Kolonien erschienenen Bücher usw.* Leipzig: Schulze, 1877–84.

Friedländer, *Chadir*—I. Friedlaender, *Die Chadirlegende und der Alexanderroman*: eine sagengeschichtliche und literarhistorische Untersuchung. Leipzig & Berlin: Teubner, 1913.

Fr. Mahall—See Firengi Maḥall.

Fulton [and Ellis]—A.S. Fulton and A.G. Ellis, *Supplementary Catalogue of Arabic printed Books in the British Museum*. London: British Museum, 1926.

Fundgr. d. Or.—J. von Hammer (ed.), *Fundgruben des Orients / bearbeitet durch eine Gesellschaft von Liebhabern*. 6 vols. Vienna: Schmid, 1809–18.

F. Wüstenfeld, *Chron.*—See Wüstenfeld, *Chron.*

G—GAL.

Garr.—See Princ. Garr.

Garr. App.—Unresolved.

Ǧārullāh (Carullah)—Roper III 348, Carullah.

Gayangos—See de Gayangos.

Ges.—Gesellschaft.

Gesch.—Geschichte.

Geschichte de Ikhshīd.—*Ibn Saʿīd, Kitāb al-mughrib fī ḥulā al-Maghrib*, Buch IV: *Geschichte der Ikhshīden und Fusṭāṭensische Biographien*, I. Deutsche Bearbeitung nebst einem Auszug aus al-Kindīs *Taʾrīkh Miṣr*, von Dr. K.L. Tallquist. Leiden: Brill, 1899.

Gesch. des Qor. III—See Bergsträsser, *Gesch. des Qorʾāns* III.

Geyer—See R. Geyer.

Geyer, *Aʿshā*—R. Geyer, *Zwei Gedichte von Maimūn b. Qais al-Aʿšā*. 2 vols. Vienna: Hölder, 1905–19.

Geyer, *Dijamben*—Idem, *Altarabische Dijamben*, Leipzig & New York: Haupt, 1908.

GGA—*Göttingische gelehrte Anzeigen*.

G. Hoffmann, *de herm.*—J.G.E. Hoffmann, *De Hermeneuticis apud Syros Aristoteleis*. Leipzig: Hinrichs, 1869.

Ghulām Sarwar Lāhūrī, *Ḥik. al-as.*—See *Khazīnat al-aṣfiyāʾ*.

Gibb Mem.—E.J.W. Gibb Memorial Series.

G. Jacob, *Berichterstatter*—G. Jacob (transl. comm., intr.), *Ein arabischer Berichterstatter aus dem 10. Jahrhundert über Fulda ... und andere Städte des Abendlandes /* Artikel aus Qazwînîs *Âthâr al-bilâd*. Berlin: Mayer & Müller, 1896 (3rd ed.).

Gl.—Gloss[es].

Glasgow [Hunt.] (Glasg.)—T.H. Weir, The Arabic, Syriac and Hebrew Manuscripts of the Hunterian Library of the Library of the University of Glasgow by, in *JRAS* 1899, 739–56; *A Catalogue of the Manuscripts in the Library of the Hunterian Museum in the University of Glasgow*, planned and begun by the Late John Young, continued and completed ... by P. Henderson Aitken. Glasgow: Maclehose, 1908, 453–523.

Gl. Ṭabarī—M.J. de Goeje et al. (eds.), *Annales quos scripsit Abu Djafar Mohammed Ibn Djarir at-Tabari*: Introductio, Glossarium, Addenda et emendanda. Leiden: Brill, 1901.

Goldziher—See Goldziher, *MSt.*

Goldziher, *Abh.*—I. Goldziher, *Abhandlungen zur arabischen Philologie*, 2 vols., Leiden: Brill, 1896–99.

Goldziher, [*al-*]*Ghāzālīs Baṭ.* (– *Bat.*)—Idem, *Streitschrift des Ġazālī gegen die Bāṭinijja-Sekte*. Leiden: Brill, 1916.

Goldziher, *Baṭ.*—See previous entry.

Goldziher, *Mél. Derenbourg*—Idem, Notices sur la littérature des *Ajmān al-ʿArab* (serments des anciens Arabes), in: *Mélanges Hartwig Derenbourg (1844–1908) : recueil de travaux d'érudition dédiés à la mémoire d'Hartwig Derenbourg par ses amis et ses élèves*. Paris: Leroux, 1909.

Goldziher, *MSt.* (– *Muhammed. Studien*, Goldziher)—Idem, *Muhammedanische Studien*, 2 vols., Halle: Niemeyer 1889–90.

Goldziher, on *Maʿānī al-nafs*—Idem, *Kitāb maʿāni 'l-nafs : Buch vom Wesen der Seele.* Abh. der Gesells. der Wissens. zu Göttingen, philol.-hist. Klasse; New Series vol. 9, no. 1. Berlin: Weidmann, 1907.

Goldziher, *Or.St. Nöld.*—See Bezold.

Goldziher, *Richt.*—I. Goldziher, *Die Richtungen der islamischen Koranauslegung.* Leiden: Brill: 1920.

Goldziher, *Vorl.*—Idem, *Vorlesungen über den Islam*, Heidelberg: Winter, 1910.

Goldziher, *Ẓāhir.* (– *Ẓāh.*)—Idem, *Die Ẓāhiriten, ihr Lehrsystem und ihre Geschichte, Beitrag zur Geschichte der muhammedanischen Theologie*, Leipzig: Schulze, 1884.

Gonzalez Palencia—See Palencia.

Gosche—R. Gosche, Über Ghazzālīs Leben und Werke, in *Abhandlungen der Königlichen Akademie der Wissenschaften zu Berlin aus dem Jahre 1858* (Berlin: Dümmler, 1859), 239–311.

Gotha (Goth.)—W. Pertsch, *Die arabischen Hdss. der Herzoglichen Bibliothek zu Gotha.* 5 vols. Gotha: Perthes, 1877–92.

Gött. [Ar.]—*Verzeichnis der Handschriften im preussischen Staate* [hsg. Wilhelm Meyer], vol. 1.3, *Die Handschriften in Göttingen* 3: *Universitätsbibliothek: Nachlässe von Gelehrten, orientalische Handschriften, Handschriften im Besitz von Instituten und Behörden. Register zu Band 1–3.*, Berlin: Bath, 1894.

Gött. Asch—This is the collection of manuscripts legated by Georg von Asch and described in Gött., pp. 22–75.

Gött. Mich.—This is the collection of manuscripts legated by Joh. Dav. Michaelis and described in Gött., pp. 181–245.

Gottwaldt—See Kazan.

Govt. Coll.—See As. Soc. Gov. Coll.

Granad[a] S.M. (Granada Sagro [Sacro] Monte, Granada)—M. Asín Palacios, *Noticia de los manuscritos árabes del Sacro Monte de Granada* (de la *Revista del Centro de Estudios Históricos de Granada y su Reino*), 30 pp. Granada: Imprenta de el Defensor de Granada, 1912.

Granad. U.—Almagro de Cárdenas, *Catálogo de los manuscritos árabes que se conservan en la universidad de Granada.* Extracto de las memorias del xi Congreso Internacional de Orientalistas celebrado en París en septiembre de 1897–3.ª Sección, Lenguas y arquiología musulmanas, págs. 45 y siguentes. Granada: Sabatel, 1899.

Gratzl—See Munich Gl.

Griffini—See Ambr. A, B, C, D, E, or F.

Griffini, *Corp. jur.* (*Corpus*)—E. Griffini, *"Corpus iuris" di Zaid b. ʿAlī.* Milan: Hoepli, 1919.

Gr. Ir. Ph.—*Grundriss der iranischen Philologie.*

Grundr. I, II—C. Brockelmann, *Grundriss der vergleichenden Grammatik der semitischen Sprachen.* 2 vols. Berlin: Reuther & Reichard, 1908–13 (vol. 1: Laut- un Formlehre, vol. 2: Syntax).

Guest—Rhuvon Guest (ed.), *The Governors and Judges of Egypt or* Kitâb el ʾUmarâʾ (el Wulâh) wa Kitâb el Quḍâh *of el Kindî : together with an appendix derived mostly from* Rafʿel Isr *by Ibn Ḥajar* (Gibb. Mem. Ser. XIX). Leiden & London: Brill and Luzac & Co., 1912.

Guidi—See I. Guidi.

GW—*Geografisches Wörterbuch*.

G. Zaydān—See Zaydān.

Hab.—'Habilitation' (German), a postdoctoral study written in qualification for a professorship at a German institution of higher education.

Ḥabīb al-siyar—See Khwandamīr.

Ḥabīb Efendi Zayyāt (collection of, Alexandria)—Not in Roper.

Ḥabīb Ḥaydar Libr.—See Shāh Ḥabīb Ḥaydar Libr.

Ḥad. al-Ḥan.—Faqīr M. Lahaurī, *Ḥadāʾiq al-Ḥanafīya* (in Urdu). Lucknow: Newal Kishore, 1906.

Hādī [(b. ʿAbbās) Āl] Kāshif al-Ghiṭāʾ (library of, Najaf)—Not in Roper.

Hādī al-Khurāsānī al-Ḥāʾirī (library of, no place)—Not in Roper.

Hadiyyat al-aḥbāb—Probably: ʿAbbās b. Muḥammad Riḍā al-Qummī, *Hadiyyat al-aḥbāb fī dhikr al-maʿrūfīn bil-kunā wal-alqāb wal-ansāb*. Lith. Najaf, 1349 (1930–31).

Haft iqlīm—Amīn Aḥmad Rāzī, *Haft iqlīm* (Persian).

Ḥājj Naṣrallāh al-Taqawī (library of)—See Sayyid Naṣrallāh al-Taqawī.

Ḥakīm Oġlū ʿA.—Roper III 329 & 349, Hekimoğlu Ali Paşa.

Halet [Efendi]—Roper III 348, Hâlet Efendi.

Halet Ilave (ʿIlāwe)—Roper III 348, Hâlet Efendi İlâvesi.

Halis (Ḫāliṣ)—Roper III 335, Hâlis Efendi.

Halle B—Manuscripts which the BDMG received as a gift from Prof. Dr. C.H. Becker.

Halle [B]DMG: H. Wehr, *Verzeichnis der arabischen Handschriften in der Bibliothek der Deutschen Morgenländischen Gesellschaft*, Abh. fur die Kunde des Morgenlands XXV.3. Leipzig: Brockhaus, 1940.

Halle, Waisenh. 37i—Halle Waisenh. Not in Roper but see: E. Pabst, *Orientalische Handschriften im Archiv der Franckeschen Stiftungen zu Halle* [Archiv der Franckeschen Stiftungen zu Halle (Saale), 2003], 72, # 29, MS AFSt/H Q 27.

Hamaker, *Spec. Cat.*—H.A. Hamaker, *Specimen catalogi codicum mss. orientalium bibliothecae Academiae Lugduno-Batavae*. Leiden: Luchtmans, 1820.

Ḥamāsa—Abū Tammām, *Kitāb al-ḥamāsa*.

Hamb. [Or. Sem.]—*Katalog der Handschriften der Stadtbibliothek zu Hamburg*, vol. 3: C. Brockelmann, *Katalog der orientalischen Handschriften der Staats- und Universitätsbibliothek zu Hamburg mit Ausschluss der hebräischen* / T. 1. *Die arabischen, persischen, türkischen, malaiischen, koptischen, syrischen und äthiopischen Handschriften*. Hamburg: Meissner, 1908.

Ḥamdallāh Mustawfī, *Taʾrīkhi gūzida*—E.G. Browne (ed. & transl.), *The Taʾríkhi-i-Guzída or 'Select History' of Hamdu ʾlláh Mustawfí-i-Qazwíní*: compiled in AH 730

(AD 1330) and now abridged in English from a manuscript dated A.H. 857 (AD 1453). 2 vols. E.J.W. Gibb Memorial Series, vol. 14.1–2. Leiden: Brill, 1910–13. The *Taʾrīkhi gūzīda* is a Persian work.

Hamdani (Hamdānī)—May refer to: 1) M. Hamdani, Some unknown Ismaili authors and their works, in *JRAS* 1933, 539–76; 2) Idem, The history of the Ismaili *daʿwat* and its literature during the last years of the Fatimid empire, in *JRAS* 1932, 126–36.

Hamel—See Zaouiyah d'El Hamel.

Ḥamīd. (Hamīd.)—*Defteri Kutubkhana-yi Ḥamīdiyye Türbe*. Istanbul, 1300.

Hammer, *GOR*—J. von Hammer-Purgstall, *Geschichte des osmanischen Reiches*. 10 vols. Pest: Hartleben, 1827–35.

Hammer, *Lettere*—J. von Hammer-Purgstall, Lettere sui manoscritti orientali e particolarmente arabi che si trovano nelle diverse biblioteche d'Italia, in *Biblioteca Italiana o sia Giornale di letteratura, scienze ed arti*, letters I to IX in vols. 42 (1826) 27–36 (I), 45 (1827) 32–41 (II), 47 (1827) 10–20 (III), 49 (1828) 15–22 (IV), 50 (1828) 158–62 (V), 54 (1829) 24–28 (VI), 56 (1829) 28–35 (VII), 59 (1830) 186–89 (VIII), 62 (1831) 306–11 (IX).

Ḥarīrī—See al-Ḥarīrī.

Harrassowitz [*Bücherverzeichnis*] (Cat. Harrassowitz)—Harassowitz's *Bücherverzeichnis* or sales catalogue is a serial publication (Brockelmann cites nos. 244, 252, 405, and 444) of which past issues are hard to come by. The addition 'NS' in Supplement 2, 730 possibly stands for 'neue Serie', i.e. 'New Series'.

Hartmann, [*al-*]*Muwashshaḥ* (– *Muw.*, Hartmann)—M. Hartmann, *Das Arabische Strophengedicht I. Das Muwashshaḥ*, Weimar: Emil Felber, 1897.

Hartmann, *Ar. Frage*—Idem, Die arabische Frage, mit einem Versuche der Archäologie Jemens. Der islamische Orient: Berichte und Forschungen, vol. II. Leipzig: Haupt, 1909.

Hartmann, *Ar. Press* (– *Press*)—Idem, *The Arabic Press of Egypt*, London: Luzac & Co., 1899.

Hartmann, *Unpol. Briefe*—Idem, *Unpolitische Briefe aus der Türkei*. Der islamische Orient: Berichte und Forschungen, vol. III. Leipzig: Haupt, 1910.

Ḥasan ʿAbd al-Wahhāb (collection of, no place)—Not in Roper.

Ḥasan al-Ṣadr (library of, no place)—Not in Roper (= al-Ḥasan Ṣadr al-Dīn ?).

Ḥasan Saʿd al-Dīn al-Kāẓimī—See next entry.

Ḥasan Ṣadr al-Dīn [al-Kāẓimī] (library of, no place)—See al-Ḥasan Ṣadr al-Dīn.

Hāshim b. Muḥammad al-Sabzawārī (library of, al-Kāẓimiyya)—Not in Roper.

Haskin, *Studies*—Ch. H. Haskins, *Studies in the History of Mediaeval Science*. Cambridge: Harvard University Press, 1924 (2nd ed. 1927).

Haupt—M. Hartmann, *Die arabischen Handschriften der Sammlung Haupt*. Halle a. d. S.: Haupt, 1906.

Ḥaydar Qulī Khān (library of, Kirmanshah)—Not in Roper.

Hdss.—Handschriften.

Hebr.—Hebraica.

Hebr. de Rossi—I.B. de Rossi, *Mss. Codices Hebraici Bibliothecae I.B. De-Rossi / accurate ab eodem descripti et illustrati*. 3 vols. Parma: Ex Publico Typographeo, 1803.

Hebr. Munich—M. Steinschneider, *Die Hebräischen Handschriften der K. Hof- und Staatsbibliothek in München*. 2nd ed. München: Palm, 1895.

Hebr. Naumann, Leipz.—See Lips.

Hebr. Paris—See Paris Hebr.

Hebr. transl., followed by a number—Refers to the § with that number in the work described in the next entry.

Hebr. transl. Steinschn. (Hebr. Steinschn.; sometimes other items are mentioned first after 'Hebr. transl.', and only then 'Steinschn.')—M. Steinschneider, *Die hebraeischen Übersetzungen des Mittelalters und die Juden als Dolmetcher*. 2 vols. Berlin: Kommissionsverlag des bibliografischen Bureaus, 1893; in the case of Fārābī, the reference may also be to Steinschneider's *al-Fārābī, des arabischen Philosophen Leben und Schriften*, Mémoires de l'Académie Impériale des Sciences de St. Péterbourg. VIIIe série, t. 13, no. 4. St. Petersburg, 1869. There is no logic here.

Heffening—See Heffening, *Fremdenr*.

Heffening, I IV, 864—Read: Heffening, *EI* IV, 864.

Heffening, *Fremdenr.*—W. Heffening, *Das islamische Fremdenrecht bis zu den islamisch-fränkischen Staatsverträgen: eine rechtshistorische Studie zum Fiqh*. Hannover: Lafaire, 1925.

Heft—German for 'number', 'issue'.

Heidelberg (Heidelb., Heid.)—J. Berenbach, Verzeichnis der neuerworbenen orientalischen Handschriften der Universitätsbibliothek Heidelberg, in ZS VI 213–237, X 74–104.

Heid. TA—Mixed Turkish–Arabic MS. See below: Heid. *ZDMG* 91.

Heid. *ZDMG* 91—J. Berenbach, Verzeichnis der neuerworbenen orientalischen Handschriften der Universitätsbibliothek Heidelberg / Schluss zu *Z.f. S.* VI 213–237, X 74–104, in *ZDMG* 91 (1937), 376–403.

Heid. *ZS*—See Heidelberg.

Hekīm Āġā—Not in Roper. Hekīm Oġlū ?

Hekīm Oġlū (Hekim Oghlū)—Roper III 329, 349, Hekimoğlu Ali Paşa.

Herrm.—C.H. Herrmann, *Bibliotheca orientalis et linguistica, Verzeichnis der vom Jahre 1850 bis incl. 1868 in Deutschland erschienenen Bücher, Schriften und Abhandlungen orientalischer und sprachvergleichender Literatur*. Halle a.S.: Hermann, 1870.

Hesp.—Hespéris.

Hidāyat al-Ḥusayn, *List of Mss.*—Hidayet Husain, *List of Arabic and Persian manuscripts acquired on behalf of the Government of India by the Asiatic Society of Bengal during 1903–1907*. Calcutta, 1908.

Hilāl, ed. Amedroz—H.F. Amedroz, *The historical remains of Hilâl al-Sâbi : first part of his* Kitab al-Wuzara *(Gotha ms. 1756) and fragment of his* History *389–393* AH *(B.M. ms., add. 19360)*. Leiden: Brill, 1904.

Hirschberg [, *Gesch.*]—J. Hirschberg, *Geschichte der Augenheilkunde* II, 1, *Geschichte der Augenheilkunde bei den Arabern*. Leipzig: Engelmann, 1905.

Hirschberg, *Lehrb.*—Idem, *Die arabischen Lehrbücher der Augenheilkunde* : ein Capitel zur arabischen Litteraturgeschichte. Berlin: Verlag der Königlichen Akademie der Wissenschaften, 1905.

Hist.—History, histoire, historia.

Hist. des Berbères—Refers to one of the two following publications: 1) de Slane, *Histoire des Berbères et des dynasties musulmanes de l'Afrique septentrionale, par Abou-Zeid Abder-Rahman ibn-Mohammed Ibn-Khaldoun*, texte arabe. 2 vols. Algiers: Imprimerie du Gouvernement, 1847–51; 2) idem, *Histoire des Berbères et des dynasties musulmanes de l'Afrique septentrionale, par Ibn-Khaldoun*, traduite de l'arabe par M. Le Baron de Slane. 4 vols. Algiers: Imprimerie du Gouvernement, 1852–56.

Hist. des croisades—See *Rec. hist. Crois., Hist. or.*

hist. lit.—historisch-literarisch.

ḤKh—*Lexicon bibliographicum et encyclopaedicum a Mustapha ben Abdallah Katib Jelebi dicto et nomine Haji Khalfa celebrato compositum, ed. latine vertit et commentario indicibusque instruxit* G. Flügel, 7 vols, Leipzig: Vogel & London: Bentley, 1835–58; Şerefettin Yaltkaya (ed.), [Kâtib Çelebi,] *Kashf al-ẓunūn ʿan asāmi 'l-kutub wal-funūn*. 2 vols. Istanbul: Maarif Matbaası, 1360, 1362 (1941–43).

Homen. Codera—D. Eduardo Saavedra (ed.), *Homenaje a D. Francesco Codera en su jubilación del profesorado*. Zaragoza: Escar, 1904.

Hoogvliet, *Div*[*ers*]*. script. loci*—M. Hoogvliet, *Specimen e litteris Orientalibus exhibens diversorum scriptorum locos de regia Aphtasidarum familia et de Ibn-Abduno poeta, ex* MSS. *codicibus biblioth. Leidensio editos, Latine redd. et annotatione illustratos*. Leiden: Luchtmans, 1839.

Hoogvliet, *Prol.*—See previous entry.

Horovitz, on Ibn Saad II, 1—J. Horovitz (ed.), *Ibn Saad: Biografien Muhammeds, seiner Gefährten und der späteren Träger des Islams bis zum Jahre 230 der Flucht*, vol. 2.1, *Die Feldzüge Muhammeds*. Leiden: Brill, 1909.

Houtsma ad Br. 980—See Br. H., no. 980.

Houtsma, *Recueil*—M. Th. Houtsma, *Recueil de textes relatifs à l'histoire des Seljoucides*. 4 vols. Leiden: Brill, 1886–1902.

[H.] Pérès [, *Le roman*]—H. Pérès, Le roman, le conte et la nouvelle dans la littérature arabe moderne, in *Annales de l'Institut d'Etudes Orientales* (Faculté des Lettres de l'Université d'Alger), vol. III (1937), 266–337.

[H.] Pérès, L'Espagne in *Publ. de l'Institut d'Études Or.* VI, 1937—H. Pérès, *L'Espagne vue par les voyageurs musulmans, de 1610 à 1630*. Paris: Adrien–Maisonneuve, 1937 (Faculté des Lettres d'Alger, Publications de l'Institut d'Études Orientales, vol. VI).

ḤS (ḤS)—See Khwandamīr *ḤS*.

hsg[b]. v[on]—herausgegeben von (published by).

Ḥu. Č[elebī]—See Bursa Ḥü. Čelebī

Hüdā'ī (Hūdāi, Khudā'ī)—Roper III 332, Hüdayî Collection.

Hudh.—J. Wellhausen, Letzter Teil der Lieder der Hudhailiten, arabisch und deutsch, in *Skizzen und Vorarbeiten* I (Berlin: Reimer, 1884), 103ff.

Hudeekat ool Ufrah—Aḥmad b. Muḥammad al-Yamanī al-Shirwānī, *Ḥadīqat al-afrāḥ li-izāḥat al-atrāḥ*. Calcutta, 1229.

Ḥuff.— See al-Suyūṭī, *Ṭabaqāt al-ḥuffāẓ*.

Hujwīrī—See al-Hujwīrī.

Hunter, *Ind. Gazet.*—W.W. Hunter, *The Imperial Gazetteer of India*. 14 vols. 2nd ed. London: Trübner, 1885–87.

Ḥūr Laylā—Unresolved.

Ḥusayniyya library—See al-Maktaba al-Ḥusayniyya.

Ḥusayn Khān (Ḥu. Ḥān)—Not in Roper.

Hüseyn Pasha Eyyub—Not in Roper. Maybe a *waqf* in Roper III 348, Eyüp Câmii Hz. Hâlid Fâtih?

Hyderabad, Jam. ʿUthm.—Roper I 403, Osmania University Library (Hyderabad).

IAR—See Ibn Abi 'l-Rijāl.

I. A. Uṣ.—See Ibn Abī Uṣaybiʿa.

ʿIbar—See Ibn Khaldūn, *al-ʿIbar*.

Ibn Abbār—See Ibn al-Abbār

Ibn ʿAbd al-Barr, *al-Istidrāk*—Probably a misprint.

Ibn ʿAbd al-Rabbih—See the correct form in the next entry.

Ibn ʿAbd Rabbih[i], *al-ʿIqd*—Ibn ʿAbd Rabbih Aḥmad b. Muḥammad, *al-ʿIqd* [*al-farīd*].

Ibn Abi 'l-Rijāl—Ibn Abi 'l-Rijāl Aḥmad b. Ṣāliḥ al-Yamanī, *Maṭlaʿ al-budūr wa-majmaʿ al-buḥūr*.

Ibn Abī Uṣaybiʿa ([I. A.] Uṣ.)—Ibn Abī Uṣaybiʿa Aḥmad b. al-Qāsim: A. Müller (ed.), *Kitāb ʿuyūn al-anbāʾ fī ṭabaqāt al-aṭibbāʾ. Taʾlīf al-ṭabīb al-fāḍil ... al-maʿrūf bi-Ibn Abī Uṣaybiʿa*. 2 vols. Cairo: al-Maṭbaʿa al-Wahbiyya, 1882.

Ibn Abī Yaʿlā [, *Ṭab.*]—Ibn Yaʿlā b. Muḥammad b. Muḥammad b. al-Ḥusayn al-Farrāʾ, *Ṭabaqāṭ al-Ḥanābila*.

Ibn al-Abbār, *Muʿjam*—Ibn al-Abbār Muḥammad b. ʿAbdallāh b. Abī Bakr, *al-Muʿjam fī aṣḥāb al-Qāḍī al-Imām Abī ʿAlī al-Ṣadafī b. Sukkara*.

Ibn al-Abbār [, *Takmila*]—Idem, *Kitāb takmilat al-Ṣila*.

Ibn al-ʿArabī, *Mawāqiʿ*—Ibn al-ʿArabī Muḥammad b. ʿAlī b. Muḥammad, *Mawāqiʿ al-nujūm wa-maṭāliʿ ahillat al-asrār wal-ʿulūm*.

Ibn ʿĀdharī, *Bayān* (Ibn ʿAdhārī, *Bayān* [*al-mughrib*])—See Ibn al-ʿIdhārī.

Ibn al-Anb[ārī] (Anb.)—Ibn al-Anbārī ʿAbd al-Raḥmān b. Muḥammad b. ʿUbaydallāh, *Kitāb nuzhat al-alibbāʾ fī ṭabaqāt al-udabāʾ* or, depending on the context, *Kitāb al-inṣāf fī masāʾil al-khilāf bayna 'l-naḥwiyyīn al-Baṣriyyīn wal-Kūfiyyīn*.

Ibn al-Anbārī, *Nuzha*—See previous entry, first part.

Ibn al-Athīr—See next entry.

Ibn al-Athīr, [*al-*]*Kāmil* (Ibn al-Athīr [(T.)])—Ibn al-Athīr ʿIzz al-Dīn ʿAlī b. Muḥammad b. Muḥammad, *Kitāb al-kāmil fī ʾl-taʾrīkh*. The abbreviation (T.) stands for the edition by Tornberg.

Ibn al-Athīr, [*al-*]*Lubāb* (– *al-Lubāb*)—Idem, *Kitāb al-lubāb, mukhtaṣar al-Ansāb lil-Samʿānī.*

Ibn al-Athīr, [*al-*]*Nihāya*—Ibn al-Athīr Majd al-Dīn al-Mubārak b. Muḥammad b. Muḥammad, *Kitāb al-nihāya fī gharīb al-ḥadīth wal-āthār.*

Ibn al-Athīr, *Usd*—Ibn al-Athīr ʿIzz al-Dīn ʿAlī b. Muḥammad b. Muḥammad, *Kitāb usd al-ghāba fī maʿrifat al-Ṣaḥāba.*

Ibn al-Faraḍī [, *Taʾr.*] (al-Faraḍī)—Ibn al-Faraḍī ʿAbdallāh b. Muḥammad b. Yūsuf b. Naṣr, [*Kitāb al-mawṣūl fī*] *Taʾrīkh ʿulamāʾ al-Andalus.*

Ibn al-ʿIdhārī, *Bayān*—Ibn al-ʿIdhārī al-Marrākushī, *Bayān al-mughrib.*

Ibn al-ʿImād, *ShDh* (– *Shad*[*h*]. *al-dhah*[*ab*])—Ibn al-ʿImād al-ʿAkarī ʿAbd al-Ḥayy Aḥmad b. Muḥammad, *Shadharāt al-dhahab fī akhbār man dhahab.*

Ibn al-Jazarī [, *Ghāyat al-nihāya*] ([Ibn] al-Jazarī *Ghāya*)—Al-Jazarī Muḥammad b. Muḥammad, *Ghāyat al-nihāya fī asmāʾ rijāl al-qirāʾāt uli ʾl-riwāya wal-dirāya*. In each case, the reference is in fact to: G. Bergsträsser and O. Pretzl (eds.), *Das biografische Lexikon der Koranlehrer von Šamsaddīn Muḥammad Ibn al-Ǧazarī : Kitāb ghāyat al-nihāya fī ṭabaqāt al-qurrāʾ, taʾlīf Shams al-Dīn Muḥammad b. Muḥammad b. al-Jazarī.* 3 vols. Leipzig: Brockhaus & Cairo: Maṭbaʿat al-Saʿāda, 1932–35.

Ibn al-Jazarī, *Ṭab. al-qurrāʾ* (– *Ṭab.*, al-Jazarī *Ṭabaqāt al-qurrāʾ*, [al-]Jazarī *Ṭab.*) = Ibn al-Jazarī, *Ghāyat al-nihāya* etc.

Ibn al-Jazarī, I/II/III (al-Jazarī I/II/III) = Ibn al-Jazarī, *Ghāyat al-nihāya* etc.

Ibn al-Jazarī, *Nashr* [*al-qir.*] (– *Nashr fī ʾl-q.*)—Idem, *Kitāb al-nashr fī ʾl-qirāʾāt al-ʿashr.*

Ibn al-Murtaḍā [, *al-Muʿtazila*]—Ibn al-Murtaḍā Aḥmad b. Yaḥyā: Al-Muʿtazila: *being an extract from the* Kitābu-l milal wa-n niḥal *by al-Mahdi lidīn allāh A. b. Yaḥyā b. al-Murtaḍā*, ed. T.W. Arnold, Part I, Ar. Text, Leipzig: Harrassowitz, 1902. See vol. 1, 253: Ibn al-Murtaḍā, II. *al-Baḥr al-Zakhkhār*, ... 3. *al-Munya wal-amal.*

Ibn al-Muṭahhar, *Khulāṣat al-aqwāl*—Ibn al-Muṭahhar al-Ḥillī Ḥasan b. Yūsuf b. ʿAlī, *Khulāṣat al-aqwāl fī maʿrifat al-rijāl.*

Ibn al-Qāḍī, *Jadhwa*[*t*]—Ibn al-Qāḍī Aḥmad b. Muḥammad b. Muḥammad, *Jadhwat al-iqtibās fī man ḥalla min al-aʿlām madīnat Fās.*

Ibn al-Qāḍī, *al-Muntaqā*—Idem, *Muntaqa ʾl-maqṣūr ʿalā maʾāthir khilāfat al-Manṣūr.*

Ibn al-Qādir, *Jadhwat*—See Ibn al-Qāḍī, *Jadhwat.*

Ibn al-Qalānisī—Ibn al-Qalānisī Hamza b. Asad, *Dhayl Taʾrīkh Dimashq.*

Ibn al-Qayrawānī, *Kitāb al-jamʿ*—See Ibn al-Qaysarānī.

Ibn al-Qaysarānī, [*Kitāb*] *al-jamʿ* (—*Jamʿ*)—Ibn al-Qaysarānī Muḥammad b. Ṭāhir b. ʿAlī al-Maqdisī, *Kitāb al-jamʿ bayna kitābay Abī Naṣr al-Kalābādhī wa-Abī Bakr al-Iṣbahānī fī rigāl al-Bukhārī wa-Muslim.*

Ibn al-Qifṭī—Al-Qifṭī ʿAlī b. Yūsuf b. Ibrāhīm: J. Lippert (ed.), *Ibn al-Qifṭī's* Ta'rīkh al-ḥukamā'. Leipzig: Dieterich, 1903.

Ibn al-Ṣalāḥ—Probably: Ibn al-Ṣalāḥ al-Shahrazūrī ʿUthmān b. ʿAbd al-Raḥmān; it remains however unclear which one from among his works is meant.

Ibn al-Sarrāj, *Maṣāriʿ*—Ibn al-Sarrāj Jaʿfar b. Aḥmad b. al-Ḥusayn al-Qāri' al-Baghdādī, *Maṣāriʿ al-ʿushshāq.*

Ibn ʿAsākir—See Ibn ʿAsākir, *Ta'r. Dim.*

Ibn ʿAsākir, *Taby. kadh. al-muft.*—Ibn ʿAsākir ʿAlī b. al-Ḥasan, *Tabyīn kadhib al-muftarī fīmā nusiba ilā Abi 'l-Ḥasan al-Ashʿarī.*

Ibn ʿAsākir, *Ta'r. Dim.* (Ibn ʿAsākir)—Idem, *Ta'rīkh madīnat Dimashq.*

Ibn ʿAsākir, *Dawḥa*—See next entry.

Ibn ʿAskar, *Dawḥa*—Ibn ʿAskar Muḥammad b. ʿAlī b. ʿUmar, *Dawḥat al-nāshir li-maḥāsin man kāna bil-Maghrib min* (*mashāhīr*) *mashāyikh al-qarn al-ʿāshir.*

Ibn Athīr, *al-Kāmil*—See Ibn al-Athīr, *al-Kāmil.*

Ibn Ayās—See Ibn Iyās.

Ibn Bashkuwāl, *al-Ṣila* (Ibn Bashk[uwāl])—Ibn Bashkuwāl Khalaf b. ʿAbd al-Malik, *Kitāb al-ṣila fī akhbār a'immat al-Andalus.*

Ibn Baṭṭūṭa—Ibn Baṭṭūṭa al-Ṭanjī Muḥammad b. ʿAbdallāh b. Muḥammad, *Tuḥfat al-nuẓẓār fī gharā'ib al-amṣār wa-ʿajā'ib al-asfār.*

Ibn Durayd [, (*Gen.-et.*) *Handb.*]—Ibn Durayd Muḥammad b. al-Ḥasan: F. Wüstenfeld (ed.), *Ibn Doreid's genealogisch–etymologisches Handbuch* [*Kitāb al-ishtiqāq*]. Göttingen: Dieterich, 1854.

Ibn Fahd, *Laḥẓ* [*al-alḥāẓ*]—Ibn Fahd Muḥammad b. Muḥammad, *Laḥẓ al-alḥāẓ bi-dhayl Ṭabaqāt al-ḥuffāẓ.*

Ibn Fahd, *Muʿjam*—ʿUmar b. Muḥammad b. Muḥammad b. Fahd al-Makkī, *Muʿjam.*

Ibn Farḥūn, *Dībāj*[*a*] (– *Dīb.*)—Ibrāhīm b. ʿAlī b. Muḥammad b. Farḥūn al-Yaʿmarī, *al-Dībāj al-mudhahhab fī maʿrifat aʿyān ʿulamā' al-madhhab.* (F.) refers to the Fez edition and (C.) to the Cairo edition.

Ibn Ḥabīb *MO* VII—Ibn Ḥabīb al-Ḥasan b. ʿUmar al-Dimashqī: Refers to P. Leander's extracts from his *Durrat al-aslāk fī dawlat al-Atrāk* in *Le Monde Oriental.*

Ibn Ḥajar, DK (– *Durar*)—Ibn Ḥajar al-ʿAskalānī Aḥmad b. ʿAlī b. Muḥammad, *Kitāb al-durar al-kāmina fī aʿyān al-mi'a al-thāmina* (see vol. 2, p. 70, no. 40).

Ibn Ḥajar, [*al-*]*Iṣāba*—Idem, *al-Iṣāba fī tamyīz al-Ṣaḥāba* (see vol. 2, p. 68, no. 1).

Ibn Ḥajar, *Lisān*—Idem, *Lisān al-Mīzān* (by Abū ʿAbdallāh al-Dhahabī) (see vol. 2, p. 68, no. 4).

Ibn Ḥajar, *Rafʿ al-iṣr*— Idem, *Rafʿ al-iṣr ʿan quḍāt Miṣr* (see vol. 2, p. 70, no. 43).

Ibn Ḥajar, *Tahdh[īb]*—Idem, *Tahdhīb Tahdhīb al-Kamāl fī maʿrifat al-rijāl* (see vol. 2, p. 68, no. 3).

Ibn Ḥawqal—Ibn Ḥawqal Abu ʾl-Qāsim al-Naṣībī: J.H. Kramers (ed.), *Opus geographicum auctore Ibn Ḥawqal … cui titulus est "Liber imaginis terrae"*, Leiden: Brill, 1938.

Ibn Ḥazm, *Faṣl*—See next entry.

Ibn Ḥazm [, *Fiṣal*]—Ibn Ḥazm ʿAlī b. Aḥmad b. Saʿīd, *Kitāb al-fiṣal fi ʾl-milal wal-ahwāʾ wal-niḥal.*

Ibn Ḥibbān, *Rawḍa*—Ibn Ḥibbān Abū Ḥātim Muḥammad b. Aḥmad al-Bustī, *Rawḍat al-ʿuqalāʾ wa-nuzhat al-fuḍalāʾ.*

Ibn Hishām, *Sīra*—Ibn Hishām ʿAbd al-Malik, *Kitāb sīrat Muḥammad rasūli ʾllāh.*

Ibn Isfandyār [, *Hist. of Tabaristan*]—E.G. Browne (transl.), *An Abridged Translation of the* History of Tabaristân. E.J.W. Gibb Memorial Series, vol. 2. Leiden etc.: Brill, 1905. The original text, the *Taʾrīkh-i Ṭabaristān*, is in Persian.

Ibn Iyās (Ibn Ayās)—Ibn Iyās Muḥammad b. Aḥmad al-Čerkesī, *Badāʾiʿ al-zuhūr fī waqāʾiʿ al-duhūr.*

Ibn Kathīr, *Tafsīr*—Ibn Kathīr Ismāʿīl b. ʿUmar, *Tafsīr al-Qurʾān.*

Ibn Khald.—See Ibn Khaldūn.

Ibn Khaldūn, *Hist. des Berbères*—See *Hist. des Berbères.*

Ibn Khaldūn, *al-ʿIbar*—Ibn Khaldūn ʿAbd al-Raḥmān b. Muḥammad b. Muḥammad, *al-ʿIbar wa-dīwān al-mubtadaʾ wal-khabar fī ayyām al-ʿArab wal-ʿAjam wal-Barbar wa-man ʿāṣarahum min dhawi ʾl-sulṭān al-akbar.*

Ibn Khaldūn, *Muq.*—Idem, *Muqaddima* (*-t Ibn Khaldūn*).

Ibn Khaldūn, *Prol.* [trad.] (– *Proleg.* trad. de Slane)—See *Prol. Not. et extr.*

Ibn Khall.—Ibn Khallikān Aḥmad b. Muḥammad b. Ibrāhīm, *Wafayāt al-aʿyān wa-anbāʾ abnāʾ al-zamān.*

Ibn Khall. de Slane (Ibn Khallikān de Slane, de Slane Ibn Khall., de Slane *Biogr. Dict.*, Ibn Khall. *Biogr. Dict.*, Ibn Khall. tr[ansl]., Ibn Khall. transl. de Slane)—Idem: *Ibn Khallikan's biographical dictionary translated from the Arabic*, by MacGuckin de Slane. 4 vols. Paris–London: Oriental Translation Fund, 1843–71.

Ibn Khall. W[üst].—See Wüst., 3).

Ibn Nājī, *Maʿālim*—Ibn al-Nājī al-Qāsim b. ʿĪsā, *Maʿālim al-īmān fī maʿrifat ahl al-Qayrawān.*

Ibn Qāḍī Shuhba, *Ṭab.*—Abū Bakr b. Aḥmad b. Muḥammad b. ʿUmar b. Qāḍī Shuhba, *Ṭabaqāṭ al-Shāfiʿiyya.*

Ibn Qut.—Ibn Qutayba Muḥammad b. Muslim; if alone, without a title, then the reference is to his *Liber Poesis et Poetarum*, ed. M.J. de Goeje. Leiden: Brill, 1904.

Ibn Qutayba, *Maʿārif* (Ibn Qutayba)—Idem: F. Wüstenfeld, *Ibn Coteiba's Handbuch der Geschichte* [*Kitāb al-maʿārif*]. Göttingen: Vandenhoeck and Ruprecht, 1850.

Ibn Quṭlūbughā, *Ṭab. al-Ḥan.* (Ibn Quṭlūbughā, Ibn Quṭlūb., Ibn Quṭl.)—Al-Qāsim b. ʿAbdallāh b. Quṭlūbughā, *Tāj al-tarājim fī ṭabaqāt al-Ḥanafiyya.*

Ibn Saad (Ibn Saʿad)—See next entry.

Ibn Saʿd [, *Ṭab.*] (Ibn Saad)—Ibn Saʿd Muḥammad Kātib al-Wāqidī, *Kitāb al-ṭabaqāt al-kabīr*. Edition by a group of scholars (C. Brockelmann, J. Horovitz, J. Lippert, B. Meissner, E. Mittwoch, E. Sachau, F. Schwally, and K.V. Zetterstéen) under the leadership of E. Sachau, *Ibn Saad: Biografien Muhammeds, seiner Gefährten und der späteren Träger des Islams bis zum Jahre 230 der Flucht*. 9 volumes in 16 parts. Leiden: Brill: 1904–40.

Ibn Saʿīd ed. Tallquist—ʿAlī b. Mūsā b. Saʿīd al-ʿAnsī al-Gharnāṭī: *Ibn Saʿīd, Kitāb al-mughrib fī ḥula ʾl-Maghrib*, Buch IV: *Geschichte der Ikhshīden und Fusṭāṭensische Biographien*, nach der einzigen vorhandenen Handschrift mit Anmerkungen nebst Auszug aus al-Kindīs *Taʾrīkh Miṣr* hsg. v. K.L. Tallquist. Leiden: Brill, 1899.

Ibn Ṣāʿid, *Ṭab.*—Ṣāʿid b. Aḥmad b. ʿAbd al-Raḥmān b. Muḥammad b. Ṣāʿid al-Qurṭubī, *Kitāb al-taʿrīf bi-ṭabaqāt al-umam*.

Ibn Taghr[ībirdī] C. ((C.), incidentally K.) I ... (– I ...)—Ibn Taghrībirdī Abu ʾl-Maḥāsin Yūsuf: Refers to one of the volumes of the Cairo (C.) edition (6 vols., 1348–55) of his *al-Nujūm al-zāhira fī mulūk Miṣr wal-Qāhira*. Sometimes C and vol. no. in reverse order.

Ibn Taghrībirdī (Ibn Taghr[īb].)—Idem, *al-Nujūm al-zāhira fī mulūk Miṣr wal-Qāhira*. See also second next entry.

Ibn Taghrībirdī (Juynb.)—See next entry.

Ibn Taghr[īb]. (Juynboll) (– (Juynb.), – (J.))—Idem: T.W.J. Juynboll et al. (eds.), *Abū l-Maḥāsin Ibn Taghri Bardii annales quibus titulus est* al-Nujūm al-zāhira fī mulūk Miṣr wal-Qāhira (until the year 365 AH). 2 vols. Leiden: Brill, 1852–61 (1852: vol. 1.1, text pp. 1–359; 1855: vol. 1.2, text pp. 359–780; 1857: vol. 2.1, text pp. 1–494; 1861: vol. 2.2, notes and indices); after Juynboll's premature death in 1861, it took almost 50 years before W. Popper picked up where Juynboll had left off, continuing the pagination of Juynboll's vol. 2: W. Popper, *Abū ʾl-Maḥâsin ibn Taghrî Birdî's Annals entitled* an-Nujûm az-zâhirâ fî mulûk Miṣr wal-Ḳâhirâ, University of California Publications in Semitic Philology vol. 2.1 (Berkeley, Sept. 1909) = *Annals* vol. 2.2 # 1 (text pp. 495–622), vol. 2.2 (Berkeley, Oct. 1910) = *Annals* vol. 2.2 # 2 (text pp. 623–791), vol. 2.3 (Berkeley, Jan. 1912) = *Annals* vol. 2.2 # 3 (text pp. 791–1028 + indices). Whenever Brockelmann in Supplement I refers to Juynboll in connection with a date *after* 365 AH, the reference is in fact to Popper's continuation of vol. 2 of Juynboll's edition (running up to and including 524 AH; double references (J.) and (Popper) at various places in Supplement I (e.g. Suppl. I p. 453) are in each case to one and the same page in *Annals* vol. 2.2, where Popper's own, continuous numbering is found at the top of the page and the continuation of Juynboll's numbering at the bottom). Subsequent parts of Ibn Taghrībirdī's chronicle edited by Popper (525 AH and following) are referred to as '(Popper)', viz. '(Popper) III' = *Annals* vol. 3.1 # 1 (524–67 AH, text pp. 1–130) (Un. Cal. Pub. Sem. Phil., vol. 3.1. Berkeley, September

1913), and V = *Annals* vol. 5.1 (746–78 AH, text pp. 1–292) (Un. Cal. Pub. Sem. Phil. vol. 5.1. Berkeley, December 1932).

Ibn Taghrībirdī I L—See previous entry, first part, vol. 1 (the 'L' stands for 'Leiden').

Ibn Taghr. (Popper)—See second previous entry, second part.

Ibn Ṭayfūr, *Kitāb Baghdād*—Aḥmad b. Abī Ṭāhir Ṭayfūr: This is an error; instead read: *Ta'rīkh Baghdād.*

Ibr. Pāshā (Ibr. P.)—There is no corresponding entry in Roper. Maybe the reference is to 'Ibrahim Efendi' mentioned in Roper III, 349?

Ideler, *Unters.*—L. Ideler, *Untersuchungen über der Ursprung und die Bedeutung der Sternnamen*. Berlin: Weiss, 1809.

I. Guidi, *Flor. de Vogüé*—I. Guidi, L'Europa occidentale negli antichi geografi arabi, in G. Maspero (ed.), *Florilegium ou receuil de travaux d'érudition dédiés à Monsieur le Marquis Melchior de Vogüé à l'occasion du 84ème anniversaire de sa naissance* (Paris: Imprimerie Nationale, 1909), 263–69.

I. Kratchovsky, Vostochniye rukopisi iz sobranii͡a V.F. Girgasa, in: *Doklady Akademii Nauk SSR* [series] B, 1927, 162–65.

'Ilāwe—For 'ilave', here: 'supplement'; Turkish, in reference to a collection of manuscripts in some library.

Ilim—Abdulhakk Adnan Adıvar, *Osmanlı Türklerinde İlim*. Istanbul: Maarif Matbaası, 1943.

IM—'Alī Manuq, *al-'Iqd al-manẓūm fī dhikr afāḍil al-Rūm*, in the margin of Ibn Khall. II.

'Imād al-Dīn, *ShDh*—See Ibn al-'Imād.

'Imād al-Fihrisī [al-Ṭihrānī] (library of, Mashhad)—Not in Roper; see also al-Muḥaddith al-'Imād al-Fihrisī and Mahdī 'Imād al-Fihrisī.

Imām Yaḥyā (collection of, Zaydī Imam, 20th cent.)—Not in Roper.

Impr. Sc.—Imprimerie Scientifique.

Ind.—Indian printing.

'Ind.—Read: Ind.

Ind. Off.—O. Loth, *Catalogue of the Ar. Mss. in the Library of the India Office*. London: The Secretary of State for India in Council, 1877.

Ind. Off. Delhi Ar.—Roper III 489. The India Office Delhi Collection has no published catalogue yet, just a hand-list. See also: https://www.bl.uk/collection-guides/the-delhi-collection (accessed 31 August 2017). The manuscripts in this collection were originally in the Mughal Library in Delhi.

Ind. Off. Ethé—H. Ethé, *Catalogue of the Persian Manuscripts in the Library of the India Office*. 2 vols. Oxford: Clarendon Press, 1903–37, with vol. 2 revised and completed by E. Edwards. Repr. London: India Office Library & Records, 1980. 2 vols. in one.

Ind. Off. II—G.A. Storey, *Catalogue of the Arabic Manuscripts in the Library of the India Office*, vol. II i, *Qur'ānic Literature*. London: Oxford University Press for the India

Office, 1930; II ii, *Sufism and Ethics*, by A.J. Arberry. London: Oxford University Press for the India Office, 1936; II iii, *Fiqh*, by R. Levy. London: India Office, 1937; A.J. Arberry, Handlist of Islamic Manuscripts acquired by the India Office Library 1936/8, in *JRAS* 1939, 353/96.

Ind. Off. III—*Catalogue of the Arabic manuscripts in the library of the India Office*, vol. II iii Fiqh (see penultimate publication in previous entry).

Ind. Off. RB—E. Denison Ross and E.G. Browne, *Catalogue of Two Collections of Persian and Arabic Manuscripts Preserved in the India Office Library*, London: Eyre and Spottiswoode, 1902.

Inst. Reg. Belg.—Institutum Regium Belgicum. This refers to the collection of Oriental manuscripts of the Royal Netherlands Academy of Sciences (Koninklijke Nederlandse Akademie van Wetenschappen), for which Brockelmann must have used P. de Jong, *Catalogus codicum orientalium bibliothecae Academiae Regiae Scientiarum*. Leiden: Brill, 1862.

ʿIqd—See Ibn ʿAbd Rabbih, *al-ʿiqd*.

Iqlīd al-Khiz. (*Iqlīd, Iql., Khiz. Iqlīd*)—See ʿAbd al-ʿAzīz Mayman.

I Revankösk—See Serāi Revan Köshk.

Irshād (*Irsh.*)—See Yāqūt.

Islam (*Isl.*)—*Der Islam*.

Islca—*Islamica*.

Ismāʿil Efendi (collection of, Istanbul)—Not in Roper.

Ismāʿīl Pāshā (library of, no place)—Ismāʿīl Pāshā Baghdādī ?

Ismāʿīl Pāshā Baghdādī (library of, no place)—Not in Roper (= Baghdadly Ismāʿīl Pāshā ?)

Ismāʿīl Ṣāʾib [Efendi] (Ism. Ṣāʾib Ef.)—Roper III 298, İsmail Sâib Collection (Ankara).

Iṣṭakhrī—Muḥammad al-Fārisī al-Iṣṭakhrī, *Kitāb al-masālik wal-mamālik*.

Ist.—Istanbul(-er).

Istanbul ʿA. Amīrī—See ʿAlī Emīrī.

Istanbul H.—See Halis.

Istanbul, Jawāʾib (Istanbul Jaw.)—Istanbul, Jawāʾib Press (founded by Fāris al-Shidyāq).

Istanbul Un. Ar. Yazma—See Ist. Un.; ʻAr. Yazma' means ʻArabic MS'.

Istanbul Un. H.—See Halis.

Istanbul Un. R[iza P.]—See Riẕā P.

Istanbul Univers. TY—The TY should refer to a Turkish manuscript in the Yildiz Collection. See Roper III 335. In fact, however, it may very well be that Brockelmann meant to refer to an Arabic manuscript on medicine in this same Yildiz collection.

Ist. Un. (Istbl. [Univ.], Ist. Ün; ʻIst. ʻUn' in vol. 1, 581 is a misprint)—Roper III 335, Istanbul Üniversitesi Kütüphanesi.

Itḥāf—ʿAbd al-Raḥmān b. Abī Bakr al-Suyūṭī, *Itḥāf al-nubalāʾ bi-akhbār al-thuqalāʾ* (see vol. 2, p. 168, # 216. ∗).

Ivanov, *Guide* (Ivanov, Ivanow)—V.A. Ivanov, *A Guide to Ismaili Literature*. London: Royal Asiatic Society, 1933.

Ivanow—See previous entry.

Izv[estija] Ak. Nauk—See next entry.

Izv. Rossk. Ak. Nauk (*Izv[estiya] Ak. Nauk, Izv. Ac. Nauk* SSR)—*Izvestija Rossijskoj Akademii Nauk*.

Jab[artī]—See al-Jabartī.

Jacob, *Bektaschijje*—G. Jacob, *Die Bektaschijje in ihrem Verhältnis zu verwandten Erscheinungen* [Abhandlungen der K. Bayer. Akademie der Wiss. Kl., Bd. XXIV, IV. Abt.]. München: K.B. Akademie der Wissenschaften, 1909.

Jadhwa—See al-Ḥumaydī, *Jadhwa* or Ibn al-Qāḍī, *Jadhwa*.

Ja. Ef. (Ya. Ef.)—*Defteri Kutubkhana-yi Jaḥjā Efendī*, Istanbul 1310.

Jaʿfar Sulṭān al-Umarāʾ (library of, Tehran)—Not in Roper.

Jahsh.—See al-Jahshiyārī.

Jaḥyā—See Ja. Ef.

Jakarta—See Batavia.

Jamh[ara]—May refer to 1) Abū Zayd al-Qurashī, *Jamharat ashʿār al-ʿArab*, or 2) Ibn Durayd Muḥammad al-Ḥasan, *al-Jamhara fī ʾl-lugha*.

Jāmiʿ—See Sarkīs, 1).

Jāmiʿ al-badāʾiʿ (*Jāmiʿ al-b.*)—*Jāmiʿ al-badāʾiʿ, majmūʿ kabīr al-qadr jalīl al-shaʾn yaḥtawī ʿalā thamānī ʿashara risāla li-amāthil al-sulaf ... kal-Shaykh al-Raʾīs ... wa ... ʿUmar al-Khayyām....* Cairo: Maṭbaʿat al-Saʿāda, 1335/1917.

Jamīl Bek [Bak], *ʿUqūd al-jawh[ar]* (– *ʿUqūd al-jawāhir*)—Jamīl Bek al-ʿAẓm, *ʿUqūd al-jawhar fī tarājim man lahum khamsūn taṣnīfan fa-miʾa fa-akthar*, vol. 1. Beirut: al-Maṭbaʿa al-Ahliyya, 1908. A second volume remained unpublished.

JAS—*JA*s. (*Journal Asiatique*).

JASB 1917 (*JASB* NS 1917)—See *JRASB* 1917.

Jaw.—See Istanbul, Jawāʾib.

Jaz.—Al-Ḥasan b. Aḥmad b. Yaʿqūb al-Hamdānī, *Ṣifat Jazīrat al-ʿArab*.

Jazarī—See Ibn al-Jazarī.

Jeni—See Yeni.

Jer[usalem]—See Jerus. Khālid.

Jer. K.—Kleopas M. Koikylidēs, *Katalogos arabikon cheirographōn tēs Hierosolymitikēs bibliothekes*. Jerusalem, 1901.

Jerus. Khālid. (Jer. Khāl., Jer. Khālidiyya, Jer., Jerusalem, Khālid.)—*Barnāmaj al-maktaba al-Khālidiyya*. Jerusalem, 1318.

Jones, *Works*—*The works of Sir Willam Jones*: in six volumes. London: printed for G.G. and J. Robinson and R.H. Evans, 1799.

Jorga—N. Iorga, *Geschichte des osmanischen Reiches*. 5 vols. Gotha: Perthes, 1908–13.

J. Th.—G. Junge and W. Thomson, *The Commentary of Pappus on Book X of Euclids Elements*. Cambridge: Harvard Press, 1930.

JRASB 1917 [Proc.]—A. al-Ma'mūn Suhrawardy, Notes on important Arabic and Persian MSS. found in various libraries in India, in *Journal & Proceedings of the Asiatic Society of Bengal*, New Series, vol. xiii (1917), lxxvii–cxxxix.

J. Rosen 245 (Supplement 2, 872)—Mistranslation; the correct rendering is: "n.p. & n.d., Rosen 245".

Jurjānī, *Kin.*—See Al-Jurjānī, *Kināyāt.*

Juweyni, the Tarikhi jehan gusha—See *Ta'rīkhi Jahāngushā.*

Juynboll, *Orient.*—T.W.J. Juynboll, T. Roorda and H.E. Weijers (eds.), *Orientalia*, 2 vols. Amsterdam: Joh. Müller, 1840–46.

K.—See Krause; in some rare cases, 'K.' stands for 'Cairo'.

k. 173 (vol. 2, p. 335, D.1, bibliographical section, line 5)—GAL first edition, vol. 2, p. 298 reveals that the reference is to Cairo^{1}, 173.

Kamankash—See Kemānkeš.

Kandilli Rasatane—See Rasadhaneküt.

Kantūrī—See Kentūrī.

Kap.—Chapter.

Karabacek, *Führer*—J. Karabacek, *Führer durch die Ausstellung Papyrus Erzherzog Rainer*. Vienna: Hölder, 1894.

Kay, *Yaman*—H.C. Kay, *Yaman, its Early Mediaeval History by Najm ad-Din 'Omāra al-Ḥakami*. London: Arnold, 1892.

Kayseri (Kaysari)—Roper III 369, Raşid Efendi Eserler Kütüphanesi (Kayseri).

Kazan, Gottw[aldt]—At *History*, Supplement 1, 900, Brockelmann refers to the "catalogue of Kazan" by Gottwaldt, by which he must mean: I. Gotval'd, Opisanie arabskikh rukopiseĭ prinadlezhavshchich bibliotek Imp. Kazanskago Universiteta, *Uchenye Zapiski, Izdavaemye Imperatorskim Kazanskim Universitetom* (*Proceedings Published by the Imperial Kazan University*), 1854 ii, 43–169; 1854 iv, 1–67; 1855 iv, 1–118.

KCs.A.—*Kőrösi Csoma Archivum.*

Kemānkeš—Roper III 332, Kemankeş collection.

Kentūrī (Kenturi, Kantūrī)—See al-Kantūrī.

Kern (F. Kern)—Between brackets, with noting added: informal statements by Kern.

kgl.—königlich.

Khadīja Sulṭān—Not in Roper; maybe the same as 'Khadīja Ṭarkhān' of the next entry?

Khadīja Ṭarkhān—Ritter, in Ruska *Or. Steinb.* 7, associates 'Hadica Tarhan' with the Yeni Cami collection = Roper III 350, Turhan Vâlide Sultan?

Khalīlallāh—See Āqā Khalīlallāh.

Khālid.—See Jer. Khālid.

Khāliṣ [Ef.]—See Halis.

Khanqāh-i Pīr (library of, no place)—Too general a name to allow any positive identification.

Khāqānī Library (Najaf)—Roper IV 229, ʿAlī al-Khāqānī.

Kharājjīz[āde]—Roper III 309, Haraççioğlu.

Khaṣāʾiṣ (*Khaṣ.*)—Abu ʾl-Fatḥ b. Jinnī, *al-Khaṣāʾiṣ fī ʾl-naḥw.*

Khazīnat al-aṣfiyāʾ—Ghulām Surūr, *Khazīnat al-aṣfiyāʾ*. 2 vols. lith. Kanpur: Newal Kishore, 1894 (repr. 1902, 1914, …).

Khazīnat al-awliyāʾ—A misprint, probably the reference is to *Khazīnat al-aṣfiyāʾ*.

Khemiri and Kampffmeyer [, *Leaders* (*Pr.* at Suppl. 3, p. 164 is a misprint)]—Ṭ. al-Khemiri and G. Kampffmeyer, *Leaders in Contemporary Arabic Literature*: a book of reference. Berlin: Deutsche Gesellschaft für Islamkunde, 1930.

Khiṭ. jad.—See *al-Khiṭaṭ al-jadīda*.

Khiz[*āna* (*t al-adab*)]—See ʿAbd al-Qādir al-Baghdādī, *Khiz.*

Khiz. Iqlīd—See *Iqlīd al-Khiz.*

Khosrev P.—See Khusraw P.

Khudābakhsh 30, 624 (Suppl. 2, 607)—See Bank.; the volume no. seems mistaken.

Khudāʾī—See Hüdāʾī.

Khusraw P. (Khosrev P.)—*Defter-i Kutubkhana-yi Khusraw Pasha.* Istanbul n.d. The addition ʻAyyūbʼ for what is apparently a sub-collection (e.g. vol. 1, p. 15) is not found Roper III 349, which mentions the Hüsrev Paşa collection among the many collections preserved in the Süleymaniye Kütüphanesi.

Khwandamīr *ḤS* (*ḤS*)—Ghiyāth al-Dīn b. Humām al-Dīn Khwandamīr, *Ḥabīb al-siyar*. Persian.

King's Coll.—E.H. Palmer and H. Bradshaw, Catalogue of the Oriental Manuscripts in the Library of King's College, *JRAS* NS vol. 3.1 (1867), 105–131.

Kl. Schr.—*Kleinere Schriften.*

König, Diss.—C. König, *Der* Kitāb muthīr al-gharām ilā ziyārat al-Quds wal-Shām *des Shīhāb al-Dīn Abū Maḥmūd Aḥmad al-Muqaddasī.* Diss. Leipzig, 1896.

Königsberg, Stadtbibl.—The municipal library of Königsberg (Kaliningrad). At the end of WW II, about 60 surviving manuscripts and some crates with books were transferred to the Russian State Library in Moscow.

Konya, Yu. Āġā—Roper III 377, Yusuf Ağa Kütüphanesi (Konya).

Köpr. (Küpr.)—*Köprülüzāde Meḥmed Pāšā Kütübḫānesinde maḥfūẓ kütübi mevǧūdenin defteri.* Istanbul n.d.

Köpr. Fāḍil A.P.—Roper III 339, Köprülü Fâzil Ahmed Paşa.

Kosegarten, *Chrest. Ar.* (*Chrest.*)—J.G.L. Kosegarten, *Chrestomathia arabica*. Leipzig: Vogel, 1828.

Kr.—Kraus, Krause, or in reference to corrections and additions provided by Kračkovsky (Supplements).

Kračk.—Kračkovsky.

Kračkovsky—See also Kratchkovsky.

Kračkovsky (collection of, no place)—Not in Roper.

Krafft (Kraft)—H. Krafft, *Die arabischen, persischen und türkischen Handschriften der K.K. Orientalischen Akademie zu Wien*, Vienna 1842.

Kratchkovsky, Intr.—I. Kratchkovsky (ed.), *Kitāb al-Badīʿ of ʿAbd Allāh Ibn al-Muʿtazz* [E.J.W. Gibb Memorial Series N.S. vol. 10. London: Luzac, 1935], Introduction.

Kratchkovsky, *Tanṭāwī*—Idem, *Šeiḫ Ṭanṭāwī professor St. Petersburgskavo Universiteta (1810/1861)* Leningrad 1929 (*Akademia Nauk, Trudi Komm. po ist. znanii*).

Kraus (Kr.)—Depending on the context, the reference can be to: 1) P. Kraus, Plotin chez les Arabes, in *Bulletin de l'Institut d'Égypte* 23/1941, 263–95; 2) Idem, *Jābir ibn Ḥayyān: contribution à l'histoire des idées scientifiques dans l'Islam.* Cairo: IFAO, 1943; 3) Idem (ed.), *Jābir ibn Ḥayyān: Essay sur l'histoire des idées scientifiques dans l'Islam* (Arabic title: *Mukhtār rasāʾil Jābir b. Ḥayyān*), vol. 1, Textes choisis. Paris: Maissonneuve & Cairo: el-Khandgi, 1935; 4) Idem, Hebraische und syrische Zitate in ismailitischen Schriften, *Der Islam* XIX, 243–63; 5) Publications by him that were mentioned shortly before the citation 'Kraus', which in addition to the four publications just mentioned may also be other works by him, e.g. in Supplement 1, 327, where 'Kraus, p. 486' refers to an article by him in *REI* IV (1933) 483–90, mentioned on page 326; 6) In some cases 'Kraus' is a misprint for 'Krause' (e.g. 'Kraus, 325' in Supplement 1, p. 901, 6b); 7) Finally there are quite many references to Kraus in connection with manuscripts from Cairo (e.g. Supplement 1, p. 986, ad p. 189) or texts or manuscripts in general (e.g. Supplement 1, p. 989, ad p. 236). Even though one cannot be absolutely sure, I think these pieces of information came via personal notes from Paul Kraus when the latter was living in Cairo (from the late 1930s until his death in 1944). And if Brockelmann did not openly thank Kraus for his help in his Postscript to vol. 2 or in the Prefaces to Supplement 1, 2 or 3, in the same way in which he had acknowledged the help of many others there, this must then have been because Kraus was a Jew with whom Brockelmann could not officially admit to having any kind of active collaboration. If true, this would put Brockelmann's National Socialist leanings into a somewhat pragmatic perspective, which would confirm Witkam's analysis in this regard. See J.J. Witkam, "Brockelmann's *Geschichte* Revisited Once More", in volume 1, p. VIII.

Krause, Hdss. (– St[amb]. Hdss., – Handschriften, – *QSB*, or just 'Krause')—M. Krause, Stambuler Handschriften islamischer Mathematiker, *Quellen und Studien zur Geschichte der Mathematik, Astronomie und Physik*, Abt. B. 3 (1936), 437–532.

Kremer—See von (v.) Kremer.

Krenkow (MS collection of)—Not in Roper.

Kroll—See W. Kroll.

Küpr.—See Köpr.

L. (l.)—'read' (from German 'lesen').

LA—Ibn Manẓūr, *Lisān al-ʿArab*.

L. Abel, ibid. 1887—L. Abel, *Abū Miḥjan poetae arabici carmina*, Leiden 1887.

Lālā Ism.—Roper III 349, Lâlâ İsmail Efendi.

Lālelī—*Defteri Kutubkhana-yi Lālelī*. Istanbul, 1310.

Lammens—H. Lammens, Le chantre des Omiades, *JA* s. 9, v. IV, p. 94/176, 193/241, 381/459.

Landb. (Landb.-Yale)—Ch. Torrey, The Landberg Collection of Arabic Manuscripts at Yale University, *Library Journal* 28 (New-York 1908), 53–57.

Landb.–Br[ill]—C. Landberg, *Catalogue des manuscrits arabes provenant d'une bibliothèque privée à El-Medina, appartenant à la maison E. J. Brill*. Leiden: Brill, 1883.

Landberg, Dathīna—C. von Landberg, *Glossaire datinois*, vols. 1–2. Leiden: Brill, 1920–23.

Landberg, *Primeurs ar.*—Idem, *Primeurs arabes*. 2 vols. Leiden: Brill, 1886–89.

Landberg, *Prov.*—Idem, *Proverbes et dictons de la province de Syrie, section de Ṣaydâ*. Leiden: Brill, 1883.

Landb.–H.—See Brill–H.

Lane—May refer to: 1) E.W. Lane, *An Account of the Manners and Customs of the Modern Egyptians*. First edition, 2 vols. London: Knight, 1836, fifth edition London: Murray, 1860, countless reprints; 2) See next entry.

Lane I, II, etc.—E.W. Lane, *An Arabic—English Lexicon*. 8 vols. London & Edinburgh: Williams and Norgate, 1863–1893

Lane-Poole—S. Lane-Poole, *The Mohammadan dynasties: chronological and genealogical tables with historical introductions*. Westeminster: Constable, 1894.

Lat. Paris.—A. Melot, *Catalogus codicum manuscriptorum Bibliothecae Regiae*. 4 vols. Paris: Imprimerie Royale, 1739–44.

Laur. [Or.]—See Flor. Ass.

La Yunta—See Madr. Junta.

L. Bl.—Literaturblatt für orientalische Philologie, herausgegeben von E. Kuhn, Leipzig 1883–8.

L. Caetani—See Caetani.

Ldbg.—Landberg.

Lecerf, Lit. dial[ectale] (Lecerf)—M.J. Lecerf, Littérature dialectale et renaissance arabe moderne, in *BEO* 3 (1933), 44–174.

Lecerf, Renaissance—See previous entry.

Leclerc—L. Leclerc, *Histoire de la médecine arabe*, 2 vols., Paris: Leroux 1876.

Lee—J. Lee, *Catalogue of Oriental manuscripts purchased in Turkey*. London: Watts, 1840.

Leid.—R.P.A. Dozy, P. de Jong, M.J. de Goeje and M.Th. Houtsma, *Catalogus codicum orientalium Bibliothecae Academiae Lugduno Batavae*. 6 vols. Leiden: Brill, 1851–77;

M.J. de Goeje and M.Th. Houtsma, *Catalogus Codicum Arabicorum Bibliothecae Academiae Lugduno Batavae*, editio secunda, vol. 1. Leiden: Brill, 1888; M.J. de Goeje and Th.W. Juynboll, *Catalogus Codicum Arabicorum Bibliothecae Academiae Lugduno Batavae*, editio secunda, vol. 2. Leiden: Brill, 1907. In the Supplement volumes these two publications are split into Leid.[1] and Leid.[2]. See below. Note: At *History* 1, 297, 'Leid. 154/6' refers to Leid.[2]

Leid.[1] ([Lugd.] Bat.)—R.P.A.Dozy, P. de Jong, M.J. de Goeje and M.Th. Houtsma (eds.), *Catalogus codicum orientalium Bibliothecae Lugduno Batavae*. 6 vols. Leiden: Brill, 1851–77.

Leid.[2]—M.J. de Goeje, M.Th. Houtsma and Th.W. Juynboll, *Catalogus Codicum Arabicorum Bibliothecae Academiae Lugduno Batavae*, editio secunda. 2 vols. Leiden: Brill, 1888–1907.

Leid. Amīn—See Landb.-Br.

Leid. Scal.—For the Hebrew manuscripts in the Scaliger collection as part of the oriental collection of Leiden University Library, see M. Steinschneider, *Catalogus codicum Hebraeorum Bibliothecae Academiae Lugduno-Batavae*. Leiden: Brill, 1858.

Leid. Warn.—Legatum Warnerianum, in the Oriental collection of Leiden University Library. In Leid.[1] vol. 6, 137ff there is a concordance between the numbering of the catalogue and the actual shelf marks. For Hebrew texts in the Warner collection, see M. Steinschneider, *Catalogus codicum Hebraeorum Bibliothecae Academiae Lugduno-Batavae*. Leiden: Brill, 1858.

Leipz. (Lips.)—K. Vollers, *Katalog der islamischen, christlich-orientalischen, jüdischen und samaritanischen Handschriften der Universitätsbibliothek zu Leipzig* / mit einem Beitrag von J. Leipoldt. Leipzig: Harrassowitz, 1906. See also Lips.

Leipz. S.S.—Leipziger Semitische Studien.

Leningr[ad] AM—See Pet. AM.

Leningrad f. Gregoire IV (Leningr. Bibl. Gr[eg]. IV)—See Pet. libr. Grig. IV.

Leningrad Fond D. Greg. IV—See Pet. libr. Grig. IV.

Leningrad, Öff. Bibl.—Leningrad Public Library, see Pet.

Leningr[ad] Un.—See Pet. Un.

Leningrad Un. Girgas—Probably: I. Kratchovsky, Vostochniye rukopisi iz sobranii͡a V.F. Girgasa, in: *Dokladij Akademii Nauk SSSR* [series] B, 1927, 162–65.

Leningr. Chr. Vost.—Unresolved.

Lévi-Pr.—See one after next entry.

Lévi Provençal (collection of)—Not in Roper.

Lévi-Prov[ençal]—See next entry.

Lévi-Prov[ençal], *Hist.* [*des Chorfa*] (– *Hist. d. Ch.*)—E. Lévi-Provençal, *Les historiens des Chorfa*: essai sur la littérature historique et biografique au Maroc du XVIe au XXe siècle. Paris: Larose, 1922.

Lib. Cl.—See al-Suyūṭī, *Ḥuff.*

Library Dahdāh—See Daḥdāḥ.

Library of Egypt—See Cairo[1] and Cairo[2], with J. Schacht, *Aus den Bibliotheken von Konstantinopel und Kairo* and idem, *Aus Kairiner Bibliotheken*.

Library of the Maronites (Aleppo)—Roper III 187, al-Maktaba al-Mārūnīya.

Library of the sultan (Fez)—Not in Roper.

Library Najafābādī—See Najafābādī.

Lindes. [Crawford] (*Lindes.* Ar.)—J.L. Lindsay (23rd Earl of Crawford) and M. Kerney, *Bibliotheca Lindesiana: Hand-list of Oriental Manuscripts : Arabic, Persian, Turkish.* Aberdeen: Aberdeen University Press, 1898.

Lips. (Leipz.)—E.W.R. Naumann, H.L. Fleischer and F. Delitzsch, *Catalogus Librorum Manuscriptorum qui in Bibliotheca Senatoria Civitatis Lipsiensis Asservantur—Codices orientalium linguarum*, Grimma: Gebhardt, 1838. See also Leipz.

Lit.–Literatur, literature, littérature.

lit. hist.—literarisch-historisch.

Littmann, *Princeton Exp.*—E. Littmann, *Publications of the Princeton Expedition to Abyssinia*, vol. 3: Lieder der Tigrē Stämme–Tigrē Text. Leiden: Brill, 1913.

Löfgren—O.A.V. Löfgren (ed.), *Taʾrīkh thaghr ʿAdan*. 3 vols. Uppsala etc.: Almqvist & Wiksell etc., 1936–50.

Longrigg—S.H. Longrigg, *Four Centuries of Modern ʿIrāq*. Oxford, 1925.

Louvain—See next entry.

Löwen (Lowen, Louvain)—H. Heffening, Die islamischen Handschriften der Universitatsbibliothek Löwen (Fonds Lefort serie B and C) mit einer besonderen Wurdigung der Mudauwanahdschr. des iv. v. x. xi Jahrhs, in *Le Muséon* 50, 85–100.

Lubāb—See Ibn al-Athīr, [*al-*]*Lubāb*.

Lubb—Al-Suyūṭī, *Lubb al-lubāb fī taḥrīr al-ansāb*.

[Lugd.] Bat.—See Leiden[1].

Lughat al-ʿArab—*Lughat al-ʿArab / Majalla shahriyya adabiyya ʿilmiyya taʾrīkhiyya*. Baghdad, 1911–14, 1927–31 (1329–32, 1345–49).

Lund—C.J. Tornberg, *Codices orientales bibliothecae regiae universitatis Lundensis*, Lund 1850. *Supplementa*, Lund 1853.

Luzac and Co., List (Luzac's Short List)—*Luzac's Oriental List and Book Review*.

Luzac, *Bibl. Or.* (– *Bull. Or.*)—*Bibliotheca Orientalis*. A sales catalogue of Luzac & Co. (London), published in the late-nineteenth and early twentieth century. Individual issues are very hard to come by.

Lyall, *Mufaḍḍ*[*l*]. (*Muf*[*aḍḍ*]. transl.)—Ch.J. Lyall (ed., transl.), *The* Mufaḍḍalīyāt, *an anthology of ancient arabic Odes compiled by al-Mufaḍḍal son of Muḥammad according to the recension and with the commentary of Abū Muḥammad al-Qāsim ibn Muḥammad al-Anbārī*. 2 vols. Oxford, 1918–21; vol. 3 Indices, by A.A. Bevan, London–Leiden, 1924.

Lyall, *Transl.*—See previous entry, vol. 2.

Maʿārif (*al-Maʿārif*)—*Maʿārif*, journal published by the Darul Musannefin Shibli Academy in Azamgar, India since 1916 and still in operation. All the issues of this journal can be consulted via www.shibliacademy.org (accessed December 2017).

Maʾāthir al-kirām—Mīr Ghulām ʿAlī Āzād Bilghrāmī, *Maʾāthir al-kirām, mawsūm beh Sarw-i āzād*. 2 vols. Agra: Maṭbaʿ-i Mufīd-i ʿĀmm, 1920 (vol. 1), Lahore: Maṭbaʿ-i dukhāni-yi Rifāh-i ʿĀmm, 1913. Persian.

Macdonald (collection of, no place)—Not in Roper.

Madr. (Madrid)—F.G. Robles, *Catálogo de los manuscritos árabes exist. en la Biblioteca Nacional de Madrid*, Madrid 1889.

Madr. Aḥmadiyya—Roper III 192, al-Madrasa al-Aḥmadiyya.

Madrasa[t] Fāḍil Khān (Mashhad)—Not in Roper. Probably: al-Madrasa al-Fāḍiliyya, q.v.

Madrasa of Samarra (library)—Roper IV 256, Maktabat al-Shaykh Aḥmad al-Rāwī (al-Madrasa al-ʿIlmiyya al-Dīniyya) ?

Madrase Nūr Aḥmadiyya (library of, Aleppo)—See Aleppo Aḥmadiyya.

Madr. Der.—H. Derenbourg, *Notes critiques sur les manuscrits arabes de la bibliothèque Nationale de Madrid*. Paris: Maurin, 1904.

Madrid, Gg.—See Derenbourg, *Notes critiques sur les manuscrits arabes de la bibliothèque Nationale de Madrid* (Paris: Maurin, 1904), p. 5 et passim.

Madr. J[unta]—J. Ribera and M. Asin, *Manuscritos árabes y aljamiados de la Biblioteca de la Junta*, Madrid 1912.

Madr. Sipāhsālār—See Teh. Sipāhs.

Madr. T[etw].—D.E. Lafuente y Alcantara, *Catálogo de los codices Arábigos adquiridos en Tetouan por el gobierno de S. M.*, Madrid: Imprenta Nacional, 1862.

Mag[azin] enc.—*Magasin encyclopédique, ou Journal des sciences, des lettres et des arts.*

Mag. für die Lit. des In-u. Auslandes—*Magazin für Literatur des In- und Auslandes.*

Mağm.—Majmūʿa

Magnesia—Manisa.

Mahā—Aḥmad Zakī Abū Shādī, *Mahā, qiṣṣa gharāmiyya sharqiyya*.

Maḥbūbjān Library (Hyderabad)—See *JRASB* 1917, p. lxxxiii, no. (16): Nawwāb Maḥbūb Yār Jang Library, Sayfābād Road (= Roper I 400, Nawab Faylsuf Jung?).

Mahdī Āl al-Sayyid Ḥaydar al-Kāẓimī—See next entry?

Mahdī ʿAbdallāh al-Sayyid Ḥaydar al-Kāẓimī (library of, no place)—Not in Roper.

Mahdī ʿImād al-Fihrisī (library of, Mashhad)—Not in Roper; see also al-Muḥaddith al-ʿImād al-Fihrisī and ʿImād al-Fihrisī.

Maḥmūd Ef.—Roper III 348, Hacı Mahmud Efendi.

Maḥmūd Efendi al-Jazāʾirī (collection of, no place)—Not in Roper.

Maḥmūd P.—Roper III 349, Mahmud Paşa.

Mai, *Nova Coll.* IV—A. Mai, *Scriptorum veterum nova collectio, e Vaticanis codicibus edita*, vol. IV.2. Rome: Biblioteca Apostolica Vaticana, 1831.

Majālis al-muʾminīn—Nūrallāh b. al-Sayyid al-Sharīf b. Nūrallāh al-Ḥusaynī al-Marʿashī al-Shushtarī (Tustarī), *Majālis al-muʾminīn*.

Majāni 'l-adab—L. Cheikho, *Majāni 'l-adab fī ḥadāʾiq al-ʿArab*. 7 vols. Beirut: Maṭbaʿat al-ābāʾ al-Yasūʿiyyīn, 1882–83 (many reprints).

Majmūʿa (sometimes: *majmūʿ*)—Does not refer to a single work but to [the title of] a collection of treatises that were jointly published.

Makr[am] (Mukr.)—See Cairo Makram.

Maktaba Ḥabībiyya (no place)—Not in Roper.

Maktaba Ḥusayniyya (no place)—See al-Maktaba al-Ḥusayniyya.

Makt[aba] Maḥmūdiyya—Roper III 26, Maḥmūdiyya Library (Medina).

Maktaba Sindiyya—Not in Roper.

Maktabat al-Ḥaram—Possibly: Roper III 16, Maktabat al-Ḥaram al-Makki al-Sharīf, or Roper III 24, Maktabat al-Ḥaram al-Nabawī (Medina).

Maktabat al-Madīna—Not in Roper.

Maktabat Āl Qaṭina (Jerusalem)—Not in Roper.

Maktabat Franki Maḥall—Not in Roper.

Maktabat Ḥabīb (no place)—Not in Roper (= Maktaba Ḥabībiyya ?).

Maktabat Ḥasan Ḥusnī ʿAbd al-Wahhāb (Tunis)—Roper II 259, ʿAbd al-Wahhāb Ḥasan Ḥusnī.

Maktabat Khalīlallāh (Madras)—Not in Roper. See also Makt. Khalīlallāh al-Madrasī.

Maktabat Maḥmūd [Muḥammad P.]—Not in Roper (= Makt[aba] Maḥmūdiyya ?).

Maktabat Ribāṭ Sayyid ʿUthmān (Medina)—Roper III 26, Ribāṭ ʿUthmān b. ʿAffān.

Maktabat Saqyzly (Medina)—Not in Roper.

Maktabat Shaykh al-Isl[ām] (Medina)—Roper III 26, ʿĀrif Ḥikmat Library.

Makt. al-Awqāf (Baghdad)—Roper II 7, Maktabat al-Awqāf al-Markaziyya.

Makt. al-Ḥaram al-Makkī—Roper III 16, Maktabat al-Ḥaram al-Makki al-Sharīf

Makt. al-Madīna—Not in Roper.

Makt. al-Maḥmūdiyya (Medina)—See Makt[aba] Maḥmūdiyya.

Makt. ʿĀrif Ḥikmat (Medina)—Roper III 26, ʿĀrif Ḥikmat Library.

Makt. Ḥalw.—Al-Maktaba al-Ḥalwiyya (Aleppo). Not in Roper.

Makt. Khalīlallāh al-Madrasī (Madras)—Not in Roper. See also Maktabat Khalīlallāh.

Makt. Maḥm.—See Makt[aba] Maḥmūdiyya.

Makt. Muḥ. (Medina)—See Makt[aba] Maḥmūdiyya.

Makt. Ribāṭ ʿUthmān—See Maktabat Ribāṭ Sayyid ʿUthmān.

Makt. Saʿd (no place)—Not in Roper.

Makt. Shaykh al-Isl[ām] (Medina)—Roper III 26, ʿĀrif Ḥikmat Library.

Makt. Sind[iyya]—Not in Roper. See also Maktaba Sindiyya.

Makt. Zanjān—Roper I 550, Muḥammad ʿIzz al-Dīn Ḥusaynī Musavī Collection ?

M. al-Ḥifnāwī, *Taʿrīf al-khalaf*—See al-Ḥifnāwī, *Taʿrīf al-khalaf*.

Manch.—A. Mingana, *Catalogue of the Arabic Manuscripts in the John Rylands Library*, Manchester 1934.

Manīnī—Abu ʾl-Najāh al-ʿUthmānī al-Manīnī, *al-Fatḥ al-wahbī ʿalā taʾrīkh Abī Naṣr al-ʿUtbī*.

Manisa Küt.—Roper III 380, Manisa İl Halk Kütüphanesi.

Mansī—Aḥmad Abu ʾl-Khiḍr Mansī, *Faraḥ Anṭūn, naqd wa-taḥlīl ʿala ʾl-nasq al-Ūrubbī al-ḥadīth*. Cairo: Maṭbaʿat al-Iʿtimād, 1923.

Maq.—Maqāla.

Maqqarī (Maqq.; Maqqārī is a misprint)—See Al-Maqqarī.

Maqr[īzī] *Khiṭaṭ* (Maqr.)—Al-Maqrīzī Aḥmad b. ʿAlī b. ʿAbd al-Qādir, *al-Mawāʿiẓ wal-iʿtibār fī dhikr al-khiṭaṭ wal-āthār*.

Maqrīzī, *Sultans maml.*—See Quatremère.

Marçais, *Takr.*—W. Marçais, *Textes arabes de Takroûna*. 2 vols. in 9 tomes. Paris: Bibliothèque de l'École des Langues Orientales Vivantes, 1925–61.

Margoliouth, *Early Development*—D.S. Margoliouth, *The Early Development of Mohammedanism*. London: Williams and Norgate, 1914.

Marquart, *Streifz[üge]*—J. Marquart, *Osteuropäische und ostasiatische Streifzüge*. Leipzig: Weicher, 1903.

Marseille (Mars.)—M. l'abbé Albanés, *Catalogue général des manuscrits des bibliothèques publiques de France, Départements, Tome VI*, 437–482 Marseille, Paris 1892.

Marzubānī—See al-Marzubānī.

Mashāhīr [al-sharq]—See Zaydān, *Mashāhīr al-sharq*.

Mashh. (Meshhed, Meshh.)—*Fihrist-i kutubkhāni-yi mubāraka Āsitān-i quds-i Riḍawī*, Mashhad, 1345 AH, with O. Spies in *Festschrift E. Littmann*, 89–100, and Ivanov, *JRAS* 1920, 535–63. The title is the title given in GAL. The actual title is: Oktai et al., *Fihrist-i kutub-i kitābkhāna-yi mubāraka-yi Āstān-i quds-i Riḍawī* (title varies from vol. 4 onwards). 13 vols. Mashhad, 1305–72 HSh (1926–1993), of which only 4 volumes had been published by the time the last volume of GAL's second edition was published, which was vol. 2, in 1949. The Roman numbers to which Brockelmann refers, e.g. 'Mashh. V, 121,$_{393/4}$' (Suppl. 1, 640 [620 German ed.]) refer to the sections into which the subjects were divided in volumes 1–3 (17 sections [*faṣl*] in all).

Mashh. al-sharq—See *Mashāhīr al-sharq*.

Maspero—G. Maspero, *Guide du visiteur au Musée du Caire*. Cairo: IFAO, 1902.

Massignon, 185–351 (Supplement 1, 343)—This is a mistake. In Massignon, *Rec. de textes* 211, reference is made to pages 158–351 of a Persian manuscript of al-Malaṭī's *Tanbīh*, a text that is referred to in detail a on pp. 218–20 of this same work.

Mass[ignon]—Massignon, Esquisse d'une bibliographie qarmaṭe, in *Or. St. Browne*, 329–33.

Massignon, *Bibl. Hall.* (*Bibl. [Ḥallāj]*)—Idem, *Bibliographie hallagienne*, in his *La passion d'al-Hosayn-Ibn-Mansour al-Hallaj*, vol. 2, chapter XV.

Massignon, *Essai*—L. Massignon, *Essai sur les origines du lexique technique de la mystique musulmane*. Paris: Geuthner, 1922.

Massignon, *Ḥallāj*—Idem, *La passion d'al-Hosayn-Ibn-Mansour al-Hallaj* : martyr mystique de l'Islam, exécuté à Bagdad le 26 Mars 922. Étude d'histoire religieuse. 2 vols. Paris: Geuthner, 1922.

Massignon, *Ḥallāj: Ṭawāsīn*—See idem, *Ṭāwasīn*.

Massignon, *Pass*[*ion*]—See second-previous entry.

Massignon, *Rec. de textes* (– *Textes* [*inéd.*], Mass. *T.*)—Idem, *Recueil de textes inédits concernants l'histoire de la mystique en pays d'islam* (Collection de textes inédits relatifs à la mystique musulmane 1). Paris: Geuthner, 1929.

Massignon, *Ṭawāsīn*—*Al-Hallaj* Kitāb al-ṭawāsīn : texte arabe publié pour la Ière fois d'après les manuscrits de Stamboul avec une introduction critique etc. par L. Massignon, Paris 1912 (transl. *Pass.* II, 830ff.).

Massignon, *Textes* (Mass. *T*[*extes*])—See Massignon, *Rec. de textes.*

Mawlānā Khalīlallāh al-Madrasī Library (Hyderabad)—Not in Roper, see Makt. Khalīlallāh al-Madrasī (where the collection is said to be in Madras).

Mawlawī ʿAbdallāh (collection of, Howrah)—Not in Roper.

Maydānī (Mayd.)—See al-Maydānī, *Amthāl.*

Maydānī, *Amthāl*—See al-Maydānī, *Amthāl.*

Mayy—Mayy (Maryam) Ziyāda.

M. b. Cheneb, *Idjāza*—See Muḥammad b. Cheneb.

Mecca—Not in this way in Roper, but see ibid. vol. III, 16ff.

Mecca Fayḍ.—Al-Maktaba al-Fayḍiyya (Mecca). Not in Roper.

Mecca Ḥabībiyya—Not in Roper.

Mecdī (Mejdī)—Meḥmed Efendi Mecdī, *Ḥadāʾiḳ uş-şaḳāʾiḳ* (Turkish translation of *ShN*, with additions). Istanbul, 1269 (1852).

méd.—médecine.

Med. (Med. Laur., Medic.)—See Flor. Ass.; in some cases, Med. may also be short for Medina.

Medina, Ārif Ḥikmat— See Makt. ʿĀrif Ḥikmat (Medina).

Medina Makt. al-Sāda—Not in Roper.

Mejdī—See Mecdī.

Meḥmed Pāshā (library [of], Istanbul)—Could refer to several collections in Istanbul, for which see Roper IV, Index 'Mehmed, Tırnovalı' and following.

Mehren, *Rhetorik* (– *Rhet.*, Mehren)—A.F. Mehren, *Die Rhetorik der Araber nach den wicht. Quellen dargestellt und mit angef. Textauszügen nebst einem literatur-geschichtl. Anhange versehen.* Copenhagen–Vienna, 1853.

Mejdī—See Mecdī.

Mél.—Mélanges.

Mél. Derenbourg—See Goldziher.

Melik Library (Tire)—Not in Roper.

Mél. Or.—*Mélanges orientaux*. Paris: Leroux, 1883.

Mél. U.J.—See MFO.

Mém. [*H.*] *Basset*—*Mémorial Henri Basset*: Nouvelles études nord-africaines et orientales publiées par l'Institut des Hautes-Études Marocaines. Paris: Geuthner, 1928.

Mercier, *Parure* (– *Trad.*)—L. Mercier, *La parure des cavaliers et l'insigne des preux.* 2 vols. Paris: Geuthner, 1924. Translation (fr. 'traduction', -> 'trad.') of the author's abridgement of Ibn Hudhayl al-Andalusī's *Tuḥfat al-anfus wa-shiʿār sukkân al-Andalus.*

Meshhed, Meshh.—See Mashh.

Meyerhof, *Ḥunayn*—M. Meyerhof (ed., transl.), *The Book of the Ten Treatises on the Eye Ascribed to Hunain ibn Ishaq (809–877 A.D.)*: the earliest existing systematic textbook of ophthalmology. Cairo: Government Press, 1928.

Mez, *Abulkasim* (Mez on Abulkasim)—A. Mez (ed.), *Abulkasim, ein Bagdader Sittenbild von M. b. A. al-Muṭahhar al-Azdī.* Heidelberg, 1902.

Mez, *Ren.*—A. Mez, *Die Renaissance des Islams.* Heidelberg, 1922.

MF (Supplement 2, 237)—This is a misprint; consulting Babinger in *Der Islam* 11, 76–7, together with GAL 1st edition, vol. 2, p. 225, note 1, it becomes clear that the reference is in fact to Quṭb al-Dīn al-Nahrawālī's *Muntakhab al-taʾrīkh* (see below, *MT*).

Mfḍḍl. (*Mfḍḍ.*)—See *Muf*[*aḍḍ*].

MFO (*MFOB*, *Mél. U.J.*)—*Mélanges de la faculté orientale* [de l'Université Saint Joseph, Beirut].

MFOB—See *MFO*.

MFO V—O. Rescher, Mitteilungen aus Stambuler Bibliotheken, *Mélanges de la faculté orientale* de l'Université Saint Joseph 5 (1912), 489–540.

M. Hartmann, Staatsverträge—M. Hartmann, Die islamisch-fränkischen Staatsverträge (Kapitulationen), in *Zeitschrift für Politik*, vol. 11 (1919), pp. 1–64.

M. Ibr. Libr. (Lucknow)—Not in Roper, see *JRASB* 1917, p. lxxxi, no. (7): Taḥsin Library Chawk, whose owner was, in 1917, a certain Muḥammad Ibrāhīm.

Mich[ael] Syrus—J.B. Chabot (ed. & transl.), *Chronique de Michel le Syrien, patriarche jacobite d'Antioche (1166–1199).* 4 vols. Paris: Leroux, 1899–1910.

Mieli—A. Mieli, *La Science arabe et son rôle dans l'évolution scientifique mondiale*, avec quelques additions de H.P.J. Renaud, M. Meyerhof, J. Ruska. Leiden 1938.

Miftāḥ al-tawārīkh—T.W. Beale, *Miftāḥ al-tawārīkh.* Agra: Messenger Press, 1849 (also Kanpur: Munshi Newal Kishore, 1284/1867–68). Persian.

Mihr Shāh Sulṭān—Roper III 349, Mihrişah Sultan.

Milan, Bibl. Ital.—*Biblioteca Italiana ossia Giornale di Letteratura, Scienze ed Arti.* Milan, 1816–40.

Mirchond, *Hist. reg. pr. Pers.*—B. Jenisch (ed., transl., ann.), *Historia priorum regum Persarum post firmatum in regno islamismum, ex Mohammede Mirchond persiche et latine, cum notis geographico-literariis*, Vienna: Kurzbeck, 1782. Persian and Latin.

Mirchond, *Sāmān*.—M. Defrémery, *Histoire des Samanides, par Mirkhond*, texte persan, traduit et accompagné de notes critiques, historiques et géographiques. Paris: Imprimerie Royale, 1845. Persian and French.

Miskawayh v—Ibn Miskawayh Aḥmad b. Muḥammad b. Yaʿqūb, *Kitāb tajārib al-umam wataʿāqub al-himam*, vol. 5.

Miskawayh, *Fragm. hist. ar.*—Ibn Miskawayh Aḥmad b. Muḥammad b. Yaʿqūb: *Fragmenta historicorum Arabicorum*, 2 vols., ed. M.J. de Goeje & P. de Jong (vol. 1) and M.J. de Goeje (vol. 2). Leiden: Brill, 1869–71.

Mitt. VAG—Mitteilungen der vorderasiatische Gesellschaft.

M.J. Müller, *Beitr.*—M.J. Müller, *Beiträge zur Geschichte der westlichen Araber*. 2 vols. Munich, 1866–78.

M. Krause—See Krause.

M. Murād—See Murād Mollā.

MO 778 (Supplement 2, p. 409)—Ms O. 778 in the Library of the Oriental Faculty of St Petersburg State University. See Pet. Un., with Roper II 694ff, Sanktpeterburgskiĭ Universitet.

Modena—Roper II 90, Biblioteca Estense.

Mollā Čelebī (Molla Celebi)—Roper III 349, Molla Čelebî.

Montfaucon—Bernard de Montfaucon, *Bibliotheca bibliothecarum manuscriptorum nova: ubi, quae innumeris pene manuscriptorum Bibliothecis continentur, ad quodvis literaturae genus spectantia et notatu digna, describuntur et indicantur*. 2 vols. (pp. 1–708, 709–1669). Paris: Briasson, 1739.

Morely—Probably: *The* Táríkh-i Baihaki*: Containing the Life of Masaúd, Son of Sultán Mahmúd of Ghaznín, being the 7th, 8th, 9th and part of the 6th and 10th vols. of the* Táríkh-i Ál-i Saboktakeen *by Abu 'l-Fazl al-Baihaqi*, edited by the late W.H. Morley Esq. and printed under the supervision of Captain W. Nassau Lees, LL. D. Calcutta: College Press, 1862.

Morgenl. Forsch.—H. Derenbourg et al. (eds). *Morgenländische Forschungen*. Festschrift Herrn Professor Dr H.L. Fleischer zu seinem fünfzigjärigen Doctorjubiläum am 4. März 1874 gewidmet von seinen Schülern H. Derenbourg, H. Ethé, O. Loth, A. Müller, F. Philippi, B. Stade, H. Thorbecke. Leipzig: F.A. Brockhaus, 1875.

Moskau Lazarew-Inst.—The Lazarev Institute in Moscow was established in 1815. After various name changes and left without students, it was dissolved in the 1930's and its library transferred to the Lenin State Library in Moscow, now Russian State Library, for which see Roper II 676, Rossiĭskaya Gosudarstvennaya Biblioteka.

Mosul [Dā'ūd] (Mosul D.)—Dā'ūd al-Čelebī al-Mawṣilī, *Kitāb makhṭūṭāt al-Mawṣil*, Baghdad 1927.

M. Rashīd—Meḥmed Rashīd, on which see Schacht, Von den Bibliotheken in Stambul und Umgegend (ZS 5/1927), 291 (XVI. Millet Kütüphanesi, *48 Meḥmed Rašīd). Not in Roper.

MS (Ms.)—Manuskript, manuscript, manuscrit, manuscriptus.

M[s]. or. [fol., ...]—See Berl. Ms. or. [fol., ...].

MSOS Was. (*MSOS Westas. St., MSOS As., MSOS*)—*Mitteilungen des Seminars für Orientalische Sprachen, Westasiatische Studien.*

MSS (Mss, mss)—Manuskripte, manuscripts, manuscrits, manuscripti.

MSt.—See Goldziher, *MSt.*

MT—Al-Nahrawālī[-nī] Muḥammad b. Aḥmad b. Muḥammad, *Muntakhab al-taʾrīkh.*

M[uḥammad] Ṭāhir Brussali—See Brussali.

Muf[aḍḍ]. (*Mufaḍḍaliyyāt, Mufaḍḍl., Mfḍḍl.*)—Al-Mufaḍḍal b. Muḥammad b. Yaʿlā (*sic*) al-Ḍabbī, *al-Mufaḍḍaliyyāt.*

Mufīd al-muftī—ʿAbd al-Awwal [al-]Jawnpurī, *Mufīd al-muftī.* Lucknow, 1326/1908.

Mughulṭāy I—Mughlaṭāy b. Qilič ʿAlāʾ al-Dīn al-Ḥikrī, *al-Wāḍiḥ al-mubīn fī dhikr man ushhida min al-muḥibbīn*, ed. O. Spies (Stuttgart, 1936).

Muḥ. (Muḥibbī)—Al-Muḥibbī Muḥammad al-Amīn b. Faḍlallāh, *Khulāṣat al-athar min aʿyān al-qarn al-ḥādī ʿashar.* 4 vols., C. 1284.

Muḥammad ʿAbdallāh Ḥifnāwī, *Taʿrīf al-khalaf*—See al-Ḥifnāwī, *Taʿrīf al-khalaf.*

Muḥammad [al-]Bashīr, [*al-*]*Yawāqīt*—Muḥammad al-Bashīr Ẓāfir al-Azharī, *al-Yawāqīt al-thamīna fī aʿyān madhhab ʿālim al-Madīna.*

Muḥammad al-Ḥafnāwī [al-Ḥifnāwī], *Taʿrīf al-khalaf*—See al-Ḥifnāwī, *Taʿrīf al-khalaf.*

Muḥammad ʿAlī (collection of Prof. –, Hyderabad)—Not in Roper (= Muḥammad ʿAlī Ḥusayn Library ?).

Muḥammad ʿAlī al-Khwānsārī [al-Najafī] (library/collection of, Najaf)—Not in Roper.

Muḥammad ʿAlī [al-]Sabzawāri (library of, Kāẓimiyya)—Not in Roper.

Muḥammad ʿAlī al-Urdubādī (library of, Najaf)—Not in Roper.

Muḥammad ʿAlī Bāriʾ (library, Lucknow)—Not in Roper, see *JRASB* 1917, p. lxxx, no. (1), Mawlavī ʿAbd al-Bārī Library.

Muḥammad ʿAlī [Bashīr] Library (Firangi Maḥall, Lucknow)—See previous entry.

Muḥammad ʿAlī Hibat al-Dīn al-Shahrastānī (library of, no place)—Not in Roper.

Muḥammad ʿAlī [Ḥusayn] Library (Hyderabad)—Not in Roper, see *JRASB* 1917, p. lxxxiii, no. (17), Mawlavī Sayyid ʿAlī Ḥusayn Bilgrāmī Library, Kūchah-i Madrasah-i Aʿizzah.

Muḥammad ʿAlī Khān Libr. (Hyderabad)—See previous entry. Not in Roper.

Muḥammad ʿAlī Khwānsārī—See Muḥammad ʿAlī al-Khwānsārī.

Muḥammad ʿAlī Library (Firangi Maḥall)—Not in Roper, see *JRASB* 1917, lxxx, no. (1), Mawlavī ʿAbd al-Bārī Library.

Muḥammad ʿAlī Sabzawārī (library of, Kāẓimiyya)—See Muḥammad ʿAlī al-Sabzawāri.

Muhammad al-Qazwīnī, *Aḥsan al-athar*—See Muḥammad Ṣāliḥ al-Kāẓimī.

Muḥammad al-Samāwī (library of, Najaf)—Roper II 40, Shaykh Muḥammad al-Samāwī.

Muḥammad al-Ṭihrānī (library of, Najaf)—Not in Roper.

Muḥammad al-Ṭihrānī (library of, Samarra)—Not in Roper.

Muḥammad al-Ṭihrānī al-ʿAskari (library of, no place)—Not in Roper (= Roper IV 229, Mehdī Muḥammad al-ʿAskari ?).

Muḥammad Bāqir, grandson of Muḥammad Kāẓim al-Yazdī al-Ṭabāṭabāʾī (library of, no place)—Not in Roper.

Muḥammad Bashīr, [*al-*]*Yawāqīt*—See Muḥammad al-Bashīr, *al-Yawāqīt*.

M[uḥammad] b. Cheneb, *Idjāza* (Ben Cheneb *Idjāza*)—Mohammed ben Cheneb, Étude sur les personnages mentionnés dans l'*idjāza* du cheikh ʿAbd al-Qādir al-Fāsy, in *Actes du xivème Congrès International Des Orientalistes* (*Alger, 1905*), Troisième partie (suite): langues musulmanes (arabe, persan et turc), 168–560. Paris: Leroux, 1908 (off-print Paris: Leroux, 1907).

Muḥammad Bek Āṣaf (library of, Cairo)—Not in Roper.

Muḥammad Ben Cheneb (collection of, Algeria)—Not in Roper.

Muḥammad b. Ṣādiq, *Nujūm al-samāʾ*—Muḥammad ʿAlī b. Ṣādiq al-Kashmīrī, *Nujūm al-samaʾ fī tarājim al-ʿulamāʾ* (Persian). Lucknow, 1303 (1885–6).

Muḥammad Hidāyat Ḥusayn Library (India 1912–14)—Read: Muḥammad Hidāyat Ḥusayn (Bibliotheca Indica, 1912–14)

Muḥammad Ḥusayn Library (Hyderabad)—See Muḥammad ʿAlī Ḥusayn Library (Hyderabad).

Muḥammad Khalīl al-Dīn Aḥmad Library (Benares)—Not in Roper.

Muḥammad Liwāsānī (library of, Najaf)—Not in Roper.

Muḥammad Majd al-Dīn al-Shīrāzī (library of, no place)—Read: al-Mujaddid al-Shīrāzī, not in Roper.

Muḥammad Muḥaddith Library (Rampur)—Not in Roper.

Muḥammad Muḥsin—See *al-Dharīʿa*.

Muḥammad Muḥsin (collection of, no place)—This is the author of *al-Dharīʿa*. Not in Roper.

Muḥammad Nāṣir al-Ḥusaynī al-Ṭihrānī (library of, Tehran)—Not in Roper.

Muḥammad Rājā Mahdī (library of, Fayḍābād)—See Rājā Muḥammad Mahdī.

Muḥammad Riḍā b. Yaḥyā al-Tabrīzī (library of, Najaf)—Not in Roper.

Muḥammad Riḍā Kāshif al-Ghiṭāʾ (library of, Najaf)—Not in Roper.

Muḥammad Ṣadr al-Dīn (library of, al-Kāẓimayn)—Not in Roper.

Muḥammad Ṣāliḥ, *Lubb al-albāb*—Muḥammad Ṣāliḥ Āl al-Suhrawardī, *Lubb al-albāb, kitāb taʾrīkh wa-adab yaḍummu tarājim ṭāʾifa kabīra min al-ʿulamāʾ wal-udabāʾ wal-siyāsiyyīn wal-shuyūkh wa-dhawi ʾl-buyūtāt fī ʾl-ʿIrāq*, 2 vols. Baghdad 1351/1933.

Muḥammad Ṣāliḥ al-Kāẓimī, *Aḥsan al-athar*—Muḥammad Ṣāliḥ al-Kāẓimī, *Aḥsan al-athar fī man adraknāhu fī ʾl-qarn al-rābiʿ ʿashar wa-huwa silsilat tarājim jamāʿa min mashāhīr al-ʿulamāʾ*. Baghdad, 1352/1923.

Muḥammad Shīr (Shubbar?) (library of, no place)—Muḥammad Shīr not in Roper. For Muḥammad Shubbar, see Roper II 42, Muḥammad Shubbar.

Muḥammad Sulṭān al-Mutakallimīn (library of, Tehran)—Not in Roper.

muhammed.—muhammedanisch(e).

Muḥibbī I, II, ..—Al-Muḥibbi Muḥammad al-Amīn b. Faḍlallāh, *Khulāṣat al-athar fī aʿyān al-qarn al-ḥādī ʿashar*.

Muḥsin al-Amīn al-ʿĀmilī (library of, Damascus)—Roper III 207, Muḥsin al-Amīn al-ʿĀmilī al-Ḥusaynī Collection.

Mujaddid al-Shīrāzī—See al-Mujaddid al-Shīrāzī.

Mukhtār—Muḥammad Badr al-Dīn al-ʿAlawī (ed.), *al-Mukhtār min shiʿr al-Bashshār, ikhtiyār al-Khālidiyayn wa-sharḥuhu li-Abī Ṭāhir Ismāʿīl b. Aḥmad b. Ziyādatallāh al-Tujībī al-Barqī*. Aligarh 1935.

Mukhtārāt al-shuʿarāʾ (*Mukhtārāt*)—Hibatallāh b. ʿAlī b. al-Shajarī, *Dīwān mukhtārāt al-shuʿarāʾ*.

Mukr[am]—See Makram.

Müller—See A. Müller.

Munajjim Bāshī—Munajjim Bāshī Aḥmad b. Luṭfallāh al-Salanīkī, *Tarīkh al-duwal*.

Munich—J. Aumer, *Die arabischen Handschriften der K. Hof- und Staatsbibliothek in München*. Munich, 1866; idem, *Die persischen Handschriften der K. Hof- und Staatsbibliothek in München*. Munich, 1866.

Munich Gl.—E. Gratzl, Die arabischen Handschriften der Sammlung Glaser in der Königlichen Hof-und Staatsbibliothek zu München, in *Mitteilungen der Vorderasiatischen Gesellschaft* vol. 21 (1916), 195–200.

Munich Pers.—See Munich.

Munk, *Mél*[*anges*]—S. Munk. *Mélanges de philosophie juive et arabe*. Paris: Franck, 1859.

Mur.—Al-Murādī Muḥammad Khalīl b. ʿAlī b. Muḥammad b. Muḥammad Murād, *Silk al-durar fī aʿyān al-qarn al-thānī ʿashar*. 4 vols., Cairo, 1291/1301.

Murādiyya Library (Magnesia [= Manisa])—Not in Roper.

Murād Mollā—Roper III 344, Murat Molla Kütüphanesi. See also Dāmādzāde.

Muradjea d'Ohsson, *Emp. ott.* III, 625—Ign. Mouradja d'Ohsson, *Tableau général de l'empire othoman* : divisé en deux parties dont l'une comprend la législation mahométane, l'autre l'histoire de l'empire othoman, vol. 4.2 (Paris: Imprimerie de Monsieur, 1791), p. 625.

Murtaḍā, *Itḥāf*—Al-Zabīdī Muḥammad Murtaḍā, *Itḥāf al-sāda al-muttaqīn*.

Muṣallā Madr.—Roper III 350, Musalla Medresesi.

Mus. L.—*Le Muséon*, vol. 50.

Muṣṭafā Kuzaybira (collection of, Aleppo)—Roper III 193, Āl al-Kuzbarī ?

Muzhir—See Suyūṭī.

MWJ—*Monatsschrift für Geschichte und Wissenschaft des Judentums*.

Mysore (Tippoo, Tippu, Steward)—Ch. Steward, *A Descriptive Catalogue of the Oriental Library of the Late Tippoo Sultan of Mysore etc.* Cambridge, 1809.

Nachtr.—See Suter, *Nachtr.*

Nadir A. (library, Rampūr; Supplement 2, p. 1001, no. 3)—There is no such library there; what is meant is the Mawlavī ʿAbd al-Bārī Library in Firangī Maḥall, for which see above: Muḥammad ʿAlī Library (Firangi Maḥall).

Nadvi—See al-Nadwī.

Nafaḥāt—Jāmī ʿAlī b. Aḥmad, *Nafaḥāt al-uns wa-ḥaḍarāt al-quds*. Persian.

Nāfiz (Nafiz, Nāfiḏ, Nāfidh, Nafīzī) [P.]—Roper III 350, Nâfiz Paşa (a collection in the Süleymaniye Kütüphanesi).

Nailī Mīrzāzāde Khalīl 363—This seems to be a confusion; for (Aḥmad) Nailī Mīrzāẓade, see Supplement 1, p. 825, line 4, together with the explanations in catalogue Vienna, vol. 3, p. 341ff. 'Khalīl 363' is possibly a reference to the Halil Serîf Paşa collection mentioned in Roper III 329, to which the name Nailī Mīrzāzāde was then accidentally added from some other, handwritten note.

Najaf—Kāẓim Dujayl (*History*, Suppl. 3, 935 'Lodjeizh'), *Maktabāt al-Najaf*, in *Lughat al-Arab* 3, fasc. 11 (1914), 593–600.

Najaf Ṣaḥn—Information on this MS probably stems from Ritter (see Suppl. I, p. 326, line 5).

Najafābādī [Library] (Library Najafābādī)—This refers to an unpublished survey of the holdings of the Najafābādī and other libraries in Najaf in possession of Hellmut Ritter (see Supplement 1, 935), which means that references to this library must be based on notes sent by Ritter from Istanbul. A Najafābādī Library in Najaf is not mentioned in Roper.

Najafāhādhī—Read Najafābādī.

Najjāshī—Read: al-Najashī.

Najm al-Dīn al-Ghazzī, *al-Kawākib al-sāʾira*—Najm al-Dīn al-Ghazzī al-ʿĀmirī Muḥammad b. Muḥammad b. Muḥammad, *al-Kawākib al-sāʾira bi-manāqib ʿulamāʾ al-miʾa al-ʿāshira*.

Nallino, *Battānī*—C.A. Nallino, *Al-Battānī sive Albatenii Opus astronomicum*. 3 vols. Milan: Hoepli, 1899–1907.

Nan.—S. Assemani, *Catalogo dei codici manoscritti orientali della Bibliotheca Naniana*, p. I, II, Padua 1792.

Napl[es]—See Cat. 199–241.

Napoli—Roper II 92, Naples, Biblioteca Nazionale. Brockelmann used the catalogue by L. Buonazia (1880) mentioned in Roper II 93 (contained in Cat., 199–241).

Naqāʾiḍ ed. Bevan (*Naq.* [Bevan])—A.A. Bevan (ed.), *The* Naḳāʾiḍ *of Jarīr and al-Farazdaḳ*. 3 vols. Leiden, 1905–12.

Nashr [*al-qir.*] (*Nashr fi ʾl-q.*)—See Ibn al-Jazarī.

Nashr[*a*] (*Nashara*[*t*])—*Nashra bi-asmāʾ kutub al-mūsīqā wal-ghināʾ wa-muʾallifīhā al-maḥfūẓa bi-Dār al-Kutub al-Miṣriyya*. Cairo, 1932.

Naṣrallāh al-Taqawī—See Sayyid Naṣrallāh al-Taqawī.

Naṣūḥī Gerğāhī (library, Skutari [Üsküdar])—Roper III 350, Nasuhî Dergâhı.

National Library of Egypt—See Cairo[1] and Cairo[2], with J. Schacht, *Aus den Bibliotheken von Konstantinopel und Kairo* ('Schacht I') and idem, *Aus Kairiner Bibliotheken* ('Schacht II').

Naumann—See Lips.

Naw[awī]—See al-Nawawī.

Nawwāb Nūr Ḥasan Library (Lucknow)—Not in Roper.

Nayl—See A[ḥmad] Bābā.

Nayl al-waṭar—See Zabāra.

Nayl al-awṭār—Read: *Nayl al-waṭar*.

Nāẓir Ḥu. Libr. (Lucknow)—Not in Roper, see *JRASB* 1917, p. lxxx, no. (3): Nāṣir Ḥusayn Mujtahid Library, Khajwah.

Nedroma—Not in Roper.

Neubauer, *Hebr. Mss.* 1886—See Bodl. Hebr.

NF—Neue Folge (New Series).

NGGW—*Nachrichten der Königlichen Gesellschaft der Wissenschaften zu Göttingen*, phil.-hist. Klasse.

Nich.—Nicholson.

Nicholson (collection of, no place)—Not in Roper.

Nicholson, *Mystics*—R.A. Nicholson, *The Mystics of Islam*. London: G. Bell and Sons, 1914.

Nicoll-Pusey—See Bodl.

Niʿma al-Ṭarīḥī (library of, no place)—Not in Roper.

Niẓām Hyderabad—Not in Roper.

NM—See al-Qādirī.

NO—*Nūru Osmānīye kütübḫānesinde maḥfūẓ kütübi mevğūdenin defteri*. Istanbul, n.d.

Nöldeke—See Nöldeke, *Gesch. des Qorans*.

Nöldeke, *Beitr*[*äge*]—Th. Nöldeke, *Beiträge zur semitischen Sprachwissenschaft*, Strasburg: Trübner, 1904.

Nöldeke, *Delectus*—Th. Nöldeke & A. Müller (eds.), *Delectus veterum carminum arabicorum*. Berlin: Reuther & London: Williams and Norgate & New York: Westermann, 1890.

Nöldeke, *Enc. Brit.* XVI—Th. Nöldeke, "Moʿallaḳát", in *The Encyclopaedia Britannica*, 9th edition vol. 16 (New York: Charles Scribner's Sons, 1883), 536–539.

Nöldeke, *Gesch. des Qorans* (– *Gesch. des Qor.*, – *Gesch. des Qs*, – *Gesch. d. Qorans* (or *Qorʾāns*), – *Gesch. d. Qor.*, – *Gesch. d. Q.*, Nöldeke)—Idem, *Geschichte des Qorāns*. Göttingen: Dieterich, 1860 (the abbreviation 'Nöldeke' refers to this first edition, e.g in vol. 1, 453). Second edition, in three parts: Th. Nöldeke, *Geschichte des Qorāns*, bearbeitet von F. Schwally, vol. 1. *Über den Ursprung des Qorāns*. Leipzig: Dieterich, 1909; Th. Nöldeke, *Geschichte des Qorāns*, völlig umgearbeitet von F. Schwally, vol. 2. *Die Sammlung des Qorāns*. Leipzig: Dieterich, 1919; Th. Nöldeke, *Geschichte des Qorāns*, 2. völlig umgearb. Aufl., vol. 3. *Die Geschichte des Korantexts* / von G. Bergsträßer und O. Pretzl. Leipzig: Dieterich, 1938. Sometimes the first and second editions are referred to by the numbers 1 and 2 in superscript, e.g. Nöldeke, *Gesch. des Qorans* $^{1}41$, $^{2}53$ (vol. 1, 178).

Nöldeke, *NB* (– *NBsS*)—Idem, *Neue Beiträge zur semitischen Sprachwissenschaft*. Strassburg: Trübner, 1910.

Nöldeke, *Übers. des Ṭab.*—Idem, *Geschichte der Perser und Araber zur Zeit der Sasaniden : aus der Arabischen Chronik des Tabari*. Übersetzt und mit ausführlichen Erläuterungen und Ergänzungen versehn. Leiden: Brill, 1879.

Nöldeke–Schwally, *Gesch.* (Nöldeke–Schwally II)—See Nöldeke, *Gesch. des Qorans*.

Not. et Extr.—*Notices et extraits des manuscrits de la Bibliothèque Impériale*. See also *Prol. Not. et Extr.*

Nouv. Mél. or.—*Nouveaux Mélanges orientaux*. Paris: Leroux, 1886.

Nufhat ool-Yumun—*Nufhat ool-Yumun ; an Arabic Miscellany of Compositions in Prose and Verse, Selected or Original*, by Shuekh Uhmud, Bin Moohummud Shurwanee ool Yumunee. Calcutta: Hindoostanee Press, 1811.

Nujūm al-samāʾ—Mawlavī Mīrzā Muḥammad ʿAlī b. Ṣādiq b. Mahdī al-Kashmīrī, *Nujūm al-samāʾ fī tarājim al-ʿulamāʾ*. 3 vols. and *dhayl*. Lucknow, 1303 (1885–6). Persian.

Nūr al-Dīn—Not in Roper. On the Turkish website Yazmalar (http://www.yazmalar.gov.tr/sayfa/collections/15, accessed December 2017) it is stated that a Nureddin Ağa collection is part of the Süleymaniye Kütüphanesi. So maybe this collection is meant.

Nuwayrī—See al-Nuwayrī.

OB—*Orientalische Bibliographie*, begründet von A. Müller, hsgb. von L. Scherman. Berlin, 1887ff.

Ob 11 or Ob 2—As part of 'Browne Cat. 160, Ob 11' or 'Browne Cat. 160, Ob 2', this refers to Browne Cat., p. 160, O. 6(7), 1 or O. 6(7), 2.

Oberleitner, *Chrest.*—A. Oberleitner, *Chrestomathia Arabica*. 2 vols. Vienna: Schmid, 1823–24.

Oct.—See Berl. Ms. or. oct.

Ode-Vasilieva—K.V. Ode-Vasilieva, *Obraztsy novo-arabskoy literatury* (*Samples of Modern Arabian Literature*) (1880–1925). 2 vols. Leningrad: 1928–29.

OJF Ak. Nauk—Unresolved.

Oppenheim 272—This refers to no. 272 of the Oppenheimer collection of Hebrew manuscripts in the Bodleian Library. See also Hebr. Steinschn., § 352.

Or.—*Orientalia*, nova series (Rome).

Orel—At *History* 1, 202, 'Orel' in 'Orel 207' (Fārābī, A. Logic) must be a misprint for 'Oratoire 107', mentioned below the description of MS no. 898 (catalogue, 155–56). The reference is to treatise no. 1 in that collective volume: 'Abrégé etc.'. For the catalogue, see above 'Hebr. Paris'.

O. Rescher, *Or. Misz.*—O. Rescher, *Orientalische Miszellen.*

Oribasius, *Med. coll.* [*ad Jul.*]—Oribasus, *Collectionum medicarum reliquiae.*

Oribasius, *Syn*[*opsis*]—Idem, *Synopsis ad Eustathium filium.*

Orient.—*Orientalia* (Amsterdam).

Or. St.—See *Or. Stud. Nöldeke.*

Or. Stud. Browne (*Studies Browne*)—Arnold, T.W. and R.A. Nicholson (eds.), *ʿAjab-nāme / A Volume of Oriental Studies Presented to Edward G. Browne*. Cambridge: Cambridge University Press, 1922.

Or. Stud. Nöldeke—See Bezold.

Osm. Müʾell.—Meḥmed Ṭâhir Bursalı, *ʿOs̱mânlı müʾellifleri.* 3 vols. Istanbul: Maṭbaʿa-i ʿĀmire, 1333–43.

O. Spies, *Beitr.*—See Spies, *BAL*.

Oud.—Roper I 436: A. Sprenger, *A catalogue of the Arabic, Persian and Hindustany Manuscripts of the Library of the King of Oudh*, vol. 1 containing Persian and Hindustany poetry. Calcutta: The Baptist Mission Press, 1854.

Ouseley—See Bodl. Ouseley.

Ouseley, *Or. Coll.* I—W. Ouseley (ed.), *The Oriental Collections.* Consisting of original essays and dissertations, translations and miscellaneous papers, illustrating the history and antiquities, the arts, sciences, and literature of Asia, vol. 1. London: Cooper and Graham, 1797.

Overs. over d. kgl. Danske Videnskab. Selsk. Forh.—*Oversigt over det Kongelige Danske videnskabernes selskabs forhandlinger* = *Bulletin de l'Académie royale des sciences et des lettres de Danemark.*

Oxf., Aula Mar. Magd.—Aula Mariae Magdalenae (Magdalen College), Oxford.

Oxf. Hunt.—Refers to the Huntington collection in the Bodleian Library; see Bodl.

Oxford, Cat. Mss. Angl.—E. Bernard & H. Wanley, *Catalogi librorum manuscriptorum Angliæ et Hiberniæ in unum collecti cum indice alphabetico.* 2 vols. Oxford: E Theatro Sheldoniano, 1697.

Oxford, Frazer—Refers to the Arabic manuscripts of James Fraser of the East India Company (d. 1754) in the Bodleian Library, Oxford.

Oxford, Neub.—See Bodl. Hebr.

Pal[at].—See Med.

Palencia—A. Gonzales Palencia, *Historia de la literatura Arabigo-Española.* Barcelona & Buenos Aires: Editorial Labor, 1928.

Palermo—Cat. Ital., 373ff.

Palermo 37, (Cat. 418/9)—The bracketed reference '(Cat. 418/19)' shows that the reference is in fact to the Biblioteca Casanatense in Rome.

Pal. Med. (Pal., Palat.)—See Med.

P. Anastase (MS collection of, Baghdad)—Not in Roper.

Pap. Schott-Reinhardt—See Becker.

Paris (de Slane)—W. McGuckin Baron de Slane, *Bibliothèque Nationale, Département des manuscrits. Catalogue des mss. Arabes.* Paris: Imprimerie Nationale, 1883–95; E. Blochet, Inventaire de la collection de manuscrits musulmans de M. Decourdemanche, in *JA* série 11, vol. 3 (1916), 305–70, 382–423.

Paris, Berb. 7, 10—Paris, Bibliothèque Nationale, *Inventaire sommaire des fonds divers orientaux* : manuscrits en langue berbère (handwritten list, accessible through BN's Gallica web-portal), 3–4, nos. 7 and 8. It seems that GAL's '10' is a misprint. For bibliographical details of other descriptions of the same copies of this text, see also: *Manuscrits, xylographes, estampages : les collections orientales du département des Manuscrits* : Guide, sous la direction d'Annie Berthier (Paris: Bibliothèque Nationale, 2000), p. 28.

Paris Blochet (Paris B): Bibliothèque Nationale. E. Blochet, *Catalogue des manuscrits arabes des nouvelles acquisitions (1884–1924).* Paris: Leroux, 1925.

Paris hebr. (Hebr. Paris)—*Catalogues des manuscrits hébreux et samaritains de la Bibliothèque Impériale.* Paris, Bibliothèque Nationale, Département des manuscrits—Manuscrits orientaux. Paris: Imprimerie Impériale, 1866. The addition 'a.f.' stands for 'ancien fonds'.

Paris, Schef.—See next entry.

Paris, Sch. pers.—E. Blochet, *Catalogue de la collection de manuscrits orientaux, arabes, persans et turcs formée par M. Charles Schefer et acquise par l'état.* Paris: Leroux, 1900.

Paris, Sch. turc.—See previous entry.

Paris, Suppl. pers.—E. Blochet, *Catalogue des manuscrits persans.* 4 vols. Paris: Leroux, 1905–34.

Parma Bibl. It.—See Hammer, *Lettere.*

Parma, de Rossi—See Hebr. de Rossi.

Par. Schefer, pers.—See Paris, Sch. pers.

Patna [Khudābakhsh Oriental Public Library]—Mawlawī ʿAbd al-Ḥamīd, *Fihrist-i dasti-yi kutub-i qalami-yi lāybiriri-yi … Khudābakhsh musammā bi-Miftāḥ al-kunūz al-khafiyya.* 2 vols. Patna: Ṣādiqpūr, 1918–22; V.C.S. O'Connor, *An Eastern Library* / with Two Catalogues of its Persian and Arabic Manuscripts compiled by Khan Sahib Abdulmuqtadir and Abdulhamid. Glasgow: Maclehose & Co., 1920. See also Bank.

Patton, Pref. 81—W.M. Patton, *Aḥmed ibn Ḥanbal and the Miḥna* : a biography of the imâm including an account of the moḥammedan inquisition called the Miḥna, 218–234 AH. Leiden: Brill, 1897. The addition 'Pref. 81' is a mistake; the *Manāqib Aḥmad b. Ḥanbal* is actually mentioned on page 8 of the 'Introductory remarks'.

Pečewī, *Taʾrīkh*—İbrahim Peçevî, *Peçevî Tarihi*. 2 vols. Istanbul: Maṭbaʿa-i ʿĀmireh, 1283 (1866). Turkish.

Pérès—See H. Pérès.

Persian Rieu—See Rieu, Pers. Cat.

Pertev P. (Pertev, Pertew P.)—Roper III 350, Pertev Paşa (Selimiye) (one of the many collections of the Süleymaniye Kütüphanesi).

Pertsch—See Gotha.

Pesh.—Maulavi Abd al-Rahim, *Lubāb al-maʿārif al-ʿilmiyya fī maktabat Dār al-ʿulūm al-Islāmiyya*. Peshawar: Maṭbaʿat Akhbār Aghrah, 1336 (1918).

Pet.—B. Dorn and R. Rost, *Catologue des manuscrits et xylographes orientaux de la Bibliothèque Impériale publique de St. Pétersbourg*. St. Petersburg: Imprimerie de l'Académie Impériale des Sciences, 1852.

Pet. AM—V. Rosen, *Notices sommaires des manuscrits arabes du Musée Asiatique* I. St. Petersburg: Académie Impériale des Sciences, 1881.

Pet. AM Buch.—V.J. Beljajev, *Arabskie rukopisi Bucharskoi kollektsii Aziatskavo Museja Inst. Vost. an SSSR* (Trudi Inst. Vost. II). Leningrad, 1932.

Pet. AM Dorn—B. Dorn, *Das Asiatische Museum der Kaiserlichen Akademie der Wissenschaften zu St. Petersburg*. St. Petersburg: Kaiserliche Akademie der Wissenschaften, 1846.

Pet. AMK—I. Kračkovskii, *Arabskija rukopisi postupivšija v Aziatskii Musei Ross. Akad. Nauk s Kavkazskavo fronta* (Izvestija Ross. Ak. Nauk) St Petersburg 1917. *Opisanie sobranja ar. ruk. pozertwowannich v Az. Musei v 1926*, Izv. Ak. Nauk 1927.

Pet. AM Nov.—These are manuscripts in the Asiatic Museum which were catalogued by C. Salemann (director of the AM from 1890 until his death in 1916) and which he gave a new numbering, starting from 1, with each number preceded by the letters 'Nov.' for 'Novissima'. He published his descriptions piecemeal in various magazine articles. These articles are not recorded in Roper but are referred to in passing on the website of the Institute of Oriental Manuscripts in St Petersburg at http://www.orientalstudies.ru/eng/index.php?option=content&task=view&id=1220 (accessed 27 April 2018). An inventory of these articles would be very welcome.

Pet. As. Mus. Buch—See Pet. A.M. Buch.

Pet. *Bull. Ac.* I, $518,_{3}$—B. Dorn, Ueber die vom wirkl. Staatsrath Chanykov dem asiatischen Museum zugekommenen Sendungen von morgenländischen Münzen und Handschriften, in *Bulletin de l'Académie Impériale des Sciences de Saint-Pétersbourg*, vol. 1 (St. Petersburg: Académie Impériale des Sciences, 1860), 513–536. The correct reference is: $518,_{23}$.

Pet. *Bull. sc.* VII, 368—M. Fraehn, Manuscrits offerts en don à l'Académie par S.E.M. de Bouténeff, in *Bulletin scientifique*, publié par l'Académie Impériale des Sciences de Saint-Pétersbourg, vol. 7 (St. Petersburg: Académie Impériale des Sciences, 1840), 367–68.

Pet. Chanykow (Pet. Chan[ikov])—B. Dorn, *Die Sammlung von morgenländischen Handschriften, welche die Kaiserliche Öffentliche Bibliothek zu St. Petersburg im Jahre 1864 von Herrn v. Chanykov erworben hat*. St. Petersburg: Kaiserliche Akademie der Wissenschaften, 1865.

Pet. Coll. [sc. VI]—See Pet. Ros., second publication.

Pet. Detsk. Selo, *Dokl. Ak. Nauk*—I. Kratchovsky, Les manuscrits orientaux du palais de Cathérine II à Detskoje Selo, in *Dokladij Akademii Nauk SSSR* 1929, 161–8.

Pet. Guirgass—See Leningrad Un. Girgas.

Pet. Instit.—Roper II 679, Institut Vostokovedeniya (Institute of Oriental Studies).

Pet. libr. Grig. IV—Roper II 683, Grēgorios IV.

Pet. Ros.—V. Rosen, *Les manuscrits arabes de l'Institut des langues orientales* (Collections scientifiques de l'Institut des Langues orientales du Ministère des affaires étrangères vol. I). St. Petersburg: Académie Impériale des Sciences, 1877; D. Günzburg, V. Rosen et al., *Les manuscrits arabes (non compris dans le no. 1): karchounis, grecs, coptes, éthiopiens, arméniens, géorgiens et bâbys* (Collections scientifiques de l'Institut des Langues orientales du Ministère des affaires étrangères vol. VI). St. Petersburg: Académie Impériale des Sciences, 1891.

Pet. Un.—C. Salemann and V. Rosen, *Indices alphabetici codicum manu scriptorum persicorum, turcicorum, arabicorum qui in Bibliotheca imperialis literarum Universitatis Petropolitanae adservantur*. St Petersburg: Tipografiі͡a Imperatorskoi Akademii Nauk, 1888; A.A. Romaskevič, Spisok persidskich, turetskotatarskich i arabskich rukopiseĭ Biblioteki Petrogradskogo Universiteta, in ZKV I (1925), 353–71.

Philadelphia—M.A. Simsar, *Oriental Manuscripts of the John Fr. Lewis Collection of the Free Library of Philadelphia*. Philadelphia: The Free Library, 1937.

Pinto—See Flor.

Pococke, *Hist, dyn.*—E. Pococke, *Historia compendiosa dynastiarum* / authore Gregorio Abul-Pharajio, Malatiensi medico, historiam complectens universalem, a mundo condito, usque ad tempora authoris, res orientalium accuratissime describens; Arabice edita, & Latine versa, ab Edvardo Pocockio. 2 vols. Oxford: Hall & Davis, 1663.

Pococke, *Spec. hist. Ar.*—Idem, *Specimen historiae Arabum*. Oxford: Robinson, 1650.

Pons Boigues (Pons B.)—Fr. Pons Boigues *Ensayo bio-bibliográfico sobre los historiadores y geógrafos arábigo-españoles: obra premiada por la Biblioteca Nacional en el concurso público de 1893*. Madrid: Establecimiento Tipográfico de San Francisco de Sales, 1898.

Popper—See Ibn Taghr. (Juynboll).

Pressb.—Roper I 176, Univerzitná knižnica (Bratislava).

Pretzl, Verz.—O. Pretzl, Verzeichnis der älteren Qirāʾātwerke, in *Islamica* VI (1934), 14–47 and 230–45 (section 4 of part A of his Die Wissenschaft der Koranlesung (*ʿIlm al-qirāʾa*), in *Islamica* VI (1934), 1–47, 230–45, 290–331.

Primeurs ar.—See Landberg, *Primeurs ar.*

Princ[e].—E. Littmann, *A List of Arabic Manuscripots in Princeton University*, Princeton–Leipzig 1907.

Princ. Garr.—Philip K. Hitti, Nabih Amin Faris, Butrus Abd-al-Malik (eds.), *Descriptive Catalog of the Garrett Collection of Arabic Manuscripts in the Princeton University Library*. Princeton: Princeton University Press, 1938.

Prol. Not. et extr.—M. [W. McGuckin] Baron de Slane, *Les prolégomènes d'Ibn Khaldoun*, 3 vols. [*Notices et extraits des manuscrits de la Bibliothèque Impériale*, vols. XIX.1, XX.1 and XXI.3], Paris: Imprimerie Impériale 1863–68.

Prüfer—C. Prüfer, Drama–Arabic, in *Encyclopaedia of Religion and Ethics*, IV (Edinburgh: Clark & New York: Scribner, 1911), 876–8.

P. Schwarz (Schwarz)—P. Schwarz, *Der Diwan des ʿUmar ibn Abi Rebiʿa*. 4 vols. in 3 tomes. Leipzig: Dieterich, 1901–09.

Pusey—See Bodl.

Qāḍī ʿAskar—See Dāmādzāde.

Qāḍī ʿIyāḍ, *Shifāʾ*—ʿIyād b. Mūsā al-Yaḥṣubī, *Kitāb al-shifāʾ fī taʿrīf ḥuqūq al-Muṣṭafā*.

Qalq.—ʿQiličʾ ?

Qaračelebīzāde—Roper III 349, Karačelebîzâde Hüsameddin.

Qara Muṣṭafā [P.]—Roper III 329, Kara Mustafa Paşa.

Qarṭās (ed. Tornbeg) (*Rawḍ al-qarṭāṣ*)—ʿAlī b. ʿAbdallāh b. Abī Zarʿ al-Fāsī, *al-Anīs al-muṭrib* (*bi-rawḍ*[*at*] *al-qirṭāṣ*) *fī akhbār mulūk al-Maghrib wa-taʾrīkh madīnat Fās*.

Qaṣ[īdağ(j)ī] S[ulaimān] Sirrī (Sulaimān Qaṣīdağī Sirrī)—Roper III 349, Kasidecizâde Süleyman Sırrı Efendi.

Qāsim b. Ḥasan [Āl] Muḥyi ʾl-Dīn al-Jāmiʿī al-Najafī (library of, no place)—Not in Roper.

Qawala (Qaw[w]āla, Qaw.)—*Fihris Maktabat Qawala*, 4 vols. Cairo: Dār al-Kutub al-Miṣriyya, 1350–51 (1931–33). In Supplement I, 973, Brockelmann seems to say that volumes I and IV were not available to him. Yet he does refer a lot to Qawala I, e.g. *History* 2, 291, and also to other volumes.

Qazwīnī, *Kosm.*—See al-Qazwīnī, *Kosm*[*ographie*].

Qazwīnī, *Taʾr. gūzida*—See Ḥamdallāh Mustawfī.

Qilič ʿA. (Qi̊li̊č ʿA., Qilič ʿAlī, Qylyč ʿA[lī] P.)—*Defteri Kutubkhana-yi Qilič ʿAlī Pāshā*. Istanbul, 1311.

Qiṣṣat al-ʿulamāʾ—Read: *Qiṣaṣ al-ʿulamāʾ*.

QS (*QSt.*)—See *Qu. u. St.*

QSB III (QS III)—*Quellen und Studien zur Geschichte der Mathematik, Astronomie und Physik*, Abt. B. 3 (1936).

QSt. Gesch. d. Nat. u. Med.—*Quellen und Studien zur Geschichte der Naturwissenschaften und der Medizin.*

Qu.—See Berl. Qu.

Quart.—*The British Museum Quarterly.*

Quatremère, *Mamlouks* (– *Maml.*)—É. Quatremère, *Histoire des Sultans Mamlouks, de l'Egypte / écrite en arabe par Taki-Eddin-Ahmed-Makrizi*: traduite en français, et accompagnée de notes philologiques, historiques, géographiques. 2 vols. in 4 tomes. Paris: The Oriental Translation Fund, 1837–45.

Qu. u. St. (*QS, QSt.*)—*Quellen und Studien zur Geschichte der Mathematik, Astronomie und Physik.*

Qylyč ʿA. P.—See Qilič ʿA.

R.—*Risāla*; see also al-Jāḥiẓ.

RA—Sharaf al-Dīn b. Ayyūb al-Nuʿmānī, *Kitāb al-rawḍ al-ʿāṭir fī-mā tayassara min akhbār ahl al-qarn al-sābiʿ ilā khitām al-qarn al-ʿāshir.* MS Berl. 9886.

RAAD—*Revue de l'Académie Arabe de Damas* (*Majallat al-majmaʿ al-ʿilmī al-ʿarabī*).

Rabat—E. Lévi-Provençal, Les manuscrits arabes de Rabat (Bibl. de l'école supérieure de langue arabe et de dialectes berbères de Rabat, vol. VII), Rabat 1922; R. Blachère and H.P.J. Renaud, *Inventaire sommaire des manuscrits arabes acquis par la Bibliothèque Générale du Protectorat Français au Maroc* (*années 1929–30*). Paris: Larose, 1931. Offprint from *Hespéris* 12 (1931), 106–31.

R. Ac.—Reale Accademia, Real Academia.

Raḍīeddīn Ṭāʾūsī—Part II of R. Strothmann, *Die Zwölferschia*: zwei religionsgeschichtliche Charakterbilder aus der Mongolenzeit. Leipzig: Harrassowitz, 1926.

Rāghib, *Muḥāḍ.*—Al-Rāghib al-Iṣfahānī al-Ḥusayn b. Muḥammad, *Kitāb muḥāḍarāt al-udabāʾ al-shuʿarāʾ wal-bulaghāʾ*, also known as *Kitāb al-muḥāḍarāt.*

Rāġib (Rāghib)—*Defteri Kutubkhana-yi Rāġib Pāshā*, Istanbul 1310 AH.

Raḥmān ʿAlī—See *Tadhk. ʿulamāʾi Hind.*

Rājā Fayḍābādī—See next entry ?

Rājā Muḥammad Mahdī [Ṣāḥib] (library of, Faizabad)—Not in Roper.

Rājā of Faizabad (library of)—See previous entry.

Rājā Fayḍābādī (library of)—See second previous entry.

Rāmp[ūr]—M. Ajmal Khān, *Fihrist-i kutub-i ʿarabi-yi mawjud-i kitābkhāna-yi riyāsat-i Rāmpūr*. 2 vols. Rampur: Aḥmadī, 1902–1928.

Ras.—*Rasāʾil.*

Rasadhaneküt (Rasath. Kütüp.)—Roper III 338, Kandilli Rasathanesi Kütüphanesi.

Rashaḥāt—ʿAlī b. al-Ḥusayn al-Wāʿiẓ al-Kāshifī, *Rashaḥāt ʿayn al-ḥayāt.*

Rashīd al-Dīn, ed. Quatremère—M. Quatremère (ed., transl.), *Histoire des Mongols de la Perse*: texte persan, publié, trad. en français, accompagnée de notes et d'un mémoire sur la vie et les ouvrages de l'auteur par Étienne Quatremère. Paris: Imprimerie Royale, 1836.

Ras. Munīr.—*[Al-]Rasā'il [al-]Munīriyya*, title of a collection of texts by Ibn Taymiyya [Aḥmad b. ʿAbd al-Ḥalīm b. ʿAbd al-Salām], published in Cairo in 1343 AH.

Rathjen (collection of, Jerusalem)—Not in Roper.

Rawā'iʿ—See *al-Rawā'iʿ*.

Rawḍ al-qarṭās—See *Qarṭās*.

Rawḍāt al-a'imma—This work could not be traced.

Rawḍāt [al-jannāt] (Rawḍāt al-j.)—Muḥammad Bāqir b. Muḥammad Naqī al-Khwansārī, *Rawḍāt al-jannāt fī aḥwāl al-ʿulamā' wal-sādāt*.

Ravaisse, *Essai*—P. Ravaisse, *Essai sur l'histoire et la topographie du Caire d'après Maqrīzī*. Paris 1890.

R. Buṭṭī—Rafā'īl Buṭṭī, *al-Adab al-ʿaṣrī fi 'l-ʿIrāq al-ʿArabī, Qism al-manẓūm, Juz'* I and II. Cairo: al-Maṭbaʿa al-Salafiyya, 1341/2 1923.

Rec. hist. Crois., Hist. or.—*Recueil des historiens arabes des Croisades*: Historiens orientaux, tome premier. Paris: Imprimerie Nationale, 1872.

Rechtsgel. Mag.—*Rechtsgeleerd magazijn*: tijdschrift voor binnen- en buitenlandsche rechtsstudie (1882–1938).

Ref.—Die Refāʿīja, in H.L. Fleischer, *Kleinere Schriften* (3 vols. Leipzig: Hirzel, 1885–88), vol. 3, 366ff.

Re'īs Muṣṭafā Faiẓullāh—Not in Roper.

Reinaud, *Aboulf.*—*Géogr[aphie] d'Aboulfeda*; texte Arabe, publié d'après les mss. de Paris et Leyde par Reinaud et Mac Guckin de Slane. Paris, 1840. Translation in J.T. Reinaud *Géographie d'Aboulfeda*: I. Introduction generale à la geographie des orientaux, II.1–2 Traduction du texte en arabe et index général. Paris: Imprimerie Nationale, 1848.

Reinaud, *Aboulféda trad.*—See Reinaud, *Aboulf.*, publ. 1848.

Reinaud, *Géographie d'Aboulfeda* [transl.]—See Reinaud, *Aboulf.*, publ. 1848.

Reinaud, *Intr.*—J.T. Reinaud, Introduction generale à la geographie des orientaux, in: *Géographie d'Aboulféda*, I, Paris 1848.

Renaud—H.P.J. Renaud, Additions et corrections à Suter, in *Isis* XVIII, 1932, 166–88; the reference can also be to Escur.[2]

Rend. della Cl. di sc. mor. e stor.—*Rendiconti della Classe di scienze morali e storiche.*

Rescher—If associated with *ShN*, the reference is to O. Rescher's translation of this work, published in Istanbul in 1927; in connection with al-Jāḥiẓ, the reference is—other possibilities excluded—to O. Rescher, *Excerpte und Übersetzungen aus den Schriften des Philologen und Dogmatikers Ǧâḥiẓ aus Baçra [1] : (150–250 H.)*; nebst noch unveröffentlichten Originaltexten. Stuttgart, 1931.

Rescher, *Abr[iss]*—O. Rescher, *Abriss der arabischen Literaturgeschichte*, 2 vols. Stuttgart, 1925–33.

Rescher 64—Idem, Mitteilungen aus Stambuler Bibliotheken I and II, in *ZDMG* 64 (1910), 195–217, 489–528.

Rev.—Revue, Revista.

Rev. Afr.—Revue africaine.

Revan (Revān, Reven, , Rēwan) Köshk (Revankösk)—See Serāi Revān Köshk.

Rev. crit. (*Rev. cr.*)—*Revue critique de l'histoire et de littérature.*

Rev. d'Ég.—Revue d'Égypte.

Rev. de l'hist. des rel.—Revue de l'histoire des religions.

Rev. des trad. pop.—Revue des traditions populaires.

Rev. d. fil. Esp.—Revista de Filosofía Española.

Rewan Köshk—See Revan Köshk.

R. Geyer, *Aʿshā*—R. Geyer, *Gedichte von Abū Baṣīr Maymūn ibn Qays al-Aʿshā nebst Sammlungen von Stücken andrer Dichter des gleichen Beinamens und von al-Musayyab ibn ʿAlas*, printed for the Trustees of the E.J.W. Gibb Memorial Trust (NS VI), London 1928. See also Geyer, *Aʿshā*.

Rhodokanakis, *Or. Stud.* I—N. Rhodokanakis, Über einige arabische Handschriften der öffentlichen Bibliotheken in Konstantinopel, in: Bezold, vol. 1, 385–92.

Riḍā P.—See Riẕā P.

Rieu—See Br. Mus., Br. Mus. Suppl., Br. Mus. Pers., or Br. Mus. Pers. Suppl.

Rieu Add.—See Br. Mus., tome 3, Addenda et corrigenda.

Rieu *Cat.*—See Br. Mus.

Rieu, Pers. Cat.—See Br. Mus. Pers.

Rieu Suppl.—See Br. Mus. Suppl.

Rieu TM (– Turk. Mss.)—Ch. Rieu, *Catalogue of the Turkish Manuscripts in the British Museum*. London, 1888.

Ritter—If cited alone, without page number, the reference is probably to a personal note sent by Hellmut Ritter from Istanbul, on which see the 'Postscript' in vol. 2, 624. But see also the separate bibliography on manuscripts in Turkey, cited ahead of the present inventory.

Ritter, Ruska, *Or. Steinb.* (*Or. St.*)—H. Ritter, J. Ruska, F. Sarre, R. Winderlich, *Orientalische Steinbücher und perzische Fayencetechnik*. Istanbuler Mitteilungen, Heft 3. Istanbul: Universum, 1935.

Riwāq Sayyidnā ʿUthmān (library, Medina)—Not in Roper.

Riẕā P. (Riza P., Riḍā P., Istanbul Un. R.)—Roper III 335, Rıza Paşa.

RMS—Royal Mail Ship.

Robles—See Madr.

Rocznik [*Rosz.*] *Or.—Rocznik Orientalistyczny.*

Rom. Ang[el].—See Angel.

Rom. Cas.—Roper II 102, Biblioteca Casanatense.

Rom[a] Vitt. Em.—Roper II 103, Biblioteca Nazionale Centrale Vittorio Emanuele II.

Roper—G. Roper (ed.), *World Survey of Islamic Manuscripts*, 4 volumes. London: Al-Furqan Foundation, 1992–1994.

Rosen, *Coll.* [*sc.*]—See Pet. Ros., first publication.

Rosen MSS Pers. Inst.—V. Rosen, *Les manuscrits persans de l'Institut des Langues Orientales* (Collections scientifiques de l'Institut des Langues orientales du Ministère des affaires étrangères vol. III). St. Petersburg: Académie Impériale des Sciences, 1886.

Rückert, *Hamasa*—Fr. Rückert, *Hamâsa oder die ältesten arabischen Volkslieder*. 2 vols. Stuttgart: Liesching, 1846.

Ruska, *Tab. smaragd.*—J. Ruska., *Tabula smaragdina; ein Beitrag zur Geschichte der hermetischen Literatur*. Heidelberg: Winter, 1926.

Rustam P. Derskhānesī (Rustam P., Rustem P.)—Roper III 350, Rüstem Paşa.

s.—series, série.

S[.]—Page (Seite).

SA—Sonderausgabe (offprint, special issue).

Saʿāda—Refers either to 1) Ṭāshköprīzāde [Aḥmad b. Muṣṭafā], *Miftāḥ al-saʿāda*, or to 2) Muḥammad b. Muḥammad (Ibn al-Muwaqqit) al-Marrākushī, *al-Saʿāda al-abadiyya fi 'l-taʿrīf bi-mashāhīr al-ḥaḍra al-Marrākushiyya wal-ishāra li-baʿḍ mazāyāha 'l-bahiyya*. 2 vols. Fez, 1336 (1918).

Sachau—E. Sachau, *Verzeichnis de syrischen Handschriften* / zweite Abteilung. Die Handschriften-Verzeignisse der Königlichen Bibliothek zu Berlin, vol. 23. Berlin: Asher, 1899.

Sachau, *Alberuni* (Sachau *India*)—Idem, *Alberuni's India*. 2 vols. London: Kegan Paul, Trench, Trübner & Co., 1910.

Sachau, *Alberunis Chron.* (in vol. 1, p. 545)—Appears the be a contamination between the previous and the next entry.

Sachau, *Chron.*—Idem, *Die Chronik von Arbela, ein Beitrag zur Kenntnis des ältesten Christentums im Orient*, Berlin: Reimer, 1915.

Sachau, *Festschrift*—G. Weil (ed.), *Festschrift Eduard Sachau*: zum siebstigsten Geburtstage gewidmet von Freunden und Schülern. Berlin: Reimer, 1915.

Sachau, *Ibn Saad*—Idem (ed.), *Ibn Saad: Biografien Muhammeds, seiner Gefährten und der späteren Träger des Islams bis zum Jahre 230 der Flucht*, vol. 3.1 *Biografien der mekkanischer Kämpfer Muhammeds in der Schlacht bei Badr* (Leiden: Brill, 1904), Introduction.

Sachau, Introduction to *Ibn Saad* [III.1 (III.a)]—See previous entry.

Sachau, *Rechtsb.*—Idem, *Syrische Rechtsbücher*. 3 vols. Berlin: Reimer, 1907–14.

Saʿd al-Dīn, *Tāj al-taw*[*ārīkh*]—Saʿd al-Dīn b. Ḥasan Hōca Efendi, *Tāj al-tawārīkh*. This is an Ottoman text.

Ṣadr al-Dīn (library of, Mashhad)—Not in Roper.

Ṣaf[*wa*]—Muḥammad Ṣaghīr b. al-Ḥājj al-Ifrānī, *Ṣafwat man intashar min akhbār ṣulaḥāʾ al-qarn al-ḥādī ʿashar*.

Ṣāḥib Mollā—Roper III 335, Sâhib Molla.

Ṣāʿid, *Ṭab.*—Ṣāʿid b. Aḥmad b. ʿAbd al-Raḥmān b. Muḥammad b. Ṣāʿid al-Qurṭubī, *Kitāb al-taʿrīf bi-ṭabaqāt al-umam.*

Salwa—See Al-Kattānī, *Salwa.*

Sam. Vostok—Unresolved.

Samʿānī, *Ansāb*—Al-Samʿānī ʿAbd al-Karīm b. Muḥammad b. Manṣūr, *Kitāb al-ansāb.*

Sánchez Pérez [, *Biogr.*]—J.A. Sanchez Perez, *Biografías de matemáticos arabes que florecieron en España.* Madrid: Maestre, 1921.

Sarāi (Sarāy)—See Serāi.

Sarajevo—Fehim Spaho, *Arapski perzijski i turski rukopisi hravatskih Zemaljskih muzeja u Sarajevu.* Sarajevo: Državna Tiskara, 1942.

Sarkīs—This may refer to 1) Yūsuf Ilyān Sarkīs, *Jāmiʿ al-taṣānīf al-ḥadītha.* Cairo: Maṭbaʿat Sarkīs, 1929ff, or 2) to the title mentioned in the next entry.

Sarkīs, *Muʿjam*—Idem, *Muʿjam al-maṭbūʿāt al-ʿArabiyya wal-muʿarraba.* Cairo: Maṭbaʿat Sarkīs, 1346/1928.

Sarton, *Hist.*—See next entry.

Sarton, *Intr*[*od*]. (Sarton [*Hist.*])—Sarton, *Introduction to the History of Science,* vol. 1: From Homer to Omar Khayyam and vol. 2 (two tomes): From Rabbi Ben Ezra to Roger Bacon. Baltimore: Williams & Wilkins, 1927–31.

Sarwīlī—See Servili.

Sayyid Aḥmad al-Ṣafī al-Najafī (library of, no place)—Not in Roper.

Sayyid Āqā al-Tustarī (library of, no place)—Not in Roper.

Sayyid Muḥammad Aḥmad al-Sabzawārī (library of, no place)—Not in Roper.

Sayyid Naṣrallāh al-Taqawī (library of, Tehran)—Not in Roper.

Sayyid Rājā Muḥammad [Mahdī] (library of, Faizabad)—See Rajā Muḥammad Mahdī.

Sayyid Sulaymān Āqā al-Tustarī (library of, no place)—Not in Roper.

Sbath—P. Sbath, *Bibliothèque de manuscrits Paul Sbath,* 3 vols. Cairo: Friedrich et Co., 1928–34.

S. Bayer. Ak. Ph.-h. Kl. (*S. Bayer.* AW)—*Sitzungsberichte der Bayerischen Akademie der Wissenschaften,* Philosophisch-historische Abteilung.

SBBA (SBBA ph.-h. Kl.)—*Sitzungsberichte der Bayerischen Akademie der Wissenschaften,* philosophisch-philologische und historische Klasse.

SB *Erl.*—See *SBPhMS Erl.*

SB *Ph. med. Soz. Erlangen*—See *SBPhMS Erl.*

SBPhMG Erl.—See *SBPhMS Erl.*

SBPhMS Erl.—*Sitzungsberichte der physikalisch-medizinischen Sozietät zu Erlangen.*

SBPMS *Erlangen*—See previous entry.

SBSGW—See *B.V.S.A.W.*

SBWA—See SB *Wien. Ak. phil.-hist. Cl.*

SBWA, *phil.-hist. Cl.* [*Kl.*]—See SB *Wien. Ak. phil.-hist. Cl.*

SB *Wien. Ak. phil.-hist. Cl.*—*Sitzungsberichte der philosophisch-historischen Classe der kaiserlichen Akademie der Wissenschaften.*

Schacht, 60 (Supplement II, p. 974 no. 50, 978 no. 101), 53 (Supplement II, p. 974 no. 530, 979 no. 105), 53,56 (Supplement II, p. 979 no. 105)—Unresolved.

Schacht, 344—In Supplement I, p. 288, this reference is to Schacht I, p 16, 3b, where al-Marwazī's death date is given as 344 AH.

Sch. I, II, or III—See Schacht I, II, or III.

Schacht I—J. Schacht, *Aus den Bibliotheken von Konstantinopel und Kairo.* Abhandlungen der Preußischen Akademie der Wissenschaften, Philosophisch-Historische Klasse, 1928 no. 8. 75 pp. Berlin: Verlag der Akademie der Wissenschaften, 1928.

Schacht II—Idem, *Aus Kairiner Bibliotheken.* Abhandlungen der Preußischen Akademie der Wissenschaften, Philosophisch-Historische Klasse, 1929 no. 6. 36 pp. Berlin: Verlag der Akademie der Wissenschaften, 1930.

Schacht III (—Bibl. III)—Idem, *Aus orientalischen Bibliotheken* (III). Abhandlungen der Preußischen Akademie der Wissenschaften, Philosophisch-Historische Klasse, 1931 no. 1. 57 pp. Berlin: Verlag der Akademie der Wissenschaften, 1931.

Schacht, *Rel. Lesebuch*—*Zu meinem Islam-Lesebuch* (Religiongeschichtliches Lesebuch, Heft 16). Tübingen: Mohr (Siebeck), 1933.

Schack—A. Fr. v. Schack, *Poesie und Kunst der Araber in Spanien und Sicilien*, 2 vols. Berlin: Hertz, 1865, 2nd ed. Stuttgart: Verlag der Cotta'schen Buchhandlung, 1877.

Schaf.—See Wüst., *Schaf.*

Scheidii Cat.—*Bibliotheca Scheidiana sive catalogus librorum exquisitissimorum.....* Leiden: Honkoop, 1806.

Schol. *Hudh.*—J.G.L. Kosegarten, *The Hudsailian Poems*, vol. 1 (London: The Oriental Translation Fund, 1854), which contains the Arabic text of Abū Saʿīd al-Sukkarī's *Sharḥ ashʿār al-Hudhaliyyīn.*

Schol. *Naq.*—Scholia on the *Naqāʾiḍ*, see *Naqāʾiḍ* ed. Bevan.

Schreiner—M. Schreiner, Zur Geschichte des Aśʿaritenthums, in *Actes du VIII*ème *congrès international des orientalistes* Sect. 1, fasc. 1 (Leiden: Brill, 1891), 79–117.

Schwally—See Nöldeke, *Gesch. des Qorans.*

Schwally on Bayhaqī, *al-Maḥāsin*—F. Schwally (ed.), *Ibrahim ibn Muḥammad al-Bayhaqī*, Kitāb al-Maḥāsin wal-masāwī. Giessen: Ricker (Töpelmann), 1902.

Schwarz—See P. Schwarz.

Script. physiogn.—R. Förster, *Scriptores physiognomonici graeci et latini.* 2 vols. Leipzig: Teubner, 1893.

Sédillot, *Matériaux*—L.P.E.A. Sédillot, *Matériaux pour servir à l'histoire comparée des sciences mathématiques chez les Grecs et les Orientaux.* 2 vols. Paris: Didot, 1845–9.

Šehīd ʿA. (Šehīd ʿA[lī] P[āš(sh)ā], ʿAlī Šehīd P., Shahīd ʿA.P.)—Roper III 350, Şehid Ali Paşa.

Selīm.—*Defteri Kutubkhana-yi Selīmīye.* Istanbul, 1311.

Selīm Ā[ġā]—*Defteri Kutubkhana-yi Ḥājji Selīm Āġā*. Istanbul, 1310. See also Roper III 332 for the collections: Hacı Selim Ağa, Hüdayî, Kemankeş, Nurbanu Sultan, and Yakub Ağa.

Selīmiyya—As stated by Ritter in ZDMG 68, referred to in Supplement 1, p. 481, this library was located between Skutari and Haidar Pasha, on the Asian side of the Bosporus. Not in Roper.

Sem. Kondek.—Unresolved.

Serāi (Sarāi)—Roper III 360, Topkapı Saray Müzesi Kütüphanesi. The addition 'A III' refers to the collection 'III Ahmed' mentioned in Roper, ibid.

Serāi Revan Köshk—Roper III 360, Revan Köşkü.

Serāy—See Serāi.

Servili (Serwīlī, Sarwīlī)—*Defteri Kutubkhana-yi Servili Medrese* Istanbul 1311.

Shāh Ḥabīb Ḥaydar Libr. (Lucknow)—Not in Roper.

Shahīd 'A.P.—See Šehīd 'A. Pāšā.

Shahrast.—See Al-Shahrastānī.

Shahrastānī, ed. Cureton—Al-Shahrastānī Muḥammad b. 'Abd al-Karīm: W. Cureton (ed.), Kitāb al-milal wal-niḥal *or Book of Religious and Philosophical Sects by Muhammad al-Shahrastáni*. 2 vols. London: The Society for the Publication of Oriental Texts, 1842–46.

Shāhzāde—Roper III 350, Şehzâde Mehmed.

Sham'i anjuman—Ṣiddīq Ḥasan Khān, *Sham'i anjuman*. Bhopal: Maṭābiʿ-i Riyāsat-i Bhūpāl, 1293 AH (1876 CE). Persian.

Shams al-ʿulamāʾ Qāḍī 'Ubaydallāh Library (Madras)—Not in Roper.

Shaq. [*al-*]*Nuʿm.*—See *ShN.*

Sharafnāme, ed. Veljaminof—V. Véliaminof-Zernof (ed. & transl.), *Scheref-nameh ou Histoire des Kourdes* : par Scheref, prince de Bidlis. 2 vols. St Petersburg: Académie Impériale des Sciences, 1860–62. Persian & French.

Shawq.—Aḥmad Shawqī, *al-Shawqiyyāt*.

Shaykh 'Abd al-Qādir (collection of, Bombay)—Not in Roper.

Shaykh Aḥmad Bāshaʿyān (collection of, Basra)—Not in Roper; relative of Yāsīn [b.] Bāshayān al-ʿAbbāsī ?

Shaykh 'Alī Kāshif al-Ghiṭāʾ—See 'Alī Kāshif al-Ghiṭāʾ

Shaykh Hādī Kāshif al-Ghiṭāʾ—See Hādī Kāshif al-Ghiṭāʾ.

Shaykh al-Islām (library of, Zanjan)—Possibly: Roper I 550, Muḥammad 'Izz al-Dīn Ḥusaynī Musavī Collection.

Shaykh Mubārak (library of, Damascus)—Not in Roper.

Shaykh Murād 187 (vol. 1, 505)—This is the only reference to 'Shaykh Murād' in the whole of GAL. The reference supposedly not being to the Murād Mollā collection and assuming there is no mistake, it could be that it stands for the Mehmed Ârif and Mehmed Murad collection, now part of the Süleymaniye Kütüphanesi, and mentioned in Roper III, 349.

Shaykh Sidia (library of)—Roper IV 286, Shaykh Sīdīya al-Kabīr (Boutilimit, Mauritania).

ShD—Probably a misprint; see next entry.

ShDh—See Ibn al-ʿImād.

Shiblī, *Sīrat-i Nuʿmān*—ʿAllāmeh Shiblī Nuʿmānī (1857–1914), *Sīrat-i Nuʿmān*. Lahore, n.d. A biography of Abū Ḥanīfa. Urdu.

ShM—See next entry.

ShN ([*al-*]*Shaq. al-Nuʿm.*)—Ṭāshköprīzāde Aḥmad b. Muṣṭafā, *al-Shaqāʾiq al-Nuʿmāniyya fī ʿulamāʾ al-dawla al-ʿUthmāniyya*.

Shükrī Ef. Ālūsīzāde (collection of, Baghdad)—Not in Roper.

Sič. Osm.—Mehmed Süreyya, *Sicilli Osmânî. Tezkire-i Meşâhir-i Osmâniyye*. 4 vols. Istanbul, 1308–15. Turkish.

Sīdī ʿAbd al-Ḥayy al-Kattānī (library of)—See ʿAbd al-Ḥayy al-Kattānī.

Sīdī Ḥammūda (library in the estate of, Constantine)—Not in Roper.

Sijilli ʿUthmānī—See previous entry.

Ṣila—See Ibn Bashkuwāl.

Simonet, *Gloss.*—F.J. Simonet, *Glossario de voces ibericas y latinas usadas entre los Mozarabes*. Madrid: Fortanet, 1888.

Skutari [Kemānkesh, Hudayi]—See Selīm Āġā (located in Üsküdar in Istanbul, formerly known as Scutari).

Smogorzewski collection (Leningrad = St Petersburg)—Not in Roper.

SMS—Seiner Majestät Schiff ('His Majesty's Vessel', prefix used for naval vessels of the German Empire).

Smyrna Milli Kütüb.—Roper III 366, İzmir Millî Kütüphanesi.

Snouck—C. Snouck Hurgronje, *Mekka*. 3 vols. The Hague: Nijhoff, 1888–89.

Snouck Hurgronje, *Verspr. Schr.* (– *Verspr. Geschriften*)—A.J. Wensinck (ed.), *Verspreide geschriften van C. Snouck Hurgronje*. 6 vols. in 7 tomes. Bonn etc.: Schroeder, 1923–27.

Sobernheim, *Mat. Corpus Inscr.* II—M. Sobernheim, *Matériaux pour un corpus inscriptionum arabicarum*. Partie 2, [section 1]: Syrie du Nord. Cairo: Imprimerie de l'Institut français d'archéologie orientale, 1909.

Socin–Br.—*A. Socin's Arabische Grammatik*: Paradigmen, Literatur, Übungsstücke und Glossar / bearbeitet von C. Brockelmann. 5th ed. Berlin: Reuther u. Reichard [et al.], 1904. Many reprints.

Sofia, Narodn. Bibl.—Sofia, Narodna Biblioteka = Sofia, Cyril and Methodius National Library. Roper I 127, SS. Cyril and Methodius National Library.

Solaqz[ade] (Ṣolāqzāde)—Probably: Meḥmed Hemdemi Efendi Solakzade, *Tārīḫ*. Istanbul: Mahmud Bey Matbaası, 1297 (1880). Turkish.

Spies—See next entry.

Spies, *BAL*—O. Spies, *Beiträge zur Arabischen Literaturgeschichte : Juristen, Historiker, Traditionarier*. AKM XIX.3. Leipzig: Brockhaus, 1932.

Spitta—W. Spitta, *Zur Geschichte Abu 'l-Ḥasan al-Ashʿarīs*. Leipzig: Hinrichs, 1876.

Spr.—See Berl. Spr.

ss—Pages, pp. (Seiten).

Stapleton—*Three Arabic Treatises on Alchemy by Muḥammad bin Umail (10th century A.D.)*. Edition of the texts by M. Turāb 'Alī, M.A. Excursus on the writings and date of Ibn Umail with edition of the Latin rendering of the *Mā' al-Waraqī* by H.E. Stapleton, I.E.S., and M. Hidāyat Ḥusain, Shams al-'Ulamā', Ph.D. *Memoirs of the Asiatic Society of Bengal*, vol. XII (Calcutta: Royal Asiatic Society of Bengal, 1933), 1–213.

Steinschn.—Depending on the context, this may refer to: 1) The name Steinschneider, followed by the title of a publication or a reference to some journal; 2) Steinschneider, *al-Fārābī*; 3) Idem, *Hebr. Übers.*; 4) Idem, *Übers.*

Steinschneider—See idem, *Übers.* and *Hebr. Übers.*

Steinschneider, *al-Fārābī*—Idem, *Al-Fārābī, des arabischen Philosophen Leben und Schriften*. St. Petersburg, 1869.

Steinschneider, *Ar. Lit. d. Juden*—Idem, *Die arabische Literatur der Juden* : ein Beitrag zur Literaturgeschichte der Araber, grossenteils aus handschriftlichen Quellen. Frankfurt a/M: Kaufmann, 1902.

Steinschneider, *Cat. libr. Hebr.*—Idem, *Catalogus librorum Hebraeorum in Bibliotheca Bodleiana*. Berlin: Friedlaender, 1852–60.

Steinschneider, *Hebr. Hds.*—See Hebr. Munich.

Steinschneider, Hebr. transl. (Steinschneider; sometimes other items are mentioned first after Steinschneider, so that the link between him and 'Hebr. transl.' is less apparent)—See next entry.

Steinschneider [, *Hebr. Üb(ers)*]—M. Steinschneider, *Die hebraeischen Übersetzungen des Mittelalters und die Juden als Dolmetcher*. 2 vols. Berlin: Kommissionsverlag des bibliografischen Bureaus, 1893.

Steinschneider, *Polem. u. apol. Lit.*—Idem, *Polemische und Apologetische Literatur in Arabischer Sprache zwischen Muslimen, Christen und Juden* : Nebst anhängen verwandten inhalts. AKM VI.3. Leipzig: Brockhaus, 1877.

Steinschneider [, *Üb(ers).*], (Steinschn.)—Idem, *Die arabischen Übersetzungen aus dem Griechischen*, Einleitung 1–24, *Centralblatt für Bibliothekswesen* Beiheft 5 Jahrg. VI, 1889, I *Abschnitt Philosophie* (25–84), Beiheift 12, Jahrg. X 1893, III *Die griechische Ärzte* § 1–34, *Virchows Archiv* 124 (1891), 115/36, 268/96, 455/87, II *Mathematik* § 85–139, §140, *Alchemie*, Index, ZDMG 50, 161/219, 357/417. Also published in one volume by Harassowitz, Leipzig 1897.

Steward (Stewart)—See Mysore.

St. Jos.—Roper II 193, Université St. Joseph.

Stockh[olm]—Roper III 171, Stockholms Universitetesbibliotek.

Storey, *Pers. Lit.* (—PL, Storey)—Ch. A. Storey, *Persian literature* : a bio-bibliographical survey. Vol. I: Qur'ānic literature, History and Biography. Two sections in one volume and four continuously numbered tomes (called 'fascicle' in section 2, which consists of three such fascicles). London: Luzac, 1927–39.

St Petersburg [VII] Bibl. Gregoire IV—See Leningrad f. Gregoire IV.

St Petersburg As. Mus.—Pet. AM Buch.?

St. R. 3071—MS 3071 of the Rizā Pasha collection in Istanbul (see above, Rizā P.).

Stras[s]burg, Spitta (Strasb. Spitta, Strasburg, Strasb.)—Th. Nöldeke, Die arabische Handschriften Spitta's, *ZDMG* 40 (1886), 305–314.

Straub—Akademische Buchdruckerei F. Straub, Munich.

Strothmann, [*Die*] *Zwölferschia*—R. Strothmann, *Die Zwölferschia, zwei religionsgeschichtliche Charakterbilder aus der Mongolenzeit*. Leipzig: Harrassowitz, 1926.

Studies Browne—See *Or. Stud. Browne*.

Subḥat al-marjān—Read: *Sabḥat al-marjān*.

Ṣubḥi golshan—ʿAlī Ḥasan Khān al-Qannawjī, *Ṣubḥ-i gulshan*. Bhopal: Maṭābiʿ-i Riyāsat-i Bhūpāl, 1295 AH. Persian.

Subkī, *Ṭab.* (—*Ṭ.*, Subkī)—See al-Subkī.

Sulāfat al-ʿaṣr—ʿAlī Khān b. Aḥmad b. Muḥammad b. Maʿṣūm b. Ibrāhīm al-Ḥusaynī, *Sulāfat al-ʿaṣr fī maḥāsin aʿyān al-ʿaṣr*.

Sulaim. (Sülaim., Sul., Sulaimān[iyya], Sulaymāniyya)—*Defteri Kutubkhana-yi Süleimānīye*. Istanbul, 1310.

Sulaimān Qaṣīdağī Sirrī—See Qaṣīdağī Sulaimān (S.) Sirrī.

Sulṭān A. [K.]—Not in this way in Roper. It is a reference to the Ahmed III collection in the Topkapi Saray Museum (see Roper III 360, Topkapı Saray Müzesi Kütüphanesi, collection 1) III Ahmed), which in Weisweiler (e.g. 153) is referred to as Top Kapu Saray, Ahmedi Salis Küt. (= Kütüphanesi).

Süssheim, *Prol.*—K. Süssheim, *Prolegomena zu einer Ausgabe der im britischen Museum zu London verwahrten Chronik des seldschuqischen Reiches*. Leipzig: Harrassowitz, 1911.

Suter *Mathem.* (– *Math.*, Suter)—H. Suter, *Die Mathematiker und Astronomen der Araber und ihre Werke* (*Abhandlungen zur Geschichte der mathematischen Wissenschaften mit Einschluss ihrer Anwendungen*, vol. 10, Supplement to vol. 45 of *Zeitschrift für Mathematik und Physik*). Leipzig: Teubner, 1900.

Suter, Nachtr.—Idem, Nachträge und Berichtigungen zu *Die Mathematiker und Astronomen der Araber und ihre Werke*, in *Abhandlungen zur Geschichte der mathematischen Wissenschaften mit Einschluss ihrer Anwendungen*, vol. 14, 157–85.

Sütlüče Mewlewī Tekke—Not in Roper. Sütlüče is a neighborhood in the Beyoğlu district of Istanbul. Right on the waterfront on the opposite bank of the Golden Horn, in the Eyüp district, we find the Mevlevi Tekke Cami. Possibly the reference is to a manuscript kept in that mosque's library.

Suyūṭī—See the lemma al-Suyūṭī and, if mentioned without a title but with a page reference, then see al-Suyūṭī, *Interpr.*

Syr. Cat.—See Sachau.

TA—Refers to either 1) Al-Būrīnī al-Ḥasan b. Muḥammad b. Muḥammad, *Tarājim al-aʿyān min abnāʾ al-zamān*, cod. Berl. Wetzst. I, 29 (Ahlw. 9889), or 2) Muḥammad Murtaḍā al-Zabīdī, *Tāj al-ʿarūs, sharḥ al-Qāmūs* (also called *Tāj al-ʿarūs min jawāhir al-Qāmūs*).

Ṭab.—*Ṭabaqāt* [in general, and not in reference to one specific title, save maybe at Suppl. II, p. 50, although it remains unclear which title containing the term *Ṭabaqāt* is meant there).

Ṭabaqāt—See al-Jazarī, *Ṭab.*

Ṭabaqāt-i Nāṣirī—Ibn Sirāj al-Dīn Jūzjānī, *Ṭabaqāt-i Nāṣirī* (Persian).

Ṭabarī (Ṭab.)—Muḥammad b. Jarīr al-Ṭabarī, *Kitāb akhbār al-rusul wal-mulūk*.

Ṭabarī, *Tafsīr*—Idem, *Jāmiʿ al-bayān fī tafsīr (taʾwīl) al-Qurʾān*.

Ṭabbākh—See al-Ṭabbākh.

Tabriz—Muḥammad Mahdī al-ʿAlawī, *Khazāʾin-i kutub-i Īrān / Khizānat al-Ḥājj al-Mollā ʿAlī Āqā fī Tabrīz* / Les biliothèques de Tébriz, in *Lughat al-ʿArab* 7 (1929), 159–60, 220–6. Note: A number following ʻTabrizʼ may also merely indicate the year of publication of a printed edition, like in ʻTabriz 1274ʼ for ʻUkbarīʼs *Fiqh al-Riḍā* in volume 1, p. 175.

Tadhk[irat] al-naw[ādir] (*Tahdk. naw.*)—Hāshim al-Nadwī, *Tadhkirat al-nawādir min al-makhṭūṭāt al-ʿArabiyya*. Hyderabad, 1350.

Tadhk. ʿul[amāʾi] Hind—Raḥmān ʿAlī, *Tadhkiraʾi ʿUlamāʾi Hind*. Lucknow, 1894. Persian.

Tadhk. ʿulamāʾi Jawnpūr—Muhammad Sana Ullah (ed. & transl.), *Tazkirat-ul-ʿUlama, or, A memoir of the learned men (of Jaunpur), by Mawlana Khair-ud-Din Muhammad of Jaunpur*. Calcutta: Abul Faiz, 1934. Persian & English.

Tāj al-ṭab[aqāt]—Muḥammad Amīn b. Muḥammad al-Ṣāliḥ al-Ayyūbī, *Tāj ṭabaqāt al-awliyāʾ al-ʿārifīn wal-ʿulamāʾ al-ʿārifīn*.

Tāj al-ṭāl.—This abbreviation does not correspond to anything in GAL.

Tāj al-tarājim—See Ibn Quṭlūbughā.

Ṭāhā Ḥusayn, *Ḥad. al-arb[aʿāʾ]*—Ṭāhā Ḥusayn, *Ḥadīth al-arbaʿāʾ*.

Takm. Naf.—ʿAbd al-Ghafūr al-Lārī, *Takmilat Nafaḥāt al-uns wa-ḥaḍarāt al-quds* (by Jāmī ʿAlī b. Aḥmad).

Talq.—*talqīn* ?

Taʿl. san.—See *al-Taʿl. al-san.*

Tanger I, II etc.—See Tangiers Gr. M.

Tanger Gr. M. [I, II etc.]—See Tangiers Gr. M.

Tangiers—G. Salmon, Catalogue dʼune bibliothèque privée, in *Arch. Maroc.* V, 134/46.

Tangiers Gr. M. I, II, etc.—P. Maillard, La bibliothèque de la Grande Mosquée de Tanger / Essai de bibliographie marocaine, in *Revue du Monde Musulman* 35 (1917–18), 107–92. The roman numbers refer to the different ʻlistsʼ (I → XI) mentioned in this article.

Taʾr.—*Taʾrīkh, taʾrīkhī, taʾrīkhiyya.*

Ṭarābulus al-Gharb—Tripoli, Libya.

Ta'rīkh—If associated with Ibn al-Athīr: Maḥmūd b. Salmān b. Fahd al-Ḥalabī, *Ta'rīkh.*

Ta'rīk al-ādāb al-ʿAr.—Most likely: Jirjī Zaydān, *Ta'rīkh ādāb al-lugha al-ʿarabiyya.* 4 vols. Cairo: Maṭbaʿat al-Hilāl, 1911–14.

Ta[ʾ]*rīkhi guzīda* (*Ta'r. gūzida*)—See Ḥamdallāh Mustawfī.

Ta'rīkhi Jahāngushā—Mīrzā Muḥammad Ḳazwīnī (ed.), *The Tā'ríkh-i-jahán-gushá of ʿAláʾu 'd-Dín ʿAtá-Malik-i-Juwayní.* 3 vols., (GMS, Old Series, xvi/1, 2, 3). Leiden: Brill, 1912–37. Persian.

Ta'rīkh Makka—Al-Azraqī Aḥmad b. Muḥammad, *Ta'rīkh Makka al-musharrafa.*

Tarrāzī (Ṭarrāzī)—Ph. de Tarrazi, *Ta'rīkh al-ṣaḥāfa al-ʿArabiyya.* 4 vols. in 2 tomes Beirut: al-Maṭbaʿa al-Adabiyya, 1913–14.

Tashk.—A.A. Semenov, *A descriptive Catalogue of the Persian, Arabic and Turkish Manuscripts preserved in the Library of Middle Asiatic State University.* Acta Universitatis Asiae Mediae, ser. II, fasc. 4. Tashkent, 1935.

Taymūr (Taymūr Pāshā)—See A. Taymūr; in Supplement III, 'Taymūr' refers to: Muḥammad Taymūr, *Ḥayātuna 'l-tamthīliyya* (Mu'allafāt Muḥammad Taymūr II), Maṭbaʿat al-Iʿtimād, 1922.

TB—Türkische Bibliothek.

T. Baghdād—Al-Khaṭīb al-Baghdādī Aḥmad b. ʿAlī, *Ta'rīkh Baghdād.*

Teh.—Y. Etessami, *Catalogue des manuscrits persans et arabes de la bibliothèque du Madjless,* vols. I and II. Tehran: Maṭbaʿa-i Majlis, 1933.

Teh. Sip[āhs].—Ibn Yūsuf Shīrāzī, *Fihrist-i kitābkhāna-yi Madrasa-yi ʿāli-yi Sipahsālār* I (Catalogue des manuscrits persans et arabes de la Bibliothèque de la Faculté de Théologie et de Philosophie de l'Iran, vol. I). Tehran: Dānishkāda-i maʿqul ō manqūl, 1315.

Tetouan—See Madr. T.

Thibaut, *Astronomie*—G. Thibaut, *Astronomie, Astrologie, und Mathematik.* Grundriss der indo-arischen Philologie und Altertumskunde, III. Band, 9. Heft. Strassbourg: Trübner, 1899.

Tiesenhausen, *Goldene Horde* (*Sbornik mater. otn. hist. Zol. Ord., Rec. de mat. rel à l'hist de la Horde d'Or*)—V.G. Tizengauzen, *Sbornik materialov, otnosjaščichsja k istorii Zolotoj Ordy = Recueil de matériaux relatifs à l'histoire de la Horde d'Or*/ par W. de Tiesenhausen. 2 vols. St. Petersburg: Stroganov, 1884 (vol. 1), and Moscow: Akad. Nauk SSSR, 1941 (vol. 2).

Tifrīshī, *Naqd al-rijāl* (Tifrīshī)—Muṣṭafā b. al-Ḥusaynī al-Tafrīshī, *Naqd al-rijāl.*

Tijdschr.—Tijdschrift (journal).

Tippoo (Tippu)—See Mysore.

Tisserant, *Spec.*—E. Tisserant, *Specimina codicum orientalium.* Bonn: Marcus & Weber, 1914.

Tkatsch, *Poetik* [*des Aristoteles*] (Tkatsch)—J. Tkatsch, *Die arabische Übersetzung der Poetik des Aristoteles und die Grundlage der Kritik des griechischen Textes.* 2 vols.

Vienna: Hölder-Pichler-Tempsky, 1928–32. The second volume was published posthumously by A. Gudeman and Th. Seif.

ṬKh—A misprint?

Tlemc. (Tlems., Tlem.)—A. Cour, *Catalogue des manuscrits conservés dans les principales bibliothèques algériennes*: Medersa de Tlemcen. Algiers: Jourdan, 1907.

Top Kapu (Top Kapu Serāi, Topqapū Sarayi, Topkapi Serāi)—Roper III 360, Topkapı Saray Müzesi Kütüphanesi. The incidental addition '[Sultan] Aḥmad III' refers to the 'III Ahmed' collection mentioned in Roper, loc.cit.

Tor. (Turin)—C.A. Nallino, I manoscritti arabi, persiani, turchi e siriaci della Biblioteca Nazionale di Torino, in *Memorie della R. Accademia delle scienze di Torino. Classe di scienze morali, storiche e filologiche*, s. 2a, L (1901), 92–101.

Tornb.—Tornberg. See Ibn al-Athīr, Lund, or Upp.

Trad.—'traduction', i.e. 'translation'.

Transact. (IXth) Congr. Or.—E. Delmar Morgan (ed.), *Transactions of the Ninth International Congress of Orientalists, held in London 5th to 12th September 1892*, 2 vols. London: The Committee of the Congress, 1893.

Tripoli, Waqf Faqīh Ḥ. (= Ḥasan)—A private library in Tripoli (Libya), mentioned in *Oriente Moderno* 8 (1928), 279 note 2. See also Roper IV 265, al-Faqīh al-Ḥasan.

Tria op.—Tria opuscula.

Trübner, Cat. 1869—One of the issues of *Trübner's American and Oriental Literary Record* from the year 1869.

Trübner, *Rec.—Trübner's Record*; continuation of: *Trübner's American and Oriental Literary Record* and *Trübner's American, European and Oriental Literary Record.*

Trudi Inst. Vostokov. Ak. Nauk SSSR—Trudy Instituta Vostokovedenija Akademija Nauk SSSR.

Tüb. (Tub.)—Chr. F. Seybold, *Verzeichnis der arabischen Handschriften der Universitätsbibliothek zu Tübingen* vol. 1. Tübingen: Schnürlen, 1907; M. Weisweiler, *Verzeichnis der arabischen Handschriften der Universitätsbibliothek zu Tübingen* vol. 2. Leipzig: Harrassowitz, 1930.

Tüb. Wetzst.—J.G. Wetzstein, *Katalog arabischer Manuscripte / in Damaskus gesammelt.* Berlin: Trowitzsch & Sohn, 1863.

Tuḥfat al-muḥtāj (C. 1282)—Al-Haythamī Aḥmad b. Muḥammad b. Ḥajar, *Tuḥfat al-muḥtāj bi-sharḥ al-Minhāj.* 4 vols. Cairo: al-Maṭbaʿa al-Wahbiyya, 1282.

Tunis [Gr. Mosq. Roy]—B. Roy, *Extrait du catalogue des manuscrits et des imprimés de la bibliothèque de la Grande Mosquée de Tunis* : Histoire, avec la collaboration de Mhammed bel Khodja et de Mohammed el Hachaichi. Tunis: Imprimerie Générale, 1900.

Tunis Ṣ. (Tunis Ṣād[iqiyya])—*Defter al-maktaba al-Ṣādiqiyya.*Tunis, 1292.

Tunis Zayt[ūna]—*Jāmiʿ al-Zaytūna, barnāmaj al-maktaba al-ʿAbdaliyya Ṣādiqiyya.* 4 volumes.Tunis: al-Maṭbaʿa al-Rasmiyya: 1326–29; O. Houdas and R. Basset,

Mission scientifique en Tunisie, deuxième partie: bibliographie, in *Bulletin de Correspondance Africaine*, vol. 3, fasc. 2 (1884), 5–65, 97–136.

Turin—See Tor.

Turin, Bibl. Acc. Sc.—Roper II 107, Accademia delle Scienze.

Türkiyat Mecm. (*Türk. Mecm.*)—*Türkiyat Mecmuasi.*

Ṭūsī, *Istibṣār*—Al-Ṭūsī Shaykh al-Ṭā'ifa Muḥammad b. al-Ḥasan, *Kitāb al-istibṣār fīma 'khtulifa fīhi min al-akhbār.*

Ṭūsī, *Tahdhīb al-aḥkām*—Idem, *Kitāb tahdhīb al-aḥkām.*

Ṭūsī (Tusy) List [of Shia Books]—See al-Ṭūsī.

Ṭūsī[1]—See al-Ṭūsī.

Ṭūsy—See al-Ṭūsī.

u.—Apart from 'und', 'u.' may at times also be short for 'unten' ('below') or 'unter' ('sub').

übers.—übersetzt (translated).

'Ulamā'i Hind—See *Tadhk. 'ulamā'i Hind.*

Ulughkhani, *Hist*[*ory*] *of Guj*[*arat*]—E. Denison Ross (ed.), *An Arabic History of Gujarat ...* by ... Ulughkhání. 3 vols. London: Murray, 1910–28 (Ulughkhani = Al-Ulūghkhānī 'Abdallāh Muḥammad b. 'Umar al-Makkī al-Āṣafī).

'Um. (Umūmi, 'Umūm.)—Kütübkhane'i 'Umūmiyye in Istanbul, where Brockelmann's data are based on the work of O. Rescher (See Supplement 1, 10), notably O. Rescher, Mitteilungen aus Stambuler Bibliotheken I and II, in ZDMG 64 (1910), 195–217 and 489–528; idem, Mitteilungen aus Stambuler Bibliotheken, *Mélanges de la faculté orientale* de l'Université Saint Joseph [MFO] 5 (1912), 489–540). Roper III 324–66 (Istanbul) makes no mention of this library/collection. Nevertheless, some of the publications listed under 'Union Catalogues and Surveys' in Roper III 271ff refer to this library as well (e.g. Rhodokanakis 1906 and Horovitz 1907).

Umm—Muḥammad b. Idrīs al-Shāfi'ī, *Kitāb al-umm.*

Umschau—*Die Umschau in Wissenschaft und Technik.*

Un. Egypt (Un. Eg.)—Roper I 210, Cairo University Library.

Univ.—See Roper III 335, İstanbul Üniversitesi Kütüphanesi.

Upps.—C.J. Tornberg, *Codices arabici, persici et turcici bibliothecae regiae universitatis Upsaliensis*, Lund 1849.

Upps. II—K.V. Zetterstéen, Die arabischen, persischen und türkischen Handschriften der Universitätsbibliothek zu Uppsala, in MO XXII (1928), 1–498; part II in MO XIXX (1935), 1–180.

Uṣ.—See Ibn Abī Uṣaybi'a.

Usāma, ed. Derenbourg—H. Derenbourg, *Ousâma Ibn Mounḳidh* : un émir syrien au premier siècle des Croisades. 2 vols. in 3 tomes (vol. I.1–2 French, vol. II Arabic). Paris: Leroux, 1886–93.

Üsküdār, Hüdā'ī (Khudā'ī), Tefs.—Roper III 332, Hüdayî (being one of the collections of the Hacı Selim Ağa Kütüphanesi, located in Üsküdar [ancient Scutari] in Istanbul).

Üsküdār (Uskudār) Nūr Bānū—Roper III 332, Nurbanu Sultan (being one of the collections of the Hacı Selim Ağa Kütüphanesi, located in Üsküdar [ancient Scutari] in Istanbul).

usw.—und so weiter (and so forth).

Utrecht Leid.—See Leiden[1] vol. 5.

ʿUyūn [al-akhbār]—Ibn Qutayba, *ʿUyūn al-akhbār*.

Van Arendonk, *Opkomst* (v[an] Arendonk)—C. van Arendonk, *De opkomst van het Zaidietische Imamaat in Yemen*. Leiden: Brill, 1919.

Van Berchem—See v. Berchem.

Vandenhoff, *Tarafa*—B. Vandenhoff, *Nonnulla Tarafae poetae carmina ex arabico in latinum sermonem versa notisque adumbrata*, Diss. Berlin: Mayer et Mueller, 1895.

Van Dyck—See v. Dyck.

v. Arendonk—See Van Arendonk.

Vat.—Brockelmann himself gives the following explanation of this abbreviation: *Bibliothecae apost. Vaticanae codd. mss. or. cat.* p. I, vol. I. Rome, 1766 (vol. 1, p. 6; see also Supplement 1, p. 11). It seems however, that such a title does not exist. There are two catalogues by Assemani that have our interest here: 1) St.E. Assemanus & J.S. Assemanus, *Bibliothecae Apostolicae Vaticanae codicum manuscriptorum catalogus*, I.1., *complectens codices Ebraicos et Samaritanos*. Rome: Rotili, 1756. But as the title shows there are no Arabic manuscripts there and the year does not fit either. Then there is 2) J.S. Assemanus, *Bibliotheca Orientalis Clementino-Vaticana : In Qua Manuscriptos Codices Syriacos, Arabicos, Persicos, Turcicos, Hebraicos, Samaritanos, Armenicos, Aethiopicos, Graecos, Aegyptiacos, Ibericos, & Malabaricos* ... (3 vols. in 4 tomes. Rome: Typis Sacrae Congregationis de Propaganda Fide, 1719–28), vol. 1, De scriptores Syris Orthodoxis. Even if this is not volume I.1 , it does contain Arabic manuscripts whose shelfnumbers do however not appear to correspond to GAL's references involving just 'Vat.' followed by a number. In the case of the reference '*Kitāb qawāʿid al-Shiʿr* Vat. 357' in vol. 1, p. 106 bottom it was the reference to Schiaparelli which put me on the right track: A. Maio, *Scriptorum Veterum Nova Collectio e Vaticanis codicibus edita*, vol. 4 (Rome: Typis Vaticanis, 1831; not included in GAL's bibliographical overviews of library catalogues), p. 481. In the case of the reference to 'Vat. $53_{,9}$' in connection with Isḥāq b. Sulaymān al-Isrāʾīlī's *Kitāb al-Usṭūqisāt* in vol. 1, p. 236, consulting Steinschneider's *Die hebraeischen Übersetzungen des Mittelalters und die Juden als Dolmetcher*, p. 391, § 225.2 it became clear that the reference should in fact be to 'Vat. Urb. 53^9'. Unfortunately, the addition 'Urb.' is not explained in Steinschneider's list of abbreviations on p. VI of this same work. But clearly it refers to the 'Urbinati Ebraici' collection of Hebrew manuscripts described in the first of the two Assemani catalogues mentioned above, where we find the text of Urbinati LIII no. 9 described on p. 446. So in this case the abbreviation in GAL was not complete, which may be something to remember in other cases as well. These are just two examples of possible complications with the abbreviation 'Vat.'

in GAL. Obviously, it was not possible to solve each and every one of them in preparing this list, but at least the reader now knows that a creative approach is likely to solve many of these problems.

Vat. Barb.—See Vat. V., sub 'Barberiniani'.

Vat. N.F.—C. Crispo Moncada, *I codici nuovo fondo della Biblioteca Vaticana*, Palermo 1900.

Vat. V.—Giorgio Levi della Vida, *Elenco dei manoscritti arabi islamici della Biblioteca Vaticana: Vaticani, Barberiniani, Borgiani, Rossiani*, Vatican City: Biblioteca Apostolica Vaticana, 1935.

Vat. V. Barb.—See Vat. V., sub 'Barberiniani'.

Vat. V. Borg.—See Vat. V., sub 'Borgiani'.

v. Berchem, *Amida*—M. v. Berchem, *Amida* (part 1), *Matériaux pour l'épigraphie et l'histoire musulmanes du Diyar-Bekr*. Heidelberg: Winter & Paris: Leroux, 1910.

v. Berchem, *Matér[iaux]* I (– *Matériaux pour un Corpus Inscr.* I, – *Mat.* I)—Idem, *Matériaux pour un Corpus Inscriptionum Arabicarum*. Partie 1, fasc. 1. Paris: Leroux, 1894.

v. Dyck—Ed. van Dyck, *Iktifāʾ al-qanūʿ bimā huwa maṭbūʿ min ashhar al-taʾālīf al-ʿArabiyya fī 'l-maṭābiʿ al-sharqiyya wal-gharbiyya*. Cairo: Maṭbaʿat al-Hilāl, 1896.

Vehbi Ef.—See Wehbi Ef.

Veliyeddīn—See *Welieddīn*.

Verspr. Geschr.—Verspreide Geschriften.

v. Hammer, *Gesch.*—See Hammer, *GOR*.

Vienna—G. Flügel, *Die arabischen, persischen und türkischen Handschriften der K. K. Hofbibliothek*, 3 vols., Vienna: Kaiserlich-königliche orientalische Akademie, 1863–7.

Vienna.—In some cases the German abbreviation '*Wien.*' (for '*Wiener*') was mistakenly changed to '*Vienna.*.'

Vienna Glaser (Vienna Gl.)—Refers to a collection of Arabic manuscripts from South Arabia which received its first description in M. Grünert, Über Ed. Glaser's jüngste arabische Handschriften-Sammlung, in *Actes du dixième Congrès international des orientalistes : session de Genève 1894, troisième partie* (Leiden: Brill, 1896), 35–43.

Vincent, *Études [sur le droit musulman]*—M.B. Vincent, *Études sur la loi musulmane [rit de Malek] / Législation criminelle*. Paris: Joubert, 1842.

Virchows Archiv—Virchows Archiv für pathologische Anatomie und Physiologie und für klinische Medizin.

Vitt. Em.—See Rom. Vitt. Em.

v. Kremer—A. v. Kremer, *Ägypten*. 2 vols. Leipzig: Brockhaus, 1863; see also von Kremer.

v. Kremer, *Syrien*—Idem, *Mittelsyrien und Damascus* : geschichtliche, ethnografische und geografische Studien während eines Aufenthaltes daselbst in den Jahren 1849, 1850 und 1851. Wien: Mechitharisten, 1853.

von Kremer, *Streifzüge* (A. v. Kremer, *Kulturgesch. Streifzüge* (*Culturgesch. Streifzüge,*), *Kulturgesch., Culturgesch., Streifzüge, Streifz.*).—A. vonKremer, *Culturgeschichtliche Streifzüge auf dem Gebiete des Islams*, Leipzig: Brockhaus, 1873.

von Kremer, *Ideen*—Idem, *Geschichte der herrschenden Ideen des Islams*. Leipzig: Brockhaus, 1868.

Vorarb.—Vorarbeiten (preparatory/preliminary studies).

Vorl.—Vorlesungen (lectures).

Vost.—*Vostok.*

Vost. Zap. Leningrad—See ZKV.

vu—von unten (from below).

Waddington–Schefer—Refers to a collection of inscriptions from Damascus that had been assembled by William Henry Waddington (1826–94) and which had come into the possession of Charles Schefer. See G. Wiet, Les inscriptions arabes de Damas, in *Syria* vol. 3.2 (1922), 153–63.

Wafā' (library of, no place)—Not in Roper.

Wājid Ḥusayn Library (Lucknow)—Even if there is one mention in *JRASB* 1917 [p. cvii, no. (52): 'Wājid Ḥu. Lib., Maḥallah, Yaḥyāganj, Lucknow'], which might seem to suggest that such a library existed in Lucknow, I think this is a misunderstanding. This is because H. Beveridge, in his "Notes on Persian manuscripts in Indian Libraries" (*The Journal of the Royal Asiatic Society of Great Britain and Ireland* 1901, pp. 69–85), p. 80, states: "Two brothers in Yahyaganj, Lucknow, named Abul Husain and Wājid Husain, carry on separately the business of second-hand booksellers, and I got some good MSS. from them". So Suhrawardy's 'Wājid Ḥu. Lib.' more likely stands for: 'Wajid Husain Librarian'. The manuscripts that Suhrawardy refers to in his article (four in all) were therefore probably for sale when he visited Wājid Ḥusayn's bookshop.

Waqf Ibr.—See Fātiḥ Waqf Ibr.

Wehbi Ef[endi] (Vehbi Ef., Wehbī)—Roper III 348, Bağdalı Vehbi Efendi.

Weil, *Gesch.* [*der Chal.*]—G. Weil, *Geschichte der Chalifen*, 5 vols. Mannheim: Bassermann, 1846–62.

Weis[s]weiler (Weisw.)—See Tüb. second part and also next entry.

Weis[s]weiler, *Ist*[*anb*]. *Hds*[*s*]*studien* (Weisw[eiler] *Trad.*, Weisw[eiler])—M. Weisweiler, *Istanbuler Handschriftenstudien zur arabischen Traditionsliteratur*. Bibliotheca Islamica vol. 10. Leipzig: Brockhaus & Istanbul: Druckerei Universum, 1937.

Weis[s]weiler, *Trad.*—See previous entry.

Weijers, *Spec. crit.*—H.E. Weijers, *Specimen criticum, exhibens locos Ibn Khacanis de Ibn Zeidouno, ex mss. codicibus Bibliothecae Lugd. Bat. et Gothanae editos*. Leiden: Luchtmans, 1831.

Welieddīn (Veliyeddīn, Walīaddīn, Wel.)—See Bāyezīd.

Wellhausen, *Das arab. Reich*—J. Wellhausen, *Das arabische Reich und sein Sturz*. Berlin: Georg Reimer 1902.

Wellhausen, *Oppositionsparteien* (*Opp.*)—Idem, *Die religiös-politischen Oppositionsparteien im alten Islam*. Berlin: Weidmann, 1901.

Wenrich—Joannes Georgius Wenrich, *De auctorum Graecorum versionibus et commentariis Syriacis, Arabicis, Armeniacis Persicisque commentatio*. Leipzig: Vogel, 1842.

Wiedemann—E. Wiedemann; problems in identifying or locating a work by Wiedemann mentioned in GAL stand a good chance of being solved by turning to D. Girke (ed.), *Eilhard Wiedemann: Gesammelte Schriften zur arabisch-islamischen Wissenschaftsgeschichte*. 3 vols. Frankfurt am Main: Institut für Geschichte der Arabisch-Islamischen Wissenschaften an der Johann Wolfgang Goethe-Universität, 1984.

Wiedem. *Ann.*—Wiedemann in *Annalen der Physik*.

Wiener (*Wien.*) *Jahrb.* [no.], Anz. Bl.—*Jahrbücher der Literatur* [no.], Anzeigeblatt für Wissenschaft und Kunst.

Wilkens, *Chrest.*—F. Wilken (ed.), *Institutiones ad fundamenta linguae Persicae cum Chrestomathia maxim partem ex auctoribus ineditis collecta et glossario locupleti*. Leipzig: Crusius, 1805.

Wiss.—Wissenschaft(en).

W. Kroll, Cat. astr. gr. v. 2—W. Kroll (descr.), *Catalogus codicum astrologorum graecorum*, t. 5. pars 2: Codicum Romanorum, partem secundam. Brussels: Lamertin, 1906.

Woepcke, *Recherches* I—F. Woepcke, *Recherches sur plusieurs ouvrages de Léonard de Pise*, découverts et publiés par M. le Prince Balthasar Boncompagni, et sur les rapports qui existent entre ces ouvrages et les travaux mathématiques des Arabes—Première Partie, Extraits et traductions d'ouvrages arabes inédits, I: Traduction d'un chapitre des Prolégomènes d'Ibn Khaldoûn. Rome: Imprimerie des beaux arts, 1856.

Wolfenb[üttel]—Roper I 361, Herzog August Bibliothek (Bibliotheca Augusta).

Wrocław—See Breslau.

Wright, *Op. ar.*—W. Wright, *Opuscula Arabica*: collected and edited from mss. in the university library of Leyden. Leiden: Brill, 1859.

Wüst.—This abbreviation may, depending on the context, refer to: **1**) Wüst. *Gesch.*, on which see below; **2**) F. Wüstenfeld, *Der Imām el Shāfiʿī, seine Schüler und Anhänger bis zum J. 300*, in *Abh. d. Kgl. Ges. D. Wiss. zu Göttingen*, Hist.-philolog. Classe, vol. 36.4 (Göttingen: Dieterich, 1890); **3**) F. Wüstenfeld (ed.), *Ibn Challikani vitae illustrium virorum* / e pluribus codd. MSS. inter se collatis, nunc primum Arabice edidit, variis lectionibus indicibusque locupletiss. instruxit … 13 vols. Göttingen: Deuerlich, 1835–50; 4) Wüst., *Ärzte*.

Wüst[enfeld], *Ac.* (– *Akad.*, – *Ak.* (*Ac.*) *d. Ar.*)—F. Wüstenfeld, *Die Academien der Araber und ihre Lehrer: nach Auszügen aus Ibn Schohba's Klassen der Schafeïten* /

bearb. von Ferdinand Wüstenfeld, zur hundertjährigen Stiftungfeier der Academia Georgia Augusta. Göttingen: Vandenhoeck und Ruprecht, 1837.

Wüst[enfeld], *Ärzte* (Wüst.)—Idem, *Geschichte der arabischen Ärzte und Naturforscher*. Göttingen: Vandenhoeck und Ruprecht, 1840.

Wüst[enfeld], *Calcaschandi*—Idem, *Calcaschandi's Geographie und Verwaltung von Ägypten*. From *Abhandlungen der Königlichen Gesesellschaft der Wissenschaften zu Göttingen; Hist.-Philolog. Classe*, vol. 25. Göttingen: Dieterich, 1879.

Wüst[enfeld], *Chron.*—Idem, *Die Chroniken der Stadt Mekka*. 4 vols. Leipzig: Brockhaus, 1857–61.

Wüst[enfeld], *Die Fam[ilie] Muḥ.*—Idem, *Die Gelehrten-Familie Muḥibbí in Damascus und ihre Zeitgenossen im XI. (17.) Jahrhundert*. Göttingen: Dieterich, 1884.

Wüst[enfeld], *Fat.*—Idem, *Geschichte der Faṭimiden-Chalifen / nach arabischen Quellen*. From *Abhandlungen der Königlichen Gesesellschaft der Wissenschaften zu Göttingen*, vols. 26, 27. Göttingen: Dieterich, 1881.

Wüst[enfeld], *Gesch.* (Wüstenf. *Gesch.*, Wüst.)—Idem, *Die Geschichtschreiber der Araber und ihre Werke*. From *Abhandlungen der Königlichen Gesesellschaft der Wissenschaften zu Göttingen*, vols. 28, 29. Göttingen: Dieterich, 1882.

Wüst[enfeld], *Gesch. Fam. Muḥ.*—See idem, *Die Fam[ilie] Muḥ.*

Wüst[enfeld], *Heerwesen der Mus.*—Idem, *Das Heerwesen der Muhammedaner*. From *Abhandlungen der Königlichen Gesesellschaft der Wissenschaften zu Göttingen*, vol. 28. Göttingen: Dieterich, 1880.

Wüst[enfeld], *Jemen im XI. (XVII.)* (*Jem[en]*)—Idem, *Jemen im XI. (XVII.) Jahrhundert: die Kriege der Türken, die Arabischen Imâme und die Gelehrten: mit einem geographischen Anhange*. From *Abhandlungen der Königlichen Gesellschaft der Wissenschaften zu Göttingen*, vol. 32. Göttingen: Dieterich, 1884.

Wüst[enfeld], *Lat. Ubers.*—Idem, *Die Übersetzungen arabischer Werke in das Lateinische*. Göttingen: Dieterich, 1877.

Wüst[enfeld], *Schaf.*—Idem, *Der Imâm el-Schâfi'i und seine Anhänger*. Zweite Abteilung: *Die gelehrten Schāfi'iten des IV. Jahrhunderds*. From *Abhandlungen der Königlichen Gesellschaft der Wissenschaften zu Göttingen*, vol. 37. Göttingen: Dieterich, 1891.

Wüst[enfeld], *Scherife*—Idem, *Die Scherife von Mekka im XI. (XVII.) Jahrhundert: Fortsetzung der Geschichte der Stadt Mekka mit einer Stammtafel der Sherife*. From *Abhandlungen der Königlichen Gesellschaft der Wissenschaften zu Göttingen*, vol. 32. Göttingen: Dieterich, 1885.

Wüst[enfeld], *Ṣūf[īs]*—Idem, *Die Çufiten in Süd-Arabien im XI. (XVII.) Jahrhundert*. From *Abhandlungen der Königlichen Gesellschaft der Wissenschaften zu Göttingen*, vol. 30. Göttingen: Dieterich, 1883.

Wüst[enfeld], *Ṭab.*—Does not correspond to his '*Ac.*' nor to his edition of Suyuti's *Ṭabaqāt al-ḥuffāẓ* (*Liber classium virorum qui Korani et traditionum cognitione excelluerunt etc.* 3 vols. Cairo: Maktabat al-Wahba, 1833–34). Unresolved.

Wüst[enfeld], *Yemen*—See idem, *Jemen im XI*.
Wüstenf., *Schafiiten* (*Schaf.*)—See Wüst., *Schaf.*
Wüstenfeld, *Geschichtenschreiber*—See Wüst[enfeld], *Gesch.*
Wyse, *Operations*—H. Vyse, *Operations Carried On at the Pyramids of Gizeh in 1837* : with an account of a voyage into Upper Egypt, and an appendix. 3 vols. London: Fraser, 1840–41 (vols. 1–2), and Weale & Nickisson, 1842 (vol. 3, containing a Survey by J.S. Perring Esq.)
Ya. Ef—Ja. Ef. ('Bešiktāš' [Suppl. 2, 335] refers to a district in Istanbul).
Yaḥyā (library, no place)—Ja. Ef. ?
Yaḥyā Efendi (library of, no place)—Ja. Ef.
Yaḥyā b. Khaldūn, *Bughyat al-ruwāh* (*sic*)—Ibn Khaldūn Yaḥyā b. Muḥammad, *Bughyat al-ruwwād fī dhikr al-mulūk min ʿAbd al-wād*.
Ya[ḥyā]Ef[endi]—See Ja. Ef.
Yāq.—Yāqūt.
Yaʿqūb Bakhsh al-Badayūnī (collection of, no place)—Not in Roper.
Yaʿqūbī, *Hist.*—M.Th. Houtsma (ed.), *Ibn Wadhih qui dicitur al-Jaʿqūbī Historiae*. 2 vols. Leiden: Brill, 1883 (Yaʿqūbī = Al-Yaʿqūbī Aḥmad b. Abī Yaʿqūb, *Hist.* = *Kitāb al-buldān*).
Yāqūt, GW (– *Geographical Dictionary*)—F. Wüstenfeld (ed.), *Jacuts geografisches Wörterbuch*. 6 vols. Leipzig: Brockhaus, 1866–73 (Yāqūt = Yāqūt b. ʿAbdallāh al-Rūmī, GW = *Muʿjam al-buldān*).
Yāqūt, *Irsh*[*ād*]—Yāqūt b. ʿAbdallāh al-Rūmī, *Muʿjam al-udabāʾ al-musammā bi-Irshād al-arīb ilā maʿrifat al-adīb*.
Yāsīn [b.] Bāshayān al-ʿAbbāsī (library, Basra)—Roper II 26, ʿAbbāsī Library.
Yatīma—Al-Thaʿālibī, *Yatīmat al-dahr fī maḥāsin ahl al-ʿaṣr*.
Yeni—*Yeni Ǧāmiʿ kütübḫānesinde maḥfūẓ kütübi mevǧūdenin defteri dir*, Istanbul n.d.
Yeni A. Ḫ(Kh)ān—Not in Roper. A subcollection of Yeni?
Yildiz (Yyldyz)—Roper III 335, Yıldız.
Yū[suf] Āġā—Roper III 377, Yusuf Ağa Kütüphanesi (Konya).
Yū. Khāliṣ—See Halis.
Yyldyz—See Yildiz.
z.—zu, zur, zum (to, towards, for).
Zabāra—Muḥammad Zabāra, *Nayl al-waṭar min tarājim nujabāʾ al-Yaman fī ʾl-qarn al-thālith ʿashar*. 2 vols. Cairo: al-Maṭbaʿa al-Salafiyya, 1348–50.
Zachs Ephem.—F.X. (Xaver) von Zach, *Allgemeine geographische Ephemeriden* (51 vols., 1798–1816).
Ẓāh. ʿIsh—See next entry.
Ẓāh.[2]—Yūsuf al-ʿIsh, *Fihris makhṭūṭāt Dār al-kutub al-Ẓāhiriyya: al-Taʾrīkh wa-mulḥaqātuhu*. Damascus: Maṭbaʿat Dimashq, 1366/1947 (Maṭbūʿāt al-Majmaʿ al-ʿilmī al-ʿArabī bi-Dimashq).

Zakī Mubārak, *al-Nathr al-fannī*—Zakī Mubārak, *al-Nathr al fannī fī 'l-qarn al-rābi'*. 2 vols. Cairo: Maṭba'at Dār al-Kutub al-Miṣriyya, 1934.

Zakī Mubārak, *La prose*—Idem, *La prose arabe au IVeme siecle de l'hégire (Xeme siecle)*. Paris: Maisonneuve, 1931.

Zakī Mubārak, *al-Muwāzana*—Idem, *al-Muwāzana bayna 'l-shu'arā'*. Cairo: Maṭba'at al-Muqtaṭaf wal-Muqaṭṭam, 1926 (repr. 1936).

Zambaur—E. de Zambaur, *Manuel de généalogie et de chronologie pour l'histoire de l'Islam*. Hanover: Lafaire, 1927.

Zanjān—Abū 'Abdallāh al-Zanjānī, *Khazā'in Zanjān (fī Īrān)*, in *Lughat al-'Arab* 6 (1928), 92–6; see also F. Krenkow, Account of some scientific manuscripts in libraries in Persia, in *BSAOS* 5.1 (1928), 201–3.

Zap[iski]—See ZKV.

Zap. Koll. Vost. (Zap.)—See ZKV.

Zap. Vost. Otd. (Zap. Vost. Otd. Imp. Russk. Arch. Ob., Zap. VOIRAO)—Zapiski Vostochnago Otdéleniya Imperatorskago Russkago Arkheologicheskago Obshchestva (ZVORAO).

Zark.—Al-Zarkashī Muḥammad b. Ibrāhīm al-Lu'lu'ī, *Ta'rīkh al-dawlatayn al-Muwaḥḥidiyya wal-Ḥafṣiyya*. Tunis, 1289.

Zarkalī—See al-Ziriklī.

ZATW—*Zeitschrift für alttestamentliche Wissenschaft*.

Zāwiya [Zaouiyah] d'El Hamel (Hamel)—R. Basset, Les manuscrits arabes de la Zaouyah d'El Hamel, in *Giornale della Società Asiatica Italiana* 10 (1896–97), 43–97; Roper IV 19, Zāwiyat al-Hāmil.

Zāw[iyat] S[idi] Ḥamza—H.P.J. Renaud, Un prétendu catalogue de la Bibliothèque de la Grande Mosquée de Fès, Appendice: Inventaire sommaire des manuscrits relatifs aux sciences de la bibliothèque de la *Zāwiya* de Sidi Ḥamza, in *Hespéris* 18 (1934), 86–99. Not in Roper.

Zaydān, *M[ashāhīr] al-sharq (Mashh. al-sharq)*—Jirjī Zaydān, *Tarājim mashāhīr al-sharq fī 'l-qarn al-tāsi' 'ashar*. 2 vols. Cairo: Maṭba'at al-Hilāl, 1902.

Zayn al-'Ābidīn b. Asadallāh al-Najafī (library of, no place)—Not in Roper.

Zeitschr. f. Math. (Z. f. Math. u. Phys.)—Zeitschrift für Mathematik und Physik.

Zenker—See BO.

Ziriklī—Zie al-Ziriklī.

ZKV *(Zapiski, Zap. Koll. Vost., Zap.)—Zapiski kollegii vostokovedov pri Aziatskom muzee Rosiĭskoĭ akademii nauk.*

Ztschr.—Zeitschrift.

Zub.—See al-Zub.

Žurn. Min. Narodn. Prosv.—Žurnal Ministerstva Narodnogo Prosveščenija.

Zuruklī—See al-Ziriklī.

Printed in the United States
By Bookmasters